# BELOVED COMMUNITY

# Beloved Community

## Critical Dogmatics after Christendom

PAUL R. HINLICKY

WILLIAM B. EERDMANS PUBLISHING COMPANY
GRAND RAPIDS, MICHIGAN / CAMBRIDGE, U.K.

Published 2015 by
Wm. B. Eerdmans Publishing Co.
2140 Oak Industrial Drive N.E., Grand Rapids, Michigan 49505 /
P.O. Box 163, Cambridge CB3 9PU U.K.

**Library of Congress Cataloging-in-Publication Data**

Hinlicky, Paul R.
Beloved community: critical dogmatics after Christendom / Paul R. Hinlicky.
pages        cm
Includes bibliographical references and index.
ISBN 978-0-8028-6935-7 (pbk.: alk. paper)
1. Theology, Doctrinal — History.
2. Dogma, Development of.    I. Title.

BT21.3.H56    2015
230 — dc23

2014041180

www.eerdmans.com

In Commemoration of the 500th Anniversary
of the Posting of Luther's *Ninety-Five Theses*

*"When our Lord and Master Jesus Christ said, 'Repent,' he willed the entire life of believers to be one of repentance. . . . Away then with all those false prophets who say to the people of Christ, 'Peace, peace,' and there is no peace. Blessed be all those prophets who say to the people of Christ, 'Cross, cross,' and there is no cross. Christians should be exhorted to be diligent in following Christ, their head, through penalties, death and hell; and thus be confident of entering into heaven through many tribulations rather than through the false security of peace"*

*and*

*dedicated, in loving esteem,*
*to the apple of her father's eye.*

# Contents

# PART TWO: PNEUMATOLOGY

Contents

## PART THREE: CHRISTOLOGY

## PART FOUR: PATROLOGY

## CONCLUSION: DOXOLOGY

# Author's Preface and Acknowledgments

I am filled with gratitude for this opportunity to present to the reader my system of theology, though it is not a seamless system but rather, as discerning readers will no doubt detect, beset with the aporia that I call the "theodicy of faith," which must accompany theology this side of the Kingdom's coming. Calling it "my system" is accordingly both a confession of sin at the idiosyncrasies, known and unknown, that afflict the presentation and a plea nonetheless for grace on the part of the reader in recognizing the work's "ecumenical intention" — a term that was in vogue in the 1970s and 1980s to describe the pre-confessionalistic motive of the Augsburg Confession (to which in the ecumenically intended sense this author freely and joyfully subscribes). In any event, what I now lay before the reader is a life's work of reflection on the troubled state and future prospects in Euro-America of the message that improbably emerged out of ancient Palestine two millennia ago and is still on its journey through the nations on the way to the coming of the Beloved Community of God. Along the way, that message found a remarkable spokesperson in a talented and troubled being, Martin Luther. While I have found many other teachers of the faith, as will be amply evident in what follows, this work manifestly stands in the tradition of theological reflection within the Western Catholic Church that arose from Luther's witness to Jesus Christ. I mention these things by way of acknowledging in a preface that none of us jumps out of our own skin; we can only live in it, and through it by grace move forward to that better world which is coming, where in loving God above all, we love all of God's creatures in and under God in the Beloved Community — a notion supremely to be credited to Augustine of Hippo, in whose tradition Luther stood.

I have some more contemporaneous acknowledgments to issue here. In writing this book, I have enjoyed the criticism and discussion of a number of theological friends. Robert Jenson graciously gave his "imprimatur" to the interpretation of his work in Chapter Two. I hope that he receives my dissent from his affection for German Idealism as a worthy attempt to sustain his own pioneering effort in systematic theology. Carl Braaten patiently and persistently read through a very rough first draft of the whole and supplied me with numerous detailed suggestions, occasionally with passionate dissents, and many illuminating and helpful suggestions for improvement. I trust that he will see his influence in much of what follows as well as the missiological and eschatological themes of his own theological work everywhere at work. Christine Helmer and Dennis Bielfeldt provided important encouragement at an early stage in the composition, and my bishop, James Mauney, did likewise at a late stage in the process. R. David Nelson engaged mightily with Part Two of this work and lent me his expertise on the subtleties of Eberhard Jüngel's sacramentology and semiotics. Joe Mangina made incisive comments on Chapter Five that turned into a helpful discussion of a broader range of issues at play in this work. I hope that he finds his own work honored in the Conclusion to this book. Rob Saler read the entire draft with charity and demanded clarity in a number of obscure places; he also provided excellent bibliographical suggestions and connections, and made many useful editorial suggestions. I trust he will see the influence of his feedback throughout. It was especially gratifying to work with these younger scholars as readers and respondents during this book's composition. My Roanoke College colleagues, Gerald McDermott and James Peterson, both offered useful comments on excerpts for which I asked their opinions. My student assistant at Roanoke College, Ms. Tiara Mehic, carefully proofed the draft — though I may have added errors since she completed her work! I am grateful to all. Whatever faults remain are the author's entirely.

I recall reading somewhere in Käsemann that the entire ministry of the Apostle Paul (for whom my parents named me) was a struggle for recognition. In this respect, I can certainly identify with my apostolic namesake, even as the apostle's declaration of personal independence *coram mundo* on account of slavery to Christ in Galatians 1:10 has played a decisive role biographically in this author's formation as a theological subject. I have tried in this respect to be an imitator of the apostle. Alas, that has also meant that like Paul the Apostle I have published my theology over the years, piecemeal and haphazard, in service to the more or less immediate needs of the church communities I have served, in various, sometimes obscure places. It is an extraordinary grace to be able, now, to retrieve various fragments of my emerging system and integrate them here into the presentation now set before the readers. Accordingly, I gratefully acknowledge permission to reprint (all or in part and in altered form) the following: Paul R. Hinlicky, "Law, Gospel and Beloved Community," in *Preaching and Teaching the Law and Gospel of God* (Delhi, NY: ALPB Books, 2013), pp. 91-114; "Problems of Evil: For Julius Filo on His Sixtieth Birthday," in *V Službe Obnovy: Vedecký zborník vydaný pri príležitosti 60. Narodením Dr. h.c. prof. Th.Dr. Júliusa Fila*, ed. M. Jurík and J. Benka (Bratislava: Evanjelická bohoslovecká fakulta, Univerzita Komenského v Bratislava, 2010), pp. 65-74; "A Lutheran Contribution to the Theology of Judaism," *Journal of Ecumenical Studies* 31, no. 1-2 (Winter-Spring 1994): 123-52; "Theological Anthropology: Towards Integrating Theosis and Justification by Faith," *Journal of Ecumenical Studies* 34, no. 1 (Winter 1997): 38-73; Paul R.

Hinlicky, "The Spirit of Christ amid the Spirits of the Post-Modern World: The Crumley Lecture," *Lutheran Quarterly* 14, no. 4 (Winter 2000): 433-58; Review of Johann Anselm Steiger, "Jonas Propheta: Zur Auslegungs- und Mediengeschichte des Buches Jona bein Martin Luther und im Luthertum der Barockzeit," *Lutheran Quarterly* 26, no. 4 (Winter 2012): 453-55; Paul R. Hinlicky, "Sin, Death, and Derrida," *Lutheran Forum* 44, no. 2 (Summer 2010): 54-59; "Whose Church? Which Ministry?," *Lutheran Forum* 42, no. 4 (Winter 2008): 48-53; "Christ's Bodily Presence in the Holy Supper and Christology," *Lutheran Forum* 33, no. 4 (Winter 1999): 41-44; "Christ's Bodily Presence in the Holy Supper: Real or Symbolic?," *Lutheran Forum* 33, no. 3 (Fall 1999): 24-28; Paul R. Hinlicky, "The Doctrine of the New Birth: From Bullinger to Edwards," *Missio Apostolica* 7, no. 2 (November 1999): 102-99; "Resurrection and the Knowledge of God," *Pro Ecclesia* 4, no. 2 (Spring 1995): 226-32; "Grace and Discipleship in the Kingdom of God," *Pro Ecclesia* 4, no. 3 (Summer 1995): 356-63; "The Presence of Jesus the Christ," *Pro Ecclesia* 4, no. 4 (Fall 1995): 479-85; "Quaternity or Patrology?," *Pro Ecclesia* 23, no. 1 (Winter 2014): 46-52.

I have twice enjoyed presenting lectures before the enormous audiences of the annual Lutheran CORE/NALC Theological Conference that were later published in the above-referenced ALPB Books and are reworked into this book. I am grateful for this work of Lutheran CORE/NALC that sustains Lutheran theology with an orthodox and ecumenical intention on a narrow pathway between predominating alternatives of fundamentalism and liberalism. Though sorely tested, I remain a member of the ELCA and accordingly, the bulk of the material in Chapter Two was first presented as lectures to the Washington, D.C. Metro Synod, ELCA, gathering at Williamsburg, Virginia, October 23-25, 2012. I am grateful to Bishop Richard Graham for his invitation and the gathered pastors and other church workers for their interest and hospitality on that occasion. Since I have conceived my books of recent years as a series of studies leading up to this system of theology, I have not repeated here the detailed argumentation that backs up some of my more controversial claims, but regularly referred the reader to those texts.

With respect to inclusive language, I endorse gender inclusivity, but not gender eliminationism, with respect to our common humanity by the strategy in English of alternating the nonspecific third-person personal pronouns between he and she, him and her. With respect to the divine, I defer to the primary language of faith in the Scriptures and the ecclesiastical terminology based on it that is useful for articulating the strong Trinitarian personalism advanced in this system of theology. Those whose way forward may be blocked by an obstacle here are urged to skip ahead to the Note on Gendered Language at the end of Chapter One and the Excursus following on Perpetua and the Fatherhood of God. My intention throughout is hardly to idolize the masculine gender but to signal a specialized usage in theology for the God who is the Father of the Son in the Holy Spirit by capitalizing "Him" or "His" when pronouns are used in reference to the

Trinitarian persons. The divine nature, being nothing but a conceptual abstraction from the Three who are the Beloved Community, could be referred to in the neuter gender, as an "It." But such an alienating innovation makes too much of a pseudo-problem that is for the most part an unfortunate distraction from relevant matters, such as the strong ecumenical case for the ordination of women made in the excursus in Chapter Four or the indication of co-humanity in marriage as the structure of love working for justice in the world argued in Chapter Eight.

I am grateful to Dean Richard Smith of Roanoke College for granting me sabbatical leave in academic year 2012-13 for work on this project. As usual, the Roanoke College library and particularly Mr. Jeffrey Martin of the Interlibrary Loan Service performed magic on my behalf with efficiency and grace. I am once again happily indebted to Norman Hjelm for his work in bringing this work to the light of day and for the vote of confidence William B. Eerdmans Jr. invested in me. I am grateful to David Cottingham for his work in copyediting the book, and Jenny Hoffman and Linda Bieze of the Eerdmans staff have been a pleasure to work with. My delight of forty some years has to my delight not been *entirely* gracious about her husband's absentminded preoccupations during the time of writing this book. I am very happy now to render to her my public thanks for her patience. This book is dedicated to my daughter, Sarah Ellen Hinlicky Wilson.

*Christmas 2014*

PAUL R. HINLICKY

# Abbreviations

| | |
|---|---|
| *ANF* | *Ante-Nicene Fathers,* ed. Alexander Roberts, D.D., and James Donaldson, LL.D. (Grand Rapids: Eerdmans, 1979). |
| *BA* | Paul R. Hinlicky, *Before Auschwitz: What Christian Theology Must Learn from the Rise of Nazism* (Eugene, OR: Cascade, 2013). |
| *BC* | *The Book of Concord: The Confessions of the Evangelical Lutheran Church,* ed. Robert Kolb and Timothy J. Wengert (Minneapolis: Fortress, 2000). |
| *CD* | Karl Barth, *Church Dogmatics,* 4 volumes, 13 parts (Edinburgh: T. & T. Clark, 1974). |
| *DC* | Paul R. Hinlicky, *Divine Complexity: The Rise of Creedal Christianity* (Minneapolis: Fortress, 2010). |
| *HD* | Adolf von Harnack, *History of Dogma,* complete in seven volumes, bound as four, trans. N. Buchanan (New York: Dover, 1961). |
| *LBC* | Paul R. Hinlicky, *Luther and the Beloved Community: A Path for Christian Theology after Christendom,* with a Foreword by Mickey L. Mattox (Grand Rapids: Eerdmans, 2010). |
| *LW* | *Luther's Works: The American Edition,* 58+ volumes (St. Louis: Concordia / Philadelphia: Fortress, 1955-). |
| *NPNF* | *Nicene and Post-Nicene Fathers,* 2nd series, ed. Philip Schaff and H. Wace (Grand Rapids: Eerdmans, 1979). |
| *PNT* | Paul R. Hinlicky, *Paths Not Taken: Theology from Luther through Leibniz* (Grand Rapids: Eerdmans, 2009). |
| *RPTD* | Brent Adkins and Paul R. Hinlicky, *Rethinking Philosophy and Theology with Deleuze: A New Cartography* (London and New York: Bloomsbury Academic, 2013). |
| *SF* | Dennis Bielfeldt, Mickey Mattox, and Paul R. Hinlicky, *The Substance of the Faith: Luther's Doctrinal Theology for Today* (Minneapolis: Fortress, 2008). |
| Jenson, *ST* | Robert W. Jenson, *Systematic Theology,* 2 volumes (New York and Oxford: Oxford University Press, 1997). |

| | |
|---|---|
| Pannenberg, *ST* | *Systematic Theology,* 3 volumes, trans. G. W. Bromiley (Grand Rapids: Eerdmans, 1991-98). |
| *TCT* | Jaroslav Pelikan, *The Christian Tradition: A History of the Development of Doctrine,* 5 volumes (Chicago and London: University of Chicago Press, 1975). |
| Tillich, *ST* | Paul Tillich, *Systematic Theology,* 3 volumes (Chicago: University of Chicago Press, 1967). |
| *WA* | *D. Martin Luthers Werke, Kritische Gesamtausgabe* (Weimar: Bohlau, 1883-). |

# Introduction

Almost twenty years ago Robert W. Jenson boldly attempted to reinvent the discipline of systematic theology by calling attention to a profound anomaly: theology, the knowledge of God in the Body of Christ, becomes impossible in a divided church. For divided knowledge is no longer knowledge but the clash of partisan opinions. Consequently, theology in any form that is conceived for the purpose of perpetuating (or that even out of mere habit de facto perpetuates) the "contrastive identity" (Radner) machineries of sectarian Christianities is to be rigorously repented and purged. So far as possible, theology is now to be undertaken in a counterfactual act of faith that anticipates the eschatological unity of the Body of the risen Lord; theology ceases to be denominational or confessional or contextual and becomes radically ecumenical as also eschatological in intention.[1] In today's hindsight of the "ecumenical winter" that set in just about the time when Jenson's *Systematic Theology* appeared, his initial proposal itself seems paradoxical. How is one to know that the Body of Christ is in fact divided, if the knowledge of God, by which one would make such a judgment, has itself become uncertain under the conditions of the divided church?

The difficulty in view here is the same one evident at the heart of the 2003 *Princeton Proposal for Christian Unity*, a document sponsored by the Center for Catholic and Evangelical Theology under the directorship of Jenson with his colleague, Carl Braaten. In calling the churches back to the doctrinal discipline of the undivided church of the post-apostolic era, we read the following diagnosis: "In every separated community the temptation has been to base the community's life on its 'distinctives,' that is, on the features of its faith and life that differentiate it from other Christian communities. The apostolic faith confessed in the ecumenical creeds, intended to differentiate the church from truly spurious 'Christian' communities, is pushed to the margins of communal self-description."[2] "Truly

---

1. Jenson, *ST* 1, p. vii.
2. *In One Body Through the Cross: The Princeton Proposal for Christian Unity,* ed. Carl E. Braaten and Robert W. Jenson (Grand Rapids: Eerdmans, 2003), p. 39.

spurious"? The *petitio principii* contained in this statement is obvious: How do we discriminate the "truly spurious" from the authentically "Christian" without continuing in theology by way of critical judgments on Christian identity, as instantiated in the very "ecumenical creeds" to which appeal was here made? In that case, however, must we not ask whether semi-Arian Origenists and Marcellian modalists, Nestorians and Monophysites, were not *victims* of the classical theological way that made judgments? Were not putatively "Christian" communities divided on the basis of "ecumenical" or "orthodox" distinctives that on examination are just as partisan as the presumably less worthy "denominational" distinctives that are dividing Christian communities today? On the other hand, if for the sake of the gospel and the true unity of the church in the gospel, we cannot in fact avoid making such "divisive" judgments of doctrine, then or now, must we not discover "in, with, and under" the sinfully divided church (then as now) access to the knowledge of God by which to make such judgments? If so, the question for the project of reinventing systematic theology that Jenson attempted is only whether we can do just this work of discriminating judgment better than we have heretofore. That requires much greater clarity today about the epistemic access of the theological subject than has been the case, even in self-consciously "orthodox" and "ecumenical" circles, heretofore.

Owning up to this difficulty, the present effort continues in Jenson's project. Indeed, the reasons that moved him then are still pressing, if not more so today. Yet this system of theology continues in the project at the cost of revisions from the way Jenson conducted his experiment, which may make it doubtful that what follows is continuous with his own endeavor. Specifically, it is not the case, according to the present effort, that theology in the tradition of Luther[3] "either would deny the name of church to all but [those of] his or her own allegiance or desecrate the theological enterprise."[4] And because this is not true of theology in the tradition of Luther, it is also not true of any theology that intends orthodoxy, that is, teaching that walks true to the gospel (Gal. 2:14) whether in the tradition of Calvin, or of Augustine or of Thomas, or of Athanasius and the Cappadocians — even as I shall try to show (at least representatively) in what follows, of a Menno Simons or a Theodore of Mopsuestia. Jenson, if I may put it this way, got ahead of himself (and many others) with too draconian a cleavage between the broken churches as in simple and obvious contradiction to the one, true (just so, *eschatological*) church that is the total Christ. Readers will recognize how much the present work derives by way of intention and example from Jenson's *Systematic Theology*. This makes our differences — few though they are (aside from differences of style and intellectual orientation that arise from being separated by a generation) — interesting and perhaps also significant.

---

3. I have tried to show how this revision of Lutheran "confessionalism" is possible in *SF*, pp. 1-10, 134-52.

4. Jenson, *ST* 1, p. vii.

The conflicted discipline of systematic theology today is torn between two epistemic requirements: one is the rational demand for a truthful acknowledgment of historical and contextual particularity, and the other is the equally rational demand for systematicity, i.e., internal coherence as also coherence with other truths to which theologians hold. "Dogma" and "system" are terms that correspond to these two demands respectively; each term has a correspondingly suspect aura in the eyes of the other. "Dogma" denotes the positivity of the particular, no matter whether we take the particular in theology as revealed truth (the "deposit of faith") or facts ("the historical Jesus") or contextual requirements (Bruce Fairchild Barton's 1925 "The Man That Nobody Knows," contextually rendering Jesus as Salesman to a gilded age, if I may use this admittedly flippant example). "System" denotes the general, the essence of the phenomena, or the logic by which ideas relate coherently to each other, again, no matter whether we take the system in theology as God's self-knowledge revealed and shared with creatures, or the pattern of development discerned in the history of salvation, or an agenda for humanization set by the progress of secular history. At worst, dogmatics revels in the chaos of pure experience according to a preference and selection from its manifold that can only be subjectively asserted, not warranted; systematicity, equally at its worst, forces all evidence, biblical and experiential, into the Procrustean bed of its own privileged insight or a priori scheme or totalizing logic. Ironically, both end in cul-de-sacs — the first in dogmatism, the second in ideology. In either case, theology suffers *rigor mortis.* The first demand leaves the world to the devil for the sake of purity and erects strong borders against the outside world. The second resolves the faith into the existing world for the sake of the unity of truth. Neither side succeeds in walking true to the gospel's claim to truth (Gal. 2:14). The would-be "purity" of the positive is always betrayed by hidden acts of selection that arbitrarily privilege some over other items and so construct its dogmas; the unity of truth aspired to in the system is likewise always betrayed as someone-in-particular's unification of truths. The question of epistemic access is left in obscurity in either case. It is to be stressed in the debased climate of today that both so-called "liberal" and so-called "conservative" theologies can fall on either side of this fault line. Indeed, the binary liberal-conservative in this respect is itself highly misleading. Conflicts in theology between locals trying to preserve community against the acids of criticism and cosmopolitans trying to force idiosyncratic forms of life into an assigned place in a conceptual totality and universal language alike betray theology into purposes that are not genuinely theological. The purpose of theology is to know God. "Critical dogmatics," as this author conceives his own "reinvention" of systematic theology, is an intentional effort to leave this debilitating syndrome with its accustomed binaries behind.

Two little notes already now, then, by way of introduction about the kinds of argumentation found in what follows. First, newcomers to systematic theology are often put off by what reads to them as but strings of apodictic assertion, that is, lofty announcements abstractly asserting identities and relationships by means of the verb "to be." To make up an example that only slightly caricatures: "God *is* unknowable. But to know God as unknowable *is* itself to know something important about God. What we know is that God *is* beyond objectification, so we cannot make an object of Him and use Him for our purposes. That God does not let Himself be used for our purposes *is* itself a revelation of the true deity of God. But as a theological formulation, even the insight that the true God is unknowable *is* in danger of being treated as a piece of objective information like other information. . . ." So an argument in theology seems to circle back around on itself in the end; it then goes on to repeat the same circle in ever-growing subtlety. Yet the newcomer is well advised to get used to this kind of argumentation and to understand what is going on in such apparently vacuous circles of predication, lacking any action verbs, when it proves fruitful and illuminating. What is going on, if we do not lose sight of the thing in the world under discussion, is *analytical* argumentation, i.e., argument that works to unpack dense and apparently nonsensical assertions about something in the world from the tradition of theological discourse (such as, "God is unknowable") by teasing out its implications ("we know God as unknowable") by patient, hence also tedious analysis. Much of systematic theology operates in this argumentative fashion, making explicit what lies packed within the dense assertions of faith received from the Bible and Christian experience.

Second, there is another feature that often puts off newcomers to systematic theology, namely, its technical vocabulary. Because systematic theology receives its material in the form of the aforementioned "dense assertions" from the Bible and Christian experience, like, say, "God is the Father almighty," or "His Son is Jesus Christ our Lord," or "the Spirit who is holy is the Spirit of the aforementioned Father and Son," it inherits also its own long tradition of "in-house" technical language that developed in order efficiently to analyze the material and debate the problems given with it. Of course, some of this traditional ecclesiastical terminology may encode profound error and may prejudice inquiry in misleading ways. The terminology provides at most a normed norm *(norma normata),* subject always to the test whether it illuminates the thing itself (the *norma normans,* the norming norm), namely, the gospel of God. On top, then, of acquiring literacy in Scripture, this ecclesiastical vocabulary with its questionable utility must simply be mastered to achieve fluency, let alone competency in theology. Just like law and medicine in the Western tradition, this specialized theological dictionary is composed of Latin terms and phrases, as just illustrated;[5] these technical terms are used in what follows, with an English translation provided in parentheses upon the first appearance of any term or phrase.

Upon reading a systematic theology, the reader should be left hungering and thirsting for more. That is so for two reasons. First, systematic theology is largely

---

5. An invaluable aid is Richard A. Muller, *Dictionary of Latin and Greek Theological Terms: Drawn Principally from Protestant Scholastic Theology* (Grand Rapids: Baker Academic, 1985).

concerned with putting a toolkit together for knowing God in the practices of Christian life.[6] While theology is also a practice of Christian life, so that knowing God occurs in the study of theology, theology is rightly focused on epistemic concerns that cannot, and should never be thought to, substitute for the holistic practices of Christian life, such as hearing the sermon as from the Lord, or joining the Eucharist to commune with Christ and His saints, or pastoral conversation and mutual consolation, or prayer, personal and communal, that is bold to address the King of the Universe as "our Father," or works of mercy, or lives of love at work in structuring justice in hope for the world, and so on. Systematic theology seeks to clarify and better enable such practices, but learning about them is no substitute for practicing them. If systematic theology succeeds, it makes readers hungry to use its tools for better living the Christian life in these manifold ways of knowing God.

Second, the production of a system of theology, it seems, can intend one of two purposes, depending upon the assessment of the spiritual situation in a missiological context. Either it intends a consolidation of existing perspectives and practices, or it intends a paradigm shift in the discipline that institutes a series of practical reforms and provokes a new research program. As announced above, in following Jenson's lead, the latter is the intention of the present endeavor. Jenson's great innovation was totally to dispense with the traditional rubric in systematic theology, *De Deo* (concerning God as such). He regarded consideration of "God as such" the Trojan Horse of the "unbaptized" deity of Greek metaphysics making its way undetected into Christian theology that ought instead arrive at its conception of this most basic and important term in theology, "God," strictly and rigorously from the gospel by which God introduces Himself to human beings as the Father of the Son in the Holy Spirit. The present effort continues in Jenson's path here in that it offers no special chapter, not only regarding God as such, but also on the Trinity as such (unless we take the Conclusion of this book as such a chapter).

There are two reasons for this. First, "Trinity" is an abstract term for, a conceptualization of, the Father of the Son in the Spirit whom we meet in the gospel. The danger of treating "the Trinity" as such is the danger of turning this abstraction into a thing in itself. This is a danger for a number of reasons. In terms of the organization of a systematic theology, it is a danger because when we treat the Trinity as a thing in itself, the chapter on it in the system does, as it were, all the work in settling upon a concept. The ironic result is that we then go on in other chapters to discuss other topics, leaving the Trinity behind. Rather, we intend that the doctrine of the Trinity permeate the whole presentation so that the whole range of topics discussed in theology should be formed and illumined by it. That means in turn that the entire work is a presentation of the doctrine of the Trinity.

---

6. For a rich survey, see *Inquiring after God: Classical and Contemporary Readings,* ed. Ellen T. Charry (Malden, MA: Blackwell, 2000).

This system's doctrine of the Trinity can only be understood in taking it in as a whole, culminating, then, in the concluding chapter. Second, there is at work in what follows another decision arising for similar reasons as the first, namely, to treat the Reformation's "chief article" of Justification by Faith in the same way. In this presentation, Justification by Faith does not get a separate chapter (nor does its cognate doctrine, the proper distinction of "Law and Gospel"). The reason is that this teaching should be (1) integrated with the doctrine of the Trinity, so that (2) it too is at work through the whole range of the topics discussed in theology. The separated treatment of the article on Justification, which forces an abstract polarization between imputative and effective righteousness, in other words, is part and parcel of the contrastive identity machinery of divided Christianity. The decision, then, to treat Justification integrally leads to the chief innovation of presentation in this system of theology, namely, to begin with the Third Article of the Creed and its provision of epistemic access and move, so to say, backwards to the First Article so that it is clear from the outset all the way to the conclusion that it is "faith, that gift of the Holy Spirit" (Luther) that forms the theological subject to know Jesus Christ and confess Him as the Son before His Father who is in heaven. In this formulation, moreover, the integration of the doctrines of justification and of the Trinity is succinctly indicated.

Tedious discussions of theological method, to be sure, have done more to destroy interest in theology than any other invention of academic theology. But so also have the traditional theological polemics of the "brutal" (Radner) Christian past and present that our modern preoccupation with method arose to overcome, already with scholasticism as we shall discuss in detail in connection with Anselm of Canterbury. One must grant this much to the modern preoccupation, tedious as it is: methodological self-consciousness in theology aims critically to disallow irresponsible talk about God, of which the religion-weary world is all too full. Even so, as a young theologian once confided to me: "I decided to study theology to learn about God, but all I was taught was what other theologians thought and how they thought — not even necessarily about God." Necessary evil in this respect that discussion of method is — thrice removed from the matter itself as systematic reflection on the practical reflection organic to the Word of God received in faith in its mission to the nations — the reader who is urgently and existentially interested in the *matter* of theology in distinction from its method may well defer the reading of Chapter One and proceed at once to Chapter Two. But that reader might also brave reading from Chapter One the subsection "The Cognitive Claim," which for heuristic reasons succinctly foreshadows the work as a whole by exploring its basic thesis or claim to truth. That reading may provide enough theological meat to fortify resolve for the continued slog through the methodological discussions in the remainder of Chapter One. One will in any case eventually have to return to these "preliminary questions." For theology today must give an account of what hope survives after full post-Christendom acknowledgment of the brutalities of our hitherto fractious unities (Radner). In just this difficult way, theology takes responsibility before our neighbors, and before God, for the manifestly dangerous act of speaking of God. That is what is at stake in discussions of theological method.

Regarding theological polemics, however, one must sharply distinguish between *ad hominem,* i.e., personal, attacks that substitute for an argument by distracting from evidence and logic given in support of a claim to truth with attacks on persons, and *critique,* the best of which rigorously advances the argument about the claim to truth by a profounder appeal to the common matter that is of concern to all in an argument. *Ad hominem* is not only a logical fallacy; it is sinful and a disgrace upon the matter that concerns theology, the coming of the Beloved Community.[7] Because in theology it is not only a matter of an author's scholarly reputation, however, but also religiously of what Paul Tillich called one's "ultimate concern," it is not always easy in the thrall of theological passion to respect this important distinction in practice, as George Lindbeck famously illustrated with his parable of the Crusader who yelps "Jesus is Lord" as he lops off the head of the infidel.[8] As "responsible talk about God" (Jüngel), theology cannot suffer such fools gladly, who speak irresponsibly and hence destructively of God; but neither can it suffer another kind of fool, the coward who remains silent when testimony of God is required. Thus theological science is and must be "critical" dogmatics (precisely not "dogmatism") in that the subjectivity of repentance and faith can never be taken for granted but must constantly be questioned and put to the test, as it is the very place in the world of theology's epistemic access; indeed, when repentance and faith are taken for granted as the secured possession of a human habit, theology transforms into religious ideology and becomes blasphemous self-justification, no matter how "orthodox" it claims to be. The method of theology (Part One) in the acquisition of theological subjectivity (Part Two) to know the object of theology (Part Three) in timely confession in the world before the audience of theology (Part Four) thus structures the presentation of this system of theology.

Finally, by way of introduction, let us now sketch out in advance the course that lies before us. Part One of this work treats the problem of the knowledge of God and the nature of the theological discipline in two chapters. In Chapter One theology is defined as critical dogmatics; this terminology intends to locate the present proposal on knowing God beyond the characteristic modern alternative of arbitrary and authoritarian dogmatism on the one side and the loss of classical and substantive content to the demand for systematic rationality on the other. It achieves this new location for theology by arguing that theology as critical dogmatics sustains a single cognitive claim regarding the identification of God for the

7. See the Appendix, "The Problem of Demonization in Luther's Apocalyptic Theology," *LBC,* pp. 379-85.

8. George A. Lindbeck, *The Nature of Doctrine: Religion and Theology in a Postliberal Age* (Philadelphia: Westminster, 1984), p. 66. See *SF,* pp. 182-83.

interpretation of experience on the way to the Beloved Community. This claim to truth is provisionally warranted by the principle of parsimony in that it accounts for the greatest data with the simplest and thus most elegant explanation. Contextual considerations — themselves constructed by the foregoing claim regarding the knowledge of God and in turn reinforcing its plausibility — depict the spiritual and intellectual situation in Euro-America today. The claim here is that theology is undertaken in a complex and uncertain situation that may be described as both post-Christendom and postmodern. How this difficult situation provides a new opportunity for theology to retrieve and advance the scriptural, patristic, and Reformation legacies is explored in Chapter Two. It develops preliminary clarifications of basic terms and concepts in theology taken up already in Chapter One. It asks a series of questions about the possibility of God, the necessity of Christ, the faith that justifies, and the power of the Scriptures to sanctify. This inquiry establishes the sense of certain usages peculiar to this system of theology and also of traditional notions deployed in sometimes-unfamiliar ways.

The treatment of the doctrine of the Spirit in Part Two of this work likewise divides into two chapters. The first inquiry into theological subjectivity requires select but detailed probes into the history of this controverted topic in order to establish the thesis that it consists not in baptismal signification alone nor in religious experience as such, but in baptismal union with, and so conformation to, the crucified and risen Jesus Christ. This union occurs by the Spirit's unification of watery tomb and the Word concerning Jesus' cross and resurrection. The second chapter in this part on the Spirit as Creator God permits more succinct and systematic argumentation for recognition of the Spirit's work in rendering theological subjectivity as that is grounded in the Spirit's immanent role in the life of the Three as the Unifier in love of the Father and the Son, the Sealer of their Beloved Community.

The Holy Spirit in time unifies the sign, the man Jesus of Nazareth, with the thing signified, the eternal Son of God, the Christ of Israel in order to create repentance and nurture faith in God the heavenly Father in those to whom, and for whom, Jesus comes in the Word and sacraments concerning Him. This work of the Spirit first becomes manifest in the anointing of Jesus at His baptism that he perform faithfully His messianic calling, although it was intimated already from conception by His birth from Mary *Theotokos* (bearer of God). As anointed in the Spirit, hence as "the Anointed One," the "Messiah" of Israel, Jesus is the subject of faith. It is He who in the power of the Spirit believed in God the heavenly Father on behalf of those to whom, and for whom, He came. The faith that forms the latter as a believer thus comes by the same Spirit through baptism into Christ's baptism of the cross and resurrection; in this way the Spirit creates the theological subject to live the life of Jesus by believing the faith of Jesus. Thus baptism by water and the Spirit is the unification of the believer with Spirit-anointed Jesus as faith in His vindicated faith. As baptism is a union of water and the Word by the Spirit, the theological subject is itself a union of sign and thing signified by the Spirit in a variety of connections: of sinner and the new birth, of believer and the Body of Christ, of this groaning earth of the common body and the coming of the Beloved Community in the redemption of our bodies.

The Holy Spirit unifies the sign and the thing signified in the world, whether for faith or for offense, on the way to the coming of the Beloved Community. The Spirit fittingly performs this work in time and space, in that within the divine and eternal life the Spirit unifies in love the Son, who is the image and expression of His Father, with the Father, who is His origin and prototype. While this personal unification in love by the Spirit comes "naturally," so to say, that is, spontaneously within the eternal and divine life, the incarnation of the Son by the Spirit into the likeness of sinful flesh precipitates a crisis in the life of God that, if the gospel is to be believed, the same Spirit at length resolves and conciliates by the resurrection of the Crucified Son from the dead. In His temporal and spatial coming from the Father and His vindicated Son, accordingly, the Spirit in mission to the nations unifies the sign and the thing signified in the justification of the ungodly by faith, the new obedience of justified sinners, the gathering of the ecclesia from the nations in and for the mission of the gospel, and at last the resurrection to eternal life at the eschaton of judgment. Until the eschaton of judgment, this unifying work of the Holy Spirit to sanctify the profane conflicts with unholy spirits that would separate what God joins together. Until the eschaton of judgment, the Spirit who is holy is only known in this mortal combat of the Word incarnate against pseudo-prophets and false messiahs that are false in separating what the Spirit unites.

As with the previous two parts of this work, Christology divides into two chapters. The first inquiry into theological objectivity requires select, but detailed probes into the history of theological objectivity to establish the thesis that it consists not in the ultimately vacuous affirmation of "real presence," let alone the unintelligible affirmation of "symbolic presence," but consists in the bread of the Eucharist as the body of Christ, when and where the Spirit unifies the sign and the thing signified for repentance and faith (or negatively, for offense in the *manducatio indignorum* — the "eating of the unworthy"). The second inquiry in Chapter Six undertakes systematic argumentation for the Christological thesis of a Cyrilian Christ for Augustinian humanity. Jesus Christ can be for us the unity of the sign and the thing signified in the world on the way to the coming of the Beloved Community because within the divine and eternal life the Son is the image of His Father, who is His origin and prototype. The Son corresponds to the Father in receiving His being from Him and returning to the Father the filial sacrifice of thanksgiving that in turn acknowledges the Father as Father. The correspondence of the Father and the Son in the Spirit is the dynamic unity of love that as such constitutes the one being of the Three as an eternal becoming in relation. So it is true to say that the Son incarnate for us is the objectivity of divine love and thus the object of faith to which the theological subject adheres. As this kind of objectivity — of the person who receives and returns love in community — the Son of God's coming in the flesh inaugurates the Beloved Community and works the creation's redemption. In this temporal and spatial advent, He comes as prophet who proclaims the imminent reign of God. He comes as priest in the decision of the man Jesus Christ to take responsibility for us before God. His earthly obedience grounds the justification of the ungodly just as His heavenly intercession works the faith and new obedience of justified sinners in the gathering of the ecclesia from the nations that is becoming the righteousness of God in the world. At the last Christ comes as judge of the living and the dead and king of creation. Until the eschaton of judgment, this work of Jesus Christ the Son of God battles structures of malice and injustice, not with sword of steel, but by Word and Spirit.

As previously, Patrology divides into two chapters. The first inquiry into the audience of theology requires a theological exposition of the faith of Jesus in the heavenly Father, given in the form of the "Lord's Prayer." This prayer, it is argued, forms the conscience of theology. But this conscience before the Father who sees in secret is not to be understood in moralistic fashion, like a Freudian superego. As faith in the reconciled God of Hosea 11:9, as faith in the Father, then, who is personally God surpassing God, it is the conscientious faith of Jesus in His own messianic mission as the Son sent from His Father to bear away the sin of the world that love might prevail in creating a community of love. The faith of Jesus is faith, we may say, in the conscience of God that will be revealed in His judgment of mercy at the eschaton of judgment. The second inquiry of this part in Chapter Eight turns to systematic argumentation for the Patrological thesis of God surpassing God in the work of creation destined for redemption and fulfillment.

As formed by the Spirit, the theological subject who knows the object, Jesus Christ the Son of God, publicly acknowledges or confesses this event before the Father on the way to the coming of the Beloved Community. This acknowledgment takes place in the world but before the Father, who is the audience of it. Confession of the faith is the church's first and foundational act of conscientious responsibility to God for the world. Theology itself is fundamentally misunderstood when these relationships are reversed, however, as if theology were responsible to the world for God. Not only is the latter pretension quite impossible ontologically, in the hubris of such an attempt theology can only end in despair, as may be observed in the deep agnosticism and creeping atheism penetrating the churches of Euro-America today. The shrill stridency of reaction testifies to the same anxiety, that somehow theology must justify God, or Christian faith in God, when in reality authentic faith justifies God in His judgment, as the eschaton of judgment, and in this spirit of penitence knows that its own talk about God must be justified by God, hence ventured conscientiously. Confusion on these relations is the deep reason why a division of the existing divisions is coming to purify the remnant of Christianity in Euro-America. Karl Barth's claim that the "first and basic act of theological work is *prayer*"[9] limns this division of the divisions that is

---

9. Karl Barth, *Evangelical Theology: An Introduction* (New York: Holt, Rinehart & Winston, 1963), p. 160.

coming in that it makes theology accountable to the Father of Jesus Christ, which accountability or its denial is precisely what is at issue in the conflicted discipline of theology today.

In any case, prayerful and conscientious responsibility to God for our speech about God in and for the world in obedience to the divine command not to take the name of the LORD in vain is possible because in Jesus Christ God the eternal Father has become our Father too. He becomes so by speaking to us by His Son's resurrection from the dead for us and sending the Spirit of the resurrection to re-form us accordingly. Theology that is not such "responsible speech about God" has no warranted claim to a hearing in communities that would claim the name "Christian." Such theologies do not intend orthodoxy.

As God the Father is the eternal origin of the Son and the Spirit, He is also the goal, Omega as well as Alpha.[10] In the Spirit the Son eternally returns to the Father giving Him the praise of His deity and the glory of His self-surpassing, merciful, and compassionate paternity.[11] As this kind of audience — of the person who freely sends and then joyfully receives love's return in community — God the Father is the eschaton of judgment that makes all things new in the coming of the Beloved Community. In the temporal and spatial beginning from the origin by the divine decree for the sending of the Son to sow, and the reaping of His harvest in the Spirit, God the Father originates the world in a word of command and blessing. This divine command and blessing remain as both a holy demand against usurping structures of malice and injustice and as inviolable promise that continuously issues in creative works of love in justice already now. Until the eschaton of judgment, the Almighty Father makes His rain to fall upon the just and the unjust alike. This hiddenness of His reign is the deep trial of faith in history.

God the Father is God surpassing God, the font of divinity within the eternal life who gives His own being in generating the Son and breathing the Spirit, infinitely to become Father in receiving the Son by the return of the Spirit in personal love. The Son and the Spirit form with the Father the whole to which the Father as person belongs and to which He also answers. The Father is responsible to the Son in the Spirit, thus for sending the Son into the world and anointing Jesus at His baptism with the Spirit to bring near in merciful words and deeds His own approaching reign against its usurpation by structures of malice and injustice. The resurrection of the crucified Son Jesus Christ from the dead, as the Father's self-surpassing transit from the wrath of love to the mercy of love, is the conscientious deed of the Father, who recognized His own love in His

10. It will be noted that in making this claim I am breaking from Jenson's idealist interpretation of the self-consciousness of the Trinity that makes the Spirit God the goal of His own being.

11. On this matter, with Pannenberg on the kingdom of *God* (*ST* 3, pp. 527-646), even though his case is not patrologically specific enough, and against Jenson's idea of the Spirit as the imminent futurity of God, as Omega to the Father's Alpha (e.g., *ST* 2, p. 339), although his reason for this speculation in the idea that there are a whither and whence, that is to say, a sequence as well as alterity in the divine life, I emphatically affirm.

Son's love for the world fallen into sinfulness, dead and buried in solidarity with the ungodly. Resolving Athanasius' "divine dilemma," the conscience of God the Father resolves for mercy and by mercy to prevail over wrath to bring about the Beloved Community. In conclusion, the Beloved Community is exposited as the Day of Judgment that forever excludes the excluders and separates the separators; that reveals the co-equal and eternal Trinity; and thus communicates to each, as harmonized with all others, a place in the eternal life of the eternal Trinity.

That suffices by way of prolepsis in a series of "dense assertions" to sketch the whole course before us now to be patiently elaborated in what follows.

# PART ONE

# Prolegomena

To know God is to enter by repentance and faith into the self-donation of the Son by the self-communication of the Spirit for new life before the self-surpassing Father of the Son on whom he breathes the Spirit.

# CHAPTER ONE

# The Knowledge of God

## The Discipline of Theology as Critical Dogmatics

Ostensibly theology is about God and about all that is not God, taken as God's creatures and "created," as Martin Luther taught in the text that best represents his own "systematic" teaching,[1] in order that God "might redeem us and make us holy . . . [by] his Son and Holy Spirit, through whom he brings us to himself."[2] Such a conception of theology is at once critical and dogmatic: critical because it *must,* and dogmatic because it *can,* discern the creative, redeeming, and fulfilling actions of God at work in the world. Yet such a conception of theology cannot be taken for granted today. Perhaps it could never have been taken for granted. While the term "theology" means knowledge of God, historically speaking theology is a contested discipline that like philosophy[3] (or perhaps as part of philosophy!)[4] is always arguing about its nature and task. And perhaps this is so because any substantive proposal in theology inevitably ventures a claim about the discipline itself, about its task and method — and vice versa, any claim about theological method betrays substantive dogmatic commitments.[5] In such a contested, not to say conflicted situation, any theology that wants to be responsible to critical readers has to launch its presentation by locating its proposal in the whirl of controversy, old and new, that attends any who dare to speak before God in the world about God in relation to the world. That is the supposition and task of these initial chapters of Part One on preliminary

---

1. On the ecclesial setting of theology and its nature as "catechetical systematics" for Luther, see Oswald Bayer, *Theology the Lutheran Way,* ed. and trans. Jeffrey G. Silcock and Mark C. Mattes (Grand Rapids: Eerdmans, 2007), pp. 65-74.

2. Martin Luther, "The Large Catechism," in *BC,* pp. 439-64.

3. John McCumber, *Time in the Ditch: American Philosophy and the McCarthy Era* (Evanston, IL: Northwestern University Press, 2001).

4. See the instructive study of Adam Drozdek, *Greek Philosophers as Theologians: The Divine Arche* (Aldershot, UK and Burlington, VT: Ashgate, 2007).

5. Jenson, *ST* 1, p. 3.

considerations *(prologoumena)* in systematic theology, or, as I prefer to put it, *critical dogmatics.*

Judging from the literature, it can seem today that Christian theology is metaphysics or art. That is, theology is presented as putative knowledge of the protological conditions for the possibility of the visible world, as in metaphysics, discovering the divine *arche* (principle of origin).[6] Or theology is presented as the construction of symbols giving expression to human experience of the ineffable ground or holy source, as in art. Certainly Christian theology shares a common world — or more primitively, what I will call in the following, a "common body" — with such metaphysical and aesthetic inquiries. Thus, theology as a discipline bears "family resemblances" to their claims and corresponding disciplines. For, like the metaphysical quest for the principle of origin of the cosmos or the religious need to figure the sacred grounding of human existence, Christian theology also speaks of the origin when it thinks of the eternal Father of the Son in the Spirit who becomes the Creator of all that is not God in the act of initiating and continuing our time-space as His creation.

According to the present proposal, however, ecumenical Christian theology in its substantive intention is not only, or even primarily, focused on origins and grounds, but rather pragmatically[7] and hermeneutically[8] on the identification of the God *of the gospel* for the purposes of public confession of and knowing collaboration in His approaching reign.[9] "We do not in any unmediated way have the gospel that we are to speak; we have it only as we receive it. . . . Theology is an act of *interpretation:* it begins with a received word and issues in a new word essentially related to the old word. Theology's question is always: In that we have heard and seen such-and-such discourse as gospel, what shall we now say and do that the gospel may again be spoken?"[10] Jenson characteristically spoke of the identification of God in the maelstrom of experience. What follows next attempts to bring out not only the acknowledged hermeneutical method but also epistemically pragmatic features implied by it (in some critical distance from Jenson's more idealistic proclivities).

---

6. See above, note 4.

7. *SF,* pp. 131-90.

8. The turn of pragmatism in a hermeneutical direction was a path not generally taken but attempted by Josiah Royce, *The Problem of Christianity* (Washington, DC: Catholic University of America Press, 2001), pp. 273-342. On an approach to theological hermeneutics that is congruent with the present effort, see Jens Zimmermann, *Recovering Theological Hermeneutics: An Incarnational-Trinitarian Theory of Interpretation* (Grand Rapids: Baker Academic, 2004). See also Monica Vilhauer, *Gadamer's Ethics of Play: Hermeneutics and the Other* (Lanham, MD: Rowman & Littlefield, 2010).

9. One may note in this sentence the deliberate use of the masculine pronoun, Him, in reference to God. For an accounting of this usage, see the note, "Gendered Language," at the end of this chapter (pp. 84-87) and the appendix to it on *Perpetua and the Fatherhood of God* (pp. 87-93).

10. Jenson, *ST,* 1, p. 14.

Pragmatism here designates an epistemic approach that is rigorously located "in the middle of things," barred from seeing (Greek: *theoria*) either origin or eschaton, but proceeding step by step from the unknown past into the unknown future with the best, i.e., most comprehensive and coherent, account of experience from across the broadest possible spectrum. Hermeneutics here means a style of argument that, while not despising but rather appropriating the logical rigor and precision afforded by more analytical modes of reasoning, holds that theological discourse as historically mediated by tradition from the inaugurating event in time and space can neither be appropriated, understood, critiqued, nor extended apart from probing inquiry into the history of the debate that the cognitive claim to truth has inaugurated. Since any contemporary understanding is itself historically situated, motivated by the concerns of the conscientious interpreter both for the truth-claim contained in the legacy and for its intelligible transmission and application in the present, tradition is just this debate, what MacIntyre once called an "embodied argument."[11] Only dead traditionalism presents its material as a fixed, finished deposit to be preserved from the erosion of time. Thus the form of argumentation in what follows will involve selective, but at times extended probes into the history of doctrinal topics as matters of contemporary theological import along the lines of David Friedrich Strauss's observation that the history of doctrine is its own criticism.

The notion of "interpretation" calls for further initial comment here. Hegel demonstrated in the opening chapters of the *Phenomenology of Spirit* that any act of understanding that would go beyond reporting sheer sense certainty to say something to others involves the construction of an object by the aid of acts of memory organized in language that enable recognition of the phenomena in the sequence of time transcending the moment of sense certainty. In this way the object of sense is taken to persist through time despite the momentary evidences of its perceived movements and relations; thus its future can be projected. Such acts of memory presuppose, however, communities formed by language by which this construction is made; hence cognition has a tacit, often unnoticed but essentially social character. Interpretation is always interpretation by a subject of an object for an audience. Taking something as true in understanding *is* discovering an object that can be verbalized or mathematized to others who can so receive and understand, test and predict. It was Charles Sanders Peirce who teased out this social nature of interpretation in language, and it was Josiah Royce who explicitly formalized the process and named it hermeneutics. Any claim to truth, i.e., any cognitive construction of an object by a subject for others is thus a socially-linguistically embedded act of interpreting the common body's sense experience in the here and now by binding past recollection with future expectation in and for communities of interpretation.

11. Alasdair MacIntyre, *After Virtue: A Study in Moral Theory* (Notre Dame: University of Notre Dame Press, 1984), pp. 216-22.

If Hegel was right at least about this, the hermeneutical procedure is not merely a method for the *studia humanitatis* (as we tend to think from Heidegger and Gadamer) but it holds in all forms of human understanding, from the natural sciences to theology. As Kuhn famously demonstrated,[12] science too is the practice of a human interpretive community, with its own history, traditions, dogmas, paradigm shifts, even revolutions, which consists in the construction of a particular object, namely the "natural" world in some particular aspect or domain of inquiry. Theology and natural science will not be differentiated in this formal way of hermeneutical understanding. Theology too is the practice of a human community in just the same way, constituted by the construction of its particular object, namely (in respect to its overlap with science), the same natural world that science knows, taken now from faith for faith as "creature" of God. If this is so, contemporary knowledge of the natural world is not the victory of a triumphant advance of untrammeled rationality over traditional prejudices by pure attention to things in one's own individual bedrock-certain sense experience (as Locke influentially imagined, especially for Anglo-American understandings of science). Rather, contemporary understandings are the ever-tested and often-contested product of a history of contending constructions of the meaning of things on many levels in various aspects in which science and faith overlap and intersect in both scientists and theologians, not infrequently one and the same person.

Christian theology, reflecting and expressing the gospel which elicits it, is an eschatological and missiological way of thinking about God and only as such also a doctrine about origins and symbolizations. Indeed its peculiar claims are subject finally to the triune God's own — critical — verification or, as the case may be if this belief proves false, the disconfirmation of nonconfirmation. Theology never transcends this riskiness of faith in the putative Word of God that inaugurates its inquiry. Its knowledge is the knowledge of risky faith. But risky faith is not blind. It can know and critically discern the God of the gospel. In the interim theological claims to knowledge of God, and of His creatures in light of the knowledge of God in the gospel, are subject in pragmatic fashion to the tests of coherence with other beliefs that we hold to be true on the basis of their demonstrated capacity to organize affects (that is, bodily experience, the experience of the common body) in the purposes of life. They are subject as well to the hermeneutical test of fidelity to the authorizing source — namely, the gospel in which Jesus Christ is believed to be truly present in faith for us (Luther: *in ipsa fide Christus adest*)[13] to do His redemptive work in us as well as for us. This context and this sourcing together always locate Christian theology somewhere and sometime in the inau-

---

12. Thomas S. Kuhn, *The Structure of Scientific Revolutions,* 2nd edition, enlarged (Chicago: University of Chicago Press, 1973).

13. Tuomo Mannermaa, *Der im Glauben Gegenwärtige Christus: Rechtfertigung und Vergottung zum ökumenischen Dialog,* Arbeiten zur Geschichte und Theologie des Luthertums, n.s. 8 (Hannover: Lutherisches Verlagshaus, 1989).

gurating gospel's mission to the nations out of which, in which, and for the sake of which theology exists. The first of these truth conditions demands humility of theologians and the second rigor.

Christian theology, then, may resemble but it is neither metaphysical speculation nor figurative construction. It is a rigorous, autonomous "science" (T. F. Torrance),[14] *fides quaerens intellectum* (Barth following Anselm),[15] "faith seeking understanding," *ut confiteamur* (Bayer),[16] "that we may confess" God in His Name against "the world, the devil and our sinful selves" (Luther) in the obedient life of eschatological expectation for the coming of the Beloved Community (Romans 8). Such faith "comes by hearing" (Rom. 10:17). If such faith knows what it believes, moreover, it knows that its path in the world is divinely fated from the outset to endure the trial of faith in Jesus and in this trial to find final vindication only in Jesus' vindication at His *Parousia* (public appearance) at the resurrection of the dead. Just that shared fate with Jesus, however, indicates the chief end and true audience of theology, as expressed in the words of the Westminster Shorter Catechism, "to glorify God and enjoy him forever." Theological knowledge is finally doxological, prayer addressed at Jesus' invitation and spoken in the power of His Spirit, ascribing to the God of the gospel now by faith, and thus in the expectation at last face to face, the "kingdom, the power and the glory, forever." For the gospel is not only God's Word to His creatures, but by the mission of the Spirit it is also God's Word spoken back to the Father in the petition, praise, and thanksgiving of those unified with Christ the Son.[17]

Jan Rohls explains: "God is glorified by the knowledge of God *(cognitia Dei)*. This knowledge is the highest good of human beings *(summum bonum hominis)*: that is, their chief end *(humanae vitae praecipuus finis)*. God has created us in order to be glorified by us, and we glorify God by knowing God. . . . The goal of human beings, that which they are ordained to do as part of creation, is to know *(cognoscere)* God according to the divine essence and will, to delight *(delectari)* in God, to honor *(celebrare)* God, to call on God *(invocare)*, to act *(laborare)* in accord with God's word, and thus to be a mirror of the divine virtues."[18] The knowledge of God the Almighty Father by the faith/faithfulness of Jesus the Son in the power of their Spirit brings and brings about on the earth the free and joyful obedience of disciples — in the mind, as theology, no less (and with no less difficulty) than in the body's new service. These "theological subjects," that is,

14. T. F. Torrance, *Theology in Reconstruction* (Grand Rapids: Eerdmans, 1975), especially pp. 46-61.

15. Karl Barth, *Anselm: Fides Quaerens Intellectum (Faith in Search of Understanding)*, trans. I. W. Robertson (Cleveland and New York: Meridian Books, 1962).

16. Oswald Bayer, *Martin Luther's Theology: A Contemporary Interpretation*, trans. Thomas H. Trapp (Grand Rapids: Eerdmans, 2007), pp. 1-14.

17. Jenson, *ST* 1, p. 5.

18. Jan Rohls, *Reformed Confessions: Theology from Zurich to Barmen* with an Introduction by Jack L. Stotts, trans. John Hoffmeyer (Louisville: Westminster John Knox, 1998), pp. 65-66.

*disciples* of Jesus, i.e., those *taught* by His Spirit, however, are and can be taught only as beloved children of the heavenly Father, adopted and made heirs by gift (see below, Part Two, on theological subjectivity). Their obedience of faith is filial and free, not the coerced obedience of slaves under compulsion in a system of rewards and punishments. It is the man Jesus from Nazareth who so knows God for us, so that it is through Him, that is, through His human faith and faithfully lived life and death for us "in the flesh" (1 John 4:2) that His own heavenly Father becomes also "ours." His Father becomes ours when, by the same Spirit that "drove" (Mark 1:12) Jesus on His way through Gethsemane, believers too are brought already now by the death and resurrection of baptismal union with the Son into the Beloved Community that this triune God is and promises to become for us. *Beloved Community* — "the needed social theory [of theology] is and can be only the doctrine of the Trinity itself."[19]

"Beloved Community" is a paraphrase of the doctrine of the Trinity. It is an expression, however, that many today will recognize first of all from the life, ministry, and Christian proclamation of the Rev. Dr. Martin Luther King Jr. Indeed this work delights in the resonances of the term from that association. Beloved Community parses a relation between church and kingdom that must exceed the visible borders in Christianity in history without obviating Christianity in history as the gospel's mission to the nations in just the ways that King activated. "Love" here is not a sentimental and falsifying gloss on social life motivated by malice and structured by injustice but creative of value for the "refuse" of "this world," yet at the same time also of creative value, though under the form of a contradiction, for their oppressors. Love here works a creative tension that reveals malice and demands truth regarding injustice. And "community," likewise, here does not mean the aggregation of atoms into a collective, which would result in nothing more than a collective egoism, but God as Christians conceive God as persons related in love.

King preached this "Beloved Community" at the conclusion of his sermon "Paul's Letter to American Christians": "Here we find the true meaning of the Christian faith and of the cross. Calvary is the telescope through which we look into the long vista of eternity and see the love of God breaking into time. Out of the hugeness of his generosity God allowed his only-begotten Son to die that we may live. By uniting yourself with Christ and your brothers through love you will be able to matriculate in the university of eternal life. In a world depending on force, coercive tyranny, and bloody violence, you are challenged to follow the way of love. You will then discover that unarmed love is the most powerful force in all the world."[20] Richard Lischer records a kindred articulation of this view of divine reality from an address King delivered at Birmingham: "God's love was poured out on the cross of Christ for unlikeable people, people who don't move us, whose ways are not our ways. With this kind of love, we, that is, all in this

---

19. Jenson, *ST* 2, p. 173.
20. Martin Luther King Jr., *Strength to Love* (Philadelphia: Fortress, 1987), p. 146.

room, will transform those who have persecuted us all these years and create a new Birmingham. But it won't happen without a sacrificial effort on our part."[21] We will have much more to say about who this "we" is in Part Two and how this subjectivity plays in the coming of the Beloved Community.

For the present we note that there is a polyvalence in the term, Beloved Community, akin to Paul Tillich's analysis of the Spiritual Community. "The Spiritual Community is unambiguous; it is New Being, created by the Spiritual Presence. But, although it is a manifestation of unambiguous life, it is nonetheless fragmentary, as the manifestation of unambiguous life in the Christ and in those who expected the Christ . . . under the conditions of finitude [though] conquering both estrangement and finitude." There is much both methodologically and substantively that distinguishes the following presentation of Christian theology from Tillich's system, yet the formal parallel here is striking and noteworthy. "As the Christ is not the Christ without those who receive him as the Christ, so the Spiritual Community is not Spiritual unless it is founded on the New Being as it has appeared in the Christ."[22] In both of these statements the "Lutheran" Tillich was correcting standard "Lutheran" teaching that had one-sidedly separated gospel from church and justification from New Being. But the "belovedness" of the Beloved Community that makes it New Being (Greek: *kaine ktisis*) in the world is its ever-new creation by the love of God breaking into time at the cross of Christ by means of its proclamation. Just so, however, this is love for the enemy, the broken, the sinner, the persecutor; thus love's victory remains contested in principle and in practice deeply entangled in the ambiguities of life. Indeed, necessarily entangled, as Tillich stressed, because "the demonic kingdom is a distortion of the divine Kingdom and it would have no being without that of which it is the distortion." Thus the "struggle of the Kingdom of God in history is above all this struggle *within* the life of its own representatives, the churches."[23] The need of critical dogmatics arises organically out of this formal description of the polyvalence of theology's subject matter, Beloved Community.

As mentioned above, the term "Beloved Community" appears to have originated from the pen of the now nearly forgotten American philosopher, Josiah Royce, who late in life converted intellectually from the monism of German idealism to a pragmatic and hermeneutical version of Pauline Christianity.[24] In his great, but unfinished testimony to this late-in-life turn of thought, *The Problem of Christianity,* Royce generated the expression as a paraphrase of Pauline theology: ". . . the idea of a spiritual life in which universal love for all individuals shall

21. Richard Lischer, *The Preacher King: Martin Luther King, Jr. and the Word That Moved America* (New York and Oxford: Oxford University Press, 1995), p. 261. See the discussion in *LBC,* pp. 348-54.

22. Tillich, *ST,* 3, p. 150.

23. Tillich, *ST,* 3, p. 381.

24. Bruce Kuklick, *Josiah Royce: An Intellectual Biography* (Indianapolis: Hackett, 1985), pp. 207, 211-37.

be completely blended, practically harmonized, with an absolute loyalty for a real and universal community, God, neighbor, and the one church."[25] Coupled with Royce's other two essential ideas of creedal Christianity, namely the "hell of the irrevocable" that burdens the individual as guilty sinner and the "need of atonement" that finds a way to reconcile just this victim-and-perpetrator of sin, we can detect here a source of King's view of Christian love as working *creative tension* for the redemption and fulfillment of life together. "Love is never merely an amiable tolerance of whatever form human frailty and folly may take. To be sure, the lover, as Jesus depicts him, resists not evil, and turns his cheek to the smiter. Yes, but he does this with the full confidence that God sees all and will vindicate his servant. The lover vividly anticipates the positive triumph of all the righteous; and so his love for even the least of the little ones is, in anticipation, an active and strenuous sharing in the final victory of God's will. His very non-resistance is therefore inspired by a divine contempt for the powers of evil."[26] In short, the theology of the Beloved Community is, according to its own light, a *militant* theology, and its militancy, as Royce exposited and King preached, has everything to do with its eschatological orientation on, and expectation of, the reign of God. Here faith is that way of life by which the just live in an unjust world; correspondingly faith's "dogma" is doctrine for this way of life, not for *theoria*, not doctrine for doctrine's sake. Beloved Community is a way of living in the world — per hypothesis, it is the *Christian* way — of knowing God in the middle of things, at the center of life, at the cutting edge that divides sin and righteousness, life and death, despair and hope.

Philipp Melanchthon set such knowledge of God at the head of the first Protestant dogmatics. "In earnest invocation of God it is necessary to consider what one wants to address, what God is, how he is known, where and how he has revealed himself, and both if and why he hears our pleas and cries."[27] This statement properly locates the preliminary question about what God is in the doxological context of prayer, as Melanchthon emphasizes. It is not that we attempt to master God with a concept, but rather that we who are not-God and in need are invited graciously by the Son to petition for true needs of daily bread and forgiveness for ourselves as for others. At stake in this inquiry into what God is, then, is "not fall[ing] into the error of addressing as God things which are not God."[28] For things that are not God cannot bear the burden of being addressed as God; they collapse under that weight back upon the petitioner. And the fall and the ruin of such "gods that fail" (Arthur Koestler) is great. So we must know what we are talking about when we use the word, God, to pray, namely, how it

---

25. Royce, *Problem of Christianity*, p. 98.

26. Royce, *Problem of Christianity*, pp. 88-89.

27. Philipp Melanchthon, *On Christian Doctrine: Loci Communes, 1555*, trans. C. L. Manschreck (Grand Rapids: Baker, 1982), p. 3.

28. Melanchthon, *Christian Doctrine*, p. 3.

is that the "Father" who becomes ours at the invitation of the Son is "heavenly," not "earthly." That is a question about the divine nature.

Even though the topic of the divine nature is in this way treated first in Melanchthon's dogmatics and is then followed by the topic on the three persons, Melanchthon makes it clear at the outset how Christian theology takes its point of departure already here in the gospel, namely in that invitation to prayer by Jesus and with Jesus (as we shall study in detail in Chapter Seven). Christians can regard that invitation of Jesus as valid in that "God has set before us his Son, Jesus Christ," so that this "God who has thus revealed himself in and through Christ is the God to whom our hearts should look and speak" precisely so that "our hearts speak to the true God, and do not address something that is not God." Moreover, Melanchthon immediately continues, for the purpose of valid "invocation" of God it is "very fitting for us to reflect on the baptism of Christ [w]here the three persons are distinctly revealed," that is, the Father's voice which sounds from heaven addressing Jesus emerging from the river as Son and sending, in the figure of the dove, His Spirit to rest upon Him. Thinking of this event, Melanchthon notes, "[W]e must contemplate God's word and revelations for an understanding of his being and will. . . ."[29] This preliminary reflection of theology on the divine self-donation in the revelation of the Three, says Melanchthon, is in distinction to the godless who scorn God's word with the result that inevitably that "which they addressed as god was a projection of their own false thoughts."[30] Just how correctly to distinguish the earthly and the heavenly natures, then, may not be so transparent a matter as first imagined, if we can only get this distinction right by a putative Word from God about God.

It is, in any case, in the light of gospel and grace that Melanchthon would take up for consideration the general or rational or natural knowledge of God, affirming that "by nature all men know that there is an eternal omnipotent being [*Wesen*], full of wisdom, goodness, and righteousness, that created and preserves all creatures. . . ." All know this, he continues on the basis of Romans 2:15, because "God implanted the knowledge of virtue in men precisely that we might know and be aware that God is, that he is a wise being, the fullness of virtues, and that he loves us and desires that we be like him, namely that we be obedient to him according to the light that he fashioned in us."[31] Carefully read, in this train of thought Melanchthon is saying that it is the common human knowledge of morality that gives rise to the thought of God as morality's author and judge. The corresponding reflection on divine nature that emerges from this line of thought

---

29. Melanchthon, *Christian Doctrine*, p. 4. He connects this also with the prologue to the First Commandment of the God of the Exodus, and comments: "With this large blazing sign he drew a distinction between himself and all the other gods who are imaginary." Melanchthon, *Christian Doctrine*, p. 5.

30. Melanchthon, *Christian Doctrine*, p. 5.

31. Melanchthon, *Christian Doctrine*, pp. 5-6.

is that the condition for the possibility of such moral authorship and judgment is the Deity's possession of essential attributes such as justice and intelligence. The quintessence of righteousness and wisdom — that is what God is.

But how then do the three persons of the gospel and the divine nature of essential justice and intelligence connect? What is the relation here between these distinct lines of preliminary theological reflection: nature and person, insight and revelation? There is the general, rational, or natural knowledge of monotheism and morality on the one side and the radical and exclusive monotheism of the triune God given in the gospel of salvation[32] on the other. As mentioned, it should not be overlooked that Melanchthon raises the question about the natural knowledge of God from within the framework of the theology of grace and revelation as a kind of reflection backward on a previous state of mind or relation to God from the newly authorized perspective of gospel-elicited faith. It is reflection outward from the gathered community of faith to the wider circle of humanity. He reasons from the particular knowledge of God in the gospel to the universal knowledge of God in morality. Otherwise, that is, if the natural knowledge of God from morality were being taken as foundational for his theological project of knowing God such that proper prayer can take place, the question seems unavoidable why this natural knowledge of God should not suffice, since Melanchthon has just so generously imputed it with the help of Romans 2:15 to the "natural man." "Is this understanding of God not enough?"

Melanchthon answers: this "legal" understanding of God by practical reason is not enough because it does not and cannot say "that God for the sake of his Son, out of grace, wishes to forgive us our sins and gives us righteousness and eternal blessedness." Not only does it not suffice for the knowledge of God in salvation, Melanchthon argues, but without this gospel knowledge of God, even that supposedly universal inference to God as author and judge from the human knowledge of morality becomes vulnerable to overwhelming doubts in the teeth of actual evil in the world. Indeed, it becomes nonfunctional or fanatical in the jaws of the structures of malice and injustice. Doubt at the surd of moral evil at loose in the world, prowling about eager to devour, multiplies to such an extent that "the natural light in wise people may become completely infatuated, and they suppose that God is neither a judge nor a helper." So Melanchthon observes with an eye to current revivals in Renaissance letters of Hellenistic philosophical theologies in the form of new Stoics, Skeptics, or Epicureans.[33] Melanchthon thus intends to correct and clarify these reviving traditions of natural theology and prevent a return to the status quo ante. With the revealed theology from the Bible he will nip in the bud the materialism, pantheism, and skepticism of pre-Christian philosophical theology with the Creator/creature distinction from the Bible. We "differentiate God from all other things . . . [as] an omnipotent eternal being, the fullness of

32. See *DC,* chapter 5.
33. Melanchthon, *Christian Doctrine,* p. 6.

wisdom, righteousness, goodness, truth and purity, and that all other things . . . are created things, are not omnipotent and are not to be invoked." Thus God is to be known as the One God over against the many that are created and thus also as author of the moral law against all doubt caused by the fractious disorder of the many. The biblical distinction between Creator and creature is thus at work also here in backing the dubious knowledge of God from morality; God the Creator is "not a physical being" and thus part of the cosmic whole, as Stoics and Epicureans think, but "a spiritual being."[34] But what kind of being is that?

Melanchthon answers this question in accord with the entire Western tradition going back to Augustine that finds singular philosophical help in Platonism's strong distinction between mind and matter over against Epicurean materialism, Stoic pantheism, Academic skepticism, and religious Gnosticism. That aid is not, at least historically, to be despised.[35] Yet it does entangle Christian theology at length in the peculiar dialectic of Platonic theology's oscillations between apophatic and kataphatic stances, that is, between denials and affirmations respectively of God's knowability. The agnosticism of academic or Platonic skepticism is a tradition that, thought out consequently, has to turn against revealed theology. Cicero's well-known *On the Nature of the Gods* had preserved for the West in the figure of Cicero's mouthpiece, Cotta, this apophatic tradition of philosophical theology. The view here is that God is theoretically uncertain but human conscience is practically sure of its own moral duty; this theological agnosticism became influential again in Kant's philosophy of religion[36] and in recent times it has been renewed with a twist by Jacques Derrida.[37] By contrast with this skeptical Platonism, a ready answer about the being of God, figured *as Mind,* comes from the tradition of dogmatic Platonism:[38] here God is to be thought as an intellectual being, as the heaven of the eternal Forms known by the Demiurge (Craftsman) of the *Timaeus,* or, in Aristotle's edition, as thought thinking itself, the perfectly intellectual being whose power is the emulation it inspires. As opposed to agnostic and apophatic versions of Platonism,[39] this more

---

34. Melanchthon, *Christian Doctrine,* p. 7.

35. *DC,* pp. 173-79.

36. Cicero, *On the Nature of the Gods,* trans. C. P. McGregor (London: Penguin, 1972). See the discussion in *PNT,* p. 216.

37. James K. A. Smith, "Re-Kanting Postmodernism? Derrida's Religion within the Limits of Reason Alone," *Faith and Philosophy* 17, no. 4 (October 2000): 558-71.

38. John Dillon, *The Middle Platonists: 80 b.c. to a.d. 220,* revised edition (Ithaca, NY: Cornell University Press, 1996).

39. Deirdre Carabine, *The Unknown God: Negative Theology in the Platonic Tradition: Plato to Eriugena,* Louvain Theological and Pastoral Monographs, 19 (Louvain: Peeters & Eerdmans, no date). Recently Knut Alfsvåg has made an intellectually powerful intervention on behalf of this tradition in correlation with a retrieval of Luther in *What No Mind Has Conceived: On the Significance of Christological Apophaticism* (Leuven, Paris, and Walpole, MA: Peeters, 2010). See the discussion below in Chapter Three.

kataphatic tradition (today we call it "ontotheology") pictures God as the Architect or Engineer who at the origin put the world into order and set it into motion before retiring from the scene.

A version of this dogmatic Platonism is at play in Melanchthon's account. Melanchthon takes up the Platonic word, being, *ousia,* and defines it to mean "something that exists in and of itself, and is not dependent on some other foundation, as a contingent thing is." Note then that by this definition of true being — in the Latin tradition, termed *substantia,* that is, *substance* — strictly speaking and also in accord with biblical theology's Creator/creature distinction, God alone would be substantial, existing *per se* (through self) and indeed *a se* (from self). All created things by contrast are contingent, coming into being by virtue of another, *per aliud* (through another), and persist in being as continually dependent on other things; creatures have then but a relative, temporary, created, and derivative substantiality. Creatures exist as compounds, then, as souls added to material bodies. As such they can fall apart again and cease any longer to exist. But as the one and only genuine substance, God is pure Mind with no need of body to exist. God in "aseity" is uncompounded, simple, "spiritual," that is, "intellectual." As intellectual, God alone is the really real precisely as Mind thinking itself, thus constituting itself as object to itself and knowing itself as such, pure self-reflective thinking without matter or body, hence without beginning or end.

Certainly usage of the abstract concept of *ousia* taken as substance *per se* and *a se* can serve simply to articulate that what God is, as Creator of all that is not God, is substantial, that is, not reducible to any of the created relations God as Creator produces.[40] So far as this usage goes, the substantiality of God is surely in accord with the strong biblical distinction between Creator and creature and serves conceptually to articulate it in a particular fashion. The theological problem, however, is that being substantial and so not reducible to external relations *also constitutes a particular kind of relationship* to creatures that are by contrast naturally vulnerable to dissolution. And the question of this particular relation to creatures is only posed, not answered, by asserting God's substantiality.

So how is that abstraction, *ousia, substantia,* to be taken in Christian theology? The apparent implication, as we have just witnessed, is that genuine substantiality — being untouched by becoming — must be purely intellectual in the sense imagined, that is, of immaterial and supersensible existence, that is to say, *ghostly* self-sameness. Or, if the dynamism of "thought thinking and knowing itself" is supplied to give life to this ghost, substantiality imagined as pure Mind may be qualified as personal as well as intellectual, as Augustine did for the Western tradition in his seminal attempt to interpret the doctrine of the Trinity achieved in the Christian East. The Father eternally thinks His Word and loves what He thinks in the Spirit; the Trinity dramatizes this eternal thought process of the one, simple, self-identical divine Mind. Fatefully, Melanchthon continues

---

40. Christopher Stead, *Divine Substance* (Oxford: Oxford University Press, 2000).

here with this traditional Western doctrine of divine simplicity that Augustine had resorted to.[41] As "spiritual," that is, as purely "intellectual being," "in God, power, wisdom, righteousness, and other virtues are not contingent things, but are one with the Being; divine Being is divine power, wisdom, and righteousness. . . ." In God, the vital distinctions apparent to us creatures between power, wisdom, and goodness are not real. In God they are simply one and the same thing. That metaphysically is how God is one. To know God, therefore, is to transcend all earthly contentions between power, wisdom, and goodness and to ascend to their heavenly identity.

Without noticing any tension, however, between quite different accounts of divine unity (as Western simplicity on the one side and Eastern perichoresis on the other), Melanchthon continues that these various perfections — supposedly one and the same divine being in the timeless, spaceless God — are proclaimed in the "first chapter of Genesis": "Because God created all things, he is not created; he is eternal and omnipotent. And inasmuch as . . . God spoke, it is clear that God is not a being without understanding and wisdom. . . . [T]he explanation of what God is comes from such statements. . . ."[42] Yet genuine perplexity arises here, as Spinoza would eventually articulate.[43] How can the eternally self-same and as such perfectly perfect Being, even if as Mind purely thinking itself and knowing itself fully and completely — how does this God ever come to act temporally and ad extra at all, let alone diversely and sequentially as these varying predications indicate that arise in the course of the seven days of creation according to Genesis 1? Does not Genesis 1, taken on its own terms, suggest on the contrary that the varying divine attributes of power, wisdom, and love can and do work externally and sequentially without any qualification of divine substantiality, but rather somehow express it? Does not the divine Fiat here express divine substantiality directly and univocally by performative utterance — "Let there be . . . and there was!" — not, then, analogically, as if a similitude of an eternal thought? In that case, the one and eternal being of the Creator of all that it is not would have to be thought more as a harmony of genuine diversities than as a static self-sameness. When the unity of God is taken as essential harmony rather than simple self-

---

41. Augustine, *On the Trinity*, trans. E. Hill (New York: New City Press, 1991). After faithfully rehearsing for the first six chapters of his treatise the Eastern church's quite distinctly different account of the perichoretic (mutual indwelling) being of the Trinity, the fateful turn occurs in Book VII, when Augustine queries whether the Pauline statement that Christ is the wisdom of God implies that God the Father is without wisdom of His own. This query shifts the direction of the entire treatise towards a monotheism of the simple divine nature and away from monotheism taken as the living, lived, jeopardized, and triumphant unity of the Three. See further the author's forthcoming *Divine Simplicity: An Ambiguous Legacy* (Grand Rapids: Baker Academic, 2016).

42. Melanchthon, *Christian Doctrine*, pp. 8-9.

43. Baruch Spinoza, *Ethics, Treatise on the Emendation of the Intellect and Selected Letters*, trans. S. Shirley (Indianapolis: Hackett, 1992), pp. 58-59. See the discussion in *RPTD*, pp. 161-62.

identity, God as such is thought in the way that makes Him capable of partaking directly, albeit externally and sequentially, in His own created space and time.

Which is it? Is God spiritual because God is the One capable of originating all other things for redemption and fulfillment? Capable then of partaking without jeopardy to divine substantiality in the creature's space and time, thus divinely "simple" in the complex way of an infinitely self-surpassing, self-donating, self-communicating life that can see these commitments through? Or is God spiritual because God is timelessly the same thing or nature or essence? Capable then of creation only and strictly (but still, strictly speaking, inconceivably) as an eternal act of determination of all that is not God? Is God's deity eternally self-surpassing, the deity of a living God, the deity that is the Beloved Community of mutually self-giving persons? Or is God's deity a natural or essential self-sameness, the deity of the simply One who as substantial is not and can never become the harmony of the many in the fulfilled Beloved Community?

In the course of time, Melanchthon's blended ways for conceiving God's spiritual substantiality more and more gave the biblical store away. As Günther Frank has shown in a number of excellent studies, the Protestant culture schooled by the teacher of Germany produced a philosophical foundation for reformed Christendom that set the political order under the rubric of God's creative work in general.[44] The concrete being of the ecclesia in mission to the nations as summoned into existence from God's particularly Trinitarian self-revelation in the gospel of salvation[45] was thus progressively eclipsed, an eclipse that continues to this day in the allegedly "Lutheran" and "anti-sectarian" notion of the "people's church" *(Volkskirche)* — an institution that is rather the Babylonian captivity of Protestantism in the ecology of the nation-state.[46] At the very least we can say that already in Melanchthon the relation between Trinity and the creative work of Genesis 1 is not adequately clarified. The consequence is that the becoming of God as outlined in the baptismal creed — as Creator, then again as Incarnate, and yet again as Temple of the Beloved Community — is not clearly seen.[47] It is not clearly seen, moreover, as expressing divinity rather than somehow compromising it (unless construed as mere rhetoric, as a way of talking rather than being). As Robert Jenson has argued, the deep ambiguity here has long troubled Christian theology both before and after Melanchthon.[48] The theologically ambiguous

44. Günther Frank, *Die Vernunft des Gottesgedankens: Religionsphilosophische Studien zur fruehen Neuzeit* (Frommann-Holzboog, 2003); *Die Theologische Philosophie Philipp Melanchthons (1497-1560),* Erfurter Theologische Studien, vol. 67 (Benno).

45. Also Trinitarian in the Christian reading of the origin according to Genesis 1, as Luther following Augustine had taught, e.g., *LW* 1, p. 9.

46. See the critique in *BA,* pp. 154-59, 166-74, 183-87.

47. Eberhard Jüngel, *The Doctrine of the Trinity: God's Being Is in Becoming* (Grand Rapids: Eerdmans, 1976).

48. Robert W. Jenson, *Unbaptized God: The Basic Flaw in Ecumenical Theology* (Minneapolis: Augsburg Fortress, 1992).

tradition of Christian Platonism in any event continues in Melanchthon. Here the philosophical argument from effect to cause to transcendent and substantial divine nature as causal agent of the world stands side by side with the theological argument that it is God's self-presentation as the Father of the Son in the Spirit by the gospel that tells who God is and thus how we may think theologically about what God is and how God is what God is.

Melanchthon to be sure concluded his opening analysis of what we are talking about in Christian theology when we use the term, God, by bringing out a further implication of exclusive or radical monotheism, namely, that there is and only can be one possessor of the divine predicates — for logically a second subject of them would limit the first and so the result would be two finite gods, neither of which would actually and without limit possess the divine perfections, i.e., as the true Infinite. Thus, he writes, "there is one unified, divine Being, and no more." There is an important differentiation that may be noted here in qualification of Melanchthon's otherwise sound argument (to be developed in Chapter Three) between the notion of *subject* as possessor of attributes over against other subjects and that of *person* as given and giving in community by the sharing and appropriation of attributes. A person is certainly also a subject, a knower; yet it is human personhood that enables subjectivity. The reverse cannot be said. Indeed a pure subject, a transcendental ego, a sovereign self that conceives and knows itself as such rather depersonalizes itself and others. Self-consciousness here replaces consciousness of others in the community of interpretation that elicits the subject in the first place and for which a subject offers its cognitive interpretations of the common body in a common cause of the community.

But here we will only trace out the way in which the notion of divine simplicity may also be taken in another, better way: as a rule of radical and exclusive monotheism, also with respect to the tri-personal God. Simplicity in this vein as a rule of faith can be rendered as incomparability, as uniqueness, as singularity. This "rule-version" is not, then, as in the foregoing argument from Platonism, a putative metaphysical insight into timeless self-identity as the natural basis of divine substantiality, an insight thought to be needed religiously to provide the natural and eternal ground for the many temporal and contingent things. In rendering simplicity as a rule, however, it becomes instead a mandate for reverent speech, derived from divine commandment. It is a rule to which Kendall Soulen has recently summoned Christian theologians when he asks them to remember, as a principle of their own theology, how believing Israel treats the Tetragrammaton (the divine Name, usually given in modern English as "Yahweh," composed of four Hebrew letters) by the pious practice of its non-utterance in respect for the Decalogue's commandment not to take the name of the LORD in vain.[49] We

---

49. R. Kendall Soulen, *The Divine Name(s) and the Holy Trinity: Distinguishing the Voice*, vol. 1 (Louisville: Westminster John Knox, 2011). See the discussion of Soulen's argument below in Chapter Seven.

shall consider Soulen's important contribution in further detail in Chapter Seven. For the moment, what matters is his insight that reverence belongs to what is strictly incomparable, the Creator of all that it is not, that is, to the Holy One of Israel, who as such cannot substantially be reduced to its external relations or made familiar by metaphors or analogies or similitudes, let alone captured in concepts. This rule recognizes the awesome singularity of the Holy One; it qualifies all speech and thought of the divine being as of that One and Only who is the Creator of all else, without any pretense of metaphysical insight into the condition for the possibility of such being.[50]

As mentioned above, Melanchthon articulated this rule of divine simplicity for the sake of radical and exclusive monotheism over against recurrent Gnostic dualism and Epicurean materialism and Stoic pantheism in divinity, stances that he acutely traces to stumbling over the question of theodicy: "When human reason beholds the great disorder and misery in human nature, it goes astray and thinks that if there were a wise and just God who could rule everything, he would not suffer such disorder."[51] Notice the language: the objection is that God should suffer human disorder; that longsuffering patience somehow contradicts God's rule as the one genuine substance. The Apostle Paul himself thinks this thought (Rom. 3:3-8, 25-26); it the question of the theodicy of faith. But how is this contradiction conceived apart from the revelation of the righteousness of God (Rom. 3:21-25)?

The rule of God over creatures, when God is conceived metaphysically as the genuine substance of timeless self-identity, has to be thought of as an eternal determination of creatures in all that happens with them through space and time; taken with radical consequence, this entails God eternally and inexorably willing the wicked along with their equally fated damnation. This implication of divine substantiality makes God the author of human disorder and its punishment as an expression of the Deity's superior order, an assertion of divine contradiction of the human contradiction. This was an implication that Huldreich Zwingli did not shy from.[52] But Melanchthon is not thinking in the cited passage above of Zwingli. He is thinking of those contemporary humanists who draw the opposite conclusion from the same thought regarding God's eternal substantiality as pure self-identity as had Zwingli's robust fatalism. That conclusion is from Melanchthon's Christian perspective tantamount to atheism. These regard this God as a moral horror, unworthy of belief — even if He is the really real![53]

---

50. Let us, however, register the clarification that in Trinitarian theology the Jewish rule of reverence in speech about God expressed in pious nonpronunciation of the Tetragrammaton is both validated and reconceptualized as the sole "monarchy of the Father," *pater est fons divinitatis.*

51. Melanchthon, *Christian Doctrine*, p. 10.

52. Huldreich Zwingli, "On the Providence of God," in *The Latin Works of Huldreich Zwingli,* 2 vols., trans. Samuel Macauley Jackson (Philadelphia: Heidelberg Press, 1922). See the discussion in *LBC*, pp. 162-69.

53. Leibniz faced this implication. In a letter to Magnus Wedderkopf in May 1671 he wrote:

Mercifully, for Melanchthon, revealed theology guides human reason away from such metaphysical quandaries towards what should be called "the theodicy of faith," as in Romans 8:18-39, by teaching instead the narrative of sin and grace, of fall and redemption, and so of nature on the way to a glorious fulfillment on account of God's self-surpassing self-determination in the economy of the Three to prevail as the God of grace, also for the dying sinner. This revealed singularity of the Three, to be reverenced in our speech of God, requires theology always to point away from itself, as earthen vessel to the treasure that it bears into the world, like the *Theotokos* (the "bearer of God," Mary the Virgin). What theology bears into the world is the gospel's truth-claim about God as the redeeming God of those in need of redemption as purportedly from the God who has created and continued these creatures in need. And this kind of substantial referentiality of theological talk to the incomparable God known in His self-surpassing, self-donating, and self-communicating is crucial to the very sense of theological statements, as Dennis Bielfeldt has argued with no little urgency today against the turn in many quarters to pure constructivism in theology.[54]

Theology in this way points by its statements through its own faltering and provisional formulations to the one and only demonstration of the promising God's existence that comes about by God's fulfillment of this world "on which stood the cross of Jesus"[55] — or not at all. No insight substitutes for this promised

---

"*Fate* is the decree of God or the necessity of events. Those events are *fatal* which will necessarily happen. Both views are difficult — that a God who does not decide everything, or that a God who does decide everything, should be the absolute author of all. For if he does decide everything, and the world dissents from his decree, he will not be omnipotent. But if he does not decide everything, it seems to follow that he is not omniscient. . . . Hence it follows that God can never be purely permissive. It follows also that there is no decree of God which is really not absolute. . . . Is this conclusion hard? I admit it. What of it? Pilate is condemned. Why? Because he lacks faith. Why does he lack it? . . . For it is necessary to refer everything to some reason, and we cannot stop until we have arrived at a first cause — or it must be admitted that something can exist without a sufficient reason for its existence, and this admission destroys the demonstration of the existence of God and of many philosophical theorems." Gottfried Wilhelm Leibniz, *Philosophical Papers and Letters: A Selection,* trans. Leroy E. Loemker, 2 volumes (Chicago: University of Chicago Press, 1956), pp. 226-27. Out of sympathy with Pilate, it appears, modernity decided against Leibniz.

54. *SF,* pp. 59-130.

55. This turn of phrase, which I will use repeatedly to underscore the "this-worldliness" of the economy of God, may be traced to the Bethel Confession of 1933, i.e., the August redrafting of an initial outline by Dietrich Bonhoeffer and Hermann Sasse. The two versions are printed side-by-side in English translation in *Dietrich Bonhoeffer: Berlin: 1932-1933,* Dietrich Bonhoeffer Works, vol. 12, ed. L. Rassmussen (Minneapolis: Fortress, 2009), pp. 374-424. Christine-Ruth Müller, *Bekenntnis und Bekennen: Dietrich Bonhoeffer in Bethel (1933): Ein lutherischer Versuch* (Munich: Chr. Kaiser Verlag, 1989), provides the German texts of all four versions (pp. 81-193). Guy Christopher Carter, *Confession at Bethel, August 1933 — enduring witness: The formation, revision and significance of the first full theological confession of the Evangelical Church struggle in Nazi Germany,* Ph.D. dissertation (Marquette University, 1987)

fulfillment of Christianity's putative Word of God by the promising God. Indeed, alleged insights that function as a substitute for the coming of the Beloved Community are not insights but alien theologies. Knowing faith in turn takes the risk of so living in the world — that is, of living *justly* — that everything comes to depend on it turning out as promised (cf. Luke 14:12-14). That perhaps is more "monotheism" than we bargained for: living towards death-*and*-resurrection *(pace* Heidegger: *Sein-zum-Tode-und-Auferstehung!)* would actually be the *knowledge of God* under the present conditions of contested reality, where God is to be *known* by faith in the *promise* of the coming of the Beloved Community.

---

## A Note on the "Historicity" of the Resurrection of Jesus

Because the originating event of the gospel continues to originate the Christian community by its proclamation in Word and Sacraments, and because this originating event bears with it the peculiar Christian knowledge of God surpassing God, we have already begun to use the primitive Christian theology of the resurrection of the Crucified Jesus. This *kerygma* (proclamation) is the inaugural form of the putative Word from God to which and for which critical dogmatics is responsible. For many centuries, however, the "beginning" of the gospel was taken at face value instead in the nativity narratives of Matthew and Luke. Modern biblical scholarship has realized that this cannot have been the case historically in the sense that only Matthew and Luke make such an attestation of the gospel's beginning; ignorance of that beginning would make the predominance of New Testament Christianity unfounded and historically inexplicable. If there is historical report in the nativity stories, then, it could only be in the form of obscure and mysterious events kept secret by Mary and/or Joseph, only to be disclosed in the post-Easter community when at last the true significance of those events was grasped. Historically speaking, it is also the case that, despite Mark 1:1, the history of Jesus of Nazareth does not as such account historically for the beginning of the gospel, since Jesus' end in ignominious disgrace and abandonment would have left Him forgotten like countless other victims of legalized injustice among the crucified of this world. Rather the history of Jesus is in fact remembered as "the beginning of the gospel" from the specific perspective of an event that early Christianity named "the resurrection." Whatever memories of Jesus survived the trauma of His death by crucifixion would not have long survived except as preserved by Easter faith in the resurrection of Jesus who was crucified. In this sense, Easter is certainly a historical event. Something happened on the third day. Apart

---

provides an English translation of all four versions (pp. 304-39). See Paul R. Hinlicky, "Verbum Externum: Dietrich Bonhoeffer's Bethel Confession," in *God Speaks to Us,* International Bonhoeffer Interpretations, 5. Edited by R. Wüstenberg and J. Zimmermann (Frankfurt: Peter Lang, 2013), pp. 189-215.

from this happening, the rise of primitive Christianity as evidenced in the New Testament literature is historically incomprehensible.

Of course, the affirmation that "something happened" is not the same as the Christian claim that "resurrection" is what happened. The more or less certain historical events that occurred were the discovery of an empty tomb, assumed to be the place where the corpse of Jesus had been laid, and the appearances of a living figure, whom followers recognized as Jesus. Since none of these followers ever claimed to have witnessed the divine event itself that connected empty tomb and appearances, "resurrection" is a theological interpretation of that something that happened. "Resurrection," whatever else it may mean, means that the God of Israel has spoken-and-acted to acknowledge the crucified, dead, and buried Jesus as indeed His own beloved Son, vindicating His faith by which He lived and in which He died by raising Him from death and exalting Him as Lord. Because of this intended meaning, Christian theology receives and passes on just this claim to truth as the putative Word from God to which and for which theology is responsible, at least so far as it intends to be "orthodox" (1 Cor. 15:1-11).

Yet to understand this very claim of resurrection as the speech-act of God, one must also consider other, indeed more plausible accounts of "what happened" in accounting for the facts of empty tomb and appearances. Edward Schillebeeckx, for representative contemporary example, argues that "Mary Magdalene may have played a part we do not know about in helping to convince the disciples that the new orientation to living that Jesus has brought about in their lives has not been rendered meaningless by his death." Having discovered the empty tomb and missing body, Mary had an audition. She heard Jesus speaking to her (John 20:16). "In other words," Schillebeeckx explains, "spiritual contact with Jesus, ruptured by death, has been restored; they can once more address each other in intimate, personal terms, death notwithstanding." From Mary who shared her experience, a contagion of such "intimate, personal religious experiences" was ignited so that followers in the mass came to "apprehend Jesus as the One who lives."[56] As a historical-critical reconstruction, this is certainly a plausible account — and for many today more plausible than "resurrection," taken as the speech-act of God. But, by the same token, it does not yield the meaning that the account, "resurrection," actually intends. It signals an act of Mary, as the Bultmann school often put it, "overcoming the scandal of the cross." Just so, it does not signal God surpassing God to reconcile the world in His Son, crucified for our sins and raised for our justification.

Embarrassment at having to intend God in this latter way is, of course, not a minor motive in modern theologians like Schillebeeckx. Theologians are entitled to their personal taste, and it is surely the case that one does not tastefully speak of "resurrection" in polite circles today — anymore than in first-century

56. Edward Schillebeeckx, *Jesus: An Experiment in Christology,* trans. H. Hoskins (New York: Seabury/Crossroad, 1979), p. 345.

Athens (Acts 17:32). N. T. Wright, in his massive study, hit the nail on the head in this connection, however, when he wrote with emphasis: "*The fact that dead people do not ordinarily rise is itself part of early Christian belief,* not an objection to it. The early Christians insisted that what had happened to Jesus was precisely something new; was, indeed, the start of a whole new mode of existence, a new creation. The fact that Jesus' resurrection was, and remains, without analogy is not an objection to the early Christian claim. It is part of the claim itself."[57] In other words, the Easter kerygma claims that here God has spoken once and for all to the world for its redemption and fulfillment. The associated problems of "miracle" and the "mechanics," as it were, of "bodily" resurrection will concern us elsewhere. For the present, it suffices to have identified the nature of the historical claim that the resurrection of the crucified Jesus is the inaugurating Word of God to which and for which Christian theology is responsible.

## The Theology of the Word

Hearing, understanding, and believing this Easter Word of God are always also at the same time interpretation of human experience in the world. Calvin famously argued that the knowledge of God and self-knowledge are correlative.[58] The Augsburg Confession had made justifying faith to turn upon a conviction about one's own self, namely, that for Christ's sake one is, in spite of sin, "received in mercy." This correlation between Word and human self-interpretation has been dramatically the case in Western theology ever since Augustine penned his *Confessions* — that remarkable probe into human self-understanding that has formed the conscience of theology ever since (Krister Stendahl's critique of the West's "introspective conscience" notwithstanding).[59] In modern theology discussion has revolved around Augustine's depiction of the "restless heart" that finds no rest until it rests in God, as if it provided an anthropological grounding of theology. But what is rather more impressive about the prayerful overture that Augustine drafted to open his remarkable work of self-examination is the correlation of this interpretation of the soul's restlessness with the coming of the Word of God. For Augustine immediately queries, "what comes first, to call for you before appraising you, or to recognize you before calling for you?" How does his restless heart become restless, knowing that it may rest in God? Augustine answers, "you have been proclaimed to us, and it is my belief in you that calls out to you — the faith

---

57. N. T. Wright, *The Resurrection of the Son of God,* vol. 3 of *Christian Origins and the Question of God* (Minneapolis: Fortress, 2003), p. 712.

58. John Calvin, *Institutes of the Christian Religion,* 4 volumes, ed. J. T. McNeil and trans. F. W. Battles (Philadelphia: Westminster, 1975), p. 35.

59. *LBC,* pp. 233-36.

that is your gift to me, which you breathed into me by the humanity your Son assumed, taking up his mission of proclaiming you." It is only in this light that Augustine proceeds to query where God is, what God is, how God is, what value God is. "Tell me by your acts of mercy, God my Lord, what you are to me," for my "soul is in disrepair — restore it."[60] Confessions of sins, confession of faith, confession of praise — it is all for Augustine a coming to the truth that is true therapy initiated by the Word of God that inaugurates faith.

Classically the first chapter in dogmatics was titled "Prolegomena," i.e., "Preliminary Matters." It dealt with questions concerning the nature and task of the theological discipline, its method, its relation to academy and church, its heritage from Scripture and tradition, its principles and sources and norms. Often it indicated a contextual account of the contemporary spiritual situation. As is evident, we have already begun to discuss these very matters in a manner reminiscent of Karl Barth's initial observation that theology is a function of the Christian church as that place in the world (thus also within the modern academy) where in fact speaking of God is ventured, thus requiring, if it is to be responsible, its own "science" with its own proper method.[61] Beginning his theology with this observation, Barth underscored what had been often obscured in the "mediating" academic theology of the nineteenth century: the oddity of Christian theology in the world as a discipline in venturing to speak rightly of God on the basis of a putative Word from God. The present proposal shares with Barth this way of locating theology as a discipline but accounts for its oddity somewhat differently.

As critics have since pointed out,[62] Barth's drastic move to theological subjectivity as "witness," that is, to the purely positive fact of the church community where human beings venture to speak normatively of God on the basis of an apparently privileged claim to truth, isolated theology — even though Barth himself was anything but a theologian disengaged from the world around him.[63] And this cognitive isolation ironically undercut the public claim to truth in Christian theology by reducing "church dogmatics" to an "in-house" discourse that would manifest

---

60. Augustine, *Confessions,* trans. Garry Wills (New York: Penguin, 2006), pp. 3-5.

61. Karl Barth, *CD* I/1, pp. 3-11.

62. The especially weighty criticism comes from Wolfhart Pannenberg that Barth, if he does not wholly replace the function of natural theology with Feuerbach's criticism of religion as illusory human projection (Pannenberg, *ST* 1, p. 104), he all too easily evades the question of whether "we are religious by nature and therefore willy-nilly absolutely dependent upon another, that other to which the religious consciousness relates . . ." (*ST* 1, p. 105). For criticism of Pannenberg's attempt to ground theology anthropologically in this countermove to Barth, see below Chapter Five. Jenson's nuanced position on this issue splits the difference: the antecedent "religious and metaphysical understandings" in the nations to which the gospel comes in its mission require both appropriation and critique as theological interpretation "both depends upon and collides with an antecedent discourse" (*ST* 1, p. 16).

63. Jeffery Stout, *The Flight from Authority: Religion, Morality and the Quest for Autonomy* (Notre Dame and London: University of Notre Dame Press, 1981).

its truth in the wider world by righteous deeds of political intervention and service rather than by public confession of its claim to truth and the corresponding argumentation.[64] Pannenberg to this extent is correct to maintain that "[a]ll talk about God must validate itself by being able to make the world of experience a proof of its power, showing what it is in everyday experience"[65] (as will be argued shortly). Yet Pannenberg goes too far in thinking that an analysis of experience as such can yield "minimal conditions for talk about God that wants to be taken seriously"[66] — as if this latter were not precisely the matter of hottest contention philosophically,[67] not to mention theologically. Indeed, Pannenberg's reliance on Cartesian-Kantian subjectivity to launch discourse regarding God as the infinity presupposed in finite self-consciousness[68] is profoundly questionable materially, in terms of philosophical anthropology itself, let alone as a stratagem of "natural theology."

The question, "What is a fitting conception of deity?," turns entirely on a deity's putative self-revelation and its reception by a corresponding community. We are learning culturally today in Euro-America at the end of Christendom, for example, that Christian "monotheism" is not obviously superior to "pagan" polytheism, as the latter theologies better accommodate the emergent pluralism. Whether and how this change is for good or for ill is precisely the matter that is disputable. But this change is our Euro-American context today. If the objection to Barth's "positivism" is that it subverts the Western tradition's pretentious belief in its own universality, that is, its legacies from Greco-Roman imperialism and the Stoic cosmopolitanism of its ruling elite, Barth is to be affirmed rather than reproached for it. The philosophical "monotheism" inherited from the Greco-Roman tradition to organize the polytheistic cults imperially is, in any case, just not the same thing as the "Christian" monotheism of Trinitarianism.[69]

The present point is accordingly different than the usual criticisms. In adopting this theological posture, Barth was following a particular strain of his Reformed heritage that laid the accent, with the Epistle of James, on the imperative: "Be ye not hearers of the word only, but doers also!" The point is not, to be even more precise, to fault this tacit reliance on a particular Christian legacy, even though I will argue that public confession, not (supposedly) righteous political interventions in the mixed society of the common body, is the fruit by which theology is known, tested, and judged.[70] This latter matter of public confession (see

64. See the critique of "political Barthianism" in *BA*, pp. 141-54.
65. Pannenberg, *ST* 1, p. 106.
66. Pannenberg, *ST* 1, p. 107.
67. *RPTD*, pp. 193-200.
68. Pannenberg, *ST* 1, pp. 114-18.
69. *DC*, pp. 159-200.
70. Paul R. Hinlicky, "Luther's Anti-Docetism in the Disputatio de divinitate et humanitate Christi (1540)," in *Creator est creatura: Luthers Christologie als Lehre von der Idiomenkommunikation,* ed. O. Bayer and Benjamin Gleede (Berlin and New York: Walter de Gruyter, 2007), especially pp. 147-66.

Chapter Eight) applies particularly today after Christendom. The church today must understand itself anew in the evangelical mission to the nations rather from within the modern nation-state, even prophetically as its "soul" or "conscience," let alone as its obsequious chaplaincy. Notwithstanding the rather traditional Lutheran-Reformed differentiations here between witness and confession or between subject and person, the present effort shares with Barth the larger point that theology is a function of the Christian church where speech about God is ventured on the basis of God's putative Word in order to articulate publicly a claim to truth. Thus, like any disciplined claim to truth, theology has its place of service in the academy, where and when opportunity presents itself.

By noting Barth's reliance on Reformed tradition, however, the point is to lift up the inescapable fact that as finite and historical in its actual iteration Christian theology is always embedded in particular — for the last millennium in mutually anathematizing — traditions of theology of a divided Christianity. This embeddedness can be obfuscated, or denied, only at the cost of honesty and self-awareness. Surely the point of acknowledging this embeddedness in a particular theological legacy is not and cannot any longer be sectarian self-promotion. Sectarian self-promotion at the expense of ecumenical Christianity has been one of the chief causes of disillusionment with Christendom, not to mention of its own internal rot. The point is rather to achieve clarity and thus also genuine self-criticism on the way to ecumenical convergence regarding the Christian gospel's claim to truth. So all Christian theology today must become critically self-aware of the particular tradition of schismatic Christianity in which it stands and give an account of the ways it will own (but also disown) it.[71]

In the present case, as is already evident, that tradition is theology in the train — or, under the shadow — of Luther. To be sure, this acknowledgment can be taken narrowly or expansively. Narrowly, as for example Mark Mattes does in his sharply argued essay against Pannenberg, Jüngel, and Jenson (with the Reformed Moltmann tossed in to boot) in the name of "the" Lutheran theology, namely one that elevates a law-gospel antinomy to theoretical status as marking the Lutheran *Sonderweg* in theology.[72] There is a profound irony embedded in the deep contradiction in which Mattes involves himself here by this narrowness, namely, that in order to attack theology as *theory* ("mapping God's being" as he puts it) he exalts a law-gospel cleavage to a status of *theoretical decisiveness* and thus remains entangled in the academic model of *theoria* for the Christian knowledge of God — even if, like most Kantians, he is then driven to *theoretical* apophaticism with respect to the knowledge of God. So in Mattes's account the thesis lived on in the antithesis.

---

71. See the appendix to *LBC* on the problem of Luther's apocalyptic demonology, pp. 379-85.

72. Mark C. Mattes, *The Role of Justification in Contemporary Theology,* Lutheran Quarterly Books (Grand Rapids: Eerdmans, 2004). Mattes has moved on from this early position.

Adapting a pragmatist model of knowledge as doctrine for life that labors to identify the God of the gospel in contest with idols and demons haunting time and space, by contrast, the present development of theology in the tradition of Luther avoids such inconsequence by drawing upon this theological tradition expansively. In the present endeavor, that will mean being as free and as critical as was Luther himself in calling on aid from, for random example, an Athanasius or an Augustine, a Bernard or a Tauler. It will mean developing theological themes from Luther as freely and as critically as do latter-day theologians — not only "Lutherans" — who in fair measure appropriate Luther, such as the aforementioned Barth, not to mention Pannenberg, Jüngel, and Jenson (Moltmann too!), as we shall shortly explore in some detail. The point of drawing upon Luther's legacy expansively is in part to defy the captivity today of theology in service to denominational identity politics and in this way contribute to a genuinely theological convergence in Christian doctrine amid these smoldering ruins of Euro-American Christendom. As we shall see, however, even drawing expansively on Luther's legacy in theology is and remains today as incisive as ever. So far as it succeeds, it will work a division of the existing divisions.

These considerations lead to a further difficulty in Barth's conception of "church dogmatics," namely the just-mentioned contemporary theological decay of the Euro-American churches into the Babel (Gen. 11:1-9) of denominational ideologies, and the genitive theologies that would supposedly replace them, all posturing for market position in the religion business. It is difficult to conceive of theology as church dogmatics when the churches themselves are no longer concerned to speak conscientiously of God but dissolve text into context and desperately repudiate even the intention of orthodoxy for the mess of pottage alleging "relevance."[73] The folly of this is evident — he who marries the *Zeitgeist* today becomes a widower tomorrow. Ironically enough, in this precarious situation it is the academy (at least insofar as it still upholds the formal universalisms of the Enlightenment) that provides theology with shelter from the suffocating political correctness and herd mentality — both left and right — that have descended upon denominational-sectarian theology. Today, it is the academy that in this way serves the freedom of theological thinking (at least where what counts is quality scholarship, intellectual honesty, broad engagement, and critical thinking). The irony of this academic location of ecumenically oriented church theology today is simply a brute fact and circumstance. This brute fact underlies the present shift from Barth's "church" dogmatics, not to mention "Christian" dogmatics,[74] to *critical* dogmatics. In this critical task, theology stands alongside philosophy

---

73. Vítor Westhelle, *After Heresy: Colonial Practices and Post-Colonial Theologies* (Eugene, OR: Cascade Books, 2010). See the review by Paul R. Hinlicky in *Lutheran Quarterly* 27, no. 2 (Summer 2013): 227-29.

74. *Christian Dogmatics,* ed. Carl E. Braaten and Robert W. Jenson, 2 volumes (Philadelphia: Fortress, 1984).

in the academy "to expose the often concealed but nevertheless functional deities or appeals to transcendence at work in accounts of our experience and require an accounting."[75] Certainly, this academic place and prophetic posture reflect an unstable situation. It is a delicate balancing act. But just so, it is a truthful account of the convolutions brought on by the collapse of Christendom, the theological irrelevance of the denominations on account of their wholesale vacuity in capitulation to the religion business, and the uncertain future of the gospel and its community in Euro-America.

There is another difficulty that has surged forward in consciousness since Barth's time. If theology is understood as thinking about God on the basis of a putative Word of God, there are as many possible theologies as there are putative revelations. Christian theology consequently appears at the beginning of this present epoch of global consciousness as a peculiar theology alongside other peculiar theologies, chiefly those of Judaism and Islam. Relations of rivalry among these Abrahamic religions have corresponded to their historical origins and ensuing histories. The theological critiques embedded in these rivalries, moreover, are not inconsequential. Thus the contemporary sense of historical relativity regarding putative words of God, along with historical knowledge of the bloody rivalry where this historical relativity has not been admitted, is a chief motive in those appalled theologians who have latched on to the more genial Platonic approach to the knowledge of God indicated above in the discussion of Melanchthon — to escape the quarreling gods, to find "God above God," as Tillich famously put it.[76] Yet this challenge to the theologies of revelation is not as new as it sometimes is said to be. Classically, in fact, we have good reason to believe that just this apophatic turn motivated the emperor Julian (the "Apostate") in pagan theology's last, great neo-Platonic effort to forestall the advance of Nicene Christianity.[77]

If, however, Christian theology proceeds with the Council of Nicea on the basis of the putative Word from God incarnate as proclaimed by the Spirit through the gospel, today these relations with Judaism and Islam might be freed from invidious rivalry, ironically enough, by the end of the Christendom that began with the defeat of Julian's cosmopolitan project. In this prospect of theology learning from historical experience,[78] the classical theological critiques of Christianity by Judaism and Islam could become principles internal to Christian theology's own reflection.[79] That is to say, the nature of Christian faith in God as knowing faith may be helpfully clarified for Christians and non-Christians alike

75. *RPTD*, p. 214.

76. Paul Tillich, *The Courage to Be* (New Haven and London: Yale University Press, 1976), pp. 186-90.

77. Hans Lietzman, *A History of the Early Church* (New York: World Publishing Co., 1961), p. 277. See the discussion in *DC*, pp. 227-28. See also Oyvind Nordeval, "The Emperor Constantine and Arius: Unity in the Church and Unity in the Empire," *Studia Theologica* 42 (1988): 113-50.

78. See *BA*, pp. 1-13.

79. See *BA*, pp. 159-63.

in coming to terms with Judaism's original dissent from the oxymoronic kerygma of the "crucified Christ"[80] as also with Islam's sharp challenge to Christianity's equally oxymoronic trinitarianism by its summons to submission to the one and only God, "who neither begets nor is begotten."[81] We will find opportunity to explore just such possibilities in Chapters Five and Seven below.

Such an explicit and critical differentiation in teaching today would be intended as a hopeful act that may move historical relations of uncomprehending and therefore murderous rivalry towards the better possibility of the friendship of achieved disagreement *coram hominibus* and perhaps also *coram Deo*. This indeed is a possibility that the Jewish philosopher Peter Ochs envisions by means of the collaborative theological project of "scriptural reasoning."[82] From the Christian perspective, such achieved disagreement in dialogue with Judaism and Islam by the modality of scriptural reasoning would manifest and enable the better, Pauline "rivalry in doing good."[83] In any event, the possibility of a critical, not vulgar pluralism with a discerning, not categorical tolerance has simply become an imperative in post-Christendom, also for Christian theology. We defer further discussion of theology's situation after Christendom to a later section in this chapter and revert now to this subsection's topic: the theology of the Word.

For its own part, Christian theology originally and continuously attends to the Easter Word of God vindicating the crucified Christ,[84] an *offense* and *folly* (1 Cor. 1:23) in that it judges as sinful the world that crucified the incarnate Son of God and continues to persecute or otherwise still scorns the same One in His earthly body. This offense of the cross of Christ makes Christian theology doubly peculiar, not merely in that it presumes to speak truthfully of the Creator God in a historically conditioned discourse, i.e., the infinite in terms of the finite, but chiefly in that it learns the Word from God about God *sub contrario* (Luther), "under the opposite," in rhetorical subversion of predominant metaphysical conceptions or aesthetic symbolizations. This latter peculiarity of gospel narrative in apocalyptic parable,[85] Pauline paradox,[86] and Johannine enigma[87] (to mention

---

80. I endeavored such a clarification in an earlier, not yet mature work, Paul R. Hinlicky, "A Lutheran Contribution to the Theology of Judaism," *Journal of Ecumenical Studies* 31, no. 1-2 (Winter-Spring 1994): 123-52.

81. E.g., Surah 112.3.

82. Peter Ochs, *Another Reformation: Postliberal Christianity and the Jews* (Grand Rapids: Eerdmans, 2011).

83. As in *A Common Word: Muslims and Christians on Loving God and Neighbor,* ed. M. Wolf, G. bin Muhammad, and M. Yarrington (Grand Rapids: Eerdmans, 2010).

84. Jenson, *ST* 1, p. 4, 42.

85. Mark 4. See below in Chapter Five the discussion of Joel Marcus, *Mark 1–8, A New Translation with Introduction and Commentary,* The Anchor Bible vol. 27 (New Haven and London: Yale University Press, 2000), and *Mark 8–16,* The Anchor Yale Bible (New Haven and London: Yale University Press, 2009).

86. *RPTD,* pp. 143-59.

87. The fourth evangelist "shows that the life and death of Jesus was not a mere visual

the chief three forms of New Testament discourse) is the inalienable form of the Word of God. Synthesizing, we can designate this form as "metaphor" in Eberhard Jüngel's sense of an innovative construction that works by means of apparent contradiction, i.e., preeminently in what is for Paul the community-constitutive proclamation of "Christ crucified" (1 Cor. 1:18–2:5). This form is not "similitude" that makes the less familiar known by means of the more familiar, as in analogical models of theological language.[88] The linguistic forms of the New Testament constitute a subversive rhetoric that is to be decoded in theology, not preached stupidly as the assertion of logical contradictions which would amount to talking nonsense gussied up as revealed mystery. As to its decoded content, however, the Word of the resurrection of the Crucified effects the reconciliation of the very world judged sinful — reconciliation to His Father's eschatological purpose from the origin for the coming of the Beloved Community on the earth. Consequently, God's Word of reconciliation through the cross is heard and believed, i.e., understood and trusted according to God's mind and purpose in the same Spirit who raised Jesus from death, who also raises the believer through a corresponding cross of repentance and resurrection to faith by means of the timely *predication* that crucified Jesus *is* the Messiah of Israel also *"for you"* (Luther).

This Spirit-wrought hearing in faith "for me" of an offensive Word that comes to us both temporally as news and spatially from outside the isolated and egocentric self,[89] bound up as it is in structures of malice and injustice, constitutes the peculiar *subject-object correlation* in the community of faith in mission to the nations. It is this correlation that gives rise to Christian theology as the "science" of critical dogmatics — if and when, that is, the *audience* of this correlation is, as Jesus proclaims in the Sermon on the Mount, the heavenly Father, whose secret seeing today will become manifest at the eschaton of judgment (Rom. 14:10-12). At the eschaton, theology *coram Deo* (before God) and *coram hominibus* (before humanity) perfectly and visibly converge, even as theology on the way anticipates this convergence. This account of the knowledge of God as ultimately prayer and praise in response to the Easter Word of God will be elaborated in detail below in Chapter Seven. For the present it may be seen to yield the following outline of epistemic access in theology.

The person who is the *subject* of theology is the Holy Spirit refashioning the mind of believers by way of dying and rising with Jesus; the person who is the *object* of theology is Jesus the crucified Jew as vindicated and revealed as the

---

or sensual manifestation of something from the supernatural sphere, but, in its very form, a manifestation by which certain unprecedented results were achieved . . ." where the enigmatic "form" in question is that the author has "presented theology in the form of a gospel. . . ." Sir Edwyn Hoskins and Francis Noel Davey, *The Riddle of the New Testament* (London: Faber & Faber, 1949), pp. 162-63.

88. Eberhard Jüngel, *Theological Essays* I, ed. J. B. Webster (Edinburgh: T. & T. Clark, 1989), pp. 16-94.

89. On the *Verbum externum,* see Luther's classic account in "Against the Heavenly Prophets," *LW* 40, pp. 146-49, and further, on his teaching of the Spirit given *per verbum,* pp. 212-14.

Messiah of Israel and Son of God by the same Spirit of the resurrection; and the *audience* of theology is the person who presides at the eschatological judgment, the Father who is heavenly and ours together, just because He sends the Son and the Spirit into the world for all. For reasons so indicated but yet fully to be explained, the presentation of topics in the three parts following the two introductory chapters of the first part of this system of theology unfold in just this order: *Pneumatology,* presenting the subject of theology; *Christology,* presenting the object of theology; *Patrology,* presenting the audience of theology; and *Doxology,* projecting the end or fulfillment of theology. If there is a "system" in this systematic theology it is just to follow the Genesis-to-Revelation narrative in the Spirit, with the Son, to the Father. While this organization around the divine Persons and their respective works of fulfillment, redemption, and creation is properly theocentric, it just so includes humanity and cosmos according to the various theologics at work in each of these divine works, taken cumulatively and together.

Faith that is true to the *Verbum externum* in the way just sketched must contest error in theology because this faith knows itself to exist in contest from the day of baptism to the day of the resurrection. In the interim, dogmatics faithful and just so critical has constantly to test both self and others who would speak of God: Which Christ (Mark 13:6)? What gospel (Gal. 1:6-9; 6:14-15)? Whose Spirit (1 John 4:1-3)?[90] At its best, this collaborative self-questioning of the Christian faith through time and across space for truthfulness to its authorizing Word from God reflects the conception of truth in Christian theology. Here truth, as in all the other sciences, is ultimately (though not penultimately) a matter of correspondence to reality. But unlike any other science the peculiar correspondence of truth in theology is not between human ideas or images and things in the presently existing and visible order of worldly relations (for such truths, theology happily defers to these other disciplines, as argued below). In theology truth primarily denotes God's own eschatological correspondence to His promise in Christ to which Spirit-given faith already now says, "Amen." Secondarily it denotes the believer's and the believing community's correspondence in faith to the promised divine faithfulness in obedience, confession, and mission. Only in the third place does it also pertain to the ongoing interpretation of experience. In this priority of seeking first the Reign of God and its righteousness, however, the interpretation of experience is both necessary and urgent. Indeed it is the kind of theological cognition that most immediately concerns Christian living and hope for the grieving world. The theology of the Word in this way cannot be nothing but an "in-house" discourse closed off from experience. It is rather the very matrix by which experience is truly known as the creation of God, being liberated and fulfilled. The Word alone is never alone, but always at work in the Spirit's interpretation of experience where it is known concretely in faith, or truly not at all.

90. Paul R. Hinlicky, "Authority in the Church: A Plea for Critical Dogmatics," in *New Directions for Lutheranism,* ed. Carl Braaten (Delhi, NY: ALPB Books, 2010), pp. 123-53.

## The Interpretation of Experience

The truth, says the Gospel of John, "sets free" (John 8:32). Truth making has causal power in the world; by the same token, truth binds consciences when it is truly known. "If revelation is understood as God's self-interpretation to the world in the life, death, resurrection and exaltation of the man Christ Jesus, then theology is this kind of cognition, the church's interpretation of God's self-interpretation to continually new human experience."[91] As the form of cognition in theology, interpretation of experience is not a superficial gloss on the hard reality of other mechanisms known in other ways; interpretation too works causally, just as Leibniz claimed in the innovative *Discourse on Metaphysics,* when he wrote that Christ's revelation of the kingdom of heaven had changed the course of history.[92] But it had long been understood that the conformation of the believer and the believing community to the Word of God includes faith's corresponding interpretation of experience during the interregnum between Christ's ascension and parousia: as the believer who believes that she is received into mercy for Christ's sake is interpreting her experience, so also her community believes that in spite of failure and woe it is the arena of the dawning new creation — and so is likewise interpreting its experience. This "regarding," "taking as" of theological interpretation (in classical language, "reckoning" or "imputation") is cognition. As knowledge of faith, such interpretation of experience causes believer and community of faith to suffer and to act differently in the world than otherwise.

This is the sense in which the article on justification by faith may rightly claim to be the chief article on which the church stands and falls in that it pertains to the authorizing interpretation of the Christian believer and so of Christian community as community of faith. United now with Christ the Son by Spirit-wrought faith, the believer is justified before His Father already now in spite of persisting sin; hence he is at peace already now with the God whose kingdom comes and therefore already now fit for new service in the mission to the nations. Such interpretation of the person- and community-constitutive experience of the *Christus pro nobis,* Christ for us, is not merely a religious perspective or noncognitive value-judgment (though it certainly is a judgment that bestows value!) as good or bad as any other, as vulgar and uncritical pluralism might think. In theology the claim is that this interpretation of human experience in the world — justification by faith alone — is the true one because it knows and articulates the divine perspective; already now it speaks and so effects the judgment of the heavenly Father whose reckoning by His almighty Word creates in the Spirit the reality it names on the way to the best of all possible worlds. This divine judgment or reckoning is appropriated and applied in faith to each one's own personal and corporate experience or it is not known truly at all. Cognitive interpretation of

---

91. *PNT,* p. 374.
92. Leibniz, *Discourse on Metaphysics* (Indianapolis: Hackett, 1991), p. 41.

experience by the Word is proper sense of the *pro me/pro nobis* principle in theology personally and communally.

This analysis of theological interpretation of experience bears a further implication. This new creative reality is spoken to our existing reality. Our existing reality correspondingly supplies the material that theology interprets as God's creating and preserving for the sake of God's redeeming and fulfilling. By the same token, the best available accounts of existing experience admit of such theological interpretation and indeed demand it. This capacity for theological interpretation, so to speak, is only possible if and when theology holds that this existing and developing world, in which the cross of Jesus stood, is God's own creation continuing in its philosophical advances to better accounts of human experience in the world. Fallen, corrupted, and subjected to vanity though it is, it is nonetheless the matter of God's ongoing blessing and the precious object of His costly love, hidden though the blessing and love seem. Groaning in futility, this is the creation destined for redemption and fulfillment, as Bonhoeffer's meditation on God's love for the world attests. "Love is the reconciliation of man with God in Jesus Christ. The disunion with God, with other men, with the world and with themselves, is at an end. Man's origin is given back to him."[93] To render this interpretation *of* the world persuasively and winsomely *in* the world, but also sharply and prophetically as needed, is the interpretive work of Christian theology for which systematic theology provides the toolkit. As we shall next see, this task entails that, in a manner carefully to be defined, philosophy is also a source — material, not formal — of Christian theology.

Notice the qualification snuck into the preceding: "our *best available* accounts of experience," i.e., philosophical accounts in their own voice according to their own integrity. Needless to say, with the diversity of human experience and the corruption of perception under predominating structures of malice and injustice, what counts as "best" will be hotly contested. Philosophy is no more settled as a discipline than theology. But philosophy, taken at its best as a discipline of critical and consequent thinking about human experience in the world, strives to "save the phenomena," that is, to account for all and to ignore nothing. A good account is maximally rich in content but simple in explanation; and it is better when more and more is explained in less and less complicated ways. In this way, philosophy keeps inquiry open by avoiding premature closures. It exposes and calls into question totalitarian ambitions at work in hidden and hence unwarranted theologies. When in the name of science someone demands closure, science has been left behind and we have entered the realm of metaphysics. Natural science in this regard does not replace philosophy, as modernity has often been inclined to think. Indeed, the natural sciences are not immune from contest and philosophical critique, since science too is a human praxis whose research can

---

93. Dietrich Bonhoeffer, *Ethics,* trans. N. H. Smith (New York: Macmillan, 1978), p. 52, pp. 17-54.

be bought and sold by nonscientific interests and whose "assured results" in the best case can and must be superseded by new and surprising paradigm shifts, as Kuhn famously pointed out, if science itself is to progress in scope through unanticipated new discoveries. Science may be self-correcting in the long run, but that is due to its embeddedness in a human culture where philosophical critique is alive and well (recall, for example, the dogmatic sterility of Soviet *Lysenkoism*).

Theology learns from philosophy the best, that is, the most *parsimonious* accounts of experience: the *simplest* explanation of the *greatest* data. The fact that this best philosophical account is further qualified as that which is "available," however, indicates the temporal and spatial delimitation mentioned above. The best available account of experience is best "here and now," fully cognizant of the fact that it will be someday superseded. The "best" accounts, knowing that they will be superseded, are content to move things forward in their own time and place. In this way they decline the totalitarian ambition to know theoretically as God is imagined to know by totalitarians. But one accepts the finitude of knowledge in the confidence, derived from revealed theology, that essentially perspectival knowledge of creatures has its particular place and time in God's creating. If the sciences do not acknowledge that limitation, and philosophy fails in critique, theology can helpfully teach the same lesson. For example, Stephen Hawking was just wrong, in Christian perspective, to speculate that a unified field theory would enable reason's knowledge of "the mind of God" (cf. 1 Cor. 2:6-16), that is, "why" the universe goes "to all the bother of existing."[94] The great philosophical question about the cosmos, "Why is there something rather than nothing?" becomes in theology the more precise question, "Why is there *this* something rather than something *else?*" where "this" world is particularly the place of the cross of the Incarnate Son of God. In this *oikonomia tou theou* ("plan of God," Eph. 1:4-14) we discover the "mind of God" who "bothers" with us in that costly act of love for the sake of the coming of the Beloved Community.

In any event, systematic theology cannot in principle resolve philosophical contests, so defined, even though theologians as subjects if not citizens of two kingdoms participate in them also. But as theologians they may only intervene in them to reframe questions theologically under the chief motif of God's costly love for the world that intends the coming of the Beloved Community. To be of service today in the foregoing ways of knowledge of God, speaking responsibly of God with the church on the basis of His Word for the sake of the cognitive interpretation of experience in the world at this critical juncture of post-Christendom Euro-American history, systematic theology has to eschew not only the temptation of systematicity but the temptation to be encyclopedic. The temptation of systematicity is to force all the evidence into a Procrustean bed; the encyclope-

---

94. Stephen Hawking, with Leonard Mlodinow, *A Briefer History of Time* (New York: Bantam Dell, 2005), p. 142. It is noteworthy that Hawking explicitly invokes *Augustine* for ruling out "God as a being existing in time" (p. 134).

dic temptation is to try to master all the evidence in a comprehensive account. Both errors attend theologies that do not want to live between the times of the Ascension and the Parousia. But theology can think dogmatically because the reign of God is inaugurated in Christ; yet it must think critically because the promised fulfillment is still future. Theology can neither survey all the evidence nor yet see how it coheres, but ventures its interpretations in faith and submits them to judgment.

Critical dogmatics in this situation can let the arts, the humanities, and the sciences speak in their own voices and it can collaborate with philosophy, taken as the discipline that argues the best available account of experience. Systematic theology does not have to do their work for them, as the various genitive theologies clumsily presume, even if for the most part they end up — embarrassed at their own presumption — merely dressing the thought of other disciplines in religious cloaking. This is a shell game, *not* the *discerning* work of *interpretation* of this wealth of material in terms of Christian beliefs in their cognitive claim — what Lindbeck called the "redescription" of the world in Christian terms.[95] In this way a "Scriptural world is thus able to absorb the universe."[96] But that is the work of all generations cumulatively and cooperatively. For its own part, systematic theology today can and should rather focus on the "theo-logic," so to say, underlying the dogmatic topics of Christian belief, as these give the rules for the proper usage of Christian beliefs to interpret experience in a world that is fundamentally contested. Indeed, this focus on theologic as the "rules of faith" *(regulae fidei)* that are also the tools for interpretation of experience by Christian beliefs is what makes critical dogmatics critical.[97] The knowledge of God in gospel faith articulated in this way by systematic theology empowers its students to live faithfully because cognizantly in the contested world of human experience.

## How Critical Dogmatics Is "Critical" and "Dogmatic"

Traditionally doctrinal topics discussed items or articles of Christian belief, for example, those listed in the baptismal creed. Thus one speaks, for example, of the doctrine of Creation, or of the Virgin Birth, or of the Atonement, or of the human creature as image of God but fallen into sin, or of the Second Coming of Christ, or of the Church as one, holy, catholic, and apostolic. It goes without saying that the nature of these traditional Christian beliefs is hotly disputed in modern theology,

---

95. George A. Lindbeck, *The Nature of Doctrine: Religion and Theology in a Postliberal Age* (Philadelphia: Westminster, 1984), p. 124.

96. Lindbeck, *Doctrine,* p. 117.

97. Robert C. Saler has correctly lifted up this element in my work in "Paul Hinlicky's Critical Dogmatics: Triune Redemption and Hope in the Beloved Community," *Dialog* 52, no. 2 (Summer 2013): 151-57.

akin to the dispute philosophically about what is a "fitting" conception of deity. Reflecting this still-unresolved situation, this system of theology, presented as critical dogmatics, does not, as, for example, Thomas Oden does in his reprise, *Classical Christianity,* attempt to preserve all the topics of traditional belief in the traditional order.[98] Still pertinent here is the objection of Rudolf Bultmann to such an endeavor, who went so far in advocating for theology as pure theologic, that is, as nothing but rules for relevant and liberating proclamation, as to deny that such venerable creedal beliefs are specifically Christian at all.[99] The question is valid, even if Bultmann's solution to it is not.

No serious theologian today, for example, holds that a historical Adam and Eve or a three-story cosmology or the existence of demonic spirits is essential to the gospel knowledge of God. Once we admit this de facto selectivity with respect to the laundry list of beliefs recorded in Scripture, Bultmann's probing question about just what makes beliefs "specifically Christian," i.e., essential to the faithful telling of the gospel in its mission to the nations, has been admitted. He offered in full consequence of this *critical* thinking in theology a program of "demythologization,"[100] which may be profitably compared to the work of *deliteralization* in the present work.[101] Demythologization regards the narrative form of biblical literature as inappropriate to knowledge of God and thus reduces it to symbolizations of states of human consciousness; deliteralization regards the narrative form of biblical literature as appropriate to the knowledge of God and thus decodes it to tell of the movement of the living God.

Demythologization aims to uncover the existential self-understanding supposedly expressed in the mythical beliefs of Christian tradition by rejecting its ostensible cognitive content. This critical program, however, led Bultmann to a modern version of Docetic Christology. Here Christ is the evanescent event of divine presence "for me" in the moment of preaching, without a narrative giving content to Christ so that He can become the object of faith that substantively forms the theological subject as a faithful person through time and in community

---

98. Thomas C. Oden, *Classical Christianity: A Systematic Theology,* previously published in three volumes (New York: HarperOne, 1992).

99. See the discussion in *DC,* pp. 49-60.

100. Rudolf Bultmann & Five Critics, *Kerygma and Myth,* ed. H. W. Bartsch (New York: Harper & Row, 1961).

101. "Thus the creation is for God just one place. And the one creation is heaven and earth together, however otherwise they differ. Therefore the difference between God's being in heaven and his being on earth can only be a difference between styles of his presence; for him to 'come' from one to the other does not require him to leave where he was or arrive where he was not." Jenson, *ST* 2, p. 254. Significantly, Jenson here approvingly "for once" cites Theodore of Mopsuestia in support, where Theodore speaks of change in God's will as the reality signified by the temporal-spatial attribution of local motion to God in the Bible. Though Jenson does not here articulate this change in divine will or style of presence as the transition from wrath to mercy, it is difficult to see how anything other could be in mind.

(as the present proposal argues).[102] As Oswald Bayer pertinently observes in this connection, "In neo-Protestantism of the neo-Kantian variety, this *pro me* has been and continues to be misused as a methodological principle, in order to eliminate anything that is objective concerning what faith believes, and to characterize faith as that which happens to each one individually."[103] In speaking of *critical* dogmatics, then, this one-sidedness of Bultmann's critical insight is both retrieved and corrected along the lines suggested by Bayer. It is corrected in that critical dogmatics remains *dogmatics,* i.e., the analysis and development of specifically Christian beliefs according to a systematic insight that unifies them to give the knowledge of the saving God of the lost and perishing creation. In the process, of course, a selection is made. For example, while it remains of historical interest and has a certain illustrative power in showing civil law reformed by the knowledge of the saving God of the Exodus, the Book of Leviticus cannot hold literally as knowledge of the structures of love and justice that God the Creator intends for the creation. Its ostensive claim must be deliteralized and decoded theologically.

In place of demythologization, the present work regularly invokes this idea of *deliteralization* of Christian beliefs by which the picture language of scriptural narrative is decoded to speak about God and to make a claim to truth about Him. A ready example of deliteralization from the history of theology is Luther's interpretation of Christ's ascension to the right hand of God, not as a spatial transit distancing the man Christ away in the sky from His earthly people, thus subverting His promised presence with them, but rather as an event within the life of God whereby the Father hands over, and the Son incarnate and now triumphant receives, the sovereignty "until he subdues every enemy under his feet" (1 Cor. 15:25).[104] To make the same point another way, the biblical language of theology literally refers to God, even though it uses terms appropriate to creatures to do so. Its similes *have reference,* and they are not correctly understood until the reference *to God* as the eternal Life with us and for us is decoded and stated, however provisionally and thus subject to revision and to final, that is, eschatological confirmation.

Theologic, i.e., rules for using beliefs is indeed one of the great, if insufficiently understood (especially by one-sided proponents, such as Bultmann) contributions of Reformation theology in that it attends not only to the apparent cognitive content of a topic, as in traditional dogmatics, but to its proper usage according to the systematic logic of the gospel's basic claim to truth about God. Theologic contends that we do not adequately know this ostensible content until

---

102. James F. Kay, *Christus Praesens: A Reconsideration of Rudolf Bultmann's Christology* (Grand Rapids: Eerdmans, 1994).

103. Bayer, *Luther's Theology,* pp. 131-32.

104. LW 37, pp. 55-64. It is interesting to observe that here Luther deploys the notion of divine simplicity as a rule of reverent speech for the Creator whose transcendence makes Him radically immanent metaphysically. He thus transcribes the literally spatial notions of divine presence and absence to notations for divine blessing and curse.

we also know how it applies to experience and how such application coheres with all the beliefs of the baptismal creed. Thus "doctrine for life"[105] (not "theory") is meant in understanding the beliefs about God taken from the Bible and organized in the baptismal creed. What is needed today from a presentation of systematic theology is a clear and comparatively succinct exposition (accompanied as needed by correction with further development) and illustrative application of the theologic at work in the essential doctrinal topics so that Christian beliefs spring to life again to sort and process information on the church's pilgrim way. This — in the author's judgment, urgent — need informs the material selected for consideration in this volume.

Alas, rules can multiply too. Examples of theologic are familiar enough from theology in the tradition of Luther. A random list includes the dialectics of Word and Spirit, of law and gospel, of hiddenness and revealedness, of sinner and saint, of destiny and freedom, of being in communion or consistent perichoresis, of joyful exchange, and so on. As doctrine for life, theology undertakes the critical analysis and further development of doctrinal topics by articulating these theologic rules of their appropriate usage. For example, theologic instructs us to speak of God's self-revelation in such a way that the Word can be heard only in the Spirit and the Spirit can be granted only through the Word. Or, again, it instructs: speak of a sinner only in such a way that she is beloved by God in Jesus Christ and made holy in that love, and speak of a saint only in such a way that he progresses in holiness by only returning to baptismal union with Jesus Christ. In appropriate usage, ecumenical Christian beliefs, e.g., about revelation and holiness as just mentioned, work cognitively to organize and interpret the mass of empirical data encountered in the mission to the nations and in the vocations of believers within them on the way to the Beloved Community of God.

As we shall see in the next section, the chief organizing "theologic" of ecumenical Christian belief for this world-absorbing mission is the Trinitarian interpretation of God as the Father who in the Son by the Spirit creates a world in order to redeem and fulfill it. To this the Reformation adds the critical rule for usage: so speak the Trinity that in the Spirit, with the Son, the auditor is returned by pure gift to the Father's waiting love already now, hence by the believer's receptivity of faith alone. In systematic theology, these two meta-doctrines of the Trinity and Justification by Faith, aside from any explicit treatment accorded to them, permeate the whole of the presentation so that they continually do the work of sorting and integrating the topics of traditional Christian belief. In this way the coherence of faith is grasped and displayed and so made available as tools for missiological praxis.

Systematic theology has the reputation, deserved in some respects, of ivory-tower theory. But this criticism must be taken more seriously and more consequently than the critics who voice it usually do. It is the very model of knowledge

---

105. Royce, *Problem*, p. 55.

as *theory,* as speculation, as gazing, as intuition of transcendent-because-self-identical reality — whether given naturally *or supernaturally* — that in fact the gospel knowledge of God calls into question. Not even the final correspondence of the world to God in the coming of the Beloved Community is to be thought of on the model of gazing, a model that is motivated by the idea of imperfect substances adhering to the perfect substance to escape the vicissitudes of becoming. But the eschatological correspondence of the world to God is rather to be thought on the model of doxology, that is, the creature's participation in the mutual glorying of the tri-personal life of God that in the Spirit with the Son glorifies the Father, even as the Father in the Son by the Spirit glorifies the redeemed and fulfilled creation. *This* final correspondence of the world to God in such a consistent and expanded *perichoresis* is a "harmony," even a "fugue," as Jenson puts it.[106] It may be so, however, because the ideal of knowledge in theology is pragmatic, not theoretic.

In this light, the negative or apophatic or anti-metaphysical theologies that arise in protest against theology as theory, justified so far as they go, merely negate in practice an ideal that tacitly remains in force as a norm: knowledge as theory. But this half-critique produces the oxymoron of "learned ignorance," i.e., of noncognitivism regarding the knowledge of God who gives Himself and communicates Himself in the gospel, providing the very charter of theology as a discipline. We can and should of course grant on grounds of reverence that to be Creator of all that is not God as He *must* be if He is *able* to promise the coming of the Beloved Community to and for all, is "infinite," that is, unbounded in relation to us, not confined by a creature's definition. As "infinite" in relation to us, God in His ability or power is eternally incomprehensible to creatures, since their comprehension cannot exceed finite perspective (even in the gift of eternal life) without abolishing their very nature as creatures, that is, as beings bounded by God. But it is the redemption and fulfillment of the creature in Beloved Community, as persons with persons, not abolition of creatureliness and absorption into the divine nature, which the gospel promises. But this negation — namely, that the infinite God of the gospel is as such "not bounded" with respect to ability, is in Christian origin dependent upon an affirmation, a positive understanding of God as Maker and Redeemer of all that is as other than Himself.

To affirm God as the infinite, concretely as the *Almighty* Father (see below, Chapter Seven) is concretely to deny that Chaos is God over God, i.e., that matter or sheer undecided potentiality is the true and infinite abyss to which even God is subjected as a finite entity — as the theogonic myths of primitive humanity envisage. If there is such an "abyss," it is in Christian perspective the very mind of God, who has all possibles as known and searched by the Spirit of God (1 Cor. 2:9-12). But to use *this* Christian affirmation of divine incomprehensibility properly is to not to distance God from creatures but rather to give eternal life as the gift to

---

106. Jenson, *ST* 2, p. 369.

creatures of an unbounded journey in God by God to God, just as Trinitarianism claims for the coming of the Beloved Community. To use the natural incomprehensibility of God the Almighty Father otherwise, i.e., to negate the gospel knowledge of God as none other than the self-surpassing Almighty Father who gives the gift of eternal life, is thus a misunderstanding, if not an alien theology.

Why one would continue at all in a discipline named theology is hard to fathom if all that one can in any case assert are denials. But in fact denials always presuppose affirmations. And in theology, affirmation is the first and constituting word of the gospel of the resurrection of the Crucified One, for in vindicating His Son God determines His own Fatherhood (see below Chapter Seven). The classical standoff here between apophatic and kataphatic tendencies in philosophical theology, or between transcendence and immanence, is something to be overcome in revealed theology by means of a better model of knowledge itself. What "system" means in theology in any case turns on the model of knowledge theology adopts and what model of knowledge theology adopts depends likewise on a putative Word of God and the community that corresponds to it. In what follows, accordingly, I subject to criticism the conceits of "system" where a theoretic model of knowledge is held in order to redeem a concept of "system" as the work of internal and external coherence in and of the evangelical mission according to a pragmatic model of knowledge.

Joyful and doxological as it surely is, theology is assuredly not in gospel perspective leisured or contemplative speculation on transcendent realities as opposed to doing and labor on the earth and in history; nor is it even reflection on practice as some separable function. It is the reflection of a specifically commissioned praxis, organic to the definite way that is named, Jesus Christ, following after the crucified but now risen Lord who presently authorizes disciples to teach the nations what He has said and done (Matt. 28:19-20). Thus all practitioners of Christianity do theology, i.e., deploy theologics to organize experience in terms of Christian beliefs and so to conceptualize the church's mission, the believer's vocation, or the prophet's advocacy. They theologize well or poorly but they do theologize. Theology done well is a disciplined thinking after the living Lord who comes to His people as promised when they gather as the ecclesia. Theology is the *nachdenken* of such faith (Jüngel) — the German verb translates as "to reflect, to consider" — but literally rendered means "to think after," just as *Nachfolge,* translated as "discipleship" (a word kin in English to discipline), means literally "following after." Theology is the discipleship of the mind, the intellectual discipline of faith following Jesus and seeking understanding in order to confess His truth publicly in the world but before God. It pertains to all believers according to each one's level of aptitude and training. With its catechetical roots thus intact, theology is academically organized as a system, as in this book, both for heuristic purposes in the church and for advancing the truth-claim of the gospel in the world.

Manifestly, then, putatively Christian faith that does not *know* Jesus Christ is *blind* faith, vulgar and uncritical thinking, a leaf blown about by every new wind of doctrine. But faith that does *know* Jesus Christ also knows how Jesus Christ — let us put this as bluntly and as provocatively as is necessary — is *to be used, objectified, made available, and appropriated as something real in the world.* To do this rightly is without doubt a massive challenge that requires consequent thinking as part and parcel of the Holy Spirit's work in forming the theological subject, so that precisely as used and appropriated Jesus Christ remains the saving Lord and does not become the figure and servant of causes other than His Father's (as has happened time and again with woeful results in the course of the gospel's journey through the nations).

Thus Christian theology is "systematic" in the foregoing sense of logical consequence required for true obedience in faith that follows and does not lead. But it is not "systematic" in the sense of pretending comprehensiveness, earthly or heavenly. Systematic theology cannot comprehend (not nearly) all the varied and diverse data that disciples encounter in mission and vocation and prophecy. Rather it provides the theologic tools in consequent thinking by which data can be processed in terms of the Christian system of beliefs. The alternative to systematic theology in this regard is not praxis, but slothful and haphazard praxis, vulnerable to capture by forces other than Jesus, His Father, and their Spirit, taken together as the One God. Taken as One God, of course, the ineffable Trinity may be beyond the grasp of human logic, but we who believe and obey are not. Theology places this demand of critical and consequent thinking on disciples who believe in time and space. If we are speaking meaningfully and responsibly in the world and before others of God and putatively in His Name, as of Him who first speaks and acts meaningfully and responsibly to us in Jesus Christ, it can only be according to logically coherent discourse. Consequent thinking of faith is needful, in that Christian discipleship in the world is ever dependent on freshly ascertaining, grasping, and understanding the coming, presence, leading, and hidden reign of Jesus, who is the object of such faith. In this respect, theology that is not intentionally and effectively *systematic* is only Christian theology *by accident.*

Taken as creation, however, reality is in the making and thus cannot be nailed down in the static transparency implied by "system" in the theoretic sense.[107] Nor is the "world" a static stage (as "nature" has been thought) on which the human drama plays out (as "history" has been thought), but it is the afflicted, contested creation, fallen under structures of malice and injustice, groaning for liberation yet ruled in a hidden way by the ascended Lord that believers struggle to discern and greet. The true problem of theology, in distinction from philosophy, lies in discerning this making new of all things — the first canon of theologic according to Galatians 6:15-16 — as it actually is at work in the world. It is at work in the world in the manifest mission to the nations that gathers the church, in the baptismal vocations of believers within the nations, by the hidden rule of Jesus

---

107. Bayer, *Luther's Theology,* pp. xv-xvi, 1-12.

Christ in the "mandates of creation" (Bonhoeffer), by prophetic voices that arise in advocacy for the sorrowing of the world so far as those creative mandates of God are violated and their divine purpose for Beloved Community frustrated. Here in the fray theology must discriminate God's new creation, as the redemption and fulfillment of the world gone astray. It must know God and His Word in distinction from prophetic frauds and messianic imposters, in this way enabling faithful discipleship.[108]

The actual cognition of theology, that is, the actual knowing of God in the world, takes place not only by thinking through a book of systematic theology. The tools, found in such a book, and learning how they work, do not themselves do this work of learning God, but rather enable it. Knowing God takes place rather in the timely exposition of the Scriptures from which the manifest event of Jesus Christ proceeds in sermon, sacrament, teaching, and conversation. By the *viva vox evangelii* the Spirit's consoling, caring, resistance, witness, advocacy, service, and whatever is needed for the mission to the nations come. Knowing God the Father takes place in sighs of thanksgiving with the corresponding service of worldly vocations on behalf of the creative mandates and by the prophetic analysis of what structures malice and injustice as opposed to what liberates creation from them for its fulfillment. For the doing of these works of the living Lord Jesus Christ by His Spirit to the glory of the Father a systematic presentation of theology, rightly understood, provides the toolkit — the theologic of the essential beliefs entailed by the gospel at work and in mission. By this knowledge the particular path of the gospel's truth-claim is cut in the world in the thoughtful and considered deliberation and collaboration of God's people extended through space and through time.

We defer discussion of the topical organization of the Christian system of belief to the next section. Suffice it to say here that because the ideal of knowledge as theory has isolated doctrinal topics from the question of usage, both the question of what beliefs are essential or "epistemically primary" (Marshall)[109] to the Christian knowledge of God and how the theologics underlying them work together as one in the Trinitarian economy of God remain unclarified. This systematic confusion is behind the Babel of contemporary Christian theologies — an unharmonious diversity that is not to be uncritically celebrated (so Westhelle),[110] however much the new attention to contextual particularity of the mission to the nations is indeed worthy of approbation and is amenable to the pragmatic model of knowledge in theology. The pragmatic model of knowledge in theology gracefully accepts the defect of our finitude, in that the point is never before the

---

108. Mark 13, as discussed in *SF,* pp. 187-89.

109. Bruce D. Marshall, *Trinity and Truth* (Cambridge: Cambridge University Press, 2000).

110. Westhelle, *After Heresy.* See this author's review in *Lutheran Quarterly* 27, no. 2 (Summer 2013): 227-29.

eschaton of judgment to try to settle once and for all the "embodied argument" that is theology in the Christian tradition, but to advance it at a particular juncture of the gospel's life in the world. This open-endedness of theology as a timely discipline, just as its procession from a definite calling and commitment in the gospel leads from the service of systematic theology in and to the ecumenical church that has been sketched heretofore to its service in and to the academy as a public claim to truth. As an academic discipline, systematic theology makes a cognitive case from the church to the world in the learned forum of the academy, notwithstanding how precarious this standing is today, given the collapse of Christendom. One can only proceed here and now in faith as opportunity is given. Theology makes its cognitive case through the entirety of its presentation. But for heuristic purposes, that whole can and should now be previewed.

## The Cognitive Claim

Critical dogmatics seeks to advance publicly the scholarly argument on the Christian knowledge of God. This is its academic service. It is a matter that concerns all, both friend, foe, and otherwise indifferent, and it is this matter that is at stake in dogmatics, traditional and critical. For no one can arise to a judgment on the worthiness of Christian belief unless one knows what such belief actually is and entails, intellectually as well as existentially, as this knowledge is proposed, articulated, and argued theologically by practitioners. Clarity concerning the cognitive claim entailed by Christian beliefs renders this service alike to believer, doubter, seeker, indifferent and even opponent. Noncognitive notions of faith and theology, on the other hand, as these have dominated academic theology after Kant, have obscured the essentially epistemic and public task of theology and hence its true academic service, in that they have regarded "knowledge" and "faith" as belonging to separate realms with boundaries between them carefully guarded, "no trespassing allowed!"[111]

Of course, this move of modern theology in its liberal iteration to noncognitivism reflected a genuine crisis that arose with the realization that the Bible or the "deposit of faith" does not simply or straightforwardly correlate with emergent scientific and historical accounts of our reality — *"wie es eigentlich gewesen ist"* (how it really happened — von Ranke).[112] In the conservative iteration, modern theology maintained the cognitive claim of traditional theology by means of a massive, undiscriminating, and a priori defense of objective revelation in a supernaturally written text reducible to a list of non-negotiable propositions (or, as in Pannenberg, a historically knowable miracle of resurrection as the proleptic

---

111. *PNT,* pp. 44-86.

112. Wolfhart Pannenberg, "The Crisis of the Scriptural Principle," in *Basic Questions in Theology,* two volumes, trans. G. H. Kehm (Philadelphia: Fortress, 1972), 1:1-14.

revelation of the whole of history) — an implausible stance for a multitude of reasons that can be maintained only at the cost of intellectual myopia and well-deserved academic isolation. Liberal theology was thus justified theologically in making necessary adjustments here. The courage of liberal theology was its concrete trust that God is active in the world as its continuing creator; in the context of modern consciousness liberal theology represented an awakening to the far wider world that God is creating than had been assumed in Christendom.

But the justified criticism of Scripture in the name of modern historical knowledge in this connection should have led an equally critical dogmatics to a purified claim to truth, as will be presented shortly.[113] Instead, modern theologies on both the progressive left (Lindbeck's "experiential expressivism") and the reactionary right (Lindbeck's "propositionalism") too often conceded, whether they regarded it as a breakthrough or as apostasy, the titanic claim of the Cartesian-Kantian subject to police all zones of public culture by a determination of what may count as knowledge. Lindbeck's own proffered "cultural-linguistic" model, however, is rightly criticized for continuing the cognitive evacuation of liberal theology in the direction of Wittgensteinian fideism, while simultaneously slighting the necessary burden undertaken by liberal theology to awaken to that wider world that God is creating in His strange present work of disassembling Christendom.

In this light, moreover, the "reconciled diversity" currently recommended by the academic scholarship of the ecumenical movement may very well be a diplomatically necessary gloss on the present Babel of Christian theologies. In its best light, "reconciled diversity" acknowledges the same theological "matter" under a variety of conceptual schemes.[114] But this affirmation of common "matter" is the assertion of pure good will, not to say blind faith. We have no access to "matter" apart from definite conceptualizations of it, and a matter that cannot be articulated in conceptually clarified language this way remains an unknown thing to us, a *Ding-an-sich*. Hence we can never achieve intellectual conviction of the reconciliation of our diverse theologies that is asserted, a sorry fate that attends the otherwise excellent fruit of this approach in the joint Lutheran-Catholic declaration on justification. Paul, for this very reason, apostolically forbade speaking in tongues in the church without interpretation that makes the "matter" manifest.

For the very sake of true convergence in ecumenical doctrine, then, systematic theology can hardly accept a principled confusion of tongues without surrendering the very "matter" that is at stake to permanent, impenetrable darkness.[115] In reality, a desire to retain possession of an ever-eroding frag-

113. There is, incidentally, a remarkable though little-known precedent for this way in the nineteenth-century theology of Isaak Dorner that Jonathan Norgate has recently excavated; Dorner's was a path not taken. Jonathan Norgate, *Isaak A. Dorner: The Triune God and the Gospel of Salvation* (London and New York: T. & T. Clark, 2009).

114. Harding Meyer, "The Ecumenical Dialogues: Situations, Problems, Perspectives," *Pro Ecclesia* 3, no. 1 (Winter 1994): 24-35.

115. Jenson, *Unbaptized God,* accordingly attempts to excavate a deep, common "flaw"

ment of ecclesiastical turf lifts up theological "diversity" as a way of avoiding the Christian claim to truth in all its penitential import for failed Christendom.[116] As Ephraim Radner has recently argued (to be further considered below at the end of Chapter Four), however, the "matter" that first gave rise to Christian theological controversy (and continues to exacerbate ecumenical incoherence in belief as is evident in contradictory doctrine and practice)[117] was the new claim to truth made with the gospel's Spirit-initiated mission to the nations. This Pentecost initiative of the Spirit[118] summoned the nations in the name of Jesus to moral conversion and new belief in God. To call the nations to repentance and faith (Luke), to appeal to Gentiles as ambassadors for reconciliation with the God of Israel (Paul), to summon one and all to come and see Israel's Jesus (John) is to make a cognitive claim, a claim to truth. But what is that? That is the "matter"!

To be sure, in comparison with ordinary knowledge and its production in the sciences, the arts, and the humanities, such knowledge of God in faith that comes by the gospel's mission to the nations is something quite extraordinary, a categorical *Novum*. It does not replace opinion with certain knowledge, as in Plato's classical scheme, but rather inchoate, blind, and servile faith with freed, knowing, and articulate faith that knows its object. Certainly this coming to knowledge of God in the freedom of faith by virtue of a report spoken in the name of God and understood according to God's intention demands an account, not a capitulation. The capitulation characteristic of modern theologies on both the left and the right takes place when theology tries methodologically to remove, as Lessing demanded, the element of historically formed subjectivity corresponding to the gospel's ineradicable temporal contingency, and instead to locate theology as a discipline in some putatively universal and necessary scheme of knowledge. But within such schemes theology can never acquire the cognitive purchase that the gospel asserts and theological subjectivity requires. It is either ghettoized in fundamentalism or devolves into wholesale religious subjectivism. We designate this capitulation and captivity of theology to universal schemes of rationality, "epistemology," the Cartesian-Kantian demand to locate any discipline of knowledge by a putatively timeless knowledge of knowledge, even as postmodern critique has exposed this epistemic policing demand as the *imperium* of the sovereign self. This "self lives in a world shorn of transcendence." There is only empty sky. "What occupies the vertical site of transcendence? The self, outside, above the

---

that produces ecumenical aporia rather than concede the framework of "reconciled diversity." See also Reinhard Hütter, *Suffering Divine Things: Theology as Church Practice,* trans. D. Stott (Grand Rapids: Eerdmans, 2000).

116. Ephraim Radner, *A Brutal Unity: The Spiritual Politics of the Christian Church* (Waco, TX: Baylor University Press, 2012), pp. 433-43.

117. Radner, *Brutal Unity,* pp. 171-219.

118. Jenson, *ST* 1, pp. 170-73.

world, a place where one rises above the 'herd' and seizes one's projects with nary a backwards glance."[119]

In its epistemic place, systematic theology as here envisioned offers its account of theological subjectivity that arises by dying and rising with Christ, known as the object of faith, and so proceeding in the world as Spirit-given discipleship of Christ, alongside of other subjectivities, but living before the Father in heaven. In this accounting, theology — also as academic theology — testifies. It bears witness concerning the self in the world transformed to faith, that is, the self called *out* from "the world" into a new community of persons as ecclesia, while at the same time remaining bodily in the mixed society of believers, half-believers, and unbelievers that is "the world" of the common body. It so remains not only by virtue of the mission of the Body of Christ in the world, but also by virtue of each believer's own abiding body that must eat and drink, work and play, make love and procreate and die, and so suffer and rejoice in and with all other bodies in the work of God's continual creating.

What matters cognitively here is not that one believes but what one believes, whether and how it is worthy of belief. And such is a matter of personal testimony in a dialogical process of mutually shared self-interpretations. If we overcome the spell of foundationalism, the question of what one believes may be seen to concern one and all in various ways, articulately in the academy where the study of systems of belief (rather than the reduction of such systems to other systems of belief) may be undertaken. Theological testimony is an accounting, then, that anyone in the mixed society of "this world" is in principle able to follow in understanding by virtue of the common body, what Heidegger, at least at one stage of his thought, meant by *Dasein,* "being there." Consequently anyone can in principle judge for themselves the Christian faith as a human possibility. Before these others, the theological account of subjectivity claims as such no privilege beyond what any other way in the world claims, that is, the common human dignity of incorrigibility with respect to the personal interpretation of one's own experience, costly though this may be under the structures of malice and injustice.[120] As testimony, such accounting is indeed the very posture of vulnerability, an ever-possible *martyria.*[121] This narrative warranting of theological subjectivity

119. Jean Bethke Elshtain, *Sovereignty: God, State, and Self, The Gifford Lectures* (New York: Basic Books, 2008), p. 204. It is questionable, however, whether the implicit critique of Nietzsche in this passage as the culmination, rather than an attempted subversion, of the sovereign self is the best reading. See *RPTD*, pp. 109-14. Likewise, to contend merely for transcendence against immanence, as in Barth against Schleiermacher, arguably does not get to the bottom of the problem. The gospel is not that there is sovereignty over humanity, but that the sovereignty that redeems and fulfills humanity belongs to Jesus, as the Son of the God of Israel, who gives His own Spirit that believers are able to do as He commands.

120. John 9:25.

121. J. Louis Martyn, *History and Theology in the Fourth Gospel,* Third Edition (Louisville and London: Westminster John Knox, 2003). Viewing the story of the blind beggar who re-

before others by testimony gives the rational (provided we see the ancient ideal of *theoria* and modern foundationalism as irrational) account of theology's "epistemic access" as personal encounter with the Word of God incarnate, though obviously it does not found theological knowledge indubitably. From it, however, critical dogmatics draws its anti-Cartesian generalization:[122] No one transcends. Everyone believes something — wisely or foolishly, knowingly or ignorantly, freely or slavishly. As mentioned above, in respect to this generalization theology alongside philosophy intervenes academically to level the epistemic playing field and reveal the hidden but unwarranted theologies at play in claims to knowledge even already in an inchoate, blind, and inarticulate state.[123] With respect to the ordinary knowledge produced in the sciences and the humanities, on the other hand, theology gratefully receives all that is good and true as works of God's hidden though continuous creating. Theology is quite properly constrained by such material although not in its own discipline formed by it.

Such an anti-Kantian account of epistemic access in theology, to be sure, does not intend a retreat to the pre-critical but a genuine advance beyond it, and thence beyond the merely critical, to a new, if chastened articulation of the Christian dogma. In pre-critical academic theology, that is, in scholasticism, a laundry-list of items of belief were extracted from Scripture and tradition and catalogued according to an underlying but generally unacknowledged conceptual scheme: an individualistic ascent of man to God (in definite tension with the Bible's testimony to the coming of God to a bound and captive humanity in the thrall of the structures of malice and injustice). On the naïve assumption of a simple unity of truth, theological attention then fell on reconciling the mass of evident contradictions in the assembled material — without sufficient awareness of the fact that the contradictions apparent in the assembled material were created at least in part by the very procedure of amassing nuggets from authoritative texts and juxtaposing them, abstracted from their biblical and patristic theological contexts and set into an alien conceptual scheme. The great and genuine advance of scholasticism in disputation and logical argument — increasingly appreciated today[124] — came

---

ceived his sight from Jesus in John 9 as a "two-level" drama interpreting the experience of the Johannine community by the Word concerning Jesus that first created it (pp. 40-45), Martyn rightly exposed the early Jewish-Christian experience of the Ban and expulsion from the synagogue as the matrix out of which the Fourth Gospel emerged (pp. 44-66). As sensitive as this discovery is for post-Holocaust Christian theology, it does neither Judaism nor Christianity nor future possibilities for theological friendship between them any good to ignore or circumvent historical knowledge. As we shall see in the discussion below at the end of Chapter Four, there is a problem here that I find in Radner's account of the original schism of Jew and Christian. See further *DC,* pp. 92-96.

122. "The problem is that of realizing the objectivity of value through the subjectivity of knowledge." Alan Richardson, *Christian Apologetics* (New York: Harper & Brothers, 1947), p. 15.

123. *RPTD,* p. 214.

124. Also by scholarship in the theological tradition of Luther: Graham White, *Luther as*

about just because of the demand to harmonize the evident contradictions in authoritative material. One may also appreciate, especially in Anselm the father of scholasticism, the requirement that theology proceed by the rationally persuasive method of questioning rather than by unquestioning submission to traditional authority. Simplistic critiques of scholasticism for "logic chopping" and "rationalism" miss its true achievement even as they miss the hermeneutical nature of its failure.

This judgment reflects Luther's humanist and anti-scholastic hermeneutical principle that "grammar precedes dialectic,"[125] that is, that rhetorical analysis of the genre of a literature is the first step in clarifying what kinds of claims are being made. Claims should not be taken *prima facie,* according to a naïve literalism or, in embarrassment at that, reinterpreted as symbols according to an allegorical invention. When dialectic, that is, logical analysis precedes grammar, however, apparent claims (i.e., statements that appear to be claims according to some tacit metaphysic in the mind of the interpreter) are extracted from texts and then assembled out of context to appear in apparent opposition to one another. Thus the "many words of God" have to be logically reconciled. The task of theology, exemplified in Lombard's *Sentences,* becomes one of harmonizing apparently contradictory claims drawn from authoritative texts. This is a false conception of the theological task, issuing in a false method.

The deep assumption of this academic procedure of logical harmonization of propositions lifted from authoritative texts was to secure the fragile coherence of Christendom as a renewed, and indeed "holy" imperial order that provided an institution of salvation for individual aspiration and appropriation. The hermeneutical futility of this procedure, based upon the impossible notion of an *imperium Christianum,* indeed as the holy *renovatio Romani Imperii,*[126] contributed not a little at length to the plausibility of the Kantian counterattack, with its delimitation of Christian belief by autonomous reason and political sovereignty[127] — the new pretenders to the imperial throne. The ambiguous epoch of liberal Protestant theology that followed this philosophical disestablishment was in retrospect, as argued above, a necessary though painful awakening to the wider world that the God of the gospel is creating. It has been a wrenching but ultimately salutary

---

Nominalist: A Study of the Logical Methods Used in Martin Luther's Disputations in the Light of Their Medieval Background, Schriften der Luther-Agricola-Gesellschaft 30 (Helsinki: Luther-Agricola Society, 1994); Christine Helmer, *The Trinity and Martin Luther: A Study on the Relationship between Genre, Language and the Trinity in Luther's Works (1523-1546)* (Mainz: Verlag Philipp von Zabern, 1999); and above all, Theodor Dieter, *Der junge Luther und Aristoteles: Eine historisch-systematische Untersuchung zum Verhältnung von Theologie und Philosophie* (Berlin and New York: Walter de Gruyter, 2001).

125. E.g., *LW* 16, p. 3.

126. *BA,* chapter 5.

127. See especially Immanuel Kant, *The Conflict of the Faculties,* trans. Mary J. Gregor (New York: Abaris Books, 1979).

deliverance of Christianity from parochialism, individualism, and the ensuing sectarian enmity of Christendom in decay.

Yet to this day, hermeneutically speaking, the scholastic model of theology continues in convoluted new forms as scholars, unwittingly, continue in the imperial project. Of course, after two centuries of probing criticism, "second naïveté" notwithstanding, one cannot honestly return to the view that Scripture and tradition preserve a deposit of revealed truths awaiting our systematic organizing or biblicistic "principling."[128] Ignored here are the hermeneutically crucial questions: For whom? What is the audience? *Quis custodiet custodem?* (Who guards the guard?), as Marx asked. The critical realization here ought to be that scholastic theology (that is, purely academic theology, old and new, in distinction from the patristic, monastic, and Reformation reading of the Bible as Scripture from within the ecclesia embarked upon its own academic service in the mission to the nations) took the *imperium* as its audience (whether as Pope or as Emperor or as today, in ideological pretext but not in reality, the *vox populi*). Consequently it never was adequately true to the evangelical sources that tell of the coming of God in the victory of the Beloved Community, where the audience of theology in making the correlation of subject and object, of faith and Jesus Christ, is and can be nothing less than the eschaton of judgment — a delimitation that fundamentally checks all claims of political sovereignty (Acts 5:29).

Thus the scholastic hermeneutic paradoxically survives even in — rather, precisely because of — the progressive de-Christianization that modernizing academic theology requires for contemporary service under supposedly "democratic" and "nonsectarian" political sovereignty. Old scholasticism or new, this purely academic procedure in theology, unconscionably still justified by a willfully naïve appeal to the substantive universalism claimed by the Euro-American Enlightenment, in fact always puts the organizer in charge: imposing her scheme on the materials, lending them a coherence not indigenous yet, not surprisingly on examination, in service precisely of her ever so breathless politics. Critical class awareness, however, rarely dawns within this spectacle of radicalized theological verbosity posing as political engagement, whether left or right, proffered by comfortably middle-class professors whose disdain for the broken, bleeding ecclesia is matched only by their presumption in expecting still to instruct it. Whatever else contemporary biblical studies are, they are an adamant display of the incoherence between what biblical texts ("It shall not be so among you . . ." Mark 10:43) actually said politically and what academic theologies have had to make them say for the sake of the imperial project of political sovereignty, also

---

128. Kevin Vanhoozer insightfully critiques evangelical reliance on ahistorical "principlizing," i.e., "abstracting the [allegedly] transcultural principles from their biblical context in order to clothe these naked principles in cultural garb that is intelligible in the contemporary context" in his contribution to *The Oxford Handbook of Evangelical Theology*, ed. Gerald R. McDermott (Oxford: Oxford University Press, 2010), p. 43.

now under the banner of "democracy," and their all-too-comfortable role within it as professional "prophets."

To cut through these convolutions of false consciousness, let us call upon Luther who puts the "matter" of Christian theology with characteristic dash: "All hypocrites and idolaters try to do the works that properly pertain to the Deity and belong completely and solely to Christ. . . . ['Hypocrisy,' i.e., the works-righteousness that substitutes civil justice for divine justice] refuses to be merely passive matter but wants actively to accomplish the things that it should patiently permit God to accomplish in it and should accept from him."[129] For in truth,

> God is the God of the humble, the miserable, the afflicted, the oppressed, the desperate, and of those who have been brought down to nothing at all. And it is the nature of God to exalt the humble, to feed the hungry, to enlighten the blind, to comfort the miserable and afflicted, to justify sinners, to give life to the dead, and to save those who are desperate and damned. For He is the almighty Creator, who makes everything out of nothing. In the performance of this, His natural and proper work, He does not allow Himself to be interfered with by that dangerous pest, the presumption of righteousness, which refuses to be sinful, impure, miserable and damned but wants to be pure and holy.[130]

In the light of Luther's claim about God's natural and proper work that theology serves to articulate, warrant, and advocate, we venture a formulation.

The Christian claim to theological truth amounts to the single thesis, proposition, or "dogma" (in fact at the heart of Scripture rightly read and tradition critically appropriated): *"God" is the self-surpassing Father who is determined to redeem the creation and bring it to fulfillment in the Beloved Community by the missions in the world of His Son and Spirit.* It is to be carefully noted that according to this formulation "God," *ho theos,* is not a personal name, but a title for the One who creates all else. This title permits, as Tillich following Luther rightly saw, theological analysis of culture even where God is not known by name, that is, wherever matters of "ultimate concern" manifest themselves.[131] Insofar as human persons are ultimately concerned, Christian theology exposes the functional if hidden deities at work and demands a rational accounting of them even as it gives its own reasons for the hope that it is in it by the open examination of its own conception of deity drawn from its own putative Word of God. This is the academic service rendered by Christian theology in the light of its single cognitive claim.

This academic procedure can be suspect, however, of special pleading and bad faith, ultimately of fideism if it admits of no possible falsification. The implausibility of conservative theology in this regard is that it can give no rational

---

129. *LW,* vol. 26, p. 259.
130. *LW,* vol. 26, p. 314.
131. Tillich, *ST* 1, pp. 12-14.

account for the incredible claims it makes and for which it requires a sacrifice of the intellect on the basis of the purely dogmatic claim that an omnipotent God can reveal in any way He, She, or It pleases. Little noticed is that in the process absolute willfulness has been thus divinized. In the light of the foregoing thesis, or truth-claim, or cognitive principle articulating the "matter" of Christian theology, however, it is evident that the pre-critical treatment of the Christian articles of faith as so many pearls gathered from the Bible and/or Christian tradition to be strung together by an imported conceptual scheme required the critical objection registered in Adolf von Harnack's great *History of Dogma*.[132] In this light, moreover, contemporary theology has openly to admit the apparent falsification of certain traditional claims made for or about its beliefs.

For painful example, as Pannenberg has written,[133] it is difficult to affirm as historical report the precious nativity stories about Jesus, and it is even more difficult to affirm the doctrine of Christ's birth from a virgin as epistemically primary in Christology. We have rather accorded epistemic primacy to the Easter kerygma of the resurrection of the Crucified Jesus, the "historical event" apart from which the rise of Christian faith is historically inexplicable. This is not to deny, Christologically, that Jesus is born from his Jewish mother, Mary, as the Spirit's New Adam nor is it to reject doctrinally her place as the *Theotokos* (bearer of God), as we shall see below. But it is to acknowledge on critical grounds the apparent lateness and relative rarity in primitive Christianity of the accounts of the nativity found in Matthew and Luke, themselves at some variance with each other,[134] though of course it is possible that memories of the unusual circumstances of Jesus' birth were lately disclosed. So it is not to deny that believers may hold as "pious opinion" to the historicity of the Virgin Birth (as Luther held to the pious opinion of Mary's perpetual virginity), only that they may not bind consciences by requiring such a doctrinal affirmation in face of such substantive criticism. As a result of this painful but truthful concession to criticism, the "doctrine of the Virgin Birth" may continue only in a deliteralized and ancillary fashion (as will be argued below in Chapter Five). The public credibility of theology as critical dogmatics vis-à-vis the academic suspicion of special pleading in bad faith requires such frank and mature acknowledgment of demonstrable falsifications over against beliefs as traditionally understood. But this is just an illustration. More profoundly, as Pannenberg also argues, the disputability of the very belief in God cannot be denied in a theology that would free itself from academic suspicion — not in order to win a grudging approval from the "cultured despisers" (Schleiermacher), but to execute its own genuine and paradigmatic self-criticism.

132. Adolf von Harnack, *History of Dogma*, complete in seven volumes, bound as four, trans. N. Buchanan (New York: Dover, 1961).

133. Pannenberg, *ST* 2, pp. 317-19.

134. See the judicious discussion of Joseph A. Fitzmyer, *The Gospel according to Luke (I–IX)*, The Anchor Bible vol. 28 (New York: Doubleday, 1979), pp. 306-9.

In a multitude of close readings Harnack revealed the incoherence and ultimate arbitrariness of pre-critical dogmatism, a point crystallized in Ernst Troeltsch's programmatic essay contrasting the historical and dogmatic method in theology,[135] and later updated in response to Barth's renewal of church dogmatics in Gerhard Ebeling's postwar essay, "The Significance of the Historical Critical Method."[136] While Ebeling's theology may be regarded as the very apex of the Kantian, noncognitive interpretation of faith as a mode of human being in the world, the more trenchant critique to be derived from this line of liberal criticism touches upon the very notion of the individual "topics" (Latin: *loci*) in theology. This method of presentation, drawn up by Philipp Melanchthon from his outline of the Epistle to Romans (and recently retrieved by Steve Paulson)[137] in order to replace the outline of ascent in Peter Lombard's *Sentences,* had the advantage of retrieving the biblical knowledge of the God who comes. But it still had the disadvantage of a "Bible Wordbook" format in which an ahistorical conglomerate of Bible verses gathered together into Pauline "topics" from Romans generated an artificial synthesis of dogmatic meaning.

In contrast to this method of listing various items of belief, each taken as supernaturally authorized by derivation from a supernatural text and awaiting only the theologian's systematization, the present effort in systematic theology regards the Trinitarian baptismal creed that evolved in early Catholicism (see Chapter Two) as giving the narrative plot of canonical Scripture taken as a whole (where, to be sure, Pauline theology plays a key role; indeed, the Letter to the Romans holds pride of place as a kind of summa of biblical theology) to render "God" as the self-surpassing Father who by the Son in the Spirit works the transformation to theological subjectivity. This is of course as "dogmatic" a procedure as Melanchthon's use of Romans as a canon within the canon. Herein lies the critical difference: the topics or articles of faith drawn from the creedal tradition can only be various articulations of one and the same Trinitarian faith in God: the Father who is determined to redeem and fulfill the creation by the missions of His Son and Spirit.[138] Thus critical dogmatics is critical in its strict concentration on

135. Ernst Troeltsch, "Historical and Dogmatic Method in Theology," in *Religion in History,* trans. James Luther Adams and Walter F. Bense (Minneapolis: Fortress, 1991), pp. 11-32.

136. Gerhard Ebeling, "The Significance of the Critical Historical Method for Church and Theology in Protestantism," in *Word and Faith,* trans. J. W. Leitch (Philadelphia: Fortress, 1964), pp. 17-61.

137. Steven D. Paulson, *Lutheran Theology* (London and New York: T. & T. Clark International, 2011), pp. 26-31. I see Melanchthon's criticism of Lombard's scholastic method, as Paulson here details, but not that which Paulson alleges of John of Damascus, whom he quite wrongly accuses wholesale of "neo-Platonic ontological philosophy" (p. 29). See my review of Paulson's book in the *International Journal of Systematic Theology* 16, no. 4 (October 2014): 489-92.

138. So Luther in his catechisms restored the Apostles' Creed to its original Trinitarian paragraphing, and hence theological function, away from the authoritarian "deposit of faith" rendering that had chopped up the Creed into twelve parts with the legend that each of the

the singular cognitive claim, or "dogma," as what is articulated in all the articles of faith.[139] In this respect it is worth mentioning that in correction of Harnack, Jaroslav Pelikan's equally monumental *The Christian Tradition* takes a properly hermeneutical approach to the history of dogma as that which the church believes, teaches, and confesses on the basis of the Word of God. Here the Word of God is not Bible verses or arbitrarily itemized principles or dogmas but the gospel of God who has created *us* for no other purpose than to redeem *us* and make *us* holy, i.e., to bring the Beloved Community.[140] While it is the task of systematic theology to articulate, exposit, and warrant this singular claim to truth regarding the identity of God by the whole of the presentation, several features of it may be lifted up immediately as signals of what is to come.

First, the Christian knowledge of God in the world is *pragmatic*. It is concerned with the identification of the God of the gospel in the maelstrom of a specified human experience — namely, the mission to the nations and the vocations of the baptized within them — where claims human, demonic, angelic, and messianic bombard us (Mark 13). Some of these claims may be correlated, others reconciled, and still others refused, but each of these varying treatments depend upon the epistemic primacy[141] accorded to what Luther called the *Verbum externum* concerning the Father's determination to save. In this way the good news and report of a true son of David comes on the scene to form theological subjectivity. As external and transformative, the gospel tells what we cannot tell ourselves but must ever learn. This continual learning fashions the theological subject who consequently cleaves to the revealed God alone in the new obedience of the mission to the nations and of the baptismal vocations within them. Rejected then, as previously argued, is any disinterested theoretical posture or epistemological attempt to ground theological knowledge a priori and universally.

Second, the God of the gospel is *self-determining*,[142] where the divine "self" is not a simple, sovereign, self-positing Ego but the complex, eternal community of persons united in love, revealed fittingly in its determination to prevail for us all on the earth in the coming of the Beloved Community: the Father who sends and the Son and the Spirit who joyfully go. The notion of divine freedom as the self-surpassing self-determination for us of the eternal community of love — with its internal costs of mutual deference and personal humility — stands in sharpest contrast to the titanic claims made for human freedom and sovereignty, especially in the modern period. Likewise the nature of divine self-determination as

---

apostles made his own special contribution to the formulation of common doctrine before they departed and went on their separate ways.

139. "The Debate on the Critical Historical Method: Correspondence between Adolph von Harnack and Karl Barth," chapter 4 in *The Beginnings of Dialectical Theology*, vol. 1, ed. James M. Robinson (Richmond, VA: John Knox Press, 1968), pp. 165-90.

140. Pelikan, *TCT*, 1, pp. 3-4.

141. Marshall, *Trinity and Truth*.

142. *PNT*, pp. 96-126.

generous and inclusive love stands in profoundest contradiction to the rapacious egocentricity and greed that are rationalized and even valorized in contemporary notions of freedom and sovereignty, as these latter are increasingly exposed in postmodern critique.

Third, creation with its redemption and fulfillment are *one, dynamic reality,* the biblical and patristic economy of God, referring to this very "earth on which the cross of Jesus stood" on the way to "the best of all possible worlds." This is not, however, as in Leibniz a philosophy of optimism based on a rational theodicy; it is rather a theology of hope based upon the theodicy of faith. "God's history with us is one integral act of sovereignty, comprehended as his decision to reconcile us with himself in Christ Jesus."[143] Rejected then are separations of creation, redemption, and fulfillment into discrete realms — especially the too-simple equation of the theological word, creation, with the "nature" known today in the physical and social sciences; likewise the reduction of "redemption" to privatized speculation, individualistic spirituality, or the self-help industry of constructing liberating metaphors for personal growth. Likewise rejected are the characteristic modern dualisms of public and private, thinking things and extended things, mind and matter, and so on. This implies that creation is not only, or even primarily, the act of origin but rather comprehensive of the new creation in Christ by the Spirit in the ultimate victory of the Beloved Community as the very end for which the world was begun.[144] Distinctions here between creation, redemption, and fulfillment within the economy of God are distinctions between kinds of divine rule and the correspondingly variegated forms of human cooperation with it — essential distinctions in power and its applications, but not segregated realms.

Fourth, as the self-determining God of the gospel made known by the economy of salvation is *self-surpassing,*[145] the knowledge of God accordingly arises in the midst of time from the divine accomplishment of reconciliation at the cross of the Messiah that the Spirit of Pentecost in a sovereign new initiative[146] is now bringing to the nations. Theology arises in this *mission* of the Spirit to bring the Word incarnate to the nations; theology ever remains tied to that original receptivity of faith constituted by this real coming of Jesus Christ by Word and Spirit — namely, the Spirit's proclaiming of the Lord's death till He comes again that constitutes the ecclesia as the Eucharistic gathering. This holy community called out by the gospel's journey to and through the nations is thus itself gift and is to be enjoyed as gift; only as gifted, thus as "patient," may the community of faith also arise to the new agency of the Body of Christ in the world. Rejected, just

---

143. Jenson, *ST* 2, p. 178.

144. So the eleventh article of the Formula of Concord teaches against the heinous doctrine of an absolute double decree of election and reprobation. See *BC,* pp. 640-56.

145. *LBC,* pp. 66-104.

146. Jenson, *ST* 2, pp. 178-79.

so, is any principled separation of "dogmatics" and "ethics" as between "theory" and "practice" or between "text" and "context" — though of course a practical division of labor here *within* systematic theology may be called for. Christian obedience in faith, including the mind's obedience in the knowledge of faith, is a fundamental *patiency* that arises with the missionary imperative to *receive* the Spirit and hence to go to the nations and teach *what Jesus has said and done*. Theology as a result does not substitute for an absent Christ but serves a present One by His Word in the power of the same Spirit that led Him on His messianic way from Galilee to Jerusalem.

Fifth, *Beloved Community* is the polyvalent term, as discussed above, that works both to name the Christian God, the Holy Trinity, and the chief end for which this God of the gospel has created the world, namely to redeem and fulfill it, that we may glorify the Father in the Son by the Spirit and by this personal participation in their eternal life enjoy God in God with God forever. It is to be noted from the outset, however, that although Christian theology articulates the eschatological creation in this Trinitarian theologic from the definite placement in the world that is the ecclesia in mission, the Beloved Community of God is greater than the presently perceptible Christian community. It is the biblical "people of God,"[147] the blessed "Israel of God," the healing of all nations, the harrowing of hell — just as it is also the eternal scourge of its would-be destroyers and defilers. This note of salvation by judgment indicates a transversal further to be explored (below in Chapter Six) of the usual alternatives between universal and particular, or personal and social, salvation.

Sixth, the redemptive mission of the Son as known in the Spirit by repentance and faith is grounded in and hence identified by Jesus Christ, more specifically, by His presence as the Crucified yet Risen Jesus in the *joyful exchange*. That is to say that the present Christ Jesus offers Himself to each one when He comes to speak His faith, faithfulness, obedience — in a word, His righteousness — in place of the pride and despair, the guile and the malice, the debt and burden of every person whom He encounters in His Word and Sacraments. Thus while the name Jesus refers to that historical human individual born of the Jew Mary and legally murdered under the Roman governor Pontius Pilate in the first century of the Common Era, this Jesus is identified from faith for faith by the evangelical narrative of His way of faithful obedience for us,[148] whether succinctly as in Paul and the catholic epistles or expansively as in the gospels. Modern historical knowledge of Jesus of Nazareth is a necessary but not sufficient warrant in theology of Christian faith in Jesus: necessary to the truth-claim that in this man, truly one of us, God surpasses God for us; insufficient because this man can only be seen as the event of God surpassing God in order to bring the Beloved Community even to the godless, that is, for us, by the Spirit of the resurrection working

147. Pannenberg, *ST* 3, pp. 463-98.
148. See the discussion in *LBC*, pp. 32-46.

a corresponding resurrection to theological subjectivity. Yet, academically, and by virtue of the common human body in the shared world, anyone of sufficient interest, aptitude, and intelligence can follow this testimony and judge its claim to truth for themselves as they too consequently venture in faith on its eschatological confirmation or disconfirmation. That is to say, the knowledge that such a systematic theology provides puts learners in a situation in which they too must risk the judgment of faith or unbelief. Suspending judgment too is possible, but only insofar as systematic theology fails to make the cognitive claim to truth articulate and otherwise compelling, thus something that can be meaningfully affirmed or denied. For that is the signature of a cognitive claim, also when it is made in faith for faith: that it can meaningfully be believed or doubted, even as its truth remains to be seen.

## Contextual Considerations

### After Christendom

We should speak in Euro-America today with more historical precision than with the commonplace "Constantinianism," as in the so-called "Constantinian fall of the church." For in the Latin-speaking "West," in any event, Christendom arose in rivalry with the Byzantine East and in reaction to the advance of Islam. With Charlemagne, a new cultural ideal of Europe as a new, now "holy" Roman empire, a *corpus christianum,* emerged. For a millennium Western theology existed within this imperial project and served its interests, whether reluctantly or exuberantly.[149] Unsurprisingly, then, given the collapse of this cultural ideal of Christendom in the course of the twentieth century, the discipline of theology is more conflicted today than ever before, though not simply across preexisting fault lines arising from the historic confessional schisms within Christendom.

For example, the reader may recognize affinities of the present project in theology with the effort of the Scottish Reformed theologian, Thomas F. Torrance, in the previous generation to reintegrate Patristic and Reformation traditions of thought for today.[150] That meant for Torrance a "reconstruction" that would enable a bold engagement with contemporary thought as informed by the natural sciences as well as a commitment to the ecumenical movement for the reunion of the divided Christian churches. But compounding the difficulties of Torrance's

149. See the discussion in *BA,* pp. 154-59.

150. I acknowledged this affinity in *DC,* x, before the publication of Torrance's two-volume Christology, *Incarnation,* ed. Robert T. Walker (Downers Grove, IL: InterVarsity Academic, 2008) and *Atonement,* ed. Robert T. Walker (Downers Grove, IL: InterVarsity Academic, 2009), came into my hands. Reading confirms this affinity, with only the nuances of traditional Lutheran–Reformed divergences in Christology, and the embrace of postmodern philosophical perspectives, separating our projects.

unfinished project of "reconstruction in theology" is the emerging recognition since his time that we in Euro-America have entered definitively into the unprecedented situation of post-Christendom.[151] Here Christianity is not only culturally disestablished but its dismembered remnants, distorted beyond recognition into mutually hostile fragments, meet the challenge of decline in cultural influence with partisan retrenchment on the one side or abandonment of traditional and ecumenical claims to theological truth on the other. Our spiritual situation reflects this decay in multiple ways. The need forthrightly to locate Christian theology in this dismal situation is the need to face the moribund spiritual and intellectual state of Christianity in Euro-America.

The same point may be put positively: Euro-American Christian theology today has the opportunity to enter into and indeed to lead the more searching thought of our times in a path between and beyond the rival post-Christian metaphysics of naturalism and idealism, not to mention inferior popular forms of behaviorism and constructivism which ultimately depend on such metaphysics. Naturalism is a metaphysics that resolves the polarity of the subject and object of knowledge on the side of the object, i.e., the natural world. It reduces the human person to an epiphenomenon of the forces at work in nature. Idealism is a metaphysics that resolves this polarity on the side of the subject, i.e., the collective human mentality in its historical evolution and dialectical play through historical time. It reduces the human person to an oracle of the *Zeitgeist*. Because in either way human persons are thus dissolved, the Beloved Community from which, through which, and for which persons who are just amid structures of malice and injustice actually live by faith, and so sustain the right kind of conflict with the loveless and hopeless world, does not and cannot appear in them as the real human possibility of God, through God, and for God.

Kant's critical revolution created the conditions for the emergence of this alternative between naturalism and idealism when he ruled out of rational bounds traditional dogmatics as cognitive discourse about God.[152] According to the precritical theological tradition, God can be known as the Creator, hence as author of both the subject and the object of knowledge, and so the ultimate basis of their unity in the temporal task of achieving knowledge by the correspondence of mind to reality. But Kant precluded this basis for cultural endeavor in the theological unity of subject and object by positing an unbridgeable gap between the sensible object and supersensible subject, tacitly thinking God along the lines of this characteristic modern dualism. He indeed made this posited gap the premise of

---

151. Tom Greggs, Scottish Reformed theologian of the generation following Torrance, takes the same stance in *Theology against Religion: Constructive Dialogues with Bonhoeffer and Barth* (London and New York: T. & T. Clark, 2011).

152. I am drawing in what follows on the insightful exposition of George di Giovanni in *Freedom and Religion in Kant and His Immediate Successors: The Vocation of Humankind 1774-1800* (Cambridge: Cambridge University Press, 2008).

genuinely critical thinking, "destroying knowledge to make room for faith," as he disingenuously but influentially claimed.[153] The gap actually excluded the Christian theological claim from cognitive consideration altogether in that it limited the domain of rationality to intra-mundane possibilities for the correlation of the supersensible subject and phenomenal object in the synthesis of "scientific" knowledge. Knowledge in turn was limited to the existing order of things, i.e., things in principle visible (sensible) today on the assumption of the static uniformity of nature. In other words, Kant privileged the prestigious knowledge of the emergent natural sciences as summed up in Newtonian physics by dehistoricizing and desocializing the human knower and universalizing and transcendentalizing the instrumental reasoning procedures of the experimental method. As indicated above, the present proposal finds in Charles Sanders Peirce's account of the triadic structure of scientific reasoning, as appropriated by Royce in turning pragmatism hermeneutically toward the questions asked in the humanities (and recently taken up the Jewish philosopher Peter Ochs),[154] a template of knowledge that rehistoricizes and resocializes human knowledge, also scientific knowledge, even as it de-divinizes the instrumental reason that Kant had venerated as theoretically normative.[155] More on Peirce's "triadic structure" will follow shortly.

But for the moment it is important to grasp that Kant's disbarment of Christian theology as a claim to truth — paradigmatic for modern culture — also depended for its effectiveness on the exploitation of a definite weakness in traditional theology: the Platonic analogy which thought of God in relation to the world like a perfect, supersensible mind over against an imperfect, sensible body. Kant too inherited this Platonizing way of thinking about God, which allowed him to retain God as the regulative idea of a Perfect Mind eternally intuiting its object in a timeless act of creativity, even as it required him to deny the possibility of any finite intuition of this noumenal divinity and hence of any human knowledge of it as something actually existing. Fundamentally, one continues to agree with Kant if one eschews as beyond the limits of reason any knowledge of God as providing a meta-account of the subject-object polarity itself, as in traditional dogmatics. Otherwise the naturalist or idealist metaphysics following the breakdown of Kantianism have tried in one way or another to fill this gap between the sensible and the supersensible. One is motivated to persist with this Kantian insistence on the limits of reason at the cost of this deep dualism of the phenomenal-noumenal gap largely for the purposes of sustaining a cultural truce that gives nature to science, morals to the humanities, and religion to the arts,

---

153. Perhaps Kant himself was confused about this. See di Giovanni, *Freedom and Religion,* pp. 1-10.

154. Ochs, *Another Reformation,* pp. 10-16, 98-102, et passim.

155. This claim may seem incongruent if we take the thought of John Dewey as the full bloom of American pragmatism. But Royce represents an alternative path and Niebuhr the theological counterstroke to Dewey's instrumentalism; see Daniel F. Rice, *Reinhold Niebuhr and John Dewey: An American Odyssey* (Albany: State University of New York Press, 1993).

with philosophy, as the Tribunal of Reason, policing the boundaries and allowing no trespassing between these domains.[156]

Today this intention is nostalgic, if not reactionary. Kant's intellectual asceticism could not in any event last, nor could his artificial segregation of human concerns into several mutually isolated domains. What has arisen from the collapse of his cultural truce, however, is not for the most part any public renewal of the cognitive claim of Christian theology in a new key (Pannenberg excepted),[157] but the rival metaphysics of naturalism and idealism which demand a choice today as between *the* rational alternatives, with theologians obediently following.

Certainly Kant's insight into the formative power of human reason in constructing its object (but not creating its object ex nihilo) renders authoritarian forms of dogmatics as may be found in the tradition impossible. One cannot rationally demonstrate God's existence. Nor can one appeal to God's Word to settle anything in theology without also asking, "Who are you who so appeals? How are you taking God's Word? How indeed could you ever recognize some finite word in the world as the Word of God?" These probing critical questions seem not only to reveal the historically conditioned subjectivities at work in the hopelessly contradictory positive or kataphatic theologies; but also the rational indemonstrability of God in principle seems to make any objective knowledge of God — precisely in face of claims to "revelation" — impossible under the conditions of finitude attending human subjectivity. Thus rationally responsible people should cease and desist with theological claims to truth — at least in public![158]

In an enormous irony, for thinkers like Hobbes, Spinoza, and Kant, Luther's critique of enthusiasm on behalf of the external news of the gospel was turned against Luther's own claim to have an external Word from God.[159] Christine Helmer, incidentally, has demonstrated that Luther cannot be made to conform to the Kantian mood of noncognitivism in theology and that nineteenth-century

---

156. So Richard Rorty put it in his *Philosophy and the Mirror of Nature* (Princeton: Princeton University Press, 1979), pp. 3-4.

157. The great merit of Pannenberg's massive theological project has been the renewal of theology's cognitive claim. So sprawling indeed is his argument for theology as the science of God that aims to provide a universal, if eschatological horizon for the many sciences, however, that it is difficult to pin down exactly why the many sciences are in serious lack and in need of theology as their critique. In other words, Pannenberg in his rationalism seems insufficiently suspicious of reason's metaphysical aspiration, if not claim to total comprehension, and this not as some inadequacy that can be met and fulfilled by theological comprehension, but as the sin of idolatry. One might trace this rationalistic element in Pannenberg to his, in the present view, insufficiently critical adoption of Descartes' account of the dialectic of the finite and the infinite, as we will discuss below in Chapter Five.

158. Immanuel Kant, *The Conflict of the Faculties,* trans. Mary J. Gregor (New York: Abaris Books, 1979).

159. Paul R. Hinlicky, "Irony of an Epithet: The Reversal of Luther's Enthusiasm in the Enlightenment," in *A Man of the Church: Festschrift for Ralph Del Colle,* ed. Michel Barnes and Mickey L. Mattox (Eugene, OR: Wipf & Stock, 2013), pp. 302-15.

Luther interpretation was quite misled in its attempt to wring out of Luther's principle of faith in "Christ *for me*" a principle of pure subjectivism in theology.[160] Bonhoeffer's "Bethel Confession" acutely diagnosed the noncognitive, antidoctrinal, anti-intellectual, and emotivist theology of the German Christian party by means of Luther's principle of the *Verbum externum,* with its sharp critique of "enthusiasm." The stark antithesis here reveals our present spiritual situation and the precise problem. How might a theology of "Trinitarian advent" (Helmer) based on Luther's *Verbum externum* reach us today, in this transitional spiritual situation that is equally after criticism and after Christendom?

Neither liberal nor neo-orthodox theologies finally overcome the difficulty here. Existential leaps of faith into unknowable supersensibles in a rapidly shrinking theological discourse evacuated of its traditional dogmatic content constitute a dead end to clear-sighted thinking. Most noncognitive forms of contemporary Christian theology think of the task as free construction of healing or redemptive metaphors arising out of religious experience, giving symbolic expression to precognitive, indeed prelinguistic feelings of the ineffable ground or sacred source of being. Rigorously considered, however, Christian theology in such Kantian modes conduces finally and purely to apophatic silence. As Ralph Del Colle put it, "Either the Christian knowledge of God identifies the very being of God in the revelation of the divine persons and in this manner preserves the transcendence of God, or trinitarian language amounts to a triadic representation of God in history according to the receptive capacity of the human subject and nothing more. In ultimate terms this latter position eventually yields to apophatic agnosticism concerning the being of God."[161] Similarly, however, the great challenge to noncognitivism represented by Karl Barth's kataphatic theology also accepted the Kantian conditions of human subjectivity. Barth thus resolved the problem by resort to a sheer miracle: incalculably God becomes the object of human knowledge without ceasing to be subject as an event that can never be captured but only described and followed, issuing in a union of moral wills for redemptive action, never any kind of cognitive synthesis by which humans can master God with their theological concepts and so put Him in service of their own causes.[162] In this respect, Barth remained a Kantian, as Bruce McCormack rightly maintains.[163]

Profound as was Barth's attempt to conceive of the God who comes rigorously as event, however, his theology too remains entangled in the sensible-supersensible dualism that Kant established as the root dogma of the modern

---

160. Helmer, *The Trinity and Martin Luther,* pp. 8-24.

161. Ralph Del Colle, "The Triune God," chapter 7 in *The Cambridge Companion to Christian Doctrine,* ed. C. E. Gunton (Cambridge: Cambridge University Press, 1997), p. 136.

162. *PNT,* p. 131.

163. Bruce McCormack, *Karl Barth's Critically Realistic Dialectical Theology: Its Genesis and Development 1909-1936* (Oxford: Clarendon, 1995). See further the discussion in *PNT,* pp. 49-57.

period in Euro-American theology (as Barth explicitly acknowledged in the Preface to the second edition of the Romans commentary).[164] In particular, as we shall see, Barth denied that the form of the Word of God in earthly language is proper to God, that it contains some fitting relation to God which theology must follow through to understanding and public confession.[165] While this denial was critically intended, it caused Barth to mistake, as we shall see, the rhetorical sense of apocalyptic parable, Pauline paradox, and Johannine enigma, i.e., how this earthly language as a subversive discourse in the world is proper to the God of the gospel, who *is* the One "bringing to naught the things that are" (1 Cor. 1:28) in order to bring about the Beloved Community. Moreover, this disconnect between the form of God's Word and its content correlates with Barth's exposition of the event of divine-human encounter with a mental/psychological model of divine personhood, the self-positing "I" of the Lord meeting and mastering the self-positing "I" of the human rebel, remaking the latter into a proper "Thou" of the one, true "I."[166] Contrary to Barth's best intentions, this model of the divine-human encounter, reminiscent of the Fichtean idealism that it theologically inverts, is still too individualistic and voluntaristic for the theology of the Beloved Community.

Such, in any event, have been the main options in Christian theology in the past two centuries. Kant's cultural truce, as mentioned, was to deed over objectivity to the natural sciences while restricting science to the world of appearances, positing an unknowable noumenal realm of "God, freedom and immortality" as ideas untouchable by scientific discovery but able at least to regulate human reason for moral and aesthetic purposes. By this regulation, Kant thought chiefly to safeguard the possibility of moral agency as spontaneous and thus morally meritorious initiative in the otherwise closed causal system discovered and known by science. Not only has the result been uncongenial to traditional Christian theology, as we have seen, it has been very unstable also in philosophy, for the simple reason that by longstanding Western tradition philosophical reason wants total explanation and cannot evidently remain reason apart from this desire for total transparency and full comprehension. Already with Fichte, the rational demand for a comprehensive explanation of reality wanted to account for the subject-object polarity itself. One had to move forward either into naturalism or idealism (later positivism or phenomenology-existentialism, today behaviorism or constructivism), even though the choice here appeared arbitrary, as Fichte himself acknowledged. At root one aspired to the comprehensive account that Kant denied, an ultimate explanation of explanation, so to say, whatever it might be.[167]

---

164. Barth, *Epistle to the Romans,* trans. E. C. Hoskyns (London: Oxford University Press, 1972), p. 4.

165. See further on this criticism of Barth, *LBC,* pp. 367-68.

166. See further on this criticism of Barth, *PNT,* pp. 133-34.

167. Di Giovanni, *Freedom and Religion,* pp. 210-25.

Thus, today various forms of behaviorism dominate the social sciences with the exception of critical theory and the sociology of knowledge where the tradition of idealism continues via humanistic Marxism. Psychology is transitioning into neurology and while neo-Darwinian intellectuals have become more axiomatically materialistic, physicists wonder at the improbability of it all. These simmering conflicts between physics and biology and between psychology and sociology thus express our post-Kantian spiritual situation. In Europe the legacy of idealism is stronger, but usually mediated by attempted syntheses of humanistic Marxism and Nietzschean genealogy. Few are able to sustain the Kantian balancing act or live on its thin diet.[168] In this vein, there have been, to be sure, (minority) versions of contemporary Christian theology still aspiring to "science." Here too the knowledge of God given in the gospel as *Verbum externum,* as Luther understood it, becomes so much window-dressing in lines of inquiry determined by quite other images or auditions than the Gospel's news of the resurrection of the Crucified and therewith the in-breaking of the Beloved Community of God. So the end of Christendom requires a deeper probe into the breakdown of the traditional symbiosis of Paul and Plato in Christian Platonism. That becomes clear when theology today is constrained by the emergent metaphysics of the continuity thesis.

## The Continuity Thesis

After the twentieth-century disasters of Hitler, Hiroshima, and Stalin there can be little doubt that the overriding perception regarding the cultural plausibility of Christian theology is nothing so abstract as the subject-object polarity of knowledge, as just argued. Rather, the difficulty appears as that which Leibniz summed up in his neologism: "theodicy" — the justification to rational minds of God's governance in nature and history.[169] Today Epicurus's dilemma — that if God is good, He is not powerful and if God is powerful, He is not good — has triumphed in terms of cultural plausibility. Specifically it has triumphed over the theodicy of faith that Augustine worked out in the opening chapters of the *City of God* on the occasion of the fall of Rome. Augustine's theodicy of faith — the essence of which Luther dramatically retrieved at the conclusion of the brilliant but vexing treatise on bound choice[170] — had prevailed more or less within the preceding epoch of Christendom, although its pre-imperial form in Augustine,

168. But see Ned Wisnefske, *God Hides: A Critique of Religion and a Primer for Faith* (Eugene, OR: Pickwick, 2010).

169. Paul R. Hinlicky, "Leibniz and the Theology of the Beloved Community," *Pro Ecclesia* 21, no. 1 (2012): 25-50.

170. Thomas Reinhuber, *Kämpfender Glaube: Studien zu Luthers Bekenntnis am Ende von De servo arbitrio* (Berlin and New York: Walter de Gruyter, 2000), p. 199. See the discussion of Reinhuber in Hinlicky, "A Leibnizian Transformation?" pp. 98-99.

with the prophetic exposé and critique of the *libido dominandi* (the lust for domination) was always in tension with the renewed imperial project's pretension to holiness in Christendom.[171] But theologically Luther and Augustine alike finally resorted to the eighth chapter of Paul's letter to the Romans: the promise of eschatological creation causes the mind to consider the sufferings of the present age not worthy to be compared to the glory to be revealed. This eschatological belief sustains sufferers in the conviction that even now all things work for this final good to them that love God and are called according to this purpose, that is, as they live in the gospel's mission to the nations and baptismal vocations within them in anticipation of the coming of the Beloved Community. We shall have occasion to consider the problems of evil more fully in this way in their proper place in Chapter Seven.

For the present it is important to see that theodicy is not unrelated to the subject-object problematic. A rational theodicy accounts for God as the unity — in Leibniz's conception, the "pre-established harmony" — of subject and object, or again in Leibniz's own vocabulary, the "harmony" of the "orders of grace and nature." On account of the human knower's bodily existence — its non-transcendable perspectival placement as finite knowledge in time and space (so decisively Leibniz differs from Kant) — the physical experience of bodily pain and the moral experiences of malice and injustice in social life cannot but seem fundamentally to challenge the supposed harmony grounded in God the Creator. The philosophical objection to God as the unity of subject and object thus takes popular form in the demand to justify God's supposed governance on the same rational grounds as God was said rationally to be the conception necessary to organize nature for final purposes of grace.

Leibniz accordingly argued that nature-and-history, taken as a whole, dynamically realize the final purposes of grace. Consequently, true reason has to proceed on this progressive or teleological assumption for science to advance. The progress of science is supported in this resolve to know the world as God's knows it, yet it proceeds step by creaturely step, by true faith, since at any point within nature and history we lack the perspective on the whole that could see final purposes in the processes of their realization. Instead of this, we proceed on faith that our tiny and faltering advances in knowledge are woven into a beneficent process directed to a worthy end. Natural faith can be confirmed in this native belief in final purpose and the harmony at work even now on account of the revelation of the economy of God in Christ. Thus it would be better to express Leibniz's "progressive" point by saying we are *on the way to* the best of all possible worlds in that it is the just and the wise who live by faith. All the same, the failure is obvious. Leibniz's rational theodicy fails satisfactorily to meet the objection that the moral evils of malice and injustice, taken as sin and as such worthy of

---

171. Paul R. Hinlicky, "Tough-Minded Augustinianism: Some Guidance for Christian Apologetics in Our Day," in *Glaube und Denken* (Sonderband, 1999), pp. 157-72.

divine wrath, are pure surds in his scheme. Nor can he meet the objection that "natural evils," as he conceptualized the vulnerabilities endemic to embodied existence, are better attributed to the utter indifference of impersonal natural regularities to human purposes, rather than to the design of an incompetent and malevolent Creator. But it is imperative to sort out Leibniz's failure in anticipation of fuller treatment of the theodicy of faith in Chapter Seven.

"I have shown," Leibniz claimed in the conclusion of the *Theodicy,* "that among older writers the fall of Adam was termed *felix culpa,* a fortunate sin, because it had been expiated with immense benefit by the incarnation of the Son of God: for he gave to the universe something more noble than anything that would otherwise have been amongst created beings . . . the opportunity to exercise their freedom, even when he foresaw that they would turn to evil."[172] This *felix culpa* is indeed possible as a theological argument, where Christ is taken as the New Adam who in the fullness of time exercised freedom for God in the obedience of faith and for humanity in the obedience of love and so not only rectified the disobedience of the first Adam, but out of it, as out of a ruin, redeemed the materials, as living stones, for the building of the Temple of the Spirit on the earth. Only so are "the sufferings of the present age not worthy to be compared. . . ." Thus we can connect the *felix culpa* to Luther's dictum from the beginning of this chapter, that God has created *in order* to redeem and sanctify. *Felix culpa,* as an element in this purpose clause, expresses the theodicy of faith stemming from Romans 8, or as in Romans 11, it expresses the revelation of God's plan, hidden from the ages but now implemented and thus made known in Christ, that God consigned all to disobedience in order that He have mercy on all. Leibniz inherited the purpose clause here, with its divine permission of evil, from the church fathers, as well as from his own (attenuated) Lutheran theological tradition.

Yet he wanted to go beyond this theodicy of faith to argue that this actually existing world is and must be known naturally as "better than every other possible universe."[173] As a philosophical experiment in thought, however, this rational theodicy fails to provide the best account of our experience, namely, of how the moral experience of captivity in and to structures of malice and injustice and the natural experience of exposure to indifferent forces of nature can and must be experienced philosophically as surds in relation to human purposes. These fatal objections were immortalized in Voltaire's bitter portrait of the ludicrous Dr. Pangloss. By the same token, however, the fruit of Voltaire's insistence upon the absurdity of natural and moral evils aids and abets the powerful tendency in thought since *Candide* towards revivals of Gnostic dualism, as Leibniz had detected already in his contemporary, the lapsed Huguenot, Pierre Bayle. If Leibniz represents the last great Euro-American effort for a philosophy of creation as

---

172. Gottfried W. Leibniz, *Theodicy: Essays on the Goodness of God, the Freedom of Man and the Origin of Evil,* trans. E. M. Huggard (Chicago and La Salle, IL: Open Court, 1998), p. 378.

173. Leibniz, *Theodicy,* p. 378.

cultural foundation of Christendom in the tradition of Melanchthon,[174] his failure has only created a vacuum filled with neo-Gnosticisms.[175]

Contemporary theological critics of Kant like the early Jacobi saw the same neo-Gnostic dualism appearing in subtle guise in Kant's sensible-supersensible scheme. Jacobi thus tried unsuccessfully to argue the Leibnizian alternative: God, understood in a rationally warranted faith as Creator of the best of all possible worlds, is author and hence unity of both subject and object, i.e., both human knowledge in its historical progression and the evolving natural world unfold together in a preestablished harmony aimed at the realization of the Beloved Community.[176] Jacobi thus pressed thought of God the Creator in teleological and progressive directions, if not yet to the view of eschatological creation advocated in this system of theology. With Jacobi, however, the cognitive force of the Leibnizian argument is already exhausted; his actual appeal amounts to special pleading against philosophy as such on ethical, humanistic, and progressive grounds. Unaided reason inevitably fails in its totalitarian ambition to comprehend all; this failure results in Kant's resignation to a foundational and unbridgeable dualism; and the consequent agnosticism eventually devolves into a destructive nihilism. That implication of nihilism is why, in the end, the later Jacobi succumbed to the Kantian expedient of the *als ob,* the "as if," that we must live *as if* the regulative ideas of God, freedom, and immortality were true. This is the brave face that rational "faith" puts on consequent to reason's destruction of pre-critical metaphysics.

Jacobi thus abandoned the rationally warranted faith in God and thus also in human progress that was based for Leibniz on the very un-Kantian and un-Cartesian doctrine of the monadological (or organic) continuity of the sensible and the supersensible. Leibniz had held to a *continuity thesis* against Descartes:[177] that conception is already at work in the most primitive of perceptions; that the most sophisticated conception is literally senseless except as an expanded and enriched perception; that each monad (or organic unit) as it emerges in the progression of the preestablished harmony is thus in its own way an integrated or harmonious whole reflecting the universe as an ordered system from its own unique perspective.[178] But Jacobi the pietist abandoned this continuity thesis in

---

174. *PNT,* pp. 24-31.

175. For a penetrating contemporary account, see Philip J. Lee, *Against the Protestant Gnostics* (New York: Oxford University Press, 1987).

176. Friedrich Heinrich Jacobi, "David Hume on Faith, or Idealism and Realism, A Dialogue" (1787), in *Friedrich Heinrich Jacobi: The Main Philosophical Writings and the Novel Allwill,* trans. G. di Giovanni (Montreal and Kingston: McGill-Queen's University Press, 2009), pp. 253-338.

177. *RPTD,* pp. 63-67, 126-33.

178. Suffice it here to cite the anti-dualist polemic of Leibniz's late "The Monadology" (1714): "This is where the Cartesians have badly failed, since they took no account of the perceptions which we do not apperceive. This is also what made them believe that minds alone are monads and there are no animal souls or other entelechies. . . . [They fell] again into the Scholastic prejudice of completely separated souls . . ." (14), in Leibniz, *Discourse on Metaphysics,* p. 69.

philosophy to become the forerunner of existential angst and cognitive fideism in modern, that is, Kantian theology.

Because of the continuity thesis, in Leibniz there is no mysterious ontological gap between percept and concept, the mysterious synthesis of which must somehow be explained and justified in a Kantian critique of reason. Even God, for Leibniz, is monadological, i.e., the organic unity that is the life of the Trinity, a dynamic harmony of power, wisdom, and love, and as such the infinite grace and giver of gifts in the continuing work of creation. What is significant for us here is how the continuity thesis connects with Leibniz's muted, but real Trinitarianism. Leibniz admits to a critic who objected to the Trinitarian conception of God for introducing multiplicity into God: "Thus in the strictest sense it cannot be said that GOD is one, so that in him in reality or before the operation of the mind distinct entities [*distincta*] do not exist. For if a mind exists, it must be that there are in it: the one who thinks, the one thought of, and the act of thinking [intellegens, intellectum, et intellectio], and those things that coincide with these: power, knowledge and will . . . there will be in GOD three really distinct foundations [tria fundamenta realiter distincta]." There is, as Maria Rosa Antognazza comments, "therefore in some way a plurality in God."[179]

Clearly this is a mental/psychological account of the Trinity in the train of Augustine. Leibniz accordingly distinguishes the nature or essence of God as the principle by which God acts as Creator in distinction from personhood in God as subject (= person, agent) of divine action.[180] He follows both Augustine[181] and Luther[182] in making the nature/person distinction by distinguishing speech regarding God taken absolutely ("the principle") and taken relatively (the "subjects"). Just like these theologians in whose tradition he stands, Leibniz therefore affirms that "the word, 'God,' is being used in another sense when we say that God is one, than when we say that there are three, any one of whom is God."[183] Having in this way avoided fatal contradiction and accounted for triunity, Leibniz in fact grasps the revolutionary metaphysical implications of the Trinitarian distinction of nature and person.

First, "multitude as such is not an imperfection, only that multitude which entails separability, and consequently, corruptibility" counts as a defect. And second, "[t]here is the greater harmony when there is the greater diversity . . . the Trinity does not destroy the unity of God if and only if this is a plurality wherein the persons are not mutually separable parts."[184] There can be little doubt then

---

179. Maria Rosa Antognazza, *Leibniz on the Trinity and the Incarnation: Reason and Revelation in the Seventeenth Century,* trans. G. Parks (New Haven and London: Yale University Press, 2007), p. 28.

180. Antognazza, *Trinity and Incarnation,* p. 32.

181. Augustine, *On the Trinity,* trans. E. Hill (New York: New City Press, 1991).

182. *SF,* pp. 201-2.

183. Antognazza, *Trinity and Incarnation,* p. 156.

184. Antognazza, *Trinity and Incarnation,* p. 29.

that Leibniz not only understands the Augustinian doctrine of the Trinity but appropriates its introduction of plurality and dynamism into a new conception of divine unity as a harmony of agents with characteristic operations. Just this is what is presupposed in the act and operation of bringing about the best of all possible worlds by selecting a world to unfold from a multitude of possible ones according to the preestablished harmony.

At the same time, however, Leibniz inherits also a certain weakness of the Augustinian doctrine of the Trinity, namely the conception of God as the perfect intellect that intuits its object purely and creatively in one timeless act, unlike creatures whose intuition is always dependent on empirical input of external data. So powerful is the similitude between the uncreated Mind of God and the created minds of creatures, that, according to Antagnozza, "Leibniz does not explicitly state that the juxtaposition of mind and Trinity is analogy."[185] Indeed not, since his continuity thesis and corresponding preference for univocity, following Scotus,[186] require Leibniz to hold that "Mind and God differ only in that the one is finite and the other is infinite."[187] Of course, that is a considerable difference. But just so the Creator God can be the ontotheological *arche* of a universe of minds, the sufficient reason why there is *this* something rather than nothing or something *else*. Human minds are the "somethings" that can emerge from the unfolding preestablished harmony as image of God; they can historically come to know and understand that the good reason for their existence in God is to fill the image with likeness to the Creator and so rejoice in God with praise and thanksgiving as they serve His cause in the unfolding of the happy Republic of Minds, the very end for which God created the world.

In Leibniz's metaphysics, God is understood as the Creator who in an eternal act thinks and wills all others into being in their providential sequence. As such, God's knowledge of the whole is the cognitive key to the order of nature that science knows, since science must always presuppose the whole that it does not see and its internal coherence that it cannot demonstrate. Consequently, theological knowledge of God's purpose, that is, knowledge of the order of grace encompassing nature, causes human minds to rise up at the right time in the predetermined sequence to embrace their exalted vocation in bringing about the Beloved Community, not least through the progress of science: "God is the Monarch of the Most Perfect Republic, Composed of All Minds, and the Happiness of This City of God Is His Principal Purpose. . . . Jesus Christ Has Revealed to Men the Mystery and Admirable Laws of the Kingdom of Heaven. . . . His gospel has entirely changed the course of human affairs; He has brought us to know the kingdom of heaven. . . ."[188] Reason and revelation harmonize, when reason is taken as true

---

185. Antognazza, *Trinity and Incarnation*, p. 29.
186. *RPTD*, pp. 157-59.
187. Antognazza, *Trinity and Incarnation*, p. 45.
188. Leibniz, *Metaphysics*, pp. 39-41.

perception arising to conception of the reign of God, and faith is taken as obedience to the monarchy of God revealed in Christ. Science participates finitely and perspectivally in God's own creative intuition of the order of nature on the supposition of its integrity and coherence as an unfolding whole, just as faith participates by obedience to God's principles and purpose in the order of grace.[189]

Traditional indeed as was Leibniz's Christian Platonism, what is distinctly modern about it is the revamped nominalism of his monadology and the corresponding historicizing of the ontological in the continuity thesis.[190] God superintends every individual, not as the atoms of irreducibly hard matter in blind and random motion as his near contemporary Hobbes had imagined, but as irreducibly complex organic wholes moving forward toward ever more complex and integrated forms of existence in an orderly development to a divinely appointed goal. Hence, Leibniz anticipates contemporary thought of emergent properties in evolution; monads do not just timelessly exist (though they are created to be immortal according to Leibniz and it would require a corresponding miracle of annihilation for them to cease to exist). But monads themselves organize into ever more rich and complex forms according to the preestablished harmony; these monadological unities develop in the sequence of time, harmonizing with vast others in a unidirectional flow. This "progress" of creation moreover can be uncovered and known in historical study of human affairs as well as in the experimental science that studies nature. Leibniz's metaphysical poetry and too-easy optimism should not obscure for us the insight into reality as history embedded in it.

Yet metaphysical poetry it is. The alternative (to Kant's) path through modernity that Leibniz represents — and which postmodern theology needs — therefore does not entail that Leibniz's own attempt to secure a philosophical discipline of natural theology could or should be resuscitated today. What is rather more salient is that Leibniz saw the need for a robust theology of creation and foresaw the ensuing vacuum in Euro-American culture, now filled with neo-Gnosticisms, that failure to meet this cultural need would create. The deeper problem here, however, is how God can be thought to originate anything not God without ceasing to be God. Correspondingly, the deeper reason, theologically, for that failure is that despite his valiant effort to introduce dynamism into the conception of divine being, Leibniz was still too much inclined by the tradition of Christian Platonism to think God analogically as Mind to Body, *intelligentia extra mundam,* supersensible to sensible. This diminished and misleading view of divine transcendence, itself based on the anthropological dualism

189. Leibniz, *Theodicy,* especially pp. 73-122, where Leibniz lays out the implications of the continuity thesis for the relation of theology and philosophy. Leibniz's place in the tradition of Melanchthon's "theological philosophy" is elaborated in *PNT,* pp. 177-22.

190. Leonard S. Smith, *Religion and the Rise of History: Martin Luther and the Cultural Revolution in Germany, 1760-1810* (Eugene, OR: Cascade Books, 2009), pp. 104, 109-11.

that otherwise he opposed, also led Leibniz into the irresolvable dilemmas of protology regarding predestination in his rational theodicy. Since God knows all in one eternal creative act, then all, also the apparent evils of malice, injustice, and punishment, must be taken as divinely willed instruments of the greater good. These apparent implications stand behind the failure of his project to secure philosophically the reconciliation of Christian Europe, for which Leibniz himself had hoped.[191]

For us today, the Leibnizian alternative means rather that the rationality of Christian belief about God as Creator can and should be argued over against naturalist and idealist alternatives in and as the critical dogmatics of the Christian theology of creation, i.e., on its own "eschatological" terms as revealed theology, not as some alleged "natural theology" that could be rationally persuasive as philosophical protology apart from the acquisition of theological subjectivity in repentance and faith. This means eschewing Leibniz's apologetic strategy, as if the alternative metaphysics of naturalism or idealism could somehow be exposed as tacitly holding at bottom Christian presuppositions, or at least requiring them in order to cohere, or to sustain ethical humanism, so that honest persons would thus be rationally forced to own up to their latent Christianity, since otherwise naturalism or idealism is shown to bear dire moral implications of nihilistic metaphysics. In fact, it was Leibniz who unconsciously smuggled in Christian dogma under the guise of natural reason, an illicit operation that the rigorous naturalisms of Spinoza and later Hume in time exposed and disallowed. Certainly, naturalism and idealism bear other moral and political implications than does the Christian theology of creation, and attaining clarity about these differences in charitable critique is imperative.

But one offers Christian interpretations of nature and theory in the conviction and to the end that these theological interpretations prove more satisfying cognitively, ethically, aesthetically, and spiritually. In the realm of theology, in any event, persuasive power is not compelling but inspiring; it is the poetry of the Spirit (not of metaphysics!) capturing our imaginations by the Word of God that tells the resurrection of the Crucified, not a deduction from first principles forcing us to supposedly rational faith. It works the other way around: knowledge of the resurrection of the Crucified as the prolepsis of God's future revises our thinking about the origin. This abandonment of natural theology for revealed theology requires thinking of creation itself eschatologically: not only as the act of origin by which all that follows is causally determined from its *arche* in a definite predetermination, but rather and indeed chiefly as the self-surpassing divine acts of redemption and fulfillment made known in the *oikonomia* of God enacted in Christ. Leibniz, to be sure, may be credited with taking an epochal step in historicizing the ontological, so to say, as well as for the modern recognition of the value of each unique individual with its own, non-substitutable and as such

191. *PNT,* pp. 223-82.

incorrigible perspective on the whole to which all belong.[192] It is substantively a vision of Beloved Community, wherein irreducible little wholes (persons) within greater wholes (communities) ought to harmonize (in love and justice).

In Leibnizian light of the continuity thesis, we also ought to be able to see how the false opposition between evolution and so-called "creationism," which has so muddled the matter of faith in God as Creator since Darwin, arose on account of a non-Trinitarian account of deity reduced to the abstract deistic notion of "intelligent design" along with an equally ahistorical view of nature.[193] Moreover, this false opposition obscured the theological problems of evil and the corresponding theodicy of faith. The massive and dangerous hubris of modernity's "sovereign self"[194] in its categorical demand to eliminate "meaningless" suffering (that is, the "natural evil," which, on Leibniz's analysis, attends any conceivable creature as finite and embodied) consequently finds theological apologists rather than prophetic critics of this ideological rationalization of privilege and greed.[195] The deistic account, which may be traced back to Aristotle,[196] makes "a happy science [= metaphysics] out of a sad creation" (Luther)[197] — an optimistic illusion spawned out of greed that powerful technologies today are all too capable of acting out. Romans 8 provides Christian theology with its apostolic alternative: the conception of a creation subjected to futility until the time of the revelation of the glorious liberty of the children of God at the coming of the Beloved Community. The creation of the triune God is eschatological; hence it has rightly suffered during this interregnum in the "theodicy of faith." Such faith justifies God in His judgment, namely, in the resurrection of the Crucified, and hence it becomes the new life obediently lived in trust that all things on the earth work for good to them that love God, who are called according to His purpose, for whom the sufferings of this present age cannot be compared to the glory which is to be revealed.

We reconstruct and reappropriate Leibniz's argument theologically as follows: The God of the gospel is antecedently and eternally the primordial Beloved Community, the love of the Father and the Son in the Spirit. It is as such that the eternal Trinity becomes the Creator of all that is other than God.[198] God, who is eternally the life of the Father and the Son in the Spirit, "becomes" the Creator

192. Smith, *Religion and the Rise of History*, pp. 103-16.

193. For the alternative, see George L. Murphy, *The Cosmos in the Light of the Cross* (Harrisburg, London, New York: Trinity Press International, 2003).

194. Talal Asad, *Formations of the Secular: Christianity, Islam, Modernity* (Stanford, CA: Stanford University Press, 2003), pp. 67-99.

195. With the notable exception of Diogenes Allen, *Christian Belief in a Postmodern World: The Full Wealth of Conviction* (Louisville: Westminster John Knox, 1989), a work discussed below in Chapter Eight.

196. Drozdek, *Greek Philosophers as Theologians*, pp. 182-83.

197. *LW* 25, p. 362.

198. So also Thomas F. Torrance, *The Trinitarian Faith* (Edinburgh: T. & T. Clark, 1993), pp. 87-89.

of the creation freely out of abundance, not out of necessity, poverty, or need. In some distinction from Augustine on whom Leibniz (and I) otherwise drew (draw),[199] this "becoming" of God already in the very act of origin as something "new" also for God makes it necessary and intelligible to ascribe to the triune God an eternity that is both "space-like" and "time-like." Fittingly, in that the triune God experiences otherness within His own eternal life and consequently movement or procession. As this kind of "temporally infinite" eternity,[200] the triune God can be intelligibly thought to come to the decision to act newly *ad extra* in one certain way rather than infinite other ways. All things are possible to God but not all things are wise or good. So Leibniz, drawing upon the trinity of attributes, namely power, wisdom, and love, reasoned against Spinoza's tacit unitarianism of power, in what in fact was his lifelong polemic against voluntarism in theology, whose lineage he traced back from Spinoza through Descartes to Occam.[201]

Certainly, Spinoza pushed voluntarism to its logical self-cancelation, arguing that it is finally too anthropomorphic to imagine God making choices like a human being.[202] God's will is rather God's infinite and impersonal desire to express all possibilities in an infinity of forms operating like an algorithm without beginning or end. In this sense, whatever is must be. It cannot be otherwise. Leibniz did not deny the lawfulness of events in time and space according to the order of nature, but argued that this very ordered sequence of the definite time and space in which we find ourselves with the world is the contingent but fitting choice of the tri-personal God, reflecting the infinite harmony of power, wisdom, and love that God is. Thus God is imagined in the very act of creation to survey all possible worlds and to choose the one of these which would be the best. The "best" metaphysically would be the one that achieves maximally compossible idiosyncrasy. The "best" morally would be the one that achieves the harmony of justice through the redemption in Christ, since the latter justice makes good out of evil, negating the negations by love and rendering even evil ultimately an instrument conscripted to the service of the coming of the Beloved Community. In all this protological reflection, the triune God "becomes" the Creator, who in the fullness of time would "become" flesh in the person of the Son, and so "become" the Temple of the Beloved Community by the outpouring of the Spirit on all flesh.

The fruitfulness of this thinking after God's decision in the act of origin is that it allows theology to render an account of natural and moral evils not only as ontologically privative, but as ontically actual, as Karl Barth endeavored to say in

199. Augustine in the *Confessions,* XI-XIII, famously found baffling the Bible's first verse: How did God begin to create before time existed?

200. Douglas Knight, "Jenson on Time," in *Trinity, Time, and Church: A Response to the Theology of Robert W. Jenson,* ed. Colin E. Gunton (Grand Rapids: Eerdmans, 2000), pp. 71-79.

201. Compare this account of the origins of nihilism to Michael Allen Gillespie, *Nihilism before Nietzsche* (Chicago: University of Chicago Press, 1996).

202. Baruch Spinoza, *Ethics, Treatise on the Emendation of the Intellect and Selected Letters,* trans. S. Shirley (Indianapolis: Hackett, 1992), and the discussion in RPTD.

his difficult teaching on *das Nichtige*.[203] Leibniz's distinction between "metaphysical evil," expressed in physical pain, and "moral evil," expressed in sin taken as structures of malice and injustice, at its best serves to clarify what these are and especially how sin is to be exposed as evil, endured in cross-bearing, opposed in prophecy, and finally defeated at the eschaton of judgment. Thus Barth rightly interpreted Leibniz's meaning: "that the real created world is the best does not mean that it is absolutely good and perfect. If this were so, it would not be the created world. From its being as such, the non-divinity of its existence, there follows necessarily its imperfection. . . ."[204] This "non-divinity" of the creation is what Leibniz means by the unfortunate terminology of "metaphysical evil," i.e., the ontological vulnerability to nonbeing of any conceivable creature which by definition (given the doctrine of *creatio ex nihilo*) arises "out of nothing" and accordingly the positive role of pain to signal danger to such ineradicably vulnerable beings. "Earth to earth, ashes to ashes, dust to dust" — any conceivable creature has come into existence and will pass again from existence. This imperfection of creation in the metaphysical sense of the non-divinity of the creature, on the other hand, "confirms the good will of God to reflect His glory in the best and most perfect way in this other being. . . ." The intended reflection of divine glory in the imperfect creature attests to the good and gracious will of God, if only in faith the creature learns to trust in it and so live justly. Just here, in turn, we detect the very origins of moral evil: we do not trust, but "we dispute both this good will of God and the actual but limited perfection of creation if we try to dispense with metaphysical evil. . . ."[205]

We ought, then, in the theodicy of faith bear the cross, i.e., that is, we ought to embrace "metaphysical evil" in order not to become "morally evil." Refusing to endure our sufferings ecologically, or to act justly for public rather than private good, we become morally evil disputants whose egocentric unhappiness fueled by envy maturing into greed drives us to rend the web of life in aggressive acts of unjust appropriation — the moral evil that is "actual" in distinction from (but not in contradiction to) the venerable privative account of evil in Augustinian tradition. And God, who identifies with His Name in the world of creatures, is in this way vulnerable to actual evil at the hands of creatures that want to be God, and do not want God to be God. He is blasphemed, no less by those who accuse Him than by those who would defend Him, by all who understand God apart from the theodicy that is the resurrection of the Crucified as the deed of divine justice that governs this world on the way to the Beloved Community. The critical and prophetic edge of the theodicy of faith (so Barth draws on Leibniz) is thus to resist blaming the body, which is good, for the evil desires of the soul and so to resist using the Name of God for human purposes,

203. *CD* III/3, pp. 289-368. See my discussion and criticism in *PNT*, pp. 107-12.
204. *CD* III/1, p. 390.
205. *CD* III/1, p. 390.

instead surrendering to God's purposes in the trial of faith, the Gethsemane of the soul. The root sin of idolatry is such abuse of God for human purposes, especially in the religion business; idolatry is not the mere misrepresentation of God by finite images, but the abuse of God, especially God's name, for contra-divine purposes, preeminently in the cult of expiation which offers sacrificial bribes to leverage the Deity.[206]

But the theodicy of faith justifies God in His judgment. The theodicy of faith is not an optimistic rationalization of moral evil on the basis of natural experience within a horizon of immanence; as in Romans 8, it is hope against hope in the God who promises to find the way to make something out of nothing, wisdom out of folly, good out of evil in the actual providence of the ever-innovating Spirit on the way to the Beloved Community. This theologic indeed takes wing when rational optimism is crushed and when pessimism seems realistic, as in Euro-America today. The theodicy of faith, as may be seen in Jesus' Sermon on the Mount, trusts in God taken as the Father in heaven who causes His rain to fall on the just and the unjust alike. It is the hopeful life of those who judge the material world "good," who accept as their own then the natural evils that attend created existence as divine limits placed upon them, who trust through their sufferings in a wisdom and benevolence that transcends their finite understanding at present, who thus believe that all things work together for good in a world that in spite of all malice and injustice is divinely determined to enter into the Beloved Community. Such believers thus enter the lists in hopeful lives of justice and love — just this mis-siological praxis that suffers the present order in the conviction of the glory that is to be revealed is the theodicy of faith. Constrained by the continuity thesis, creation must be taken as eschatological.

## Neither Univocity nor Analogy

By means of such believing interpretation, the theodicy of faith offers a cognitive path between and beyond idealism and naturalism for the interpretation of experience. Yet it does so without the terrible cost of sheer denial of the truths in fact and theory that these alternatives represent, rather more fruitfully putting these truths into its better perspective of the approaching reign of God known through faith in Jesus Christ. Theology can do this because most basically it thinks the God of the gospel in the Trinitarian way, as the self-donating and self-communicating God who by His own Word and Spirit both gives Himself to faith and makes Himself known as this Gift. Fundamentally, however, this move to theological cognition as interpretation claims — controversially — to resolve a fundamental

206. See René Girard, *Violence and the Sacred,* trans. Patrick Gregory (Baltimore: Johns Hopkins University Press, 1979), and the critical distinction between expiation and propitiation in *LBC,* pp. 96-104.

ambiguity in the history of Christian thought: as we have hinted throughout, it models God not as a disembodied Mind to be known in theoretical contemplation but as the advent/event of Beloved Community, whose coming by the gospel brings the new and saving interpretation of nature and history, beginning with the fact that it causes us to think of ourselves as sinners nevertheless included and destined for life and good along with all the others for whom Jesus lived and died. This is a pragmatic knowledge of God that aims not to comprehend God in His essence but rather to enjoy Him in the fellowship of His own personal relations by obedient confession and mission, anticipating the eternal doxology that ascribes all power, wisdom, and love to the God of the gospel as to the One who triumphs for one as for all.

As mentioned, Leibniz, who rightly maintained the organic continuity between the sensible and supersensible, misconstrued the significance of this biblical holism, insofar as he continued to think God on the Platonic analogy of mind to body, an *intelligentia extra mundam.* Despite this, the Trinitarian knowledge of God is present in the monadological vision, informs it in important ways, and qualifies Leibniz's Platonism. In this respect, Leibniz was drawing on a particular Melanchthonian theological tradition descending from the Augsburg Confession. Here the traditional *via negativa,* "eternal, incorporeal, indivisible," was employed to identify God as other than all that is not God, as Creator to creature (not as mind to body). Hence the traditional *via eminentia,* "immeasurable power, wisdom, and goodness," was next used to identify God as "the creator and preserver of all things, visible and invisible," linking the essentially other God existentially to this world where such words are spoken and heard. Crucially, the trinity of attributes in their harmony was immediately correlated by the Augsburg Confession with the "three persons," the Father, the Son, and the Holy Spirit, noting explicitly that the term "person" here means "not a part or a quality in another but that which subsists in itself." Thus deity is not thought as a quality that can simply and essentially be predicated of a simple substance, God, and participated in lesser degree by other, lesser (not simple but compounded) substances. But as the Three agents ("subsistences") of the gospel narrative, God is here thought as the primordial Beloved Community, the Trinity of persons whose unity is not a metaphysical given grounded in static, natural self-identity (as per the ambiguous doctrine of divine simplicity)[207] but an eternal action and passion of love in the Spirit of the Father and the Son.

To succeed in making such a claim today, the knowledge of God has to be distinguished properly from the various knowledges of the world and then rightly re-

---

207. See the running critique of the doctrine of divine simplicity in the counter-titled *DC,* especially pp. 167-83. The Lutheran Leibniz was similarly heir in this regard to the 11th Article of the Lutheran Formula of Concord, which presented the gathering of the Beloved Community in Christ as the Trinity's eschatological goal over against contemporary Calvinism's protological speculation about an absolute double decree predestining the saved and the damned.

lated to them. Spinoza, as mentioned, represents the real challenge here,[208] with his resolute repudiation of all anthropomorphism in theology and insistence that God, like anything else, be thought univocally, i.e., strictly on the "plane of immanence" (Deleuze).[209] Then "God" becomes nature conceived as acting rather than as acted upon. While theology in the tradition of Luther can fruitfully enter the lists here, taking immanence as the mask of God, the theological tradition has predominantly, in rejecting pantheism such as had been known from Stoicism, tried to make this distinction between the knowledge of God and the knowledge of the world by rejecting univocity and affirming analogy. Univocity forces God to be an object, like any other object, in the world; that is, it reduces God to His kataphatic appearances — to what Deleuze and Guattari call the "figures" of religion.[210] But the resulting anthropomorphism in theological language amounts to an ontological reduction to polytheistic absurdity, if anything is intended like the traditional One and Only, who is Creator in relation to all others as creatures. Under univocity, God becomes the quarreling gods, reducible then to philosophical concepts by demythologization, hence ultimately to atheism in theology and nihilism in philosophy. Under univocity, strong Trinitarianism becomes suspect of tritheism.

Caught on the horns of this dilemma — either the quarreling gods or self-identical divine Nature — analogy held that God as Creator is somehow like the creation, but not identical with it. How? God is *intelligentia extra mundam,* a Mind without body, hence Perfect Mind, Pure Actuality, thought thinking itself. Thus analogy de facto articulated a mental-psychological model of transcendence: God is to the world as the mind is to the body, but purified of all imperfections entailed by the creature's embodiment. God causes the effects in the world without being one of its effects or intra-mundane (secondary) causes by thinking-willing-and-acting things out according to His eternal creative intuition in a single eternal act of protological determination. Strictly speaking, however, this model of divine transcendence as pure Mind excludes the missions of the Son and the Spirit in the world as genuine appearances of divine nature. Truth be told, it also excludes the almighty Father, who just as much *becomes* Creator of heaven and earth as the Son *becomes* Incarnate and the Spirit *becomes* the earthly Temple of God. It must at the least impugn the true deity of the Son and the Spirit in mission or make the mission no more than a temporal signification of an eternal state of affairs. But that lands theology back in the company of Arius, even worse, of Eunomius.

The *intention* of analogy to affirm that the God of the Bible is like the creation though not identical with it is certainly correct. The Trinity is the Creator,

208. See *PNT,* pp. 76-82.

209. For clarification of this "plane" as the way critical thought "slices" the chaos as philosophy — no different for theology as critical dogmatics — see *RPTD,* pp. 105-9.

210. Giles Deleuze and Felix Guattari, *What Is Philosophy?* trans. H. Tomlinson and G. Burchell (New York: Columbia University Press, 1994), pp. 91-92.

according to Christianity, who cannot be conceived unfaithfully to create a world unsuited to His own living harmony of power, wisdom, and love. The problem is that under the conditions of the existing order of reality we do not know ourselves truly as God's creation and hence this analogy of the *imago Dei* becomes unavailable to us. In fact, "we want to be God and do not want God to be God."[211] Moreover, then, under the assumption that analogy is available to us, we are led, if not to crude and brutal projection of human fantasies for domination, then to the Platonic model of transcendence as Disembodied Mind, the Aristotelian "thought thinking itself" in rapt self-possession untouched by any other and considered divine just because timelessly self-possessed. Aside from the Trinitarian objection just alluded to, this venerable model of transcendence founders on powerful objections today from both naturalism and idealism, which are equally anti-dualist and as such undermine from within philosophy the very point of the traditional analogy that took for granted the mind's ontological superiority to the body.

For naturalists, matter comes to think in an evolutionary development. For idealists, thought thinks itself, indeed, as history, generating its own material embodiment in the course of its progressive dialectical unfolding. If these alternatives to theological analogy were not sufficiently powerful objections to the fantastic idea of perfect being as Mind without body, the mental model of divine transcendence is pressed from within by its own essentially negative dialectic, stemming from the Platonic tradition, which achieves transcendence by negating the alleged imperfections of immanence.[212] This logic pushes talk about God ultimately to apophatic self-cancelation, to the God beyond Thought and beyond Being, the reification of a "No-thing" that Nietzsche both abhorred and mocked.

The region of theology in the landscape of human knowledge, however, need not be imagined as giving nothing but the unhappy choice between kataphatic polytheism and apophatic silence. The social model of the Trinity,[213] derived from the kataphatic figures of the gospel narrative, represents a model of God's creative transcendence as *imminence* to the things that are, i.e., the existing world, as the promised and in faith effected *coming* of the Beloved Community.[214] In that case, the region of theology is indeed not the metaphysician's *arche,* the protological first cause at the beginning, logically or temporally, of all effects that one posits and pursues in the quest for metaphysical totality in knowledge of the cause of causes. Pragmatically speaking, the quest for origins constitutes a "genetic fallacy" on a massive scale that fails to recognize the reality and value of emergent properties.

211. *LW* 31, p. 10.

212. Jenson already executed this "dialectical self-cancelation" of Christian Platonism in his early work, *God after God: The God of the Past and the God of the Future, Seen in the Work of Karl Barth* (Indianapolis and New York: Bobbs-Merrill, 1969).

213. Cornelius Plantinga Jr., "Gregory of Nyssa and the Social Analogy of the Trinity," *The Thomist* 50, no. 3 (1986).

214. *DC,* pp. 26-27.

The region of theology, in any case, is eschatology, the region of putative final causes for which the world exists, the possible fulfillments that connect the dots of time into a coherent and saving narrative — or not. It is only and strictly by making this differentiation between the light of nature and the light of glory that Christian theology can criticize naturalism and idealism appropriately in the light of the presence of grace in Jesus Christ as the light that lightens the world. As mentioned previously, such eschatological theology does not compete with fact or theory, offering an alternative Christian "worldview" as if theology were philosophy, like naturalism or idealism. Rather, it interprets fact and theory as historical creations of God (including discernment of corruptions of God's creation) in an ongoing work of discernment; it tests its own belief by its coherence with these other beliefs that we hold as true on the theological ground of God's continuing creation as well as by the test of fidelity to theology's authorizing discourse in the gospel of the resurrection of the Crucified One. Incarnation requires the first affirmation of this earth in its history as God's creation, while the cross of the Incarnate One requires the second posture of critical discernment. Theology ever negotiates this dialectical interplay of affirmation and critique in conceiving of creation as eschatological.

The gospel's philosophically odd discourse about the imminent God takes canonical form in apocalyptic parable, Pauline paradox, and Johannine enigma. This peculiar discourse does not fit with the dialectics of either univocity or analogy; it is a rhetorical form that must be allowed to interpret itself on its own terms or be misunderstood entirely. The biblical basis for the foregoing argument lies in a Luther observation, which is conceptually congenial to Leibnizian perspectivalism: God-in-His-Word comes into the world to be known as the Word-made-flesh by the Spirit's act of creating a new knower of this innovative reality. Hence, fittingly, the form of the Word of God serves as a subversive rhetoric — "breaking into a strong man's house to bind him and plunder his goods" (Mark 3:27), according to the parable of Jesus, who thus scandalously likened His messianic task with that of a thief. The apparent contradiction — Messiah comes covertly as a thief — exposes the real thievery of the "strong man," i.e., the dominant discourse that ensnares and enslaves into lives of blind greed and insatiable egocentricity by capturing desire in structures of malice and injustice. The apocalyptic parable works a reversal or inversion of dominant meaning, a revaluation of values from within the dominant order; this linguistic action is taken up in extended ways in Pauline paradox and Johannine enigma. "God on a cross," Nietzsche exclaimed in apt horror, "the transvaluation of all hitherto existing values!" In critical dogmatics, everything depends on observing and following this subversive form of the gospel discourse as *befitting* the God of the gospel.

The reference of apocalyptic parable is to the coming of the Reign of God, but it is made *sub contrario* in the figure of Jesus who had no place to lay His head; the reference of the Pauline paradox is to the presence already now of the future Messiah whom it figures as the man on the Roman gibbet; the reference of the Johannine enigma is to the glory of divine love penetrating the very heart of the world's darkness in the flesh of Jesus lifted up on the cross for the sight of the new eyes of faith. That is to say, in all its major forms in the New Testament the meaning of the Bible's theological language is to break through the dominant discourse to break in with the promise of the One God who is determined by His incarnate Word and life-giving Spirit to redeem and fulfill the very world in which this subversion of language sounds and is heard. Therefore the worship of the eschatological assembly takes the signs of bread and wine as Jesus risen in such a way as to be present as promised in His transfigured body and blood at its communal meal: "This is my Body."

Apocalyptic parable, Pauline paradox and Johannine enigma thus make cognitive claims. Metaphors have reference[215] and the sense of a metaphor, as in any other kind of language, lies in deciphering its reference to something other than its own sound or sign; the truth of the metaphorical sign is the thing signified (even if ascertaining such truth is elusive and signification pragmatically is not a matter of adequation or correspondence but of effective guidance). As Luther observed against Zwingli, "that which represents is always inferior to that which is represented; and all signs are inferior to the thing they signify. Even fools and children know that quite well."[216] Naturally, then, there can be many varying metaphors for the thing signified, "indeed all the figures of speech in Scripture refer to Christ, the one and only Savior. He is called a lamb, a rock, a cornerstone, sun, morning star, wellspring, bridegroom, householder, teacher, father; indeed, each and every expression points to him and speaks of him, each in its own way."[217] What concerns theology is not the variety of metaphors but the novelty they indicate, Jesus who was Crucified as Messiah. Consider, "Christ is a flower," Luther asks. "All grammarians say that 'flower' here has become a new word and has acquired a new meaning, and now no longer means the flower in the field but the child Jesus. They do not say that the word 'is' here has become metaphorical, for Christ does not represent a flower but is a flower, yet a different flower from the natural one."[218] So Jesus is the Messiah, yet a different kind of Messiah than expected and His Body is bread, yet a different kind of bread than usual. In this way the characteristic metaphorical language of the gospel narrative is deliteralized and decoded theologically to refer to the novelty of the Word made flesh among us and for us. This matter will be more fully discussed below in Chapter Five.

Logical analysis in theology is imperative, but only after the cognitive claim of biblical discourse is clarified and understood on its own terms grammatically and historically. Understanding the truth-claim of the gospel narrative does not reduce to something its original authors had in mind (though interpretation is

---

215. Janet Soskice, *Metaphor and Religious Language* (Oxford: Clarendon, 1987), p. 70.
216. *LW* 37, p. 174.
217. *LW* 37, p. 164.
218. *LW* 37, p. 172.

controlled by a test of coherence with what the original authors had in mind and the first auditors would have heard). Rather, it is to require theological interpretation of the biblically and historically clarified meaning of gospel discourse by asking in terms of canonical and creedal principles what the Holy Spirit intends to say in such and such a way that faith may be rightly formed and thus knowingly obedient in our present steps on the pilgrim way to the Beloved Community of God. That is the marching order of critical dogmatics, to appropriate and use rightly the Bible's subversive rhetoric of God under the battle conditions of the apocalyptic conflict of the ages in one's own time and place.

But how can biblical rhetoric be understood on its own terms and not in terms of some alien metaphysic that would instead tell us what counts as a claim to truth in the first place? This is another crucial challenge first posed in modernity by Spinoza, who required that nature interpret the Bible, not the Bible nature. Needless to say, the very assertion that the canonical Bible coheres and can as such be understood on its own terms is tantamount to the assertion that the God who appears as a figure within its pages is also its ultimate author, or, that the Spirit-inspired Scripture can and must be interpreted according to the Spirit, i.e., according to the mind of its divine Author. Is this circle — the Word requires the Spirit to be understood, the Spirit comes through the Word and not apart from it — vicious? Only if it were offered as some kind of foundationalist epistemology with which rationally to convince a theoretical doubter. But that is not the Bible's epistemic function in critical dogmatics, which presupposes faith as the Spirit's sovereign gift of theological subjectivity and accordingly never uses the Bible philosophically, as if rationally to convince an imaginary neutral observer. The use of the Bible as the first authority and norm in critical dogmatics is theological, i.e., it is gospel faith under way in mission seeking its own understanding for the sake of its own public and intelligible articulation as confession in the world but before God.

Within this circle of faith, on the other hand, the claim to understand the Bible on its own terms, according to the Spirit's intention, does not amount to an idle, self-validating claim to private truth, but has cognitive traction in the public of the community of faith in mission to the nations. It has long been acknowledged that the Bible's notion of truth is "personal," though this insight today is often taken in the debased form of existentialist leaps in the dark, precisely then as some individual's "private truth": an "objective uncertainty embraced with infinite subjective passion" (Kierkegaard). The meaning of this distinction is rather that the Bible is not particularly interested in truth as the impersonal and intra-mundane correspondence of image or idea to thing, the kind of truth that can be universalized just because it is impersonally verified by any mind with appropriate skills on the assumption of the static uniformity of nature.

Rather, the kind of truth that interests the Bible is the correspondence of a person to her word through time and across space, hence "personal" truthfulness. God is true in fulfilling His Word, the promise of the coming into the world of

His Reign. People are true by the bodily obedience of their lives that works by trusting God to fulfill His Word even already now within the existing order of things, even though such truthfulness makes martyrs of them. Theology is true, then, in thinking-after the subversive God-in-His-Word to identify Him for such true faith and confession and missiological obedience. Theology is not true in and of itself as a correct and impersonal representation of God, taken as a thing, to which any neutral mind within the existing order of things might rationally be led without regard to its own truthfulness in repentance and faith. But theology is true in bearing true witness to God, who alone can finally verify His Word by the fulfillment of His promises, who alone in the interim by sovereign grace bestows the gift of theological subjectivity *ubi et quando Deo visum est* ("where and when it pleases God" — Augsburg Confession V).

Certainly this answer to Spinoza begs the question of how anyone in the world becomes a believer and thus a theological subject. Like Barth it asserts what to Spinoza is "out of this world," incomprehensible and potentially authoritarian by the light of nature: theological subjectivity descends freely and incalculably from above without regard to human merit as befits the God of the gospel. That makes theological subjectivity a surd to rigorous immanentism, which *a priori* excludes the possibility of extramundane visitations. There is a real tension here. Every rigorous form of immanentism knows with Darwin that there are no free lunches. Grace is and must be excluded on the strict ground of the lawfulness of events and the sole merit of survival in the contest of competing forces. This conflict remains, even when theology for its part de-Platonizes its model of transcendence as timelessly disembodied Mind in favor of the social Trinity, the Beloved Community drawing near in the subversive rhetoric of apocalyptic parable, Pauline paradox, and Johannine enigma. For this "folly" of preaching the resurrection of the Crucified and the faith that corresponds to it is professedly not in the control of critical dogmatics, which proceeds on the fact that the Christian community of faith exists in the world and ventures to speak of the coming God on the basis of His Easter Word, itself the oxymoronic assertion of a Christ Crucified for our sins.

Yet, in some distinction from Barth, who understood the *sub contrario* principle of biblical language so as to deny that the "form" of the Word of God in the Bible has any suitability in itself to inform the theological content it bears,[219] the present endeavor in critical dogmatics takes the forms of apocalyptic parable, Pauline paradox, and Johannine enigma to fit or suit its content. The "is" in "This is my Body," is an *est,* not a *significat.* Likewise the "I" in "I believe" (as in the Credo, see below, Chapter Two) is the empirical self actually wed and formed into Christ by His joyful exchange, not an elusive, dialectical "event." The "hypostatic communication of properties" (as classical Christology interpreted the Incarnation) is not merely a way of speaking; it is to be understood as Christ's way

---

219. Barth, *CD* 1/1, pp. 165-74. See the discussion in *LBC,* pp. 367-68.

of being for us, His "*pro me* structure" (Bonhoeffer), and accordingly now also of believers in Him, their being *for Him* (1 Cor. 6:13) as the Object of their faith.

Admittedly, also this understanding of the fittingness of the *sub contrario* to its divine referent as God surpassing God in order to come in grace to us who are sold under sin continues to beg Spinoza's question about the seemingly "absurd" appearance of grace in the world, within the existing order of visible things, as ruled according to law and merit. But it does make a counter-question to Spinoza possible: not whether the believer is justified before the Tribunal of Reason, but whether Christ is justified here and now in claiming the believer, otherwise un-godly and a sinner, and this by the right of divine grace. For Christian theology, that claim of Christ to enact grace already now, within the existing order, is what is at issue: "Who do you say that I am?" (Mark 8:29). The right use of the Bible's rhetoric, as the matrix of theology (*prima,* not *sola scriptura;*[220] see Chapter Two below), is to follow the form of its language in this way right back into Galilee (Mark 16:7). Theology decodes this form of language, not in order to replace it with abstractions, but to make clear its cognitive claim regarding the knowledge of God who comes in grace for sinners. Decoding is a feedback reflection that occurs here between "first" and "second" orders of theology to sharpen usage of biblical language in the world.

There is price for this proposal, which I trace back to Luther, that the region of theology is eschatology in distinction from the protological orientation of the metaphysical tradition, whether naturalistic or idealistic. It is the sharp cognitive delimitation that has been argued for throughout this chapter: the *single* cognitive claim of the Christian gospel is that true God is to be identified as the One who is (self-)determined by His Son and Spirit to redeem and fulfill the very world on which the cross of Jesus stood. The truth of this claim is the actual coming of the Beloved Community. This is the Christian dogma to which critical dogmatics attends, and it stands in a determinative relation to the various articles of tradi-tional dogmatics, which in turn are to be understood according to their respective theologics as expressive of this singular cognitive claim. In other words, there is no independent doctrine of, say, the Virgin Birth, or of Original Sin, or the Sec-ond Coming of Christ, and so on, which confront us as revealed facts demanding recognition as "fundamentals," then to be assembled like pearls on a string or systematized on the basis of some other foundational metaphysics. Rather, all such traditional doctrines are received as beliefs justified in, cohering with, and in some particular way articulating the single dogma concerning the God of the gospel who is determined by His Son and in His Spirit to redeem and fulfill the creation. Each doctrinal item from the legacy must be tested and received in this way (or reformed or even rejected in this way).

As a result, this system of theology is not organized as are traditional dogmat-ics, working through a list of beliefs that are, or have been, identified somehow

220. Paul R. Hinlicky, "The Lutheran Dilemma," *Pro Ecclesia* 8, no. 4 (Fall 1999): 391-422.

as items of Christian faith. Neither is it organized around a systematic principle from which one draws out implications deductively. It shares the "positivity" of traditional dogmatics in receiving the baptismal creed as the identification of the God of the gospel; it acquires "systematicity" in following strictly after the Trinitarian movement. Insofar as there is a "system" in this "systematic" theology, it is the intention and resolve of the ecclesia to know God in the Spirit with the Son as our Father on the basis of the Father speaking the Son to us in the Spirit through the gospel. Cognitively speaking, this entire work makes just this claim and nothing else. The hybrid conception of theology as critical dogmatics in this way takes from traditional dogmatics the historical contingency of the Christian faith in attending to the gospel as the putative Word of God that authors and authorizes the mission to the nations, and it borrows from philosophical criticism the rational demand for coherence and warrantability in articulating a public claim to truth. Thus it seeks at the same time to avoid the authoritarian dogmatism of the former and the epistemological conceit of the latter.

To put the matter epistemically: Christian beliefs about God do not reduce to the percepts that inform naturalism nor the concepts by which idealism constructs them into usable objects, but exist as interpretive articulations of the new perspective that arises from audition of the gospel, where faith comes by this hearing. For example, Jesus in His person marks a new beginning in humanity (i.e., the doctrine of the Virgin Birth), or Jesus in His death is not merely a victim, nor punishment bearer, but divine love's innocent and voluntary bearer of the sin of the world with all its consequences as His own (i.e., the doctrine of the Atonement). Neither of these truths can be known naturally or historically, but only theologically, that is, precisely as the (divine!) interpretation of the Jesus of nature and history in the perspective of His resurrection from the dead in which theology participates, however falteringly. This new perspective of the gospel, taking form in such basic Christian beliefs, in turn yields further theological interpretations of fact and theory in the common world, where facts or theories are now seen as creatures of God (or, perhaps, as actual evils, diabolic corruptions of God's creation in actualizing possibilities that God has rejected). For example, Jesus' new beginning of humanity in His person forbids us to think of existence any longer as being-towards-death but instead requires us to think of authentic existence in space-time as being-towards-death-and-resurrection. Or, Jesus' bearing the sin of the world forbids us any longer to evade or project onto others the evil consequences of our sin, but rather to be saved from them and from sin itself by dying with Him in the Spirit to rise, forgiven and freed, to newness of life. That is what the dogmatic beliefs of the Christian creed are: theologic articulations of the new perspective of the gospel that interpret common experience, first, of Jesus, by the Father's speech-act of resurrection, and then, of believers in Jesus, by the Spirit's corresponding speech-act in baptism causing repentance and faith.

This delimitation of theology's cognitive claim reflects the relative autonomy of Christian theology as a human, but nonspeculative "thinking after" *(nachden-*

ken) the gospel's discourse about God even with respect to its own, often ambiguous tradition. The right relating of theology to philosophy in this connection is, as we have argued, first, to distinguish metaphysical, historical or natural claims, which have their own integrity and relative autonomy, from theological claims, but then, second, to bring theological claims to bear cognitively as interpretation of them in view of the promised coming of the Beloved Community. Critically that forges a way between the Scylla of naturalism and the Charybdis of constructivism. Such ongoing, pragmatic, cumulative but revisable interpretation of experience in light of the Christian knowledge of God would or could result in a kind of Christian philosophy, an explication of the new perspective of Christian belief in the world, such as I called for in the conclusion of *Paths Not Taken*.[221] Critical dogmatics, as I envision it, provides a "toolkit" for this task, which might also be conceived as Christian ethics or as Christian aesthetics, if attending strictly and rigorously to the extended argument about the knowledge of God given rise by the gospel. Critical dogmatics as the embodied argument about how to pass on what has been first received arises in the Easter re-visioning of the executed Jesus who died as a blasphemer, *sub contrario,* to bring the Beloved Community to the unloved and unlovable. This cognitive task of interpretation, as identified in the conclusion of *Luther and the Beloved Community,*[222] reflects the new self-interpretation of the theological subject as a sinner nevertheless justified by faith in Jesus, the saving Agent of the Beloved Community. We conclude this introductory chapter with two final notes on the triadic structure of the following presentation of the system of Christian doctrine and another on the use of gendered language for the Father, the Son, and the Holy Spirit.

---

## A Note on the Triadic Structure of Theological Knowledge

In proper Trinitarian theology the so-called "monarchy" of the Father is to be acknowledged in the order of reality. This does not mean "patriarchalism" or the "divine right of kings" as alleged in fashionable but uncomprehending critiques. It means monotheism — though not in the sense of the Western church's habit of privileging the self-identical nature or essence of deity in its ontologically simple self-identity. It means ontological monotheism in the sense of the Eastern church that the eternal and unbegotten Father of His own "natural" Son and breather of His own "natural" Spirit is the sole principle of origin in the one divine life. The self-surpassing Father begets and breathes from all eternity, even as the Son eternally returns the glory in the Spirit, to constitute the one divine *life,* the true "eternal return of the same" (if I may so outbid Nietzsche). But this precious insight of Trinitarian theology into the inner basis and reality of monotheism is

---

221. *PNT,* pp. 293-94.
222. *LBC,* pp. 373-74.

but a hint of the eternal doxology to which theology, as oriented by the economy of God, comes and indeed rests in wonder and praise; it is not the basis of further speculation that takes theology far afield from the earth on which the cross of Jesus stood, the very object of redemption and fulfillment in the coming of the Beloved Community. In the order of knowledge, according to the economy, therefore, it is advisable especially today in the ruins of Christendom to follow the opposite sequence of the order of being. It is by the Spirit that we are united with Christ the Son and so come to knowledge of our heavenly Father. Because this epistemic access in Christian theology is so little comprehended today, we adopt in what follows the drastic device of inverting the traditional order of the creeds which present Christian doctrine in the sequence creation, redemption, sanctification. Yet I stress here that this sequence is a matter of epistemic access, not divine ontology.

If knowledge in Christian theology is pragmatic and hermeneutical, not theoretical gazing (let alone reveling in pure experience), it is because of the triadic organization of knowledge first uncovered by Charles Sanders Peirce but developed in a hermeneutical direction by Royce. Embracing the continuity thesis, they joined in critiquing the dualism of perception and conception that dominates modern thought since Descartes on behalf of the social and historical dynamism of cognition, taken as interpretation by a motivated subject of an interesting object to and for a relevant audience in the present of historical passage. The root insight of the continuity thesis here is that nature is history and history is natural, that nature and grace are alternating perspectives on one and the same world that theology interprets as God's creation destined for redemption and fulfillment. In Royce's words: "if we view the world as everywhere and always recording its own history, by processes of aging and weathering, or of evolution, or of stellar and nebular clusterings and streamings, we can simply define the time order, and its three regions — past, present, future — as an order of possible interpretation. That is, we can define the present as, potentially, the interpretation of the past to the future. The triadic structure of our interpretation [i.e., subject-object-audience] is strictly analogous, both to the psychological and to the metaphysical structure of the world of time."[223] The irrevocable past, the urgency of its interpretation for well-counseled action in the present, and the openness of the future constitute or structure knowledge as interpretation, both of self and of other selves in communities of interpretation, in an open process pending the eschaton of judgment.

As we appropriate this insight theologically, it seems clear in the light of the foregoing that the theological subject is the person who is formed by Spirit-wrought faith in Christ, thus the subject who exists in the world as crucified with Christ and in just this way raised to membership in the community of interpretation that is the ecclesia drawn to faith from the nations through the ages.

223. Royce, *Problem*, p. 288.

Likewise, it seems clear that the object that interests this theological subject is Jesus as the Christ, the Son of God, a union of the sign and thing signified, who is as such believed, known, and confessed before the world as the good reason for this new subjectivity-cum-community as the way of life in the world that is the mission to the nations and baptismal vocations within them. And while it is certainly true that the proximate audience of this act of interpreting Jesus as the Messiah of Israel and savior of the nations, and just so the true Son of the eternal Father, is the very "nation" in which and to which these subjects and communities are in mission and vocational service, the final audience of this action is the eschaton of judgment, the day of judgment before the eternal Father. As a matter of conscience and conviction, as Paul paradigmatically attests in Galatians 1, theology confesses Jesus Christ in the world in order to be found in Him at the eschaton when the secrets of every heart will be revealed. Wherever this conscientious anticipation of the final audience of theology *coram Deo* goes missing, however, theology becomes self-justification, religious ideology, and ecclesiastical triumphalism.

In this presentation of the cognitive system of Christian theology for the situation after Christendom in Euro-America, accordingly, we follow the order of knowledge as triadic interpretation just sketched. We begin with the third article of the creed, and move through the second, to conclude with the first: Pneumatology, Christology, Patrology in the order of knowledge leading to the concluding doxology of eternal life in the eternal Trinity. The divine Word of promise as appropriated in theological subjectivity in decoding the paradoxical predication, Christ crucified, as the promise of God to which faith is correlated is articulated in a corresponding threefold form: I believe that, united with the Son by Spirit-given faith, I too am a beloved child of God. I believe that Jesus is the Messiah of Israel, the Son of God. I believe that with all the common body, I am the creature whom God the Almighty Father is creating, redeeming, and bringing to fulfillment in the Beloved Community. This is one faith structured in three articles. The dynamic unity of the three expresses the dynamic unity of the one eternal God, whose incomparable being is the ineffable harmony of power, wisdom, and love.

## A Note on Gendered Language

Finally, as readers have undoubtedly noticed heretofore, traditional gendered language for the God of the gospel has not only been adopted in this work but accentuated by the use of capitalization of the masculine pronouns, His and Him. As previously mentioned, the messianic faith of Jesus in His God and heavenly Father is and remains ontologically primary. Just so, however, it goes on to include faith in this very Father's Easter re-cognition of the Crucified as indeed His beloved and faithful Son; indeed, it further continues to the appropriation of these judgments of the Father and the Son in Spirit-given theological subjectivity. But the ontological primacy of faith in the Father has not only come under attack in Nietzschean fashion for thinking of God as Past, Origin, Pure Simplicity, Ground of Being, and so on. More potent, at least in the popular life of the churches, is a feminist critique to the effect that calling God Father makes fathers God, i.e., that it is an ideological mystification of patriarchal power.

This feminist critique can be prophetic in the way that Feuerbach's critique, to which these feminist claims of today may be traced, was prophetic. But then it requires the hard work of theology to explain the paradoxical, not univocal or analogical nature of theological language. In place of this, however, the feminist critique of the Bible's gendered language for God can take place, and predominantly heretofore has taken place, in the fashion of consistent apophaticism. This makes illicit the cognitive claim of theology bound to the gospel; indeed it makes it idolatrous anthropomorphism. God must be and be thought to be beyond thought and being. But just such an ontologically primary commitment to negative theology — as opposed to the faith of Jesus in His God and heavenly Father — is deeply, indeed fatally problematic, according to the argument of this book. It puts God "beyond" in the lethal way of hostility to embodied life that Nietzsche so potently criticized. That is why some feminist theologians do not want to abolish the parental reference to God as Father, but rather to deliteralize it, treat it as a symbol, and supplement it by complementary symbols ranging from invoking God as Mother or the Holy Spirit as the feminine Hebrew *ruah* or the divine principle incarnate in Christ by the Greek feminine, *sophia*. Even this more considered revisionism, however, cannot but meet profound resistance anywhere that the language of the Bible is the primary language of Christian theology, its very *matrix*. Even with apt modernizations, the awkwardness and artificialness of such proposals is liturgically inescapable. But this aesthetic objection cannot be the dogmatic basis as such for rejecting revisionism.

The reason why such proposals are awkward and artificial is that the theological assumptions made in the critique of allegedly patriarchal language are those of negative, not Trinitarian theology. That is to say, the function of doxological language is assumed to be the projection of our own virtues, powers, identities onto the blank screen of the unknown divine for admiration and inspiration — a *via eminentia* that must be qualified apophatically to avoid idolatry. If that were so, rather to the extent that that is so, the feminist critique of exclusively masculine images for God surely has traction. But that is not how Trinitarianism understands the language about God in the gospel narrative, as Jenson crisply put the matter some years ago: "The assumption that it is a deprivation not to address God in one's very own gender is a case of humankind's general religious assumption of direct analogy from human perfections to divine qualities. In the faith of the Bible, this direct line is, for our salvation, broken. Indeed, Christianity's entire soteriological message can be so put: God's self-identification with the Crucified One frees us from having to find God by projection of our own perfections."[224]

In this pioneering study of what I am articulating as the *pragmatic* approach to cognition in theology, Jenson took the doctrine of the Trinity as doctrine *for life,* not for *theoria,* that is, for identifying the God of gospel in the maelstrom of experience. Holding to this essential conviction of revealed theology as central to the case for theology's cognitive claim, as that has been made and developed in this chapter, one must simply and boldly proceed with this traditional gendered language, building the case for it along the way and safeguarding it against the general religious assumption. Such has been our procedure. There are several ancillary arguments, however, that may be reinforced here.

First, as mentioned, the Bible provides the elemental and incorrigible language of Christian faith. While legitimate concerns about human inclusiveness and apt translation are and should be welcome in theology, the massive fact of the Bible's, more specifically, the Trinity's gendered language calls for the hard and patient work of theological interpretation, not a draconian act of substitution — a violent stroke of the sword that actually substitutes for theology in the life of the church. Second, not only are the typical contemporary objections to this gendered language based on the false premise that Christian language about God in its particularity is or should be taken analogically — the false assumption that misses the subversive nature of evangelical rhetoric, as argued above — the vexed discussion of the past generation has been an enormous and polarizing distraction from contextually legitimate concerns for justice and love in the church and beyond. As the best feminist theology[225] readily acknowledges, however, substantively the doctrine of the Trinity endorses and warrants the Christian intuition of divine reality as relational and capable of history that is dearest to feminist concerns (though this very affirmation is frequently in great, if poorly understood, tension with analogy and its principled apophatism). Rather than undermine the biblical and rhetorical basis of that intuition of God as "being in communion" by liturgical experimentation that belies the cognitive commitment of theology, one should make use of Trinitarianism to interpret experience theologically, including the prophetic exposé of the sick, mutually reinforcing dynamics of masculine privilege and feminine cunning that still plague us even after the forward strides of the last generation.

These arguments are well known, but have issued in a dreary stalemate that falls short of penetrating insight into the captivity of theology to theoretical ideals of knowledge and a corresponding breakthrough to the pragmatic and hermeneutical model for the knowledge of God. This chapter has made the case for the latter. The following excursus attempts to show how the pragmatic and

224. Robert W. Jenson, *The Triune Identity* (Philadelphia: Fortress, 1982), p. 16.

225. E.g., Elizabeth A. Johnson, *She Who Is: The Mystery of God in Feminist Theological Discourse* (New York: Crossroad, 1994), where the apophatic reserve is quite explicitly maintained, p. 33.

hermeneutical argument for the Bible's gendered discourse regarding Jesus, His Father, and their Spirit has a basis in the actual history of early Christianity. If it succeeds in demonstrating this as an original Christian possibility of relevance to contemporary feminist concerns in the community of interpretation that is Christian theology, however, it will entail the ethos as well as the theology of the martyrs.[226] But that implication correlates with the concurrent diagnosis of our spiritual situation as post-Christendom.

---

## EXCURSUS: PERPETUA AND THE FATHERHOOD OF GOD

Jenson's thesis can be tested empirically; we can look and see how the naming of God as the almighty Father actually worked for Christians, and for women who were Christians, in incipient normative Christianity as attested in *The Martyrdom of Perpetua and Felicitas,*[227] a remarkable third-century account of the death of two Christian women with their comrades in the arena at Carthage. The document apparently preserves Perpetua's own prison diary. The context has been succinctly laid out by Cecil M. Robeck Jr. Perpetua "had been arrested as a relatively young Christian during a period of persecution in North Africa ordered shortly after A.D. 200 by Septimius Severus. His target was the catechumens, with the anticipated outcome of breaking the will of those arrested. . . ." In prison, while "awaiting her hearing on the charges, Perpetua, a well-educated daughter of an influential family, asked the Lord for a vision that would reveal the outcome of the hearing. She received a vision and concluded from it that she was to be martyred. In resolute fashion, she prepared herself. . . ."[228] The text has attracted interest in recent times because of the window it gives into the patriarchal structures of Roman family life. Perpetua's preparation for martyrdom involves her not least in disobedience to her father, as we shall shortly track in detail. At the same time, taken theologically, what the heavenly Father gives to His sons and daughters in Christ is the Spirit as a real agency that overcomes the world. What God declares these sons and daughters to be in the Word spoken in Christ, God also effectively gives them to become here and now, on the earth, by the Spirit: a new creation capable of resistance to structures of malice and injustice. The visions recorded by Perpetua and Saturus and preserved for the edification of the community of faith by the

---

226. *DC*, pp. 124-39.

227. *The Martyrdom of Perpetua and Felicitas,* trans. Herbert Musurillo, Oxford, 1972 at http://www.pbs.org/wgbh/pages/frontline/shows/religion/maps/primary/perpetua.html

228. Cecil M. Robeck Jr. *Prophecy in Carthage: Perpetua, Tertullian & Cyprian* (Cleveland: Pilgrim Press, 1992), p. 39.

redactor function as promises of the future with God and so strengthen the resolve of witnessing faith in the present trial. The true depth of that trial is going on also within Perpetua and her comrades: the struggle to give up old self-identifications in order to sustain the new identity of *filia dei* (daughter of God) in Christ.

A community has recorded and preserved this text with this witness to the God of the gospel for the purposes of *fidei exempla et Dei gratiam testificantia et aedificationem hominis* (1:1: of giving an example of faith and testimony of God's grace and the edification of humanity). In being written down, any text intends to transcend its immediate occasion and thus create for itself a history of reception and interpretation. We may thus begin our analysis with the redactor's theological purpose. In the opening paragraph, the prophecy of the prophet Joel, taken up in the Book of Acts to explain the Pentecost gift of the Spirit, is reiterated. It stands as a motto over all that follows: "For in the latter days, says the Lord, I will pour out my Spirit on all flesh, and your sons and your daughters will prophesy, and on my man-servants and maid-servants I will pour out my Spirit; and your young will see visions and your old dream dreams." In the text's conclusion our redactor tells us that "these new deeds of heroism" are no less significant than the "tales of old. For these new manifestations of power [*virtute* — not "virtue"!] will be witness to one and same Spirit who still operates. . . ." References to the Spirit's work thus open and close the text. The redactor, who has taken up the written accounts from the diaries of Perpetua and Saturus, makes a point of telling us that it is the Spirit who "permitted the story of this contest to be written down and by so permitting willed it." This makes his own undertaking, carrying out Perpetua's wish to preserve her diary and then to finish the story of her martyrdom, also a work in the Spirit of the Spirit.

In the redactor's theology, God endows the martyrs with the Spirit. Felicitas rebukes the mocking prison guards: "another will be inside me who will suffer for me" (just as earlier Perpetua had recorded the growing perception by the prison guards that "we had some great power within us," and was assured in her second vision in the figure of the deacon Pomponius, "Don't be afraid. I am here, struggling with you"). Dramatically, according to the redactor's account, Perpetua is in a state of spiritual ecstasy when tossed by the mad heifer *("in spiritu et in extasi fuerat")*. Refusing to don the clothing of the pagan goddess, the redactor tells us, "she was already treading on the head of the Egyptian." Judith Perkins is thus right to characterize the redactor's story as "a narrative of empowerment": "To the end Perpetua is represented refusing objectification, refusing to be a spectacle for the crowd's gaze. In the course of her experiences and her narration of them, she has fashioned an understanding of herself as powerful, empowered by her sufferings . . . death is no punishment; it is a victory. By not recognizing her punishment, by not naming it, Perpetua embodies a transcendence of both the punishment and the hierarchical structures it purports to support."[229]

---

229. Judith B. Perkins, "The Passion of Perpetua: A Narrative of Empowerment," *Latomus: Revue d'Études Latini* 53, no. 4 (1994): 845.

In this vein, the redactor has Perpetua upbraiding the prison guards' cruelty with the ironic counsel that prisoners should rather be kept in good condition more fitly to perish in the arena on the celebration of the emperor's birthday. The redactor has the martyrs turning their last meal into a love feast, preaching to the curious mob about God's coming judgment and finding joy in suffering. "You have condemned us, but God will condemn you" — a message of defiance which enrages the mob, but causes joy among the martyrs who in this way "obtain a share in the Lord's suffering." They march joyfully to death as to heaven, Perpetua's radiant face at the lead, figuring the "beloved of God, wife of Christ," meeting — and defeating — one and all with her own intense gaze. In their last words, Perpetua and Saturus speak to believing kin and catechumens that they must stand fast and not stumble on account of the suffering that they have witnessed. Dying, they gather themselves for the kiss of peace and then Perpetua guides the sword to her throat. Supreme agency, in the redactor's representation, has undone the evil purposes of the persecutors. "It was as though so great a woman, feared as she was by the unclean spirit, could not be dispatched *nisi ipsa voluisset,* unless she herself willed it."

If we take Tertullian's *Ad Martyras* as a contemporary or near-contemporary witness to the Carthage community's theology of the Spirit, we hear the same: "O blessed, grieve not the Holy Spirit, who has entered the prison with you . . . let him lead you thence to your Lord." Or again, ". . . the Holy Ghost is your trainer. . . . Therefore, your Master, Jesus Christ, . . . has anointed you with His Spirit, and led you forth to the arena. . . ." So the redactor's story is indeed a narrative of empowerment, of the heavenly Father who by the Word of Jesus gives the Spirit to them who ask to follow Jesus. Theologically, the Spirit is down payment of God's future, convincing the martyrs of their promised inheritance and so freeing them from bonds that hold them to the past.

In this light, we can now turn to the testimony that Perpetua herself has left behind. What is the theology of Perpetua? We will follow the narrative course of her diary to answer that question. What we will see is that Perpetua's interaction with her father is considerably more complex than a too-simplistic identification of him as some villainous *paterfamilias* allows. That becomes evident when we outline Perpetua's account and see how in every case an exchange transpires between the remonstrations of Perpetua's father and the assurances given her in visions of her heavenly Father.

SCENE ONE: PERPETUA'S NEW IDENTITY

Perpetua's account begins with her father's earnest attempt *pro sua affectione* to dissuade her while still at home under house arrest. The issue for Perpetua, however, is simply the truth of her new identity as *christiana,* which like a vase, she replies to him, cannot be called by any other name than what it is. This attestation of the truth of his daughter's new identity so angers her father that he almost plucks out her eyes before turning away defeated. But notably Perpetua claims victory, not over her father, but over the argument of the devil, namely, that her identity should consist in being this father's daughter rather than *christiana*. This is standard early Christian teaching.[230]

### SCENE TWO: WELCOMED BY THE HEAVENLY FATHER

Perpetua now records a vision, which consists in a collage of biblical images and allusions: Jacob's Ladder, the dragon, treading on the head of the monster, overcoming "in the name of Christ Jesus." Naming this name, Perpetua triumphs over her own fear of death and torture and ascends to heaven. There she encounters another gray-haired man. In his garden he addresses her as *teknon,* a Greek word for child (Saturus in his vision sees Perpetua speaking Greek). This gray-haired man is represented as a shepherd who nurtures Perpetua. Unlike the earthly father, this one is pleased with her decision to be and to be called *christiana.* Thousands around clothed in white robes welcome Perpetua when she drinks of the Shepherd's sweet milk with a hearty Amen. Here Perpetua has found a new family and a new father. Awakening with this sweet taste in her mouth, she realizes that the imprisoned have no hope for reprieve in this life — an indication, incidentally, that there had been hope among these persecuted Christians of legal remedy and a desire for it.

### SCENE THREE: EARTHLY FATHER WITHOUT HOPE

Back on earth now the gray-headed earthly father returns. He pleads on the basis of the fatherly favor he has shown to Perpetua over all her brothers, the disgrace he will suffer before others, the pain relatives will feel. Then he plays his trump card: the about-to-be-orphaned child over whom Perpetua suffers so much motherly anxiety. Change your mind, he implores, shedding all the supposed dignity of the Roman *paterfamilias,* kissing her hands, falling on his knees, tears in his eyes, addressing his daughter as *Domina,* my Lady. At this, Perpetua claims no victory, but instead tells: "I, I myself grieved at my father's state *(ego dolebam casum patris mei)."* She tries to comfort him with the very theology that is robbing him of her: "Our case is not in our own power but in God's." All the more reason that he is disconsolate: his daughter has a new father.

230. E.g., "For I have come to set a man against his father, and a daughter against her mother, and a daughter-in-law against her mother-in-law; and a man's foes will be those of his own household. He who loves father or mother more than me is not worthy of me; and he who loves son or daughter more than me is not worthy of me; and he who does not take his cross and follow me is not worthy of me. He who finds his life will lose it, and he who loses his life for my sake will find it" (Matt. 10:35-39).

## SCENE FOUR: CHRISTIANA SUM

So the earthly father acts desperately. He reappears at court with Perpetua's baby, asking pity on himself and the infant. The judge too implores pity. It is nothing, a trifle: sacrifice for the welfare of the emperor. But Perpetua reiterates: *Christiana sum,* "I will not worship another." After making yet further spectacle of himself, her father is punished with the rod by the court. She identifies with him in his suffering and grief. Perpetua does not claim victory over him but grieves for him *quasi ego fuissem percussa,* "just as if it were I being beaten." After the judge pronounces the death sentence, however, her father refuses to give the baby back to the condemned daughter, who is no longer in his eyes fit to be a mother.

## SCENE FIVE: VICTORIOUS DAUGHTER

As the appointed day of death approaches, the father comes again and protests his daughter's resolve with such "words as would move all creation" including Perpetua, who says, "I myself grieved on account of this misfortune of his old age." Purely structuralist accounts of this text, which render such poignant depictions of real human conflict and grief invisible and inaudible to focus attention instead on some underlying power relations, dehumanize these human characters and in the process obscure Perpetua's actual experience of inner conflict, making any understanding of its true nature impossible. Not accidentally, however, Perpetua's final vision follows immediately upon this last, heart-rending encounter with her father. The mysterious deacon Pomponius leads Perpetua to the arena and assures her that she will not struggle alone. Instead of meeting beasts, Perpetua is surprised to confront an evil-appearing Egyptian — why the surprise? Because in this entire ordeal, as Perpetua expressly tells us at the end, she has been facing not merely the anticipated loss of earthly loves or prospect of physical torments. In all these things she is fighting with the Devil/Dragon/Egyptian. It is upon that head she will finally tread when winning the wrestling match. The giant trainer, marvelously clad, welcomes victorious Perpetua: *"Filia, pax tecum!"* Transformed into a male in order to do combat with the Egyptian, she takes her trophy nonetheless as *filia dei.*

As the Spirit is the source of Perpetua's action in passion, her struggle is not primarily with "flesh and blood," but with the unholy spirit, who tests her inwardly by playing upon her own fear and her own grief, so that she might renounce her identity as *christiana.* We may not without violence to Perpetua's personhood dismiss from consideration this rhetorical and indeed in her own mind substantial opposition between Holy Spirit and unholy spirit. The primary opponent of Perpetua is not the authority of the *paterfamilias* nor the authority of the Roman state; what Perpetua fears is not primarily physical death or painful torture, let alone the anger of her father. What she fights against and finally triumphs over is the argument of the devil *(cum argumentis diaboli)* making its powerful appeal within her own torn heart that she renounce her identity as a Christian. She prevails against this by the greater power and authority of the Spirit who grants a vision of her new identity confirmed in its final victory. Certainly, the argument of the devil is made through earthly father's frantic attempts to dissuade deluded daughter from committing suicide under the influence of an exotic new cult. But Perpetua can distinguish between her human father, indeed grieve for him and sympathize with the sorrow of his old age, and the devil with his arguments. Her struggle is not "with flesh and blood" but with structures of malice and injustice, figured in the unholy spirits.

The dragon at the foot of the ladder, the Egyptian squared off before her in the arena, are precisely not earthly enemies; they represent forces at work within her own conflicted sense of personal identity that would prevent her from following through on the new self-identification as *christiana*. Perpetua herself expressly tells us this: "I was inspired by the Spirit not to ask for any other favor after the water [of baptism] but simply perseverance [*sufferentiam*] of the flesh." This prayer for perseverance is the clue to her visions. Thus Perkins is surely right to observe: "Through her dreams, Perpetua fashions a powerful conception of herself. She climbs to heaven; she cures others' pain; she vanquishes a strong and evil male opponent in a triumphal context." It may also be true that "this self-conception empowers her daily life where she consistently defies the patriarchal authority of her father and the state," but that would be a consequence of Perpetua's primary intention. Perpetua intends to be *christiana,* whatever that brings. That is primary. She shares the faith of Jesus in the heavenly Father, and with Jesus she stands in the time of trial, in this Gethsemane of her own soul, because the same Spirit has steeled her for battle.

Our text is a vivid sampling of the gospel claim that God in Christ has identified with humanity in the depths of its plight in order that human beings by the power of the Spirit identify themselves in Christ as children before God the heavenly Father and so be enabled now to live by faith justly and in defiance of earthly structures of malice and injustice. In this great exchange God takes on the predicates of humanity (like suffering and struggle), and humanity takes on the predicates of deity (like agency and joy). What transpired once and for all in the cross and resurrection of Christ now also transpires in the cross and resurrection of the saints as they are led by the Spirit from the waters of baptism into the wilderness of testing to "participation in the sufferings of the Lord." What stands out, as we have seen, are the identity transactions.

At the center of Perpetua's visions we see her, who had incriminated herself before the earthly authorities as *christiana,* in turn identified by the heavenly father/shepherd/grayhead as *teknon* in the heavenly garden, or again, addressed by the Lord, *filia,* upon defeating the Egyptian. For the redactor also, Perpetua's martyrdom tells of this great exchange: we see Perpetua put off her worldly anxiety (for her baby), grief (at her father's hopeless sense of loss), and fear (of her own torture) and put on certainty, joy, and ecstatic agency in the Spirit. She radiates the glory of God. She is the Spirit's new creation. She is formed by the Spirit as daughter of God. She is a sign of the fulfillment to come ". . . when [the Son] hands over the kingdom to God the Father, after he has destroyed every ruler and every authority and power. For he must reign until he has put all his enemies under his feet. . . . When all things are subjected to him, then the Son himself will also be subjected to the one who put all things in subjection under him, so that God may be all in all" (1 Cor. 15:24-28). This is how the "fatherhood of God" works in the project of eschatological creation by the Son in the Spirit (just as the rhetoric of "lordship" worked to subvert the *Führerprinzip* in the Barmen Declaration).[231] The origin is but the beginning of the end. Evil is permitted its full fury in order to be defeated, if wills other than God's are to exist and through many trials and tribulations nevertheless enter the kingdom of God (Acts 14:22).

---

231. Thanks to Dr. Rob Saler for suggesting this apt parallel.

# CHAPTER TWO

# Preliminary Clarifications

## Odd Questions — I

In the light of the previous chapter's articulation of theology's basic cognitive claim, we now turn to complications in regard to it demanding clarification. For we have employed language that begs many questions. As a preliminary matter, scholarly analysis of the gospel's claim to truth involves four central questions about it: Is God possible? Is Christ necessary? Does faith justify? Are the Scriptures holy? To answer these questions affirmatively in preliminary fashion is in customary terms respectively to give the source, the norm, the subject, and the method of systematic theology. But these customary terms are still too much entangled historically speaking in the ideal of knowledge as *theoria* (knowledge as intuition, as vision) inherited from the tradition of Christian Platonism. Richard Rorty, certainly no friend of theology, puts the point polemically: "The word *knowledge* would not seem worth fighting over were it not for the Kantian tradition that to be a philosopher is to have a 'theory of knowledge,' and the Platonic tradition that action not based on knowledge of the truth of propositions is 'irrational.'"[1]

The conceit of theoria is not worth fighting for. But "knowledge" is worth fighting for in theology, if knowledge itself can be delivered from the hubris of claiming to be lord over humanity by supposedly founding or grounding in timeless and direct vision and become again a servant of the promise of creation to humanity that is the revealed wisdom of God (1 Cor. 2:6-16). For there is faithful reasoning and there is faithless reasoning, though both know one and the same world. Here "knowledge" is not self-justifying intuition but knowing how to be "fruitful and multiply, and fill the earth, and subdue it, and have dominion over it" (Gen. 1:28) in acquiring likeness to the Creator of all that is not God. Here "knowing" God is hearing and believing and obeying this calling of humanity

1. Richard Rorty, *Philosophy and the Mirror of Nature* (Princeton: Princeton University Press, 1979), p. 356.

as image of God, and reason is the wisdom by which this calling is fulfilled in acquiring likeness to God. Just such redemption of reason by restoration to true creatureliness theology offers and illustrates, if it knows in its own place what it is doing.

In the light of this pragmatic conception of knowledge in theology, it will be better to think of the Scriptures as the canonical matrix of theology, of faith as forming the knowing subject of theology, of Christ given to be the object of faith's knowing and of His Father as its audience in endless acts of interpretation. Over against the ideal of theoria, this amounts to a "horizontalizing" of the knowledge of God in view of the coming of the Beloved Community. What this entails in detail will be made clear in what follows as we work through these four questions successively.

Admittedly, these are odd questions. Usually we ask not whether God is possible but whether God exists. Likewise we ask whether Christ somehow or another helps, not whether Christ is necessary. If we ask the question about justification at all today, nothing seems more evident in churches both left and right than that it is the doer of the Word, not the hearer only, who is justified in our sight (perhaps also God's, though who can be sure?). The question about the Bible in recent times has been whether it is true in its report of the mighty acts of God in history, not whether it is healing and sanctifying in its proper use by the Spirit to render Christ present for the formation of theological subjects who already now live before God. While we must take seriously the changed circumstances that lie behind such characteristic objections to the tradition of Reformation theology in the ambiguous present of modernity's wane, we dare not in systematic theology capitulate to their all too self-evident force.[2] In any case, the modern critique of Christianity is at the very apex of its spiritual power today, having now been internalized in theology itself.

Consider the Reformation's "exclusive particle" from Melanchthon's *Apology,* later expressed in the motto "Christ alone, grace alone, faith alone, Scripture alone."[3] Originally intended to repudiate the self-boot-strapping natural theology

2. E.g., Philip Clayton, *Transforming Christian Theology for Church and Society* (Minneapolis: Fortress, 2010). It will be evident that I share neither this author's characterization, nor his sanguine view, of postmodernity, only the fact that we have entered it. His manifesto for a "progressive" Christianity — *"in this new situation, here and now, to participate in God's bringing about the kingdom of God in ways that reflect Jesus' transformative responses to the situations he encountered in his ministry"* (p. 31, italics original) — sounds suspiciously like the old liberalism, particularly in Christology. Consequently, I worry that Clayton's egalitarian constructivism — "I invite you to become *producers* of Christian theology and not merely *consumers* of theologies" (p. 124, emphasis original) — not only perpetuates the root economic metaphors of modernity, but also presupposes a theology still captivated by it. In other words, this approach is not radically enough *post*modern.

3. *BC,* p. 132. This paragraph and the following one have been adopted from Paul R. Hinlicky, "A Leibnizian Transformation? Reclaiming the Theodicy of Faith," in *Transformations*

of the late medieval "modernists," it came to refer instead to the Spirit's means in the Word and sacraments to create and sustain the theological subjectivity of faith.[4] But how problematic the sixteenth-century exclusivism seems today! Global consciousness of the world religions makes the claim for salvation in Christ alone sound mean-spirited and ethnocentric. If we have learned anything from Darwinian evolution, we have learned that everything must be paid for; there really is only merit in the competition for survival. After Hitler, Hiroshima, and Stalin, it is criminal to take things on authority or to affirm without evidence. As for Scripture, after criticism it has become Kierkegaard's "objective uncertainty." Theology rightly wrestles with religious pluralism on a rapidly shrinking and increasingly stressed planet, as well as scientific cosmology, endemic political crises, and a historical consciousness that makes biblicism impossible.[5] If we think that we can disown all these problems by a simple return to the Bible, or to the fathers, or to Luther, we deceive ourselves. Bultmann was wrong about *how* theology modernizes, but he was certainly right to insist that no one chooses their own worldview, which is rather given to them by their place in history.[6]

To use a vague and confusing designator of our place in history, we are "postmodern" in Euro-America today. I take this designation in Robert Ericksen's sense that theologians in Luther's tradition today suffer a "double crisis of modernity."[7] First, we suffer the rationalist subversion of Europe's antecedent religion and morality (hence we are "post-Christendom") and second, at the hands of the rebellious children of rationalism (preeminently Ricoeur's "masters of suspicion," Marx, Nietzsche, and Freud), we suffer the anti-rationalist subversion of the Tribunal of Reason. "Post-Christendom" — "been there, done that!" Such is the overwhelming cultural and spiritual fact that Euro-American Christians deal with every day of their lives. It is also a self-evident assumption in much of the contemporary academy. In its depth, it is not simply that the church as institution is regarded as passé — as if somehow these bones could yet live if only the church were *relevant!* Rather, it is that the biblical tradition as it has been appropriated in the church's theology in the cause of Christendom seems discredited by the crushing weight of accumulated failures. Alfred Loisy's witticism, "Jesus promised us the Kingdom and what we got was the church," puts the matter succinctly.[8] The faith is actively repudiated by prominent and persuasive

---

in *Luther's Reformation Theology: Historical and Contemporary Reflections,* vol. 32, Arbeiten zur Kirchen- und Theologiegeschichte, ed. C. Helmer and B. K. Holm (Leipzig: Evangelische Verlagsanstalt, 2011), p. 86.

4. *BC,* p. 132. I will cite the Latin version of the *Augsburg Confession.*

5. So also Roger Haight, as cited by Clayton in *Transforming,* p. 31.

6. Rudolf Bultmann and Five Critics, *Kerygma and Myth,* ed. H. W. Bartsch (New York: Harper & Row, 1961), p. 3.

7. Chapter 1 in Robert B. Ericksen, *Theologians under Hitler: Gerhard Kittel, Paul Althaus and Emanuel Hirsch* (New Haven and London: Yale University Press, 1985), pp. 1-27.

8. Cited by Jenson in *ST* 2, p. 170.

public intellectuals, regularly mocked on TV comedy, unwittingly parodied by loud and outspoken fundamentalisms, or revised beyond recognition by their liberal opponents, ignored politically except when usefully exploited, greeted more and more with indifference and incomprehension, if not hostility by the rising generation (which has its own set of issues, to be sure).

At the same time, however, change is in the air. "Postmodernism" is sharply qualifying both the alleged objectivity and comprehensiveness of the natural and social sciences and the exaggerated claims for human subjectivity that have characterized the modern Cartesian-Kantian turn to the subject. These modern claims about universal and objective but nonmetaphysical science and the transcendence of the human subject go together hand-in-glove; the "modernity" that we have known stands and falls with the cultural plausibility of this symbiosis. The Kantian alliance of instrumental reason and human self-transcendence, however, is increasingly exposed and critiqued today as the most sublime expression of the will-to-power, Augustine's *libido dominandi,* "ontotheology," the distilled quintessence of classical metaphysics expressing itself in the sovereign self of the modern West that posits itself as *summum bonum* and whips into shape whatever stands in the way — including the common body in the juggernaut of biopolitics. There is thus a certain continuity between the pre-critical Augustinian tradition and the post-critical critique of the sovereign self of modernity that is explored in the following excursus.

## EXCURSUS: AUGUSTINE, LUTHER, AND THE CRITIQUE OF THE SOVEREIGN SELF

At the end of her Gifford Lectures, published as *Sovereignty: God, State, and Self,* the late Jean Bethke Elshtain invoked Augustine as a resource against the sovereign self of modernity. "Augustine's fear would be that as we give up God's sovereignty, other forms of human sovereignty — not of the chastened or limited sort — drive to become superordinate and destructive. . . . The Augustinian pilgrim is one who can challenge the idolatries of his or her day without opting out (as if one could) or fleeing into a reality at least theoretically removed from the vortex of social and political life. The pilgrim of Augustinian Christianity offers up that possibility, as the late antique world makes startling contact with late modernity."[9] Elshtain's attempt to retrieve the Augustinian pilgrim for today thus comes by way of a parallel detected between late modernity and the decline and fall of the Western Roman Empire. Elshtain is thus thinking of the Augustine of the *City of God* — not of an earlier Augustine, certainly not the Manichaean Au-

9. Jean Bethke Elshtain, *Sovereignty: God, State, and Self* (New York: Basic Books, 2008), pp. 240-41. See further her *Augustine and the Limits of Politics* (Notre Dame: University of Notre Dame Press, 1995).

gustine, but also not the neo-Platonist philosopher whose intellectual conversion to scriptural reasoning by way of the close reading of Israel's history with God that occupies the *City of God* was a more protracted process than is evident in the drama of the conflicted heart recorded in the *Confessions.*

This observation concerning *which* Augustine it is that Elshtain invokes makes the relation of Augustine to the sovereign self of modernity rather a more complicated question. It is well known that Descartes retrieved Augustine's own argument against skepticism — to wit, that I cannot doubt that I doubt — in his invention in the *Meditations* of the thinking thing that essentially transcends extended things and rules over them with the aid of the knowledge of the God who in turn is in the very busy business of coordinating thoughts to events. By retooling Anselm's so-called ontological argument for the existence of God, Descartes had inferred from my self-knowledge as an imperfectly thinking thing the notion of a perfectly thinking being that conveniently serves to bridge the parallel worlds of thinking things and extending things. While these moves give the appearance of continuity with Augustinian tradition in modernity's "turn to the subject," in fact they invoke the earlier Augustine's relation to neo-Platonism more than his mature relation to the Bible. This differentiation is important in that the neo-Platonic paradigm of the mind's coming to self-consciousness (i.e., thought thinking itself and willing itself) is a, perhaps *the* singular classical source of modernity's sovereign self.

As Carol Harrison has noted, the intellectual drama of Augustine's long career plots right along this fault line: "The very spirituality of the Platonists, which had resolved so many problems for [Augustine in overcoming Manichaeism], seemed to be totally irreconcilable with a doctrine of the Word made flesh, of his bodily resurrection and of faith in him as the only means for fallen man to grasp truth."[10] Along the same lines we could add to Harrison's list of items from the Bible Augustine's own report in the *Confessions* of his bafflement at the God of the canonical narrative, beginning with the first verse of the Bible, "In the beginning, God created. . . ." The ascent of the soul to its divine source by the acquisition of self-consciousness and the descent of the biblical God to creation, to history, to incarnation and redemption seem indeed to run in different, perhaps "irreconcilable" trajectories.

We who are children of the Western cultural tradition still align along this fault line. Some contemporary thinkers — let me mention representatively only the significant Protestant theologian Wolfhart Pannenberg — find Descartes' retrieval and modernization of Augustinian insight into the dynamics of human self-consciousness essential for indicating the theological horizon of ineffable infinity against which the finite self sees and knows its world in space and time and so comes to thematic awareness of itself as subject of knowledge hungering

10. Carol Harrison, *Augustine: Christian Truth and Fractured Humanity* (Oxford: Oxford University Press, 2000), p. 33.

for the wholeness of knowledge that is God.[11] Others, however, see in Descartes' invention the modern founding of a nightmarish *superbia* that "dreams of radical transcendence," as Elshtain put it,[12] in that it must finally and decisively turn against human embodiment itself as obstacle and enemy. Descartes' construct of a purely mental self, and its claim to sovereignty over extended things as something alien and inferior, is criticized here as an intoxicating illusion of power. It is the *sicut Deus eritis.* Not only does it institute an invidious mind-matter dualism, but in the process configures God as but the transcendental ground of this immanent claim to sovereignty over inferior things. Yet others, like Louis Dupré, try to mediate a chastened modernity,[13] though his critique of Descartes' merely apparent Augustinianism is concise and precise. "For a moment," Dupré writes, "the French philosopher reminds us of Augustine's self-examination before God. But only for a moment, because Descartes's introspection reverses the traditional order from God to the soul. All ideas — including the idea of God — have their formal basis in the mind which envisions all beings as *cogitata.* . . . God has to be proven, and to be proven on the basis of the prior certainty of the self." The road to German idealism's creative, self-positing *ego* opened up by Descartes' *cogito, ergo sum* thus marks a deep inversion of the mature Augustine, not his retrieval.[14]

Critics of the sovereign self today can be thinkers as widely divergent from Jean Elshtain as Gilles Deleuze. Whether from the side of dynamic nature *(natura naturans)* or the robustly Trinitarian God of Christian tradition *(esse deum dare),* such thinkers deny that the human mind, conceived as something ontologically other than its material body with all its organic links to the entirety of creation, is, can be, and/or ought to be "sovereign" — or rather, they argue that the notion of "sovereignty" is itself fraught and in need of genealogical investigation and critique, such as undertaken by Giorgio Agamben's *Homo Sacer* (a text discussed in greater detail below). For these the danger of the sovereign self of Cartesian modernity, unthinkingly taken as a matter of course in the modern politics of identity (as Hasanah Sharp has shown in an insightful Spinozist critique),[15] is manifest in modernity's ecologically unsustainable juggernaut together with its morally unacceptable pauperization of masses of people, ideologically perpetuated and reinforced by the inferiorization of the sensual to the mental.

As powerfully as such critiques of the sovereign self may resonate across a spectrum of contemporary dissent, it is very much unclear in this time of transition, ambiguously called "postmodernity," what can take the place of the profound Cartesianism of the modern project, on which philosophically the tri-

11. Pannenberg, *ST* 1, pp. 113-18.

12. Elshtain, *Sovereignty,* pp. 203-26.

13. Louis Dupré, *Passage to Modernity: An Essay in the Hermeneutics of Nature and Culture* (New Haven and London: Yale University Press, 1995), pp. 249-53.

14. Dupré, *Passage to Modernity,* pp. 117-18.

15. Hasana Sharp, *Spinoza and the Politics of Renaturalization* (Chicago and London: University of Chicago Press, 2011).

umphs of Western political economy in technology are predicated and its hopes nourished. But Augustine would teach us that technology cannot save us from our greed, *concupiscentia* in his language, nor deliver us from the fatal dynamics of political sovereignty, the *libido dominandi*. Technology rather empowers these dark forces. As C. George Benello has written in an essay on Jacques Ellul, "the domination of technique has little to do with different political ideologies. Both the Marxist and the liberal-democratic versions of progress are equally uncritical of technique's domination."[16] The sovereign self who would dominate extended things becomes dominated by the techniques of domination. This dilemma or rather juggernaut requires us to probe more deeply.

This digging takes us back to Augustine. In an incisive article published in the journal *Zygon,* Phillip Cary argues that "[t]he inner self was invented as a place to find God."[17] Its roots thus lie, he claims, "in the history of the Western religious tradition and its long involvement with philosophical issues, especially (in this case) epistemology."[18] Turning his focus on the "inner" self, that is, the sheer privacy that Descartes creates by the method of doubt in inventing the sovereign self, Cary traces the genesis of "the mythic reality of the autonomous individual" all the way back to the inner world of Plato and Plotinus. Yet their inner world is not yet a private world as in the purely subjective "ideas" of the isolated, individual mind studied by Descartes and Locke. These ancient philosophers rather discovered in the soul "the unchanging realm that is the same for all souls. In essence, they all share one and same inner space" when looking inward, just as by looking outward from their discretely embodied souls upon the infinite multitude of bodily phenomena in the exterior world, they "are diminished and drawn from that primal unity by their diverse interests. . . ."[19] Hence the Platonic soul finds itself suspended between the One and the Many; here intellectual ascent leads to the One from whom the soul fell into the individuated, and thus conflicted existence of the body, where it is driven haphazardly by diverse material allures and dispersed, fragmented, torn into many.

A transition in the Platonic tradition towards the modern privacy of the individual soul, Cary argues, comes from Augustine, who is "both deeply attracted to the Plotinian inward turn," and yet finds that as a Christian "he cannot simply accept the inner divinity of the soul, as if deep within us there was no real difference between the Creator and the creature." Thus the turn inward to the "space of soul," is not just so for Augustine, as for Plotinus and Plato, a looking upward

16. C. George Benello, "Technology and Power: Technique as a Mode of Understanding Modernity," in *Jacques Ellul: Interpretative Essays,* ed. Clifford C. Christians and Jay M. Van Hook (Chicago: University of Illinois Press, 1981), pp. 92-93.

17. Phillip Cary, "The Mythic Reality of the Autonomous Individual," *Zygon* 46, no. 1 (March 2011): 122.

18. Cary, "The Mythic Reality," p. 122.

19. Cary, "The Mythic Reality," p. 126.

into "the eternal realm of the divine Mind" that is the same for all rational souls. Instead, with Augustine — think only of the narrative of his own soul's painful wanderings in the *Confessions* — the one who turns inward enters into "the changing inner world of the individual human soul." This is an "inner space with no roof, open to the light above" as in Plotinus and Plato. All that remains to the wandering soul from Augustine's Platonic sources "is the memory of God" as "our long lost happiness," as the "Truth by which all things are true." Just so the soul in Augustine is "not an absolutely private space." For God as Creator remains present to His absentminded creature even though it has forgotten God; the result is that "[o]nly sin separates us from the public realm of inner wisdom. . . . Conceptually speaking, then, the private inner self is born in sin."[20] What Augustine considers to be born in sin, then, is what Descartes discovers as the sole source of certitude: the self-positing self, the sovereign self.

The soul itself has become historical in Augustine. As Jean-Luc Marion has recently written in a trenchant analysis, Augustine's realization of the lack of definition for the human soul made in God's image for likeness to the ineffable Creator "implies that I do not reside in any essence, but that on the contrary I resemble what has no semblance, God, without form, indescribable, incomprehensible, invisible. . . . Or, more exactly, that . . . I appear each time myself according as I move up (or down) on the invisibly graded scale of my resemblance . . ." to the inimitable Creator.[21] Though Cary does not explicitly note the historicization of the soul that is occurring in Augustine's treatment of the soul's movement in time, as sketched in *Confessions* Book X, it is a notable implication of Augustine's break with Platonism, as Marion sees it. If Platonism considers divinity to be a quality that can be participated in to greater or lesser degrees, Augustine thinks of the creature's relation to its Creator in the drama of a temporal history — the plot of which is a contest of sovereignties, so to say, between the proud creature who would ascend and the Creator who humbled Himself to descend. Jesus Christ therefore is the likeness of God. By knowledge of His love the sinful soul is both cleansed and restored to its true history, the destiny of the City of God.

If Augustine initiates such a historicization of the soul, however, moderns like Locke and Descartes have not only wholly privatized the soul so that all that is present to it are its own subjective ideas with no certain relation to the external world beyond the inner experiences of the senses. They have all the same radicalized the tacit claim to sovereignty by claiming truth, indeed bedrock and indubitable truth, for private "intuitions of the unmediated presence of things," taking this foundationalist claim as a "religious idea" with "deep religious meaning for those who believe in it . . .," even though the "ultimate provenance" of this

---

20. Cary, "The Mythic Reality," pp. 130-31.

21. Jean-Luc Marion, "Resting, Moving, Loving: The Access to the Self according to Saint Augustine," *The Journal of Religion* 91, no. 1 (January 2011): 32.

remarkable claim to a private sovereignty over extended things "is not," as Cary concludes, "the Biblical gospel but Platonist metaphysics."[22]

Can Augustine's properly differentiated theological reflections on the self, forged not only in his quarrels with skeptics and Manichaeans to affirm human agency but also with Pelagius to deny an ahistorical and autonomous human sovereignty, be brought forward in an alternative trajectory today by way of Martin Luther's teaching on the servility, not sovereignty, of free choice in a fallen world? That experiment in thought would only be possible if Luther was in fact an Augustinian — there are those who actually deny this. It is indeed something of a cottage industry in modern German Protestantism; it has fellow travelers in the ranks of Roman Catholic scholarship all too eager to agree with these adversaries that Luther was no Augustinian. Even the new Finnish Luther research[23] follows Anders Nygren[24] in seeing a decisive break between Luther's view of Christian love as purely other-regarding *agape* in distinction from Augustine's *caritas,* a hybridization with happiness-seeking eros that makes God over as highest good in a hierarchical order that supposedly undervalues creatures. Luther's Augustinianism, as a matter of historical truth, upsets all these camps.

The plausibility of denying of Luther's Augustinianism consists in the fact that Luther's well-known diatribe against Erasmus does not in a disciplined way distinguish *voluntas, arbitrium,* and *libertas.* Terminological imprecision, if not equivocation, as a result, produces confusion about just what agency Luther ascribes to human creatures, though in other of his writings, for example, "Two Kinds of Righteousness,"[25] his teaching on human agency is adequately clarified; there he speaks of "our proper righteousness, not because we alone work it, but because we work with that first and alien righteousness" of Christ, given as a gift to faith in Christ.[26] We may stipulate as noncontroversial that Luther contends for God's sovereignty, more precisely, for the sovereignty of the Holy Spirit in enlightening the soul to behold the righteousness of Christ and so receive it as a gift in faith. What is controversial is how Luther reconciles this divine sovereignty with human agency, as manifestly, indeed indignantly he claims to have done in the same treatise against Erasmus. The echo here of Augustine, moreover, is unmistakable: "Yet God does not work in us without us; for He created and preserves us for this very purpose, that He might work in us and we might co-operate with Him, whether that occurs outside His king-

22. Cary, "The Mythic Reality," p. 133.

23. Antti Raunio, *Summe des Christlichen Lebens: Die 'Goldene Regel' als Gesetz der Liebe in der Theologie Martin Luthers von 1510 bis 1527* (Helsinki: Reports from the Department of Systematic Theology XIII, 1993).

24. Anders Nygren, *Agape and Eros,* trans. Philip S. Watson (New York and Evanston, IL: Harper & Row, 1969).

25. *LW* 31, pp. 296-306.

26. *LW* 31, p. 299.

dom, by His general omnipotence, or within His kingdom, by the special power of His Spirit."[27]

The matter can be sorted out as follows. *Voluntas* connotes the personal dignity of each person's uncoerced willingness or desire; *voluntas* denotes each embodied soul's natural desire that spontaneously seeks the good and averts from evil. Marion, not incidentally, discovers exactly the same notion in Augustine, of the love of the soul "trigger[ing] in the heart the same spontaneity that gravity unleashes in the body."[28] Note that the creaturely freedom of *voluntas* is, like gravity, bounded; the soul *must* naturally seek the good and avert from the evil. We would regard a person who averted from good and sought evil instead as pathologically ill just as we regard a good imposed coercively upon us as a tyrannical imposition upon our natural freedom to love what we love. The creature's freedom, then, is the freedom to desire what one naturally desires rather than be constrained unnaturally by exterior force, as if coerced to desire what one takes no pleasure in. Luther thus agrees not only with Augustine but with the ancient truism that forms the first sentence of Aristotle's *Nicomachean Ethics,* "All by nature seek the good"; he disputes about *what* goods are to be sought. "It is certainly true," he wrote in his early *Commentary on Romans,* "that the law of nature is known to all men and that our reason does speak for the best things, but what best things? It speaks for the best things not according to God but according to us, that is, for things that are good in an evil way. For it seeks itself and its own in all things, but not God. This only faith does in love."[29] By the same reasoning, Luther denies what is impossible, that free will in the sense of *voluntas* can "freely turn itself in any direction, yielding to none and subject to none." That kind of freedom, Luther says, belongs only to the Creator, not the creature — one must say further for Luther, the self-surpassing Creator of the canonical narrative who dramatically enough can will to love the sinner in Christ.

In any event, "the condition of this life" of the creature in time, again quoting from the *Commentary on Romans,* "is not that of having but of seeking God." Yet by the same canonical narrative, true desire for God — Luther is commenting on the Pauline statement, "no one seeks God" — is not any longer in the creature's power. As with Augustine, it is lost and remains as but a dim memory and faint rebuke. It must and does come anew with the power of divine grace to reorganize the soul's affects: "the very love of God which makes us will or love what our understanding causes us to know. For even if one understands and believes, yet without the grace of God he cannot love and willingly do what he believes and understands."[30] So *voluntas* is freely willing love of the God who alone can

---

27. Martin Luther, *The Bondage of the Will,* trans. J. I. Packer and O. R. Johnston (Grand Rapids: Fleming H. Revell, 2000), p. 268.

28. Marion, "Resting, Moving, Loving," p. 37.

29. *LW* 25, p. 344.

30. *LW* 25, p. 225.

make Himself lovely again to the estranged soul by pouring out His love into its heart — Romans 5:5, surely Augustine's favorite Bible verse. Infused love in this Augustinian way is not a remnant of Luther's pre-Reformation theology; the notion, theologized as the work of the Spirit, saturates *De servo arbitrio,* a book that could equally have been titled *De Spiritu sancto.* It means both God's love for us in Christ and our love for God with Christ in the Spirit. In his paradoxical formulation of a *servile free choice,* which he perhaps might better have conceptualized as a *filial* free choice sold into bondage under sin, Luther based himself not only negatively on Augustine's anti-Pelagian writings but also positively on Augustine's Pneumatology.

To follow Luther's retrieval of Augustine, one must cleanly break with the nominalist narrative in which Luther is far too conveniently cast by opponents, left and right, of his Augustinianism. The nominalist theology imagined free will thinking of the perfect being as its highest good and acting on that thought to leverage divine approbation. But merely to understand Luther, one must adopt instead the framework provided by the biblical canon's narrative of the self constituted in its dramatic history with God: of freedom, fall, bondage, redemption, struggle, and final liberation. Henri de Lubac, to be sure, denied that Luther had rightly understood Augustine's teaching on graced nature.[31] We can hardly blame him for taking predominant Luther interpreters of his time and place at face value. But in fact de Lubac read Luther through the lenses of the Jansenism controversy and either did not know, or did not weigh, the pregnant formulations of theological anthropology in the Genesis lectures where Luther linked the rational human *person* and the Holy Spirit: in the state of original righteousness, Luther writes that "man was righteous, truthful, and upright not only in body but especially in soul, that he knew God, that he obeyed God, with the utmost joy, and that he understood the works of God even without prompting."[32] Indeed, Luther continued, this "original righteousness" was a "part of nature," not some "sort of superfluous or superadded gift." Acquiring likeness to God is humanity's essential calling and destiny; there would be no need for the coming of the New Adam, that is, "if the original righteousness, like something foreign to our nature, has been taken away and the natural endowments remain perfect."[33]

---

31. Henri de Lubac, S.J., *Augustinianism and Modern Theology,* trans. Lancelot Sheppard (New York: Crossroad, 2000), p. 11, but see the odd concession to Luther's actual teaching made in passing on p. 37.

32. *LW* 1, p. 113.

33. *LW* 1, p. 166. The anthropological linkage here between the human as person and its relation to the person of the Spirit is highly significant for the interpretation of Luther's mature theological anthropology, for he comes to this late formulation in the Genesis lectures after the outbreak of controversy and confusion in his own camp whether sin is substantial or accidental, reflecting a metaphysical scheme from Aristotle that overwhelms the theological distinction from Trinitarianism between nature and person, between image and likeness. Historically speaking, Luther's thinking in the Genesis lectures was overshadowed by the ensuing conflict

If probes into the theological past along the foregoing lines prove illuminating, what can interrupt, if not dislodge modernity's sovereign self, is the coming of the beloved community that Augustine envisioned theologically as the eternal love of the Father and the Son in the Spirit now emerging among creatures as the *civitas Dei* in struggle with the *civitas terrena*. A very promising correlation in this connection is the contemporary philosopher Giorgio Agamben's discovery of Luther's translation of Paul's Greek verb *katargeo* with the German *aufheben* to indicate the way in which Jesus' death on the cross cancels the sovereignty of law as condemnation by fulfilling the law as love and in this way creating a renewed humanity in the image of God for likeness to God:[34] in Agamben's words written against "negative dialectics": "restoring possibility to the fallen."[35] This sovereignty of grace, that is, of the God who gives, comes by way of a "positive dialectics" in sharp contrast to, indeed conflict with, the "negative dialectics" of political sovereignty *(civitas terrena)* founded on the state of exception, in which the lawless impose law and include by excluding — all in the name of the sovereignty of the modern self, as Agamben argued against modern Hobbesianism in his penetrating *Homo Sacer*[36] (discussed below, pp. 146-52).

---

## Odd Questions — II

Luther's way of retrieving Paul's theology[37] via the "blessed Augustine" is a precious resource for us today in this complex situation, at once post-Christendom and postmodern, where the contextually immediate theological task is to jam a stick into the spokes of the juggernaut that is the sovereign self of modernity. It is a resource if, that is, we are as willing to be as *assertive* theologically as was Luther in confessing the Christian claim to truth. "Away, now, with Sceptics and Academics from the company of us Christians. . . . Take the Apostle Paul — how often does he call for that 'full assurance,' which is, simply, an assertion of conscience, of the highest degree of certainty and conviction. In Rom. 10 he calls it 'confession.' . . . Nothing is more familiar or characteristic among Christians than assertion. Take away assertions, and you take away Christianity. *Why, the Holy*

---

between Flacius and Melanchthon and obscured by the compromise formulas codified in the Book of Concord for Lutheran Orthodoxy. See *BC,* pp. 531-42.

34. Giorgio Agamben, *The Time That Remains: A Commentary on the Letter to the Romans,* trans. P. Dailey (Stanford, CA: Stanford University Press, 2005), p. 108. See the discussion in *RPTD,* pp. 200-206.

35. Agamben, *The Time That Remains,* p. 38.

36. Giorgio Agamben, *Homo Sacer: Sovereign Power and Bare Life,* trans. D. Heller-Roazen (Stanford, CA: Stanford University Press, 1998). See the discussion of "biopolitical captivity" in *RPTD,* pp. 114-20.

37. *LBC,* pp. 221-57.

*Spirit is given to Christians from heaven in order that He may glorify Christ and in them confess Him even unto death. . . .* [But you, Erasmus, are likewise *asserting*] that religion and piety and all dogmas are just nothing at all."[38]

Not by accident, the first three of our four announced questions for clarification in this chapter regarding the single cognitive claim of Christian theology are drawn from a significant text on theological method by the early Luther. On September 4, 1517 — that is, less than two months prior to the posting of the Ninety-Five Theses — Luther wrote his inaptly named *Disputation against Scholastic Theology.* It is "inaptly" named because in it Luther himself argues in the scholastic way of disputation,[39] which lends the document logical force. It is also inaptly named because Luther's target is not so much the *via antiqua* of St. Thomas Aquinas (who had been dead for 300 years at Luther's time — ancient history!) as the *via moderna* in which he had been schooled.

Nuance is critical here. As Sammeli Juntunen has noted in his insightful study "Luther and Metaphysics," "The education which Luther received can be called Ockhamist [= modernist] only in a limited sense."[40] More broadly, as Theodor Dieter has recently taught us,[41] one must carefully distinguish between scholasticisms, i.e., methodologically between advances in logic by means of the disputation genre[42] and inept hermeneutical procedures as criticized in the previous chapter. But one must also distinguish dogmatically. In several rich and carefully argued studies,[43] Bruce Marshall has demonstrated doctrinal conver-

38. "Take away assertions and you take away Christianity!" Martin Luther, *The Bondage of the Will,* trans. J. I. Packer and O. R. Johnston (Grand Rapids: Fleming H. Revell, 2000), p. 67.

39. In *The Trinity and Martin Luther: A Study on the Relationship between Genre, Language and the Trinity in Luther's Works (1523-1546)* (Mainz: Verlag Philipp von Zabern, 1999), Christine Helmer has shown that Luther "loved" the medieval "disputatio" (p. 41). "[S]tudy of the disputatio opens up a view of Luther's understanding of the activity of reason that is illuminated by faith" (p. 42) and "the importance of academic formulation as a theological necessity of disputing not the event of revelation but its truth . . ." (p. 45). Luther "was not satisfied with the role of exposing the error, but wanted to learn how to express the affirmative, to resist the enemy but also to care for the weak, defending the borders against the adversary by articulating the truth at the center" (p. 47). "What one learns in the academic genre can be converted to the other genres of prayer and praise" (p. 48).

40. Sammeli Juntunen, "Luther and Metaphysics," in *Union with Christ: The New Finnish Interpretation of Luther,* ed. Carl E. Braaten and Robert W. Jenson (Grand Rapids: Eerdmans, 1998), pp. 129-60.

41. Theodor Dieter, *Der junge Luther und Aristoteles: Eine historisch-systematische Untersuchung zum Verhältnis von Theologie und Philosophie* (Berlin and New York: Walter de Gruyter, 2001).

42. Graham White, *Luther as Nominalist: A Study of the Logical Methods Used in Martin Luther's Disputations in the Light of Their Medieval Background,* Schriften der Luther-Agricola-Gesellschaft 30 (Helsinki: Luther-Agricola Society, 1994).

43. Bruce D. Marshall, "Faith and Reason Reconsidered: Aquinas and Luther on Deciding What Is True," *The Thomist* 63 (1999): 1-48; "Justification as Declaration and Deification," *International Journal of Systematic Theology* 4, no. 1 (March 2002): 3-28.

gences between Luther and Thomas Aquinas in their mutual oppositions to the semi-Pelagian theologies of each one's time. In fact, the modernists were concerned that Thomas, like Augustine before him, had conceded too much to divine sovereignty and predestination and, as a result, had undercut human freedom and responsibility. For them, God had created a happy world in which human freedom to desire, to choose, and to do was both real and decisive, so that if only creatures do what is in their power *(facere quod in se),* God is obligated by His own graciousness as well as by His tacit covenant with creation to do the rest for their salvation.[44]

One might very well with Elshtain see in medieval modernism the seeds of modernity's sovereign self.[45] The line of thought ran something like this.

> I can realize that I did not create myself; that I am a creature, imperfect, that is, in a state of becoming, not being. I can consequently infer that there is a Creator, perfect, that is, in a state of being. I can likewise reason that this perfect being is worthy of my highest love; the love of God would be my highest good, leading to my own perfection in life eternal by adherence to the perfect being of God. I can therefore want to love God above all, even if I do not succeed in loving God above all. On the other hand, God, being perfect, does not need my love but may rather be presumed to want His own creature's salvation and thus, as the creature's Creator, God would be freely obligated, so to say, by a kind of parental responsibility to reward the creature so far as it freely turns by its own natural powers towards Him. Thus God gladly counts the creature's mere wanting to love as if it were full and complete doing of love. In this way the free human person is justified and accepted by God by doing the minimal that is in her own natural powers.

In this scheme — eerily familiar as it is in contemporary American religiosity — there is no necessary place for Christ. He will serve here as an example, or model, or revelation of the human who saved himself along self-bootstrapping lines. Here Christ is the author and pioneer of free human agency realizing its highest potential in gaining its highest good, achieving nothing less than obligating God. Nor is there place here for the Spirit but as a gloss on one's eminently natural desire to escape the restless state of becoming and arrive at the rest of heavenly being. This was the modernist theology of the *quid pro quo* "good deal" — what I will call the "religion business" — at which Luther took aim in the *Disputation against Scholastic Theology* with the aid of the anti-Pelagian writings of the "blessed Augustine" and his fresh reading of the Pauline epistles in that light.

---

44. Heiko A. Oberman, *The Dawn of the Reformation: Essays in Late Medieval and Early Reformation Thought* (Edinburgh: T. & T. Clark, 1986); *The Harvest of Medieval Theology: Gabriel Biel and Late Medieval Nominalism* (Grand Rapids: Baker Academic, 2000).

45. Elshtain, *Sovereignty,* pp. 1-55.

From Luther's critique, we lift out three statements corresponding to our preliminary questions. First, "By nature we want to be God and do not want God to be God." That is to say, the actual God of the gospel is impossible for us as we actually are, not then as the free natural agents that the medieval modernists imagined vis-à-vis the perfection in being they projected as divine. Rather we are in bondage to structures of malice and injustice and unable to free ourselves from them, subtly but especially *in our religiosity,* in the conduct of the religion business. If so, the question then becomes: How does the actual God of the gospel become possible for us? Second, "God cannot accept man without His justifying grace." That is to say, God cannot simply become possible for us as we actually are in that there is no reconciliation of the contradiction between willfully ignorant slaves to self-sovereignty and the usurped God. Rather there must be a rectification; accordingly, there cannot be the good will of forgiveness without atonement, nor gift free to us without cost to God. Hence Christ, more specifically, the *crucified* Christ, is necessary as the very gift of God's justifying grace. If so, the question then becomes: How is Christ necessitated? Third, "The grace of God makes justice abound through Jesus Christ because it causes one to be pleased with the law." That is to say, faith justifies as faith in Christ Crucified because it causes us to love the divine law — in true obedience to which Messiah Jesus underwent His passion — that previously we had hated as a limit imposed upon our sovereign desires and choices. In other words, faith justifies when it *causes* change at the core of our historical way of being as creatures; faith *is* the new birth,[46] a Gethsemane of the soul, a co-crucifixion-and-resurrection with Christ the Crucified by the same Spirit that once for all led Jesus in true obedience through Gethsemane and Golgotha into the true death of utter patiency. If so, then, the question becomes: How is the new birth to faith given as this passage in Christ after Christ from death to resurrection? (We will add to this series of statements from the *Disputation against Scholastic Theology* another text from Luther at the appropriate place to inform the fourth question in the series, "Are the Scriptures holy?")

## Is God Possible?

If, as argued in the preceding chapter, testimony (always disputable and often controversial) is in fact a way of accounting for epistemic access in theology, permit me to begin answering the question "Is God possible?" with a little anecdote from my own theological journey. During my year of pastoral internship on Long Island, New York, in 1977-78, I made friends with an atheist Jew, Larry, who greatly enjoyed sparring with me about the existence of God. When I became a

---

46. Paul R. Hinlicky, "Staying Lutheran in the Changing Church(es)," Afterword in Mickey L. Mattox and A. G. Roeber, *Changing Churches: An Orthodox, Catholic and Lutheran Theological Conversation* (Grand Rapids: Eerdmans, 2012), pp. 281-314.

graduate student at Union Theological Seminary in New York, Larry would visit me in my Manhattan apartment to continue our great debate about the existence of a perfect being. Unlike the medieval modernists, Larry thought that the postulation of a perfect being corresponding to my imperfect being created more problems than it solved. How could God be possible in a world that recently witnessed the systematic murder of Europe's Jews? How could God be possible, if belief in God required a sacrifice of the scientific mind to an ultimate mystery beyond rational comprehension and the sacrifice, to boot, of those pleasures of the flesh that make life good (Larry, with the approval of his girlfriend, was in the midst of a torrid affair with the lonely wife of a Long Island medical doctor)? I myself felt the force of these arguments.

I had been reading Paul Tillich in recoil against resurgent fundamentalism in the Lutheran Church–Missouri Synod, in which I had been reared. I was just about in love with Paul Tillich. So when Larry proposed that his college philosophy professor join him on a visit and explain to me the compelling arguments for the nonexistence of God, I agreed. But at once I began to lay my plot. The trap was sprung on the unsuspecting professor of analytic philosophy when in reply to his critique of theism I proudly announced in my own effort to speak Tillich-ese: "God does not exist."[47] That is to say, God is *das Unbedingt,* the unconditioned condition of all that does exist or could exist, the creative ground of essence and existence, of finitude and self-transcendence. "A conditioned God is no God."[48] God is beyond the categories of existence and essence that apply to finite things. As Tillich preferred to express the absolute transcendence of the divine, God is the ground of being, Being Itself. Never mind that my bombastic and equivocating use of the verb, to be, in this odd affirmation of God, who is as nonexistent, involved me in logical nonsense. Larry's professor was quite impressed that my attempt to preempt him had relieved him of any need to argue at all. Agreed: God does not exist. Already I had joined the ranks of those theologians of modernity who have labored to give the unbeliever less and less in which to disbelieve.

I discovered in these years Karl Barth and his American Lutheran interpreter, Robert Jenson, and with them the renewal of Trinitarian theology that Barth had pioneered as an alternative to the sterile modern impasse between theism and atheism on which Tillich's theology so heavily traded. I learned from Barth that the "doctrine of the Trinity is what basically distinguishes the Christian doctrine of God as Christian, and therefore what already distinguishes the Christian concept of revelation as Christian. . . ."[49] Barth to be sure dialectically agreed with

---

47. See Tillich, *ST* 1, pp. 236-37.

48. Tillich, *ST* 1, p. 248.

49. *CD* I/1, p. 301. It is to be noted that for Barth the "doctrine" is not the revelation itself, but provides by "analysis of this statement ['God reveals Himself as Lord'] . . . what it denotes . . . a work of the Church, a record of its understanding of the statement or of its object . . . only indirectly, a record of revelation." *CD* I/1, p. 308.

Tillich, that God does not exist for us modern people — apart, that is, from the incalculable event of God's self-revelation in which God makes Himself an object of human apprehension in faith,[50] that is to say, where and when the Father in sovereign freedom to love sends the Son who is revealed by the Spirit as our gracious and liberating Lord. This "revelation" is the coming of the reign of God.[51] It always initiates a particular "history between God and certain men."[52] This coming of the free and incalculable event of "revelation," the "self-interpretation of this God"[53] as humanity's saving Lord, is that to which the church in its particularity bears a historical witness, also today under the conditions of objectively godless modernity. Theologians, as noted above, are witnesses. Notice with Barth, then, that you cannot express this dynamic of God becoming God for us, who are objectively godless, in the free event of revelation apart from the Trinitarian names and the gospel story they parse. In the doctrine of the Trinity the church analyzes and describes this event so that it may be known and recognized as God at work in the world and attested in faith.

The doctrine of the Trinity is the church's work, a descriptive analysis of the gospel event.[54] In Barth's shorthand, "God reveals Himself as Lord"[55] — grammatically a subject with a double object, that is, the eternal Father who begets the Son and breathes the Spirit. We come to know this God because now, in time, God "repeats" this eternal being, becoming "God a second time in a very different way, namely, in manifestation, i.e., in the form of something He Himself is not."[56] Turning to us in the human creature, Jesus Christ, that is, in temporal and spatial acts so denoted by this human name as Him who was *crucified under Pontius Pilate,* the eternal Father sends, the Son obediently goes, and the Spirit brings us to the Son and in the Son to the Father. God speaks. God is spoken. God is heard — really heard if and when we become new beings of repentance and faith as grasped by God's self-revealing that is at the same time God's self-giving in Jesus Christ. The "God who reveals Himself in the Bible must also be known in His revealing and His being revealed if He is to be known. . . . Again He Himself is not just Himself but also what He creates and achieves in men . . . the revealing God and the event of revelation and its effect on man."[57]

In this light we can see what it means to want to be God and not to want God to be God; it is a predicament in which objectively we are bound to such an extent that it is not known and cannot be recognized as a predicament; rather it is affirmed

50. *CD* I/1, p. 315.
51. *CD* I/1, p. 306.
52. *CD* I/1, p. 298.
53. *CD* I/1, p. 311.
54. See above, note 20.
55. *CD* I/1, pp. 296, 314.
56. *CD* I/1, p. 316.
57. *CD* I/1, pp. 298-99.

as the very essence of humanity.[58] The Promethean myth redeems Adam from the "sinfulness" of the *sicut Deus eritis* and valorizes his desire to be God without God. Consequently, this concealed predicament is uncovered — just as Saul of Tarsus discovered his true predicament on the road to Damascus and Peter likewise discovered as he went out from the High Priest's courtyard and wept bitterly — if and when, that is, we are discovered and recovered in Christ by the Spirit. Taking these divine and saving actions of the gospel given by the narrative interactions of the Father, the Son, and the Holy Spirit as truthful expression of true deity, then, the doctrine of the Trinity provides the specifically Christian thing to say about deity, namely that "God" (a title for the Creator of all that is other, not a proper name) is the eternal Father who does not take the No of human ignorance, sloth, and indifference for an answer, but rather seeks in the Son until He finds in the Spirit on the way to the coming of the Beloved Community for us all.

What for Tillich was at bottom a matter of metaphysical principle, *finitum non capax infiniti est,* revealed by the intellectual progress of modern thought, was subjected to a Luther-like twist in Barth. As we shall shortly see, God does not exist for us, *not only* because God is in principle the Infinite that cannot be adequately expressed in the finite, let alone captured: the Unconditioned, the Absolute, the Beyond. Barth *does* agree with Tillich in this respect. "Godhead in the Bible means freedom, ontic and noetic autonomy,"[59] and it is "thus of the very nature of this God to be inscrutable to man. . . . God is always a mystery." As the Creator of all that is not God, "this God is different from the world, i.e., as the One He is, He does not belong to the sphere of what man as a creature can know directly."[60] As in Tillich, this echo of Kant and German idealism necessarily leads to a highly paradoxical dialectic of revelation: "Revelation in the Bible means the self-unveiling, imparted to men, of the God who by nature cannot be unveiled to men."[61] Barth claims that this noumenal account of *das Unbedingt* is the equivalent of the ancient church's vocabulary for the "essence of God," the "being of God as divine being . . . the Godhead of God,"[62] because this transcendent divine nature is and remains "the basis of the distinction of the essence of God as such from His essence as the One who works and reveals himself . . . [so that] the triunity of God, too, is revealed to us only in God's work."[63] Here Barth adopts

---

58. This epistemic inability is not some uniquely "Calvinist" fixation on human "depravity." The anti-Calvinist Formula of Concord concludes its discussion of original sin citing Luther, "Whether we call original sin a quality or a disease, it remains true that the greatest evil is this: to be a victim of eternal wrath and death and not even to realize one's terrible lot" (*BC,* p. 542). The doctrine of sin so expressed executes a total critique just as it requires a correspondingly radical soteriology.

59. *CD* I/1, p. 307.

60. *CD* I/1, p. 320.

61. *CD* I/1, p. 315.

62. *CD* I/1, p. 349.

63. *CD* I/1, p. 371.

a position reminiscent of the later Orthodox distinction in Palamas between the essence and the energies of God. By it, Barth asserts simultaneously that God remains essentially unknown and that this unknown essence only reveals itself in its works in and with us. The difficulties for intelligibility here are evident, as is the subtle displacement of the "nature–person" distinction in Nicene Trinitarianism by the later "nature–energy" distinction. The questions thus raised remain the crux of interpretation, as we shall see.

In any case, there *is* a further, Luther-like reason that Barth gives for our godlessness that in fact presupposes a knowledge of the Creator already *willfully* ignored, a truth *suppressed* (Rom. 1:18-23), but now exposed in the confrontation between God and humanity that happens in the event of divine self-revelation by the coming of the Word and Spirit. God does not exist for us because "by nature we want to be God and do not want God to be God." Here the gospel's "point of contact" with *homo religiosus* is the society of the sacrificial system that structures malice and injustice; that sacrifices victims to leverage favor; and by this trade in cruelty erects a Babel, poses as a Leviathan, gathers as "the City of Man" (Gen. 11:4). We purport to speak of deity. We make a claim to ultimate truth. It is admittedly a minor theme within Barth's initial exposition of the doctrine of the Trinity, and it has been obscured further by Barth's quarrel with Emil Brunner regarding natural theology. But it is there and it arguably expresses notions of central importance to his theology as a whole. In Barth's own words, "All else we know as lordship can only be a copy, and is in reality only a sad caricature of this lordship. Without revelation man does not know that there is a Lord, that he, man, has a Lord, and that God is this Lord. Through revelation he does know it."[64] The "point of contact" for the gospel of the reign of God is confrontation with political sovereignty.

The "knowledge" in question here, in context of the hiddenness of God's essence that Barth like Tillich has insisted upon so strongly is the knowledge of *faith.* Our objective godlessness, then, is revealed as *sin* in the sense of disbelief in the lordship of the Creator by the coming of the knowledge of God in faith, exposited in the truth-claim "God reveals Himself as Lord." Our godlessness then is not, as the modern narrative would have it, the loss of innocent belief in fairy tales,[65] but it is the unwillingness to acknowledge the Giver in the gifts of creation; to live under the "lordship" of divine generosity; to take up the task of care of creation in structures of love and justice, but rather we project cruel caricatures of divine lordship in structures of malice and injustice animated by the *libido dominandi.*

64. *CD* I/1, p. 306.

65. So Daniel C. Dennett at the conclusion of his *Darwin's Dangerous Idea: Evolution and the Meanings of Life* (New York: Touchstone, 1996), alluding to Santayana's witticism, "There is no God and Mary is his mother": "But how many of us are caught in that very dilemma, loving the heritage, firmly convinced of its value, yet unable to sustain any conviction at all of its truth?" (p. 515).

God is impossible for us, then, because we resist and reject the coming of *the reign* of God the Giver, just as God's self-revelation institutes His reign by revealing and establishing His good and gracious lordship. God is impossible for us because we are in rebellion against His deity, the particular infinite of the Trinity that at Bethlehem and Golgotha showed itself all too capable of the finite in the advent of free grace as freedom to love even the godless. God becomes possible for us rebels in the free event of God's self-revelation, when, my enmity exposed, I am shown my true and merciful Lord in the cost of His seeking and finding love at the cross. The singular destination of the Son of God's journey into a far country is to seek and find us as we actually are, not as we fancy ourselves. This coming of God to dwell among us godless as God, that is, the gospel narrative, is thus "the root of the doctrine of the Trinity."[66]

From the foregoing we derive a thesis: the God who can and does exist for us is the Trinitarian God, more specifically, the *socially* Trinitarian God.[67] With the latter qualification, "social," we move beyond Barth's great contribution to the renewal of Trinitarian theology under the conditions of modernity and towards the continuation of this renewal under our "postmodern" conditions. Shortly we will focus on the further contributions to this renewal in our times by three great theologians in the tradition of Luther: Pannenberg, Jüngel, and Jenson. With their help, we will see how certain metaphysical truisms from the Greek philosophical tradition subvert our cogent telling of this God of the gospel, that is, how the ambiguous Platonic axiom of divine simplicity[68] can render the Trinitarian apprehension of deity inert and thus make God once again impossible for us. We will see consequently how Trinitarianism, not bare theism, provides the true counterpoint to contemporary disbelief, since Trinitarianism gives us a deity that includes the crucified Messiah Jesus as an essential moment in God's own surprisingly self-surpassing life, unlike theism for which God's history with us has no bearing on our understanding of the being that is divine. And we will see how modeling the Trinity as a society of persons whose unity is the "dramatic coherence" (Jenson) of love rather than the psychological processes of a single subject is not only more authentic to the New Testament and patristic witnesses, but works today to orient us to the coming of the Beloved Community as our destiny of redemption and fulfillment of this very earth on which stood also the cross of Jesus. We have already made use in the preceding chapter, accordingly, of a characterization of divine nature as *self-surpassing* to express the metaphysics of the *esse Deum dare*. For self-giving is always a self-surpassing that changes not only the recipient and beneficiary of a gift; but in a way carefully to be specified, particularly when the

---

66. *CD* I/1, p. 34.

67. Cornelius Plantinga Jr., "Gregory of Nyssa and the Social Analogy of the Trinity," *The Thomist* 50, no. 3 (1986).

68. See forthcoming Paul R. Hinlicky, *Divine Simplicity: An Ambiguous Legacy* (Grand Rapids: Baker Academic, 2016).

gift in question is the gift of one's self, giving changes the giver also. This topic will be explored in detail in Chapter Seven. For the present this much can laid out.

Divine *self-surpassing* is a terminology introduced to take up and develop the stunning argument of the early chapters of Robert Jenson's *Systematic Theology*. His thesis in this connection is that the "biblical God is not eternally himself in that he persistently instantiates a beginning in which he already is all that he ever will be; he is eternally himself in that he unrestrictedly anticipates an end in which he will be all he could ever be."[69] The theological opposition to mythology and the metaphysics that rationalize it here are categorical. In a passage that could have been cribbed right out of Mircea Eliade, Jenson writes: "The gods of the nations are guarantors of continuity and return, against the daily threat to fragile established order; indeed, they are Continuity and Return: the archtypically established order of Egypt was the very damnation from which the Lord released [Israel]. . . ." Here "God is not salvific because he defends against the future but because he poses it."[70]

Jenson's case for this thesis may be summarized as follows.[71] God is not what is eternally self-identical. Rather God is whoever raised Jesus from the dead. Whoever raised Jesus from the dead is identified as God not only by raising Jesus but by identifying in the very act with Jesus as His Son. Whoever is identified by His identification with Jesus as His Son is further identified as the One who had sent the Spirit to remain on Him for His mission of proclaiming this One's reign that in fact led to the cross. Whoever is identified by His identification with Jesus as His Son on whom His Spirit rested for His messianic work is identified as the Father of the Son and Breather/Sender of the Spirit. The God who is "one" God as the Father who sends the Son and the Spirit into the history of His creatures is thus "one," not by the reiteration of simple and eternal sameness, but by achieving the final, i.e., eschatological coherence of these three agencies and actions. God is in this true history with creatures, as God is eternally in Himself, a self-surpassing life. The coherence of this God was put in crisis at the crucifixion of the Son. Somehow this abandonment had to be integrated or the unity of the Father and the Son in the Spirit disintegrates into a mutually betraying pantheon, as in the cosmogonic myths of the nations. In this respect, then, the proclamation of the resurrection is a promise of this very integration to all creatures. So the Lord's identity along the way with creatures consists in anticipation of His future with them, not self-persistence that returns to the origin, leaving history behind in oblivion. On the other hand, the fulfillment of this promise cannot take place according to the immanent and existing laws of nature and history but only by the actual coming of God to share His own eternal life with creatures, the Beloved Community of God. Theosis is the culminating act of God surpassing God:

69. Jenson, *ST* 1, p. 66.
70. Jenson, *ST* 1, p. 67.
71. Jenson, *ST* 1, pp. 63-89

"the Lord's Spirit is his life as he transcends himself to enliven other reality than himself."[72] A more categorical repudiation of even lingering fragments of the metaphysics of divine simplicity can hardly be imagined.

In Barth himself, however, the problematic ambiguity of Christian Platonism's doctrine of divine simplicity remained and took its toll. It is evident in the essence-energy distinction that Barth adopted to separate the unknowable divinity in its inscrutable freedom from its knowable-because-created effects of love. This distinction plays no little work in Barth's theology as a whole. "It is not the form, but God in the form, that reveals . . .," he claims, because "God's self-unveiling remains an act of sovereign divine freedom. . . . In it God cannot be grasped by man or confiscated or put to work."[73] This intention to safeguard against idolatry — also if not especially in the ranks of the Christians — is undoubtedly justified. Any criticism of Barth here must find another way to erect this safeguard. But Barth's denial that the *form* of God's self-revelation suits its content cannot but make the cross of the Messiah, "Christ crucified," strictly incidental to another paradox than God's passage for us from wrath to mercy, hence also our passage from the subjectivity of malice and injustice to the subjectivity of Christ for us and in us. This *other* paradox tells of the divine Subject asserting His transcendent subjectivity to us and for us in the world of objects in order that we acknowledge divine Subjectivity in its incomprehensible freedom and learn to recognize and follow it as the free event of grace. This *other* paradox bears several deleterious consequences that in fact subvert Barth's pioneering retrieval of Trinitarianism. These may be succinctly enumerated.[74]

First, because God as subject is sharply distinguished from the form of the Word of God incarnate, the externality of the *Verbum externum* cannot be located in the *humanitas Christi* (humanity of Christ) as Barth expressly notes, but is rather indicated by the so-called *extra-Calvinisticum* (the Lutheran polemical characterization of Reformed Christology, meaning "Calvin's outside" of the humanity): "the Godhead is not so immanent in Christ's humanity that it does not also remain transcendent to it."[75] Second, Barth makes a strong argument *against* the modalist deviation in classical Trinitarian theology (i.e., that Father, Son, and Holy Spirit are not true persons of God, but modes of His appearance to creatures), yet he does so in the form of an argument *for* the unity of God as Subject in His self-objectification in Christ and self-communication in the Spirit;[76] Barth thus understands the Trinity on a mental/psychological model as the threefold

---

72. Jenson, *ST* 1, p. 86.

73. *CD* I/1, p. 321.

74. See the detailed critique in *PNT*, pp. 129-42.

75. *CD* I/1, p. 323.

76. That is, he argues against the "Sabellian idea of three mere manifestations behind which stood a hidden fourth[.]" *CD* I/1, pp. 354, 382. Thus, Barth takes the case against modalism primarily as a contention for the truthfulness of God in His self-revelation, rather than as against modalism's denial of the real distinction of persons in the deity as such.

modality of one act of divine subjectivity in its eternal self-knowledge, now "repeated" in time in the event of Jesus Christ. That "God is One in three modes of being, Father, Son and Holy Ghost, means, therefore, that the one God, i.e. the one Lord, the one personal God, is what He is not just in one mode" but in the three just listed.[77] The appearance in the gospel narrative of sociality (which Barth impugns as "tritheism") is but a way of speaking; sociality cannot be attributed to God ontologically, but is rather the temporal-spatial refraction of God's oneness as the eternal event "repeats" in the temporal and spatial events that bear witness to it.[78] Third, even though Barth is right to criticize the modern conceit in the notion of "scientific" history as that which is "apprehensible by a neutral observer" — claims to "neutrality" are among the most ideological claims that can be made, even if not especially when the theological predicament of human knowledge as finite and sinful is not acknowledged! — he is surely wrong to conclude that the question of historical certainty is "ignored in the Bible itself . . . as obviously and utterly inappropriate to the object of its witness."[79] This indifference to "history" (in the sense of knowledge of the spatial and temporal particularity) goes hand in glove with Barth's denial that the "form" of the Word of God is material to its content.

Before we go on then to further developments in Pannenberg, Jüngel, and Jenson, let us linger a little longer on our oddly formulated question — is God possible? Is God possible for us? By a longstanding tradition of Western thought going back to Aristotle, we think it wise to determine first that something exists before we inquire into what it is. Existence, as St. Thomas Aquinas exposited, is the first question and then follows immediately the next question about essence.[80] If we do not follow this order, we begin inquiry with merely possible beings of our

77. *CD* I/1, p. 359.

78. The issue is subtle. Barth correctly understands his usage here of "mode" as translating the *modus entitativus,* as the Latin translates the Greek *hypostasis* in the Cappadocian sense as a concrete way of being in distinction from a nature, *ousia.* But Barth differs from the Cappadocians, as Western theologians classically do, in regarding the "essence" of God, not semantically as an abstraction that classifies sets of possibilities, but as a metaphysical reality that can be articulated in terms of self-identity, as the uniquely divine *simplicity.* "The subject of revelation is the subject that remains indissolubly subject. One cannot get behind this subject. It cannot become object" (*CD* I/1, p. 381). Although Barth in this way dynamizes his concept of divine nature in terms of his celebrated "ontology of act," the problem of the Western tendency to modalism remains. In the West, a contention for Trinitarian personalism can only appear as heretical tritheism, as in Roscelin of Compiègne, who was condemned for that "heresy" in the eleventh century. See the brief discussion in Stanley J. Grenz, *The Named God and the Question of Being: A Trinitarian Theo-Ontology* (Louisville: Westminster John Knox, 2005), p. 60. Roscelin evidently lacked the Cappadocian doctrine of internal relations so that the correct denial of generic deity could not but appear as tritheism.

79. *CD* I/1, p. 325.

80. Joseph Bobik, *Aquinas on Being and Essence: A Translation and Interpretation* (Notre Dame: University of Notre Dame Press, 1965), pp. 1-48.

imagination, say, like unicorns or leprechauns or Platonic forms — beings that we can imagine to exist without a self-contradiction (unlike, say, a round triangle, an impossible being because it involves a self-contradiction). But if instead we begin by determining that something exists in the world, we avoid such flights of fancy and can more carefully inspect this definite, really existing something, analyze it and classify it by the determination of what it is, that is, by ascertaining the essence of this really existing something. Notice, however, that even in determining that something exists, we already and inevitably presuppose at least vague ideas about what this something might be by virtue of which we ascertain that such an apparent essence exists as a particular something yet to be precisely classified. If I ask whether unicorns really exist, for example, I must employ existing ideas of horses and horned beasts, so that I have some sense of what in the world I might be ascertaining. If, on the other hand, I apprehend a horse that by some mirage appears to have a single horn stemming from its brow, I recognize a possible unicorn. So the sequence, "existence first, then essence," is not so tightly ordered either in reality or in our knowledge of reality. There is a continuum extending between percept and concept, between sensible and supersensible. Percepts are primitive concepts; concepts are sophisticated percepts.[81] The recommended sequence that stems from Aristotle's rejection of Platonic Ideas, as taken up by St. Thomas, it is basically a methodological recommendation on sound scientific procedure.[82]

Now if we apply this recommended methodological procedure of inquiry to God, even if we follow Aristotle and Thomas in thinking that the first question would be whether God exists, we will still presuppose vague but general or common notions of deity by means of which we ask whether a divine something or other actually exists. Generally speaking, these are various notions of perfection that metaphysical analysis can unfold and articulate. An indication of this is that Thomas concluded each of his classical demonstrations of God's existence, whether of a first cause or a first mover or a necessary being grounding the contingency we experience in the flux of becoming and so on with the statement: "and this is what everybody understands by God."[83] Thus all such classical discussions about God's existence already presuppose ideas about what God possibly is, about the essence or whatness of deity, as we just heard: whether as the cause of causes or ground of being or prime mover or the infinite perfection of being corresponding to our imperfection in finite being. At the same time, however, if we inspect these vaguely presupposed ideas about what God possibly is, we discover that they are answers to questions framed by us finite beings and asked

---

81. *RPTD,* pp. 63-65.

82. Bobik, *Being and Essence,* p. 25.

83. St. Thomas Aquinas, *Summa Theologiae: A Concise Translation,* ed. Timothy McDermott (Allen, TX: Christian Classics, 1991), pp. 12-13. McDermott's contemporary paraphrase of the *Summa* is highly useful for students of systematic theology.

naturally if naïvely enough in relation to *our* reality: Do *we* have a first mover, a first cause, a ground, an archetypal perfection to mirror or copy? Is there a cause of us effects, a Creator of us creatures?

The perspective is naturally enough anthropocentric. The epistemic problem caused by this naïve supposition of the human perspective was overlooked by Thomas. Living as he did in an enchanted universe of "graced nature," Thomas simply took his perspective for granted in a way that begs the question whether humans can so naturally relate themselves to the divine in a cognitively truthful way. Yet already from ancient times, this is a possibility that the tradition of negative theology denies. Thomas, to be sure, felt the force of this objection. He employed negative theology to negate the imperfections inevitably attributed to God by naïve projections of creaturely excellences as qualities of divinity. This naïveté is what makes his classic approach to the basic question of God's existence "pre-critical," even if the apophatic element anticipates critical thought. It is also why modern proponents of Thomism insist on "the analogy of being" as the indispensable procedure in theology for today. Analogy combines the ways of eminence and of negation, as if to say that as we exist, so God exists yet in a way that infinitely exceeds the existence of creatures. As existence is taken to be the first question in inquiry, God must be thought to exist in some eminent way analogous to the existence of finite things, though infinitely transcending them, and thus as Creator to bear some relation to really existing creatures, even if we cannot say what it is. We can and must say *that* God exists, even if we cannot say *what* God is, as must be the case when we deny to God any imperfections. Apart from this procedure, modern Thomists argue, theology cannot get off the ground. In just this way, however, the apophatic cancelation of kataphatic features ultimately takes its revenge on language about God, also in Thomas.

For us today Thomas's analogy of being is a problem because we cannot take the human subject for granted, especially in theology. At the font of modern atheism, as in Ludwig Feuerbach who pioneered this sad denouement of Western theology, such unexamined but presupposed notions of God as the supremely existent one who anchors us are seen to be as not really about God as such, according to His own voice and intended reality. Rather they are exposed as covert statements about us, that is, about what grounds us, what causes us, what grasps us, what inspires us — those "regulative ideas" of Kant that in Feuerbach became the "ideals" we unconsciously project of our own, alienated human essence as if objectively real in God. "Man — this is the mystery of religion — projects his being into objectivity, and then again makes himself an object to this projected image of himself thus converted into a subject."[84] Marx's oft-cited words capture the radical import of Feuerbach's exposé of the religious subject: "Religious misery is in one way the expression of real misery, and in another a protest against

---

84. Ludwig Feuerbach, *The Essence of Christianity,* trans. George Eliot (New York: Harper Torchbooks, 1957), pp. 29-30.

real misery. Religion is the sigh of the afflicted creature, the soul of a heartless world, as it is also the spirit of spiritless conditions. It is the *opium* of the people. The abolition of religion as the *illusory* happiness of the people is the demand for their *real* happiness."[85]

When speaking of "God," then, theology cannot take for granted the questions, Who wants to know? and Why? Divine qualities turn out to be, upon examination, projections of our varying needs or aspirations.[86] They thus beg the question of the suffering subject in history who asks such questions — a human subject with a definite biographical narrative forged in history, not the abstraction of a merely existent creature pondering the mystery of existence as such. But if Christianity is at all true in Luther's reading, the subject who asks about God cannot possibly occupy any such stance of disinterested neutrality, metaphysically reduced to mere existence and asking about an equally abstract essential existence. According to the canonical narrative, we are already born into a state of exile from that paradise of childlike "dreaming innocence" (Tillich). That is why, in turn, Karl Barth in response to Feuerbach always insisted that we rigorously set aside as the idols or demons of an alienated humanity all preconceived notions of deity and learn in Christian theology who and what God is strictly from God's revelation that is at the same time His self-donation and self-communication. That in turn specifies the theological subject as one for whom God has become possible by the Spirit through the Word.[87]

Thus, there are two severe difficulties attending this Aristotelian methodological procedure that inclines to treat God's existence as the first question in theology — likewise in those anthropocentric theologies of modernity after Kant that begin with the impossibility of the proofs of God's existence and accordingly convert, after Feuerbach and Marx, theology into anthropology. First, we never come in this way to any knowledge of what God is in and for God, minimally how God is spirit and love, to recall the ontological claims of the Fourth Gospel. Indeed as mentioned above, consequent theologians in Thomas's tradition readily acknowledge, at least after Kant, that we can only know vaguely that God is, never concretely what God is. That is to say, we cannot infer from what God is for us, from His existence as Creator to creatures, anything specific about God's being for God, what God is essentially. As God's causality is a transcendent causality, we cannot infer directly from effect to cause in the case of God. Why

85. Karl Marx, *On Religion*, trans. Saul K. Padover (New York: McGraw-Hill, 1974), pp. 35-36.

86. See the discussion in Paul R. Hinlicky, "Luther's Atheism," in *The Devil's Whore: Reason and Philosophy in the Lutheran Tradition*, ed. J. Hockenberry Drageseth (Minneapolis: Fortress, 2011), pp. 53-60.

87. Thus also from the Thomist tradition and on behalf of all three Abrahamic faiths, David B. Burrell, C.S.C., *Freedom and Creation in Three Traditions* (Notre Dame: University of Notre Dame Press, 1993), pp. 1-6; see also his "Creator/Creatures Relation: 'The Distinction' vs. 'Onto-theology,'" *Faith and Philosophy* 25, no. 2 (April 2008): 177-212.

should this cease to be the case in regard to revelation, where too God is known from inferring from an effect in the world back to its cause? The Thomistic theology of the analogy of *being* (that is, of *existence,* not essence) quite properly (so it is claimed) leaves us in ultimate ignorance, or apophaticism, which not even revealed theology overcomes. By the same token, however, contemporary Thomisms today are not and cannot be Thomas's Thomism, since no one today seriously argues that God's existence can be argumentatively determined as the first step in theology.[88] One puts a good face on this gap, arguing that analogical theology both precludes fundamentalist idolatry that takes earthly language for God literally and at the same time preserves an aura of genuine mystery around the transcendent being of God. Nevertheless, a gulf threatens to open wide here between God as He exists for us and what God is essentially. This gap leaves us haunted by the question whether God is true in this relationship with us, given the admitted relativity of human analogical language to the finite domain of our experience in the common body.

The late Catholic theologian Ralph Del Colle thus wrote critically of the Aristotelian methodological procedure in theology by reinvoking strong Trinitarianism: "[T]he trinitarian naming of God points to the Christian understanding that the event of Jesus Christ and the sending of the Spirit reveal the loving mystery of the saving God whose transcendence in the mystery is the basis for its communication and invitation to the creature."[89] That is to say that the eternal Father who begets the Son and breathes the Spirit in His own eternal life of divine becoming is the same One who sends the Son and the Spirit to do the works of the redemption and of the fulfillment of the creation in space and time. He is the same One, of course, but not in the same way. Karl Rahner's "rule," that the economic and immanent Trinities are one and the same God is, thus, *prima facie* correct, according to Del Colle, but a lack of clarity attends the thought. What is the point here of a distinction, though not a separation? The relation of immanent to economic Trinity is not a relation of cause to effect, but one of self-manifestation, of self-donation, of self-communication *ad extra.* As Christine Helmer has put the matter, following Reiner Jansen, albeit in Kantian idiom: "The immanent Trinity is the condition for the possibility of its economy; the economy is the 'noetic' revelation of God as three persons in salvation history, and on the basis of this revelation, the triune essence of God is known to be a necessity of the divine nature."[90] The doctrine of the Trinity thus explicates how God is possibly what He is actually. Antecedently by virtue of a divine harmony of power, wisdom, and love appropriated respectively to the Father, the Son, and

---

88. See Fergus Kerr, *After Aquinas: Versions of Thomism* (Malden, MA: Blackwell, 2002), for a fruitful exploration of this problematic.

89. Ralph Del Colle, "The Triune God," chapter 7 in *The Cambridge Companion to Christian Doctrine,* ed. C. E. Gunton (Cambridge: Cambridge University Press, 1997), p. 121.

90. Helmer, *The Trinity and Martin Luther,* p. 24.

the Spirit, God is able to make, keep, and fulfill the temporally enacted and communicated commitments made in Christ by the Spirit through the gospel. But if we do not begin with the gospel and reason thusly to the condition in God for its possibility, Del Colle worries, the Trinity becomes merely a nugget of revelation, a supernatural puzzle beyond understanding as such taken on mere authority, put on an altar to be adored but otherwise ignored. As a result, even the Trinity comes to be qualified by other ideas of God's essential or natural transcendence, like first cause and prime mover and necessary being, that make God over as the ineffable Ground, the Origin, the Protological Principle. The result of adopting Aristotle's procedure is that theology joins in the classical metaphysical quest for the divine *arche* and leaves unexamined the problematic of human perspective and theological subjectivity in discourse about God; the irony is that to affirm that like us creatures God too exists, though we know not how — leads to the "conundrum" that in the final analysis "the redeemed human creature does not actually know or participate in the actual being of God."[91]

As a result, even this ultimately "learned ignorance" (Cusa) of God is vulnerable to the Feuerbachian critique of projection, as Del Colle puts it: "Either the Christian knowledge of God identifies the very being of God in the revelation of the divine persons and in this manner preserves the transcendence of God, or trinitarian language amounts to a triadic representation of God in history according to the receptive capacity of the human subject and nothing more. In ultimate terms this latter position eventually yields to apophatic agnosticism concerning the being of God."[92] This penetrating analysis and Catholic self-criticism make it abundantly clear that if we can no longer say with sense and with conviction that and how "God is spirit" and "God is love," but only weakly affirm that so it seems to me and works for me, we have in fact said that God as God is impossible for us, that He does not really but only apparently exist for us, we know not how. Thus, in our theology and earnest religiosity — piously rejecting fundamentalism and affirming transcendent mystery — we confirm Luther's suspicion that we want to be God and do not want the actual God to be God — the God of the gospel, the One who comes to us, too close for comfort, in and as the "disruption of grace" (Hunsinger).[93]

That leads to a second difficulty with the classical procedure stemming from Aristotle. Not only is the question of essence, about what in the world the word "God" means, vaguely assumed on the basis of unexamined common notions rather than warranted. But furthermore, in this way what God means for us becomes the purely academic question whether some kind of Perfect Being, we know not how, exists. This procedure thus displaces the urgent existential, social,

---

91. Del Colle, "Triune God," p. 133.
92. Del Colle, "Triune God," p. 136.
93. George Hunsinger, *Disruptive Grace: Studies in the Theology of Karl Barth* (Grand Rapids: Eerdmans, 2000).

and cosmological question about the God of the Bible who comes amid the contingencies and particularities of temporal existence to disrupt and reconstruct all things. So Luther said thematically of the Letter to the Romans, "The chief purpose of this letter is to break down, to pluck up, and to destroy all wisdom and righteousness of the flesh."[94] This bespeaks a total, radical critique that goes to the root of structures of malice and injustice and demands correspondingly a total conversion to the justice of living by faith, that is, living by the possibility of restoration for the fallen, the possibility of God for us, the possibility of the coming of the Beloved Community. So the possibility of God is and must be controversial in the world. As Pannenberg has so rightly argued in this connection, *dubitability* about the existence of the disruptive God of the gospel is built right into the world that this God is creating in order that the final demonstration of God's existence consist only in God's own fulfillment of His Word by the coming of the Reign at the eschaton of judgment.[95] Theology, in the interim, has *both* to prosecute this total disruption *and* to participate in the controversy it opens, testing its claims to truth about what makes God to be God for us.

Our biblical problem with God is not then a philosophical quandary whether or not a first cause exists but rather a structured and deeply entrenched enmity with Him who comes with the rightful claim to be Lord and Giver of life. Malice and injustice have become second nature. For us, then, to speak with the Bible in these ways about God is to learn anew to speak the coming of the Reign, our inclusion in the Beloved Community, resurrection to life in the life which is eternal — that of the Father and the Son in the Spirit. Is God possible? Concretely, is God possible for us? God is possible for God as the love of the eternal Father and the Son in the Spirit. That eternal life is the condition for the possibility of the divine life at work and so revealed in the gospel narrative. This God is possible for us, then, in promising communion in that very divine being by the life, death, resurrection, and exaltation of Jesus Christ; we become possible for God in turn by the outpouring of the Spirit that confers theological subjectivity by baptismal union with Christ. Thus it is evident that we are only in a position to believe or disbelieve the God of the gospel, that is, to entrust ourselves to His promised demonstration of His existence, insofar as we know what we are talking about. But we only know what we are talking about in response to a putative word from God, a divine self-introduction.

This "theological circle" is not a vicious nor self-privileging one, so far as it is transparent to the vulnerable posture of testifying faith alongside other such vulnerable postures in the world. It is not "special pleading" in the sense of making a claim to truth that could and should have traction apart from acquisition of the particular subjectivity that is both needed and granted to receive it that consists in the patiency of living by faith. Indeed, the appeal to be reconciled to God (2 Cor.

94. *LW* 25, p. 135.
95. Pannenberg, *ST,* 1, pp. 58-59.

5:18-20), i.e., to receive this new subjectivity, because of God's reconciliation in Christ, comes on the scene as a spiraling motion: the Word pointing to the Spirit and the Spirit to the Word. That, in any case, is what the gospel is existentially, a putative word from God by which God introduces Himself as the One who has surpassed wrath at our bondage to sin to achieve liberating mercy and who thus invites the hearer into His care and keeping for the fulfillment of the divine cause. This word from God is not just any word, not even any of the many words of God found in the Bible, but the one Word of the eternal Father's determination to redeem and fulfill the creation through the missions of His Son and Spirit. Thus in regard to God the question "Who?" orders the questions "What?" and "How?" For the question *Who?* is the question of personhood that asks about a subject in relation to us.

Jenson has rigorously carried through on the insight of Luther and Barth that neither existence nor essence can be privileged in the question of God; that it is rather the Bible's personal and social, historical and narrative identification of God in our world that tells — as of first importance — *who* God is for us. At the same time, the understanding of the *who* brings a new understanding of the *what* and the *that* of God, as Jenson puts it: ". . . the gospel's God can be an object for us if and only if God is so identified by the risen Jesus and his community as to be identified *with* them."[96] The differences Jenson articulates here between the *who,* the *what,* and the *that* are important for our question.

A *who* is always a corresponding, that is, personal "other," a possible equal that claims my acknowledgment as a moral agent, that is, my respect and good will as befits a fellow person, not a thing over which I dispose, a *that* in the world that I make into a useful *what.* Because of this acknowledgment of another's freedom, when I ask who one is, I am asking about what possibilities for me this other brings. When I ask, Who are you?, I am asking for self-manifestation, a disclosure of how you will be for me in determining your freedom in this particular way. The questions of the *what* and the *how,* by contrast, lend themselves to my agency and instrumentalization — perfectly apt in relation to the things of the world given for our free use and generous sharing. As an agent who causes things to happen in the world, I properly want power over things to use them as I see fit, and thus it comes about that I want to know that something exists, how it works, and what it is good for. We can of course in this way try to *thing-ify* God, so to speak; we can attempt to instrumentalize God — treat God as an object and use this objectified God for our own purposes, as regularly happens in the religion business. But if I meet a true *who,* my naïve will-to-power is at least in principle checked. Here I must reckon with another who wants the same recognition, respect, and power in the world as do I, whom then I am obligated to honor as I honor myself, if we are to live side by side in the same world in love and in justice. So to know God truly, Jenson is arguing, is in the first place not to know the *what* and the *that* of

96. Jenson, *ST* 1, p. 13.

God by which I master things in the world. Rather to know God is first of all to meet another who speaks and addresses me and whose claim to truth awakens me to the proffered relationship. "God" is the One who speaks to us, Jenson argues, by the speech-act of the resurrection of Jesus from the dead, news that recurs, so to say, in the ongoing telling of it. It is God's self-introduction that comes on the scene as God's personal promise to the auditor: as I have raised Jesus from death, so I will also raise you and all together who die with Jesus by repentance and faith. I am God who gives life to the dead and calls into being worlds that do not yet exist. This is who I am and claim to be, also, for you.

We have thus far seen how important the *who* is; how it must, according to Jenson, be the first question in theology. Yet the matter is not quite so simple. This *who* of the God of the gospel turns out to be complex not simple, social not individual, persons in community not a self-positing subject. The God who is identified by Jesus raised from the dead in this report and promise claiming me with many others with this proffered truth involves two others, the just-mentioned Jesus and the Spirit of Jesus and His Father. At the very least, as a result, God as "identified by the risen Jesus" in the complex not simple story that the gospel tells comes across more like a society — "Jesus, his Father and their Spirit," as Jenson frequently expresses it — than a single, sovereign self, "the Lord," as American Protestants like to say. Thus we could be saying the very same gospel, if we alternated the voice of the Son, saying, "I am yours and you are mine. Give me your sin and take my righteousness." Or if we alternated the voice of the Spirit in the bath of Christian initiation, saying, "You too are a beloved child of God, who has died as Adam and been born anew in Christ." Or, we could be saying the very same gospel when we articulate the coordinated works of the Three: God so loved the world that He gave His only Son that all those born anew from above by His free-blowing Spirit should enter His own eternal life.

According to Cornelius Plantinga Jr. these variable ways of speaking one and the same God in the event of His self-surpassing that is also His self-donation and self-communication are indications of what he calls "strong Trinitarianism." This would hold that "1) Father, Son and Spirit are conceived as persons in a full sense of 'person,' that is, as distinct centers of love, will, knowledge and purposeful action (all of which require consciousness), and 2) who are conceived as related to each other in some central ways analogous to, even if sublimely surpassing, relations among members of a society of three human persons."[97] It is to be noted that the social Trinity, like the psychological Trinity, provides but a model, just as the accompanying notion of person as a distinct center of agency is likewise but a model in this context. A model is not the thing itself but a map of it. An accurate map is not a mere symbol but a true and workable guide to navigation, just as the thing itself is not a static reality that can be mastered by a representation but the living God who invites to life together. Moreover, the social Trinity is not

97. Plantinga, "The Social Analogy," p. 325.

the theological sentimentalism that frequently accompanies it in contemporary theology, the projection onto God of middle-class hunger for better relationships while happily coexisting with structures of malice and injustice. The social Trinity comes into our world on the attack, as an "invader" ( J. Louis Martyn) "to break down, to pluck up, and to destroy all wisdom and righteousness of the flesh" (Luther).

Just this social complexity of the divine in strong Trinitarianism presses us on to new understandings of the divine *what* and *that*. While we may be willing to concede that this complex *who* of strong Trinitarianism is biblically grounded in gospel narrative and indeed generates the classically Christian way of talking about God for us in our time and space, we might well wonder whether it is also a true way of eternal being — of divine being, that is, of God being God for God. The difficult question arises here of whether and how we might close the apparent gap between God hidden and God revealed and why we would want to close it. The knowledge of God is the knowledge of faith in still-contested reality, not the knowledge of sight that sees in the light of glory. Thus we can parse the problem of God's hiddenness and revealedness in one of several ways. We can regard this gap as essential and ontological or as economic and historical, that is, as a gap between Transcendence and any possible human speaking of It, or, as a gap in God surpassing God in historical passage from blessing to wrath to mercy to victory. This is a difficult problem that we will take up in Chapter Seven in the section "God Surpassing God." We cannot in the interim, however, avoid indicating in a preliminary fashion a position on the "ontological" status of faith's language about God hidden and revealed.

A who without a *what* and a *that* would be a ghost — and God in the non-cognitivism of Kantian theology has indeed become ghostly in much modern theology when we decline to think the ontology of God but speak only indirectly of God by means of His supposed created effects (but then how do we know our supposedly absolute or categorical feelings as *divine* effects rather than *infantile fantasies?*). So, the question whether this economic Trinity in history is one and the same as an eternal and immanent Trinity and how it may be the one God has to be thought through, if the reality of this God is to be understood in faith and distinguished from ambiguous human feelings. Does this way of talking about God according to the gospel also indicate how it is possible to be God — for God? Or what is the same, is God true to God in this Trinitarian self-revelation?

Despite the *homoousios* of the Nicene Creed, affirming that Jesus and His Father are of "one being," much Christian theology over the centuries has choked on the thought — too hard to swallow (cf. John 6:52-60)! The reason lies in Jenson's further claim that the God who is identified by Jesus' resurrection as Father to Son in the Spirit is identical *with* those events; that makes the one true God the eternal and holy Trinity at work, without reserve yet specifically, in the space and time of His creation. This latter tells something about *what* God can be, as somehow, and despite the proper personal and natural distinctions, the same in being as the man crucified under Pontius Pilate. The *who* then does not only identify God in the complex way of a society of Father, Son, and Holy Spirit but implicates God essentially in this specific human existence in the world: the One eternal God is somehow capable of time and space, capable of the Incarnation and the Cross, capable of being shed abroad in human hearts by the Holy Spirit, capable of prevailing for us in the coming, even to us, of the Beloved Community as the very fulfillment of this creation that we actually are.

If God is not identified with the historical event Jesus Christ, Jenson writes, then "the identification would be a revelation ontologically other than God himself . . . [giving] clues to God, but would not be God." Why is that a problem, one may wonder, rather than a blessed relief (as the apophatic tendency in theology has always found)? Here the ante is upped and the stakes become very high. The space left between the revelation in history and the presumably essential and atemporal being of the deity, Jenson writes, "is exactly the [empty] space across which we make our idolatrous projections" — above all, for Jenson, the great and subtle idol of a timeless, hence ontologically otherworldly eternity. As a result, the gospel's revelation in time becomes "mere occasions and triggers of the religious quest, of a journey to what lies behind them." This capture of the gospel by the antecedent metaphysics of Platonic ascent has Christological consequences. Rather than *being* God *for us,* the man Jesus is thought to tell us — not what the invading God can and will be for us — but timelessly "what God is like," a waxen nose to be sure. Jesus then becomes a similitude of varying utility for the religious projects of self-transcendence and ceases to be the stone of stumbling, the paradox of the Christ of Israel crucified for us godless Gentiles. Jesus becomes the Christian idol alongside others, in a complacent and tolerant polytheism, featuring Christian tribalism as the heretofore highest evolutionary development of cosmopolitan human religiosity — or not. It also has Pneumatological consequences. Rather than the Spirit being God in believers, and they in turn the Temple of the Spirit in their new life together, the ecclesia becomes a voluntary organization, like the ancient funeral society. Closing any gap between God's being and God's self-revelation, Jenson accordingly notes, is the "conceptual move" on which the "whole argument" of his *Systematic Theology* depends.[98]

Nor does Jenson shy from the draconian existential implication that closing this gap entails for complacent Christian polytheism and its comfortable racketeering in religion. A true preacher of the gospel, he says, can only say: "We are not here to entice you into our religion by benefits allegedly found only in it. We are here to introduce you to the true God, for whatever he can do with you — which may well be suffering and oppression."[99] So little can the true God identified with the Crucified One be instrumentalized ("he had no form or majesty that we should look at him, nothing in his appearance that we should desire

98. Jenson, *ST* 1, p. 59.
99. Jenson, *ST* 1, p. 51.

him," Isa. 53:2b); so little likewise can this God's true becoming as an object for us entice without a corresponding transformation of human desire by the conferral of a new theological subjectivity. That further gift of the same Spirit, who led Jesus obediently into conflict with demonic powers for us and thence to the ignominy of the cross, is how the God of the gospel becomes possible for us. In sum, for Jenson, the starting point of theology in God's self-identification with the Crucified One frees us from the need to find God by the projection of our own preferences or ideals on the basis of our own perceived needs — needs that in fact are shaped all the way down by the structures of malice and injustice into which we are born as exiles from the paradise that is our destiny. If desire is captivated, nothing less can save us than a new birth into a new world.

Eberhard Jüngel's magnum opus, *God as the Mystery of the World,* is a sustained critique of the binary of theism and atheism, that is, of the theist's "God is a necessity for us," and the atheist's rejoinder, "God is not necessary for us." In either case, under analysis is the concept of God as the philosopher's necessary being, ground of the contingent beings of the world of becoming, whose function is to be Leibniz's *ultima ratio rerum* (ultimate reason of things) in answer to the question, Why is there something rather than nothing?[100] The problem with necessary being from the perspective of theology in the traditions of Luther and Barth is that a merely necessary being seems bound and chained by its own essential predicates of immutability and simple self-identity and thus can do nothing new, such as assume flesh in the Incarnation, or bind together in love a human temple of the Spirit, let alone originate a world of creatures in a genuine beginning. Any of these divine becomings threaten to shift ground and so destabilize the cosmos. As Jüngel puts it: ". . . God so understood, as the goal of man so understood, has no possibilities anymore. In him, everything is completed, in accordance with the metaphysical concept of deity whose essence is simple *(haple),* "because it is activity without potency." Of course, in a deity conceived as reality without possibility, the possibility of surrendering oneself to another is excluded. . . ."[101] It is just such mutual actions of surrender in love, however, that lie at the heart of the Trinitarian drama of the gospel narrative and thus also, if the drama is true to the agents, the eternal being of the God of the gospel who thus can be God for us in time and space. That this destabilizing narrative "brings to naught the things that are" (1 Cor. 1:28) is, to be sure, the very point.

The new-creative possibility of God for us in the gospel is, in Jüngel's oddsounding refrain, "more than necessary."[102] This formulation aims to "explode the entire concept of one who grounds" on account of its affirmation of the "more,"

---

100. Eberhard Jüngel, *God as the Mystery of the World: On the Foundation of the Theology of the Crucified One in the Dispute between Theism and Atheism,* trans. D. L. Guder (Grand Rapids: Eerdmans, 1983), p. 29.

101. Jüngel, *God as the Mystery,* p. 339.

102. Jüngel, *God as the Mystery,* p. 24.

i.e., the superabundance of creativity, the "groundlessness" of creation in the self-surpassing God who freely makes and values creatures as goods for their own sakes such as to redeem and fulfill them.[103] Thus at the same time Jüngel's formulation does *not* affirm the opposite thesis of the ungrounded contingency of all things, the sheer arbitrariness of events. It does not affirm the apparently opposite denial of the atheist, that "God is not necessary in the world,"[104] i.e., that the world just is. The reason why the atheist's affirmation is not entailed by the "explosion" of Leibniz's theistic thesis, according to Jüngel, is the curious "fact" that Leibniz's basic question, why "something exists at all and not nothing," is "in and of itself ambivalent." It is ambivalent because the things that in fact exist are not so clearly "not nothing." In other words, Leibniz's question poses an alternative that is itself not free from aporia. In fact what exists, fleeting as it is, exists as ever exposed to the nonbeing from which things have arisen and to which they return. What "is" is the flux of becoming. Thus "this experience of possible nonbeing can also summon up anxiety and nothing more." The philosophical question leads *only* to the "dimension within which the question of God is raised, but it does not lead to God as the necessary ground."[105] For that matter, neither can it lead to the denial of God as the necessary ground. It leads to the "contemporary aporia in the traditional concept of God."[106] The root of the perplexity, however, is that a true God cannot be derived from the needs of the world; the metaphysical deity, for all abstraction, will always be nothing but such a conceptual idol. Rather, a true world of others together in time can only be given by a free God and ever received as a gift by a freed creature in the doxology of a fulfilled creation. But a free *"God comes from God"*[107] so that "the point of *Christian* talk about God" is that God comes from God "in[to] *the midst* of this contradiction" between being and nonbeing as the redeemer and fulfiller of the threatened creation.[108]

Jüngel's formulation recognizes the biblical God of promise and hope as the decisive *presupposition* of theological thought and this God indeed as something, not as little as, least of all as less than, but rather as something "more than" the metaphysical deity. Reminiscent of Luther's important distinction of theology from philosophy as "the new thinking of the Spirit," Jüngel argues that "responsible talk about God," i.e., "responsive to the crucified man Jesus as the true God," i.e., the conscientious theology of the God of the gospel, *evangelical* theology "single-mindedly and unswervingly, based on its specific task . . . attempts to think God from the encounter with God . . . a possibility already determined by the existence of biblical texts and claimed already by faith in God."[109] This way of

---

103. Jüngel, *God as the Mystery*, p. 33.
104. Jüngel, *God as the Mystery*, p. 30.
105. Jüngel, *God as the Mystery*, p. 34.
106. Jüngel, *God as the Mystery*, p. 35.
107. Jüngel, *God as the Mystery*, p. 34, emphasis original.
108. Jüngel, *God as the Mystery*, p. 35, emphasis original.
109. Jüngel, *God as the Mystery*, p. 154.

theological understanding arising from the experienced encounter with the crucified Christ of God bears three methodological implications worthy of note here.

First, one owns up to one's presuppositions as given in history by testimony. No one can arrive at a responsible conception of God without presuppositions (i.e., without a putative Word of God); even speculation working by free imagination responds to some antecedent speech regarding God. One first listens to testimony, beginning with "biblical texts" and thinks conscientiously in the confessional form of response, doxologically. Of course, any such act of hearing and responding by creatures is *ipso facto* a new cognitive synthesis in history that itself becomes an artifact for further interpretation in the continuing tradition of the gospel and its Spirit-guided understanding. Equally such hearing and responding may abort in unbelief. In any case, one speaks of God only in response to a Word from God, even in denial.

Second, the one who thinks this way in faith unabashedly appeals to and testifies of standing in the historical train of gospel tradition and hence of a "very special experience of God . . . with a special relationship of God to human thought which claims to have general validity." That is to say, the one who so listens and thinks as a theologian is first and ever formed in the Spirit by the Word into a theological subject while remaining in the world of the common body to which the gospel's claim refers in referring also "for me." As theology interprets the believer's individual experience of the world, *pars pro toto,* theology interprets the experience of the world by the unveiling of its mystery as the God of the gospel.

Third, this formation of the theological subject is guided by the biblical texts from which and in terms of which the putative Word of God is articulated. The biblical texts are those that historically crystallized around the originating claim to the truth that God made in the speech-act of the resurrection of the Crucified and received as the Spirit's rule of faith for the mission to the nations. In sum, "the place of the conceivability of God is a Word which precedes thought" and "[o]ur access to God is thus really understood as God bringing us to himself."[110] It is not epistemology, then, but epistemic access warranted by the specific claim to truth of the putative Word of God concerning Jesus as God's Son (Rom. 1:2-3) as received in trusting faith that gives us the prolegomena to dogmatics.

Jüngel went on to parse the acts of mutual surrender in the life of the Trinity which make the God of the gospel "more than necessary."

> Whereas the Jesus who exists totally from the Father made it possible to believe in God as the Father, the God who identifies with Jesus in his death makes it possible to believe in God the Son. To believe with Jesus in God (the Father) means, with all the necessity of Easter, to believe in Jesus as God (the Son). But this faith is not derived from man; it is possible only in the power of the Spirit who comes to man. To believe in God with Jesus, and to believe in Jesus

110. Jüngel, *God as the Mystery,* pp. 154-55.

as God, means thus to believe in the Holy Spirit. Since it is solely the Holy Spirit who makes faith in God the Father and in God the Son possible as one faith, faith in the Spirit is necessarily faith in God the Father, the Son, and the Spirit: faith in a triune God.[111]

The Trinity so sketched by Jüngel is a living chain of love that has reached out of its eternal and blessed life to include us in Jesus Christ by the Spirit's mission in His name. To be this God is not to realize all possibilities necessarily, let alone to have eternally realized all possibilities. Its almighty potency consists rather in having access to all possibilities, yet its wisdom consists in choosing among them wisely and well, in order in goodness freely to give life to the dead and existence to worlds not yet in being. The *what* of God, the being of God, as known from the *how* of God in the economy of salvation is thus an ultimate harmony of power, wisdom, and love — this is the mystery of the world as gift of God.

Jüngel's motto, "God is more than necessary," indicates that the Trinitarian God is to be thought preeminently in the category of possibility, of what God can be, ever opening up the tomb, the closed mind, and hardened heart. God the Father is the God of possibilities, not necessities, the self-surpassing One, whose act of origin is forward looking to its fulfillment in a new creation. To be sure, as we will see, this demands a rigorous account of the gospel as the actualization of a possibility that overcomes necessity by the cross and resurrection of the Incarnate Son.

Jüngel's insights into a renewed Trinitarianism as the way beyond the modern theist-atheist impasse have a context. In Jüngel's account, it was the emergence of the Cartesian-Kantian subject in the transcendental "I think" that undermined the metaphysically conceived God from within and made it no longer conceivable, as it was, for example, in Anselm's so-called ontological argument. By interposing between God's existence and God's essence to derive the certainty of the perfectly thinking thing's existence as the correlate and ground of the imperfect existence of the human thinker, hence without regard to *what* God was so interrogated, modern thought "destroyed the [metaphysical] concept of God understood as the unity of essence and existence." It is, consequently, no solution to this destruction simply to assert by fiat the simple unity of existence and essence as God. Rather, we must ask now, Who is it who asks about God? With what access?, and, Why? For Anselm, as many have recognized since Barth's justly celebrated study,[112] the God under consideration in the so-called ontological proof is the one to whom he prays, whose Trinitarian essence had been established for thought in the preceding reflection of the *Monologion,* and whose existence as such was discovered to be analytical to that particular essence, conceived as Trinity, in the *Proslogion.*

111. Jüngel, *God as the Mystery,* p. 368.

112. Karl Barth, *Anselm: Fides Quaerens Intellectum (Faith in Search of Understanding),* trans. I. W. Robertson (Cleveland and New York: Meridian Books, 1962).

But a god — any God — whose existence can be questioned and thus verified or disconfirmed solely by the creature's "I think" is no longer thought metaphysically as true God at all, even as the necessary being whose very essence it is to exist. Nor is the "more" of the Trinity, whose essential existing is ecstatic and self-surpassing and so active in superabundant charity thinkable by the Transcendental Ego of modernity. When Descartes silently severed the *Proslogion* from the *Monologion,* the Christian element in Christian Platonism was utterly subordinated to the Platonic element, and the marriage of the two traditions, never a happy one, ended in divorce. In principle, if not yet in clear understanding, the metaphysical deity thus became inconceivable in the very process of Descartes' proof that divinizes in its place the *ego cogito.* Thus as modernity ran its course, God became a nothing for us other than our own coming to self-consciousness. The logic of this analysis is valid for the entire episode of modernity, even with the important mutations of the Cartesian "I think" into the Marxist "I work" or the Nietzschean "I will."[113] All are permutations of Fichte's self-positing Ego, versions of modernity's "sovereign self."[114]

Rather than lamenting this modern denouement in aporia, if not atheism, however, Jüngel sees in it an "opportunity": "it is possible that the thinking which decides about the existence of God could be replaced by thinking which accords with the existence of God, and such thinking could lead to a new constitution of the thought of God,"[115] even if that "new thinking" turns out to be a recovery of the old dogma about the Trinity. In tandem with this important "opportunity" that Jüngel so describes is yet another one that accompanies it: one of liberating Christian theological thought on Creator and creation from its captivity in protology, giving even the act of origin a new orientation as eschatology, so that the beginning is always and clearly the beginning of the end and the new creation is not the end of time but the advent of the time of the end — a task to which we will return below in Chapter Seven.

Finally, in consideration of the question, "Is God possible?," let us consider Pannenberg's contribution to this emerging consensus on the renewal of Trinitarianism in the tradition of theology stemming from Luther. While, to my knowledge, Pannenberg does not use the terminology of the "social" Trinity, and while he is cautious with regard to the anthropomorphism of attributing self-consciousness to the Trinitarian persons, Pannenberg in fact has offered in his *Systematic Theology* an outstanding case for the social Trinity. Acknowledging as we did above Barth's great new beginning for postmodern theology, Pannen-

---

113. Thanks to R. David Nelson for this observation (personal correspondence, 9/10/13).

114. Frederick C. Beiser, *The Fate of Reason: German Philosophy from Kant to Fichte* (Cambridge, MA: Harvard University Press, 1987). George Di Giovanni, *Freedom and Religion in Kant and His Immediate Successors: The Vocation of Humankind 1774-1800* (Cambridge: Cambridge University Press, 2008).

115. Jüngel, *God as the Mystery,* pp. 152-53.

berg sharply criticized Barth for his still-too-Western reliance on Augustine's psychological model of the Trinity as faculties at work in the self-consciousness of a single intellect. Instead, he argued that the Father, Son, and Holy Spirit appear in the Bible "as living realizations of separate centers of action,"[116] i.e., as agents "in such a way that each of the three persons relates to the others as others and distinguishes itself from them." Hence "[r]elations among the three persons that are defined as mutual self-distinction cannot be reduced to the relations of origin in the traditional sense. The Father does not merely beget the Son. He also hands over his kingdom to him and receives it back from him. The Son is not merely begotten of the Father. He is also obedient to him and he thereby glorifies him as the one God. The Spirit is not just breathed. He also fills the Son and glorifies him in his obedience to the Father, thereby glorifying the Father himself."[117] Pannenberg does not reject the distinction that comes by relation to origin, i.e., the "monarchy of the Father," but rather the way that it becomes in Barth the One Subject enacting His subjectivity by the modes of His self-objectification and self-communication. In place of this psychological model, Pannenberg finds the unity of the Three in the Johannine *perichoresis* or *circumincessio,* i.e., the "mutual indwelling" of the Three, such that agency itself is exchanged among them and Spirit and Son also act upon the Father as upon each other.[118]

This is *strong* Trinitarianism, Trinitarian *personalism,* as we might call this understanding that personal individuality is constituted in the social mutuality of the three: this Father cannot be the Father that He is apart from this Son, nor can this Son be the Son that He is apart from this Father, nor can the Father and the Son so relate to each other apart from the Spirit who binds them in love, nor can the Spirit be the Holy Spirit that He is except as the Spirit of the Father and the Son in their mutual love. In this divine life of joyful exchanges, God is God for God, and so also becomes truly God for us in creation, its redemption and fulfillment.

Possible, not necessary! The social Trinity *is* a free action of love for community, not the narcissistic egoism of the "development of an absolute subject after pattern of self-consciousness," the "logically necessary self-development of the Absolute in producing a world of the finite." So Pannenberg alludes to Hegel's heterodox account of the Trinity,[119] according to which God is driven by lack, by the need to acquire self-consciousness and thus unfolds as Trinity

---

116. Pannenberg, *ST* 1, p. 319.

117. Pannenberg, *ST* 1, p. 320.

118. Verna Harrison, "Perichoresis in the Greek Fathers," *St. Vladimir's Theological Quarterly* 35 (1991): 53-65. A notable contribution of this study is Harrison's correlation of perichoresis with the ubiquitous and immediate presence of God in *creatio continua* in strong distinction from the neo-Platonic scheme in which a mediating Logos is required to bridge the gap between transcendent Deity and the creaturely world.

119. Lewis Ayres, *Nicea and Its Legacy: An Approach to Fourth-Century Trinitarian Theology* (Oxford: Oxford University Press, 2006), pp. 384-429.

in time in humanity coming to self-consciousness. In the beginning was the undifferentiated Father, so to speak, who was not other than nothingness. Thus to acquire distinctiveness the Father estranged Himself and became finite as the Son. The finite but estranged Son at last realized His unity with all and so became the Spirit, the world achieving self-consciousness. This atheistic interpretation of the Christian Trinity in Hegel's footsteps, first argued forcefully by Alexandre Kojève,[120] is today powerfully voiced by the Marxist philosopher Slavoj Žižek: for him, the Spirit, arising from Christ's defeat at Golgotha after the realization that He was abandoned because there was no heavenly Father there to save Him, now lives on in the militant (but endlessly ironic and thus impotent)[121] revolutionary community.[122] As Cyril O'Regan has shown, this entire reading of Trinitarianism is predicated upon a Gnostic theology of divine neediness that derives in part from Jacob Boehme.[123] As Pannenberg points out, "if we think of the life of the Trinity in terms of the mutuality of the relations of the trinitarian persons, no such necessity [as Hegel imagines, for the Absolute to acquire self-consciousness] arises. For each of the persons, self-distinction from the others is a condition of their fellowship in the unity of the divine life. . . . Thus the divine life is a self-enclosed circle, which needs no other outside itself."[124] Because God is eternally the Trinity of love, God is not needy nor is God greedy. To be this God is freely to give, out of abundance, for God and so also for us. The world therefore is not God's ego-trip, the instrument by which God achieves self-consciousness, but His beloved creation on the way to redemption and fulfillment in the Beloved Community which comes as the sharing His own true and eternal life with creatures other than Himself. Thus, over against Hegel and Žižek, we see how Trinitarianism, not mere theism, is the Christian answer to the challenge of contemporary atheism. Indeed, we may dialectically affirm the atheistic critique of the theistic idol of timeless eternity as a step on the way towards the renewal of Trinitarianism.

Jenson, Jüngel, and Pannenberg are each criticizing the merely theistic idea that what makes God God is timelessness, hence changelessness or metaphysical simplicity, such that God as the necessary being eternally grounds changing beings immersed in time. God's job here is grounding. Thus any hint of change in God quite literally shifts ground and threatens the cosmos with destabilization. But disruption of the fallen creation by the free advent of grace is exactly what

120. Alexandre Kojève, *Introduction to the Reading of Hegel: Lectures on the Phenomenology of Spirit,* trans. James H. Nichols Jr. (Ithaca, NY and London: Cornell University Press, 1996).

121. Thanks to Robert Saler for this parenthetical observation.

122. Slavoj Žižek and John Milbank, *The Monstrosity of Christ: Paradox or Dialectic?* ed. Creston Davis (Cambridge, MA and London: MIT Press, 2009), p. 60. See the critique in *RPTD,* pp. 133-42.

123. Cyril O'Regan, *The Heterodox Hegel* (Albany: State University of New York Press, 1994).

124. Pannenberg, *ST* 2, pp. 28-29.

the God of the gospel does as it gives the One who breaks in Christologically to bind up the strong man and plunder his goods; who comes to seek and find Pneumatologically when we are not seeking but had gone astray. Of course, this God is also believed to be the origin and continuing creator and preserver of the created world just as the God of the gospel is believed to be "eternal" — otherwise the Incarnation and the sending of the Spirit would be notions from nowhere and any sense of salvation as the redemption and fulfillment of the creation beyond its immanent possibilities would be lacking a competent agent. The eternal Trinity as the divine way of being backs the economic Trinity as the divine way of acting to redeem and fulfill the creation from origin to eschaton. Or else, just as Hegel intimates and Žižek argues, the Trinity kenotically dissolves into the world's self-conscious coming of age. The difficulty that arises here — how God's eternity is to be conceived, if not timelessly — is one that must be tackled step by step throughout this presentation of the system of Christian belief and cannot fully be answered until the conclusion of it. But an indication may be given here.

When strictly the Trinity as subject (that is, not as fourth entity, the divine ousia, over against the Three, but also not as the Trinity taken as a collective noun, but the Father of the Son in the Spirit) governs the predicate, eternity, we see that eternity cannot be conceived by pure negation of the creature, as the abstract opposite of time, as sheer timelessness. As Trinity, there is sequence as also alterity in the eternal God: the unbegotten Father begets, the Son is begotten, and the Father of the Son breathes His Spirit on Him so that in the Spirit the Son returns this glory to the Father — and so God lives *ad infinitum*. The Trinity is this "temporally infinite" (Jenson) going out and return, a divine motion or dance *(perichoresis)*, hence time-like and space-like.[125] Just so it is the fittingly unbounded or infinite being of the Creator of a time and place for creatures. "To be God is always to be open to and always to open a future, transgressing all past-imposed conditions."[126] We learn this "revision of metaphysics" from the redemptive and fulfilling missions of the Son and Spirit because these show that the same eternal God and Father is not bound to the origin and its simple perpetuation but rather is from the beginning free to innovate in accord with His original intention and in just this way to redeem the fallen world of creatures for a fulfillment that had been forfeited. "Consider not the former things, nor consider the things of old. Behold, I am doing a new thing!" "If anyone is in Christ, behold! New creation!" "And He who sat upon the throne declared, 'Behold! I make all things new!'"

In the Bible, these novelties are the insignia of true deity (Rom. 4:17) as not bound slavishly to the past, even His own past, but as self-surpassing freedom. In them we see that the power of God includes the Father's freedom to entrust His reign to the Son and the Spirit, just as the Son's freedom had been to abandon Himself to His Father's vindication, as now the Spirit's freedom is to glorify the

---

125. Jenson, *ST* 1, pp. 214-18.
126. Jenson, *ST* 1, p. 216.

Father in the Son by making this God possible for the dying sinners that believers are and remain in solidarity with the common body from baptism day to resurrection day. Hence power is not having no further possibilities as the already perfect being who has decreed once and for all but infinitely having all possibilities on the way to the coming of the Beloved Community. Wisdom is not using any and all possibilities but only those that creatively love. Love is not realizing all one's own possibilities but surrendering to another's in the daily miracle of trust. In these ways, the Trinity is the free subject of its own divine predicates, not the slave of any one of them, so that the unity of the Trinity as the one God is a life of infinitely novel harmonization. The Trinity — once again, more like a society than an individual ego — governs its attributes and is not governed by them. The *who* determines the *what* and the *how* and is not determined by them. *What* God is — this glory of the divine being is revealed in the interaction of the three: in their *perichoresis,* dance, rhyme and rhythm, their harmony. If we think this way about what makes God God for us, it is not timeless, immutable, and essential qualities of a single, unrelated subject (or of a dynamic subject coming to self-consciousness), but rather the Father's self-determination to redeem and fulfill the creation by the missions of the Son and the Spirit. The essential harmony of power, wisdom, and love, the divine attributes appropriated respectively to the almighty Father, the Incarnate Word, and the life-breathing Spirit, will be revealed by the coming of the Reign and in just this way demonstrate the triune God's existence when God becomes all things to all people (1 Cor. 15:28).

This possibility of God exists for us now in faith. Faith is faith ultimately in God's existence taken as the coming of the Beloved Community, already now ecstatically and doxologically singing the eternal song of the victory of God for us. In this interim, as-yet-embattled faith is active in love and in hope. "But when you give a banquet, invite the poor, the crippled, the lame, and the blind. And you will be blessed because they cannot repay you, for you will be repaid in the resurrection of the righteous" (Luke 14:13-14). So the just live — really live — by their faith in such a way that everything here and now comes to depend on the existence of God who gives life to the dead and calls into being worlds that do not yet exist. God's eternity is in this way timely for us or it is not at all.

## Is Christ Necessary?

We recall now Luther's statement, directed against William Occam, that "God cannot accept man without His justifying grace." Occam had affirmed this possibility in terms of a distinction he drew between God's absolute power and God's ordered or ordained power. According to the former, God essentially is absolute freedom. God is the unbounded will who can do anything God pleases and is thus essentially inscrutable to creatures according to this libertine conception of divine "good pleasure." Even in His ordained acts, then, we cannot follow God's choices or make sense of God's decisions. God could equally have created a world in which sins are not counted, debts not accumulated, and acceptance is unconditional. To be sure, that is not the world that God has in fact created, this lawful order in which human creatures are obligated to do what is in their power and God is obligated in turn to accept those who try. Our world in fact reflects God's ordered power in this covenant of creation. But, Occam held (so Luther infers), even in this world it cannot be ruled out that the Deity, which is and remains essentially absolute and inscrutable power, can simply by a new act of will suspend existing rules and thus abrogate the divinely instituted *quid pro quo* by which He ordinarily rules the creation. So it is not only or even chiefly the tit-for-tat system of God's ordered power that Luther rejects. Indeed, Luther denies equally, if not more so, the possibility of understanding grace as an arbitrary miracle that magically suspends the instituted rules, as though grace were an act of pure power apart from divine wisdom and love. Rather, the God who is possible for us is God in Christ in whom God's justifying grace is enacted, achieves the right, and is as such delivered in temporal and spatial actions of new creativity that surpass the instituted rules to render them "old." Apart from Christ, God remains impossible for us, not only de facto as enforcer of a *quid pro quo* that crushes those helplessly in bondage to structures of malice and injustice, but also by the way Occam imagines grace. In sheer and arbitrary grace, God appears as an abyss of absolute power and apparent caprice, though in reality this speculation of our terror is an idol, a manipulative and brutal construction of the *deus absconditus.*

Occam, of course, had intended his speculation optimistically, on the assumption that the absolutely free God would and could be presumed to be gracious. Luther, however, does not find this optimistic assumption warranted; indeed he finds it to be presumptuous, given the malice and injustice that prevail over creation and make ruin of it. In pride, as we learned from Jenson in the previous section, the gap between God as such and God in His self-revelation becomes the blank screen on which we project our own fantasies for domination. Or, in despair this gap between the free God and His self-binding Word to us becomes an abyss of uncertainty for the troubled in conscience, that is, for those who "grieve over the ruin of Joseph" (Amos 6:6). As Luther later put it in his polemic against Erasmus, "God hidden in Majesty [is God] who neither deplores nor takes away death, but works life, and death, and all in all. . . ."[127] Occam's purely voluntaristic deity thus survives in Luther's *deus absconditus:* a kind of nightmare hovering in the background of faith in the *deus revelatus.*

Whatever we make of Luther's "God hidden in majesty," the grace of justification is not in any case for Luther an act of raw power, or a whim of divine good pleasure, magically disappearing sins into thin air by the wave of a wand. To be sure, the grace of justification is an act of divine power, but also of divine wisdom and love, never one of these without the others. At this early stage of his

127. Luther, *Bondage,* p. 170.

theological career, Luther is primarily thinking with Augustine that the grace of justification is the new birth given by the Spirit that empowers in us true love of God for God's sake, hence a real if inchoate rectification of the sinner, who has come in true, Spirit-given *ex corde* contrition to justify God in His judgment on sin. In this way, the humbled sinner actually fulfills the law, like the Publican in Jesus' parable (Luke 18:13-14), by assenting to its condemnation of sin and of the sinner as sin's agent, thus satisfying its demand for truth. Thus by this humility the sinner becomes justified before God, who mercifully demands only truth in order to be truthfully merciful. Later Luther will come to a fuller realization and integration of something he also already holds: that it is Christ who brings the justice of justification in person by a "joyful exchange": "Christ bears all sins, if only they displease us," as he wrote in the early *Commentary on Romans* from the same period, "then they are no longer our sins but his, and his righteousness is ours in turn."[128]

Here grace comes on the scene as the truthful expression of the Father's good-pleasure, the *favor Dei,* resting on Christ the beloved Son who goes on to give His *precious* life as a ransom for many. Hence it rests also on those who now at the same Spirit's initiative and invitation rest by faith in this incarnate and obedient person in His deed of love, giving to Him their sin, taking in turn His justice, and giving all the glory to the Father's boundless mercy. In the joyful exchange we see the Three at work in the divine harmony of power, wisdom, and love in a narrative that theology can follow and understand. Thus it is in this costly way of the Incarnation, to the Cross and the Resurrection, and by the Spirit's folly of preaching of it in which this person of Christ and His work recurs "for me," that God the Father of the Son and breather of the Spirit provides the justifying grace that is needed in the Lamb who takes away the sin of the world. In this way, God both creates the believer who justifies God in His judgment and justifies this believing sinner who now newly exists in a life of repentance, entrusting herself to the Christ present in faith for the future of God's reign.

*Christ's role is essential here.* Christ mediates the joyful exchange between the reconciling God and reconciled sinner, which mediation does not exist apart from Christ. The law's condemnation is canceled not by authoritarian or capricious *obiter dicta* from beyond, but by being fulfilled on the earth by Christ for us and then by Christ in us, even as this transaction happens now, as an event in time, to and with human persons, on the earth. Here Christ is not the mere occasion or instrument of a justice other than Himself, that takes place in heaven rather than on the earth, but He Himself is the justice achieved in His life of faith, faithfulness, righteousness. This is a justice from God that interposes as the self-donation of the one obedient man who loved God above all by loving sinners as Himself. In this account, this Christ, the One "crucified for our sins," is *necessary.*

128. *Luther: Lecture on Romans,* trans. Wilhelm Pauck (Philadelphia: Westminster, 1961), p. 121.

It is certainly another odd question, Is Christ necessary? If there are two commonplaces in Protestant preaching in Euro-America today they would be the ideas stemming from Occam that God can do whatever God wants and we cannot box Him, Her, or It with our dogmatic ideas; but thankfully Christ as a paradigmatic figure of *us* helps *us* to accomplish *our* own *self*-realization projects. To ask disruptively whether Christ is *necessary,* however, is to throw a monkey wrench into the gearbox of the religion-as-usual business, that, by the cunning device of the asserting the unknowability and unfollowability of God by nature, removes the self-giving and self-communicating God from consideration and divests conscience of its true audience. Indeed, the necessity of Christ poses a question that reframes Christian theology entirely, away from the religious search for the unknown God as the ultimate form of narcissistic self-realization to the prophetic indictment of the religion business, in collusion with political sovereignty, for the buying and selling of God for purposes of imperial domination with its manufactured distractions in bread and circuses.

I gratefully acknowledge my debt for this disruptive question to my seminary professor, the sainted Robert Bertram, who discovered this line of argument in Melanchthon's masterpiece, the *Apology of the Augsburg Confession.* Let us trace out the case. Melanchthon charged that his opponents in the papal party confuse civil and philosophical justice with divine and theological justice, that is to say, under the term "sin," they see only the visible crimes that transgress civil order, unlike the God of the Bible who searches and judges the heart. Hence as we heard in the previous section, these "modernists" in theology imagine a free human being who without the Holy Spirit can elicit, at least in principle, an act of love for God above all things — naturally enough, a reasonable expectation if and when people realize that, if there is a perfect being, it would be their highest good somehow to affiliate with It. But this line of thought is a flight of fancy, untutored by the Holy Spirit's Holy Scriptures, from which we learn that we are "truly to fear God, truly to love God, truly to call upon God, truly to be convinced that he hears us, and to expect help from God in death and in all afflictions . . . so that we do not flee or avoid these things when God imposes them."[129] That is to say, we are to live truly as creatures on the earth and not in religion fly away from the becoming of creation but rather to learn trust of God in its slings and arrows. Ignoring this demand of God here and now for all our fear, love, and trust even amid sufferings and the cross as the true justice and good will required of creatures before Him, Melanchthon's opponents are said to have invented all sorts of religious exercises and devotions as aids in the project of "religious" self-realization, "good works" so-called, that demonstrate that the pilgrim is doing her part by doing what is in her power to ascend beyond this veil of tears.

Melanchthon regards all of this religion business as both swindle and distraction from the truly good works of faith operative in love and hope here on

---

129. *BC,* p. 121.

the earth where neighbors need love's solidarity amid sufferings and the cross. "Many great and destructive errors," he writes, "lurk behind this opinion." But, he continues, "let the discerning reader consider only this: if this is Christian righteousness, what is the difference between philosophy and the teaching of Christ? If we merit the forgiveness of sins by these elicited acts of ours, what does Christ provide? If we can be justified through reason and the works of reason, why do we need Christ or regeneration?"[130] Indeed, just why is Christ necessary? And why is it wrong as a result "to bury Christ" — that is, to put the risen and present One whom truly we need back into the tomb — "so that people do not use him as a mediator and on account of him believe that they freely receive the forgiveness of sins and reconciliation"?[131]

From such passages, Bertram taught us that the task of theologically informed preaching is so to execute the prophetic critique of religiosity that we realize our need of a Messiah, so deeply indeed that we perceive our need of the crucified Messiah, as the Apostle Paul had first reasoned: "If justification were through works of the law, then Christ died to no purpose" (Gal. 2:21). But instead, "Christ died for our sins and was raised for our justification" (Rom. 4:25). If we take this reframing of our thinking by the gospel as giving the very possibility of God for us, then theology itself becomes in central part the discipline of necessitating Christ. From the foregoing, then, we derive a thesis: Christ the Crucified is made necessary when the prophetic critique of this world in the name of God is so penetrating — striking with the Baptist's ax to the root (Luke 3:9)! — that nothing less than Messiah's cross can accomplish genuine reconciliation with Luther's "real, not fictitious sinners." In this way the relation between possibility and necessity in philosophy is inverted in theology. The God who is "more than necessary" necessitates Christ the Crucified truthfully to make Himself possible for us as truly we are, not as we fancy ourselves: victims and perpetrators of structures of malice and injustice. Before moving to a demonstration of this thesis, let us amplify it a bit further with some further thoughts from Luther and then from a series of more contemporary thinkers, beginning with Bonhoeffer.

As noted, Luther emphatically rejected the possibility entertained from within the thought-world of the medieval modernists that the omnipotent God can simply set aside the instituted order, namely, this creation He is creating and preserving in order to redeem and fulfill. The reason for this rejection historically speaking is that Luther's contemporaneous reading of Augustine on God's trinity of power, wisdom, and love is step by step overcoming the virtually unitarian voluntarism in which he had been trained at Erfurt under the *via moderna*. Or to cash in this historical point theologically: Luther is realizing that the divine self-determination to redeem and fulfill this creation is integral to God's very being since God is the triune God, the One who can pledge and has pledged His very

---

130. *BC,* p. 122.
131. *BC,* p. 123.

deity (Gen. 15:7-21)[132] on the accomplishment of this purpose — and fittingly so. It could have been otherwise. But it cannot now be otherwise on account of God's faithfulness to His own work. As Luther later put it in the Large Catechism in the words cited at the outset of this book, "For this very purpose He has created us, so that he might redeem us and make us holy."[133] The purpose clause is essential. It remains in force in spite of the defection from God's purpose in Adam. Now, to be sure, God does an *opus alienum* (alien work) against Adam in the Law *ut faciat opus proprium* (in order to do a proper work).[134] Luther thus rejects any magical suspension of the rules of the game; accepting the sinner without justifying grace would involve God in a fatal contradiction to His own intention in creating the world, given the purpose to which God has pledged His deity. Involving God in a true contradiction — having God affirm and deny the same thing in the same sense under the same conditions — would entail divine self-destruction. Then God would be impossible not only for us but also for God. God would be against God and no longer be God. Hence the contradiction between judgment on sin and redemption of the sinner who is an agent of sin requires innovation on the part of God, a self-surpassing engagement that creates a *Novum*.

God cannot then simply and freely forgive sins. Sin is what God righteously hates, what truly opposes God in his decision from eternity to realize beloved community with us in time and space; sin is what ruins God's work and creation; it is therefore what God condemns and what must be judged once and for all and forever if creation is to be redeemed and fulfilled in God's eternal life. Without justifying grace that makes the sinner just, God cannot — and should not — accept the hatred, the rebellion, the pride and despair, the greed and the envy that ruin the sinful person whose desire is captured by malice for service in structures of injustice. A God who would not say No! to this ruin would be our idol, not true God. Therefore God's true and truthful Yes! to the sinner cannot simply bypass or ignore this No! of love and justice arising against what is against love and to judge that which is against justice. There can be no reconciliation without truth; no forgiveness without atonement; no gift free to us without cost to God; no restoration of fellowship without the deed that repairs. The genuine miracle of the Christ event is the news that is good; that we do not already know; that we must ever learn again and again in wonder and praise: God provided the Lamb (Genesis 22). God undertook our true need and made it His own in a human life of love that surpasses the condemnation of God's own just judgment on our slavery to malice and service of injustice. In Christ, this divine self-surpassing

132. Otto Kaiser, "Traditionsgeschichtliche Untersuchung von Genesis 15," *Zeitschrift für die alttestamentliche Wissenschaft* 70 (1958): 107-26.

133. *BC,* p. 439.

134. On this purpose clause, see Paul R. Hinlicky, "Law, Gospel and Beloved Community," in *Preaching and Teaching the Law and the Gospel of God,* ed. Carl E. Braaten (Delhi, NY: ALPB Books, 2013), pp. 91-113.

comes not by power alone but by right, by right of fulfilling the holy demand for love precisely on behalf of those unworthy of love.[135]

Rather than retrace further Luther's teaching here — a teaching that we will encounter throughout the following, but especially below in Chapters Six and Seven — let us next add to this mediation of the necessity of Christ the Crucified, the voice of another notable, latter-day Lutheran theologian, Dietrich Bonhoeffer. What necessitates Christ is our true (not perceived) need of a new humanity. What "sheds the clearest light on the fundamental difference between Adam and Christ," the young Bonhoeffer wrote in his dissertation, *Sanctorum Communio,* is Jesus' "function of vicarious representative."[136] "God does not 'overlook' sin; that would mean not taking human beings seriously as personal beings in their very culpability; and that would mean no re-creation of the person, and therefore no re-creation of the community." The penal suffering of the representative Christ is therefore the ultimate act of divine sharing, *koinonia, communio.* So, "though innocent, Jesus takes the sin of others upon himself" and "in the death of Jesus on the cross God's judgment and wrath are carried out on all the self-centeredness of humanity. . . . Because he was made sin for us, and because he was accursed by the law for us, Jesus died in solitude." This representative work for us of Jesus alone is Jesus' alone. By it God accepts the sinner by provision of His own justifying grace. Consequently in obedient faith to Christ's gracious command, "I take your sin, I give you my righteousness," we ought to share in turn; as Bonhoeffer continues, "we ought to let our sin be taken from us, for we are not able to carry it by ourselves; we ought not reject this gift of God." Just this passive obedience of faith brought about by Christ's proffered robbery of our sins, as it were; just this trusting and obedient surrender to this divine Robber enacts "the reality of the divine love for the church community" by which it is called out from the world of mendacity and united in the shared gift of Christ's own, to us alien, righteousness.

135. Thomas F. Torrance, *Incarnation: The Person and Life of Christ,* ed. R. T. Walker (Downers Grove, IL: InterVarsity, 2008), and *Atonement: The Person and Work of Christ,* ed. R. T. Walker (Downers Grove, IL: InterVarsity, 2009). In *LBC,* I explained in detail how Luther thinks of the atonement as the Christological work that backs up the sinner's justification by faith, on account of which *(propter Christum)* sinners can *rightfully* believe in their forgiveness as also their rebirth as graciously adopted sons and daughters of God. I won't repeat that argument here, except to note that Luther shares with Anselm the conviction that Christ's sacrifice is *necessitated* by the debt of sin that we owe but cannot ourselves repay, even though he differs rather dramatically from Anselm in thinking of Christ, not as having gained by His active obedience a treasury of surplus merit from which the sinner may draw to pay down his debt of guilt, but rather of Christ by His passive obedience as He who bears away the sin of the world, in whom Adam dies in order that in Christ a new humanity may arise.

136. Dietrich Bonhoeffer, *Sanctorum Communio: A Theological Study of the Sociology of the Church,* Dietrich Bonhoeffer Works I, trans. Reinhard Kraus and Nancy Lukens, ed. Joachim von Sooten and Clifford J. Green (Minneapolis: Fortress, 1998), p. 145. All citations from Bonhoeffer to the end of this chapter are drawn from chapter 5, pp. 122-57.

The church of forgiven sinners lives in this obedient separation from the world that is dying only because it holds on to its sins and does not yield them to Christ but rather suppresses the truth. The church of forgiven sinners lives together in sharing, in turn: not by bearing one another's sins, the work of Christ alone that first and ever binds one and all together, but by sharing one another's burdens. Just this new field of force in the world, this community of joyful exchanges in Christ, is harbinger of the new humanity that truly is needed, if the promise of creation is to be redeemed and fulfilled. Faith and beloved community thus go together. So Bonhoeffer: "Faith is based on entry into the church-community, just as entry into the church-community is based on faith."

In the proclamation of the gospel the Holy Spirit makes the crucified Christ present to us as the Risen One who comes to rob us of our sins so that we may surrender to this divine Thief by the faith that reckons this thievery as God's own new and stunning deed of justice, giving precisely what is not deserved. This, according to Bonhoeffer, is how Christ is necessitated, as giving what is needed in truth but in truth not deserved. In the New Adam we discover our true need by coming to see ourselves as that old Adam who wanted to be like God and did not want God to be God. The rupture of the bubble of perceived needs in Adam by the revelation of our true need at the Messiah's cross — that is how, according to Bonhoeffer, Christ the Crucified is necessitated as the Thief who breaks into the strong man's house to bind him and plunder his goods. To necessitate Christ is prophetically to burst the bubble of apparent needs to uncover true neediness before the God whose will for one and all is and remains to all eternity the Beloved Community. It is of *this* that we fall short.

From Bonhoeffer's contribution to our theme we now turn to the contemporary Methodist theologian, Daniel Bell. A student of Stanley Hauerwas, Bell has, with the help of the philosophy of Gilles Deleuze, described the bubble of perceived needs in the contemporary manipulation and capture of human desire in Adam that is Euro-America. He does this in his account of "savage" capitalism in his *Liberation Theology after the End of History: The Refusal to Cease Suffering*.[137] Capitalism is not, for Bell, primarily an economic system; it is an ontology of the constitutive human power, which, following Deleuze, Bell regards as originally innocent, productive desire.[138] As an ontology, however, capitalism "captures" desire for the market in the form of consumerism and "disciplines" it to conform to the imperatives of increased efficiency for the sake of maximal wealth extraction. This sounds like a version of the Marxist surplus theory of labor value. Indeed, it bears a family resemblance to it. But Bell draws far more on Deleuze and Foucault than on Marx and Engels. He follows their rigorously

---

137. Daniel M. Bell Jr., *Liberation Theology after the End of History: The Refusal to Cease Suffering* (London and New York: Routledge, 2001). An earlier version of this analysis of Bell appeared in the online *Journal of Lutheran Ethics* 10, no. 10 (October 2010).

138. Bell, *Liberation Theology*, pp. 9, 13, et passim.

non-teleological, anti-Hegelian account of capitalism. This "savage" capitalism (Hinkelammert) is the now aimless but dominant juggernaut of mindless production and consumption, "savage" in that it relentlessly works the commoditizing of all things.[139] Nothing is sacred; everything has a price; greed replaces charity as the categorical imperative of our age. In the process the masses reduced to *Lumpenproletariat* become so much excess, garbage really, fit only to be discarded. They are the banned, *Lebens unwertes Lebens* (life not worthy of living). Such capitalism is not, as Marx imagined, dialectically creating the industrial and technological presuppositions of socialism through the conquest of nature by science; benevolent socialism will not emerge from this gathering storm right on schedule when the contradictions of capitalism become unsustainable and implode, giving revolutionary birth to a new order of the ages. Least of all will this happy end state emerge by peaceful evolution, as "progressives" who still believe in Progress assume. Rather, as an ontology, *victorious capitalism*[140] is something far more sinister: it is the "undulating snake," an overwhelming seduction to evil only to be resisted with no worldly guarantee of success.

Every attempt to co-opt capitalism fails — Marxism-Leninism being the prime example. Savage capitalism captures all: the nation-state and civil society[141] cannot control the market but are turned into its instruments. The pathetic contemporary church becomes its chaplaincy,[142] lending succor to the battered selves who live by selling themselves day in and day out. Hence politics as statecraft, community organizing, church ministry to the neighborhood, even proclamation are all hopelessly compromised as unwitting agents of the "undulating snake."

The only hope to be found in this bleak Deleuzian picture is that underneath the ontology that has so captivated desire, desire itself remains innocent:[143] anarchic, revolutionary, generative.[144] Following John Milbank, Bell assimilates this Deleuzian doctrine of primal, innocent desire to de Lubac's doctrine of "graced nature,"[145] Augustine's restless heart hungering for God, righteousness, and life. Captivated desire can thus in principle be liberated and redirected to God as its true object. This theological move permits Bell the worry, as well it might, that Deleuze's post-Marxist (i.e., non-teleological) account of purely savage capitalism leads only to "madness beyond madness," which cannot fund any real resistance. He asks whether "madness intensified," as Deleuze seems to commend, "finally collapse[s] back into the black hole of nihilism, where life becomes death and an absolute violence is unleashed."[146] The theologian thus asks the philosopher, "Is

139. Bell, *Liberation Theology*, p. 31.
140. Bell, *Liberation Theology*, p. 10.
141. Bell, *Liberation Theology*, pp. 70, 74.
142. Bell, *Liberation Theology*, p. 98.
143. Bell, *Liberation Theology*, p. 151.
144. Bell, *Liberation Theology*, p. 33.
145. Bell, *Liberation Theology*, p. 58.
146. Bell, *Liberation Theology*, p. 33.

there a path beyond madness to health . . . ? a therapy that will heal desire of the distortions and deformities inflicted by capitalist discipline?"[147]

To this acute and timely question, Bell proposes the "bold" answer that "Jesus Christ, and the body of Christ that is the church of the poor, is about the work of liberating desire from the clutches of capitalism."[148] This is theology: "forgiveness as a means of resistance to capitalism remains a claim about who God is and the way God in Christ is working in the world to overcome sin."[149] This admirable theological assertion signals the reformist claim of Radical Orthodox ecclesiology, specifically: "if it is to fund resistance to capitalism, Christianity must shed its (modern) identity as an apolitical custodian of abstract values and preferential options and assume its proper place in the temporal realm as the true politics, the exemplary form of human community."[150] How can the church return to its true life as harbinger of the Beloved Community in the flow of time? Not easily. The church is paralyzed by the modern metaphysics of divine voluntarism into which it has unwittingly bought, together with the putative objectivity and comprehensiveness of science and the correspondingly exaggerated claims for the human subject. Theology has to help the church think itself out of this debilitating entanglement in order to learn again how to resist the master that presently it serves.

Again, following Milbank's case against modern metaphysics of divine voluntarism that encode violence ontologically, the alternative Bell offers is the Christian-Thomist-DeLubacan vision of desire as the naturally graced thirst for the supernatural. This latter, provided it can be redeemed from capitalist captivity, can "fund" real resistance to capitalism,[151] since it provides the true therapy for disordered desire in the paradoxical refusal to cease suffering. This refusal of authentic resistance bears the cross of forgiveness of offenders, "redirecting desire toward its true end: the shared love that is friendship in God"[152] — the coming of the Beloved Community.

With a little bit of translation, we may discern just how profoundly Bell has led us into the communitarian worldview of medieval Catholicism. Capitalism, shorn of Marxist teleology, is exposed as just old-fashioned greed, now elevated to a motive power and de facto virtue; capitalism is systematized *concupiscentia*, disordered desire which takes the place of the love for God as one's *summum bonum*. "Capitalism" here, let it again be stressed, is not capitalism in the Marxist sense, but rather names modernity's complex of individualism, materialism, atheism, and secularism. The therapy of such disordered desire is equally old-fashioned

147. Bell, *Liberation Theology*, p. 35.
148. Bell, *Liberation Theology*, p. 35.
149. Bell, *Liberation Theology*, p. 162.
150. Bell, *Liberation Theology*, p. 144.
151. Bell, *Liberation Theology*, p. 161.
152. Bell, *Liberation Theology*, p. 171.

confession and penance: "deconstruction of desire in its agonistic, proprietary (capitalist) modality that occurs in confession and repentance is accompanied by the construction of new, participatory relations in penance."[153] Finally, there is a similarly medieval summons to a new asceticism: ". . . penance will undoubtedly entail the redistribution of goods. Indeed, the liberationists stress that entering into solidarity with the poor entails voluntary poverty, the loving renunciation of privilege and assumption of the condition of the poor for the sake of struggling against it."[154]

This turn to the medieval model provides Bell with a penetrating, though somewhat ironic theological critique of Latin American Liberation Theology, namely, that it remains too entangled in modernist assumptions about justice and rights and so blinded to its own Catholic tradition's better insights. The liberationist's "vision is insufficiently radical . . . remain[ing] circumscribed by the very capitalist order they hope to overcome. . . ."[155] How is that? "Rights" are a capitalist invention, a cunning stratagem that eviscerates the needed forms of social solidarity in the struggle to resist with atomizing individualism.[156] Liberationists argue for social justice as equal rights, and unwittingly assume with liberalism that the sum of justice is the individualistic *suum cuique* (to each her due). But this is to overlook the crucial fact that "without shared love, the general virtue of justice has no end and hence is defunct";[157] it reduces to endless procedural wrangling, the chaos of democratic parliamentarianism. Under these conditions, capitalism always wins by reducing all substantive questions of the common good to procedural justice. It always reduces the universal struggle for the common good in a just order to the desire of partial communities for a bigger piece of the pie as their "right" and "due."

The deeper, theological problem behind this debilitating entanglement with the enemy lies in the "liberationists' understanding of the Church" as an abstract repository of value and hence its corresponding "misplaced" hope in politics as statecraft to force redistribution of goods. Bell argues instead for recovery of the Church as public in its own right,[158] constituted by the message and practices of forgiveness.[159] Poignantly, he concludes acknowledging the "risk of forgiveness" as an act of faith, not sight,[160] a risk which he elucidates with the powerful idea that forgiveness is a "refusal to cease suffering," i.e., not to be bought off with the palliative of "rights" and "development," but rather to bear Christ's witness to those whose greed harms, seeking their reconciliation, not just a piece of their

153. Bell, *Liberation Theology*, p. 182.
154. Bell, *Liberation Theology*, p. 183.
155. Bell, *Liberation Theology*, p. 42.
156. Bell, *Liberation Theology*, p. 126.
157. Bell, *Liberation Theology*, p. 110.
158. Bell, *Liberation Theology*, p. 72.
159. Bell, *Liberation Theology*, pp. 85-86.
160. Bell, *Liberation Theology*, p. 189.

goods. This bearing of the offender's sin "liberates desire from capitalism not simply by opposing its destructive force with an equally destructive force but rather by meeting it with a refusal, a refusal to cease suffering by shifting suffering onto others by embracing the terror of [retributive] justice."[161] This practice of Christ in the "church of the poor" is "costly," an "act of hope," a "wager on God," namely, that "God is who the Gospel proclaims God to be."[162] It constitutes a defenseless "witness" in the train of the martyrs of old.

Though Bell might likely bridle at the comparison, his concluding meditation is not unlike the young Reinhold Niebuhr's thought about the "sublime madness of the soul" required of the "agents of redemption"[163] when Niebuhr too, though benefiting from Marxist insights into "capitalism," abandoned Marxist teleology. Like Niebuhr's work in his own day, Bell has issued a profound restatement of the Christian doctrine of the sinfulness of a fallen creation that does the work of *necessitating* Christ the Crucified. It is especially delicious if nominally Lutheran theologians today would have to learn about this again from a Methodist! There are some "existentialist" and "antinomian" versions of the "Lutheran" doctrine of justification current today that make deliverance from "the law" — not in a movement beyond God's holy judgment on sin, but merely as release from the legalism of the religion business — more central to the gospel narrative than salvation from sin, both from its guilt and from its power. We do not need Christ, however, to be liberated from fundamentalism and legalism; "the" Enlightenment does that divine work well enough without any Christian theological help. What we need Christ and Him crucified for is liberation *from ourselves* in our own *willing bondage* as perpetrators and victims of structures of *malice and injustice*.

We conclude this section on the necessity of Christ by turning to a converging line of thought from another, surprising contemporary source, the post-Marxist Italian philosopher, Giorgio Agamben. His work is best among the contemporary philosophers who are rediscovering the Apostle Paul's line of thought: "If justification were by works, then Christ died to no purpose."[164] The stunning thing is how Agamben discovers this relevance of Paul after the collapse and failure of Marxism as a viable human future, leaving us, as Bell has so acutely diagnosed, helpless and paralyzed before the juggernaut of savage capitalism. The hope of liberal democracy is founded on the state as the only institution capable of keeping the market in the marketplace against a relentless and totalizing desire to expand and take over all of life. But the probing question that today necessitates Christ is whether this desperate hope in the liberal democratic state is well grounded.

Agamben traces political sovereignty back to the ancient practice of the ban

161. Bell, *Liberation Theology*, p. 190.

162. Bell, *Liberation Theology*, pp. 190-93.

163. Reinhold Niebuhr, *Moral Man and Immoral Society: A Study in Ethics and Politics* (New York: Charles Scribner's Sons, 1960), p. 277.

164. Agamben, *The Time That Remains*.

as the constituting power by which a polity is formed through mechanisms of inclusion and exclusion. The "exception" that institutes polity is the originating act of sovereignty. It is not called exceptional just because it is the power to decide who is excepted from civil membership by being placed beyond the ontological and legal boundaries of the state. It is called the state of exception because precisely in making this determination, constituting sovereignty itself also and continually steps outside the rule of law. A double exclusion occurs in the ban, which renders the law inoperative on either side. The sovereign is above the law in determining to whom the law applies; the banned are placed outside the law by the sovereign's lawless determination of boundaries. The banned are in this way stripped of all vestiges of pre-political social relations that make for more than bare life, like the man on the road left to die by the bandits in Jesus' parable (Luke 10:29-37). They are bereft of neighbors. They cease to be comrade, friend, sister, brother, boss, colleague, barbarian, or Greek and are reduced to biological existence as such, to *Lebens unwertes Lebens.* These slogans from the Nazi eugenics regime give the sense of Agamben's odd term "bare life," *blosses Lebens,* taken over from Walter Benjamin. It is a concept by which one determines that those who do not count as neighbors to whom love is owed, as equally precious and good creatures of the same Creator, are rather a common body that can as such be commoditized and so disposed of.

"This is the structure of the ban that we shall try to understand here, so that we can eventually call it into question."[165] We need not delve into Agamben's erudite genealogical investigations. His point in any case is properly philosophical: to demythologize the "Hobbesian mythologeme of the state of nature," not as a "real epoch chronologically prior to the foundation of the City but a principle internal to the City. . . ."[166] The political state, in other words, is always also this "state of exception," the sovereign above the law who determines who is outside of the law. If that is so, Hobbes's "state of nature" is not so much a literal *bellum omnes contra omnem* in a prehistorical state of nature from which the social contract with the election of a sovereign rescued once upon a time. Theologians in any event should be expected to recognize in Hobbes's famous thought-experiment a pointed reversal of the biblical saga of origins in Genesis 2–11: a "fall" from the community of paradise into the society of coercion and retributive justice (Gen. 9:2).

But Agamben shows how Hobbes's state of nature is a continuing "condition in which everyone is bare life . . . for everyone else." The constituting of sovereignty does not come about by "the subjects' free renunciation of their natural right but in the sovereign's preservation of his natural right to do anything to anyone. . . ."[167] Thus the exceptional suspension of rights in a state of emergency is always latent in the City as the very presupposition of the order of rights instituted

165. Agamben, *Homo Sacer,* p. 29.
166. Agamben, *Homo Sacer,* p. 105.
167. Agamben, *Homo Sacer,* p. 106.

by the drawing of legal and ontological jurisdictions — which must be defended, precisely, in the ever-threatening circumstances of an emergency. The sovereign retains his own exceptional right to do anything to others as needed in order to perpetuate the instituted order. Thus "sovereign violence is in truth founded not on a pact but on the exclusive inclusion of bare life in the state."[168] Thus the "first foundation of political life is a life that may be killed, which is politicized through its very capacity to be killed."[169] The power of the State is the sword and its jurisdiction is the human body. (The only thing truly shocking, in this light, is the naïveté embedded in our liberal outrage at the Obama Administration's spying operations, kill lists, and predator drone campaign, not to mention Bush-Cheney renditions and waterboarding).[170]

The principle of the rule of law, "which today seems inseparable from our conception of democracy and the legal State, does not at all eliminate the paradox of sovereignty."[171] Any state, qua constituted order, is always also this monopoly on the means of coercion that enables and executes the self-exception of sovereignty to constituted law and rights. What is deeply troubling about Agamben's analysis, we may now see, is that it opens up an ontological zone of indiscernibility between modern democracy and equally modern fascism (or Leninism) notwithstanding the important ontic differences between them.[172] *Habeas corpus* — you have bare life, mere body. This legal rule of modern democracy is "its strength and, at the same time, its inner contradiction . . ." since "[c]orpus is a two-faced being, the bearer both of subjection to sovereign power and of individual liberties."[173]

As conceptually reduced to mere physical existence, to the bare life of mere bodies, persons are *equalized* and thus entitled to the *same* rights. At the same time this egalitarian reduction to base rights on the naked equality of bodily life in turn compels state and "law to assume the care of this body" as a matter of securing rights. The state enables and secures the basic necessities of bodily life

168. Agamben, *Homo Sacer*, p. 107.

169. Agamben, *Homo Sacer*, p. 89.

170. So former president Jimmy Carter, "A Cruel and Unusual Record," *New York Times,* June 25, 2012. "Revelations that top officials are targeting people to be assassinated abroad, including American citizens, are only the most recent, disturbing proof of how far our nation's violation of human rights has extended. . . . Recent legislation has made legal the president's right to detain a person indefinitely on suspicion of affiliation with terrorist organizations or 'associated forces,' a broad, vague power that can be abused without meaningful oversight from the courts or Congress. . . . Despite an arbitrary rule that any man killed by drones is declared an enemy terrorist, the death of nearby innocent women and children is accepted as inevitable. . . . We don't know how many hundreds of innocent civilians have been killed in these attacks, each one approved by the highest authorities in Washington. This would have been unthinkable in previous times."

171. Agamben, *Homo Sacer*, p. 30.

172. See *BA*, pp. 183-87.

173. Agamben, *Homo Sacer*, p. 125.

within its constituted order. Just this exposes the inner contradiction of modern liberal democracy: the mere body that is presupposed as the bearer of rights cannot in fact care for itself without the protection of the sovereign to which it must then submit for the sake of security along with acceptance of the sovereign's self-justifying exception to the rule of law. Consequently, in "biopolitical" modern democracy, "the physician and the sovereign seem to exchange roles."[174] Just as politicians can now appear as healers, so also physicians can now occupy the sovereign place of exception in determining who belongs and who will be the banned, the triage involved in determining *Lebens unwertes Lebens.* The gruesome icon of this is the SS medical doctors making their "selections" as disoriented Jews and others disembarked the train wagons upon arrival at state-of-the-art, dual-function death and slave-labor machines. Nor can this underlying medicalizing of politics — also under modern democracy — call a halt. It rather relentlessly expands with the creeping emergency created by the ecologically unsustainable and morally inferiorizing project of modern self-transcendence, hand in glove, with savage capitalism. "The life that, with the declarations of rights, became the ground of sovereignty now becomes the subject-object of state politics (which therefore appears more and more in the form of 'police') . . . its own principal vocation as the formation and care of the 'body of the people.' "[175] Modern democracies thus enter into "a lasting crisis and the State decides to assume directly the care of the nation's biological life as one of its proper tasks."

Thus, the presupposition of Nazi racial politics in modern biopolitics is shared by the democracies. "In modern biopolitics, sovereign is he who decides on the value or the nonvalue of life as such. . . . The Führer represents precisely life itself insofar as it is he who decides on life's very biopolitical consistency."[176] In terms of this shared modernity, Agamben writes provocatively that there "is no reason to doubt that the "humanitarian" considerations that led Hitler and Himmler to elaborate a euthanasia program immediately after their rise to power were in good faith. . . ."[177] Indeed, the Nazi "laws concerning the Jews can only be fully understood if they are brought back to the general context of National Socialism's legislation and biopolitical praxis."[178] *Mutatis mutandis,* in "the fight against the external and internal enemies of the State, and . . . the care and growth of the citizen's life, National Socialist biopolitics — and along with it, a good part of modern politics outside of the Third Reich — cannot be grasped" — that is, apart from the fusion of policy and policing required by the sovereign state of exception also in its democratic sublimations.[179] If the democ-

174. Agamben, *Homo Sacer,* p. 143.
175. Agamben, *Homo Sacer,* p. 148.
176. Agamben, *Homo Sacer,* p. 142.
177. Agamben, *Homo Sacer,* p. 140.
178. Agamben, *Homo Sacer,* p. 149.
179. Agamben, *Homo Sacer,* p. 147.

racies differentiate from fascism, it is only because and to the extent that they still ask and permit answering the question "Who is my neighbor?" differently. Or perhaps better, fascism answered this question with greater exclusiveness, clarity, resolve, and ruthlessness, given the progressive displacement by biopolitics of competing notions of sovereignty and membership that in the Western tradition descend from Paul, the Apostle of Jesus Christ. Not least of Hobbes's contributions to the constitution of modern political sovereignty was his banning of Pauline competition.[180]

If these analyses of Bell and Agamben have salience, we do not *need* Christ to keep this juggernaut rolling, as chaplains of the state of exception (ambulance chasers, really, with our churches as the funeral societies it needs and at the same time despises). We rather need Christ, in Bonhoeffer's famous expression, to jam a stick into the spokes of the wheel.

Thus, Agamben's purpose in turning to Paul is to restore the Letter to the Romans "to the status of the fundamental messianic text for Western tradition."[181] It is fundamental, because of Agamben's discovery of a *positive dialectic* in Paul,[182] which we may recognize as the Reformation's dialectic of law and gospel. "Paul is able to set the *nomos pisteos,* the law of faith, against the *nomos ton ergon,* the law of works. Rather than being an antinomy that involves two unrelated and completely heterogeneous principles, here the opposition lies within the *nomos* itself, between its normative and promissive elements. There is something in the law that constitutively exceeds the norm and is irreducible to it, and it is this excess and inner dialectic that Paul refers to by means of the binomial *epangelia/ nomos. . . .*"[183] When we recall that the Decalogue is founded on the promise of the Exodus God's faithfulness, its claims and prohibitions are therewith relativized and ordered to the sustenance of the community of liberated Israel. When, however, the commandments become universalized (say, as "the law of works," as "natural law," or as "categorical imperative," i.e., when the second table is decoupled from the first and its prologue, Agamben's "promissive" element in the unilateral and unconditional divine indicative, "I am the LORD your God"), it becomes a deceiver that blinds us to our deep entanglements as perpetrators in structures of malice and injustice; or, if we are victims, those "normed," the "bare life" included as excluded, the commandments become tyrants that only accuse and reveal the incapacity to live and work as freed people. It is this latter law of

180. On Hobbes's banning of Pauline-Augustinian-Lutheran "enthusiasm," see Paul R. Hinlicky, "The Use of Luther's Thought in Pietism and the Enlightenment," in *Oxford Handbook to Martin Luther,* ed. Robert Kolb, Irene Dingel, and Lubomir Batka (Oxford: Oxford University Press, 2014), pp. 540-50.

181. Agamben, *Time That Remains,* p. 1.

182. See further, *RPTD,* pp. 179-86.

183. Agamben, *Time That Remains,* p. 95. Cf. also pp. 114, 118. This is, as Agamben points out, by no means a dialectic imposed on the Jewish law from the outside. The Kabbalists also distinguish between the law of creation and the law of the unredeemed world (p. 49).

works, decoupled from promise, that accomplishes no good work, as the commandments intend, but only blinds and hardens on the one side and reveals impotence on the other. The reason is that in demanding good works, it treats separated, presumably sovereign individuals as if in principle meritorious agents *(sicut Deus eritis)*. Since this very project of self-transcendence by the works of the law contradicts immanence, somatic existence, and solidarity, it in fact accomplishes only presumption, self-righteousness, and contempt for sinners (even the self that is sinner), hence indictment, conviction, and sentence of death on one and all in turn. If this juggernaut of legally sanctioned destruction is to be halted, the law of works must be rendered inoperative. The symbiosis of sin and law that leads to death must be now put to death, and a division of the division rendered. That really is what we need and what we are given in the Christ crucified.

The Pauline verb, *katargeo,* is a word virtually created by Paul, as Agamben discovers, and it yields "substance for reflection . . . particularly surprising for a philosopher."[184] The surprise is this: Luther translates this verb meaning to deactivate, as in Romans 3:31, into German with the verb *"aufheben* — the very word that harbors the double meaning of abolishing and conserving used by Hegel as a foundation for his dialectic!" Thus, a "genuinely messianic term expressing the transformation of law impacted by faith and [the gospel] announcement" was "secularized" into a "key term for the dialectic" of negativity and thus for anti-messianic purposes: "Hegel used a weapon against theology furnished by theology itself" albeit ironically, since "this weapon [Paul's *katargeo* and Luther's *aufheben*] is genuinely messianic." The implication, needless to say, is that theology can fight back by reclaiming Paul's positive dialectic of the Law battling the Law in order to be liberty for all, as Luther classically put it.[185] This is theology, which tells of "God" as God surpassing God in Christ crucified, constructing from our ruin a new sovereignty and subjectivity of the Beloved Community at work in the body of Christ. "For our sake he made him to be sin who knew no sin, in order that in him we might become the righteousness of God" (2 Cor. 5:21). Agamben thus sees the theological function of Christ crucified in Pauline theology as "rendering the law inoperative while carrying it to its fulfillment."

On the one hand, Paul radicalizes the law until it becomes "entirely unobservable, and, as such, only functions as a universal principle of [accusatory] imputation."[186] *Lex semper accusat* (The law always accuses). But he does so in order to "fulfill and recapitulate the law in the figure of love."[187] Consequently, the "new testament" is not in the first place the text named after it, "but the very life of the messianic community, not a writing, but a form of life. . . ."[188] Paul's

---

184. Agamben, *Time That Remains,* p. 95.
185. *LW* 26, pp. 277-90; see *LBC,* pp. 249-54.
186. Agamben, *Time That Remains,* p. 108.
187. Agamben, *Time That Remains,* p. 108.
188. Agamben, *Time That Remains,* p. 122.

Israel of God, the Beloved Community, comes on the earth bringing the free use of all good things in joyful exchange, since the rule or canon here (Gal. 6:16) is to know Christ crucified as the mediator of a self-surpassing love that by cunning bans the ban in order to include the excluded. The operative presence in the world of this messianic community in just this way detoxifies and humanizes not merely the religion business, working on behalf of savage capitalism, but above all works to wrest the state free to resist the savagery and put the market back into the marketplace where it serves in just exchanges rather than dominates by exploitative ones.

If, as purveyors of what Bonhoeffer called "cheap grace," we think like Occam that God can accept us without justifying grace, we do not penetrate to the necessity of Christ crucified, because in a flight into counterfactual speculation we evade rather than penetrate our true predicament as creatures bound by the common body to the earth in some particular time; we do not discover how desire here and now is captivated by savage structures of malice and injustice, but live as passively as the dead under political sovereignty that increasingly and openly violates the very law that it claims to protect. In such a world, the just will live by their faith (Hab. 2:4; Rom. 1:17), even as faith does not conform to this world but transforms to render new service in the body (Rom. 12:1-2).

## Does Faith Justify?

In the previous section, we heard Bell affirm the practice of Christ in the "church of the poor" as the refusal to cease suffering. This is "costly," an "act of hope," a "wager on God," namely, that "God is who the Gospel proclaims God to be."[189] This, then, is the faith in God by which those made just in the word concerning Christ Crucified live as only they can: in the power of the Spirit as the "church of the poor." To explore that claim by asking how faith justifies is the task of this section. We begin once again by recalling a statement of Luther from the 1517 *Disputation against Scholastic Theology:* "The grace of God makes justice abound through Jesus Christ because it causes one to be pleased with the law." As indicated earlier, in a formulation like this Luther is still largely under the influence of Augustine — not that that is a bad thing. He has, however, still not quite broken through to his mature insight that justice abounds in the redeemed because God now speaks — and hence sees — them baked into one loaf with Christ the beloved Son, by virtue of Christ's own joyful exchange of His righteousness for their sin, where and when the Spirit evokes the faith to receive the Crucified One as the Christ by creating a community that now lives in joyful, not exploitative exchanges. Here each person says *ex corde* (from the heart) with the *Theotokos,* "Yes and Amen, Let it be unto me as the Lord says,"

189. Bell, *Liberation Theology after the End of History,* pp. 190-93.

and thus freely and joyfully enters into these ecstatic new relationships in Christ with God and with others.[190]

Eberhard Jüngel published his *Justification: The Heart of the Christian Faith,* with an excellent Introduction by John Webster for the English translation,[191] accentuating this latter point in the heated discussion that attended the reception of the Lutheran-Catholic *Joint Declaration on Justification.*[192] Jüngel had come to endorse the *Joint Declaration* after first opposing it in no little blaze of brilliant light and searing heat.[193] He found (I would submit) that he could in fact deliver this latter point about *transformative* faith only in the space that the *Joint Declaration* opened up within the tradition of theology descending from Luther for resisting the reduction from Christology to anthropology[194] that pervades contemporary existentialist Lutheranism.[195] Only where Christ is present by the Spirit in the joyful exchange, as we shall see, can the proper, i.e., inseparable relation between the passive faith that receives pure gift from God the Giver and active faith that freely and joyfully circulates the gift in glory to God and good for others be clarified and sustained.[196] But that will further require that faith itself be understood Pneumatologically, as *divine* faith, work, and gift of the Spirit that moves the human heart to will the will of God and to love the love of God. Just this *Augustinian* contention was at the heart of Luther's volcanic diatribe against Erasmus: we "completely exclude the Holy Spirit and His power as if superfluous and unnecessary,"[197] if we imagine creatures that can move themselves to the love of God. "Fallennesss" denotes nothing but this crippling, indeed lethal loss of the "Holy Spirit and His power."

To make the same point from another direction: even when he came to clarity about the mediation of justice in Christ, Luther never repudiated what he had first learned from Augustine, namely, that transformative faith causes one to be pleased with the law. One becomes pleased with the law in a double sense: one comes both to justify God in His judgment on sin in one's own person (what

---

190. Eberhard Jüngel, *Justification: The Heart of the Christian Faith,* trans. J. F. Cayzer (Edinburgh: T. & T. Clark, 2001), pp. 247-59.

191. Webster incisively concludes that "the clear separation of the work of Christ and the work of the Christian may indicate to some a pneumatological deficiency. Anxieties about synergism may be relieved if the bond between Christology and anthropology is a function of the Spirit's action, rather than (as Jüngel fears) of an overdeveloped moralism or sacramentalism" (p. xv).

192. *Justification and the Future of the Ecumenical Movement,* ed. William G. Rusch (Collegeville, MN: Liturgical Press, 2003).

193. Daphne Hampson, *Christian Contradictions: The Structures of Lutheran and Catholic Thought* (Cambridge: Cambridge University Press, 2001), pp. 214-22.

194. So also Bo Holm; see the discussion in *PNT,* pp. 162-70.

195. Jüngel, *Justification,* pp. 238-42.

196. E.g., Risto Saarinen, *God and the Gift: An Ecumenical Theology of Giving* (Collegeville, MN: Liturgical Press, 2005), pp. 70-79.

197. Luther, *Bondage,* p. 142. See the discussion in PNT, pp. 141-53.

else than this is Luther's theology of the cross?)[198] and at the same time begins
to participate in the truly good work received from and so revealed by Christ's
fulfillment of the law, i.e., not for one's own benefit but on behalf of and for the
sake of others. So by faith, according to Agamben's positive dialectics, the Law's
condemnation is satisfied and so surpassed precisely because its ethical content
is Christologically fulfilled, even, so to say, super-fulfilled. The believer's faith in
the vindicated faith of the man Christ *already now* comes into force by the grant
of the Spirit's persuasion in a discipleship that refuses for the sake of others to
cease suffering.

Strictly speaking, then, faith justifies the sinner on account of *(propter)*
Christ's righteousness, that is, by virtue of His obedient love on behalf of the
enemy helplessly at the mercy of her enmity (Rom. 5:6-11). That is to say, God
does not justify on account of the believer's faith, embattled, thus often weak and
wavering, but on account of Christ's faith, which vindicated *already now* comes
and bestows itself by the Spirit, mercifully giving the very thing required for
anyone *already now* to enter into *His* victory and peace, that is, *ahead of its time.*
As surely as the Spirit proceeds from the Father of the Son, then, God justifies
— speaks-and-so-enacts this "rectification"[199] — *already now* for the sake of, but
not on account of, faith alone in Christ alone. Certainly this righteousness of
Christ does not prevail "for me" as person here and now on the earth except by
the appropriating faith that apprehends Christ *pro me,* "for me," and so comes
to entrust the concrete, biographical, and hence sinful self with its abiding and
indeed ineradicable membership in the common body to Him as saving Lord.
God's justice in Christ thus prevails *already now, ahead of its time,* wherever and
whenever it comes to be trusted in "the time that remains" (Agamben) between
the ascension and parousia of Christ, when at last it will prevail uncontested
forever and for all (Phil. 2:10-11). The eschaton of judgment thus reaches *into
the present already now* in the Spirit-wrought faith that receives the Crucified as
Christ; that is the eschatological "justification" that takes place *already now* in
"justification by faith." The lame paraphrase of this in existentialist theology as
"acceptance" by God hardly does justice to the sharp paradox articulated here,
namely, that the merciful justice that will prevail visibly and universally is *already
now* appropriated and enjoyed by faith in the Christ crucified for our sins and

198. See *LBC,* pp. 358-63.
199. This terminology is proposed by J. Louis Martyn in his exegesis of Galatians as a way
to unite the favor of the Father and the empowerment of the Spirit in justification by faith alone
in Christ alone, who breaks the power and the grip of the structures of malice and injustice.
J. Louis Martyn, *Galatians: A New Translation with Introduction and Commentary,* The Anchor
Bible, vol. 33A (New York: Doubleday/Random House, 1997), pp. 249-60. "Rectification" refers
to "God's making right what has gone wrong" (p. 250, emphasis original) so that "God's means
of rectification is solely the divine act of Christ's faith. Now, however, in a decidedly secondary
place, Paul does speak of placing one's trust in this faithful Christ, a matter no less significant
for being secondary" (p. 252).

raised for our justification, who is thus believed and obeyed in the struggling life of the emergent Beloved Community *already now* amid the "undulating snakes" of malice and injustice. The Augsburg Confession Article IV nicely captures both of these poles, the objective *propter Christum* and the subjective *pro me,* in its precisely formulated statement: "But they are justified as a gift on account of Christ through faith when they believe that they are received into grace and that their sins are forgiven on account of Christ, who by his death made satisfaction for our sins. . . ."[200]

This is the classical statement and chief contention of theology in the tradition of Luther, yet in the course of Protestant history many latched onto the first part of this statement in sloganistic fashion, "justification *by grace* through faith," and then further reduced this slogan to an intellectual principle: grace being the idea that God is gracious and faith being the idea that we can adopt as a principle the idea that God is gracious — so that if we know these ideas we have what Bonhoeffer called, *in place of the transformative encounter* with Christ crucified in Word and Sacrament to form the theological subject as member of the Beloved Community, a religious ideology providing a "cheap covering for our sins."

> Cheap grace means grace as a doctrine, a principle, a system. It means the forgiveness of sins proclaimed as a general truth, the love of God taught as the Christian "conception" of God. An intellectual assent to that idea is held to be itself sufficient to secure remission of sins. The Church which upholds the correct doctrine of grace has, it is supposed, ipso facto a part in that grace. In such a Church the world finds a cheap covering for its sins; no contrition is required, still less any real desire to be delivered from sin. Cheap grace therefore amounts to a denial of the living Word of God, in fact, a denial of the Incarnation of the Word of God.[201]

This deformation — the Lutheran heresy of "cheap grace" — happens, according to Bonhoeffer's diagnosis, when we turn grace into an idea, even a true idea, rather than the ever timely and contextually apt theological *interpretation* of something actually transpiring in time and space when and where the Spirit works the encounter with Christ crucified by His Word and Sacraments. Luther, in any case, had a clear account of this temporal and spatial encounter. He called it, as we have previously heard, the *joyful exchange.*[202]

Consider his words from a letter to George Spenlein dated April 8, 1516. It comes early on in Luther's career but articulates the consistent pattern of

---

200. *BC,* p. 41, Latin version.

201. Dietrich Bonhoeffer, *The Cost of Discipleship,* trans. R. H. Fuller (New York: Simon & Schuster, Touchstone Edition, 1995), p. 43.

202. Johan Anselm Steiger, "The *communicatio idiomatum* as the Axle and Motor of Luther's Theology," *Lutheran Quarterly* 14, no. 2 (2000): 125-58.

thought, or model,[203] of the life of faith in Christ which stands behind Luther's development of the Reformation doctrine of justification. This Christology can be left behind and forgotten only at the cost of turning justification by faith into a caricature of itself:

> ... learn Christ and him crucified. Learn to praise him and, despairing of yourself, say, "Lord Jesus, you are my righteousness, just as I am your sin. You have taken upon yourself what you were not and have given to me what I was not." Beware of aspiring to such purity that you will not wish to be looked upon as a sinner, or to be one. For Christ dwells only in sinners. On this account he descended from heaven, where he dwelt among the righteous, to dwell among sinners. Meditate on this love of his and you will see his sweet consolation. For why was it necessary for him to die if we can obtain a good conscience by our works and afflictions? Accordingly you will find peace only in him and only when you despair of yourself and your own works. Besides, you will learn from him that just as he received you, so he has made your sins his own and has made his righteousness yours.[204]

Luther had not, of course, invented this account of the encounter with Christ out of thin air. He was appropriating and giving a personal-existential accent to Paul's own Christological basis for the reconciliation of the world with its Creator: "For our sake he made him to be sin who knew no sin, so that in him we might become the righteousness of God" (2 Cor. 5:21). He was developing the patristic *admirabile commercium,* "He became what we are that we might become what He is,"[205] that probably he absorbed from John of Damascus, whose *On the Orthodox Faith* was known in the Latin West.[206] Indeed, Luther's mature Christology strongly affirms the classical *communication of idioms in the one person* of the incarnate Son, especially against the outbreak in the course of the 1520s of neo-Nestorian tendencies to separate the Son of God and the Son of Mary into two persons, as we shall have occasion to study in detail below in Chapter Six.

If we neglect these Christological affirmations at the basis of Luther's doctrine of justification by faith — which point always to the living presence of Jesus Christ in Word and Sacrament as the Spirit's place on the earth of joyful exchange — we turn the good news of the justification of the ungodly back into the ideological "good deal" of the religion business that trades in ever-cheaper grace. Moreover, having turned justification into an idea, we then indulge in a

---

203. See further *PNT,* pp. 145-48.

204. *LW* 48, pp. 12-13; LW 31, p. 343; LW 35, p. 49.

205. Hans Urs von Balthasar, *Theo-Drama: Theological Dramatic Theory, IV: The Action,* trans. G. Harrison (San Francisco: Ignatius, 1994), p. 284.

206. Manfred Schulze, "Martin Luther and the Church Fathers," in *The Reception of the Church Fathers in the West* (Leiden and New York: E. J. Brill, 1997), pp. 573-626.

misleading and divisive polemical caricature: "Protestants teach grace but Catholics teach works."

To make this point with students, I often read the following paragraph and ask how well it expresses the Protestant principle of grace against Catholic works-righteousness. "If anyone says that man can be justified before God by his own works, whether done by his own natural powers or through the teaching of the law, without divine grace through Jesus Christ, let him be anathema. If anyone says that divine grace through Christ Jesus is given for this only, that man may be able more easily to live justly and to merit eternal life, as if by free will without grace he is able to do both, though with hardship and difficulty, let him be anathema. If anyone says that without the predisposing inspiration of the Holy Ghost, and without His help, man can believe, hope, love or be repentant as he ought, so that the grace of justification may be bestowed upon him, let him be anathema."[207] Almost universally students respond in the affirmative, that here we have a fine statement of the Protestant principle of grace. I then announce that I have just read the first three canons of the Decree on Justification from the Council of Trent. The point of the exercise is that grace, that is, the *ecumenical* teaching[208] that Christian salvation comes as free gift of God, was *never* in dispute between the sixteenth-century parties. What was at issue was whether this gift for us prevails in us by faith alone in Christ alone or by faith activated and informed by love. In many respects, as the *Joint Declaration* has clarified, this actual dispute was the product of semantic confusion and polemical overstatement.

The language of the Augsburg Confession and its Apology is actually quite precise in speaking of justification by faith, meaning by "faith" the Spirit's grant of new birth, regeneration, adoption into the family of God, the Spirit's persuasion *ex corde* of the Father's favor upon those who are already now united with Christ by baptism as indeed the children of God, hence already now "pleased with the law." Faith is a *conversion,* then, not merely a new human opinion or attitude but a transformative divine gift, not Platonic "faith," i.e., mere human opinion, the lowest form of knowledge taken on authority. But "God has sent the Spirit of his Son into our hearts, crying, 'Abba! Father!'" (Gal. 4:6). Accordingly, faith is actual in us as the Son's own cry to the Father by the coming of their Spirit upon human hearts gathered together in the inchoate Beloved Community; faith is not and cannot be a mere human opinion, let alone a meritorious one for accepting blindly on authority. Nor can it be understood as an individual decision, let alone a pious feeling. Faith is precisely the work of the Spirit impressing Jesus in and on the assembly that gathers so that with Him the glory is given to the Father who out of love has sent the Son to them and for them. Christ embodies the

207. "On Justification," in *Canons and Decrees of the Council of Trent,* trans. Rev. H. J. Schroeder, O.P. (St. Louis and London: Herder, 1960), p. 4.

208. Cf. the condemnation of Celestius alongside of Nestorius in the fourth canon of the 3rd Ecumenical council. *NPNF* 14, p. 229.

righteousness that comes from the outside as help to the helpless and so as truly good news that makes His body in the world.

Consequently faith also believes something about one's own self, namely, that in spite of all on Christ's account one too is received into mercy. In this most primitive act of theology, faith interprets experience. This personal accent reflects Luther's celebrated *pro me,* which distinguishes justifying faith from that *fides historica* that even the devils have but which does not apply the knowledge of God in Christ to one's own experience. The Augsburg Confession definition holds both aspects together, although in the course of Lutheran history, as we shall shortly take note, these elements came apart into the sibling rivals of orthodoxy and pietism and then further into liberalism. But Melanchthon affirms in the Apology *both* that righteousness is imputed *on account of* Christ (the objective pole, Christ's work of righteousness not ours) *and* is imputed *to* faith (receiving by the Spirit the new self, the subjective pole of regeneration). They can be held together because these poles have as their common audience the joyful judgment of God the Father whose reign approaches. "And because faith receives the forgiveness of sins and reconciles us to God, we are first regarded as righteous by this faith on account of Christ before we love and keep the law, although love necessarily follows. And this faith is no idle knowledge, nor can it coexist with mortal sin; but it is a work of the Holy Spirit that frees us from death and raises and makes alive terrified minds. . . . [O]n account of Christ and by faith alone we are justified, that is, out of unrighteous people we are made righteous or regenerated."[209] Thus, the faith to receive the gift of Christ's righteousness is itself gift, the regenerating work of the Holy Spirit's *ubi et quando Deo visum est* ("where and when it pleases God," AC V).

Yet astonishingly enough some fifty years later the Formula of Concord, Solid Declaration, Article III:19, obscured all this. It launched the career of Lutheran orthodoxy when it expressly rejected *any* notion, however carefully defined, of justifying faith as regeneration and thus confounded the teaching of the Augsburg Confession and the Apology that faith is itself the Spirit's gift of regeneration. So it canceled the plain meaning of the Apology, as just cited. The reasons it did so are complex,[210] but fear of Catholic reform and its accommodation of early Lutheranism's critique surely played a role in a process of polemical polarization (as may be seen already in AC XX, p. 53: 6-7). What had been a matter of bringing to light something obscured (AC XX, p. 53: 8) became a matter of fixed polemical antitheses (as in the apocalyptic invective of Luther's later Smalcald Articles).[211]

209. *BC,* p. 128.

210. Olli-Pekka Vainio, *Justification and Participation in Christ: The Development of the Lutheran Doctrine of Justification from Luther to the Formula of Concord (1580)* (Leiden and Boston: Brill, 2008).

211. But see the careful nuance provided by William R. Russell, *The Schmalkald Articles: Luther's Theological Testament* (Minneapolis: Fortress, 1995), pp. 94-95, 115-16.

The stage was now set for the eventual Pietist reaction, which with evident justice tried to retrieve Luther's *pro me* in the form of the religious experience of the new birth over against the arid and disputatious proclivities of Lutheran orthodoxy. So Philip Jacob Spener concluded in his manifesto, *Pia Desideria,* "Hence it is not enough that we hear the Word with an outward ear, but we must let it penetrate to our heart, so that we may hear the Holy Spirit speak in them, that is, with vibrant emotion and comfort feel the sealing of the Spirit and the power of Word. Nor is it enough to be baptized. . . . Nor is it enough to have received the Lord's Supper externally. . . . Nor is it enough to pray outwardly with our mouth. . . . Nor, again, is it enough to worship God in an external temple. . . ."[212] *Non satis est* to believe the right doctrines or practice the right sacraments. Spener's justified reaction against Orthodoxy on behalf of the personal interpretation of experience by faith did not come without bringing along its own set of problems, to be sure.

There was no dispute and never was about justification by grace. We all can and should agree on the first three canons of Trent as the 2001 *Joint Declaration on Justification* shows. Thus we should forthrightly acknowledge that Catholics never doubted the primacy and sufficiency of divine grace in human salvation. The precise question posed by the sixteenth-century dispute was whether faith — indeed, faith *alone* — justifies. Gratis — to be sure, but the disputed question was whether the gift of Christ comes home and achieves giftedness, so to speak, in a person coming to believe something. In fact two things: something about Christ and accordingly something also about oneself. First, Christ lived and died and lives for others — also then for me. Just so, second, Christ's purpose is accomplished *already now, ahead of time,* when I believe that the righteousness of His messianic life avails for me the undeserving sinner and will prevail over me the doubting believer. When I believe that my sins are thus already now borne away by the Lamb of God, then, something has happened with me. I have passed from wrath and condemnation and death to favor and justification and life. Already now I stand before my judge as our merciful heavenly Father. Another way to say the same thing is to say that the faith that justifies is faith formed or better, informed by Christ in the sense of the joyful exchange: it is the faith that surrenders sins to Christ on His promise to take them as His own burden and responsibility and receives in turn His righteousness as ours to trust and to obey. In this concrete and biographical way faith interprets experience by spiritually reenacting Messiah's cross and resurrection in respect to one's own person. In this way, Christ crucified and risen forms, informs, reforms, and transforms the person who believes, that is, by *faith,* faith *alone.*

By contrast the opposing idea in the sixteenth-century dispute was that the faith that justifies is the one activated by and formed in love. This opposing view took faith as Platonic opinion, the lowest form of knowledge, i.e., taken on mere

212. Philip Jacob Spener, *Pia Desideria,* trans. T. G. Tappert (Philadelphia: Fortress, 1964), p. 117.

authority and apart from understanding, let alone application. This alternative view of faith as submission to mere information that does not per se transform the person represents an entirely different scheme, where faith can have no saving significance until the opinion is acted upon and applied to make a real difference in a person's life. And so far as this goes, it is certainly true: if faith is opinion taken on authority, without works of love it is dead and barren faith.

Underlying this, there is to be sure a dispute between two schemes about the nature of grace, but it is subtle. Grace can be understood as favor but also as gifts of empowerment: as *charis* or as *charismata*. If we make this distinction, we can say that as the Spirit proceeds from the Father, so the grace of God's fatherly good-pleasure logically precedes and governs the gift of the Spirit that empowers the new life of faith in Christ, although materially these are inseparable as we see in the story of Jesus' baptism. Charismata are the concrete empowerments given with the Spirit so that those who have passed from wrath to favor may now live as beloved children. These empowering gifts of the Spirit are not the reason why beloved children are loved. Christ the Son is the gift of the Father's love and so the good reason that the adopted, who may not be so lovable nor live as they are empowered to live, are nevertheless loved. Yet the problem raised here goes even deeper. If the faith to receive Christ is itself the Spirit's coming and gift, is not faith in God's fatherly favor by virtue of union with Christ the Son already now, as maintained above, the new birth, regeneration, adoption into the family of God? Never mind the gifts or fruits of the Spirit; isn't the very coming of the Spirit to bestow trusting faith one and the same thing? Is justification by faith not already "sanctification"? If the Spirit presents crucified Jesus as the Risen One in the joyful exchange, is not the same Spirit at the same time opening the closed mind and hardened heart to hear, understand, believe, and obey? In historic Lutheranism, as noted at the outset, there is a real knot of confusions here.

To sustain the understanding of grace as Christ's life-deed of goodness or righteousness for others that triumphs when and where a sinner comes to believe that it avails and so will prevail for her, we have to have strong and vital Christology, affirming that Christ is alive, present, and active in faith, as Tuomo Mannerma and his students in the Finnish school of Luther research have shown.[213] Shrinking from this Christological affirmation, from the beginning some Lutherans — especially following Melanchthon — were tempted to explain justification by faith instead as a psychological process.[214] First we are terrified by the law. Then we remember that Christ died for sinners. At length we cry out for mercy. God in heaven hears our plea and forgives our sins for Christ's sake. Then, and only then, God sends the Spirit to renew our lives. Justification takes place as nonimputation of sins first, then sanctification follows as our human response

213. *Union with Christ: The New Finnish Interpretation of Luther,* ed. Carl E. Braaten and Robert W. Jenson (Grand Rapids: Eerdmans, 1998).
214. *PNT,* pp. 148-54.

of new obedience — strictly in that order! But notice what happens in this psychological account. Not only does it force all human experience of God's grace into one rigid pattern untrue to Christian life and experience; not only does it require preachers to be spiritual terrorists before they can be spiritual consolers; ironically and against all intentions it turns the initial act of faith, the terrorized sinner's plea for mercy, into a purely human and natural act of will that separates some sinners from others as worthy of receiving grace. At what cost! Christ is only present in this psychological account as a memory of something someone supposedly did for us long ago.

So how can faith justify without turning faith into a new "good" work or "religious" work, decision, feeling, or activism? That happened in Lutheran history, as we shall describe in the excursus following this section. Orthodoxy made faith into an intellectual work of holding to right doctrine. Pietism turned faith into experience rather than the interpretation of experience, having right emotions according to the palpably felt new birth. Liberalism turned faith into making right decisions ethically and politically for socially activist engagement for justice in the world — with ambiguous results, when measured by this very clarion call.[215] To answer this question how faith can justify without turning faith into a new, and hypocritical, work, we return to the beginning.

We have all heard the cliché about the anxious monk's search for a gracious God. In this way twentieth-century existentialists painted a picture of Luther's *Anfechtung* but in reality projected their own angst in the double-crises of modernity (Ericksen) onto him. When we study Luther's earliest writings, especially the theology of the cross from the Heidelberg Disputation of 1518, what we find instead is an angry young man executing a prophetic critique of cheap grace. Luther rails against spiritual *securitas*, the complacent presumption that God's grace can be bought or bribed or easily earned, be it by indulgences purchasing the meritorious works of others or by one's own effort. To cut through the fog and smoke of the religion business, Luther posed a radical question that he had actually learned from Augustine though he developed it more sharply, namely, whether we can love God for God's sake.[216] He aimed this question directly at the medieval modernists, who, as we recall, assumed that we can naturally love God as our highest good. But, Luther asked, when we love God as our highest good, do we love Him truly, for His own sake, or rapaciously, *amor concupiscentiae*, for our own sakes, seeking self in all things, even in God? Here is the test, Luther proposed, of whether we are in the religion business or in the Kingdom business: *resignation to hell*. Would one be willing to be damned

---

215. A devastating lesson drawn in *BA* lies in the discovery made by Jewish historians of the role that the liberal, progressive theology of the nineteenth century played in welcoming Adolf Hitler and National Socialism. See especially the discussions of Richard Steigmann-Gall and Susannah Heschel, *BA*, pp. 39-45.

216. See Wilhelm Pauck's "Introduction," to *Luther: Lecture on Romans*, p. lv.

to the glory of God? Then one can be sure that one loves God not for one's own sake, but for His!

After he had made this case in the Heidelberg Disputation, Luther anticipated an objection. Is not this thought-experiment about resignation to damnation in *odium sui* (self-hate) a counsel of despair? Who then can be saved? Luther denies that it is a counsel of despair. He says that it is meant as a prod toward a salutary despair of self that prays for grace. But is not just this prodding still aimed at producing a human work, namely, despairing of self and praying for grace? Is not this line of thought going to lead eventually to the anxious bench and the altar call?[217] Is there not a very real danger in the theology of the cross that self-hatred — taken psychologically rather than socially as the breach with the structures of malice and injustice[218] — becomes the last, desperate refuge of works-righteousness, as if one could merit God's love by hating oneself?[219] In fact, this dubious implication is one of the reasons Luther left his theology of the cross behind. Luther completed this early thought-experiment and moved on when he came to the further realization that already Christ was the One who went to hell for others in obedience to God, who thereby triumphed on behalf of those others over hell, and now, as the vindicated One present in Word and Sacrament, comes joyfully to exchange our sin for His righteousness and His heaven for our hell. In that case, we surrender our mistrust, distrust, unbelief and are given in turn His own faithfulness and faith as He breathes His Spirit on us to receive and then to circulate. That is how faith comes and why faith can justify without being turned into a human opinion or meritorious work or a religious exercise. In this respect, faith is passive obedience, receptivity, patiency that lets Christ be Christ also for us and in just this permission justifies God in His judgment on sin that nevertheless mercifully justifies the sinner and awakens trust. "So it happens that faith alone makes a person righteous and fulfils the law. For out of the merit of Christ it brings forth the Spirit. And the Spirit makes the heart glad and free, as the law requires that it shall be. Thus good works emerge from faith itself. That is what St. Paul means in [Romans] chapter 3[:31]; after he has rejected the works of the law, it sounds as if he would overthrow the law by this faith. "No," he says, "we uphold the law by faith; that is, we fulfill it by faith."[220]

For Luther's joyful exchange to be true, such that faith in Christ justifies in this way, Christ must be present in the first person to speak this invitation and promise, "I am yours and you are mine." The joyful exchange is a nuptial image. Like the wedding vow, it effects what it speaks as individuals are re-formed continuously by their mutual pledging. According to the joyful exchange, we "have" Christ as a spouse "has" the other in love: not as objects to be possessed and

---

217. See the discussion below of John Nevin's *The Anxious Bench* in Chapter Four.
218. Hampson, *Christian Contradictions,* pp. 239-40.
219. *LBC,* pp. 363-67.
220. *LW* 35, pp. 368-69.

used like inanimate things, but rather "to have and to hold," where the having and holding continually re-form each one according to the structure of beloved community. Amid the changes and chances of life, the appropriating or having of faith *structures* love as justice that gives and receives what is not our due but is gift. Such is the "having" of Christ in faith: trusting His promise to be there for me, "one flesh" for better or for worse, "baked into one loaf" in the Eucharistic assembly, as Luther put it, in spite of unworthiness.

The nuptial analogy finally breaks down, however, because Christ and the believer are not equals like husband and wife. The otherwise unsavory aspect of this nuptial imagery going back to the prophet Hosea's marriage to Gomer the prostitute is intended to accentuate the inequality when applied to the Creator-creature relation. Christ is the Lord, the Creator, the Head of the Body; He makes unilateral promises that depend on Him, not on us, for their persistence and fulfillment. He makes these promises not on account of our faith but for the sake of faith so that believers can give Him nothing in return but their sins, on the one hand, and honor as the Mediator, on the other. Thus, the reciprocity suggested by the nuptial metaphor requires the supplementation of the law-court metaphor of justification to remind that we are not talking about a deal or *quid pro quo,* not even a just and reciprocal marriage covenant between equals. Rather we are talking about how the creature and the sinner stand before the holy God and Creator who comes wroth to judge over the ruin of creation. When we hold together both the Christological metaphor of nuptials in the joyful exchange and the apocalyptic metaphor of the law-court in judgment and justification, however, we see how justification by faith alone does not assert some legal fiction, but rather the divine speaking of the new covenant reality of God's own making: new creation, new birth, the righteousness of God in Christ prevailing on the earth. In this respect, faith becomes active obedience — agency, human cooperation with God, synergy, joyful exchanges in that structure of love and justice that is the Eucharistic assembly, where the gift of God is purely received and *just so* circulated in fervent love for one another and joyful sacrifice of praise.

Consequently Luther without any sense of self-contradiction can also speak of faith as a living, mighty, active thing.[221] He can practically personify faith as an agent capable of doing things, new things and great things. Thus one might object in the name of the psychological version of justification discussed and rejected earlier, "Is not active trust in Christ's promise our own necessary human contribution to justification? Who else believes but you or me, one by one? How else

---

221. "Faith, however, is a divine work in us which changes us and makes us to be born anew of God, John 1[:12-13]. It kills the old Adam and makes us altogether different men, in heart and spirit and mind and powers; and it brings with it the Holy Spirit. O it is a living, busy, active, mighty thing, this faith. It is impossible for it not to be doing good works incessantly. It does not ask whether good works are to be done, but before the question is asked, it has already done them, and is constantly doing them. Whoever does not do such works, however, is an unbeliever." *LW* 35, p. 369.

can faith believe in Christ for me? Who else believes but me?" Interestingly, this was the first actual point of Catholic dissent, as expressed in Canon 4 from Trent: "If anyone says that man's free will moved and aroused by God, by ascribing to God's call and action, in no way cooperates towards disposing and preparing itself to obtain the grace of justification, that it cannot refuse its assent if it wishes, but that, as something inanimate, it does nothing whatever and is merely passive, let him be anathema!" Is not this insistence on the involvement of our own free will and personal consent in justification what most of us nowadays think? Are we not then all good Tridentine Catholics — certainly not radical Lutherans insisting on extrinsic righteousness and the monergism of grace? Note the irony of this complaint: Luther, who railed against faith in mechanical ritual, implicit faith in whatever the authoritarian church says, impersonal or merely historical faith that doesn't bring Christ home "for me," is here accused of making faith something inanimate and merely passive.

But it is a troubling question that presses to the heart of the classical controversy. How does each believer indeed "cooperate," that means, work with God, so that we can truthfully say about ourselves: "I, yes I, freely and joyfully believe that Christ prevails for me"? Paul can indeed say passively, "I have been crucified with Christ; it is no longer I who live, but Christ who lives in me. . . ." But he can also immediately add actively, "and the life I now live in the flesh I live by faith in [or, by the faithfulness of] the Son of God, who loved me and gave himself for me" (Gal. 2:20). To address this vexing question of the unity of justifying faith in its passive and active dimensions, we might recall Luther's take on Romans 7 as a description of the *Christian's* conflicted life on the battle-line between the ages. For it is here that we come to ask which "me" we are talking about when we say, "I believe." The old "me" who is stubbornly the rebellious Adam that keeps reviving and will not accept his death sentence? Or the new "me" of Christ living in me, that is, the me who lives by faith in/the faithfulness of the Son of God who loved me and gave himself for me? And which "me" is that? Which "me" is the "me" of faith, both the helpless one for whom Christ gave Himself but also the agent of the new humanity, who loves the law of God, in whom justice abounds, who actively cooperates with the Spirit in the warfare against sin, death, and the power of the devil — what Paul calls "the flesh" — that is, against one's own body insofar it is penetrated by, and so enslaved to, entrenched structures of malice and injustice that still claim allegiance? All this is involved in the problem of theological subjectivity, to which Chapter Three is devoted. Here we can approach the solution developed there by way of preview.

The unity of human and personal participation by faith, passive and active, fairly demands a correspondingly vital doctrine of the Holy Spirit to that which Luther gives in his account of the Christology of the joyful exchange. As the Augsburg Confession puts it in Article V: "For through the Word and the sacraments as through instruments, the Holy Spirit is given, who effects faith where and when it pleases God. . . ." This persuasion or full conviction coming from outside the self

164

to the self is necessary. Psychologically, we do not see that we are a new creation and often we do not feel that we are a new creation; indeed, we ought to have doubts about believers, beginning with oneself, who believe above all in their own feelings. It is indeed a matter — even regarding oneself — of faith, not sight; not of experience, but of the interpretation of experience. For by the solidarity of my body with the common body I still belong to this corrupt and dying system of things and I cannot extract myself from it. Indeed the structures of malice and injustice that dominate in the world continue to infiltrate me, their conduit being my inalienable bodily existence in the same world over which they reign. I am caught up intimately in a war of worlds, fought out in and over my own body, and often enough I — the new "I" who loves the law of God — am defeated in the to and fro of battle between the Spirit and the flesh. "The good that I would I do not, and that which I would not, that I do" (Rom. 7:19). Even as agent of the new humanity, then, the believer never transcends the passive obedience of faith in the Christ who loved the sinner, who is this failure before God; who gave Himself for this bound body that I am. The agency of faith indeed can arise only from this ruin which Christ in the tomb made His own.

It is telling from the perspective of theology in Luther's tradition that so many interpreters of Paul are befuddled by Romans 7 and against all exegetical reason regard it as some kind of interruption in the flow of the epistle — a sudden, unmotivated retrospect on Paul's former life as a Pharisee from which his new life in Christ has delivered him. Luther sees things quite differently. He attacks "the metaphysical theologians [who] deal with a silly and crazy fiction when they dispute about the question whether there can be opposite appetites in one and the same subject, and when they invent the notion that the spirit, i.e., reason, is something absolute or separate by itself and in its own kind an integral whole and that, similarly, opposite to it also sensuality, or the flesh, constitutes equally an integral whole." These eisegetical imaginations "cause them to lose sight of the fact that the flesh is a basic weakness or wound of the whole man which grace has only begun to heal in his reason or spirit."[222] Falling between the account of the Spirit's coming by baptism in Romans 6 to assert a liberating lordship over life in the body and the eager longing of the frustrated creation for the glorious liberty of the children of God yet to come in Romans 8, Romans 7 describes with genuine existential insight and psychological depth the conflict in and over the body between the structures of malice and injustice on the one side and the new subjectivity of the Spirit given by baptism into Christ in conformation to His cross and resurrection on the other. This is a battle now inaugurated, one that still awaits the final victory of God, precisely and nothing less than the Pauline "redemption of our bodies" (Rom. 8:23). In this dynamic way, consequently, we should understand Luther's *simul iustus et peccator,* that is, that baptism removes the guilt of sin and so makes already now peace with God but does not yet remove

---

222. Luther, *Lectures on Romans,* p. 214.

the body from the sinful world and thus the world's continuing penetration of the body in capturing desire for sin. This makes life in the body that is not only my own but also belongs to others the very scene of the warfare between the creative love of God and the destructive seductions of the powers.

Hence to sustain the Christian life as battle of the Spirit against the flesh in this dynamic way, we need a Pneumatology that does as much and as vital work as does Luther's Christology. As justification is practical Christology, so battling faith is practical Pneumatology. To make this point with students when we are reading Luther's treatise against Erasmus, *The Bondage of the Will,* I tell them to open to any page at all. "Now take a red pen," I say, "and circle every occurrence of the Holy Spirit." Inevitably, the students will hold up their given page filled with red markings. Luther called the treatise *De servo arbitrio,* but it could have equally been called *De spiritu sancto.* It is truly one of the great mysteries of Lutheran history that the Holy Spirit disappeared,[223] ironically and in part as a victim of Luther's own critique of "enthusiasm," during the Enlightenment.[224] The twentieth-century Danish theologian, Regin Prenter, in his great book *Creator Spiritus,* set the record straight in recent times, at least in regard to Luther's own theology.[225]

As the Spirit once and for all made alive again the crucified Jesus on the first Easter, so now the same Spirit makes crucified Jesus really present as the risen One in the preaching of the gospel through sermon and sacrament. Hence auditors may encounter Him truly, in the first-person pronouncement of His promises. Just so they may die with Him and rise with Him. For Luther, the Holy Spirit's work is "objective," not "subjective," in the sense that the Spirit works in the public of Word and Sacrament, not privately and apart from Word and Sacrament in some region of modern interiority. But in the public place in the world that is the ecclesia, the Spirit works to remove the historical or ideal distance that exists between contemporary auditors and Jesus, a distance from which Jesus can appear as no more than model, example, revelation, demand — as such "dead." Only by overcoming this distance and becoming really present to speak His nuptial promise in the first person, "I am yours and you are mine," does the "dead" Jesus pass from state of distant exemplar or heavenly ideal to become alive to the auditor, the present savior who gives as a gift what is otherwise merely a demand that humiliates auditors who are powerless to fulfill it. The Spirit is not then some anonymous, impersonal, subjective inspiration supporting the main agent or actor, an autonomous human ego in an individual decision of will. By

223. *PNT,* pp. 127-76.

224. Paul R. Hinlicky, "Irony of an Epithet: The Reversal of Luther's Enthusiasm in the Enlightenment," in *A Man of the Church: Festschrift for Ralph Del Colle,* ed. Michel Barnes and Mickey L. Mattox (Eugene, OR: Wipf & Stock, 2013), pp. 302-15.

225. Regin Prenter, *Spiritus Creator,* trans. John M. Jensen (Philadelphia: Muhlenberg Press, 1953). See the helpful recent reintroduction of Christine Svinth-Voerge Poder, "Why Read Regin Prenter?" *Lutheran Forum* 47, no. 3 (Fall 2013): 52-55.

the same token, faith is divine faith, participation by trust in the Father's love for the Son and the Son's for the Father, precisely not an existentialist leap into the void by a daring human decision. Here the Spirit is the resurrection power of God who makes Jesus present in the preaching of the gospel about Him, so that faith comes about in shattering the self-determining ego which is Adam, refashioning it into Christ.[226]

Presentation of Jesus Christ as the risen and contemporaneous Lord who in this way gives what God demands to form the theological subject — this is the, so to say, *objective* work of Christ's Spirit in Luther's understanding. Just so, the objective work of the Spirit bestows theological subjectivity as membership in the Beloved Community of God. My faith is mine as the gift of the Spirit, who brings the gift of the Son home to me, so that the Son may now give me to the Father as part and parcel of the sacrifice of praise rendered by the Eucharistic community to which I am joined in the Son, harbinger on earth of the Beloved Community of God. Faith is each person's personal Pentecost, divine faith that in the power of the Spirit unites with Christ in new life to the glory of the Father and for the bearing of each other's burdens. Note well the Trinitarian structure of these statements. It is indispensable. Note as well that such faith is not anything corresponding to our preconceived religious or political needs. It becomes necessary only when a disruptive preaching of the crucified Messiah makes plain to us what structures of malice and injustice we merrily or miserably serve; what true need we have for a new righteousness endowing a new humanity not of our own making but just as surely of our own partaking.

---

## Excursus: On the Three Lutheranisms

It is illuminating here to take a short detour on the conflicted, but for Protestantism paradigmatic, history of Lutheranism in the light of the foregoing, insofar as all descendents of the Reformation today in all sorts of conscious and unconscious ways are still playing out these debilitating quarrels. The *Confessional Period (1517-1580)* came to an end with the signing of the Book of Concord, a compromise formula that bought Lutheran church unity at the cost of persecuting Anabaptists, disowning any relation to Calvinists, and pledging eternal opposition to Rome. Recent research is showing how uncertain and fluid the Confessional Period actually was. Olli-Pekka Vainio has shown that during this time there were at least five contending interpretations of the doctrine of justification among those who

---

226. It is worthwhile to note here that Helmut Thielicke, *The Evangelical Faith*, vol. 1, trans. G. W. Bromiley (Grand Rapids: Eerdmans, 1974), in his *anti-Cartesianism* similarly contends against reducing the work of the Spirit to human subjectivity's new self-understanding and describes it instead as the grant of "a new history and existence in and through which I am taken up into the history of Christ" (p. 152).

identified with the tradition of Luther.[227] Jill Raitt, on the other hand, shows how far Melanchthon's students had traveled from Luther's doctrine of bound choice in her delicious portrait of Calvin's successor, Theodore Beza, wagging a copy of Luther's *De servo arbitrio* to spite Melanchthon's student, Georg Major, in a public debate on predestination in the 1570s.[228] In this whirl of confusion that lasted for fifty years we can see the seeds of all three future Lutheranisms. The elements of each are found in that very definition of justifying faith of AC IV: "when believers believe they are received into mercy on account of Christ." Orthodoxy would make the *propter Christum* the standard of real Lutheranism, the doctrine that Christ's death on the cross makes satisfaction for sin. Pietism would seize upon the *pro me* of living faith, regeneration, not the dead *fides historica* which even the devils have, even in regard to Christ's vicarious representation on the cross. Liberals would reclaim the *merciful compassion* of God as the leading motif, saying that it is not God who needs to become merciful, nor is it merely we as individuals who need mercy, but the world that needs to be transformed into the Beloved Community that God in His compassion wills and works.

*Orthodoxy* reigned from 1580 until it declined in the course of the eighteenth century. It was the official theology of the legally established Lutheran church in various provincial alliances of throne and altar. These were the awful years of the Wars of Religion, when European Christianity committed a fratricide that amounted cumulatively to its moral and spiritual suicide. But the theological problem of Orthodoxy was that the issue had shifted far away from Luther's rediscovery of the Pauline apocalyptic question, i.e., God's prophetic rebuke to His own lost and wayward creation, pitched pointedly against spiritual *securitas*. Justification by faith, as we recall, is an answer to the question of justification, that is, judgment, as argued above. How will we justify ourselves before God whose kingdom comes? But in Orthodoxy this question lost its primary power to frame theological debate. Rome succeeded in making ecclesiastical authority as such the leading question. The problem now became: Which is the true, i.e., rightly authorized church? The Orthodox Lutherans were boxed into the corner of claiming that an inerrant, miraculously dictated Bible was pope, not the bishop of Rome, and that the Lutheran church, because it supposedly reads that Bible without interpretation, is the true church.

De facto, the problem with this argument was that the multiplication of Protestant sects and theologies all claiming to read the same inerrant Bible without any human admixture produced multiple, contradictory theologies and so am-

227. Vainio, *Justification and Participation in Christ,* pp. 223-25. Moreover, "[i]t is plain at any rate that 16th-century Lutheran theology did not employ a purely forensic doctrine of justification, except for Flacius.... For this reason, christology is not reduced to the mere acquisition of legal merit since Christ's being is the being of the believer, which forms the cause of justification" (pp. 207-8).

228. Jill Raitt, *The Colloquy of Montbéliard: Religion and Politics in the Sixteenth Century* (New York and Oxford: Oxford University Press, 1993), pp. 154, 210.

plified sectarianism, just as the papists had predicted and now taunted. Some few Orthodox Lutherans around Calixtus understood how they had been boxed into a corner and sought in patristic tradition a way out of the dead end. Gottfried Leibniz, schooled in the tradition of Melanchthon and belonging to the Calixtus school, was the last great lay thinker who worked out of the tradition of moderate Lutheran Orthodoxy to heal the breach of the sixteenth century.[229] But he failed in this as in other endeavors. In futile and stubborn apologetics, most Orthodox sought to shore up the inerrant Bible with circular arguments that appeared increasingly as little more than special pleading. With the rise of rationalism and historical criticism of the Bible, Orthodoxy collapsed and survives only as a reactionary force. Reactions, to be sure, are sometimes and to some degree justified. This depends, however, entirely on what folly is being resisted.

*Pietism,* which is usually dated to Philip Jacob Spener's previously cited treatise in 1675, *Pia Desideria,* was for the most part a churchly movement of renewal, not separation. Carter Lindberg has done a great service in putting together a collection of studies, *The Pietist Theologians,*[230] which brings the features of the original movement back to life as a recognizable "second" Lutheranism. For it was here that Luther's original teaching of the righteousness *of faith* was rediscovered and appropriated anew — that "living, mighty active thing," regeneration according to the Augsburg Confession, divine faith and gift of the Spirit. Yet how the Orthodox — God's cops, so to say — feared the Pietist movement! They hunted out and punished the prayer circles and Bible studies as schismatic *ecclesiola in ecclesia.* This fear, like most fears, had its justifications. Here in these intimate groups, the contrastive identity machinery of Orthodoxy constantly policing confessional boundaries was challenged by the lived experience of living faith in and among confessional "others" from the Reformed, the Anabaptists, and Spiritualists, even the Roman Catholics. In Pietism's grass-roots ecumenism Orthodoxy's attempt to turn Christian dogma into a fixed and comprehensive worldview controlling all aspects of culture was undermined from within. Moreover, here the urgency of the mission to the nations was rediscovered, both inner-mission as urbanization and industrialization increasingly eroded traditional forms of settled church life, but also mission abroad, riding the wave of European immigration and colonialism in search of new souls to gain for Christ with new chances to get Christendom right. Therein, however, lay the weakness of the second Lutheranism. Its turn away from the critical cognitive task of Christian theology towards a theology of the heart made it quietistic and largely uncritical towards the colonial project. So far as it was individualistic and otherworldly, Pietism made a deal with the devil: the princes and the universities would have the public world of politics,

229. G. J. Jordan, *The Reunion of the Churches: A Study of G. W. Leibnitz and His Great Attempt* (London: Constable, 1927). This is a research topic in need of renewed effort.

230. *The Pietist Theologians: An Introduction to Theology in the Seventeenth and Eighteenth Centuries,* ed. Carter Lindberg (Oxford: Blackwell, 2005).

economy, and science, while Christians claimed for Christ the interior regions of the soul and domesticity. Halle Pietism and Prussia's enlightened despotism were thus yoked.

*Liberalism* too was an authentic development of Lutheranism's desacralization and demystification of the cosmos that made the groaning of the creation the very place of service for renewed lives of holy secularity. Both the social and this-worldly orientation of Luther's evangelical ethics[231] (now modernized as the "social gospel") and its courageous intellectual honesty that applied critical reason to the study of its own Scriptures are tokens of liberalism's Lutheranism. Of course, this latter move was also forced upon Lutheranism by the breakdown in the plausibility of Orthodoxy's authoritarian claims about an inerrant and uninterpreted Bible and the cognitive force of new studies of Scripture pioneered by rationalists intent on showing the unmistakable humanity of the Bible's authorship. All of this was codified in Lutheranism's most influential philosopher, Immanuel Kant, who gave the marching orders for the liberal Protestant theology of the nineteenth century. Kant took up Luther's apparent fideism but gave it a new twist: reason cannot know God, so that even if there were a revelation of God, reason could not recognize which claim would be authentic among all the putative, and mutually contradictory, words of God.[232] Thus, Kant famously declared that he had destroyed knowledge to make room for faith. By faith, however, he meant not Luther's divine faith in Christ as saving Lord but practical reason's postulate of a heavenly reward for those who do their rational duty. Christ accordingly becomes for Kant the Prototype of the morally dutiful life. The duty is to build the kingdom of God on earth according to ethical reason.

In this development we travel a very far distance from Luther, yet we can still recognize a third Lutheranism when we see how Kant and his followers had to discredit their predecessors in Orthodoxy and Pietism for failing to complete the Reformation, as the liberals now claimed they would do. We can also see, however, especially in a figure like Ritschl a genuine retrieval of a *Leitmotif* of Luther's theology: divine love, *Barmherzigkeit,* compassion as the motive in all God's ways — as also in our times Christine Helmer has urged in her Luther interpretation along renewed liberal lines.[233] The polemical strife of Orthodoxy and the alienated oth-

---

231. For modern restatements, see George Forell, *Faith Active in Love* (Eugene, OR: Wipf & Stock, 2000); William H. Lazareth, *Christians in Society: Luther, the Bible and Social Ethics* (Minneapolis: Fortress, 2001).

232. Immanuel Kant, "The Conflict of the Faculties," in *Religion and Rational Theology,* The Cambridge Edition of the Works of Immanuel Kant, trans. A. W. Wood and G. Di Giovanni (Cambridge: Cambridge University Press, 2001), p. 283.

233. Helmer, *The Trinity and Martin Luther,* on the eternity of divine compassion *pace* Oswald Bayer, pp. 148-49: "I challenge the interpretation that locates the turn from wrath to mercy in the inner-Trinity" since "the movement unfolds from the lament, heard by God in eternity, to the heartfelt compassion compelling God to remember God's mercy and desire to help . . . an inner-trinitarian turn [that] precedes Christ's advent" (p. 164).

erworldliness of Pietism alike fall short of the main thing, divine love for the world. Wasn't liberalism right about that? To be sure it was, as none less than Dietrich Bonhoeffer affirmed in his early work, *Sanctorum Communio*. But, as the same Bonhoeffer realized, with the loss of scriptural authority, the *propter Christum*, and the living faith of the regenerate taking worldly shape in new lives of discipleship, liberalism's correct intuition that the gospel is concerned with reclaiming the world for the Beloved Community of God was bound to collapse after its critique had been executed. Fundamentalism lives on, as a reactionary force, but it is intellectually bankrupt and theologically dead. Now what? One fears that, just like Orthodoxy and Pietism before, the third Lutheranism feeds like a vulture on the decomposing corpse of divided and theologically incoherent Christendom.[234]

The moral of the sad story is that we today should cease and desist playing out these family quarrels, none of which penetrate to the true radicalness of the Reformation breakthrough. But all of these partisanships proceed parasitically and one-sidedly: exhausting the resource, failing to arise anew to the mission to the nations or discover afresh the true unity of the ecclesia in Spirit-given faith in Christ to the glory of the Father for the good of this suffering world by the coming of the Beloved Community of God.

---

## Are the Scriptures Holy?

We begin to answer this final question of our preliminary clarifications regarding theology's cognitive claim by recalling Jüngel's statement, left undeveloped above, that the formation of the theological subject who knows Christ as saving Lord is guided by biblical texts: "the place of the conceivability of God [is] a Word which precedes thought." Here, however, a pertinent differentiation from the earliest years of the Reformation is needed.[235] Luther tried to answer a critical objection to his Bible-based critique of the sale of indulgences, which asked: "By what right do you contradict customary teachings and practices of the church and presume to correct or purify them?" Luther famously appealed to the Word of God and offered straightforward exegetical arguments from the Bible about the meaning of texts to justify reformatory teachings, namely, that (1) repentance, or turning to God, concerns the whole life of the believer, (2) that divine mercy cannot be bought or sold but only received in faith as a free gift, and (3) that therefore the true treasure of the church is the gospel of the grace and glory of God in the crucified and risen Christ, which should be openly exhibited, freely offered, and purely explained for the sake of the penitent.[236] In this way, Luther

---

234. See the meditation on Bonhoeffer's "Inheritance and Decay," in *BA*, pp. 188-92.
235. The following paragraph is drawn from *DC*, pp. 7-8.
236. *LW* 31, 77-252.

sought to liberate the Bible for its proper, i.e., Spirit-intended usage simply by using the Bible properly to critique the religion business and commend news from God that is truly good.

Luther quickly discovered, however, that opponents could challenge his interpretations of Scripture by construing texts differently, questioning his selection of texts, or pointing to contradictions in the Bible leading to endless disputation that could only be settled in turn by the teaching authority invested in the papacy.[237] In consequence, after some back and forth in the course of controversy the question was refined in Luther's mind. He took the question opponents were asking at bottom to be: "How can you appeal to the Word of God when there are so many words of God?" To this more nuanced question respecting religious pluralism, Luther replied that he was speaking of the word from the God of Israel that first of all speaks to us Gentiles making us people of God, namely (citing Rom. 1:3), "the gospel concerning his Son. . . ."[238] This answer, *with its supposition of a pluralism of putative words from God,* informs the answer to the question posed in this section, "Are the Scriptures holy?"

A theology is "biblical" accordingly if, and when, it thinks with the Bible taken as a canonical narrative that tells of the eternal Father who is determined by the costly missions of His Son and Spirit to redeem the creation and bring it to fulfillment. Theology is then thinking after God's thinking (Mark 8:33, followed by 9:7), counting the cost that is the Christ crucified that makes grace free to sinners and their faith alone to justify. On the other hand, no matter how peppered with Bible verses, if a theology tells some other story to think some other thoughts it is not biblical. To set such boundaries for faith's thinking by telling the story of God's history with humanity and to direct theological attention to the narrative coherence within it is the authoritative function of the Bible in theology. Yet this boundary setting of canonical normativity is but an implication of the Bible's primary work as the Spirit-given language shaping faith to conformity with God's purpose in a world surfeit with religious options; here the canonical narrative identifies the God of the gospel by revealing His oikonomia for the obedience of faith in a world where many other schemes of liberation and summons to obedience are available. So the Bible is much more than a theological norm, and its normativity is misunderstood if this broader role in the hands of the Spirit holistically to form the theological subject in instruction, mediation, prayer, and so on is neglected. The Holy Scriptures are holy in making their readers holy.

In this rendering of its theological authority as deriving from its power to sanctify, the Bible is received in faith as its own elemental language that as such provides the *matrix* in which Christian theology takes place. It is received in faith as a gift from God the Holy Spirit bound up with the Spirit's sovereign initiative at Pentecost, delaying the parousia of the Lord for the sake of the mission to the

---

237. See Luther's account of the debacle in *LW* 31, pp. 307-25.
238. *LW* 31, p. 346; *LW* 35, p. 358.

nations (Mark 13:10), to tell and to teach all that Jesus, sent by His Father, has said and done.[239] The process of biblical canonization as the Spirit's selection and integration of texts is bound up with the mission to the nations just as the mission to the nations provides the hermeneutical key to the Bible's theological function. With the Bible theology can thus tell whether the discourse and the iconography are about Jesus, His Father, and their Spirit and so know that we are in that place in the world among many others called out by the gospel in order to be gathered and sent on as the Body of Christ. If the discourse and iconography are other, we simply are someplace else in the world. The Bible in this way authoritatively maps the ever-open, ever-fluid economic distinction between the ecclesia and the nations from which it is gathered. Just so the Bible ever challenges every form of *Kulturchristenheit* (acculturated Christendom) and every formation of *Volkskirche* (church of the ethnic group) as blurring injuriously the most fundamental of dogmatic distinctions.

Be it crude or sophisticated, on the other hand, "biblicism" is the deformation of "proof-texting" without the preceding appreciation for the Scripture as matrix of theology or critical dogmatic reflection on the emergence of the Scriptures from God's history with His people to serve as the primary rule of faith; biblicism attempts "to bypass logical, hermeneutical, and metaphysical questions probing the truth-value of Christian beliefs by direct appeal to arbitrarily selected texts of Scripture."[240] The proof-texting method of Protestant orthodoxy is well known and mercifully abandoned by all today who would intend to talk responsibly about God and the world before God and the world — also, then, by contemporary evangelicals.[241] But modern historical criticism too, in spite of uncounted and significant advances in understanding the genres and occasions of biblical texts that can be ignored only at the cost of cognitive seriousness, does not in principle avoid this arbitrariness. In some ways it exacerbates it. Historical criticism is, or too often operates as, biblicism of a higher order.

Insofar as historical criticism discovers the past and leaves what it discovers there, of course, it cannot be accused of arbitrariness, but rather of precision. Just this is what historical criticism is supposed to do, i.e., critically to know the text by discovering its historical origin and contextual sense. This necessary critical work

239. Jenson, *ST* 2, p. 178.

240. *DC*, pp. 228-31.

241. Kevin J. Vanhoozer, *The Drama of Doctrine: A Canonical Linguistic Approach to Christian Theology* (Louisville: Westminster John Knox, 2005), particularly on *scientia,* knowledge of God, pp. 265-305. As much appreciation and indeed honor that will be rendered below to Johann Gerhard for his work in Christology and the Trinity in Chapters Five and Six, it behooves me to record with equal seriousness the uselessness of Gerhard's attempts to save the Bible from criticism in *On the Nature of Theology and Scripture: Theological Commonplaces,* trans. Richard J. Dinda (St. Louis: Concordia, 2006). See the unsurpassed deconstruction of "inerrancy" by Arthur Carl Piepkorn, "What Does 'Inerrancy' Mean?" *Concordia Theological Monthly* 36, no. 8 (September 1965): 577-93.

at the same time is not and cannot be theology, knowledge of God. It is rather knowledge of the second Isaiah, or the Yahwist writer, or the redactor of those traditions we call the Deuteronomic, and so on. The problem of sophisticated biblicism arises here for two reasons.

First, historical criticism in its pretense to atheological, trans-confessional objectivity forgets that it has an audience to which it is accountable as it forgets that the Scripture that it studies is preserved for the sake of an audience. The very existence of these writings as something for us to examine presupposes a decisive historical event, namely, their deliberate preservation in writing and further as canon, as rule of faith. Thus, second, the particular content of canonical texts, both in their own voices and in their interactions with one another by virtue of their written preservation in the emergent canonical tradition, articulate *claims to truth regarding God*. In other words, the texts are theological in their very content and this content as theology is not reducible to originating occasions. These texts intend theology, knowledge of God, not only for their own moment but for the future. This theological content is what made the texts eligible in the first place, so to say, for inclusion in the genre, Scripture, while the genre of Scripture itself arises from sorting and selecting such particular theological claims to truth in a discerning process of tradition, just as Paul remarks regarding the Easter testimony he both records and develops in 1 Corinthians 15:1-8. Being written down and preserved for the instruction of future readers in the continuing community of faith, then, Scripture as genre denotes selected texts that are held to transcend their immediate historical context. Indeed, joined with other such theological testimonies as Scripture, they acquire new meanings by their canonical interactions, as they must, when theology itself is taken as "scriptural reasoning" (Ochs) that produces knowledge of the God of the Bible for us today. In just this way the canonical text is not merely or even primarily a record of something in the past, but theological scripture that aims to engage us as sanctified subjects, making us its thinkers in our own missiological situation.

How then can historical criticism say anything whatsoever about the claims to truth the text bears, since that claim to truth cannot be a matter only of what was said but also and indeed chiefly of what is being said through the tradition of scriptural reasoning up to today in and for the community that believes with the Scriptures? Historical criticism surely can debunk abuses of the Bible that claim proof where only a sign from faith for faith is given; it can surely expose eisegesis (reading into the text) in distinction from exegesis (drawing out from the text). It can test the coherence of contemporary claims by comparison with original meanings. But it is arbitrary if on the basis of historical-critical expertise biblical scholars opinionate regarding contemporary theological questions emerging out of the ecclesia's use of the biblical canon as the scriptural matrix of its contemporary thinking about God and creatures. This is especially so if such opinionating takes place by lifting up favored texts, or rather favored scholarly constructions of texts, without critical dogmatic labor in logical, hermeneutical, and metaphysical testing of claims. The last two centuries are fraught with such episodes of sophisticated biblicism that for example favored prophet over priest, or narrator over sage, or the faith of Jesus over the faith of Paul, or eschatology over apocalyptic, and so on. This kind of expert but hermeneutically arbitrary opinionating frequently becomes the ersatz substitute for critical and consequent theological thinking in contemporary Euro-American Christianity. Acute minds within biblical studies have regularly borne witness to this fundamental confusion, for example, Albert Schweitzer in his demythologization of the "quest for the historical Jesus" or Johannes Weiss in his exposé of the confusion of Jesus' proclamation of the imminent reign of God with nineteenth-century progressivism.[242] Sophisticated biblicists facilely quote the Bible, but their deliverances turn out on examination to be oracles of the *Zeitgeist.*

The Arian controversy in the fourth century of the Christian era is a classical demonstration of this claim about the "failure of biblicism."[243] In that controversy a consistently Platonic doctrine of transcendence, suffusing Hellenistic culture and undisrupted by the gospel of the incarnate and crucified Son, had ontologically to separate rather than personally to distinguish the deity of the Father from that of the Son. In this way Arians rendered the saving deed of the divine Son's incarnation nugatory and in the process triggered a crisis in theological thought regarding the very nature of divine transcendence. Even though Arians, claiming "the Bible alone," had significant proof-texts on their side, they had forgotten in their naïve appeal to various things said in the Bible the hermeneutically critical fact that the canonical collection of Hebrew Scriptures combined with apostolic and evangelical literature of the New Testament had come into existence as early Catholicism's "martyrs' canon."[244] Howsoever tacit and informal in comparison to later decisions by council, this canon was the first and constitutive dogmatic decision of Christian theology against docetism in Christology and Gnostic dualism in theology.[245] Historically this decision in principle also "closed" the canon in the sense that it made a definitive selection of texts regarded as theologically apostolic as well as publicly attested and handed down openly in the churches over against rival texts newly appearing with theologically incompatible claims based on allegedly secret inspiration and transmission.

It is easy then to see how a readily misunderstood *sola scriptura,* such as the Arian biblicists claimed, can forget what the Bible actually is and consequently open wide again the door to the perennial theological temptation to dualism,

---

242. Christopher Morse, " 'If Johannes Weiss Is Right . . .': A Brief Retrospective on Apocalyptic Theology," in *Apocalyptic and the Future of Theology: With and Beyond J. Louis Martyn,* ed. Joshua B. Davis and Douglas Harink (Eugene, OR: Cascade, 2013), pp. 137-53.

243. *DC,* pp. 228-31.

244. William R. Farmer, *The Formation of the New Testament Canon: An Ecumenical Approach* (New York: Paulist, 1983). See also Arland J. Hultgren, *The Rise of Normative Christianity* (Minneapolis: Fortress, 1994).

245. *DC,* pp. 96-106.

transposed in the Arian case from the doctrine of God as in Gnosticism now to a Platonizing doctrine of the Logos. Remembering this history and its theological sense in the correlation of public church, as normed and known by the baptismal creed, with the canonical unity of the Testaments, it is better to speak of *prima scriptura*,[246] i.e., the canonical Scriptures as the *matrix* of theology that intends orthodoxy in the sense of precluding the aforementioned invidious separations of God and creation, soul and body, Jesus and faith, Spirit and sacrament, grace and community, and so on. As Philip J. Lee wrote in his impassioned and insightful clarion call against the new Gnosticisms that have now more or less captured the Protestant churches in Euro-America: "It is indeed in the *Church* where the Gospel is proclaimed and within the context of the Church where the Gospel is received. Nothing is more important for North American Protestantism than the reassertion of that axiom of orthodoxy."[247]

Forgetting the history and thus ignorant of the genre, Arians had therewith also forgotten the "joyful exchange" at the soteriological heart of this dogmatic decision against Docetism and Gnosticism: the Word became what we are in order that we become what He is. It was for the sake of this belief in salvation as divine redemption of the human body, and it was in the power of this belief in the Logos made flesh, that martyrs in the maw of empire resisted as their shed blood seeded the church. The very existence of the Bible as canon in the sense of this assemblage of texts written from faith for faith and now combined to form the Genesis-to-Revelation narrative developed through the second century, especially in Irenaeus. It came to the point that it could be received more or less as a given, say, by the time of Origen, who was, among other things, a great biblical scholar. Yet in principle it is already, as mentioned above, de facto "dogma" in Ignatius of Antioch, indeed in the Fourth Gospel.[248] Though Athanasius published a canonical list of recognized texts in an Easter letter, it is sometimes objected that it was not until the Council of Trent that such a list was dogmatized. But this counts as an objection only to a legalistic, proof-texting, biblicistic mentality that we are presently rejecting. What is biblical is not a list of canonical books, but the books that proved canonical from Pentecost on by their power to sanctify in the name of Jesus, sent by the Father in the Spirit's power for human redemption and fulfillment, now proclaimed to the nations. That function gives also the hermeneutical key to the proper use of the Scriptures, as Luther later maintained, to necessitate Christ *(was Christum treibet)*. Necessitating Christ in and by the apt use of biblical texts both exposes God's controversy with His creation fallen prey to structures of malice and injustice and gives God's merciful solidarity with victims and penitent perpetrators to redeem them and bring the liberated creation to fulfillment.

---

246. Paul R. Hinlicky, "The Lutheran Dilemma," *Pro Ecclesia* 8, no. 4 (Fall 1999): 391-422.

247. Philip J. Lee, *Against the Protestant Gnostics* (New York and Oxford: Oxford University Press, 1987), p. 251.

248. Lee, *Protestant Gnostics,* pp. 69-108. See *DC,* pp. 69-108.

Under the pressure of imperial Platonism during the epoch of the semi-Arian emperors, culminating in the renewed paganism of Emperor Julian, these preceding commitments to the canonical narrative as dogmatic decisions against docetism in Christology and dualism in the doctrine of God yielded further doctrinal explications that matured in the articulated teaching on the Trinity at Constantinople in 381: to know God as the one deity of the three persons is to interpret canonical Scripture rightly with respect to its theological content. The God of the Bible *is* the Trinity, and *mutatis mutandis,* the Bible is read rightly according to the Trinity. It is to be stressed that the claim here is *analytical* of the prior canonical decision against dualism. Moreover, as such, the decision regarding the Trinity became the basis for the future dogmatic decision on the unity of divine and human natures in Christ's person, i.e., as the Second of the Three, at Chalcedon in 451. This Christological dogma too continues the theological decision against dualism that is originally the decision for the unity of the Testaments to make one canonical story of one God determined to redeem and fulfill the creation by the missions of His Son and Spirit.

Here then we come to the heart of the matter. A theological decision against dualism entails something with comprehensive implications in theology, as just noted, but exceedingly difficult to understand, let alone to trust: substantial divine participation in the creation that is not God, just as Nicea's *homoousios* indicated when it was predicated of the person, Jesus Christ, born of a human mother and executed on the Roman stake. That substantial divine participation in creation further entails, as we think about the nature of the Christian Bible that enables it to be Holy Scripture, the insight that the Bible is precisely *not* spoken from heaven intact as a whole in a miracle of dictation (the view that Mohammed initiated and adopted in criticism of what he perceived to be the corrupted scriptures of Jews and Christians). But the Bible emerges humanly and historically from the God of Israel's originating pledge of His own divine life to keep the promises He had made to Abraham and his offspring, as the dramatic symbolism of the smoking fire pot passing through the lane made of slain beasts in Genesis 15 indicates — God invoking a curse upon God if He fails to keep His word.[249] Talk about substantial divine participation in creation! This evangelical promise and divine commitment or covenant is from the beginning of the canonical narrative therefore the hermeneutical key to its right reading and usage: to identify God in His costly grace for the obedience of faith.

Such substantial divine participation in the creation indeed tells how and in

---

249. Von Rad regards the covenant ceremony recorded here as "probably one of the oldest narratives in the traditions about the patriarchs." Gerhard von Rad, *Genesis: A Commentary,* revised edition (Philadelphia: Fortress, 1973), p. 189, but he cautions against overinterpretation: "By subjecting it to a meaning that appears reasonable, one loses the meaning of the whole, which is simply the gift of quite a real guarantee" (p. 188). R. R. Reno follows Luther in allegorizing the ceremony as a prophecy unveiling God's plan, in *Genesis,* Brazos Theological Commentary on the Bible (Grand Rapids: Baker, 2010), pp. 160-61.

what sense the Scriptures are holy: in forming the obedience of faith as they are read and received according to the Spirit's mind and intention to redeem and sanctify the "profane" that its Creator has claimed for the Beloved Community.[250] As Lindbeck wrote now almost a generation ago, "The primary function of the canonical narrative . . . is 'to render a character . . . , offer an identity description of an agent,'" namely, God as the One who is determined by His Son and Spirit to redeem and sanctify. It does this, "not by telling what God is in and of himself, but by accounts of the interaction of his deeds and purposes with those of creatures in their ever-changing circumstances. . . . The primary focus is . . . on how life is to be lived and reality construed in the light of God's character as an agent as this is depicted in the stories of Israel and Jesus."[251] To understand "God" in the way that entails our sanctification, we get to enter the scriptural world and learn there of this supervening order of costly grace. The "Creator" is the almighty Father who through his Word and Spirit creates all things for the Beloved Community and is self-determined, by the pledge of His own divine life, to bring it to pass — a pledge made to Abraham and fulfilled on Golgotha, hence also in each believer's own Gethsemane of the soul when and where in the matrix of the Scriptures she is born anew to holiness of life.

But does entering "the strange new world within the Bible" (Barth)[252] mean leaving the common world behind? Lindbeck denied this inference and spoke of the common world theologically "redescribed in Christian terms."[253] But how do we account for this very distinction that Lindbeck seems to take for granted between the scriptural world and the common world? Have we here no more than

---

250. According to Luther's *Disputation on the Divinity and Humanity of Christ,* we do not surpass biblicism until we achieve theological interpretation that makes the claim to truth for the sense intended by the Spirit for us today: "heresy lies in meaning not in words" (#57) because heresy consists in "understanding the Scriptures other than the Holy Spirit urges" (#64). See Paul R. Hinlicky, "Luther's Anti-Docetism in the *Disputatio de divinitate et humanitate Christi* (1540)," in *Creator est creatura: Luthers Christologie als Lehre von der Idiomenkommunikation,* ed. Oswald Bayer and Benjamin Gleede (Berlin and New York: Walter de Gruyter, 2007), pp. 184-85; cf. also pp. 169-80.

251. George A. Lindbeck, *The Nature of Doctrine: Religion and Theology in a Postliberal Age* (Philadelphia: Westminster, 1984), p. 121.

252. Karl Barth, *The Word of God and the Word of Man,* trans. Douglas Horton (New York: Harper & Brothers, 1957), pp. 28-50.

253. Lindbeck lifts up Augustine as the model for this kind of theology: "the whole of his theological production can be understood as a progressive, even if not always successful, struggle to insert everything from Platonism and the Pelagian problem to the fall of Rome into the world of the Bible" (*Doctrine,* p. 117). Theologians like Augustine "redescribe" extrabiblical reality in distinctly biblical terms. Lindbeck consequently claims that the "reasonableness" of Christianity is not found in its conformity with some other discourse of "secular rationality" (Milbank) that is regarded as more "true," but is "primarily a function of its assimilative powers, of its ability to provide an intelligible interpretation in its own terms of the varied situations and realities adherents encounter" (*Doctrine,* p. 131).

a version of Barth's initial observation of the positive fact that the Christian community exists as that form of life in the world that ventures to speak of God on the basis of a putative word from God? Bluntly, that the Bible exists and purports to tell of God? Certainly, a pragmatically oriented account of theological knowledge affirms, as did Bonhoeffer in *Creation and Fall*,[254] that we are not at the beginning nor at the end but in the middle, *in medias res*. We cannot and do not transcend and should not try to. If so, however, can we communicate outward a claim to truth from the Word that forms us in our theological particularity? How so? If not, has the mission to the nations become impossible and theology as scriptural reasoning ghettoized? Then, contrary to the present hypothesis, the originating claim for the Scripture as a *missiological* gift of the Spirit has been undermined. A ghettoized theology of the Bible alone contradicts what the canon is as rule of faith for the gospel's mission to the nations.

Forms of life presuppose life, that is, the common body. Ned Wisnefske therefore is on to something when he proposes a reconceived discipline of natural theology oriented to the common perils and prospects of natural existence,[255] even if the relation of his natural theology to Christian theology remains unclarified and, according to the present argument, if thought out consequently, his naturalism leads away from Kantian transcendentalism to the consistent naturalism of Deleuzian metaphysics, as Adkins and I recently argued.[256] In fact, Biblical theology does make a remarkable claim about the common body that cannot but interest anybody who hears it, namely, that it is the precious creature of God, the material bearer of the human person, destined for the redemption of resurrection and glorification in the Beloved Community of God. Making this claim that common human existence is a being-towards-death-and-resurrection, the "strange new world within the Bible" engages the mind of the common world (cf. Paul at Athens in Acts 17).[257] These considerations help to answer a critical objection put to Lindbeck's theory on the nature of doctrine, namely, that it isolates theology from the world and makes cognitive engagement impossible. We are to this extent incorporating Lindbeck's position in arguing that the authority of the Bible in theology for the church's obedience of faith lies in its holiness, not in its "truth," that

---

254. Dietrich Bonhoeffer, *Creation and Fall,* Dietrich Bonhoeffer Works, vol. 3, trans. D. S. Bax (Minneapolis: Fortress, 1997), pp. 28-31.

255. Ned Wisnefske, *Preparing to Hear the Gospel: A Proposal for Natural Theology* (Lanham, MD: University Press of America, 1998).

256. See *RPTD.*

257. "The meaning is quite simple: If the Gentiles understand that there is one God, the Creator, and if they repent, then they do indeed believe. And then they know that they should always have understood this. Here Luke provides an insight into the structure of faith: he knows that independent of our comprehension, God has always been near at hand; thus unbelief cannot be blamed on God's alleged distance." Hans Conzelmann, *A Commentary on the Acts of the Apostles,* trans. James Limburg, A. Thomas Kraabel, and Donald H. Juel (Philadelphia: Fortress, 1987), p. 148.

is, in the claim of God that it makes and effects, not yet in the fulfillment of this claim. It engaged Athenians very much to hear the common body redescribed as precious creature of God, destined for life. Reflection on what would be required for this to be true brought them, whether in faith or unbelief, to the knowledge of God who gives life to the dead and calls into being new worlds.

It is certainly true that Lindbeck's argument reflected his judgment — in principle separable — on the collapse of Euro-American Christendom and the consequent de facto marginalizing of the Christian community into a sociologically sect-like existence, even if in its theological self-understanding this sectarian existence is ecumenical in orientation and its theology's redescriptive ambition is world-encompassing. That is a judgment on our spiritual situation in Euro-America today that the present work also shares, as explicated in the previous chapter. But, bearing in mind that we are speaking of scholarly theology as an academic discipline that devises and polishes tools of praxis — not preaching strategies that must be as flexible as context demands and opportunity affords — we may meet the objection. By no means is this approach to the Bible as matrix of theology and norm of theology ghettoizing, if theology takes clear account of the *double existence* of the theological subject as a member, though not citizen of two kingdoms, by virtue of the *common body. The common body is our shared world.* If there is a "point of contact," then, it is not modern self-transcendence, but the common body that all share in the common world; this is the suffering and desiring and frustrated body that groans for redemption, as redescribed by the eighth chapter of Romans.

It is this specifically theological act of interpretation of the body as creature of God destined for resurrection as known from biblical texts that actually gains rational attention as something pertinent, interesting, and worthy of consideration. In words that Josiah Royce composed against *both* theological apologists *and* cultured despisers, the Christian claim to truth about the common body may be taken "at least provisionally, not as the one true faith to be taught, and not as an outworn tradition to be treated with an enlightened indifference, but as a central, as an intensely interesting, life-problem of humanity, to be appreciated, to be interpreted, to be thoughtfully reviewed, with the seriousness and striving for reasonableness and for thoroughness which we owe to every life-problem whereupon human destiny is inseparably interwoven."[258] That is not only a matter of philosophical hermeneutics. Theology itself understands that the intelligible interpretation of the common matter of the common world — our experience as body — bridges between theology and other forms of knowledge.

By the same token, the realities of this shared world of bodily existence constrain what a canonically shaped theology says in this process of interpretation. Scientific discovery simply rules out as antiquated, for example, the predom-

---

258. Josiah Royce, *The Problem of Christianity* (Washington, DC: Catholic University of America Press, 2001), p. 7.

inant opinion in theology just several centuries ago of a six-day creation that had occurred about five thousand years before. The discoveries of the sciences, the events of history, and whatever else is of human significance in the common world of the human body as known in our best available accounts provide the real material of this real world that is to be interpreted and so integrated into a growing, ever-modernizing theology, as the theology of the church (ectypal theology) progressively anticipates the knowledge that God has of God and the world (archetypal theology).[259]

What may rationally persuade nonadherents to consider the theological truth-claim of Christian theology is that they find themselves with their worlds cogently interpreted by such "accounts of the interaction of God's deeds and purposes with those of creatures," so that they are won over to the gospel's vision of "how life is to be lived and reality construed in the light of God's character," as we have heard Lindbeck say. At its existential depth, as Wittgenstein knew, it is particularly the experience of suffering redescribed as the "Gethsemane of the soul" (where "soul" means the Hebrew "heart" of the body, not a disembodied intellect) that may lead to a kind of rational persuasion: "Life can educate one to a belief in God. And experiences too are what bring this about: but I don't mean visions and other forms of sense experience which show us the 'existence of this being,' but e.g., sufferings of various sorts. These neither show us God in the way that a sense impression shows us an object, nor do they give rise to conjectures about him. Experiences, thoughts, — life can force this concept on us."[260] This is so because, biblically understood, bodily life at its depth, in the "soul," is through the particularities of one's time the experience of being created by God — "suffering God," as Reinhard Hütter provocatively put it.[261]

The theologian who inspired Hütter to this formulation was Oswald Bayer, who himself took inspiration from the Enlightenment gadfly and dissident, Johan Georg Hamann. "Knowledge of God and knowledge of self are not to be separated" but are mediated together "in a specific linguistic medium ... in the exchange of words between God and the human." Once again, we are not talking here about "visions," but about experience and its interpretation. Just as in Lindbeck, the biblical Word and human self-interpretation arising from it are ...

... literally "world-shaping." One's own life-story is not only reflected in it but has its very existence in it, is formed in it and experiences its unity in it.

---

259. Heinrich Schmidt, *Doctrinal Theology of the Evangelical Lutheran Church,* 3rd edition (Philadelphia: Lutheran Publication Society, 1899), p. 16.

260. Cited in *The Christian Theology Reader,* ed. Alister E. McGrath (Oxford: Blackwell, 1999), p. 24.

261. Reinhard Hütter, *Suffering Divine Things: Theology as Church Practice,* trans. D. Stott (Grand Rapids: Eerdmans, 2000).

This unity is not that of an "individual substance of reason" that would accidentally have a history. No "I" that I myself would be is at the basis of my life-story. The fact, however, that the human is not an amoeba that dissolves and dwindles away in ever-changing shapes and relations, that in the midst of these changes a continuity nevertheless persists without there being any inherent power to change the self or integrate its changes, as with Proteus — all this results from the fact that God is primary motif and motive of my life-story. He is the Poet in the radical sense; he is Author. God — an author! God — a writer! This is Hamann's answer to the question [of Bonhoeffer], "Who am I?"[262]

The Bible, Bayer claims on behalf of Hamann, "forms the a priori, thoroughly accidental, but a posteriori necessary condition for understanding self and world . . . one can speak of [the Bible] as a historical a priori"[263] — what we are calling the "matrix" of theology, when theology itself adopts a pragmatic, rather than theoretical, ideal of knowledge of God for the interpretation of experience.

This knowledge of self as creature of God is paradigmatically the case in the human experience of becoming the creature God intends by dying and rising with Christ. "Therefore, man in this life is the simple material of God for the form of his future life. Just as the whole creation which is now subject to vanity is for God the material of its future glorious form. And as earth and heaven were in the beginning for the form completed after six days, that is, its material, so is man in this life for his future form, when the image of God has been remolded and perfected" (Luther).[264] "Nature" is the "material" of grace in scriptural reasoning. The book of revelation in this way interprets the book of nature even as the book of nature presents the material that cries out for true interpretation — a dialectic immanent to Scripture itself as may be seen in the canonical inclusion of Wisdom literature as a kind of counter-testimony to the predominant testimony to Yahweh's saving deeds in history (Brueggemann).[265] If Scripture cannot work in this way to sanctify experience, however, it possesses no authority that theology might otherwise create for it. On the contrary, the use of Scripture in theology as norm is derivative of its sanctifying function as matrix. As Bayer articulates the primacy of the Bible as matrix: the Bible's "*auctoritas normativa* follows from its *auctoritas causativa* — because of the authority that it has to create faith."[266] Concretely, the faith that interprets experience as the creation of

---

262. Oswald Bayer, *A Contemporary in Dissent: Johann Georg Hamann as Radical Enlightener,* trans. Roy A. Harrisville and Mark C. Mattes (Grand Rapids: Eerdmans, 2012), p. 49.

263. Bayer, *A Contemporary,* p. 65.

264. *LW* 34, p. 138.

265. We will discuss Brueggemann's important contribution in this connection below in Chapter Seven.

266. Oswald Bayer, *Martin Luther's Theology* (Grand Rapids: Eerdmans, 2007), p. 77.

God, by conformation to the resurrection of the Crucified One, in this way and by this Word sanctifies the secular. The "truth" of the Bible is not the Bible, but the gospel it bears into the world of experience; and the "truth" of the biblical gospel's interpretation of experience is the coming of the Beloved Community it promises.

If, on the other hand, the primary questions in theology were whether and how the Scriptures are as such "true," wittingly or not we subject the Scriptures to contemporary notions of "truth," themselves historically conditioned, as we surely ought to know and acknowledge, living today in our condition of cultural vertigo that is the criticism of criticism in postmodernity. The denouement of this line of thought is in such aporia — what Horkheimer and Adorno called the "dialectic of Enlightenment" in their bitter obituary of National Socialism: "The principle of immanence, the explanation of every event as repetition, that the Enlightenment upholds against mythic imagination, is the principle of myth itself . . . which critically determines the limits of possible experience."[267] We ought to trace this subjugation of Scripture to the myth of immanence to its origins in Baruch Spinoza's seminal treatise on Scripture on the basis of his rigorous philosophy of immanence.[268] This progressively more radical dialectic has crystallized in recent years in the attack by the contemporary History of Religions school on the very principle of canonicity.[269] We conclude our treatment of the holiness of Scripture by responding to this challenge.

The "canonical delimitation of the textual sources of theology," as I put it some years ago, is repudiated as "arbitrary vis-à-vis the variety of early Christian voices." The result is that the canon itself has come "more and more to appear as the very essence of the retrospective imposition of a dogmatic framework, the founding act of orthodoxy."[270] This is true, though the epigones of the History of Religion School hardly grasp its significance correctly. While contemporary figures like Elaine Pagels or James Robinson might come to mind in this regard, the searching probe along these lines was first made by Walter Bauer in his incisive *Orthodoxy and Heresy in Early Christianity*.[271] This culminating objection to Christian theology in the line that runs from Spinoza

---

267. Theodor W. Adorno and Max Horkheimer, *Dialectic of Enlightenment,* trans. John Cumming (London and New York: Verso, 1997), p. 12.

268. Baruch Spinoza, *Theological-Political Treatise,* trans. S. Shirley (Indianapolis: Hackett, 1998).

269. In several footnotes, Jenson carries on guerrilla warfare against Helmut Köster in his *ST* 1, p. 5n5, p. 32n28.

270. Paul R. Hinlicky, "Secular and Eschatological Conceptions of Salvation in the Controversy over the Invocation of God," in *This Is My Name Forever: The Trinity and Gender Language for God,* ed. Alvin Kimmel Jr. (Downers Grove, IL: InterVarsity, 2001) p. 222.

271. Walter Bauer, *Orthodoxy and Heresy in Early Christianity,* ed. R. Kraft and G. Krodel (Philadelphia: Fortress, 1971; reprint Sigler Press, 1996).

through the History of Religions School to Bauer strikes at the heart of the matter and as such actually contains a valuable insight. It implies that if, contrary to the intention of the objection, we receive the canonical Scriptures as holy, i.e., in their selection by the Spirit for formation of theological subjects in conformity with the cross and resurrection of Christ, then their holiness is to be sought and found in nothing other than this *selection*, i.e., this *sanctification* of texts from out of the mass of contending voices. In just this holy selectivity, concerning which historical criticism richly informs us, moreover, we discover the Bible's aptitude today to discriminate between voices contending for authority in the life of the people of God in mission to the nations. The historical critical interpretation of the thirteenth chapter of the (historically) first gospel, significantly, uncovers just this motive already in the seminal construction of the gospel narrative[272] — if we are willing to trace "early Catholicism" back that far![273]

Too often historically the "assured results" of criticism instead betray not only a fallible construction but an intention to make the critic invulnerable to theological criticism by rendering null and void the truth of the Word of God in Scripture and its claim in creed and confession, also on the biblical critic. But biblical criticism does not have to fall into this anti-theological trap.[274] Nor must a canonical theology that thinks consequently in a post-critical way beg the question of the true humanity of the Scriptures. The best theological criticism of the History of Religions scholarship lies in showing, not merely its incapacity as theology to provide for such critical judgments that test the spirits today, but its utter vulnerability to capture by spirits other than the Holy Spirit of Jesus and His Father.[275] In other words, reorientation of the doctrine of the authority of Scripture by pointing in the direction of the proper or holy use of the canon is not necessarily to lapse into pre-critical naïveté but rather to have become justifiably skeptical about the "assured results" of the modern criticism of Scripture after several centuries of experience with it.[276] The hermeneutical

272. Joel Marcus, *Mark 8–16,* The Anchor Yale Bible (New Haven and London: Yale University Press, 2009), pp. 864-923, esp. pp. 875, 896, and 922-23.

273. In the same dialectical fashion as the treatment of Bauer's valuable insight, then, we can take a study like Burton L. Mack, *A Myth of Innocence: Mark and Christian Origins* (Philadelphia: Fortress, 1988), as valuable for the critical insight into "early Catholicism" beginning already in Mark's "historicizing of the eschatological." This discussion continues below in Chapter Five, tracing Rosemary Ruether's brief against "historicizing the eschatological" back to a worthy patristic theologian, Theodore of Mopsuestia. Our interpretation of Mark, by contrast, is informed by the apocalyptic reading of Joel Marcus, also discussed below in Chapter Five.

274. Leander E. Keck, *A Future for the Historical Jesus: The Place of Jesus in Preaching and Theology* (Philadelphia: Fortress, 1981).

275. Susannah Heschel, *The Aryan Jesus: Christian Theologians and the Bible in Nazi Germany* (Princeton: Princeton University Press, 2008), is a devastating exposé of the scientific and disinterested history of religions inquiry of Walter Grundmann into Jesus "the Galilean" in service of "racial science."

276. So also Walter Brueggemann, *Theology of the Old Testament: Testimony, Dispute, Ad-*

approach[277] to this problematic, on the other hand, welcomes the opportunity to trace historically the decisions of the community of faith, taken as the inspiration of the Spirit, in deciding for and against texts and in ordering selected texts into the canonical whole to discover their integration in issuing knowledge of God.

Indeed, this latter inquiry also seems better justified historically and thus also critically. As I put it in an essay some years ago:

> In that very act of writing down and passing on the historically concrete words of prophets or apostles, sages or scribes, the Word of God is made to transcend its immediate occasion and to extend its meaning into the projected future of the community — yet without ever abandoning the primacy of the historically specific occasion which is preserved and handed on in just this fashion. In this light, we can say that a scriptural community in the world exists in that it stands before (what come to be assembled in time as) canonical texts in disciplined listening to their distinctive, historically specific and precisely as such untranslatable witnesses of the Word of God. Thus — and this is the critical point — this community exists by relying on the Spirit, who once spoke by these prophets, to speak to today's community anew. The community survives and flourishes if, and only if, this reliance on the same Spirit to speak anew is justified. So far as such confidence is justified, the canonical biblical narrative and the eschatological community of the ecclesia imply one another, "for whatever was written in former days was written for our instruction, so that by steadfastness and by the encouragement of the scriptures we might have hope" (Rom. 15:4).[278]

I would only add to this account today the further qualification, argued above, that in being placed into a canonical whole the phenomenon of intertextuality arises by means of which Scripture comes to interpret Scripture according to some implicit or explicit key. This too historically and critically has been demonstrated by the best contemporary biblical scholarship.[279]

---

*vocacy* (Minneapolis: Fortress, 1997), pp. 61-114. "*We now recognize that there is no interest-free interpretation, no interpretation that is not in the service of some interest and in some sense advocacy.* Indeed, it is an illusion of the Enlightenment that advocacy-free interpretation can exist" (p. 63, emphasis original). This judgment also reflects disagreement with Pannenberg, who rightly understood the "crisis of the Scripture principle," but wrongly sought to resolve it by the historical-critical knowledge of the resurrection. See Wolfhart Pannenberg, *Basic Questions in Theology,* two volumes, trans. G. H. Kehm (Philadelphia: Fortress, 1972), 1:1-14. To be clear, the Easter experience of the disciples is historically knowable. What is not knowable historically is their interpretation of this experience as resurrection, in that just this interpretation is the gift of theological subjectivity.

277. Such as attempted in *DC,* pp. 1-24.

278. Hinlicky, "Secular and Eschatological," p. 224.

279. Donald H. Juel, *Messianic Exegesis: Christological Interpretation of the Old Testament in Early Christianity* (Philadelphia: Fortress, 1988).

In Christian theology "the" Scriptures, i.e., the canonical Scriptures form a hermeneutical whole with creed and confession,[280] answering respectively the questions: What is the narrative? Who are its agents? What is its import for us? In answering these questions, or what is the same, in reading Scripture theologically, the Scriptures in this extended way work to critique the fallen world, to create in its maw the obedience of faith, to build up the community of this faith called out from the nations and so made holy by the gospel, and to absorb the world of common bodily experience in the cumulative play of ever-new interpretation. To quote the Bible in isolation from this hermeneutical complex — as barbaric, supersessionist, and triumphalist notions of *sola scriptura* attempt — proves nothing in an epistemological sense; in a theological sense, moreover, it less proves a point than puts the testimony of a theological subject under the judgment of the Word of God. To be sure, taking the Scriptures canonically may be for some "postliberals" today a pretext for begging the critical question of their human and historical origin, as happened in pre-critical theology. Some contemporary iterations of Ricoeur's "second naïveté" seem willfully pre-critical rather than genuinely post-critical.[281] "God said it, I believe it, that settles it" is the motto of theological barbarism. Over against this barbarism, the "destructive" work of modern criticism is fully justified. It is justified in demanding that the words of Scripture be known, at least in first part, by their original sense as human words in their own historical and social contexts. At its best such critical historical knowledge checks arbitrary, unethical, and ideological appropriation as that occurs in biblicism, crude or sophisticated. It is justified in requiring that present-day users take responsibility for their own appropriations of Scripture and not hide behind the authority of the sacred text that they allege to assert as if without any act of theological interpretation on their own part. The biblical author's own meaning in time and place is one thing and the meanings created by the Spirit in incorporating that authorship into the ensemble of the Scriptures for the use of the present community of faith in knowing God is another. Knowing this distinction further requires that these latter usages of texts be compatible theologically with the original sense as responsible developments of it, even as new usages cannot but exceed that original sense.

This "excess" is always the risk of faith, but it is not arbitrary. In appropriating texts in theological testimony, the invocation of authoritative Scripture may be likened to taking an oath, summoning the God of the Bible as a witness, projecting God as the ultimate audience of one's theological testimony, and thus submitting that testimony to the eschaton of divine judgment. To be sure, the proximate audience of theology is the people of one's own time and place, just as it was for the biblical authors. Before fellow human beings, consequently, one

280. See Hinlicky, "Luther's Anti-Docetism," pp. 147-49.

281. Luke Timothy Johnson, "Interpretive Dance: How the Brazos Biblical Commentary Falls Short," *Commonweal* 2, no. 18 (2012), accessed online at commonwealmagazine.org.

does not cite the Bible to make one's theological testimony invulnerable to criticism, but on the contrary to subject it to the proper criticism with one and all who likewise submit to the canon of the Scriptures. It is to invite those who do not to join this theological circle. This is the sense in which all theology that intends to be orthodox is and must be under the Holy Scriptures.

We conclude now with a reprisal. What are "the Scriptures," the canonical ones deemed "holy"? As previously mentioned, the bare-boned plot line and *dramatis personae* of them are given in the early Christian baptismal creed that sketches the story from Genesis to Revelation of the creation, redemption, and fulfillment of the one world by the One God through the missions of His Son and Spirit. If we supplement this admittedly hyper-succinct summary statement with the insights of modern biblical scholarship, we could perhaps flesh out the content of the Scriptures (thus answering the question, what is the narrative?) as follows:

> ... [T]he canonical narrative of human salvation tells of the gift of God's Reign which comes mercifully to lost and perishing children of Adam from the heavenly Father through the missions of Christ and the Spirit. Elect Israel was trained by God to expect salvation as the coming of the Reign, which would bring about the divine judgment and redemption of human history. In the fullness of time, Jesus, a son of Israel endowed with the Spirit of God, came proclaiming the advent of the Reign. He called upon that coming king, the God of Israel, as his own Father and freely invited others, but notably sinners, to join him in this same invocation of God. For this two-sided act of self-identification, at once with the Father as his own Son, and at the same time with the godless, Jesus was at length condemned and executed as a messianic pretender. The One whom Jesus called on as his Father, however, revealed the nearness of his kingly power by raising the Crucified from death and exalting him as Lord over all. In this very act, God re-cognized the crucified Jesus as His own beloved Son and validated His mission of mercy to sinners. The Father and the exalted Son sent their Spirit, creating the Church to be the body of the Christ in the drama of the history of salvation till every contra-divine power is subdued and God becomes all things to all people.[282]

Needless to say, details here can vary significantly,[283] but the general plot-line stands. Given the canonical boundaries, Scripture is a really existent collection of writings that cohere as such a narrative of the world's destiny as God's eschatological creation. To enunciate this narrative, not another, *is* the authority of the Bible in theology.

Yet this putative word of God appears amid many words of God. As a result

---

282. Hinlicky, "Secular and Eschatological," p. 213.
283. See the alternative formulation of Scripture's narrative content in *DC,* p. 13.

the Word of God as drawn from the Bible by the hermeneutical key of the gospel may be eschatologically fulfilled in such a way that falsifies any of our own particular theological claims about it. We live in and still belong to a religiously and philosophically pluralistic world, having in common the human body, its experience, and the contending accounts of this with the consequent confusions in the minds also of theologians. The problem of the Holy Scriptures as source and norm of particularly Christian theology belongs precisely in this pluralistic context of contending voices and contradictory claims and confused formulations in space and time; here a critical, not vulgar pluralism is demanded of all of us today on the earth as globally we are engaged in truly a life-and-death struggle for human survival itself. Here the burning question is not whether sacred texts inform, but what texts should inform as sacred, why and how diverse texts may be compatible and, where not, how rationally satisfying and ethically edifying disagreement can be achieved. If we would be theologians in the living tradition of Luther, this is how rigorously we are to think today about the "disputable" (Pannenberg) existence of the biblical God[284] on the basis of the prolepsis in Christ made known through the Scriptures. "The fact that reality and the revelation of God are debatable is part of the reality of the world which dogmatics has to consider as God's world."[285] Critical dogmatics attends rigorously to who it is that speaks and invites to faith, thus also to whose we are as theologians, namely and with the non-substitutable specificity that the Scriptures attest when read as evangelical narrative: the Father in the Son by the Spirit.

This knowledge of God from the Scriptures is — with a twist — Tillich's famous "theological circle": "a person can be a theologian as long as he acknowledges the content of the theological circle as his ultimate concern."[286] This circle is not the vicious circle of foundationalist epistemology, but the eternal circle of the love of the Father and the Son in the Spirit that becomes temporal in the gift and task of theological subjectivity. When theological subjects are themselves thus interpreted by the faith of Christ, the Bible may be understood on its own terms in accord with the Spirit's holy intention in the timely way that is both needed and required; here the audience of understanding and confession is the Father of the incarnate Son known in the Spirit. As holy testimony read by those being made holy, moreover, the Bible yields the principal doctrines of the *fides catholica,* which must be considered as analytic of the singular truth-claim that the God of the Bible is the One who is determined by His Son and Spirit to redeem and fulfill this creation.

284. "But dogmatics may not presuppose the divine true which the Christian doctrinal tradition claims. Theology has to present, test, and if possible confirm the claim. It must treat it, however, as an open question and not decide it in advance. Its concern must be that in the course of all its thinking and arguments the rightness of the claim is at issue." Pannenberg, *ST* 1, p. 50.

285. Pannenberg, *ST* 1, p. 49.

286. Tillich, *ST* 1, p. 10.

These doctrines that make a normative and ecumenical claim as "normed norms" *(norma normata)* on all Christian theology that intends to be orthodox and ecumenical, that is, to work within the matrix of Scripture in the "theological circle" are as follows. (1) The Genesis-to-Revelation canon telling the story of the creation to its consummation in the Beloved Community from the revealed perspective of the Father's *oikonomia*. (2) The Trinity, identifying the author of the canonical story in the divine project of eschatological creation: the Father with His Son and Spirit as the one God. (3) The Second of the aforementioned Three as He who became a servant in order to liberate the enslaved. And (4) the free and unmerited love of the Spirit of the Father and the Son by which creation is graciously given, preserved, redeemed, and fulfilled in the coming of the Beloved Community. These four doctrines stemming from the originating canonical decision against dualism are normative for ecumenical Christian theology in the forms of canon, creed, and confession, even though (and despite significant recent progress) the fourth of them is still in dispute.[287] The canon of the Genesis-to-Revelation narrative gives us the divine *oikonomia,* revealing the divine self-determination from before the foundations of the world to love us in the Beloved, making a Beloved Community in the act of eschatological creation. The ecumenical creeds provide us with the dramatis personae, the Father who does all things in the Spirit through the Son who became a Servant, the man Jesus Christ, to give His righteousness and life in place of sin and death. The confession tells us how dying sinners are rightly or justly included in the Beloved Community by the event, not the principle or idea, but the biographical event of grace, that is, by the surplus of love that is eternally and also externally the Spirit proceeding from the Father of the Son *ad extra* to reach a particular person in a particular history. To the exposition of this body of doctrine in its systematic coherence we are now prepared to turn.

287. See the previous section, "Does Faith Justify?"

# PART TWO

# Pneumatology

Jesus is the Son who in the power of the Spirit believed in God as our Father. Whoever believes does so by Spirit-imparted participation in the faith of Jesus, hence by the Spirit's impartation of the cross of the Messiah, working the spiritual death of the sinner.

# CHAPTER THREE

# The Theological Subject

## The "Natural" Man (1 Cor. 2:14)

"I believe in God." With this pronouncement of the new and theological subjectivity, the doctrinal standards of ecumenical Christianity begin, as in the familiar Apostles' Creed that evolved from the old Roman baptismal formula.[1] This action is twice repeated, constituting a formal declaration of belief in the Father almighty, Christ Jesus His only Son, and the Spirit of the aforementioned Father and Son. Who speaks here? Who is the agent here making an *assertion* about deity, taking "assurance of things hoped for, conviction of things not seen" (Heb. 11:1) in this threefold confession? Faith is not bodily sight, which believes the present evidence of one's senses, though it includes such seeing and indeed turns into fantasy if it does not essentially presuppose bodily sight — and hearing, touching, tasting, and smelling (1 John 1:1-4). Rather, faith sees what the common body sees, the same present evidence of the senses as anyone else. But it sees in a new light and from a new perspective that has come upon the believer, the very gift and work of the Spirit that the New Testament calls *faith*. Accordingly the subject here is not Paul's "natural man," the one struggling to survive in the order of (fallen) nature as an exile from paradisiacal existence (Gen. 3:16-19), who does not "accept the things that come from the Spirit of God, for they are foolishness to him, and he cannot understand them, because they are spiritually discerned" (1 Cor. 2:6-16).

Yet in the order of nature there is also the need and will to believe, even if only the aforementioned evidence of one's own senses — e.g., witness the not infrequent experience of cognitive dissonance, as in "I can't believe my own eyes!" More often, however, indeed regularly we believe authorities who interpret the evidence apparent to all in broader, better-tested, and thus truer perspectives

---

1. J. N. D. Kelly, *Early Christian Creeds,* 3rd edition (New York: David McKay, 1972), pp. 100-66. The Nicene Creed, constructed to establish the doctrinal consensus of regional churches in Eucharistic fellowship, begins in the plural, "We believe. . . ."

than any individual set of eyes can acquire. Our scientific ability to question our own immediate sense experience; the moral experience of having our naïvely egocentric perspective called into question; our cultivated need as citizens to trust (but also verify) the opinion of experts and political leaders in the complex and manifold challenges of civilized life; our philosophical scrutiny that queries whether apparent goods are truly good or claims to truth are really so — all these critical ruminations work, not to do away with trust, but rather to make trust viable by critically ascertaining trustworthy beliefs. Faith is thus an imperative also of natural existence, and with it comes also critical scrutiny upon "animal faith" (Santayana) and its would-be objects of trust.

From this anthropological datum[2] of the ubiquity of basic faith in human existence arises an apparent *sensus divinitatis* (Rom. 2:15), the posit of an ultimate basis and object of faith. So Calvin taught: "all men have a vague general veneration for God. . . . There is within the human mind, and indeed by natural instinct, an awareness of divinity."[3] It is a "natural law, as St. Paul says (Rom. 1:20), that the Gentiles also know that there is a God," wrote Luther, that is, that there is an author of existence who by right is also author of the moral imperative to trust and be trustworthy. Theologians following Paul have thus distinguished between the innate moral sense (Rom. 2:15) and the acquired cosmological knowledge of God by inference from nature as from effect to its transcendent cause (Rom. 1:20). By means of the latter reasoning the basic trust endemic to human life together in the common body arises critically in search of a worthy conception of deity as the supreme source and object of trust. Such theologians have thus spoken of the "natural theology" that comes from the reflective correlation of these two paths: the starry heavens above and the moral sense within, as Kant articulated this tradition for modernity.

According to Luther, evidence that such reflection is not mere speculation but an important rational inquiry derives from "the fact [that] all the heathen have set up gods and arranged forms of divine service, which would have been impossible if they had neither known nor thought about God."[4] In large part, "philosophy" in ancient Greece arose in criticism of the "myths of the gods" in search of worthier conceptions of deity in support of more rational forms of social existence. Yet Luther's criticism of religion is not quite the same as that of the philosophers who sought to break the spell of cosmogonic myths that seemed to encode violence by distancing deity from humanity, albeit from within a cosmic totality that encompassed both. But Luther could famously assert that "to have a god is to have something in which the heart trusts com-

---

2. From a sociobiological perspective, see Matt Ridley, *The Origins of Virtue* (London: Penguin, 1997), pp. 247-65.

3. John Calvin, *Institutes of the Christian Religion,* vol. 1, trans. F. L. Battles (Philadelphia: Westminster, 1975), p. 43.

4. *LW* 40, p. 97.

pletely"[5] — even if that be something as small as one's own self and its powers (as is common today, for example, in Robert Bellah's "Sheilaism").[6] So also Luther could make the philosophically interesting argument that "having a god" in the sense of basic trust in something worthy of trust is at the root of human life, no matter whether we parse that task as living well, or virtuously, or dutifully, or effectively.

The need to believe of the "natural man" gives Christian theology at least these three avenues of epistemic *access* to the faiths of the common body: the moral sense, the cosmological wonder, and the phenomenon of the cult. Christian theology finds human creatures already wondering about, feeling obligated by, and trying to relate to "the divine." When they do so deliberately and critically by striving to arise to a worthy conception of the divine, they are doing "natural theology," even if covertly and by terminology other than "God." "Access" is thus provided to Christian theology, that is to say, common topics for dialogue and disputation, not "foundations," as if to erect on a common natural knowledge of God a superstructure of revealed theology.

"Access" is itself the Christian theological conviction that believer and non-believer share a common world, the very creation that is the object of God's redeeming love and destined for fulfillment in the Beloved Community. So indeed it must be, if, as Augustine famously prayed in the light of revelation, "Thou hast made us for Thyself and our hearts are restless until they find their rest in Thee." Augustine's insight here is a precious one: basic trust is requisite to the common body because its life is never complete in itself but always one of desire; in humanity that becomes desire for righteousness, desire for knowledge, desire for blessing, supremely and in sum desire for life itself, the source of life, for the life that is eternal. That remains so even if enlightened reason regards this desire as infantile, renounces it, and adopts a tragic view of life of always wanting more than it can possibly have — as the figures of Nietzsche and Freud emblematize for emergent postmodernity. The revealed truth, however, is that human beings "do not live on bread alone, but on every word that comes from the mouth of God" (Matt. 4:4) and that all needful, though temporary, desires will be satisfied for those who "seek first the Reign of God and its righteousness" (Matt. 6:33). Of course, desire can be captured by bread and circuses, palpable satisfactions, but unable to bear the weight of infinite desire.

So Pannenberg was right to ask Karl Barth, famous or notorious for his categorical repudiation of natural theology, whether "it is not a feature of God's revelation in Christ that it presupposes the fact that the world and humanity belong to, and know, the God who is proclaimed by the gospel, even though a wholly

---

5. *BC*, p. 387.

6. Robert N. Bellah, Richard Madsen, William M. Sullivan, Ann Swidler, and Steven M. Tipton, *Habits of the Heart: Individualism and Commitment in American Life* (Berkeley: University of California Press, 1985).

new light is shed on this fact by the revelation in Christ. . . ."[7] Just so, however, the foregoing reflections on de facto theologies of the natural man, as upon one lost in wayward desires captivated in various ways by lesser goods, do not arise as the natural man's spontaneous self-analysis. Just as little does the natural man know himself as "natural" as opposed to "spiritual." Rather these are interpretations of humanity by revealed theology. Indeed knowledge of captivity to lesser goods than true God, that is, captivity to idols or bondage to demons, would call the entire existence of the natural man into question. Such a total critique is as inconceivable as unmotivated apart from the intervention of the gospel. So at the least it is an incautious statement when Pannenberg further adjudges, "The natural theology of the philosophers had formulated a criterion for judging whether any God could be seriously considered as the author of the whole cosmos, and Christian theology had to meet this criterion if its claim could be taken seriously that the God who redeems us in Jesus Christ is the Creator of heaven and earth and thus the one true God of all peoples."[8] It is highly questionable, that is to say, whether natural theology in the Greek tradition ever conceived of God as the Creator of all that is not God, hence Creator *ex nihilo;* equally questionable then is Pannenberg's tacit equation of "nature" (physis) and "creation" (ktisis).[9] In fact, we shall argue, "creation" is the Christian theological interpretation of the common body (= "nature"). And it is the Spirit who unifies this sign (nature) with thing signified (creation) where and when the Spirit wills by revealing the creative Word of God in the flesh of the common body, Jesus Christ, the man who is the Son of God.

The very categorization here of "natural" thus presupposes a new theological subjectivity that ought rather to account for itself before it accounts for others by writing a natural theology on their behalf — as if theology could do philosophy better than philosophers. If theology forgets this newness of its own inquiry, on the other hand, it forgets its own epistemic access by way of the Word of God and becomes lost in the welter of phenomena being explored in morality, cosmology, and religious studies; moreover, in this forgetfulness theology indulges in an invidious categorizing of natural goods as "lesser," conveniently arranged into a teleology leading naturally enough to the theologian's highest good. The three traditional ways to conceptions of deity in "natural theology" of morality, cosmology, and the cult are rather to be understood as retrospective reflections of faith. Within Christian theology, these explorations are more "theology of the natural man" than "natural theology." The revealed God in the process of giving and revealing Himself to faith also reveals His lost and dying human creature in bondage to religiously sanctified structures of malice and injustice in worldviews,

---

7. Pannenberg, *ST* 1, p. 75.

8. Pannenberg, *ST* 1, p. 79. See also his early formulation of the problem in *Basic Questions in Theology,* 2 vols., trans. G. H. Kehm (Philadelphia: Fortress, 1972), 1:119-83.

9. Pannenberg concedes the latter point to Jüngel in a footnote, *ST* 1, p. 79n46.

in moral orders, and in the business of religion. Such diagnoses are the creatures of revealed theology. As theological constructs, that is, as knowledge of God, they are not "natural" at all!

Such natural awareness of God as exists cannot be conscripted, then, to serve as an anthropological foundation for theology, as for example in the contemporary systematic theologies of a Pannenberg or a Rahner. The latter writes: "This unthematic and ever-present experience, this knowledge of God which we always have even when we are thinking of and concerned with anything but God, is the permanent ground from out of which that thematic knowledge of God emerges which we have in explicitly religious activity and philosophical reflection . . . [in which] we are only making explicit for ourselves what we already know implicitly about ourselves in the depths of our personal self-realization."[10] Pannenberg is arguably more cautious here than to issue a blank check this way to unthematized human religiosity. Yet, the rationalism of his basic approach requires that the finite self-reflection of human consciousness against a vague screen of infinity — fittingly enough drawn from Descartes — be established as a modernized natural theology. This anthropological foundation gives traction to the initial claim of revelation in speaking of God. "God" is a naturally intelligible concept as the articulation of the vague but presupposed Infinite. "God" is the articulate thematization of Rahner's unthematized awareness in the depths of our self-realization. Notice that this makes human consciousness, more precisely modern self-consciousness rather than the common body, into an epistemological basis of theology. But it is rather, as presently proposed, the common body that is the place of epistemic access for the cognitive claims that revealed theology goes on to make in regard to common humanity and its ersatz knowledges (note the plural) of God.

There is, as indicated, a proper concern for faith in Rahner and Pannenberg, since the gospel comes as liberating news to beings who are in captivity. This proclamation of freedom, it is argued, falls on deaf ears if there is no preexisting awareness of the miserable state of captivity or of human responsibility to God in it.[11] Such precisely is the experience of many a preacher nowadays. How does one liberate the captive who does not know or acknowledge captivity but is rather bewitched or enthralled, knowing nothing better than the nation-state as object of ultimate allegiance? How does one proclaim the forgiveness of sins to pawns of malice and injustice who feel no responsibility for their plight — for whom, as Nietzsche pilloried, the forgiveness of sins is an imaginary solution to an imagi-

---

10. Karl Rahner, *Foundations of the Christian Faith: An Introduction to the Idea of Christianity,* trans. William V. Dych (New York: Seabury, 1978), p. 53.

11. This concern was argued with passion and insight by Gustav Wingren in *Theology in Conflict: Nygren, Barth, Bultmann* (Philadelphia: Muhlenberg, 1958): "We have emphasized that the gospel in the New Testament implies a liberation from bondage, and that it is questionable whether this aspect of the gospel appears clearly in modern theology" (p. 151).

nary problem? Must one not prepare the ground for the preaching of the gospel by an immanent and thus incisive analysis of the human condition that reveals its unquenched thirst for the supernatural (Milbank), or its moral paralysis before urgent imperatives to save the earth (Wisnefske), or its impending eternal ruin (evangelicalism), or its terror in the night and at the approach of death (existentialism), or its oppression under sexism, racism, or classism (liberationism)? Such approaches today are legion. As mentioned, they do address a proper concern of faith.

But this very problematic turns out to be far more profound than these various modern attempts in anthropological foundationalism imagine. So Luther: "I believe that I cannot by my own reason or understanding believe in my Lord Jesus Christ or come to Him, but the Holy Spirit has called me by the gospel. . . ." "The crooked man thinks crookedly and speaks crookedly even about his own crookedness" (Barth) because, once again with Luther, "This inherited sin has caused such a deep, evil corruption of nature that reason does not comprehend it; rather, it must be believed on the basis of the revelation in the Scriptures."[12] The depth and true misery of human captivity is that we do not and cannot know it or acknowledge it or take responsibility for it unless, and until, someone breaks in to bind up the strong man in order to plunder his goods (Mark 3:27), as per a brief but key apocalyptic parable. The parable portrays, in echo of the Red Sea and Sinai, "a God who destroys the captivity of human beings by placing them in a higher captivity to himself."[13] As right as Jürgen Moltmann was when he wrote in his seminal *The Theology of Hope* that "[w]ithout apocalyptic a theological eschatology remains bogged down in the ethnic history of men or the existential history of the individual," forfeiting the "vistas of the cosmos,"[14] he did not yet have the problem of the acquisition of theological subjectivity in view. Rightly trying to move beyond the transcendentalisms of Bultmann and Barth, Moltmann was able to take the ferment of the 1960s in Euro-America as a sign of the Spirit stirring and leave the matter at that. Today, however, after the "end of history" when everything appears to be more of the same, Euro-American postmodernity grimly assesses its "biopolitical captivity" and owns up, if at all, to its objective hopelessness.[15] There appears to be no change in which we can believe. But Moltmann saw that theological strategies to meet modern self-consciousness halfway are part of the problem, not the solution.

If Pannenberg was right to trace modern self-consciousness to Descartes, there is no way that the preceding paragraph can fail to offend what Reinhold

---

12. *BC*, p. 311.

13. Joel Marcus, *Mark 1–8, A New Translation with Introduction and Commentary*, The Anchor Bible vol. 27 (New Haven and London: Yale University Press, 2000), p. 283.

14. Jürgen Moltmann, *The Theology of Hope: On the Ground and the Implications of a Christian Eschatology*, trans. James W. Leitch (New York: Harper & Row, 1967), p. 138.

15. On the theological interpretation of "biopolitical captivity" see *RPTD*, pp. 114-20.

Niebuhr called "the easy conscience of modern man" (including this "modern self-consciousness" who has just penned it). The notion of sinfulness strikes us as a morbid idea and a literally useless one that only humiliates and cripples — useful only as a mechanism of social discipline by "priestcraft," as the epigones of the Enlightenment complained. Yet recalling the discussion of Daniel Bell's thesis about the captivation of desire from the previous chapter, there is a compelling rationale for receiving the notion of human sinfulness precisely in its abiding offense to modern self-consciousness. Anyone today who, like Agamben, is concerned that the failure of Marxism-Leninism to provide a plausible human future has left the world at the mercy of a self-validating juggernaut merrily hurtling towards catastrophe with hapless Euro-America holding the reins, will in principle have to sympathize with the notion that the depth of our captivity consists in a strangely willful ignorance of it. Theological fellow-travelers like Agamben, who try to break the spell of our false consciousness by genealogical explorations that uncover the sources of it, are not far from the kingdom of God — indeed much nearer than cheerleading theologians of unembarrassed optimism.

Within modern theology itself, it was the father of the social gospel theology, Walter Rauschenbusch, who maintained that, although "many modern theologians are ready to abandon this doctrine [of original sin], and among many laymen it seems to carry so little sense of reality that audiences often smile at its mention[,] I take pleasure . . . in defending it. It is one of the few attempts of individualistic theology to get a solidaristic view of its field of work . . . [namely, of the human] race as a great unity, descended from a single head, and knit together through all ages by unity of origin and blood."[16] Rauschenbusch was mainly interested in the socio-ethical dimension of the "corporate personality" view embedded in the Adam-Christ typology in Romans 5. Yet he recognized the ever-accumulating web of sin and guilt fueling and refueling the structures of malice and injustice that he named apocalyptically the "Kingdom of Evil."

To anticipate a little: these malicious episodes of organized chaos are the incursions of actual evil into the web of life when and where the possibilities that God has rejected in electing our world for the coming of the Beloved Community are selected, bursting out as lethal dynamisms sweeping up all in their paths. They leverage sin unrepented and guilt unacknowledged and death denied to live parasitically in anticipation of the insatiable satisfactions of the revenge fantasy. The malice of envy becomes actual in structures that pervert what is a good creature of God into organized chaos — think the unholy trinity of "modern self-consciousness": Hitler, Hiroshima, and Stalin.

So there are both philosophically and theologically urgent reasons to question the offense that modern consciousness takes at the notion of sinfulness — namely, that we are both victims and perpetrators of structures of malice and in-

16. Walter Rauschenbusch, *A Theology for the Social Gospel* with an Introduction by Donald W. Shriver Jr. (Louisville: Westminster John Knox, 1997), p. 57.

justice and so in forfeit of humanity's divine calling, even though the faithful God continues to create and preserve what He has vowed yet to redeem and fulfill. Is there a plausible way of retrieving the content Rauschenbusch identified for aid in exposing our contemporary blindness about which Agamben worries? Notice that the question so posed is not about "relevance," but rather "true" relevance, not on the basis of borrowed insight from other disciplines but with knowledge produced by theology itself. In this way Niebuhr praised Rauschenbusch's social gospel, despite a certain soteriological shallowness, as eminently more realistic than the individualistic revivalism that had preceded it in American history (as we shall discuss in detail later in this chapter). If the theological subject, then, is not to be found "naturally" in a world under the "unnatural" but formative sway of structures of malice and injustice, when and where does it appear? Entering into the matrix of the Scriptures, let us look and see how the cognitive organization of the theological subject is given as God heard understands God spoken and so recognizes God who speaks.

## John 20: Hearing Is Believing Is Seeing in a New Way

The story of Easter day in the Gospel of John[17] addresses the question of the subject of faith and its knowledge of God in the way that it depicts the self-revelation of Jesus to grieving, hopeless disciples after the shattering events of His death and burial. The dramatic center of each of the main episodes found in John 20 and 21 is the moment of recognition when the identification of the Risen One as crucified Jesus of Nazareth, who had died and been buried, takes place. This new perception correlates with the genesis of faith. In each case that recognition does not consist in the sheer appearance of the Risen One, but rather comes about by means of some significant act of speech on His part which establishes the speaker's personal continuity with the activity and fate of the crucified "king of the Jews" (John 19:19-22).

Mary Magdalene is called by name. She hears in this the voice of the Good Shepherd who lays down his life for the sheep, the One who said, "My sheep hear my voice. I know them, and they follow me. I give them eternal life, and they will never perish. No one will snatch them out of my hand" (John 10:27-28). At the sound of her name, Mary recognizes the figure that stands beside her in the garden as her *Rabboni,* the one whose missing body she had been seeking in her distress. Likewise, upon the greeting "Peace be with you," the disciples in hiding see the marks of the nails on the hands and of the spear in the side of the One who has suddenly stood before them in the shuttered room — and so the disciples rejoiced when they saw that He who now speaks peace to them was indeed the

---

17. An earlier version of this exegesis appeared as "Resurrection and the Knowledge of God," *Pro Ecclesia* 4, no. 2 (Spring 1995): 226-32.

Lord. The Beloved Disciple similarly perceived that the stranger on the shore of the Sea of Tiberias, who had directed their fishing nets to a great shoal of fish after a luckless night, was the Lord, i.e., the same one who had so richly provided for them before, in these same whereabouts, when in a great sign he showed them aforetime that His glory would be to give His flesh as meat to eat and His blood as drink (John 6).

The human recognition of the Risen One as Jesus of Nazareth, who was crucified under Pontius Pilate, dead and buried, is the effect of the self-revelation, which is in turn always the *act* of the Risen Lord's *speech* from the enigma of his apparition. The mysterious and unseen event of Easter itself, i.e., "the resurrection," expresses the judgment of God about Jesus. The resurrection of Jesus from the dead is God's speech-act who so recognized His beloved Son and thus confirmed His own divine Fatherhood of this Son who had truly died for others, the innocent wrapped up in the guilty.[18] Faith in Jesus, if it is to be true faith, can only consist in the perception and appropriation *of the same divine judgment* regarding crucified Jesus, yet now as mediated by this very One as risen from death, and so appropriated as faith *in* Jesus Christ, the Son of God. In the Johannine resurrection appearances, the crucified Lord *reveals* Himself to Mary, Peter, and the Beloved Disciple as He now exists — vindicated, exalted, glorified — because of the Easter judgment of His God and their God, His Father and their Father (20:17). Thus He elicits among human beings *true* faith in Him, i.e., that *validly* leads to the eternal life which Jesus now enjoys and has the right also to share. Whoever knows and believes that *Jesus* is the Christ, the Son of God, knows what God knew when the grave was vacated and Jesus awoke to new existence in and as this now glorified humanity. Christology, therefore, insists that the question of who Jesus is *for God* frames the question of who Jesus is *for us* and only so can be soteriologically valid and truly transformational, that is, making believers in Jesus relevant to the project of God for the coming of the Beloved Community. The one who believes, then, is the one to whom the Father reveals the vindicated Son; the one who hears vindicated Jesus' promise addressed personally; the one who in coming to believe has passed by the Spirit from death to life.

Dietrich Bonhoeffer put the point thematically: "My sin is forgiven, I am no longer in death, but in life. All this depends upon the person of Christ, whether his work perishes in the world of death or abides in a new world of life. But how can the person of Christ be comprehended other than by his works, i.e. otherwise than through history? This objection contains a most profound error. For even Christ's work is not unequivocal. . . . There is no point in the life of Jesus in which one could say with unambiguous conviction that here we see the Son of

---

18. ". . . God defines himself when he identifies with the dead Jesus. At the same time, he defines the man Jesus as the Son of God." Eberhard Jüngel, *God as the Mystery of the World*, trans. D. L. Guder (Grand Rapids: Eerdmans, 1983), pp. 363-64.

God, proved to be such by one of his works."[19] In this way, Bonhoeffer makes the predominant Jewish unbelief in Jesus a principle internal to Christian theological reflection itself. With Israel, Bonhoeffer denies that any of Jesus' reported works or fulfillments of prophecy in the passage from Nazareth to Jerusalem prove His identity as the Son of God. On the contrary, the earthly course of the man Jesus, though surfeit with signs, according to John, had provoked a theological crisis — a crisis not merely in Israel but in Israel's God, who by Jesus' own testimony had led Him (or, as in Mark, abandoned Him) to the cross. Easter morn dawns to reveal the resolution of this crisis in the life of God, how God has surpassed God in order to find the unholy and ruined, the dead and buried, to reclaim these as His own in the body of Jesus and sanctify them in and with Him once and for all. It follows that soteriology is a function of Christology, in the sense that if crucified, dead, and buried Jesus is divinely vindicated, then the human salvation that He now brings as the Risen One is communion of the *dead* with God, reconciliation of the *sinner* with God, liberation of the oppressed from the oppression *of the devil* — *only* the dead, *only* the sinner, *only* the maniac. The declaration of the Risen Lord to failed disciples is not a narcotic of inner tranquility but a militant's shout of victory: "Peace be with you."

Recall now the episode of the footrace of Peter and the Beloved Disciple to the emptied tomb on Easter morn and of the confession of doubting Thomas on the following Sunday evening. The striking thing in the first case is that the Beloved Disciple grasps the significance of the emptied tomb and believes, that is, *without* the help of the Scriptures as is expressly noted, *without* the help even of the appearance of the Risen One (as we may infer on the basis of Mary's "secondhand" report that the grave had been vacated). Is there a connection between this perplexing picture of the Beloved Disciple's coming to faith within the emptied tomb at the sight of emptied grave clothes and the Thomas story? The Beloved Disciple is said here to see, and believe upon seeing, the emptied *grave clothes* in the vacated *tomb,* just as Thomas will finally believe in grasping the significance of *the wounds* that still scar the Risen One. In both cases, the reports of others attesting the Easter Word from God regarding the Crucified led to perception of evidence — not that a Risen one had indeed risen but rather that the Risen one who had appeared was indeed Jesus, that is, the man they knew who had truly been crucified, died, and buried. The theological point is not proof of the resurrection. The point is Christological and *anti-docetic.* Thomas and the Beloved Disciple understand the significance of these signs of true death and burial that had happened and come to believe that the Father of Jesus has gloried His Son, as had been told them. It is this *anti-docetic, virtually materialistic identification of Jesus as corpse with the risen Lord proclaimed to them by the witness of others* that connects the Beloved Disciple's seeing and

19. Dietrich Bonhoeffer, *Christ the Center,* trans. E. H. Robertson (San Francisco: Harper & Row, 1978), p. 38.

believing to the Thomas story and clarifies sharply the Johannine sense of the new subjectivity of faith.

The Thomas story, in other words, is not an object lesson about coming to a decision of Easter faith that "overcomes" the scandal of the cross based on the Word alone, without the aid of sight and sign, as Rudolf Bultmann thought.[20] For John, faith always consists in the theological judgment that Jesus of Nazareth (who remains an object of common sight, and as such an object of the disciples' testimony about Him, and thus also an object of historical inquiry in the common world of the body) — this *Jesus* is the Christ, the Son of God. In the world of the Gospels (in this there is no difference between John and the Synoptics), Jesus' ministry provokes the acute question of his identity and authority. A true judgment about Jesus, however, proves to be one that only God can make and that only upon "the world's" fierce and definitive rejection of Jesus at Golgotha. Over against *that* rejection of Jesus by the world, God's affirmation of Jesus is precisely the joyful tiding of Easter morn. The purpose of the appearance narratives is to establish this divine identification of Jesus *for us* so that faith *in Jesus* is established and believers are invested with authority *in His Name* to carry out God's mission (John 20:21-23).[21] The point of the Thomas story is accordingly that the doubting disciple traces the visible wounds of the Risen One to discover that He is indeed the *same* Jesus *who was crucified.* The result is that he falls before the crucified but now glorified Man and worships *Him* as his *Lord and God.* This picture of worshiping Thomas gives John's readers an icon of the rightly believing community over against docetist rivals invoking the apostolic authority of Thomas.[22] The rightly believing community is the one that has been led to the same judgment of Jesus as His God and Father had made on Easter morn.

The dominical blessing therefore falls upon those who will afterward come to believe that which Thomas came to believe, though they do not themselves see the Risen One in the same immediate way that he saw, but rather envision Jesus through the testimony of these historically unique and divinely appointed witnesses. For that reason, those who follow in faith are dependent on this unique testimony, so that through it they perceive and believe the very *same* Jesus, albeit in derivative fashion. The stress then does not fall on the power of eyewitness experience to overwhelm a hypothetical skeptic with physical evidence of the resurrection miracle, taken as a return of Jesus to earthly vitality. The speech of the risen Jesus governs the seeing so that seeing consists in the personally *invited* recognition of the crucified but now risen Christ *as one and the same person.*

20. Rudolf Bultmann, *The Gospel of John: A Commentary,* trans. G. R. Beasley-Murray (Philadelphia: Westminster, 1976), pp. 693-99.

21. Sir Edwyn Clement Hoskyns, *The Fourth Gospel,* ed. Francis Noel Davey (London: Faber & Faber, 1947). See the discussion in *DC*, pp. 87-92.

22. Gregory J. Riley, *Resurrection Reconsidered: Thomas and John in Controversy* (Minneapolis: Fortress, 1995).

As Bruce Marshall has argued: "When the Father has done his work on the dead Jesus, and the Spirit has done his work on us, whether our belief that Jesus is risen is true depends on Jesus himself, on his free self-presentation, his spontaneous creative willingness that the belief that he is risen be true."[23] The stress here falls upon the *personal freedom* of the crucified but risen Jesus Christ — what early Lutheranism called the *"ubivolipraesens Christi"* — being present where and when He freely wills.[24] Marshall further calls attention to the Trinitarian structure of this event. "The Father brings about the true belief that Jesus is risen by raising Jesus. The Holy Spirit brings about the true belief that Jesus is risen by enabling people to hold this belief true. The Son Jesus brings about the true belief that he himself is risen by freely presenting himself such that when this belief is held true, it is true."[25] For the same reason, however, early Christians understood that testimony of the resurrection could in principle be doubted (John 14:22). Thus, for John, the nonapologetic and rather dogmatic accent falls on establishing the *content* of Easter faith among those who believe, however imperfectly, and belong to the new community of faith, however precariously. What matters here is that we see one and the same *Jesus*. The issue is the *content* of Easter faith as faith in *Jesus*. The function of these stories is *to specify* for those who afterward come to believe "that *Jesus* is the Christ, the Son of God" (20:31). So faith comes about in response to *His* greeting of victory peace, a greeting which in *His* very Breath *converts* the hearer (John 20:22) by the gift of the Spirit — or there is no faith at all.

We may entertain briefly an objection to the foregoing account of the rise of theological subjectivity as encounter with the crucified and risen Christ by the apostolic testimony to Him. It is certainly the case that the Johannine resurrection narratives come later in the primitive Christian theological development and that historically we have traveled a definite distance from what Adolf von Harnack called the "simple gospel" of Jesus' own faith in the heavenly Father. *"The Gospel, as Jesus proclaimed it, has to do with the Father only and not with the Son."*[26] Roughly true, in all probability. The problem, however, is that we have no simple, that is to say, direct access to Jesus' own faith as a possibility for us. His faith, such as it was, was defeated and so refuted on the cross, so far as we can see historically and critically. We have access to Jesus' own faith only by the way of faith in Jesus' *vindicated* faith — the gift of the Holy Spirit that comes by proclaiming His vindication in the Father's Easter speech-act with the result that we too come to know Jesus as the Christ, the Son of God. We will at length come

23. Bruce D. Marshall, *Trinity and Truth* (Cambridge: Cambridge University Press, 2000), p. 251.

24. Martin Chemnitz, *The Two Natures of Christ,* trans. J. A. O. Preus (St. Louis: Concordia, 1971), p. 278.

25. Marshall, *Trinity and Truth,* p. 256.

26. Adolf von Harnack, *What Is Christianity? Sixteen Lectures Delivered in the University of Berlin during the Winter Term, 1899-1900,* trans. Thomas Bailey Saunders (New York: G. P. Putnam, 1901), p. 144.

to Jesus' own faith in His heavenly Father (in Chapter Seven below), but we must travel to that faith of the man Christ by the mission of the Spirit. It is the Spirit who leads us to the mission of the Son of God. This we too must engage in the acquisition of theological subjectivity before we can properly understand and appreciate the faith of Jesus in the heavenly Father who sent and anointed Him to serve the coming of His reign.

Long before the Fourth Evangelist wove these tales of Easter morn, the message of Easter from God concerning His crucified Son had been given the name in primitive Christianity "the gospel," the powerful speech-act of God to save all who believe (Rom. 1:16). This power to save when proclaimed in the Spirit did not refer to some purely future or otherworldly state. It refers to an actual event on the earth, working in its auditors conformation to Christ by imparting to them His death and resurrection. John's gloss on this term, gospel, is the "word of life" (20:31), yet importantly it is not simply or obviously so. It is good news for retirement accounts that the stock market goes up, but that is not the "gospel." I may find it liberating to hear that "God is dead" and that "anything is now possible." But neither is that "the gospel." That one regards this particular message *about Jesus who ended on the imperial stake* as good news is already sign of the Spirit's calling that has challenged previous convictions and altered antecedent values in working a *conversion*.

As the Apostle Paul wrote to Gentile *converts* in his earliest preserved letter: ". . . you have *turned* to God from idols, to serve a living and true God, and to wait for his Son from heaven, whom he raised from the dead, Jesus, who rescues us from the wrath that is to come" (1 Thess. 1:9b-10). Or in John's idiom: "But to all who received him, who believed in his name, he gave power to become children of God, who were born, not of blood or of the will of the flesh or of the will of man, but of God" (John 1:12-13). The "gospel" of the living God, who gave life to His crucified Son and promises to give the *same* life to believers, just so "converts" hearers to "faith" by bestowing on them the same Spirit working a transformation of the self, the conferral of a new subjectivity. With reception of this "good news," there comes about also the repudiation of previous theological beliefs as "bad news." For that is what conversion to a new theological subjectivity is: the weaning of the heart from the milk of idols and of the mind from attractive beliefs that in fact are now judged toxic. Theological subjectivity therefore can neither be bought nor sold nor inherited. It is not a cultural legacy. So the opening salvo of Luther's Ninety-Five Theses: "When our Lord Jesus Christ said, Repent!, he meant for the entire life of the believer to be one of repentance" — life now lived in total turning to the Lord who has turned to us. This is the life then that ever advances into the baptism in which it had first begun. If the entire life of the Christian is one of turning to the Lord who is returning to finish the work of redemption and fulfill the oppressed creation, then the malady of the earth, sick to death with malice and injustice, is far profounder than moralism, including pious and even highly Christological moralism, imagines.

## Sinfulness

The confession of sinfulness is a necessary but not sufficient condition (Luke 5:8) in the acquisition of theological subjectivity. That is not to say that it is a human work that prepares the way for, i.e., somehow "merits" grace. The "condition" here is logical and analytical. Forgiveness cannot be received apart from the acknowledgment of sin, nor justification apart from the knowledge of ungodliness, nor resurrection apart from the knowledge of death to God. It is to say, then, that the confession of sinfulness is part of the gospel, a true self-knowledge that corresponds to the knowledge of God who gives life to the dead and justice to the ungodly — only the dead, only the ungodly. Yet such knowledge is not sufficient because if, as readily happens, sinfulness is conceived apart from the justification of the confessed sinner by faith in the vindicated faith of the Friend of Sinners (Luke 5:10), something vital for the truthfulness of that confession is not made clear and left in dangerous ambiguity.

For the Spirit makes sinners, i.e., convicts of sinfulness *in order to* make them righteous; He does an *opus alienum ut faciat opus proprium* (an alien work in order to do a proper work). The ambiguity becomes lethal, if the sinner thinks that by her work of self-hatred she makes herself acceptable. That is the work of the unholy spirit, a parody of the Spirit's work of sanctification. So the acquisition of theological subjectivity swims in dangerous waters, where the religion business of the *sicut Deus eritis* captures and deploys even a pseudo-knowledge of sinfulness as its most cunning leverage in the manipulation of guilt. Here everything depends on the clear teaching that true knowledge of sinfulness comes upon the newborn believer as the Spirit's work rather than as a desperate ploy of the sinner to preserve itself in sinfulness by sinful self-hatred. For an act of apparent self-accusation is not necessarily a reception of God's merciful love; it may well be the cunning new assertion of sovereignty against God that is the essence of sinfulness, "to be like God, knowing good and evil" (Gen. 3:5). This cunning to be sure leads to death, to the religious illusion of sovereignty that culminates in self-destruction when the self must turn against the self to sustain the illusion.

Such manipulative self-accusation in the religion business may be readily observed in the canned lamentations in worship services today put on the lips of the people of God that amount to a thinly disguised partisan cheerleading in the demagogic politics of Euro-America. The community of forgiven sinners should be an alternative to this demagoguery, not a prime instance of it — a place of truth-telling secured by the merciful love of God, not of truth-manipulation. There can be no reconciliation without truth, just as there can be no forgiveness without contrition nor resurrection without death. But these things are a matter of Spirit and conscience, not instruments of propaganda in the business of religion as usual.

We asked at the conclusion of the section preceding the previous, "Is there a plausible way of retrieving the content Rauschenbusch identified for aid in exposing our contemporary blindness about which Agamben worries?" Derek R.

Nelson makes a sound beginning when he advocates at the conclusion of his survey of the doctrine of sin in modern theologies a "closer connection of Trinitarian relationality with human selfhood . . . [theology's] next goal [ought to be] the reinterpretation of human relationship along the line of the imago dei."[27] This assessment of a Trinitarian deficit in modern theology's account of sin is accurate enough. It is inherited from the traditional theology of the West, as we shall see.

In a classical treatise on this topic, *The Virgin Conception and Original Sin,*[28] Anselm of Canterbury, heir of Augustinianism and the father of Latin scholasticism, sought to understand the necessity for Christ's birth from a Virgin in the plan of salvation. The problem is thus posed from the perspective of salvation in Christ as inquiry into the necessity of God's acting for us as He has done and communicated in the evangelical narrative. Like all theologians in the Western tradition, Anselm's thinking has been shaped decisively in this respect by Augustine, indeed sharpened to a knife's edge by the bishop of Hippo's polemic against Pelagius. Augustine's resort to the Adam-Christ typology of Romans 5 has thus been definitive for Western theology. It is, in Augustine's words, ". . . the matter of the two men by one of whom we are sold under sin, by the other redeemed from sins — by the one have been precipitated into death, by the other liberated unto life; the former of whom has ruined us in himself, by doing his own will instead of His who created him; the latter has saved us in Himself, by not doing His own will but the will of Him who sent Him: it is in what concerns these two men that Christian faith properly consists."[29] In this overriding contention, Augustine was undoubtedly in the right, that is, so far as Paul was in the right.

Carol Harrison has aptly written of the Augustinian theology of sinfulness that Anselm is appropriating in all its radicalness: "Christ is not only an example and lawgiver, but mediator of grace welling up within man by the Spirit, who not only informs of the good, but also moves the will to desire it, love it and delight in it. Obedience motivated by fear or hope of reward, such as the Pelagians urged, is servile when compared. . . ."[30] But is Augustine's radical theology of sin and grace so radical that it actually destroys nature? "Is man truly free when his every good action is attributable solely to the irresistible inspiration and operation of grace?"[31] Is radical grace irresistible, compulsive, coercive? Harrison rightly replies on behalf of Augustine and his tradition with a counter-question. Is divine grace irresistible because "it overrides, coerces, and controls the will

27. Derek R. Nelson, *What's Wrong with Sin? Sin in Individual and Social Perspective from Schleiermacher to Theologies of Liberation* (London and New York: T. & T. Clark, 2009), p. 186. This summons has deep roots in theology in the tradition of Luther. See *PNT,* pp. 24-31.

28. Anselm of Canterbury, *Why God Became Man,* and *The Virgin Conception and Original Sin,* translation, introduction, and notes by Joseph M. Colleran (Albany, NY: Magi Books, 1969).

29. *NPNF,* V, pp. 246-47.

30. Carol Harrison, *Augustine: Christian Truth and Fractured Humanity* (Oxford: Oxford University Press, 2000), p. 111.

31. Harrison, *Augustine,* p. 111.

or because it unfailingly, irresistibly calls forth a response which corresponds with man's deepest desires and motivations, with his true identity and being as a creature of God . . . enabling him to fulfill his being as it was created to be?"[32] Harrison's leading question certainly leads in the right direction. Grace does not destroy nature but fulfills it, when nature comes to understand itself as from its origin intended for love of the Creator and of all creatures in and under Him. But coming to understand just this comes about in no other way than by dying with Christ to egocentric Adam and arising in Christ the New Adam to the ecstatic life liberated to give God all the glory and neighbors all our love on the way to the Beloved Community of God.

Nonetheless there are two special features of Augustine's pioneering formulation of the doctrine of original sin that were and remain contentious. The first is a tendency to naturalize the understanding of sin. Often this tendency in Lutheran theology is blamed on the employment of the Aristotelian distinction between form and matter, which required Luther's ardent follower, Flacius, baldly to assert in neo-Manichaean fashion that in Adam human nature is formed into sin,[33] as if it had become substantively an evil creature rather than remaining the good but corrupted creature of God. But this tendency to depersonalize sin and understand it naturalistically is already at work in Augustine. He was misled in part by the Vulgate's translation of Romans 5:12 ("*in whom* all sinned" where the Greek is better translated "*in that* all sinned").[34] Thus, commenting on this passage in a treatise against Pelagius, Augustine states that in Adam "the entire mass of our nature was ruined beyond doubt, and fell into the possession of its destroyer. And from him no one — no, not one — has been delivered, or is being delivered, or ever will be delivered, except by the grace of the Redeemer."[35]

Clearly the intention even here in speaking of the *massa damnata* is to magnify the grace of the Redeemer by *magnifying* the plight of the redeemed without Him. But that rhetorical strategy is not identical with *conceiving* the predicament rigorously in light of the Redeemer and His deed. Thus even though the conceptuality (nature and grace) differs from medieval Aristotelianism (form and matter), the same naturalizing reduction of sin occurs here when Augustine imagines a lump of diseased semen inherited from Adam and passed on by sexual procreation. Unlike Flacius, and at the cost of logical consistency, however, Augustine hastened to deny that man's nature "is changed into a beast's nature." God, he continues, "condemns man because of the fault wherewithal his nature is disgraced, and not because of his nature, which is not destroyed in consequence of its fault."[36]

---

32. Harrison, *Augustine*, p. 112.

33. E.g., Friedrich Mildenberger, *Theology of the Lutheran Confessions,* trans. E. Lueker (Philadelphia: Fortress, 1986), pp. 154-55.

34. For the exegetical and grammatical issues, see C. E. B. Cranfield, *A Critical and Exegetical Commentary on the Epistle to the Romans* (Edinburgh: T. & T. Clark, 1975), vol. 1, pp. 274-81.

35. *NPNF,* V, p. 249.

36. *NPNF,* V, p. 254.

Augustine's notion of evil as privation of being would have better served him here to conceive of sinfulness, not as diseased semen, but as the failure of Adam to become the person who images God in the work of beloved community (Gen. 1:26-28) and hence he bequeathed the loss of this possibility to all his children born henceforth in exile from paradise.

So we have a complicated picture. Even though Augustine's grammar is wrong, and his naturalizing explanation of biologically inherited guilt is exegetically unjustified and theologically misleading, Augustine's overall sense of the drama of Adam's redemption in Christ is superior to that of his self-bootstrapping opponent: "[T]he Mediator, who was stronger than the angels, became weak for man's sake. So that the pride of the Destroyer is destroyed by the humility of the Redeemer; and he who makes his boast over the sons of men of his angelic strength, is vanquished by the Son of God in the human weakness which He assumed."[37] Even though the good intention is to surpass the individualistic framework of moralism in conceiving the corporate unity of humanity in the figure of fallen Adam, what may be faulted, then, is simply the attempt to explain sin by a biological mechanism of natural inheritance and, correspondingly, to think of physical death as the simple equivalent of death to God, caused by a corruption of physical nature by sin taken as a genetic disorder. What is the same, the fault lies in equating "nature" with "creation": not only are these distinct concepts, but nature as we know it is nature known and oppressed by the fallen creature of God in which sinfulness has become an acquired, habitual, unnatural "second nature." In us who are persons, nature itself is fallen.

A second special feature of Augustine's doctrine of original sin is the understanding of the sinfulness of sin as Adam's loss of love of God for God's sake and thus of all creatures in and under God, the *ordo caritatis*. This was Augustine's reading of Jesus' double love-commandment which he conceived as giving an "order" or structure in which all created things are loved properly, including the self, when loved in and under God. But creatures are loved improperly when loved apart from or in place of God. So the believer can rightly love herself with God's love in entering into and abiding in the Beloved Community. As a result of this understanding of Adam's loss of true or original righteousness, then, Augustine understands the grace of Christ to consist not only in the divine favor shown in the forgiveness of sins but also in the gift of the Holy Spirit who pours love for God into the hearts of believers whence comes as well proper love for all creatures. The believer "receives the Holy Ghost, by whom there is formed in his mind a delight in, and a love of, that supreme and unchangeable good which is God. . . ."[38]

This is the Spirit of God, Augustine further writes, "by whose gift we are justified, whence it comes to pass that we delight not to sin — in which is liberty; even as, when we are without this Spirit, we delight to sin, — in which is

37. *NPNF*, V, p. 254.
38. *NPNF*, V, p. 84.

slavery. . . . [T]his [is] the Holy Spirit, through whom love is shed abroad in our hearts, which is the fulfillment of the law" and hence the justice really possible now for believers on their pilgrim way, even if it is not perfected until the resurrection.[39] The old law was written on tablets and came externally to the soul of the creature fallen away. The new law of the gospel is the Holy Spirit, writing the law, that is, the love for God and His creatures, upon hearts, within the soul, that is, really transforming human affections. It is not difficult to see that Augustine's favorite Bible verse is Romans 5:5. Indeed, commenting on this verse Augustine can even say that this love is the believer's justice not because the Spirit "loves us, but because He makes us lovers of God. . . . This is that righteousness of God, which He not only teaches us by the precept of His law, but also bestows upon us by the gift of the Spirit."[40] The Spirit, who is the person of the love of the Father and the Son, gives Himself in His love to place the believer into these relations and so be filled with the same love that animates them.

This complex of Augustinian ideas became controversial in Lutheran theology, though it would not be difficult to document multitudinous examples of Luther himself employing Augustine's idiom: no Spirit, no true love for God without which the law is merely kept, not truly fulfilled. Following Anders Nygren,[41] however, many have sharply criticized the eudaimonism that allegedly contaminates Augustine's understanding of charity in the name of Luther's supposedly pure agape ethic. Contra Augustine, they argue, God's love for the world does not return to God; least of all is the sinner's Spirit-worked progress in righteousness to be understood as growth in the love of God above all and thus all things in and under God. So the issue has been joined. Is the sinner's justification only and purely the divine favor of the forgiveness of sins, the nonimputation of guilt, the cancelation of punishment, an alien and imputed righteousness that does not justify because it touches the desires of the heart? Or is it not also the healing of the soul's disordered loves, a real if inchoate rectification of the heart's desire so that it eagerly longs for "the hope of righteousness" (Gal. 5:5)? Is justification in Christ a remedy for the guilt of sins and liability to punishment or deeper still for the sinfulness that makes one guilty and worthy of rejection? Does it merely cancel the Law that accuses or does it root out the evil desire that the Law accuses? Is the enemy of God the Law or the sinfulness that the Law condemns? Is the gift of the Spirit subsequent to justification — sort of an option for those interested — or is the gift of the Spirit already the very faith, active in love for God and all His creatures, that justifies?

As argued in Chapter Two, Luther goes beyond Augustine's teaching Christologically in his teaching of the "joyful exchange," but he never abandons what

---

39. *NPNF,* V, p. 95.

40. *NPNF,* V, p. 108.

41. Anders Nygren, *Agape and Eros,* trans. Philip S. Watson (New York and Evanston: Harper & Row, 1969).

he inherited from him in this regard. He does so when he distinguishes but does not separate passive and active faith, anthropologically applying the Trinitarian sequence manifest in the paradigm provided by the baptism of Jesus of the pronouncement of the Father's favor followed by the anointing in the Spirit in the figure of the dove. In this distinction, Luther actually corrects the tendency in Augustine's theology to naturalize sin. Luther re-personalizes the gift by parsing grace in terms of Trinitarian personalism, so that the love of God poured into the hearts of believers by the Holy Spirit is *an anointing of the body* that causes it to *partake* in the *relationships* at once given and communicated in the gospel narrative: both the Father's love for the Son, the favor of God now resting on believers united with Christ, and the Son's love for the Father, the new obedience that rises up in the power of the Spirit to return all the glory to the Father for all His rich mercy in Christ. The grace spread abroad in our hearts by the Spirit personally (uncreated grace) is thus *both* the favor of love received *and* the empowerment to love as one has been loved. But it is grace in this Trinitarian sequence of patiency that gives rise to new agency. In the same way, Luther re-personalizes the notion of inherited sin when he interprets sin, not as the erotic desire of animal flesh, but as unbelief in the promise of God in and by the soul's highest powers of reason and will. By the same token he sees the righteousness of Christ, the new Adam, precisely in His own faith and faithful obedience in the power of the Spirit to live by giving Himself on behalf of others, indeed, on behalf of sinners, culminating in the awesome surrender of love to the Father's will at Gethsemane.

So also Anselm understood. In particular, he understood Christ's birth from a virgin as an act of new creation by the Spirit within the fallen creation.[42] Because Christ is born as perfect man, endowed by the Spirit with the original justice that Adam had lost, He is able as man perfectly to obey God and to fulfill the divine law not for His own sake, but for the sake of others. In this way of gratuitous surplus, He can supply satisfaction for the sins of others or make payment for their debt of guilt out of sheer mercy.[43] Anselm wants further to demonstrate that there is no other true solution to the burden of human sin in debt and guilt before God than Christ's sacrifice for us.[44] If this need is so profound, human nature must have been radically damaged, incapable any longer of acquiring the justice it needs to make peace with God, whom it has offended precisely by losing this capacity for justice. Original sin is thus the loss of original integrity, the very capacity for righteousness, let alone the performance of it.

Such original justice is defined personally, as keeping the will rightly ordered on the will of God, for its own sake, in true filial obedience, not then in blind obedience or by the mechanical performance of good deeds.[45] This true obedi-

---

42. Anselm, *Virgin Conception,* pp. 187, 189, 201.
43. Anselm, *Virgin Conception,* pp. 192, 195.
44. Anselm, *Virgin Conception,* pp. 198, 203.
45. Anselm, *Virgin Conception,* p. 173.

ence entails the recognition that sin does not originate in feelings, passions, or desires of the body, which are good creatures of God.[46] It is not the feeling but the will's consent to it, when it is evil, which makes a sin.[47] Evil passions arise from the seduction of the vulnerable body by external forces captivating desire.[48] The location of evil desire is not in the body per se, then, but in the fallen world and each one's willing consent to its false goods as goods lesser than willing the will of God. Anselm thus employs the nature/person distinction from Trinitarian theology[49] to say that sin can only be the personal act of a will, not a property of human nature. How is it then that all children of Adam inevitably sin and become themselves personally Adam the sinner? It is because they have been bequeathed a status as lost to God on account of Adam's originating disobedience. All the children of Adam are beings born in exile from Paradise, having lost the original capacity for obedience that was available there, capable now only of a slavish and perverted obedience motivated by fear of punishment and hope of reward, not the filial obedience that delights in the law of the Lord.

Lacking Paradise, humans inherit from Adam a lack of confidence in the will of God. By default, then, they seek security instead in lesser goods. So the creature inevitably sins. This is no trivial matter; the disintegration of this human nature begun in sin completes itself in death — the physical death that now becomes the sign of death to God. Exiled from paradise, the creature is born to die, lest sinfulness be eternalized. Adam's sin at the origin of the human race had this fateful consequence for all his children.[50] Adam lost for himself and all his posterity the paradisiacal possibility of willing the will of God in spontaneous love of children for their heavenly Father, and with this loss, human nature itself became disordered and, no longer wanting what God wills, sinful. Anselm's parable of the lost estate illustrates the idea: if parents by some outrageous crime lose their property, so also do all their descendants after them.[51] The property here, however, is not accidental, but essential to the human person, since to be human is to constitute a personal identity by personal acts of will in obedience to the will of God through the course of time. The loss of the will's spontaneous subjection to God's will is at the same time the loss of the life that God wills for the person. Thus the Pauline conclusion follows: "the wages of sin are death," where "death" means not primarily the physical termination of an organism, but "death to God," "spiritual" death, becoming a "person" whom God does not will, lost to God eternally.

So original sin is a state of "natural destitution"; for human "nature" is noth-

---

46. Anselm, *Virgin Conception*, p. 176.
47. Anselm, *Virgin Conception*, p. 175.
48. Anselm, *Virgin Conception*, p. 191.
49. Anselm, *Virgin Conception*, p. 183.
50. Anselm, *Virgin Conception*, p. 188.
51. Anselm, *Virgin Conception*, p. 209.

ing but the human capacity to become the person who in its own history knows, loves, and does the will of God.[52] This failure in becoming true person before God is what all inherit from Adam. This destitution includes the "necessity" of sinning, both failures to act in sloth and the commission of actual deeds of injustice. Incapacitated by worldly anxiety and indebted to God for an accumulating history of personal deficit,[53] the disordered human will cannot overcome this state in which it finds itself. Instead, desperately it rationalizes it. Reason becomes the ideological instrument of its disordered desires and unbearable burden, disowning responsibility, hating the thought of God and thus deepening the darkness. Here, as said above, enters the most profoundly disturbing point of the doctrine: all being born into an impossible situation become willfully ignorant of it merely in order to survive, even if survival means living as dead to God — like the zombies that haunt the popular consciousness of postmodern culture. "Humankind-sicut-deus is dead, for it has cut itself off from the tree of life; it lives out of its own treasures, yet it cannot live. It is compelled to live, yet it cannot live. That is what death means" (Bonhoeffer).[54] So Anselm comes to the conclusion: the absence of original justice[55] can only be overcome for us by the coming of the New Adam, born of the Virgin Mary, re-creating human nature to reclaim by personal obedience the destiny Adam lost for his descendants, making satisfaction to the holy God for the debt of infinite guilt and so making the reconciliation of sinful humanity available by the aid of unmerited mercy.

Objections to the classical teaching of original sin, as represented by Anselm, are several, modern and traditional, and similar to those made against Augustine. Adam, even though a literary figure, is seriously meant as a symbol of something that fatefully happened at the origin of the human race and so in this sense the figurative Adam nonetheless indicates *a historical event.* But the historicity of the Fall seems impossible to affirm in the light of modern scientific knowledge of human origins. A related objection, then, is that, if historically shown to be untenable, the doctrine of the loss of original righteousness in Adam amounts to a defamation of humanity, as per the slogan of Darwinian theology: "We are not fallen angels, but rising beasts." We can set aside here as a pseudo-issue (even though in its damaging effects, it has hardly been an innocuous error) the associated, so to speak, "venereal" theory of sin's transmission that derives from Augustine's naturalizing explanation.[56] Damaging as this aspersion cast on sexual love

52. Anselm, *Virgin Conception,* p. 197.

53. Anselm, *Virgin Conception,* pp. 181, 185.

54. Dietrich Bonhoeffer, *Creation and Fall,* Dietrich Bonhoeffer Works, vol. 3, trans. D. S. Bax (Minneapolis: Fortress, 1997), p. 135.

55. Anselm, *Virgin Conception,* p. 208.

56. So also Bonhoeffer, following Holl, credited Luther for overcoming the biological view. Bonhoeffer, *Creation and Fall,* pp. 149-51. But in Anselm, as in Augustine, the matter is not so simple; Bonhoeffer himself could write: "That church dogmatics has sometimes seen the essence of original sin in sexuality is not as absurd as Protestants have often declared on the

has been, taking the Christian doctrine of sinfulness at its best, as in Anselm, we see that the biblical figure of Adam is taken in the first place not as the biological progenitor of humanity, but as a corporate personification of the human race who comes into focus only in the light of Jesus' Spirit-wrought obedience as the New Adam. We can thank modern science for the knowledge that sin is not biologically transmitted from one generation to another like some kind of flawed gene, even if some today think on the basis of this science that human dysfunction admits of genetic therapy, as in the new eugenics. Ironically enough, today it is theology that warns against this venereal theory of sinfulness![57]

The intention of Augustine's unfortunate speculation was in any case genuinely Pauline: to undermine the legalistic prejudice of superficial moralism, with its myopic focus on the individual fault and merit of human beings, who are presumed still to possess the paradisiacal possibility of true and filial obedience to God. Humanity as a totality is caught up under the *power* of sin, willing but unwitting heir to the failure of becoming which Adam is. Sin encompasses all as an overwhelming power, as we see figured in the story of Adam followed by the spiral of violence and decay that follows in Genesis 2–11; Adam signifies a fateful human defection from its divine calling at the origin. The humanity we know exists in universal defection (Rom. 3:9-18, 23) from the command-and-promise of God (Gen. 1:26-28) that humanity should arise and grow by faithful obedience into its status as God's image on the earth by becoming like God. Is the teaching of a historic defection from that vocation, then, a defamation of humanity or rather a way of insisting in spite of all historical experience to the contrary on humanity's exalted and indeed indelible status, which it can refuse in sin but never erase?

Bonhoeffer pointed the way forward when he undertook the theological exposition of the story of the fall of Adam at the beginning of the human race under the rubric of "hope projected backwards"[58] in his commentary *Creation and Fall* — a pointed, though indirect critique of the theology that was welcoming Adolf Hitler at the time as the new Adam of the Aryans. If history admits of a fall from God's calling, it also admits of a new creation in its midst. More precisely, since in Jesus Christ the New Adam had appeared, we can now see how Adam, who is each of us and all of us together in the common body, defected from his calling to rise up and fill out the image of God on the earth in true likeness to God.

This starting point of interpretation in the Adam-Christ typology of Romans 5 is adhered to rigorously: ". . . as those who live and have their history through

---

basis of a moralistic naturalism" (pp. 124-25). Like all things human and created good, sexuality too is in the thrall of malice and injustice.

57. See the penetrating analysis in Fritz Oehlschlaeger, *Procreative Ethics: Philosophical and Christian Approaches to Questions at the Beginning of Life* (Eugene, OR: Cascade Books, 2011).

58. This turn of phrase appears in Dietrich Bonhoeffer, *Sanctorum Communio: A Theological Study of the Sociology of the Church,* Dietrich Bonhoeffer Works I, trans. Reinhard Kraus and Nancy Lukens, ed. Joachim von Sooten and Clifford J. Green (Minneapolis: Fortress, 1998), p. 61.

Christ alone we are enabled to know about the beginning not by means of our own imagination but only from the new center, from Christ."[59] Speaking against the social Darwinism in the air, Bonhoeffer argued that the "attempt — with the origin and nature of humankind in mind — to seek to know for ourselves what humankind was like in the original state and to identify our own ideal of humanity with what God actually created is hopeless. It fails to recognize that it is only from Christ that we can know about the original nature of humankind."[60] With Luther, original sin, like original righteousness, must be believed on the basis of the revelation in Scripture. "Man no longer lives in the beginning — he has lost the beginning. Now he finds he is in the middle, knowing neither the end nor the beginning. . . . No one can speak of the beginning but the one who was in the beginning."[61] Because we see in Christ the New Adam, hence the true *imago Dei,* we can see in the story of Adam the antitype: "Imago dei, sicut deus, agnus dei [image of God, like God, lamb of God] — the human being who is God incarnate, who was sacrificed for humankind sicut deus, in true divinity slaying the false divinity and restoring the imago Dei."[62]

This procedure has sweeping implications for theology itself. Bonhoeffer sees that it was the serpent who asked pious, but speculative questions whether God had really said thus and so, in order to create doubt about God's motives. Bonhoeffer contemporizes: "Did God really demand the sacrifice of Christ — the God whom I know better, the God whom I know to be the infinitely good, all-loving Father?"[63] But knowing the Lamb of God, theology knows that "in the Bible God speaks to us" in order for us to hear and so to understand. "And one cannot just proceed to think about God under one's own steam; instead one must ask God questions."[64] One understands God's Word when one comes to understand in faith why God has said what in fact God has said.

What such theological inquiry leads Bonhoeffer to is the rejection of the venerable way of the analogy of being that reasons to God as from created effects to transcendent cause; for the optimistic presumption is that the being we now know is transparently the good creature of the good Creator. But this bypasses the biblical revelation of the creature's fall into sin, its corruption in structures of malice and injustice, and above all, its redemption in Christ and the promise of its fulfillment in the Spirit. As a result, "The likeness, the analogia, of humankind to God is not analogia entis but *analogia relationis.*"[65] It is not in the mere fact of existing, but rather existing in the Christ-relationship, "being in Christ," that

59. Bonhoeffer, *Creation and Fall,* p. 92.

60. Bonhoeffer, *Creation and Fall,* p. 62.

61. Bonhoeffer, *Creation and Fall,* p. 29.

62. Bonhoeffer, *Creation and Fall,* p. 113.

63. Bonhoeffer, *Creation and Fall,* p. 107.

64. From a letter to Rüdiger Schleicher, cited in the Afterword in Bonhoeffer, *Creation and Fall,* p. 153.

65. Bonhoeffer, *Creation and Fall,* p. 65, emphasis original.

manifests likeness to God. This is the "relationship" given and disclosed in Christ's dwelling graciously in the company of sinners as in a joyful wedding banquet (cf. Mark 2:19); in its light, moreover, we can now clearly see that the likeness of God of Genesis 1:26-28 consists not in some essential quality, like the rationality which it presupposes, but in the divinely instituted co-humanity of the male and female in partnership as the primal structure of love and justice in creation. "The human being is not alone. Human beings exist in duality, and it is in this *dependence on the other that their creatureliness consists.*"[66] This is knowledge of our creaturehood, of the human dignity and its creative task in the world — as of something lost to sinfulness but redeemed in Christ for fulfillment yet to come.

To the objection from the venerable tradition of the analogy of being that the analogy of relationship — that is, of Christ divinely dwelling with sinners or the male and female in the embrace of sexual love for a partnership in justice — depicts God as community, as "being in relation," Bonhoeffer replies that "anthropomorphism in thinking of God, or blatant mythology, is not more irrelevant or unsuitable as an expression for God's being than the abstract use of the generic term, 'deity.' On the contrary, clear anthropomorphism much more plainly expresses the fact that we cannot think of 'God as such' whether in one way or another. The abstract concept of God, precisely because it seeks not to be anthropomorphic, is in actual fact much more so than is childlike anthropomorphism."[67] The generic approach naturalizes and depersonalizes the God known in Scripture; but this naturalization is in fact human instrumentalization which by a concept distances the God who strolls in the garden in the cool of the evening, calling "Adam, where art thou?" In that case the metaphysical deity, arrived at by the ascent of reason from effect to cause, is not only the illusionary reification of an abstraction. It is the sublime idol of the thinker who would think *sicut deus.* Original sin thus finds its most refined expression in "pious talk," in theology itself — so much for the modern objection to the doctrine of original sin. When it objects to the doctrine of original sin it is protecting its own way of life.

The classic theological objection to the teaching of original sin from Eastern Orthodoxy differs from the foregoing account of modern and typically Western objections. Even if one were to grant the idea of the inherited corruption of human nature, can that truly be called sin which is passively inherited? Is the corruption not instead the liability to death that a more natural reading of the Greek in Romans 5 suggests? What is inherited from Adam is not sin but death, so that in anxiety over death each person inevitably succumbs to sin as their own deed. The oxymoron of inherited guilt is simply unintelligible. How can what I am rather than what I do be called and truly be sinful? How can nature, not person, sin? Can anyone really be guilty for the failure of another, let alone a legendary ancestor, apart from actual personal fault of our own? Is original sin really *sin?*

---

66. Bonhoeffer, *Creation and Fall,* p. 64.
67. Bonhoeffer, *Creation and Fall,* p. 75.

And if it is really sin, does not Flacius simply think through in logical consistency the crypto-Manichaeism that Augustine and Luther actually thought?

While the guilt of original sin is unequal — Adam is obviously personally responsible for his sin in a way that his newborn baby is not personally culpable — yet the sinfulness of the fallen nature is the same in the one who actively commits sin and in the one who passively fails to will and to do God's will. Sloth too is sinful. Sinfulness lies, not first in what we do, but in what we fail to do because we do not will to do it because we do not love the neighbor as ourselves because we do not love God above all and thus for God's own sake. What we fail to want and therefore to do is to become the just creature of creative love whom God created us to be. This failure in becoming, this "falling short of the glory of God" (Rom. 3:23), this absence of righteousness, this loss of the very possibility of filial obedience is universal. So the guilt of original sin is universal and is true guilt, not because everyone is equally criminal, but because, being born in exile, desire is captured in structures of malice and injustice. Yet the point of this total diagnosis of sinfulness at the root of our acquired and now habitual way of being in the world is only to necessitate Christ as the New Adam who comes to recapture desire lost to God and thus to justice and love.

So Anselm reasons: the virginal conception of Jesus denotes the divine initiative of a new creation out of this human failure. Anselm's biblical exegesis is exceptionally good here, for he rightly sees that the point of the birth narrative in Luke is not to prove Jesus' divine Sonship, but to account for His sinless humanity. Because His human nature is taken from our fallen nature, He can represent us who are fallen and offer Himself to the Father in our place and for our good. Because His human nature is a new creation, on the other hand, He can do what we cannot do ourselves. Since His rational human soul is united from conception by the Spirit to the person of the eternal Son, Jesus does not inherit from Adam the corrupted human will bent away from God to self-will. Jesus has no "self-consciousness," no autonomous "personality" like the *sicut deus* Adam acquired in wanting to know good and evil for himself; but from conception His human will is formed by personal union with the Word of God, who has taken this human nature as His own and anointed it with the Spirit. Thus, Jesus, born of the Virgin Mary, is the new human being who regains the paradisiacal possibility — otherwise lost to humanity in Adam's fall — of living a righteous life of perfect love for God and others. Even more astonishing, He has this new possibility not in Eden, but here and now, on the earth, in the likeness of sinful flesh. Of course, Jesus born of the Virgin Mary must go on to actualize this possibility in His life's way by fulfilling the double love commandment. He must actually learn obedience by testing. Thus His human nature is led by the Spirit on His life's way, in whom He is anointed as the Messiah. It is the Spirit who likewise leads Jesus into testing and leads him through it. In this actual historical obedience of the Son incarnate, we may then say, human nature is being created anew and actualized as God intends. Jesus Christ is the true man, the new Adam, through whose obedience righteousness and life come about for many. In His birth from the Virgin, the Spirit works the first fruits of eschatological creation.

Anselm's reflection is radical. It is radical in that it subverts individualistic, moralizing thinking of sin as vice stemming from the unruly bodily passions and instead thinks of actual evil stemming from a trans-individual, perhaps trans-human, power opposed to God and His purpose for humanity. It is radical, more-over, in that it necessitates Christ as the New Adam who comes from above. What is really at stake, then, in the doctrine of original sin is the anthropologically normative notion of original righteousness, lost in Adam but restored and indeed expanded in Christ as the New Adam. It is this revelation of the human life of love and justice that is constitutive of theological anthropology, sinfulness being noth-ing but its deprivation — no matter how cruelly actual this deprivation in being transpires. This normative notion holds that humanity in its very "essence" — the philosophical notion of "essence" theologically reconceived now as divine calling or vocation, *imago Dei* — is the creature *filled with the Spirit* to live, to work, and to prosper on the earth in the knowledge of God.

So Luther put it in his Genesis lectures: ". . . righteousness was not a gift which came from without, separate from man's nature, but it was part of his nature, so that it was Adam's nature to love God, to believe God, to know God, etc." Original sin is the deprivation, the "falling" away from this creaturely *calling* as made by God for the God who is determined to give, redeem, and fulfill the creation in a communion of beloved persons. But now sinful "man not only does not love God any longer but flees from Him, hates Him, and desires to be and to live without Him."[68] In sinfulness, the human creature wants to be God without God and thus becomes a caricature of itself. This flight from God issues in all the actual evils that fill the world and, if indeed it is human "nature" to love God, it is this corruption that makes death spiritual, death to God, the eminently just wage of sinfulness.

Notice that according to this brief sketch from Luther, building on Anselm, the sin of origin has nothing to do with casting suspicion on human sexuality as the special conduit of sinfulness. The tendency will be just the opposite: it is sinfulness that casts suspicion on the sexual union and life's partnership of male and female in receiving and extending the divine work of creation. It is sin that disdains the vocation of humanizing the earth in the structure of justice that is erotic love in the partnership of marriage that raises children born of love.[69] Note also that historical literalism regarding the story of the Fall is not only beside the point, but becomes detrimental to the theological point that "in Adam we have all been one, one huge rebellious man,"[70] if historicity is insisted on as the essential

---

68. *LW* I, p. 165.

69. On Luther's rehabilitation of marriage as a structure of love and justice, see *LBC,* pp. 191-201.

70. Martin H. Franzmann, "In Adam We Have All Been One," *The Lutheran Book of Wor-ship* (Minneapolis: Augsburg/Philadelphia: Lutheran Church in America, 1978), #372.

point. Above all, note that this fractious unity in Adam becomes visible from the vantage point of the lonely Christ, the Man for Others (Bonhoeffer), whose obedience of faith made Him smallest of all and servant of all, God without God on the cross for the sake of truly identifying with the plight and predicament of *sicut deus* Adam before God. "So it is Christ that reveals the true nature of man. Man's nature in Adam is not, as it is usually assumed, his true and original nature; it is only truly human at all insofar as it reflects and corresponds to essential human nature as it is found in Christ."[71]

Along such lines the success of this reflection of faith backwards upon the state from which divine rescue has delivered matters, not least because it clarifies who this new subject of faith properly is: the new Adam, the true Adam. Here the King James Bible translates what the Greek of Paul actually said in Galatians 2:20: "I am crucified with Christ: nevertheless I live; yet not I, but Christ liveth in me: and the life which I now live in the flesh I live by *the faith of* the Son of God, who loved me, and gave himself for me" (emphasis added). The Son of God incarnate had faith, lived faithfully as the New Adam.[72] And this obedience of faith was His righteousness,[73] a righteousness acquired by the living of the particularly messianic life that Jesus did in love for God above all by loving others more than Himself — in "taking responsibility for us," in Friedrich Gogarten's apt formulation of the obedience of Christ (as we shall further explore below in

71. Karl Barth, *Christ and Adam: Man and Humanity in Romans 5,* trans. T. A. Smail with an Introduction by W. Pauck (New York: Macmillan, 1968), p. 112.

72. Richard B. Hays, *The Faith of Jesus Christ: The Narrative Substructure of Galatians 3:1–4:11,* 2nd edition (Grand Rapids: Eerdmans, 2001).

73. R. Michael Allen has made a compelling case for this rendering in his *The Christ's Faith: A Dogmatic Account* (London: T. & T. Clark, 2009). It is made all the more compelling in his *Justification and the Gospel: Understanding the Context and the Controversies* (Grand Rapids: Baker Academic, 2013) in arguing the thesis that "obedience is part of [Christ's] nature" (pp. 77-96). Allen holds to classically Calvinist notions of divine immutability and strict forensic imputation in justification per se. It will be evident that I would prefer to say that obedience is an expression of Christ's person, in that I qualify immutability by a doctrine of consistent perichoresis as required by strong Trinitarian personalism; and further that I parse "imputation" by the Christological model of the joyful exchange, the patristic *admirabile commercium,* in rigorously anti-Nestorian fashion. Lutheran anxieties that the traditional rendering of the genitive to mean faith in Christ is being excluded are ill-founded for two reasons. First, faith in Christ as per the argument above is divine faith, "that gift of the Holy Spirit," who is the Holy Spirit in person communicating the Father's love to the Son (and to those sinners now united to the Son in faith) and the Son's love to the Father (in those unbelievers now reborn by union with Christ in faith). The alternative to this view *of Luther* is the typical incoherence of Lutheran theology (see *PNT,* chapter 4) in thinking of justifying faith as somehow a free decision and human act (to avoid double predestination) that nevertheless is credited to grace alone (to avoid Pelagianism). Second, the faith of Christ, as Allen so rightly sees, provides theological understanding with the actual obedience of the life that the Son of God lived in the flesh that costs God but just so justly wins the right powerfully to claim those not in the right as nevertheless God's own.

Chapter Six).[74] As vindicated by His resurrection from a death undertaken in faith as responsibility for us before God, the acquired or achieved righteousness of Messiah Jesus in His human life and death becomes communicable. Vindicated by the Easter event and present by the Spirit in the Word, the faithful obedience of Jesus exchanges for our human failure. In the faith of the faithfulness of the Son of God in the flesh, Jesus believed for us all, both on behalf of all and for the sake of all. As the vindicated Son of God's own faithfulness, this truly human faith of Jesus comes and gives itself to those very humans whose burden He bore once and for all. *So Jesus is the subject of faith in whom believers partake insofar as they believe at all, when by the Spirit they are spiritually crucified with Christ and raised to His own newness of life.* And so they become members of the new and true humanity, citizens of the kingdom of God, loved and lovers in the dawning Beloved Community.

That means: *not* the pious human being,[75] who crowns her striving for health, wealth, and status with God's well-merited recognition; who will receive nothing as a gift but takes everything as merit and reward; for whom believing in Jesus, unlike others, is a small price to pay to go to heaven, a really good deal; for whose discipline or decadence God exists to extort or to heal as the case may be; for whom God is the supernatural guarantor of a sublimely egocentric existence that is not "faithful to the earth" (Nietzsche), but is always wanting something "beyond,"[76] even when as today the "beyond" drops the guise of piety and steps into the open to show itself as ruthlessly "secular" greed, wanting nothing but more stuff. This is the humanity, religious *or* secular, whose corrupt desire must be "overcome" by the creation of an ecstatic new humanity, "faithful to the earth" as that strange hammer of God Friedrich Nietzsche had his Zarathustra proclaim: "Once the sin against God was the greatest sin; but God died, and these sinners died with him. To sin against the earth is now the most dreadful thing. . . ."[77] But sin against God's earth on which the cross of Jesus stood is sin against the God who comes to redeem and to fulfill. The theological subject arises in dying to this sinfulness, whether in religious or in secular guise.

Zarathustra prophesied in a bitter polemic against the Kantian Christianity

---

74. Friedrich Gogarten, *Christ the Crisis,* trans. R. A. Wilson (London: SCM, 1970). The German title is *Jesus Christus Wende der Welt* — a perhaps penitent allusion directed against Gogarten's own hailing of the National Socialist claim in 1933 of the "turning point" of history.

75. Eberhard Busch, *Karl Barth and the Pietists: The Young Karl Barth's Critique of Pietism and Its Response,* trans. D. W. Bloesch (Downers Grove, IL: InterVarsity, 2004).

76. Not even the rigorous, quasi-ascetic moral philosophy of Kant escapes this criticism, since respect for others as bearers of reason is grounded in one's own self-respect as bearer of reason, and thus finally is a fundamentally dualistic form of self-love as the bearer of reason that must be scrupulously suspicious of all motives stemming from bodily "inclination," as if from another realm.

77. Friedrich Nietzsche, *Thus Spoke Zarathustra,* First Part, Prologue, #3 in *The Portable Nietzsche,* trans. and ed. W. Kaufmann (New York: Viking, 1969), p. 125.

of modernity that Nietzsche quite aptly dismissed as "Platonism for the people" — the very transcendentalism valorized as an anthropological foundation in theologies like Rahner's and Pannenberg's. Nietzsche's polemic is a strange mix of incisive critique and wild swinging at shadows on the wall, which in its own radical individualism and dangerous forays into social Darwinism[78] is vulnerable, if not itself a direct path, to fascism.[79] Nonetheless Nietzsche's critique of pious existence under the conditions of modernity as covert egocentrism, a dishonesty paid for at the price of a dualistic hostility to the earth and the body, as also his proclamation of the death of the God of Christian Platonism (as we shall see),[80] may serve postmodern Christian theology. That is particularly the case regarding the topic of this chapter and the next, the Spirit of the Father of the Son and the concrete form of theological subjectivity the Spirit renders. For Nietzsche's critique destroys faith as a human possibility. Faith as the obedience that gives up all to follow Jesus is not a human possibility, but the Spirit's possibility. As the gospel narrative attests: pious Peter denied, pious disciples fled, pious Judas betrayed, pious women watched from a distance, while Jesus the blasphemer died alone in the company of bandits. With Adam "it is impossible" (Mark 10:27); not even religion helps. If it is "true faith, that gift of the Holy Spirit,"[81] it is not human piety, even at its best, but the very obedience of faith of the man Jesus Christ. Believers participate ecstatically in the faith of Jesus by the coming of the Holy Spirit, when and where it pleases God to unify the sign and the thing signified in pronouncing the Crucified arisen, thus the object of faith, and so the sinner justified as the newly formed subject of faith. Faith is possible for us, where and when God becomes possible for us, by the coming of the Holy Spirit who creates and ever gives the obedient faith of Jesus in exchange for Adam's unfaithful disobedience. This joyful exchange begins with baptism into Christ by the Spirit through the Spirit's unification of water and the Word.

## Early Christian Baptism

Who is the subject of faith? In early Christian baptism the one who professed in response to the gospel, "I believe," was one who said simultaneously: "I renounce you Satan, your pomp, your service, your works" (Chrysostom); "I renounce

---

78. Richard Weikart, *From Darwin to Hitler: Evolutionary Ethics, Eugenics, and Racism in Germany* (London: Palgrave Macmillan, 2004). See the discussion in *BA*, pp. 117-24.

79. Steven E. Aschheim, *The Nietzsche Legacy in Germany 1890-1990* (Berkeley: University of California Press, 1994).

80. Robert W. Jenson, *God after God: The God of the Past and the God of the Future, Seen in the Work of Karl Barth* (Indianapolis and New York: Bobbs-Merrill, 1969). See also Paul R. Hinlicky, "Luther's Atheism," in *The Devil's Whore: Reason and Philosophy in the Lutheran Tradition,* ed. J. Hockenberry Drageseth (Minneapolis: Fortress, 2011), pp. 53-60.

81. *LW* 34, p. 109.

the devil and his work, this age and its pleasures" (Ambrose). These formulas renouncing Satan preface the profession of the thrice-repeated "I believe" of the creed in early Christian baptism. The second-century baptismal creed of the Roman church likewise couples the act of profession of faith with renunciation of the Evil One. Though consigned to oblivion by squeamish modern editors, Luther too in his "Baptismal Booklet" had the officiating minister declare: "Depart, you unclean spirit, and make room for the Holy Spirit!"[82] This action of renunciation and new allegiance did not happen overnight or in a vacuum. Pastor-bishops gave "catechetical lectures," delivering basic texts (the Commandments, the Lord's Prayer, the Baptismal Creed) and explaining the "mysteries of faith" in the course of a holistic preparation over a period of time, attending as well to the new ethos and spirituality incumbent upon the converts. "Preceded by authentic proclamation of the risen and exalted Christos-Messiah and by conversion, Spirit baptism by water at apostolic hands initiates one into the full life of the community in which the gospel has begun to become praxis."[83] We can briefly survey a sample of such an address[84] to the newly baptized from an eastern bishop, Cyril of Jerusalem (315-386), to see how early Christian "catechetical" theology worked in the formation of the theological subject.

Cyril wrote "in order that the baptized may know the effect wrought upon [them] on that evening of [their] baptism . . . the symbolical meaning of the things which are there performed." First the candidates assemble and, facing the West where the sun disappears in darkness, they renounce Satan. This is a declaration of personal independence, as it were, a claim of liberation: "I fear your might no longer; for Christ has overthrown that, having partaken with me of flesh and blood, that through these He might by death destroy death, that I might not be subject to bondage forever. I renounce thee. . . . I renounce thee." Renounced are not only the works of the devil, that is, sin, but also the devil's "pomp," i.e., the cultural ceremony of the surrounding world: "the madness of theatres and horse-races," the meat-markets associated with idol worship, the incantations and pharmacology of occult healing arts, sorcery, and divination. Now turning to the East, the place where the sun rises, a sign of paradise, the candidates confess the Father, the Son, and the Holy Spirit as the one, true God.

In this double act of renunciation and profession, a public transfer of allegiance is both signified and put into effect. In the "holy bath of regeneration," as Cyril tells the baptized, "you have put off the old man and clothed yourself in the garment of salvation, even Jesus Christ." As the candidates entered the church,

---

82. *BC,* p. 373. Kolb and Wengert to their credit have restored this material in their translation.

83. Aidan Kavanagh, *The Shape of Baptism: The Rite of Christian Initiation* (New York: Pueblo, 1978), pp. 22-23.

84. *NPNF* Series Two, VII, all citations drawn from pp. 144-50. I have taken the liberty of modernizing the archaic English of this nineteenth-century translation.

they removed their tunics, "an image of putting off the old man with his deeds." Naked, "imitating Christ who was stripped naked on the Cross," and made like the dead by being anointed with oil for burial, they are then "led to the holy pool of Divine Baptism, as Christ was carried from the Cross to the Sepulcher." Immersed three times as Christ lay in the grave for three days, Cyril instructs: "at the self-same moment you were both dying and being born; and that Water of salvation was at once your grave and your mother." Cyril thus sees the transfer of allegiance taking place by the unification of the believer with the death and resurrection of Christ. Here the salvation from death that Christ won for humanity by death is transferred to the baptized, snatching them from Satan's grip. Celebrating the *pro nobis* (for us), Cyril exclaims: "Christ was actually crucified, and actually buried, and truly rose again; and all these things He has freely bestowed upon us, that we, sharing His sufferings by [ritual] imitation, might gain salvation in reality. O surpassing loving-kindness! Christ received nails . . . while on me without pain or toil by the fellowship of His suffering He freely bestows salvation."

"Let no one suppose, however," Cyril continues, "that Baptism is merely the grace of the remission of sins, or further, that of adoption." The one who by baptismal union becomes a recipient with Jesus of the Father's unconditional love immediately becomes a subject in Jesus of new life to the Father's praise. For, as Baptism means putting on "Christ," i.e., the one anointed by the Spirit, it also means being endowed with Christ's own Spirit. Baptism "ministers to us the gift of the Holy Spirit," just as Christ himself was anointed with the Spirit at his baptism in the River Jordan. This is symbolized by the anointing in oil, the chrism or unction, which followed emergence from the pool of water, "the antitype of that with which Christ was anointed, and this is the Holy Spirit." Therefore the newly baptized are equipped for messianic battle. Just as "Christ after His Baptism, and the visitation of the Holy Spirit, went forth and vanquished the adversary, so likewise you, after Holy Baptism and the Mystical Chrism, having put on the whole armor of the Holy Spirit, are to stand against the power of the adversary and vanquish it. . . ."[85]

Surveying Cyril's address and others like it from East and West, Hugh M. Riley writes that what hearing the gospel did to candidates for baptism was to work "a turning from evil works to good works. It is rising from slavery and all forms of human degradation and captivity. It is joining the entire universe in acknowledging Christ's Lordship. It is a prayer for help and grace and an admission of universal sinfulness and redemption excluding and favoring no one. It is a serious moral choice, irrevocable because of its eschatological overtones. . . . It is

---

85. So also Martyn writes of Galatians 3:27 about ". . . equipping the baptized for participation in apocalyptic warfare. Recognizing the danger of its being understood as a cultic act that merely replaces circumcision as a rite of entry (1 Cor. 1:11-17), Paul sees in baptism the juncture at which the person both participates in the death of Christ (Rom. 6:4) and is equipped with the armor for apocalyptic battle (1 Thess. 5:8-10; 1 Cor. 15:53-54; Rom. 13:12)." *Galatians,* p. 376.

a rejection of all in the world which pertains to slavery and exploitation through fear, and it presents a new freedom and partnership with a new kind of Master in the struggle for good."[86] Theologically speaking, the "I" in the "I believe" is Jesus Christ who in the Spirit believed His own Sonship in profoundest solidarity of love with those in bondage to sin and subject to death. Historically speaking, then, the "I" in the "I believe" of the early baptismal creed is the early Christian convert, whose conversion was this dramatic passage from evil to good, ritualized in the baptismal ceremonial that has been described as union with the Christ who had first united with her. This convert has been moved by hearing the gospel to prepare for the event of unification by learning the faith in the living and true God which the gospel brings in bringing Jesus, and at the same time unlearning, so to say, contra-divine notions, sensibilities, ethics, and rituals to which he or she had previously adhered.

## A Note on Apocalyptic Demonology

We must briefly consider here the Spirit's narratively rendered opponent, the *unholy spirit(s)* (cf. Mark 1:12-13), whom the theological subject renounces by way of preface to her or his descent into the watery tomb. In the depiction of the unholy spirits in the gospel narrative, we discover a subjectivity that seizes possession of what is not its own, and abuses and destroys it. How, without superstition, may we account for this rhetorically indispensable figure of apocalyptic theology, a figure that when taken literally becomes ethically lethal — as it did also in the case of Luther?[87]

The originator of moral evil is figured in the Bible variously as the accuser, the tempter, the devourer of souls; it is variously named Satan, Beelzebub, the devil, the prince of this world. This unholy figure, unmasked, is the legion (Mark 5:9) spirit of envy, wanting not what God in His power, wisdom and love has chosen but rather what God has just so rejected. As corrupted desire curved in upon itself, envy has nothing of its own to receive and enjoy but only wants what belongs to another and that, not as something to be enjoyed for itself, but only as something enjoyed because taken from another. Envy is parasitical in this way. It is also desperate and desperately active in this neediness, until it collapses in exhaustion and despondency, weary of desire itself, in final form a death wish, a suicidal assertion of the sovereignty usurped from God. It has nothing of its own because it only wants what is another's. It won't have anything of its own to enjoy because it won't have anything as a gift. Full of cunning and frantic in activity, desperate envy cannot regard labor as gift and calling to service, and therefore will not work justly for a fair

---

86. Hugh M. Riley, *Christian Initiation* (Washington, DC: Catholic University of America Press, 1974), p. 84.

87. See the appendix to *LBC,* pp. 379-85.

wage because it rather wants only what another has earned, all the more delectable if what is taken has been earned justly. Envy is poisoned desire that sickens the earth; it is the glue of malice that holds together structures of injustice.

Whether, then, by the blessing and free favor of God, or by the ruthless exploitation of the poor and powerless, the rich are rich *unjustly*. If blessed, that is to say, it is by undeserved gift and in order that those blessed may become a blessing to others in turn. If rich, however, by the legal thievery of the privileged, it is by the sin of greed meriting nothing but divine wrath "over the ruin of Joseph" (Amos 6:6). For this reason Jesus pronounced eternal woe upon the rich (Luke 6:24-25). Envy or covetousness, however, is ontologically prior to greed; envy is the corruption of desire that fills the vacuum in the human heart vacated by true faith in the true God, almighty giver of gifts. The last of the Ten Commandments (Exod. 20:17, Deut. 5:21) circles back to the first; it is the commandment that probes and searches the heart (Rom. 7:7) to expose the concupiscence that organizes a heart void of love for God above all. Greed is nothing but the envy of the rich towards competitors, real and imagined, in mindless, soulless accumulation. At the base of greed lurks this envy; it is the origin of moral evil in the world. Envy is at theological root the desire for those possibilities that God has not chosen but rejected in determining to create, redeem, and fulfill this world as the Beloved Community. Envy is the *sicut Deus eritis* of Genesis 3:5. Envy is the creature's knowledge of good and evil that is not the good that God has elected but rather the evil that God has rejected, now taken as good in place of God. Such rejected possibilities are in theological truth a nothingness, Barth's *das Nichtige*,[88] the "idols" that have no real existence but nevertheless are actual as "demons" (1 Cor. 10:19-22). Rejected possibilities become devastatingly actual when creatures who by dint of their imaginative and creative capacities grasp after these ideas and resolve to act on them within the world that God is creating for the coming of the Beloved Community.

Envy is what is uncovered in the best theological accounts of the "fall of the devil." According to Nyssa's learned speculation (The Great Catechism, VI), having discovered that the lowlier human being had been appointed God's covenant partner, the prince of the angels and child of light in a fit of envy vowed to spite God's election and to destroy the earthly rival. The unholy spirit is moved by envy to defy God's choice and destroy God's works by seducing those works themselves, the human creatures, into paths other than God has determined by arousing envy also in them (Gen. 3:5-6). The power of this devil to entice, so figured, is the power of envy both over creatures in structures of malice and injustice and the power within human beings in the Pauline "desires of the flesh." The medie-

---

88. *CD* III/3, pp. 289-368. See the illuminating study of Wolf Kroetke, *Sin and Nothingness in the Theology of Karl Barth,* trans. P. G. Ziegler and C.-M. Bammel, Studies in Reformed Theology and History, New Series, Number 10 (Princeton: Princeton Theological Seminary, 2005). See also the discussion in *PNT,* pp. 104-12.

val term for this power is concupiscence, Augustine's lust for domination *(libido dominandi)* that fills and dominates the heart that has lost its true love of God as for the free Giver of gifts in the joy that haves and holds what is freely given.

In talking about "the devil," theology is talking about a creature (*City of God,* XI, 13-15), yet a creature superior in power and cunning that captivates human desire and organizes these less capable creatures for service in structures of malice and injustice. The figurative interpretation is necessary, not because of any doubt about the actuality of evil, but because "the devil" is an unthinkably willful self-corruption; it lives as violation of the principle that all by nature seek the good. It is a sheerly pathological entity, a *"subjectivity that despises"* the creation God is creating with a hatred that must include the most profound self-hatred.[89] If we interpret the figure of the devil theologically as personifying this virtually unthinkable thought of personally willful destruction, as that figures the experience under structures of malice and injustice into which bondage human creatures are born and nurtured before ever having any choice to think or do otherwise, we are entitled to continue with the biblical rhetoric of "the devil," whose wicked works and ways the theological subject renounces in order to be a theological subject at all. "You cannot drink the cup of the Lord and the cup of demons. You cannot partake of the table of the Lord and the table of demons" (1 Cor. 10:21). The danger of superstition notwithstanding, as Rauschenbusch noted, theology needs to figure "the super-personal forces of evil," and to interpret this figure as a veritable "Kingdom of Evil"[90] just as theology at the same time needs to decode this figure as the corruption of desire in the power of envy. This is especially so for theology that appropriates Pauline apocalyptic — lest we perpetuate Luther's sin of demonizing theological opponents.[91] Sinners are at once victims and perpetrators of sinful envy just as in Christ they become righteous as recipients of gifts, even as this righteousness consists in a struggling renunciation on the basis of divine forgiveness in the time between Ascension and Parousia. The baptismal renunciation of Satan that demarcates the formation of theological subjectivity is *sine qua non:* renunciation of victimhood as of violence, of envy and despair as of pride and greed. In the power of the Spirit, this renunciation is a declaration of independence and the commencement of apocalyptic warfare.

---

## Baptism as Rebirth into the Ecclesia — I

Before there was a canonical Bible and a common creed, there was this ritual practice of water baptism into the ownership of Christ and the triune God that

89. Jenson, *ST* 2, p. 130.
90. Rauschenbusch, *Social Gospel,* pp. 81-87.
91. *LBC,* pp. 379-85.

separated the holy ecclesia from this sinful world of malice and injustice. It was a ceremony indicating a public transfer of loyalty, which joined gospel believers to the new people "called out" by God from their previous identities among the nations. Baptism "called them out" of their previous social world and "called into" the *ecclesia,* the church. The ceremony ritually abolished the previous web of worldly identities and established the newly baptized as members of Christ's people. So Paul states in Galatians 3:27-28, "As many of you as were baptized into Christ have clothed yourselves with Christ. There is no longer Jew or Greek, there is no longer slave or free, there is no longer male and female; for all of you are one in Christ Jesus." The implication of this attractive statement is that no one can individually be united with Christ without at once also being united to all the rest of Christ's people throughout time and space in this gathering new humanity. For early Christian baptism, one not only dies spiritually as a sinner before God in dying with Christ. One simultaneously dies socially as a person defined by the ethnic, economic, or sexual identifications of the fallen world. One not only arises spiritually as a believer in rising with Christ. One becomes a member of God's new humanity, a neophyte in God's new culture of agape love, a newborn child of the family of God, an instance of the dawning new creation, Temple of the Spirit and Body of Christ.

To be "born again" therefore did not refer to some inner or private event in the individual's consciousness, let alone coming to "self-consciousness," as something separable from the ceremony of the body's water baptism, though of course the new birth did denote utter and radical transformation from the heart outwards, the Pauline "circumcision of the heart." But this profound change of the heart's affections referred to one's actual, indeed physical, bodily adoption into the new covenant people of God by the washing with water in the name and thus by the authority of the Three. This social change, renouncing one's previous identification as a worldling under the hegemony of Satan by putting on Christ in its place, effected in the individual believer the profoundest transformation, but, so to say, from the outside in. That is to say, the identification of the ceremony of water baptism into Christ with the regenerating work of the Spirit of Christ meant that one is born again *from above* by the Spirit when the Spirit puts one into the company of Christ and his people *on the earth,* in this way locating the neophyte believer within the relations of love between the Father and the Son. The believer's "inner" (lifelong, not instantaneous) transformation comes from the outside in, from the new company into which the Spirit puts the believer with other believers within the very life of God: hence truly a "new birth."

Such notions are very hard for modern people to understand, not only on account of the self-consciousness that has radically individualized us, but also because of the long and ambiguous history of Christendom and its various practices of baptism. Recall Francis Ford Coppola's great movie, *The Godfather,* the story of a Mafia family with its climactic scene of betrayal and murder powerfully juxtaposing the baptism of the murderer's child in an ornate Catholic church with alternating scenes of gangland execution: in the world a treacherous murderer, in the church a pious father baptizing his baby. *Simul iustus et peccator?* How can anyone think that this ceremony of water baptism, standing for incorporation into the institutional church, changes anything, let alone transforms from the thrall of envy to the struggle of righteousness for righteousness?

In the unreflective stance of faith in the early church, where costly renunciation of the Satanic empire discouraged baptisms of convenience, however, few systematically inquired about the possibility of insincere or hypocritical baptism — abuses that could cast doubt on baptism's efficacy as the work of the Spirit. True, the ecclesia did so implicitly in that it tested candidates for baptism and developed a rigorous catechumenate to this end. Just so, given the ever-present possibilities of persecution and martyrdom, the decision to become a Christian was not taken lightly (recall the excursus on Perpetua at the end of Chapter One). What was rather envisioned in these circumstances was the possibility of apostasy, i.e., of denying the faith under duress. The Epistle to the Hebrews addressed this specific situation and warned with apodictic severity that "it is impossible to restore again to repentance those who have once been enlightened [i.e., baptized],[92] who have tasted the heavenly gift, and have become partakers of the Holy Spirit, and have tasted the goodness of the word of God and the powers of the age to come, if they then commit apostasy, since they crucify the Son of God on their own account and hold him up to contempt" (6:4-6). This interpretation of the unforgivable sin (Mark 3:29) as forsaking the Spirit's work in one's baptism had unforeseen consequences as the delay of the Parousia stretched into long-term residency of the church in the still unredeemed world. It led many in the early church to delay baptism until death was imminent, in order not to risk squandering the one-time offer of remission of sins. It led others to refuse reconciliation with Christians who had failed during episodes of persecution, just as the Hebrews text indicates. We shall explore these complications below. In both cases, the presupposition is that baptism is valid and effective from God's perspective as forgiveness, adoption, and gift of the Spirit. But precisely so, it can be betrayed, as Judas betrayed, from the human side — an act for which there is no repair and no forgiveness. Just because the Spirit works in water baptism, apostasy by the baptized is unforgivable. This being the "naïve" understanding — God's gift in baptism could really be disowned, with force equal to God's gift, once and for all — no one considered the possibility (taken for granted in modern self-consciousness) that water baptism could be an empty sign that did not effectively convey the grace of forgiveness, adoption, and the Spirit.

---

92. Justin Martyr uses the same term, borrowed from the mystery religions, to denote baptism: "And this washing is called *illumination,* because they who learn these things are illuminated in their understandings. And in the name of Jesus Christ, who was crucified under Pontius Pilate, and in the name of the Holy Ghost, who through the prophets foretold all things about Jesus, he who is *illuminated* is washed" ("First Apology," chapter 61, emphasis added, in *ANF* 1, p. 183).

To gain perspective on this, we can ask what can be known about the origins of this water rite as initiation and incorporation into a new community, the ecclesia in Christ. It is significant that the gospel narrative in all its iterations finds the origin of the gospel in the preaching and practice, not of Jesus, but of John the Baptizer, to which Jesus submitted. Traditional purification rites with water and the proselyte baptism of Gentile converts to Judaism are well attested in the Judaism of the Second Temple period. The scandal and affront in the message of John the Baptist, however, was his demand that fellow Jews also submit to baptism, i.e., a public act of repentance and purification in hope of forgiveness on the impending day of the Lord, the eschaton of judgment. John demanded this act of the children of Abraham, heirs of divine promise, the elect of God and keepers of the holy Temple in Jerusalem. This demand seemed to challenge the very basis of the covenant, God's gracious election of Israel. "He said therefore to the multitudes that came out to be baptized by him, 'You brood of vipers! Who warned you to flee from the wrath to come? Bear fruits that befit repentance, and do not begin to say to yourselves, "We have Abraham as our father"; for I tell you, God is able from these stones to raise up children to Abraham. Even now the axe is laid to the root . . .'" (Luke 3:7-9).

In submitting to John's baptism, Jesus of Nazareth indicated assent to this message. Indeed in his fateful controversy with the Temple authorities Jesus asked whether or not they would acknowledge that John's baptism came from God and bore divine authority (Mark 11:27-33). John's radical critique of Judaism from within Judaism, then, is the historical presupposition of Christian baptism. It indicates from the very start that, howsoever we understand Christian baptism, we cannot understand it as a guarantee of salvation based on the presumption of election without fruits that befit repentance. The Spirit indeed promises both to believers and to the community founded on baptism a certain indefectibility. The gates of hell will not prevail against the community that confesses Jesus as the Son of the blessed One; this God who has begun a good work in believers will bring it to conclusion. But this infallible election of the Spirit does not work by magic, *ex opere operato* (mechanically) or naturalistically, but by repentance and faith transforming the person as a theological subject. The promised Paraclete at work in baptism is the One who convicts the world concerning sin and righteousness and judgment (John 16:7-11). A false understanding of the Spirit as magical privilege or a natural inheritance is precisely the false understanding of Israel's election that John and Jesus alike reject — and this, be it noted and underscored, as a position *within* Second Temple Judaism (not then the expression of triumphal Christian supersessionism).

What was decisive for early Christian understanding was what actually transpired in Jesus' baptism, i.e., how the Holy Spirit led Jesus to do battle with the unclean spirits, culminating in His death in the very place of the helpless sinner under abusive power and cruel dominion. One cannot underestimate the theological attention that the early church gave to the gospel texts regarding Jesus' baptism, for these, coupled with the actual practice of water baptism into Jesus' name from the earliest days (Acts 2:38), guided the church through its earliest ethical and doctrinal contests with Docetism, the Christological heresy that taught that Jesus was only apparently human, and Gnosticism, which denied that the Father of Jesus was the creator of this palpable world where bodies wash with water and drown in raging floods.[93] The origin of Christian baptism in John, in other words, identifies the *Holy* Spirit as the one who had "spoken by the prophets" of Israel to summon repentance and faith, precisely not the Gnostic coming to self-consciousness of our supposedly true selves from deep within. The Spirit is not the lost depth of the human self dramatically expressing itself, but the depth of the triune God (1 Cor. 2:9-10) who comes from without to the self by the Word incarnate to bring ensouled bodies to their true human calling, its redemption and fulfillment in the Beloved Community on this very earth on which stood the cross of Jesus.

First, consider how the practice of baptism into Jesus Christ guided the church ethically. Baptismal transfer to the sphere of Christ's saving Lordship did not signify the end of moral struggle, as Gnostics thought, but its true beginning. For Gnostics, to be born again meant a *katharsis,* a decisive breakthrough to true self-consciousness as a spark of divine light, trapped within an earthly body and covered over by a socially formed psyche. This breakthrough, in plausible echo of the "illumination" claim for the baptized (Heb. 6:4), supposedly overcame the false consciousness of worldly existence. But what is illumined in baptism into the Christ who came in the flesh (1 John 4:2-3) is the challenge of knowing and doing God's will on the earth, in the body (1 John 4:7) — *God's* will, which is other than ours and revealed as *love* in Jesus' bearing the cross for the sake of others (1 John 4:7-8). Baptismal illumination thus conducted one into His Spirit-led, lifelong battle against sin, death, and devil. This new way of life was known from the narrative of Christ's baptism. Just as the anointing with the Spirit "drove" Jesus into the wilderness confrontation with Satan and thence into the trial of His life's path from the wilderness through Gethsemane to the ignominy of the cross, so also the impartation of the Spirit to the baptized, signified by the anointing with oil following immersion in and emersion from the drowning water, now "drives" the baptized into a lifelong battle of the Spirit against the flesh, faith against doubt, hope against despair, love against apathy and resignation. The gift of the Spirit is then no narcotic, no tranquilizer, but implantation into this militant life of Jesus in the power of the Spirit, His lifelong battle of faith to love and to hope here and now, on the earth.

Second, recall how the practice of baptism guided the church doctrinally. Here, for the first time in salvation history, the Trinity is openly revealed. In the story of Jesus' baptism, the Father, the Son, and the Holy Spirit appear simultaneously, each in His own distinct person playing His own role, yet in harmony

93. See *DC,* pp. 96-106, 133-58.

of purpose. Inspired by this text, the early Christian baptismal confessions or statements of faith connected Father, Son, and Holy Spirit as the one God, not three deities each doing their own thing. They connected the three by means of their essential relations to one another, so that no matter what one person especially does, it necessarily involves the others, each in its own characteristic way. The Father sends, the Son is sent. The Father imparts the Spirit to the Son, in the Spirit the Son returns obedience to the Father. The Father creates, but through the Son and in the Spirit. The Son redeems, but is sent by the Father to His own creation to become truly human, hence truly dependent on the Spirit's guiding. The Spirit gives life, the eternal life of the Father triumphant over death through the obedience of the Son to death, death upon a cross. And so on. In such ways, the Trinitarian baptismal creeds, which evolved out of the elementary baptismal interrogation,[94] articulated the dynamic unity of salvation history as the complex, internally differentiated but singular work of the one God in and by the three mutually related persons.

By contrast, Gnostics and Docetists in various ways depicted a Christ "principle" descending on the earthly Jesus at His baptism but departing Him again before the crucifixion. In this way they implied that matter is evil and the work of an evil deity; that Christ was only apparently a physical being; that salvation is shedding this body of suffering like the butterfly shedding its cocoon to fly away to some distant world of pure light. That is the scheme by which they subverted the narrative conveyed in the canonical gospels. But the Trinitarian connection of the Father and the Son in the Spirit meant that this visible creation could not be regarded as the inferior work of a demon. Salvation is not escape from this evil world of matter. Jesus is a true flesh-and-blood human being whether in his mother's womb or dying on the cross — and in this true human God in the person of the Son was reconciling the world to Himself; in Him the eternal Word became flesh and dwelt among us; in Him we too expect the redemption of our bodies. God creates the world in order to redeem it. The world Jesus comes to redeem is none other than this visible world, which His Father creates and preserves, is creating and will yet fulfill. Jesus' baptism revealed this dynamic unity of God, the unity of creation and redemption in the harmony of divine love, combating not matter but Satan and his envy. All this doctrine arises out of the gospel conviction that, because of Jesus' baptism by John in solidarity with penitent sinners, those who in public ceremony now renounce Satan and are physically, bodily washed by the Spirit into the ownership of Jesus Christ are just so spiritually born anew into God's new humanity. For the opponent of the Holy Spirit is not matter but the devil, not dirt but sin, not social and bodily consciousness but death and destruction, malice and injustice. The sphere of the Spirit is not private consciousness but the ecclesia, for "God has sent the Spirit of His Son into *our* hearts, crying, Abba! Father!" (Gal. 4:6, emphasis added).

94. Kelly, *Early Christian Creeds,* pp. 30-61.

Since it is *hearing,* as in God hearing God spoken, that is, the Spirit proclaiming to us and for us the Word incarnate, that brings the new seeing that is believing in Jesus as the Christ of Israel, the Son of God, Christian theological subjectivity had its real, organic beginnings in this missiological work of preparing catechumens for baptism, in training this new "I" in and for the statement of faith to be made publicly in the Credo, spoken like a pledge of allegiance. It is striking for us today to realize that before there was a canonical Bible, or an ecumenical council, or even a developed Credo to fix the form of faith, it was this gospel-inspired and Spirit-effected ritual practice of water baptism into the ownership of Christ and membership in His Body that generated Christian theological thinking as the reflection of newly birthed theological subjects. If that genesis remains a clue, however, it suggests that Christian theology is always in the first place thinking through this public transfer of loyalty at the root of the new Christian life, always thinking with the new people "called out" by God from previous identities and allegiances among the nations to gather and form the "church" of the gospel.

To grasp this as an *event,* indeed as the *primary event of rebirth into the harbinger of Beloved Community,* we should always qualify the unfortunate English word "church" with a paraphrase of the Greek word that it translates, *ecclesia,* a "calling out," an "assembling" from the nations in the world by the Holy Spirit. Only so can the predicate "holy" be made of the "church" without blasphemy or contradiction to modify the Spirit's new creative work rather than suggest some palpable quality of a religion making a manifestly false claim about itself before God, let alone before the world. Baptism as the initial act of the Word of God "calls out" of the antecedent social world and calls into the ecclesia as into a new society, a new social form, *communio sanctorum,* harbinger of the Beloved Community. It can do this because baptism by the Spirit is baptism into Christ, that is, an impartation by effective imputation of the faith of the messianic man, Jesus, who dwelt in the midst of unclean people and perished between transgressors to bring God near to them.

---

## EXCURSUS: THE JEREMIAS–ALAND DEBATE ON INFANT BAPTISM

What does the social interpretation of baptism as rebirth into the ecclesia suggest for the division in modern Christianity between those who baptize infants and those who baptize believers? Joachim Jeremias was a significant biblical scholar among the pioneers who studied the New Testament in light of its Jewish and Rabbinical background. He wrote an impressive book in which he tried to prove historically that from the earliest days of the church infants were baptized.[95] When all is said and done, his argument boils down to the claim of a parallel

---

95. Joachim Jeremias, *Infant Baptism in the First Four Centuries,* trans. David Cairns (Philadelphia: Westminster, 1962).

between the Jewish ritual practice of circumcision on the male baby's eighth day of life and the new Christian ritual practice of initiation, baptism. Since Christian baptism is incorporation into the new covenant community, Jeremias argued, it follows that early Christians would follow the same practice as with circumcision, incorporating the infant children of believers by the new covenant ceremony of baptism. All the various evidence Jeremias collects is then interpreted in light of the supposition that circumcision and baptism are ritual equivalents for initiation into covenant communities. Kurt Aland, a fellow Lutheran, responded to Jeremias with a powerful critique,[96] patiently unraveling all Jeremias's evidence and showing how in every case this supposition of the ritual equivalence of circumcision and baptism as initiation rites colored his judgment. Jeremias took what is in reality highly ambiguous evidence to indicate the practice of infant baptism. Aland is skeptical that the early church baptized infants, but not quite conclusive. He puts the results of his study in a negative form: there is no proof of infant baptism before the end of the second century, while the prevailing picture in the first two centuries is that of the conversion of adults as we have seen presupposed in Cyril's catechetical lectures. As importantly, Aland really advanced the discussion theologically with three valuable theological insights emerging from his historical study.

First, Aland shows that Jeremias was so eager to defend the practice of infant baptism as apostolic that he did not notice the heavy price he paid theologically for treating Christian baptism in parallel to circumcision. In fact there is only one New Testament text that seems to do this, Colossians 2:11-14, which reads: "In him also you were circumcised with a circumcision made without hands, by putting off the body of flesh in the circumcision of Christ; and you were buried with him in baptism, in which you were also raised with him through faith in the working of God, who raised him from the dead. And you, who were dead in trespasses and the uncircumcision of your flesh, God made alive together with him, having forgiven us all our trespasses, having canceled the bond which stood against us with its legal demands; this he set aside, nailing it to the cross." At first sight, this text seems to provide impressive proof that Christian baptism was understood as a ritual that supersedes circumcision. But on more careful examination we see that this text does not say that at all. It is Judaism's ritual practice, characterized as the "circumcision made with hands" i.e., as a human action, that is instead contrasted with baptism, the "circumcision of Christ," i.e., divine action of the Spirit. This divine action, moreover, is explicated in the familiar Pauline way as the spiritual death and burial of the old man in the watery grave of baptism by which God conforms believers to His crucified and risen Son.

The Colossians text thus agrees with Galatians 6:15, that the root issue is not whether we are for *or against* the ritual practice of circumcision as practiced in

---

96. Kurt Aland, *Did the Early Church Baptize Infants?*, trans. G. R. Beasley-Murray (Philadelphia: Westminster, 1963).

Judaism. Paul never disputes circumcision for Jews as custom, as human work or even as divine tradition, only the imposition of this practice on Gentile converts, as if it were the divine deed that does the decisive thing of effecting death and resurrection with Christ. Paul therefore never polemicizes in the form: Baptism is superior as an initiation rite to circumcision, since, say, it includes girls not just boys, or uses water instead of scalpel. Rather, insofar as we are in Christ there really is no more "Greek or Jew." The very alternative between circumcision and uncircumcision has been by-passed in baptism into Christ. The only question is the canon of Galatian 6:15, whether we have become the new creation, whether "God has made us alive together with Christ" by incorporating us into the new humanity, the *ecclesia;* precisely here the old contrast of Jew and Gentile no longer holds valid. Finally, Aland argues, if baptism was regarded as superseding circumcision as a covenant initiation ritual, one would expect to find Jewish Christians abandoning circumcision for baptism. But there is no evidence of that. Consequently, one can draw no conclusion from the Colossians text for the ritual practice of early Christian baptism, since it manifestly does not stand in any simple parallel to circumcision. Theologically, viewing Christian baptism as a ceremony of initiation to the covenant community, like circumcision, does not suffice to bring out either the divine action claimed in Christian baptism in contrast to "the circumcision made with hands" nor its particular content as union with Christ by Spirit-worked death and resurrection.

Second, Aland makes an important distinction between infant and child baptism. Much of the evidence Jeremias marshaled from the first four centuries can in fact rightly be read to indicate something that conforms neither to infant nor to believer baptism as we know these practices today. Children of believers who had reached the age (three years is a figure proposed by Gregory of Nyssa) when they were capable of speaking for themselves in the ceremonial renunciation of Satan and confession of the Trinity were admitted to baptism. This incidentally gives an important clue to how the early church tested preparation of candidates for baptism: Was the candidate capable of participating in the public liturgy? Given this distinction, in any case, it can be granted that Jeremias has proven that at least in some places in the first two centuries *child* baptism was practiced in early Christianity. But this practice of child baptism may not be taken to imply *infant* baptism on the basis of a faulty parallel to circumcision.

In this connection, Aland indicated two further important points for the history of early Christian baptism. First, practices of admitting children (possibly also infants, though that is not proven) most likely were not at all uniform across the early church, but reflected local circumstances and traditions from the very beginning. Second, the practice of infant baptism began to prevail at the end of the second century with little controversy and quickly became the standard across the church. Tertullian weakly protested against infant baptism in favor of child baptism, but otherwise we can find little serious opposition to this shift. Jeremias had suggested that it was the development of the doctrine of original sin, as we can see in the third-century fathers Origen and Cyprian, that resolved all doubts about the legitimacy of infant baptism: unbaptized children were unforgiven children, destined for perdition. Once this danger was understood, Jeremias suggested, opposition to infant baptism collapsed. But Aland suggests another explanation.

What lies behind the transition to the standard practice of infant baptism at this time was the victory of early Christianity over the ascetic doctrines of Gnosticism (which disdained marriage and discouraged sexual intercourse even in Christian marriage). Having repudiated Gnosticism, and on account of the rapid growth of the church at the beginning of the third century, Christianity was confronted with the presence of masses of children in its ranks whose true status and relation to the community of faith were unclear. For baptism effected incorporation into the church. Of what status then were all these unbaptized children? Were they joined to Christ or not? Now the text about Jesus' blessing the children and rebuking those who would forbid them to come to him (Mark 10:13-14) played a significant role in convincing the church that the Spirit of the Gospel now required in new circumstances the admission to baptism even of those infants brought forward by believing parents. These could not be excluded. Note that the motive for admitting infants in Aland's account is to secure union with Christ and his church, not chiefly to remit the guilt of original sin and to escape from eternal perdition, as Jeremias suggested.

This leads to another contribution. Surprisingly enough for one who has just demolished Jeremias's historical claim to have proved the practice of infant baptism in the earliest church, Aland concludes that the practice of infant baptism nevertheless might be justified theologically, given the church's freedom in the Spirit and the circumstances in which it finds itself. "The New Testament undoubtedly makes statements about the character and significance of baptism for the Christian, but it makes these statements without providing any binding prescription as to the manner in which it is to be carried out, and in particular without any clearly binding directions concerning the *time* of its administration."[97] What is mandated clearly by the New Testament is the bath into the name of Jesus Christ, invoking Him with His Father and their Spirit. Beyond this, arguments for infant, child, or believer baptism depend on theological reasoning that goes beyond this evangelical mandate (Matt. 28:19). Aland thus argued in conclusion that in the course of history the church has been led to a "profounder understanding of the teaching of the New Testament." He cites as still valid the dictum of Cyprian in support of infant baptism, "The mercy and grace of God is not to be refused to any human being."[98] Whether one follows Aland in making such an *inference,* however, the deeper point is that there is and can be no administration of baptism whatsoever that is preserved from making some such inference in

97. Aland, *Did the Early Church Baptize Infants?*, p. 113.
98. Aland, *Did the Early Church Baptize Infants?*, p. 113.

Christian freedom and in the light of the circumstances. Advocates of infant and believer baptism stand on the same footing (or rather, lack of it!) with respect to the clear New Testament mandate. But this does not imply arbitrariness. It implies that we are not yet asking the right questions.

---

## Baptism as Rebirth into the Ecclesia — II

As argued above, the faith of the Christian is originally and properly the faith of the man Christ who believed for us once and for all and, as the Risen One, comes to believe in us, when by the Spirit the old Adam is slain by immersion into the watery tomb and the new person in Christ arises. Much more needs to be said about this faith of Jesus, both in Christology concerning the way in which the Spirit led Jesus to take responsibility for us and in Patrology concerning Jesus' proclamation of the heavenly Father and the Father's self-surpassing proclamation of Jesus as His Son. For the present, however, the focus in Pneumatology falls on the new subjectivity of this Spirit-imparted faith of Jesus bequeathed to believers, which is and effects, as Bonhoeffer argued, the supersession of the humanity of Adam by the coming of "Christ existing as church-community."[99]

In his dissertation, *Sanctorum Communio*, Bonhoeffer executed an acute critique of the individualism (and its antipode, the sociology of collectivism) of the transcendental Subject of Kantianism according to which "the knowing I becomes the starting point of all philosophy."[100] He saw that any union of such knowing subjects "never leads to the concept of community, but only to the concept of sameness . . . ,"[101] that is, of objects known as the same in the same way by interchangeable subjects. Where this paradigm reigns, the existence of persons in community becomes an enormous enigma. Whether the transcendental scheme is even an apt characterization of experimental science would surely be contested by the hermeneutical pragmatism utilized in this book; Peirce's philosophical reflection on the actual practice of science exposits science as a human community of interpretation, historically "traditioned" and socially determined "all the way down." But the transcendental construal of the knowing subject is a perfectly apt characterization of the Cartesian-Kantian subject of modernity, based on the dualism of thinking things and extended things, sensible and supersensible notions. Bonhoeffer's intention in his analysis of depersonalized knowledge was to set off "the specifically Christian concept of person in order to clarify how it differs from that of idealism."[102] The

---

99. Bonhoeffer, *Sanctorum,* p. 121.
100. Bonhoeffer, *Sanctorum,* p. 40.
101. Bonhoeffer, *Sanctorum,* p. 43.
102. Bonhoeffer, *Sanctorum,* p. 45.

difference is that it is "impossible to reach the real existence of other subjects by way of the purely transcendental category of the universal,"[103] that is, the epistemological universal of the knowing I, which knows only objects, never other subjects, since for it other subjects are formally interchangeable. Purely conceived, they exist as the impersonal "I think" that attaches to every claim to objective truth. To know one is to know all, and anything that deviates from the formal sameness in knowing the same objects in the same way is an idiosyncrasy, an accidental accretion of time and place deriving from suspect bodily inclinations or parochial loyalties.

To be sure, then, personal knowledge of other subjects would be another kind of knowing altogether — akin to what we have termed "hermeneutical" or "interpretive" knowing in which a subject "knows" another subject as its "object" in view of an audience of fellow subjects, offering to them an interpretation of another to which others in turn respond, offering interpretations of interpretation that in turn become artifacts begging new interpretations to new audiences *ad infinitum.* This never-finished circulation through time forms communities of interpretation in the world, since by the giving and receiving of information, interpreters also give and reveal themselves as specific perspectives in space and time. From this personal giving and receiving there emerges the phenomenon of persons in community knowing each other by the mediation of their reciprocating interpretations as opposed to interchangeable subjects timelessly knowing sameness. Thus we know persons as particular "identities" in the world by learning the history of their communities of interpretation in which they have received themselves, interpret their own experience, and so give themselves to others. "The person does not exist timelessly; a person is not static, but dynamic. The person exists always and only in ethical responsibility; the person is re-created again and again in the perpetual flux of life."[104]

In terms of the present work, where and when these essentially personal exchanges are gifts joyfully given and received and their circulation as such is infinite we may speak of *the Beloved Community* of God. Notions of person and community, then, are correlative, as Jenson sees: "[A] person is one with whom other persons — the circularity is constitutive — can *converse,* whom they can *address.*"[105] As such, the notion of the person is not reducible to human "nature," though it presupposes a set of distinct possibilities. A willful, but ontologically violent reduction of person to nature (to "mere life") produces in the place of person and community *individuals* and *aggregates;* here communication becomes a historyless transcendence of intelligence over the chaos of matter in motion and knowledge an instrument of domination for the imposition of order. But God, angels, and even animals (such as are we) can be persons that interchange

103. Bonhoeffer, *Sanctorum,* p. 43.
104. Bonhoeffer, *Sanctorum,* p. 48.
105. Jenson, *ST* 1, p. 117.

in communities of interpretation. Indeed, Bonhoeffer acknowledges, the human person — elusive as it becomes under the structures of malice and injustice, reduced to manipulated nature — emerges *"only in relation to the divine"*[106] whose image it bears, when God speaks, addressing it as a Thou corresponding to the divine I for the sake of establishing beloved community.

In summary, Bonhoeffer writes, *"[T]he person is willed by God, in concrete vitality, wholeness, and uniqueness as an ultimate unity. Social relations must be understood, then, as purely interpersonal and building on the uniqueness of separateness of persons."*[107] Not interchangeable subjects in timeless sameness, but unique historical persons receiving and achieving community — or fatefully failing to do so in the spiritual death that is human isolation. We note here with emphasis the difference between historical persons relating to other persons in a shared world of intersubjectivity and transcendental subjects relating to objects in a world of sameness and repetition. This distinction is a distant descendant of the Trinitarian distinction between person and nature worked out by the Cappadocian fathers in the fourth century, as we shall see. It plays a subtle role in the Christological divergence between Bonhoeffer and Barth, as we shall also see. For the present, however, it sheds much light on the claim that the Christian theological subject is born anew into the ecclesia, when the ecclesia is taken as forming one person with Christ, the new Adam, that is, the total Christ of Head and Body, the Spirit's temple made of bodies unified to become the earthly body of the risen Lord (1 Cor. 6:12-20).

In this light, then, we return to the primitive Christian water ceremony ritually abolishing antecedent identities that had reduced persons to instances of supposed natures: Jews or Greeks or Barbarians, slave or free, married or unmarried. By disrobing the denizens of the world of their familiar costumes and clothing them in Christ, baptism composed "Christ existing as community." For early Christians, according to J. L. Martyn's exegesis of the pregnant text of Galatians 3:26-28, one not only dies spiritually as a sinner before God in being crucified with Christ. One simultaneously dies socially as a person defined by the ethnic, economic, or gender binaries of the fallen world. "To pronounce the nonexistence of these opposites is to announce nothing less than the end of the cosmos . . . ,"[108] that is, the world as organized by malice and injustice, the world as contrastive identity machine, the world that reduces persons to representatives of supposed essences or natures. Paul's interpretation of baptism as a work of mortification is thus "an implied reference to new creation";[109] it is the Spirit's crucifixion that prepares the ground for the Spirit's resurrection. In Christ, one arises to membership in God's new humanity, "a newly created unity. . . . Members of the church

106. Bonhoeffer, *Sanctorum,* p. 49.
107. Bonhoeffer, *Sanctorum,* p. 55.
108. Martyn, *Galatians,* p. 376.
109. Martyn, *Galatians,* p. 377.

are not one *thing;* they are one *person,* having been taken into the corpus of the One New Man."[110]

How do believers become in baptism one person with Christ? Clearly the question depends on firmly grasping that the "I" in the "I believe" is by no means an isolated "I," although it is truly and profoundly personal, a trusting appropriation "for me" of the Christ who is *the* Person for others. This social change, mediated by the body's free submission in a public ritual of spiritual drowning signified and effected the profoundest transformation, yet *from the outside in.* That is to say, whatever various, complex, ambiguous, or even contradictory motives we may imagine psychologically, fundamentally the *baptized is here exposed utterly as patient* even in regard to its human agency and *the Spirit* in turn is given and revealed as *agent* of this new patiency-cum-agency. What the baptized does she does in the obedience of faith to the call of Jesus heard in the gospel, giving God the glory for whatever God may now do with this human life in the body. That is why, as Jüngel rightly observed, what Paul, Augustine, and Luther call the *"inner man,* in total contrast to an 'I' shut up in its 'inwardness,' [is the one that] can *allow himself to be called out of himself* and can actually *come out* of himself so as to become a new man."[111] Persons exist ecstatically within time and space as they become conscious of others; they are not impersonal subjects transcending time and space in self-consciousness. Communities are places of joyful exchange making history through time, not collectivities organized around some arbitrary claim to realize essence or nature ("the Aryan race," the "proletariat," the "market"). Concretely, the old "outer man" is the deformed psycho-social self formed by malice and structured by injustice that survives by crude or sublime self-seeking in all things. In just this way, Bonhoeffer later parsed discipleship: "When Jesus calls a man He bids him come and die and in dying to find his true life."[112] The agency of discipleship arises from the patiency of the call, when the Spirit makes Jesus present as the Christ to unite the auditor to Himself by the death of repentance and resurrection to the new obedience of faith.

Thus Paul's identification of the ceremony of water baptism into Christ with the regenerating work of the Spirit to form the "one person" of what Augustine later called the "total Christ" is the basis on which the apostle can both logically and ontologically warn the Galatians that they are in danger of falling from grace if they seek to justify themselves by anything other than *what Christ has done for them* and what His Spirit has subsequently and accordingly effected in them *from the outside in.* The one who is changed from the heart outward and from the outside in is the one born again *from above, by the Spirit's free descent.* Faith is

---

110. Martyn, *Galatians,* p. 377.

111. Eberhard Jüngel, *The Freedom of a Christian: Luther's Significance for Contemporary Theology,* trans. R. A. Harrisville (Minneapolis: Augsburg, 1988), p. 63.

112. Dietrich Bonhoeffer, *The Cost of Discipleship,* trans. R. H. Fuller (New York: Simon & Schuster, Touchstone Edition, 1995).

thus located *spatially and temporally* in the tangible company of Christ among his people: "Thus out of utter isolation arises concrete community, for the preaching of God's love speaks of the community into which God has entered with each and every person — with all those who in utter solitude know themselves separated from God and other human beings and who believe this message."[113] As the "inner" or better, personal transformation comes from the outside in, that is, from the new company that believers now keep in Christ as *communio sanctorum*, just so the gospel message itself, which awakens and sustains faith in each person, does this just as it assembles into *communion* those so Spirit-ed.

"This cup of blessing that we bless, is it not a sharing in the blood of Christ? The bread that we break, is it not a sharing in the body of Christ?" (1 Cor. 10:16). The meal of the baptized is their communion with Christ and through Christ with one another. This calling out and calling together for sharing of gifts ever comes about by this news of the righteousness of Another, on whom the Spirit rested and remained, the One who actually lived for others even to death for others. Hence, this faith and its community exist on account of Christ's righteousness, coming to them as "extrinsic" righteousness, accomplished bodily and so coming as gift of His very body and blood. Faith and its community endure from moment to moment in the world by hearing of that which they could not have known in themselves, let alone have acquired by themselves privately, in their own isolation, or collectively, by their own self-sanctification. The historical continuity of the church through time is the Spirit speaking the Word, namely, of the "community in which God has entered" with the isolated, a veritable harrowing of hell.[114] The holy ministry, then, is the Spirit's work of continuity that provides for fresh speaking of just this Word of God. By the same token, the holy order of prophetic and apostolic ministry of the Word remains under this Word and is to be tested for fidelity to it. Such testing is in the competence of the baptized who hunger and thirst to hear the voice of the Shepherd, not of a hireling (John 10:4-5). For the union of the sign and the thing signified is always gift, inseparable from the Giver. The Spirit's advent in the world is not an institution; it is event faithfully given from above, that forms holy tradition, not dead traditionalism.

This *ecclesiology* is the crucial point that divides a theology of the cross from a theology of glory: a theology of the cross is one of theological subjectivity[115] in

---

113. Bonhoeffer, *Sanctorum,* p. 149.

114. Bonhoeffer continues in the same passage: "Serving the law [the execution of God's judgment on false and idolatrous association] leads Jesus to the cross, truly leads him into the most profound solitude that the curse of the law brings upon human beings. When Jesus is arrested all the disciples forsake him, and on the cross Jesus is quite alone. In the death of Jesus on the cross God's judgment and wrath are carried out on all the self-centeredness of humanity, which had distorted the meaning of the law," i.e., to secure false and idolatrous forms of association. Bonhoeffer, *Sanctorum Communio,* p. 150.

115. To this extent *with* Gerhard O. Forde, *On Being a Theologian of the Cross: Reflections on Luther's Heidelberg Disputation, 1518* (Grand Rapids: Eerdmans, 1997), pp. 9-11.

which those graced with faith as the Giver's gift ever recognize their profoundest solidarity with the sinful and perishing world on account of Christ crucified
*(propter Christum),* even as the world in unbelief refuses to recognize its sinfulness, sees no need of Christ and His cross, and thus separates from the community of faith that is open to, indeed seeking all ( John 3:17-20). A theology of glory
is one in which faith is taken as the pious act of those who just so separate themselves from sinners and boast of this lovelessness as if it were righteousness before
God.[116] Thus the subject of faith, when and where faith is personal conformation
to Christ by the Spirit in the new community of joyful exchanges, is and remains
this very isolated sinner by virtue of the common body to which it still belongs,
although in its broken grip and no longer in its thrall. The point is, then, that the
faith of Christ becomes "ours" only with others, in this solidarity with the *Christus
pro nobis* where the equally sinful body that I am is still member of the common
body captivated by structures of malice and injustice. Apart from this, even if we
think of faith as "mine," even if we gather together in an association of those who
think similarly of faith as each one's own individual mark of distinction from the
world, we in fact fall back into the isolation of the self-justifying self *incurvatus
in seipsum.* Is not this illusion of individual piety the motor that drives religion in
its grim business of trading in sacrifices?

To understand this point with the sharpness it deserves, we must take note
here of Schleiermacher's influential characterization of the difference between
Catholic and Protestant ecclesiologies. Protestantism, he said, "makes the indi-

---

116. Busch, *Karl Barth and the Pietists,* pp. 77-78. In the conclusion of this fascinating
study, Busch speaks of two principles of communication for theology in the framework of
the church — what we are calling theological subjectivity. "First, such a dialogue between
Christians, even if it has the form of an argument with each other, occurs in the brackets of the
assumption that both are in the church of Christ." One can only exclude from this dialogue "an
arch-heretic who is totally lost even to the invisible church as well," though Barth, according to
Busch, immediately adds that we lack the ability to discern such an arch-heretic. The second
principle continues in the train of this qualification of the first. A boundary is drawn right
through theologians in "the fact that God's truth and my understanding of it are always two
completely different things. At the moment I forget this border . . . the other person and I no
longer stand before our common judge, rather I become the judge of the other" (p. 289). The
modesty here is commendable; it is indeed the case that whoever appeals to the Word of God
more puts herself under judgment than proves a point against another. Yet Busch's formulation
is overdrawn. It is not coherent with the cognitive claim of critical dogmatics in which just
such discernment is the sine qua non of theology. If God's truth and my understanding of it
are in principle "two completely different things," God's truth is in principle unknowable. My
theological understanding will be inadequate to the eschatological fullness of God's truth,
to be sure, but it will be adequate to this time and place that I occupy, by the Spirit's own
promise to lead to truth, if my Spirit-given intention is in fact *sentire cum ecclesia* (thinking
with the church). Charitable critique, just as Barth commends it, in fact exposes the fault line
that de facto runs through decaying Christendom and necessitates the realignment that this
work advocates.

vidual's relation to the Church dependent on his relation to Christ, while [Catholicism] contrariwise makes the individual's relation to Christ dependent on his relation to the Church."[117] This misleading characterization, however, makes "Catholics" out of both Luther and Calvin (indeed, they *are* "catholics"!) since they spoke of the church as the *mother* of all who believe. For here the Spirit's Scriptures are at work as the matrix of theological subjectivity. According to the great Reformers, faith comes from the down-to-earth "hearing" of the gospel, *Verbum externum,* through the ordered ministry of the church (*rite vocatus,* AC XIV) in the Spirit's mission to the nations, just as theology is thinking with the church, not with modern self-consciousness. By contrast, Schleiermacher advocates as a proper "Protestant" ecclesiology the view that "the Christian Church takes shape through the coming together of regenerate individuals to form a system of mutual interaction and co-operation."[118] The ministry of the church, as the work of the Spirit ministering the Word that it be heard, falls out of the picture here. How people are then "regenerated," let alone formed into theological subjects without the ministry of the Word is something of a mystery passed over here in imperceptive, if not embarrassed silence.

Of course, by the light of the present argument, Schleiermacher was not wrong to try to accent the new birth as the Spirit's basis of the community of faith; he erred in setting the new birth in opposition to the church's ordered ministry to the *Verbum externum.* As a result of this error, he also frightfully underestimated the persistence of sin in the life of the redeemed, including the sinfulness that still afflicts their life together. At the tension-filled juncture between continuing membership in the dying world by virtue of the common body and the new subjectivity of belonging to Christ and His people in faithful anticipation of the Beloved Community, the righteousness of faith is not and cannot be in any sense the believer's independent experience, let alone doing. Regeneration is rather faith in Christ's experience and doing for others, hence also "for me," according to the new synergy of the union of faith with Christ by the Spirit. The doing of Christ in the believer is first of all manifest by the gift of Spirit-wrought and hence embattled faith in the world. So a worldling claimed and formed in baptism now lives as one claimed by Christ in the battle initiated by the Spirit against "the world, the devil and our sinful flesh." In just this way and only this dynamic way of an inaugurated eschatology, faith active in love effectively transforms that penitent but believing self step by step *(partim et partim)* as the self that now lives into the righteousness of Christ by means of the righteousness of Christ given as gift. Sanctification therefore is an active synergy of the renewed human will of the believer in the Holy Spirit, an active striving to follow the Logos incarnate in every aspect of life, as Luther, in his most anti-Pelagian tract of all, expressly

---

117. Friedrich Schleiermacher, *The Christian Faith,* two volumes, ed. H. R. MacKintosh and J. S. Stewart (New York and Evanston: Harper & Row Torchbooks, 1963), 1:103.

118. Schleiermacher, *The Christian Faith,* 2:532.

teaches.[119] It is a juncture that is made fresh and traversed anew every day from baptism day to resurrection day. In this dynamic sense, the theological subject is *simul iustus et peccator* (at the same time righteous and sinful). Because the subject of faith, Jesus Christ, was made to be sin in order that in Him we might become the righteousness of God, so also those who believe by His faith are dynamically becoming righteous even as they remain sinners by their organic solidarity with the world.

Thus, as Ephraim Radner maintains, "there is no looking to Christ apart from the sinful Church."[120] As in Luther's dictum that "the true people of God are they who continually bring to bear the judgment of the cross upon themselves,"[121] the communal being of sinners in Christ is, echoing the first of Luther's Ninety-Five Theses, "continually *penitent* and hence truly 'holy' from a human perspective just because the truly 'righteous' are those who are humbly contrite."[122] It "is not possible to identify the one Church except as she is given over to those who would divide. *Simul iusta et peccatrix* properly describes the Church. . . ."[123] The new imperative Radner draws from this state of affairs is that we cannot accordingly separate ourselves even from the sinful separatism that would seduce and de facto has seduced all divided Christians; even less can we dualize in principle the sign that is this assembly of sinners gathered around Jesus and the thing signified, the Temple of the Holy Spirit, in order to carve out a countercultural colony of the truly regenerate, howsoever we parse that allegedly authentic community. But the church "is born in time" and "exists in time" and exists precisely there as an "evangelical antinomy, the juxtaposition of contraries in the assertion of which lies the disclosure of God's redemptive power."[124] The Spirit unifies the sign and the thing signified as somehow in, with, and under the dark, brutal, opaque covering of sinfulness that is given as the community of sinners and tax-collectors united to Jesus.

If we can say that Luther's view of purgatory was the whole present life of the repentant Christian, we may also say that this Christian life is based upon his view of the Incarnation at its depth as the harrowing of hell. So he deliteralizes and theologically decodes these motifs. Jesus Christ crucified and risen is the present and active *subject* of faith in believers because he has once and for all "descended into hell" in solidarity with sinners — also this "hell" of our post-Christendom as also into all the other false or distorted "objectifications" of His

119. Martin Luther, *The Bondage of the Will*, trans. J. I. Packer and O. R. Johnston (Grand Rapids: Fleming H. Revell [Baker], 2000), p. 268.

120. Ephraim Radner, *A Brutal Unity: The Spiritual Politics of the Christian Church* (Waco, TX: Baylor University Press, 2012), p. 153.

121. *Luther: Lecture on Romans,* trans. Wilhelm Pauck (Philadelphia: Westminster, 1961), p. 120.

122. Radner, *A Brutal Unity*, p. 154.

123. Radner, *A Brutal Unity*, p. 154.

124. Radner, *A Brutal Unity*, p. 157.

more or less faithful people through the ages.[125] He meets us in these "hells" of our corrupt and dysfunctional church life as the living *subject* of faith or he meets us not at all. In the literarily central motif from the Apostles' Creed of the *harrowing* (i.e., the emptying) *of hell* by the victorious Christ, Christianity's early adherents confessed faith at once in the depth of the Incarnation and the breadth of God's saving love. Very probably entering the Apostles' Creed of the West "under Eastern influence," according to Kelly, "the Descent was explicitly mentioned by St Ignatius, St Polycarp, St Irenaeus, Tertullian and others . . ." in the martyrological line that developed early Christian orthodoxy in contest with docetist and Gnostic dualisms. Its meaning was controverted.[126] By the time it became part of the Creed, "a rather different complex of ideas [than deliverance of the dead from Hades] was being associated with it according to which Christ's activity consisted in completely subjecting hell and the ruler of the underworld . . . [for Rufinus] the underworld meant hell, and the Descent was coming to be viewed as the occasion of the redemption, not just of the patriarchs of old, but of mankind in general."[127] It was exposited in terms of the Christus Victor motif reclaimed and made famous in modern theology by Gustaf Aulén:[128] the Lion of Judah "hunts us to save us, He captures us to release us, He leads us captive to restore us liberated to our native land."[129] But it was also understood to underscore the "reality of His death," which "proved His participating in the fullness of human experience."[130] The descent could thus indicate both Christ's drinking the full cup of God's wrath as the innocent victim of sin for others and of His routing of Satan to set the prisoners free as God's righteous victor over sin, death, devil, and indeed the very wrath of God.

Luther characteristically manages to unite both accents.

> For when we were created by God the Father and had received from him all kinds of good things, the devil came and led us into disobedience, sin, death and all misfortune. As a result, we lay under God's wrath and displeasure, sentenced to eternal damnation, as we had merited it and deserved it. There was no counsel, no help, nor comfort for us until this only and eternal Son of God, in his unfathomable goodness, had mercy on us because of our misery

---

125. *LBC,* pp. 356-57.

126. "The main difficulties . . . were that the Old Testament saints scarcely needed illumination, since they had foreseen Christ's coming, and that it seemed inappropriate that the unconverted should receive a second opportunity for repentance in the other world." The alternative view "placed the accent on the deliverance of the saints and the defeat of Satan. . . ." Kelly, *Creeds,* p. 381.

127. Kelly, *Creeds,* p. 381.

128. Gustaf Aulén, *Christus Victor* (London: SPCK/New York and Toronto: Macmillan, 1931).

129. Kelly, *Creeds,* citing St. Caesarius of Arles, p. 382.

130. Kelly, *Creeds,* p. 383.

and distress and came from heaven to help us. Those tyrants and jailers have now been routed, and their place has been taken by Jesus Christ, the Lord of life, righteousness, and every good and blessing. He has snatched us, poor lost creatures, from the jaws of hell, won us, made us free, and restored us to the Father's favor and grace. As his own possession he has taken us under his protection and shelter, in order that he may rule us by righteousness, wisdom, power, life and blessedness . . . the little word "Lord" simply means the same as Redeemer, that is, he who has brought us back from the devil to God, from death to life, from sin to righteousness, and keeps us there.[131]

Christ liberates from the tyranny of the anti-divine powers precisely by his *penal* suffering of the plight of sinful humanity, though Himself innocent. The law's illegal overreach in this case gives Him the right in turn, not merely the power, to undo their tyrannous usurpation of the creation.[132] In "snatching" He has won us, and "winning" us He has snatched us free. In power and in justice, this only and eternal Son has enacted the Father's grace and favor who, by this deed of His Son in turn, has surpassed His own wrath on the way to the Beloved Community.

The early Pannenberg took up this position on the penal suffering of Christ from Luther and the fathers: "To be excluded from God's nearness in spite of clear consciousness of it would be hell. This element agrees remarkably with the situation of Jesus' death: as the one who proclaimed and lived the eschatological nearness of God, Jesus died the death of one rejected."[133] That account of sin's punishment in the rejection borne by Jesus surely indicates love's *depth*. But it also indicates the *breadth* of the saving Incarnation: "the concept of Jesus' descent into hell, of his preaching in the realm of the dead, affirms . . . that men outside the visible church are not automatically excluded from salvation. Who participates in salvation and who does not remains, to be sure, open."[134] The *depth* and the *breadth* of Christ's truly divine and universal victory belong together. When we understand this about Christ as the subject of faith, in whose faith believers partake, not only is the ecclesia of His solidarity with sinners part of the gospel He brings, but this ecclesia has no boundaries other than marked by the one doctrine that so proclaims and understands Christ the boundary-breaker, sent from the Father to the depths of hell and effective for us in the free-ranging Spirit. Here, in other words, we meet the *single cognitive claim* of theology under the aspect of the Spirit that is holy and makes holy by proclaiming the sinless Christ in solidarity with "real, not fictitious sinners" (Luther).

This scope of the Spirit in proclaiming salvation in Christ as ours together

131. *BC,* p. 434.

132. *BC,* p. 434.

133. Wolfhart Pannenberg, *Jesus: God and Man,* trans. L. L. Wilkins and D. A. Priebe (Philadelphia: Westminster, 1975), p. 271.

134. Pannenberg, *Jesus: God and Man,* p. 272.

when we know together that we are sinners is decisive for the formation of theological subjectivity by *catechesis,* by learning to know Christ aright in the depth and truth of His saving incarnation. There is no hell of God's rejection that God has not for humanity's sake first endured in the person of His Son. There is no humanity outside the scope of God's saving Incarnation in the Jesus who, alone innocent, willingly knew also the fate of the sinner who is us, one and all, in Adam. The centrally located article of the Creed, which in one image unites Christ the victim who takes on himself God's rejection of humanity's moral evil and Christ the victor who sets free all those so forgiven by His own powerful act as saving Lord, has much to say to fragmented and dis-spirited contemporary Christianity.

For modern Christianity in Euro-America has separated the sign and the thing signified in multitudinous ways and consequently fractured into a thousand contending schemes of self-salvation supposedly justified by a thousand different objectifications of Jesus *that take the honor away from Him*[135] as "the only and eternal Son" and harrower of hell, and award it instead to pious man, or existentially authentic woman, or whoever is the greatest victim, or contrariwise whoever is most healthy and wealthy, or perhaps whoever is the least religious and most socially concerned, or alternately, those true believers who will be rapt out before the Final Woes take their revenge on the rest, those liberal Christians especially, *et cetera ad infinitum ad nauseum.* It is no good to bless this spiritual mayhem as some liberating "new pluralism" in theology when it is in truth a symptom of inner decay. All this salvation-mongering and liberation-pandering turns theology into religious ideology by which one stakes out a preferred identity for oneself in the sick dynamics of modern self-consciousness and identity politics and heaps scorn on others by means of "contrastive identifiers" (Radner) other than the one identity that is revealed as needful and normative: the placement of the theological subject on the apocalyptic battlefront between the Holy Spirit and the unclean spirits of the malicious structures of injustice that hold all in bondage by virtue of universal sinfulness. If we turn aside from this battle of faith against sinfulness in solidarity with sinners, we turn Jesus into a cipher at the mercy of His human users and abusers, all the while never maturing to the seriousness of a commitment to theological truth and the corresponding boldness of the risk of self for others. The true subject of faith in this way disappears into a morass of pious subjectivity — a delusional state of mind justly pilloried by the likes of a Nietzsche.

The truth is that the self does need to be reinvented — as the same Nietzsche knew, who also demanded a human "self-overcoming." But the reinventing is never radical enough when the sinful self attempts its own reformation. The excruciating work of the truth-telling Holy Spirit in conforming the sinful self to the mortifying judgment of the cross of Christ is needed. In this sense, the church is to be *die Zone der Freiheit* (the "place of freedom" — the claim made for the church

135. *BC,* pp. 224, 338, 496, 567.

in the former German Democratic Republic). The Spirit's reinventing of the self comes through the cross of contrition as learned in a lifelong journey with the pilgrim people of God or it does not come about at all. Alasdair MacIntyre has made the general point here unforgettably in his discussion of the once-upon-a-time Nazi turned literary critic, Paul de Man, who effortlessly reinvented himself to tack to prevailing winds after the war. MacIntyre argued that the antinomian moralist — that is, the one who eschews the question of the truth of God's judgment on the person who has given himself in obedience to structures of malice and injustice — "faces grave difficulties in constructing a narrative of his or her past which would allow any acknowledgement in that past of failure, let alone a guilty failure, which is also the failure of the same still-present self. ..."[136] Disowning the question of truth in matters of human good and evil — this is what antinomianism as a doctrine is — human beings inevitably forfeit moral agency as well, washing their hands like Pontius Pilate of the wicked deeds those very hands commit. But owning the question of truth — true judgment, the eschaton of judgment — is the decisive political intervention of the church that consists of forgiven and struggling sinners.

"To pass critically beyond Nietzsche is to pass into recognition of the necessity and yet the ungrounded character of some sort of metanarrative, some privileged transcendent factor, even when it comes disguised as the constant element in an immanent process."[137] By "ungrounded" John Milbank rightly underscores that a master narrative is taken up in an act of faith to hold epistemic primacy for certain forms of life such as Christian living; here there are no "knock-down" arguments establishing one "myth" and refuting another. Rather in ethical responsibility one makes a choice, what existentialist theologians of the previous generation called a "decision of faith." Although all narratives are subject to the cognitive test of their capacity fruitfully to interpret experience and finally depend for their truth on the eschaton of judgment, the matter of adherence to any one of them is a matter of faith, "the assurance of things hoped for, the conviction of things not seen."

Yet even epistemologically "ungrounded" faith is not faith in faith (fideism). It is assuredly not mere traditionalism; nor are the choices between narratives

---

136. Alasdair MacIntyre, *Three Rival Versions of Moral Inquiry: Encyclopedia, Genealogy and Tradition* (Notre Dame: University of Notre Dame Press, 1990), p. 213. Calvin classically connected true knowledge of God with knowledge of self in just this way: "It is certain that man never achieves a clear knowledge of himself unless he has first looked upon God's face, and then descends from contemplating him to scrutinize himself. For we always seem to ourselves righteous and upright and wise and whole — this pride is innate in all of us. ... As long as we do not look beyond the earth, being quite content with our own righteousness, wisdom, and virtue, we flatter ourselves most sweetly and fancy ourselves all but demigods." John Calvin, *Institutes of the Christian Religion,* trans. F. L. Battles (Philadelphia: Westminster, 1975), pp. 37-38.

137. John Milbank, *Theology and Social Theory: Beyond Secular Reason* (Oxford: Blackwell, 1997), p. 2.

blind and those between communities empty. Christian faith is *theological,* or it is not Christian at all, or rather, it is only Christian by *accident.* The theological subject knows the One in whom it believes. Knowing faith arises from hearing the (putative) Word of God in such fashion (by the Spirit!) that the conversion of the subject by death and resurrection with Christ takes place and the newborn believer is accordingly placed in Christ by the Spirit and just so into the relations of love between the Father and the Son articulated by the Spirit. This place is *on the earth,* in the body, through time's passage, so that the believer who "endures to the end will be saved" (Mark 13:13). Just so, the well-educated theological subject seeks understanding of what is heard and welcomes the opportunity to test itself against alternative narratives, even exposing itself to the possibility of the conversion that would be apostasy, in the confidence of the Spirit who promises to lead to all truth (John 16:13). So knowing faith can find ways to make the disbelief of others fruitful for its own ever-new self-understanding. It continually tests itself to see whether it is true to the gospel story by which it was given birth, now lives, and continually modernizes, simultaneously under the obligation of coherence with all the other truths held in the common world by virtue of the common body, taken as fallen creature of the common Creator. This double-focus of knowing faith is one that any non-Gnostic, non-docetic, non-dualistic theology of orthodox intention must adopt. This double-sided *sentire cum ecclesia et in mundo* is the discipleship of the mind, where the Spirit's sanctification of the body (its mind included) is *paideia,* lifelong theological learning, the catechesis of the theological subject born anew into the ecclesia in mission to the nations.

In the next three sections on the doctrine of baptism in Luther, Menno Simons, and Barth, we make intense probes into particularly influential episodes in the history of theological subjectivity organized around the *crux intellectum:* whether and how baptismal unification with Christ *separates* from the world in captivity to structures of malice and injustice; whether and how, then, theological subjectivity in Christ is apocalyptically *new.* The tension here goes to the heart of things in Christianity, where on the one hand the doctrine of the Incarnation of the Son of God affirms the common body as the good creature of God destined for redemption and fulfillment (Rom. 8:19-23), but, on the other hand, the doctrine of the crucifixion of the Incarnate Son condemns this world as the dark place of malice and injustice from which good creatures are to be rescued from the wrath that surely comes (1 Thess. 1:9). The argument is that the theological subject knows how to sustain both of these judgments in the time that remains, in this time of the end. Ultimately, however, that is possible when on the level of metaphysics we apply to theological anthropology the nature-person distinction worked out in Trinitarian theology. Then we see how the redemption of nature by the reformation of the person hangs together.

## Luther's "Baptizatus sum!"

Apocalyptic theology — Oberman's *"man between God and the devil"*[138] — frames Luther's teaching on baptism. In "The Baptismal Booklet," an instruction Luther attached to the *Small Catechism* on how the ceremony of baptism was to be performed, Luther characterized baptismal regeneration or new birth as "being freed from the devil's tyranny and loosed from sin, death and hell, becom[ing] children of life, heirs of all God's possessions, God's own children, and brothers and sisters of Christ."[139] As in the ancient church, Luther understood new birth to refer to translation from Satan's dominion to the Spirit's, concretely, into the ecclesia gathered from the nations. Even more provocatively for modern sensibilities, as mentioned above, Luther retained the exorcism, "Depart you unclean spirit and make room for the Holy Spirit!" Quite consistently he speaks of the "infant possessed by the devil, a child of sin and wrath" who is lost but for the dramatic saving action about to transpire in the ritual of water baptism in the name of the triune God. But, he laments, we do not grasp or appreciate what is really going on here.

Luther ventures that so "many people turn out so badly after baptism because we have dealt with them in such a cold and casual way and have prayed for them at their baptism without any zeal at all." Blame for the failure of infant baptism is thus laid at the feet of the cold and slothful church, which neither feels nor comprehends the great stakes involved in wresting a child from the kingdom of Satan for the kingdom of Christ. Thus Luther imagines that baptism involves a reorganization of communal affects. In proper understanding the ecclesia fervently engages in the apocalyptic warfare of prayer on behalf of the child that the Word incarnate may bind the strong man and in this child's case plunder his goods. A church reformed according to the Word of God, which really knew again the apocalyptic battle-line, would rather come before God "with all earnestness, on the child's behalf setting themselves against the devil with all their strength . . ." and hence in the power and purpose of the Spirit.

In the *Large Catechism*,[140] Luther justified the baptism of infants on the following grounds: (1) God had confirmed the practice by making so many Chris-

---

138. Heiko A. Oberman, *Luther: Man between God and the Devil,* trans. Eileen Walliser-Schwarzbart (New Haven and London: Yale University Press, 1989). Likewise Gustaf Wingren, *Luther on Vocation,* trans. Carl C. Rasmussen (Philadelphia: Muhlenberg Press, 1957): "Man is set between God and the devil. When he is bound by God, he is free against the devil. When he is bound by the devil, he is free against God. . . . Before God man can be free only as evil. He cannot be separated from God and independent of God without being a captive to God's adversary and foe, a slave of the devil" (p. 105). "Man would be free from the bondage of the will only if the will were free and unengaged, with the ability to choose its rider or to pursue existence with no rider at all" (p. 106). "In God's power man's entire status is called freedom; in the devil's power it is called thralldom" (p. 106). Man "has to take God as he is and suffer him" (p. 107).

139. *BC,* p. 373.

140. *BC,* pp. 456-67.

tians on this basis for centuries; (2) the unbelief of some does not render their baptism invalid, but rather redoubles the guilt of those who despise God's mercy; (3) in principle, abuse does not disqualify proper use; and finally, (4) the proper use of baptism for "slaying the old Adam and the resurrection of the new creature in Christ" applies also to little ones, just as the gospel is addressed to all people. Undoubtedly Luther's profound sense for the objectivity of God's gospel promise, signed and sealed in the Christ who is present in faith, dominates in this justification of infant baptism. In times of testing, the adult believer may be driven to the sheer, naked fact of Christ's claim to ownership: "I am baptized." "God made his promise once for all in baptism — no matter at what age it is carried out for the individual. God does not lie. In this regard baptism takes on an indelible character *(character indelebilis)* — irrespective of what happens later in the life of the person who is baptized. It is not a guarantee of salvation, but it is the action of God in the life of the person, which continues to have its effect and behind which I can never go. . . ."[141] Notice in this summary statement by Bayer that it does not matter at what age baptism is carried out. That is not the chief thing. Chiefly Luther's *baptizatus sum* gives his account of theological subjectivity as the Spirit's "objective" rendering of the new person by conformation to Christ's cross and resurrection.

Gustaf Wingren similarly explained Luther's account of theological subjectivity grounded in the Spirit's objective work in baptism.[142] The "gospel is thus an eschatological message," for "the kingdom of God is given us as a promise." The believer lives as one suspended between this promise and its fulfillment: "nothing is lacking in that righteousness which Christ has acquired by his death and resurrection, but which he has not yet fulfilled in us." So the believer lives into the righteousness of Christ on the basis of the righteousness of Christ given as gift. Knowingly, faith "looks to things which are invisible and unknowable . . . because they are not yet visible, not yet knowable. Faith directs itself to that which is to come — faith is the proper way to wait." This patiency of the theological subject is formed by daily baptismal dying to what is and what is visible. So "baptism is the church's fundamental sacrament. . . . This takes place day by day through the putting to death of the old man and the rising of the new man out of sin. This is completely effected in death, when the body of sin withers, and God's new creation appears in the consummation. . . . God must help man to die daily. . . . Christ died on the cross, and one who is baptized unto death with Christ must be put to death by the cross." "Baptism is therefore completely fulfilled only in death. . . ."

Luther defines sacramental baptism as God's Word making use of water to

---

141. Oswald Bayer, *Martin Luther's Theology: A Contemporary Interpretation,* trans. Thomas H. Trapp (Grand Rapids: Eerdmans, 2007), p. 269.

142. Gustav Wingren, *Luther on Vocation,* summarizing pp. 20-31 for the following. As baptism is God's work in Christ, there are and can be no self-chosen crosses: "the cross comes to us uninvoked in our vocation" (p. 53), "not in deserted places apart from the company of people, but right in the social and political order" (p. 57, from WA 43, 214).

inaugurate what is therewith visibly signified for the sake of faith — notice that faith is *not* part of the definition of the baptismal work but rather seen as the purpose and effect of it. The faith that justifies is thus the faith that receives this divine action in Christ so signified by the water as the thing itself. Such faith is the product, then, of the Spirit's unification of the sign, body in bath, with the thing signified, the death and resurrection of Christ. As this creature of baptism, living faith appropriates the thing itself by putting it daily to use. A *valid* or true baptism, by this definition, is simply and solely the extension by name, in personal address, of the gospel promise of salvation from death by death. This personal address in the church's action of immersion in and emersion from water *signs* the dying and rising with Christ thereby promised as *the thing itself.* The Spirit's unification of water and the Word in the action of baptism is welcomed and received in the Spirit-given passion of faith that takes the sign made on one's own body as the thing itself — where and when it pleases God.

In "promissory narration" by this kind of "visible Word"[143] that picks out a body from the common body, "God the Promisor promises to be present in all the affairs of life, and death, and destiny in the manner of the Crucified and Risen Christ."[144] Since such *promising* is what baptism objectively *is* as a public

143. Robert W. Jenson, *Visible Words: The Interpretation and Practice of Christian Sacraments* (Philadelphia: Fortress, 1978).

144. Christopher Morse, *The Logic of Promise in Moltmann's Theology* (Philadelphia: Fortress, 1979), p. 132. Morse's critique of Moltmann's critique of Barth's transcendentalism affirms with Moltmann that the ordinary language form of the Word of God as promise yields a logical account of God who promises to be present according to a narrative content, namely, present "in the manner" of Christ crucified and risen. At the same time, Morse's book is a Barthian critique of Moltmann's foray in *The Crucified God* into Hegelian patripassianism as vastly and even dangerously exceeding "what can be established by appealing to revelation as a promissory 'passion narrative of Christ' " (p. 121). While it will be clear that I prefer to speak of the promised presence in "the person" of Christ rather than "in the manner of Christ," I share Morse's caution against "the deification of any human state of affairs [as leading] to its dehumanization" (p. 121). I try to guard against lethal idolatry, however, by stressing the sovereignty of the Spirit in uniting the sign with the thing signified in giving faith *ubi et quando Deo visum est* to receive and appropriate the person of Christ in the joyful exchange, rather than by the neo-Nestorian tactic of the *extra-Calvinisticum.* Morse tends towards this classical Reformed stance when he articulates "the conviction that in Jesus of Nazareth God identifies *with* the world in such a way that the world cannot be identified *as* God" (p. 121). That would perhaps hold if the Christian identification of Jesus of Nazareth intended but a revealed analogue of God's transcendent and eternal identity as the One who loves in freedom, say, as opposed to the lovelessness of this world. But such a revelation of timeless truth, no matter how "eventful," is not the gospel, nor can it help me; rather it exposes and condemns my loveless captivity to structures of injustice. The knowledge that God is love, even as revealed by God, can in fact only condemn me, if in fact I am helplessly — all the more so because willingly and willfully ignorant — a puppet of structures of malice and injustice. If Jesus is to be identified by the Spirit for the liberating faith of such bound sinners, He is identified as the Christ, the Son of God, as sign to thing signified "for me." This is the "event," better "advent," of Christ through the gospel that reaches me, the

performance that narrates this Christological content for the candidate, Luther reasons, we do not baptize on account of the faith of the candidate, even if the candidate has already come to faith. Rather, also in the case of a believer's baptism, we baptize for the sake of it, i.e., to create, nurture, and direct faith so that it is formed as union with Christ crucified and risen and in no other way. Objectively grounded in the promised presence of a competent Promisor of good will, as the church that knowingly baptizes in the Triune Name perforce believes, the baptismal enactment of divine promise by ritualized narrative creates faith and forms it into Christ, where and when the Promisor wills. Faith in turn is just this personal conviction that the putative Promisor is willing and able to do as promised, hence a true and human willingness so to die and be raised into the new identity of the reborn child of God. Baptism, then, just *is* the gospel of the resurrection of the Crucified One in the specific form of the rite of initiation into the ecclesia in the Spirit's mission to the nations.

If we bear in mind the Spirit's work in the resurrection of the Crucified, Christopher Morse, whose words we just cited, explains the logic of this claim (in his cogent and still illuminating analysis of Moltmann's "theology of hope"): "The resurrection, as the 'setting-in-force' of God's promise, cannot properly be said to have taken place *in* history; rather it *makes* history. In the language of the narrativists to *make* history is to *generate* a story. . . . [T]he resurrection does not conform to the generally accepted criteria for determining historical events; rather, it is narrative-generating in such a way that it gives historical significance to events, such as the life and death of Jesus and the mission of his followers, for which there is documentary evidence." While Morse is not directing this analysis to the logic of sacramental baptism for the formation of theological subjectivity, his analysis serves to explicate how baptism is the form that the Spirit's resurrection work takes in the initiation of believers into the story of Christ crucified that is the ecclesia in mission to the nations. The Spirit at work in baptism to generate the theological subject is no more visible in the water than the resurrection of Christ is visible in the empty tomb; visibility in either case consists in the new history that is generated by the Spirit's setting-into-force of God's promise by uniting its sign, water and empty tomb, with the thing signified, death and resurrection in Christ. To believe in one's baptism and to believe in Christ's resurrection, then, is one and the same Spirit-given faith in His resurrection from the dead for us all, so also "for me."

Thus Luther could rightly argue that, if we were to baptize on account of

---

sinner, to make me the beloved in the promissio that takes concrete form as the joyful exchange. In turn, where and when it pleases God, faith is personal conformation to Christ's death and resurrection as signified by water baptism. If such unifications hold "for us and for our salvation," as the *homoousios* of the Nicene Creed commits us to hold, then in the case of one particular creature in the world, Jesus Christ, we must affirm an identification with the world *as* God, though God in the way of being Son.

the visible evidence of the Spirit, we would never baptize anyone at all since the Spirit's work in history is not visible to us as such but only in the ambiguous visibility of its sign. What we see is the activity of faith apparent in love that arises, according to personal testimony, from the conviction that God's promise has effectively overtaken one. With Augustine, however, even such believers, if not especially believers, know that only God knows who really has faith; since faith is truly the work and gift of the Spirit, faith is not faith in faith but in God and His Word working in the Spirit. All such probing of the interiority of candidates behind the willing public confession of faith must therefore lead down a blind alley into a labyrinth in search of what can only be signed and trusted, so far as evidence before our eyes in the common body allows. Faith does not transcend the putative Word of God putatively working the new birth, but it holds fast to the earth. If we reflect on what we actually do in the mission to the nations, however, we see that we do not ever share the gospel promises *because* we see that someone believes, but rather *in order* that someone believe, also among believers. If baptism simply *is* the gospel itself in the specific, mandated form of promising salvation from death by signing death in the public washing into the ownership of Christ, it is to be administered, just as the gospel itself is to be preached, inclusively ("to all nations") to the end that faith be created and/or strengthened. As we shall see, the only question can be whether anything prevents a candidate from being baptized. Otherwise public confession of informed faith is the sufficient condition for admission to baptism as baptism into the ecclesia.

From this perspective, it makes no difference in any individual case whether one comes to faith before or after the Spirit provides for water baptism. Whoever has come to faith through the preaching of the gospel prior to baptism has faith precisely in anticipating his or her baptism by water and the Word. He or she submits to baptism in order to hear personally, with divine authority and in the presence of the ecclesia, the gospel promises addressed by name to her and to acknowledge in principle and in power death to the world of malice and injustice, Yes and Amen to the saving dominion of Christ. Saving faith is always objectively ordered to the gospel promise of resurrection of the dead and justification of the ungodly as it is individuated in the once-and-for-all ceremony of water baptism. In baptism the promise is solemnly and ceremoniously addressed to me by name and so becomes valid *pro me,* so that it holds with continuing force and I may at every step along life's way return to it. Consequently this gospel promise is daily to be reappropriated in living faith. *Baptizatus sum.* Faith returns to this event in remembrance when tested, oppressed, failed, or exhausted, proceeds from it ever anew into the world to live the life of Jesus in the priesthood of all believers that transforms stations in life into vocations of service. Thus the new birth is to recur *daily* in the interim time between baptism day and resurrection day. *Daily* the old man is crucified. *Daily* the new man arises as the gospel promise of baptism is recalled and appropriated afresh.

In all this, then, Luther is not precisely responding to, let alone repudiating, what we have come to call since his time "believer's baptism." The target of his polemic is rather the practice of *rebaptism* that had arisen among Zwingli's followers in Zurich. Zwingli himself (1484-1531) occupies an interesting and ambivalent position in the history of baptism. Zwingli was a consistent Platonist. He took up Augustine's *distinction* between baptism as the external sign and the internal new birth as the thing to which it refers and turned it into a thoroughgoing *dualism*. The starting point of this theology of baptism, targeting Catholic "sacramentalism," is thus the claim that the external washing of the body with water cannot of itself cleanse from sin within; it is only a covenant sign, on analogy with circumcision in the old covenant, which it replaces.[145] Quite unlike Augustine, however, Zwingli rejected the doctrine of inherited guilt and thus a traditional justification for infant baptism. "Anabaptists are without doubt most indebted to Zwingli as far as theology is concerned; to that extent, they can be considered his disciples."[146] Anabaptists — literally rebaptizers — carried Zwingli's dualism of sign and thing signified through to its logical conclusion, arguing that infant baptism was a corrupt practice, neither necessary to forgive an infant's inherited guilt nor useful as a sign, since the infant cannot perceive or understand it. When some of his followers began to rebaptize, however, Zwingli opposed the sectarian political implications of this innovation. Rebaptism threatened the political unity of the reforming church and society in Zurich that in an undifferentiated unity of Word and Sword still thought, consciously or not, on the model of Christendom.[147] So he tried to substantiate the validity of infant baptism. But, as George W. Bromiley put it, Zwingli failed "to show any compelling necessity for infant baptism on theological grounds. . . ."[148] His only arguments for retention of the practice were practical and political ones.

Like Zwingli, Luther also saw in the practice of rebaptism a threat to the visible unity of the church (as per the "one Lord, one faith, *one* baptism" of Eph. 4:5), and like Zwingli Luther too wants to reform, not abolish Christendom — although he configures the relation of Word and Sword according to the rather different theologic of God's two regiments. In any case, to rebaptize one who had been baptized previously is inescapably to assert that the first baptism was fraudulent and so also the church which administered a fraudulent baptism. The point

---

145. Ulrich Gäbler, *Huldrych Zwingli: His Life and Work,* trans. Ruth C. L. Gritsch (Philadelphia: Fortress, 1986), p. 128.

146. Gäbler, *Huldrych Zwingli,* p. 127.

147. Gäbler, *Huldrych Zwingli,* p. 130.

148. Bromiley continues: "Zwingli himself seems to lack the beliefs or presuppositions which make infant baptism logically necessary. He does not accept an original guilt in infants of which baptism is the means or sign of remission . . . [he] seems to separate too rigidly the sign from the thing signified. He grasps clearly the basic duality of the sacrament, but he is in danger of losing the essential and underlying unity." *Zwingli and Bullinger: Selected Translations,* ed. G. W. Bromiley, The Library of Christian Classics, vol. 24 (Philadelphia: Westminster, 1953), p. 126.

at issue here is not the relation of baptism and new birth per se. The so-called *ordo salutis,* order of salvation, which tried to sketch out one normative psychological pattern for the religious experience of conversion and then shoehorn all experience into one pattern is a speculation that opens the door and plunges headlong into the labyrinth of interiority. Luther's speculations on infant faith — which, however, he never made into a theological basis for infant baptism — also fall into this category. Rather the issue is ecclesiology, that is, what Christ's community is to which one is joined by baptism. Different views of baptism imply different ecclesiologies. Ecclesiologically viewed, rebaptism can only mean a principled, theological repudiation of the church in which and by which one had been previously baptized — entailing a principled separatism based upon an apocalyptic judgment.

For all his criticism of the Roman papacy, this was a step that Luther was in principle never willing to make.[149] He did not and could not regard the Roman Catholic *Church* as apostate, even if he did regard the contemporary *papacy* so.[150] Note the distinction. Luther refused to identify the Roman church with the papacy — for that would have meant *agreeing* to the *false* claim of the papacy to speak for the church. Indeed he viewed the Roman church, like himself, as a victim of papal oppression. Just so, he quite consistently maintained against the rebaptizers (in the 1528 tract *Concerning Rebaptism*) that just because "Antichrist" is to "take his seat in the temple of God . . . , [so] the Christendom that is now under the papacy is truly the body of Christ and a member of it. If it is his body, then it has the true spirit, gospel, faith, baptism, sacrament, keys, the office of the ministry, prayer, holy Scripture, and everything that pertains to Christendom. So we are all still under the papacy and therefrom have received our Christian treasures."[151] Luther could no more deny that the Roman church is Christ's church than he could deny that Christ had been active there for the past thousand years, also in the practice of infant baptism. So Luther affirms an ecclesiology that admits of continuity through time, though he denies that this continuity is given or guaranteed by the innovation in recent history of papal sovereignty. Rather, he finds in Spirit-baptism by water and the Word the continual generation of theological subjectivity that makes the church the church through time and space. To be sure, baptism issues in specific callings, one of which provides ministry to the Word, so that the Word can continually be spoken in time and space. If this basis for ministerial authority in serving the Word were clear and clearly agreed to so that claims to authority in the church could be tested by the Word being served, Luther acknowledges, he would kiss the pope's feet.

By contrast with Luther, then, the consequent repudiation of the preceding

149. *TCT,* IV, pp. 176-77.
150. Scott H. Hendrix, *Luther and the Papacy: Stages in a Reformation Conflict* (Philadelphia: Fortress, 1981).
151. *LW* 40, pp. 229-62.

church history was a step that the early Anabaptists were willing to take. It was a step for which Zwingli's Platonizing cleavage between the sign and the thing signified had prepared the way. It is possible that still today one sees here nothing but a choice.[152] But the discussion to this point should allow us to consider another possibility for contemporary ecumenical doctrinal convergence that is too rarely considered. What offends against the unity of the church is not the new (or, renewed) practice of believer baptism, which is arguably the better pastoral practice in our post-Christendom situation. What offends against the unity of the church is the practice of rebaptism, for this act anathematizes the other church and its practice with apocalyptic finality. Repudiating rebaptism as a divisive practice says nothing strictly speaking to the question regarding the more appropriate practice of baptism today at the end of Christendom. The assumption here would be that admission of candidates at any age to baptism is a matter of pastoral freedom and churchly discernment. That the baptism of infants may be valid under certain circumstances does not entail the conclusion that it is or should be the predominant way that baptism is administered. Indeed, the unqualified practice of infant baptism today betrays a pastoral sloth that declines any instruction of candidates or sponsors and, worse, justifies this sloth as signifying a grace so cheap it cannot be given away. This is perverse. "Grace" offered and received as ritual leniency rather than as the miracle of the sinner's costly forgiveness and the gift of the Holy Spirit for newness of life is not baptism into Christ but baptism into empty air.

Towards the conclusion of his discussion of baptism in the *Large Catechism,* Luther makes a statement that cuts in every direction because it restores baptism to the hands of the Holy Spirit: "Baptism remains forever. Even though someone falls from it and sins, we always have access to it so that we may again subdue the old creature. . . . Repentance is nothing else than a return and approach to baptism, to resume and practice what has earlier been begun but abandoned. I say this," Luther continues, "to correct the opinion which has long prevailed among us, that baptism is something past that we can no longer use after falling back into sin. This idea comes from looking only at the act that took place a single time."[153]

---

152. Contemporary Baptist theologians can quite agree in the ecclesiological implications of the choice between infant and believer's baptism. The "one thing" the European state churches "cannot endure and permit: the baptism of believers. To her it denotes the rejection of the foundations of the State Church, a denial of the right of that Church system to exist at all. And so it is. Biblical baptism has, therefore, at the present time not only the permanent meaning which is stated in the New Testament and is confirmed in the experience of believers, but in addition it has — what did not count in primitive Christianity — its significance as a protest against the mass-Christianity of the 'Christian' world, against the world-conformed Christianity of Christendom." Johannes Warns, *Baptism: Studies in the Original Christian Baptism in Its History and Conflicts to a State or National Church and Its Significance for the Present Time,* trans. G. H. Lang (London: Paternoster, 1962), p. 308.

153. *BC,* pp. 456-67 for this and the following.

Luther blames the church father Jerome (342-420) for the view that "penance is the second plank on which we must swim ashore after the ship founders," i.e., when a Christian sins after baptism. This view is incorrect, Luther holds, because "it takes away the value of baptism, making it of no further use to us." Jerome's image is all wrong. It is not that we make shipwreck of a boat loaned to us so that, fallen again into the watery chaos, we must now extricate ourselves under our own powers. Rather we have fallen overboard from an ark that remains there to deliver us. This being the true state of affairs, "those who do fall out should immediately see to it that they swim to the ship and hold fast to it, until they can climb aboard again." Notice that in either Jerome's view or Luther's, the lapsed believer is expected to be active and, for Luther, can be active because this fallen Christian remains a Christian who can cooperate with the Spirit. The difference is not in the fallen believer's responsible action to overcome the failure, but what action is to be taken in this situation.

Luther in these words is abolishing the sacrament of penance as something independent of baptism; he does so in order to make the entire life of the baptized one of repentance, that is, of conversion, of transformation of the self, of growing into Christ's righteousness on the basis of Christ's righteousness, of acquiring theological subjectivity. "Baptism," he declares, "both by its power and by its signification, comprehends also the third sacrament, formerly called penance, which is really nothing else than baptism." By doing this, he was also clarifying the real meaning of baptism. Baptism is not a magical cleansing of sin that is forfeit once the baptized sins again. Baptism is *the Spirit's* abiding attack on the old creature and *the Spirit's* resurrection in its place of a new creation. The sign effects what it signs with enduring force, when it is *the Spirit's* sign. Thus human repentance is, and can be, nothing but the life lived returning to this divine action by faith that can and does in just this returning cooperate with it.[154] "What is repentance but an earnest attack on the old creature and an entering into a new life? If you live in repentance, therefore, you are walking in baptism." Or again, "If we want to be Christians, we must practice the work that makes us Christians, and let those who fall away return to it. As Christ the mercy-seat does not withdraw from us or forbid us to return to him even though we sin, so all his treasures and gifts remain."

It helps here to think a little more about the error Luther attributed to Jerome. The old teaching based on Hebrews 6 is that baptism forgives all sins up

---

154. Luther does not hesitate to speak of the new creature's Spirit-enabled *cooperation* with God, as Wingren makes clear: "In *The Bondage of the Will* Luther distinguishes between the free will's 'own power and efficacy' and its 'co-operation.' The former is denied, and the latter affirmed. Man has not ability of his own, independent of God, with which he can act before God. . . . Even the ungodly co-operate with God, for God alone has made all things and set all in motion. . . . The righteous are moved by the Spirit of God and co-operate with God . . . co-operating with a righteousness not our own but given to us by God . . . consists of three things: the putting to death of the flesh, love to others, and humility before God." Wingren, *Luther on Vocation,* p. 131.

to the time of its administration and gives the Holy Spirit, who is thought, as it were, physically to replace in the human heart all the unclean spirits and sinful desires that previously dominated there. One was expected, then, to live a sinless life under the dominion of the Spirit. So long as we live in the common body, however, the believer's body remains vulnerable to the counterdominion of malice and injustice, giving the old Adam access by which to revive and reassert his dominance. Situated here between the contending headships of Christ and Adam over the common body, the redemption of the believer's body is thus the matter of a lifelong struggle of the Spirit against the flesh, whose every progress depends on the constant mercy of divine forgiveness. The baptismal sequence of the Father's free divine favor and the sending of the Spirit to renew is as crucial to the theology of baptismal grace as rejecting their separation. With regard to its own body, then, the theological subject is righteous *in spe sed non in re,* as Augustine taught in correction of the teaching that Luther attributed to Jerome.

This idea of Augustine about the persistence and power of sin in the life of the baptized was difficult for many to accept. How can the Holy Spirit coexist with the Old Adam in one and the same body? One or the other must rule, just as Paul teaches in Romans 6. We must be holy or sinful, not both at once. So if the Holy Spirit really is given in baptism, doesn't that mean that He drives out sinful desires and replaces them with godly ones? How can lust, greed, concupiscence, malice remain? How can the old Adam, crucified in baptism, return to life and plague us? In a complicated process through the course of a thousand years, questions like these led to the development of penance as that second plank after baptism that Luther rejected. The sacrament of penance was officially enshrined in the Council of Trent. Reviewing Trent's doctrine in this connection brings the contrast with Luther into full view.

Trent[155] called the baptismal gift of "true and Christian justice" the "first robe," i.e., the forgiveness of all sins committed hitherto. Yet what happens when Christians "through sin have forfeited the received grace of justification? [These can] again be justified, when, moved by God, they exert themselves to obtain through the sacrament of penance the recovery, by the merit of Christ, of the grace lost.... [It is] a second plank after the shipwreck of grace lost.... Hence it must be taught that the repentance of a Christian after his fall is very different from that at his baptism...." How is it different? Penance includes sacramental confession and absolution, "as well as satisfaction by fasts, alms, prayers and other devout exercises of the spiritual life, not indeed for the eternal punishment . . . but for the temporal punishment . . . of those who, ungrateful to the grace of God which they have received in baptism, have grieved the Holy Ghost." The whole life of a Christian thus comes to be dominated practically by the work of making satisfaction. As the result of such a dutiful life, "eternal life is to be offered, both as a grace merci-

---

155. All citations from the council of Trent here are taken from H. J. Schroeder, O.P., *Canons and Decrees of the Council of Trent* (St. Louis and London: B. Herder, 1941), pp. 39-40.

fully promised to the sons of God through Christ Jesus, and as a reward promised by God himself, to be faithfully given to their good works and merits." In a church that practices infant baptism, however, Trent's doctrinally correct, anti-Pelagian account of grace arousing desire for justice before God which leads one to baptism, and of the need for penance after post-baptismal sin, is purely theoretical. In fact, as soon as a child becomes conscious of itself, it discovers that it has already lost baptismal innocence and needs to regain lost grace. Thus it finds its relation to God wholly structured by the sacrament of penance, that is, by the demand to confess sins and to make satisfaction for them, and so to gain back the forfeited state of grace. In this practice of piety, it is psychologically impossible not to draw the conclusion that the believer earns or gains grace through pious practices.

"Baptism remains forever." There is no difference between Trent and Luther on the lifelong struggle of the Christian to live into the righteousness of Christ. The difference is that Trent thinks this struggle is *completed* in baptism, and so in need of supplementation in the case of post-baptismal lapse, while Luther thinks of this struggle of the Spirit against the flesh as *inaugurated* in baptism and sustained by the same Spirit on the same basis. It is the difference on the level of personal discipleship between a realized and an inaugurated eschatology — both of which are dealing realistically with the persistence of sin in the life of the redeemed. For Luther, the daily battle against the old Adam that refuses to die, far from separating the believer from God, is the very sign of the Spirit's presence in his or her life. It must be so, because in the believer's body God is reaching out to reclaim not only an individual but the common body and to return the entire world to His dominion. But that entails the abiding membership of that Christian's body in the world still dominated by structures of malice and injustice, permeable then to new incursions of its despair and pride, its envy and malice. Because of faith in Christ, however, the abiding sinfulness of the old Adam in this way is not reckoned or imputed, but rather forgiven. Thus in spite of its presence, the whole Christian life joyfully proceeds on the basis of the Father's free and unconditional favor vouchsafed by baptism into Christ into the new obedience dominating sin and not being dominated by it.

One lives by faith in the *state* of grace, *at peace* with God whose future judgment has already been executed. As baptism remains forever as the inauguration of the eschaton of judgment, all sins, past, present, and *future* are forgiven: "Therefore, since we are justified by faith, *we have peace* with God through our Lord Jesus Christ" (Rom. 5:1, emphasis added). The assurance of faith as faith in the vindicated faith of Jesus is given as an enduring status signed and effected by the Spirit in baptism. This status of the child of God is not the uncertain goal, but the abiding basis of the Christian life, even as Christian life on this basis is a daily and lifelong struggle of the Spirit against the flesh.[156] *Baptizatus sum* therefore

---

156. Heiko A. Oberman, *The Dawn of the Reformation: Essays in Late Medieval and Early Reformation Thought* (Edinburgh: T. & T. Clark, 1986), p. 124.

means that I am not my own, that I have been bought with a price, freed to glorify God in the body (1 Cor. 6:19-20) already now as the dawning on the earth of the Beloved Community of God.

## Menno Simons on the New Birth

Luther's contemporary, Menno Simons, became the spiritual and theological leader of the Anabaptist movement that arose *after* the debacle of Thomas Müntzer's militant agitation of the Peasants' Revolt in 1525. His teaching decisively renounced Müntzer's violent fantasies for religious revenge (e.g., "For the godless person has no right to live when he is in the way of the pious").[157] In recent theology John Howard Yoder,[158] and to some degree Stanley Hauerwas,[159] have ably retrieved Menno's theological vision of the apocalyptic antinomy of the kingdoms of God and Satan, taken in a way that requires a principled and consistent ecclesiology of separation and an ethically consistent pacifism. There is an important overlap here with the fashion in which the present project of theology in the tradition of Luther works in respect to the apocalyptic antinomy.[160] There is also, however, considerable conflict with respect to the doctrine of creation, the mandates, and the vocations.[161] As noted above, the Magisterial Reformation led by Luther, Calvin, and all others who retained the practice of infant baptism aimed at the reform of *Christendom,* not the restoration of a lost, primitive, New Testament *Christianity.* It is crucial historically to grasp this difference in self-understanding, even if not especially because theology in Euro-America lives and works at the end of Christendom and thus in new openness to the critique of Christendom voiced by Menno. *Christendom* — the word speaks of a *political* kingdom, the *Holy* Roman Empire, divinely legitimated by the Christian religion. This is the ideal of a civilization based on the co-identity of the citizen with the baptized, which (with difficulty) traces itself back to (a certain Carolingian reading of) Augustine.

Menno rejected this very ideal. He sought a separated, holy, intentional Christian community, which would be a countercultural force. Menno thus absolutely refused to collaborate with the secular sword. He wanted a church that fights its spiritual battles against the dominant culture with the Word of God alone, just

157. *Christianity and Revolution: Radical Christian Testimonies 1520-1650,* ed. Lowell H. Zuck (Philadelphia: Temple University Press, 1973), p. 37.

158. John Howard Yoder, *The Politics of Jesus* (Grand Rapids: Eerdmans, 1972).

159. Stanley Hauerwas, *The Peaceable Kingdom: A Primer in Christian Ethics* (Notre Dame: University of Notre Dame Press, 1983).

160. Johannes Heckel, *Lex Charitatis: A Juristic Disquisition on Law in the Theology of Martin Luther,* trans. Gottfried G. Krodel (Grand Rapids: Eerdmans, 2010), is the best defense of the apocalyptic interpretation of Luther's so-called Two Kingdoms doctrine.

161. See Steffen Lösel, "The *Kirchenkampf* of the Countercultural Colony: A Critical Response," *Theology Today* 67 (Fall 2010): 279-98.

as that Word is evident in the transformed lives of those truly regenerated by it. Menno's social critique and his consistent pacifism are admirable, if not wholly convincing theologically. For given the delay of the Parousia and the Spirit's mission to the nations, theology that rightly wants to indigenize the gospel into the cultures it finds must also in good faith accept the acculturation of the gospel that such syntheses produce as the price paid for indigenization. Theology lives in this tension at the heart of its Christological teaching. Christian theology affirms culture as God's creation and the object of His redeeming love *in the Incarnation;* just the same, it exposes culture as structuring malice and injustice by proclaiming *Christ crucified.* It is no small art to theologize wisely and well in this tension and not to fall into a false optimism or a false pessimism, but rather to have eyes and ears to speak the Incarnation and to speak the Cross as the times demand. There should in any case be no doubt about Menno's personal courage and conviction of faith in proclaiming the cross against the incipient Protestant triumphalism of the magisterial Reformation. Nor should there be any doubt about the stain of inhumanity and cruel intolerance that the magisterial Reformation, not to mention Rome, brought upon itself in hounding him and his followers to death.[162]

That being said, Menno's vision is highly problematic in some regards. Disastrously he rejected the new learning associated with Renaissance humanism;[163] this made him first in a long line of Protestant biblicists, who in failing to study philosophy as if it were some kind of poison to the pious soul, simply blinded themselves to their own extrabiblical philosophical assumptions (e.g., Menno's anthropocentric analysis of religious experience,[164] and, more broadly, his Platonizing dualism of matter and spirit, as we shall see in detail). His moralism, which does not distinguish between drinking a stein of beer, say, and failing to feed the hungry and clothe the naked, coupled with a rigorism willing to destroy families by enforcing the ban against backslidden spouses, is not obviously closer to the Spirit of Christ, not to mention Christ's example. Menno, like Luther or any other important figure in Christian history, is complex and not so easily pigeonholed. So let us seek a more nuanced appreciation and criticism than either villainization or hagiography provides.

Menno appealed to the experience of new birth, being "baptized with the Spirit and fire . . . inwardly fired by this fire of love,"[165] which he defined "not

---

162. *Healing Memories: Reconciling in Christ,* Report of the Lutheran-Mennonite International Study Commission (Geneva and Strasbourg: Lutheran World Federation and Mennonite World Conference, 2010). See John D. Roth, "Mennonites and Lutherans Re-Remembering the Past," *Lutheran Forum* 44, no. 1 (2010): 38-42. I am grateful to Sarah Hinlicky Wilson who brought these materials to my attention in her account: "Joyful Exchanges, Part I," *Lutheran Forum* 44, no. 2 (2010): 2-6 and "Joyful Exchanges, Part II," *Lutheran Forum* 44, no. 3 (2010): 2-6.

163. *The Complete Writings of Menno Simons c. 1496-1561,* trans. L. Verduin, ed. J. C. Wenger (Scottdale, PA and Kitchener, ON: Herald Press, 1984), p. 260.

164. *Writings of Menno,* pp. 266-67.

165. *Writings of Menno,* p. 246.

[as] water nor in words, but . . . the heavenly, living, and quickening power of God in our hearts, which flows forth from God, which, by the preaching of the divine Word, if we accept it by faith, quickens, renews, pierces, and converts our hearts, so that we are changed and converted from . . . the wicked nature of Adam to the good nature of Jesus Christ."[166] Menno had no independent interest in the new birth as a religious experience per se. As the citation shows, it was the ethical transformation of the person to the peaceable lifestyle of the truly born-again child of God, with the willingness to suffer martyrdom before resorting to violence and coercion,[167] that mattered most to him. Surely the violent rhetoric of Müntzer precipitated this accent, but for Menno it really goes much deeper than mere condemnation of the utopian fantasies of the first Anabaptists. As I shall stress in conclusion, personal transformation for Menno is really a kind of *transubstantiation,* as we shall see, from the fleshly *nature* to a spiritual one; it leads directly from reliance on the sword to reliance on the Spirit alone, conceived *substantively not personally.* Pacifism sounds utopian to the unregenerate — but that is precisely Menno's point. For one truly born again from above, who now participates in the heavenly nature, pacifism becomes viable as a way of life already now amid the structures of malice and injustice, not least as a living Word and prophetic protest against them that exposes their demonic nature. Pacifism and new birth are thus correlative concepts in Menno's theology, the latter being the supernatural foundation of the former way of life on earth.

It is not by accident then that Menno rejects as a contradiction in terms the very notion of Christian empire, where crusades, inquisitions, and persecutions are used by Christians to advance the cause of God. Menno likewise rejected the Augustinian doctrine of sin, which, as we recall, legitimated the practice of infant baptism for the remission of original sin (though not the later correlation of baptism with political membership in Christendom). What is at stake for Menno in the attack on infant baptism is true recognition of the decadent Christianity of the Empire, which degenerated in the very act of undertaking the project of constructing a Christian civilization.[168] As this is a contradiction in terms, defenders of infant baptism are the "true heretics,"[169] architects of a false Christianity, according to Menno, for "the holy Christian church is not an assembly of unbelievers, carnal or brazen sinners, even if they falsely appropriate the name of Christ Jesus, and think of themselves to be the true Christian church."[170]

"[W]hat a secret, hidden snare of soul and what a terrible, fearful idol infant baptism is[!]"[171] If so, rebaptism is *required* if one is to renounce the "terrible,

---

166. *Writings of Menno,* p. 263.
167. *Writings of Menno,* p. 232.
168. *Writings of Menno,* pp. 249, 251-52, 256-57, 259, 280.
169. *Writings of Menno,* p. 231.
170. *Writings of Menno,* p. 234.
171. *Writings of Menno,* p. 257.

fearful idol" and honor God alone. Menno is not simply name-calling; for him, infant baptism is rightly characterized as an *idol* because "it is administered without the Word and commandment of God; righteousness is sought therein; and because of this infant baptism the true baptism of Jesus Christ, that is, believer's baptism, is so lamentably rejected and trampled upon by all men as an heretical baptism. . . ."[172] It is interesting to observe that in the just-cited summary of the case against the idolatry of infant baptism Menno is virtually parroting Luther's earlier criticism of Catholic practice — although the critique is now redirected against Luther himself. In the famous initial case, Luther had held against *indulgences* that these were religious or pious works invented without scriptural basis by means of which people sought to become acceptable to God, in this way obscuring the actual means God provides in the gospel to make people acceptable to him. Menno takes up this criticism popularized by Luther and applies it to Lutheran baptism of infants, saying that the latter is founded on nothing but human tradition which obscures the new birth as the real gospel means of making Christians. Menno thus hoists Luther by his own petards!

The theological difference between the two is that, as we have heard, Luther regards baptism as God's Word making use of water to give and effect what is thereby signified; baptism is thus the gospel itself in the ritual form through which the grace of adoption into the ecclesia is extended. From here it is a natural extension of the implicit theologic to baptize little ones when they are presented for baptism by believing parents — since the alternative is a de facto exclusion of them. For Menno, in an unconscious echo of Augustine's teaching on the love of the Spirit poured into the believer's heart, the grace of God is understood as a purifying fire burning away the idols of the heart as it infuses the soul. Grace comes when the Holy Spirit effects conversion by infusing God's love into the soul. This is in fact one of Menno's most basic ideas and dearest convictions, that regeneration does not come by "signs but by grace,"[173] i.e., not by the "external" ceremony of baptism but by the direct, unmediated presence and action of the Holy Spirit who burns away the sinner's unholy desire and replaces it with holy desire.

"It is verily altogether vain and empty to read, to call, to teach, if the Holy Spirit of God, the true teacher of all righteousness, does not quicken, pierce, and turn the hearts of the believers by the only God-given means to this end, which is the Word."[174] It is the "seed of the Word of God" that germinates in the new birth, in which one "born of the corruptible seed" is purged and takes on the "divine nature of the Father who has begotten them."[175] So in another unconscious echo of Augustinianism, Menno likewise naturalizes the understanding of sin and grace.

172. *Writings of Menno*, p. 249.
173. *Writings of Menno*, pp. 261, 267, 277.
174. *Writings of Menno*, p. 271.
175. *Writings of Menno*, p. 58.

While rejecting the notion that the *guilt* of original sin is inherited from Adam and is to be remedied by infant baptism, Menno like Flacius virtually demonizes human nature. This is a plight that can only be remedied by the birth in us of a new nature at the Spirit's coming, attested by believer's baptism. Accordingly, we may say that in Menno's understanding a carnal child of Adam is *transubstantiated* into the newborn child of God. Once again, we cannot but be impressed by the rhetorical overlap between Menno and Luther on the Spirit's work of converting the heart, the seat of desire; also for Luther the Augustinian this comes as an "infusion" of the Spirit through the Word in the sense that for him justifying *faith* is already *the new birth* and the beginning of the new creation. We do not, however, penetrate to what truly divides these theologians until we grasp how Menno conceives the event of the new birth substantially but Luther personally.

Yet there are still more remarkable similarities in the theologies of Menno and Luther that are worth noting. For both, death of the sinner and the spiritual resurrection of the believer are the true content of baptism,[176] as for both the Holy Spirit is the actual actor in this regeneration. For both the mark of authentic discipleship is cross-bearing. For both the Christological and Pneumatological content of baptism/new birth must be utterly clear in the church's piety and practices, so that the gospel is not obscured or corrupted by human traditions. Indeed, for both sinfulness remains,[177] and so the life of the Christian is a struggle of the Spirit against the flesh. Moreover, both agree in principle on the Two Kingdoms, according to which the sword is only to be used in secular matters, while in spiritual questions the Spirit is to be relied on working through the Word. Luther's criticism of crusades, inquisitions, and violent revolution is of a piece with Menno's plea for toleration of dissent and his repudiation of recourse to the sword. In fact, an earlier Luther made the same plea for religious toleration of dissidents.

Menno was aware of his greater similarity to Luther than to the other reformers in all these ways. He pointed out very acutely that Protestant defenders of infant baptism did not agree among themselves about its theological basis: "some seek the washing away of original sin; others [say] that children should be baptized on account of their own latent faith. Or, to train them in the Word and commandments of God. And others again, to have them included into the covenant of God. And others again, to incorporate them into the church of Christ. Kind readers, in this way each of the before-mentioned writers follows his own and not a common course. If they were supported by the Word of God in regard to this matter, they would be unanimous."[178] Menno finds all these rationalizations inconsequent, but devotes considerable attention in particular to refuting Luther's speculations about infant faith. Why this concentration on Luther's error? From Menno's own perspective, we can see that if it were in some way reasonable

176. *Writings of Menno*, pp. 53, 59.
177. *Writings of Menno*, p. 247.
178. *Writings of Menno*, p. 279.

to ascribe true faith to infants, his arguments against infant baptism would fall since true faith is precisely the effect of new birth, as Menno in fact understands the new birth. The very divergence on infant faith as possibly a supernatural gift of the Spirit indicates just how close Menno is to Luther on the necessity for a living, personal, appropriating faith, itself a gift of the Spirit. Such faith is the very heart of regeneration, the spiritual resurrection. The difference, in Menno's mind, is simply that such faith cannot be ascribed in any way to infants since they cannot yet experience and know.

One might object, however, in a rather traditional Lutheran way that Luther and Menno conceive of living, vital faith in fundamentally different ways. For Menno the heart of faith is obedience to a divine demand: God "demands, yes, demands, us not to follow our own opinion, but to hear, believe and obey His voice."[179] When this demand becomes real to us in the regenerating work of the Spirit, faith as *obedience* is born. In this vein, Menno teaches that faith is the source of all true virtue[180] and can even say that "the affectionate eyes of the Lord," i.e., divine favor, fall on the truly regenerate "*because* they have sincerely and fully denied themselves, and have obediently followed the will of God to live according to the will of Him who has graciously called them, Christ Jesus."[181] But does not Luther think in exactly the same way? Christine Helmer has pointed to the decisive command of God the Father in the Transfiguration story, *Listen to Him!*, which for Luther becomes the divine command to think after God's Word in theology and not follow one's own opinion.[182] Luther's entire polemic against the "self-chosen" works of the monks is founded on his derivation from the Bible of God's revealed Word and command given for our good. When we take

---

179. *Writings of Menno,* p. 237.

180. *Writings of Menno,* p. 238.

181. *Writings of Menno,* p. 274, emphasis added.

182. The difference from Menno then would lie in Luther's robust Trinitarianism. As Christine Helmer, *The Trinity and Martin Luther: A Study on the Relationship between Genre, Language and the Trinity in Luther's Works (1523-1546)* (Mainz: Verlag Philipp von Zabern, 1999), explains: "By hearing the Son and obeying the Father, both Son and Father are acknowledged to exist in an intimate relation. The relationship between Father and Son is secured by the dogma that articulates their natural unity. . . . The church's dogma is placed under the authority of the Father's speech, a position already implying a trinitarian theological claim of a natural unity between Father and Son . . . the issue of authority, however, does not turn on the disjunction between privileging either dogma or Scripture as the authoritative ground of the trinitarian article" (p. 59). "[W]hat Luther conceptually executes is to orient both scripture and the church to the relation between the Father and the Son. . . . Luther succeeds in demarcating the theological region inside which no disputations are necessary. If, on the contrary, the Father's voice is disobeyed, a cloud of suspicion is moved over the Father's natural unity with the Son, and the issue becomes the subject for dispute" (p. 60). The demonic attempt is always to separate the Father and the Son, against which "the disputation becomes a form of speech to demonstrate obedience to the Father in a defense against those who, like the devil, attempt to separate the Father from his word" (p. 61).

into account the etymology of the Greek verb *hypakouo,* literally, "to give ear," which is translated as "obedience," what is the "obedience of faith" other than the theology of the Word and faith taken in the active rather than the passive sense?

Certainly there is a tendency in Menno to see Christ primarily as a revealer, model, and teacher of God's will for righteousness, who *also* graciously gave Himself to pay the debt of sinners.[183] Certainly for Luther, demands — even God's own demands — cannot create true faith or the obedience of faith, since demands only reveal and accentuate impotence and bondage to sin. Faith comes by the word of *promise,* delivered home personally by the Spirit in baptism, which wins the new self-entrusting life based on God's free favor in Christ. In the first place for Luther the gospel is no demand to be righteous like Jesus, but the command to believe in Christ's righteousness as valid for me, the sinner, such that united with Christ by baptismal faith I am, in spite of continuing sinfulness, also God's beloved child. Divine favor falls upon faith *alone,* which trusts in Christ *alone* and lives by God's free favor (the baptismal grace as adoption) *alone.* Such faith as *trust* apprehends Christ as Savior not just at the chronological beginning of Christian life in the experience of new birth, but daily reappropriates Christ and his promises of forgiveness, life, and salvation at every step along the disciple's way. Faith is pleasing to God because of Christ whom faith appropriates, just as Christ is seen here preeminently as the victorious Redeemer of the creation fallen prey to sin, death, and devil. Christ's righteousness is also ethically effective in believers, but inchoately; the full realization of it waits upon the coming of the kingdom. But all this divergence of Luther from Menno on the basis of a common account of the necessity of the Spirit's new birth can only be accounted for — not with an artificially exaggerated dualism between the rhetoric of demand and that of promise — but with the insight that Menno thinks of the transformation of the believer substantially rather than personally.

Menno and Luther finally part ways ethically, not in their common view that a distinction between the two kingdoms is necessary, but on the question of what this distinction is and how the two are now to be related to each other. For Luther, the temporal kingdom is not only created by God but is the object of God's redeeming love. "God so loved the *world....* God was in Christ reconciling the *world...."* The *sinful, fallen, estranged* world usurped by structures of malice and injustice! Thus Luther can positively relate the earthly and heavenly kingdoms in his idea of salvation from death by death, and in this new, much more dialectical way continue to support the idea of Christendom, as a civilization based upon a positive relation to Christianity. For Menno, this thought is quite impossible. The visible, earthly world is created by God but it is irredeemably fallen and must be substantially replaced. It is temporarily tolerated by God and used by God, for the sake of a new, spiritual creation that will replace it, its members being plucked from the flames that will soon engulf Christendom like Sodom and Gomorrah.

183. *Writings of Menno,* p. 283.

Consequently Menno refuses the possibility of any Christian collaboration between the two kingdoms, because the two kingdoms are ultimately based on two antithetical origins in the flesh and in the Spirit.

For Menno "the true being is in Christ,"[184] while "according to [the] first birth and origin after the flesh . . . , the first or old Adam . . . [is] ungodly or wicked, that is, one without God, a stranger to the divine nature."[185] The old nature or creation cannot be redeemed, it must be replaced. This dualism of the two natures led Menno to the idiosyncratic Christological view, verging on docetism, that Christ did not take his human nature from Mary, since that would have had to have meant that Christ partook of this nature "ungodly or wicked, that is, without God, a stranger to the divine nature." He argued that by a miracle God created a new, pure human nature in the womb of Mary, so that Christ's humanity originates not *from* Mary, but only *in* her. *Separation* from the old nature in the relation of church to society, in the experience of the new birth and even in the doctrine of the Incarnation is Menno's consistent demand for a radical reformation, a veritable transubstantiation. Ironically, despite the fact that he calls for a restoration of primitive Christianity, on analysis he continues in a medieval theological conceptualization of salvation as transubstantiation.

If we follow Luther, the theological subject is the *person* baptized into Christ, where "Christ" denotes the vindicated faith of the man Jesus who had been crucified. In that case, baptism must be taken as a Spirit-worked conformation that crucifies the old Adam and from its ashes raises up the new creature of faith, hope, and love. The old Adam *is* the *sicut Deus eritis*. In the words of Eric W. Gritsch, then, "all of life is ruled either by ego power or by gospel power. Ego power is manifested in the enduring human desire to exercise unlimited control, 'to be like God.' Gospel power is disclosed in God's unconditional promise that in Christ we are reconciled and returned to never-ending fellowship with God."[186] Just so, baptism by conformation to the judgment of the cross of Christ on the old Adam "is the uncomfortable and, at times, offensive reminder that my salvation must come from outside myself if it is to be really effective against the original sin of taking charge of my life without any interference."[187]

Just here, however, we are confronted with a new, dynamic, and ambiguous alternative that Gritsch tagged "born againism." It arose in American evangelicalism, though it can trace its lineage back through Bullinger to Zwingli's Zurich Reformation[188] with its axiomatic dualism of the sign and the thing signified. It

184. *Writings of Menno,* p. 232.

185. *Writings of Menno,* p. 55.

186. Eric W. Gritsch, *Born Againism: Perspectives on a Movement* (Philadelphia: Fortress, 1983), p. 94. For this author's detailed account, see Paul R. Hinlicky, "The Doctrine of the New Birth: From Bullinger to Edwards," *Missio Apostolica* 7, no. 2 (November 1999): 102-99.

187. Gritsch, *Born Againism,* p. 95.

188. Charles S. McCoy and J. Wayne Baker, *Fountainhead of Federalism: Heinrich Bullinger and the Covenantal Tradition* (Philadelphia: Westminster, 1991).

lacks the redeeming features of Menno's prophetic social critique and consistent pacifism, taken as a public witness against the world. Indeed, it inhabits a modern place of interiority that passively leaves the world to the devil. From there "born againism" has come to influence global Christianity.

Evangelical "born againism" has Lutheran parallels in Halle Pietism.[189] August Hermann Francke's account of his conversion shows, as R. W. Meyer pointed out, that his "religious dilemma becomes identical with an intellectual dilemma unknown to Luther." In place of Luther's learning to despair of the striving self under the judgment of Messiah's cross, Francke was wracked with doubt, wondering "whether the Scriptures are truly the Word of God. Do not the Turks make this claim on behalf of their Koran, and the Jews on behalf of the Talmud? And who shall say who is right?"[190] The early modern Pietist worries as much, if not more, about historical relativism than about finding a gracious God. Francke's answer to this question, moreover, is not theologically reasoned; rather his intellectual doubt is overwhelmed in the experience of the New Birth: "So great was his fatherly love that he wished to take me finally, after such doubts and unrest of my heart, so that I might be more convinced that he could satisfy me well, and that my erring reason might be tamed, so as not to move against his power and faithfulness. He immediately heard me. My doubt vanished. . . . I was assured in my heart. . . . Reason stood away; victory was torn from its hands, for the power of God had made it subservient to faith."[191] In this way, religious experientialism came to trump reason with its critical questioning and expelled rational doubt about the Christian claim to truth from Pietist theology. Likewise in American evangelicalism, the quest for the new birth is a quest for an experience of felt assurance in a Christendom awakening in the Enlightenment to a much bigger world than ever before imagined.

Typically following upon a season of "evangelical sorrow in which sin becomes grievous to the saintly person purely because it is sin," the struggle for assurance was crowned "with the grace of heartfelt, voluntary, joyful obedience": a reorganization of affects for the lifelong walk of sanctification.[192] The price paid for this experience of felt assurance, however, was the same banishment of critical questioning that is theology as critical dogmatics and in its place a studied labor in the manipulation of feelings into states of psychological terror by means of which an experience of felt assurance might be contrived.

---

189. See further Paul R. Hinlicky, "The Reception of Luther in Pietism and the Enlightenment," *Oxford Handbook to Martin Luther,* ed. Robert Kolb, Irene Dingel, and Lubomir Batka (Oxford: Oxford University Press, 2014), pp. 540-50.

190. R. W. Meyer, *Leibniz and the Seventeenth Century Revolution,* trans. J. P. Stern (Cambridge: Bowes & Bowes, 1952), p. 76.

191. August Hermann Francke, "Autobiography," in *The Pietists: Selected Writings,* trans. P. Erb, Classics of Western Spirituality (New York: Paulist, 1983), p. 105.

192. E. Brooks Holifield, *A History of Pastoral Care in America: From Salvation to Self-Realization* (Nashville: Abingdon, 1983), p. 27.

While contemporary evangelical theology shows signs of distancing itself from the legacy of revivalism,[193] the present argument about the Spirit's baptismal formation of the theological subject must be related and distinguished from this widespread, vague, but extraordinarily influential modern doctrine of the New Birth. This relation and distinction is possible because all forms of Western theology draw upon Augustine's seminal analysis of the affections with his insight that the human creature is motivated in all things by this love of the heart — with reason obediently following. There is no difference in this respect between Luther's baptismal account of the theological subject, Menno's and the one in "born againism." Indeed, if we recall here Luther's lament over the "coldness" with which baptism is practiced, it seems that the evangelical doctrine of the New Birth validly criticizes much habitual practice of sacramental baptism touching on: (1) the indiscriminate baptism of infants; (2) the lack of catechetical preparation of parents and sponsors; (3) the removal of the sacrament from the framework of the Eucharistic worship service and the context of Christian community (since that contradicts the essence of baptism as the rite of entrance into the ecclesia); (4) the corresponding reduction of the soteriological content of baptism to the forgiveness of original sin (let alone the reduction to today's welcoming ceremony/rite of passage), which neglects the central meaning of the sacrament as establishing fellowship with the cruciform Christ in His community by the gift of the Spirit; and (5) finally, the failure to preach and teach baptism as the Holy Spirit's electing act, not only to the community in general as the foundation of its common life (Gal. 3:26-28), but to each child as it grows, so that the message of what God has already done for it in baptism is actually the source and inspiration of the child's developing faith.

It is no part of the authentic doctrine of sacramental baptism to imagine that it "works" automatically, that is to say, *impersonally*. Rightly understood, as we have seen, it is the foundation of personhood as membership in the New Adam. There is no place here for a dualism between the sacramental sign and the new birth signified, and for the same reason, no place for any notion of magical efficacy *ex opere operato*. Baptism is the gospel itself; it is *the Word* in a visible form and specific function, namely, of uniting one personally to Christ crucified and

---

193. See the recent *Oxford Handbook of Evangelical Theology*, ed. Gerald R. McDermott (New York: Oxford University Press, 2010). It is a safe generalization regarding the assembled theologians writing in this volume to say that they are united in search of a new evangelical future "after revivalism" (pp. 209-10), beyond the Calvinist-Arminian standoff towards a "theology of religious experience that is grounded in the sovereign priority of God's grace and yet takes human volition seriously as Spirit-inspired response to God's initiative" (p. 214). That coordination of Word and Spirit points to a fuller Trinitarianism than either Calvinism or Arminianism historically knew. Concretely and in tandem with that latter point, a fuller Trinitarianism means an evangelical turn to Word and Sacraments as the means of the Spirit (p. 216). I note that this is a turn towards what the nineteenth-century American Reformed Mercersburg theologian John Nevin called, in criticism of revivalism, the "catechetical method."

risen and calling by name into *this* Body. *Baptism "works" in the act of its being communicated and it is communicated as the Spirit intends where and when it elicits repentance and faith.* Or, what is the same, baptism works as the means of the Spirit. Just as it is not the legal documents granting custody that make an adopted child a member of the family, but the actually nurturing and raising and loving of the child inaugurated with the legal document, so also the sacramental act of baptism establishes the new relation to God in Christ. But that relation is only realized in the course of its being lived out. Baptism creates personal faith in the continuing event of bringing to remembrance what God has done for us before we had any faith, weak and godless, and on this basis of what God continues to do now in nurturing faith in us, and what God will yet do for all in Christ in fulfillment of His purposes. Baptism includes all of this; the whole Christian life is founded in baptism, which remains forever as it is the will and work of the Spirit of the Father and the Son. Such baptism had better transform us personally! If not, something has gone terribly wrong!

## Karl Barth's Second "Nein!"

According to Karl Barth, something has indeed gone terribly wrong. This is a diagnosis all the more weighty because it comes from the great twentieth-century representative of theology in the tradition of the magisterial Reformation. Barth is famous, among other things, for his resounding *Nein!* to Emil Brunner's interest in an evangelistic point of contact with the "natural man," a quest that Barth took as the "Trojan horse" of systematic apologetics opening the doors of the church wide to the new humanity of National Socialism. Barth understood that an error in the beginning lays the foundation for a multitude of errors later on. The way in which questions are framed predetermine the kinds of answers that can be supplied. If Christian theology allows the questions and concerns relevant to the "natural man" to frame its questions in a systematic method of correlation (Tillich), everything theology says will turn out to be but recirculation of existing opinions, worldviews, idolatries, and demonologies — a fact confirmed for Barth by the contemporaneous spectacle of the Nazi-uniformed German Christians singing *Sieg Heil!* to the tune of *Ein Feste Burg.*

Less well known, and less understood, is a second *Nein!* Barth came to late in life, in fact, in the last published installment of his multi-volume *Church Dogmatics.* This *Nein!* arose in large part out of frustration and even disgust at the failure of the Protestant "people's church" *(Volkskirche)* to draw the right lessons from their failures during the Hitler time. It was a radical *Nein!* designed to strike at the heart of an ecclesiology that had now managed to survive without reformation even with the full exposure of its theological vacuity during the Hitler time. This was Barth's *Nein!* to the practice of infant baptism.

Barth speaks of faith as an adult act of human decision. In this respect, Barth sounds just like the existentialists whom he normally opposes. He defines the issue this way: "We have to be clear that the faithfulness to God here at issue must be understood as a human act, the Christian life as the life of a man. The question is how this man himself *becomes the subject of this event,* of faith in God, love for Him, of hope in Him, a man who wills and acts in this positive relation to Him, a friend instead of an enemy. . . . [Here] man himself is at issue . . . as one who for his part is a faithful partner in the covenant of grace."[194]

We will return to this definition of the subjectivity of faith by which a person is a Christian, for here is where criticism of Barth will find its proper target. It is, all the same, a very subtle matter. Barth thinks of the "I" in "I believe" as a relatively autonomous subject over against an object given for belief, where the object in question — God! — can never be captured; hence this "I" is always subject as "witness" to others of what is present as event, not thing. This very epistemic scheme — subject, object, audience — has also been adopted in the present work, as it or something like it must be adopted, if theology is *knowledge* of God. The overlap here is significant and important.

Yet Barth does not think of the "I" in "I believe" as the *person* baptized into community; hence he is not thinking of the person united in faith by the Spirit with the Person of Christ, who is also the object of belief, in relation to others, the "family of God" (Mark 3:31-35). The subtle difference here regarding the ego in the credo between the abstracted epistemological subject and the concrete person in community, as already signaled, takes on its full significance in Christology, as we shall explore in Part Three of this system of theology. But even in Pneumatology it has the effect of reinforcing in Barth a dualism of the sign and the thing signi-fied, which must remain in an oscillating dialectic of convergence and separation that never settles into a concrete union of person. Of course, such a capture of the event of God is just what Barth wants to avoid, for the good reason of saying *Nein!* to the Wehrmacht trooper with *Gott mit uns* stamped on his belt-buckle. This "No" to union includes a No to the Spirit's work in the baptismal union of the sign of watery tomb with the thing signified, dying with Christ, which Barth accordingly dualizes into the human work of water baptism and the Spirit's bap-tism as the free and incalculable event of coming to the knowledge of God's grace and thus becoming "a man who wills and acts in this positive relation to Him." By contrast, we will argue that water baptism, properly qualified, *is* Spirit baptism, where and when the Spirit wills, in which a union of the sign and the thing signi-fied takes place though in different respects for the baptized, for the ecclesia, for the nations, and for God. We leave this thesis aside until the beginning of Chapter Four in order to see now how Barth differs from his existentialist opponents, in spite of the activist definition of human faith that he shares with them.

Barth asserts that the human decision of faith comes as a miracle, namely, through the "baptism in the Holy Spirit," which he exposits as "the change in

194. *CD* IV/4, p. 4, emphasis added.

which man himself is free to become what he was not and could not be before."[195] Christian life has its "true source in this change which God brings about in man." This divine "change," which may even be called "supernatural," does not abolish human freedom or subjectivity with a mystification, as existentialist critics claim. Rather it enables "free partnership with God" in "man himself, man in his own most proper subjectivity," who "voluntarily and by his own decision" "is enabled to participate not just passively but actively in God's grace as one who may and will and can be set to work too."[196] The *miracle* of God's *causal* act here must be maintained against the reductionist tendency of existentialist theology to resolve faith into a purely human decision and act, yet in such a way that this divine act does not eliminate human freedom but actually elicits it. God draws, the man turns. God calls, the woman responds. God decides for us, we decide for God. As God changes the man, he returns to God in service. This change of woman or man into God's covenant partner is the "baptism in the Holy Spirit" — the thing itself signified but not caused by the sign, "baptism in water."

In speaking of the change in the human being this way as baptism in the Holy Spirit, Barth is criticizing classical Catholic and Lutheran, and to a lesser extent, Reformed doctrines alike. He agrees with the Catholics that a real change comes about in the believer, but not by infused grace impersonally dispensed through the sacrament, which Barth polemically characterizes as a "magical infusion of supernatural powers by whose proper use man [supposedly] can do what he cannot do in his own strength, namely, be faithful again to the faithful God."[197] He agrees with the Lutherans that God's decision for the human being in Christ precedes man's decision. But God's decision is not a forensic, external imputation of Christ's righteousness that leaves the believer unchanged. God's decision really touches and affects and so changes and gives a new Christian being; it is not merely "something external, not to speak of a mere Christian appearance, a hood which is pulled over him and under the concealment of which he can be the same as he always was."[198] So, a pox on both Lutheran and Catholic houses! "The Christian life begins with a change which cannot be understood or described radically enough, which God has the possibility of effecting in a man's life in a way which is decisive and basic for his whole being and action, and which He has in fact accomplished in the life of the man who becomes a Christian."[199]

Barth in this way joins his voice to the development of the doctrine of the New Birth,[200] though he is most careful not to let the new birth metaphor fly off

195. *CD* IV/4, p. 5.
196. *CD* IV/4, p. 6.
197. *CD* IV/4, p. 4.
198. *CD* IV/4, p. 6.
199. *CD* IV/4, p. 9.
200. It would be an interesting exercise in Barth scholarship to compare this turn of the elder Barth to the sustained critique of Pietism in the younger Barth that Eberhard Busch, *Karl Barth and the Pietists,* has uncovered for us.

into various figurations of felt assurance or cathartic experience. He anchors the image of new birth in the gospel's core message of dying and rising with Christ: "The life of one who was dead but who is raised from the dead is the Christian life."[201] Indeed, it is especially necessary to identify the specifically Christian event of new birth as dying and rising with Christ nowadays in the cornucopia of spiritualities available at the end of Christendom, "at the annual fair of philosophies and panaceas, of disguised or undisguised religions, with the very different, yet confusingly similar, foundations of life which they espouse and proffer."[202] The connection of the change, the New Birth, with Christ's death and resurrection, disallows as authentic Christian conversion in particular any generic notion of man's breakthrough from a restless, anxious state of discontent with creaturely life to some higher, superhuman state. After Hitler's experiment in "political religion,"[203] Barth wanted Christian theology to be on guard against all general talk of salvation, all general buying and selling of spiritual experiences. He wanted Christian theological talk of the New Birth strictly to refer to "the history of Jesus Christ."[204]

In accord with his total theological program, Barth's meaning is that the new birth of believers has already taken place in the historical life of Jesus, in whom "the turning of all from unfaithfulness to faithfulness took place." Barth teaches that Jesus is our Representative, not only extrinsically, so to say, but intrinsically. He *is* the New Adam, in whom our human nature itself has been created anew. All that he did and accomplished before God is truly done for us and accomplished on our behalf; and further, in the case of the Christian who actually and actively believes, it is done also in us. This precisely is what a Christian *knows* concretely, that his or her conversion has already occurred in Jesus' obedience on his or her behalf so that she or he may now simply live as one who has already been converted. A Christian knows this because the Holy Spirit has disclosed to him Jesus' historical life as the Representative of all people before God; this is the "decisive event which establishes his existence as a Christian."[205] A Christian "sees himself as one of those for whom and in whose place Jesus Christ did what he did."[206] This representation happened supremely in Jesus' death on the cross, while we were yet weak and ungodly and so incapable of converting ourselves. There, in his own body, Christ by his human obedience converted sinful humanity back to God.

So the new birth of human nature has already taken place in Christ's historic act of obedience on our behalf. Yet one immediately wants to ask, "What has this Other, who there and then was born in Bethlehem and died on Golgotha,

201. *CD* IV/4, p. 9.

202. *CD* IV/4, p. 11.

203. A concept with which Michel Burleigh has brilliantly illuminated the phenomenon in his *The Third Reich: A New History* (New York: Hill & Wang, 2000). See *BA*, pp. 101-2.

204. *CD* IV/4, p. 13.

205. *CD* IV/4, p. 13.

206. *CD* IV/4, p. 14.

what has He to do with me? . . . And what have I to do with Him? How can it be that . . . He can be one with me and I with Him? How can that which He was and did *extra nos* become an event *in nobis?*"[207] How does the conversion of human nature in Christ now happen in me? The question indeed comes down to a certain kind of union with Christ. In answering this question, Barth rejects what he calls christomonist and anthropomonist solutions, according to which there is no real encounter and convergence, but one party or the other takes over. Here either Christ or the believer is the one true subject of the new life of the regenerate person. The christomonist is the Christ-mystic who says, "It is no longer I who live, but Christ who lives in me," thus abolishing the human partner. The anthropomonist (Barth is thinking of Schleiermacher) teaches that a human's God-consciousness is clarified by the illuminating paradigm of Christ's, turning Christ into little more than an inspiring model for the human subject in its own spiritual striving. "No," says Barth, to both.

The newborn believer and Christ are united as "two different partners"[208] — personally, one might say, as persons in community, not naturally — such that "[the reborn human partner] freely, of himself, and by his own resolve, thinks and acts and conducts himself otherwise than he did before."[209] Of course what Christ did for him comes first, but it comes first in order to "come with revolutionary force into the life of each and every man" so that "in spite of the unfaithfulness of every man He creates in the history of every man the beginning of this new history, the history of a man who has become faithful to God."[210] So a kind of union with Christ, initiated by Christ himself and put into effect by the baptism in the Holy Spirit, comes about as a new life lived together in covenant partnership: a personal not a mystical union.

Barth does not envision either Christ alone or the believer alone, then, but the newborn believer and Christ newly covenanted into a partnership *with a history yet to unfold,* "a true intercourse between God and man,"[211] in which man fulfills his own humanity, realizing "his own faithfulness, decision and act" in "answer to the Word of God" in the adventure of dynamic Christian service. Union with Christ thus comes in living out the *moral* harmony of wills inaugurated by the baptism in the Holy Spirit at Christ's own behest. It is therefore a union that may be recognized and tested by the fruit that it bears. How does this change of man into a covenant partner, this new birth for new life in moral partnership with God, come about?

Its basis is the resurrection of Jesus Christ from the dead. As the risen One, Christ is always contemporary. His past, which "happened once for all, is pres-

---

207. *CD* IV/4, p. 18.
208. *CD* IV/4, p. 19.
209. *CD* IV/4, p. 18.
210. *CD* IV/4, p. 21.
211. *CD* IV/4, p. 22.

ent to all later times and indeed to all earlier times." Because Christ lives and reigns, "one may see how it can come about that the history of Christ which took place once in time becomes in the life of a man again once in time the event of his renewing." Barth sounds here very much like Luther, with his ubiquitous Christ, representing the first-person speech of the risen Christ approaching in the proclamation of the gospel to say, "What I was and did, I was for you and did for you. Through me your sins are forgiven. In Me you are God's child. In Me you are justified before Him, sanctified for Him, called to His service. It is also a promise to all . . . with Me, after Me, as the man who is reconciled to God in Me, you, too, shall and will rise again from the dead and come totally and definitively to light."[212] Indeed, the universal presence of Jesus Christ as our contemporary allows Barth to claim, "To be a man is to belong to Jesus Christ as an addressee and recipient of the Word in which Jesus Christ presents Himself and His work to every man." The union is thus a union that comes about by address and response. "In the work of the Holy Spirit the history manifested to all men in the resurrection of Jesus Christ is manifest and present to a specific man as his own salvation history."[213] The Holy Spirit makes Christ in His past history real and as such personal to the auditor as her own true history. The really present Christ in turn baptizes with the Holy Spirit.

Barth's teaching can be summarized as follows: (1) The Spirit initiates — "He, He alone, acts as the author of faith, just as He, He alone, is its finisher."[214] No one becomes a believer "through his human decision or his water baptism. . . . Jesus Christ Himself, and He alone, makes a man a Christian. He Himself is the divine change in this man's life . . . as he becomes an event in the life of a man. . . . He baptizes, as only He can, but as He can and does, with the Holy Spirit." (2) "Baptism with the Spirit is effective, causative, even creative action on man and in man. . . . It cleanses, renews and changes man truly and totally. . . . All this is to be taken realistically, not just significantly and figuratively . . . so that at all times and in all circumstances [the believer] will remember this divine change in his life; he will take comfort and glory in it." (3) Baptism in the Spirit emphatically "*demands* gratitude. . . . In it man effectively acquires his Lord and Master . . . obedience is effectively demanded of him." No excuses, no laments of inability, the weakness of the flesh, the overwhelming power of the world, the devil and our sinful selves! Nor can one now resort to a "separate freedom of choice," as if nothing had changed. But man's will has been freed and reoriented by the Word that has overtaken him. This is the change in man. Thus "the only way open for him . . . is obedience." (4) As the one baptized in the Spirit receives Christ as Lord, so also she receives all other Christians as brothers and sisters in community, incorporated into the communion of saints. The isolation of the one who

212. *CD* IV/4, p. 25.
213. *CD* IV/4, p. 27.
214. The summary statements in this paragraph are all drawn from *CD* IV/4, pp. 31-32.

seeks is overcome by the community of those who have been sought and found. (5) As one baptized in the Spirit, one has not arrived but rather started out. This is a "real beginning. It is not perfect. . . . It is a commencement which points forward to the future." It leads to daily repentance as it joins the pilgrim people of God on their journey to the glory of Christ yet to be revealed.

Always a courageous thinker, Barth ended his long writing career in this final fragmentary volume of the *Church Dogmatics* with a pointed attack on the practice of infant baptism in the Protestant and Catholic churches of Europe. Many of his admirers thought him senile to end his magnificent life's work in this embittered way, but even a cursory reading of *Church Dogmatics* IV/4 belies this *ad hominem*. The writing and the argument are as vivid and persuasive as any other that Barth produced. Barth's doctrine of the Baptism in the Holy Spirit is the positive teaching in light of which he makes his criticism of sacramental baptism and its extension to children. True, given Barth's great admiration of Thomas, Calvin, and Luther, this final turn in his thought took many by surprise; it was as if the great contemporary champion of the mainstream Protestant theological tradition, who early on supported the ecumenical movement and in particular took Catholic theology seriously, had now switched sides in his old age and gone over to the Anabaptists!

But Barth perceived that Europe had changed, so that faithfulness to Europe's Christian tradition now required the liberation of the church and its sacred ordinances from their captivity to the political and cultural needs of what had in fact become a pagan society again. The unquestioned baptism of all infants, without regard to their upbringing in faith or the motive and commitments of their parents, was sign of this appalling servility of the discredited church in post-Hitler Europe. So for Barth, after the catastrophes he had witnessed in his lifetime, there could be no going back to business as usual for the church in so-called Christendom. The project, traced back to Augustine in the West, of building a new civilization from the ruins of Imperial Rome on a Christian basis through the universal baptism of infants, had now been refuted historically by the Nazi ranks filled with these nominal but sacramentally baptized Christians. Whatever good part Christendom had once played in God's economy, the role of Christianity as the West's cultural overseer was now played out. Under Hitler, the remnant of faithful Christians had come to see their true situation. From the catacombs, a call went out, "To the theology of the martyrs! To the catechumenate! To the miracle of the Holy Spirit's sovereign work in calling and converting, with water baptism taken now as an obedient public sign of true conversion."

So, Barth lifted up the baptism in the Holy Spirit as the radical "change to the Christian life." This conversion event has "its outward attestation in their baptism with water," which "brings to light the once-for-allness of the event [of conversion], and is not, then, to be repeated."[215] From this prohibition of rebap-

215. *CD* IV/4, p. 39.

tism, we see that while Barth regarded infant baptism as an erroneous practice, he withheld approval of rebaptism on the grounds that the ceremony of water baptism signifies God's effective calling of a particular person through the gospel. As one is born again but once, so one should be baptized but once. In this way sign and the thing signified should find some semblance of correspondence. But they should not be confused, fused together, united. The sign of baptism stands, even when erroneously administered according to a false theological understanding of it. But it stands as a sign, pointing away from itself to the thing itself.

In this way Barth avoided the ecumenical blind alley of denying the validity of baptism in other churches, even as he tried to persuade Calvinists, Lutherans, and Catholics to change their understanding and practice of baptism. In this complex stance, Barth envisioned a new post-Christendom Christianity of ecumenically reconciled Calvinists, Lutherans, and Catholics, who in any case were being pressed together by the forces of secularism and of Europe's new paganism. These would be mature, adult, freely committed Christians, whom God has taken seriously "as the creature which is different from God, which is for all its dependence autonomous before Him, which is of age." This new, true Christian adult is "man come of age" — a phrase Bonhoeffer had made current in the postwar discussion. The Christian baptized in the Spirit to live as God's partner is this adult, the mature human being who freely and joyfully takes up his or her place of responsibility in God's reconciliation of the world in Christ.

Barth's prophetic analysis of Euro-American civilization is only further confirmed with the passage of time. The vitality of religious life in America, compared to Europe, is no refutation of it. For the vitality of religion and the vitality of Christianity are not the same things. This is especially so in America where Christianity is a mile wide and an inch deep. With the main thrust of Barth's teaching, understood historically this way, one may accordingly agree, with but one proviso. The Augustinian project — freed from its capture by the Carolingians to construct an ideology, the political theology of Christendom — is neither wrong in principle nor yet utterly defeated historically. It would be best both for Western civilization and for Christianity if a positive relationship between the eschatological faith of the gospel and the work of human civilization in the West could be developed afresh from these ruins and sustained. This may not be given to us, but it is surely to be hoped for, provided that the prophetic critique of the modern "sovereign self" that this new relationship requires is not sacrificed. But whatever the Euro-American future, it *is* today just as Bonhoeffer put it: "The *corpus christianum* is resolved into its true constituents, the *corpus Christi,* and the world. In His Church Christ rules not by the sword but solely with His Word. Unity of faith exists only in obedience to the true word of Jesus Christ. But the sword is the property of the secular government, which in its own way, in the proper discharge of its office, also serves the same Jesus Christ."[216]

---

216. Bonhoeffer, *Ethics,* pp. 94-95.

Stating the disagreement with Barth, as already hinted, is difficult in that it focuses on a point where most alternatives in Christian theology, even those otherwise quite hostile to Barth, seemingly concur with him: his activist definition of the Christian's faith as the human subject's free and voluntary faithfulness, an adult response to God's faithfulness. One hastens to agree, of course, that this action of faith as a Spirit-given synergy is an important and indeed essential aspect of Christian life. Such faith, according to Luther's famous *Preface to Romans*, "is a living, mighty thing," working with God in the Spirit for witness and service in love and hope. It is especially important here, to be sure, to speak of the Holy Spirit as the actor in us of this active faith, as Barth readily does in pointing to the baptism in the Spirit as the thing signified.

Yet, to register Luther's lonely but essential dissent from a widespread consensus: the faith that makes anyone a Christian is not in the first place this active faith of cooperation with God in the power of the Spirit, but faith as the pure *receptivity* by which the Holy Spirit makes watery baptism into the tomb of the Risen One. This death is first and ever first in sequence; this shows and showers the mercy unconditionally promised to the helpless. Citing Luther ("the righteousness of faith is passive in that we allow God alone to work in us and we ourselves, with all our powers, do not do anything"), Bayer comments: "Faith is a divine work within us that changes us and brings us to a new birth from God [John 1:13] and kills the old Adam; he makes of us a completely different human being in the heart, mood, mind, and in all powers" (cf. Deut. 6:5). Faith is thus the work of God, through and through, with nothing accomplished by the human being; rather, it can only be received and suffered."[217] This is personal faith — personal in willing, assenting, surrendering, permitting, allowing this strange gift of dying with Christ, along with the further gift of faith by the Spirit to welcome it. It corresponds to Christ's own passive obedience in the power of the Spirit at Gethsemane. And this correspondence is a real union of the sign and the thing signified, of the watery tomb of baptism and the union with Christ crucified and risen.

Barth's activist definition of faith tends systematically to overlook this crucial primacy of faith as reception that in wonder and praise rises up as from the grave to give God all the glory and just so all love to the neighbor in need and all hope for this groaning earth. The same faith that goes on actively to do great things for God and creation always begins in the watery tomb of baptism, receiving, allowing, suffering but, just so, ever refreshed because ever resting in the life that Jesus lived for us who would not and could not live for others and in the death He died for us that we too may die in His company. For Jesus Himself, as we shall see in the next chapter, took responsibility for us by first receiving His own destiny as the most strangely beloved of sons. Only so is it Jesus, then, who comes to us by the Spirit and only so does Jesus come to live His life of agape love in us by the bap-

217. Bayer, *Martin Luther's Theology,* p. 43.

278

tism of the Holy Spirit and fire, the same thing as our washing with water in the Name of Jesus and of the Father who sent Him and of the Spirit who has brought us to Him. That means, of course, that for human persons who assent to this watery baptism, who allow it and suffer it, the very union that Barth denied: not just of water and the Word, not only of sacramental baptism with Spirit baptism, but of believer and Christ in "a mystical union," as it were, by a "joyful exchange."

That being the case, the connection between water baptism and Spirit baptism need not be dualized, as Barth imagines, in what in fact turns out to be one more spin of the tired Western song of the dialectic of the sign and the thing signified. There is a deep reason for Barth's neglect of the receptive side of faith, as that is articulated in sacramental baptism, especially accented in the case of infants. It points forward to the next chapter on Christology but may be registered here. In Barth the Protestant version of Anselm's doctrine of satisfaction was brought to its logical conclusion. Because Jesus really is God, and so as incarnate, as Man, He represented *all* humanity in his Godforsaken death on the cross, He is the Judge judged in our place. It follows that *all* sin is really judged, atoned for, and so truly forgiven in Him, whether anyone knows this or believes it or not. The only difference between a Christian and a non-Christian is that the Christian *knows* what also obtains for the nonbeliever but which the nonbeliever does not yet know, namely, that because of Christ all is forgiven and everyone is reconciled with God. Thus, the preaching of the gospel does *not* bring into temporal and spatial effect the forgiveness of sins; preaching is the subject's witness, not the personal address that elicits divine faith by the communication of Christ's promise in the first person to a person who now accordingly passes, as one crucified and risen with Christ, from wrath to mercy. Rather preaching as witness to the past event becomes a present event that awakens those already forgiven and reconciled to their new lives of active Christian service. Faith does not in the first place receive mercy, since all people already are under mercy because of the objective atonement accomplished by the divine Son of God on the cross. Faith rather denotes the active, Spirit-awakened faithfulness to the God of grace, which comes about when a person with joy and gratitude becomes aware of the grace in which he and all people already stand because of Christ. The subject's knowledge of universal grace, not the person's passing into grace, is the decisive sign of the Christian life.

There are immense difficulties involved here in spite of something that is to be appreciated and affirmed, namely, that in the atonement God is the actor so that those who are sought are found in their abiding solidarity with the sinful world with which they remain linked by the common body. On Barth's side is the simple but powerful argument that if Jesus is true God, then His sacrifice for sinners is divinely, universally, and already now valid, no matter whether anyone accepts it or not, though certainly God wills also this subjective reception in the baptism of the Spirit. Opposing this line of thought is the difficult idea that in coming to faith an individual passes from wrath to mercy and so from a state of rejection to a state of acceptance. In the latter case, our Spirit-wrought dying and rising with Christ in baptism into the ecclesia, not the adult awakening of European "man come of age" to the theological datum of Christ's divine and universal deed of reconciliation, marks the decisive change. The choice here is a matter of immense import. Clearly, what we think of the Spirit's work in baptism will depend almost entirely on whether it is taken as an awakening to a state of affairs that has already come objectively to obtain or as a conversion within a reality that is itself contested, where conversion remains itself the Spirit's *contestation* of reality, the Paraclete's *prosecution*.

If the Christian's faithfulness to God in renewal is or can be little more than inchoate in still-contested reality, moreover, then the faith that makes and marks a Christian cannot be tested on the basis of his or her active renewal in witness and service since these deeds as such remain ambiguous, just as Christ the Crucified Himself remains ambiguous, a "stumbling block" and a matter of dispute, in the world. Witness and service even as corresponding to Christ are and remain ambiguous because the Christian-cum-ecclesia remains vitally linked to the common body, as is the incarnate Christ. They wrestle against but also amid and within the structures of malice and injustice, just as did the Christ who broke like a thief into the strong man's house, in such fashion that no umpire, least of all an interested partisan, can see clearly and definitively who is who and what is what until the eschaton of judgment. There are many secrets now that then will be revealed, as Paul says in Romans 2:15-16. What believers know is not the single righteous action required in the concrete hour, but in Spirit-given faith they believe and know the One righteous man, whose surprising but also offensive righteousness is to give what is not deserved by taking upon Himself what others deserved and He did not.

This light of agape shining in our moral darkness and confusion lightens our darkness before God but does not give us any clear commandment specifying the right deed in the concrete situation from the infinity of possibilities on the earth, where the moral agent perforce chooses one and only one of them in the risk of faith that remains, as it must, under the promise of mercy. As Paul Tillich pointed out: the unconditional moral demand to acknowledge every other as a person is fraught "with countless ambiguities, many of which put before us painful decisions" to sacrifice the acknowledgment of one for the sake of attending to another.[218] To think that any political judgment, however informed by the covenant of Christ and His people, is and can be the fruit of the Spirit and the test of Christian authenticity is the illusion avenged upon realized eschatology that is living as if already in heaven. But if, on the other hand, the Christian's Spirit-given faith is a receptivity that confesses Christ as the savior of helpless sinners before God, then what can be tested and examined theologically on the earth is Word and Sacrament as the public confession of the gospel by which faith lives

218. Tillich, *ST* 3, p. 47.

its new life together as ecclesia — also "sinning boldly" in the inevitable political judgments of baptismal responsibility to God for the world.

To make the same point from another angle: there is no devil to figure actual evil in Barth's theology, that is, to figure the malice of envy at work in the structures of injustice that still attacks and assails faith at the root, in the primary place of its receptivity, where undeserving it receives as its own what is and can only be gift. Faith boldly claims "for me" the favor of God, despite sinfulness. This gift of undeserved favor is the special object of the devil's envy, and the inevitable sinfulness that still accompanies one so gifted is the special evidence it uses to attack and assail and drive to despair. But such apocalyptic contest between God and the devil over tenuous human loyalty is too absent in Barth's theology. Yet if faith as receptivity of mercy is precious as a gift undeserved, it is just so fragile in this as-yet-unredeemed world. It is daily dependent on the offered mercy of Christ as remembrance of the baptism that remains forever as it is also daily exposed to doubt and despair by its abiding exposure in the common body. The preacher-pastor who is not attuned to this apocalyptic warfare over human conscience cannot know how to afflict the comfortable or to comfort the afflicted.

Finally, then, we must question whether Barth is right to say that Spirit-baptized Christians have no real choice but obedience, that the alternative to obedience is a *nihil,* a sheer nothingness. One wonders whether this is an echo of the old Reformed teaching on irresistible grace, just as one wonders whether a Saul or a Judas is not a sign to us that the freedom of the Christian also creates new possibilities for evil. It is worth pondering whether a Hitler, former altar boy, or a Stalin, former seminarian, could only have arisen on the soil of Christendom, their evil exceedingly evil just because premised on a knowing and willful repudiation of the merciful Christ. But the issues raised here already press us on towards Christology. It suffices here to say that Barth's *Nein!* to the indiscriminate baptism of infants as the foundation of a corrupt and perishing Christendom may be received by theology in the tradition of Luther, even if all that Barth thought needed to accompany that rejection need not be received.

## Concepts of Theological Subjectivity

The concepts of theological subjectivity with which we have been working are nature, person, and corruption. By means of them, the preceding survey of significant doctrines of theological subjectivity has conducted a running argument for the thesis that the theological subject is formed by baptism into Christ, where and when the sign of drowning is unified by the Spirit with the thing signified, crucifixion of the old Adam. In the process we have deployed these concepts to analyze the material. The concepts are traditional ones in theology, although their precise sense today can hardly be taken for granted. In any event, the traditional warrants for these concepts will now be summarily presented and then the case made for their viability in terms of Trinitarian theology, particularly the doctrine of the Spirit.

The concept of essence *(ousia)* or nature *(physis)* as found in the philosophical world of so-called Middle Platonism was revised when it was predicated by the First Ecumenical Council at Nicaea in 325 equally of the heavenly Father and the incarnate Son Jesus by the anti-Arian neologism, *homoousios,* to assert that these two are "of the same essence, substance, nature, being." Consequently, it could be said of the Son that He was "begotten not made," hence "God of God, light from light, true God from true God." Yet further, while sustaining that identification in nature there was need also to clarify the equally salient distinction between the Father who begets and the Son who is begotten. The concept of personhood (Greek: *hypostasis,* Latin: *persona*), taken as a concrete way of being in distinction from and in relation to other concrete ways of being within a natural set of common possibilities, had to be invented and developed. For example, Peter and Paul are two concrete ways of being human. Thus began a process of distinction and conceptual revision that culminated in the Second Ecumenical Council at Constantinople in 381, where the formula "one being in three persons" emerged as a succinct summation, when the Holy Spirit was affirmed as the third of the three persons of the one divine essence.

In a kind of loop, these conceptual developments and inventions of Trinitarian theology also came to serve in conceptualizing Christology and theological anthropology. So the notion of nature was put to work to sort out the possibilities of experience and action that classify creatures into sets, that is, in distinction from and relation to the Creator with its own distinct set of natural possibilities, divine nature as distinct from human nature. Just as Father and Son formed correlative concepts of personhood as begetter and begotten, so God and human being formed concepts of divinity and human being. To be God, one might say, is to be unchanging and to be human is to be mutable. In Christology, accordingly, one could say that in the Incarnation Christ, the divine way of being, or, person, that is the Son, unites to Himself by the Spirit a human nature, that is, the particular set of creaturely possibilities characterizing humans, such as the capacity to suffer and die, to accomplish His Father's will for the redemption of the creation at the cross. So the Incarnate Son has the possibilities of both Creator and human creature available to accomplish His messianic mission, which as person He both experiences and enacts in His actual and particular history in the common body from Bethlehem through Golgotha. In the unity of His person, there is in Christ a real circulation of these divine and human attributes, so that characteristics of either set can truthfully be predicated of the concrete person, Jesus Christ the Son of God, where and when the Spirit presents Him for faith to apprehend, appropriate, and confess.

In the same way, for the theological understanding of the human being one could speak of it both as a specific creature by human nature and as a concrete person by calling in distinction from and in relation to other persons of other natures, such as God or the angels and of course also other humans. Vladimir Lossky spelled out the anthropological implications of the revolutionary Trinitarian distinction of nature and person that we have adopted and utilized along these lines. "Man is not merely an individual of a particular nature, included in the generic relationship of human nature to God the Creator of the whole cosmos, but he is also — he is chiefly — a person, not reducible to the common (or even individualized) attributes of the nature which he shares with other human individuals. Personhood belongs to every human being by virtue of a singular and unique relation to God who created him 'in his image.'"[219] According to Lossky, then, the human being exists naturally as the animal having reason and language; that is its nature by virtue of which this animal can respond intelligently to God, if and when God speaks to it. But an individual of this nature exists personally in and as the response it actually makes in its biographical journey to the concrete calling of God. By this lived history, it actually fulfills its human nature by becoming from birth day to death day an actual and particular person. By this whole life lived in response to God's calling, each one in its own idiosyncratic way loves God above all and all creatures in and under God — or does not. When a community of such persons comes about which loves God above all and loves one another in and under God, we have the eternal Sabbath for which God created the world, the Beloved Community, the City of God (Augustine), the Kingdom that Jesus proclaimed.

Only the one made in the image of God for likeness to God can sin and die the personal death that is death to God. To state further how the human being could personally fall from its high calling into the corruption of sin with its wages, death, and yet not cease even in this depravity to be the good creature of the good Creator, Lossky takes advantage of the exegetically arbitrary but conceptually convenient variation of terms in Genesis 1:26, "image" and "likeness." The human creature is created in the image of God as the animal nature that has language and reason, for likeness to God, the personal being in community of love. This biblical language provides for saying theologically that the "nature" of the human creature is that of the created image of God; that is, it is that creature of all the creatures that is able to mirror the Lord God its Creator in ruling over the creation rationally, by virtue of the power of language. So in the garden Adam named all the animals (Gen. 2:19-20) and cried a cry of exultation when he recognized Eve as his true partner (Gen. 2:23). The human creature would do so by fulfilling the divine calling to care for the earth as the Lord cares for the cosmos, as God had commanded and blessed in Genesis 1:27-28.

In acquiring likeness to God by this obedience of faith in response to the divine command and blessing, the image of God becomes through its history the person that God created it to become. And history is necessary for this becom-

---

219. Vladimir Lossky, *In the Image and Likeness of God,* ed. J. H. Erickson and T. E. Bird (Crestwood, NY: St. Vladimir's Seminary Press, 1985), p. 137.

ing to take place. So God leaves the human couple in the garden with His Word so that they may make it their own in obedience and in this way arise to their personhood. The cunning serpent intervenes. It takes advantage of the apparent withdrawal of God to cast doubt upon the command and God's good intention for the couple in it. It fills the human imagination with other possibilities, more precisely with the possibility of being like God without God, "knowing good and evil" for itself in place of the command of God (Gen. 3:5) who has given all things provided that He is truthfully recognized as the Giver (Gen. 2:16-17). The created image of God can thus fill the mirror that it is with likenesses to what are the idols of pride and the demons of despair in the course of realizing its own project. Or in the obedience of faith it can achieve likeness to God by giving things to others in recognition of the Giver. In either fashion, this creature actualizes personhood by a concrete way of living out in its history the mirror that it is, that is, by filling it with images, whether of God or not-God, becoming like or unlike its Creator.

It does not cease being the good creature as the created image of God called to become like God even in its waywardness (Gen. 9:6), though it fulfills its personhood henceforth in a state of exile (Gen. 3:24) in an accursed trajectory (Gen. 3:14-19) of sin spiraling down through perpetual violence to eternal death (Genesis 4–11). So actual evil terminating in eternal death is a fatal corruption of something actually and abidingly good, the set of possibilities that comprises the created image of God that human beings possess by nature and which singles them out from all other creatures on the earth as created for likeness to God with God and in God. Corruption in sin and death is thus a *privatio boni,* a deprivation of the good. Actual evil is thus something parasitical upon its host, the good creature of God, feeding on it until, exhausted, both parasite and host die in a death that is irreversible and hence eternal (Gen. 2:17).

Thus far, then: a summary of traditional concepts in theology of nature, person, and corruption with classical warrants derived from the Christian reading of Genesis 1–3. But now we come to contemporary interpretation, reflecting on the viability of these traditional concepts for theological service today. What needs to be said clearly and sharply in this regard, even though it is already implicit in the crucial Trinitarian distinction of nature and person and was haltingly grasped by Luther, is that, over against the tradition of Christian Platonism and its tendency to reify abstractions, only "persons" are anything real. "Nature" is a semantic or conceptual reality only, a useful abstraction, a way of referring to concrete ways of being or specific actualizations of possibilities by abstract sets, classifying them according to shared and thus common possibilities.[220] There is, then, no divine "nature" as a really real something that transcends the Father, the Son, and the Holy Spirit and exists separately as some kind of really real fourth thing underly-

220. Graham White, *Luther as Nominalist: A Study of the Logical Methods Used in Martin Luther's Disputations in the Light of Their Medieval Background,* Schriften der Luther-Agricola-Gesellschaft 30 (Helsinki: Luther-Agricola Society, 1994).

ing the three persons. Rather it is these persons, each as together, that are alone really real, i.e., "deity" or "divinity." The "deity" is what these three actually do as one, both for themselves and for all others, that is, for creatures. And what must be said here about divine nature when we characterize it strictly on the basis of the self-surpassing Father, the self-donating Son, and the self-communicating Spirit is *esse Deum dare:* to be God is to give. Not that there is a fourth entity of giving, but rather that the Father who begets the Son and breathes the Spirit gives all things in creating through the Son in the Spirit.

If we reify the notion of "nature," on the other hand, and treat it as if it were something really real, we get the classical idea of "substance," that is, of an individual being that exists *a se* (from itself) and *per se* (through itself) and not *per aliud* (through another substance), an entity which is therefore capable of pure agency *(actus purus),* of acting without being acted upon. The problems created by this reification for theology are both theological and anthropological. First, creatures clearly do not exist in this substantial way, and whatever agency they acquire is the product of their patiency, that is, of their being continually created by God. On the other hand, if we insist on working with the concept of substance, only God is and can be substantial. But that entails the pantheistic idea that only God is truly active, *natura naturans* ("nature naturing" — Spinoza), that everything in creation is only a modality of God's universal agency that produces all effects *(natura naturata* — "nature natured"). Against just such pantheistic implications that rob creatures of *any* agency at all, Augustine had argued that God is the cause of all causes but not the maker of all choices, i.e., that God empowers all creatures, but only personal creatures make the evil choices that are sinful — and this not in spite of but just because of their calling to become like God. On the plane of theology, moreover, the concept of substantiality causes the critical Trinitarian insight that God exists *per alium* (through the other), i.e., in the personal relations of Father, Son, and Holy Spirit, to be obscured. As we shall see, Augustine was not as perceptive on this plane, but instead made a philosophical notion of divine substantiality into a virtual fourth entity in the Christian God that undermined the Trinitarian insight and blocked the way forward to a consistent doctrine of the eternal life of God as *perichoresis* (mutual indwelling).

"Nature" is a concept of concepts, a "meta-concept" telling what concepts are and how they work. Concepts exist in the human mind for thinking a coherent set of possibilities from its creaturely perspective; they are built up practically and refined by experience for the swift and efficient processing of the infinity of data in the work of inductive generalizations. Concepts thus effectively organize the chaos of experience into a predictable and thus habitable human cosmos. As such, concepts are indispensable tools of language. But they are not anything real in themselves. There is no idea, say, of "chairness" populating a Platonic heaven that is more real than the wood and metal device on which I am sitting as I key these words. Concepts are mentally "real," we could say, that is, real in the minds of really existing persons who think them. But what is real, that is, what takes up time and place in the cosmos, are the things and the persons that populate the world in a dynamic infinity of instances and interactions. Applying this (today commonplace) criticism of Platonism to theology, we have to say that it is a metaphysical illusion to imagine that the dynamic cosmos is anchored in a really real divine nature that can be comprehended as timeless, spaceless self-identity, in a word, as simplicity, the One as opposed to the many. Such a philosophical ascent to the divine "nature" by the metaphysical mind is sharply to be distinguished from the God and Father of our Lord Jesus Christ, who eternally begets the Son and eternally breathes on Him His Spirit, who lives eternally as this divine *complexity* and *becomes* with the initiation of time and space the Creator of a creation that is destined for redemption and fulfillment in the history limned by the canonical Genesis-to-Revelation narrative. The "reality" of this God as a possibility for us is the actual coming of His kingdom in the fulfillment of His promise.

Even if we do not claim metaphysical insight for our ordinary language about the "nature" of things, or even if we are among those few who, feeling ungrounded in ordinary experience, obsess over the inadequacy of ordinary language to the really real, it indeed matters practically that our concepts of the nature of things work for common human purposes of organizing experience. Survival depends on it. But there is no need purely to ground the things appearing to us by means of such conceptual sets so that we may ascertain why it is that they "really" belong there. Nor worse, is there any need in an abstraction of an abstraction to conceive the conception of possibility in itself and as such. The transcendental move of modern metaphysics of conceiving the condition for the possibility of some factual phenomenon dualizes the subject from the object of knowledge as the supersensible or noumenal knower of sensible or phenomenal things,[221] making a gap that repeats itself in every effort to bridge it. But the move is unnecessary. Trial and error of common experience in shared language evolving over time works well enough in producing inductive generalization continually to correct our conceptions of the natures of things. Practical life in the common body awash in the flood of becoming has no need to found knowledge in this theoretical way and may well find the attempt to do so a useless distraction from the tasks swimming in the stream of life — including our theological tasks.

The real critical scrutiny ought rather to be focused upon the very need for transcendental anchoring and the purposes or projects such anchoring tries to secure. Much critical attention in modern thought has gone to the problem of "essentialism," not only regarding its descriptive inadequacy but also its prescriptive imperialism. The latter occurs when an a priori definition of what a thing is in and for itself is then imposed on its embodiment as if the standard of its rational realization — an idea that falsely divinizes creatures but also imprisons them in this pseudo-divinity. Essentialism as an ideal demanding actualization in existence works as a norm by which the actual idiosyncrasies of genuine evolutions in

---

221. *RPTD,* pp. 11-19.

nature and of genuine persons innovating on the way to their destinies are oppressively policed. That is bad enough humanly. But worst of all, theologically, such metaphysics block the theological perception of human "nature" as the "hope projected backward" of the *imago dei* and thus of human personhood as the gift and task forward to Beloved Community. Thus, if we probe more deeply, we uncover a protological bias in classical metaphysics towards what Jenson called the "God of the Past,"[222] or what Tillich named the *Blut und Boden* "myth of origin."[223]

If then we speak of divine or human natures in contemporary theology, all we are conceptualizing is what a Creator of all that is not the Creator on the way to the Beloved Community would be able to experience and to do, so that we may know God to pray, praise, and give thanks, to trust and obey. In the same way with humans, statements about human nature say no more than what this human creature is able to experience and to do, so that we may know how to operate and to cooperate, how to feel and to share ourselves with others, and so on. No metaphysical insights are required into how experiencing as such and doing as such are possible to make such inquiry and resolve such problems.

To sum up, then: "natures" are nothing real, except in the language of the common body, at work in the common "mind" by which the common body communicates. Aside from things, that is, unintelligent ways of being in the world that impersonally actualize according to physical laws, only persons, that is, concrete ways of intelligent being that actualize vocational possibilities according to moral laws, are real. Because only concrete persons, whether divine or human, are real, moreover, they can also be ruined; that is, they can actualize in such contradiction to their own calling — what Royce analyzed as self-betrayal[224] — or that of other persons (as in Cain's paradigmatic fratricide in a fit of envy at the acceptance of his brother Abel's sacrifice, Gen. 4:1-16) that they corrupt, decay, and disintegrate as persons. That can happen if persons actualize in ways that contradict their own goals, as in God's case, or their divine calling, as in the case of human persons. Even the divine person of the Son can go to ruin and find Himself in strange contradiction to His Father, if we are to believe that truly He who was made man was crucified, dead, and buried because He took upon Himself the sin of our world and made it His own. If, as per our cognitive claim, God has created the world and especially humanity in it to lead it freely and joyfully to His kingdom by the way of Spirit-given faith in the Crucified as His Son, theology has all the reason in the world to consider humanity as "essentially" historical in being in the sense that our nature, taken as our species-typical possibilities for life, is

222. Robert Jenson, *God after God: The God of the Past and the God of the Future, Seen in the Work of Karl Barth* (Indianapolis and New York: Bobbs-Merrill, 1969).

223. Paul Tillich, *The Socialist Decision*, trans. Franklin Sherman (New York: Harper & Row, 1977).

224. Josiah Royce, *The Problem of Christianity* (Washington, DC: Catholic University of America Press, 2001), p. 153.

fulfilled — or not — in the concrete person we become by the lived obedience of faith to the calling of God — or not.

Abstractly put (that is, bracketing the calling of God that ought to be the goal of intentional human life), we can say that to be a person is to lead a life to completion in death in the light of, and so as judged along the way by, a personal goal. To pit Aristotle against Aristotle,[225] then, personally adopting a goal (not realizing an essence) is a matter of faith and history, not insight into one's timeless essence. Teleology is grounded not in essentialist metaphysics but by social narratives that construct the self precisely by giving goals and tasks that are personally sifted, selected, and actualized. Such is the *gift* of narrative; it forms what MacIntyre called the "moral starting point" of anyone's life.[226] But narratives are many and gifts can be refused. So it is by a decision of faith that human beings project themselves into a future that is not in their control on the basis of beliefs about the worthiness and viability of the goods that are intended as provided by the narrative they appropriate. This actual living of intentional life thus requires that one constantly face new, unexpected challenges. Faithfulness to the goal through the vicissitudes of time constitutes one's "identity," one's personal "coherence" or "integrity," just as a change of goals in the course of life signifies nothing less than a conversion, a surrender of the coherence one previously knew and the beliefs that informed it. For good or for ill, the dramatic narrative of life lived by faith (or weak faith, or breach of faith, or false faith, or converted faith) through time yields personal identity, even if only in fragments of meaning.

So we speak whenever we speak historically of human personhood. Judas is the one who betrayed Jesus. Julius Caesar is the one who crossed the Rubicon and marched on Rome. Dietrich Bonhoeffer is the one who returned to Hitler's Germany to share in his people's fate. This is how we actually identify personal agents, ourselves as well as others, made known in the fateful faith-decisions, which in turn dramatically determined each one's personal biography in face of the changes and chances of life that are in no creature's control. Human persons are their stories of passion and action, meaningful stories if the coherence of remembered past with the future anticipated by faith can be sustained. Lacking either a past to remember or a future for which to hope, or suffering an impossible contradiction between the past we have and the future we hope for, life becomes incoherent and collapses into the slough of meaninglessness and despair. Even this misery of despair, however, pathetically witnesses to the hope by which human creatures must live. Human beings as historical beings have that nature from among all the other creatures, a nature that is in this way essentially oriented to the future, even if for the most part human beings can hardly bear the tension of

225. This, I take it, is the real though understated import of Alasdair MacIntyre's much-discussed *After Virtue: A Study in Moral Theory* (Notre Dame: University of Notre Dame Press, 1984).

226. MacIntyre, *After Virtue,* p. 220.

courageously facing the future that they do not and cannot control and instead do everything to evade the risk of projecting themselves forward by adopting a goal in a clean and consistent decision of faith. Indeed, much of human religiosity is nothing but such an evasion, an attempt to make life cycle back to a mythical past that anchors becoming in an illusion of transcendence.

But "faith is the substance of things hoped for," according to Hebrews 11:1. The attribution of substantiality to God, when God is understood according to the doctrine of the Trinity as the God of hope, the God of the future, forces a re-vision of the concept, substantiality, as "being in communion" (Zizioulas). Lewis Ayres cogently argued in *Nicea and Its Legacy*, however, that the attribution of substantiality also helps to preserve the doctrine of the Trinity from another kind of absurdity. Here, he argues, the idea that helps is the metaphysical insight that what exists a se and per se exists *simply*, that is, as an irreducible whole, not compounded of parts that can come apart and disintegrate. The doctrine of the Trinity is thus delivered by this idea of simplicity from the very real appearance of tritheism (as like three individuals, Peter, Paul, and James, who could quarrel and separate) by the qualification of its language about "being in communion" as nevertheless simple. The Father's begetting of the Son and breathing of the Spirit is thereby purified of all corporal images and associations to be thought of as an eternal and ineffable state: "[T]he order we perceive in scriptural discussion of the Trinity does not involve spatial or temporal separation of sequences because of the unity and simplicity of the divine essence."[227] There is manifest truth in Ayres's argument that expresses and sustains the biblical distinction between Creator and creature. The corresponding doctrine of the "two natures" is not only a Christological conceptuality. It articulates the axiomatic and inviolable biblical distinction by thinking out the sets of possible experience and action by which we distinguish in the abstract deity from creaturehood. God is by nature one and simple as compared with the nature of creatures, which in multiple ways is compounded: of form and matter, of soul and body, of male and female, of individual and society, and so on.

Yet there is also an obvious difficulty here. How is God's natural oneness or simplicity to be understood? Can it be understood at all, or rather only believed in time and enjoyed in eternity? The doctrine of the Trinity, which surely does say that God's being is in becoming and in communion so that it is and remains one

---

227. Lewis Ayres, *Nicea and Its Legacy: An Approach to Fourth-Century Trinitarian Theology* (Oxford: Oxford University Press, 2006), p. 362. Whether Ayres himself understands or would agree to the distinction I am making between simplicity as metaphysical insight and simplicity as rule for creatures speaking reverently of their Creator is not germane to his important observation. There is a not inconsiderable danger in the Hegelian doctrine of the Trinity (cf. chapter 16, "In Spite of Hegel, Fire and Sword," pp. 384-429) of reducing divine substantiality to the immanent world process that justifies his caution, though it is finally no solution to try to revert to the pre-critical doctrine of God that asserts simultaneously being in communion and divine substantiality.

by communion (what I shall term, in conclusion, consistent perichoresis), rather than by static self-sameness, and hence by achievement of its goal with creatures, indicates just how it is that the triune God is and can be Creator of all that is not God, namely, by natural generosity, surplus, self-surpassing, self-donating, self-communicating ecstasy. Being already a fulfilled communion of love, God does not create out of need or greed but out of surplus, and does not cease creating until the creation is redeemed and fulfilled. But no creature in all eternity comprehends the "how" of this dynamic divine unity, even when knowingly they participate in it, love, and enjoy it. Just this ultimate ignorance of the "how" of God on the basis of knowledge of the "who" of God revises "what" we think of God. Simplicity, then, is the Christian way of observing a rule of reverent speech regarding the incomprehensible singularity of God as Creator of all that is not God. All it accomplishes is to erect a boundary for thought beyond which it may not ascend, a sheer reference that consists purely in pointing to an irreducible singularity in relation to us.

Metaphysically, then, theology would have to say today in revision of "unbaptized" notions (Jenson)[228] of divine substantiality that God the Creator, taken as the triune Life, is alone the Life that lives in and for itself eternally as the Father of the Son in the Spirit, the one true "substance," whose giving of a world of creatures can be and is motivated by surplus of love, not any kind of neediness. In just that light, however, we see that no creature, as Luther interprets the First Article of the Creed, exists or can even be conceived to exist in and for itself: "Thus we learn from this article that none of us has life — or anything else that has been mentioned here or can be mentioned — from ourselves, nor can we by ourselves preserve any of them, however small and unimportant. All this is comprehended in the word 'Creator.'"[229] Creatures exist in and for other creatures, where the mutuality of love and the harmony of justice are "essential" to each person's flourishing, to their "blessing" as opposed to their "curse." Indeed, only so are they individuated persons at all, concrete biographical "actualizations" of human "nature" by way of communion, or by the perversion of communion, with other such persons through the sequence of their interactions and outcomes in time. The communal "essence" of human beings as history consists in personhood, the personal identity humans acquire from birth day to death day by love and justice — or by want of love and justice — in sharing, exchanging, circulating, communing with other creatures as finally settled at the eschaton of judgment. Or, to say the same, the substantiality of humanity is not already given but promised and so acquired in and by the coming of the Beloved Community. The concept of *nature* in theology is thus "baptized" by the appearance of the person, Jesus

---

228. Robert W. Jenson, *Unbaptized God: The Basic Flaw in Ecumenical Theology* (Minneapolis: Augsburg Fortress, 1992); "An Ontology of Freedom in the *De Servo Arbitrio* of Luther," *Modern Theology* 10, no. 3 (July 1994): 247-52.

229. *BC*, pp. 432-33.

Christ, the new Adam now to refer to this promise of origin straining forward for its fulfillment at the eschaton.

Another feature of the problem of the Christian theology of subjectivity has been the massive failure, especially in liberal theology, to grasp the revision of metaphysics achieved in patristic theology, which was far more, as Pelikan held against Harnack, an evangelization of Hellenism than a Hellenization of the gospel.[230] As John D. Zizioulas has argued, the ontological bombshell of Trinitarianism brought the insight that for God, not to mention for creatures fitly made by God: "*To be* and *to be in relation* becomes identical."[231] To be sure, as noted above, in God this *being that is in becoming related* is qualified as an eternal and ineffable one, as befits the One who is uniquely the Creator of all that is not God. This patristic "ontology of communion" allows theology today aptly to solve urgent contemporary difficulties. For example, if "nature" is but an abstract description of certain sets of possibilities, "essences" may be seen as evolving sets and hence flexible and adaptable. Fundamentally that permits recognition of the "emergent property," as evolutionary theory speaks, of a "passive aptitude"[232] for personal relation with God and all His creatures that actually anticipates in space and time the communion of the Beloved Community. On this basis, as previously noted, theology should now teach that human "nature" is but a divine promise of the fulfillment of creatures' obedience of faith by the Lord and Giver of life. By faith in the "natural" promise of creation, persons come into being. The actual individual's lived vocation in some particular way images God (or disfigures God) on the earth. This is the original calling of the common body of humanity that stands behind the original sin of defection from this calling. The calling to live out the individual nature (i.e., the inherited and acquired set of human possibilities at any given place in the sequence) that is uniquely one's own in one's particular time and place is thus redeemed by the faith, hope, and love of Jesus Christ, the New Adam, the true *eikon tou theou* that it may be fulfilled by the Lord and Giver of life.

*Faith* is therefore the human, historical way of life by which God creates persons from the lump of nature, in that these persons actually live historically, in anticipation of the fulfillment of God's promises. "The just will *live* by their faith" (Rom. 1:17) says the Apostle of the New Testament, quoting a Hebrew prophet (Hab. 2:4). Christian beliefs are "doctrine *for life*." By the same token, false faiths, of which the world is full, corrupt persons, making them loveless and unjust; they disappoint and end in the ruin of despair. True faith lives every moment on the way by receiving the gospel story of Jesus as its pledge of hope in the world not

230. Jaroslav Pelikan, *Christianity and Classical Culture: The Metamorphosis of Natural Theology in the Christian Encounter with Hellenism* (New Haven and London: Yale University Press, 1993).

231. John D. Zizioulas, *Being as Communion: Studies in Personhood and the Church* (Crestwood, NY: St. Vladimir's Seminary Press, 1993), p. 88.

232. Luther, *Bondage,* p. 105.

beyond it, for the redemption of the body, not escape from it, for the coming of the Beloved Community to this very earth on which stood the cross of Jesus. It is by following Jesus in the Spirit, that is, in the patiency of faith, that human beings become genuine agents, created substances, makers of history, persons with other persons in the mission of the gospel to the nations and the vocations of service within them.

## On the Plane of Immanence

Because — contrary to the Cartesian-Kantian construal of subjectivity in the modern epoch — no one actually transcends the common body either with metaphysical insight into nature or by religious evasion of the body's historical existence, life itself compels us to believe in something. No one withholds belief in a coherent way, as the easy refutation of skepticism has shown again and again. In this situation in which we always find ourselves *in medias res,* everything depends on what and/or in whom we hope. It would be a true saint of secularism[233] who could live without hope, in true detachment, ascetically and passionlessly withholding assent from any and all beliefs on which engaged living depended. For just this reason of psychic survival in an unsustainable Euro-America that has lost its narrative, as Jenson argues, but hurtles on towards catastrophe, as Agamben urges, neo-Gnosticisms abound, as Lee shows. But life "saved" on such terms of private survival in worlds of fantasy is not worth living. It is just more of the same self-obsession from which ostensibly it would escape.

Rather, through every moment of life, the truth of personal identity is staked instead on the actual coming of that particular future in which one hopes; it is staked on whether, then, a goal proves worthy and redeems faith's investment of life lived on a journey to it. Because Christians hope in the God "who justifies the ungodly, gives life to the dead and calls into being things which are not," they are required to disbelieve[234] anything less as *by nature* idols, false saviors, unreal (utopian) futures, or demonic deceptions. In representative self-criticism, penitent Christians disbelieve even the sincerity of their own faith, the integrity of their own lives, the authenticity of their own risky decisions; these pious virtues too will fail, and those whose faith proves only to be faith in faith will perish along with their fideistic illusions. The will to believe, moral sincerity, and existential authenticity are but formal truths regarding human "nature" and are of no material help here. Only parasitically can one continue to live in Euro-America today *als ob* the Christian claim were true. There were and still are many sincere

---

233. W. K. Clifford, *The Ethics of Belief and Other Essays* (Amherst, NY: Prometheus Books, 1999).

234. Christopher Morse, *Not Every Spirit: A Dogmatics of Christian Disbelief* (Harrisburg, PA: Trinity Press International, 1994).

Nazis and Stalinists in the shadows, and Stimsons at the reins, making their own risky leaps of faith. If human hope for the world of our common body is not to shipwreck on the shoals of the indifference of nature, the moral evil of our own kind and the hiddenness of true deity in a putative Word, everything depends on faith's knowledge of the one, true God; this is the One who truly gives Himself from "essential" hiddenness of divine singularity to be known and trusted in the "existential" fog and friction of life in space and time. Only this true God — such is the Christian cognitive claim — is the proper object of human hope as the One who judges and redeems and fulfills created life, weaving each one's historical journey, blunders and blind alleys too, into a meaningful whole with all the others on the way to the Beloved Community. To know God this way, however, is a veritable participation in God's own self-knowledge, as the Spirit of the Father and the Son teaches (1 Cor. 2:9-13) when He imparts Himself in the formation of the theological subject. For that to happen to the natural man, however, on the plane of immanence One is needed who breaks into the strong man's house to bind him and then plunder his goods (Mark 3:27).

# CHAPTER FOUR

# Creator Spiritus

## Toward the Ecumenical Doctrine of Baptism

From the discussion in the previous chapter, we call to mind the following points regarding baptism as the work of the Spirit in the world, giving a new birth to form the theological subject.

First, the Spirit is the earnest of God's promised future which provides the assurance of faith that God will prove to be the God who God has promised to be. The gift of the Spirit grounds the assurance of God's faithfulness not in a metaphysical insight into God's "nature" as immutable, as if God absolutely *could* not do otherwise because God *cannot* do otherwise. Rather the gift of the Spirit grants to faith the full wealth of conviction by revelation of God's personal self-relation as the eternal love of the Father and the Son, who as such commits Himself to us in the "new covenant" of Jesus' body and blood. What assures is the commitment of love, taken as a true expression of God's "nature" as the God who gives and in Christ has found in faith the way to give Himself in the person of the Spirit even to the perishing sinner. The Spirit of the Father and the Son is in person that "surplus" of the divine life of love, now turned freely to the creation which is other than God and estranged by sin.

Second, the new and truly human possibility that is actualized in Jesus' human obedience to God in face of genuine trial is grounded in His baptism in the Spirit that was inaugurated at His baptism in water by John (Mark 1:9-11 and parallels, or, as we may also in ancillary fashion put it, by his conception from Mary the Virgin by the power of Spirit), marking him as the New Adam. This specifies the *true* humanity (the *likeness* to sinful flesh, Rom. 8:3) of the Incarnate Son "without sin" (Heb. 4:15), and thus the *true* freedom of His human will, *by elaborating true freedom as love of God above all and all others in and under God.* To be truly human is to love this way, only possible, to be sure, so far as the Spirit communicates Himself to the creature. The Spirit's self-communication to the human for the obedience of faith is what is truly "natural"; sin and death are ultimately "unnatural." It is the "natural man," discussed at the beginning of the previous chapter, who is not truly "natural." These confusing equivocations are unavoidable rhetorically. Theologically clarified, "nature" is here being redescribed in Christian terms as the promise of eschatological creation, given and revealed in Jesus as the New Adam. In precise analogy, the same new creation by the same Spirit is conveyed by the sign of water baptism into Christ where the thing signified is the creature's new birth into the ecclesia, with all that this entails.

Third, the church as creature of the Spirit and as body of the Risen Lord, consequently, is not differentiated from the world as the exclusive object of divine love as opposed to the unloved world. Rather the ecclesia is that place of the common body that has become subject in the Spirit by the passivity of receiving God's redemptive love for all creatures, thus in repentance and faith; the ecclesia shares divine love given and made known in Christ who lived and died and lives for all. The atonement of the Incarnate Son is "unlimited" in scope. The transformation to theological subjectivity, however, marks a true differentiation between church and world (Rom. 12:1-2), reflecting the "personal" differentiation between the Son who gives Himself for all and the Spirit who communicates Himself in "bestow[ing] faith where and when it pleases God" (Augsburg Confession, Article V). This differentiation is not of the triumphalist and invidious type of ecclesiology, where either the Son's atonement is limited or the Spirit's sovereign communication of faith is hijacked. For the wrath of God is revealed from heaven against all ungodliness and wickedness (Rom. 1:18–3:20), including the ungodliness and wickedness of the ecclesia when it limits the scope of the Son's sacrifice or presumes to replace the Lord and Giver of life with its own piety, insight, deeds, rules, or feelings. Rather, its theological subjectivity consists in knowing just this solidarity in sinfulness with the world that is loved nevertheless by the costly love of the Incarnate Son, knowing penitently that just this penitence is the sovereign work and gift of the Spirit.

So the ecclesia is truly ecclesia in acknowledging that the Holy Spirit communicated to it exceeds its own theological subjectivity; it knows the Spirit, then, as Lord and God.[1] Accordingly, Pneumatology, not Christology, is the proper place for the concern expressed in the *extra Calvinisticum,*[2] i.e., Calvin's teaching

---

1. Leopoldo A. Sánchez M., "More Promise Than Ambiguity," in *Critical Issues in Ecclesiology: Essays in Honor of Carl E. Braaten,* ed. Alberto L. Garcia and Susan K. Wood (Grand Rapids: Eerdmans, 2011) speaks of the priority of the "Spirit-Word relationship over the Spirit-Church relationship in establishing ecclesial authority" for "discerning the spirits" (p. 211). This priority is echoed by the Institute for Ecumenical Research in Strasbourg, "The nature of the community's life in communion must constantly indicate that its communion is communion in the Lord and depends on the Lord for its life. Thus, word and sacrament have theological priority over other forms of communal life because they are the events in which we have the promise of the presence of the communion-creating Christ." *Baptism and the Unity of the Church,* ed. Michael Root and Risto Saarinen (Grand Rapids: Eerdmans, 1998), p. 2.

2. Joseph L. Mangina, "The Cross-Shaped Church: A Pauline Amendment to the Ecclesiology of Koinonia," in *Critical Issues in Ecclesiology,* pp. 68-87.

that the divine Son of God exceeds the man Christ. In teaching this, Calvin properly intended to keep faith subject to the God who is believed, yet this unfortunate formulation worked classically to limit the scope of the Son's atonement to the "elect." The problems here will be further attended in Part Three of this work. For the present, we acknowledge Calvin's concern as legitimate by arguing that it is the Spirit who freely unifies the sign and the thing signified, whether for faith or for offense, where and when He pleases (John 3:8). So the Spirit of the Son may in ways unknown to the ecclesia unify the sign and the thing signified in a baptism hidden from its eyes, in realms over which the exalted Christ reigns incognito in His own continuing battle against contra-divine powers. In turn, the very real distinction between the nations and the ecclesia drawn from them, *but also for them,* requires a church vicarious, believing on behalf of, interceding for, and performing the works of Christ's mercy as the sign of God's love for the sinful and unbelieving world.

Fourth, the work of the Spirit incognito, as the work of the *same* Spirit *of the Son of the Father,* is testable by the Christological question about Jesus Christ having come in the flesh, i.e., whether the common body as creature of God destined for redemption and fulfillment is acknowledged, recognized, and embraced as the place and time of the Spirit's working to fulfill the lost promise of creation. "Proscribed and disbelieved by the confession of this life 'in Christ' is any spirit that claims that the full inclusiveness of love and freedom is not the full rejection of all that opposes love and freedom" (Morse).[3] True inclusion therefore also excludes exclusion. True acceptance rejects rejection. Resurrection entails a crucifixion because love is against what is against love. This test question after the *militancy* of the Spirit who is *holy* corresponds to the examination of the candidate for baptism, who now submits his body to the drowning water as the place and time believed to be, as the Spirit wills, unification with Christ crucified and risen for redemption and fulfillment.

The theological subject is the person formed by baptismal union with Jesus Christ, that is, with His crucifixion and resurrection effecting the turning point of repentance and faith. As advent of the Spirit, the union of sign (water baptism) and thing signified (Spirit baptism) is spoken and put into effect in the specifically theological mode of discourse, "I baptize you in the Name of the Father, of the Son, and of the Holy Spirit." This linguistic performance is in accord with Luther's dictum that in philosophy the sign indicates the absence of the thing but in theology the sign indicates its presence. This differentiation between philosophy and theology reflects on the one side the finitude of natural discourse in philosophy as our best available account of experience in the flux of becoming. It reflects on the other side the Incarnation, the Son's full embrace of the flux of becoming that we creatures are. In the theological mode

---

3. Christopher Morse, *Not Every Spirit: A Dogmatics of Christian Disbelief* (Harrisburg, PA: Trinity Press International, 1994), p. 244.

of discourse, the resurrection of the Incarnate Son does not disincarnate Him or remove Him, but makes Him present — bodily and thus recognizably — in a new way on the way to the coming of the Beloved Community. This latter accounting in theology is both necessary and critical, as we have argued, because the unaccustomed and indeed novel union of the sign and the thing signified in sermon and sacrament and confession is dynamic and personal; it materially concerns the daunting gospel paradox of God's love for enemies, for Luther's "real, not fictitious sinners."

At base, the union of the sign and the thing signified in baptism is the divine speech act of the resurrection of the Crucified. In application of Christ crucified to us and for us by the same Spirit of the resurrection so that the baptized become theological subjects, this union is the justification of the ungodly, the sanctification of the sinner, the resurrection of the dead, *creatio ex vetere* (out of the old) in service of the eschatological *creatio ex nihilo* (out of nothing). The vigilance of theology as critical dogmatics on this basis would not be needed if the union in question were impersonal, static, and merely expressive of natural love for one's own kind — even as just this is what the promiscuous practice of infant baptism has de facto reduced to under Christendom. In that case, theology would be nothing but the self-serving ideologies of partisan collectivities and individualist projects in pseudo-sanctity. Critical dogmatics, on the other hand, cannot begin to rise to its calling and task unless this theological subjectivity and its task of testing the church by the gospel, and the world in its works, are themselves grounded in the very doctrine of God who calls them into service, that is to say, grounded in the personal being and consequent work of the Holy Spirit. Anything less surely falls back into mere criticism or mere dogmatism, of which partisanships the suffering world is already too full.

Accordingly, we come to a proposal for a doctrinal definition. *Water baptism in the Triune Name is Christian initiation as the Spirit's formation of the theological subject in Christ with enduring force in time and into eternity.* This is the very baptism with which Jesus was baptized, now applied and put into effect by the same Spirit in believers who will follow Him. It is a kind of unification of persons (Gal. 1:19-20), more than but not less than imitation of an example or participation in a timeless idea. For it cuts deeper than *theoria* can know or imagine; it is the radical reorganization of bodily affects. It touches the heart, wellspring of desire, not with a literal knife but with the sword of God's Word incarnate. The Spirit's gospel-mandated rite of symbolic drowning in water before God and the world *signifies, and just this way puts into public effect, both a disunion and a new union.* It works a renunciation of "the world," i.e., understood as the structures of malice and injustice bequeathed in Adam and captivating the existing self at the stem of its bodily desire. Thus working this self's spiritual death as crucifixion with Christ, baptism works rebirth into the new creation of being "in Christ." In this interim time of inaugurated eschatology, this being in Christ is faith in His promise to have taken sin and given righteousness, and so to have been placed into the new community of those redeemed, the ecclesia drawn and gathered from the nations in order to be sent again into the nations in anticipation of the promised Beloved Community, living in its light and spreading news of its coming.

Notice that this definition of baptism says nothing explicitly about the common body, the one "world" that old and new humanities alike inhabit, understood theologically as God's continuing creation destined for fulfillment. Yet baptism washes over a particular body, that is to say, a select member of the common body. This definition therefore can be explicated by analysis of the distinct ways in which baptism is the Spirit's union of the sign and the thing signified in the many relationships pertaining in the common world of visible bodies, occupying space and a sequence in time. For the baptizer, that is, for the Spirit working through the rite, baptism is a union of water with the Word incarnate to effect His own messianic anointing, the new birth. For the baptized, baptism is a union with Christ crucified and risen that receives the new birth. Hence the newborn child of God becomes a sign for the ecclesia, and in this relation baptism is a union of neophyte with existing members. In the same way, the Body of Christ becomes a sign for the world, and in this relation its one baptism for the forgiveness of sins bespeaks the solidarity of the elected with the rejected in priestly intercession, that is to say, in the priesthood of all believers at work living the life of Jesus in the world. Now this intercessory solidarity of the ecclesia with the common body in turn becomes a sign for God, and in this relation baptism is a union of Christ's body with the groaning creation that proclaims back to the Father His own purpose of Beloved Community, as in the prayer that Jesus taught us (see below, Chapter Seven).

In the preceding progression through the various relationships in which baptism expresses the Spirit's unification of the sign and the thing signified, we have been presented with the traditional doctrinal topics of (1) justification by faith, (2) the new obedience, (3) the mission to the nations, and (4) the eternal glorification of God by the resurrection of the dead to life eternal, that is to say, the traditional topics of the Third Article of the Creed. The theological subject, accordingly, is one who, received into divine and fatherly favor by faith alone in Christ alone by the Spirit's gracious work alone, offers herself in service of the ecclesia in service to the nations to the glorification of God as our heavenly Father.

It must be stressed that this Spirit-worked union of the sign and the thing signified is not only variegated as laid out above but always also dynamic and personal; it exists as event and it persists through time by the faithfulness of its agent, God the Holy Spirit, in giving this event of His own coming and abiding to do specific work with various gifts as promised — not then by any kind of natural endurance that persists apart from repentance and faith, apart from truth and reconciliation. It persists in the form of joyful exchanges; where there is neither joy nor exchange, the baptism, the baptized, the *sanctorum communio,* the mission to the nations gathering the praise of God — all these are but dead and empty signs absent the thing signified, fume and vapor of an empty bottle. The Word without the Spirit is not theologically possible, even as there is no Holy Spirit but the Spirit of the Word incarnate. The Spirit's union of the sign and thing signified persists as a living form only as perpetually enlivened by the Spirit, who as the Lord and giver of life is trusted to bring to completion what He has begun. The persistence of this baptism in the Spirit signified and put into effect by baptism with water is as living growth as opposed to the stubborn persistence in self-identity of a dead stone. It remains gift and grows by the nurture of the same Giver and does not become a routine or habitual possession, which would be the bad faith of trading the Giver for the gift.

But baptism is possessed in faith, as the Pauline "having as having not," not then as a substance owns its essential qualities but as a person lives into its destiny by ever-new and self-surpassing episodes in a historical journey. An event that has enduring force, like a Greek verb in the perfect tense, is grounded at an event of origin. For us to persist in its enduring force we must have knowledge of this grounding that we can remember and ever freshly appropriate. The alternative to such knowledge of faith is fideism on the one side and fanaticism on the other. Who and what then is the Holy Spirit that He can unify the sign and the thing signified with enduring force, so that whoever in His power endures to the end will be saved? Who the Spirit is for us turns on who He is in and for God. Only so can His extraordinary work in us be grounded in His divine and personal reality and thus the believer's confidence in the Spirit be a confidence that is true to the reality promised in Christ of entry into the Beloved Community of God that fulfills the promise of creation in the redemption of our bodies.

There is thus a broad and growing consensus today in ecumenical theology that describes baptism as "participation in Christ's death and resurrection."[4] But, as New Testament scholar James D. G. Dunn observes, the connection here with the water rite is not immediately evident. "As Christ had spoken of *his death* as a *baptism,* so Paul could speak of the beginning of salvation as a *baptism* into *Christ's death,* in which case it is relevant to note . . . that the metaphor of baptism had been quite far removed in conception from the actual performance of the baptism in water."[5] The result of this distance is that, as André Birmelé points out in his contribution to the same collection, *Baptism and the Unity of the Church,* this consensus about participation in Christ's death and resurrection, important and indeed far-reaching in its consequences, suffers from a certain equivocation. In striving "for a mutual recognition of baptism," the consensus misperceives the real problem of Dunn's distance between the water rite and dying with Christ

---

4. *Baptism and the Unity,* p. 107. Birmelé is describing the World Council of Churches' document "Baptism, Eucharist and Ministry" (Faith and Order Paper 166 [Geneva: WCC Publications, 1994], pp. 247ff.).

5. *Baptism and the Unity,* p. 97, emphasis original.

by trying too hard, as it were, to accommodate the practice of so-called "infant baptism" to so-called "believer baptism" in a visibly reconciling church.

"Theologically it is a matter of two different understandings of [water] baptism," Birmelé writes, "which are prior to the problem of infant baptism: Ultimately it is a matter of what adult baptism means for each. The different traditions do not always mean the same thing when they use the word 'baptism'"[6] — even though they intend to speak of "participation in Christ's death and resurrection." The real problem is how the water rite is theologically related to the Spirit's action in Christ, drowning the old Adam to make way for the New Adam. Rightly tracing the source of these divergent understandings to the dispute running through Protestantism from the fonts (as represented by the figures of Luther and Zwingli[7] as argued in the previous chapter), Birmelé clearly, if perhaps too simply, parses this difference as "the understanding of Baptism either as God's deed or as the deed of human obedience."[8] Surely "participation in Christ's death and resurrection," however, is *both* the self-donation of the Word incarnate *and* the deed of human obedience in faith by the Spirit's self-communication. A fuller Trinitarianism would perceive in a stark alternative between God's gracious gift and the human person's autonomous response a Pneumatological deficit on both sides of a false antithesis.[9]

Welcome, and ecumenically significant at this juncture, is the intervention of the astute Pentecostal theologian, Veli-Matti Kärkkäinen, in his *One with God: Salvation as Deification and Justification*. Following Lyle Dabney, Kärkkäinen tries to cut through the "the old dichotomy" grounded on the modalistic tendency in the West (the thesis of Colin Gunton to be discussed below) to operate along the lines of a "nature-grace opposition" as opposed to a nature-person distinction — that is, where the corruption of nature in Adam as fallen is not properly distinguished from the nature designated *imago Dei* and destined as such for likeness to God by redemption in Christ and fulfillment in the Spirit. The way out of this dilemma is the doctrine of the Holy Spirit, Kärkkäinen argues, which represents

6. *Baptism and the Unity*, pp. 108-9.

7. *Baptism and the Unity*, p. 115.

8. *Baptism and the Unity*, p. 114.

9. Birmelé himself (*Baptism and the Unity*, p. 117) tries to bridge the gap between "a causative and a cognitive understanding of baptism" by the performative "magic," if you will, of *promissio*. This is all too typical a move by which a modern Lutheran theology of the "Word alone" tries to make the Word dynamic and communicative of itself without a fuller retrieval of the Trinitarian dialectic of the Word and the Spirit and at the terrible cost of the narrative-cognitive Christological content denoted by the name, Jesus, who evaporates into the kerygmatic event of performatively uttering a promise of goodness in general. To be sure, Christ crucified is *promissio;* equally sure, no one can say that this first-century Jew dying on an imperial stake is *promissio Dei* apart from the Spirit of the resurrection who communicates this Jesus as God's self-donating promise, where and when this Spirit pleases in accord with the Father's missionary purposes, as Romans 9–11 expressly teaches.

"continuity through discontinuity which begins its witness to Christ with the Holy Spirit, is rooted in the Trinitarian event of the cross, and then defines the Christian community in those categories" (Dabney). A pneumatological concept of grace, anchored in the cross of Christ and a trinitarian vision, might help to reassess the traditional dilemma." That is surely right, although the swipe taken in passing at "the strict Lutheran view of human beings as almost as inactive as a 'stone or log of wood' "[10] is based on a caricature, albeit the caricature historically that Lutheran theology made of itself.[11] It is rather the case that the "strict," i.e., Lutheran orthodox view of the monergism of divine grace (to avoid Pelagianism) *and* the free assent of the will in faith (to avoid Gnosticism) is not a "paradox" but a conceptually incoherent self-contradiction.[12] It is so just because of the Pneumatological deficit in respect to full Trinitarian personalism that Kärkkäinen diagnoses as a general malady of Western theology. In that accounting of things, Pentecostalism may be understood, as he suggests, as the eruption within the West and its theological history and categories, of the suppressed Spirit of the Father and the Son. In Kärkkäinen himself and his work, we can detect the first stirrings of the return of the Spirit to the theology of the Word. And that is what ecumenical theology should want, a proper dialectic of the Word and the Spirit, not a false choice between them.

What is at issue, then, in a renewed, ecumenical teaching on baptism in the post-Christendom situation of Euro-America is not the question of infant or adult baptism, nor even the associated alternative between theologies of the monergism of divine grace and semi-Pelagian ones of free human obedience. Other studies in the collection, *Baptism and the Unity of the Church,* confirm this diagnosis. Baptist theologian S. Mark Heim writes that what "Baptists cannot recognize in infant baptism is full initiation into the church of Jesus Christ, in both the spiritual and the structural sense. Those churches which put emphasis upon confirmation express in essence a similar view."[13] Surely this is right. The separation in the West of water baptism and chrismation brought about by the development of widespread and indeed promiscuous baptism of infants, and the consequent evolution of confirmation as a rite of young adult ownership of baptism, bears witness to the truth of Heim's claim. The alternative to Heim's Baptist claim regarding the normativity of adult baptism as knowledgeable and responsible ownership of the Christ who has claimed the believer for Himself by the Spirit's proclamation of the gospel is elaborated in the painful contribution of

10. Veli-Matti Kärkkäinen, *One with God: Salvation as Deification and Justification* (Collegeville, MN: Liturgical Press, 2004), p. 128.

11. *PNT*, pp. 127-76.

12. On the Lutheran self-contradiction, see Paul R. Hinlicky, "Staying Lutheran in the Changing Church(es)," Afterword in Mickey L. Mattox and A. G. Roeber, *Changing Churches: An Orthodox, Catholic and Lutheran Theological Conversation* (Grand Rapids: Eerdmans, 2012), pp. 281-314.

13. *Baptism and the Unity,* p. 161.

Swedish theologian Ragnar Persenius. He actually has to pose the "crucial question" about the, evidently, purely accidental relationship between "the Church of Christ and the Church in Sweden";[14] here, just as Heim's analysis predicts, infant baptism has devolved into a secularized, Volkskirche ideology of civil inclusiveness — the quintessence of Christendom sans the Christianity. Transformative encounter with the crucified and risen Jesus Christ in one's history dissolves into the "prevenient grace of God" that usurps lived history.

All this is not to deny a theological justification for the baptism of infants. It is to say that, with Dunn in echo of Karl Barth, "the water ritual always stands at the center of 'baptism,' no matter how much we insist that the focus is on God's action. And the water rite is what *we* control. By *our* decision to baptize X or Y in water, we in effect dictate to God to act upon X or Y in accordance with the fuller theology of the sacrament of baptism we confess. We say it is *God* who acts in baptism, we delight in a sacrament (infant baptism) which mirrors the initiative of grace, but the actual initiative is all *ours*." With not unjustified sarcasm, Dunn continues, "Of course, we can make theological capital from the situation by meditating humbly and gratefully on a God who thus commits himself to act in a sacrament whose happening is at our command."[15] Pointing to the reception of the Spirit prior to the rite of water baptism in the Book of Acts, as well as Paul's allusion to it in Galatians, Dunn argues that the real theological problem is Pneumatology. "[A]re we subordinating the Spirit to a rite which we humans decide to administer?"[16] This *is* the right question, even if Dunn's formulation here is somewhat flat-footed. The fact that those who received the Spirit went on to submit to water baptism indicates that the Spirit in question is and must be known as the Spirit of the incarnate Son, the One who led the Son to cross and through grave to the newness of God's own life, and likewise leads believers to die with Him and be reborn into the ecclesia of God.

The alternative between infant and adult baptism represents a question that is transcended by the collapse of Christendom and the new missionary situation in which Christian theological thinking finds itself in Euro-America. The theological question is whether all humanity is in need of saving union with the crucified and risen Jesus Christ presented in the gospel in its mission to the nations, hence whether a person comes to see her true need for the kind of personal union with Christ that is dying and rising with Christ. Where Christ is thus necessitated, the Holy Spirit has been preveniently at work. If in principle we affirm the universal validity of salvation in Christ as death to death by His death for us, the church accordingly has *the freedom* in pastoral practice and ecclesial discernment to administer baptism where and when *nothing hinders* the proffered baptismal unification offered in Christ by the Spirit through the gospel. Baptism of infants,

---

14. *Baptism and the Unity*, pp. 187-88.
15. *Baptism and the Unity*, pp. 81-82, emphasis original.
16. *Baptism and the Unity*, p. 85.

children, or adults then becomes a question of church discipline in the concrete historical situation.

Oscar Cullmann argued for this disciplined freedom in the administration of baptism in a study that he published in response to Karl Barth's critique of infant baptism. He detected "traces of an ancient baptismal formula" in the texts of Acts 8:36, "As they were going along the road, they came to some water; and the eunuch said, 'Look, here is water! What is to *prevent* me from being baptized?'; in 10:47, "Can anyone *withhold* the water for baptizing these people who have received the Holy Spirit just as we have?"; in 11:17, "If then God gave them the same gift that he gave us when we believed in the Lord Jesus Christ, who was I that I could *hinder* God?"; and in Matthew 3:14, "John would have *prevented* him, saying, 'I need to be baptized by you, and do you come to me?' " He also found a parallel in the second-century Gospel of the Ebionites (Epiphanias 30:13). Here the Greek verb, *koluo*, "to hinder, forbid, withhold," regularly appears in connection with baptism. On the basis of this observation, Cullmann asked, "Would not the question, whether anything prevents the Baptism of this or that candidate be put from time to time in the first century before the completion of Baptism, so that gradually it became a ritual question?"[17] Indeed so. The church *had to test* whether a candidate for baptism was appropriately prepared, where "preparation" turns precisely on fundamental questions of theological subjectivity: How does the candidate understand his desire of the crucified and risen Christ? How does she understand her own need to die and rise in union with Christ? How is incorporation into the church taken, as called out from the nations, called together in anticipation of the Beloved Community, and called forth again in mission to the nations? Is one prepared in every respect to answer to the Father by confessing His Son in the power of their Spirit before the world? Has one counted the cost? Just such a Trinitarian confession of the God of the gospel stands at the ritual crossroads where the candidate renounced Satan and turned "from idols to a living and true God and to wait for his Son from heaven, whom he raised from the dead — Jesus, who rescues us from the wrath that is coming" (1 Thess. 1:9-10).

The early church addressed this problem of testing theological subjectivity by developing the catechumenate, the *paedeia* prior to baptism. Today we should probably reconceive this *paedeia* as lifelong learning in theology, taken as critical dogmatics, yet a task that is still elicited and shaped by the early church's liturgical interrogation of the candidate before immersion into the water. Those questions and answers spelled out who Jesus Christ is, in whose name and into whose ownership the baptized is given; more fully elaborated, it spelled out who is the Father who sent this Son in the power of the Holy Spirit, claiming to be the Creator of all now at work in redemption and fulfillment of creation. At the heart of the baptismal ceremony, following fast upon the solemn renunciation of Satan,

---

17. Oscar Cullmann, *Baptism in the New Testament,* trans. J. K. S. Reid (London: SCM, 1964), pp. 72-73.

his works and pomp, come the questions: Do you believe in God the Father? Jesus Christ? The Holy Spirit? In answering these questions, the candidate for baptism publicly identifies the God of the Gospel, naming the Name of the One as the Three and of the Three as the One in whom she believes.

As Jenson has pointed out, this naming — *theological* naming as befits address in prayer,[18] not philosophical naming to capture and control, let alone magical naming along the same lines — is accompanied by elementary articulations of Christian doctrine in the grammatical form of relative clauses, i.e., "who" clauses that work as "identifying descriptions"[19] to specify how the personal name is to be taken, e.g., the Father *who* made heaven and earth; the Son *who* suffered under Pontius Pilate; the Spirit *who* gives resurrection to the dead. The cognitive claim is that the Three so identified constitute the one God in coming to us as our own future too, as the "eternity" that embraces time and renders its sequenced passage both meaningful and salutary.[20] *Already now,* however, this future comes to faith because *already now* one of the Three has lived a human life among us and for us to make us fit for the coming of the Beloved Community. "But we address *this* Father in that and only in that we pray *with* Jesus *in* their Spirit. The particular God of Scripture does not just stand over against us; he envelops us. And only by the full structure of this enveloping do we have this God."[21] Baptism by water and the Word that is baptism in the Spirit, then, inaugurates already now that future promised as our enveloping destiny.

As Luther captured with great existential insight, the theological subject may now correspondingly identify herself: "I believe that God has created me. . . . I believe that Jesus Christ, God's Son is my Lord. . . . I believe that the Holy Spirit has called me. . . ." In the light of these reciprocating identifications, Christian initiation in baptism is formative of the theological subject. The new birth into the ecclesia is not to be understood as some independent event in the interiority of the soul, apart from baptism so defined, but rather as the public transfer of the loyalty, allegiance, or conscience of the baptized from the claim of this dying world into the church under the claim of Christ for the Beloved Community that is coming. Of course people came to faith from hearing this gospel prior to the ceremony of baptism. This is the presupposition of the whole matter, as we have seen, for baptism is nothing but a specific form of proclamation. But when we understand that true faith is the faith which believes the "pro me" of Christ's life, death, and resurrection, and more broadly the "pro nobis" of God who creates in order to redeem and fulfill, then faith from the outset is objectively ordered to baptism, so defined, as union with Christ. Water baptism in the Triune Name is

---

18. Robert Jenson, *The Triune Identity: God according to the Gospel* (Philadelphia: Fortress, 1982), pp. 16-18.

19. Jenson, *The Triune Identity,* p. 3.

20. Jenson, *The Triune Identity,* pp. 22-23.

21. Jenson, *The Triune Identity,* p. 51.

the specific form of the gospel in which its promises are concretized and individualized, that is, personally signed and sealed before the community, before the world, and before God. It is the public rite of origin, the sacrament of the new creation, the inauguration of eschatological destiny.

The post–Vatican II Roman Catholic Church would quite agree with the stand the nineteenth-century American Reformed theologian, John Nevin, took against revivalism's "anxious bench." The way to prepare for entry into the kingdom of Christ, where water baptism is received in and for faith as Spirit baptism, is by the "system of the catechism."[22] This system, according to Nevin, re-forms human character with steady, persistent teaching of the gospel and its way of life in the context of the church's corporate life. The revivalist "system of New Measures has no affinity whatever with the life of the Reformation," Nevin urged, "as embodied in the Augsburg Confession and the Heidelberg Catechism."[23] Indeed he did not hesitate to speak of "the heresy of New Measures."[24] He attacked the revivals so induced as pretentious hysteria: "Finneyism and Winebrennerism, the anxious bench, revival machinery, solemn tricks for effect, decision displays at the bidding of the preacher, genuflections and prostrations in the aisle or around the altar, noise and disorder, extravagance and rant, mechanical conversions, justification by feeling rather than faith, and encouragement ministered to all fanatical impressions . . . have no connection in fact with true serious religion . . . but tend only to bring them into open discredit."[25] Ethically he charged the engineers of revival with deceit and manipulation, since they "rely far less on the presentation of truth to the understanding than they do upon other influences to bring people forward. Pains are taken rather to raise the imagination, and confound judgment. Exciting appeals are made to the principle of fear," especially preying upon women and the young.[26] All the New Measures amount to nothing but a "mere show of force" unworthy of the gospel.[27] That the New Measures are undertaken in a good cause is no justification: "Quackery in the church is not confined of course to Rome."[28]

Nevin acknowledged that the old forms are "liable to be abused" and neither "ritual" nor "creed" guarantees the "inward life and power of true religion"; but

---

22. *Catholic and Reformed: Selected Theological Writings of John Williamson Nevin,* ed. C. Yrigoyen Jr. and G. H. Bricker (Pittsburgh: Pickwick, 1978). The follow paragraphs on Nevin are adapted from Paul R. Hinlicky, "The Doctrine of the New Birth: From Bullinger to Edwards," *Missio Apostolica* 7, no. 2 (November 1999): 102-99. See the powerful comparison and analysis of Derek R. Nelson, "Charles Finney and John Nevin on Selfhood and Sin: Reformed Anthropologies in Nineteenth-Century American Religion," *Calvin Theological Journal* 45 (2010): 280-305.

23. Nevin, *Catholic and Reformed,* p. 12.

24. Nevin, *Catholic and Reformed,* p. 19.

25. Nevin, *Catholic and Reformed,* p. 30.

26. Nevin, *Catholic and Reformed,* p. 41.

27. Nevin, *Catholic and Reformed,* p. 44.

28. Nevin, *Catholic and Reformed,* p. 46.

the "friends of the new measures . . . discard [these] old forms, only to trust the more blindly in such as are new." With this observation Nevin came to the heart of his position: "They have no faith in ordinary pastoral ministrations . . . no faith in the Catechism."[29] Accordingly Nevin says that the New Measures come as a "strong temptation . . . to ministers. They are endangered of being seduced by the appeals which this system makes to their selfishness and sloth. It offers to their view a 'short method of doing God's great work,' and a sort of 'royal road,' at the same time, to ministerial reputation."[30] Behind the New Measures Nevin sees a profound loss of faith in the Holy Spirit working through the church's ministry to the Word by the catechetical work of formation, the *paideia* of the Spirit and the practice of pastoral ministry. Along these lines, Nevin taunted the "American theology" of Samuel Schmucker and his followers with the not merely rhetorical question, "Why do you call yourselves Lutheran?"[31]

Nevin's critique can be summarized in the following seven sharply formulated theological points. (1) The anxious bench creates for the awakened sinner "a false issue for the conscience," to wit, whether he or she will come forward in the revival on the basis of an "artificial, arbitrary form and [of] ambiguous authority" rather than "inwardly . . . lay down the weapons of his rebellion and cast himself on the mercy of God in Christ Jesus."[32] (2) Emotionalism creates and fosters an anti-intellectualism that ironically casts aspersions on the truth-claims of the gospel itself, thus hindering serious contemplation of the Christian message's claim to truth. (3) The very notion of coming forward at the revival reinforces a false view of man as an autonomous individual who "gets religion" and henceforth "holds it as a property or means for some other end."[33] "A low, shallow, pelagianizing theory of religion runs through [revivalism] from beginning to end. . . . All stress is laid upon the energy of the individual will (the self-will of the flesh) for the accomplishment of the great change in which regeneration is supposed to consist. . . . The heresy lies involved in the system. . . . Religion does not get the sinner, but it is the sinner who 'gets religion.'"[34] (4) The long-term results are actually harmful to the corporate life of the ecclesia in the loss of souls. Convictions and experiences so artificially produced cannot but be resented and disowned when one returns to her senses, with the result that "often disgust and irritation towards the whole subject are the unfortunate consequences."[35] Thus Nevin prophesies the coming of "burnt out districts": the so-called decisions,

29. Nevin, *Catholic and Reformed*, pp. 48-49.

30. Nevin, *Catholic and Reformed*, p. 57.

31. On Schmucker and his program of "American Lutheranism," see David A. Gustafson, *Lutherans in Crisis: The Question of Identity in the American Republic* (Minneapolis: Fortress, 1993).

32. Nevin, *Catholic and Reformed*, pp. 59-60.

33. Nevin, *Catholic and Reformed*, p. 64.

34. Nevin, *Catholic and Reformed*, pp. 98-99; cf. pp. 105-6.

35. Nevin, *Catholic and Reformed*, p. 69.

vows, or pledges of the revival "spring from excitement rather than reflection [and] are to be considered fanatical, and as such neither rational nor free."[36] (5) Revivalism destroys all sense of the holiness and otherness of God, promoting a "vulgarism of feeling in religion that is always injurious to the worship of God, and often shows itself absolutely irreverent and profane . . . the pulpit is transformed, more or less, into a stage. Divine things are so popularized as to be at last shorn of their dignity as well as their mystery. Anecdotes and stories are plentifully retailed, often in low, familiar, flippant style. . . . The preacher feels *himself,* and is bent on making himself felt also by the congregation; but God is not felt in the same proportion."[37] The preacher becomes a religious virtuoso, a celebrity, a personality with a fan club rather than mouthpiece of the crucified and risen Christ. (6) The demagogic indulgence of the lowest feelings to garner popularity for the preacher has terrible social consequences: "Wanting true reverence for God, it will be without true charity also toward men. It is likely to be narrow, intolerant, sinister and rabidly sectarian."[38] The popular revival preacher is dependent on currying favor with the crowd, not free to challenge their prejudices in the name of the gospel. (7) The true nature of sin and sanctification is obscured by revivalism's sole focus on conversion-experience at the expense of the new, lifelong struggle of the redeemed, for "the true theory of religion carries us continually beyond the individual" to consider the corporate humanities of Adam and Christ, so that we understand that "as born of the Spirit . . . salvation begins, and thus it is carried forward till it becomes complete in the resurrection of the great day."[39]

What Nevin offered in place of the New Measures was the "system of the catechism," the classical curriculum organized around the Ten Commandments, the Creed, and the Lord's Prayer, taken respectively as answers to the questions, What does God require of us? What does God do for us? How then shall we live as children of God? Ministers of the Word in this classical model should be "apt to teach"; they should give "sermons full of unction and light; faithful, systematic instruction; zeal for the interests of holiness; pastoral visitation; catechetical training; due attention to order and discipline; patient perseverance in the details of ministerial work; these are the agencies by which alone the kingdom of God may be expected to go steadily forward among any people."[40] In this way the ministry of the Church to the Word mediates Christ to any individual: "individual Christianity is the product, always and entirely, of the Church as existing previously and only revealing its way of life in this way . . . [here] it is altogether natural that children growing up in the bosom of the Church under the faithful

36. Nevin, *Catholic and Reformed,* p. 81.
37. Nevin, *Catholic and Reformed,* pp. 92-93.
38. Nevin, *Catholic and Reformed,* p. 94
39. Nevin, *Catholic and Reformed,* pp. 106, 108.
40. Nevin, *Catholic and Reformed,* p. 101.

application of the means of grace should be quickened into spiritual life in a comparatively quiet way. . . ."[41]

The motives of the Second Vatican Council in restoring the catechumenate — the ancient church's order of instruction and spiritual formation of converts seeking baptism and membership in the church — were not identical to Nevin's motives. If revivalism was parasitic upon Christendom, i.e., precisely a strategy for *reviving* what had become tacit, implicit, dormant in a supposedly Christianized culture, the restoration of the catechumenate is recognition that Christendom is now dead and buried under the smoldering ruins of the Euro-American catastrophes of the twentieth century. This is a tacit recognition of reversion to the status quo ante, of the repaganization of Euro-American culture that has occurred, a "revival" of Greco-Roman imperialism without the veneer any longer of Christian "holiness." The restoration of the catechumenate, in this missiological situation, made clear that while infant baptism can be accepted and even statistically speaking remain the "normal" practice, adult baptism is and ought to be regarded as *normative,* i.e., provide the model of what it means to become of a member of Christ's body. Catholic theology today speaks in this connection of three integrally related sacraments: Baptism, Confirmation, and Eucharist.[42]

The first sacrament pardons sins, rescues from the power of darkness, and brings the dignity of adopted children; it is a new creation through water and the Holy Spirit. Baptism incorporates into Christ and so forms the baptized into God's people. Hence they are called and indeed are the children of God. Baptism is a bond of unity, linking together all who have been signed by it. Thus work for the church's visible unity flows directly out of baptism. The baptized are made the children of God by being joined to Christ's death, burial, and resurrection. As superior to the purifications of the Law, the bath of baptism produces these effects by the power of the mystery of the Lord's passion and resurrection. Those who are baptized are united to Christ in a death like His; buried with Him in death, they are given life again with Him and with Him they rise again. For baptism recalls and makes present the paschal mystery itself, as in baptism we pass from the death of sin into life with God. We receive the Spirit of filial adoption.

By signing us with the gift of the Spirit, the next sacrament, confirmation, makes us more completely the image of the Lord and fills us with the Holy Spirit, so that we may bear witness to Him before all the world and work to bring the Body of Christ to its fullness as soon as possible. Consequently we come to the table of the Eucharist, that is, to the third sacrament. We eat the flesh and drink the blood of the Son of Man so that we may have eternal life and show forth the unity of God's people. By offering ourselves with Christ, we share in the univer-

---

41. Nevin, *Catholic and Reformed,* p. 111.
42. *Rite of Christian Initiation for Adults* (Chicago: Liturgy Training Publications, 1988).

sal sacrifice, that is, in the entire community of the redeemed offered to God by their High Priest. In this sacrifice of ourselves in Christ to the Father we pray for a greater outpouring of the Holy Spirit, so that the whole human race will be brought into this unity of God's family.[43]

With this theology of the integral sacramental life laid out, the new, post–Vatican II Rite of Christian Initiation for Adults envisions a three-step process in the conversion of adults by the catechetical method. The first step is initial conversion. Wishing to become a Christian, one is accepted as a catechumen by the church. After having progressed in faith and nearly completed the catechetical instruction, a second step follows: one is "elected" by the church and accepted into a more intense, final preparation for the sacrament of initiation. The third step is actually receiving the sacraments of Christian initiation with admission to the Eucharist.[44] A few words of commentary about each step are in order.

"The Period of Evangelization and Precatechumenate" is a time for hearing the living God proclaimed and Jesus Christ whom He has sent for the salvation of all. Thus those who are not yet Christians, their hearts opened by the Holy Spirit, may begin to believe and be freely converted to the Lord and commit themselves sincerely to Him. Acceptance into "The Order of Catechumens" presupposes such beginnings of spiritual life and that the fundamentals of Christian teaching have taken root in the candidate. Thus there must be evidence in the sense of personal testimony and pastoral examination of an initial conversion and corresponding intention to change life and to enter into a relationship with God in Christ. During the catechumenate suitable catechesis is provided by priests or deacons. This catechesis leads the catechumens not only to an appropriate acquaintance with doctrine and moral precept but also to a profound sense of the mystery of salvation in which they desire to participate. Thus formed by theological and moral teaching, the catechumens set out on a spiritual journey. Already sharing through faith in the mystery of Christ's death and resurrection, they pass from the old to a new nature made perfect in Christ. A progressive change in outlook and conduct should become manifest as it develops gradually during the period of the catechumenate.

Upon completion of this period of instruction, Election, or Enrollment of Names, completes the period of the catechumenate proper. In this act of election, the church judges the candidate's state of readiness and decides on advancement toward the sacraments of initiation. Thus the church makes its "elections," that is, its choice to admit those catechumens who have the dispositions that make them fit to take part, at the next major celebration, in the sacraments of initiation. The time of Purification and Enlightenment, with which the rite of election begins, customarily coincides with Lent. In the liturgy and liturgical catechesis of Lent, preparation for reception of baptism, as well as the theme of repentance, renews

---

43. *Rite of Christian Initiation,* p. xiv.
44. *Rite of Christian Initiation,* p. 3.

the entire community preparing to celebrate the paschal mystery by the baptism of the new sisters and brothers. This period is intended as well to enlighten the minds and strengthen the hearts of the elected with a deeper knowledge of Christ the Savior. At the conclusion of Lent, on Holy Saturday at the Easter Vigil, the Celebration of the Sacraments of Initiation takes place, thus dramatically signifying death and resurrection with Christ. This has as its center and high point the baptismal washing in invocation of the Holy Trinity.

This carefully thought out rite precludes the false understanding that the sacraments work automatically or mechanically: adults are not "saved" except as they come forward with the free desire to accept in faith God's gift through their own profession of belief that is one with the prophetic and apostolic belief of the universal Christian community. The faith of those prepared for baptism is not simply the doctrine of the church to which they impersonally or implicitly submit, but it is knowingly learned and personally appropriated. Therefore the renunciation of sin and the profession of faith form an apt prelude to baptism. The questions are posed: "Do you reject sin so as to live in the freedom of God's children? Do you reject the glamour of evil, and refuse to be mastered by sin? Do you reject Satan, father of sin and prince of darkness?" The affirmation of the triune God in the three articles of the Creed follows. There still follows a season of Postbaptismal Catechesis or mystagogy during the Easter Season. The distinctive spirit and power of this catechesis or mystagogy derive from the new, personal experience of the Eucharist to which the baptized are now admitted, just as the community in this way actively incorporates the newly baptized into its Eucharistic way of life.

There are many profound reasons why all Christians, who are in truth personally bound to one another by their baptismal bond with Jesus Christ, should especially now, after Christendom, repent of separatism and with all their hearts and minds work for the visible unity of the church in a new formation along the lines of Nevin or the Roman Catholic Rite of Adult Initiation. This would be a kind of *evangelical catholicism* waiting to be born from "the ruins of the church" (Reno). As noted above, many contemporary evangelicals are catching up with Nevin's warnings about the dangers of the individualistic and sectarian tendencies latent in theologies that systematically dualize God's actions in Word and Spirit, separating the new birth from the gospel ceremony of water baptism, the sign from the thing signified — all the while trading tacitly upon a Christendom that they would "revive." Likewise, one can see that the restoration of the catechumenate concedes considerable truth to the evangelical, more precisely, Baptist, argument: while infant baptism may be "valid," the model of adult conversion is *normative* for our understanding of what is involved in "new birth."

As we draw to a conclusion here, it is useful here to recall one of the first doctrinal dialogues that took place in the post–Vatican II ecumenical opening of the Roman Catholic Church, side by side with its restoration of the Catechumenate. In their second U.S. encounter, *One Baptism for the Remission of Sins*

(1966),[45] Lutheran and Roman Catholic theologians made rapid progress on the relatively noncontroversial teachings between the two traditions about baptism as a divine action of salvation from which infants cannot arbitrarily be excluded. The agreement in the Pauline teaching of "one baptism" exposed a foundational unity between Lutherans and Roman Catholics. Both reject any kind of serious dualism between the sacramental baptism with water and a spiritual baptism signifying some other invisible or interior event. Lutherans and Roman Catholics think of sacramental baptism as the one baptismal work of the Spirit which has significance for all of life. For all the historic enmity between the two churches, they have always recognized each other's baptisms as valid. Trent even anathematized those who deny the validity of the "heretic's" baptisms. Insofar as baptism is nothing other than admission to the church, however, mutual recognition of baptism was always implicitly mutual recognition of one another as Christian communities. The deep incoherence of officially anathematizing but de facto recognizing each other was thus penitently acknowledged. Building upon the radical implication of the mutual acknowledgment of baptism (and the discovery from the previous dialogue of how "much in common [is] their attitude toward christological dogma," as we shall see in the next two chapters), the occasion was given in this dialogue to reflect self-critically on failures in their respective traditions. For baptism becomes effective as truth and reconciliation.

Warren Quanbeck, speaking for Lutherans, criticized the Lutheran tendency to reduce the essential content of baptism to forgiveness of sins for the individual, overlooking its wider "eschatological and ecclesiological significance" as "union with Christ in his death and resurrection" and imparting "the gift of the Holy Spirit."[46] Acknowledging that the Council of Trent had condemned a caricature of Luther's actual teachings on baptism,[47] Godfrey Diekman ironically discovered a parallel error in post-Tridentine Roman Catholicism to what Quanbeck saw in Lutheranism, i.e., a "failure to situate all these doctrines [about baptism, penance, etc.] positively in their fuller context, namely Christ and his redemptive mysteries now operative in the church." As a result, Diekman wrote, the decision of the Council of Trent "permitted if it did not actually encourage a spiritual pragmatism, concerned predominantly with the sacraments as channels of grace profiting the individual. It was not until the liturgical movement of our own century, supported in recent years by the biblical revival, that the ecclesial dimension of the sacraments has been, as it were, rediscovered . . . and that their nature as a personal faith encounter with Christ within the ecclesial community is again being stressed."[48] Diekman went on especially to lift up the Second Vati-

---

45. *Lutherans and Catholics in Dialogue I-III* [hereafter *LCD*], ed. Paul C. Empie and T. Austin Murphy (Minneapolis: Augsburg, n.d.).

46. *LCD* II, p. 72.

47. *LCD* II, pp. 64-65.

48. *LCD* II, p. 65.

can Council's *Constitution on the Sacred Liturgy* as a source of "reform" that "can promote union among all who believe in Christ." Here it becomes absolutely clear that for Roman Catholicism today "the source and continuing root of sacramental efficacy are 'the Paschal Mysteries,'" centered "in Christ the High Priest." This focus on Christ in turn "underscores the role of faith."[49] But, as we have argued, it is the Holy Spirit who focuses the theological subject on Christ, beginning with baptism into Christ as abiding in Christ to the Parousia of Christ at the eschaton of judgment. Who the Spirit is for us in this way turns on who the Spirit is for God; understanding who the Spirit is for God clarifies the works of the Spirit as one work of unifying the sign and the thing signified, paradigmatically as the good pleasure of the Father that rests upon the Son incarnate.

In sum, then, the sign of water is not mere washing but death to death by drowning the old Adam in a watery tomb, there to be joined to Jesus Christ in His death for one and for all, to rise with Him into His new life in the Spirit. The Spirit intends and puts into effect this union in water baptism as inauguration of the reign of God and initiation into the ecclesia of the Beloved Community. Since baptism is this inauguration and initiation into the apocalyptic warfare of the Spirit against the flesh, its administration requires discernment of the spirits by a holistic catechetical formation. This discernment and discipline in turn entail a magisterium, that is, a teaching office among those baptized who have been especially set aside to minister *to* the Word and sacraments in support of the priesthood of all the baptized, who minister *from* the Word and the sacraments to the suffering creation. A teaching office that does not quench the Spirit, or conscript the Spirit to serve ecclesiastical partisanships, but rather knows and follows the Spirit, depends on a much clearer doctrine of the Spirit than has obtained in Western Christianity for a millennium. Hence we now turn to the doctrine of the Holy Spirit.

## The Way to Ecumenical Convergence on the Spirit[50]

If the foregoing holds, the church has no other existence than as the mission of the Spirit, sent by the Father of the Son to *cause* the Son's redemption to come into effect in the world by causing a *division* within it. Its causal agency in the Spirit is to unite persons with Christ's death and resurrection as sign to the world of the coming Beloved Community and against the loveless individualisms and collectivities of the structures of malice and injustice. Pending the eschaton of judgment, that entails a carefully articulated *disunion* with the world. Such new

49. *LCD* II, p. 69.
50. The next two paragraphs are drawn from Paul R. Hinlicky, "The Spirit of Christ amid the Spirits of the Post-Modern World: The Crumley Lecture," *Lutheran Quarterly* 14, no. 4 (Winter 2000): 433-48.

agency requires a critical stance, one skeptical of the undifferentiated embrace of all conceivable spiritualities that no longer distinguishes between God and Caesar, Creator and creation, sin and righteousness, or law and gospel because it no longer thinks theologically at all, that is, to convict concerning sin, righteousness, and judgment. Thinking theologically, however, is one fundamental manifestation of life in the Spirit among intelligent creatures, who are critically to test the spirits to see whether they are of God (1 John 4:1). Judgment begins in the household of God. Critical dogmatics will require of all today a painfully self-critical look at accustomed ways we have of thinking of, that is to say, domesticating the Spirit in the service of our sectarianisms. Our many, divergent denominational theologies of the Spirit actually conspire individually and collectively to quench the Spirit.

If the sacraments are not taken as magical rites that automatically dispense grace as some kind of impersonal medicine, but are understood simply as mandated ritual forms (chiefly Baptism and the Lord's Supper) of the gospel itself, then it is both true that the Spirit works through sacraments and that the Spirit remains sovereign in His own work, the Lord who works faith through these means "where and when it pleases God."[51] Just so, the associated questions stemming from five hundred years of Protestant division and multiplication may be swiftly and drastically resolved. The Spirit works through the external word and sacraments, but not as its bound and indentured servant, for the Spirit is the free and sovereign Lord. Baptizing with water, with new birth, with fire, with angelic utterance, and heaven knows with whatever else — the point of any and all baptism consists in dying and rising with Christ to engender and sustain Christ-formed faith. *This* baptism into Jesus' death *is* the life-giving work of the Spirit of the resurrection. "Sanctification" beginning ever with the faith that receives this baptism is the *life* that ever arises from such death into the resurrection life of *Jesus,* so that it is *His* faith that is active in the love and hope of the baptized in the world. In this way, Jesus is and remains in all of Christian life and to the hour of death faith's *only* righteousness, also of the second type of righteousness that is biographically our own personal histories as the faith of Jesus becomes operative in the world as my love and my hope. All the artificial "orders of salvation," all the *competing* psychologizing schemes laying out how calling, justification, regeneration, and sanctification follow one another, must then simply *collapse* into irrelevance once the Spirit's personal and divine reality in presenting Christ for us and in us is grasped as incorporation into the ecclesia in mission to the nations. If Word and Spirit are distinct in person yet inseparable by cooperation, there is no gap between them to be filled with psychology. There is no place in their operation left open to be filled in by our self-invented religious ingenuity looking for a pretext to organize yet another new sect and/or spirituality. *All* of

---

51. Augsburg Confession, V: "Nam per verbum *et sacramenta tamquam per instrumenta donatur spiritus sanctus, qui fidem efficit,* ubi et quando visum est Deo. . . ."

Christian existence in the Spirit is in *every* respect the very same dying to Adam and rising with the New Adam into His body. In this way every believer joined with all others becomes "the righteousness of God" (2 Cor. 5:21), since holiness does not lie in attaining an individual perfection apart from others but in becoming a vital member of the Risen Lord's earthly body, in the world but not of the world, against the world for the sake of the world, the militant advocacy in the Spirit of the coming Beloved Community of God. For the Holy Spirit is the One who convinces the world concerning sin, and righteousness, and judgment.

Recall as well all the chief controversial questions from Christian history: Does the Spirit come from the Father only or from the Father and the Son? On one level, this dispute can be rapidly resolved in the light of the foregoing. The Greek fathers were thinking of the eternal Trinity when they said that the Spirit proceeds from the Father only, for otherwise, if the Son is added to the Father as some kind of immanent collaborator in the Spirit's eternal origin, one posits a double source of origin in God and that would be polytheism: two originators. Of course, this argument reflects their strong Trinitarian personalism that excludes even tacitly taking the divine nature or substance as a fourth and more basic reality. In other words, only the persons really exist and only one of them can be the personal origin in the life of God, assuming Trinitarians wish to be monotheists, not bitheists or tritheists. And the one source is the Father of the Son and Breather of the Spirit. The Latin church fathers were thinking of the Spirit's mission in human history, where it matters immensely that the divine Spirit really is and thus may be recognized as the Spirit of Jesus, the Son of the Father. Miscommunication based on these contrary presuppositions at length engendered the great schism of the Eastern and Western churches, finalized in 1054. But today we can see that these two interests are readily reconciled. One can but slightly alter the Latin *filioque* clause, "who proceeds from the Father *and* the Son," to the words "who proceeds from the Father *of* the Son" or "who proceeds from the Father *and rests upon* the Son." Such an amendment would make clear that in eternity the Father alone is the source both of the Son and of the Spirit. At the same time it identifies the Spirit who appears in history as the Spirit of that God who is eternally the Father of Jesus Christ, His only Son, the incarnate Word. But that appearance in history nonetheless seems contingent and to many implies tritheism.

## Tritheism?

Recalling the previous discussion in Chapter Three of the resurrection narratives in the Gospel of John, we may well wonder whether contemporary theology can get past the useless argument whether and how the primal Christian kerygma of the resurrection of the Crucified is "true" — that is, "true" according to the variety of truth conditions assumed or asserted under Cartesian-Kantian subjectivity —

and learn again to ask for the truth of the resurrection theologically. This quest would not be Bultmann's demythologization, which reduced the biblical narrative to alleged states of human self-understanding, but a deliteralization that interprets biblical narrative as knowledge of God. In that case, the truth of the resurrection of Jesus as the Christ, the Son of God by the Holy Spirit, does not consist in the first place on how the reference to the corpse of Jesus is to be taken in the report of the empty tomb and the appearances of the living One who was recognized by followers as the same person. Rather the truth of the resurrection refers in the first place to what it means for God as Father to have recognized in the corpse of His beloved Son His own love for His own world that hates Him.

Yet there is another obstacle to this kind of theological inquiry in critical dogmatics that does not arise out of the titanism of the modern epistemological project. In fact it is as old as Christian theology itself. When we ask for the truth of the resurrection in the biblical sense of God's faithful correspondence to His own word of promise, we are immediately delivered by the gospel narrative into an unnerving reflection that totters on the brink of tritheism: the theological truth of the resurrection purports to be the unification of the sign, the Crucified King of the Jews,[52] with the thing signified, the eternal Son of God (cf. Rom. 1:3-4), not only for those who believe but indeed first of all also for God, whose own deity, that is, whose own unity had been jeopardized by the Son's taking on the likeness of sinful flesh. Pannenberg sums up a certain consensus of the chief postwar Lutheran systematic theologians: "As the resurrection of Jesus was seen as a divine confirmation of the claim implied in his earthly ministry, Jesus in the light of Easter had to appear as the Son of the Father whom he proclaimed. . . . By his resurrection from the dead, says Rom. 1:3-4, Jesus was instituted [by the Spirit] into the dignity of divine sonship."

It is clear enough from this that for us it will be the Spirit of the resurrection who unifies the sign with the thing signified, where and when we come to faith in Jesus as the Christ, the Son of God. The Apostle makes the unification of the Christological unification with believers explicit: "If the Spirit of him who raised Jesus from the dead dwells in you, he who raised Christ from the dead will give life to your mortal bodies also through his Spirit that dwells in you" (Rom. 8:11). Käsemann aptly comments: "For us the Spirit is obviously regarded as the true resurrection force. . . . For us he is the pledge that we shall be made like the resurrected Christ (Asmussen) — and this in new corporeality as the sign of creation which is no longer subject to assault."[53] This consensus in fact goes back to Luther, as Regin Prenter has shown. "In connection with Romans 1:1-4, Luther

52. For the historical argument in support of this theological claim, see Nils Alstrup Dahl, *Jesus the Christ: The Historical Origins of Christological Doctrine,* ed. Donald H. Juel (Minneapolis: Fortress, 1991).

53. Ernst Käsemann, *Commentary on Romans,* trans. and ed. G. Bromiley (Grand Rapids: Eerdmans, 1980), p. 225.

often points out that work of the Holy Spirit is to proclaim the divinity of Jesus Christ in the resurrection. By the incarnation the Son of God humbled himself and assumed the *forma servi*. He became *humiliatus* so that his divinity was emptied out and hidden in the flesh . . . the public proclamation of the divinity and power of Christ is done *per spiritum sanctificationis,* which was not given before the resurrection of Jesus. . . ."[54] Or again: "By the work of the Holy Spirit the resurrection is really taken from the hidden sphere of God into the message of the gospel, so that the risen Christ lives his risen life in our midst in this message . . . the center in the Word of God is the risen Christ himself . . . the outward Word does not become the Word of God until the Spirit causes the risen Christ to live his life in that Word. . . ."[55] Thus the appearance of the Spirit, as also the divinity of the Son, seem to be contingencies.

But, as Pannenberg continues, "the Son of God was also at the side of God from all eternity. The idea of preexistence does not contradict the fact that his divine sonship will be revealed only eschatologically or that it is already manifest in a historical event, which like the resurrection of Jesus, anticipates the eschatological consummation. . . . Only thus can we understand why the idea of preexistence appeared so early in primitive Christianity."[56] This unification is for us by way of the Spirit's baptismal conformation to Jesus Christ, crucified and risen; but it is this for us only if it is also and indeed primarily an event for God, namely, the event of reconciliation between the Father who abandoned into the hands of sinners and the Son of the Garden of Gethsemane who surrendered. To all appearances these parted ways in life-threatening separation at Golgotha. Yet this unification of the Father and the departed Son by the Spirit at the resurrection in turn presupposes some "preexistent" non-contingent relation of unity in the Spirit, one that can be both jeopardized and yet surprisingly enriched by the Son's taking on the likeness of sinful humanity. This surprising enrichment comes about, if the divine wrath of love against the lovelessness of the human creature that ruins creation, and the mercy love for the human creature made unlovely by sinful lovelessness, are and so can be reconciled in the self-communicating love of the Spirit who unites cross and resurrection into the triune act of reconciliation.

In this case, unification entails a preceding differentiation, if not disjunction. Just the same, it also presupposes at least the immanent possibility of a profounder preexisting unity, namely, of a communion in being that is divinely capable of incorporating disjunction in a self-surpassing act, just so expressing the true deity

54. Regin Prenter, *Spiritus Creator,* trans. John M. Jensen (Philadelphia: Muhlenberg Press, 1953), p. 111.

55. Prenter, *Spiritus Creator,* p. 112. "If the presence of Christ in the Word shall be nothing else than the presence of his image or the presence of a correct doctrine about him, then there naturally will be no space for a sovereign Spirit and his free work. In that case the Spirit becomes a synonym for warm feelings or superfluous accompaniment to the natural influence which comes from the figure of Jesus or the correct doctrine about him" (p. 125).

56. Pannenberg, *ST* 1, pp. 264-65.

of God as infinite Giver even for the weak and ungodly (Rom. 5:6). Just this latter would be affirmed by the truth-claim that "God" is the one who is self-determined to create, redeem, and fulfill the world. This truth-claim indicates a specific difference in being between Creator and creature, a "natural" difference that is preserved in all unifications, between Giver and gifted. In Christian theology the ontological description of the Giver's "nature" would come by way of understanding the immanent possibility of the self-surpassing reconciliation given and revealed in the resurrection of the Crucified, an "immanental induction,"[57] as it were, of the eternal Life of the Three as the final "mystery of the world" (Jüngel). It would come to this conception of the immanent, co-equal, and eternal Trinity as its last thought in order to stop there in wonder, prayer, and praise.

Be that as it may, the gospel narrative itself brings us to the brink of tritheism — the specter of "polytheism" that strong Trinitarian personalism always seems to evoke. For it would seem that the Father abandoned the Son to ignominious death. It would seem that the Son died in despair. It would seem that this mutual alienation is the end of the story. Without the Spirit, what other conclusion can the "natural man" draw? If otherwise, however, an intercession is needed and has been in fact supplied to break this lethal and apparently final impasse. So the Easter kerygma must be thought theologically. The Spirit sent from the Father led the Son to this strange and awesome strife. Here the holy love of God in the person of the Father judged sin in the flesh of Jesus who assumed it as His own by virtue of the forgiveness He pronounced in God's own name. The same Holy Spirit of the Father, resting on the Son though dead and buried, now completes the sending with returning. He presents the Crucified to the Father as the true and sufficient sign on the earth, in the world of creatures, of His own love for the sinners in whom and for whom the Son perished, the true and indeed eternal judgment against malice and injustice notwithstanding. And the Father receives Spirit-risen Jesus as heir to His own throne, declaring the sign sealed in the Spirit, "This is my beloved Son. Listen to Him!" (Mark 9:7). Now the love that personally sent, and the love that personally went, unite anew in the love that personally returns the Son to the Father and the Father to the Son. Our reconciliation is first of all thus reconciliation in the life of the Three.

Love returns, just so, with this enormous and consequential difference not only for us but also for the life of God: the Spirit is now bringing with the Son those that had been lost to love whom the Son has claimed and made His own. If, theologically, on Easter morn the Father beheld the Son truly dead and dead truly on account of his solidarity in love with the sinful and dying, and the Son was consequently exalted from this true death by the Father's vindication of this love as right in His sight, powerfully confirming that the Son's love for the enemy is also His own, it has been the Spirit who once again has freed the Father and the Son for one another by His active intercession. The intra-divine event that tran-

57. *RPTD,* pp. 209-11.

spires because of the enormous incongruity that occurs in the divine assumption of sinful flesh in the person of the Son is figured for us as the resurrection of Jesus from the dead, a figure that is theologically decoded as the revelation of Jesus' true and singular divine Sonship, hence of His true and divine self-donation for us in the supreme obedience of the cross.

Two theological implications are noteworthy. First, on the grounds of loving compassion divine unity must be capable of voluntarily undertaking suffering physical and spiritual, body and soul, of the sinful and perishing creature. However interpreted theologically, the statement of the self-revealing LORD from the burning bush to Moses in Exodus 3:7-8 is axiomatic: "I have heard the cry of my people. . . . Indeed I know their sufferings and I have come down to deliver them. . . ." It is a categorical rejoinder to all theologies — for notable instance those of Epicurus and Aristotle — that make the apathy of narcissism the signature of true deity. Second, divine unity so understood is personal, not natural, or better, it is the living unity of the "being in communion" of persons that reconceives the category of the natural as such. If God's being is in eternal Trinitarian becoming, the conception of God's "nature" is dislodged from the classical metaphysical quest for an underlying stasis or continuity at the origin of things to the discovery of faithful being in the dynamism of becoming that presses on to a promised end. What God is and how God is what God is are then functions of the life together of the Three. A doctrine of the divine perfections as the freedom to love wisely will result, as we shall see in Chapter Eight of this system of theology. This ontological claim about divine "nature" is what the doctrine of the Trinity asserts, when thought through consequently by staying faithful to the gospel narrative that elicits it and whose understanding it serves strictly to clarify. *Esse Deum dare:* divine nature is divine in self-surpassing love, the Father's giving of the Son in the ecstasy of the Spirit. He becomes our Father too by unification with the Son by the same ecstasy of the Spirit that is faith taking us out of ourselves and enveloping us in this life of the Three.[58] Divine "being in communion" is thus understood as the fitting origin and goal of the creation, revealed in the middle of things by the resurrection of Jesus Christ from the dead.

The appearance of tritheism here is unavoidable, then, but it only so appears to the sight of the common body that has not yet been transfigured in the Spirit (Mark 9:2-3). It necessarily appears as a real disjunction — not merely the abstract riddle of three personal agencies in the one deity — but as a real disharmony, signed by the erstwhile Beloved Son's cry of dereliction (Mark 15:34) that is the rendering of the veil that separates the Holy of Holies from the sinful world (Mark 15:38), the thing signified. For the Son has in faith in His own Beloved Sonship obeyed as true Servant of the Lord (Isaiah 53), undertaking the sinfulness of the world: every caravel carrying slaves, every transport shipping Jews, every death march, every rape, every incineration of cities whether by napalm or by nuclear

---

58. Jenson, *ST* 1, p. 122.

devices, every bullying of the weak, every molestation of a child, every lying politician, every Wall Street thief, every bigoted, benighted, corrupt preacher trading in the religion business *ad infinitum ad nauseum*. This sinfulness the Son of God has taken into the divine life itself, swallowing the poison. In the eternal moment that is hell, this poison the Father vomited out as the poison that it is, albeit wrapped together with the Beloved Son. The disjunction here is real, as real as the Incarnation, and so it appears: "Then Jesus died screaming" (Mark 15:37, my translation).

A brief digression: if we let this text stand without flinching, we may accordingly de-Platonize and re-Messianize Christian theology.[59] That begins with the affirmation of God's creative immanence in all things, even though that must appear as an impersonal chaos to us. "For it is God who creates, effects, and preserves all things through his almighty power. . . . For he dispatches no officials or angels when he creates and preserves something, but all this is the work of the divine power itself. If he is to create and preserve it, however, he must be present . . ." (Luther)[60] — also, then, in evils of natural-historical experience (Matt. 5:45). So Jesus experienced His death as abandonment by the One whom He, the Beloved Son, had known as Father. In a world where becoming is the constant and being is the appearance, that is, in a genuine creation, *esse est percipio*. Epistemological quests for foundations of knowledge are vain but not innocent attempts to transcend the flux; they are titanic attempts of the *sicut Deus eritis*, to know as the Creator knows above the flux as its origin and mover rather than under God in solidarity with the flux. Perspectivalism, by contrast, puts creatures back on the earth again, where the epistemic issue is access, not foundation. Perspectivalism holds, then, that knowledge is what appears to be in any finite perspective; that no one transcends this embodied state of the soul where knowledge changes with perception; that the Platonic attempt to transcend, the quintessence of Cartesian-Kantian subjectivity, kills bodies for the sake of an illusionary, disembodied soul. Science here is the gain of better perspective by collaborative and methodical acquisition of broader scope that is thus able to account more comprehensively for greater phenomena with progressively simpler explanations. When we parse things this way, we discover that the alleged conflict between science and religion[61] is a conflict between a specific — Platonic — rationality and specific — theistic or deistic — theologies, howsoever dominant such rationalities have been, especially in the modern period. Just so, however, a valid change in perspective — one that works successfully to negotiate the flux — is a change in being itself, a true becoming, even a new creation.

59. *RPTD*, pp. 144-47.

60. *LW* 37, p. 58.

61. John Hedley Brooke, *Science and Religion: Some Historical Perspective* (Cambridge: Cambridge University Press, 1993), p. 275. David C. Lindberg, *The Beginnings of Western Science: The European Scientific Tradition in Philosophical, Religious, and Institutional Context, Prehistory to A.D. 1450,* 2nd edition (Chicago and London: University of Chicago Press, 2007).

In this light, the resurrection of the Crucified purports to signify a universal fulfillment latent in the becoming that is otherwise perceived as aimless drift or organized in bad faith into a static cosmos theistically or deistically grounded in a timeless deity. Just this perception of the sign, the Crucified as risen and His faith as vindicated, is the work of the Spirit, disclosing, sharing, and putting into effect the Father's now settled view of His Son. So effected, such a person is "raised by the Word so that he may perceive in the Spirit how Christ, precisely through his suffering and death has attained true life and glory. And whoever does this properly, whoever is able to do this, is a new creation in Christ, endowed with new spiritual knowledge."[62] The appearance of tritheism — of deity with multiple personality disorder, as it were — is valid as the perception of *unbelief.* The understanding of the unity of the Trinity is the "new spiritual knowledge" of God *in faith.*

Returning now to the matter at hand, namely, the disjunction that comes upon the divine Life by virtue of the Son's taking on the likeness of sinful flesh. This disjunction is *not* to be conceived as immanent to the divine life of the Trinity, which is eternally light and blessedness of being in communion of love. The Lamb who was slain before the foundation of the world, the *Logos incarnandus,* the preexistent Logos "intending to become flesh," is to be thought with the divine decision and self-determination to redeem and fulfill a creation. But this very decision and self-determination are not necessary to the divine Life, which, precisely as community of being in love, has no need of a world other than itself; which therefore rather gives a world out of surplus, and indeed, at cost to itself. If incarnation and cross were immanent, there could be no true and salutary Incarnation, but only the symbolic representation of a universal process of negative dialectics, as in Hegelian theology, where symbols are finally replaced by philosophical comprehension of the necessity of contingency, including the contingency of human minds coming to understand the necessity of it all: a bleak nihilism.

But the dialectic of the Word and the Spirit in Christian theology is a "positive dialectic" that does not arise out of lack, but out of surplus. The Word gives "Christ crucified" as a rhetorical, not logical contradiction; as metaphor that generates a new meaning in the world, i.e., the reference in Mark 10:45 to the Messiah who comes not to be served but to serve by laying down His life for others as a liberating ransom, where and when the Spirit enlightens. This is not simile that enlightens a lesser-known thing by comparison with a better-known thing, as if to say the crucified of the world are really Messiah, or Messiah is really a loser in the world. That would be purely natural reasoning, not the Spirit's. It is the Spirit who makes the letter spirit, and apart from whom the letter is a dead letter (2 Cor. 3:6), just as the letter of the Cross is a ministry of condemnation, but the ministry of the Resurrection of the One crucified for us is a ministry of justification (2 Cor. 3:9). The positive dialectics of speaking the letter in the Spirit to the situation here and

---

62. *LW* 37, p. 202.

now is the art of ministry. For the term "Christ" indicates God's merciful gift of justice, just as the term "cross" indicates the critical demand for justice, so that the paradoxical combination, "Christ crucified," spawns a dialectic (a reasoning that proceeds *sic et non*) of judgment and justification, of critique and reconciliation, of division and new unity until the *krisis* of the world is settled at the eschaton of judgment. We re-messianize Christian theology — the Messiah is the Anointed One on whom the Spirit comes and remains (John 1:32) — when we learn this art of the Spirit who convicts the world concerning sin and righteousness and judgment to afflict the comfortable and comfort the afflicted.

So the Lamb slain before the foundation of the world is already the movement of this immanent divine life outward, into the economy, in the free decision to create a world of creatures in order to redeem and fulfill it that in the fullness of time would cost the Father the death of the Beloved Son and the Son the loss of the Father's favor when hell itself came between them. Yet this happened by their own initiative; it did not happen to them. It happened on account of the conflict that comes to divine love for "real, not imaginary sinners" (Luther, cf. Hosea 11, and the discussion, especially of Brueggemann, in Chapter Eight). This disjunction happened and must have happened with a true Incarnation into our world, such that One of the Three truly suffered and died, groaning together with us under the structures of malice and injustice to which one and all we personally yield, though He did not and did not precisely for the sake of redeeming us who do. This disjunction in the divine life is the necessity for us of Christ crucified; it is the necessity Jesus knew when He knew that He "*must* go up to Jerusalem" to be rejected; it is the necessity of consequence, given God's love for creatures such as ourselves. Thus the disjunction in God's own life happens once and for all, not then in order to remain in this state of rupture but in order to own it once and for all and just so to *surpass* it.

God communicates God by the personal life and work of the Holy Spirit, who in eternity breathes the favor of the Father upon the Son and sings back the glory of the Son to the Father. So also in time the Spirit recalls the favor of the Father upon the Son who had glorified the Father by truly dying in solidarity of love with the enemies of God's reign of righteousness, life, and peace. So also in time the Spirit opens the Father's heart in welcome to the returning Son in company of His newly won people, now in the right by the righteousness of that loving deed of the Son for them. So also on the earth this reconciliation is a matter of truth concerning sin, righteousness, and judgment. Just this is the ministry of the Holy Spirit for us.

The appearance of tritheism resolves into a new understanding of the "nature" of divine unity with the emergence of a consistent doctrine of *perichoresis,* i.e., of the Johannine "mutual indwelling" of the Three such that none of the Three can be the one that personally it is except in relation to the others, where this relation is one of other-regarding love. Thus the Three dwell in one another in love as the eternal Beloved Community. This doctrine of consistent perichoresis may be connected with Augustine's flash of insight into the Spirit as the *vinculum caritatis,* the chain of love, insofar as it makes the Spirit the personal agent of perichoretic love between the Father and the Son.[63] This is to say, Augustine's exegetical insight here is to be appreciated but sharply distinguished from the tendency in his thought to reduce the Spirit to the erotic relationship he saw binding the Father and the Son in "natural" divine charity.[64] The Spirit is rather to be taken as the active agent of love who personally unifies the image with the prototype, the sign with the thing signified.

Then just as the origin of the persons is the Father who begets and breathes the Son and the Spirit, the personal indivisibility of these Three distinct by way of origin is the eternal act of the Spirit, showering the Father's love on the Son and returning the Beloved Son to the Father in love, as active anticipation of God's ever-new future. In this respect, the Father is Alpha and the Spirit is Omega in God, as Jenson has argued in trying to think God's eternal being as time-like, as "infinite temporal duration."[65] By this he intends to give a different — personal, not natural — account of divine "simplicity" as the ever-achieved indivisibility of the Three by the complexities of mutual fidelity rather than by the timeless self-identity of the metaphysical One of the Platonists. Jenson argues that such an account derives from strictly theological reflection on revelation, not metaphysical speculation on perfection in being. We defer discussion of this difficult problematic to the conclusion of this system of theology, adopting Jenson's position as a working hypothesis on the way there, as we shall discuss from time to time in what follows. The hypothesis asserts that if divine indivisibility is based on the eternal now of perfection in being, Trinitarian theology will be destabilized in the oscillation that in fact characterizes Western theology in its "modalistic tendency" (Gunton, see below): between a binitarianism that depersonalizes the Spirit into the mere force field or erotic attraction of the Father and the Son on the one side and a quaternity that makes the divine and impersonal substance God absolutely and the three persons God relatively. But let us look and see in the matrix of the Scriptures.

## The Paraclete of John 17

The Farewell Discourse in John 13–17 serves to clarify all this because it is the source of all this in early Christian theological *Nachdenken.* Commenting on the culminating words of John 17:26, C. H. Dodd wrote, "That which is from all eternity is the unity of the Father and Son, in a 'mutual knowledge,' an 'indwelling,' of which the real character is *agape.* This is the ultimate mystery of the Godhead

---

63. Jenson, *ST* 1, pp. 146-49.

64. Colin Gunton, "Augustine, the Trinity and the Theological Crisis of the West," *Scottish Journal of Theology* 43, no. 1 (February 1990): 52.

65. Jenson, *ST* 2, pp. 29-35.

which Jesus revealed to the world. . . . The human career of Jesus is, as it were, a projection of this eternal relation (which is the divine agape) upon the field of time."[66] Augustine's Trinitarian synthesis was to identify this relation of love between the Father and the Son, arising out of close reading of the Johannine Farewell Discourse, with the Spirit. The Spirit, he reasoned, is the relation of love that binds together the Father and the Son eternally, just as also in time the Spirit binds believers together in love to the Son and through the Son to the Father and to one another. And surely this is right, provided only that we do not in the process reduce the Spirit to the relationships that He works, as if a kind of impersonal eros. Rather, we are to treat Him, like the Father and the Son, as a concrete person who relates, whose work is relating in love rather than in the many other ways in which persons can be related. Indeed, love is against what is against love. And this observation serves to bring out the other side of the Johannine witness to the Spirit as love's prosecuting attorney at work in the world.

Raymond Brown has observed that the role of the promised Paraclete is intimately bound up with the delay of the parousia.[67] The Johannine Paraclete is a theological interpretation of the Spirit who comes as "the personal presence of Jesus in the Christian while Jesus is with the Father."[68] While there is sufficient textual evidence to distinguish Jesus from the Spirit as "another Paraclete" (14:16), numerous parallels between the work of Jesus and the work of the Spirit show that "John is interested in the similarity between the two."[69] In Brown's exegesis we may thus detect the legitimate Western concern that stands behind the ontologically ill-advised *filioque:* that the Spirit is identifiable as the Spirit of Jesus, whose coming decisively was and ever remains a coming in the flesh (cf. 1 John 4:2). Eduard Schweitzer makes a similar case: "John regards the Spirit as nothing other than the power of the proclamation of Jesus as Redeemer, a proclamation in which man encounters the divine world,"[70] where audible words sounding in time-space powerfully sign and effectively communicate the thing signified. In distinction from competitor ideas current in Second Temple Judaism of the Spirit as either an angel or an impersonal heavenly substance or energy, "for John, as for the whole Church, the Spirit could only be the power which makes it possible for man to recognize Jesus as the Redeemer, in whom he encounters God . . . [who is] now present in the preaching of the Church, moulding the life of the Last-Age people of God, and so challenging and judging the world."[71] Nils

---

66. C. H. Dodd, *The Interpretation of the Fourth Gospel* (Cambridge: Cambridge University Press, 1995), p. 262. See also pp. 284, 348, 419-20.

67. Raymond E. Brown, S.S., *The Gospel according to John (xiii–xxi)* (Garden City, NY: Doubleday, 1970), pp. 1142-43.

68. Brown, *John,* p. 1140.

69. Brown, *John,* p. 1141.

70. Eduard Schweitzer and others, *Spirit of God,* trans. A. E. Harvey (London: Adam & Charles Black, 1960), p. 97.

71. Schweitzer, *Spirit,* p. 97.

Alstrup Dahl accordingly spoke of the Paraclete in connection with John's foren-sic conception of history, in which the Spirit of Jesus now puts the world on trial through the preaching of the gospel of the resurrection of the Crucified.[72]

The traditional translation of Paraclete as "comforter," then, is somewhat misleading. The Spirit comes upon the world as God in the role of prosecuting attorney, usurping the usurper, the Satan, now exposed as the "father of lies" (John 8:42-47).[73] This "comforts" the people of God in the sense that they have in their trials an advocate — though the Spirit can also turn against them if they abandon the materiality of Jesus who binds them to visible love for one another. C. H. Dodd sums up the case: Paraclete "is properly a forensic term." The pros-ecuting attorney convicts the world (John 16:8-11) in the "same procedure as in ix.35-41, only with the Spirit in the place of Christ. Thus the coming of Christ after His death, which for the disciples means the attainment of eternal life, means for the world the Last Judgment. . . . The crucial event has now happened (has happened, that is, in spiritual intention) — the death and resurrection of Christ, which is the judgment of this world, issuing in the expulsion of the Archon of this world (xiii.31). This judgment is made effective through the work of the Spirit in the Church" (John 16:11).[74] While Dodd has often been accused of advocating a "realized eschatology," this account of John, which retains the decisive thing of the apocalyptic battle of the Spirit against the unholy spirits, would be better described as an *inaugurated* eschatology: because of the victory of Christ in His resurrection, His Spirit is already now convicting the world concerning sin, and righteousness, and judgment through the preaching that announces the resurrec-tion of the Crucified. The Spirit's preaching is the *krisis* of the world, as Bultmann rightly characterized it:[75] apocalypse *now*.

The *peace of Christ* is therefore not inwardness or equanimity based on an otherworldly transcendence of the troubles of life. It is the victory peace of the reign of God breaking in upon the closed world with the sundering of Jesus' tomb. It is the peace that gives courage to the martyrs of Jesus. It is the peace of Jesus' victory over the lies and death-threats of this world: "Peace I leave with you; my peace I give to you. I do not give to you as the world gives. Do not let your hearts be troubled, and do not let them be afraid" (John 14:27). The *love of Jesus* is not a manipulative summons to ecclesiastical conformity. It is the militant love that is against what is against love; it bears witness to the truth and endures all things to gain and keep another in truth: "Those who love me will keep my word, and my Father will love them, and we will come to them and make our home with them"

72. Nils Alstrup Dahl, *Jesus in the Memory of the Early Church* (Minneapolis: Augsburg, 1976), p. 117.

73. This text is bound up with the terrible history of the Christian demonization of "the Jews." Here we have a case in which theology must correct the biblical text in terms of *Sachkritik*.

74. Dodd, *Fourth Gospel*, p. 414.

75. Rudolf Bultmann, *Faith and Understanding*, ed. Robert W. Funk, trans. Louise Petti-bone Smith (Philadelphia: Fortress, 1987), pp. 165-83.

(John 14:23). So distant likewise from conformity to this world is *the unity of the believers:* "My sheep hear my voice. I know them, and they follow me" (John 10:27). The love of the new covenant would be vacuous sentimentalism — it *is* vacuous sentimentalism in the funeral societies today that pose as congregations of Christ — did it not take its measure from the truth about Jesus: "I give you a new commandment, that you love one another. Just as I have loved you, you also should love one another" (John 13:34). Witness to the love of Jesus that binds disciples to one another in love is not introspective inventory but public testimony in the trial of the world: "You also are to testify because you have been with me from the beginning. I have said these things to you to keep you from stumbling. They will put you out of the synagogues. Indeed, an hour is coming when those who kill you will think that by doing so they are offering worship to God" (John 15:27–16:2).[76]

In all this it is evident that the identification by the Spirit of crucified Jesus as the Risen One in the Easter appearance narratives establishes a community under the cross. The new order of the Spirit is the very existence of that community of Jesus' love amid the hostility of the world. Because the disciples follow Jesus, on the other hand, they can be hated as He was hated and suffer as He suffered in the world. The very real peace, love, and unity in Jesus which attends the believers' way in the world inevitably entails conflict: against "the world" outside to be sure, but also against "the world" that invades the community in dissensions, schisms, and apostasy; against "the world" that continues to creep and seep in to assert its powerful claim from within each wavering disciple. The community's new relation in the Spirit to God therefore must constantly be regrounded in the victory of Christ on behalf of all, the Word of which makes the disciples clean: "You have already been cleansed by the word that I have spoken to you. Abide in me as I abide in you" (John 15:3-4). In spite of all failings, the embattled community is nevertheless the new order of the Spirit precisely insofar as it lives every day on the basis of Jesus' victory for all. The Lord's final words are spoken to a troubled and embattled community: "I have said this to you, so that in me you may have peace. In the world you face persecution. But take courage; I have conquered the world!" (John 16:33).

The One who speaks in the Farewell Discourse has *already* "conquered the world" (John 16:33). His glorification is the theological presupposition of the entire Johannine presentation (John 13:31). The literary function of the Farewell Discourse is to establish the benefit of Jesus' glorification for the disciples who otherwise anticipate nothing but the loss of the One who loves them in the name of God and speaks to them the words of eternal life. Disciples do not and cannot have the same unmediated knowledge of the Father as the Son has, and for that reason they cannot bear the thought of Jesus' departure after having brought God

---

76. On the martyriological *Sitz im Leben,* see J. Louis Martyn, *History and Theology in the Fourth Gospel* (Louisville and London: Westminster John Knox, 2003).

close to them in love and in this way having made God known (1:18). Nevertheless, in His final testament Jesus bequeaths to His disciples — by remembrance
of His Word in the power of His Spirit — the same knowledge of the Father as is
His own. Jesus gives believers the authority to become the children of God. That
authority is the knowledge of God that faith in Jesus already possesses. It needs
only to be explicated. In knowing that God has sent Jesus to them and for them,
they have come to know the Father of the Son who sends Him even as they have
come to know Jesus as the Son of the Father. "Have I been with you all this time,
Philip, and you still do not know me? Whoever has seen me has seen the Father"
(John 14:9). The prayer of consecration, "Righteous Father, the world does not
know you, but I know you; and these know that you have sent me" (John 17:25)
seals the new covenant.

Craig R. Koester points to the reversal that takes place in the course of the
Farewell Discourse: the "Gospel's understanding of the Spirit takes a surprising
turn. As Jesus goes to prepare a dwelling place *(monĕ)* for the disciples to abide
in the future, the Spirit discloses that Jesus and his Father come to make their
dwelling place among believers right now. . . . The Jesus who rose in the past
continues to be present; the Jesus who will come again is already present; and
the Spirit now makes the presence of Jesus and his Father known within the
community of faith"[77] — the community that simply is, albeit in the form of
an embattled anticipation, the Beloved Community of God. The Spirit of this
community is a militant advocate, not a pious tranquilizer, just as divine love is
not the apathy of tolerance, but zeal for the truth that is divine agape (cf. Rom.
12:9). Thus this "advocate" will "prove the world wrong about sin and righteousness and judgment" (John 16:8, Koester's translation), the idea being "that the
Spirit will enable the believers to see the truth about the world even if the world
cannot see the truth about itself"[78] (recall here the discussion of sinfulness in
Chapter Three).

Koester unpacks this claim as follows. First, sin is unbelief that fails to see
in the sign, Jesus, the thing signified, the divine Son who as human becomes
the Lamb who takes away the sin of the world. By unifying the sign and thing
signified for faith, the Spirit enables believers to resist the world's unbelief "since
it manifests the world's sin and alienation from God." Second, the absence of
Jesus is also a sign that signifies His exaltation, that is to say, His vindication as
the very righteousness of the Father who sent the Son into the world, onto the
cross. "In the eyes of the world, Jesus was crucified because he was an unrighteous opponent of God; and his adversaries can argue that no one sees Jesus
now because he is dead and gone. . . . The Spirit enables believers to see that
the world has judged Jesus wrongly, and that by laying down his life Jesus has

---

77. Craig R. Koester, *The Word of Life: A Theology of John's Gospel* (Grand Rapids: Eerdmans, 2008), p. 151.

78. Koester, *The Word of Life*, p. 153.

acted in righteousness." Third, "Satan operates through deception, hatred, and death . . . [but] the Spirit . . . enables people to see that the crucifixion was not a victory for Satan but the point at which Jesus overcomes him by the power of truth, love and life. . . ."[79]

Thus, "this is eternal life, that they may know you, the only true God, and Jesus Christ whom you have sent" (John 17:3). The Johannine Jesus directs us to the self-revelation of the triune God in the economy of salvation. This knowledge of God is not speculative or theoretical; it is evoked in the mission of the Spirit and strictly serves the missionary cause of God to give life to the world by gathering together into one flock under one shepherd the scattered children of God. Evocation of the knowledge of God is the work of the Spirit of God: "When the Spirit of truth comes, he will guide you into all the truth. . . . He will glorify me, because he will take what is mine and declare it to you. All that the Father has is mine" (John 16:13-15). Christian faith knows God personally in this gift and calling of service to God, by this mission of the Spirit of the Father and the Son.

Indeed, such mission to the nations gathering into one the scattered children of God, in place of near-expectation of the Parousia, *is* the gift of the Holy Spirit in John's theological interpretation of the earlier Synoptic traditions. The risen but not yet ascended Jesus tells Mary Magdalene, "Do not hold on to me, because I have not yet ascended to the Father. But go to my brothers and say to them, 'I am ascending to my Father and your Father, to my God and your God'" (John 20:17). Easter evening, the risen Son commissions the disciples, "'As the Father has sent me, so I send you.' When he had said this, he breathed on them and said to them, 'Receive the Holy Spirit'" (20:21b-22). The enigmatic prohibition spoken to Mary in the garden on Easter morn points the reader of the Gospel back to the teaching of the Farewell Discourse that Jesus *must* depart in order for the greater good of the coming of the Spirit to occur. The meaning is that the resurrection appearances have served their purpose when the anti-docetic identification of Jesus as the risen Lord has been made. The appearances do *not* stand for resumption of the previous relation, but as testimony to and promise of the new order of the Spirit about to be inaugurated. That new order is made manifest on Easter eve. Established anew in the power of Christ's victory peace, the scattered, frightened, and failed disciples now receive as a body the same mission from the Father with the same Spirit to accomplish it, as had Jesus in His time. The disciples become branches of the Vine who bear much fruit; they become the love among one another reaching out to the nations in which Jesus has loved them. Their existence in the Spirit will therefore enable the world to see Jesus. Yet they too will experience how the divine offer of life and salvation provokes a lethal crisis in the world.

79. Koester, *The Word of Life*, p. 154.

## The Spirit as Unifier of the Sign and the Thing Signified

From the foregoing sojourn in the matrix of the Scriptures, we may now put forward a thesis: the Spirit who ever gives birth to the church through the Word is the Spirit who convinces worldlings of sin and righteousness and judgment. This is the preaching of the gospel of the resurrection of the Crucified, *where the preaching of the gospel is understood theologically as unification of the sign and the thing signified.*[80] Here, crucially, the sign is something available to all in the world of the common body: "*Jesus* is the Son of God," "the Three of the gospel *narrative* are the one God," "you washed by this *water* with the Word are washed by the Spirit and are a newborn child of God," "*you* are mine and I am yours." Such unification is the Spirit-given conviction (Heb. 11:1) — centrally, about Jesus as Son of the Father and the corresponding assurance that in Him we too have become the children of God — that is authoritative in the sense of being constitutive for the life of the church, taken as the creature of this Word when proclaimed by the Spirit. Whatever else we go on to say about authority in the church, critical dogmatics tests whether this authorizing work of the Holy Spirit by the Word is and remains primary so that all other claims to authority are relativized by it. The referential element is what the gospel says about Jesus as someone in the world; the illocutionary element is the hope and love which this report narrated as God's promise elicits when taken in the Spirit, thus by faith, as the Word of God. These stand and fall together. Without the report, the proclamation is empty; without the import, the proclamation falls on deaf ears. Only together do they constitute the Word of God as the Spirit intends, speaking to author and to authorize the church-in-mission by creating the faith that already now justifies before God in a world still in the thrall of malice and injustice.

The referential element gives the sign, Jesus, and the illocutionary element the thing signified, the Son of God's love for us, when the Word is spoken in the Spirit and according to the Spirit on the way to the Father's Beloved Community. Protestant reformers were not wrong to think of the Word of God as a causative power that creates the church; but as a rule they did not adequately grasp that the Word "alone" (as causative power) is never alone, but always bundled, so to speak, with the Spirit who speaks it truly. Only in this way does the Word perform as *promissio* that unifies the sign with the thing signified for faith. By contrast, making promises apart from the Spirit's work of unifying with the cross and resurrection of the Son can be and often is the work of the "father of lies": the *sicut Deus eritis* of Genesis 3:5.

The pertinence of this thesis is that dysfunctional Western Christianity has dualized and indeed polarized the sign and the thing signified, in order to protect itself from ecclesiastical authoritarianism on the one side and charismatic fanaticism on the other. But evacuating the gospel by divorcing Word and Spirit

---

80. *LAD*, pp. 147-66.

is no true protection; indeed, it is a kind of surrender to the Liar, whose work is to separate what God joins together. If Colin Gunton is correct, this dualizing tendency may be traced back to the great Augustine himself. He calls attention to passages from Augustine's *De Trinitate,* such as in XV:20, where Augustine wrote that "the word which sounds outwardly is a sign of the word that shines inwardly, and to this latter the name of 'word' is more appropriate."[81] Gunton goes on to argue on the basis of such passages that the inner word is taken as foundational in Augustine and that this foundation is in fact the neo-Platonic philosophy of the rational soul in its coming to self-awareness. Certainly, as argued above, such a distinction between inner and outer word became a matter of dualistic principle in the theology of Zwingli many centuries after Augustine. But such a distinction is not necessarily a dualism. A distinction can equally provide the basis for a profounder unity. How we negotiate difference is the deep problem exposed by the gospel and made a topic for thought in the world by Christian theology — if and when it remembers the gospel in sufficiently self-critical fashion!

Thus difference may be taken as the Trinitarian distinction of Word and Spirit in their mutual referencing to one another. It may serve to make the existential point accordingly that the sign is not grasped truly until it is grasped in its significance "for me," so that faith in the sense of personal trust is specified as the true cognition of the sign. Just such faith is itself understood as the Spirit-given unification of the sign and the thing signified, where and when He wills. In that case we have a clear distinction and relation of persons between the self-donating Word and the self-communicating Spirit of the one God who is Father of the Son and breather of the Spirit. Indeed, in this case there is theological need to maintain the distinction between the sign and the thing signified, not least so that the Protestant error of thinking that the Word "alone" works all, as it were, is avoided. More material to the present discussion, however, is that monocausal theologies of the Word render nugatory the essential work of the Holy Spirit in that it is the invocation *(epiklesis)* of the Spirit that gives the unification of the sign and thing signified by the Word, where and when it pleases God. So Regin Prenter in interpreting Luther: ". . . it is the Holy Spirit which unites the promise and the sign. It is the Spirit that causes Christ to be truly present in the Word and that makes it a gospel which kindles faith and supports it. . . . The sacrament as the living unity of *promissio* and *signum* received by faith is created by the work of the Spirit."[82]

Thus the Spirit may be invoked and must be invoked by the theological subject, who lives in dependence on His free coming and working. By the same token then we must wait, and wait patiently bearing one another's burdens, for the Spirit's coming. The Spirit freely and personally witnesses to the Word incarnate, faithfully awarding the patiency of faith the reconciliation that is needed at some particular juncture of the gospel's progress through the nations. But if,

81. Gunton, "Augustine, the Trinity and the Theological Crisis," p. 47.
82. Prenter, *Spiritus Creator,* pp. 160-61.

impatiently, we think that the Spirit is, as it were, naturally yoked to the Word as some kind of alter ego, we fall into modalism (thinking the Spirit as but another variable mode of divine presence, just as the Word once was). Then we will be forced to choose between the Spirit yoked to the text of Scripture or to the contemporary lightning-bolt of existentialist preaching. Conversely, if we think impatiently that the Word of God is yoked to the Spirit, we fall into enthusiasm and have to choose between the divinely endowed institutional church and the latest charismatic preacher. All four of these familiar options are deformations. Protestants have claimed to possess the Word of God in an inerrant book or, more recently, in the event of proclamation (not even noticing how the dictation theory survives here in admittedly rarified form). Catholics have claimed to possess the Spirit of God in an inerrant papacy, while Pentecostals have inverted the same enthusiastic claim about possessing the Spirit in chaotic episodes of prophecy. In these false antitheses, each has struggled to carve out a fragment of the bleeding corpse of Christianity as represented by its own true church in antithesis to others as the false church. What we have in common is rather the disease of dualizing or synthesizing the sign and the thing signified by confusing or separating the Word and the Spirit.

It is no accident that the modern ecumenical movement arose on the mission field from the sobbing wounded of this conflict and the dysfunction as the missionaries handed it on to the younger churches. There the church of the Spirit was being rediscovered in the work of mission to the nations just as the scandal of mutual anathemas became perceptible after centuries of uncomprehending animosity. Carl Braaten drew the lesson: "The doctrine of the church needs to be reconceived within the horizon of the eschatological mission of God in world history. The very being of the church is shaped by its missionary calling to go into the uttermost parts of the world. . . . The church is sent by the Spirit, the Spirit is sent by the Son, and the Son is sent by the Father."[83] Nothing is more reactionary in contemporary Euro-American theology than the desire, scarcely concealed in some instances, to perpetuate the schisms for the sake of various fractured identities and peculiar traditions that resist Braaten's call to reintegrate ecclesiology into the Trinitarian *missio Dei*. The alternative is in fact some version of church as established chaplaincy of political sovereignty, "Christendom." Braaten was saying already almost a generation ago: apart from the "missionary drive" that befits church in the time from "the appearance of the Easter Jesus to his final manifestation as the Lord of the cosmos . . . it becomes the religious shell of the dying culture of Christendom."[84]

But the lethal entanglement here is perhaps deeper than Braaten himself realized in 1977. The seductive desire for political relevance in imperial projects,

83. Carl E. Braaten, *The Flaming Center: A Theology of Christian Mission* (Philadelphia: Fortress, 1977), p. 55.

84. Braaten, *Flaming Center,* p. 44.

as understood by critical dogmatics, began already with the Carolingian invention of the *filioque* as a contrastive identifier for Western Christendom over against Byzantium. So our interest in this section in the Spirit as divine person converges with a critique of the Western *filioque* — *not* for its legitimate underlying concern to identify the Spirit in history as the Spirit of the incarnate Son — but as prime instance of the schismatic tendency to depersonalize the Spirit. This can happen either by the modalist assimilation of the Spirit to the Word or by the enthusiastic assimilation of the Word to the Spirit, ironically enough in either case producing a revelation handed over to the control of sinners rather than subjecting them to its judgment. In either case the assimilation destroys the Trinitarian dialectic of Word and Spirit and thus serves to capture the gospel and put it to work ideologically for other purposes. Strong Trinitarianism that undergirds the "theological circle" of Word and Spirit requires a knowing dialectic[85] instead of such assimilations in order to keep the church true to its gospel mission to the nations.

At the dogmatic center of the ecumenical movement within Western theology since the Second Vatican Council in the aftermath of the Second World War is the remarkable work of the Lutheran–Roman Catholic dialogue on all the aspects of the Third Article of the Creed: baptism and Eucharist, justification by faith, the church as communion, the holy life — all these freshly understood and appropriated under the rubric of the person and work of the Holy Spirit as Lord and giver of life.[86] We shall take advantage of this work, as already we have done above, from time to time in what follows. But the "ecumenical winter," that is, the stasis and inertia into which these very promising doctrinal dialogues have now fallen, is witness to the unquestioned and hence unrecognized error embedded in the Western dissent from the actual teaching of the second ecumenical council at Constantinople in 381, namely, that the Spirit proceeds from the Father of the Son *also as person* in the *identical sense* that Father and Son are person, that is, concrete particular "identities" ( Jenson) in communal relations that are essential to each one's actual being in its world. Indeed and as such, the person of the Spirit "completes" the deity, where deity is simply what the Father and the Son are in and through and for one another.

This completion in the Spirit snaps forever the bridge built in neo-Platonic, Hegelian, or Process theologies in which the cosmos is the third in the triad, yoking the One with its mediator Logos to the world of becoming in an eternal system.[87] But since the Father and the Son live for one another eternally in the

---

85. *LAD,* pp. 169-80.

86. For an account, see Paul R. Hinlicky, "The Lutheran Dilemma," *Pro Ecclesia* 8, no. 4 (Fall 1999): 391-422.

87. J. N. D. Kelly, *Early Christian Creeds,* 3rd edition (New York: David McKay, 1972), p. 331; cf. also Pelikan, *TCT* 1:211 and *PNT,* pp. 233-36. Jenson made this point powerfully in *Triune Identity:* "The legitimate theological reason for the immanent/economic distinction is the freedom of God: it must be that God 'in himself' could have been the same God he is, and so triune, had there been no creation . . ." (p. 139). He intends to observe this rule also in

Spirit, the cosmos is not necessary to complete God.[88] Rather the completed God gives being to the cosmos as a free and spontaneous act of love out of its own surplus. The cosmos is not necessary, and God's love in freely giving a creation is "more than necessary" (Jüngel). In that case the mutual referencing of Word and Spirit is not a natural yoking but the ever-free giving and receiving of persons in community that can and does extend also to creatures. In that case, the Word cannot be for us the incarnate Word that He is without the Spirit nor can the Spirit be the Holy Spirit that He is for us without the Word who became flesh, nor can either Word or Spirit live in this dialectic of mutual deference for us except as equally and alike in nature begotten and breathed respectively of the Father. Just so and only so are they sent into the world for us in the Father's own self-determination to redeem and fulfill the very creation that is, in part, I writing and you reading these words.

Sustaining the Trinitarian distinction between nature and person always meets its test case in relation to the Spirit, where the temptation to depersonalize the Spirit and to rob Him of true deity combine. The Spirit who comes from above to effect the personal transformation of believers by conforming them to Christ in baptism is no mere instrument of God, but God in person, third in the sequence of the Father who sends, the Son who is sent, and the Spirit who returns the sent Christ to His sending Father with all those whom He has gained. That means that the Spirit of God is emphatically *not* conceived as an arbitrary, independent, merely supernatural display of impersonal power. The conception of the Spirit's

---

his *ST,* though his concern to follow Barth and Rahner and at times, it seems, Bruce McCormack, stretches this rule to the breaking point, e.g., *ST* 1, p. 65, where he calls the distinction a "sheer counterfactual." I will tackle this most difficult issue of the gospel's revision of the time-eternity relation in the conclusion of this work. Suffice it to say for the present that I hold that the immanent/economic distinction is not a "sheer counterfactual" but what I have called, parodying Kant, an "immanental induction" (*RPTD*, pp. 209-11). In other words, in God the Father theology comes to the limit of its thinking in all eternity, even as, with Jenson, in God the Spirit eternity is this infinite encounter with the Father who remains other even in the ultimate personal relation that is sharing His eternal life by union with the Son.

88. This point is exposited with passion and insight in Thomas F. Torrance, *The Trinitarian Faith: The Evangelical Theology of the Ancient Catholic Church* (Edinburgh: T. & T. Clark, 1993), pp. 105-9. Likewise, John Meyendorff: Creation "is an act of the will of God, and will is ontologically distinct from nature. By nature, the Father generates the Son — and this generation is beyond time — but creation occurs through the will of God, which means that God remains absolutely free to create and not to create, and remains transcendent to the world after creating it. The absence of a distinction between the nature of God and the will of God was common to Origen and Arius. To establish this distinction constitutes the main argument of Athanasius." John Meyendorff, *Byzantine Theology: Historical Trends and Doctrinal Themes* (New York: Fordham University Press, 1979), p. 130. The only question here is whether Athanasius, or Meyendorff, or Torrance see that in just this way the conception of "nature" is itself revised so that however ineffable divine generation is, it indicates an eternity that is time-like, hence a creation in which eternity can truly enter time and time itself can be truly divinized.

divine person and His specific divine agency cohere, but this coherence is only intelligible in terms of strong Trinitarian personalism. Hence we cannot understand the personhood of the Spirit without reflecting on the Spirit's place in the divine life in a brief anticipation here of the conclusion of this system of theology.

As Basil argued in his seminal treatise on the Holy Spirit, because the church experiences the Spirit as the divine person in whom the Father and the Son live for one another in love and just so reach out in this very love beyond their own immanent, sublime, and eternal relations to create, redeem, and fulfill the creation, the Spirit together with the Father and the Son is to be worshiped and glorified — *already now.* For truly the Spirit comes as the *arrabon,* the "down payment" (2 Cor. 1:22) of the eschatological victory. Even *now* the church in mission, which journeys in the Spirit, with the Son, to the Father, anticipates the eschatological victory and sings the eternal doxology to the co-equal Trinity: "Glory to the Father, and to the Son, *and to the Holy Spirit,* now and forever. Amen!"[89] This exuberant shout of praise to the co-equal Trinity indicates that the notion of eschatological glory by participation in God's eternal life is governed strictly by the gospel insight into the advent nature of deity as event, the eternal becoming that is true and divine being now becoming possible for us. This "induction" of God's immanent Trinity from the economy[90] is an instance of the biblical "hope projected backwards." What eternal life, communion with God, theosis or divinization, could possibly mean in any case depends wholly on the identification of the deity involved.

The triune God's deity (or spirituality), as we have just heard, is *not* some kind of supernaturally imagined intellectual stuff abiding unchanged in a static state of perfect self-satisfaction, which shows itself *ad extra* in arbitrary displays or effects of power while for itself it glories in immunity from suffering. Indeed this very idea of spirit as the idealistic negation of natural life was first exposed, not by Nietzsche, but by Trinitarian theology itself. It was exposed in writings of Athanasius (that probably precede the Arian controversy) as a demonic glorification of nothingness, as worship of the dead, melodramatic deism, the god of the philosophers, a gilded abstraction made into a splendid conceptual idol concealing a secret despair of created life.[91] But the deity of the living God of the Bible is *event,*[92] not only for us in the coming of God's reign, but also for God in

89. Basil, "On the Holy Spirit," *NPNF* 8, pp. 1-50.

90. *RPTD,* pp. 209-11.

91. Khaled Anatolios, *Athanasius: The Coherence of His Thought* (London and New York: Routledge, 2005), pp. 38-39.

92. Taken to an extreme, i.e., without subjects of the event who relate to each other by the event of their community, however, "God as event" would come to a new reduction in precise parallel to the Western reduction of the persons as subsistent identities to the mere registration of relation. "The decision for the covenant of grace is the ground of God's triunity and, therefore, of the eternal generation of the Son and of the eternal procession of the Holy Spirit from the Father and the Son." So Bruce McCormack in "Grace and Being," chapter 6 in *The Cambridge*

the becoming of His own immanent and eternal life that further becomes with time and space in the origin of the creation, its redemption by the Incarnation and its fulfillment by the coming of the Beloved Community. The eternal Trinity of love is the true "eternal recurrence of the same" — not the mindless play of brute force, as Nietzsche and his lesser minions darkly intimate.

As this eternal *life,* God's own, i.e., immanent Omega[93] is the Holy Spirit's return in whom the Father and the Son live for one another and now through Jesus Christ live also for us. God is spirit, that is, being in communion, and the Spirit is the person in whom the persons of the Father and the Son exist for one another and so also, thus truly, for us as well. Jenson has argued that God's own internal telos is the Spirit of the Father and the Son.[94] We take this to mean that He is the unity of the Son with the Father, of the image with the prototype, of the sign with the thing signified. He is this unity, not as some kind of naturally divine stuff, but this unity as person, where person indicates a specific way of being in relation to other persons with their own ways of being. The specific way of relating to others that is the person of the Holy Spirit is to shower in person the Father's favor upon the Son and to return in person the Son's thanksgiving to the Father in filial, not servile obedience. For us, the Holy Spirit is just so the one who in person convinces the world concerning sin, and righteousness, and judgment. He does just this by showering in person the Father's favor on those worldlings found crucified and risen with Christ and bringing them in Christ to the Father in new lives. This dynamic unification by love of the sign in the world with the divinely signified thing is the person at work who is the Holy Spirit of the Father and the Son.

---

*Companion to Karl Barth,* ed. John Webster (Cambridge: Cambridge University Press, 2000), p. 103. If we accept an ontology of act, *given* the Augustinian understanding of the doctrine of the Trinity in which the unity of God's being governs the conception of the triad of persons, then, God as the event of the world, rather than the event of the eternal Trinity who becomes Creator of a creation other than itself, i.e., a right-wing Hegelianism, seems unavoidable. *Esse Deum dare.* We can accept an ontology of act, decoupled from the Augustinian tendency towards modalism, as a way of bringing the Cappodocian theology to a more consistent perichoresis and in line with deeper insight into the distinction between philosophy as protology and Christian theology as eschatology. Then it will be the Father who ever surpasses Himself in breathing the Spirit on the Son on the way to new futures, just as these new futures always consist in the Son's return to the Father by the Spirit enriched with new experience. This eternal becoming of the same is ever generative, also for creatures in giving life to the dead and calling into being the things that are not (Rom. 4:17).

93. Jenson, *ST* 1, pp. 156-61.

94. This "eschatological" interpretation of Trinitarian being is the interpretation of God as event that dances close but arguably avoids the Hegelian reduction criticized in McCormack in note 92. It derives from Robert W. Jenson, who already in his seminal response to the "death of God" theology of the 1960s maintained that "the Spirit is the goal of the Trinity . . . God-future, God as what we may live *for.* . . ." *God after God: The God of the Past and the God of the Future, Seen in the Work of Karl Barth* (Indianapolis and New York: Bobbs-Merrill, 1969), p. 173.

## Overcoming the Western "tendency towards modalism"[95]

In a seminal article from 1990 already referenced several times, Colin Gunton identified a complex of concerns that we are addressing throughout this system of theology: the Kantian turn of modern thought that exacerbates the latent modalist tendencies in the Western theological tradition into widespread agnosticism, not only in Western culture, but in theology itself. This modalism, which regards the three persons of the gospel narrative as but temporal and spatial figures accommodated to creatures, matures today, Gunton argued, into contemporary "atheism" (more precisely, *agnosticism*) by virtue of the "thought of the essential unknowability of God" that is embedded in the very construal of Father, Son, and Holy Spirit as masks, modes, or mere figures of an unknowable Beyond.[96] This modalist trajectory towards theological apophaticism stands in evident contradiction to "glorifying in the being of a God whose reality as a communion of persons is the basis of a rational universe in which personal life may take shape."[97] Building upon Harnack's acerbic comment that "Augustine only gets beyond Modalism by the mere assertion that he does not wish to be a Modalist . . . ,"[98] Gunton made the case that the modalist tendency of Western theology can be traced back to Augustine by a detailed analysis of the Western church father's influential treatise *De Trinitate.*

The Holy Spirit, Augustine taught, "is a kind of inexpressible communion or fellowship of Father and Son."[99] He is not "one of the two, since he is that by which the two are joined to each other, by which the begotten is loved by the one who begets him and in turn loves the begetter. . . . We are bidden to imitate this mutuality by grace. . . . In this way those three are one, only, great, wise, holy, and blessed God. . . . So the Holy Spirit is something common to Father and Son, whatever it is, or is their very commonness or communion, consubstantial and eternal. Call this friendship, if it helps, but a better word for it is charity. And this too is substance because God is substance, God is charity. . . ."[100] The ambiguity of Augustine's teaching due to his uncritical embrace of metaphysical simplicity is that one can never quite tell whether he conceives of this love between the Father and the Son impersonally as the divine substance that God as love simply is or personally as the Holy Spirit who as agent relates Father and Son to each other in

---

95. Colin Gunton, "Augustine, the Trinity, and the Theological Crisis of the West," *Scottish Journal of Theology* 43, no. 1 (February 1990): 45. See also the similar analysis by Jenson, *ST* 1, pp. 110-13.

96. Gunton, "Augustine, the Trinity, and the Theological Crisis," p. 33.

97. Gunton, "Augustine, the Trinity, and the Theological Crisis," p. 34.

98. Gunton, "Augustine, the Trinity, and the Theological Crisis," p. 35, cited from Harnack, *HD* 4, p. 131.

99. Saint Augustine, *The Trinity*, trans. E. Hill, O.P. (Brooklyn, NY: New City Press, 1996), V:3,12; p. 197.

100. Augustine, *The Trinity* VI:1,1; p. 209.

love. Because for Augustine, as for modalists generally, it was more important to assert the equal, hence essentially identical deity of the Son to that of the Father, it does seem clear that the specific contours of this Jewish humanity executed as a messianic imposter and its narrative role in the gospel do not and cannot serve to reveal to faith's understanding the particular Sonship by which the creature Jesus is concretely affirmed as a way of being God in relation to two other ways of being God, namely, that of His Father and of their Spirit. This concern with the timeless self-identity of God as God, furthermore taken as the very unity of being as God that the Three have equally, neutralizes the *sedes doctrinae* (the doctrinal seat in a biblical text) in the Baptism story.

There the Son receives His specific mission in the power of the Spirit to proclaim the imminence of His Father's reign in conflict with the demonic powers. Gunton notes Augustine's reaction to this: "It would be utterly absurd for us to believe that he received the Holy Spirit when he was already thirty years old . . ."[101] since by nature the Son is already God who has the Spirit and so brings the Spirit along, so to say, from the moment of His conception from the Virgin. Thus, a prior conception of the simplicity of the divine nature overrules the specific witness of the text to the concrete way in which the creature Jesus is the divine Son, namely as man receiving the Holy Spirit at about the age of thirty years as seal of His Sonship in the commission to undertake His messianic mission. To be sure, there are Christological concerns at work here regarding adoptionism; but Gunton's focus is on how the understanding of divine Sonship in its personal particularity manifest in the obedience in faith of the man Jesus is sacrificed to a greater interest in securing its natural equality as God with the Spirit and the Father.

In a word, Gunton writes, Augustine appears to treat the Spirit, "in anticipation of a long tradition of Western thought, substantially rather than personally and relationally: as if the Spirit was a substantial presence, given in the womb and, so to speak, pre-programming his life, rather than the means by which his humanity is realized in relationship to the Father"[102] — namely, this human being in his history of obedience in faith realized as the coming of His own eternal Son in the flesh. Thus Augustine prepared the way "for the later, and fateful, *definition* of the person as a *relation*,"[103] i.e., as a reduction of person to a function of mental life (as in the triad memory, understanding, and will).[104] This "fateful" reduction of a concrete particular way of being in relation to concrete and particular others forming a social life, to its function within the metaphysically simple operations of the divine Mind, indicates, Gunton argues, Augustine's deep reliance on neo-Platonic philosophy.

---

101. Gunton, "Augustine, the Trinity, and the Theological Crisis," p. 39, cited from *De Trinitate* XV, 46.

102. Gunton, "Augustine, the Trinity, and the Theological Crisis," p. 40.

103. Gunton, "Augustine, the Trinity, and the Theological Crisis," p. 43.

104. Gunton, "Augustine, the Trinity, and the Theological Crisis," p. 48.

But the Spirit is to be understood as the divine and personal reality of the love of Jesus and His Father, the freedom in which they live for one another, as Jenson in particular has stressed in contemporary theology.[105] Building on the renewal within the Western tradition of the Eastern way that proceeds from the economy to the divine ontology,[106] Jenson has shown that the traditional topic of the divine attributes in Western theology, deployed to construct a foundational doctrine of divine nature, must be drastically revised if the Trojan Horse of deity as timeless immutability is not to be snuck in. This latent modalism systematically undercuts the revealed economy — for modern example, in the way that Tillich influentially maintained in rejecting the traditional notion of the Incarnation: strictly speaking the one thing God cannot do is cease to be God by becoming a creature, as per the classical assertion of John 1:14 that Tillich regards as a "literalistic distortion."[107] It is not surprising then that Tillich expressly came to a sublimely modalist quest for "God above God."

Yet it may also be noted here that Jenson's scattered remarks on the divine attributes (by design, be it noted),[108] with 1) his retention of the putative metaphysical insight that in God the attributes are one and the same eternal thing (probably in deference to Aquinas and in the interest of Lutheran-Catholic convergence), and further, 2) with his dependence on Barth's binitarian scheme of divine ontology as the freedom to love (that is, omitting *wisdom* as a co-equal perfection at play in the freedom to love), do not quite succeed in carrying through his own intention to rethink divine ontology strictly in the light of the Trinitarian revision of classic metaphysics. It is not an accident that Augustine stumbled precisely over the Pauline text that Christ is the wisdom of God. Augustine feared that this implied that God the Father had no wisdom of His own, but only in the relation to His Son. "Some people find it difficult to accept the equality of Father and Son and Holy Spirit because of the text, *Christ is power of God and the wisdom of God* (1 Cor 1:24). Equality seems to be lacking here, since the Father is not himself, according to the text, power and wisdom, but the begetter of power and wisdom."[109] The discussion of this problem is actually the turning point in Augustine's treatise on the Trinity. Up until this point he had more or less faithfully reproduced the Eastern doctrine, albeit via Hilary with a strongly Athanasian polemic against Arianism that is not attuned to the opposite problem of modalism

105. Jenson, *ST* 1, pp. 146-61.

106. Meyendorff, *Byzantine Theology*, pp. 180-81.

107. Tillich, however, is right to find the problem of the traditional Christological dogma in the "inadequacy" of the term "nature" (*ST* 1, p. 142) and also to strive accordingly for a revision of Chalcedon adequate to the "justification of the sinner . . . a Christology of the participation of the Christ in sinful existence, including, at the same time, its conquest. The christological paradox and the paradox of the justification of the sinner are one and the same paradox. It is the paradox of God accepting a world that rejects him" (*ST* 2, p. 150).

108. Jenson, *ST* 1, p. 223.

109. Augustine, *On the Trinity* VI:1,1, p. 205.

(which Athanasius himself finally realized in recognizing the Cappadocians). But from here on Augustine introduces the distinction between absolute and relative predications regarding God, where "absolute" equates with the doctrine of divine simplicity, the divine nature taken as unfathomable timeless self-identity. Inevitably this absolute relativizes the persons as but expressions of that unfathomable self-identity, whose personal differences and relations can only be noted but in fact make no sense and do no theological work. For if we cannot see how Christ is the wisdom of God; how God can be God as a Son; how God as a Son can be the faithful creature Jesus of Nazareth, hence as the Logos incarnate, we do not actually understand the gospel theologically at all.

The modalist tendency of Western theology embedded in Augustine's distinction between absolute and relative predications causes us to think of God's unity as substantial, intellectual, simple, and timelessly eternal where all properties are convertible and hence to us creatures unknowable. This tendency cannot be overcome, however, by sheerly dispensing with the rubric concerning the divine perfections, all the while tacitly holding to such a doctrine via Barth's ontology of act. Trinitarian theology has to give some alternative account, however obliquely, of *what* God is and *how* God is what God is as the eternal Life that shares its own life with creatures, if our de facto agnosticism regarding God today is truly to be met and overcome. The clue to this alternative account lies in this: the freedom to love that the triune God displays in the origin, the redemption, and the fulfillment is a *harmony* mediated by divine *wisdom.* It is not "reckless," as Barth in his more antinomian moods would characterize it.[110] Rather, God's freedom is the freedom to love *wisely,* just as justice is the charity of the wise (Leibniz),[111] issuing in provisional *orders* of love and justice as real and rational effects in the world, however much contested. In terms of pastoral practice and proclamation, wisdom gives the Spirit's art by which the gospel is spoken concretely in the situation to afflict the comfortable but to comfort the afflicted; zealously to change what can be changed for the good but serenely to accept what cannot yet be changed and to know the difference (Niebuhr); to tear down

110. *CD* II/1, pp. 297-321. Barth's polemical purpose in this is to be appreciated and affirmed: "But He is who He is as the One who loves, *not as a substance* in which He can be more or less or something other than the living God" (*CD* II/1, p. 321, emphasis added). Nevertheless, to privilege freedom in God, i.e., as the very deity of God by which God decides what God will be, even when this decision is in fact, i.e., in its positivity, the freedom to love is to think of a Father, or origin, in the divine life that could be other than the Father of the Son and breather of the Spirit. This inevitably leads — in spite of Barth's intentional dialectic that resists this reduction — to making God's relation to the world necessary and God's love for the world in Christ coercive in that it collapses the person of the Spirit into the person of the Son as the deed manifesting freedom's love. But the wisdom of Christ's divine self-donation and the love of the Spirit's divine self-communication are distinct, if inseparable divine operations.

111. Patrick Riley, *Leibniz' Universal Jurisprudence: Justice as the Charity of the Wise* (Cambridge, MA: Harvard University Press, 1996), pp. 158-59.

only what can better be rebuilt in the present circumstances. We shall see this fleshed out in Chapter Eight, following Bonhoeffer's attempt to rehabilitate the concept of "nature" in theology as that which in the wisdom of God, after the fall, is redirected by Christ to Christ: the *mandatum Dei*, the "mandates of creation" (marriage, labor, worship, and political service), provide the "arenas of responsibility" (Benne) for Christian vocation that transform stations in life into anticipatory structures of love and justice preparing to greet Christ's coming in glory. Noting this here in anticipation of the treatment of the divine ontology as descriptive of the *life of perfect harmony in love of power and wisdom* at the conclusion of this system of theology, for the present we are focusing on the person of the Spirit, who personally harmonizes power and wisdom by love, the attributes appropriated respectively to the almighty Father, His Logos/Son, and their Spirit.

To be sure, following Jenson's pioneering path, this schematization of the divine perfections dispenses altogether with the traditional division between metaphysical and moral attributes by which Christian Platonism arbitrarily tried to fuse together two heterogeneous theologies. Likewise it contemplates a certain creative tension in the divine Life itself that is ever generative, always innovative, given the free decision to initiate a world of creatures. But this approach to the divine "nature" of the Trinity as the harmony of power, wisdom, and love aims to redeem Augustine from himself (i.e., from Gunton's severe indictment that neo-Platonist philosophy of the Mind is the true foundation of his Trinitarian theology). "The Trinity is not an identity," Jenson rightly notes. If it were, we would be right back to modalism, with a fourth identity, the "Trinity as such," as a more basic identity behind the three in the economy, as absolute to relative. Rather the Three identify each other as the One that is the Beloved Community of eternity becoming temporal in the three-act drama of creation, redemption, and fulfillment. In that case, we may intelligibly describe an eternity becoming actual in time this way as the dynamic harmonization of power and wisdom by love that arrives at the eschaton of judgment. In this way divine "nature" would be attained in theological understanding by way of induction from the economy, and not by a transcendental argument about the conditions for the possibility of some idea of God as perfect being.

Unfortunately, then, Jenson with the help of German Idealism proceeds directly from his correct affirmation that the "Trinity is not an identity" into the speculation that if the Trinity were an identity, "contrary to the primal fact of his own being as God, the Father of the Son, he would be a sheer transcendental consciousness, unidentified and unidentifiable also to himself"[112] — unless this unconsciousness, somehow feeling its lack, would objectify itself in initiation of a negative dialectic driving an unfolding history on the way to the attainment of self-consciousness. Thinking he can preclude the Hegelianism by treating it as a counterfactual thought-experiment, Jenson pays an extraordinary price for

112. Jenson, *ST* 1, p. 122.

this flirtation with the enemy. He thinks it necessary to say that — despite the acknowledged, and in the present view, salutary postmodern deconstruction of this titanic self-consciousness of Cartesian-Kantian subjectivity — it "should always have been obvious that Father, Son and Spirit could not each be personal in quite the same way."

This statement is either a redundancy, in that the concept of person *is* to be a concrete and particular identity in essential relation to *other* such identities, or it subverts the very notion of concrete and particular identity by allowing a person to be, as it were, a double-agent, wearing masks behind which a hidden actor lurks. Just this latter, it seems, is the course Jenson takes. He asserts "different personalities of the Father as Father [i.e., of the Son] and the Father as the Trinity" where the latter can be parsed by the idealist scheme "transcendental unity of consciousness, ego, and freedom." Thus the entire neo-Platonic dialectic of Mind thinking itself and loving itself recurs. "The Trinity is here indeed understood as a person, and Father, Son, and Spirit as the poles of the inner life that makes him personal." This is exactly, in the perspective of the present system of theology, the wrong way to "rescue" Augustine, a way already tried by Karl Barth and not improved here by Jenson.[113] It is the source of all the baffling dialectics of past, present, and future in Jenson's doctrine of God that in the process depersonalize the persons into poles of consciousness of a divine Mind in a vain attempt to avoid articulating a doctrine of the "nature" of God. But persons are person as other-conscious, not self-conscious, at least where the harmony of love prevails; self-consciousness is a fall away from that true ecstasy of life in Beloved Community into agonistic, other-disregarding contrastive identity, into the malice of self-love at the expense of others.[114] The "nature" of Beloved Community is not this tautological self-asserting self coming to consciousness of itself by the instrumentalization of others, but a dynamic harmony creative of the new, infinitely selecting and realizing the possibilities of love, if indeed *esse Deum dare.*

This work of a divine ontology can be accomplished more simply and more elegantly by the traditional doctrine of Trinitarian appropriation of the perfections of power, wisdom, and love to the persons of the Father, the Son, and the Spirit respectively. In this way even the aroma of German idealism's negative dialectics is avoided,[115] itself a revival of neo-Platonic philosophy of Mind,

---

113. Jenson, *ST* 1, p. 123. Cf. *PNT,* pp. 52-57, 128-42.

114. Vladimir Lossky makes this point incisively: ". . . the subject who defines himself by opposition to all that which is not 'I,' is not the person or hypostasis who shares nature in common with others and who exists as person in a positive fellowship to other persons. Self-will (combated by all Christian asceticism) is not identical to the will of the new creation — to the will which one finds in renouncing oneself, in the unity of the Body of Christ, wherein the canons of the Church make us recognize a common and undivided will." *In the Image and Likeness of God,* ed. J. H. Erickson and T. E. Bird (Crestwood, NY: St. Vladimir's Seminary Press, 1985), p. 186.

115. *RPTD,* pp. 179-86.

grounding instead (as Jenson also clearly wishes) the eternal Life of the Father and the Son *in the Spirit* and thus also grounding the freedom of the act of origin as per Jüngel's "more than necessary." The eternal *perichoresis* in this respect is the primal *communicatio idiomatum:* the "natural" interchange of divine properties that harmonizes the three persons as one living organism, the eternal Beloved Community. As antecedently Beloved Community God is God who can and does give Himself to creatures in the free act of creation out of infinite alternatives, and again in redemption by the folly of God wiser than the wisdom of men, and at last in fulfillment that gives life to the dead — only the dead. To give in this way, God must be conceived to have available all possible worlds, the wisdom to know them and choose the one that best accords with the surplus of love that God is, and the surplus of love to initiate and actualize such a world of creatures. Following Kendall Soulen, this would extend to consideration of the divine "nature" the "most appropriate way of naming the persons of the Trinity . . . precisely in the three patterns together, as mutually illuminating, nonidentical repetitions of each other."[116] *Esse Deum dare* by the concrete particular agents of Father, Son, and Holy Spirit in the three distinct acts of creation, redemption, and fulfillment according to the divine perfections of power, wisdom, and love as the One God who will be God for us in the coming of the Beloved Community that antecedently He is and consequently He becomes for us.

In this light the naturally divine harmony of power, wisdom, and love provides the profoundest alternative to thinking of the economic appearances of God as manifestations adapted to varying temporal circumstances of a divine being that is in itself static and beyond apprehension, *because it makes the "nature" of God knowable* (in a pragmatic, not theoretical sense), even if not in all eternity comprehensible. This knowability of divine "nature" cuts the ground from under the modalist move. This solution that locates God's unfathomable and ineffable singularity in the *harmony* that is promised, moreover, happily corresponds to Jenson's difficult speculation of divine glory as akin to a musical fugue. All this preceding, however, is but a note sounding in anticipation of the conclusion of this system of theology.

## "Sanctification": Holy Secularity in Fulfillment of Creation

As we transition now to consideration of the work of the Spirit, we note that heretofore we have avoided the traditional terminology of "sanctification" to describe the work of the Spirit of the Father of the Son, not indeed to leave it behind, but to resituate it according to the present system of theology in which the Spirit brings creation to its eschatological fulfillment by communicating the

---

116. R. Kendall Soulen, *The Divine Name(s) and the Holy Trinity: Distinguishing the Voices,* vol. 1 (Louisville: Westminster John Knox, 2011), p. 255.

redemption that is in Christ the Son. So we have spoken of the Spirit's work as the fulfillment of creation, therewith also taking creation itself as divine promise of things to come by the faithful obedience of humanity, the image of God on the earth, the New Adam, Jesus Christ. This resituating is necessary to link the Spirit to creation as the promise of its origin and as the innovation of its preservation under, but also against, the usurping structures of malice and injustice; here resistance to the wrong kind of change is as imperative as recognizing the Spirit's creative innovation. This move makes it both possible and desirable to conceive of "holy secularity" well beyond the walls of our funeral societies — literally and figuratively. For the Spirit is everywhere at work in creation, making holy wherever the sign is unified with the thing signified as He intends and gives, even if faith alone sees this and knows it, joins in and celebrates it, as the very work of creation being fulfilled. Such holy secularity happens in creative labor, faithful marriage, also in organized religion and even by means of political sovereignty, where these serve rather than exploit. Here justice and love structure life in holy secularity against the structures of malice and injustice; such is the "sanctifying" work of the Holy Spirit on the way to the coming of the Beloved Community. For, it is not a creative work but an idle tautology if the Spirit sanctifies only the holy rather than the profane.

Beloved Community also makes it necessary to decouple "sanctification" from a narrow, bigoted, and often legalistic quid pro quo of the religion business that sacrifices the body in order to gain the soul — in truth no holy work of the Spirit at all, but the cunning of the religious will-to-power and source of a special *ressentiment* that poisons life with the profoundest, most sublime, and spiritual *malice*. But, as Cheryl Peterson has concisely and effectively argued, for theology in the tradition of Luther sanctification is communal, not individualistic;[117] it is gift and missiological task of the Spirit, not the preservation of an ever-shrinking religious legacy in decomposing Christendom.[118] By asking, *Who* is the church?, and theologically answering by "starting with the Spirit"[119] (parsing "Spirit" as Spirit of the Father and the Son in the Trinitarian way, not as the independent operator of enthusiasm), Peterson in quite exact parallel to this system of theology grounds theological subjectivity as the ever-learning common mind of the ecclesia in mission to the nations. Just this move makes it both possible and desirable to reconceive "sanctification" as the communal progress of faith in true and so life-transforming knowledge of God on the way to the coming of the Beloved Community.

The work of "sanctification," of making holy, is as such *life*-giving, so that

117. Cheryl M. Peterson, *Who Is the Church? An Ecclesiology for the Twenty-First Century* (Minneapolis: Fortress, 2013), pp. 123-28.

118. Peterson, *Who Is the Church?*, pp. 143-47. On the end of Christendom, see pp. 83-97.

119. Peterson provides an excellent narrative exposition of the Book of Acts, *Who Is the Church?*, pp. 99-120. Notice the conceptual transition from substance with essential attributes, the "what" question, to the description of church as "who," the baptismal subject united with its object, Jesus Christ, by the Spirit to constitute His earthly Body in mission to the nations.

creation comes to fulfillment in a free, joyful, and articulate praise of God in and by a redeemed humanity. This anticipated participation in God's own eternal life is thus personally mediated by faith in new lives of Christian discipleship. It is not an impersonal, mechanical, or automatic process.[120] The Spirit comes as personal reality, as the liberating Lord who frees from idols and demons for Himself, not as an impersonal source of divine energy to be tapped and deployed willfully at the whim and art of private individuals or abusive institutions. It is the Spirit who blows as He will, bestowing faith when and where it pleases God. Precisely so, the Spirit is in His very person the gift itself that changes everything. The Spirit is God Heard as the Father's spoken love for the Son as also for us, God Heard in the Son's life lived returning in love to the Father as also in us, God Heard now in human faith that freely and joyfully receives with Jesus the Father's favor and with the same freedom and joy rises with Jesus from the baptismal waters for combat with the anti-divine powers. In the Spirit, the anthropocentric, egocentric distortion of the created image of God which in its fit of envy leads to deathly violence against others as also against self is crucified by the Spirit, precisely *not* by means of self-devised pious exercises, meditations, devotions, deprivations, and so on. Rather the Spirit works this work by the Word, a lifelong and daily conversion of the heart to the new and ecstatic existence of faith in God, love for the neighbor, and hope for the world. The Spirit comes to reorganize affects, and if affects are not reorganized, only the shell of faith exists, precisely not its beating heart; in Luther's words, the Spirit "illuminates and inflames hearts so that [people] grasp and accept [the Word], cling to it and persevere in it,"[121] indicating once again how artificial a solely forensic account of imputed righteousness must be. But in the Spirit, a new eccentric humanity arises that lives outside of itself by faith in God and love of neighbor and hope for the world. This new life in the Spirit is a kind of ecstasy or rapture; faith is always the personal freedom to give life away in divine confidence of its return, patiently to suffer one another in divine confidence of our final blessedness, always to rejoice and to hope against hope in every adversity: all in all to give glory to God and just so to come to true life, to share in God's life, the only eternal life of which the Spirit is harbinger. True "sanctification" is this doxological ecstasy, new life as freed and joyful Eucharist, the self-offering of Jesus made also ours by the gift of the same Spirit of faith in His own faith vindicated on our behalf.

We can and should speak just here with Luther of two kinds of righteousness,[122] so that against any appearance of "theopanism"[123] from the perspective

---

120. As some traditional theological terminology may unfortunately suggest: "infused grace," "medicine of immortality," "divinization" — all easy targets of liberal theology, impugned as elements of a "physical theory of redemption."

121. *BC,* p. 436.

122. *LW* 31, pp. 293-306.

123. Edward T. Oakes assumes this criticism by Przywara in his otherwise illuminating account of how von Balthasar — a Catholic theologian in substantial proximity to Luther —

of traditional substance ontology, it is quite clear that a "substantial individual" (if we must speak this way), that is to say, the biographical human and creaturely patient-agent is transformed and made new, not by shedding historically concrete personhood and being absorbed into some transcendent and ineffable substance. This is the "mystical" misinterpretation of Luther that began in Osiander and fatefully traumatized Lutheranism into the reactionary doctrine of solely forensic imputation in justification; it is perpetuated by Catholic polemics to this day — even by such luminaries as de Lubac.[124] But the new being in Christ lives "in the flesh" by faith, that is, in the new relation of trust in God given in Christ by the Spirit, living a specific time-space biography uniquely its own, replete with all the changes and chances of life, proceeding at every step by faithful and fateful decisions covered by the forgiveness of sins and in no other way becoming one historically concrete person in union with Christ on the way to the Beloved Community. In this perspective our "own proper righteousness" is nothing other than each believer's own Christian life from baptism day to resurrection day by virtue of a particular body in its own particular temporal sequence, member like all others of the common body. This life in and as body is uniquely and preciously each one's own, not as the product of a self-determining agency, but as the patient who becomes agent by faith and lives justly — since it is the just who *live* by their *faith.* It is divinely valued as such a body and the body is the very place of the Spirit's coming to lead in the world. What this personal life in the body is not, theologically, is any kind of an autonomous, that is to say, purely self-determining agency. Nor is its inevitable suffering as body a tacit imperative to become a sovereign power, ultimately and ironically but catastrophically one that eliminates the body itself as source of suffering. As body, this vehicle of new agency is first patient of God's creating. It is patient with Christ in the mortification of the flesh on the way to redemption. As mortified, it becomes an agent of the life-giving Spirit and His gifts and so agent of its own proper righteousness in the actual life it lives in love and hope. Thus this agency is as member of the Body of Christ.

We have already called attention to the subtle but crucial distinction between the *Alleinwirksamkeit Gottes* (sole agency of God) and the *Alleswirksamkeit Gottes* (universal agency of God), following Augustine's dictum that God as Creator of all that is not God is the cause of all causes but not the maker of all choices, having crowned creation with human creatures that have wills of their own, howsoever fallen into bondage under the structures of malice and injustice.

---

was influenced by the dialogue and debate between Barth and Przywara; see his *Pattern of Redemption: The Theology of Hans Urs von Balthasar* (New York: Continuum, 2002), pp. 33-39.

124. Henri de Lubac, S.J., *Augustinianism and Modern Theology,* trans. Lancelot Sheppard (New York: Crossroad, 2000), pp. 231-32, even after conceding, "It is true that Jansenius begins by rejecting energetically the opinion 'of Luther and Calvin,' by which original righteousness was as natural to the first man as health is to the animal or coldness to water" (p. 37).

In that case these human creatures must be won freely and joyfully to will the will of God and in this way learn true obedience as faith in the holy yet unfailing love of God. The gospel tells of God who out of love for perishing humanity sent the Son in order to bestow the life-giving Spirit, so that in the Spirit, with the Son, a new humanity might live to God now and forever. In the gospel narrative the Spirit is manifest as the One sent by the Father to lead Jesus into His life's contest with the unclean spirits and finally to raise Jesus from death's grip. In precise parallel with this *sovereign* and personal role in the life, death, and resurrection of Jesus, the Spirit is sent again from the risen Lord to create His earthly body and to endow it with gifts for its messianic mission in the world. The risen Lord baptizes with the Spirit and fire. The Spirit in turn makes the risen Christ really present in the preaching of the gospel in such a way that hearers of the Word spiritually die in this encounter with Christ that they may rise with Him to new life as doers of the Word, just because first of all they are remade and remain open-minded and open-hearted hearers of it. Thus the faith wrought by the Spirit as obedience is not any human spirituality; it is quite specifically this spirituality of the Father and the Son that is bestowed upon creatures as a real participation in the crucified and risen life of Jesus. It is not *our* faith that incorporates Jesus into *our* projects, but Jesus' Spirit-wrought faithfulness that finds the echo in us of our little faith and draws us by that personal appropriation into *His* way of life. Sanctification is thus no arbitrary, self-chosen human act of self-improvement according to the prevailing sentiments of moral majorities or, for that matter, moral minorities. Spiritual gifts and spiritual fruits befitting the life of Jesus are rather given for the building up of His community of life in a world stigmatized by death. In this community the Spirit is revealed as Lord and as Giver of *God's* life — giving life to the dead, justifying the ungodly, calling into being new worlds out of the ruins of one dying. Being so gifted and actually so living *is* the sanctified life.

There is a price to be paid theologically for this dialectic of the Spirit and the Word that brings about faith and offense alike in the gospel's course through the nations; it is the rejection of all too-easy doctrines of *apokatastasis* (universal reconciliation) that have become commonplace today in theology. As there is sanctification, so also there *is* a hell of God's eternal rejection, though we may hope for Christ's sake that it in the end it will be lightly populated, even unpopulated but for "the devil." But we need not speculate about the final future to see this unnerving implication of the Spirit's sovereignty in His work through the Word. We see already now how the gospel creates and nurtures faith but also how it offends and hardens hearts, anticipating the eschaton of judgment. Oriented to such present experience, Luther insisted on the paradox of the *resistibility* of the *sovereign* Spirit's work with his (inconsistent) teaching on the hiddenness *(deus absconditus)* and revealedness *(deus revelatus)* of God. At times this appears as a virtual dualism between God revealed in the economy as universal savior and God hidden in majesty decreeing and working a double predestination. Karl Barth objected to this apparent dualism of Luther's teaching on the grounds that any reference to some other God than God revealed in Christ destabilizes revelation itself as God's truthful self-donation and self-interpretation to the world. From this Barth drew out the natural implication of the universal scope of Christ's atonement, hence the accomplished fact of the world's reconciliation with God. It can certainly be granted that some of Luther's formulations in this respect are unguarded, as he himself evidently came to realize;[125] but the dialectic of Word and Spirit of inaugurated eschatology that we are affirming against realized eschatology that collapses together Spirit and Word allows for the genuine experience in faith of God's hiddenness in the as-yet-unredeemed world that still groans in frustration, sighing for God's promised future. And it does so without positing a hidden will of God, a God beyond God. It rather affirms that the Word cannot be understood truly, that is, "for me," apart from the Spirit's grant of faith. Yet this is a grant that is not in human power, and evidently, moreover, not made to all but only as the Spirit decides in the gospel's course through the nations, as Romans 9–11 teaches. Even so, just here the final thought is the hopeful one that God "consigned all to sin that He might have mercy on all" (Rom. 11:32). With the apostle we must leave the matter here in the genuine tension of faith that is not yet sight, of knowledge that sees in part and knows in part.

Luther's *deus absconditus* is thus best interpreted not as nominalism's *deus absolutus,* but as faith's own perception of God's creative determination of the world as it variously appears in the differing lights of nature and of grace and of glory, since the believer remains a member of the common body and continues to see things in the light of nature. Reinhard Hütter thus argued against Barth the general point made by post-Barthian theologies of hope that "the decisive problem is not the still-outstanding vision, but the as-yet-incomplete redemption and renewal of the creation."[126] The embattled work of Christ continues in His hidden reign and in the Spirit's manifest mission to the nations in conflict with the unholy spirits, but neither of these is yet the actual redemption and fulfillment of creation but only the inauguration of the latter by the coming of the former. As already indicated, the criticism of Barth in this connection is that he cannot understand the Holy Spirit's work other than as a private "internal" or "subjective" attestation of the objective revelation of an already accomplished reconciliation. He does not have in view the temporal event of the coming of the personal Spirit to call, gather, enlighten, and unite by means of the physical, creaturely event of the church's proclamation and gathering to faith from the nations. But just this is the Spirit's work of convicting the world concerning sin, righteousness, and

---

125. Robert Kolb, *Bound Choice, Election, and Wittenberg Theological Method: From Martin Luther to the Formula of Concord* (Grand Rapids: Eerdmans, 2005), pp. 166-69.

126. Reinhard Hütter, *Suffering Divine Things: Theology as Church Practice,* trans. Doug Scott (Grand Rapids: Eerdmans, 2000), p. 114.

judgment. Thus, to this extent the dualism of the sign and thing signified remains in force for Barth and he cannot really carry through on his Trinitarian intention[127] but ends up with an inconsistent "binitarianism."

It is in this connection — namely of the Spirit as down payment of God's promised future in whom the eschaton of judgment already now is breaking in — that the traditional Lutheran distinction between God's Word as law and as gospel may be usefully, even vitally retrieved, that is, when taken as the Spirit's art of making the folly of God wiser than the wisdom of the world, pitting the law against the law in order to make liberty for all. This is not a psychologizing distinction to the effect that only those terrorized by the preaching of the law can appreciate the consolation of the gospel. That particular deformation has been the ruin of many a preacher and even more auditors. Neither is it some kind of ontological distinction between the Gods of the Old and New Testament, or a re-pudiation of Torah as expressing the will of God for righteousness on the earth, as neo-Gnostics think in antinomian versions of the doctrine of justification. Rather the distinction is between the Spirit's uses of the one Word of God to afflict the comfortable and comfort the afflicted by the proclamation of the incarnate Son, Jesus Christ. This is an art in which preachers of the Word must be trained and become practiced if they are to preach wisely and well.

Christ may be proclaimed as the true model of the human being whom God intends, the very fulfillment of the law, who in the power of the Spirit loved God above all and neighbor as Himself, our New Adam. When used this way, how-ever, the brilliant light of Christ is "law," that is, God's holy will for us and thus the demand placed upon us to be perfect even as the Father in heaven is perfect. When used properly this way, moreover, the holy demand placed upon us by the Spirit holding up Christ as model of divine Sonship reveals our impotence to will the will of God, let alone to do it and to live as beloved creatures doing the blessed works of the divinely appointed image. This prophetic usage of the Word of God reveals sinfulness and necessitates Christ, no longer as model but now as Redeemer; so it gives way to the gospel use of the same Word of God in-carnate to give what God commands, namely, the righteousness that is this same Christ for us with the Spirit to receive Him. The proper distinction between law and gospel is thus an "instruction to preachers" (Jenson) to know what they are doing and to know to whom they are speaking. The rule is that they so proclaim Christ that mere trust in Him suffices to put "real, not fictitious" sinners right with God and just so to convince the world concerning sin, righteousness, and justice. At the same time, this rule also stipulates that preachers recognize that the grant of this trust in Christ's mercy is not in their power — for all the reasons that Nevin inveighed against the "anxious bench." The grant of faith belongs to the Spirit who blows where He will, who unifies the sign, "Christ crucified," with the thing signified, "Christ also for me, a sinner, together with these others," as

---

127. Hütter, *Suffering Divine Things,* p. 110.

God pleases. The church's ministry to the Word serves but does not ever master, for this conviction is contested by the unholy spirits until the eschaton of judgment. The Spirit who unifies the sign and the thing signified for faith just so divides the world — at least provisionally. To this divisive work of the Spirit on the earth we now turn.

## The Spirit's Mission to the Nations

We can borrow here a formulation made elsewhere recently: "The end of Christendom in the theological recognition of the disputability of the Christian claim to truth demands reconstruction of Christianity from its present debased state as chaplaincy to political sovereignty (as Volkskirche or as denominationalism) to its true being in the missionary act of the Spirit to bring the Son to the nations as the One sent by the Father for the world's reconciliation. The communion so drawn from the nations is both harbinger and agent of the coming in fullness of the Beloved Community that is from all eternity and to all eternity the blessed life of the Holy Trinity."[128]

As creedal faith in the "one, holy, catholic, and apostolic" church is faith in the Holy Spirit unifying, sanctifying, keeping whole, and keeping faithful, the church cannot become an independent item of theological investigation without missing an essential and inherent dynamism, namely, that the church exists in the Spirit's gospel mission to the nations as both foretaste and agent. In other words, concern with the church, theologically, is concern with the Holy Spirit whose chief work is to gather from the nations and to send to the nations on the way to the Beloved Community. To say that "God" is the coming of the Beloved Community, as this system of theology proposes in its singular cognitive claim, is thus to say not only that "God is missionary *in se,*" not only that this *missio Dei* brings the Beloved Community to our world, but that this *missio* of the Father who sends the Son in the Spirit "cannot ever come to an end. There must, therefore, be an eschatological continuation of God's mission. For all eternity, the Father will continue to send his Son and Spirit to bring peace and joy to creation" (Holmes).[129] At the fulfillment the church will no more be something separated out of and in conflict with the unholy world, as Revelation 21:22 and 1 Corinthians 15:28 indicate. In the interim, moreover, the "means of missionary witness [are to be] congruous with its end; that is, the witness to the reconciliation in Christ demands an actual reconciled fellowship with Christ." "This life in Christ," Lesslie

---

128. *BA,* p. 166, altered.

129. Cited in John G. Flett, *The Witness of God: The Trinity, Missio Dei, Karl Barth, and the Nature of Christian Community* (Grand Rapids: Eerdmans, 2010), p. 76 from Stephen R. Holmes, "Trinitarian Missiology: Towards a Theology of God as Missionary," *International Journal of Systematic Theology* 8, no. 1 (2006): 89.

Newbigin continues, "is not merely the instrument of the apostolic mission, it is equally the 'eschatological end and purpose of reconciliation.' "[130]

In this way the sterile alternative between so-called "classical" and so-called "ecumenical" missiologies is transcended, that is, between saving individuals by recruitment to church membership under the model of extending Christendom on the one side and seeing in secularization and urbanization, underwritten by capitalist homogenization, immanent progress toward the kingdom of God on the other. John Flett has smartly parsed this false dilemma and opened up the theological alternative to it by reading Barth's renewal of Trinitarian theology in ways that contravene the preceding critique of Barth's incomplete, "binitarian" theology. In Flett's own words, "Mission is something the Christian community must receive in order to be, and any attempt to seize control of this act threatens her being."[131] That is all to the good, if Flett's reading proves convincing to the guild of Barth scholars. It is not wholly convincing theologically, however, if the notion of God's being missionary *in se* amounts to a gospel that is nothing more than a repetition in time of God's eternal self-identity, even when this self-identity is parsed as Trinity.

The gospel is certainly nothing less than the coming of the triune God. But if that is all that is understood — that God as missionary *in se* becomes missionary *pro nobis* — such an account, as previously argued, has to sustain the Western dualism of the sign and the thing signified to avoid capture of God by the religion business for its own purposes of chaplaincy to political sovereignty and domestication of the Spirit. In just this well-intended way, however, it renders the actual and indeed essential work of the Spirit nugatory. As a result, it cannot adequately reckon the cost to God of originating a creation with a mind of its own; becoming flesh in the person of the Son and so subject to the creature's willfulness and hostility; and yet seeking and finding a way in the Spirit of making holy those who are and remain by virtue of the common body members if no longer subjects and citizens of the structures of malice and injustice. In other words, the apocalyptic framework of theology has dropped out here in favor of an accomplished reconciliation, so that the contested nature of the *missio Dei* is insufficiently recognized. Nor can such thinking reckon with the genuine problems of mission in this world, where creatures do not know and do not want to know that they are creatures; where therefore the offered redemption of the creature is resented and rejected as an answer to a question that no one is asking; and where the new sanctity ascribed to secular callings, no less than the disruption of grace that gathers and empowers forgiven sinners, are found inconvenient if not subversive.

The difference indicated here between the blessedness of the eternal Trinity and the woe of the economic Trinity is the test of what we mean by *missio Dei*, that is, whether our conception of the eternal Trinity discloses as signature of

---

130. Flett, *The Witness*, pp. 71-72, cited from Lesslie Newbigin, *The Household of God: Lectures on the Nature of the Church* (London: SCM, 1953), pp. 147-48.
    131. Flett, *The Witness*, p. 73.

deity the self-surpassing capacity of the Creator for the creature. Flett cites Barth in conclusion, "What value would His deity be to us if — instead of crossing in that deity the very real gulf between Himself and us — He left that deity behind Him in His coming to us, if it came to be outside of Him as He became ours?"[132] True enough, but the alternative here is not the abject kenosis against which Barth rightly protests. The alternative is to take Barth's own notion of deity as "event" further in terms of its Trinitarian interpretation so that God's becoming "outside" of Himself — *God surpassing God* — is not a negation but an expression of the Trinity's eternal being in becoming. Then the Spirit comes and is made known in the unification of the sign and the thing signified. So Luther: "But the glory of our God is precisely that for our sakes he comes down to the very depths, into human flesh, into the bread, into our mouth, our heart, our bosom; moreover, for our sakes he allows himself to be treated ingloriously both on the cross and on the altar. . . ."[133] This true "glory" of deity makes the bread the Body of Christ, Jesus of Nazareth the Son of God, the water-drowned sinner the newborn child of God. This work is the glory of the Spirit of God and His specific mission in the world, communicating the self-donation of the Word for us by communicating Himself as Lord and Giver of the life of God for the life of the world (2 Cor. 3:17-18).

For present purposes, however, Flett has another contribution to make: an incisive critique of German Lutheran missiology in the 1920s and 30s. By reconstruction of Barth's correspondence with significant missiologists, Flett shows how the concept of *Volkstum* was made by these missiologists into a foundation for Christianization of "primitive" cultures in the sense of extending and indigenizing Christendom. "The grounding of mission in *Volkstum* leads to the method of Christianization, and together these define the whole of the missionary task." Interestingly, so far as Barth challenged this uncritical and "totalizing logic," he was taken by the missiologists to be denying "the very possibility of missions."[134] The missiologists defended their *völkisch* approach to Barth by pointing at the pincer movements of Anglo-Saxon colonialism on the one side and Bolshevist revolutionary leveling on the other as the actual alternatives to their model of indigenization of the gospel in new cultural contexts by way of nation-building. As one wrote to him, "What is the larger danger today: that we turn our nation into an idol, or that we are submerged by the floods of internationalism and are Americanized or bolshevized?"[135] But the price paid for the *völkisch* approach that assumes the construction of an articulate ethnic culture based on primal revelation, and so the agonistic experience of God's law before the gospel can be proclaimed and appreciated, is a heavy one. It is not only the obvious blindness to the danger of idolizing the nation, as would be revealed shortly in the course

132. Flett, *The Witness,* p. 199, cited from *CD* IV/1.
133. *LW* 37:72.
134. Flett, *The Witness,* p. 118.
135. Flett, *The Witness,* p. 119.

of the Third Reich. But theologically, as Flett sees, this missiology aims at "the true idea of the *Volkskirche* as the historical goal of the missionary undertaking"[136] — note well, not the Beloved Community, but the ethnic community of blood and soil as foundation for the community of faith. This kind of neo-Arian subordination of the second and third articles to the first turns mission upside down and inside out. Nor does it get "creation" right, the promise of which is frustrated and yet to be fulfilled and so in need of redemption.

As Carl Braaten had similarly pointed out, the evolution here from Pietist to Liberal required but a small step: "The aim of mission is no longer to confront individuals with the preaching of Christ for repentance and faith with a view to eternal salvation, but rather to spread Christian culture, morality and religion to other people as a whole, and thus to raise them to a higher point of development."[137] Braaten lifted up the challenge to the false antithesis of Pietist soul-saving and Liberal nation-building missiologies by Martin Kähler, who asked the "decisive question . . . whether Christianity points to a suprahistorical message valid for every religion, something which can be truly called 'the word of God.'" "On a purely human plane," Braaten asked, "what right do Christians have to claim any religious superiority over others"[138] according to either "classical" or "ecumenical" missiologies? Missiology without a definite word from God addressed to all, however contestable, self-destructs not only abroad but at home. In fact contemporary religious and cultural pluralism mean that "it can no longer be taken for granted that everyone knows what Christianity means, or that Christianity holds the inside track in commanding people's interests and loyalties."[139]

Carl Braaten has been a theologian in the tradition of Luther who has risen to the missiological challenges of post-Holocaust/post-Christendom theology by arguing for a rigorous return to the eschatological orientation of the Christian kerygma as a promise of the coming of the reign of God announced to the world in the divine speech-act of the resurrection of the Crucified. The deep affinity of the current project in systematic theology with Braaten's themes should be evident. Braaten for his part met Kähler's demand for a genuine word of God with "the universal promise that is signed and sealed by the life, death, and resurrection of Jesus . . ." where the signing and sealing is the missiological work of the Spirit. This is a promise addressed to all peoples and so "sets in motion an historical mission to announce and celebrate the universal future that has been opened up for all people, nations, cultures, and religions. None are too bad to be saved or too good to be damned. None are left out of the covenant which God has made and promises to keep on account of Christ."[140]

---

136. Flett, *The Witness,* p. 120.
137. Braaten, *Flaming Center,* p. 25.
138. Braaten, *Flaming Center,* p. 27.
139. Braaten, *Flaming Center,* p. 64.
140. Braaten, *Flaming Center,* p. 54.

Thinking this promise through as divine self-donation and divine self-communication, Braaten comes both to the doctrine of the Trinity and to the reconceptualizing of the church in this context of the Trinitarian *missio Dei*. "The church is sent by the Spirit; the Spirit is sent by the Son; and the Son is sent by the Father."[141] In the spirit of critical dogmatics, Braaten accordingly wrote that "the church has to struggle for the realization of the kingdom of God on the model of its definitive arrival in Jesus Christ." Thus he asked the test question: "Is the present-day church norming its mission on such a model, or does it make up a program of convenience to suit itself?"[142] Just so he likewise locates the theological task of "norming" in the mission to the nations, in accord with the foregoing critique of the dualism of the sign and the thing signified: "We would differ from the Barthian way by placing eschatological salvation into the stream of the unfinished historical process. It is not a *fait accompli* above and beyond history, but is at work in the events of history, transforming it from within. This eschatological salvation is not so much *ganz anders* (totally other), as Barth said, but *ganz änderndes* (totally transforming), as Moltmann holds."[143] So Braaten joined the ranks of the post-Barthian theologies of hope aiming to restore the outstanding, still-conflicted, inaugurated, but not yet fulfilled eschatology attested in the New Testament.

Congruent with this historicizing of the eschatological, the polarization between personal salvation and social salvation is to be overcome. "Mission will assume the role of advocacy, tracking down the causes of global injustice and violence ... [also] how the American system itself, in which we are enmeshed, is involved in a conspiracy with other big powers to control and channel the world's limited resources to our own advantage."[144] But just this public advocacy it will do *as theology*: "What, then, is the point of the church's mission if the grace of salvation is possible without it? The church [rather] becomes a sign of salvation, at her best bringing to light what is hiddenly present, proclaiming and interpreting what God is doing everywhere, discerning the power of salvation at work everywhere it can be found in the world."[145] Because the church exists in receiving the Spirit manifest, who is the Spirit of the Father and the Son, the church in mission can recognize the Spirit incognito in the world, at work in the common body structuring orders of love and justice in contest with the structures of malice and injustice.

Braaten's pioneering work along these lines has borne fruit. A festschrift, *Critical Issues in Ecclesiology*,[146] appeared in 2011, making a fitting tribute to this happy warrior who has spent the last twenty years of his illustrious career battling *pro*

141. Braaten, *Flaming Center,* p. 55.

142. Braaten, *Flaming Center,* p. 79.

143. Braaten, *Flaming Center,* p. 106.

144. Braaten, *Flaming Center,* p. 89.

145. Braaten, *Flaming Center,* p. 113.

146. The following discussion of *Critical Issues in Ecclesiology* in part first appeared as a book review in *Lutheran Quarterly* 27, no. 1 (Spring 2013): 104-6.

*ecclesia,* "for the church" as "sent by the Spirit, sent by the Son, sent by the Father." Ironically, however, working for the unity of the divided churches on the normative basis of biblical canon, ecumenical creeds, and Reformation confessions (including today the reforming documents of Vatican II and the Joint Declaration on Justification!) is *divisive* of today's pseudo-theological unities, whether in North American denominationalism or the European *Volkskirche.* Braaten has labored to see a realignment of the forces intending Christian orthodoxy emerge out of these ruins. The beginnings of that new synthesis may be glimpsed in the more significant contributions to this volume from across the ecumenical spectrum.

UCC theologian Gabriel Fackre argues cogently that a "full doctrine of the at-one-ment is inseparable from the at-one-ment of the Church,"[147] meaning that the three traditional motifs of satisfaction of divine wrath, moral example, and victory over contra-divine powers should not be played off against one another but thought together theologically in the converging church bringing the redemption that is in Christ Jesus to the nations in the Spirit's holistic mission. Evangelical Timothy George takes to task Konrad Raiser's attack on theology as such, noted above, by recalling the splendid statement on the *verbum externum* from the Orthodox delegation to the 1991 Canberra assembly of the World Council of Churches: "We must guard against a tendency to substitute a 'private' spirit, the spirit of the world or other spirits for the Holy Spirit who proceeds from the Father and rests in the Son. Our tradition is rich in respect to local and national cultures, but we find it impossible to invoke the spirits of 'earth, air, water and sea creatures.' " Pneumatology is inseparable from Christology or from the doctrine of the Holy Trinity confessed by the church on the basis of divine revelation."[148] Anglican Joe Mangina's contribution, "A Cross-Shaped Church," makes the "Pauline-Lutheran" qualification of *communio* ecclesiology (expertly limned in this volume by Roman Catholic Susan Wood) better than do most Lutherans. He asks the critical dogmatic question: "[C]ommunion in what? Participation in whom?" and answers missiologically: "The church may be thought of as the death of Jesus stretched out across time, not by way of repeating or supplementing that death — the Reformation is very clear about this — but by way of attesting and confirming it. The unity of the church is not an end in itself. Its particular *koinonia* serves the larger covenant in which God is involved with the world as a whole."[149] In an encouraging parallel to Cheryl Peterson's work,[150]

---

147. *Critical Issues,* p. 7.

148. *Critical Issues,* p. 61.

149. *Critical Issues,* pp. 79-80.

150. Peterson provides here a helpful and well-researched summary of her case for Pneumatological ecclesiology, previously discussed. She criticizes the Protestant tendency to reduce the Spirit's work to inwardness in the experience of pious subjectivity (*Critical Issues,* p. 159). From Luther's catechism she draws the counter-thesis that "[s]anctification is more than a new existential awareness for the believer and includes a communal element . . . 'holy people' corporately lives out and experiences the new existence" (*Critical Issues,* p. 161).

LCMS theologian Leopoldo A. Sánchez M. takes up the work of Roman Catholic Yves Congar on the dialectic of Word and Spirit in his impressive essay. He fleshes out a view of the church as a corporate reality from the perspective of a Trinitarian pneumatology, that is, of "the Spirit as a personal agent in its own right" and shows how this strong Trinitarian personalism opens the divided churches to ecumenical engagement and convergence.[151] Frank Senn of the Society of the Holy Trinity crisply reminds Lutherans of the ecumenical orthodoxy at the heart of their claim: "The very way the article on justification is presented in the Augsburg Confession shows that it is a theological implication of established church dogma. . . . [I]f God is as holy as the doctrine of the Trinity affirms, if original sin is as virulent as the Augustinian tradition holds, and if Christ is as necessary for salvation as the Christological doctrines imply, then the only way to talk about the human relationship to God is to hold" to justification by faith alone.[152]

This inventory of new theological probing of the theological subjectivity of the ecclesia inspired by Braaten over against the mass of dysfunction that is the contemporary, and de facto divided, churches suffices to make the present point. If the cognitive claim of Christian theology is that "God" is the coming of the Beloved Community, the ecclesia has no other existence than to serve Christ in the Spirit to a world captive to and groaning under the structures of malice and injustice. As discussed earlier, Cheryl Peterson advances a thesis that accords well with the present argument: "A central claim of this book is that the church finds its identity in the activity of the Holy Spirit. This makes the starting point of ecclesiology the triune God and what God is doing, rather than the church and what its members do. . . ."[153] Peterson articulates this thesis contextually in North America by sharply contrasting it with the "voluntary association concept." This starting point of ecclesiology in what the Spirit is doing through the gospel by baptism into Christ permits her to expose the presumption of righteousness that infects ecclesiologies that start with their own agency or their members' agencies. By contrast, the community of the Spirit "embodies new life, albeit imperfectly; that is, echoing Luther's dictum that the true people of God is the one that brings the judgment of the cross to bear upon itself, as a community who lives out the gift of reconciliation and forgiveness before the world, as people who are *simul iustus et peccator.*"[154] Likewise, in parallel with the present effort's starting point in baptism as the formation of the theological subject, she begins with the Spirit's novelty in the ecclesia in its witness to Jesus and "the centrality of forgiveness of sins." Her reading of Luther's Large Catechism shows a "narrative structure, drawing out the story of salvation in which the Holy Spirit acts as the character who enables the church to live out the new life given in Christ's resurrection as

---

151. *Critical Issues,* p. 190.
152. *Critical Issues,* p. 31.
153. Peterson, *Who Is the Church?,* p. 6.
154. Peterson, *Who Is the Church?,* p. 92.

"the communion of saints" and the "forgiveness of sins."[155] In the Spirit, communion and forgiveness coalesce and do not polarize, because in the Spirit we share the Word incarnate. Indeed in the Spirit we become words of the Word incarnate spoken to one another, speaking together to the world in a common speaking of salvation that is at the same time a common doing of salvation.

There is a further implication of taking the Spirit's work as formative of a community of forgiven sinners in the world. If the church, as Bonhoeffer argued in *Sanctorum Communio,* is "Christ-existing-as-community," then the baptismal calling of all the people of God is articulated as renewal of the *imago Dei* in Jesus Christ, the Lord who became a servant. This is the thing signified in what Luther signed as "the Priesthood of All Believers." It is the Christian service within the people to which the gospel has come and made for itself a dwelling in the gathering of the ecclesia. By virtue of the common body to which the gathered in Christ still belong, their "ordinary" stations in life now become the vocations of what Robert Benne called "ordinary saints" in his important and influential book by that title. We will take up Benne's reconceptualization of the old Lutheran doctrine of the "orders of creation" as "places of responsibility"[156] to locate "Christian life in the everyday, common world"[157] in Chapter Eight. In that chapter we consider holy secularity on this earth, on which the cross of Jesus stood, as the place of God's redeeming and fulfilling graces recovering the structures of life from malice and injustice and making them, however provisionally, into structures of love and justice. For the present purpose, however, the point is that Benne retrieves the great insight of Luther in his Reformation treatise on *The Freedom of the Christian* that holiness is wholly secular just as priesthood is not the bribing of God for our own benefit by a hired hand, but serving Christ in the Spirit by serving Christ to the neighbor in need, body and soul. In Benne's words, "[W]hen we in faith hear and receive — and are nurtured in — the gracious word of God in Christ, we enter into union with Christ. Christ's faith, love, and hope are bestowed on us. This is part of the 'happy exchange' that Luther talked about when Christians receive Christ in faith. Christ's gifts to us in the Spirit become effective in our lives."[158] This — not private spirituality — is the "priesthood of all believers."

## The Ministry of the Church — I

Priests, pastors, bishops, deacons, popes, and preachers are also "laypeople" in this sense, who by baptism are called in the Spirit to be Christ to their neighbors

155. Peterson, *Who Is the Church?*, p. 121.
156. Robert Benne, *Ordinary Saints: An Introduction to the Christian Life* (Minneapolis: Fortress, 2003), p. 63.
157. Benne, *Ordinary Saints*, p. 95.
158. Benne, *Ordinary Saints*, p. 99.

in the common world. That means that the clergy also have secular lives that are to be sanctified in the world by the ordinary virtues of competence, integrity, and personal excellence no less than by faith, hope, and love. It is a disgraceful abuse of the special calling to the ministry of Word and Sacrament to disown these common standards in the common body of competent service and personal excellence that pertain to all the baptized on account of the special nature of or-dination. It is part of the decay of Christendom to have clergy rosters populated with sexual predators, unfaithful spouses, distracted parents, slothful and needy parasites sucking congregations dry, "company men" who can think neither crit-ically nor theologically, and/or special pleaders who substitute lament for argu-ment. It is also part of the decay of Christendom in response to this widespread breakdown in clergy discipline to regard the ministry as a job like any other, a "professional career" that may be turned off at five and back on at nine. But the ministry of Word and Sacrament for the pastoring of a flock of God is a calling that indelibly alters the person ordained to it; it is not a "function" that can be switched on and off any more than baptism itself can be switched on and off. Rather, precisely as the indelible stamp of the Spirit marking the cross of Jesus on one's person in baptism, clerical ordination as a specific form of the priesthood of all believers may be resisted, despised, disowned, abused, and rejected but never erased. And just as with baptism, the ordained minister that disgraces her ordination will be held doubly accountable for scandalizing the weak.

There is a distinction, then, to be made within the people of God on the com-mon basis of the one baptism for the forgiveness of sins. In lay vocations most are called into service *from* the Word served in the gathered ecclesia into the world and to the neighbor there in need. Here, as mentioned above, their stations in life become transformative vocations. But some are called into service *to* the Word, for the gathering of the ecclesia, for the building up of the Body of Christ locally and trans-locally, contextually and universally. This is the "ordained" ministry whereby the ecclesia in a lawful procedure (*rite vocatus,* AC XIV) elects one of the baptized to serve the Word in a theologically competent way. This service may be conceived in a variety of concrete forms. It can be conceived as preaching, as teaching, as caring, as presiding, as overseeing, for example, or a mix of these. But in all these forms — inevitable as functions but flexible in organization — there is but one ministry "ordered" *to* Word and Sacrament. Converging on this point, once again the Lutheran-Catholic dialogues of recent times pointed the way forward.

In the 1970 doctrinal dialogue, *Eucharist and Ministry,* Roman Catholic Harry J. McSorley called the Roman Catholic attitude toward the celebration of the Lord's Supper by separated Christian communities the most "neuralgic" problem of ecumenical theology. Ecumenical progress still faces, McSorley wrote, the "serious problem . . . of the competence of a person to lead the Eucha-rist who has not been ordained by a bishop who is himself rightly consecrated."[159]

---

159. *Lutherans and Catholics in Dialogue IV: Eucharist and Ministry* (USA National Com-

McSorley himself took the lead in tackling this "serious problem." In his study, "The Roman Catholic Doctrine of the Competent Minister of the Eucharist in Ecumenical Perspective," he established that the Council of Trent never committed itself on the ontology of ordinations in separated churches, judging only on their illegitimacy or illegality in terms of canon law. In other words, according to McSorley, Trent did not comment on what God does in Protestant celebrations of the Lord's Supper. Trent only denied that these ministrations were legal according to its own ecclesial understanding, and that therefore believers could not possess the full certainty of receiving a valid Sacrament. Moreover, "Trent neither discussed nor rejected the argument of the Lutheran Book of Concord that, when bishops negligently fail to ordain priests for a given Christian community, the pastor of that congregation, himself an ordained priest, can validly ordain priests. . . ."[160] McSorley's acknowledgment here is part of the general perception among Roman Catholics, as it developed in the course of the dialogues, that much of Counter-Reformation theology was based on false or inadequate information. Better historical knowledge reopens issues long thought to have been closed. As McSorley put it, Roman Catholics must reckon with a new "basic principle in interpreting Trent: because Trent condemns something do not conclude that the Reformers were teaching it."[161] In any case, McSorley continued, the view that Protestant Eucharists are wholly void of reality, "a non-efficacious sign" because the clergy who lead them lack proper ordination, was rejected by the Second Vatican Council.[162] It is the Spirit who effectively unifies the sign and the thing signified as promised, not the canon law.

New historical knowledge thus profoundly challenges the traditional Roman Catholic perception. It also raises sharply the question of the pastoral negligence of the papacy at the source of the schism of the Western church in the sixteenth century, as McSorley implied. We are entitled then to venture the thought that the papacy's claim to pastoral oversight over the whole church is undermined by the failure of the papacy (thus far) pastorally to understand dissent and persuade dissenters otherwise. In that case, at fault for schism would be less the stubborn dissent of dissenters than the pastoral failure of overseers. The Roman Catholic theologians who participated in this dialogue in any case issued a public summons for the recognition of the Lutheran ministry; it deserves to be quoted at length:

> As Roman Catholic theologians, we acknowledge in the spirit of Vatican II that the Lutheran communities with which we have been in dialogue are truly Christian churches, possessing the elements of holiness and truth that mark

---

mittee of the Lutheran World Federation and the Bishops' Committee for Ecumenical and Interreligious Affairs, 1970), p. 120.

160. *Eucharist and Ministry,* p. 133.

161. *Eucharist and Ministry,* p. 296.

162. *Eucharist and Ministry,* p. 135.

them as organs of grace and salvation. Furthermore in our study we have found serious defects in the arguments customarily used against the validity of the eucharistic ministry of the Lutheran Churches. In fact, we see no persuasive reason to deny the possibility of the Roman Catholic Church recognizing the validity of this ministry. Accordingly, we ask the authorities of the Roman Catholic Church whether the ecumenical urgency flowing from Christ's will for unity may not dictate that the Roman Catholic Church recognize the validity of the Lutheran Ministry, and correspondingly, the presence of the body and blood of Christ in the eucharistic celebrations of the Lutheran Churches.[163]

This appeal, so noteworthy from the Roman Catholic side, was based upon the following two convergences that the dialogue achieved.

First, the traditional charge that the Lutheran churches are "defective" in lacking the "apostolic succession through episcopal consecration" is mitigated by the greater importance of "apostolic succession in doctrine." The dialogue process demonstrated to the Roman Catholic theologians involved that "despite the lack of episcopal succession, the Lutheran Church by its devotion to gospel, creed and sacrament has preserved a form of doctrinal apostolicity."[164] Second, Lutherans have been found to hold that "ordination to a sacred ministry in the Church derives from Christ and confers the enduring power to sanctify,"[165] precisely, of course, in the ministration of Word and Sacrament through which the Spirit has promised to work as through means. These two convergences on the apostolic and sacramental aspects of the ordained ministry constitute the foundation for a Roman Catholic recognition of the validity of the Lutheran ministry today.

At the conclusion of this dialogue, the Lutheran theologians also asked their churches to confirm the historic conviction that the "Roman Catholic Church is an authentic Church of our Lord Jesus Christ." The difference in form is striking. From the Lutheran point of view, it had never been denied that the Roman Catholic Church, for all its errors under the papacy, is the Church of Jesus Christ. On the contrary, from the Lutheran point of view, the only cause of the schism of the sixteenth century, strictly speaking, had been papal negligence that led to the withdrawal of recognition of its ministry, further compounded by the abusive authority claimed in support of this negligence and disregard. From the Lutheran perspective, Roman Catholic recognition of its ministry would be essentially, if not fully, a restitution of the Church's visible unity. Just this potential breakthrough, however, has been obscured since the time of the dialogue by the growing rift over the ordination of women that had developed in the interim.

163. *Eucharist and Ministry*, p. 32.
164. *Eucharist and Ministry*, pp. 26-27.
165. *Eucharist and Ministry*, p. 29.

## EXCURSUS: THE ORDINATION OF WOMEN[166]

In 2005, my denomination, the Evangelical Lutheran Church in America (ELCA), celebrated the thirty-fifth anniversary of the ordination of women. Today the ELCA has approximately 11,000 ordained ministers active and in good standing. Of these, approximately 2600 are women. In the conclusion of this excursus, I will comment on how the practice has fared in these years. But first I need to set a context because I will argue we do not usually grasp the import of such data. Much more than "women in the ministry" is at stake. *What the ministry is to which they are ordained is the real question.* We should frankly acknowledge that the practice has been ecumenically controversial and remains so, though not always for the same reasons for everyone. Examining the practice theologically provides a context for understanding the nature of the experiment.

Let me begin then with a brief statement of a theological rationale for the ordination of women. It is a culturally appropriate modernization for us in the USA; it conforms with our biblical and confessional norms, when these *norma normata* are themselves normed by the *norma normans,* the Word of our free justification by the Son and reconciliation to the Father in the Spirit, whose living temple is the church and where ordained ministry serves the Word and Sacraments of Christ the Son. Let me explicate this statement step by step.

First, the church under the Spirit is always "modernizing," since it lives in time and can never "go back" to some golden age of the past — if one actually ever existed. Some look back to the blessed fellowship of the first apostles (Acts 2:42-47) but the entire purpose of the Book of Acts is to show how the Holy Spirit does not let the church stand idly by (Acts 1:11), but pushes it forward from Jerusalem to Rome and beyond (Acts 28:8) through many changes in understanding (Acts 10:14-15) and practice (Acts 15:19-21). Second, modernization must be culturally appropriate; after all, the evangelical point of modernizing is to remove false obstacles in the minds of contemporary people (Acts 15:10) so that they can hear the Christian message, and thus come to faith and enter new life at the calling of the aforementioned Spirit of the Father and the Son. Importing culturally inappropriate mandates for modernization from the outside, on the other hand, is a form of neocolonial imperialism, even, if not especially, in the name of a "good cause." This can happen when the Western European or North American experience of feminism is simply imposed on cultures that do not share the same historical development but are nevertheless expected to adopt a Western trajectory of development. Who is to say, what, when, or whether modernization is appropriate? The local churches themselves must decide in a dialogue with other churches who share the same biblical and confessional norms, as we see modeled in the Great Council in Acts 15.

166. This excursus originally appeared as "Whose Church? Which Ministry?," *Lutheran Forum* 42, no. 4 (Winter 2008): 48-53.

Third, there is a subtle but decisive point concerning the relation of the Spirit and the Letter (2 Corinthians 3). One can read the "letter" of the Bible and the confessional documents with perfect historical and grammatical correctness (or deep critical insight) but get the "Spirit" all wrong, if one takes the historical circumstance in which "the Word became flesh and dwelt among us" as giving a so-called "biblical worldview" that ought to be normative for us. This is a version of the Lutheran Church–Missouri Synod repristination theology, which leads to all kinds of embarrassments (e.g., "creationism" versus evolutionary science) and in practice to all kinds of arbitrary selections of what aspects of the "biblical worldview" are still supposed to be authoritative (e.g., should women be required to cover their heads in church?). The text of Scripture and its interpretation in the confessional writings are, on the contrary, historical acts conditioned by their own times, which are not our times. The real theological art is reading the letter of Scripture in the Spirit who once inspired those prophetic and apostolic witnesses of the Word made flesh, Jesus Christ, so that He may speak clearly and truthfully from these Scriptures to His people today.

Concretely, in both biblical times and in the sixteenth century the biological imperative of reproduction defined the role of women in society, including the church (where the practical alternative to marriage and children in the household economy was nunnery or whoredom). How striking then in this very historical context that the Spirit at work in the ministry of Jesus treated women with equal dignity to men (especially evident in the Gospel of Luke); made of Mary Magdalene the first witness of the Empty Tomb and apostle of the Resurrection (John 20) to the men in hiding; and put women to work in the fluid ministries of the earliest churches (Romans 16). When the text of Scripture is read in the light of the Spirit, it becomes clear that women are not only equal recipients with men as hearers of the Word, but potentially equal agents with men as speakers and doers of the Word in service of Word and Sacrament.

Therefore, fourth, we enjoy the gospel freedom in our changed historical circumstances of modern medicine with birth control technology and expanding economic opportunity to redefine the role of women in society, including the church (and its ordained ministry). Indeed, the apostolic imperative (Gal. 5:1) not to surrender Christian freedom may even require us to do so. Just as Paul opposed Peter for excluding Gentiles from table-fellowship with Jewish Christians (Gal. 2:11-16), we may in Christian freedom oppose those who arbitrarily, out of prejudice or even out of manifest hostility to women (misogyny) bar ordained service to them. As Spirit, the doctrine of justification has always had this critical, reformatory edge as *norma normans,* breaking up human traditions that put Christ back in the tomb; in just this way the freeing Spirit frees the New Testament community of Jesus (Gal. 6:15) to be in its own time and space the harbingers of God's new humanity (Gal. 3:26-28).

Let us now consider two possible lines of objection to the preceding argument. First, *from the left,* one could argue that justice for women oppressed by eons of patriarchy demands as a gospel imperative the relentless agitation for the ordination of women as a symbol of the liberation of women generally — no matter what the cost, since smashing the patriarchal church is itself part and parcel of the liberation. The Spirit belongs to those oppressed and seeking liberation. They are the ones who have insight into the hidden sense of Scripture; indeed they may even set the literal text aside in the light of new revelations. This is the well-known hermeneutical claim of Liberation Theology. Second, *from the right,* one could argue that the Spirit who promised to guide the church to all truth cannot have been away on vacation during these past two millennia, but in fact has exhibited divine guidance in the unbroken tradition of what has everywhere been accepted by everyone at every time. Heresy is whatever deviates from this massive consensus. In this case, the Spirit belongs to the tradition, including the male-only clergy who are its guardians. From this perspective, the church has neither authority nor even permission to innovate by ordaining women. This is the well-known stance of the Roman Catholic magisterium, and also (though less officially) of Eastern Orthodox churches.

In my judgment, we ought to refute both these objections by heeding instead Luther's insightful diagnosis in the Smalcald Articles, where in principle he tied together these apparently radical opposites of the "left-wing" (Müntzer) and the "right-wing" (the "papists") as alike "enthusiasts."[167] "Enthusiasts" are those who claim to have come into possession of the Spirit as authority for new or old practices but neglect "to test the spirits" (1 John 4:1), i.e., to identify the Spirit as the Holy Spirit of Jesus and His Father. They claim spiritual authority at the expense of theological argument and hence to the injury of theological subjectivity. They do not labor to persuade the community theologically, winning free and rational assent by demonstrating the Word in the Spirit and the Spirit from the Word. But how could that happen? The Holy Spirit's justifying and liberating work, as was said above, consists in our reconciliation to God the Father and inclusion in the holy community of Jesus Christ, His Son. How does that apply to the question of the ordination of women?

In this perspective, the first objection about eons of patriarchal oppression from which follows an urgent mandate for social liberation requires a critique. It is in fact true that women on the whole have been more vulnerable to physical and sexual abuse on account of relative lack of power in comparison to men. The New Testament is well aware of this and is fighting against it within the horizon of possibilities available to that time in history (Eph. 5:25; 1 Tim. 3:2, 12; 5:1-16, et al.). It is also true (as pioneering feminist theorist Simone de Beauvoir recognized in *The Second Sex* when she wrote of the "cruel tyranny of biology" that subordinates women to the reproductive function of the race)[168] that women

---

167. *BC,* pp. 322-33.

168. See the discussion in Paul R. Hinlicky, "Havens from the Heartless Home," *dialog* 28, no. 3 (Summer 1989): 175-82.

have been in this position of relative inequality because of the biological fact of their reproductive role. To put the matter plainly: men can walk away from sexual intercourse without bearing its consequences in their bodies in a way that women cannot. Until modern medicine neutralized this "inequality" in consequence of sexual intercourse, all societies in history and across cultures have needed (for survival itself) to bind men to the mothers of their children by the social institution of marriage — hardly then a simple instrument of "patriarchal" oppression.

Our theology ought then instead to follow the melancholy analysis of the moral ambiguity that inheres in marriage according to Genesis 3: as a consequence of their equal disobedience to God, Adam is subordinated to the soil just as Eve is subordinated to Adam (who came from the soil). In other words, the vulnerability to sinful abuse (men in the economic struggle with the soil for sustenance, women in the domestic struggle for the man to provide) is a consequence of sinfulness, a corruption of the good creation, a perversion of a structure intended for love and justice into one of malice and injustice. To use a scholastic distinction, this double subordination is God's consequent, not antecedent will. Accordingly in Christ, God's original intention for the human couple as expressed in the *imago Dei* passage of the first creation story (Gen. 1:26-28) is restored, and the double subordination expressed in the curse of Genesis 3 may be mitigated. We are freed in Christ to fulfill the image of God in the partnership of male and female, concretely in marriage but also more broadly in the economic, religious, and political structures of society.

Indeed the Lutheran Confessions lift up marriage along these lines of the true *partnership* of male and female, overcoming the idealization of sterile virginity in the monastic tradition, as may be seen for example in their treatment of monastic vows, clerical celibacy or, more positively, in Luther's exposition of the sixth commandment. In addition to this basic line of interpretation stemming from Reformation theology, we may further argue that the modern usage of reproductive technology to control fertility is permitted in Christian freedom as part of the task assigned to the human couple to "subdue the earth and have dominion over it." At the same time, this new power (like all our technology) creates new challenges. Even more so than in the past, we should identify male bullying of women physically, emotionally, or sexually as a particularly loathsome and regressive behavior; at the same time we should be aware that modern conditions of sexual equality and gender flexibility create new possibilities for female sin. To put the matter plainly: in modern Euro-America, women can act as badly as men ever did.[169]

From the same perspective of Luther's analysis of enthusiasm, the claim that the Spirit belongs to the tradition likewise merits a critique, along the lines of Jaroslav Pelikan's well-known aphorism: "Traditionalism is the dead faith of the

---

169. Islamic critics of American culture, particularly of feminism, see this clearly. Dinesh D'Souza, *The Enemy at Home: The Cultural Left and Its Responsibility for 9/11* (Garden City, NY: Doubleday, 2007), p. 137.

living; tradition is the living faith of the dead." The living faith of the dead in the "tradition of the gospel" (1 Cor. 15:3) is the work of the life-giving Spirit in guiding the church into all truth, according to the promise of Jesus in John 16:5-16. Now *this* guidance of the Spirit of the Father and the Son cannot simply be equated with Vincent of Lérins's dictum *quod ubique, quod semper, quod ab omnibus creditum est,* for the simple reason that not all of us have yet been gathered into the church. His dictum then is biased towards the past. So long as history lasts, however, the gathering by the Spirit through the Word in mission to the nations continues and thus includes all the requisite "modernizations" mentioned at the beginning of this excursus. Thank God that it does! Aren't we glad that unlike Aristotle and his erstwhile theological followers in Christian tradition we do not believe any longer that some people are by nature fit for slavery? Or that women are maimed men? Luther inveighed mightily against such corruption of Christian doctrine on woman, "that most beautiful creature of God," under the influence of Aristotle's biology and politics.[170]

But the Spirit rather leads to truth (John 16:13) through the ministry of the Word, in particular through the preaching of law and gospel exposing sin, revealing grace, and overthrowing the devil: "And when [the Paraclete] comes, he will prove the world wrong about sin and righteousness and judgment: about sin, because they do not believe in me; about righteousness, because I am going to the Father and you will see me no longer; about judgment, because the ruler of this world has been condemned" (John 16:8-11). *Such* preaching about *Jesus* is the work of the ordained ministry, through which *His* Spirit leads to all truth in doing just this work of convincing and convicting. Theological truth then is not whatever the church everywhere once believed (as though we could ever settle on this), but truth is what the Spirit reveals through the entire — as-yet-*unfinished* — tradition, by preaching Jesus as our righteousness, sin as our unbelief in Him, and liberation as belonging to Him.

In this light, the question is: Could the ordination of women be true to God's gospel purpose? How could we ever tell? Not by asking about "women," but by asking about "ordination"! The theologically prior question is about ordination. Just what is it to which we are ordaining (or refusing to ordain) women? The controversy is not in the first place about "women in the ministry" — a very vague and dubious expression in Lutheran perspective, since by virtue of baptism and the priesthood of all believers, women have always had ministries in the church and from the church to the world in keeping with Luther's great paradox: "A Christian is a perfectly free lord of all, subject to none; a Christian is a perfectly dutiful servant of all, subject to all."[171] If women are baptized, then all that is said

170. See further Paul R. Hinlicky, "Luther against the Contempt of Women," *Lutheran Quarterly* 2, no. 4 (Winter 1989): 515-30.

171. *LW* 31, p. 344. See also Eberhard Jüngel, *The Freedom of a Christian: Luther's Significance for Contemporary Theology,* trans. R. A. Harrisville (Minneapolis: Augsburg, 1988).

and included in this paradox of Luther applies to them. The controversial question of today — precipitated by the largely unreflective modernization process in the West — really has to do with what we mean theologically about ordination in distinction from the general priesthood of believers in Christ, bestowed in baptism.

We can confirm this analysis from an opposing point of view. To begin with, Paula D. Nesbitt's decade-old *Feminization of the Clergy in America* provides a careful sociological analysis of the difficult time many ordained women have experienced in mainline American Protestant denominations (she focuses particularly on Episcopalians and Unitarians) and comes to the conclusion that the liberationist mentality of many in this first generation of ordained women conflicts with existing understandings of the pastoral office. She interprets this conflict purely in terms of an alleged patriarchal "right to dominance and control"[172] embedded in traditional Protestant understandings of the office and correspondingly speaks of rather dramatic possibilities of reconfiguring "religious leadership." She speaks, for example, of: "greater inclusivity with regard to sexual orientation"; a "more relational, interconnected understanding of religious authority and divine immanence, socially from women's experience on the margin of power and essentialistically from women's differing biological experience connected with menstruation and childbearing"; radically reconstituting "notions of purity or diminish[ing] their traditional importance"; "wider legitimation of socialization experiences," new "paradigms of interdependency," and so on. While there are ideas here worthy of consideration, it is not difficult to see that taken as a whole the traditional understanding of the ordained minister as administering the Word and Sacraments of Christ to form and guide a flock of Christians could hardly survive reconfiguring under Nesbitt's "liberationist ideal."[173]

Let us understand why. A beautifully written and deeply moving account of such an experience of conflict in ministry by a contemporary woman is provided in Barbara Brown Taylor's *Leaving Church*. It is an autobiographical account of Taylor's sense of The Mysterious Presence (a.k.a., "God") in experiences of natural beauty;[174] her discovery of the Episcopal Church; and her gradual path to ordination as a priest. She lovingly portrays the trials and joys of a contemporary urban pastor in Atlanta and then of her move to a rural parish in the north of Georgia. She tells of a vibrant growing ministry there, truly a "love story" — yet

172. Paula D. Nesbitt, *Feminization of the Clergy in America: Occupational and Organizational Perspectives* (New York and Oxford: Oxford University Press, 1997), p. 175.

173. Nesbitt, *Feminization of the Clergy*, p. 176.

174. Barbara Brown Taylor, *Leaving Church: A Memoir of Faith* (San Francisco: HarperSanFrancisco, 2007), pp. 22-25. I mention this to underscore, in Lutheran terms, the theological "enthusiasm" that informed Taylor theologically from the beginning of her journey: "If anyone had tried to tell me that creation was fallen or that I should care more for heaven than earth, I would have gone off to lie in the sweet grass by myself" (p. 23, cf. pp. 80, 82).

then of estrangement, separation, perhaps even divorce (not from her husband, but from the church).[175] *Leaving Church,* as the title indicates, is an important theological interpretation of a contemporary American woman's difficult experience in the ministry because in the end the author construes the ordained ministry as an experience in false consciousness and inhumane separation from ordinary people. Painfully Taylor's is a tale of exhaustion, of disillusionment, and finally renunciation.

Midway through the book, Taylor is telling of the sad days after she had resigned her beloved country-parish call. She recounts how she awkwardly attended a pool party in the town where she had been the priest for five years. Things got rowdy and folks were getting tossed into the pool. Finally someone threw her in. She certainly wasn't the priest anymore. "I looked around at all of those shining people with makeup running down their cheeks, with hair plastered to their heads, and I was so happy to be one of them. If being ordained meant being set apart from them, then I did not want to be ordained anymore. I wanted to be human."[176] This revealing episode raises the question: What did Taylor think she was getting into in the first place? To what ministry had she been ordained? What inhuman thing had she imagined priesthood to be? This question actually haunted her from the beginning. Earlier on in the story, Taylor asked: "If the purpose of the church were to equip all God's people for ministry in the world — as I was learning in seminary — then what sense did it make to designate one of those people 'the minister' in a congregation? The minute you set someone apart like that, didn't you give everyone else license to say, 'Don't look at me — she's the minister'?"[177] Over time it was to be exactly this sense of separation from others that defeated Taylor. Is this the "separation" that sanctification is, the holiness of the Holying Spirit? How can we make sense of this?

Theologically, Taylor tells us in words that could have come straight from Nesbitt, "my faith is far more relational than doctrinal. . . . God is found in right relationships, not right ideas."[178] It is popular nowadays to speak this way of right relationships instead of doctrine, but it actually begs the question of doctrine. Her statement is itself an assertion of doctrine. Yet for Lutheranism, the chief "doctrine" is about the "right" relationship to God and others signified by the sinner's justification by faith alone in Christ alone on the sole account of God's almighty, all-sufficing grace. Taylor's anti-doctrinal confusion (which actually degenerates into polemic, e.g., "defending the dried ink marks on the page becomes more vital than defending the neighbor")[179] does not then penetrate to the heart of the matter. The heart of the matter is, as her story actually reveals,

175. Taylor, *Leaving Church,* p. 113.
176. Taylor, *Leaving Church,* p. 120.
177. Taylor, *Leaving Church,* p. 31.
178. Taylor, *Leaving Church,* p. 107.
179. Taylor, *Leaving Church,* p. 106.

that she burned herself out trying to be Christ to others ("compassion fatigue").[180] In other words, she thought of her pastoral ministry as substituting for an *absent* Christ. A "priest . . . ," she expressly affirms, "is someone willing to stand between a God and a people who are longing for one another's love, turning back and forth between them with no hope of tending either as well as each deserves."[181] Given this hopeless (!) task, Taylor felt it was up to her to be Christ in people's lives, apart from whom Christ would not be there for them. She, not He, then became the real operative priest, the mediator, in her story. Unsurprisingly, she at last realizes that "the demands of parish ministry routinely cut me off from the resources that enabled me to do parish ministry."[182] Intriguingly she links this understanding of ordination with her gender identity: "I had such a strong instinct for rescue that my breasts fairly leaked when I came across those in need of rescuing. Mother Church gave me a way to bring this instinct under God's roof. . . . Feeding others became my food."[183] Starving to death as a result, Taylor left the priesthood and her congregation to survive. Hence: *Leaving Church.*

In Luther's understanding, the ordained minister is the representative of the *present,* not absent, Christ. The risen Christ entrusts His own priestly ministry to ordained human beings, but does not abandon it to them. In turn, the ordained proceed in faith that the crucified and risen Christ by His Spirit causes the growth (1 Cor. 3:6) by the faithful (1 Cor. 2:2) preaching of the Word and administering of the Sacraments. Only God, so to say, can make grace come true; in this very faith, as Eberhard Jüngel has so rightly emphasized, the believer in general, and the ordained as the example and model of this faith for the community, is "set free from a sham existence"[184] — even, painfully enough, the kind of religious sham that Taylor found herself living by trying to be Christ rather than believe Christ, to do Christ rather than to share Christ in Christ-existing-as-community by virtue of the one baptism giving union with Christ by joyful exchanges of the Spirit.

So we return to the prior, genuinely theological question: To what do we ordain? What is the public office, the special ministry of the church? The tensions that Taylor records in her story indicate deep confusion on this question in American Protestantism, compounded by the gender interests and "enthusiastic" theology that informed her as she recounts. What is the ministry of all the baptized? It is a ministry *from* baptism *to* the world, the vocation of the people of God in society to transform stations into vocations of love and justice. What in contrast is ordained ministry? It is a ministry *from* baptism *to* the church, *for* the church. Indeed, but that is not precise enough. In the New Testament we see

180. Taylor, *Leaving Church,* p. 102.

181. Taylor, *Leaving Church,* p. 44.

182. Taylor, *Leaving Church,* p. 98.

183. Taylor, *Leaving Church,* p. 50.

184. Eberhard Jüngel, *Justification: The Heart of the Christian Faith,* trans. J. F. Cayzer (Edinburgh and New York: T. & T. Clark, 2001), p. 262.

a variety of functions ranging from diaconal service to the apostolate. We cannot derive a settled, normative doctrine of ministry from this variety appearing on the pages of the New Testament, since the very problem of a doctrine of the ordained ministry is a by-product of the Spirit's decision indefinitely to delay the parousia of the Lord for the sake of the mission to the nations. In this light, we can see that by the second Christian century the threefold pattern of diaconal service, presbyterial leadership, and episcopal oversight had evolved. This pattern is still useful to us. Certainly any vital church will feel the need to fulfill these three functions of (1) organized charity and prophetic advocacy in society on behalf of the ecclesia to "the least of these"; (2) pastoral leadership of the congregation by serving Word and Sacrament; and (3) the ministry of oversight and unity between local Christian communities.

To what do we ordain? The preacher is to be pastor of a community and the pastor pastors by preaching,[185] when and where the community understands itself as the temple of the Holy Spirit because the preaching is of Christ and Him crucified.[186] In these "right" relations, the special office of ordination to ministry of Word and Sacrament denotes a calling by the Lord of the Church to attend to His own Word and Sacraments and to "rule" the church (AC XXVIII:5-18)[187] with them (only them!) in His Name. That women are essentially capable of doing this (having brains and mouths like men), and are freed to do this (Gal. 3:26-28), seems to this contemporary American Lutheran theologian sufficiently evident that the burden of proof now falls on opponents. Having said that, I am far more concerned that the "right relationships" just designated are actually maintained, encouraged, and enhanced in the life of my drifting denomination. I am in fact worried that the sort of theological understanding of ministry we saw articulated by Taylor is eclipsing Luther's, also in the ELCA.

Ecumenically, the ordination of women is still a venture in faith, a holy experiment testing the Spirit's guidance to see "whether it be of God" (Acts 5:38-39). The ecumenical and hence genuinely theological issue is not in the first place whether women are fit to be ordained, but rather what our theology of ordination is. If ordination to the church's ministry descended from the apostolate is understood as the living tradition of the gospel message, and if otherwise in the eyes of local churches cultural circumstances permit, the burden of proof falls upon those who find barriers preventing women from presenting themselves for ordained service. In the interim, we can conclude with this much of an affirmation: where women undertake the ministry of the gospel as servants of the risen and present Lord Christ, there they fare as well as men do. Where women (or men), however, think of ministry as filling in for an absent Christ, not only is personal

185. Steven D. Paulson is particularly instructive here in his *Lutheran Theology* (London and New York: T. & T. Clark International, 2011), pp. 18-34, 61-86.

186. Paulson, *Lutheran Theology,* pp. 35-60.

187. *BC,* p. 92.

burnout predictable. So finally is "leaving church." It is fitting to recall again the words of Saarinen and Root: if the "nature of the community's life is in the Lord and depends on the Lord for its life[, then] word and sacrament have a theological priority over other forms of communal life because they are the events in which we have the promise of the presence of the communion-creating Christ."[188] In that case the matter of doctrine — to be sure provisionally formulated doctrine *for life* and doctrine *strictly organized by the single, universal or "catholic," cognitive claim* that God is the Father who by the Son and the Spirit redeems and fulfills creation — and how the church decides doctrine, can hardly be avoided if we are to discern "right relationships," even if it is not possible to formulate definitive solutions once and for all short of the eschaton of judgment.

---

## The Ministry of the Church — II

How does the church ever decide such matters? That, for example, the ordination of women is "of God" or that "justification by faith alone" rightly accounts for Christian existence as *simul iustus et peccator?*[189] Can it? Can it without schism? Can the true unity of the church be understood not as assimilation of Word to Spirit or of Spirit to Word[190] but as a dialectical dynamism of unifications that must constantly test novelty both in the sense of experimentation and in the sense of discrimination? What kind of "reformation" of teaching authority would that entail?

Already the call for immediate mutual recognition of ministries at the end of the fourth round of the U.S. Lutheran-Catholic dialogues in 1970 proved to be premature. One can forgive the enthusiasm of those first years of the dialogue, which so rapidly seemed to be rolling back the accumulated misunderstandings of centuries. Warren Quanbeck stated the paradox of "the closeness and distance of Roman Catholic-Lutheran relations" in the fitting analogy of a conflict in the family: "Ours is a quarrel within the family, and like many family quarrels a very bitter one which seems to defy the possibility of reconciliation."[191] The call for mutual

---

188. *Baptism and the Unity of the Church*, p. 21.

189. Paul R. Hinlicky, "Staying Lutheran in the Changing Church(es)," Afterword in Mickey L. Mattox and A. G. Roeber, *Changing Churches: An Orthodox, Catholic and Lutheran Theological Conversation* (Grand Rapids: Eerdmans, 2012), pp. 281-314.

190. Yves Congar, *The Word and the Spirit,* trans. David Smith (San Francisco: Harper & Row, 1986), who perhaps better understood Luther and Calvin on this point than do their putative contemporary followers! "This position of the two greatest Reformers is close to the heart of my own investigation, which is concerned with the links between the Word and the Breath, the Word and the Spirit . . . there was, however, a certain danger of individualism. History shows that this was no imaginary danger" (p. 32).

191. *Papal Primacy and the Universal Church*, ed. Paul C. Empie and T. Austin Murphy (Minneapolis: Augsburg, 1974), p. 180.

recognition of ministries at the end of the fourth round immediately required attention to a topic that indeed seemed to "defy the possibility of reconciliation," namely the papacy, an institution which Martin Luther had branded the Antichrist. Yet once again the theologians surprised even themselves in uncovering convergences in *Papal Primacy and the Universal Church* (1974). New historical and biblical studies led the way.

A study group of Roman Catholic and Lutheran biblical scholars published a volume, *Peter in the New Testament,* which established the existence in the New Testament writings, not of traditional Roman Catholic claims to derive the papacy directly from the institution of Jesus in Matthew 16, but rather of what they called a "Petrine function." By this, they meant the special ministry associated in the New Testament writings with the Apostle Peter for the unity and faithfulness of the whole church. These biblical studies established that the New Testament witness to Jesus Christ could not be made without reference to Simon Peter, and that in the primitive church Peter was accordingly looked upon as "missionary fisherman, pastoral shepherd, martyr, recipient of special revelation, confessor of the true faith, magisterial protector and repentant sinner."[192] This multiform image of Simon Peter provided a biblical starting point for a "continuing trajectory"[193] in the post–New Testament development. While it is quite a few lengthy steps from here to even the moderate early papalism of Cyprian or Leo the Great, these biblical studies did establish a basis for, and thus also a norm for the critical evaluation of, later development of papal doctrine.

On this basis of the biblical study, the fifth round of the dialogue offered a working definition of the "Petrine function": ". . . a particular form of Ministry exercised by a person, officeholder, or a local church with reference to the church as a whole . . . [which] serves to promote or preserve the oneness of the church by symbolizing unity, and by facilitating communication, mutual assistance or correction, and collaboration in the church's mission."[194] It is to be noted that this biblically derived Petrine function is not immediately tied to the papacy. Accordingly, the definition expects that even in churches not acknowledging the Roman claim to Petrine ministry, some exercise of the Petrine function will occur. Christianity essentially requires this Petrine function, this special ministry for the unity of the whole. The concept of "Petrine function" thus enabled the Lutheran–Roman Catholic dialogue to transcend the old argument about whether the "papacy is biblically warranted," i.e., established by "divine law *(ius divinum)*." Clearly, in this dialogue, Roman Catholic theologians have conceded that the institution of the papacy experienced a long development that cannot be derived directly from the pages of the New Testament. On the other hand, in

---

192. *Peter in the New Testament,* ed. Raymond E. Brown, Karl P. Donfried, and John Reumann (Minneapolis: Augsburg / New York/Paramus/Toronto: Paulist, 1973), p. 166.

193. *Peter in the New Testament,* p. 168.

194. *Papal Primacy,* pp. 11-12.

light of the Biblical notion of "Petrine function," Roman Catholics in the dialogue could and did maintain, though not uncritically, that the papacy emerged in history as a divinely willed gift of God for the unity of the whole church under the Spirit's promised guidance to lead the church to truth.

Thinking of the papacy in terms of the Petrine function provides contemporary Roman Catholic theologians a way to criticize the medieval development of an imperial papacy, climaxing in Boniface VII's bull *Unam Sanctam,* which asserted the papacy's "spiritual but also temporal dominion over the whole earth."[195] Citing Luke 22:25-26, the Roman Catholic theologians in the dialogue made this self-criticism explicit: "The doctrine concerning the papacy must be understood in ways that recognize the church's total subordination to Christ and the gospel and its obligation to respect the rights of all individuals, groups and offices both within the church and beyond its limits. Monarchial absolutism in the church would violate the command of Christ."[196] Such Roman Catholic self-criticism unfolds in a pattern not unlike the Lutheran principle of *simul iustus et peccator:* "the papal office can be seen both as a response to the guidance of the Spirit in the Christian community, and also as an institution which in its human dimensions is tarnished by frailty and even unfaithfulness."[197]

As a result of such insights, Lutherans and Roman Catholics are today in a position to ask together about what a reformed papacy could be, that is, a papacy in service of the gospel for the unity of the church, rather than a monarchial papacy in symbiosis with the new Roman imperialism, the Western form of "Constantinianism," the political ideal of Christendom. Here the dialogue asserted unequivocally: "The ultimate source of authority is God revealed in Christ. The Church is guided by the Spirit and is judged by the Word of God."[198] Quoting Vatican II, the Dialogue emphatically reiterated: "The Church's teaching office is not above God's Word; it rather serves the Word."[199] Under the norm of the Word of God, a renewed and reformed papacy would possess no arbitrary or subjective power, but only the power of service. Two principles taken up from Vatican II make this vision more concrete: The principle of *collegiality* protects against curial centralization and assures a process of deliberation appropriate to "a worldwide Church." The principle of *subsidiarity* likewise ensures "that what can properly be decided and done in smaller units of ecclesial life ought not to be referred to church leaders who have wider responsibilities."[200]

In view of such a structurally reformed papacy, placed under the Word of God, and committed both to the integrity of local churches and to the unity in

---

195. *Papal Primacy,* p. 18.
196. *Papal Primacy,* p. 36.
197. *Papal Primacy,* p. 19.
198. *Papal Primacy,* p. 19.
199. *Papal Primacy,* p. 20.
200. *Papal Primacy,* p. 20.

mission of the whole church, Lutheran theologians added the comment, "The one thing necessary from the Lutheran point of view is that papal primacy be so structured and interpreted that it clearly serve the gospel and thus unity of the church of Christ, and that its exercise of power not subvert Christian freedom."[201] Presumably the Lutherans meant here the freedom to experiment according to contextual considerations in the mission to the gospel, as Paul experimented in dispensing with kosher requirements and circumcision in bringing the gospel to the nations. "Testing the spirits" has a double connotation: not only testing for fidelity to the Word incarnate, but testing for the Spirit's sense in speaking the Word incarnate in a historically specific context. Freedom in this latter sense does not mean freedom from authority as such, including ecclesiastical authority, but the freedom that the gospel itself authors and authorizes in sending the church in service of Christ by serving Christ to the nations.

By the same measure, the very consideration of the possibility of a reformed papacy for the future entailed a serious Lutheran self-criticism over a kind of riot of uncontrolled experimentation no longer ordered by the gospel in mission to the nations: "We Lutherans consider the need for symbols and centers of unity to be urgent. We believe that we must try more energetically than we have in the past to give concrete expression to our concern for the unity of the whole empirical church. . . . Some form of the papacy, renewed and restructured under the gospel, may be an appropriate visible expression of the Ministry that serves the unity and ordering of the church."[202] Lutheran self-criticism also reflected a positive appreciation of some aspects of the existing papacy: "Lutherans can appreciate the papacy's assertion of the church's right to be independent of state control, the serious social concern exhibited by modern popes, the liberating insight into the way in which the Bible should be studied . . . and the efforts which modern popes . . . have devoted to the cause of peace."[203]

Roman Catholic theologians commented on this Lutheran self-criticism: "Our Lutheran partners in dialogue acknowledge that their independence from the papacy has not freed them from all abuses of ecclesiastical authority. They acknowledge that officers and assemblies on various levels in any church body are themselves capable of violating the rights and freedoms of the faithful and of resisting God's will for his church."[204] Conceivably, then, Lutherans could likewise be able to entertain the related but distinct question of "Roman primacy," i.e., the claim that for providential reasons the Church of Rome became the locus of the Petrine function. Robert Jenson helpfully elaborated on this question: "the congregation in which Peter and Paul finally united their witness, and which maintains the memorials of their martyrdoms for that witness, was for the an-

201. *Papal Primacy*, p. 21.
202. *Papal Primacy*, p. 28.
203. *Papal Primacy*, p. 32.
204. *Papal Primacy*, p. 37.

cient church just so a Spirit-chosen 'touchstone . . . and point of reference for the apostolic faith.' "[205] In that case, Roman primacy actually grounds a critical hermeneutical supposition, i.e., the canonical unity of Pauline and Petrine witnesses to Jesus Christ as touchstone of right faith. Of course to ground Roman primacy in this way, once again, puts it under this very canon, that is, rule of faith. Even so, the identification of the sign, the diocese of Rome, with the thing signified, the Petrine function, remains another, controversial step and not only with the children of the Reformation.

The root dilemma concerning authority in the church is, however, exposed here. It is the manifest disunity of the sign and the thing signified captured in the paradoxical theologic of the Reformation affirming that Christian existence, personal and communal alike, is *simul iustus et peccator.* How can a sinful church exercise divine authority in teaching that binds consciences? One false but all-too-Lutheran answer to this question is to assert that the sinful church cannot exercise authority except in authoritatively denying any claim of the church to exercise authority. In that case, the paradox of the church as *simul iustus et peccator* is understood by its own proponents, not only in the caricatures of its opponents, as the nonsense of a contradiction. The real problem embedded in the paradox has been advanced in exactly this easily misunderstood way. For pertinent example, in a significant document of Lutheran-Catholic ecumenical convergence, *Justification and the Church,* the "critical function" of the Reformation doctrine of justification of the simultaneity of sinfulness and righteousness is said to prevent ever receiving the "binding doctrine" of the church "without reservation," i.e., "with no questions asked." The reason is that even "this ministry [of magisterium], like every church institution, is carried out by human beings who are capable of error[. Then] not only would the danger of error be increased thereby, because the error would then take on binding force for the church, but also and above all a sovereignty and ultimate binding force would attach to the decisions and stipulations of this ministry and its representatives which are reserved for the gospel alone. That is why what people teach in the church must ultimately be measured against the gospel alone. Only then is it certain that the church relies on God's word and not human words."[206] On examination this not a little familiar argument proves to be perplexing.

In place of a forthright Lutheran statement that surely would intend to bind the conscience of Roman Catholic ecumenical partners — for example, that the modern Marian and papal doctrines are false doctrine that wrongly burden Christian consciences and are unacceptable — we have here instead a kind of transcendentalizing of "the gospel" into a noumenal principle above and beyond the fray

205. Jenson, *Unbaptized,* p. 85, citing Paul VI.
206. "Justification and the Church," Joint Evangelical Lutheran–Roman Catholic Commission (1993), #211-12. Accessed online at http://www.prounione.urbe.it/dia-int/l-rc/doc/e_l-rc_church.html.

of human confusion.[207] This will not do. The gospel too is a word that emerges in the conditionedness of all things historical. By what right or logic does this elevation occur of "the gospel" into an absolute principle able to relativize other doctrines in their binding claims? What goes unsaid here — though it needs to be said and warranted — is that the "Reformation conviction" about the gospel as *the* gracious Word of God functions too as binding church doctrine, even though it is just as much the product "of human beings capable of error." What access here on the earth do we have to the "gospel" apart from its ministration by sinful human beings — for example Paul the Apostle or Mark the Evangelist or the unknown prophet we call the Second Isaiah — with claims to authority that forthwith bind consciences by stipulating in language what the event of Jesus Christ is about — as for example that the grace of Christ is "gift," not "merit and reward"? Are not also *we* who maintain the "pure" gospel of grace human beings as well who are capable of error in our putative purifications? Have we from the side of the Reformation really gotten to the heart of the problem — the material disunity of the sign and the thing signified captured in the Reformation teaching that believers, in and as their community of faith, are *simul iustus et peccator?*

Certainly the "Reformation conviction" itself can by way of such abstraction all too easily devolve into the Lutheran heresy of cheap grace and become an ecclesiastical ideology in its own way, as Bonhoeffer famously exposed.

> Cheap grace means grace as a doctrine, a principle, a system. It means the forgiveness of sins proclaimed as a general truth, the love of God taught as the Christian "conception" of God. An intellectual assent to that idea is held to be itself sufficient to secure remission of sins. The Church which upholds the correct doctrine of grace has, it is supposed, ipso facto a part in that grace. In such a Church the world finds a cheap covering for its sins; no contrition is required, still less any real desire to be delivered from sin. Cheap grace therefore amounts to a denial of the living Word of God, in fact, a denial of the Incarnation of the Word of God.[208]

It does not help to appeal to the gospel as the ultimate authority if no one can say in the formulation of conscience-binding doctrine, i.e., the catechesis that informs the theological subject, what on earth we are talking about when we

---

207. In "Justification and the Church," #214, the statement identifies the "independence of the gospel and of its ultimate binding nature" as "nothing other than the independence and binding nature of the grace of God." But we have seen that appeal at this juncture to "grace" is question-begging. Certainly the statement is correct to insist that "the Reformation doctrine of justification therefore requires that the church's ministry and its decisions should as a matter of principle be open to examination by the whole people of God" (#213), but this protest against uncritical dogmatism and authoritarianism hardly meets the classical Catholic objection head on.

208. Dietrich Bonhoeffer, *The Cost of Discipleship,* trans. R. H. Fuller (New York: Simon & Schuster, Touchstone Edition, 1995), p. 43.

assert the apparent contradiction of simultaneous sinfulness and righteousness that is at the material center of the Reformation witness to Christian existence. "Grace" or "gospel" taken as an absolute and turned into an epistemically inaccessible principle seems to obliterate the Reformation witness rather than to assert in full tension the real contradiction of simultaneous sin and righteousness as a claim binding on Christian conscience regarding the truth of their standing before God. In the process, this ideological trick does nothing but exorcise the Spirit who comes to convict the world concerning sin, righteousness, and judgment by leading the church to all truth.

In the background of such curious contemporary Lutheran arguments lies the model of knowledge in theology as *theoria* and the convoluted attempts accordingly both to express as ultimate the grace of divine favor and yet to avoid claiming binding knowledge of the ultimate being that is gracious: the latter, formulated in human language, would constitute beliefs about God binding on human conscience and constitutive of the church in its temporal and spatial existence. Much of the problem here disappears when we adopt the pragmatic and hermeneutical model of knowledge proposed in this book: in that case the articulation of binding doctrine is not a once-and-for-all set of propositions that are timelessly valid because they correspond like replicas to divine reality. Certainly, if taken in that theoretical way, such formulations cannot be made binding on Christian conscience without violence towards others and presumption over against God. The protest registered above in the name of the critical function of the doctrine of justification is valid in this respect. Yet protest is only protest and "protestant-ism" is a parasitical phenomenon that finally exhausts its host and dies with it. In the manner argued above, it even misses the nuance of the Reformation's actual position against doctrinal innovation by the papal party, namely that we dare to speak and teach and confess the Word of God in conscience-binding claims to truth. This is not because we possess holiness that qualifies us to be its conduit, but because Christ has won us by His Spirit in that word of God from the Bible that is gospel, sinners that we are, and made us His own; just so, only so, He has commissioned to speak in His name the same gospel to the nations.

Binding doctrine is the Spirit's work in progress following the gospel in its progress through the nations. Hence previous formulations of doctrine can become outdated and inept. But new formulation of doctrine is required to account for this outdating and to preserve material continuity with the past in order to demonstrate that it is speaking the same gospel under new circumstances and according to better understanding — just in the way that quantum mechanics, for example, transcends Newtonian physics while preserving the truth that it had once expressed about gravitation.

Hence we have striven to explicate the Lutheran *simul* in the dynamic sense of a battle inaugurated. The declaration of the sinner's justification by faith (*pars pro toto,* the community of justified sinners) is the already now of the eschaton of judgment. As such it inaugurates the battle of the Spirit against the flesh in a conflict that stretches from baptism day to resurrection day, from Pentecost to Parousia. Even so, indeed just so, the pertinent objection arises how such an embattled sinner, strictly speaking righteous only by an extrinsic determination, could ever actually live with the certainty of faith at peace with God. The manifest disunity of the sign and the thing signified here seems intolerable; it belies the very claim to truth. With Feuerbach one has to ask how this Reformation conviction of a "gracious God" in spite of sinfulness can be anything other than an illusion of alienated existence, if faith does not experience newness of life but rather sinfulness. Hence the profound Catholic resistance to the critical principle of the justification of the sinner by faith alone, also for the sake of the certainty of faith: in some real, if inchoate way, in justification the sinner must truly pass from sin to righteousness. This is not, as earlier stressed, a conflict between grace and works righteousness, but rather between grace, taken as divine favor-declaring, and grace, taken as divine gift-effecting, righteousness. On the other hand, this Catholic claim to real, ontic sanctity for the believer-cum-church as such seems to require us to don rose-colored glasses, overlooking the "brutality" (Radner) of the long history of *forced* unifications of the sign and the thing signified. So we seem to be caught on the horns of a dilemma, what Daphne Hampson exposed as "Christian contradictions" in her extended critique of the *Joint Declaration on Justification* between Lutherans and Catholics.[209] We will continue this discussion shortly in considering the alternative to the present proposal in Ephraim Radner's work.

We may summarize up to this point as follows: we are all modern Christians in a secularized but not sanctified world. Both Lutherans and Roman Catholics experience profound pressures toward fracturing and the loss of Christian identity. In this new situation, in which Lutherans see their need of a ministry for unity, and Roman Catholics have renounced secular instruments and imperial images of papal ministry, the possibility arises of a renewed papacy. From the Catholic side, this is possible because of the emergence of so-called *communio* ecclesiology from the Second Vatican Council.[210] From the Lutheran side, it is possible because "most contemporary Lutherans no longer believe that the papacy is unalterably the Antichrist" — an idea that belongs to an unsavory turn in Luther's thinking towards the demonization of his theological enemies.[211] It is also possible because many contemporary Lutherans will see that something like "the Petrine function" is biblically warranted and also an urgent need in the post-Christendom situation of the church. This does not mean that agreement on Roman primacy or on what a reformed papacy would entail with regard to the usurped right in modern times of local churches to elect their bishops, let

209. Daphne Hampson, *Christian Contradictions: The Structures of Lutheran and Catholic Thought* (Cambridge: Cambridge University Press, 2001).

210. *Papal Primacy,* pp. 152, 167, 188.

211. *LBC,* pp. 379-85.

alone agreement on the binding claim of the modern Marian and papal dogmas, has yet been reached. It only means that Lutherans, not only for the sake of the Roman Catholic Church nor only for their own sake, but for the sake of the whole church in mission to the nations, must make the case for papal reform in Rome by entertaining the possibility of it also for themselves. George Lindbeck expressed the dialogue's idea in an apt and clever formulation: "Lutherans, one might say, are conscience bound not to 'submit' to the papacy until it has been so thoroughly renewed that the language of submission is totally inappropriate."[212]

Is such openness to a future reformation of the papacy a genuine Roman Catholic possibility? In a study published in 1983, Roman Catholic theologian J. Michael Miller accurately summarized the meaning of the dialogue's claim for Lutherans: "The early Lutherans rejected the papacy they knew, not the ministry of unity that Jesus willed for the universal Church. . . . Even though there is no dominical guarantee that the Petrine office must coincide with the office of the bishop of Rome, an orthodox Lutheran can now hold that a permanent Petrine function is desirable as an ecclesial ministry."[213] Miller went on to say that for Roman Catholics the dialogue allows them to think "that papal primacy developed in response to the Holy Spirit's guidance of the Church . . . the papacy is more accurately held to exist by divine design *(ex ordinatione divina)* rather than by immediate divine institution."[214] This thinking has "at least two advantages." First, "it eliminates the idea of the papacy as an absolutely immutable structure . . . considerable room is left open for development. . . ." Second, this thinking "allows theologians to pinpoint precisely where their respective interpretations of the papacy agree and disagree."[215] Miller concludes by venturing just such a statement regarding the remaining disagreement: even if "Lutherans [were] to acknowledge a papacy by divine design, they would not thereby hold it to be an absolutely constitutive element of the church. This difference between a Catholic and Lutheran theology of the papacy remains unresolved and is not overcome by adopting the same term to describe papal primacy."[216]

We must also ask whether such openness to a reformed papacy is truly "Lutheran." It is useful here to cite the important study of Scott H. Hendrix, *Luther and the Papacy: Stages in a Reformation Conflict,* which was stimulated by this very dialogue between Lutherans and Roman Catholics. Hendrix found in Luther both a changing empirical assessment in response to the treatment he received from the papacy and an underlying standard of judgment that remained remarkably uniform. Luther's judgment about the papacy as an institution changed from

212. *Papal Primacy,* pp. 201-2.

213. Michael J. Miller, *What Are They Saying About Papal Primacy?* (New York/Ramsey: Paulist, 1983), pp. 88-89.

214. Miller, *What Are They Saying?,* p. 89.

215. Miller, *What Are They Saying?,* p. 90.

216. Miller, *What Are They Saying?,* p. 91.

youthful veneration to early skepticism to open defiance and finally to the condemnation of the papacy as Antichrist. Given the unjust treatment Luther received from the papacy, these judgments are historically understandable. Luther became convinced by the end of his life that the papacy was incorrigible.[217] This conviction, reinforced by the deafness and blindness of the Counter-Reformation "papal party" that gathered at Trent to what the Lutherans were actually saying, had massive influence on "the Protestant cause" and its self-understanding.[218]

What Hendrix brings out, which is not so well known, is Luther's underlying criterion of judgment in all stages of his life: *the papacy is by divine right a pastoral office "of nourishing people in the church with the Word of God."*[219] This pastoral function is for Luther "the criterion for claiming legitimate authority in the church."[220] True pastors are "servants of the present Christ and not vicars of an absent Christ."[221] Even repudiation of the papacy is based on this criterion.[222] Luther's outrage is directed "at the perversion of the pastoral office."[223] Hendrix in this way corrects the predominant neo-Protestant misinterpretation of Luther as a forerunner of modern freedom rather than as a reformer of Christendom. But in fact Luther "was protesting against the usurpation of the church by an unfaithful hierarchy on behalf of the faithful people, not against the church on behalf of the individual."[224] Notwithstanding Luther's own empirical judgment about the papacy's incorrigibility, in light of his own "pastoral principle" do we not have to ask whether Luther would have welcomed and celebrated a faithful hierarchy with a renewed papacy that would properly exercise its pastoral office? Wouldn't his own principle compel him to rejoice to be proven wrong?

A recently published study, *How Can the Petrine Ministry Be a Service to the Unity of the Universal Church?,*[225] inclines in the direction of an affirmative answer. *Tolles assertiones, et christianismum tulisti* ("Take away assertions and you have taken away Christianity"). When Luther's *De servo arbitrio* can be thus cited positively by a Roman Catholic ecumenical partner[226] as entrée into this subject matter, a new ecumenical situation has surely emerged. Indeed the common need to find an authentic way to formulate binding definitions of evangelical truth in face of contemporary challenges within and without the churches is what inspired

---

217. Scott H. Hendrix, *Luther and the Papacy: Stages in a Reformation Conflict* (Philadelphia: Fortress, 1981), p. 148.

218. Hendrix, *Luther and the Papacy,* p. 159.

219. Hendrix, *Luther and the Papacy,* p. xi, emphasis added.

220. *Papal Primacy,* p. 21.

221. *LW* 48, p. 342.

222. Hendrix, *Luther and the Papacy,* p. 70.

223. Hendrix, *Luther and the Papacy,* p. 136.

224. Hendrix, *Luther and the Papacy,* p. 134.

225. *How Can the Petrine Ministry Be a Service to the Unity of the Universal Church?,* ed. James F. Puglisi (Grand Rapids: Eerdmans, 2010).

226. *How Can the Petrine Ministry?,* p. 8.

the improbable project of this book to keep the flame from the 1970 dialogue lit even in the dark cold of this ecumenical winter. This collection of contributions to the (chiefly) Lutheran–Roman Catholic "Farfa" discussion group in the past decade provides a "snapshot" of deliberations on the issue that all parties agree is "the" most difficult obstacle to further progress: the Roman claim to Peter's ministry for the papacy. It provides an education in sophisticated ecumenical method and seriousness of purpose regarding the renewal of Christianity after modernity.

With frequent references to an increasingly "secularized" world, the threat of which had first motivated the highly problematic decrees of Vatican I in the nineteenth century, the Lutheran theologians appearing in these pages manifestly now sense such danger to their own witness in post-Christendom Euro-America as well. Catholic theologian Jared Wicks thus helpfully clarifies: "The problem the Petrine ministry claims to help resolve is not knowing the apostolic gospel from the New Testament, but rather how to discern what in a contemporary formulation is a proper expression of that gospel in this later age."[227] Lutheran contributors agree formally with Wicks's statement: contemporary confession, i.e., the power of the church "to judge doctrine" (*potestas clavium,* AC 28) is what is at issue. Nørgaard-Højen accordingly lays out how the Lutheran category of *status confessionis*[228] parallels papal teaching *ex cathedra:* "an extraordinary (in terms of category and complexity) and previously not-experienced situation that calls for an exceptional decision and claims a new version of at least some of the traditional confessional statements, lest the credibility — or even the very existence — of the church as a community of faith and obedience should be endangered."[229] Because of this parallel between the Lutheran *status confessionis* and the papal statement *ex cathedra,* the problem of magisterium, of binding conscience in new situations by new formulations of doctrine, is exposed as a common problem that can now be rethought together rather than in opposition to one another.

The task of such mutual rethinking would be moot if a Roman Catholic rejection of the "maximalist," Ultramontane interpretation of Vatican I were not

---

227. *How Can the Petrine Ministry?,* p. 356.

228. See Paul R. Hinlicky, "Status Confessionis," *The Encyclopedia of Christianity,* vol. 5 (Grand Rapids: Eerdmans / Leiden: Brill, 2008), pp. 198-201.

229. *How Can the Petrine Ministry?,* p. 205. To this mutually acknowledged contemporary need, especially noteworthy advances in understanding may be claimed for Birmelé's application of the methodology of the Joint Declaration on Justification to the matter of papal primacy in search of a "differentiated consensus," Legrand's deconstruction of contemporary papal revanchism, and Brosseder's systematic subordination of infallibility to indefectibility. The historical contributions by Catholic scholars on the origin and development of the papacy (Meier, Minnerath, Pottmeyer) move the contemporary debate definitively beyond the sixteenth-century binary *de jure divino/humano.* In turn, historical reflections by Lutheran scholars on the forms of magisterium that have de facto existed in Lutheran confessionalism (especially Root, Meyer, and Nørgaard-Højen) complement serious attempts here by Catholic authors to rethink papacy.

a compelling Catholic theological possibility.[230] Neither would it be possible if consideration in some form of the "Petrine function" were not a real possibility for Lutheran theology.[231] Are these moves possible?

Considered in best light, Catholics have seen three great advantages in the development of the papacy: the link of historical continuity with Jesus and the apostles; the specific ministry to the unity of the churches highlighting the universal (i.e., the aforementioned Jesus as proclaimed by the apostles) in the particular or local; and the defense of this universal church's autonomy in every local situation against the claims of the state or of the ethnic group. Today, as mentioned, the first claim has been relativized by historical criticism to such an extent that apostolic succession in history, whether of episcopal or primatial orders, can only be honestly received as a "sign, not a guarantee" of the continuity that is claimed, with the acknowledgment therewith that there have been other forms of apostolic succession in Protestantism. The second claim is and remains controversial, although the Catholics represented here regard the maximalist interpretation of papal power as actually undermining the Petrine function. The third claim, by contrast, finds an interesting echo of Lutheran assent throughout this book, as Lutherans look self-critically at their own history of obsequiousness to temporal power and temptation to ethnic-nationalistic idolatries. Likewise Catholic contributors, struggling against their own history of mimicking temporal power in the monarchal papacy, sharply challenge Ratzinger's arguments that the universal church has ontological priority over the local churches and that the papacy represents this principle of universality. More than once we see contemporary Catholic theologians taking up Melanchthon's statement as their own: *non est transferendum ad pontifices quod dicitur de ecclesia* ("that which is said of the church is not to be transferred to the papacy")! To the extent that Catholics themselves are saying this, one must agree with Harding Meyer that a corresponding new reception of Petrine ministry is indeed now a "possibility for Lutheran theology"[232] as the Spirit's sign of the unification of the universal church and the local churches.

The problem of authority in the church between the times is thus not solvable once and for all, even under a renewed papacy, but only piecemeal. The authoring and authorizing of the gathering of the church in the gospel's mission to the nations occurs step by faltering step, as Spirit-given unifications of the sign and the thing signified.[233] In this true interim between Pentecost and Parousia,

230. As indeed Pottmeyer, Kasper, Lüning, Legrand, and Wicks variously argue along with editor Puglisi in the Introduction.

231. As especially Birmelé, Gassmann, and Meyer urge, under the condition — a tall order to be sure — that Lutheran theology would no longer be obsessed by "antipapal phobia" (Gassmann).

232. *How Can the Petrine Ministry?*, p. 226.

233. Portions of the following paragraphs first appeared in "Authority in the Church: A Plea for Critical Dogmatics," in *New Directions for Lutheranism*, ed. C. Braaten (Delhi, NY: ALPB Books, 2010), pp. 123-53.

critical dogmatics emerges as the disciplined, argumentative process by which the church under the Word tests the spirits that speak in the present hour to see whether they are of God. Critical dogmatics probes the words of God to find the Word incarnate, the sense that the Spirit intends, and by the Word incarnate seeks to recognize the Spirit at work in the world. In the pilgrim church on the way to the Reign, there is no other solution to the outstanding problem of the contested Lordship of Jesus Christ than this demanding, ongoing intellectual labor in the Spirit's battle for our minds, reading Scripture rightly that we may believe, teach, and confess Jesus Christ as Lord to the glory of God the Father, in every new day, in every new neighborhood.

How institutionally might that be put into practice? The opportunity before us is to use the present disintegration of the Euro-American Volkskirche denominational system for the forging of a new Christianity after Christendom. How do we get there? We have to begin with the brutally honest acknowledgment that not everyone is competent, especially not in our debased churches. By the argument made in these chapters, only the catechized are competent — those who by baptism and its practice have been formed into the theological subject.[234] Just so, this is not a competency to judge as an individual; it is rather a competency to participate in theological deliberation. The church is to become the forum of theological intersubjectivity, as normed by canon, creed, and confession. That it is not so is clear enough today from the manipulation of the guileless that occurs at every denominational assembly. It is also a question for us: What would credential one as a competent theological interlocutor, recognizing that the laity and the clergy need different forms and levels of theological discourse? Certainly it would entail a far more serious doctrinal subscription and a far more serious theological education than currently we practice — also for the laity. "My sheep hear my voice and will not listen to the voice of a stranger," Jesus says. The laity have the baptismal right and catechetical power to assess doctrine for its fidelity to Jesus, to probe and to test for this, and, as needed, to judge. By the same baptismal token, however, this right is not a private or unqualified right on the basis of simple, shared humanity. It is the right and duty of the *baptized,* as those who have been *evangelized and catechized,* who *know what they are talking about* in the Spirit's struggle against the world, the devil, and our sinful selves.

This then presupposes another, deeper question. Are we willing to be and to

234. "During the time in which the church and the culture are separating but not separated, this ambiguity cannot be avoided or denied. Much of the late modern church has dealt with the ambiguity by capitulating to it, by mitigating the church's liturgy, morality, and theology to accommodate 'seekers' and incompetent members. That way lies apostasy from the faith, which in broad stretches of Western Protestantism has already occurred. However it is to be managed in times of uncertain boundaries, the church must not dilute or estrange her sacramental culture but instead train would-be believers in its forms, not dispense with God's *torah* but instead reform would-be believers' moral structure, not succumb to theological relativism but teach would-be believers the doctrine of the Trinity." Jenson, *ST* 2, p. 305.

work for theological community, for an ecclesial communion where the process of theology decides questions rather than otherwise? Where, as Jenson once noted, we might actually be led by the Spirit to *new* thoughts rather than the uncomprehending repetition of past thoughts in the form of mere slogans that reinforce old failures? Where utilizing the theological heritage is a service on behalf of the ecumenical hope of the Lord's high-priestly prayer that "they may be one," not a defensive circling of the wagons to shore up an ever-shrinking cultural legacy?

Jenson talked about two possibilities for democratic polity in the church: "A group's decision may represent an average of the opinions held anyway by the individuals who make up the group. Or a group's decision may be a new thought created by discourse in the group — the conclusion of a common mind that does not exist except as the group argues within itself. . . ."[235] The latter procedure, of course, is the "how" of the Spirit entailed by the "what" of the Word in a church polity where theology is the very mechanism of its life together on the way to the Beloved Community. In a paragraph worth quoting in full, Jenson argued that the choice between these two "is one of the few that are unambiguously decided for Lutherans by their confessional position" on the *Verbum externum* as the means of the Spirit.

> The Reformation-era "enthusiasts" taught — as have all their like before and since — that the Spirit comes to each individual of the elect equally, privately, and in principle independently of the outward word, that is, of actual discourse among believers. The Lutheran Reformation found in this understanding a perversion worse than any at Rome, and vehemently attacked it, also in confessional writings. The Spirit, said the Lutherans, is the Spirit of the actual outward word, spoken by believers to each other and the world, and comes to no one independently of this discourse in and of the church. On the basis of enthusiasm, it will indeed be possible to discover the mind of faith by polling the opinions of individual believers. But by Lutheran understanding, what could thus be discovered would be at best the mind of the religious Old Adam; the church's mind, the mind of the Spirit, is given only as the living mutual word of the gospel constitutes an actual congregation of the Spirit.[236]

Such deliberation is impossible without substantive ground rules articulated in critical dogmatics: (1) canon, saying what the story of God's saving Word tells; (2) creed, saying who the saving God is; and (3) confession, saying how we sinners are included in the foregoing by repentance and faith.

The entire argument of the preceding two chapters, then, assails cheap and

---

235. *The New Church Debate: Issues Facing American Lutheranism,* ed. Carl E. Braaten (Philadelphia: Fortress, 1983), p. 48.
236. *The New Church Debate,* p. 49.

disgraceful appeals to our one baptism as uniting us no matter what, *ex opere operato,* as if baptism were a magical trump card that abrogates the doctrinal ground rules as just laid out that specify exactly what baptism is and entails as conformation to Christ's cross and resurrection by the Spirit. Why is such an appeal to unity not only bogus, not only a shameless ideological abuse of the sacrament of God to shore up denominational identity politics that are collapsing from their weightlessness, but in the merely logical sense *question-begging?* Baptized into Whom? Baptized for what? We have been baptized into the one, holy, catholic, and apostolic church of Jesus Christ, not into a denominational sect positioning itself in the religious marketplace over against other such sects, vultures feeding on the decaying corpse of Christendom.

We cannot have such deliberation without mutually trusted umpires, even if umpires will be as fallible as you and I. What would an evangelical episcopate be, which ruled the church according to the gospel, as per AC 28? It doesn't matter whether we call them referees, umpires, adjudicators, superintendents, presidents, or bishops. The point of AC 28 is that the episcopal function of oversight for the sake of true unity is an exercise of evangelical authority. It is the use the office of the keys to credential the competent, uphold the ground rules of churchly discourse, and lead ever-new debate forward through the *consensus fidelium* to the discernment of the Spirit's meaning, who speaks from the Scriptures by the Word Incarnate Jesus Christ to the glory of the Father. If we are willing to work for such a theological community as the mind of truly ecclesial community, then we must work concretely today for the realignment of the churches in Euro-America today.

## An Alternative: Ephraim Radner's *Brutal Unity*

Ephraim Radner's recent treatise[237] is a brutal confrontation with the brutal truth about the forced unifications that attend the history of the gospel through the West and beyond the West to the extremities of massacres of Christians by Christians, for example, in Radner's case study of Rwanda in the 1990s. Whatever else the "end of Christendom" means and portends, it means coming to terms with this brutal history within the household of God, whatever that may now portend. The book deserves a full and wide-ranging discussion,[238] but it is selected here

237. Ephraim Radner, *A Brutal Unity: The Spiritual Politics of the Christian Church* (Waco, TX: Baylor University Press, 2012).

238. Of particular merit as well as pertinence are Radner's critique of "bound conscience" (Radner, *A Brutal Unity,* p. 325) and his corresponding justification of a genuine sacrifice of conscience in imitation of the divine self-surpassing that takes place in the forgiveness of sins (p. 396); his corresponding critique of "dialogical reciprocity" in the ecumenical dialogues and of the model of visible unity as "reconciled diversity" (p. 433); his affirmation of political liberalism as necessary but not sufficient by itself to break the power of the self-privileging of the

to articulate an alternative to the Pneumatological and ecclesiological proposal that has been developed to this point regarding the theological subject as formed by baptism for ecclesial existence in the Spirit's mission to the nations. Hence we can isolate that feature of Radner's book that is relevant to this purpose. The point of engaging Radner in this way is not to refute him. The point is to advance the argument about who believes, knowing whom they believe by considering a powerful alternative to the argument conducted thus far.

This argumentative engagement is possible because of a profound agreement between us on the nature of the problem such that we diverge only — and that subtly — in what we propose to do about it. The agreement is this: *the church qua church is sinful.*[239] All illusions to the contrary must be rigorously banished in order to see this reality of the *simul peccator.* "There is no looking to Christ apart from the sinful Church."[240] Further in agreement: it is the one, holy, catholic, and apostolic church that is sinful, the same church that cannot fatally err and against which the gates of hell cannot prevail and that can and must teach truth binding consciences. It is, following Luther's dictum on the true people of God, "continually *penitent* and hence truly 'holy' from a human perspective just because the truly 'righteous' are those who are humbly contrite."[241] This agreement makes a diagnosis of the type represented by Menno Simons, as we have seen, on how to take the sinful church — namely, by separation from it as false church — impossible for Radner and myself. It "is not possible to identify the one Church except as she is given over to those who would divide. *Simul iusta et peccatrix* properly describes the Church . . ."[242] provided, as we have argued, that we take this formula of Luther in the dynamic sense of new life in the Spirit in constant turning to the returning Lord.[243] We cannot separate from the manifest sinfulness nor can we dualize in principle the sign and the thing signified in order to carve out a countercultural colony of the truly regenerate. For the church "is born in time" and "exists in time" and exists there as an "evangelical antinomy, the juxtaposition of contraries in the assertion of which lies the disclosure of God's redemptive power."[244] Thus we must find the Spirit's unification of the sign and

---

powerful (p. 441) and the church's obligation in turn to take responsibility within liberalism for the health of liberalism (p. 462), even as liberalism is received by the brutally divided church as divine judgment on the brutal politics of Christian disunity (p. 462). In all these matters, so far as I correctly understand Radner, we are in agreement with the possible exception of the first item above, his call for the sacrifice of conscience. In any case, I wish to parse the matter of conscience differently, as may be seen below especially in Chapter Seven.

239. Radner, *A Brutal Unity,* pp. 146-54.

240. Radner, *A Brutal Unity,* p. 153.

241. Radner, *A Brutal Unity,* p. 154.

242. Radner, *A Brutal Unity,* p. 154.

243. The "chasm between the two is real; we shall say as well, that it is spanned somehow and overcome" (Radner, *A Brutal Unity,* p. 167).

244. Radner, *A Brutal Unity,* p. 157.

the thing signified somehow under the dark, brutal, opaque covering of sinfulness that is given with the sign. And we must find a way of doing just this that does not perpetuate the sickness of Christendom but breaks through again to knowledge of the ecclesia as gathered, united, and sent forth in the Pneumatological *missio Dei.* "For if the Church is not to be simply the replication of the sins of the past, a porous community 'bound to violence . . . ,' normative and directive claims need to be given."[245] Critical dogmatics, thus, comes forward as the piecemeal solution to the insolvable problem of authority in the church between the times of Pentecost and Parousia in today's specific situation: in Euro-American post-Christendom under the hegemony of liberalism, where "modern political efforts have rightly come to [be seen] as necessary means of ordering and perhaps controlling religious self-deception."[246]

How then do we diverge? Radner makes the same dialectical argument criticized above that the Lutheran side made in the ecumenical document *Justification and the Church.* He transcendentalizes grace in order to embrace "the godless, even the godless within the Church's own nominal membership," that is, in order to continue the *Volkskirche,* albeit contritely. And he makes the same perplexing claim that the chief doctrine, "the solidarity of God with the godless," "the embodied act and purpose of God," is "from an institutional or social perspective impossibly ordered" with respect to its "unitive function." Hence the "procedures of the Church" up to and including its formulations of binding doctrine "will never guarantee or provide either unity *or* truth." Instead they may "offer the necessary framework of life together" in which "God's own self-giving" gives truth in unity and unity in truth. The consequence of this interpretation of church as institution incommensurate with church as creature of the Word is a summons to radical surrender, up to and including the sacrifice of "conscience," to the "place of divine solidarity," even there where the "truth of God suffers blasphemy."[247] Schism thus emerges as the unforgivable sin when knowing and contrite solidarity with the blasphemous becomes the article on which the church stands and falls.

If we ask Radner for his account of Christian history that corroborates this stunning denouement, it turns on the original schism of Jews and Christians, when Christians ceased to abide the blasphemy of Jewish disbelief in Jesus on account of Jesus' blasphemous self-identification as the Son of God in solidarity with sinners. So Jews and Christians separated and constructed contrastive identities in an "Epiphanian" logic that continually divides and separates. To distinguish our accounts of Christian history in this connection, let me recall that in the present argument we have found quite prior to this "Epiphanian paradigm" of "contrastive identities" over against Judaism a strong case for continuity with

245. Radner, *A Brutal Unity,* p. 165.
246. Radner, *A Brutal Unity,* p. 165.
247. Radner, *A Brutal Unity,* p. 445.

Israel, as known from the Hebrew Scriptures, in the original and formative conflict with Christological docetism and the theological dualism of Gnosticism. That difference in historical theology in turn requires of us differing accounts — or rather differing accents in the account — of theological subjectivity.

For Radner love subordinates knowledge, so that "the Christian self is not a self apart from such self-giving, and such self-giving manifests the character of the relationship that sustains Christian self-hood."[248] To be sure, this self-giving, this offering of the self, "is given only in the complete possession by Christ of the self. . . . The material and formal meet here, for it is Christ's own abandonment to the will of the Father, in the Spirit, that is taken hold of or takes hold of the self in this sanctifying life. Our selves become like and one with his self, a oneness that finds its substantive unity in the giving away of self to God with Christ."[249] The reader will recall that this conception of the *fides Christo formata* (faith formed by Christ) violates, according to the present argument, the sequence in baptism of extending the Father's favor and on this assured basis empowering in the Spirit the new Eucharistic life of Christ's oblation. Here knowledge in faith of the Father's free favor subordinates love, in the sense that we love *because* He first loved us, and indeed that we know love in that we who remain sinful "have an advocate with the Father, Jesus Christ the righteous; and he is the atoning sacrifice for our sin, and not for ours only but also for the sins of the whole world" (1 John 2:1-2). We do not rise to the new Pneumatological agency of self-giving in Christ until in the knowledge of faith we sink to the contrite surrender of our sins to the Lamb of God who bears them away. This sinking is what is entailed when theological subjectivity is rendered by the Spirit under the drowning wave of baptism. If we do not find here the unification of the sign and the thing signified in the pure receptivity of faith that joyfully exchanges sin for righteousness we surely will never find it in the actual doing of Jesus' self-giving.

Our divergence here is subtle and perhaps even reconcilable. As it stands, however, it sends us in differing directions in responding to the crises of expiring Christendom. For Radner there is no way forward but a radical surrender to the ruin, bearing the disgrace in Christ-empowered sacrifice, purely awaiting the new coming of the Spirit, surrounded by blasphemy, not in the secular city, but in the ruined churches. I confess that understanding escapes me how this (if I may say so, Radner's "Lutheran") dogma of God's solidarity with the godless somehow transcends the mediation of theological argumentation to appear as some kind of meta-truth overriding the evident contradictions. The paradox is so severe it totters on the edge of unintelligibility. So this "Lutheran" must say to this "Anglican" that while he finds the patiency affirmed in his stance admirable and is willing to concede that it may even be the right course practically, he cannot find it persuasive theologically. According to the present proposal,

248. Radner, *A Brutal Unity,* p. 394.
249. Radner, *A Brutal Unity,* p. 417.

the theological subject knows in whom she believes because theologically she decodes the metaphor, Christ crucified, to interpret the justification of the ungodly as the vindication of Messiah Jesus' faith and faithfulness for us and for all. And this knowledge is articulated in the formulation of the binding beliefs of the ecumenical church through which, as Perpetua knew, *Christiana sum*. She would not and could not sacrifice her conscience. So distinctions must be made, even here. That knowledge leads me to call for the realignment of all fragmented and distorted Christian forces who intend Perpetua's orthodoxy in a new Christianity — one that has given up its privileged chaplaincy in Christendom in order to live the *missio Dei* also in Euro-America, even if, God forbid, that entails a renewed theology of the martyrs.

## A NOTE ON THE ESCHATON OF JUDGMENT

We reserve discussion of the eternal destiny of Beloved Community for the conclusion of this system of theology on the topic of the Eternal Life and the Eternal Trinity, only recalling here concerning it that, once decided, the *missio* of the Father who sends and the Son and Spirit who freely and joyfully go "cannot ever come to an end. There must, therefore, be an eschatological continuation of God's mission. For all eternity, the Father will continue to send his Son and Spirit to bring peace and joy to creation" (Holmes).[250] The *missio Dei* is thus eternal; it comes in forms scarcely imaginable under the current duress. What else must be briefly noted here to bring this chapter to conclusion is simply this: there is a resolution to the ambiguity of history at the eschaton of judgment. In this resolution the unification of the sign and the thing signified prevails forever and unambiguously, as also do the refusals of this unification. So Schüssler Fiorenza: "No compromise with the imperial cult is possible because God and Christ are the true rulers of the world. . . . John advocates an uncompromising theological stance towards the imperial religion because, for him and his followers, the dehumanizing powers of Rome and its vassals have become so destructive and oppressive that a compromise with them would mean an affirmation of 'those who destroy the earth' (Rev. 11:18)."[251]

This judgment of the nations so envisioned does not have in view "Christianity and the World Religions," as we commonly think of these today. We do not rightly think theologically about this eschaton of judgment if we think it turns on whether someone has accepted Jesus as their personal savior. Rather it turns on whether we have loved (Matt. 25:31-46), a judgment fulfilled for us already now where and when in faith Jesus is received as Him on whom the Spirit remained,

250. See above, note 126.

251. Elisabeth Schüssler Fiorenza, *The Book of Revelation: Justice and Judgment* (Philadelphia: Fortress, 1985), p. 196.

who came not to be served but to serve and to lay down His life a ransom for many (Mark 10:45). Since the Spirit is universally active in the promise of creation and since genuine signs of His sanctification appear in all nations and among all "religions,"[252] Christian theology can only think that those in whom the signs of sanctity appear, but who have not encountered Jesus Christ through the gospel between Pentecost and the Parousia, will nevertheless recognize their true and saving Lord as this One on whom the Spirit remains when He comes to judge the living and the dead. That would be the eschatological unification of the sign with the thing signified.

The teaching of the Bible's final book, the interpretation of which is highly problematic, is theology of the martyrs. It is written from the perspective of the persecuted. The seer tells us how he "saw the souls of those who had been beheaded for their testimony to Jesus and for the word of God. They had not worshiped the beast or its image and had not received its mark on their foreheads or their hands. They came to life and reigned with Christ a thousand years" (Rev. 20:4). On them the special privilege and blessing is pronounced: "Blessed and holy are those who share in the first resurrection. Over these the second death has no power, but they will be priests of God and of Christ, and they will reign with him a thousand years" (Rev. 20:6). Their exaltation to millennial reign corresponds with the defeat of the anti-divine powers: "Then I saw an angel coming down from heaven, holding in his hand the key to the bottomless pit and a great chain. He seized the dragon, that ancient serpent, who is the Devil and Satan, and bound him for a thousand years, and threw him into the pit, and locked and sealed it over him, so that he would deceive the nations no more, until the thousand years were ended" (Rev. 20:1-3). It is noteworthy that the wickedness of the Evil One here is understood as deception, untruth, lying; consequently, once again, "when the thousand years are ended, Satan will be released from his prison and will come out to deceive the nations" (Rev. 20:7-8). Resolution of the conflict of history requires that this possibility of deception is forever barred; thus in final defeat "the devil who had deceived them was thrown into the lake of fire and sulfur, where the beast and the false prophet were, and they will be tormented

---

252. See the discussion of "dispositional soteriology" in Gerald R. McDermott, *Jonathan Edwards Confronts the Gods: Christian Theology, Enlightenment Religion, and Non-Christian Faiths* (Oxford: Oxford University Press, 2000), pp. 133-38. If we take "disposition" as the universal work of the Spirit of the Son in working faith, hope, and love in the world, we can ground recognition of this Son, Jesus Christ, at the eschaton of judgment. McDermott speaks in the traditional Augustinian way of the Spirit's work "by infusion of grace into the whole person" creating a disposition (p. 223). So McDermott is justified to observe that "Edwards could have opened the door for a more hopeful view of the salvation of the heathen. The advance he made in typology, the extensive use he made of *prisca theologia,* and his development of a dispositional soteriology . . ." (p. 143) all tend in this direction. He drew back from this, interestingly, because "to affirm the salvation of the heathen on the grounds of moral sincerity alone would have conceded the argument" to his Deist opponents in a way too easily co-opted (p. 145).

day and night forever and ever (Rev. 20:10). Only then is hell harrowed in the seer's end-time drama: "And I saw the dead, great and small, standing before the throne, and books were opened. Also another book was opened, the book of life. And the dead were judged according to their works, as recorded in the books. And the sea gave up the dead that were in it, Death and Hades gave up the dead that were in them, and all were judged according to what they had done. Then Death and Hades were thrown into the lake of fire. This is the second death, the lake of fire; and anyone whose name was not found written in the book of life was thrown into the lake of fire" (Rev. 20:12-15).

Now the drama is finished. "It is done! I am the Alpha and the Omega, the beginning and the end. To the thirsty I will give water as a gift from the spring of the water of life. Those who conquer will inherit these things, and I will be their God and they will be my children. But as for the cowardly, the faithless, the polluted, the murderers, the fornicators, the sorcerers, the idolaters, and all liars, their place will be in the lake that burns with fire and sulfur, which is the second death" (Rev. 21:6-8). History is thus finally resolved at the eschaton of judgment, if what we do in the body through time matters. As persons we are what is done to the body and what we do in the body from birth day to death day. If God is God who gives life to the dead, the eternity of this salvation is secured because the deception that began with the serpent's *sicut Deus eritis* is undone by the God whose dwelling comes to be with His people. So deception is now and forever precluded. Only so can there never be a return to the status quo ante — the cycle is broken and the redemption of our bodies has been fulfilled.

In Christianity, the opposite of love is not hate but the indifference of apathy (Rom. 12:9). Those who by the Spirit will not become the sinner for whom the Lamb lived and died and lives forever instead remain forever the loveless that in reality they are and still wish to be. Those who will in their lovelessness not be loved will go unloving and unloved into the judgment of eternity. For love is against what is against love. Grace, which *is* the love of the Father for the Son and the Son for the Father, can be truly offered *and* therefore just as truly resisted, because this Holy Spirit as Person is not an impersonal, coercive force but One who calls from love for love by the Word spoken in the decisiveness of real history. It is heard when and where the same Spirit unifies the sign with the thing signified in faith, for hope and for love, the last of which endures forever to know as it has been known.

There is thus a cost of this doctrine of eschatological personhood, human and divine: history is decisive.[253] The human person qua person is paradoxically

---

253. According to McDermott, Edwards "conceived of all religion as a response to revelation" (p. 89) and thus he "believed it was historical in its very nature, while deists refused to take history seriously" (p. 92). "For the classical writers and the deists, whose view of history was basically cyclical, progress occurs within larger cycles, which recur endlessly. For Edwards, on the other hand, repeating cycles or patterns contribute to long-term historical progress. . . . For

unfree in election, since the Spirit blows where He will, but just so freed thereby also to reject election. The harrowing of hell is the promise that there is no depth into which the living Jesus Christ does not descend to establish solidarity and from there to proclaim His victory for all. The judgment of the nations is in His hands and therefore it will be a judgment of mercy that shows mercy. Yet it is not an Origenist *apokatastasis* that renders the biographies of embodied persons nugatory but rather a judgment that lifts the veil of ambiguity covering them. The Son's atonement is potentially universal; history in its depth dimension includes the Son's proclamation of His victory for one and for all, who sends the Lord and Giver of life that all may believe. Just so history is decisive, grace can be resisted, the Spirit may be spurned and the Son declined. This hellish possibility of deciding eternally against the free and universal grace of God gained for all by the Son and offered to all by the Spirit is the cost of personal existence. It is the ontology of disunion, the ultimate dualism of the sign and the thing signified, eternal death.

---

Edwards the historical view was critical to understanding the work of redemption, God's nature and being itself" (p. 98). Thus he conceived a " 'new body of divinity in an entire new method, being thrown into the form of a history . . .'" (p. 100), which speaks accordingly of "Divine self-enlargement" (p. 101). The affinities are evident with the present system of theology, for which as well God is historical, and the Incarnation into the likeness of sinful flesh is at once a crisis in the divine Life and, upon its Easter resolution, an enrichment.

# PART THREE

# Christology

Jesus is the Son who believed in His vindication as Messiah, making Himself the object of His own Messianic faith. Whoever believes does so by Spirit-directed belief in the vindicated faith of Jesus, hence by the Spirit's conviction of the righteousness of Jesus Christ, crucified for our sins and raised for our justification, working the spiritual resurrection of the believer to the Beloved Community of God.

# CHAPTER FIVE

# The Objectivity of Faith

## Historicizing the Eschatological?

In *Faith and Fratricide,* Rosemary Ruether's influential and in some respects incisive critique of the toxic symbiosis of anti-Judaism, ecclesiastical triumphalism, and Christendom ideology displacing the theology of the martyrs, she came to the conclusion that the "Chalcedonian doctrine of the two natures in one divine person is only a pure compromise indicative of the Church's inability to sort out the duality between Jesus' historical existence and his mediation of eschatological presence." Indeed, she argues, "as soon as this eschatological presence is regarded as already realized in his historical existence — i.e., he already was the Messiah — then the historical Jesus as a human person must be abolished." For Jesus to remain a historical being for us, she continues, requires the realization that Jesus "can only be nonfinal in himself, not only in the sense that he becomes a mediating presence for some but not for others, but also in the sense that he himself is not 'the One,' but points beyond himself to the 'One who is yet to come.'" To repudiate Chalcedonian Christology is to affirm that "this dualism between . . . the historical and the eschatological is not overcome for [Jesus] or for us."[1]

One might take Ruether's claim, however, to mean something that Chalcedon precisely affirmed, namely, that the natures of divinity, taken biblically (Rev. 1:4) as the "eschatological," and of humanity, taken biblically as the "historical," are not to be confused in thought or fused naturally into a hybrid being even in their personal union. In that case, it would be the "personal" union that Chalcedon affirms, not the "natural" confusion it rejects that she critiques. While the feisty rhetoric Ruether employed in making her case often gave the impression that something new and radical was being thought over against a monolithic theological tradition, in fact she expressed in this concluding judgment what

---

1. Rosemary Radford Ruether, *Faith and Fratricide: The Theological Roots of Anti-Semitism* (New York: Seabury, 1979), p. 243.

have come to be certain truisms of modern theology[2] that themselves have long precedence in Christian tradition stretching back through Nestorius to the Antiochene school of Theodore of Mopsuestia and its so-called "Logos-anthropos" Christology.[3] This Christology was more precisely, in Jaroslav Pelikan's words, a Christology of the "indwelling Logos," that is, of the divine Person, as it were, co-inhabiting a human person, Jesus of Nazareth, to work out the human obedience by which salvation comes. In contrast, the Alexandrian alternative culminating in Cyril was a Christology in which the person of the divine Logos personally unites a human nature to Himself to accomplish the redemptive mission commissioned by the Father in the power of the Spirit.

In this light, then, Ruether's claim perpetuates a longstanding tradition of Christological "dualism" cutting right through what was in fact, historically, a "compromise" at Chalcedon. It is true that the Chalcedonian formula, acknowledging two natures in Christ "without confusion, without change, without division, without separation . . . combining in one Person and *hypostasis* — not divided or separated into two Persons, but one and the same Son and only-begotten God . . . ,"[4] is not a stable doctrine in the sense of an intelligible synthesis. It is rather little more than a marking of boundaries within which Christology that intends to be orthodox must think. As a result, however, something very much like the soteriology of the Antiochene school of salvation by the divinely assisted human person can be read out of Chalcedon, in Robert Jenson's acerbic words: "Thus what finally is supposed to make Christ savior is not *achieved in* the hypostatic union, but rather is given to the human *picked out* by the hypostatic union."[5] That is to say, salvation is not given as a gift in the person of Christ to those who cannot save themselves; salvation is modeled in the human obedience of the Jesus for those who can and would imitate Him.

While Jenson's assessment may be overstated in underestimating the force of the notion of personal or hypostatic union in the text of Chalcedon, it is true, as we shall later examine in some detail, that contemporary defenders of Chalcedon, not only in the West, accentuate Pope Leo's moderate qualification of the "dualism"[6] — the very "dualism" that Ruether wants in an exaggerated form to lift up in the spirit of Antiochene Christology against the "compromise" at Chalcedon. In the process they affirm the two-nature distinction as expressive of the

---

2. Aloys Grillmeier, S.J., *Christ in Christian Tradition,* vol. 1, *From the Apostolic Age to Chalcedon (451),* 2nd, revised edition, trans. J. Bowden (Atlanta: John Knox, 1975), pp. 345-91.

3. Pelikan, *TCT* 1, p. 247, pp. 251-56.

4. *Christology of the Later Fathers,* ed. Edward R. Hardy (Philadelphia: Westminster, 1954), p. 373.

5. Robert W. Jenson, *Unbaptized God: The Basic Flaw in Ecumenical Theology* (Minneapolis: Augsburg Fortress, 1992), p. 124.

6. Grillmeier speaks of a blending, *circumincessio,* of the natures according to Leo in distinction from Nestorius's juxtaposition of two persons in the same place. Grillmeier, *Christ in Christian Tradition,* p. 537.

biblical Creator-creature distinction and thus as proper antidote to an opposite error, namely, the fusion in fact and confusion in thought of the sign and the thing signified in Alexandrian Christology of the so-called "Logos-sarx" type.

That being said, the decree at Chalcedon was unstable and remains unstable to this day; it had to elicit the so-called neo-Chalcedonian response of the fifth ecumenical council, which affirmed that in the person of Jesus Christ "one of the Trinity suffered."[7] The latter is, as is evident, the stance adopted and argued in the present system of theology. The so-called "neo-Chalcedonian" Christological thesis is twofold: that "person" in the Christological "personal" or "hypostatic" union is to be used in precisely the same sense as gained by the antecedent Trinitarian distinction of person and nature, that is, that Chalcedonian Christology is to be taken as a function and implication of the doctrine of the Trinity; and that the danger of a confusion of natures in thought, let alone a fusion in reality, is safeguarded when it is strictly understood that it is by the ministry of the Spirit that the historical sign and the eschatological thing signified are unified for baptismal repentance and faith, not otherwise or for purposes other than performing the Son's redemptive mission in the economy of the Father on the way to the Beloved Community of God. The Word incarnate without the Spirit's enlightening does not give the *Machtwort,* the powerful Word of God, but its inefficacious sign, *fides historica.*[8] The Spirit apart from the Word incarnate, by the same token, is not the Holy Spirit but some other spirit, *Schwärmerei,* "enthusiasm."[9] Or, to put the matter positively: *opera Dei ad extra sunt indivisa* (the external works of God are not divisible), but Word points to Spirit points to Word.

This thesis by no means implies dismissal of Ruether's contemporary critique nor of the classical concerns of Antiochene Christology for the true humanity of the historical Jesus, but rather requires that these be received in a better Christological synthesis. Indeed, the conceptual ability to take these concerns more seriously than these proponents do is the test of any claim to such a synthesis. If we revert, then, from the rather crude and vacillating theologizing of Nestorius to his teacher, Theodore, we find themes and accents that are valuable Christologically in spite of his failure ultimately to unify the person. This is ecumenically important today because not only liberal Catholic theology but also Reformed theology continues in this Christological line and at its best warns against any unification of the person that obscures its counterfactual *(sub contrario)* nature under the conditions of malice and injustice and thus falls short of the visibility of the eschatological victory. Correspondingly a necessary accentuation on the *obedience* of faith comes along with this construction of Christology, although it often skates on thin ice with respect to the saving significance that Christology

7. Pelikan, *TCT* 1, pp. 266-77.
8. *LW* 37, pp. 180-82.
9. *LW* 40, pp. 146-49.

must claim for Jesus Christ. This eschatological reserve in respect to Christology and accent on obedience is at the heart of Theodore's teaching, who ties human glorification to the victorious obedience of the man Christ as something still to be achieved for us in fullness and power: "We are expecting to enjoy these pleasures in which Christ our Lord became our first fruits, whom God the Word put on, and who through the close union that he had with him became worthy of all this glory and gave to us also the hope of communion with him."[10] We can summarize Theodore's Christological teachings as follows.

Theodore was a Nicene theologian: the "teaching of the persons . . . is the true teaching of the Christian faith and the true knowledge for those who become disciples of Christ."[11] Thus, if God "is called Father of men, He is not called their Father because He created them, but because of their proximity to Him and relation with Him. This is the reason why He is not called Father of all men but only of those who have relation with Him . . . by *special favor.*"[12] It is grace — *eudokia,* good pleasure — by which God relates to creatures as Father, who is eternally Father of His own Son by nature and so *becomes* Creator of creatures and likewise also Father to obedient creatures by further grace through their communion with Christ the Son. Correspondingly the union of the eternal Son with humanity in Christ will be a union by *eudokia:* the Son *becomes* human in an act of grace to save by grace-empowered obedience in the assumed humanity. "Paul frequently says 'preordination' and 'good pleasure' and 'will,' teaching that the grace is deliberate and free. And so it was that God preordained and wishes those things done on our behalf in such a way, without our contributing anything of our own."[13]

This Pauline insight led Theodore into a theological struggle to understand divine transcendence as unbounded will, a predicate that belongs exclusively to the Creator: "[A] creature is not able to free us nor is a servant able to renew us . . . no other nature can create, renew and free except Divine nature, which is neither created nor made, but is the cause of everything . . . *according to its will . . . as it wishes.*"[14] It is a struggle to think in this way that God's will determines all, because that self-determination apparently includes also divine nature. God's nature does not determine the divine will, because essentially God is free will. God is the One who is self-determining. One does not have to claim that Theodore is conceptually successful in this recognizably biblical struggle to free himself from the determinism of the natural in Hellenistic metaphysics, but only to recognize the significance of it: "If he were present everywhere by good pleasure, he would

10. Theodore of Mopsuestia, *Catechetical Homilies,* Woodbrook Studies, vol. 5, trans. A. Minguna (Cambridge: W. Heffer & Sons, 1932), p. 78.

11. Theodore of Mopsuestia, *Catechetical Homilies,* p. 27.

12. Theodore of Mopsuestia, *Catechetical Homilies,* p. 32, emphasis added.

13. Theodore of Mopsuestia, *On Ephesians,* as quoted by Joanne Dewart, *The Theology of Grace of Theodore of Mopsuestia* (Washington, DC: Catholic University of America Press, 1971), p. 24.

14. Cited in Dewart, *The Theology of Grace,* p. 101, emphasis added.

be seen to be subjected in another way to external necessity, since he would no longer effect his presence by will, but by the boundlessness of his nature and his will would be subservient to that. But since he is present to all by nature, and is separated from whom he wishes by will, no one who is unworthy is profited by God's presence, while the true and pure limitlessness of his nature is preserved to him."[15] As Luther might have put the same point: it is one thing for God to be present; it is another for God to be present for you.

This inchoate conception of divine transcendence as grace (as opposed to the predominant contemporary conception in Hellenistic metaphysics of the divine as *nous,* as mind suffusing the cosmos) in turn guides Theodore in his polemic against the Alexandrian theologian, Apollinaris of Laodicea, who, as Richard Norris exposits, by way of the Hellenistic analogy of mind subsumed "under the single category of *pneuma* both the human soul and the divine Logos."[16] Indeed, for Apollinaris the rational soul "possesses a natural affiliation and community of nature with the Divine."[17] As a result, Apollinaris attributes to the divine-like mind of the human creature precisely that freedom of will that Theodore, following Paul, ascribes uniquely to divine good pleasure. On account of this high view of the rational soul's self-determining power, Apollinaris denied that in the Incarnation the Logos was united with the whole human being of body and soul and taught rather that the Logos united only with body, with flesh. The rational soul by virtue of its natural affinity for the divine and its freedom of self-determination does not need the grace of a new will but rather reinforcement; moreover, a union of the rational soul with the Logos would destroy the soul's autonomy, undercutting its grace-assisted but meritorious sanctification. Thus the human problem for Apollinaris is that the "human spirit cannot control the flesh with which it is joined; and the point of the Incarnation was to alter this state of affairs."[18]

By contrast, for Theodore the "soul is not 'divine' in the same sense as its transcendent source."[19] Moreover, as Theodore comments on Romans 1:28-31 to his catechumens, it "is indeed clear that the strength of the sin has its origin in the will of the soul . . . [and that] the majority of [sins] are not born of the passions of the body, but exclusively of the will of the soul."[20] If the Incarnation is to help, it is the obedience of the man Jesus in His own human soul that must win the victory for us and in us whose souls, not bodies, are the source of sin. Christologically, then, for Theodore the union of the Logos and the whole human being Jesus of Nazareth, body and soul together, cannot be a "natural" union (*kat' ousian,* as he takes Apollinaris's fusion of the Logos with human flesh) but rather one

15. Theodore of Mopsuestia, *On the Incarnation,* Fragment 6 from the unpublished translation of Richard Norris, p. 19.

16. Richard Norris, *Manhood and Christ* (London: Oxford Press, 1963), p. 98.

17. Norris, *Manhood and Christ,* p. 101.

18. Norris, *Manhood and Christ,* p. 115.

19. Norris, *Manhood and Christ,* p. 101.

20. Theodore of Mopsuestia, *Catechetical Homilies,* pp. 56-57.

according to grace *(kat' eudokian)* in the public appearance *(prosopon)* of Jesus Christ: "indwelling him as of a son" by grace to work out grace in this human life and through this human life conveying the accomplished grace of Jesus Christ to others. Thus the human life of Jesus in His decisions of obedience acquires soteriological significance: if Jesus did not have a human soul, but it was the deity occupying the place of the rational soul in Him that won the victory, then what was accomplished could not benefit us in our own true need: ". . . all things happened to the human nature: things through which God wishes his Economy to be accomplished on our behalf. And he who was assumed for our salvation bore upon himself all things affecting mankind, and became worthy of perfection and a source of benefits for us though our communion with him."[21]

In sum, two persons, the son of Mary and the Son of God, converge as one *prosopon* in the world by the *eudokia* of the "indwelling" Son who "perfected through sufferings and made immortal and immutable in everything the form of a servant which was assumed as His temple."[22] This is a functional *(kat' energeia)* union of persons by grace, not a natural *(kat' ousian)* fusion, for the Son of Mary could not have tasted "the trial of death if [the Godhead] were not cautiously remote from him, but also near enough to do the needful and necessary things . . . to perfect with sufferings the Head of the life of the many children whom he brought to his glory."[23] If we bear in mind, however, that for Theodore God is God, that is, transcendent by the free will of His grace or good pleasure, this union by grace rather than of "natures" intends to express a *free* unification of the sign, the man Jesus, and the thing signified, the eternal Son, in the concrete *prosopon* or *persona,* the figure of Jesus Christ as rendered in the evangelical narrative for the obedience of faith. Yet, at the same time, as is evident in the preceding citation, Theodore seems to retain yet another notion of divine nature that requires him to affirm a divine Son of God "cautiously remote" from the sufferings of His man.

Let us take this Christology of Theodore as the best possible challenge within the theological traditions that intend orthodoxy to the case to be made in this chapter for Cyrilian/Alexandrian Christology — so good that it can only be met by incorporating its insights about the soteriological significance of the human obedience of Jesus into a better synthesis. To be sure, the issues that Ruether raised in her book are urgent and on point today, as already indicated from the opening chapters of this system of theology and as will be further addressed in what follows. But it is doubtful that Ruether has actually contributed something new to their solution. She has rather repeated a characteristic false antithesis, exacerbated in the Western tradition that she otherwise rejects, by reiterating its modalist tendency to take the appearance of Jesus in the world as but a figure alongside others of a hidden and unknowable divine essence. Nor has she

21. Theodore of Mopsuestia, *Catechetical Homilies,* p. 73.
22. Theodore of Mopsuestia, *Catechetical Homilies,* p. 87.
23. Theodore of Mopsuestia, *Catechetical Homilies,* p. 87.

articulated a Christology on the level of Theodore's Nicene commitment to the nature–person distinction that in Theodore's case distinguishes the persons of the Son of Mary and the Son of God in order to preserve their unification as a gracious, Spirit-given *event,* a union of moral will and action, as for example in the "critically realistic dialectical" (McCormack) Christology of Karl Barth. As such, for Theodore as for Barth, Christ is not *objectifiable* for purposes of ecclesiastical triumphalism but comes freely to press us forward in the obedience of faith to the coming of the Beloved Community. This resistance to the ecclesiastical domestication of Christ within a world still groaning with malice and injustice is the invaluable contribution of this Christological tradition. Unlike Ruether's blunt recommendation of "dualism," however, it depends on a notion of the Christological union as an event freely and incalculably given by grace for the obedience of faith.

Even as its best, as in Theodore, however, an economic union of persons does not break another spell: that of imprisoning God in a divine "nature," as Theodore put it, "cautiously remote" from human suffering and only drawing "near enough" to succor. This criticism remains even though Theodore has pushed the concept of nature to its limits by conceiving, with the Bible, the deity of God as self-determining freedom. Deity as "self-determining freedom" would be a virtual "anti-nature" in the sense that it is affirming that God's deity cannot in principle be captured in any conceptual definition; such capture is precisely the semantic function of the concept of "nature," as if to say paradoxically, then, that the nature of God is not to have any fixed or capturable nature. That is well and good, but it does not yet give us this divine freedom as freedom to love wisely and well. It does not yet give us God surpassing God, that is, the Father sending the Son, in order to include also the ungodly in the coming to this earth of the Beloved Community. It does not give Jesus Christ the Son of God as savior of those helplessly because willingly bound to structures of malice and injustice. It does not give Jesus Christ as the known object of faith, by which a new theological subjectivity is forged in the Spirit. It rather gives a transcendent Word that is occasioned by Jesus as a model or pattern of obedience, thus, one that is illuminated by Him but is not He Himself, the Person who came in our flesh to serve us and give His life for us in His own self-donation of love, and this very One as now vindicated, to be received, believed, and obeyed in baptismal transformation.

Modalism, we recall, is the prior theological problem in Trinitarianism that does not take the personal distinctions between Father, Son, and Holy Spirit, as evident in the gospel narrative, as true to God's being but as varying accommodations of the self-same but in-itself unknowable divine being in communicating to various creaturely circumstances. To hold that the Son and the Father, being personally or hypostatically different, yet alike and together true expressions of divine being is the substance of Nicea's *homoousios.* To complete the "triad," so that the divine life together of the Father and the Son is complete in their own Spirit and eternal as such — not, then, as neo-Platonism imagined, complete and eternal in the cosmos thus forming an eternal system — is the mature doctrine of the Trinity articulated at Constantinople in 381. To employ just this distinction between person/hypostasis and nature/ousia/physis in articulating the incarnate life and work of Jesus Christ is what is here termed a "Cyrilian Christ," after Cyril of Alexandria. But to retrieve this Cyrilian Christ today, we need fully to articulate and utilize the Pneumatology worked out in Part One that makes the presentation of Jesus Christ the Son of God the Spirit's free and personal act for the obedience of faith, beginning with Jesus Himself. It is this dialectic of Word and Spirit that safeguards against the danger of a confusion of natures that has been the legitimate concern of the Antiochene tradition.

Developing a new Christological solution that I have elsewhere pegged "a Cyrilian Christ for Augustinian humanity"[24] is the task of this chapter, which will argue that Western Christologies betray a modalistic tendency that requires at length Christological choices between Apollinarian confusion of natures on the one side and Nestorian division of the person on the other. Ruether, manifestly, falls squarely into the latter tendency to divide the person into two, the nonfinal Jesus of history and the coming One to whom He points: a textbook example of the dualism of the sign and the thing signified. What goes begging in this characteristic antithesis is the Western habit of forgetting the prior question of what Christology is for and thus what kind of cognitive claim is being made on the basis of the accumulating dogmatic precedents of the canonical decision against docetism and dualism and the decision for the Trinity of persons against Arian unitarianism. All this dogmatic development is analytical of the identification of God as the One who is determined by the missions of His Son and Spirit to redeem and fulfill the creation as known from the primitive kerygma of the resurrection of the Crucified. In pursuing this thesis, then, we first orient ourselves in the matrix of the Scriptures by asking what possibly could be meant by their unification of the sign, Jesus of Nazareth, and the thing signified, the Son of God, in presenting the *one* Lord Jesus Christ the Son of God from faith for faith. Indeed, let us begin at the point of great possible contemporary offense to see that things may not be as they appear, not only to Ruether, but to the tradition of Western Christian theology in which her putatively radical but forthrightly (traditional!) "dualistic" Christology in fact stands.

## The "Theotokos" and Her Child

The birth narratives of Matthew (Matt. 1:23: "Look, the virgin shall conceive and bear a son, and they shall name him Immanuel, which means, God is with us") and Luke (Luke 1:35: "The Holy Spirit will come upon you, and the power of the

24. Paul R. Hinlicky, "Theological Anthropology: Towards Integrating Theosis and Justification by Faith," *Journal of Ecumenical Studies* 34, no. 1 (Winter 1997): 38-73.

Most High will overshadow you; therefore the child to be born will be holy; he will be called Son of God") have played a massive role in the history of Christology. Mark has in common with John, however, that he does not know the birth narratives (or, if these latter evangelists do know these traditions, they ignore or even suppress them; the same may be said for Paul and his tradition). Ignatius, it seems, was the first to combine traditions of Mary's virginal conception by the Holy Spirit and the Pauline and Johannine doctrines of the coming into flesh of the heavenly Son or the Incarnation of the Word when he wrote that Jesus Christ our Lord is at once "flesh and spirit, born and unborn, God in man, true life in death, both from Mary and from God."[25] From Ignatius' time onward few in the early church felt the tension in the combination of these two (at least historically) distinct accounts of the origin of Jesus' person. Rather, as we see in Ignatius, they were felt to complement each other.

The Johannine doctrine of the incarnation prevented one from thinking that the Son of God first came into existence when Mary conceived (an impression Luke's account could give), since the eternal Son had existed with the Father from the beginning as the creative Logos of God. The birth from the Virgin Mary prevented one from thinking that the Incarnation began at some point of achievement in Jesus' career, say, His baptism, transfiguration, or resurrection, with the danger that the man Jesus would then be thought to have attained divine status by Himself for Himself rather than having proceeded from it in filial obedience to do His saving work for others. The virginal conception thus made it clear that the incarnation determined the totality of Jesus' historical existence from the beginning. It also concretely pictured the reality of the *egeneto sarx* of John 1:14: so human had the divine Word become that once He grew in Mary's womb and suckled at her breasts, then as a boy grew in wisdom and understanding (Luke 2:52).

According to this traditional synthesis, it is necessary in teaching the personal union of humanity and deity in Christ to speak not only of the divine Word's act of assuming a human nature, but of the Spirit's forming of the assumed human nature to befit the assuming Word, including the formation of Mary's faith to give her assent as the servant of the Lord (Luke 1:38). The humanity of Jesus thus appears as the new creation of the Spirit in the midst of the old, a "real existence of God in Him"[26] who is God's true human image, the New Adam. In this respect the Christological miracle is sought and found in the new humanity that appears in Jesus, *from* our fallen stock yet *not by* our fallen stock, from our sister, Mary, then, *as Virgin,* that is, *without* the natural causality of the male-female sexual union. The curious point, then, is that even though it can be harmonized as in

---

25. Ephesians 7:2 in *The Apostolic Fathers: Revised Greek Texts with Introductions and English Translations,* ed. J. B. Lightfoot and J. R. Harner (Grand Rapids: Baker, 1984), p. 141.

26. Friedrich Schleiermacher, *The Christian Faith,* 2 volumes, ed. H. R. Macintosh and J. S. Steward (New York: Harper & Row, 1963), p. 397.

Ignatius with the Johannine doctrine of the Incarnation, the birth from the Virgin has to do with the true humanity of Jesus: "true" in a twofold sense as truly one from the common body but now true as the human being whom God intends. That was why docetists found the Nativity stories just as offensive as the passion narrative: hanging on a Roman stake and passing through Mary's birth canal were equally repulsive to them who sought salvation by shedding the body as a snake sheds its skin. So even as harmonized with John, the testimony to Jesus' true humanity in Luke and Matthew survived in the traditional synthesis, though its specific witness was muted.

Deliteralized, as with Schleiermacher, it indeed became the foundation of modern Christologies. Rejecting the help of the doctrine of the Trinity,[27] because like Ruether they found an impossible confusion in the "two natures in one person" Christology of Chalcedon,[28] these modern Christologies have instead taken the Nativity stories as expressive of the disciple's experience of Jesus' pure "God-consciousness."[29] This humanity is something that can be historically investigated and still mediated to us today by historical inquiry, deliteralized and critically purified. In the perspective of the present attempt in Christology, these modern Christologies amount to half-truths in which the traditional synthesis of Johannine incarnation and the Synoptic Nativity stories has fallen apart. That hardly means that one can simply reassert the traditional synthesis uncritically. It rather means that one must with the help of the doctrine of the Trinity discern more profoundly the role of the Spirit in the Incarnation, not of deity in general, but of the Logos who is God in the way of being the Son. In the matrix of the Scriptures, let us now probe the Matthean account as a first step in this direction.

An assumption of benign divine presence in general, so to say, easily erases the concrete features, not always attractive to us Gentiles, of the material *body* of Christ and its *Jewish* lineage — a prerequisite for the office it fulfills as the Christ of *Israel*, the One "in whom the Gentiles [are to] hope" (cf. Matt. 12:17-21). The distinctive Matthean[30] accent on the "good news" of the Gospel assures readers of the abiding presence of *Jesus* the Christ. It is *He* who will "be with" disciples whenever they gather in His name (18:20), as they faithfully herald the reign of *His* Father to the nations (28:20). The Gospel's final verse thus forms an inclusion with 1:23 where the nativity narrative had told of the royal birth of

---

27. Schleiermacher, *The Christian Faith,* 2, p. 399.

28. Schleiermacher, *The Christian Faith,* 2, pp. 391-94.

29. Schleiermacher, *The Christian Faith,* 2, p. 389.

30. An earlier version of the following exegesis of Matthew appeared in Paul R. Hinlicky, "The Presence of Jesus the Christ," *Pro Ecclesia* 4, no. 4 (Fall 1995): 479-85. Literature consulted includes Karl Barth, "The Miracle of Christmas," in *CD* I/2, pp. 172-202; Raymond E. Brown, *The Birth of the Messiah: A Commentary on the Infancy Narratives in Matthew and Luke* (New York: Doubleday, 1977); Ulrich Luz, *Matthew 1-7: A Commentary,* trans. Wilhelm C. Linss (Minneapolis: Augsburg, 1989).

"Immanuel," "God with us." In the nativity narrative the evangelist introduces, as in an overture to the whole, his particular theological accent on the hidden but effective presence in the world of Messiah Jesus, its coming king. This *particular* presence, however, is neither obviously nor unambiguously a source of balm. It serves poorly for stilling modern anxiety. It is something disturbing and intrusive. The "saving" significance of it is by no means obvious. What Matthew's Jesus saves Gentiles together with Jews from is their "sins" (1:21).

Salvation from sin plays a subversive role over against political sovereignty. Matthew's second chapter gives voice to Christological protest against the closure of political sovereignty to God and the coming of the Reign. Herod the king "trembles at" (2:2-3) word of Messiah's entry into his world. The presence of Jesus precipitates in turn the dreadful acts of massacre, rescue, and judgment recorded in 2:1-23, recalling Pharaoh's slaughter of the male babies of Israel at the time of Moses' birth. More broadly, these events call to mind the Passover of Israel from bondage in Egypt, just as they anticipate the suffering and vindication that lie ahead for the newborn "King of the Jews" as also for His people. Precisely in this ferment, however, the pattern of God's cross-and-resurrection providence is disclosed. Matthew's readers are to discern the presence of their Lord in the thick of fierce opposition. In the figure of the Magi, Matthew lifts up Jesus as the divinely given child, who will finally be adored by all nations as the only Son of the heavenly Father (2:11). This action of the worship of Jesus in the church (cf. 14:33; 28:9, 17) thus signifies a decisive public breach with the butchers of this world who pose as saviors of the people. The iconographic juxtaposition is stunning: vulnerable infant Jesus and bloodthirsty Herod. Worship of the vulnerable child is an act of messianic hope and protest.

Thus the presence of Jesus as the Christ according to Matthew is not a matter of whether He is sheerly there as God in general, but of His coming to reign in the worship, confession, and service of His new humanity — not like that of Pharaoh or Herod — where He lives "for" us as "against" this world structured by malice and injustice.

This nuance of meaning regarding Jesus' presence reflects Matthew's place in the second Christian generation, i.e., after the Roman destruction of Jerusalem in the first century. For Matthew, the end of the worship in the Temple had resolved the disputes that had raged earlier in the days of Peter, Paul, and James. The question about the relation of the Christian mission to the true Israel had been settled in a terrible divine judgment on the Temple in Jerusalem — so Matthew sees things (cf. 23:28). Consequently the gospel mission to the nations which had been foreordained in God's plan of salvation and carefully woven into the unfolding of Israel's history (1:1-17) has now become manifest. From the moment of His earthly origin Jesus is seen as the designated heir of David's throne, "the Christ" (1:17), "the Son" whom God "called out of Egypt" (2:15), the "Nazorean" (2:23, i.e., the stem from Jesse's root, consecrated from the womb to do the Lord's will, who sums up all the Scriptures of Israel). This scheme of recapitulation of Israel's history concludes by locating Jesus the "Nazorean" in Nazareth, in "Galilee of the Gentiles" (4:15), the interface of Israel and the nations. All this providential stage-setting indicates that as Jesus' human existence is directly created by God in a unique act by His Spirit, so also God's Spirit determines this human existence at every step along its earthly way.

With precisely these *Jewish* themes, Matthew's Gospel is especially a Gospel for the *ecclesia,* i.e., for the community ever sent to the nations from Israel, by the mediation of Israel's Scriptures, even though now increasingly drawn from the nations. In the new situation of his generation, Matthew perceives the urgent need of the ecclesia to continue to understand itself in the matrix of the Scriptures of Israel and thus to be taught by them to think aright concerning the Christ, Israel's anointed One of God. The ecclesia dare never forget that Jesus was born a Jew (1:1-17) and that he has saving significance for Gentiles as, and only as, the "king of the Jews" (2:2, which forms an inclusion with the statements in the Passion narrative, 27:11, 29, 37). That is the significance of Matthew's characteristic "fulfillment of Scripture" formula. The "fulfillment of Scripture" in Jesus the Christ is not intended apologetically as some proof from predictive prophecy refuting the disbelief of emergent normative Judaism, even if it is colored by such polemics. It is dogmatically motivated. It intends to instruct *Gentile* converts what it means to call upon Jesus as *the Christ, the Son of God who is also the son of David.* It is the church itself which has to search the Scriptures of Israel in order to understand who its Lord is and what is obedience to His will, so that it manifests His messianic reign in and to the world. Here, as in the New Testament generally, the Old Testament "Scriptures were used not to prove that Jesus was the Christ but to explain what that confession means and what the implications are."[31]

What then is the precise sense of the "Immanuel" proclaimed in the nativity? Matthew, thanks to the Greek of the Septuagint, misunderstood the Book of Isaiah's language in the much-disputed passage which he cites in 1:23. The Hebrew text is rightly translated, "Therefore the Lord himself will give you a sign. Look, the young woman is with child and shall bear a son and shall name him Immanuel" (Isa. 7:14). With the Septuagint, however, Matthew reads "virgin" in place of the Hebrew, "young woman." This reading allows him to apply the "Immanuel" designation to the child miraculously born of Mary seven centuries later. The prophet Isaiah was clearly not envisioning such an event in the distant future. He was speaking to his faithless contemporary, King Ahaz (Isa. 7:11-17). This Ahaz sits on the throne of David, but does not reign as a true son of David who would trust in the Lord and forego faithless political scheming and intrigue (Isa. 7:9). Most probably, the "sign" with which Isaiah confronted Ahaz was meant ironically. Temporary relief from Assyrian military pressure is coming, for which a newborn child will be gratefully named, "God is with us!" Nevertheless, before

---

31. Donald H. Juel, *Messianic Exegesis: Christological Interpretation of the Old Testament in Early Christianity* (Philadelphia: Fortress, 1988), p. 87.

this ironically named child comes of age, devastation and divine judgment will fall upon Ahaz's kingdom and throne.

Compounding his creative misunderstanding of Isaiah, then, Matthew has taken the name Immanuel as a message of salvation that Isaiah meant in bitterest irony as harbinger of doom. Matthew's confusion, only possible on the basis of the Septuagint's Greek, has led many modern exegetes to regard the story in which Matthew's citation of Isaiah 7:14 is embedded as a late, purely theological construction. The angel's announcement to Joseph of the child's miraculous conception from Mary the Virgin was first inspired, in this critical reconstruction, by the church's appropriation of the "Immanuel" passage. The desire of Christians to acclaim Jesus as "God with us" found a proof-text in ancient Scripture, and this need together with the discovery of a proof-text overwhelmed the previous restraint imposed by the tradition's historical silence regarding Jesus' infancy. It generated the story of Mary's virginal conception of Jesus on the basis of the prediction thought to have been discovered in the Septuagint Greek version of Isaiah 7:14.

This well-known critical reconstruction, however, takes for granted what really stands in need of explanation. It assumes the transparency of the "Immanuel" designation as a "high" title of honor for Jesus, requiring a virginal conception or at least indicating the birth of a God by means of one. But this assumption does not sense the problem involved in the application of "Immanuel" to the infant Jesus on account of the peculiar messianic sense which this application bears for the evangelist. That is to say, Matthew most probably associates the "Immanuel" of Isaiah 7:14 with the messianic birth foretold in Isaiah 9:6: "For a child has been born for us, a son given to us; authority rests upon his shoulders; and he is named Wonderful Counselor, Mighty God, Everlasting Father, Prince of Peace." In that case, the association of Isaiah 7:14 with 9:6, together with the application in this sense of the designation Immanuel to Jesus, would lead Matthew and his readers immediately to pressing questions like: How does Jesus fulfill this messianic function to reign as the shepherd-king? To enlighten the nations? To deliver His people? To establish justice and peace forever? We have to ask consequently whether the Evangelist's point is to raise such questions at the outset of his Gospel as orientation for understanding what is to follow. The nativity, in any case, does not replace the ensuing Gospel-narrative but serves to introduce it in a theologically pointed way. Matthew, we know, wants to teach his community to be suspicious of any use of the title "Lord" that is not an acknowledgment of Jesus' messianic reign over all of life, but only accolade, no doubt deeply felt, but devoid of narrative and hence of ethical content (e.g., 7:21). Matthew's use of the "Immanuel" designation belongs in the context of expectations of a specifically messianic salvation (cf. 2:2-4). By the same token, the sense of such a predication of the obscurely born infant Jesus is not immediately obvious. It creates the tension of anticipation that the reader must read on to resolve. The conflict with Herod prefigures the whole.

Much contemporary exegesis, not to mention proclamation, misses this tension. In biblical faith, titles of honor are not mere honorifics, more or less exchangeable expressions of religious emotivism. They are designations that bear specific conceptions of human salvation. Whether we are looking for a "sage," say, or a "messiah" makes a world of difference.[32] "Messiah" bears the force of the historically particular, Jewish expectation of a true son and heir of David anointed by the Spirit of God to do the work of justice in and among the nations. The question is not whether Jesus is so dear to us that we honor Him with superlative titles but whether He actually brings about the reign of righteousness promised by God to David as the Shepherd-King who will rule the nations with equity. The function of the nativity narratives is to point us to Jesus as this very Christ of Israel, also now for Gentiles. But so designating Jesus means we have to be asking (just as Matthew in fact clues us) Isaiah the prophet's questions about how the Lord, the God of Israel, will fulfill His promises to the throne of David in view of the historical failure of David's line. If, then, in spite of misunderstanding the Hebrew, Matthew's appropriation of the "Immanuel" designation is intended to pose this question, his appeal to Isaiah is apropos.

In spite of the apparent ineptitude of Matthew's citation in 1:23, then, the evangelist's constant (3:3; 4:14; 8:17; 12:17; 13:14; 15:7) appeal to Isaiah's messianic preaching is cogent both historically and theologically. This becomes evident as we bear in mind that the historical Isaiah's ministry was to expose the failure of the house of David to shepherd God's people as it ought. In view of the persistent failure of the line of David, Isaiah in fact began to offer the hope of a true son of David whom the Lord himself would send (cf. Isa. 9:2-7; Matt. 4:13-16). On closer examination, moreover, the citation in 1:22-23 appears to be the evangelist's *comment* on a story that he had inherited concerning the angel's announcement to Joseph of the meaning of Mary's scandalous pregnancy. In that case we can see how the Greek word from the Septuagint, "virgin," triggered for Matthew an illuminating connection between the story of the angel's announcement to Joseph and Isaiah's oracles of messianic expectation. The point of Matthew's allusion to Isaiah, in that case, is not the so-called proof from prophecy of Mary's virginal conception. Rather, Matthew wants to link the terse story he has received of the angelic announcement of Jesus' birth to Joseph with Israel's experience of the failure of the Davidic dynasty and Israel's consequent hope for a Spirit-endowed heir to the Davidic promises whom the Lord would send at last (cf. 12:17-23). The "Immanuel" designation therefore does not signify an abstractly conceived "high" Christology, honoring Jesus as if He were a God. It designates most particularly Israel's expectation of the new David, the God who as man undertakes to fulfill the promised reign of justice and peace that redeems the good creation groaning under the structures of malice and injustice.

---

32. Reinhold Niebuhr, *The Nature and Destiny of Man,* two volumes, *Human Destiny* (New York: Charles Scribner's Sons, 1943), 2:6-34.

The birth of this Immanuel is represented in the nativity story as a new, divine initiative within the course of the generations of the people of Israel. This child has been created in a sovereign act of the Creator Spirit. In fact Joseph, the literal descendant of David (1:16), must graft Mary's child into his line by naming the child as a father does and thus making it his own by adoption. Joseph does this in obedience to the angelic command. Every form of Christological adoptionism is thereby excluded: it is not God who adopts the man Jesus, but Joseph who adopts the newborn Son of God. The concomitant notion of virginal conception strictly corresponds with the foregoing. While the reader trained in Scripture will recall barren Sarah, Hannah, and others, virginal conception is unprecedented. It finds its analogues in the biblical notions of *creatio ex nihilo* (or at least *ex vetere*) and resurrection of the dead, the uniquely creative acts of God particularly associated with the power of the Spirit. It is the miracle of a new beginning of humanity within humanity. Thus the theological sense of this miracle is not unintelligible. It is precisely a sign. It signifies that the existence of the Messiah child from the first moment of His human origin is determined by the Creator Spirit. It signifies that God here undertakes as man to fulfill all righteousness. In that work — which now includes the ecclesia as the place in the world in which this righteousness is being realized — we are to discern the saving presence of Jesus the Christ.

A brief digression on "miracle": "Primitive Christian miracle stories testify to a revelation of the holy, to its power to break into the normal course of the world. That is their only message." But much modern exegesis, Gerd Theissen continues, is nothing but an attempt "to minimize the importance of the miraculous in the miracle stories" by "the history of religions, redaction criticism and tradition history, and with historical and interiorizing interpretations."[33] To ask about the "how" of a miracle, as Luther understood, is precisely to misunderstand the claim to truth expressed in it as a summons to faith in God to whom all things are possible, if not also wise or good. Miracle stories express belief in the God who is "more than necessary," the God of hope who comes on the scene when all immanent possibilities are exhausted, especially for the poor and oppressed under the structures of malice and injustice. Theissen makes this point quite powerfully: "It is totally impossible to describe belief in miracles as superstition without reference to sociological categories unless one simply calls superstition anything that is obscure to oneself. Historical analysis, however, requires a term which does not make value judgments, but describes the value judgment contained in the term 'superstition.' On such a definition, 'superstition' is a belief rejected in society, and 'religion,' to put it ironically, the officially recognized superstition. . . . In order to understand this conflict between Christians and pagans we must distinguish different forms of beliefs in miracles,"[34] that is to

---

33. Gerd Theissen, *The Miracle Stories of the Early Christian Tradition,* trans. Francis McDonagh (Philadelphia: Fortress, 1983), p. 291.

34. Theissen, *The Miracle Stories,* p. 232.

say, between contending theologies — as in the classic biblical confrontation between Moses and the magicians of Pharaoh's court (Exod. 7:8–11:10) or that battle between Jesus anointed in the Spirit and the unholy spirits in the Gospel of Mark (e.g., Mark 1:12-13, 23-25).

What this divine initiative in the "miraculous" birth of Messiah Jesus portends for the future is depicted by means of the varying responses to the word announcing Jesus' birth. These responses are figured in Joseph, the Magi, and Herod the king. The homage of the Magi (2:11) anticipates the adoration by the nations of the exalted Lord (28:9), who will be present as the divine Savior of the storm-tossed ship of the church (14:33). Like righteous Joseph (1:24-25), disciples will be called and equipped to play indispensable roles in the unfolding drama of salvation, as the envy of the Herods of this evil age rage against them (2:16). When the pretense of political sovereignty to piety dashes on the rock of divine providence (2:8), the true purpose "to search for the Child, to destroy him" (2:13) becomes manifest. Thus, as Matthew shows us, the epiphany of the Son of God also always precipitates as well an epiphany of actual evil, springing forth from the shadows in which it otherwise hides. For that reason the sound of Rachel weeping will be audible (2:18) again and again. But the gates of hell will not prevail against the people of Jesus (16:18), for the Jesus who is always "with them" is God's royal "Son, the beloved, with whom [God] is well pleased" (3:17). "His authority shall grow continually, and there shall be endless peace for the throne of David and his kingdom. He will establish and uphold it with justice and with righteousness from this time onward and forevermore. The zeal of the Lord of hosts will do this" (Isa. 9:7; cf. Matt. 28:18). So Matthew portends by the "miracle" of Messiah's birth a contest of contending theologies/sovereignties.

There is no further role for the remarkable events of the nativity in the course of Matthew's Gospel narrative. That is as it ought to be. The presence of Jesus in fact brings with it salvation "from sin" (1:21), but this deliverance depends entirely on who the baby Jesus proves to be and how His office as the Christ actually is realized on this earth. Such questions are not yet answered in the infancy narrative; rather they are pointedly posed by it. How shall this Jesus reign as David's heir, to whom the nations are turning? Sharing the scriptural expectation that God will bring forth a true son of David to "fulfill all righteousness" (3:15), Matthew wants to teach Gentiles what they must hope for, namely, nothing less than the reign of Israel's God and its righteousness. To grasp this grounding of hope, they shall have to follow Jesus as he "fulfills all righteousness." The nativity has prepared us to understand the work of Christ, by teaching us His person from the mystery of its origin.

"The novelty," Lindbeck wrote of his rule-theory approach to the nature of doctrine, is that "it does not locate the abiding and doctrinally significant aspect of religion in propositionally formulated truths, much less in inner experiences, but in the story it tells and in the grammar that informs the way the story is told and used."[35] Revising that rule-theory to bring out the singular cognitive claim to truth that the canonical narrative bears in promising the coming of the Beloved Community, we may say that "born of the virgin Mary" tells the gospel story in such a way that believers are led to expect *messianic* salvation from the child born of Mary in fulfillment of the prophet Isaiah's promises, for knowledge of which they must turn to Israel's Scriptures. That is its "grammatical" function *as doctrine;* we can say that its first-order doxological function is found in Mary's exuberant hymn of praise to the God who casts down the mighty from their thrones (Luke 1:46-55). "Born of the virgin Mary" consequently shapes the faith of the community in Jesus in a conscience-binding way as true knowledge of God. By it, the community learns to see itself in the narrative figures of Matthew's adopting father Joseph as also in Luke's Virgin Mary, hearing, bearing, receiving, singing the Word of God into the world by faith which concurs in the Spirit with God's new creative initiative, breaking into doxology at the God who has exalted them of low degree.

The dominant icon of this is Mary's virginal conception. She is the archetypical *Theotokos,* in whom the church exists in the matrix of Israel's Scriptures for mission to the nations, which in turn come with the Magi to worship the infant God she cradles. This iconography can be *true* in that "in our christological synthesis the person of Jesus Christ himself is not limited to the historical Jesus" (Braaten).[36] What *truth* is that? How can Jesus be *true* God and *true* human in one person? One of us in all things except sin, and just so, an object in the world for faith to know? These questions are and continue to perplex, even as they are answered in Christology.

Turning now from the Scriptures to their normative interpretation in the ecumenical creedal tradition, this birth of the New Adam from virgin Mary was explicated by the terse formulation of the Chalcedonian decree: "of the same reality as we ourselves as far as his humanness is concerned; thus like us in all respects, sin only excepted . . . born of Mary the Virgin, who is God-bearer *(Theotokos)* in respect of his humanness." The birth from Mary the Virgin, in other words, tells how to take our co-humanity with Christ in the aforementioned twofold way. He who is co-divine *(homoousios)* with His Father but personally obedient to Him comes *voluntarily* to dwell with us, even as *innocently* bearing the sin of our world for us in assuming as His own our humanity. This divine and personal act stands out for faith to apprehend, rightly grasping it as the Son of God's *personal* act of self-giving — hence "sinless" — love in His own human body-and-soul. Thus in this body-and-soul God, who created humanity, now re-creates it in the person of the incarnate and obedient Son of God coming and dwelling even in the midst of our

35. George A. Lindbeck, *The Nature of Doctrine: Religion and Theology in a Postliberal Age* (Philadelphia: Westminster, 1984), p. 80.

36. Carl E. Braaten, "Sixth Locus: The Person of Jesus Christ," *Christian Dogmatics,* vol. 1, ed. Carl E. Braaten and Robert W. Jenson (Philadelphia: Fortress, 1984), p. 481.

alienation and corruption. He freely comes in love, so He is truly the Man intended from the beginning of creation. He freely comes to us in His own body-and-soul, so He is truly one of us, even to prenatal life and birth, hunger and thirst, death and burial. The doctrine thus provides a rule, a regulation for thinking, preaching, and praising: so sing the humanity of Christ as of "a new rootstock, a new beginning" of fallen humanity within fallen humanity (Cyril of Alexandria).[37] So speak of this "sinless" humanity of Christ that it becomes our own righteousness as those who are also born anew from above in the power of the same Spirit by which Mary conceived Him. So speak of this humanity that no one can have this man's heavenly Father who will not also have His earthly mother, Mary, *Theotokos,* icon of "mother church" who "begets and bears every Christian through the Word of God" (Luther). Speak then of Mary, daughter of Israel, who bears the Word of God into the world, of faithful Mary the source of the humanity of Christ made new in Christ, Mary the archetype of the hearing, believing, and so also acting, worshiping, and confessing church in mission to all nations.

Deliteralized, as argued above, the doctrine of the Virgin Birth is to be taken as gospel knowledge *of God;* that means that it is received as an instruction of the Spirit to receive the humanity of Christ *from Mary,* daughter of Israel who gives Him birth by the special will and electing counsel of God, in order to give her Son up *for others.* As instruction of the Spirit, the story of Messiah's birth from the Virgin Mary is doctrine binding the conscience particularly of preachers in their preaching and in this way also of hearers of the Word who would count as believers and doers of it. It binds conscience not as a historical report, on which critical opinion differs, but as the Spirit's instruction that both preacher and auditor pronounce with Mary their own "Let it be, Amen!" to the Word incarnate offered by the Spirit who in just this way gives to them also the New Birth. "Because she gave to Jesus the human flesh he has now transformed," Mary's flesh is the first to experience the overflow of that transforming power for itself. But what the faithful now confess as realized in her, as well as in the humanity of Jesus, this "Mystery of the Virgin, now being accomplished," is "our lot, too," Andrew [of Crete] insists, "set aside for human nature from the beginning." "This is our frame that we celebrate today," he writes in another place, "our formation, our dissolution." So for every Christian who hopes in Christ, death becomes a "falling asleep" rather than an experience of terror and "demonic subjugation."[38] Or, as Luther put it: If Mary "had not conceived Christ spiritually in her heart [by faith in the angel's pronouncement], she would never have conceived him physically. God could have made Christ's body from her body in her sleep, without her knowing it, as he made Eve from Adam, but then she would not have been his mother, just

---

37. St. Cyril of Alexandria, *On the Unity of Christ,* trans. J. A. McGuckin (Crestwood, NY: St. Vladimir's Seminary Press, 1995), p. 64.

38. *On the Dormition of Mary: Early Patristic Homilies,* trans. Brian E. Daley, S.J. (Crestwood, NY: St. Vladimir's Seminary Press, 1998), p. 32.

as Adam was not Eve's mother."[39] Just so, Mary is the mother of all believers, the icon of the matrix of the Scriptures of Israel received from faith for faith.

In this deliteralized but genuinely instructive way, in view of the singular cognitive claim of Christian theology, the doctrine of the Virgin Birth further serves to indicate against docetism old and new the common body as the good creation of God in spite of its sinfulness and liability to corruption. This body is the very object of the redemptive mission of the Son and the fulfillment of the Spirit in making matter new to be the dwelling place of God. It can do this work just because it makes the *humanity* of Jesus Christ, the bodily Son of God, the *object* of faith. Note well the anti-docetic accent: we are to believe in the *body* of Christ, the human body that was, is, and ever remains Jesus of Nazareth. We believe the Son of God in the flesh or we do not believe Him at all. It is very easy to believe in a free-floating spirit or Christ principle just because it cannot be objectified. Cheap faith, like cheap grace, floats above the suffering body and sinful soul and never settles into the solidarity of love. Costly grace demanding and giving divine faith descends deeply into the flesh and stays there with the suffering and the sorrowing until all things are made new, bound in conscience even as bound bodily to others in love.

Such is the way in critical dogmatics of articulating the doctrine of Christ's birth from Mary the Virgin, i.e., as Theotokos, the iconic figure of "mother church" receiving and passing on the Word of God from faith for faith in the world in order that the Word incarnate *be used, known in the flesh, objectified.* It is to objectify this good earth, our other mother in the common body, as the good creation of God, destined for redemption and fulfillment. It is to objectify the sinful and sorrowing human soul, the failed person that every human body bears, as the heart whose desire the Creator wants for Himself and wins for Himself in the Beloved Community. It is to objectify the Christ of Israel, the eternal Son of God at Bethlehem and at Golgotha, lying in our desolate manger and dying on the imperial stake in our place. In these ways it articulates one aspect of the singular cognitive claim of Christian theology. It does not dissolve the narrative figure of Mary, even as it deliteralizes the narrative by decoding it theologically and applying it existentially. It resolves the narrative of Mary into an icon or figure of the coming of God in free grace to redeem and to fulfill this time and space creation. For that is what an icon or figure is: an object of human knowledge constructed from the maelstrom of experience by a purposeful subject for an intended audience. The language of icon and iconography seems less abrasive than that of object and objectification. Icons skirt on the edge of idolatry, to be sure,[40] just as objectifications manhandle God. But the reality is the same.

---

39. *LW* 37, p. 89.

40. Jean-Luc Marion, *God without Being,* trans. Thomas A. Carlson (Chicago: University of Chicago Press, 1995), pp. 7-24. See also Jan-Olav Henriksen, *Desire, Gift and Recognition: Christology and Postmodern Philosophy* (Grand Rapids: Eerdmans, 2009).

Contrast this illustration of the nature of doctrine with the two major modern understandings of it represented by fundamentalism and by liberalism.[41] For fundamentalism, doctrine is a proposition of commonsense realism[42] about something that happened in the world, the sense of which is literal reference. When the Creed says of Jesus, "born of the Virgin Mary," the meaning of that doctrinal statement is affirmation binding on conscience of the miraculous event in history to which it refers, the conception and birth of Jesus without human father about 2000 years ago in ancient Palestine, which now must be thought and intended as a simple historical fact, if faith is to be true to reality.[43] Its rationale

41. George Hunsinger, *Disruptive Grace: Studies in the Theology of Karl Barth* (Grand Rapids: Eerdmans, 2000), pp. 210-25.

42. Following here is Nicholas Wolterstorff's penetrating dissection of Locke's teaching: "It was [Locke's] conviction that trying our best to get in touch with reality requires that our beliefs be grounded on what we 'perceive.' 'To the facts themselves' was his motto." But Locke's notion of pure attention to the objects given in experience does not hold up. It turns out that subjects formed by different cultural-linguistic traditions, even empirical scientists formed by disciplinary traditions of inquiry, in service of different research projects financed by nonscientific interests perceive things differently. That is the monkey-wrench gumming up the works. "Now it turns out that false beliefs we already have inhibit either 'perception' itself or its efficacy in producing the relevant first-order and second-order beliefs. The beliefs we already have either obstruct our direct access to the facts or render that access irrelevant for our purposes, since the corresponding beliefs are not evoked." Nicholas Wolterstorff, *John Locke and the Ethics of Belief*, Cambridge Studies in Religion and Critical Thought (Cambridge: Cambridge University Press, 1996), pp. 96-97. The capacity of the autonomous subject for perception of what is given to any unprejudiced observer fails to stand up to scrutiny because the seeing self turns out to be embedded in traditions of discourse that incline it to see according to inherited preconceptions. Nor can one extract oneself from this linguistic web into some stance of neutral disinterestedness above this fray of contending perspectives, as Locke's experientialism imagines that a truly secular culture would and could do. As a result, secularism and positivism, and the modern theological appropriation of this culture in commonsense realism, which thought of itself as founded by appeal to direct experience as an alternative to dogmatism, turn out to be nothing other than conversion to a new dogmatism. Wolterstorff concluded rightly: "Locke's proposal will not do. Our problems with traditions remain, however. Traditions are still a source of benightedness, chicanery, hostility and oppression. And our moral, religious, and even theoretical traditions are even more fractured today than they were in Locke's day. In this situation, examining our traditions remains for many of us a deep obligation, and for all of us together, a desperate need. But we shall have to acknowledge what the thinkers of the Enlightenment would have found appallingly unpalatable; namely, that examination of tradition can take place only in the context of unexamined tradition, and that in our examination, our convictions as to the facts are schooled by our traditions. The thinkers of the Enlightenment hoped to bring about a rational consensus in place of fractured tradition. That hope has failed. In my judgment it was bound to fail; it could not succeed" (p. 246).

43. I am roughly following Lindbeck's influential analysis here, with the following qualification. The term "fundamentalism" is bandied about in the loose way that all clichés are. Its pejorative usage should be abandoned in favor of precise language for actual positions taken by real theologians. The same applies to "liberalism." By fundamentalism, I mean the theologically

as Christian doctrine is secondary to its acknowledgment as a positive fact of revelation. Fundamentalism at least has the merit of wanting and daring to make a public claim to truth, even if this merit is betrayed by its vast overconfidence in the "commonsense" which is in fact, theologically, the opinionating of Adam who wants to be God and does not want God to be God — at work, also, in all too self-assuredly "orthodox" Christian theologians.

For liberalism, on the other hand, such doctrinal assertion of revealed truths referring to miraculous facts in the world is impossible for historical, scientific, existential, and indeed theological reasons. There is little early evidence for it. The claim defies all scientific understanding of how conception works to generate a human individual. The demand to receive this putative fact of history as doctrine binding conscience cannot be harmonized with a positive estimation of human sexuality and in fact presupposes a venereal theory of sin's transmission; nor can it be harmonized with the understanding of faith as trust in the unconditional love of God. It rather crushes trust with a tyrannical demand to sacrifice both mind and conscience. Finally, like the doctrine of the Incarnation itself, the Virgin Birth gives an "icon" that is indistinguishable from an idol if taken literally, capturing God as an object at the disposal of creatures. Hence the meaning of "born of the Virgin Mary" is to be sought elsewhere than in the world of commonsense realism. Liberalism arises as a general theory of the symbolic nature of religious language as expressive of modern interiority. "And in like manner each one of us beholds in the birth of Christ his own higher birth whereby nothing lives in him but devotion and love; and in him too the eternal Son of God appears."[44] "Born of the Virgin Mary" is not to be taken literally, to be sure, but the decoding is anthropological rather than theological in diligent obedience to the Kantian proscription of knowledge of God. It does not and cannot tell something of God to be known in the world of the common body. Indeed, it makes a virtue of this Kantian necessity.[45] The story works as a symbol of the religious experience of

---

uncritical appropriation of "commonsense realism," a version of Lockean empiricism. By liberalism, I mean the theologically uncritical appropriation of Kantianism, an apophatic philosophy of religion. By the critical dogmatic alternative to these modern methodologies in theology, I adopt and adapt the pragmatist critique of either camp without in any sense using pragmatism as a philosophical foundation for theology but rather borrowing its tools for purposes that arise in theology as the reflection organic to the gospel's mission to the nations in critical appropriation of the tradition of classical dogmatics.

44. "Christmas Eve," in Keith W. Clement, *Friedrich Schleiermacher: Pioneer of Modern Theology* (London: Collins, 1987), p. 202.

45. According to Rudolf Bultmann's influential interpretation of the Gospel of John, e.g., the "Evangelist rejects any concept of God by means of which God can be thought of as the object of human or suprahuman knowledge. God ceases to be God if he is thought of as an object." In the preceding sentence Bultmann had denied that the Evangelist was motivated by Kantian principles of "the inadequacy of the human faculties to perceive him." Rudolf Bultmann, *The Gospel of John: A Commentary,* trans. G. R. Beasley-Murray (Philadelphia: Westminster, 1976), p. 81. The juxtaposition provokes the Shakespearean suspicion, "Methinks thou dost protest too much."

coming to a new awareness of kinship with the divine. It thus carves out a space of interiority or existential authenticity over against the public world of the common body where subjects know objects in addressing audiences and interpreting social experience.

That is the characteristic modern choice: we are to take doctrine with fundamentalists as reference to an unusual fact in the world or symbolically with the liberals as evocation of self-transcendence, under the assumption shared by both sides that the sense of the doctrinal statement "born of the Virgin Mary" is provided by its anthropological reference, be that to a miracle in history that happened to Mary or to a miracle in consciousness that happens in religious experience. But in fact *Jesus* is the referent of the statement "born of the Virgin Mary." He is the one identified by this clause as sign signifying the coming of the Son of God in the flesh, the New Adam. "Born of the Virgin Mary" may or may not also refer to something that actually happened or happens in history, be it Mary's or the believer's. A truth of history preserved privately and only lately disclosed by Mary "who pondered all these words in heart" (Luke 2:19) is not precluded by the critical dogmatic understanding of doctrine. Nor is a religious experience of regeneration. But the meaning *as doctrine* does not depend on such reference, either to history or to interiority, other than as reference to Jesus as object of faith for the theological subject who confesses Him as Christ, the Son of God, by joining with Mary in her hymn of praise (Luke 1:46-55). Its meaning as doctrine depends, then, on its coherence with the singular cognitive claim of theology and its aptitude in this coherence for articulating some aspect of it or its utility for interpreting experience in the world; the sense as doctrine thus presupposes faith in Jesus Christ as present and made known as the Son of God sent in the Spirit from His Father to us and all nations. The ultimate reference of each and all theological doctrine together is strictly to the promised coming of the Beloved Community of God at the Parousia of Jesus Christ.

Let us probe further. "Jesus Christ, the Son of God" is integral to the truth-claim that God is the One determined to redeem and fulfill, where the mission of the Son is identified and thus made known by His Father's vindication at the Spirit's raising Him from death and now speaking that very act to the world in the proclamation of the gospel. When we take that Christological statement as integral, then an ancillary statement like "born of the Virgin Mary," as it occurs in the Creeds, is first of all a matter of denoting the particular, Jesus, of our common world who is acclaimed Christ and Lord by the gospel. "Born of the Virgin Mary" helps to specify who in the world this *Jesus* is. Of course, one might object that the statement as it stands is "out of this world" where virgins do not conceive and give birth. The point is well taken. If "born of the Virgin Mary" is to specify a member of the set, humanity, theology cannot in this way "cook the books" by sneaking in an uncommon qualifier to specify the individual Jesus.

Yet, as we have seen in our study of Matthew, we are guilty of a certain speculation in falling into a trap like this. We have assumed that already we know what the Scriptures must mean when they proclaim virginal Mary the Theotokos who bore Jesus Christ, the Son of God into the world; we have assumed that "born of the virgin Mary" is a modalist honorific, indicating a "high" Christology, that is, a claim without Trinitarian differentiation of persons that Jesus is God. So, we had to return to the matrix of the Scriptures to learn again what they are talking about. So the fresh thesis arises: born of this Jewish woman named Mary yet without aid of a natural father, Jesus is thus denoted as the *new* human being created directly by the God of Israel but from Mary, just as Eve had been created directly by the same God but from Adam. As Irenaeus saw, this reversal made by the new beginning occurs in order to recapitulate Adam's history and so fulfill Israel's hope for a true son of David, Immanuel, God with us. "Born of the Virgin Mary" is then about the *Jewishness* of Jesus, linking the gospel narrative about Him to the narratives of Israel's Scriptures. Or, to put the same point another way: it was not as though even Mary already knew what her virginal conception meant and had to mean. It is not as though the New Testament looked to the Old to find its preconceptions fulfilled and the Old superseded in the process. Rather, not knowing what the Holy Spirit had intended by the Theotokos, the New Testament looked to the Old to understand its newly given object of faith, the man Christ Jesus.

The same applies to the other appellation of the Nativity story in Matthew's version, calling the newly born Son of God in the flesh, Immanuel, God-with-us. It is indeed the unspoken assumption of much contemporary theology in the West — albeit in continuation of its long-term modalist trajectory — that the sheer *presence* to us of God as such is the Christian message of salvation. Against this, as Luther pertinently noted, "it is one thing for God to be present, another for God to be present for you."[46] In a contribution to the Lutheran-Catholic dialogue on Mary and the Saints that is pertinent to this question, Robert W. Bertram expounded Luther's Christological challenge to this modalist assumption:

> Quite a different danger that neither Melanchthon nor Luther seems to have reckoned with, nor yet needed to, is the sort of reductionist Christology in which the saints are not so much promoted to christological responsibilities as Christ is demoted to theirs. In this alternative all Christ does is what the saints admittedly do, too: transmit, communicate, reveal us-ward — in that sense, mediate — a pre-assured divine grace that would have obtained anyway, with or without Christ, except that we might not have known about it. On such a view, from the outset there never was any real alternative to divine mercy like divine judgment or wrath, which only in Christ — that is, in God as a human being — is historically overcome for all other human beings. Against such tepid christological background the danger of the saints competing with Christ is probably a non-problem because by contrast with more classical Christologies

46. *LW* 37, pp. 67-69.

this revelationist Christ has little to do that is all that unique and might not just as well be shared or delegated among his members.[47]

A meager construal of the gospel as mere presence, just like a meager interpretation of the gospel as but the repetition in time of an eternal truth, tells much about the "soul of man under secularism" (C. Lasch) who desperately wants to know that he or she is not finally alone in the vast, indifferent cosmos. But it tells little of what the presence of *Jesus* the Christ of *Israel* signified to early Christians or should signify for us, what is the very thing so signified. For Luther, certainly, the "real presence" that mattered was the very presence of the body that had been born from Mary the Virgin and suffered under Pilate for us in order, with Matthew, to "save from our sins." Saving is the presence of that human body in which the deed of divine reconciliation was and is accomplished, when the Spirit makes it an object for faith to know.

---

## EXCURSUS: ON JEWISH PERPLEXITY
## AS A PRINCIPLE INTERNAL TO CHRISTOLOGY[48]

The preceding argument that the story of Mary's virginal conception of the Lord is to be received as doctrine binding conscience when taken as an instruction to receive Jesus as the Christ, Israel's Messiah, acutely raises the issue in post-Holocaust Christian theology of the theological sin of anti-Judaism. It also shows what considerable lack of clarity still surrounds the question of exactly what anti-Judaism is and how it can be overcome as a matter of principle in Christian theology. To achieve clarity, we need to establish a historical context that reveals why the theological truth that "Jesus Christ was born a Jew" (Luther)[49] could not

47. *The One Mediator, the Saints, and Mary: Lutherans and Catholics in Dialogue VIII,* ed. H. George Anderson, J. Francis Stafford, Joseph A. Burgess (Minneapolis: Augsburg, 1992), p. 261.

48. Portions of what follows in this excursus first appeared in Paul R. Hinlicky, "A Lutheran Contribution to the Theology of Judaism," *Journal of Ecumenical Studies* 31, no. 1-2 (Winter-Spring 1994): 123-52.

49. *LW* 45, pp. 195-229. As Luther was also the victim of lies and heresy-hunting at the hands of his opponents, he undertook in 1523 to write "something useful" not only in his own defense but "also to win some Jews to the Christian faith." He says that he will "cite from Scripture the reasons that move me to believe that Christ was a Jew born of a virgin." He wants to win Jews, then, by rational persuasion, not as the "fools . . . the crude asses' heads have hitherto so treated the Jews" as if "they were dogs rather than human beings," deriding them and depriving them of their property. Luther empathizes: "If I had been a Jew and had seen such dolts and blockheads govern and teach the Christian faith, I would rather sooner have become a hog than a Christian" (p. 200). He even invites his heresy-hunting opponents "to seize the opportunity" he gives them by publishing this tract "of denouncing me as a Jew" (p. 201). Two statements even mitigate the apparent triumphalism in Luther's traditional desire to win Jews to the Chris-

stand up to the sin against Jews, not to mention against that Christological truth, of the smear "On the Jews and Their Lies" (Luther).[50]

---

tian faith, as if their Jewish faith in the coming Messiah were simply false. First, following Paul (Rom. 9:1-2), Luther situates his desire that Jews "will become genuine Christians," i.e., not like the "dolts and blockheads" previously mentioned, by "turn[ing] again to the faith of their fathers, the prophets and patriarchs." For Luther, "conversion" is really a matter of bringing Jews back "to their own true faith, the one which their fathers held" (p. 213). This is precisely the Pauline position — that Judaism consists not in the works of the law of Moses but in the promises given to Abraham and preached by the prophets — though it is just this alternative, of course, that normative Judaism rejects. Against de-Judaizers, Luther thus argues that "Jews will only be frightened away . . . if their Judaism is so utterly rejected that nothing is allowed to remain and they are treated only with arrogance and scorn." So Christians ought "to treat the Jews in a brotherly manner," remembering that the gospel was first brought to them by Jews (p. 200). Second, Luther says of "conversion" that "even we ourselves are not yet all very far along, not to speak of having arrived." Winning the Jews, presumably, returns Christians to their own profound need of "conversion" (p. 201).

50. The cited excerpts are drawn from Luther's late 1543 tract, "On the Jews and Their Lies," *LW* 47, pp. 137-306. Martin Gilbert began his harrowing account drawn from the oral testimonies and written memoirs of survivors citing as the "first steps to iniquity" Martin Luther's "'honest advice' as to how Jews should be treated. 'First,' he wrote, 'their synagogues should be set on fire. . . .' Jewish homes, he said, should likewise be 'broken down or destroyed.' Jews should then be put under one roof, or in a stable, like Gypsies, in order that they may realize that they are not masters in our land.'" Martin Gilbert, *The Holocaust: A History of the Jews in Europe during the Second World War* (New York: Holt, Rinehart & Winston, 1986), p. 19. Luther's xenophobic venom in this tract actualizes the worst possibilities in traditional Christianity, rooted in the recourse to demonization found in John 8:44. The tract was a source of embarrassment to Luther's friends already in his lifetime and was quickly buried on library shelves, forgotten from living memory. This now-notorious 1543 tract has a peculiar reception history. Johannes Wallman has shown that "practically all the writers of Hitler's time who, by making references to Luther's opinions about the Jews attempted to legitimate the national socialist enmity against them, voiced the complaint that Luther's struggle against the Jews was unknown, that it had been concealed by the Lutheran Church for centuries, and that Luther's writings on the Jews had completely fallen into obscurity." "The Reception of Luther's Writings on the Jews from the Reformation to the End of the 19th Century," *Lutheran Quarterly* 1 (Spring 1987): 73-74. In any case, even here Luther's frame of reference remains religious, not racial. It is the devil, not genetics, that lies at the basis of his vicious language, even though we should see that this religious demonization forms the slippery slope to racialism; this slide may be witnessed in the use of Luther's newly appropriated tract against the Jews made by German Christians in 1941: ". . . Dr. Martin Luther, after harsh experiences, demanded the most severe measures against the Jews and their expulsion from German lands. Since the crucifixion of Christ and up to the present day the Jews have fought against Christianity or have misused and falsified it for the attainment of their selfish ends. Baptism in no way changes the racial traits of a Jew, his nationality or his biological characteristics." Cited by Ernst Ludwig Ehrlich, "Luther and the Jews," in *Luther, Lutheranism and the Jews,* ed. J. Halperin and A. Sovik (Geneva: Lutheran World Federation, 1984), p. 46. The problem in Luther is the same as in John 8: recourse to demonization in the face of theological disagreement. As Mark U. Edwards rightly observes: "Neither the vulgarity nor the violence nor the charges of satanic motivation nor the sarcastic mocking is unique to

Without being conscious of it, most modern Christians have in mind the following "triumphalist" picture of the historical development of their religion. First there were the great Hebrew prophets, but then there were Ezra, Nehemiah, and the famine of the Word of God, i.e., Judaism. Then Jesus appeared, but after him came Paul, early Catholicism, and the Dark Ages. Then Luther arose, but after him came orthodoxy and the wars of religion. Then the Enlightenment cleared the air. But after that came the Nazis. Now we are existentialists. But the fundamentalists are at the gates. And so on. In this scheme, Judaism was never much to begin with and lost its role in the march of progress a long way back with terrible consequences for enduring Judaism. Appalled at that shabby treatment, we might want to correct the scheme by exposing the crimes and follies of overrated Christianity and restoring to Judaism some legitimate role, perhaps now as catalyst of the Enlightenment and harbinger of secular culture.

Christian triumphalism is a specific, datable tradition that begins in the Greek-speaking East with the semi-Arian celebration of the Constantinian establishment;[51] in Jewish theologian Jacob Neusner's words: "For Christians, the meaning of history, commencing at Creation, pointed toward Christ's triumph through the person of the emperor and the institution of the Christian state."[52] As argued above, in the West this conception of Christian empire was further developed by the Carolingians, where Jews were regarded as fellow travelers with the Muslims colonizing Spain. But today we in Euro-America live after two hundred some years of Enlightenment and the apparent victory of the liberal democratic order over against the failed dream of Christian empire. We have long since entered post-Christendom. Theologians who think themselves just now to be saying something fresh, bold, and radical against the tradition by denying *Jesus as Lord* are thus vulnerable to the charge that they have become mere cheerleaders of the secular liberal order, busy at work building new "ideological triumphalisms" with which grandly to denounce those who bind themselves to the faith of the Scriptures — believing Israel too (not to mention believing Islam). Therefore Christian recognition of Judaism's divine vocation today dare not be merely a matter of post-Holocaust emotional release, drummed with Christian breast-beating, but must be taken to the theological heart of the matter: the doctrine of the Person who is head of the church, the Jew Jesus, in His messianic office, born of His virgin Jewish Mother, yet positively disbelieved by believing Israel.

Jacob Neusner's scholarship is most instructive at this point. He discovers a

---

these treatises [against the Jews]. . . . In all these respects Luther treated the Jews no differently than he treated his other opponents." Mark U. Edwards, *Luther's Last Battles: Politics and Polemics, 1531-46* (Ithaca, NY: Cornell University Press, 1983), p. 141.

51. See Oyvind Nordeval, "The Emperor Constantine and Arius: Unity in the Church and Unity in the Empire," *Studia Theologica* 42 (1988): 113-50.

52. Jacob Neusner, *Judaism and Christianity in the Age of Constantine* (Chicago: University of Chicago Press, 1987), p. 17.

precedent in Jewish writings (*Genesis Rabbah, Leviticus Rabbah,* and the *Talmud of the Land of Israel*) of the fourth century, the era of the Constantinian establishment, and contemporaneous Christian literature. For a brief passing moment as it were, a real argument, a real engagement between them occurred. This was possible theoretically because of the unique bond between Jews and Christians: "Scripture taught them both that vast changes in the affairs of empires came about because of God's will. History proved the principles of theology. In that same Torah prophets promised the coming of the Messiah, who would bring salvation. Who was, and is, that Messiah, and how shall we know? And that same Torah addressed a particular people, Israel, promising that people the expression of God's favor and love. But who is Israel, and who is not Israel? In this way Scripture defined the categories shared in common, enabling Judaism and Christianity to engage."[53] Neusner insists upon another, practical precondition of such an authentic engagement, namely, that brief historical moment in the fourth century of rough social and political equality such that Jews could no longer dismiss the claims of ascendant Christianity as little more than an "irritating heresy," nor could Christians dismiss the nagging, recalcitrant witness of "the existing Israel, the Jewish people, which revered the same Scriptures and claimed descent, after the flesh, from ancient Israel."[54] The stakes were high in this for both sides, and, as we know, settled into mutual anathematization with fateful consequences. It is not, of course, Neusner's purpose that we should repeat this history. Rather, he wants to make us aware by means of it that our present political circumstances provide a similar precondition, not that we repeat the old condemnations, but in the better hope that the argument "may now go forward once more."[55]

Neusner conducts us through a rich maze, teasing out all the fascinating exchanges over the meaning of history and the identity of the Messiah and of the people Israel, showing how for each party these exchanges served the internal clarification of the faith. What Neusner means by a real argument, as opposed to polemic, may be crisply illustrated in this example: "Keep the law and the Messiah will come[, the Talmud argued.] This forms an exact reply to Chrysostom's doctrine: do not keep the law, for Messiah has come."[56] Yet even if this kind of exchange took place, Neusner comments, "Judaism as we have known it was born in the matrix of triumphant Christianity as the West would define that faith."[57] The key words here are "triumphant" and "as the West would define that faith." In this perspective, the Talmud's rejection of Christian triumphalism, i.e., the claim to find faith in Christ vindicated by Constantine is cut from the same cloth as Judaism's internal criticism of political messianism, as represented earlier by

53. Neusner, *Constantine,* p. 14.
54. Neusner, *Constantine,* p. 112.
55. Neusner, *Constantine,* p. 152.
56. Neusner, *Constantine,* p. 82.
57. Neusner, *Constantine,* p. ix.

Bar Kokhba's disastrous revolt in 131-35, and more contemporaneously by fourth-century Jews, whose expectations for the rebuilding of the Temple in Jerusalem under the Emperor Julian (the Apostate) were disappointed.

From this renunciation of political messianism, i.e., triumphalism, Neusner argues, Judaism as we have known it derives: "Keeping the commandments as a mark of submission, loyalty, humility before God is the rabbinic system of salvation. So Israel does not save itself. Israel never controls its own destiny, either on earth or in heaven. The only choice is whether to cast one's fate into the hands of cruel, deceitful men, or to trust the living God of mercy and love. . . . Israel can free itself of control by other nations only by humbly agreeing to accept God's rule. . . . There is no such thing for Israel as freedom from both God and the nations, total autonomy and independence. There is only a choice of masters, a ruler on earth or a ruler in heaven."[58] Perhaps we should qualify: this is Judaism as Judaism has known itself, not as Christians have known it. Yet it is a picture that Christians ought to be able to recognize.

David Novak insists that the essential point of any theological anthropology is that anything other than theonomy is idolatry. "The choice, then, is not between hearkening to God's voice and not hearkening to God's voice. The choice is, rather, hearkening to God's voice or hearkening to the voice of that which is not God."[59] Idolatry is not so much, as the Platonic tradition would have it, the confusion of the conditioned and the unconditioned, but the "supreme act of unfaithfulness to the covenant. . . . Unfaithfulness involves the substitution of another beloved for the Lord."[60] The significance of this, of course, is that "the Lord" is the one who has revealed himself in history, not, as Clemens Thoma puts it, "an isolationist, imperialist, static Being but one who lives in himself, holds mysterious exchange within himself, manifests himself to man in free affability and is even affected by events among men."[61] Thoma concludes from this — Jewish, not Platonic — understanding of deity that a "christological perception of God — apart from its historical realization — is not unJewish."[62] Idolatry lies not in the naming of the Lord, it being understood that only God can first provide the name of God; rather, the First Commandment requires "exclusivity, singularity, and the fervor for YHWH and his demand for special, unadulterated cult (monolatry). For that reason, Judaism is a towering sign against cheap, overhasty religious ecumenism."[63] Understood biblically this way, the First Commandment is what at once unites formally and yet materially divides Judaism and Christianity.

58. Neusner, *Constantine,* pp. 70, 75.

59. David Novak, *Jewish-Christian Dialogue: A Jewish Justification* (New York and Oxford: Oxford University Press, 1989), p. 144.

60. Novak, *Jewish-Christian Dialogue,* p. 38.

61. Clemens Thoma, *A Christian Theology of Judaism,* trans. and ed. Helga Croner, with a Foreword by David Flusser (Mahwah, NJ: Paulist, 1980), p. 126.

62. Thoma, *A Christian Theology of Judaism,* p. 127.

63. Thoma, *A Christian Theology of Judaism,* p. 44.

What is immensely clarifying, at least for contemporary Christians, is that this new historical picture of the emergence of Judaism as a co-claimant alongside Christianity of the heritage of Israel helps shatter the grotesque caricature of Judaism, to speak very precisely now, as the dead religion of the Old Testament, spiritually exhausted, legalistic, cunning conjurer of a wrathful God, self-righteously separatist, but now supplanted by the new religion of reason and mercy. This caricature of the "teaching of contempt" exists in two versions, the classical, so to say, and the Enlightenment's. The logic of the classical version Neusner reconstructs, not from already-triumphant Greeks like Eusebius, but from an as-yet-embattled Mesopotamian, Aphrahat, who wrote in Syriac. The classical argument Neusner draws out of Aphrahat is straightforward: "Once the new people formed out of the peoples enters the status of Israel, then the old Israel loses that status. And how to express that judgment? By denying the premise of the life of Israel after the flesh, that salvation for the people of God would come in future time. If enduring Israel would never enjoy salvation, then Israel had no more reason to exist."[64] This line of thought, in which seeming logic overrules life, meant that for Christians Judaism existed as an anomaly, a surd. Henceforth in times of misguided Christian zeal for Jewish souls, this posture would produce staged "disputations with the Jews" aimed at convicting them out of the Scriptures. Of course this failed in the mass, but the failure, instead of calling into question the logic of triumphalism, now called into question the humanity of "obstinate" Jews: "That the Jews could know the truth of Christianity and still reject it seemed such extraordinary behavior that it could scarcely be human" (Johnson).[65] Disappointed missionary zeal frequently enough then descended into the sheer zealotry of forced conversion "for their own good" and eventually into the downward spiral of expulsion or pogrom. Luther's evolution from 1523 to 1543 certainly follows this pattern.

Nevertheless, even in this classical teaching of contempt, one finds a positive point of contact in the mutual esteem accorded the Scriptures, which in principle makes rational argument meaningful, given also social and political equality and a theologically principled forswearing of proselytism. But ironically, it was precisely this long-dormant and unique bond between Jews and Christians in the Scriptures of Israel that was to be undercut in the age of emancipation, at the dear cost of a new, even more deadly version of the teaching of contempt. In the Age of Reason, Judaism is no longer the promise to be fulfilled in Christianity as in the classical teaching of contempt, but becomes the antithesis of Christianity, a position classically expressed by Adolf von Harnack's call in his study of the second-century Marcion's semi-Gnostic Paulinism to decanonize the Old Testament. True, there emerged in nineteenth-century liberalism a paradigm that still commands widespread assent today, "of the new type of modern religious

---

64. Neusner, *Constantine*, p. 86.
65. Paul Johnson, *A History of the Jews* (New York: Harper & Row, 1987), p. 207.

man, whether Christian Protestant or liberal Jew, [who] ultimately sprang from the religious ideals and energy of the Jewish Bible."[66]

This paradigm is justly associated with the name of Julius Wellhausen, the father of Old Testament historical criticism, who first argued that between the summit of Hebrew prophecy and its renewal in the spirit of Jesus stood "late Judaism." As Blenkinsopp explains: "In keeping with nineteenth-century moral idealism and certain dominant emphases in German Evangelical Christianity, the prophets were read as exponents of ethical individualism, an unmediated approach to God without benefit of priesthood and sacrificial ritual and, in brief, a religion in which personal experience counts for more than institutions and the traditions which they mediate."[67] Wellhausen, as cited by Blenkinsopp, eagerly executed the liberal Protestant anti-Catholic polemic by means of an anti-Jewish smear: "The Church is not [Christ's] work, but an inheritance from Judaism to Christianity."[68] With just cause traditional Jews detected in the higher criticism of Wellhausen "the higher anti-Semitism." For "the new type of modern religious man" justified by liberal Protestant scholarship is surely not the anachronism of an observant Jew, just as little as he is or could be a creedal Christian. "The living Hebrew tradition . . . could not be fitted into the master plan of the Enlightenment"[69] any more than the classical Christian dogma could be. Novak's observation is incisive: "If Jesus had been de-Christologized, as it were, then the Torah had to be delegalized."[70] Ironically, however, this "new, more secular emphasis on Jesus' ethical teaching often led to a new denigration of Judaism as 'legalism,' as opposed to the Christian ethics of love."[71] But in truth, the liberal, secularizing, syncretistic project "distorts both traditional Judaism and traditional Christianity in the service of the secular state, that, in truth, require[s] neither faith."[72]

It was this brief for a "new type of modern religious man," which produced the new caricature of classical Judaism (but also, of classical Christian dogma as "Hellenizing of the Gospel"), in E. P. Sanders's words, of "rabbinic religion as legalistic works-righteousness." In this allegation that Judaism is legalistic

66. Johnson, *A History of the Jews,* p. 406.

67. Joseph Blenkinsopp, "Tanakh and the New Testament," in *Biblical Studies: Meeting Ground of Jews and Christians,* ed. Lawrence Boadt, C.S.P., Helga Croner, Leon Klenicki (Mahwah, NJ: Paulist, 1980), p. 104.

68. Blenkinsopp, "Tanakh and the New Testament," p. 105.

69. Johnson, *History of the Jews,* p. 338.

70. Novak, *Jewish-Christian Dialogue,* p. 76.

71. Novak, *Jewish-Christian Dialogue,* p. 75.

72. Novak, *Jewish-Christian Dialogue,* p. 123. Clemens Thoma likewise traces an "unfortunate" Jewish apologetic beginning in Moses Mendelssohn (*A Christian Theology of Judaism,* p. 32), which took themes of the Enlightenment to the advantage of Judaism: "[N]ineteenth century Jews, for example, very one-sidedly emphasized that Judaism was a rational alternative to romantic, mystical, mythical Christian religion. Judaism does not know original sin, ideas of expiation, irrational mysticism, dogmas or mysteries" (p. 92).

works righteousness, the difference between the classical anti-Judaism, which had focused on questions of identity, and the Enlightenment's version, becomes sharply focused: in the past Jews had appeared to Christians as not-yet-fulfilled, i.e., as potential candidates for baptism. But now, as remaining religious, they appeared to the secularized as the living dead. Conversely, as secularized Jews (in Spinozism, Freudianism, Marxism, and Zionism), they appeared to the traditionally religious (both Christian and Jewish) as particularly strident proponents of the "acids of modernity."[73] With this shift in modern times from traditional Christian anti-Judaism, Jews become not merely a surd, but an impossible surd. Sanders traces the evolution and deployment of the "legalistic works righteousness" motif through F. Weber, Bousset, Bultmann, Billerbeck, and other major figures. In sum, he writes, "The principal element is the theory that works earn salvation; that one's fate is determined by weighing fulfillments against transgressions. Maintaining this view necessarily involves denying or getting around in some other way the grace of God in the election. . . . [Other aspects are] that of establishment of merit and the possibility of a transfer of merit at the final judgment . . . uncertainty of salvation mixed with the self-righteous feeling of accomplishment . . . that God was inaccessible."[74]

Sanders then summoned a richly detailed, point-by-point refutation of this caricature through a careful study of the Mishnah, the rabbinic body of teaching that developed after the destruction of the Jerusalem temple in the year 70. Sanders's well-regarded conclusion is: "[The] general prevalent and pervasive pattern of religion to be found in Rabbinic literature . . . is based on election and atonement for transgressions, it being understood that God gave commandments in connection with the election and that obedience to them, or atonement and repentance for transgression, was expected as the condition for remaining in the covenant community."[75] Classical Judaism then is every bit as much as Christianity a religion of grace; the two divide Christologically, that is, in understanding how grace is objectified for us. From the contemporary standpoint, Novak states pointedly, "Both Judaism and Christianity affirm that redemption, like revelation, is ultimately dependent on God's grace, not man's works."[76] If Sanders is in the large historically right,[77] and Novak in the right theologically, then the liberal,

---

73. This is the grain of truth that Uriel Tal uncovers in his otherwise unsatisfactory interpretation of the attitudes of those Lutherans who opposed Nazism towards "the Jewish problem," namely, how they saw "both the Völkisch and Nazis as well as the Jews, especially modern and liberal Jews, [as] proclaim[ing] the human being's self-redemption through works, through its self-sufficiency, and through its *Selbstherrlichkeit* — thus worshipping creation rather than the Creator." "On Modern Lutheranism and the Jews," in *Lutheranism and the Jews*, p. 53.

74. E. P. Sanders, *Paul and Palestinian Judaism* (Philadelphia: Fortress, 1977), p. 54.

75. Sanders, *Paul and Palestinian Judaism*, p. 236.

76. Novak, *Jewish-Christian Dialogue*, pp. 88-89.

77. Sanders has been criticized for trying to "distill an essence of early Judaism" in his concept of "covenantal nomism." George W. E. Nickelsburg, with Robert A. Kraft, "Introduc-

evolutionary paradigm of religious development does not work: the evidence from primitive rabbinic sources defies its theoretical expectations. The whole scheme collapses, though, of course, its pervasive influence remains: a lethal misrepresentation of Judaism as stalking horse for Catholicism by Protestant progressivism.

This deconstruction of the liberal paradigm bears two important implications: it requires a better historical portrait, not of the emergence of Christianity from Judaism, but of the dual emergence of Christianity and Judaism from . . . from what? Historically speaking, emergence from an argument that had been going on about the legacy of the Scriptures ever since Ezra returned from Babylonian exile. And second, if in this context the dispute between Jewish and Christian claims to that legacy is not to be regarded as an "accident of history," a better theological understanding is required of what is at stake in that conflict than the hidden agenda of vindicating liberalism's "new type of modern religious man" over against "legalistic works righteousness" or, for that matter, creedal Christianity (which in precise parallel is caricatured and impugned as a dogmatic faith righteousness: "Good deeds are what saves, and not a particular historical revelation" — Ruether).[78]

A sketch of the first implication, in S. David Sperling's words, "that Judaism and Christianity are eisegetical variations on the themes of the Hebrew Bible rather than plain sense interpretations,"[79] looks something like this. Long since Hellenized, i.e., incorporated into the cosmopolitan world of Greco-Roman civilization,[80] religion in Palestine at the time of Jesus witnesses a bewildering contest of partisanships: Pharisees bringing the Holiness Code to daily life, scribes teaching Torah in local synagogues, Zealots conspiring by force of arms to bring in the Kingdom, Sadducees resisting innovation to preserve the Temple cult, Herodians grasping for Solomon's glory, Diaspora Hellenizers proselytizing Gentiles, the Essenes withdrawing as a righteous remnant to the wilderness, apocalypticists dreaming dreams and seeing visions. What holds all this disparate activity together, however, positively or negatively, is the worship at the Temple in Jeru-

---

tion: The Modern Study of Early Judaism," in *Early Judaism and Its Modern Interpreters,* ed. Robert A. Kraft and George W. E. Nickelsburg (Philadelphia: Fortress, 1986), p. 20. That is not quite fair because Sanders's heuristic model gives a "pattern of religion," not an "essence of religion." Whether the pattern Sanders discovers in the Mishnah, however, can without further ado be projected back to the time of Paul, let alone Jesus, is a reasonable question. Too easy a projection here could overlook the revolutionary impact of the destruction of the Temple and the transformation of Pharisaism from one party among others to the position of rabbinic responsibility, just as it makes Jesus' crucifixion as a messianic pretender and Paul's suffering of the lash historically incomprehensible.

78. Ruether, *Faith and Fratricide,* p. 236.

79. S. David Sperling, "Judaism and Modern Biblical Research," in *Biblical Studies,* p. 43.

80. Martin Hengel, *Judaism and Hellenism: Studies in Their Encounter in Palestine during the Early Hellenistic Period,* 2 volumes, trans. J. Bowden (Philadelphia: Fortress, 1981), p. 252.

salem which, despite everything, is the living source of the people's religious identity. Even where the Temple is denounced as corrupt, as in the Qumran community, the denunciation is in terms of what the Temple ought to be. By the same token, the intense competition of the time is a family quarrel, a living argument about the legacy of the Scriptures: Who is Israel?

In this context, when Jesus is identified by the first Christians as the Son of God, it is an answer to this most hotly contested question of the hour. *Jesus* is the true Israel! Even if that identification of Jesus is rejected in the mass, however, the issue does not come to head. The new partisans of Jesus can coexist, "worshiping in the Temple," one Jewish sect alongside of others. But, remove the Temple, and the question about who Israel is comes to a boil and must be resolved. It is from this juncture that our Jacob and Esau emerge: Judaism and Christianity emerged as co-claimants to the name of Israel.

The shared point of reference in these competing "eisegetical variations" on the Hebrew Scriptures is the destruction of the Temple in Jerusalem in 70, an event that gives birth to rabbinic Judaism no less than catalyzes the formation of the canonical Gospels, as Neusner explains: "The entire history of Christianity and Judaism alike flowed across the abyss of that catastrophe. Each religious tradition had to make sense of what it meant to worship God in ways lacking all precedent in the history of Israel, of which each religious tradition claimed to be the natural outcome and fulfillment."[81] This event was a "theological challenge," which required both interpretation and reconstruction of religious life that in effect would transfer the atonement and sanctification that the Temple worship had provided to the now scattered community's life in the world. The old Temple built with hands would now be rebuilt in the sacred community. Neusner's account of the rabbis' task applies no less to the post-apostolic Christian community.

Thus we can see how Mishnah and later Talmud in relation to Hebrew Scripture form the proper parallel in Judaism to the relation of the Testaments in the Christian canon: the rabbinic writings are the oral Torah, just as the New Testament is the kerygma, the *viva vox evangelii,* written down not only as the definitive hermeneutical orientation to the Scriptures of Israel, but written down in the very act of taking up the Scriptures of Israel to comprehend the Gospel theologically. Martin A. Cohen, from a classical Jewish perspective, explains this beautifully: *Torah min ha-Shamayim,* "Torah-given-from-heaven," the key hermeneutical concept created by the rabbis, denotes the "one fully authentic revelation, original, unrepeated and supreme,"[82] which includes both the written Torah in the narrow sense (the Pentateuch), the other biblical writings, and the Oral Torah. This *Torah min ha-Shamayim* is "the central concept in Judaism," not

81. Jacob Neusner, *Judaism in the Beginning of Christianity* (Philadelphia: Fortress, 1984), p. 89.

82. Martin A. Cohen, "Record and Revelation: A Jewish Perspective," in *Biblical Studies,* p. 150.

"chosenness or covenant or an amorphous and infinitely interpretable general revelation,"[83] as "central and indispensable to Judaism as the Incarnation is to Christianity."[84] This is for Judaism the *da'at 'elohim,* the knowledge of God that God gives in revelation.

From the Christian side, Donald Juel, following his teacher Nils Dahl,[85] has executed a methodologically brilliant study of primitive Christian "messianic exegesis," demonstrating rather more precisely that the "central concept" of Christianity is that of the crucified Messiah: "The confession of Jesus as Messiah is the presupposition of NT theology."[86] By this Juel means that the death of the man who had been hung on the Roman stake as a messianic pretender defined for the earliest Christians "in the realm of history" the very terms in which His Easter vindication had to be understood, even though Jesus had apparently not, or at least not obviously, interpreted Himself in the royal terms of current messianic motifs. The claim becomes comprehensible in fine detail as Juel examines the "messianic exegesis" of the New Testament in the light of contemporary Jewish canonical presuppositions and exegetical methods which, as such, expressed "the conviction that the God who raised the crucified Messiah from the dead is the God of Abraham, Isaac and Jacob."[87] That the Messiah was to be crucified cannot be found, nor inferred from those Scriptures, in any simple way; yet the meaning of the cross of the Messiah could only be gleaned from that field. "Behind the grim reality stands the will of God: Jesus goes 'as it has been written of him.' "[88] Insofar as Juel himself has demonstrated the equivalence, or rather, the association and openness of Sonship and messianic terminology[89] (against Schillebeeckx's essentially liberal Protestant claim to find "the critical moment in Jesus' unique God-consciousness"), it is theologically right to conclude that "the only course is to begin with the cross as the moment of disclosure and then work forward and back."[90] Juel's study contents itself with this formal though radical point:

83. Cohen, "Record and Revelation," p. 158.

84. Cohen, "Record and Revelation," p. 152.

85. Nils Alstrup Dahl, *Jesus the Christ: The Historical Origin of Christological Doctrine,* ed. D. H. Juel (Minneapolis: Fortress, 1991): "The real explanation, however, is to be sought in the historical event itself; the inconsistency stems from Jesus' crucifixion as the Messiah, although he never made an express messianic claim. He did not deny the accusation that he acted the role of Messiah when it was raised against him. This fact had a determinative significance for the Christian kerygma and thus for the ideas of the evangelists. The end of Jesus' life stands at the heart of the gospel; the historical Jesus, like the kerygmatic Christ, is the crucified Messiah. There is no gap between the historical Jesus and the preaching of the church; rather, there exists a close and inseparable connection" (p. 44).

86. Donald Juel, *Messianic Exegesis: Christological Interpretation of the Old Testament in Early Christianity* (Philadelphia: Fortress, 1988), p. 81.

87. Juel, *Messianic Exegesis,* p. 26.

88. Juel, *Messianic Exegesis,* p. 96.

89. Juel, *Messianic Exegesis,* p. 62.

90. Juel, *Messianic Exegesis,* pp. 174, 176.

the correlation of cross and the kingdom is the (Easter) presupposition of New Testament theology.

This new historical portrait, emerging from the side of both Christian and Jewish scholars, leads us to a second implication of what it must mean for Christians to let the witness to God of Judaism into its own process of theological reflection. It is past time to recognize afresh the scandal that the Christian gospel is, first of all, to the Christian. The old, classic triumphalism was not wrong to perceive that the issue between Jacob and Esau was the question of identity: Who is the Messiah? It erred rather, when in answering this very question, it left out the signature of the cross. The "stumbling block" of proclaiming the *crucified* Messiah as the very best of news from God, as Leonard S. Kravitz glosses, "while the world remains in sadness and pain,"[91] is not only a "stumbling block to Jews and folly to the Greeks." It remains the obstacle to every form of Christian triumphalism, whether in secular or religious guise. "This is the true people of God," wrote the early Luther, "who are always bringing to bear the judgment of the cross upon *themselves*" — note well, the very principle the old Luther violated in his sinful abuse of Jews.[92] Kravitz is right, however, to see that the notion of a "crucified Messiah" is the real, theological bone of contention between Ju-

---

91. Leonard S. Kravitz, "A Jewish Reading of the New Testament," in *Biblical Studies*, p. 97.

92. Luther's sin against the Jews derives not from his theology, particularly not from his Christology cum-doctrine-of-justification, but rather from his forfeiture of it and headlong dive into religiously charged politics, which caused him to shut off dialogue, abandon reason, resuscitate and deploy every vile slander of the Jews, finally to invoke the secular sword against them. As despicable as this was, it is of a piece with his stance on the pope as the Antichrist and the peasants' revolt under the leadership of Thomas Müntzer as the work of the devil (as I showed in the Appendix to *LBC*, pp. 379-85). All this manifests a demonological turn in Luther's thinking following upon his excommunication, which is in theological principle separable from his prior theological conviction in Christology and justification. Indeed, it had been perhaps the most politically promising implication of the Reformer's theology to deny in principle, for the sake of faith itself, that the secular sword had either competence or authority in the realm of conscience, where the Word of God alone must carry the day. Indeed, all of his reformatory theology might be summarized as the gospel protest against the fusion of spiritual and temporal power in Christendom, as the hermeneutically decisive Article 28 of the Augsburg Confession shows. Thus Luther's reverting to the Sword against the Jews proves to be at once a betrayal and a recapitulation of the previous history of Christian triumphalism with enduring ecumenical and ethical implications. Heiko Oberman comments: "The solidarity in sins shared by 'us wicked Christians' and the Jews loses its penitential and reformational force when 'Reformation' comes to be understood as the achieved exodus from Babylonian captivity. This Protestant triumphalism leaves behind heretics, popes, Jews and 'us wicked Christians' in the landscape of a past that has been overcome." Heiko A. Oberman, *The Roots of Anti-Semitism: In the Age of Renaissance and Reformation* (Philadelphia: Fortress, 1984), p. 124. Oberman demonstrates in the manner of *Sachkritik* the material, theological contradiction between Luther's venomous statements of 1543 and his own gospel: "Our heinous crime and weighty sin nailed Jesus to the cross, God's true Son. Therefore, we should not in bitterness scold you, poor Judas, or the Jewish host. The guilt is our own" (p. 124).

daism and Christianity. The issue is not the polemics of which the Jews of that period are equally capable,[93] nor is it forced exegesis of which the rabbis too are guilty, but rather the messianic authority ascribed to Jesus who died disgraced and abandoned, indeed, cursed by the God whom He had invoked.[94] Nor is the bone of contention ethics as such,[95] nor even the resurrection, since faith in it would be tantamount "to a belief in the mission of Jesus and the new meaning of Messiah."[96] The dispute over table fellowship, and the Pauline controversy regarding justification that arises from it, come close because they touch upon the communal identity of true Israel (Gal. 6:16),[97] but the heart of the matter is that for Jews the messianic "promises are yet unfilled. . . . The meaning of the term Christ or Messiah is the crux of the different views of the Synagogue and the emerging Church."[98]

As perplexing as Jews find faith in the crucified Messiah — and, pray God, may their perplexity afflict many Christians with perplexity! — it does not mean that Judaism in living dialogue with Christianity today cannot recognize its divine vocation. Cohen states: "The dissemination of Torah has . . . primarily been the work of the Christian world. . . . Torah values prismed through the Bible provided the rule by which faithful Christians have measured their societies, churches, communities, homes and personal lives . . . [this] has kept ever present the consciousness of the biblical Hebrews, the Jewish foundations of Christianity, and the special role that appears to have been assigned to the Jewish people by history or history's Source."[99] Many other such Jewish voices could today be added to those above. Novak brings the point to bear upon Judaism: "the necessity of Christianity for Judaism, then, is that it has the capacity to include all nations in the revealed relationship with God."[100] We may include Islam in this new fellowship of the erstwhile rival children of Abraham — but that is a topic in its own right (see the note on Islam below in Chapter Seven).

Jewish perplexity about the sense of the predication Messiah to defeated Jesus should become a principle internal to Christian theology, especially in the construction of Christological doctrine. For Christians today to recognize the

---

93. Kravitz, "A Jewish Reading," p. 77.

94. Kravitz, "A Jewish Reading," p. 84.

95. Kravitz, "A Jewish Reading," p. 86.

96. Kravitz, "A Jewish Reading," p. 89.

97. Kravitz, "A Jewish Reading," p. 92.

98. Kravitz, "A Jewish Reading," p. 82.

99. Cohen, "Record and Revelation," pp. 163-64. Likewise, Pinchas Lapide: "No Jew living today doubts that Jesus has, as the Christ so convincingly proclaimed by Paul, become the Savior of the Gentile church; nor do we question the messianic mission of Christendom in this as yet unredeemed world. . . . [T]he Christianizing of millions of Gentiles is a significant, if not redemptively essential, interim station on our pilgrimage to the last days." Pinchas Lapide and Peter Stuhlmacher, *Paul: Rabbi and Apostle* (Minneapolis: Augsburg, 1984), pp. 50, 55.

100. Novak, *Jewish-Christian Dialogue,* p. 108.

divine vocation of Judaism — not least in posing this question to them — is thus to recognize before God a true partner in conversation "in our pilgrimage to the last days." Because of our unique relation to the Scriptures of Israel, it is living Judaism that provokes Christians to authenticity; because Judaism has borne the cross of which too often Christians have merely made an ornament (Forde), it asks us the most penetrating questions; because Judaism endures, it also inspires us to faith beyond adversity that we today only dimly sense. This has ecumenical implications for the church. As Radner argues,[101] Christian disunity may be traced to Christian confusion about its "messianic vocation" that arose in precise correlation with that triumphalism that wanted to make of the gospel a new law with which to rule the world and just so turned a deaf ear to the dissenting voice of Judaism. If for no other reason than that the conversation with Judaism will bring into focus again for Christians, at the very historical moment when the Euro-American church is again tempted to plunge into Gnosticism, true unity under the gospel that paradoxically proclaims in the crucified Messiah the very best of news in a world as yet not redeemed, then Jewish-Christian conversation on the way to friendship intending the Beloved Community will prove the good and gracious will of God indeed.[102]

---

## A NOTE ON THE MODERN MARIAN DOGMAS

As argued, "born of the Virgin Mary" is to be deliteralized and theologically decoded to refer in an ancillary way in Christology to the Jewishness of Jesus and the messianic nature of His saving work as fulfilling Israel's offices of prophet, priest, and king. As such it is doctrine that can and does bind consciences by instructing them to refer to the object of faith, Jesus, in this specifically scriptural way, the Christ, the Son of God. Just so, this affirmation of critical dogmatics makes the modern Marian dogmas of the immaculate conception and bodily assumption that were promulgated in the nineteenth and twentieth centuries by Rome[102] a

---

101. Radner, *Brutal Unity*, p. 80.

102. Leon Klenicki and Richard John Neuhaus, *Believing Today: Jew and Christian in Conversation* (Grand Rapids: Eerdmans, 1989).

102. For a sympathetic and irenic exploration see Jean Guitton, *The Virgin Mary*, trans. A. Gordon Smith (New York: P. J. Kennedy & Sons, 1952). The beautiful coherence of the Virgin as model of adoration, mediation, and redemption may be granted as pious opinion; it may not be accepted as dogma binding on conscience at pain of salvation nor accepted theologically as a proper development of the creedal Christological statement that, as argued, points rather to the Jewishness of Jesus and His office and thus alludes to the divinely willed contradiction of Jewish disbelief as a check against Christian triumphalism and realized eschatology.

matter of *conscientious* objection. The basic trouble with the Marian dogmas is that Mary ceases to be Jew and becomes a Baroque Catholic.

First and most obviously, it is a matter of authoritarianism. No one can be asked rightly — on pain of salvation no less — to submit in faith to something that at the same time is thought of as untrue — unless in the name of mystery or by appeal to paradox the law of noncontradiction is to be tossed and any possibility of rational theology as faith seeking understanding jettisoned. Only with Tertullian's "I believe because it is absurd" could one have recourse to a faith *known* to be in contradiction to reason (a fideism that Catholic polemicists otherwise impute to Luther). But such a servile sacrifice of the intellect is no true surrender of faith to the mysteries of God. Indeed the real theological problem of faith in the *Jesus* who was born of the Virgin Mary as Christ, the Son of God, as argued above, is not even acknowledged when blind submission is demanded and worse, passively conceded. If there is no way to understand what one believes, an affirmation of faith is vacuous. One may as well make up any absurdity, "Triangles are octopuses," acknowledging that it is a "paradox" or "mystery" to which faith submits by divine authority, puts it on an altar and reverently adores having no idea how in the world it works or is to be used — as must happen in any true knowledge of an object, also faith's knowledge.

In the second place, the speculative expansion of the creedal "born of the Virgin Mary" assumes things that critical dogmatics cannot take for granted. Consider the sober objection of as ecumenically minded a theologian as Wolfhart Pannenberg. In a review of the new *Catechism of the Catholic Church,* he wrote: "The statements concerning the virginity of Mary too superficially dismiss all doubt about the historicity of the tradition at this point. . . . Surely dubious is the representation of the church's tradition on Mary as a 'perpetual Virgin,' as if we are not dealing here with a symbolic expression of Mary's relation to God rather than an historical matter."[103] If the virginal conception is an essential datum of revelation that must be believed as a fact of history, then Paul, Mark, John, and any number of the Catholic Epistles are deficient for ignoring it; and if her perpetual virginity is a matter of dogma even Matthew, who makes mention of Jesus' sisters and brothers from Mary (Matt. 13:55-56, cf. Luke 4:22), becomes suspect. Certainly the church comes to theological clarity about the gospel in the course of time through dogmatic development, but this does not mean that it is free just to make things up.

From what standpoint, then, could we judge the truth or falsity of further development of the creedal doctrine of Christ's birth from Mary the Virgin?

First, it must be clear that it is not the mere assertion of a biological singularity, nor the low level of historical probability, that creates the problem. An assertion that from the perspective of biological or historical science may seem

---

103. Wolfhart Pannenberg, "Catechism of the Catholic Church: An Evangelical Viewpoint," *Pro Ecclesia* 4, no. 1 (Winter 1995): 55.

simply incredible may rightly invite faith, or cause offense, from the perspective of theology — for prime example, the fundamental Christian message of the resurrection of the Crucified. The prior question is how the assertion of such an event could be true or false with respect to the Christological proposition for which it is summoned in support, that is, whether the alleged miracle is, or can be understood as, a fitting articulation of the person of Jesus Christ who is believed in Christian faith as the objectification of God's determination to redeem the creation. Islam's Qur'an, for pertinent example, can and does appropriate the Virgin birth tradition stemming from Luke (or perhaps the *Proto-Evangelium of James*), while suspending, if not disputing the creedal use of this reference to denote Jesus born of Mary of Israel as the Son of God incarnate, savior of the world. That is to say, Islam holds to the historicity of the miracle of Jesus' birth from Mary the Virgin and yet denies that the "truth" of this event concerns the person of Jesus who was crucified for our sins as the only Son of God and raised for our justification.[104] In Christian theology we are talking about the identity of Jesus, the Son of God, as the one who saves from sin, and it is in this respect that reference is made to His birth from Mary the Virgin. But what is that *reference?* What *in the world* are we talking about?[105]

If Christ's person is to be known in terms of other notions of truth than the cognitive claim to truth of Christian theology — for example, current understandings of biology — He cannot Himself be received as "the way, the truth, and the life," as the gospel represents and theology understands. One cannot meet such objections from outside theology without getting entangled in the way the question is being posed — from outside the theological circle, apart from the guidance of "dogma," no longer within the canonical narrative. This recognition of the "theological circle" is not dogmatism, except where the Kantian conceit, itself a dogmatism, of the Tribunal of Reason is still in force. It is a clear-eyed recognition of the finitude of reason and its dependence on what Gadamer called the "prejudice" of tradition, not only for theology.[106] Slavoj Žižek, in his debate with

---

104. Kenneth Cragg, *Jesus and the Muslim: An Exploration* (Oxford: Oneworld Publications, 1999), p. 19. In Cragg's words, "the clear commitment of the Qur'an to virginal conception (which is, of course, the very heart of 'annunciation') in the case of Jesus marks his birth as coming from within a divine initiative and as an expression of God's directly creative power... celebrating a unique status belonging to Jesus — albeit for the purposes of prophecy — which gives him a significance altogether his own as 'God's Word'" (p. 32). Thus the Qur'an can hold to the miracle in the very way that offends scientific sensibilities without holding to the Incarnation as the divine assumption of flesh, let alone of sinful flesh. But for Christianity, the theological issue is whether in the Incarnation God assumes a human nature without sin, and how this assumption of the flesh is then related to Jesus' bearing of the sin of the world.

105. One might consider Lindbeck's cultural-linguistic model as a thoroughgoing effort to dodge just this question of reference.

106. "Does the fact that one is set within various traditions mean really and primarily that one is subject to prejudices and limited in one's freedom? Is not, rather, all human existence, even the freest, limited and qualified in various ways? If this is true, then the idea of an absolute

John Milbank, made the point powerfully: "[A] pure confrontation of positions is never possible: no formulation of differences is neutral, every attempt to delineate the confronted positions already formulates them from the standpoint of one position."[107] This simply is a marker of our finitude that goes all the way down. One must meet an external objection, then, not by demonizing it but instead by reframing the problem it poses from within the scriptural world, according to the analogy of faith. Nor is this reframing an innovation. The problem of reference is the problem of Christology itself from the angle of epistemic access. We cannot know what we believe unless we know what in the world we are talking about.

For it has never been obvious at first sight that Jesus is the Messiah of Israel, the Son of the One whom He addressed as *Abba,* Father. Indeed Israel on the whole has from the beginning disbelieved the gospel's claim about Jesus, as argued above, on the eminently reasonable ground that the Lord's Anointed does not end defeated, disgraced, and forsaken, leaving the world unredeemed. Indeed, it is not even apparent what such a title from Israel's prophetic history could mean, when predicated of the man who died *sub Pontio Pilato.* How does *this* tortured, dead, and buried man fulfill rather than fail Israel's offices of the "prophet [who] shows God to us, the priest who leads us to God, and the king [who] joins us together with God, and glorifies us with him," thus "healing our ignorance, forgiving our sin, and making us royal children"?[108] This objection from within the biblical tradition by believing Israel poses the even more fundamental problem about the nature of the truth that can bind the Testaments together into one scriptural narrative of God who creates, redeems, and fulfills the world and so in turn binds the consciences of those believers entrusted with the care of this biblical gospel.

We cannot gain clarity about the referent of the virginal conception of the Lord Jesus from Mary His mother — and thus control speculative development of the doctrine — until we relocate the question this way. If the humanity of Christ, the New Adam, is to be our "road to God" (Thomas Aquinas), this humanity must refer to a true son of David, a prophet like Moses, the High Priest who offers himself as

---

reason is impossible for historical humanity. Reason exists for you only in concrete, historical terms, i.e. it is not its own master, but remains constantly dependent on the given circumstances in which it operates. . . . In fact history does not belong to us, but we belong to it. Long before we understand ourselves through the process of self-examination, we understand ourselves in a self-evident way in the family, society and state in which we live. The focus of subjectivity is a distorting mirror. The self-awareness of the individual is only a flickering in the closed circuits of historical life. That is why the prejudices of the individual, far more than his judgments, constitute the historical reality of his being." Hans-Georg Gadamer, *Truth and Method* (New York: Seabury, 1975), p. 245.

107. Slavoj Žižek and John Milbank, *The Monstrosity of Christ: Paradox or Dialectic?,* ed. C. Davis (Cambridge, MA and London: MIT Press, 2009), p. 94.

108. François Turrettini, cited in Alister E. McGrath, ed., *The Christian Theology Reader,* 3rd edition (Oxford: Blackwell, 2007), p. 153.

victim once and for all. Christ's threefold office derives from Israel. Christ is the fulfillment of Torah and Temple because "Christ's flesh, which comes from the Virgin Mary, has theological significance because by it Christ belongs to the people of Israel."[109] The Creed's reference to Mary the Virgin, and through her, to Israel, thus raises the problem of the human mediation of God's salvation to an acute level, namely, "what kind of mediating function the church has in salvation . . . the question of human institutions in mediating."[110] The problem is acute, because the first and enduring form of the church, believing Israel, disbelieves in Jesus precisely as born from the Virgin Mary, that is, as the Spirit-anointed Messiah. Indeed, what is Christologically decisive is not modernity's glib disbelief in miracles but faithful Israel's scripturally reasoned disbelief in Jesus' Messiahship. Speculation in the further development of the doctrine is not to be licensed by an a priori dogmatism to the effect that God, who can do anything, can also cause virgins to conceive and bear but is rather to be controlled by Israel's objection to a Messiah born to die. Christian triumphalism and supersessionism is to be checked by the apparent contradiction that "born of the Virgin Mary" refers Jesus, the object of Christian belief, to the very people of the covenant who disbelieve this claim to truth.

Can such disbelief mediate the gospel? Yes, indeed, as we have seen above that today Jewish disbelief in the Jew Jesus as the Messiah of Israel must become a principle internal to Christian theology so that the dubitability of the Christian claim to truth is acknowledged within the ecclesia. Israel's disbelief forces Christian theology to refer to the crucified and dying man rejected by all, abandoned by His own, as the object in the world denoted by the name, Jesus, born to Mary whose heart would be thereby pierced (Luke 2:35), even — no, *precisely* — when by the Spirit of the resurrection it speaks of *this* Jesus as the Christ, the Son of God. Only in this way can the knowledge of faith remain Spirit-given knowledge of *faith;* therewith the *risk* of faith *ethically* as a way in the world is sustained in the posture of humility of a broken community that still awaits the coming of the Beloved Community as the visibility of its own claim to truth. Belief in the birth of Christ from Mary the Virgin can and must bind consciences only in this way, as a claim for the Jewishness of Jesus, impaled on the imperial stake, and an even more precarious claim to the messianic nature of His work as salvation from sin. Just so, disbelief in the modern Marian dogmas (that is, as anything more than pious opinion, as something authoritative that would bind consciences) is and remains a matter of conscientious objection in that they make faith and the community of faith themselves the object of faith in a grand and triumphalist fideism and in this way obscure the true objectivity of faith given in the sign, Christ crucified, decoded theologically as God's own propitiation for the sins of us wicked Christians, *pars pro toto,* the sins of the world captive to malice and injustice.

---

109. Matthew Levering, *Christ's Fulfillment of Torah Temple: Salvation according to Thomas Aquinas* (Notre Dame: University of Notre Dame Press, 2002), p. 68.
110. *Lutherans and Catholics in Dialogue VIII,* p. 37.

The modern Roman Mariologies that tends to make of her, as separated from Judaism and turned into Catholicism, co-redemptrix with Christ, are not possible as true developments of doctrine; the open wound in Mary's heart is and remains the original schism of normative Judaism and early Catholicism (John 19:25-27).[111] This Mary never had need to be preserved from the stain of original sin in order to bear the Son of God, who came to take on the likeness of sinful flesh in order personally to take on Himself the sin of the world, His mother's too. This Mary fell asleep in death in perfect solidarity with all her children, awaiting the Lord's call on the last day. All such triumphalistic developments in Mariology to the contrary forget the original schism and tacitly regard Judaism as simply superseded. Mary of Israel like her Son is and remains a Jew. Salvation is from the Jews. Gentiles are grafted in. Yet believing Jews do not believe in Jesus as the one Redeemer of the world and do not recognize the Mary who bore Him as one of their own. This perplexity is at the root of things and must abide by divine decree (Romans 9-11) so that Christians cannot and may not regard their own faith in the person of Jesus Christ as a superior insight, work, decision, or anything along such lines, but rather what it is: the sovereign work and election of the Holy Spirit who gives to each the new birth as once He gave to Mary Theotokos the conception of the Son of God.

The Spirit calls each from spiritual death to new life in faith as once He called the crucified and buried Jesus from the grave. We accordingly have the Spirit in no other way, Mary too, than by knowing Christ put to death for our sins and raised for our justification. Mary is not to be made into the functional equivalent or even surrogate of the Holy Spirit, the true co-redeemer with the Son; rather she is iconically the exemplary human instrument of Him and fitting symbol of the church's mediation of the gospel in the power of the Spirit. But the church which mediates the gospel is wounded from the beginning by its separation from Judaism, just as it is not yet the Beloved Community of God. It has its treasure in an earthen vessel. Mary too, earthen vessel, a true *tokos,* is and remains one of us children of the earth, coming from Adam, and only so does she aid us as the paradigm of obedient faith.

---

## Modalist Confusions in Christology

The latent modalism of the Western tradition, as critiqued in the preceding, has a Christological implication that touches upon the task of Christological doctrine as such; that implication is the supposition that Christology is concerned with the highest possible predications of honor to Jesus culminating in His identification, for example, as God, or near God, or like God — just as if divinity were an essen-

---

111. *Pace* Raymond E. Brown, *The Gospel according to John, xiii–xxi* (Garden City, NY: Doubleday, 1970), pp. 992-97.

tial quality pertaining to a substance that can be predicated in varying degrees. Because modalism fails to make the crucial distinction between nature and person, it takes Christology to be the work of conceptualizing the natural relation of Jesus and God as, for example, one of identity, or of proximity, or of similitude (univocity, equivocity, and analogy respectively). In fact it is possible Christologically to speak of Jesus, the New Adam, as the true similitude of God, the *eikon tou theou* (2 Cor. 4:4; Col. 1:15) and so also of believers who have put Him on in baptism (Eph. 4:24). This is the grain of truth in the Western approach that, as indicated, finds its denouement in the modern theology of liberal Protestantism.

Even at its best, however, Western modalism in all its iterations is strangely imperceptive of the New Testament and patristic way of Christology in seeing the personal identification of Jesus as the only *Son* of the almighty *Father* who breathed upon Him the *Holy Spirit* for His messianic mission and vindicated this *Sonship* at length by raising Him from the dead. Instead of thinking after this revelation of the Three from Jesus' baptism on, in modalism one asks, "Does Jesus affect us in ways that are divine?" and answers, "Then Jesus must be divine," i.e., functionally divine, effectively divine in such and such a way or to such and such a degree. By the same token, in this line of thought the notion of what is "divine" is taken for granted as what more or less supplies such and such a need of the human inquirer. "God" becomes more and more whatever I or my group need ultimately or maximally to survive, advance, be set free, and/or to triumph over foes real and imagined and just so less and less a concrete reality that exists independently of my perceived need, a personal Life in its own right that exists in and for itself naturally and only as such also by grace for us — thus in a way that this very objectivity becomes in its advent to us and for us transformative of human subjectivity.

The entire modalist procedure is a systematic transgression of the *theologia crucis,* taken as a theological rule: *vera theologia et cognitia dei in Christo crucifixo sunt* ("true theology and knowledge of God are in Christ crucified"). The first question in Christology is not whether believers recognize Jesus as "divine," under the dubious assumption that He meets their "needs" as only "God" can (cf. John 6:14-15), i.e., that already they know what are their true needs and what "God" must be to meet them. The first and decisive question of Christological doctrine is whether the One whom Jesus addressed as His Father and into whose communion He invited others also recognized this One Crucified, truly dead and truly buried, as truly His Son and thence imparts to believers by the same Spirit the same knowledge in faith, making crucified Jesus as the object of His vivifying love the object of their vivifying belief. Certainly, such an objectivity of faith's knowledge is transformative for them. It trans-values their existing values — their loves — as well as their perception in a work of conversion by the gift of the same Holy Spirit who led Jesus to Gethsemane and through it to His risen glory. This objectivity works a radical reorganization of affects. As God can be known only by God, only the theological subject can know the theological object. And the conjunction of these is the *theologia crucis,* taken as the resurrection of the *Crucified* — this One *alone.*

Because the narrated story of Jesus referenced in the ecumenical creeds is a "passion story with an extended introduction" (Kähler), it is in fact singularly ill-suited to issue in the "effect" on us from which in turn the highest-possible value ascription might be elicited so that we award the man Jesus the honorific titles of functional equivalence to, or even identity as, deity as we conceive deity. Mark's Gospel — which invents the genre of gospel narrative — contradicts just this expectation by having no human being rightly identify Jesus as the Son of God until in an apocalyptic moment the words fall from the lips of the executioner seeing "how Jesus died" (Mark 15:39). Just so, the relative clauses that identify the Son Jesus in the creeds do so by narrating first a series of things that *happen to Him,* i.e., things that He *suffers.*[112] The divine Son of the Father is to be identified in events of *humiliation:* highlighting the natural prenatal habitation in and issue from a human womb and then the unnatural humiliation and torture at the hands of Pilate, followed by death and burial. Only from this point onward does the Creed make use of active verbs: now this humiliated One is said in the active voice to have "descended into hell, on the third day rose again from the dead, ascended to heaven, and seated at the right hand of God the Father almighty, whence He will come to judge the living and the dead."

He *acts* as a personal agent only as the one who has first suffered patiently, as a patient, as a personal patient. If this person is the Son of God, clearly this designates a way of being God as Son, who exists as God in receiving being from His Father, who lives in returning glory to the Father who gives.

Clearly here, personhood or subjectivity is not to be identified simply with agency, just as agency is not to be understood apart from personhood. It is the person who works, a subject that in the first place emerges in a nexus of sociality that cannot admit of a real isolation of "the individual." In the totality of His existence, the Son is therefore to be known in the definite narrative sequence as the humiliated-and-exalted One, the crucified-and-risen Jesus. In this sequence, He who lived and died now lives again His own definite, particular, concrete life. Instead of distinguishing two sons, one of Mary and one of God, or in modern idiom, a Jesus of history and a Christ of faith, under the assumption that the first produces an effect upon us and the second arises as a consequent value judgment, or alternately, that the first signs the second by way of an ascent from below to above, the Creed distinguishes the passion and the action of the "one" same person, the "one" Lord Jesus Christ both patient and agent, victim and victor, the one Son from Mary and from God.

Such Christology is *not* soteriology though it issues in one;[113] it is the knowledge that faith — "that gift of the Holy Spirit" — has of Jesus, Son of God in the

---

112. Hans W. Frei, *The Identity of Jesus Christ: The Hermeneutical Basis of Dogmatic Theology* (Philadelphia: Fortress, 1975).

113. Dietrich Bonhoeffer, *Christ the Center,* trans. E. H. Robertson (New York: Harper & Row, 1978), pp. 37-38.

flesh, given by the Father for us and at work in us by the Holy Spirit. This Christology in turn provides the basis for right understanding of true, not perceived human need — Matthew's salvation *from sin* — in accordance with the saving work that Jesus has done as the *prophet* of God's reign, is doing as high *priest* in the Temple of the Spirit that is the gathering ecclesia, and will yet do as the messianic *king* of creation (the threefold office of the Christ of Israel) in the final victory of the Beloved Community of God. Carl Braaten rightly maintains therefore that "despite the current preference for doing christology from below, starting with what can be known about the historical Jesus, christological reflection is a hermeneutical process in which the movements 'from above' and 'from below' are not so much mutually exclusive as dialectically related in a comprehensive understanding of the identity and meaning of the person of Jesus Christ."[114] That is to say, the alternative of "above" and "below" reflects the framework of the modalist tendency of Western Christology. The question to be put in its place is Bonhoeffer's "*Who* is Jesus Christ?" This question is first of all a question for God and only so also a question for us. Hence it cannot be answered within a modalist framework that is interested in degrees of deity that can be honorifically ascribed to Jesus no matter whether such ascription is from human experience and insight (from below) or comes as supernatural truth that must be revealed (from above).

In modern attempts to do Christology "from below" the modalist thesis of Western supernaturalism lives on in its antithesis to the West's traditional "high" Christology. These attempts represent according to Braaten a "type of rationalistic criticism which wants to get rid of the Christ of the creeds in order to return to a historical Jesus whose moral principles, it is thought, would be directly relevant to modern times."[115] More sophisticated in Braaten's view are attempts to "translate" the supposedly archaic thought-forms of the creedal affirmation of Christ's person into accessible categories of modern thought, under the tacit assumption of the self-evident superiority, or in any case, inevitability of current forms of thought in comparison to "substance metaphysics" and its "physical theory of redemption," not to mention the antique "mythology" standing behind the creedal statements of the ancient church. The critical potential of creedal theology to execute an insightful critique of modernity's insubstantial and unnatural modes of thought in its own "mythologies" is therewith squandered. "What is at stake is not the questionable philosophical terms and categories of Chalcedon," Braaten states, "but quite simply the Christian confession that the person of Jesus Christ unites the reality of God with humanity in a way sufficient for salvation."[116] In our terms, what is at stake most basically in the Chalcedonian doctrine is the Spirit's unification of the sign and the thing signified for us by the Word creating and sustaining faith (or giving offense), with the result that we think that "the

114. Braaten, "Sixth Locus," p. 479.
115. Braaten, "Sixth Locus," p. 511.
116. Braaten, "Sixth Locus," p. 513.

earthly Jesus and the risen Christ are one and the same person."[117] This bring us to a salvation inextricably linked to this One who has experienced once for all the depth of Godforsakenness in His own history of humiliation. Consequently, His exaltation can only mean justification and life for all the Godforsaken who now forsake their Godforsakenness. Christian faith is faith confessed — publicly articulated, ecumenically shared — in this *person,* the *one* Lord Jesus Christ, the Son of God, the Word made flesh, born of the Virgin Mary as true human being, the victimized but now vindicated Lord.

"When I know *who* he is, who does this [suffers this!], I will know *what* it is he does"[118] and only so, what it *really* means for me, not what I *want* it to mean for me. "Who Jesus is" is not a function of "what Jesus means to me." But what Jesus means for me and for all is the saving consequence of what Jesus means *for God,* that is, what the Son's incarnation and dwelling with sinners means for the Father who sent Him. He is, as we shall see, the "death of death and hell's destruction" as the event, once for all, of God surpassing God in order to save us "from our sins." This line of thought, to be sure, entails the notion that somehow God suffers, i.e., that something *happens* to God that *determines* God, albeit at God's own *initiative* in the *trinitarian* dialectic of the persons in their history together with creatures. This event of Christ is not known then by a modalist dialectic of divine and human natures alternately touching and repelling in Christ (or elsewhere) — as a free-floating "event" rather than as the definite, indeed bodily object known in faith as the Spirit's unification of the sign and the thing signified: Jesus Christ the Son of God. Moltmann rightly speaks in this connection of determining the Christo-logical "who," as we shall explore in greater detail below, of "active suffering, the suffering of love, a voluntary openness to the possibility of being affected by out-side influences," and rightly tries to bring this insight about the passion of creative agape into relation to the doctrine of the Trinity.[119] The notion here is similar to the patristic "passionless passion" of the incarnate Logos (so important for Cyril of Alexandria, as we shall see, in his campaign against Nestorianism). Some such notion of creative agape was also at the center of Luther's Christological vision.

In the cross of Jesus, we may say, *God suffers God, God affects God, God de-termines God* in order to love us who as unloving are offensive to love. By this intra-divine event which can only be explicated as the interaction of the persons of the gospel narrative — Jesus, His Father, and their Spirit — God determines the salvation of the world as liberation from the anti-divine powers, reconciliation of sinners in Christ to the holy God, and fulfillment of the frustrated promise of cre-ation by the resurrection of the dead. Salvation from sin is central here, but does not fill up the whole circle; but it is salvation from sin that pries loose the demonic grip of the structures of malice and injustice and so bears implications for political

117. Braaten, "Sixth Locus," p. 524.
118. Bonhoeffer, *Christ,* p. 39.
119. Cited in McGrath, *Reader,* p. 118.

sovereignty as well for the wholeness and healing of the earth in the sanctification of the secular. Christology asks about the *truth* of human salvation in this *theocentric* way, in this *trinitarian* perspective, in this *cosmological* scope. What is true *for God?* Jesus the Crucified is truly known *as the Son sent by the Father in the Spirit to the cross for one and all,* as the Easter message asserts. Take away this assertion and you have taken away Christianity. To explicate and warrant this objectivity of theological knowledge is *alone* the problem of Christological doctrine — doctrine that expresses theology's cognitive claim to truth and thus *binds the conscience* of believers to the public confession of Jesus Christ before the world, especially the consciences of those called to minister to this Word by ministering it to others in the public that is the ecclesia in mission to the nations.

## Realignment: The Christological Division of the Divisions

One of the ironic outcomes of the Western tendency to modalism in its contemporary liberal phase is the tendency to disqualify doctrine as binding on conscience. This disqualification is undertaken in the name of "the gospel" or "the Word of God," taken as a noumenal principle somehow superior to its doctrinal understanding and articulation in public confession. Understanding articulated in doctrinal "formulation" is thus relativized as the inferior "word of man" or "church regulation." Doctrine is but the variable mode in which the transcendent Word appears refracted, as it were, to understanding by finite minds under varying historical and material circumstances. One hardly notices in this ubiquitous move today that the very distinction between doctrine and Word of God is itself a human construction, hence a doctrine, hence also a particular response to a particular historical context — the one we are identifying as the end of Christendom in Euro-America. This collapse brings with it a loss of theological nerve regarding the gospel claim to truth; if seriously meant, any claim to truth *eo ipso* binds consciences as truth purportedly does, human formulations and all. Moreover, we do not need to bow down to the Platonic idol of timelessness and universality here. As God's truth is His truthfulness to His Word of promise, thus His faithfulness in time and space, the truth of doctrinal formulation is timely, not timeless; it is contextually apt, not above and beyond the fray, truth in our own time and place *in statu confessionis* (in the state of confession, i.e., called upon the witness stand). It is one thing to acknowledge that we strive to understand and articulate the confession of faith for our times and place — including first of all our understanding of today's faith in unity with the tradition of the gospel that we have received — and it is quite another to abandon this very struggle for true doctrine to hopeless theological pluralism.

Harding Meyer, the distinguished Lutheran ecumenist, has written that "the message of the gift of salvation free from all human conditions is not to be thwarted by a view of the Church and its unity which makes human factors and statutes appear to be in the strict sense 'necessary,' i.e., constitutive, for the being and unity of the Church." This is a version, much imitated today, of Augsburg Confession VII's *satis est* claim: that agreement on the gospel and the ministration of the sacraments in accord with that gospel "suffices" for the true unity of the church. While the Augsburg Confession had in view papal demands for additional agreement on ceremony and orders, Meyer extends the notion beyond ceremonies to doctrinal formulation, as if the article were affirming a theological pluralism. Since doctrine — presumably including the doctrine concerning Christ's person now under discussion — is in this way regarded as a human work of the Church, in principle nothing more can be secured or required, Meyer argues, than a "fundamental consensus" in teaching, which would itself be "internally differentiated" between matters that are essential and matters that are secondary.[120] Meyer acknowledged in passing how contemporary awareness of historical relativity undergirds even this minimalist interpretation of doctrine binding the conscience to an internally differentiated fundamental consensus that would still be able to bind the church together conscientiously by common confession of the faith. "To the extent to which we recognize that no aspect or area of the church's life is totally exempt from being humanly and historically conditioned, not even the normative teaching of our churches, the consensus necessary and sufficient for unity cannot be but such a 'fundamental consensus' ... differences in the area of church Confession and church doctrine (doctrinal conceptualities, forms of expression, images, perspectives, or emphases) do not hinder church fellowship provided there is a consensus 'in the right proclamation of the gospel,' in 'fundamentals,' 'in the basic view of the gospel,' in the 'heart of the message of salvation.'" Agreement in the "one and the same apostolic faith," Meyer consequently says, can find expression in "a multiform confession. . . ."[121] Meyer correlates this notion of multiform doctrinal expression to the model of church fellowship as *reconciled diversity.*

Perhaps this is the best that can be done; for Meyer's stated task as an ecumenist working to restore the visible unity of the church, it perhaps even suffices. It is true, moreover, that pre-critical Christian dogmatism choked on an ever-accumulating wealth of dogmatic convictions that could no longer order itself critically in terms of the "one thing needful" but instead had to resort to the competing authoritarianisms of inerrant Bible or inerrant papacy or inerrant Holy Tradition or the inerrant charism of authentic proclamation to order the chaos in a manner that, contrary to intention, only multiplied it. The modern Marian doctrines previously critiqued are a prime instance of this undisciplined speculation, just as the modern Christological reductions of Jesus to similitude who shows what God is like attempt the necessary pruning of this luxuriant growth

120. "Fundamental Consensus and Church Fellowship," in *In Search of Christian Unity: Basic Consensus/Basic Differences,* ed. Joseph A. Burgess (Minneapolis: Fortress, 1991), p. 113.

121. Burgess, *Search,* p. 113.

with hedge-clippers rather than a scalpel. Nevertheless, it is hard to see how "reconciled diversity," supposedly articulated in terms of an admittedly slippery "basic consensus," amounts to anything more than an endorsement of the existing situation of spiritually exhausted and theologically vacuous Euro-American Protestantism — too tired to change and at the same time too tired to argue any longer about the truth of the gospel regarding the gift of salvation as a matter binding consciences, especially of those who would teach in the churches. The objection is obvious: Why should *any* claim for "fundamental consensus" — including the Protestant principle "of the gift of salvation free from all human conditions" — be immune from the same acids of relativism?[122] Does not "unconditional gift of salvation" here operate precisely as a human formulation of doctrine? It is questionable in systematic theology (as opposed to ecumenical diplomacy) whether Meyer's doctrinal minimalism represents a coherent idea at all, since even this claim for "fundamental consensus" cannot strictly be held necessary and so as publicly binding on churches conscientiously living together as the one church of Christ.

It is not surprising consequently to learn that a Roman Catholic counterpart to Meyer, Walter Kasper, did not concur with contemporary Protestantism's incoherent doctrinal minimalism, in that it leaves aside the question whether in fact a "different understanding of the common core" remains unarticulated, one that will surface to divide the church again in spite of the incoherent claim to a fundamental, if "differentiated" consensus. Against this diplomatic ambiguity, Kasper points to the fact that doctrine, among other things, *refers* to something in the world, an objectivity, and so has truth conditions. It identifies God one way or another in the world. Doctrine is thus more than the various "doctrinal conceptualities, forms of expression, images, perspectives, or emphases" of theological subjectivity; theological subjectivity does not license a vulgar pluralism of the object, the identification of the God of the gospel. On the contrary, as the work of the indivisible Spirit of the Father and the Son in the world, reference is made and thus objectivity constructed into a standard of teaching that makes a claim to truth that can and does bind consciences. "Jesus Christ is the same yesterday, and today, and forever" (Heb. 13:8). Consequently, critical dogmatics, acknowledging the necessary plurality of contexts attending theological subjectivity, nevertheless intends and can intend to assess adequacy to the self-donation

122. This is the objection that then Professor Joseph Ratzinger registered against the proposal under discussion in the 1970s whether the Church of Rome could receive the Augsburg Confession as a legitimate expression of the faith. He argued that it is not at all clear that the Augsburg Confession actually governs the lives of Lutheran churches since there is no order capable of exercising this doctrinal discipline and that in fact it has been the view of Luther as charismatic prophet that historically fulfills the Petrine function in Lutheranism. As Luther faded from consciousness and as changing times demanded new theological thinking, the evolution to the abject doctrinal pluralism that in fact holds in today's Lutheranism was inevitable. See the discussion in *LBC,* pp. 275-81.

of God in Jesus Christ by the self-communication of God in the Holy Spirit in the formulations of doctrine. This is urgently needed, moreover, because faith does not justify of itself, as faith in faith or faith in one another's sincerity or authenticity, as fideism or collective fideism. Faith justifies in view of its object, which for church fellowship, or theological intersubjectivity, that is, among those who in good faith intend orthodoxy, is "Jesus Christ, the same yesterday, and today, and forever." Just so, claims for a literally *useless* "fundamental consensus" that cannot be tested by reference to Jesus Christ provide no real help, let alone solution, if in fact contradictory understandings of that to which the "fundamental consensus" *refers* remain or remain unclarified. Different or confused understandings of the object of the consensus inevitably generate contradictory practices with regard to what being the church in fidelity to the object of faith actually involves.

Both Protestants and Roman Catholics, Kasper argued, have to regard as "untenable a unity achieved purely by pragmatic means. Indifference to the question of truth can never be acceptable to the church. If only to be humanly acceptable, unity presupposes agreement. Finally, any church unity that does not arise from obedience to the truth of the gospel, but is instead put into operation arbitrarily 'from below,' would actually have an apocalyptic dimension opposing God and could only be called the worst perversion of what is ecumenical. Unity can only be unity in the truth. Above all, one cannot do the same thing together during worship and yet think differently. Such pretended unity would be deeply dishonest and could not last for long."[123] Affirming Kasper's intent here, we may leave aside here this passage's untenable equation of pragmatism with relativism that supposedly suspends the question of truth but for the following brief correction.

We have no way to avoid relativism and pursue truth in a wholly historical world except by the pragmatist way of ascertaining objectivity by the test of successful practice. We have no access to the unconditional gift of the gospel in any case apart from the disciplined articulation of its truth in mutually binding doctrinal formulations just because successful practice in the gospel mission to the nations turns upon the common mind of conscientious practitioners in what is essentially collaborative labor, where the fellowship of love in and through Jesus Christ is integral to the labor itself. When our binding doctrinal formulations conflict, our access to one another in church fellowship is to that degree hindered by conflicting consciences, and our capacity for cooperation in the mission of divine love is accordingly diminished. What the pragmatic perspective does underscore, however, is that common doctrine is in perpetual development as the gospel progresses through the nations and the times. Much is decided and new decisions must account for their continuity with previous progress in doctrinal development since there is a trajectory of orthodoxy that forms the starting point of theology in every new situation of every new generation. Yet nothing is finally settled until the eschaton of judgment resolves the ambiguities of history. So in a

123. Burgess, *Search,* p. 23.

pragmatic approach there is and must be a continuing dialectic of the Word and the Spirit, of openness and commitment, of testing for fidelity and freedom to experiment.

Kasper in any case seemed more willing than many contemporary Lutherans to hold up the doctrine of justification, rightly understood, as a matter binding consciences. Rightly understood, he argued that it entails in fact a critique of a certain one-sidedness in contemporary Lutheran formulations of its own chief article. "The basic Reformation concern, formulated in the article on justification, i.e., on the unconditional sovereignty of God, does not at all have to be understood as that which cannot be assimilated by the Catholic tradition. To the contrary! But it cannot be the only and exclusive Catholic concern. For the temptation to idolatry rejected by this doctrine, i.e., the idolizing of created objects because the distinction between God and the world has not held, is not the only temptation. Opposed to it stands the other, equal temptation to blasphemy, i.e., disparaging the holy by radically secularizing, instrumentalizing, and functionalizing signs and means of salvation instituted by God himself."[124] Kasper thus pinpoints the dualism of the sign and the thing signified that, truth be told, under the banner of Zwingli rather than Luther, captivates the theological mind of liberal Protestantism today. Kasper's correct concern here should not be seen as something alien to the sixteenth-century Lutheran doctrine, including the doctrine of the *satis est* of church unity. Melanchthon made it quite clear in the Augsburg Confession: "[W]e reject the notion of merit. We do not exclude the Word or sacraments. . . ."[125] If that is so, Kasper's concern is manifestly legitimate. If it is Luther's ecstatic Spirit-wrought faith that justifies, and accordingly sanctification is not the goal, but the source of all good works, it is because the Holy Spirit makes holy by "the signs and means of salvation instituted by God himself." One must therefore wonder if the "codicil" that Roman Catholic Carl Peters offered to the convergence statement on justification in the American dialogue is nothing other than a reminder to Lutherans of their own forgotten doctrine: "God's promise provides for Word and Sacraments and guarantees their indefectibility in Christ's church for the sake, among other things, of the forgiveness of sins."[126]

Kasper went on along these lines to ask whether there must not be "a teaching office of the church that makes binding decisions about the interpretation of Scripture and tradition." This question of the Spirit's "office" of teaching, leading to all truth by recalling the word of Jesus, exposes "perhaps even the decisive ecumenical problem . . . how a basic consensus can ever be reached and how binding

124. Burgess, *Search*, p. 38.

125. *BC*, p. 132. David S. Yeago, "The Church as Polity? The Lutheran Context of Robert W. Jenson's Ecclesiology," in *Trinity, Time, and Church: A Response to the Theology of Robert W. Jenson,* ed. Colin E. Gunton (Grand Rapids: Eerdmans, 2000), pp. 201-37; R. David Nelson, *The Interruptive Word: Eberhard Jüngel on the Sacramental Structure of God's Relation to the World* (London and New York: Bloomsbury / T. & T. Clark, 2013), pp. 2-7.

126. Burgess, *Search*, p. 311.

it can be."[127] "How does the church speak authoritatively? Is it even capable of speaking authoritatively? The issue is not the superiority of the gospel over the church. Both churches agree on that. The issue is rather how this actually works and actually is transmitted."[128] How is truth lived communally as church, Christ-existing-as-community? Who in and as this community decides?

As argued in the previous chapter, the papacy as we have known it is not obviously the answer, even if Kasper's question is incisive. The problem is Christological, since most basically Jesus taken as the Christ, the Son of God is the objectivity of the faith. There were and can be many other relations to Jesus than that in the so-called "Great Tradition" of those intending orthodoxy. This fact is reflected in the bewildering variety of Christological titles already embedded in the New Testament, each reflecting some relationship to Jesus. The would-be orthodox church's constituting confession, however, is that Jesus is the Christ of Israel, the Son of God (Matt. 16:16), culminating in the Trinitarian dogma of the *homoousios* of this Son and His Father and their Spirit. This confession specifies the relation to Him that obtains in the church catholic, since it is held here as the relation to Him that is true to God. Can we be such creedal Christians today?

This decisive question forms the increasingly visible fault line, not between the officially divided churches of post-Christendom Euro-America but rather within the divided churches themselves. It is not an accident that the presenting issue in the great divide that began in the confrontation of Cyril and Nestorius was the honoring of the Virgin Mary as *Theotokos,* the iconic figure of the one of us who as a daughter of Israel bore the Son of God to be the savior of the world. This was a stance that Luther and Calvin could still and in fact did sustain. The great reformers could take Mary as the icon of the church "who bears every believer by the Word of God" (Luther), so that he "who will not have the church as his mother cannot have God as his Father" (Calvin). We who descend from the Reformation may in fidelity to the Reformation's catholic claim thus execute what de facto is already the case today: a division of the division for those who intend orthodoxy in the sense of taking Jesus the Christ, the Son of the living God, as the objectivity of faith. The test of this realignment will be whether we can come together to state in doctrine binding on conscience here and now who Jesus Christ is for us today. On the other side of this division of the division will be those who do not intend orthodoxy because they are unwilling (in distinction from being unable or incapacitated) to confess before the world Jesus Christ, the person in the work, as that cruciform object in the world that is true to the God who promises in Him to come for us all as the Beloved Community and thus true also to us who still labor and groan under structures of malice and injustice. To that "divisive" task of Christological objectivity our inquiry now turns by returning again to the matrix of the Scriptures.

127. Burgess, *Search,* p. 33.
128. Burgess, *Search,* p. 34.

## New Testament Objectifications

The objectifications of Jesus Christ in the literature of the New Testament are, according to the present proposal, *normative* for theology, taken as critical dogmatics, that is, where "normative" means taking the canonical Scripture uniting the Testaments as the Spirit's matrix in forming the theological subject who knows God as the One determined in His Son and by His Spirit to redeem and fulfill the creation. Asserting this, however, is not to solve the problem of Christological objectification but to state it. One assured result of the historical criticism of the New Testament is to make inescapably plain the range of objectifications of Jesus Christ that cannot be artificially harmonized as happened in pre-critical dogmatics.[129] This critical insight stands behind Meyer's model of "reconciled diversity," as criticized above. It was argued with great critical acumen by Ernst Käsemann at the beginning of postwar ecumenical theology in a classic essay, "The Canon of the New Testament and the Unity of the Church"; there he came to the conclusion that "the New Testament canon does not, as such, constitute the foundation of the unity of the Church. On the contrary, as such (that is, in its accessibility to the historian) it provides the basis for the multiplicity of the confessions."[130] For example, one may think of the commonplace generalizations about the Johannine spirit of Eastern Orthodoxy, or the Pauline spirit of the churches of the Reformation, or the Matthean spirit of Roman Catholicism, or Pentecostalism's predilection for the Book of Acts, and so on.

The task of this section in surveying significant instantiations of Christological objectivity in the New Testament, as understood by contemporary scholarship at its best, is to acknowledge this truth so far as it goes, but also to transcend

129. We may observe the root of this artificial harmonization in the argument of Johann Gerhard. He takes the "canon" of Galatians 6:16 no longer as the gospel of the resurrection of the Crucified, so that all that matters now is "new creation," but as an authority principle "applicable to the rest of the books of the Old and New Testaments," that is, as conferring on them the same authority. In the process authority within the canon becomes undifferentiated and the Scripture principle accordingly requires harmonization of diverse materials in order to sustain its block authority, as Gerhard repeatedly but futilely attempts in face of the rise of historical-critical scrutiny. Johann Gerhard, *On the Nature of Theology and Scripture,* trans. Richard J. Dinda (St. Louis: Concordia, 2006), p. 408. On the other hand, Stephen J. Hultgren offers a post-critical reading of Gerhard on Scripture. He takes the aforementioned equation of Galatians 6:16 with the canonical Bible in accord with the present proposal to see recovery of the authority of canonical Scripture as a "matter of regarding Scripture as a unity, in which the literal sense of every text is understood with reference to the Holy Spirit's intended sense, as summarized in the articles of faith." Stephen J. Hultgren, "Holy Scripture and Word of God: Biblical Authority in the Church," *Seeking New Directions for Lutheranism: Biblical, Theological, and Churchly Perspectives* (Delhi, NY: ALPB Books, 2010), p. 89. See also in this connection that valuable study of Arland J. Hultgren, *The Rise of Normative Christianity* (Minneapolis: Fortress, 1994).

130. Ernst Käsemann, *Essays on New Testament Themes,* trans. W. J. Montague (London: SCM, 1971), p. 103.

it by uncovering for us today the supervening canonical unity. Recalling the argument made above in Chapter Two about the holiness of the Scriptures, that transcendence of diverse objectifications of Jesus Christ comes by discernment of the Spirit's unification in the selection of these apostolic constructions of Jesus as the Christ the Son of God to modify one another in giving Christ to faith today. Unification presupposes difference and does not abolish it or artificially harmonize it. Scripture in its pluralism of testimonies to Jesus Christ must be allowed to speak, each in its own voice. Jesus Christ is given to faith today as these witnesses combine to contest from diverse perspectives our recurring docetism and dualism by identifying God as the One who is determined by the Son incarnate to give us His Spirit and bring us in this way to the Beloved Community.

On the other hand, Käsemann's valuable insight should lead us to recognize the poverty of biblicism as Protestantism's *sola scriptura* unravels in the contradictory "multiplicity of the confessions." It should spur us, not to forced and artificial harmonizations based upon an arbitrary choice of a "canon within the canon," but rather to receiving the complex canon as a rule of faith against docetism in Christology and dualism in the doctrine of God. When we take the New Testament representations of Jesus Christ as the object of faith together in this way, we discover the supervening harmony of the second-century "martyr's canon"[131] that permitted the combination of this diverse literature in the first place. The Jesus who is presented as Christ and Lord in these various ways is by virtue of His membership in the common body and His place in it on the imperial stake the objectivity of His Father's determination to redeem the very earth on which that cross once stood. In this Christological objectivity Paul, the Synoptics, and John concur in spite of diversely articulated theological subjectivities. And that dogmatic convergence in spite of diverse rhetoric and even conceptualization reflects a common bond with the Hebrew Scriptures as the "old" of their own "new."

In this section, then, we first dispute with the help of Peter Stuhlmacher the influential neo-docetic interpretation of Paul in Bultmann's rendering of the apostle's Christology. We next concur with Joel Marcus that the first iteration of the gospel genre objectifying the Christ event by narrative is an appropriate development in accord with Pauline apocalyptic Christology, rightly understood in the aforementioned anti-docetic way. Finally we concur with Udo Schnelle's reading of the Bread of Life discourse in John 6 that Johannine theology is likewise marked decisively by an anti-docetic turn. We discover as a result how the chief New Testament witnesses unite in presenting Jesus Christ as the *material* object of faith by specifying this crucified Jewish *body* from the first century as the time and place in the world in which God was reconciling the world to Himself (Paul), by laying down that body of His own Son as a ransom for many (Mark),

---

131. William R. Farmer, *The Formation of the New Testament Canon: An Ecumenical Approach* (Mahwah, NJ: Paulist, 1983).

in order to build from it a new temple of the Holy Spirit (John). We are working to divide these divisions by uniting them in the greater synthesis of the church on the way to the Beloved Community of God. Without gainsaying the problem of historical-critical skepticism, our purpose is to vindicate theologically the move from Pauline kerygma to Marcan narrative to Johannine glorying in the flesh that the Son of God became once and for all.

## Stuhlmacher against Bultmann on Pauline Christology

"Bultmann's appropriation of the Pauline and Johannine *Christus praesens* amounts to a reformulation of the liberal doctrine of the presence of Jesus. The saving efficacy and contemporary agency that liberals attributed to the personality of the historical Jesus, Bultmann now attributes to Jesus Christ as God's speech act, an act continually occurring in and through the kerygmatic occasion of Christian proclamation. . . . Christ is our contemporary, present and acting for us, in and through the proclaimed kerygma."[132] James Kay aptly describes in this way the gravamen and the genealogy of Bultmann's rendering of Paul's Christology. Bultmann was not wrong to see the proclaimed Jesus Christ as God's speech act, as previously argued, more precisely as the Spirit's unification for us of the sign and the thing signified. Indeed, in this Bultmann vastly exceeds his usual critics in theological depth and rigor. The present criticism will be rather that he fails to see that this speech act of God, proclaimed contemporaneously in the Spirit, consists in the Father's recognition of His crucified Son whose antecedent life in the Spirit had taken Him not accidentally to the cross. In this way *the scandal of the cross is epistemically embraced* — in resurrection faith as also by God who raised Jesus — as revealing the mystery of creation's redemption and fulfillment.

While Bultmann speaks of God's speech act, he is actually thinking of a human decision of faith to speak in God's name that, as he expressly notes on many occasions, "overcomes" the scandal of the cross. This account of the primitive Christian kerygma amounts then to sheer assertion: God or faith "overcomes" the crucifixion by asserting resurrection in the sense of getting past the cross's force as disconfirmation of faith. It is pure decision, moreover, for which no worldly reason can be given. For that would undermine its authenticity as the new self-understanding of faith. Kay rightly queries: "If we are to continue to speak of the presence of *Jesus* Christ, as Bultmann clearly wants to do, how can we do so meaningfully without referring to his *identity as narrated* by the New Testament?"[133] Bultmann strongly resists — on theological, not merely historical-critical grounds of skepticism — the objectification of Christ rendered in gospel narrative. He

---

132. James F. Kay, *Christus Praesens: A Reconsideration of Rudolf Bultmann's Christology* (Grand Rapids: Eerdmans, 1994), pp. 122-23.

133. Kay, *Christus Praesens,* p. 140, emphasis added.

must regard it as "bad faith," an attempt to ground the authentic decision in knowledge of the historical Jesus rather than to take the genuine risk of faith.

In his essay in *Faith and Understanding,* "The Christology of the New Testament,"[134] Bultmann criticized the tacit notion of teaching or doctrine used in systematic theology which, he says, is based on the concept of science in Greek philosophy. In this conception of science, we know an object when we apprehend it by seeing it and locating it in "a connected whole determined by law, as a 'system,' a 'cosmos.'" If we are thinking in this theoretical way about knowledge, however, we will understand "the statements of the New Testament about Christ as statements about a world phenomenon," i.e., as an object to be seen like any other object in the world and related one way or another to all else. But that way of seeing and locating Christ in the world would fundamentally misunderstand Christ as the eschatological event. To be sure, this is a misunderstanding, Bultmann believes, that has in fact dominated the church's creedal Christological teaching from the beginning. Bultmann takes up a polemical statement of the early Melanchthon against creedal Christology, "To know Christ is not to know his natures or the mode of his incarnation, but to know his benefits." For Melanchthon this had meant that true, saving faith does not consist in doctrinal information about Christ intellectually grasped but in the personal trust that this Christ (as identified by the doctrines) elicits in my case and to my benefit. Bultmann radicalized Melanchthon's polemical statement (from which the later Melanchthon distanced himself) against scholastic theology. It is a worldly, scientific, objectifying thinking, Bultmann claims, that thinks that to know Christ is to "discern his natures, his modes of incarnation." That is a false, nonexistential approach to the knowledge of Christ who is the eschatological event that tears one loose from all worldly security founded on secular and scientific knowledge.

As it happens, Bultmann writes, the historical research of the nineteenth century has shown what an illusion this approach really is. None of the glorious titles given to Jesus in the growth of Christological doctrine are anything "new; they come from old mythologies. . . ." Christ, Son of God, Son of Man, Logos, Lord, King, and all the rest are nothing but precipitates of old myths now attributed to Jesus. Indeed, "the christology of the New Testament contains nothing specifically Christian, but simply shows the process by which ancient mythology was transferred to a concrete historical figure so as to conceal his individual features entirely." Bultmann acknowledges that this conclusion of historical-critical research leads to a "shock." He illustrates this by the example of his teacher, Johannes Weiss.

Weiss inferred from this negative criticism that theology and the church must turn away from teaching about Christ in the form of antique myths to a real experience of the man Jesus. The significance of those mythological titles cannot

---

134. Rudolf Bultmann, "The Christology of the New Testament," in *Faith and Understanding* (Philadelphia: Fortress, 1987), pp. 262-85. All following citations are from this chapter.

be found in their own apparent content but in their function of ascribing soteriological value to the experience of the historical Jesus from the perspective of existential interest. They are honorific expressions, whose real sense is uncovered in the existential possibilities they disclose. Words like "Christ" or "Son of God" tell us nothing about Jesus as such. Rather they represent, as Weiss wrote, a "multiform expression for one conviction, the conviction that in the person of Jesus was given the highest that can be thought . . . how powerful his personality must have been to inspire men to such faith!" With this thought, Weiss epitomized the liberal method of inferring the ineffable cause from the phenomenal effect, all the while acknowledging that this inference can tell us nothing about the cause in itself, only that It, whatever It is, has so affected us. Disillusioned thus of procuring the cognitive content of the honorific titles, Weiss undertook a quest for the historical Jesus, i.e., a new demythologized picture of Jesus' *Persönlichkeit* that can replace the mythological Christ of creed and dogma for honest faith today. Weiss thus imagined a historical Jesus who inspired others to faith in God. This Jesus gave them courage to believe in their own salvation. We really believe in Jesus, the person, when we experience this same or kindred effect in us, as occasioned by the historically reconstructed and thus mythologically purged memory of Him.

Bultmann, however, now proceeded with a criticism of Weiss: the New Testament nowhere talks about imitating Jesus nor does it preserve an inspiring portrait of the "personality" of Jesus. Even if it did, "the most that such an image can effect would be to make faith in God and love of neighbor appear to me as beautiful and desirable. It can never give me that faith and love. . . ." Howsoever beautiful, a picture of love does not perform love and so elicit love. It is a picture, not a deed, an event, a gift. Yet the gift of faith and love is exactly what the New Testament attributes to God's saving work in Christ. Christology must serve to *deliver* faith and love to us, if it is in fact to function as did Christology in the New Testament. Weiss's analysis of the problem is valid, but his liberal solution of the historically reconstructed portrait of Jesus' inner life cannot help us.

Bultmann next turned to the significant study of Wilhelm Bousset, *Kyrios Christos,* which argued that the so-called "Christ cult" of the early Hellenistic Christian communities is the "real backbone of the Christian religion and the driving force in its development." This study claimed that what actually happened historically in the evolution of New Testament literatures had little to do with memories of Jesus of Nazareth. Mythological needs overruled the memory of the historical figure. The real event was the spread and growth of "the community assembled to worship the Lord Christ who was present in it." "Jesus Christ" thus names not a figure in past history but "the divine power which rules in the community. . . ." Christology is "simply the theoretical explanation of this piety. . . ." Bousset's study represented real progress over against the dubious historical picture drawn by Weiss and the older liberalism; it overcame the false idea that historical memory of Jesus' personality as such, and apart from faith in Him as the Risen and Present Lord, plays a role in New Testament traditions.

Yet Bultmann protested against Bousset's reconstruction. In one decisive way Paul does not conform to Bousset's scheme. In Paul Christology "designates not a mystic, but an eschatological fact." That distinction between mystic and eschatological means, according to Bultmann, that Paul's talk about Jesus Christ is not intended to transfer old or new titles of glory onto Jesus of Nazareth as the hero of a cult and so turn Him into one idol among many. Rather, Jesus, with reference to the one, concrete historical fact, namely, His cross, represents for Paul God's *judgment* on all human "boasting," especially boasting in religious guise. This divine judgment of the cross unmasks and defangs mythological attempts to manhandle God as an object in the world that human beings can know, bribe, cajole, invoke as a hero, or for that matter ignore. In Bultmann's technical vocabulary, the "eschatological" judgment is not apocalyptic. Apocalyptic is the fantastic mythology of a future world coming from which "the eschatological" judgment is distilled. Eschatology designates the true Beyond of this space-time reality, transcendence of the world of objects and the human self-understanding based upon it. Thus eschatological judgment asserts ungraspable Transcendence against human attempts to storm heaven; it is pure Negation of all that is.

The Pauline preaching of Christ and His cross thus effects a transformation of human self-understanding insofar as humans crave worldly security and deceive themselves into thinking they have secured existence by grasping even God like an object in the world, that is, as an idol. The eschatological proclamation of Jesus' cross and resurrection is an event in time and space, to be sure. But this is an event that announces the end of human self-understanding on the basis of one's position in time and space; it therewith opens the new possibility of faith as embracing the unsecured existence of the creature who is not God. In Jesus' cross, God calls human beings to become creatures before Him in the risk of the decision of faith, not in self-worked security. Creatures cannot in truth secure the means or the meaning of their own lives in the world of objects but can only live in love and hope as they cast themselves by faith upon the announced judgment and grace of God. Such radical faith does not look for any historical or mythological supports. Such support compromises radical faith. It does not look upon Jesus Christ as a worldly object that supports certain beliefs about Him that make Him, so to say, the best idol of all. In the message of the cross, faith hears a call from beyond time and space summoning to live without assurance in the world by assurance of a transcendent love beyond all that is perceptible.

Because the Christ-event effects this divine judgment on worldly existence, Christology is radically concentrated by Bultmann into Paul's doctrine of justification. The human person "is asked whether he is willing in the light of this fact of Christ to understand himself as a sinner before God and to surrender himself and all that externally he is and has, to take the cross of Christ and at the same time to understand himself as the justified one who shares the new life in the resurrection of Christ." Such preaching of judgment and justification through the cross of Christ is the only actual sense of Christology. "Paul's teaching of justification is, it could be said, his real christology . . . christology does not consist in speculation on the nature of Christ." The titles given to Jesus therefore have no other meaning than to express this eschatological judgment of God against the sinful human attempt to take possession of God with ideology, philosophy or theology by means of concepts, worldviews, religious myths or theological dogmas.

The critical force of Bultmann's thinking thus becomes fully evident. The "*titles* of Jesus were not meant as definitions or descriptions[,] but as a confession of faith" in the eschatological significance of Jesus. The titles in any case express "secondary" concepts "which depend on the world-view connected with the titles." Thus "the mythological picture of Christ as a pre-existent heavenly being served Paul as a way of saying . . . that God's act confronts us. We no longer need that particular image; yet we do still hold the christological belief of Paul." That is on reflection a stunning claim — as stunning as this essay's opening salvo: "the christology of the New Testament contains nothing specifically Christian." The mythological form of Christological doctrine can, indeed *must* be deconstructed in order to discern and retrieve its underlying anthropological or existential sense. Its real intention is to serve as vehicle for the proclamation of God's judgment effecting justification as a new existential possibility for human living. If we share the same existential understanding of ourselves as justified sinners, that is, as humans who have sought to secure existence rather than to live in openness, and if we have now come to realize and abandon this sinfulness by virtue of the proclamation of the Cross and thus have resolved henceforth to live openly, we share the same Christology, even if we discard something like Paul's notion of the "pre-existence" of Christ.

This critical renunciation applies, however, not only to mythological titles of honor; it applies as well to the historical knowledge of Jesus of Nazareth. The nineteenth-century quest for the historical Jesus committed the same sin as the one committed by orthodox dogmas about Christ as the preexistent divine Son. Both turn Jesus into an idol by which human beings try to secure themselves religiously; neither takes the Crucified Jesus as God's judgment against human security and God's justification of living without security, by faith alone, unsecured in the world. What matters then is only the historical fact of Jesus' coming, the fact of Jesus' call to the decision of faith: "What is decisive is not *what* he proclaims but *that* he is proclaiming it." This de-narrativized and contentless "that" of the historical Jesus' summons to faith is the sole presupposition of the proclamation of God's judgment in His cross as the cross of Christ. The real task of Christology today does not lie in retrieving the titles of the past let alone the historical personality of Jesus of Nazareth, but in executing the same call to decision. To this end, "every age and every culture must re-state the decisive act in its own terms."

Despite considerable strengths in laying bare existential motives at work in New Testament Christology, a fundamental objection to Bultmann's procedure is that he knows *a priori* a great deal about God. Bultmann knows that God is categorically ineffable; that God therefore cannot become an object of human knowledge — that is, identified temporally as an object in a narrative, the cognitive synthesis of which is understood and articulated in doctrine; that faith is essentially an answer to the universal problem of the human individual's anxiety about the meaning of existence in its faithless fear of risking the decision to live openly. How does Bultmann know all this, indeed, with such axiomatic force that it is entitled to control his reading of the Christology of the New Testament?

We have seen in Part One of this work that it is baptism that inaugurates eschatological existence in the New Testament precisely as baptism into the ownership of Jesus Christ, by unification with His death and the gift of newness of life in the Spirit that anticipates the resurrection of the body. The early traditions that led to the formation of the baptismal creed identify the God of this gospel by renouncing Satan; this act of identification *prima facie* contradicts each of Bultmann's a priori assumptions.

God is not utterly ineffable because the God of the gospel *lives* (a kataphatic attribution!) as the eternal love of the Father and the Son in the Holy Spirit reaching out and taking hold in baptism. God's mysterious incomprehensibility is not that of abstract, absolute transcendence but of inexhaustible love encompassing the world in spite of its malice and injustice, indeed re-taking it as the good creation destined for redemption and fulfillment. Because God *is* this love as given and communicated in the evangelical narrative, God can indeed become truly, if not only or simply, the object of human knowledge, indeed, truly the object of human maltreatment in every way, as the cross of the incarnate Son brutally exhibits. Correspondingly, faith in Jesus as the Christ, the Son of God, is not essentially a cipher for the existential decision before universally felt human anxieties; faith is not merely or even chiefly a new self-understanding that changes the individual's interiority but leaves the world as it is. Faith in Jesus does not "overcome" the stumbling block of the cross but is rather a conversion to a new world that is coming; a conversion that looks for radical change beginning with the self now claimed by Christ, a change of worlds and a transfer of lordships, displayed in, but not reducible to, the new and theological subjectivity.

Peter Stuhlmacher's work may be regarded in many respects as a correction of Bultmann's neo-docetism in Christology and his apophaticism in theology while continuing Bultmann's insight into the doctrine of justification as expressive of salvation through the cross and resurrection of Christ.[135] He detects in Paul's

135. I have previously analyzed the so-called "New Perspective on Paul," which in its strengths resembles Käsemann's critique of Bultmann's individualism and loss of the cosmic scope of apocalyptic theology and Stuhlmacher's critique of its anti-Judaism. In its weaknesses, it reasserts a deservedly discredited progressive view of history as revelation and makes a hash of Paul's apocalyptic "antinomies" (Martyn). See *LBC*, pp. 221-57. See also the especially detailed and precise argument in Stephen Westerholm, *Perspectives Old and New on Paul: The "Lutheran" Paul and His Critics* (Grand Rapids: Eerdmans, 2004). The incisive comment made by Timothy J. Wengert, "The 'New' Perspectives on Paul," orally at the International Luther Congress in Helsinki in 2012 is now printed in *Lutheran Quarterly* 27, no. 1 (Spring 2013): 89-91. Hence I am

letters "three christological thought patterns that are related to one another: [first,] the pattern of Jesus' mission, [second,] of his sacrifice on the cross, and [third,] of the fulfillment of God's work of reconciliation through the Risen One."[136] Taking these three together as a whole, Stuhlmacher concludes that for Paul, Christ "is the personification of God's salvation-creating righteousness . . . [i.e.,] the way that God acts to set the world on the path to salvation." As this person at work, Paul's Christ is thus known by means of His story — howsoever abbreviated in Paul that story appears: He is the One sent "from above," who offered Himself on the cross once for all, but now lives and reigns as exalted and coming Lord at work both manifest in the church and incognito in the world. That is a narrative, however bare-boned. It is as such no more or less "mythical" in principle than the plot of the Synoptic Gospels in speaking of One sent from God; indeed it is no less mythical than Bultmann's bare-boned retention of the word "God" to indicate a rupture of our immanence, a disruptive breach in the paradox of the eschatological event of the resurrection of the Crucified. Taken this way as God's personification of salvation-creating righteousness as known in the narrative of His coming to us, Stuhlmacher says emphatically, "Christology is the real central theme of the Pauline gospel"[137] — Christology — not self-understanding.[138] In our conceptuality: the theological subject, which Bultmann rightly lifted up, lives in knowledge of the theological object, Jesus Christ the salvation-bearing righteousness of God.

The gospel is about Jesus, who Jesus is, who God says Jesus is. Whatever good news there is for humanity depends on who Jesus really is. Jesus is the new, true Adam, the human creature God intended and for Paul at the same time the "preexistent" Son equal with God but sent into the likeness of sinful flesh. He is both of these, since Paul is not speaking of two different persons. As such, He is the model whom Paul imitates and calls on others to imitate. Jesus' self-sacrifice on the cross, moreover, enacts His Father's self-surpassing love that extends now even to enemies, while at the same time it executes God's judgment on unbelief — again, not two different acts but one and the same baptism into Christ's death. The risen Jesus' reign in the world through the Spirit is at work in the mission of the church to the nations and remains so until the dawning of the promised new age in the resurrection of the dead. Eschatology is inaugurated but just so not completed. Paul's narrative gospel with these world-changing intentions and effects can hardly be reduced to the individual's new self-understanding as unsecured openness.

---

able here to stay with the Bultmann school's attention to the doctrine of justification as Paul's "practical Christology."

136. Peter Stuhlmacher, *Reconciliation, Law, and Righteousness: Essays in Biblical Theology,* trans. Everett R. Kalin (Philadelphia: Fortress, 1986), p. 174.

137. Stuhlmacher, *Reconciliation, Law, and Righteousness,* p. 175.

138. So also for Luther, if Bernard Lohse is correct, *Martin Luther's Theology: Its Historical and Systematic Development,* trans. Roy A. Harrisville (Minneapolis: Fortress, 1999), p. 259.

The first pattern in Paul's Christological thinking is the mission of Jesus. Jesus has His own relation to God from the outset. He exists as the one sent from God. "Pauline christology includes Jesus' preexistence from the start."[139] From the very beginning of creation, the mission of Jesus was the plan of God. In this way the continuity of salvation history and the coordination of creation and redemption are affirmed.[140] Explicit evidence of this pattern is to be found in passages that Paul probably composed himself, such as 1 Corinthians 8:6: "for us there is one God, the Father, from whom are all things and for whom we exist, and one Lord, Jesus Christ, through whom are all things and through whom we exist." We also see this in the tradition that existed before Paul and which he passed on, for example, the famous hymn in Philippians 2:6-11, which begins with the statement that Christ Jesus, "though he was in the form of God, did not regard equality with God as something to be exploited. . . ." Paul's Christology makes no sense apart from the idea that the mission of Jesus originates in God and as such expresses God's own eternal being, whether this is stated in "mythical" or "historical" form. It is vacuous, as previously mentioned, to criticize the notion of the Son's preexistence as mythological while retaining language of God or the Father as if these were not in the same way objectifications of the Beyond (as Bultmann at least in part defined "myth") that historicize the eschatological in speaking of an eschatological event in time and space. As post-Bultmannians realized, to be consequent both should fall to the same critique. In this light, the truly striking thing is not the notion of the Son's preexistence as such, but that it is conceived *personally,* as the Son's *obedience* to His Father's will in strange conflict with the Law that was given by the same God through Moses. "One speaks of Christ in the style of and by appropriation of the Old Testament–Jewish wisdom theology . . . to put a stop to the claim of total supremacy put forward by the Mosaic law and by sin, the perverter of the law."[141] This divine, preexistent figure is a person, the same One who personally obeyed His Father's will when He came "in the likeness of sinful flesh."

Paul stresses three things in connection with the mission of the eternal Son. First, Jesus "appeared in Israel as a descendant of David and as Messiah" in continuity with God's promises of salvation to and through Israel (Rom. 1:3; 9:5; 15:8; 2 Cor. 1:20). Second, Jesus' missionary "existence was totally determined by the

---

139. Stuhlmacher, *Reconciliation, Law, and Righteousness,* p. 172. For confirmation of Stuhlmacher's thesis of the Christological thematic of Pauline theology from a different theological perspective, see N. T. Wright, *The Climax of the Covenant: Christ and the Law in Pauline Theology* (Minneapolis: Fortress, 1991), pp. 56-98.

140. See here also Käsemann's discussion of the problem of continuity and discontinuity in salvation history in his *Commentary on Romans,* trans. G. W. Bromiley (Grand Rapids: Eerdmans, 1980), pp. 253-321.

141. The following discussion of Paul's Christology is drawn from Stuhlmacher's chapter, "On Pauline Christology" in Stuhlmacher, *Reconciliation, Law, and Righteousness,* pp. 169-81. Unattributed quotations come from these pages.

love that sacrificed itself for others in obedience to the will of God" (Rom. 5:18-19; 14:15; 15:3, 8; 1 Cor. 8:11; Gal. 1:4; Phil. 2:5ff.). The very love that induced God to create and sustain the world now comes to new expression in the self-surpassing divine act of God's unprecedented love for the sinner. Third, "by virtue of this obedience Jesus' life was sinless . . ." so that he could be the "spotless sin offering for the guilt of the world" (2 Cor. 5:21; Rom. 8:3) in fulfillment and hence also cancelation of the rites of atonement instituted for the Jerusalem Temple. Paradoxically Jesus' righteousness was His radical love for sinners in apparent conflict with their condemnation under the Law yet in obedience to his Father, since love is the fulfillment of the law. This achieved righteousness made His human life and death the atonement of God for the "ungodly." This atonement was the purpose of His mission as the High Priest of God's new humanity.

This second Christological pattern of sacrificial death calls for a little further theological explication — with the help of Luther — than Stuhlmacher himself provides.[142] When Paul wrote in Galatians 3:13 that on the cross Jesus became a curse for us, he was thinking of Deuteronomy 21:22-23, "When someone is convicted of a crime punishable by death and is executed, and you hang him on a tree, his corpse must not remain all night upon the tree; you shall bury him that same day, for anyone hung on a tree is under God's curse. You must not defile the land that the LORD your God is giving you for possession." If Jesus truly died this accursed death on the cross because of love that made Him "who knew no sin to be sin" (2 Cor. 5:21), then His resurrection can only attest that Christ is indeed the "end of the law" (Rom. 10:4), not in the ethical sense of law as expressing God's moral will for love, but in the juridical sense as the final forum of the divine-human relation. So the eschaton of judgment occurs already now in Christ's death, making way in the resurrection for a new relation of God and humanity that moves from curse to blessing.

Luther understood the difficult paradox that attends Paul's thinking here about atonement: Jesus' love fulfilled the law of love by extending love precisely to those undeserving of love on account of the just judgment and condemnation of the law upon their lovelessness. This transmoral love for sinners, whom juridically the law justly curses, condemns, and excludes, invoked the just condemnation of Jesus as the friend of "real, not fictitious sinners." For the law must condemn sin or it is no true law at all; all the more so, to enforce its jurisdiction, the law must condemn those who subvert the law's authority to pronounce definitive judgment, not as mere transgressors, but as rebels. Law, for Paul, is not merely moral legislation; it is not merely an expression of God's ethical will to which human beings may or may not respond as they please to their personal credit or

---

142. I draw here from Robert W. Bertram's Luther-interpretation, "Luther on the Unique Mediatorship of Christ," in *The One Mediator, Mary and the Saints: Lutherans and Catholics in Dialogue VIII,* ed. H. George Anderson, J. Francis Stafford, and Joseph A. Burgess (Minneapolis: Augsburg Fortress, 1992), pp. 249-62.

discredit. Law, for Paul, is preeminently God's activity as Lord and Judge over His own creation (Rom. 3:4-6). It is an aspect of God's kingly sovereignty, God's juridical activity by which God thwarts, accuses, indicts, and finally condemns the malice and injustice that structures the creation into lethal and ruinous juggernauts of organized evil. It is God's juridical activity by which God also protects the innocent, preserves the blessing of creation, and finally vindicates the innocent.

In this light, Jesus' ethical love for sinners in fulfillment of the law is so intimate a union in His personal solidarity with them that He makes their burden His own, not as the One committing the sin but as the One taking responsibility for it. His sovereign word of forgiveness is not magic. He does not wave a wand and make the malice and injustice that he forgives disappear into thin air. Christian preaching that superficially preaches this Jesus magic and calls for faith that disbelieves the reality of sin in sinners and the power of evil over them mocks the "hell of the irrevocable" (Royce) in which sinners are helplessly ensconced. It is this shallow sentimentalism that evoked Nietzsche's scathing rebuke that the forgiveness of sins is a false solution to a false problem. But Sin is not sins and forgiveness is not closing eyes and believing that it is not there anymore. Sin is a power, yet it is overthrown not by power alone but also by right, the powerful right of self-surpassing love on the part of the offended; it is creative love that triumphs for the offenders by the deed of divine power that can and does enter into their state to reach and rightfully reclaim them. Nor is this deed of self-surpassing divine love a revelation of a timeless truth, telling us what God is like. The love of Christ is a wholly personal love, which elicits in turn the personal act of entrusting oneself to Him, i.e., faith. This is always the faith of the helpless sinner to whom Jesus comes and joins Himself, to take sin away by taking it upon Himself. Jesus appropriates the sin of the sinners whom He forgives, relieving the one who is crushed before God under the load. Jesus' love, which the law itself requires in the sense of God's ethical will, therefore comes into direct conflict with this just condemnation of the law, in the sense of God's juridical activity that must condemn lovelessness. It is not just the deeds of lovelessness, then, but the sinner, the loveless subject who must die and gets to die in union with Jesus who united Himself in love with just this one.

Not only does Jesus' love for sinful subjects violate the prohibition against associating with sinners, seeming, as it does, to condone their sin by partying with them (Mark 2:15-20). Jesus' love for sinners directly speaks against, that is, contradicts the holy judgment of God in His law in "the mighty duel" of jurisdictions, the "law battling the law in order to become liberty for me" (Luther).[143] In this way the entire legal system of predication by merit and demerit is exploded by the anomaly in its teeth of Him who knew no sin, but was made to be sin. The Law of God, the holy Law, may thus be overthrown from within the divine Life itself as the final forum of the divine-human relation. The new testament of pred-

---

143. *LW* 26, pp. 277-90, 370-71.

ication by grace is established in its place by the joyful exchange.[144] In this way, Christ is both the ethical fulfillment of the moral purpose and the eschatological termination of the juridical function and jurisdiction of the law. Jesus Christ becomes in person the eschaton of judgment.

In sum, returning to Stuhlmacher, "Jesus' mission arose from God's intention to save the world by the sacrifice of Jesus' life on the cross. God's saving decree, already comprehended before all time in Christ the Son, finds its soteriological climax in the mission and sacrifice of this Son." To demonstrate this, Stuhlmacher stresses the *hyper hemon* ("for us") statements that are embedded in the earliest traditions about Jesus' death, such as 1 Corinthians 15:3 where Paul reminds, "For I handed on to you as of first importance what I in turn had received: that Christ died *for our sins* in accordance with the scriptures," or as in 1 Corinthians 11:24: ". . . when he had given thanks, he broke it and said, 'This is my body that is *for you.*'" By means of such "for you" formulae, the "incomprehensible enigma of Jesus' death on the cross was penetrated and became comprehensible as an essential part of God's work. . . ." So the "scandal of the cross" was not "overcome" but rather embraced as the key to understanding. The earliest Christians thereby realized that "God not only had turned the evil of Jesus' death into its opposite by the resurrection, but also had effected salvation already in the death of Jesus, precisely through the vicarious sacrifice. . . ." The atoning death of Jesus, known to be sure in the light of Easter morn, inaugurates eschatological existence in accordance with God's eternal plan now unfolding in time. Other important texts that seem to express pre-Pauline tradition, such as Romans 4:25, 1 Corinthians 1:30, and 2 Corinthians 5:21, all speak of God as the merciful source of atonement. God does not wait for human beings to reconcile themselves to Him. Rather, God creates the conciliation. God provides the lamb. Such is the salvation-creating righteousness of the God of Israel, the justice of the kingdom of God, which does not annul the law by fiat, but ethically fulfills its moral purpose and thus satisfies it juridically so that God's justice can give freely as a gift exactly what the sinner does *not* deserve.

Paul's special theological contribution to this complex of Christological doctrine about Christ's saving death which he inherited from the primitive church was to correlate it with "faith apart from the works of the law." "The atonement effected by God in Christ can be appropriated only in faith, that is, in the thankful and also obedient acknowledgement of that saving work of God to which the sinner, fallen from the creative glory of God, can contribute absolutely nothing." All people, both Jews and Gentiles, are thereby placed under the same judgment of God and offered the same justification before God. "Christ is the reconciler of the world and not of Israel alone." Critically that means that there is no advantage in the way of the law, which may lead to worse self-assertion against God as Paul now looks back on his own previous life as a Pharisee. In Romans 10:3, Paul writes

144. Robert W. Bertram, "The Human Subject as the Object of Theology: Luther by Way of Barth," University of Chicago Ph.D. dissertation, 1964.

about those who are, as he once was, "ignorant of the righteousness that comes from God, and seeking to establish their own, have not submitted to God's righteousness." For "Paul knows precisely from his own faith experience that the law does not save even the pious Jew"; that seeking justification on the basis of works of the law "can even make that person an enemy and opponent of God," as he had once thought to serve God by persecuting Christians. Only Christ's atoning death really breaks the sinner free from the powerful and subtle hold, sublimely at work in the business of religion, of sinful self-assertion against God, "when the guiltless Son of God took over the fate of sinners — death — and precisely thereby put the law with its deadly claim of dominance in its place." So Romans 10:4: "For Christ is the end of the law so that there may be righteousness for everyone who believes."

That leads to the third pattern of Christology in Paul, according to Stuhlmacher, in answer to the increasingly obvious question about the "delay" of the Parousia: How does the Christian community continue to live on this basis, when surely it fails again and again to live up to the merciful righteousness of God? Eschatological existence is inaugurated; it is not yet fulfilled or even completed from the side of Christ; certainly not then from the side of Christ's own people, bought with a price, who must be exhorted continually to "glorify God in the body" (1 Cor. 6:20). But the body of the Christians, still linked organically to the common body, is thus constituted a field of battle between the Spirit and the flesh. Were it not for the misperception of modernity in carving out a privatized realm of interiority, one could say, with Luther, that Christ now reigns as saving Lord in the "conscience," that is, in "faith," not yet sight, "before God," in anticipation of the eschaton of judgment, not yet its public coming. Thus Paul thinks of "Christ, the crucified and risen Son of God, the Lord, *who is to finish the still incomplete work* of God" in the world in at least two ways. First, through the Spirit-led mission of the church to the nations announcing the gospel, Christ "must reign until he has put all his enemies under his feet" (1 Cor. 15:25). The righteousness of the Christian community is not of a legal/ethical nature, as if it were an island of genuine ethics in a sea of barbarism; it is misunderstood if it is either sought or found wanting by this measure. Rather the church's righteousness is its conscientious place in the Spirit's mission to spread the gospel of Christ in which the risen and exalted Lord is active with His all-sufficient righteousness coming to bear for these others. The church's faithfulness, that is, biblically, its righteousness is tested then by its obedience in spreading the message of forgiveness, life, and salvation in Christ's name. In the interim, the full renewal of humanity in the redemption of the body awaits the final victory of God.

The goal of Christ's reign is the resurrection of the dead, which comes from God, when we all shall "be changed" (note the passive voice, 1 Cor. 15:51-52). This surpassing power comes from God (2 Cor. 4:7). It is not in the church's power to enact the resurrection, to build the kingdom of God on earth, to change human nature. Indeed, such Christian heresies have an apocalyptic dimension to them of opposing God in titanic fashion. It is veritable apostasy for the church to look for salvation in anything or anyone less than Christ coming in final glory for the redemption of the body, including especially in the much lesser good of its own embattled and ambiguous life as a *corpus permixtum.* Rather the church is to reflect the reality of the resurrection in the world by following Jesus in the humility of service, bearing the cross, spreading the gospel, living together in community under Jesus' hidden reign. It is the new and common life of mutual love and care in Jesus' name always in mission to the other that realizes righteousness, not any individualistic super-saintliness or the collective egoism of ecclesiastical triumphalism. So the Beloved Community already now breaks into the structures of malice and injustice, and, as we shall see in Chapter Eight, breaks their grip to restructure life in love and justice.

So second, Romans 8 shows how the "Risen One, on his way to the subjection of the universe, is to uphold believers in their existence as justified sinners." Simply by receiving Christ's love and living on the basis of it, believers have become "doers of the true will of God" who are "made strong precisely in weakness, suffering for Jesus' sake." The Risen Christ is the strong advocate and intercessor of His people. Nothing can separate them from His love. He shall complete the good work begun in them and bring them safely to the glory of the age to come. In short, "instead of a justification narrowly restricted to baptism, Paul proclaims justification through Christ as a process that controls the life of people and history in general right on through to judgment day." That is to say with Luther, "baptism remains forever." For people who now *live* to follow Jesus in the Spirit by faith, the word of their free justification for Jesus' sake apart from their deserving is the word that they rejoice to hear at every step along the way. For this word of mercy is the true taste of the world to come, the merciful eschaton of judgment already now. That is why in Paul the church as a worshiping community, as the Temple of the Holy Spirit, is part of the gospel, gathering the nations and in this way unifying humanity in the new song of praise to God.[145] The church as Eucharist is the paradoxical presence of that future world, for the church is essentially the worship of God already sounding now the praise that will obtain forever.

With this tense expectation of the saving work that the risen Lord Jesus has yet to accomplish as messianic king, we have come to the crux of the Christological problem in Paul. In Christopher Morse's words: "The Resurrection and Parousia as the destiny of Jesus Christ are confessed in faith to be the universal future to which all that actually happens is ultimately related. . . . Worldviews that rule out this promised destiny of Jesus Christ as off-limits to reality are themselves thus called into question and challenged. . . ."[146] The Christological tendency of

---

145. See Käsemann's penetrating essay, "The Theological Problem Presented by the Motif of the Body of Christ," Chapter IV in *Perspectives on Paul,* trans. Margaret Kohl (Philadelphia: Fortress, 1971), pp. 102-21.

146. Christopher Morse, *Not Every Spirit* (Harrisburg, PA: Trinity Press International, 1994), p. 165.

the Pauline gospel, beginning with the Easter message itself, is to hold together the one concrete personal life, Jesus Christ Son of God, and accordingly to understand God as God who truly can be the one who sends and is sent in Jesus, who just so finds the human echo of praise and thanksgiving in the Spirit. Yet the difficulty in understanding Jesus Christ, son of Mary and Son of God as one, concrete, indivisible life is real, i.e., it is rooted in the peculiar fact that this one, concrete life is *not yet finished.* We still await the great change (1 Cor. 15:51-57), the "redemption of our bodies" (Rom. 8:23), the public manifestation of Christ's kingly rule by the cosmic defeat of the last enemy, death. Though we are "beloved," and "God's children now," we cannot yet describe fully "what we will be" (1 John 3:2), as if by looking back upon a completed matter. With believing Israel we are still awaiting the end of the story — of Jesus as the Christ. What matters is that we so speak of Jesus as the Christ that we are able by means of this Christological teaching on His person to enter upon the life of hope in His destiny, till at last "every knee should bend, in heaven and on earth and under the earth, and every tongue should confess that Jesus Christ is Lord to the glory of God the Father" (Phil. 2:10-11).

## Marcus's Commentary on Mark

From a variety of angles, the publication of Joel Marcus's two-volume commentary on Mark[147] ought to be a major event in contemporary Christian theology that reconfigures the relationship between theology and biblical exegesis away from the usual modern polarizations. First and foremost, it is testimony to the continuing importance of sober historical critical exegesis that, out of rigorous, imaginative, but also disciplined hearing with the ears of first auditors constructs for us today a critical baseline of knowledge against speculative and abusive appropriations of the biblical text,[148] whether in history or in theology.[149] No one can appeal to Scripture, whether for or against a theological claim to truth, without controlling their appeal by inquiry into what claim to truth was made in the hearing of a text's first addressees. This is so particularly because gospel narrative is never a pure event in itself but always an event as addressed to someone, in the

---

147. Joel Marcus, *Mark 1–8, A New Translation with Introduction and Commentary,* The Anchor Bible vol. 27 (New Haven and London: Yale University Press, 2000) and *Mark 8–16, A New Translation with Introduction and Commentary,* The Anchor Bible vol. 27A (New Haven and London: Yale University Press, 2009). Pagination in the second volume is continuous from the first.

148. Leander E. Keck, *A Future for the Historical Jesus: The Place of Jesus in Preaching and Theology* (Philadelphia: Fortress, 1981).

149. In contrast to reader response speculation, as W. R. Telford commented in his review of the first volume, "the approach taken is a purely historical-critical one." Review, *Journal of Theological Studies* 53 (2002): 191.

case of texts, by authors and to readers/auditors. Marcus's method, learned from his teacher J. Louis Martyn, of hearing the gospel of Mark in the ears of its first auditors is thus fruitful. It exposes the distinctive historical and theological nature of the gospel narrative — the genre Mark is inventing — as a "two-level drama." As M. Eugene Boring put it in his review of the second volume, Marcus in this way captures "the evangelist's simultaneous double focus on the revelatory and salvific event of Jesus' life, death and resurrection, and the theological narrative that retells this story in terms of the events and concerns of the evangelist's own time."[150]

The appropriation of the traditions about Jesus and their production in a narrative to interpret the present situation in the world for believers, in other words, is an interpretive objectification of who Jesus is for contemporaries and in this very way a normative model of Christian theologizing: "remind[ing] that we are dealing with a layered text, that Mark was not free to compose ex nihilo, but saw himself as an interpreter of a tradition he respected but felt no obligation simply to repeat."[151]

This tradition that Mark receives, develops, and passes on, moreover, is thus greater than memories about Jesus of Nazareth; in fact, the memories about Jesus are themselves already layered, if not saturated by the motifs and theology of the Hebrew Scriptures. Thus the Markan Jesus rendered by Marcus, as reviewer J. R. Daniel Kirk put it, is "scripting Himself" with the Hebrew Scriptures. The Jewishness of Jesus in this way could not be more firmly established. What is precious in Marcus's commentary is his exposure of this deep intratextuality, as it were, running both backwards and forwards. Backwards, Marcus shows how motifs from the Exodus and from the second Isaiah provide the narrative plot line of the gospel that assembled the various units of Jesus tradition, and forwards, how the resulting Marcan narrative functioned liturgically to form the evangelist's own Eucharistic community in a time of terror.[152]

Needless to say, Marcus's commentary is not without several difficulties, which we may note and acknowledge here, before continuing with our own interpretation and appropriation for the purposes of systematic theology. First, his historical locating of the Marcan community in the proximity of the Jewish revolt against Rome that culminated in the destruction of Jerusalem and the Temple, together with his identification of the persecutors of Mark's Christians in this context as Jewish "zealots,"[153] has not gone unchallenged on both historical and

---

150. M. Eugene Boring, Review, *Interpretation* (April 2011): 198. "Mark thus serves as a hermeneutical model for the modern interpreter: interpret Mark as Mark interpreted his tradition, but let Mark be Mark" (p. 199).

151. Boring, Review, p. 200. Telford criticizes Marcus on just this point of the gospel narrative as history scriptured, however, defending Crossan's dichotomy between history remembered and prophecy historicized (p. 375). See the discussion in Marcus, *Mark,* pp. 927-98. I will defend Marcus's position.

152. J. R. Daniel Kirk, Review, *Horizons in Biblical Theology* 32 (2010): 99-127.

153. Marcus, *Mark,* pp. 766, 896.

literary grounds, especially by W. R. Telford. The historical objection is that Marcus's claim is an argument from silence: we do not have independent evidence of Zealot persecution of Christians during the revolt. The literary objection is that certain Hellenistic features of the text speak against too close an identification with a Jewish Christian community escaping Jerusalem during the revolt. But it is enough for present purposes that Marcus has identified the Gospel's *Sitz im Leben* as a time of terror, in which contemporary disciples are summoned to watchfulness (13:37). That is surely correct. Second, just because of the canonical scope and theological interest informing his historical-critical scholarship, Marcus is faulted in numerous instances with "overinterpretation," that is to say, with making suggestions that exceed the evidence.[154] This is akin to Telford's objection that we cannot prove with certainty the setting of Mark in the Jewish revolt. But "overinterpretation" is a "sin" only in the eyes of empiricist foundationalism. Underinterpretation is no less interpretation. What Marcus does in these so-called "overinterpretations" is to play out his well-grounded hypothesis to explore possibilities for which evidence is lacking and in just this way to stimulate further research. The disciplined construction of a model that extends into areas for which evidence is lacking is hardly a fault; it is how science progresses into new research. If this is speculation, it is well-disciplined speculation that fruitfully fills out the picture for broadly hermeneutical, not narrowly empirical purposes. Perhaps just this shading into theological concerns is what makes Marcus's critics nervous.

Finally, and most pertinent to our purposes, is the difficulty that, while Marcus acknowledges the three soteriological motifs evident in Markan Christology — namely the divine Warrior Christ who comes as victorious liberator, the Suffering Christ who comes as ransom, and the moral example of Christ who calls disciples to follow him — it is not wholly clear how these three cohere in Mark according to Marcus's interpretation. Telford put the objection to the bold paradox crisply in his review of the first volume: "The Markan Jesus is said to have won the decisive holy war victory when he was rejected by his own people and executed on a Roman cross, but there is little explanation of how the second evangelist understood this to happen."[155] Theologically, this is indeed the Christological *crux intellectum*. But this objection asks the historian Marcus to do what only theological interpretation of Mark can accomplish, since Mark is written from faith for faith and his paradox cannot be understood apart from disclosure to faith (Mark 4). It is highly unlikely historically that Mark would have had an

---

154. Robert H. Gundry's review of Volume 1, in *Review of Biblical Literature*, pp. 386-91.

155. Telford, Review, *Journal of Theological Studies*, p. 195. The passage continues: "This may come out in the second volume, however." In his review of the second volume, Telford is content when Marcus himself admits that "we are left with the impression that Mark has a genuinely ambivalent attitude toward the Davidic image" of the apocalyptic holy warrior (p. 374). As we shall see, Marcus has more to say than that.

integrated theology of the three motifs. But that is akin to saying the doctrine of the Trinity is not found in the New Testament because the conceptuality of the three persons and one being is not articulated there, when the conceptuality had to be developed to understand how Jesus, His Father, and their Spirit together constitute the one complex event of the coming of the Reign. It is likewise no objection to the observation of the three atonement motifs in Mark to point out that Marcus has not yet conceptually integrated them. It is enough to establish historically and literarily that they are there in the text and somehow modify one another. That is how Scripture works as matrix of theology in critical dogmatics.

Let us begin with a crucial discovery regarding the well-recognized matter of the so-called "messianic secret" within Mark's narrative (it is, of course, no "secret" to readers of Mark who are clued in from the beginning, 1:1, to the identity of Jesus Christ the Son of God), which goes beyond typical apologetic or psychological interpretations[156] to the heart of the matter — as Marcus puts it — "that human puzzlement is a necessary part of the revelation of divine mysteries."[157] This is the "Jewish" (*pars pro toto,* the human) perplexity at the strange message of salvation by the cross of the Messiah that, as argued above, must become a principle internal to Christian theology, particularly of Christology, insofar as Mark and his commentator are able to "reproduce the situation of the disciples and place themselves on the road that leads to understanding."[158] Narratively figured, this is the road that passes from Galilee to Jerusalem, on which the three passion predictions are delivered by Jesus to uncomprehending followers. On the one hand, Mark is telling a story in this way about "what happened way back when" in Jesus' earthly ministry, "when the full truth about him could not yet be revealed because the epistemological revolution created by the crucifixion and resurrection had not yet occurred." On the other hand, this narrative "inevitably shades off into a reflection on who Jesus *is* now, in the post-Easter period, for Mark and his community" — as becomes more than evident in Mark's asides to his auditors/readers that lift the narrative veil (e.g., especially 13:14, 37). The secrecy motif is thus neither an apology for the historical Jesus' lack of "messianic consciousness" nor an account of Jesus' own slowly emerging "messianic consciousness." It is rather Mark's theological account of the apocalyptic shift in perspective that comes and prevails as the knowledge of faith in the crucified Son of God — the "revelation," humanly implausible, placed on the Centurion's lips after he watched how Jesus had died.[159]

As the apocalyptic genre turns on the need for divine revelation to see the world in proper perspective, it is a fitting term to describe coming to faith as an "epistemological revolution" in that faith comes to see and to think as God

156. Marcus, *Mark,* p. 525.
157. Marcus, *Mark,* p. 81.
158. Marcus, *Mark,* p. 81.
159. Marcus, *Mark,* pp. 71-73.

does (so literally the Greek, though in the negative, of Mark 8:33) about Jesus. Humanly, this thinking and speaking after the Word of God (Mark 8:31) is faith (or offense). Christologically, this Word of God is the "open" — that is to say, not "secret" — teaching of the passion predictions and their fulfillment in the narrative at the apocalypse of the death on the cross of the Son of God. Such is revelation in apocalyptic — at least in Mark's modification of the Jewish genre by making its content the Crucified Christ; it is not a mere disclosure of a timeless, transcendent truth or state of affairs but is rather the *Novum* on the earth of a divine self-donation that is also a divine self-communication.

Beginning with his interpretation of Jairus who, *seeing* Jesus, pleads for the healing of his daughter in 5:22-23, Marcus makes note of this "first instance of the language of perception that will permeate" the Gospel.[160] "The God whom Jesus proclaims, therefore, is the one who grasps mind as well as heart and thus brings a new type of perception into the world."[161] The old type of perception sees but does not understand — "perception of Jesus' striking words and deeds ('looking' and 'hearing') may lead not to faith but to rejection of him."[162] The "hypocrisy" of those who reject Jesus' teaching of the divine will is "not conscious dissimulation but the reflection of a deep malady that results in a tragic split between claim and reality" in the business of religion, "under the sway of human tradition that has emptied the divine word of its force and blinded its possessors to God's true will."[163] (The Pauline warning, "do not be deceived," finds an echo in the Marcan Jesus who asks the Sadducees, "Aren't you deceived . . . ?" [12:24], intimating the role of the apocalyptic prince of deceivers[164] in their thinking about the Scriptures.[165] This "old" thinking knows the letter but not the spirit, the text but not the divine intention.)[166] By contrast, the restoration of sight to blind Bartimaeus is "reminiscent of early Christian baptism . . . as 'illumination.'"[167] Accordingly, the exhortation to those illuminated by baptism into the baptism in which Christ is baptized[168] is to Watch! Look! Stay Alert![169] All this contestation about perception comes to its climax, of course, for auditors/readers as the executioner voices the Markan claim to truth precisely upon seeing how Jesus died: "an unexpected character to enunciate the radical inversion of values that sees a dying criminal as God's true Son."[170] The theological subject is thus the one who, hearing what

160. Marcus, *Mark,* p. 365.
161. Marcus, *Mark,* p. 844.
162. Marcus, *Mark,* p. 379.
163. Marcus, *Mark,* p. 451.
164. Marcus, *Mark,* pp. 832-33.
165. Marcus, *Mark,* p. 830.
166. Marcus, *Mark,* pp. 822-23.
167. Marcus, *Mark,* p. 795.
168. Marcus, *Mark,* p. 754.
169. Marcus, *Mark,* p. 878.
170. Marcus, *Mark,* p. 1057; cf. p. 1067.

Mark tells, sees Jesus in the same apocalyptic way, the crucified One as the object of faith, the sign unified with the thing signified in the event of revelation.

Bultmann, following Bousset, was not wrong to see that like Paul's own Christology, the Christologies of the Synoptic Gospels, beginning with Mark, are one and all determined by the "Hellenistic" congregation. They were wrong, however, in polarizing in history-of-religions fashion Hellenism and Judaism which in this period suffused one another.[171] They were further mistaken — the Apostle Paul himself being direct evidence to the contrary — in thinking that Hellenistic Judaism could not have embraced "cosmic apocalyptic eschatology." Marcus is correct historically in seeing instead "a line of Christian apocalyptic thinking [that] can be traced back to Jesus himself, through the earliest Christians, and on to Paul and other first-generation Christians" that reaches also to Mark (without, however, claiming direct dependence on Paul).[172] Precisely in this connection, moreover, it is also right to see Mark, like Paul in 1 Corinthians, fending off a docetic reading of Christology. Marcus endorses broadly the view of scholars who have claimed that "the purpose of Mark's gospel is to prevent the Pauline kerygma from floating off into space by grounding it in the story of Jesus of Nazareth. . . . Mark mobilizes the Jesus tradition as well as the theology of the cross to fight against incipient docetism."[173] In that case, the real "correction" of Christology going on in Mark is not that of the original disciples with their wonder-working "divine man" Christology (supposedly depicted in the first half of the gospel but then corrected in the second half). The Christological correction is rather of those already now claiming to have full union with the heavenly Christ[174] in a message of escape from suffering as opposed to conformity with Christ by believers' bearing of their own crosses in the time that remains before Christ's Parousia. Just like Paul in 1 Corinthians, Marcus sees Mark connecting the real presence of the risen Lord[175] as continued penetration into the world under the structures of malice and injustice by way of the paradoxical signs of the broken bread and poured wine,[176] signs unified with the thing itself, the crucified and risen body of Christ, that forms believers into the Body of Christ in the world. In a further blow against incipient docetist ecclesiology, this Eucharistic presence means that Christ "does not exist primarily as a solitary individual but as a being-in-communion, and living the Christian life means 'being with him.' "[177]

The connection Marcus makes here, as we shall see, accords with Schnelle's reading of John 6, provided we keep the apocalyptically paradoxical nature of

---

171. Hengel, *Judaism and Hellenism,* systematically dismantles this taxonomical fiction.

172. Marcus, *Mark,* pp. 73-75.

173. Marcus, *Mark,* pp. 75-76.

174. Marcus, *Mark,* p. 76.

175. Marcus, *Mark,* pp. 237-38, 435.

176. Marcus, *Mark,* p. 78.

177. Marcus, *Mark,* p. 267.

perception in mind. "Even the blind derision of Jesus as king [in the mocking of 15:29-32] reflects the kingship of God, and thus, by implication, that of Jesus. The 'looking' of the priests and scribes is a form of myopia — blindness to the upside-down way in which God's purposes work themselves out in a world where the cross may truly become a throne. And the leaders' demand that a miracle be performed in order that they may 'believe' reverses the Markan and NT dynamic in which faith in God's dominion, which sometimes hides under a contrary appearance, precedes the miracle that brings it into the light."[178]

All this attention to perspective applies centrally to the figure rendered in Mark's gospel narrative, the *prosopon* or *persona,* Jesus Christ the Son of God. The apocalyptic cosmic battle scenario indicates how Mark conceives Jesus' "divine Sonship" in connection with "his effective opposition to the power of Satan" in that Jesus "participates in God's sovereignty over evil supernatural forces."[179] He comes as the new Joshua, the divine holy warrior against the demonic legions. Yet He does so in human fashion, like a farmer sowing seeds, seeds that are mere human words. Commenting on the parable of the Sower in 4:13-20, Marcus writes: "For in the apocalyptic Markan worldview, the identity of the sower of the word of God is not a simple matter, since proclamation is not an autonomous human action in which a person merely decides to open his mouth and forms words about God; it is, rather, a complex act in which divine and human factors are inextricably and confusedly mixed up together . . . Jesus' words, then, are not just *his* words but God's, and they will become the words of the Markan community."[180] The Word of God on the lips of human beings is a union of the sign and the thing signified by the Spirit, where and when it pleases God. God's Word comes as a "disruptive word" that "establishes the self from outside of the self and thus apart from any of its works, including the modern epistemological subject's sovereign construction of its object" (Jüngel).[181] The theological subject, beginning with Jesus Himself, is not then a mere external witness to an event that happens alongside of him or outside of her. The coming of faith deprives the subject of such security. Rather, the witness of the Word of God is formed as person within that event of the Word that is its advent in human language (Jüngel's "analogy of advent");[182] the event of the Word is narrated by the temporal sequence of cross and resurrection, suffering and vindication, tribulation and salvation as the "two sides of the complex, divine-but-human

178. Marcus, *Mark,* p. 1052.

179. Marcus, *Mark,* p. 261.

180. Marcus, *Mark,* p. 311.

181. Eberhard Jüngel, *God as the Mystery of the World: On the Foundation of the Theology of the Crucified One in the Dispute between Theism and Atheism,* trans. D. L. Guder (Grand Rapids: Eerdmans, 1983), pp. 169-84. R. David Nelson, *The Interruptive Word: Eberhard Jüngel on the Sacramental Structure of God's Relation to the World* (London and New York: Bloomsbury / T. & T. Clark, 2013), pp. 22-27.

182. Nelson, *Interruptive Word,* pp. 28-37.

identity of the Son"[183] and also of the Son's disciples who will be baptized in His baptism by the grace of adoption.[184]

The subtle but significant alternatives here are between the theological subject as a witness exterior to Christ and as the person formed in Christ by the Spirit in baptism, that is, Christologically, between Christ as the person Jesus giving voice to the divine Word in His human obedience and Christ as the divine Word in His human obedience of faith. This is a distinction that will become important in the next chapter. It is the difference between thinking of the "person" as a Kantian subject, the noumenal condition for the possibility of the act of knowledge, and thinking of the "person" as person-in-relation, thus as existing with others in some time-like and space-like world. For the present, Marcus is uncovering the roots of classical Christology in the pioneering gospel narrative that juxtaposes Jesus' transcendent glory and His human vulnerability as "inseparable characteristics of God's new age."[185] Marcus achieves this by exposing the location of this unification of naturally different characteristics of Creator and creature — this *communicatio idiomatum* — within the apocalyptic conflict of the ages (citing Dostoyevsky's *Brothers Karamazov*): "God and the devil are fighting for mastery, and the battlefield is the heart of man."[186] To enter the lists and to fight upon this battlefield, the Son of God came as the Son of Man.

It is in the context, then, of God's confrontation with the structures of malice and injustice that we are presented with the one person, Jesus Christ the Son of God, who exhibits characteristics of both divine and human natures in the accomplishment of His messianic mission to redeem the creation for the sake of its fulfillment. This latter motif of the good creation as object of redemption to be liberated as a structure of love and justice emerges in Mark's Gospel in the tenth chapter's discussion of marriage and the little episode that Mark appends to it of Jesus' blessing of the children. Concern with sexual malice and injustice "is only the reverse side of a 'high' view of marriage and of the sexual act, one that ascribes transformative significance to that act and the relation it creates. When one body enters or is entered by another, a transaction of eternal significance has taken place — one that, in its merging of opposites and resolution of contradictions, mirrors the ones of God with the world in the new age inaugurated by Jesus' advent,"[187] who likens His presence to that of the Bridegroom (2:18-20). In this respect, as a redeemed structure of love and justice that goes back to the Creator's intention from the beginning of creation, marriage is "inextricably linked with the divine gift of children . . ."[188] who as such are those especially

---

183. Marcus, *Mark,* p. 641; cf. also 983, 1051.
184. Marcus, *Mark,* p. 754.
185. Marcus, *Mark,* p. 988.
186. Marcus, *Mark,* p. 988.
187. Marcus, *Mark,* p. 713.
188. Marcus, *Mark,* p. 713.

singled out for blessing by Jesus on His messianic way. The acute apocalyptic conflict — the dualism of the ages — inaugurated in Jesus' battle with Satan thus does not abolish "nature" but redeems it for its fulfillment in the coming of the Beloved Community.

Indeed, God's own unity is not to be conceived as a timeless self-sameness above and beyond the many in space and time. God's oneness in this coming is an event of unification occurring in this Person at work, on His way, in His mission: "In the Markan narrative, then, the Shema's acclamation of divine unity is not a static description of a condition that has always existed but an announcement of an event, the eschatological fusion of the world below with the world above that occurs as Jesus extends God's dominion from heaven to earth (cf. Zech. 14:9: 'And the LORD will become king over all the earth; on that day the Lord will be one and his name one')."[189] God *is* the coming of the Beloved Community, the unification of the sign, creation, with the thing signified, the Creator, not as a natural fusion but as a historically initiated joyful exchange and an eternally achieved perichoresis of persons in the harmony of love.

But this event of unification meets opposition, not merely from Satan, or hypocrites, or stumbling disciples, or fickle crowds, or hostile clerics. In a strange and wondrous turn of Mark's narrative, Jesus in obedience to God meets opposition from God in the personal confrontation of the Son and the Father. Jesus Christ, the beloved Son of God called at His baptism and proclaimed at the Transfiguration, is abandoned, not merely by disciples, but by the God whom still He called Abba, Father, in Gethsemane. The "cup" that Jesus must now drink alone is "the beaker of divine wrath that is to be poured out on the recalcitrant earth in the end-time. . . . [Jesus] quails not just before the termination of his life but also before the prospect of the outpouring of the divine wrath. . . . The true horror is not just to face death but to face it under the wrath of God."[190] In the dimension of its depth, the coming of the Beloved Community as the "eschatological fusion" of heaven and earth must unify the eschaton of judgment with, in Paul's words to which according to Marcus, Mark would have agreed, "Christ being made sin for humanity's sake (2 Cor. 5:21)."[191] If this unification is possible, in turn, the "suffering and death of the Servant [of Isaiah] cannot be separated from the victory of the Divine Warrior [like Joshua]"[192] — nor for that matter from the renewed and effective command of the vindicated Servant Warrior to "come, follow me."[193]

Mark, to be sure, does not explain how this "ransom" (10:45) works here to unify the Son and the Father, or the victim and the victor, or the ransom and the ransomed; he only proclaims that in this way the ransomed are redeemed from

---

189. Marcus, *Mark,* p. 845.
190. Marcus, *Mark,* p. 985.
191. Marcus, *Mark,* p. 990.
192. Marcus, *Mark,* p. 746.
193. Marcus, *Mark,* p. 167.

Satan's dominion for God's Beloved Community. His commentator, Marcus, is likewise reticent. He only points to the effect this objectification of Christ as the ransom of God would have had for his audience in reversing the predominant theology of revenge: "God will deliver sinful nations into the hands of the Son of God/Son of Man, and it is likely that the Jewish revolutionaries whose militant theology forms the backdrop of our Gospel fervently embraced such expectations. Jesus . . . , however, announces the opposite: the Son of Man is about to be delivered into the hands of sinners. By doing so, he will accomplish a different kind of salvation, taking upon himself the divine judgment. . . ."[194] Christ as crucified, the apocalyptic Son of Man handed over to sinners, the divine Judge judged in our place — in this way theology receives from the initial and formative gospel narrative its Christological object, the divine person at work in suffering and death and despair, under the apocalyptic outpouring of the wrath of God. How that is to be understood for us today, whose desire is also still captured by structures of malice and injustice, is a central task of Christology. Such soteriology is a function of this Christology.

## Schnelle's John 6

Of all the objectifications of Christ in the New Testament, none rivals Mark's "ransom" in its potential to offend the conscience of modern people like John 6:53: "Very truly, I tell you, unless you eat the flesh of the Son of Man and drink his blood, you have no life in you." The text, not surprisingly, has played a central role in the Eucharistic controversies of Western theology regarding the so-called "real presence," as we shall see. According to the important study of Udo Schnelle,[195] John 6:53 in its "surprising sharpness" and "emphasis on the Eucharist as the

---

194. Marcus, *Mark,* p. 990.

195. Udo Schnelle, *Antidocetic Christology in the Gospel of John: An Investigation of the Place of the Fourth Gospel in the Johannine School,* trans. Linda M. Maloney (Minneapolis: Fortress, 1992). I do not concur with Schnelle's critique of Martyn's theory regarding the expulsion of Jewish Christians from the synagogue following the destruction of the Temple (e.g., p. 25). It seems to me that the matrix of the gospel is so overwhelmingly Jewish and preoccupied with Jerusalem, its festival and rites and images and texts as the very terms in which the newness of Jesus Christ must be expressed, that at the formative stage of this tradition the Johannine community must have known an "acute conflict with contemporary Judaism." One would have to defeat Martyn's brilliant reading of John 9 as a two-level drama to show otherwise (J. Louis Martyn, *History and Theology in the Fourth Gospel* [New York: Harper & Row, 1968], pp. 35-68). That does not preclude a rapid integration thereafter with nascent early Catholicism, as may be detected in John 21. But for my theological purposes, I can leave this dispute between historians to the side. Against Raymond Brown, however, I do concur with Schnelle's important conclusion about locating the "Fourth Gospel" (perhaps not in its earliest stages but certainly in its final form) not on the fringes but "at the center of the theological history of earliest Christianity, at a point where important currents in developing Christian theology converged" (p. 238).

indispensable condition for salvation gives the impression that the Evangelist is deliberately placing an antidocetic accent on his words at this point. It is only the Eucharist,[196] so devalued by the Docetists, that mediates the saving gift of eternal life. . . ." The passage continues: "[I]t is not a symbolic 'eating' of the bread of heaven or a spirit-filled 'eating' of the Son of man that gives eternal life, but only the real eating and drinking of the flesh and blood of Jesus Christ in the Eucharist."[197] As I have made the scholarly argument for the importance of this text and Schnelle's interpretation of it elsewhere,[198] we can succinctly conclude our survey of the normative objectifications of Jesus Christ in the major literature of the New Testament on this note and then turn our attention on this basis to the theology of the Eucharist, where the drama plays out of whether and in what sense Jesus Christ the Son of God becomes present for us as the object of faith, that is to say, as the Spirit's unification of the sign and the thing signified for faith (or offense).

The Johannine theology of the "sign" (Gk: *semeion*) "at this point becomes the hermeneutical key to the Fourth Gospel."[199] Similarly as Marcus defended the Christological unity of the first and second halves of the Gospel of Mark, Schnelle argues that "it is no accident that the wedding at Cana and the raising of Lazarus frame Jesus' public appearance" in John.[200] In these "signs," that is, "miracles," "the one *doxa* [glory] of the Father and the Son is revealed in order to evoke faith . . ." although the sign "also provokes disbelief." As such, these signs "stand at the center of Johannine christology" just as "seeing of the *doxa* is connected with a visible and tangible event in space and time."[201] As with the Markan Jesus of the first half of the Gospel, "the power of Jesus over life and death that is present in the miracles occasions the evangelist's present-eschatological statements."[202]

196. Schnelle has argued for continuity between the docetism combated by the apostolic father, Ignatius of Antioch, and the docetism rejected in the First Epistle of John, connecting both to the schism reflected in John 6. The telling passage from Ignatius reads: "Mark those who hold strange doctrines concerning the grace of Jesus Christ which came to us, how that they are contrary to the mind of God. They have no care for love, none for the widow, none for the orphan, none for the afflicted, none for the prisoner, nor the hungry or thirsty. They abstain from the Eucharist and prayer, because they do not allow that the Eucharist is the flesh of our Savior Jesus Christ, which flesh suffered for our sins, and which the Father in his goodness raised up" (Epistle to the Smyrneans, 6 in *The Apostolic Fathers*, p. 189). Here the truth of the Incarnation is tested by the present surrender of faith to Christ and thus the transfer of lordship over one's body that makes of believers members of the Body of Christ and so of one another.

197. Schnelle, *Antidocetic Christology*, p. 204.

198. See *DC*, pp. 69-108.

199. Schnelle, *Antidocetic Christology*, p. 139.

200. Schnelle, *Antidocetic Christology*, p. 134.

201. Schnelle, *Antidocetic Christology*, p. 134.

202. Schnelle, *Antidocetic Christology*, p. 135; cf. Mark 2:18-22. Marcus comments: "Thus both elements, absence/death and presence/life, are given their due weight within Markan Christology: Jesus has been physically absent since his death, but that absence is, paradoxically,

Schnelle observes that "the subject of all seventeen occurrences of *semeion*" is Jesus, indicating the "exclusively christological meaning of this concept." While the Markan Jesus rejects the demand for a "sign" as a faithless demand for proof of His authority to heal and forgive (Mark 8:11-12), the Johannine *semeion* "is given a positive sign character. It points to Jesus, who is the true Temple (cf. 2:19-22) and real food (cf. 6:31-35)."[203] That is to say, in John the signs of Jesus signify Jesus as the Son sent from the Father to save — a sign in which faith may rest. They are not "proofs" because they can and do provoke hostile unbelief as well as elicit faith in the Son's saving mission from the Father. And this "contrast" between unbelief in the face of Jesus' signs, i.e., denying His glory and divine Sonship in spite of the signs, and the faith affirming His divine Sonship in spite of His evident humanity, is to "be attributed to the evangelist." The presentation of Jesus in His signs is his "deliberate theological, that is, christological, tool for interpretation."[204] "The miracles, as works of Jesus, have both the quality of revelation and the function of legitimation (cf. Matt. 11:2-6) and are the palpable expression of the unity of the Son with the Father."[205] Jesus is the unity of the sign and the thing signified, where and when the Spirit pleases. How so?

The point of this deft and convincing account of the Johannine theology of the sign is not that faith sees miracles where unfaith does not. Both faith and unbelief see the same thing, the wonders that Jesus performs in God's name for the purpose of making whole the broken and fulfilling the lost promise of creation. What distinguishes them is that faith sees the *doxa* that the signs reveal, where unbelief does not. And this *doxa* is Jesus' relation to God as Son to Father, namely then, as the incarnate Son who brings this very relation to humanity, to give those who believe in His name the power also to become the children of God (1:12) in the new birth of faith. "Faith in Jesus Christ as the Son of God is not only the goal of John's Gospel writing; it is the whole purpose of the Incarnation (1:7, 12) and thus of the whole event of salvation." Against Bultmann's influential interpretation of John, Schnelle writes that the *doxa* "encompasses both Jesus' fleshly and heavenly existence. Thus its content is not only the 'that' of revelation; instead, the miracles describe, with a virtually unsurpassable palpability and reality, the activity of the Revealer within history,"[206] that is, bringing salvation as redemption and fulfillment of the creation. The *doxa* is the thing signified by the sign for faith (or offense). Because the signs — that both faith and unbelief see — reveal visibly this *doxa* of the Incarnate One for faith, "they emphatically

---

the means by which his presence is achieved. For it is through the eschatological events of his death and exaltation to God's right hand that he has gained the power to be dynamically present with his church everywhere" (p. 238). Is the matter otherwise in John?

203. Schnelle, *Antidocetic Christology,* p. 145.
204. Schnelle, *Antidocetic Christology,* p. 148.
205. Schnelle, *Antidocetic Christology,* p. 149.
206. Schnelle, *Antidocetic Christology,* p. 169.

secure the identity of the Preexistent One with the fleshly, suffering and exalted Jesus Christ"[207] — the anti-docetic point.

Certainly, this revelation of the glory of Jesus is not, for the readers of the Fourth Gospel, their own firsthand experience. They do not see as the people of Jesus' time saw but rather through them, that is, through their testimony as the first generation of theological subjects. Their own seeing is mediated by the sign of the sign that is the testimony of the Beloved Disciple handed down to them, in whose testimony, now codified as the Fourth Gospel, they too have been formed as theological subjects as in the matrix of the Spirit who gives them new birth — so little do the "signs" function as "proofs" — as if offered to a neutral observer for contemplation and independent verification. Rather in knowing the unity of the sign, Jesus, with the thing signified, the only Son of the Father full of grace and truth in the world for the world, they have come to know God's costly and incarnate love for the world of flesh-and-blood human beings even in all its darkness and mendacity. The signs sign the objectivity of the Father's love for the world in "giving" His Son, just as the sign of the signs, the written Gospel, is written that readers may believe and themselves be unified with the beloved Son in beloved community, becoming the children of God.

Is it problematical that with John the church thus becomes the community that knows God's love over against the hostile world that continues in darkness and hostility, as if a sphere outside divine love? Is this present-eschatology in the field of the community of faith just another religious self-privileging at the expense of those outside? So it has seemed to important critics of the Gospel, preeminently Ernst Käsemann. But it is important for a moment to suspend this ready criticism — truth be told, animated by modern resentment against pietism and evangelicalism — to see how the issue here was actually experienced in the Eucharistic schism that Schnelle detects behind John 6. In this light the salvation-history dualism of the children of light and the children of darkness has a rather different import.

He argues that "the Docetists within the Johannine school denied the soteriological importance of the Lord's Supper" and that accordingly the evangelist "was guided exclusively by a christological interest: in the Lord's Supper the identity of the exalted Son of man with the Incarnate and Crucified One is made visible. In its eucharistic practice, the community confirms this identity, but it is denied by those who absent themselves from the Lord's Supper."[208] As the strange note in the Johannine passion story about "the outflow of both blood and water" from the dying Jesus "furnishes proof of Jesus' real human body" in 19:34, it also indicates that baptism as the gift of the Spirit and union with God points to union with Christ the crucified in the Eucharistic fellowship of His Body and Blood. That would cohere well with the evangelist's critique of the Docetists, who can easily be imagined to think that by baptism in the Spirit they have already arrived

207. Schnelle, *Antidocetic Christology,* p. 175.
208. Schnelle, *Antidocetic Christology,* p. 207.

in a heavenly existence with no need of continued conformation to Christ in His cross by gathering with the less spiritual in sharing the common cup and broken loaf — and this as the essential act of worship!

If Schnelle is right about this, the hostility of the unbelieving world is not only to be found outside the community of faith but arises again and again within it. As Tillich, previously cited, once wrote, the battle for the kingdom of God is fought first of all within the life of its ostensible representatives, the churches, i.e. there, where the sign that is Jesus is signified. On the one hand, the Incarnation is taken seriously in theology as the abiding objectivity of the faithful God's eternal-become-temporal love for this world upon which the cross of Jesus stood as His own creation destined for redemption and fulfillment. Here the community simply is that part of the world where the sign, intended for all, is unified with the thing, preeminently in the Word, "This is my body, given for you" or, as John theologically rephrases it: "The bread that I will give for the life of the world is my flesh" (6:51). Here faith leaps to life at this tangible Word of divine-and-human promise, where and when the Spirit convicts by means of it concerning sin, righteousness, and judgment (16:8). Here also unbelief is provoked in refusing this tangible unification, in covert fashion within the visible community of faith, by separating the sign from the thing signified: "Is not this Jesus, the son of Joseph, whose father and mother we know? How can he now say, 'I have come down from heaven'?" (6:42).

The incredulity that insists on the evidence of one's senses and that alone is precisely what unbelief is — not a theoretical perplexity or epistemological skepticism, but a resistance to the new community from God that Jesus signals in the world and the Spirit effects. It takes Christological form as questioning Jesus' authority to give the thing signified, a self-justification that the Johannine Jesus consistently defers to His Father and their Spirit. Both faith and unbelief see the same thing in the world, Jesus son of Joseph. Both hear the same claim to truth, "I am the Bread of Life," having perceived the same sign, Jesus' feeding of the multitude in the wilderness, redolent of a New Exodus as a type of the Eucharistic assembly. This battle over the interpretation of the same perception is not then a contest between a pure sect and the wider world. It is conflict within the world for the sake of the world, within the church for the sake of the church, where the ecclesia gathered around the Bread of Heaven is taken as true harbinger of the promised land, the coming Beloved Community of God. This community of the Beloved Disciple believes in God's love for the world on behalf of all who do not believe it, in the creative tension of love that is against what is against love.

## The Truth of the Incarnation

Schnelle's case carries us a long distance in showing how, theologically, the Fourth Gospel acquired its privileged theological position, so important for the future development of Trinitarian and Christological doctrine, as the "bridge" (James

Dunn) between Paul and the Synoptic Christologies (pioneered in Mark, as we have seen from Marcus) and that of the later ecumenical creeds. For Schnelle's interpretation of John shows how anti-docetic Christology culminating in the doctrine of the Prologue, that the divine Logos became flesh, is the material decision at the fonts of Christian theology. As such it reveals the internal theological unity of the literature collected as the New Testament in union with Hebrew Scriptures as its "old." Christ is to be thought of as the One who saves by His coming in the flesh and in no other way than as the particular instance of human flesh that the Jew Jesus of Nazareth was and is and will be forever. Henceforth "God" as well is to be thought as God His Father, who in the person of this Jesus, in His own Son's flesh and blood, suffered death at the hands of His own unbelieving creation and just so, i.e., as this Spirit-endowed man, overcame with omnipotent love the world that opposed the coming of God to dwell in and as the Beloved Community. This victory of Jesus over the world is unified with faith by the Spirit so that faith itself may be called the victory over the world (1 John 5:4-5; cf. John 16:33).

That is *in nuce* the theological sense of anti-docetism; it has next to nothing to do with imagining or wanting a realistic psyche in Jesus, as modern theology imagines. It has everything to do with the Spirit's unification of the Son with us in faith, and of us all in the Son with the Father forever, when faith gives way to sight.[209] These are implications of the Spirit's unification Christologically of the Logos with the flesh in the person of Jesus Christ, and by sacramental extension of the believing human body-and-soul with crucified and risen Jesus in baptism, and yet again these baptized with one another in the *koinonia* of His Body and Blood itself unified with blessed cup and loaf. These Spirit-wrought unifications of sign and thing signified are the truth of the Incarnation in its manifold articulations. This divine action of unification is necessary. The Spirit's free coming to present Jesus Christ the Son of God can be trusted but not coerced, relied upon but not taken for granted. It is and remains Gift of the Giver, not a given. The same Spirit has withheld these unifications on the whole from God's ancient

209. See Schnelle, *Antidocetic Christology,* pp. 63-70, and Paul R. Hinlicky, "Luther's Anti-Docetism in the *Disputatio de divinitate et humanitate Christi* (1540)," in *Creator est creatura: Luthers Christologie als Lehre von der Idiomenkommunikation,* ed. O. Bayer and Benjamin Gleede (Berlin and New York: Walter de Gruyter, 2007), pp. 139-85. In reality the modern use of the concept of Docetism to criticize the New Testament and its theological tradition in early Catholicism for lack of interest in the psyche of Jesus is without historical foundation. In fact it masks a material dispute in modern theology. A preference for Jesuology over the Christology of the *fides catholica* is disguised by a historically baseless confusion of terms. Here we may recall Raymond Brown's helpful clarification that "docetism" does not stand for the sheer denial that the Logos had a real human body and soul. Rather the docetism which the First Epistle of John attacked is the belief that "the human existence of Jesus, while real, was not salvifically significant . . . [but] only a stage in the career of the divine Word and not an intrinsic component in redemption." Raymond E. Brown, *The Community of the Beloved Disciple: The Life, Loves and Hates of an Individual Church in New Testament Times* (Mahwah, NJ: Paulist, 1979), p. 113.

people and can withhold them again if foreigners grafted into Israel forget their adoption by grace, in the free advent of the Spirit. That indeed is what is occurring today in post-Christendom, where pathetically the church losing its privileges loses its faith.

This brings us to a critical juncture in our Christological inquiry in this chapter into the objectivity of faith. What can be the truth of the Incarnation, and so faith in the person of Jesus Christ, if it cannot be treated as a given but only and ever received as a gift, as attested by our reception today — as a principle internal to Christian theology — of the testimony of faithful Jews who for very good messianic reasons refuse Jesus this recognition? How can God's truth be so, as it were, internally contested? In theological shorthand the answer is already apparent: the Incarnation is inaugurated, not completed eschatology. The man who is the Son of God is a Jew, as only a Jew can be crucified as a messianic pretender. "The end of Jesus' life stands at the heart of the gospel; the historical Jesus, like the kerygmatic Christ, is the *crucified Messiah.* There is no gap between the historical Jesus and the preaching of the church; rather, there exists a close and inseparable connection."[210] This thing in the world — the empire's instrument of torture and degradation — marks the objectivity of the Incarnation, where "incarnation" refers to the coming of God as Beloved Community in Trinitarian advent. Jesus' crucifixion as Messiah or pretended Messiah is and remains the stumbling block of this disruptive objectivity that is never "overcome" but only received in faith or refused in offense. Faith understands this paradox just because it understands it to assert, as it does, an otherwise impossible contradiction. (For that is what a paradox is, a strong metaphor that works to generate a new meaning in the world by assertion of an apparent contradiction in terms.) The truth of the Incarnation is the unification of the antinomy, "the Christ" and "the Crucified" — a disruptive or absurd objectivity in the world as real as Pilate's contemptuous placard placed over the head of the impaled man.

Of what is this placard a sign? Believer and unbeliever are alike talking about the same thing in the world, whether they decode the sign ironically or Christologically, for offense or for faith. Thus faith's confession of the crucified Jew Jesus as the Son of God is not and cannot be a modalistic valuation of Jesus as more divine than other figures from the world's religions, or as divine in the same way as all the other figures, or as idolatrous in the same way. It is rather a moment in trinitarian advent: the Easter gospel of God about God, of God surpassing God by the affirmation of the One of the Three who for us and our salvation suffered to redeem us from suffering. It is a claim in the first place about Jesus as person and this person's place in the life of the Three who are the God who can and does come to the creation. In this movement of the living God, the gospel continues to call all, both Christians and adherents of other religions, to conversion of faith in the

210. Nils Alstrup Dahl, *Jesus the Christ: The Historical Origins of Christological Doctrine,* ed. D. H. Juel (Minneapolis: Fortress, 1991), p. 44.

person of Jesus Christ, as it must, because the crucified Jesus Christ is risen from death and universally active, also in the world religions, incognito yet personally. The call is heeded to the extent that Christians, first of all and bearing the burden of proof as bearers with Mary of this truth to the world, submit themselves to its claim, i.e., precisely not as a claim for the superiority of the Christian religion but of the God of the gospel who is still trying to convert "us wicked Christians" (Luther) as well as all others to new life in His kingdom.

Moreover, Christ's universal saving work — what He has done as prophet, what He is doing as priest, what He will yet accomplish as king — is in every respect the harrowing of hell. If those bound in chains could free themselves they would have no need of a liberator. Just the same, if those so liberated could not in any case have freed themselves, not merely out of weakness but out of captivity of heart and mind to the unclean spirits of malice and injustice, it would be arbitrary to exclude salvation from anyone else as worse and undeserving. Such triumphalist Christian exclusion would be just the same old malice and injustice. Because in His person, He is the God who has undertaken Godforsakenness and so has become the heavenly man who reigns in God's name until those deathly enemies that are malice and injustice are defeated, the work of Jesus Christ is the emptying of hell. This is the truth, the objectivity, of the Incarnation. Ultimately, none can be excluded except those who by invincible willfulness exclude themselves in the unforgivable sin, not against Christ who forgives all, but against the Spirit who offers but does not compel salvation as unification by repentance and faith with the Christ who unilaterally forgives.

There is, to be sure, an absurdity in this thought of final loss that must be faced — but not until the end. The visible truth of the Incarnation, well grounded but still expected, is that it will be the merciful Christ who judges the nations at the eschaton of judgment. Aforetime the truth of that judgment of mercy is the believer's justification by faith already now. That too is the truth of the Incarnation for sinners still oppressed within and without by the structures of malice and injustice. In this struggle the consolation of the Lord's Supper is given to them as manna in the wilderness, attesting already now the objectivity of grace that is Jesus Christ, the person at work on the way to the Beloved Community of God.

## Eucharistic Controversies regarding the Objectivity of Christ's Presence for Faith

Cyril of Alexandria spoke in Johannine spirit when he wrote:

> Indeed the mystery of Christ runs the risk of being disbelieved precisely because it is so incredibly wonderful. For God was in humanity. He who was above all creation was in our human condition; the invisible one was made visible in the flesh; he who is from the heavens and from on high was in the like-

ness of earthly things; the immaterial one could be touched; he who is free in his own nature came in the form of a slave; he who blesses all creation became accursed; he who is all righteousness was numbered among transgressors; life itself came in the appearance of death. All this followed because the body which tasted death belonged to no other but to him who is the Son by nature.[211]

It is this Christ for *us* — *we* who yield our members and minds to the structures of malice and injustice — that we now want to understand in what Bonhoeffer called "the pro me structure of His existence."[212] And we understand Him this way not "theoretically" but by coming to the Eucharist to meet Him bodily there as the objectivity of God's love for the world. There we come to understand theologically the glory of Jesus as the Father's Son coming to the depths to find us as really we are and not as we fancy ourselves.

If the body of Jesus belongs forever to the Son of God as the One anointed in the Spirit to be for us, and so is the One for us by and in His true obedience to death, even death upon a cross (Phil. 2:8), it is a docetic abstraction even to speak of the "real presence" of Christ in the Eucharist,[213] a redundant formulation that only has a kind of polemical sense as a contradiction to the oxymoronic notion of "symbolic presence." What matters for John, if Schnelle is right, is Christ's *bodily* presence as that flesh that once was crucified but is now vivified. To be sure, Christ can be present bodily in the Eucharist only if His body is transfigured, glorified, exalted, divinized[214] (as Paul teaches expressly in 1 Cor. 15:35-50, a passage that deeply offended Bultmann and those who follow in his train), so that it really now participates in the omnipresence of divine nature in such personal fashion as voluntarily to make itself available according to personal intention and promise, as in the *Verba,* "The Words of Institution," taken as Christ's testament. As such, the bread of the Eucharist, which signs this particular crucified but risen Body of Christ, is no longer only natural food that creatures by consuming transform into themselves as fuel for their own organisms. But those who eat the Body of

211. Cyril of Alexandria, *On the Unity of Christ,* trans. John Anthony McGuckin (Crestwood, NY: St. Vladimir's Seminary Press, 1995), p. 61.

212. Dietrich Bonhoeffer, *Christ the Center: A New Translation,* trans. E. H. Robertson (New York: Harper & Row, 1978). Bonhoeffer is critical of Chemnitz's *ubivolipraesens* in this passage; we shall pursue this difficult question regarding the personal freedom of the ascended Christ to manifest Himself in the next chapter.

213. Surprisingly, then, *pace* Jenson *ST* 2, pp. 212-20, who falls victim to an abstraction, taking body as "availability for others" rather than "availability for others" as a conception of body, as if the personal identity of Jesus Christ could be something without the particular "availability" that is His crucified and risen organism. This abstraction allows Jenson to adopt a theory of "real presence" as impanation, i.e., that the abstracted subject, Jesus, by virtue of His deity as the Logos of God, comes to make the bread His own, and thus becomes by this other body in the world available for us, as if His "body."

214. *LW* 37, pp. 195-97.

Christ are instead transformed by it to become anew and anew Christ's Body in the world. This food transforms its consumers into itself.[215] It is, therefore, as Ignatius of Antioch said, the "medicine of immortality" no less than the assurance of the forgiveness of sins. "The Eucharist is the flesh of our Savior, Jesus Christ, which suffered for our sins and which the Father by his goodness raised up."[216] As this *bodily* presence, it is the objectivity of Jesus Christ for us in that gathering in and from and for the world that is the ecclesia.

In the previous chapter, we already endorsed the Eastern view of the necessity of the *epiclesis,* the invocation of the Spirit who unifies the sign of broken bread and poured wine with the thing signified, the crucified and risen Lord Jesus in His glorified body. This invocation of the Spirit indicates the theological subjectivity of the ecclesia, that those who gather for this meal are the baptized, thus truly catechized to know the One in whom they believe. In receiving Him as promised, they discern His Body into which they are incorporated into His life's oblation, by the Spirit presenting their own bodies in Christ as living sacrifices to the Father's glory, the neighbor's good, and in hope for the world. Where this invocation of the Spirit goes wanting, however, the paradoxical nature of the bodily presence of Christ in a world where His death must be proclaimed until He comes again is forgotten. His presence then becomes a mere wonder, a supernatural trick whose significance as Word of God in conflict with the word of the serpent is forgotten, for which then we have to find a use or invent an abuse in that factory of idols that is the religion industry. Since theology in Luther's tradition was polemically forged over against such a distorted and magical view of Eucharistic sacrifice — not then as the Spirit's work as indicated by the epiclesis, but, as the old Lutherans perceived it, a profitable human work of religious bribery — it has been a long and difficult struggle to reclaim the proper meaning of Eucharistic sacrifice as a work of divine grace by the ministry of the Spirit. Assuming that gain,[217] however, it is every bit as necessary today also to reassert and argue for the classical Lutheran view of the Supper as the objectivity of God's mercy bodily given for us in the crucified and risen and therefore *bodily* present Jesus Christ — for us who are and ever remain body.

As we saw in the previous chapter, the "sacraments" so-called are not independent themes in critical dogmatics; they are the practices of faith in its particular Trinitarian articulations. Just as the practice of baptism is our practical Pneumatology, the observance of the Lord's Supper is our practical Christology. We acknowledge and receive the objectivity of God's love for the unlovely world we have made in our sin and to which we still belong in our bodies in the Lord's Supper — or we do not.[218] Paul wrote normatively: "The cup of blessing that we

---

215. *LW* 37, p. 101.
216. *The Apostolic Fathers,* p. 189.
217. Here, with Jenson, *ST* 2, p. 267.
218. An earlier version of the following material appeared in Paul R. Hinlicky, "Christ's

bless, is it not a sharing in the blood of Christ? The bread that we break, is it not a sharing in the body of Christ? Because there is one bread, we who are many are one body, for we all partake of the one bread" (1 Cor. 10:16-17). Regarding this text Werner Elert acutely observed, "From even the most ancient documents of Christianity, the Sacrament of the Altar towers like a cliff that can always be seen. This doctrine is set forth in its entirety in the First Epistle to the Corinthians. It is neither capable of nor in need of further development. It mocks every effort at spiritualization. If it actually were a hindrance in the path of justification, the question would be whether the latter would not sooner founder on it than be able to push it aside."[219] Elert rightly suggests that the encounter with the crucified and risen Christ in the feast of the Eucharist is the reality that the theological idea of justification by faith interprets — not the reverse! Christ's "unspiritualized" presence in the Supper is not a "theory." It is the phenomenon that creates the theories — even "justification by faith" — that attempt to grasp it. It gives and enacts the covenant renewal of every gathering by the nuptial vow of Christ to His gathered people, "I am yours, soul and body, and you are mine, body and soul." Paul's koinonia in the cup and loaf is the very place in the world of the joyful exchange.

On reflection, then, the traditional dogmatic title, "real presence," is not a little odd, for the notion of presence, "being there," entails reality in the concrete sense of occupying some place in the world. To be present then means that "something" is there in "someplace." Thus the combination of words, "real" and "presence," sounds redundant. What other kind of presence could there be than "real," that is, circumscribed, mapable, locatable in the world? Even when Paul the Apostle warns the Corinthians that in spite of his physical absence, he will be present in Spirit to judge their behavior (1 Cor. 5:3), his meaning is that he nonetheless will be there in the power of God's Spirit — so that they had better behave! So the idea is that by the Spirit there are ways of being circumscribed, mapable, locatable beyond natural human powers. We can doubt that Paul's claim to be present "in the Spirit" is possible. Or we can imagine that not every kind of presence has to be corporal. But these questions about the "mode" of presence are logically secondary to the fundamental consideration, namely, that presence as such implies concrete reality, i.e., simultaneity in time and proximity in space of something in relation to something else. If this is not what we mean by "presence," we are using the term in confused and equivocal fashion, as for example, in the oxymoron "symbolic presence" to say that by means of a sign I am thinking of an object that is absent. But in fact that is the nature of signs as such, which are linguistic tokens for discussion of items apart from their immediate presence

Bodily Presence in the Holy Supper: Real or Symbolic?," *Lutheran Forum* 33, no. 3 (Fall 1999): 24-28.

219. Werner Elert, *The Structure of Lutheranism,* trans. Walter A. Hansen (St. Louis: Concordia, 1962), p. 320.

to the senses. That is why Luther could specify that in philosophy the sign marks the absence of the thing, but in theology the sign is its presence. For theology is knowledge of God in the Spirit by His sign, the man Jesus.

If we say that the body and blood of Christ are present in the Lord's Supper, it is grammar and exegesis, not theology let alone metaphysics, to elucidate that claim this way: in this ceremony, with this bread and wine, the *man* Christ is present, i.e., as His *body-and-blood human reality born of Mary and suffered under Pontius Pilate* — or, He is not there as such at all. How this may be true is quite another question, and whether we should have to believe it in the sense of a binding conviction of faith is yet another question. But that this is the promise and claim being made in the instituting words of Christ, "This is my Body," or in the Johannine paraphrase, "The bread I will give for the life of the world is my flesh," is fundamental. According to Luther's conviction, as we shall see, the man Christ wills to be present according to His concrete humanity, "in His body and blood." Everything will be distorted if this claim to truth is not firmly grasped as promising what in fact it promises, however scientifically or metaphysically difficult we find that promise to be.

The traditional usage of "real presence," then, seems to represent a kind of emphatic polemical rhetoric that wants to insist: not just "apparently" as in an apparition, or "verbally" as in a sign as usual filling in for an absent referent, or "symbolically" as in an image resembling the original as a replica, but "really" present, present in the basic sense of the word, simultaneous in time and proximate in space, here and now. The oddly emphatic rhetoric of "real presence," then, unsurprisingly betrays a history of theological controversy. Under the influence of neo-Platonic dualism, Augustine introduced into Western Christianity the idea of a "symbolic presence" to interpret the Lord's Supper as a sign pointing away to the thing signified.[220] To be sure, in Augustine himself this recourse to neo-Platonism in regard to the Lord's Supper is far from the fully ramified symbolic doctrines found in later Eucharistic theologies that appeal to him. Augustine, as we shall shortly note, does not yet face a decision about what the signs of bread and cup actually refer to, what "body" of Christ they are signing, but can leave the matter vague.[221] In the history of theology, the emphatic notion of "real" presence, as just discussed, in any case originated in order to contradict this neo-Platonic theory of "symbolic" presence that appealed to Augustine's authority and a somewhat selective reading of his thought on the matter.

Augustine himself was originally motivated to introduce symbolism because he found repulsive the realistic impression that Christ is physically sacrificed

220. Bernhard Lohse, *A Short History of Christian Doctrine,* trans. F. Ernest Stoeffler (Philadelphia: Fortress, 1978), pp. 136-41. I am summarizing Lohse's account of Augustine in this paragraph.

221. I am grateful to Joe Mangina for a clarifying discussion of this issue of Augustine's responsibility for doctrines of "symbolic presence" (personal correspondence, 12/8/2013).

anew on the altar, then taken into the mouth, chewed, eaten, and digested. The Greek verb in John 6 means "gnawing" — a repulsive, cannibalistic image. In Augustine's reading of John 6 he found a contrast between fleshly and spiritual eating that seemed to support a rejection of realistic gnawing on Jesus' flesh. Augustine took Jesus' statement at the end of the Bread of Life discourse as the hermeneutical key: "It is the spirit that gives life; the flesh is useless. The words that I have spoken to you are spirit and life" (John 6:63). Augustine understood this to mean that "faith" in the Word of Jesus as such is the true, spiritual eating and drinking of Christ. Such faith feeds on Jesus' words, which are spirit and life, not literally on His body and blood. Indeed, to imagine a literal eating and drinking of His body and blood, as did the Jews in Capernaum (John 6:59) who took offense at Jesus' teaching, is to commit the same error. So Augustine regarded as error any realistic understanding of Jesus' words, "my flesh is true food and my blood is true drink. Those who eat my flesh and drink my blood abide in me, and I in them" (John 6:55-56), and from his time on this error was named "Caperneticism," after the Jews in Capernaum. Thus the West's greatest father, Augustine, taught that in the Eucharist Christ is not really, but rather symbolically present. The symbols of broken bread and poured wine, that is to say, call to mind the Word of Jesus to which faith adheres, passing mentally from the sensible symbol to its prototype, His sacrifice on Calvary, for the soul's edification.

If the notion of "real" presence sounded odd, the notion of "symbolic" presence is odder still. The notion depends on a series of kindred distinctions, indeed on a series of ontological gaps: between a sensible impression and a supersensible mental conception; between the external message regarding grace and the internal experience of grace; between the physical element and the spiritual blessing; between Jesus who was crucified and the risen Lord. For Augustine, the term "body of Christ," properly speaking, refers to the glorified body of Jesus of Nazareth which resides circumscribed in heaven (until the last day when Jesus Christ visibly returns in glory). This body of Christ in heaven is the thing signified in the Lord's Supper, the sign pointing us away from itself to the thing signified as something other than itself. This sign that points to Jesus Christ in heaven is the broken bread and poured cup of the Lord's Supper, illustrating physically and so reminding mentally of His earthly sojourn and sacrifice as the path He trod among us on the way to His present heavenly reality, the way in which we are now to follow.

As a result, the signs of bread and cup are and should be appropriate signs that can serve as effective pointers to the intended reality. As visible signs they should correspond to the reality somehow, picturing the reality to which they point in some effective and illustrative way. For example, if we served pizza pie and Coca-Cola in the Lord's Supper, it would be grotesque parody, because these foods have inappropriate associations. Signs, especially visible signs, images, icons are fluid but not arbitrary. A good, strong visible sign that illustrates would be similar enough to the thing signified that the sign and the reality would have something in common. There would be some analogy in being between them — as we see in the Bread of Life discourse of John 6: as bread feeds the body for temporal life, the Bread of Life feeds the embodied soul for eternal life. Consequently, through this analogy or partial correspondence between the intended reality and the sign, it can be said that to some extent the reality is present in the sign — functionally, efficaciously. The reality "participates" in the sign by virtue of the common being they share. That would be the sense of speaking of symbolic presence: the heavenly or spiritual reality expresses itself to a degree through the earthly image or picture of it and puts itself into effect accordingly. So a sign is neither arbitrary nor empty.

But here symbolic presence stumbles upon a fundamental theological ambivalence. What is to be illustrated by the visible words of wine and bread? The past event of Golgotha? Or the present reality of the Lord's heavenly life? Are they symbols of the broken body and shed blood of Jesus who died? Or of heavenly food in the heavenly banquet with the exalted Christ? Of course, the thing signified is both. But it is hard enough for an image effectively to illustrate, taking a snapshot so to speak of some fixed thing. It is even more so when the objectivity intended is personal and dynamic, and there is a lack of clarity about the way in which a person can and indeed must also be an object in the world. The words inherited in the biblical tradition point to the present gift of the very body born of Mary that hung on the tree as itself foretaste of the heavenly feast, but the theory of sign and thing signified would seem to have to choose between the traditional signs of broken bread and poured cup illustrating Jesus' bodily death and the present reality of His heavenly life, that is, between Zwingli and Calvin. For the main purpose of the idea of symbolic presence is to draw attention to the distance between the sign and what it signifies, the reality. In this fundamental intention, symbolism contradicts the intention of realism, which wants to point to the unification of the sign and the reality, concretely, the bread of the Supper and the Body of Christ.

Yet as applied to the Lord's Supper, the symbolic approach remains attractive for several important theological reasons. First, to our sight the bread and the wine of the Eucharist remain bread and wine, a fact that the symbolic approach does not obscure but rather insists upon. That fact could be theologically important in accenting the distinction between the present time of hope and expectation in our yet untransformed existence and the future time of fulfillment and glory in the kingdom of God. In other words, the symbolic approach wants to insist that the true body of Christ is still future for us, still distant from us, and thus will only come and so become visible on the last day. So Calvin taught that in the Supper the Spirit raises us to Christ in heaven by way of anticipation of the glory to come. The distinction between the sign of mere bread and the reality of Christ's glorified, risen body thus serves to emphasize that our real hope of salvation must look forward to nothing less than sharing in His resurrection. The Lord's Supper points us to, and encourages us toward, that eschatological hope by proclaiming the Lord's death until He comes again by the figures of bread and wine. The Lord's Supper should not then become a false alternative to the true hope of the future resurrection, as if in eating the bread and the wine we already had reached salvation in its fullness.

A second example of the theological value of the symbolic approach: if the sign has significance insofar as it corresponds to the thing signified, this requires that our liturgical practice carefully attend to this correspondence for the sake of clear communication of the gospel. We must be liturgically careful to see that the signs make sense, that they function as "visible words" illustrative of the reality intended. Given the ambiguity and fluidity of signs, the capacity of the sign to signify the saving, spiritual reality depends on this liturgical attentiveness. To illustrate: if we use little wafers or bit-sized diced cubes of Wonder Bread prepared in advance for individual consumption, this "sign" signifies that the Lord's Body is not a partaking of one loaf which unites all in a common meal. Rather it signifies that the Lord's Body is intended from the beginning for individual consumption and private use. The use of individual wafers then signifies something other about the Lord's Body than does the use of a whole loaf. The sign that is given this way is not an indifferent thing; it communicates. The use of bread is supposed to signify our common belonging to the one Lord who in His own body on the tree reconciled us and in this way points to our unification with Him. It follows that the use of individual wafers would be a *false* signification insofar as it contradicts Paul's express teaching on the significance of the symbol of the one loaf.

It is ironical that realists are often indifferent, even blind and deaf, to the liturgical import of such practices. The reasoning is not hard to discover. They think that it "really is" the body and blood of Christ, no matter how we treat or use or practice the Supper. The signals we give liturgically make no serious difference provided we verbalize "real presence." It is truly and validly Christ's body and blood, no matter whether the people hear and understand Christ's promise in the words of Institution; no matter whether our posture, our prayers, our preaching, our bodily attitudes correspond to the reality or not. No possible liturgical malfeasance or incompetence in the Supper can invalidate its reality as body and blood of Christ.

By contrast, symbolists have to take the illustrative correspondence between the sign and our liturgical practice very seriously because the significance of the Lord's Supper depends on it. (This is true also of Zwinglians, whose folksy practice of the Supper shouts out disbelief in Catholic hocus-pocus.) To continue the previous illustration: Because, in the first place, the eschatological redemption that Christ will bodily bring is still future, and because, in the second place, our true relation to that future redemption is symbolized in the signs of the Lord's Supper by which "we proclaim the Lord's death until he comes," it follows that we need those signs to communicate this hope accurately and clearly to us in our present trouble. It is through these signs that we are established in and directed toward our true hope. Our salvation does not consist in the bread and wine of the Supper, but in the coming Christ to whom they point. Therefore, this bread and wine must clearly, effectively, and exclusively point away from themselves to Christ who died once for all and will come again in power and great glory. That is precisely their function as signs.

We can and should grant the theologically important reasons for appreciating certain emphases in the symbolical approach. Nevertheless there are objections to this approach, beginning with the fact that, Augustine notwithstanding, it does not cohere well with the faith of the church (Apology X).[222] The Middle Ages witnessed extended disputes between realists and symbolists in which the tension between the faith of the church based on 1 Corinthians 10:16-17 and Augustine's neo-Platonic hermeneutic came to expression. Luther, to my knowledge, was the first to state a strictly grammatical objection to the dualism of the symbolic approach. He objected to any attempt to take the verb "to be" as itself symbolical or metaphorical, as if "to be" really meant "to signify." According to this latter thinking, as we have been discussing, "This [bread] is my body" really means "This [bread] signifies my body." For Luther, the grammatical sense is rather "This [sign of bread broken and distributed] is my body."

Luther's objection to symbolism begins with grammar and exegesis where the Bible is the matrix of theological knowledge. The basic claim of symbolism, that the verb "to be" here means "to signify," involves us in a grammatical confusion which makes all biblical interpretation arbitrary. In this way Luther opposed Zwingli at the Marburg Colloquy in 1529. Zwingli had argued (in the Augustinian, symbolic way) that the body of Jesus had literally risen through the clouds on Ascension Day and was physically located in heaven above at spatial remove from us. That is the reality. Therefore, the words "This is my body" must mean "This [earthly] bread signifies my body," namely, it points away to the one that is now above in heaven. Luther's objection to Zwingli's reasoning sometimes seems quite stubborn. "It is written, Take, eat, this is my Body, and for this reason one must do it and believe it at all costs. One must do this! One must do this!"[223] Repeatedly he refused to budge beyond the rejoinder, "Dear Zwingli, you cannot assume that 'to be' means 'to signify,' you have to prove it!" Whether and how "body" here is figurative has to be demonstrated, not assumed as a matter of principle. "Many metaphors are found in Holy Scripture. This I grant. But that here — 'This is my body' — a metaphor is present — this you must prove."[224] (Let me note for the sake of semantic clarity that all parties here use the term "metaphor" loosely for what contemporary theory distinguishes as "simile," namely, a comparison in which the lesser known is illuminated by the better known. In contemporary

---

222. *BC,* pp. 184-85.

223. "The Marburg Colloquy," in *Great Debates of the Reformation,* ed. Donald L. Ziegler (New York: Random House, 1969), p. 79.

224. "The Marburg Colloquy," p. 79.

theory, metaphor is taken more precisely as a rhetorical contradiction that references a new meaning in the world.)[225]

Luther's basic contention in this apparent stubbornness is hermeneutical. To argue *a priori* that "to be" must mean "to signify" is fundamental error, for it conceals the fact that in a wholly arbitrary way in regard to theology as interpretation in the biblical matrix Zwingli has taken the story of the Ascension literally in order to deliteralize the *Verba*. But how does Zwingli know that heaven is a local place above in which Jesus now physically resides so that Jesus cannot be simultaneously present in the Lord's Supper in His own body and blood? Such assumptions must be tested. Zwingli asserted, "One and the same body cannot possibly be in different places." To which Luther again with apparent stubbornness replied, "I ask you, why not accept a figure of speech in the words, 'He ascended into heaven' — and let the text of the Lord's Supper stand as it is?"[226] In fact, Luther is not being stubborn. A basic theological choice is involved. Should we interpret the Ascension to heaven symbolically in light of the bodily presence of Christ in the Lord's Supper? Or should we interpret the Lord's Supper symbolically in light of a literal Ascension to heaven? How could we ever decide this? Luther's grammatical and hermeneutical point is that it cannot be decided *a priori* on the basis of the confused idea that "to be" is itself a metaphor that really means "to signify." For by this principle one could as arbitrarily insist that Zwingli's contention that Christ is at the right hand of God is symbolic.

So Luther actually taught. God does not literally have a right hand. This simile signifies God's majestic power. The meaning is that the man Jesus is invested with God's royal authority. From this we see that Luther's objection was not against symbolic interpretation as such, which he himself was willing to use to deliteralize biblical language if and when required by consequent theological thinking according to the analogy of faith. His objection was against arbitrary procedure concealing the theological agenda of the neo-Platonic dualism of God and world. Whether something is simile or metaphor or not has to be decided case by exegetical case. Theological interpretation would otherwise become completely arbitrary, and worse, to overcome such chaos it would have to be governed by other, hidden, unexamined ideas of what is appropriate or possible for God to do. Ultimately it is this *a priori* reasoning or philosophizing about who and what God is apart from the divine self-donation in Christ that Luther opposes. All true theology, he argued, proceeds *a posteriori* from the divine self-communication regarding what God in fact has done and given in Christ. In this connection Luther made a fascinating statement to which we shall return, "I wish to avoid distressing arguments about *whether the presence is real or not*. This is no concern of mine. It is not argument of this nature, based on reason, but scriptural passages

225. *RPTD,* pp. 153-59.
226. "The Marburg Colloquy," p. 91. See Jenson, *ST* 2, p. 254.

of clarity and certainty that are called for."[227] Note that Luther here associates the long medieval Western dispute between realists and symbolists with philosophical reason, which he wishes to leave behind. Instead of this disputation, Luther repeatedly pressed Zwingli and his colleagues on the basic hermeneutical question: If certain texts "seem to you to stand in opposition to the words of the Lord's Supper, why not find a figure of speech in them rather than in the words of the Lord's Supper?"[228] Why indeed? By what principle of biblical exegesis do we decide whether any given predication is literal or figurative?

Among figures of speech, we should distinguish minimally between metaphor, similitude, and synecdoche. In ordinary language, we usually decide whether a figurative interpretation is required on the basis of the practical import of a particular predication within a context of possibilities. If I say to my sweetheart, "We will fly on the wings of our love," I am not likely suggesting that we jump off the roof to travel through the air. As Janet Soskice has taught us, the very incongruity of that literal interpretation is what makes the metaphor effective as a figure for the ecstasy of love.[229] We are compelled to the metaphorical interpretation because of the real incongruity between the subject (our love) and the predicate (wings to fly on) which is created precisely by the direct, straightforward meaning of "to be" to assert univocally an identification. If the verb "to be" were not working univocally to assert a straightforward identification, there would be no surprising incongruity generating a delightful new meaning of love as ecstasy. But this is precisely what metaphors do by making unusual, paradoxical, apparently contradictory assertions. Metaphor consists in such jarring identifications. And this metaphorical work in turn depends on the nonsymbolic, literal meaning of the verb "to be" to put terms into positive relations of proximity and simultaneity. For the same reason, metaphors rightly decoded have reference in the world. If I speak about flying with my sweetheart, I am really denoting our erotic desire and characterizing it in an intelligible way. If we jumped from the roof, however, we would have both literally and fatally misunderstood the reference.

We can compare this understanding of metaphor to synecdoche. Synecdoche is a figure of speech in which the part is designated by the whole, the general by the particular or vice versa. Synecdoche also depends on the nonsymbolic, ordinary meaning of the verb "to be" to assert an identification in time and space. In the following passage from Luther in the Marburg Colloquy, he is not understanding "metaphor" in the way Soskice has explained, but rather taking "metaphor" as similitude, as comparison by which the lesser known is made clearer to understanding by relating it to something better known. So we should read his term "metaphor" as "similitude" in the following passage.

227. "The Marburg Colloquy," p. 93.
228. "The Marburg Colloquy," p. 94.
229. Janet Soskice, *Metaphor and Religious Language* (Oxford: Clarendon, 1987).

When the king says to the servant, "Bring me my sword," he really wants the scabbard brought along with it, even though he did not expressly command this in the words that he used. Or one speaks of the mug and means the beer. Hence the words, "This is my body" are an encompassing mode of expression. The body is in the bread as the sword is in the scabbard. The text compels this mode of expression. Metaphor, however, obscures the main point — the body, [which it treats as a] figure of the body . . . ! [This] is not the effect of synecdoche. . . . A figurative mode of expression obscures the essence and leaves the empty form. The synecdoche is not a comparison — no; this is here in this place and it is within that. So it is here, "This is my body."[230]

Note, then, that Luther actually rejects "transubstantiation" by appeal to synecdoche in order to assert a co-presence of bread and Body of Christ. By contrast, in the similitude a sign stands for something that is absent, as if we were to say, "The bread is like the body of Christ to which it points." That is precisely what symbolists in the Augustinian line want to say theologically. But in synecdoche a sign stands for something that is present with another, in it, or under it. The beer is there, inside the mug that we asked for at the restaurant when we said, "Mr. Waiter, Please bring me another mug!" According to Luther philosophy thinks in similitudes since it only knows the closed system of being in which better-known things can illuminate more obscure things; but theology thinks in synecdoche because it learns of the new and coming world of God inaugurated in Christ who is paradoxically present *sub contrario* to bring to naught the things that are. In this tense existence between the already and the not yet, theological subjectivity is sustained in the community's eschatological meal, a sharing of the body of the One whose death is proclaimed until He comes. This is a hermeneutical principle of theology. It cuts both to the left and to the right. It means that the ministry of the church is not a substitute for an absent Lord, but service to the Lord who is coming and who as such becomes present in a paradoxical predication in and against the conditions of malice and injustice; the Christ as the crucified body, the risen One's Body as broken bread and wine poured out.

With this argument, Luther certainly must be understood to sympathize with the tradition of realistic interpretation of the Lord's Supper. Luther, never known to avoid hyperbole, once declared that he would rather drink Christ's blood with the pope than mere wine with the fanatics.[231] Yet in fact Luther's argument in a decisive way transcends the traditional conflict between realists and symbolists. The statement of Bernhard Lohse's influential textbook on the history of dogma, which represents a fairly common understanding today, is simply wrong. He writes that during the post-Augustinian, medieval Eucharistic

---

230. "The Marburg Colloquy," p. 95.
231. *LW* 37, p. 317.

controversies "the two basic interpretations of the Supper which are actually possible had been thought through, and clearly articulated. Even the Reformation could not go beyond the two leading motifs, namely, realism and symbolism."[232] Lohse sees here an exclusive alternative in which the notion of the sacrifice of Christ in the Mass is associated with realism while the sacrifice of praise is associated with symbolism.[233] This is indeed how Zwingli saw things — who went so far as to accuse Luther with his perceived realism of "reviving the Papacy" and restoring the sacrifice of the Mass. But Luther's actual position cannot be fit into either of these categories.

In the Marburg Colloquy Luther did not so much argue for a realistic doctrine of the (redundant) Real Presence (which he would have had to try to make theoretically intelligible) as assert that Christ is present according to His promise *in His own, hence, true body and blood.* These two contentions are not the same. Recall the comment earlier, "I wish to avoid distressing arguments about whether the presence is real or not. This is no concern of mine." Luther repeatedly insisted that the "mode" of Christ's bodily presence is beyond human comprehension so that, strictly speaking, any attempt to comprehend how it is possible misses the point of the "miracle." The point is not how Christ is present, whether "really" or "symbolically," but rather that He promises to be present "in His body and blood," that is, according to His specifically crucified, but now risen humanity. The latter is an explication of the belief, not an explanation of it; it tells what is believed, not how it is possible. With this subtle shift, however, what we have from Luther is not so much another version of the realistic theory as opposed to the symbolic. What we have is a doctrine of Christ's *bodily, creaturely presence* in the Lord's Supper. The point is not to say that somehow Christ really, really, really is present, but that the Jesus who died for us all under Pontius Pilate is present. Peter Brunner has expressed this subtle accent pointedly:

> The particular feature is, first of all, the concreteness of this communion with the *Christus pro nobis* vouchsafed in Holy Communion. The selfsame true humanity of Jesus which He received from His mother Mary becomes present to us under the Eucharistic food. Here Jesus Christ steps into our midst not only in the omnipresence of His deity . . . now He actually gives His bodily humanity in substantial identity with His earthly body, to everyone who receives the bread and the wine in the Holy Communion. The Eucharistic real presence vouchsafes to the congregation of disciples the continuation of the physical presence of Jesus' true humanity in a new, transformed, end-time manner. In the Eucharistic real presence the congregation of disciples has in its midst the same Jesus who lay in the manger, who traversed Galilee, who suffered in Jerusalem, and who died on Golgotha . . . [who at the same time

232. Lohse, *A Short History*, p. 145.
233. Lohse, *A Short History*, p. 141.

is] the exalted Christ who is seated at the right hand of God and who will one day return visible to all.[234]

The gospel of Jesus Christ does not consist simply in the fact of the coming to us of God, but in the coming to us of God *as man, as this man, as Jesus* who lived for sinners, by His death made peace for them, and by His resurrection comes to them as He promises in the meal of the new testament to renew them until He comes again in final glory. Likewise, the evangelical significance of the Lord's Supper does not simply consist in the real presence of Christ, howsoever that may be understood, but this presence "in His body and blood," His presence *as the Man* who lived and died and reigns for us. This is certainly a doctrine of "presence." As Brunner stresses polemically, "Holy Communion is the opposite of a festival commemorating a dead man! It is a meal fellowship with Him who lives, and who, by reason of His resurrection victory, is actually present among His followers through the administration of Holy Communion."[235] Yet if He is present because He is risen from the dead, then He is present in and as this risen humanity. The accent does not fall on the reality of the presence as such. It falls on the *bodily* reality of the One who becomes present in, with, and under the bread and the wine. With this accent, the old conflict between realism and symbolism is in fact transcended.

For surely the bread remains bread and as such it signs the body of Christ as something substantially other than itself. The bread is not substantially transformed into the body of Christ (as the theory of transubstantiation teaches). Rather the two concretely coexist, the bread indicating as a sign the Body which has come, in the action of the Lord's Supper, by virtue of the Body's Head, who has promised so to come to the community of faith, namely, the very community that calls upon the Spirit now to unite for them the sign and the thing signified in the epiclesis. To be sure, just as Jesus signs the Son of God and becomes Jesus Christ the Son of God where and when the Spirit unites the sign with the thing signified for faith or offense, so also the bread becomes the Body of Christ for faith's edification (or poison for unbelief). Neither Jesus nor bread is a substance in itself that persists unrelated when the Spirit unites it with the thing signified. A "realistic" understanding of the presence of Christ in the Lord's Supper therefore does not have either to argue for transubstantiation of the elements or to dispute the important truths expressed by the symbolic approach. Indeed, it can and should incorporate the valuable eschatological and liturgical accents of the symbolist tradition. Luther's companion Melanchthon basically became a symbolist, who laid the stress on the bread and wine of the Supper as efficacious signs. He regarded the bread and wine as signs that give precisely what they represent, the

234. Peter Brunner, *Worship in the Name of Jesus,* trans. M. H. Bertram (St. Louis: Concordia, 1968), p. 183.

235. Brunner, *Worship,* p. 171.

body of Christ, through the divine power of the Word of God. Luther never denied or rejected these accents of the symbolist approach, especially when symbol was understood in this dynamic and efficacious way. As he said at Marburg: "But when something is said by the Supreme Majesty, by God, then this is not merely to 'signify,' but to achieve and bring forth that which is signified. . . ."[236] Certainly the almighty power of God's eternal Word is the ultimate ground of Christ's presence in the Eucharist, as we shall see in considering the Christological doctrine of the *communicatio idiomatum.* But Luther has something even better to teach us. What that is cannot simply be identified with the previous, medieval tradition of Eucharistic realism.

Rather than speak of Luther's doctrine of the Real Presence (and thus perpetuate the essentially Augustinian frame of reference in the dualism of sign and thing signified) we should speak of *the doctrine of Christ's bodily presence* in the Lord's Supper. If we look at the actual language of the confessional writings, this is what we will find. In the Large Catechism, Luther defined the Sacrament of the Altar as "the true *body and blood* of our Lord Christ in and under the bread and the wine which we Christians are commanded by Christ's word to eat and drink" (the *manducatio oralis*).[237] In the Smalcald Articles, following upon the fierce attack on the sacrificial Roman Mass, Luther writes, "We hold that the bread and the wine in the Supper are the true *body and blood* of Christ and that these are given and received not only by godly but also by wicked Christians" (the *mandicatio indignorum*).[238] Augsburg Confession X declares concisely, "the true *body and blood* of Christ are really present in the Supper of our Lord under the form of bread and wine and are there distributed and received."[239] The Apology points to the chief Pauline text, 1 Corinthians 10:16, and notes that "the bread would not be a participation *in the body of Christ but only in his spirit* if the Lord's *body* were not truly present."[240] What is to be affirmed with the Roman Church and the Eastern Church is "the *bodily presence* of Christ."[241] Melanchthon says that Lutherans too defend "the doctrine received in the whole church — that in the Lord's Supper the *body and blood* of Christ are truly and substantially present and are truly offered with those things that are seen, bread and wine." Importantly, he adds that "we are talking about the presence of the living Christ, knowing that 'death no longer has dominion over him'"[242] — a reference to Christ in His risen glory. Later, the Formula of Concord will pick up the accent on "the bodily presence of Christ": "if *the body* of Christ were not truly and essentially present and were received only according to its virtue and operation, then the bread

---

236. "Marburg Colloquy," p. 88.
237. *BC,* p. 447, emphasis added.
238. *BC,* p. 311, emphasis added.
239. *BC,* p. 34, emphasis added.
240. *BC,* p. 179, emphasis added.
241. *BC,* p. 179, emphasis added.
242. *BC,* p. 179, emphasis added.

could not be called participation in the body but in the spirit, the virtue, and the benefits of Christ, as the Apology argues and concludes."[243] There is no need to belabor the point with further quotations. The sixteenth-century confessional doctrine prefers to speak of "the bodily presence of Christ" in the Supper rather than the "real presence." Two questions need to be posed about this. Why this new emphasis on the bodily presence of Christ in the Supper? And how is this "bodily" presence to be taken without absurdity?

Historically, the first question is extremely important because to Zwingli, Bucer, later Calvin, and most Protestantism thereafter (including much Lutheranism since the Enlightenment and Pietism), it seemed that the conviction about Christ's bodily presence in the Supper contradicted justification by faith alone. If faith alone feeds on Christ alone, what further need is there of the body of Christ in the Lord's Supper? If spiritual communion with Christ is made to depend once again on physical sacraments, baptism, the Lord's Supper, the Church's ministry, and so on, is that not precisely what Zwingli alleged against Luther, a revival of the papacy? Melanchthon, as Elert points out, had already clarified the question in the Apology. Faith alone means that "we rule out the thought of merit. We do not rule out the word or the sacraments, as our opponents falsely allege."[244] The Spirit gives justifying faith in Christ through the external word and sacraments, because here Christ comes to give Himself according to His promise. But that implies, does it not, that faith is concretely based on the gospel-in-the-sacraments? More precisely, that true faith is faith in *that* Christ who concretely gives Himself *in His bodily existence for us* through the Eucharist? If we are not thinking of Christ who is and can be present "in His body and blood," are we not thinking of *some other* Christ? Is not the issue here Christological? Is not the question *what* faith justifies, *who* Christ is whom faith believes?

Luther thought so. He feared that the emergence of a general "Protestant" front against Rome would prove to be only an apparent consensus. Luther explicitly noted at the outset of the Marburg Colloquy, in reference to the Arian and Nestorian tendencies evident in Bucer's Strasbourg: "without unanimity in these matters, it would be pointless to discuss the real significance of the Lord's Supper."[245] Why? Because faith only justifies on account of the One on whom faith depends, Jesus Christ the Son of God, present as the person at work in the faith that depends on Him by the joyful exchange. The disagreement about the Lord's Supper in the final analysis betrays divergent Christologies. Elert noted in this connection how reluctant Luther was to give any rationalistic justification for the necessity of his doctrine of the Supper against the criticism "that the real presence of Christ is neither profitable nor necessary."[246] As Luther put it in

---

243. *BC,* p. 579, emphasis added.
244. *BC,* p. 117; Elert, *Structure,* p. 320.
245. "Marburg Colloquy," p. 74.
246. Elert, *Structure,* p. 316.

Marburg, "my Lord Jesus Christ can easily do what he wishes, and that he wishes to do this is attested by his own words."[247] Only on this basis can we proceed to discuss why the bodily presence is necessary and profitable. One must reason in theology by *nachdenken, a posteriori* not *a priori;* theology is not speculation but *faith seeking understanding.* One must look and see what Christ does and gives in this His self-donation and theologically "think after" the gift to comprehend our true, not apparent need of it. From this angle, Elert detected four "effects" of the bodily presence of Christ in the Supper, as the early Lutherans understood it.

First, the innermost nature of the Church as a communion in Christ's body is therewith established. "The church is not a society, but a communion." It is *Gemeinschaft,* not *Gesellschaft* according to its true being in Christ, though it is also as member of the common body an organized polity in the world. Second, the remembrance of Christ is itself the work of God, "not the thought of man." How we are to remember Jesus is not an arbitrary matter at our free disposal. We are to remember Jesus as He wished to be remembered, not as we wish. When we gather as the church we are to remember Jesus by celebrating the Lord's Supper, *in this mandated way* proclaiming His death until He comes again. Third, over against preaching which is addressed to the public, in the Supper Christ's salvation is "individualized in an unambiguous manner" in the act of distribution. The body and blood of Christ are given "to me" and "for me" in particular. Fourth, and most importantly, the forgiveness of sins is not understood as some concept or idea that the believer appropriates intellectually. Rather forgiveness, bringing life and salvation, simply is the fruit of fellowship with the man Jesus, who lived for sinners and died for sinners and reigns for sinners. Forgiveness is to be appropriated personally and concretely through fellowship with Jesus "in His body and blood." We have His benefits when, and only when, we have Him, this Man for Others. And we have Him in the actual act in space and time in which He gives Himself to us — the Holy Communion.[248]

Reasoning in this *a posteriori* way, we can say that the doctrine of Christ's bodily presence in the Supper articulates a conception of salvation as occurring in space and time in a public and social encounter with Jesus Christ. Brunner puts it this way: "Jesus' Savior-activity, His Savior-suffering, His Savior-victory achieved for us, are *in His Body and are His Body* which we receive with the Bread."[249] His Deity helps only in and as this body-and-blood humanity. The Gospel, Luther says in the Large Catechism, is "embodied" (German, *gesteckt ist;* Latin, *conclusus est*),[250] that is, circumscribed in the Lord's Supper. In that act of embodying the gospel, the church of the baptized is gathered as the Pauline fellowship *(koinonia)* in the Body of Christ. Oecolampadius, Zwingli's colleague in the dispute with Luther,

247. "Marburg Colloquy," p. 93.
248. Elert, *Structure,* pp. 316-19.
249. Brunner, *Worship,* p. 175, emphasis added.
250. *BC,* p. 450.

had said at Marburg, "The church is founded on the words, 'You are the Son of the living God' [Matt. 16:16], not on the words, 'This is my body' [Matt. 26:26]," in this way basing the church on the human act of confession of faith in response to revelation, overlooking the fact that Baptism and Eucharist are the concrete acts of revelation that engender faith and bear fruit in faith's action of confession (as we shall more fully discuss below in Chapter Eight). The church, in other words, is already there for the individual believer as the offered "sacraments," that is, as Christ existing as community, before any individual is drawn into this community and enabled personally to confess the faith — provided that by "church" and "community" and "sacraments" we truly are denominating Christ as saving Lord, not conscripting Christ to the religion business. As it is the Baptism into Christ's ownership that admits persons to the meal of the New Covenant, the meal is the gospel itself in one of its distinct forms — the meal practice that sustains and renews the life together of the justified in the interim between Ascension and Parousia.

From these differing starting points, therefore, follow diverging conceptions of what the fellowship of the church really is. Zwingli rejected the Lord's Supper celebrated by an unworthy pastor or received by unworthy people and called it "absurd" that the ungodly could produce the body of Christ. But in the Large Catechism, Luther wrote "that it is the highest wisdom to realize that this sacrament does not depend on our worthiness . . . on the contrary, we come as poor miserable men, precisely because we are unworthy."[251] Just such a joyful feast of reconciled and reconciling sinners in the fellowship of Jesus is what the church of the gospel really is and ought to be. Precisely in receiving Jesus in "His body and blood," we become His community of mercy, His body of the forgiven and forgiving. That joyful transaction really, actually, physically occurs in the Lord's Supper. In eating Christ's body, we become the body of Christ.

So what is at stake in the question of the nature of the Lord's Supper is ultimately our understanding of who Jesus Christ is by the practical test of what it means to be His people who gather as the church for the koinonia of His body and blood. At the Marburg Colloquy, Oecolampadius had argued that "Christ is always and everywhere present in his divinity, grace and power. When, however, he says that he would be absent, it must be his human nature that is absent. But if his human nature is absent, then he cannot be present in the Lord's Supper in a bodily sense."[252] On this basis, Oecolampadius exhorted Luther, "Don't cling so fast to Christ's humanity and flesh! Raise your thoughts to Christ's divinity!" To which Luther replied, "I know God only as he became human, so I shall have him in no other way."[253] At this *Christological* juncture, we reach the root of the conflict. For Luther, the saving gospel is not just that God somehow comes into contact with us, but that God becomes the particular man Jesus and so connects

---

251. *BC,* p. 473.
252. "Marburg Colloquy," p. 93.
253. "Marburg Colloquy," p. 94.

with us and thus remains connected with us forever who have fallen by sin into the destiny of death.[254] Apart from this flesh, even the Spirit of God is of no help. The Eucharistic meal is a saving communion in Jesus Christ because and only because in it Christ becomes present for us *objectively* as His own concrete body-and-blood humanity, the innocent in place of the guilty. "These leaders of the blind," Luther wrote in a parallel discussion of sacramental baptism, "are unwilling to see that faith must have something to believe — something to which it may cling and upon which it may stand. Thus faith clings to the water and believes it to be baptism. . . . Now, these people are so foolish as to separate faith from the object to which faith is attached and secured, all on the grounds that the object is something external. . . ."[255] As in the water, so in the bread and the wine Jesus Christ as promised comes as the objectivity of faith, where and when the Spirit wills.

Can this be understood without absurdity? The offense taken by the Jews at Capernaum is as old as Christianity. But the scandal of this Eucharistic teaching about feeding on the flesh and blood of Christ is not essentially different than the scandal of the Word made flesh, as the same Evangelist John emphatically teaches. As we have seen, for the early Lutherans the doctrine of Christ's bodily presence in the Supper is the concrete extension and practical actualization of their Christology. It is the practical truth of the Incarnation. Here it is not abstract contact between humanity and divinity that is saving, but the concrete life that the Son of God lived in human obedience that saves those who cannot save themselves. Apart from this particular life of self-sacrificing love, God and Son of God are of no help to us at all, no matter how close we get to them. Without this humanity, they will rather burn us alive. But Jesus in His body and blood given for us is the presence of God in the way of being the Son that truly helps. Here is the God who comes to us in Jesus, as Jesus, forever and ever Jesus. That is why Luther said at Marburg, "We hold the flesh of Christ to be very, indeed to be absolutely, necessary. No text, no interpretation, no employment of human reasoning can take it away from us."[256] This absolute insistence on Jesus as the concrete humanity of God for us who are not for God was the reason why Luther had to say to Bucer in the end, "Our spirit has nothing in common with your spirit."[257]

The difficulty of the doctrine of the bodily presence of Christ in the Eucharist is nothing but an acute because practical formulation of the difficult problem of the redeeming Incarnation itself. Whether we regard it as absurd finally stands and falls with how we regard the classical Christology that the Lutheran Eucharistic doctrine took over but also advanced. Without doubt that is how the early Lutherans tried to explain themselves, as can be seen in the Formula of Concord's Articles VII and VIII, and the Catalogue of Testimonies from the church fathers

254. Cf. Brunner, *Worship*, p. 191.
255. *BC,* p. 460.
256. "Marburg Colloquy," p. 93.
257. "Marburg Colloquy," p. 106.

appended to the Book of Concord. They appealed to the Christology of the Greek Fathers, especially Athanasius and Cyril of Alexandria and to the (neo-)Chalcedonian notion that the two natures in Christ exist in one concrete and indivisible personal union, so that each nature shares in the other by the will, the decision, the act of Christ the person at work in His messianic mission. In particular, they taught that the human nature of Christ participates in the divine predicates of majesty *(genus maiesticum),* where and when the person wills. This means that Jesus according to His human nature is established at the right hand of God's power, meaning not that He is spatially removed but rather invested with God's reign. Thus all that pertains to executing the reign of God is given to the man Christ. This in particular accounts theologically for the capacity of the one person Jesus Christ to be present in the Lord's Supper in His "body and blood," that is, according to His glorified, exalted, now majestic humanity.

For the same reason, the early Lutherans consistently and emphatically denied that in the Eucharist believers eat dead meat magically multiplied for countless Eucharists. They earnestly repudiated "Capernetic" conception of a "gross, carnal presence," because the body is given according to its new mode of existence in the resurrection as "divinized," as the "spiritual body" of 1 Corinthians 15. The body which is given in the Supper is the identical body of the man born of Mary and hung on the cross, yet it is this body according to its new, glorified, spiritual existence as they understood it, trying to follow Paul's thinking. At this point, to be sure, human imagination fails. We cannot conceive what the "spiritual" body of the Risen One is. We can only simultaneously assert its continuity in being with the earthly body that was "sown perishable," and its qualitatively new mode of existence through its personal participation in God's eternal life, as now "raised imperishable." It is pointless, once again, to ask "how" this may be. It is meant as "miracle" — though again "miracle" not as an unintelligible assertion of supernaturally warranted truth for purposes of the religion business, but rather as God's self-donation, intelligible precisely when deliteralized and decoded theologically as knowledge of God.

It is a serious question, however, whether this entire Christological development represents a mythologizing of Jesus, in which His real humanity has been irretrievably lost from sight. From the beginning that had been the fear of Luther's opponents, when they insisted that a human body cannot cease to be spatially limited without ceasing to be human. A body that participates in God's omnipresence, they said, can no longer be really human, nor is it intelligible why it should continue to be called a body. A body that ceases to be located definitely in space is no longer a body. This objection, modern as it sounds, is actually as old as Theodore of Mopsuestia, who so distinguished between the human and the divine in Jesus Christ that he virtually created two persons, the Divine Son who can be omnipresent and the human Christ who sits locally above "in heaven." We have seen how Oecolampadius voiced the same objection. But that kind of Christology was rejected in principle at Chalcedon because it tears into pieces the basic datum of faith, namely, the one concrete person Jesus Christ the Son of God, who appears in the Gospel and accordingly gives Himself to us in the Lord's Supper as the objectivity of faith.

So the argument returns again to Luther's fundamental hermeneutical stand, that all theological reasoning follows *a posteriori* from the actual act of salvation — the particular salvation, however, that redeems rather than destroys creation and so recaptures reason for service in the knowledge of God. From this angle we can say that the absurdities that are urged — about eating Jesus' flesh like a sausage, gnawing on the sandwiched Deity in our mouths — are actually quite coherently met, if one grants the appeal to the old Christology of the two natures in one Person, thought through consequently. In that case, it is the glorified body of the Risen Lord suffused with divinity that feeds believers, just as it is the very glory of the eternal Son to have descended once and for all into our sinful alienation, in order to embrace us once and for all, finally to wipe every tear from our eyes. To be human, in this Christological vision of reality, does not mean finally to be mortal, restricted, ontologically alone, a body in the sense of an absolute individual marked off from others, a profoundly walled being that ceases with death, when the walls crumble, making death the ultimate boundary of life. As the Greek fathers insisted, and Augustine too: God made us for eternal fellowship with Himself, for participation in His own eternal life — *us,* who are our bodies. This view that God has created in order to redeem and fulfill includes the "body" as the fit and inalienable vessel of the person destined for community and designed for the joyful exchanges of love. In this vision, the human body is not finally the sign signifying the reality of our ultimate aloneness before the absurdity of Lord Death. Rather the body is the sign of our destination for beloved community in the joy of the resurrection.

To be human then is to become "divine," i.e., not by a fusion of natures but in a communion of persons, that is, as creatures who come to partake in God's tri-personal exchanges of life, already now by conscientious union in faith with the Son, in fulfillment by the Spirit's glorious work of the resurrection of the body. Jesus in the interim has not ceased to be human in being raised from the dead and glorified. To the contrary, it is we sinners who cease to be human when we die in sin and perish without God. It is the fulfillment of humanity — Jesus' own, but also ours in Him and with Him, one Body through the cross — that this man in His body and blood, triumphant over death, still freely and joyfully imparts Himself to hungry, needy folk and just so makes them forever His own. In this Eucharistic self-giving, Jesus is perfectly man and perfectly God by becoming the saving Lord of perishing sinners, even as we become the Body we were meant to be in personal union with our Head — God's forever in the coming of the Beloved Community. If that is "absurd," it is the "absurdity" of God's omnipotent love for the material of this creation, object of redemption for the purpose of fulfillment. It is the "absurdity" of joyful not exploitative exchange, enjoyed already now in the Eucharist gathered from the nations on the way to the coming of the Beloved Community of God.

# CHAPTER SIX

# Christology

## Toward the Ecumenical Doctrine
## of the Eucharistic Meal

The old Lutheran theologians from the period of Orthodoxy held that the theology of the Lord's Supper is analogous to the doctrine of Christ's person. As the bread is to the Body of Christ, so the human nature is to the divine nature of the Son of God. Rejecting "Romish transubstantiation" because of its docetic implications for Christology according to this analogy, they "taught the sacramental union of the substance of the unchanged bread with the body of Christ," analogous to the personal or hypostatic union of divine and human natures in Christology: "In the same way, the passage, John 1:14, 'The Word was made flesh' [along with parallels like Col. 2:9, Acts 10:38, 2 Cor. 5:19] . . . declare[s], viz., that by the incarnation the divine essence was not changed into the human nature [nor the human essence into the divine], but that the two natures are personally united without confusion."[1] Thus a certain reading of Chalcedon that places the accent on the personal union as opposed to a natural fusion or conceptual confusion or mere conjunction provided the model of the sacramental union of bread and the Body of Christ in the Eucharist. This insight into Eucharistic doctrine as practical Christology, so to say, both gathers up the arguments from the preceding chapter and advances the case to be made in this chapter for Trinitarian Christology, i.e., for the doctrine of the *personal* union as a function of Trinitarian theology — of strong Trinitarian *personalism* as made known in the economy of salvation.

Contemporary Lutheran theologians are thinking along these lines. Because the grace to receive a gift gracefully is no less gift than the gift itself, the urgent requirement for the restoration of Eucharistic fellowship among the divided churches is, on the level of doctrine, the need for such Trinitarian Christology.

---

1. Heinrich Schmid, *The Doctrinal Theology of the Evangelical Lutheran Church,* 3rd edition (Philadelphia: Lutheran Publication Society, 1899), pp. 559-60.

Jesus Christ, who gave Himself for others once and for all, now also gives the Spirit to these others that they receive Him in repentance and faith. The Spirit, who was given to the Son by the Father that He might live for us while we were yet weak and still sinners, gives this incarnate Son to faith that believers might now live before God in love for others and hope for the world. In this reciprocity or mutuality of giving and receiving, the Spirit and the Son work out for us the self-surpassing grace of the Father in true expression of their eternal perichoresis in the divine Life. In light of such reciprocity of Word and Spirit both within and without the life of the triune God, Risto Saarinen asks, "Can it be that so much of Western theological reflection has been misguided in its focus on receiving rather than giving, or on anthropological preconditions rather than God's donative self-revelation?"[2]

In pursuing critically this question, what may be called today the Scandinavian "theology of gift"[3] works past the Pneumatological deficit of a one-sidedly forensic interpretation of the doctrine of justification. The one-sidedness of the "Word alone" in this respect had forgotten that Christ alone is never alone, but is always also the One sent to us by the Father and received by us in the Spirit along with all others gathered into the ecclesia in mission to the nations. Needing to have the Word alone do all the saving work, so to speak, in order strictly to exclude any human contribution to justification, an ironic reduction of the saving encounter with Jesus Christ to the assertion of grace as an almighty fiat forgot the centrality of the Christological "joyous exchange" in Luther[4] and correspondingly "the concept of divine self-giving [as] central to Luther's understanding of the *triune* God."[5] This polemically overwrought one-sidedness incoherently held that

---

2. Risto Saarinen, "Theology of Giving as a Contemporary Lutheran Theology," in *Transformations in Luther's Reformation Theology: Historical and Contemporary Reflections,* vol. 32, Arbeiten zur Kirchen- und Theologiegeschichte, ed. C. Helmer and B. K. Holm (Leipzig: Evangelische Verlagsanstalt, 2011), p. 148.

3. See the excellent survey in *Word-Gift-Being: Justification-Economy-Ontology,* ed. Bo Kristian Holm and Peter Widmann (Tübingen: Mohr Siebeck, 2009), pp. 1-16. See further Risto Saarinen, *God and the Gift: An Ecumenical Theology of Giving* (Collegeville, MN: Liturgical Press, 2005) and Jan-Olav Henriksen: *Desire, Gift, and Recognition: Christology and Postmodern Philosophy* (Grand Rapids: Eerdmans, 2009). In his chapter, "Anselm's *Cur Deus Homo* and Beyond," Henriksen executes a sympathetic critique of Kathryn Tanner's treatment of the atonement (pp. 269-94) that so far as I can see much parallels my own treatment of the topic in *LBC,* pp. 66-104. To put the point of the *theologia crucis* perhaps too tersely: the "penal" aspect of the atonement is not to be discarded but rather integrated with the other motifs from the New Testament, and this is possible where the "death of the sinner" in the Spirit by union with Christ crucified is received as the good news of the birthpangs of the new creation and correlated as such with Romans 8 and the theodicy of faith. I discussed Bo Holm's important contribution to this "transformation" of Lutheran theology — redeeming even Melanchthon! — in *PNT,* pp. 166-68.

4. *Word-Gift-Being,* p. 2.

5. *Word-Gift-Being,* p. 3, emphasis added.

"faith alone" justifies without a consequent accounting of faith itself in terms of the gift and self-giving of the Spirit.

This Lutheran self-criticism today may be seen to have been anticipated in the third session of the Lutheran–Roman Catholic dialogue in the USA, *The Eucharist as Sacrifice* (1967). The partners discovered that Roman Catholics in general have not distinguished between the Lutheran confession of the so-called "real presence" of Christ's body and blood in the bread and wine of the Supper and the general Protestant rejection of such a "bodily" presence. Lutherans in turn have emphatically rejected Roman Catholic sacrificial language of "offering Christ" in the Mass, "because they believed that only thus could they preserve the once-for-all character and the full sufficiency of the sacrifice of the cross and keep the Eucharist from becoming a human supplement to God's saving work, a matter of "works-righteousness."[6] By contrast with this latter dispute over the Eucharist as sacrifice, convergence on Christ's Eucharistic presence seemed not so difficult to achieve.

Both traditions acknowledge a "manifold presence of Christ," but specifically "that in the Sacrament of the Lord's Supper, Jesus Christ, true God and true man, is present wholly and entirely, in his body and blood, under the signs of bread and wine."[7] The common position entailed a "rejection of an understanding of the Sacrament as only commemorative or figurative." Rather, "the Lord's Supper is an effective sign: it communicates what it promises . . . ," not through "the faith of the believer, or through any human power, but by the power of the Holy Spirit through the word."[8] The Lutherans could even agree that "as long as Christ is sacramentally present, worship, reverence and adoration are appropriate,"[9] though disagreement continued to exist about any adoration of the consecrated elements outside the purpose for which the Supper was instituted. The sense of the Lutheran rejection of "transubstantiation," as a speculative philosophical explanation of the Eucharistic presence not to be imposed on consciences, was clarified and understood by Roman Catholics in the dialogue who themselves today search for other models of understanding than the substance/accidents scheme derived from Aristotle. Lutherans, without committing themselves to any such "theory," were willing to say: "God acts in the Eucharist, effecting a change in the elements."[10] That affirmation minimally satisfies the Roman Catholic concern to teach doctrinally that a real encounter with the crucified but risen Lord Jesus occurs in the Eucharist.

Far more problematic, then, was the idea that early Lutheranism so emphat-

---

6. *Lutherans and Catholics in Dialogue I-III,* ed. Paul C. Empie and T. Austin Murphy (Minneapolis: Augsburg, n.d.), III:189.

7. *Lutherans and Catholics in Dialogue,* III:192.

8. *Lutherans and Catholics in Dialogue,* III:193.

9. *Lutherans and Catholics in Dialogue,* III:194.

10. *Lutherans and Catholics in Dialogue,* III:195.

ically rejected as idolatry, namely, that in the Eucharist the church, or the priest on behalf of the people, offers Christ to God as an expiation for sins by right of the power "to confect" the transubstantiation, a right and power provided by God in sacerdotal ordination. Here it helps to recall the precise complaint of the Augsburg Confession in Article 24. Melanchthon wrote:

> The Mass came to be misused . . . by turning it into a sort of fair, by buying and selling it, and by observing it in almost all churches for a monetary consideration . . . such mercenary Masses and private Masses . . . were discontinued in our churches. . . . At the same time the abominable error was condemned according to which it was taught that our Lord Christ had by his death made satisfaction only for original sin, and had instituted the Mass as a sacrifice for other sins. This transformed the Mass into a sacrifice for the living and the dead, a sacrifice by means of which sin was taken away and God was reconciled. . . . [But] there is no sacrifice for original sin or any other sin except the one death of Christ. . . . [It is] a misuse of the Mass [to] think that grace is obtained through the performance of this work. . . . The holy sacrament was not instituted to make provision for a sacrifice for sin — for the sacrifice has already taken place — but to awaken faith and comfort our consciences when we perceive that through the sacrament grace and forgiveness of sin are promised us by Christ. Accordingly, the sacrament requires faith, and without faith it is used in vain. . . . *The Mass is not a sacrifice . . . but should be a communion.* . . .[11]

Melanchthon's *intention* to identify the Lord's Supper as *the Lord's,* i.e., as the risen Christ's gracious self-impartation to His people is clear enough. But it is equally easy to imagine how his language was confusing to opponents. Clearly Melanchthon, in denying that the Mass is a sacrifice, is *not* denying that the crucified but risen Christ truly encounters the assembly in the Holy Supper. The sacrificed Christ, who identifies Himself by His true body and blood given for sinners, encounters us in His Supper to awaken and nurture faith. Christ's Eucharistic presence as the One who gave Himself in His body and blood is accordingly the very presupposition of Melanchthon's criticism of abuses which, as he argues, blaspheme this body and blood of the Lord. The purpose of the Sacrament is communion with Christ and all believers, forgiveness, mutual love and unity, in a foretaste of the eternal feast to come. Yet how confusing to Roman Catholic ears, untutored in the new vocabulary and conceptual scheme of Lutheran theology, it must have sounded to hear that the Mass is not a "means by which sin is taken away and God reconciled"! We note the further irony that for most of Lutheran history the Lord's Supper has been understood *reductively as nothing but* a "means by which sin is taken away and God reconciled"!

The Reformers understood the problem this way: false use had made of the

11. *BC,* pp. 68-72.

Mass a commercialized profit-making instrument (a critique with which Trent concurred in no uncertain terms). This trade seemed to be based on the theological idea of satisfying an angry God by the priestly work of offering Christ's body and blood to Him as an appeasement. Dogmatic lack of clarity about the saving work of Christ as the work of the Trinity had allowed the church to relapse into the essentially pagan notion of seeking to expiate an angry God by offering sacrifices, even if the Christian God was thought to have mercifully provided a sacrificial system and an acceptable victim. Especially among the later medieval "semi-Pelagian" theologians, the thinking seemed to have been that God had made a deal in Christ with sinners, on very lenient terms, with the institutional church as the broker. The new covenant was that God had given Christ's treasury of merit to the Church. The Church through the sacrificial Mass could offer these merits back to God to compensate for the sins of penitents. The terms were very generous. It was not necessary for the penitents to eat or drink. It was not necessary to gather as an assembly. It was not even necessary personally to understand or actually to be changed in life. What mattered theologically was that the priest offered the unbloody sacrifice of Christ in the Mass back to God on behalf of the sinful people. Witnessing the elevation that offers Christ to God, not eating and drinking together, became the ritual center of the Lord's Supper. The original Eucharistic meaning of the Lord's Supper as the Christian assembly's joyful thanksgiving to the Creator, communion in Christ, and unification by the Spirit in Christ's life of love and praise, had been obscured. This late-medieval theology and practice had lost sight of the nature of the Mass as gift, as communion, and as thanksgiving.

What Melanchthon is denying in the Augsburg Confession is that we can use the Christ present in the Sacrament for other, alien purposes. Rather, the Holy Supper belongs to Christ and remains subject to His intention. It is Christ's feast; He is the host. According to such "a pure understanding of the Gospel," a gracious God freely offers anew and anew to believing and repentant sinners the personal reality of Christ in His own crucified but glorified existence *pro nobis*. The Sacrament of Christ's Body and Blood is the Gospel itself in the particular form of nurturing the community of faith. The Eucharist *is* the New Covenant in Jesus' blood in which the church as church exists. It communicates the gracious forgiveness that Christ established once and for all in the form of a communion between Christ and His people. It is therefore a time of joy and praise. Assembling, eating and drinking, and believing reception are requisite, not as legal demands, but as analytic of what by divine institution Holy Communion is. The Supper belongs in the communal context where Christ and faith encounter each other. The proper use of the Holy Sacrament to awaken and nurture faith belongs to a gathering of the community for a service of God's promises and a corresponding sacrifice of praise. Holy Communion belongs in the Eucharist just as the Eucharist ought to be such a communion in Christ with one another.

When Melanchthon therefore wrote in Article 24, "We are unjustly accused of having abolished the Mass. Without boasting, it is manifest that the Mass is observed among us with greater devotion and more earnestness than among our opponents," he was reflecting Luther's own stance and mature Christology. Indeed, as we saw in the previous chapter, Luther ardently insisted on the tight correlation between Christological doctrine and the doctrine of the Eucharistic presence of Christ in the Lord's Supper. The Jesus Christ who can and does graciously give Himself anew to His people in the Eucharist, and thereby brings them in the power of the Spirit to service of His Father's reign, can only be true God, Son of the Father from eternity; true man, born of the virgin Mary, and just so, saving Lord, as Luther taught catechumens to say.

Returning to the dialogue, we can see once again how Roman Catholic self-criticism in the light of Vatican II led to a "breakthrough," as the Lutherans actually claimed at that time. A brilliant study by the Roman Catholic theologian James McCue established that for Luther the notion of the church as community, as *communio* "of all things between Christ and the faithful," is what the Lord's Supper as "sacrament both signifies *and effects*."[12] The ecclesia exists in the actual event of eating of the one loaf and drinking of the one cup, for this action of sharing is the communio in Christ which the ecclesia essentially is (as *creatura Verbi,* where the Word is inseparable from the Spirit who speaks it). Precisely so, Jesus is adored and worshiped to the end that He willed in instituting the Supper: in Him, with Him, through Him, wholly by grace, exclusively in the power of the Spirit, His forgiven and freed people *get to* offer themselves to the Father in praise and for service. They are *freed* to do this and do this *joyfully* on account of the joyful *exchange* enacted by the invitation, "This is my body, given for you."

The Eucharistic prayer, accordingly, does not offer Jesus to God in place of sinful people. On the basis of God's gift to the world of His Son, which is celebrated in its praises, this prayer rather has believers consecrate themselves in the Spirit as Christ's people, freed and forgiven, to do the Father's will. On this basis, McCue explained, it is "a basic distortion to make of the Mass something that we offer to God," and he cites Luther himself: ". . . we do not offer Christ as a sacrifice. . . . Christ offers us. And in this way it is permissible, yes, profitable to call the mass a sacrifice; not on its own account, but because we offer ourselves a sacrifice along with Christ. That is, we lay ourselves on Christ by a firm faith in his testament and do not otherwise appear before God with our prayer, praise and sacrifice except through Christ and his mediation."[13]

With this opening to the traditional Roman Catholic concern provided by Luther himself, McCue went on to argue that the genuine Roman Catholic teaching about the Mass as sacrifice "is rooted in the community or fellowship of Christians with Christ."[14] McCue's argument thus implicitly grants Melanchthon's

---

12. *Lutherans and Catholics in Dialogue,* III:51.
13. *Lutherans and Catholics in Dialogue,* III:58, cited from *LW* 35, p. 99.
14. *Lutherans and Catholics in Dialogue,* III:53.

rejection of private Masses; at the same time, it suggests that Lutheranism's polemically inspired "antithesis between receiving and giving, between testament and sacrifice, proves to be overly simple" — just as the new Scandinavian theology of gift also urges. Rather, McCue concluded, "we *receive* the fruits of Calvary in an act in which we say yes to Calvary by offering ourselves along with Christ to the Father."[15] We actually receive the mercy of Christ in the Spirit-wrought act of giving thanks to the Father for it; that confession of praise is the first and chief work of faith. Faith exists publicly in the world as this communal act of worship at the Eucharist. Faith is not a private, interior experience of isolated individuals. Personal, justifying faith in Christ is manifest in the world in a public event, as giving thanks with Christ to the Father in the power of the Spirit, even as Christian life is ultimately this doxological existence before God. We may note here how a fuller use of Trinitarian theology integrates the legitimate concerns of both parties, so that the gift-character of Christ's self-impartation in the Supper includes also the gift of the Spirit who draws believers out of themselves to live new lives of praise to the Father and love for others and hope for the world. As Christ has donated Himself with His Spirit to us, so with Christ and in the power of His Spirit, we offer ourselves to the Father whose kingdom comes.

This fuller use of Trinitarianism should, in principle, not strike Lutherans as some categorical innovation. Mauer writes in exposition of the faith that justifies:

> What Christ does for us is closely tied to the works of God the Creator and the Holy Spirit; faith opens itself to these works and then acknowledges them by praising and honoring God. Thus confession is not merely the recounting of biblical truths and events; faith is itself a divine gift by which believers are adorned, raised from the dead, freed from sin, and made joyful and confident, free and secure in their conscience. That Trinitarian approach makes it possible for Luther to join the objective side of salvation history with the personal experience of salvation. . . . [These] elements in the process of belief, that have steadily lost contact with one another since Pietism and the Enlightenment, maintain an inner connection with one another through the Trinitarian connection of faith.[16]

Consequently, one has to wonder to what extent contemporary Lutheran resistance to restoration of the Eucharistic prayer, in its manifestly Trinitarian structure, is not in reality based upon a tacit theological Unitarianism.[17]

---

15. *Lutherans and Catholics in Dialogue,* III:67.

16. Wilhelm Mauer, *Historical Commentary on the Augsburg Confession,* trans. H. George Anderson (Philadelphia: Fortress, 1986), p. 322.

17. The connection here is not gratuitous polemic. See the seminal sermon of modern Unitarianism, "The Lord's Supper," *Ralph Waldo Emerson Texts* at http://www.emersoncentral .com/lordsupper.htm.

McCue, in any case, pointedly emphasized that his reinterpretation of Eucharistic sacrifice excludes the idea that "we take Christ, as a pre-Christian might take a sacrificial animal, and 'slay' him (even symbolically) as a sign of our dependence on God or our desire for community with him, to appease his wrath, to gain forgiveness. . . ."[18] The "mass is not propitiatory in the sense that it somehow wins over a hostile God." In this spirit, the dialogue cited Karl Rahner's rule: God's "gracious will is not newly constituted in the sacrifice of the mass; it is appropriated."[19] If this statement holds for today's Roman Catholicism, the fundamental contradiction with Lutheranism regarding the Eucharist as sacrifice has been substantially overcome. The teachings of the two churches are not in contradiction. In McCue's conclusion,

> We have seen that the Roman Catholic view is rooted in the idea of the Church as the body of Christ, and thus in the idea that Christ is not only God's word to mankind but simultaneously the representative high priest of mankind before God. . . . [Luther, we have also seen, taught that] we share with Christ and are at least inchoately conformed to him. Luther does not go on to add that, since the mass is our participation in Calvary, our sharing and being conformed to Christ takes the form first of all of joining ourselves with him in the sacrificial act which is the center of his as of our life. Luther does *not* add this; but I do not see that he *could* not have done so; and if he had, he would have been saying substantially what Trent was to say.[20]

The Lutheran partners in this dialogue found McCue's argument persuasive and grounds for claiming that a "breakthrough" in understanding had occurred.

In fact both Lutherans and Roman Catholics are recovering more a patristic understanding of the Lord's Supper in the context of the joyful "sacrifice of praise." Since prayers of thanksgiving, on the model of the biblical psalms, consist in celebrating God's saving deeds by remembrance of them, they are proclamation in the form of prayer and praise, giving God all the glory for all His rich mercy in Christ. Setting Jesus' word of promise into the doxological form of a prayer of thanksgiving to the Father does not detract from its nature as address and promise spoken to the congregation, but rather recovers the trinitarian structure of the Lord's Supper. In other words, the objection — that in speaking to the Father one cannot simultaneously be speaking to the congregation — presupposes a non-trinitarian, merely theistic idea of God as something external to the event of the Christian assembly. In fact the whole New Testament urges the opposite. Inasmuch as the assembly really exists "in Christ," as communio in Christ, it exists within the life of the Father, the Son, and the Holy Spirit.

18. *Lutherans and Catholics in Dialogue*, III:66.
19. *Lutherans and Catholics in Dialogue*, III:8, n. 45.
20. *Lutherans and Catholics in Dialogue*, III:70-71.

Concretely, at the same time that the Son proclaims Himself to His people in His words of self-donation for us in the Lord's Supper, His people in the power of His Spirit are acknowledging this donation of the Son before the Father in an act of praise and thanksgiving, that is, Eucharist, giving Him the glory. That the church whose motto had been *soli Deo gloria* should have a problem with this only testifies to the power of malice structuring injustice also in the polemical theologies of schismatic Christianity.

In the joint statement, Lutherans and Roman Catholics were thus able to agree that "Christ is present as the Crucified who died for our sins . . . as the once-for-all sacrifice for the sins of the world," and that "the celebration of the Eucharist is the Church's sacrifice of praise and self-offering or oblation."[21] On the historical controversy whether the "worshiping assembly 'offers Christ' in the sacrifice of the Mass," the joint statement was able to insist *"that Catholics as well as Lutherans affirm the unrepeatable character of the sacrifice of the cross. . . . The events are unique; they cannot be repeated, extended or continued."* But because the risen Christ is present as the one who was sacrificed for all, believers *"become participants in his worship, his self-offering, his sacrifice to the Father* . . . the eucharistic assembly 'offers Christ' by consenting in the power of the Holy Spirit to be offered by him to the Father."[22]

The implications of the convergence — noting that a convergence is not a complete theological harmony but a trans*form*ation of doctrine in which previously contradictory *form*ulations have been reconciled and cease to be mutually exclusive — are powerful and far-reaching. Roman Catholics were quick to point out that the practical reforms, authorized already in the Second Vatican Council's *Constitution on the Sacred Liturgy,* restored the communal context of the Sacrament, and asked: Does not this reform satisfy Martin Luther's concern that the mercy of Christ be clearly and freely offered in the rites and proclamation of the church? At the same time, Lutheran recognition of the new Roman Catholic understanding of the Eucharist as the church's self-offering in, with, and through Christ to the service of the Father on the model (so dear to their own tradition) of Romans 12:1-2, challenges the widespread loss of the Eucharist as the normal form of Christian worship within Protestantism. Contemporary Protestantism can hardly claim Melanchthon's words in the Augsburg Confession as their own: "We are unjustly accused of having abolished the Mass. Without boasting, it is manifest that the Mass is observed among us with greater devotion and more earnestness than among our opponents." But Christ offering Himself in His Body and Blood is the objectivity of justifying faith, just as the faith that receives this gift returns to the Father with

21. *Lutherans and Catholics in Dialogue,* III:188.

22. *Lutherans and Catholics in Dialogue,* III:189, emphasis added. See also John Reumann, *The Supper of the Lord: The New Testament, Ecumenical Dialogues, and Faith and Order on Eucharist* (Philadelphia: Fortress, 1985).

joy and thanksgiving in Spirit-born theological subjectivity. The practice of the Lord's Supper is our practical Christology.

If we turn in the other direction on the ecumenical spectrum from this Lutheran-Catholic convergence on Trinitarian Christology, we find a noteworthy effort along the same lines in the work of the not-easily-categorized Reformed theologian Jürgen Moltmann, even though it is not particularly focused on the Lord's Supper. At the beginning of his celebrated authorship he offered in *The Crucified God*[23] a systematic *theologia crucis* that attempted to derive the divine ontology from the suffering of love as revealed in the Father's pain of infinite loss at the death of the Son. The charge of "patripassianism," so easily committed in the context of the Western tendency to modalism, had to be brought against him in this, since his Christology seemed to obliterate the narrative drama of the gospel that specifies not only the personal uniqueness of the Son's incarnation and therewith His suffering in and as the assumed humanity, but also the personal uniqueness attending the hiddenness and indeed abandonment of the Abba, Father. It is not so much, then, that the gospel gives a crucified God-in-general, but rather a crucified Son of God in solidarity with the world in its sinfulness over against the Father's *No!* to sin as the ruin of the good creation. Ironically enough, the Jesus of the Garden of Gethsemane and of the Cry of Dereliction was eclipsed by the picture Moltmann drew of the helpless, hapless, but intensely pained heavenly Father.

To what extent Moltmann received these criticisms we may leave for other scholars to decide. The fact is that in his 1989 *The Way of Jesus Christ*[24] Moltmann undertook a new approach to Christology that wanted to take the Jewishness of Jesus with far greater cognitive seriousness in understanding both His historical humanity and His messianic office. This move accords well with the intention of this chapter to incorporate the biblical perspective of Theodore of Mopsuestia's contention for Jesus in His true humanity within a higher, "Cyrilian" synthesis. Moltmann sought to avoid thinking "statically" in Christology, either according to the "one person in two natures" of classical Christology or according to the "historical personality" of liberalism — a necessary dialectic that we are rather pursuing by way of the theology of the Spirit who freely unifies the sign and the thing signified, first of all in constituting the person of Jesus Christ for faith, beginning with the faith of Jesus Himself who in faith took responsibility for us all before God.

Moltmann parsed this difficulty of the tension between sign and thing signified eschatologically. He acknowledged the doxological Christ as the "wonder of the God who has become human and the human Christ who was deified," but

23. Jürgen Moltmann, *Der gekreuzigte Gott* (Munich: Chr. Kaiser, 1976).

24. Jürgen Moltmann, *The Way of Jesus Christ: Christology in Messianic Dimensions,* trans. Margaret Kohl (San Francisco: Harper, 1990). The citations following in this and the next paragraph are all taken in summary from the Preface, pp. xiii-xiv.

insisted with Theodore and the Reformed Christological tradition that we "who are living in the exile of history, and who are searching for life, need a christology for pilgrims *(christologia viatorum)* . . . a christology of the way *(christologia viae)*, which points beyond itself and draws people towards the future of Christ, so that they remain on Christ's path, and move forward along that path." This "provisional knowledge" of Christ — in that it still expects a future work of redemption from Him at the eschaton of judgment before the full doxology can truthfully be sung — also accords well with the present approach of "doctrine for life" according to a pragmatic ideal of knowledge. Moltmann's eschatological framing of Christology comports with the present effort so far as we take the Spirit's work of unifying the sign and the thing signified for faith in anticipation of the eternal doxology. This approach to the Person at work wants to know Christ's *way* in the world, His *mission,* "from His birth in the Spirit and His baptism in the Spirit to His self-surrender on Golgotha" as the marks by which His present work as risen and coming Lord of all are recognized.

As Moltmann saw, this missiological knowledge of Christ is hampered, even paralyzed by certain features of the inherited theological tradition. This paralysis entails the critical endeavor to "free the Christian doctrine of God from the confines of the ancient metaphysics of substance, and from the modern metaphysics of transcendental subjectivity, in order to develop a social doctrine of the Trinity in the different context of a metaphysics of community, process and relation" of today. This latter development in metaphysics from the historical predominance of Parmenides via Plato and Christian Platonism to Heraclitus via the wrenching victory of Darwinian evolution in contemporary thought further indicates the shift to a "post-modern christology, which places human history ecologically in the framework of nature." Yet Moltmann expressly notes that this "transition" from the "static" doctrine of the "two natures in one person" of classical Christology "does not have to be a breach." Indeed, as argued in the previous chapter on the Eucharistic controversies surrounding the *bodily* presence of Christ, Moltmann's newer perspective turns attention "towards Christ's bodily nature" since "embodiment is the existential point of intersection between history and nature in human beings."[25] That indicates that there are resources in the tradition for the needed "transition" that evince continuity as well as discontinuity, as indeed we argued in treating the Eucharistic controversies surrounding the objectivity of Christ's presence in His body.

How successful Moltmann was in this purpose in this book is also a question that we may here leave aside. It is apparent that there is much of great value in it, and its affinities with what follows in the remainder of this chapter will be

---

25. And with caution, Niels Henrik Gregersen's cosmic-Christological "Deep Incarnation." See Ted Peters, "Happy Danes and Deep Incarnation" and Gregersen's response, "Deep Incarnation and *Kenosis:* In, With, Under, and As: A Response to Ted Peters," in *dialog* 52, no. 3 (Fall 2013): 244-62.

everywhere evident. The present proposal differs from Moltmann's, if we have understood him correctly, on three points. First, the problem of Christological dogmatism that we inherit from the Western tradition is less to be found in the alleged substance metaphysics of the classical "two natures in one person" Christology of Chalcedon in the Western tradition's subsequent modalist construal of that legacy. Indeed to take "nature" metaphysically as substance rather than semantically is the chief move made by modalism. Over against this Western tendency, the "substance metaphysics" that tacitly divinizes creatures by according to them a "substantial" nature rather than by grace calling them as *imago Dei* to likeness to God, and in the fullness of time incorporating them as persons into the Person of the Son, is already in principle overcome in Eastern Trinitarianism's strong distinction between nature and person. Moreover, this Trinitarian personalism is presupposed in the classical Christology of "two natures in one person." This difference will, predictably, make for rather traditional Lutheran–Reformed divergences on the "unity of person" in Christ between the present (neo-Chalcedonian) Christological proposal and Moltmann's eschatological Christology, though hopefully in ways that move this old argument forward.

Second, we differ from Moltmann surprisingly enough in wanting to see a clearer fulfillment of Theodore of Mopsuestia's demand that Christology acknowledge and respect the human obedience of the Jew Jesus of Nazareth as the very event of the Son of God's coming to us in order to take upon Himself the sin of the world and so into the life of God: as an apocalyptic crisis, then, not only for the world but also for God. Moltmann asks polemically, "To whom is he supposed to have sacrificed himself . . . ? If he wanted to sacrifice himself to the God of Israel as a 'ransom for many,' did this force him to draw on the assistance of Pilate and the Roman torturers?"[26] This rhetorical *tour de force* in the name of political correctness only fends off the most serious problem of Christology, that is, how doctrine here serves to indicate God surpassing God for us and for all. Such, in any event, will be the understanding of the person of Christ at work that overcomes Theodore's tacit dualism of the Son of Mary and the Son of God by virtue of a higher synthesis — one, we may note here, articulated by Maximus the Confessor and retrieved in Lutheran Orthodoxy by Johann Gerhard (as we shall see): theologians who alike labored to fend off the Apollinarian, Eutychian, and Schwenckfeldian "monophysite" take on Cyrilian Christology by affirming the human will in the one Person of Christ.[27]

---

26. Moltmann, *The Way*, p. 166.

27. Commenting on the prayer in Gethsemane (Matt. 26:39), Maximus unites the antidocetic accent of the Antiochene tradition with the deification soteriology of the Alexandrian tradition: "So his flesh was acknowledged by those who saw him not to be a phantom deceiving the senses, but he was in truth and properly a human being: to this his natural will bears witness by his pleas to be spared from death that took place in accordance with the economy. And again, that the human will is wholly deified, in its agreement with the divine will itself, since it is eternally moved and shaped by it. . . . Not mine, but your will be done. . . . Thus he

Finally, these differences with aspects of the Christological proposal of Moltmann on the objectivity of Christ for faith indicate, third, a difference in epistemic warrantability in theology. For Moltmann, as cited above, it is apparent that the need of postmodern Euro-Americans not only provides the context but sets the agenda for Christology. We have agreed with the liberal theological tradition that historical context provides the proximate audience of theology, and we avowedly stand with Moltmann in the same Euro-American situation of post-Christendom. But surprisingly for a post-Holocaust theologian who is alert to the eschatological horizon of specifically Christian theologizing, I do not see this attention to *context* sufficiently balanced methodologically in Moltmann by the conscientious recognition that the final audience of theology is the Father in heaven, whom Jesus proclaimed in the Sermon on the Mount as the One who sees in secret and knows in secret, pending the eschaton of judgment. This is a methodological point, not a personal criticism of Moltmann. It is a methodological point that takes context more seriously than do the contextualists in regarding context as the work of the Father's continuous creating, not an autonomous source of revelation. After the woeful performance of theologians under Hitler, who sold their souls along these lines for the sake of politically "progressive" *Lebensbezug*,[28] the importance *as a matter of conscience* of recognizing the judgment seat of God as final audience in theology cannot be gainsaid.[29] Indeed, confession of Christ in the world but before God is the *ratio ultima* of Christological doctrine (Matt. 10:32-33; Rom. 10:9-10). A tendency to abject trendiness can be easily documented in contemporary "contextual" theology.[30] In this regard, Moltmann certainly towers above lesser theologians in his responsibility to the tradition of the gospel and his passion for Jesus Christ. But the problem of the conscientiousness of theology before God will be the matter of the next chapter. Now we turn to the heart of the chapter's Christological proposal of a *Cyrilian Christ for Augustinian humanity.*

## The Unity of Christ's Person

A twelve-point memorandum on Christology derived from Cyril of Alexandria "Third Letter to Nestorius"[31] was formally approved by the ecumenical council at Ephesus in 431 and again at Chalcedon in 451 (although its anathemas against

---

possesses a human will . . . only it was not opposed to God. But this will is not at all deliberative, but properly natural, eternally formed and moved by its essential Godhead to the fulfillment of the economy." Andrew Louth, *Maximus the Confessor* (London: Routledge, 1996), pp. 186-87.

28. Robert B. Ericksen, *Theologians under Hitler: Gerhard Kittel, Paul Althaus and Emanuel Hirsch* (New Haven and London: Yale University Press, 1985).

29. *BA,* pp. 180-83.

30. E.g., perusal of any current catalogue of books from Fortress Press.

31. *Christology of the Later Fathers,* ed. Edward R. Hardy (Philadelphia: Westminster, 1954), pp. 353-54.

Nestorius were deleted in 451). Chalcedon may therefore be read as endorsing Cyril's views in somewhat mitigated fashion in accord with a further clarification about how the technical term, *physis,* is to be distinguished from *hypostasis* (which Cyril still tended to treat as synonyms in his pioneering attempt to apply Trinitarian personalism to Christological problems). Frequently overlooked in the ensuing controversy about the application of the Trinitarian nature-person distinction to Christology is the antecedent gravamen of anti-docetism expressed in Cyril's twelfth and final point: "If anyone does not confess that the Word of God suffered in the flesh and was crucified in the flesh and tasted death in the flesh, and became the first-born of the dead, although he is as God Life and life-giving, let him be anathema."[32] The words could have been penned by Ignatius of Antioch. They indicate the "higher synthesis" that we are aiming at: that the human Jesus' experience of dereliction just *is* the coming of the Son of God into the likeness of sinful flesh. In any case, this is how Chalcedon itself was read (or reread) at the Fifth Ecumenical Council in light of the Theopaschite controversy, where it was affirmed that "one of the Trinity suffered." Cyril is thus the chief theologian of normative ecumenical Christology just as the gravamen of his thought falls on the unity of Christ's person: Christ is "the one and only Son, not one son alongside another son, considered in this way to be one person *(prosopon).* In this way we can gather into a true unity, though one that transcends speech and understanding, realities which were unlike one another and separated because of their respective natures."[33]

In the aside made in passing in the citation just given, Cyril acknowledges the ineffability of the Christological union of the truly different natures of Creator and creature; therewith Cyril makes a point about the nature of doctrinal knowledge as hermeneutical and pragmatic, not theoretical. Knowledge is always a well-warranted selection of material from the chaos of experience for the construction of an object that works to accomplish a task in a world structured by a vast multitude of such constructions contrasting, contesting, combining, and repelling. The good description that an object of knowledge provides serves for recognizing something through passing time and in new places, distinguishing it from frauds, imposters, and deceptions. That discrimination, as in Mark 13, is the critically dogmatic task of Christology as the objective aspect of the knowledge of God.

It is not the immediate task of Christology, then, to know the How of the Incarnation. If we begin Christology with the thought of two different natures, taken as really existing "substances," we will never be able to unite them adequately to the figure — the one *prosopon* — who appears in the gospel narrative. Rather we begin with this figure, the Who (the person) as revealed in His history with us, and accordingly proceed to the What (the two natures) that are manifest

---

32. *Christology of the Later Fathers,* p. 354.

33. St. Cyril of Alexandria, *On the Unity of Christ,* trans. J. A. McGuckin (Crestwood, NY: St. Vladimir's Seminary Press, 1995), p. 83.

in His mission; and then, and only then, do we come to the ineffable How (that is, the "miracle" of the personal union in the communication of properties). The reasoning is thus *a posteriori.* It is theological *Nachdenken,* according to the principle that what is in fact the case must also possibly be the case. Beginning always with the concrete figure of the gospel narratives with *its* question, Who? (Mark 4:41; 8:27-28; 14:61), knowledge in faith of Jesus' divine Sonship both constrains and informs thinking about the How of this union of human and divine for the accomplishment of the mission on which Jesus is sent by His Father and empowered by His Spirit. Accordingly we must think of the Son of God as capable of the Incarnation, as also of the finite as capable of the Infinite, if we are to think of the Son of God incarnate. Thus we are thinking of God as Trinity and of the human as its creature; so, further, in Christology we are thinking of that One of the Three who in some fitting way became one of us in order to redeem the creation and bring it to fulfillment, by right powerfully sharing His own Spirit.

That line of reflection in that sequence is not a speculative flight but an analytic and descriptive ontology arising from the gospel's presentation to us of Jesus Christ the Son of God as object of faith, the One whom faith knows as sent by His Father and sending their Spirit. It does not answer the question, How, in a theoretical way as the theory of gravity explains the moon's pull on the ocean's tide, but in a hermeneutical way, like coming to understand a novel, or an artifact uncovered in an archeological dig, or one's spouse in the heat of a passionate argument. So Cyril's contention for the strict "unity of person" in Christ prioritizes the Who and thus aims to nip in the bud any and every speculative theory about the What and How of the union that takes flight into theory by eschewing the primary hermeneutical task of Christology. That task arises in response to the living encounter with Jesus Christ in His Word and sacraments, declaring, "I am yours and you are mine." Who speaks to us in this sovereign yet saving way, reminiscent of the Prologue to the Decalogue (Exod. 20:2-3)? By what right? With what competence?

Behind Cyril's contribution to Christological doctrine we may not see merely contending schools of theological thought, but far-reaching and indeed rival conceptions of what Christology as knowledge of God is to be about that divide the divisions today. Christology answers precisely these questions in this sequence because it begins in faith in this one Lord Jesus Christ the Son of God given for us and our salvation; this is the figure coming from the Scriptures in Word and Sacrament as promised to His baptized people in their Eucharistic assembly and so through this ever-nurtured and newly assembled Body pressing on to all nations. Dissent on this level is simply to conceive of some other assembly with some other mission under some other authority. Those who conscientiously fail to make this confession of faith should not presume to teach in the ecclesia, nor have they a right to teach. Indeed also those who conscientiously make this confession of Jesus Christ the Son of God do not have a right to teach in the church but rather a duty, indeed a cross, is laid upon them.

To substantiate that claim, we now consider the debate between historians of dogma, beginning with Jaroslav Pelikan's account of the Christological difference between the Alexandrian *(Logos-Sarx)* model of Cyril and the Antiochene *(Logos-Anthropos)* model of Nestorius. "The Antiochene and the Alexandrian traditions were in agreement that salvation was the purpose of the coming of Christ and that immortality and impassibility were the consequence of that salvation. It was also agreed on all sides that there had to be a theological congruence between the person of Christ and the doctrine of the work of Christ."[34] Both parties agreed on the ontology of the Creator/creature distinction. Theodore of Mopsuestia could write: "It is not possible to limit and define the chasm that exists between the one who is from eternity [the eternal Son] and the one who began to exist at a time when he was not [Jesus of Nazareth]."[35] Cyril of Alexandria could likewise affirm: "God whose existence transcends all reason and who rises above all beginning and all passing away, is superior to change."[36] Nevertheless, for Cyril "no mere association, nothing less intimate than a union between the Logos-Creator and the one who was born and crucified would have been sufficient . . . if salvation was to be the gift of impassibility and immortality, the Savior had to be the Logos himself, not only a man assumed by the Logos."[37] In contrast, Theodore spoke of a "conjunction" of divine and human wills in Jesus, not a "personal [= hypostatic] union" of divine and human natures. In Cyril's theology Christology accounts for the divine person who comes as savior of humanity in humanity. In Theodore's theology Christology accounts for the work that saves, the God-assisted human obedience of Jesus.

Adolf von Harnack's formal account of Cyril differs little from Pelikan's. But thinking that a psychologically plausible portrait of the historical personality of Jesus of Nazareth is the point of a Christological account of the saving work, Harnack none too subtly favored the Antiochenes who saw in Jesus' willing the will of God that human conformity to God in which salvation consists. Harnack accordingly regarded the classical Christological dogma of the incarnation of the divine Logos, whether already in Paul's "preexistent" Son or the Logos doctrine of theologians like Athanasius or Cyril following John, as tacitly or naïvely docetist. Belief "in the real incarnation of God was only capable of the treatment which [the heretic] Apollinaris had given it,"[38] Harnack pronounced. That is to say, if one takes the personal distinctions in God of Father, Son/Logos, and Spirit as the starting point of Christology, then the personified divine being of the Logos must actually supplant the rational human soul of Jesus in a true incarnation. Harnack is thinking that this model has the Logos in place of the rational soul immediately animating the physical body, which in turn has become its instrument

---

34. Pelikan, *TCT* 2, p. 232.
35. Pelikan, *TCT* 2, p. 229.
36. Pelikan, *TCT* 2, p. 231.
37. Pelikan, *TCT* 2, p. 234.
38. Harnack, *HD* 4, p. 174.

of communication with mortals. By the time of the conflict between Nestorius and Cyril, Apollinaris's teaching that the Logos replaced the rational human soul in Jesus had been rejected as soteriologically inadequate. If the Logos did not also assume the rational human soul in Jesus, then the soul could not be healed (or is regarded as not in need of healing). Since Apollinaris's teaching had been repudiated in this way, Harnack contended, any possibility of a "scientific" account of the Incarnation had become impossible. The doctrine of a genuine incarnation of God maintaining a genuine union of incommensurable natures was an impossible muddle — a jerry-rigged conceptual contraption passed off as a revealed mystery but in truth prime evidence of the intellectual Hellenizing of the gospel.

As mentioned, Cyril occasionally used the terms for "nature" and "person" synonymously, thus giving rise to the (false) impression, as scholarship since Harnack has established, that he tended toward the monophysite (the "one nature") Christologies of Apollinaris, later Eutyches at the time of Chalcedon, and Schwenckfeld at the time of the Reformation.[39] But Harnack took for granted Cyril's monophysitism, on the grounds that his faith does not "start from the historical Christ" but with the divine Logos "and is occupied only with him," who "incorporated within himself the whole human nature and still remained the same . . . the one indivisible subject which merely added something to itself. . . ."[40] It does not seem to occur to Harnack that this critique of Cyril on behalf of his truly human Christ also expresses a "monophysite" Christology, so to speak, from below. In any case, what especially is damning in Harnack's assessment is Cyril's "express rejection of the view that an individual man was present in Christ, although he attributes to Christ all the elements of man's nature."[41] All this is true, but tendentiously expressed.

Cyril's Christ does not have an independent human personality as an "individual" that is then to be somehow conjoined to the equally independent personality of the Logos by acts of will on either side. Rather from His conception, Jesus' human nature coheres — organizes, holds together — in the personhood of the divine Logos that has made this human being its own, producing also the theonomous mind of the man Jesus.[42] This is, of course, just as Jesus appears in the evangelical narrative as the messianic man on a mission. The question of Jesus' human "personality" is of no interest whatsoever — quite in contrast to the display, for example, Paul makes of himself in his letters. This is important to

---

39. In *On the Unity of Christ,* a late work looking back on the whole course of the Nestorian controversy (p. 30), Cyril explains the notion of the personal union, not as confusion of substances, but as a "concurrence in one reality" (p. 73): "I say that we must call him God made man, and that both the one and the other are this same reality . . ." (p. 76, see p. 91). In "the case of Christ[,] they came together in a mysterious and incomprehensible union without confusion or change" (p. 77).

40. Harnack, *HD* 4, p. 175.

41. Harnack, *HD* 4, p. 176.

42. Pannenberg, *ST* 2, p. 389.

soteriology, because the anhypostatic (= without an independent human personality) union of human nature with the person of the Logos, as Harnack himself sees, "forthwith purified and transfigured human nature generally. Christ can be the second Adam . . . the real beginner of a new humanity."[43]

Tied up with Cyril's notion of Christ as new and true, so "sinless," Adam on account of personal union, Harnack continues, is the "realistic thought of redemption," i.e., "the Logos suffers in His own flesh and was born of Mary as regards His own humanity. He is thus God crucified. . . . What belonged to the Logos thus became the property of the humanity, and again what belonged to the humanity became the property of the Logos."[44] This is, in Harnack's considered judgment, the "perverse" line of thought, namely, the *commercium admirabile,* the joyful exchange, the *communicatio idiomatum.* Indeed, any idea of Christ that rejects Jesus' individual existence as an independent human personality and instead depicts the "perfect humanity" of the New Adam in its place can no longer "reconcile the Christ of faith with the picture of Christ given in the Gospels; for the idea of the physical unity of the two natures and of the interchange of properties, which Cyril had worked out in a strict fashion, swallowed up what of the human remained in him."[45] Sneaking in the adjective "physical" here to modify Cyril's conception of a union that is the personal act of the Son of God, Harnack would thus vindicate Nestorius and the Antiochene tradition to bury not only Cyril, but Luther also, as we shall see in the excursus below.

Harnack's influential critique was misled by his supposition that the term "nature" represented two equal — "physical" — magnitudes somehow "poised in an uneasy balance in Christ," as the Cyril scholar J. A. McGuckin writes. Rather "the one [nature] was the nurturing matrix of the other [so that] union with God would not cramp individuality but rather liberate personhood and enhance it."[46] The nineteenth-century cult of personality as the antithesis of nature[47] is the source of Harnack's misunderstanding. Like the Gospels themselves, which present Christ only as a public *persona,* Cyril in fact "refused to reduce the notion of person to those psychic experiences . . . on the contrary, consciousness was the effect of a divinely created personhood." According to McGuckin, Harnack has thus fundamentally misunderstood the profoundly anti-Platonic motive represented by Cyril's theology of "the real Incarnation of God": as the Arians warred against the Logos in His glory equal to the Father, so the Nestorians "war[red] against the Word even in his Incarnation . . . [and] dare[d] to criticize his loving grace toward the human race. . . ."[48] For Cyril, "the Timeless one engages with

43. Harnack, *HD* 4, pp. 176-77.
44. Harnack, *HD* 4, p. 177.
45. Harnack, *HD* 4, p. 179.
46. *On the Unity of Christ,* p. 37.
47. *PNT,* pp. 76-82.
48. *On the Unity of Christ,* p. 52.

history,[49] and "impassively suffers . . . adding to the deity" the "personal experience of a lifeform."[50]

In this light, the actual fear of the Nestorians, given their theoretical, that is, Platonic take on the knowledge of God, is that a real Incarnation would entail substantial change in God's being; in this sense, "they are of the opinion that the term 'became' [in the Johannine, 'The Word *became* flesh'] inevitably and necessarily signifies change or alteration"[51] of a substantial sort, such that God would cease to be God and morph into something else in a genuine and hence fatal divine kenosis. So Cyril asks, "Has the one of whom we sign laid aside his being as God and through some transformation passed over into becoming a refuge? Has he changed by nature into something else which at first he was not?" And he answers: We must "preserve the immutability and unalterability as innate and essential to God."[52] Clearly this answer to the Nestorian anxiety amounts to a merely formal or logical notation: an incarnation that cost God His divine being would be pointless, if the saving point is that the Logos became what we are in order that we become what He is. It is rather this latter soteriology itself, just as Harnack detects, that offends the Antiochene theologians. The real question that arises here, and one not to be taken for granted on the basis of natural theology (especially the default Platonism of the tradition), is not whether God is God eternally, but how the immutability and impassibility of the eternal God is to be known and hence conceived: by the ascent of negative theology or by the descent of divine love? In the latter case, the question of the "what" and the "how" of God arises, not speculatively and *a priori,* but theologically and *a posteriori* to account for the What of the Incarnation (the two natures) and the How (the being in communion of the Trinity) that takes Christological form as the *communicatio idiomatum.*

The Logos is the real active agent in the incarnation,[53] who becomes flesh not by virtue of an ontological *kenosis* that violates divine immutability but by the eternal Son's personal act of humility in entering the creature's time and space for the sake of the loving act of obedience there, giving His body for the life of the world. Cyril thus understands this "becoming" of the Incarnation not as the laying aside of divine power but rather as an expression of it, albeit astonishing to the depraved mentality of creatures formed by the structures of malice and injustice. It is divine power exercised in the fashion befitting the divine person who is Son. As Son, God is God immutably, inalterably, impassibly, and thus freely out of love, undertaking vulnerable human nature and hence living a life

49. *On the Unity of Christ,* p. 43.

50. *On the Unity of Christ,* p. 44.

51. *On the Unity of Christ,* p. 53. The real motive is that "they are afraid to attribute human characteristics to him in case he might somehow be dishonored by them, and brought down to a dishonorable state" (p. 98, see also pp. 112, 129).

52. *On the Unity of Christ,* p. 54.

53. *On the Unity of Christ,* p. 86.

of human woe as His very own in order to deliver.[54] "As God he wished to make that flesh which was held in the grip of sin and death evidently superior to sin and death. He made it his very own, and not soulless as some have said, but rather animated with a rational soul, and thus he restored flesh to what it was in the beginning . . . in his own person to reveal our nature honored in the dignities of the divinity."[55] How can Jesus' *body* give us life? Cyril asked, How can His blood cleanse from sin? The equivocation of the Nestorians on this provocative point in fact makes them guilty of Jesuolatry, Cyril charged. They "are found to be worshipping not the true and natural Son made man, the Word who shone forth from God the Father's very being, but rather some other person apart from him, a man of the line of David. . . ."[56] This telling point puts Nestorianism on the long road that culminates in Ruether's repudiation of her own theological tradition's piety towards Jesus as idolatrous.

Cyril's doctrine of the Great Exchange takes "a real incarnation of God" as involving neither a substantial change in God nor the conceptual destruction, so to say, of the humanity of Christ, as in docetism. Recalling the Pauline "He who was rich for our sakes becomes poor," Cyril wrote: "He made our poverty his own, and we see in Christ the strange and rare paradox of Lordship in servant's form and divine glory in human abasement. . . . The Only Begotten did not become man only to remain in the limits of emptying. The point was that he who was God by nature should, in the act of self-emptying, assume everything that went along with it." The kenosis is not a natural one resulting in divine powerlessness, but a personal one of humiliation for the sake of others; that is to say, it is the voluntary appropriation of human woe by One by nature blessed, undertaken to overcome human woe.

> Indeed the mystery of Christ runs the risk of being disbelieved precisely because it is so incredibly wonderful. For God was in humanity. He who was above all creation was in our human condition; the invisible one was made visible in the flesh; he who is from the heavens and from on high was in the likeness of earthly things; the immaterial could be touched; he who is free in

---

54. *On the Unity of Christ,* p. 88. The voluntary *kenosis* is undertaken for our sakes: "necessarily born of the flesh, taking all that is ours into himself so that all that is born of the flesh, that is us corruptible and perishing beings, might rest in him" (p. 59). The body of Jesus is thus the divine bond of the new covenant, "abasing himself to our condition out of tender love" (pp. 59, 123).

55. *On the Unity of Christ,* p. 55. The Logos "became man, appropriating a human body to himself in such an indissoluble union that it has to be considered as his very own body and no one else's" (p. 63). "All that is human has become his own" (p. 76). In this "economic appropriation" (p. 110), He became not flesh, but man (p. 57).

56. *On the Unity of Christ,* p. 71. ". . . for then he is not truly God but someone who has fellowship and participation with God, and is thus a falsely named son, a saved savior, a redeemed redeemer" (p. 89).

his own nature came in the form of a slave; he who blesses all creation became accursed; he who is all righteousness was numbered among transgressors; life itself came in the appearance of death. All this followed because the body which tasted death belonged to no other but to him who is the Son by nature.[57]

At the zenith of the Son of God's voluntary descent into our humanity, He became the Godforsaken.[58]

"This same Jesus is one and single. . . . Are we to say then that all things were made through a man, and that he who undergoes this birth from a woman in these last times of this age is the Creator of heaven and earth, the sum of all that they contain?"[59] Is this still Jesus, our brother, one of us? Just as we may not speculate on divine nature a priori but only reflect *a posteriori* in disciplined thinking after the divine self-donation of the Word and divine self-communication in the Spirit, so also in theology we are not to speculate about human nature, as if in the sinful and contested world we already and easily knew ourselves, the truth of our predicament, and the vocation we have forfeited in the lost promise of creation. Human "nature" is plastic as creature of the continually creating God who consistently intends the fulfillment of life together of persons in the Beloved Community. Divine love makes hearts of stone into flesh anew, and the finite capable of the infinite.[60] Joyful exchanges are the beating heart of creation — creation as the promise of God redeemed in Christ and fulfilled in the Spirit.[61] Just so, to be truly human is not only to die as creatures die, but to live in faith and to rise from death as the human creature destined as the image for likeness to God. To be human is to be nature as promise, and so promise redeemed and fulfilled by grace in the community of persons in the love performed, and so made known, in this Person at work, Jesus Christ the Son of God.

As that one of the Trinity who suffered, this same Jesus is the one of us creatures of God who uniquely but for us all subsists in God the Son, one Person, the God who suckles at Mary's breast, the Man who created the universe. From eternity He came not to be served but to serve and lay down His life a ransom for many, then to take it up again, victorious, with all whom He has won, to present to His Father as the trophies of their love. So far from Jesuolatry is the adoration by the redeemed of this Person, the victorious Lamb, with the Father in the Holy Spirit that it can be affirmed only on the final horizon still hoped for: the "appearance" (Parousia) visibly of the Object to which every knee will bow, the new humanity that every tongue will confess. Just this one who judges the nations

57. *On the Unity of Christ,* p. 61.

58. Cyril emphatically takes up the Marcan cry of dereliction, *On the Unity of Christ,* pp. 102-6.

59. *On the Unity of Christ,* p. 87; see also pp. 92-93.

60. *On the Unity of Christ,* p. 79.

61. Oswald Bayer has taken up this interpretation of creation as promissio in *Schöpfung als Anrede* (Tübingen: J. C. B. Mohr [Siebeck], 1986).

with the justice of the mercy that He lived on earth is Jesus, our brother, one of us — as will be visible bodily when we too rise from death, made fit, to hail Him.

In critical dogmatics, Christology is a function of the doctrine of the Trinity in the sense that the Trinitarian distinction between nature and person is presupposed by it, just as Cyril's great struggle is to come to this Christological application and extension of the metaphysical revolution. Only after Christian theology has clarified to itself that (1) God *is* God's self-donation and that God *is* God's self-communication, and (2) that these self-givings of God are not impersonal energies vaguely reaching us from an unknowable transcendence but the personal acts of the Three, by which (3) God is God to God and for God eternally so that (4) God can and does truly become God for us and in us in space and time — only now can the question properly be raised about the relation of the Person of the Son to the appearance in the world of the man, Jesus of Nazareth. Of course, loosely, that is to say, uncritically and not-yet-theologically we can talk about christologies as the ways in which Jesus and His work of salvation, or conversely, the work of salvation and its relation to Jesus (or not) can be variously conceived. But the matter is normatively determined for Christian theology by the appearance of this man, according to the gospel narrative, that crescendos in His bold promise of self-donation at the climax of His earthly sojourn: "This is my Body, given for you."

This is a promise that only a human body can offer and it is at the same time a promise that only a divine agent can keep. Here the human object in the world and the divine self-donation so interpenetrate one another that they become distinguishable only abstractly as reflecting respectively the sets of possibilities that we semantically group as human and divine respectively. But to know the mission of the Son and the Son in His mission is to know Jesus Christ the Son of God in this personal promise of divine self-giving of His own human body, in time and space. And this is to know the person, one with us and at the same time One of the Three.

To retrieve the Cyrilian Christology in contemporary fashion: the object of faith is (1) that human body-and-soul in the world that may be historically and critically named Jesus of Nazareth born from Mary and crucified, dead, and buried under Pontius Pilate; (2) taken as the Christ, the Son of God by the Spirit and so by virtue of divine self-communication in theological subjectivity; (3) in the sense that in this body the divine self-donation for us and our salvation took place; (4) where "divine" is taken as the Father who so loved that He gave, the Son who so loved that He went, and the Spirit who so loved that He returned the Son, with all those whom He loved, to the Beloved Community of God. Although expressed in the mythological language of the Son spatially descending and ascending from heaven to earth and back, deliteralized and decoded theologically, the aspect of the one cognitive claim of theology that is articulated here is the identification of the Son in His mission of redemption as the body given once and for all at Golgotha.

Manifestly, this Christology cares as much about the inner life and development of the self-consciousness of Jesus as did Jesus, that is to say, not at all. Jesus
has no "personality" like us who give ourselves body and soul to the structures of
malice and injustice to form a consciousness of self over against others as inferiors
and superiors, enemies and allies, consumers and consumed, doers or done-to.
But Jesus, as revealed in the decisions He made in his life's journey to Jerusalem
to proclaim God's coming near to reign, appears conscious only of His mission as
the beloved Son who inaugurates the Father's reign. He appears as nothing but
this man on a mission. His human *decisions* — I repeat, *not* His *self-consciousness* —
but His human *decisions* along this messianic way are indiscernible from the Son
of God's self-donation. That is the claim of the Incarnation. What is indiscernible
is the same thing, or better, the one same person, the one Lord Jesus Christ the
Son of God. How this can be is the proper mystery of the Incarnation; that this
is what the Incarnation is and claims to be, however, is the theological decoding
of the Christological objectivity of faith.

In corroboration of this Cyrilian claim, we may call upon the eminent Orthodox theologian John Meyendorff and his instructive *Christ in Eastern Christian
Thought,* as we shift now to the contemporary debate in systematic theology regarding the legacy of Cyrilian Christology. Meyendorff began by pointing out the
interesting Christological parallelism between Arius and Apollinaris, even though
the latter was assertively Nicene in his theology. But "both taught that in Christ
the Logos had taken the place of the human intellect; both understood Christ as
one being or nature." Arius accomplished this by diminishing the divinity of the
Logos, who was for him a superior, i.e., angelic mind; Apollinaris did the same
by taking Christ as a heavenly man "whose whole vitality and dynamism resided
in the Logos." While Antiochenes cut their theological teeth opposing Apollinar-
ianism by "their insistence on the fully *human* reality of Jesus," and while Alexandrians "remained for a long time insensitive to the Apollinarian deviation" in
their "fundamentally anti-Arian" commitments, in the end it came to "ultimately
contradictory Christologies."[62]

They diverged not over the "fully human reality of Jesus," but on the questions of (1) the unity of this full humanity with the divine Logos, and (2) how
this united humanity is true humanity, not our corrupted humanity. On the latter
point, Meyendorff detects an air of "Pelagianism" (to use the Western term for
the heresy of works righteousness that was in fact condemned in the person of
Celestius at Cyril's council at Ephesus in 431) in the notion of the autonomous
personality of Jesus, as conceived by the Antiochenes, with "free will and . . .
an independent development and activity." Indeed, "to this human nature the
Antiochenes attributed the merit of our salvation."[63] (So with the nineteenth-

---

62. John Meyendorff, *Christ in Eastern Christian Thought* (Crestwood, NY: St. Vladimir's
Seminary Press, 1975), p. 15.
63. Meyendorff, *Christ in Eastern Christian Thought,* p. 17.

century British theologian, Charles Gore, it is not wrong to speak of the Nestorian Christ as "the fitting saviour of the Pelagian man"[64] — the converse of the present proposal of a Cyrilian Christ for Augustinian humanity.) In contrast, Meyendorff sees in Cyril a "positive and theologically creative concept: that of a Christic humanity wholly human, wholly 'appropriated' by the Word, and constituting the principle of the deification to which all those who are 'in Christ' are destined."[65] Christ is, by virtue of the personal union, the New Adam and those who are in Christ are members of this New Adam's Body; this life together in Christ now is true, not fallen and corrupt humanity, and so humanity redeemed and destined for resurrection to the eternal life of the Beloved Community. But this participation is Christologically possible just because "the flesh of Jesus did not possess an independent existence but was truly 'the flesh of God.' "[66]

Cyril's insufficiently critical habit of using emergent technical terms in Christology, *physis* (nature) and *hypostasis* (person), interchangeably confused the point he was trying to make, namely, that as Person *(hypostasis)* the Son of God makes human nature His own to form the particular way in the world that is Jesus from Bethlehem through Golgotha. The union is a personal or hypostatic unification, an appropriation, making something to be one's own. In this way, Cyril was attempting to deliteralize and decode the mythological language of John 1 about the Word *becoming* flesh — a point perhaps obscured by his exuberant delight in the biblical paradoxes and his corresponding comfort with the primary language of faith. But for Cyril the Logos neither morphs into another nature, nor hybridizes, nor absorbs another nature into its own by a process of natural assimilation — all consequences that the Antiochenes rightly feared so far as a strong distinction between nature and person is not articulated and sustained. Rather the Person personalizes the human nature (not anything real but the set of species-typical characteristics) to become the concrete human being we have figured for us in the biblical narrative. As Son of the Father on whom the Spirit abides He makes this life of one of us, in distinction from all other human lives, His own human life in which He gives Himself for all those gripped in physical and mental chains to structures of malice and injustice, in every nation, to the end of days.

That is what is at stake in an articulation of "the clear distinction between the Word, as person or hypostasis, and the divinity as a nature impassible, unchangeable, and common to the whole Trinity," though Meyendorff immediately qualifies this "clear distinction" with the apophatic note that it serves to express, not explain the "mystery of redemption."[67] What is perhaps surprising today is

---

64. Cited in Alister E. McGrath, ed., *The Christian Theology Reader,* 3rd edition (Oxford: Blackwell, 2007), p. 314.

65. Meyendorff, *Christ in Eastern Christian Thought,* p. 21.

66. Meyendorff, *Christ in Eastern Christian Thought,* p. 21.

67. Meyendorff, *Christ in Eastern Christian Thought,* p. 22.

that Meyendorff in this early work (1975) of his distinguished career credited the intervention of Pope Leo in his "famous Tome to Flavian" at Chalcedon for supplying the conceptuality that Cyril lacked clearly to articulate the unity and the distinction of the two natures in Christ "without being in any way Nestorian." Moreover he credits this Western contribution at Chalcedon to its tendency to "see Christ above all as a mediator between God and humankind, based on a conception of redemption [that] was more juridical, based on the idea of sacrifice and reconciliation rather than on the Eastern concept of deification."[68] Thus, we would have a Cyrilian Christ for Augustinian humanity.

We should not too quickly today dismiss this account, say, as the offering of an ecumenical olive branch back in the optimistic days following Vatican II. Meyendorff argues that Leo's intervention offered "no mere juxtaposition" of divine and human but rather "the identity of subject in the divine and human activities of Christ: the same is God and man." This "identity of subject," Meyendorff concludes, is there in Leo's text in "a clear concept of the *communicatio idiomatum,* the very thing that was the stumbling block for all the 'nestorianizing' theologians of Antioch." The communication of natural properties as the personal act of the Logos in appropriating human nature to undertake the reconciliation of sinners and give life to the dead makes it possible to say that the Son of God died without losing His deity: "God, without ceasing to be God, made human nature *his own* to the point of mortality."[69] Hence, thanks to the Western intervention of Leo, the Formula of Chalcedon was able to preserve the "two natures" precisely in the "unity of *subject* in all actions, whether divine or human, of Christ. The word *Theotokos,* implying the *communicatio idiomatum,*" is therewith also affirmed.[70] Because the Christological union exchanges not only our death for God's life in theosis, but also our sin for Christ's righteousness in justification, the identity of subject in both the act of Incarnation and in the living of the Incarnate One's life in obedience to His mission, even to death on the cross, is necessary.

How remarkable, then, today to compare this account of Meyendorff with Robert Jenson's culminating argument in his *Unbaptized God* where the Tome of Leo represents the incoherent "compromise" that, as we recall from the beginning of Chapter Five, Ruether alleged in her own summons to a new and thoroughgoing Nestorianism. In reality, we enter now into the densest thicket of problems troubling contemporary Christology, especially in the tradition of Luther, where both the Reformer's predominant allegiance in Christology to Cyril[71] yet also his peculiar sympathy for the Nestorian theme of abandoned Jesus'

68. Meyendorff, *Christ in Eastern Christian Thought,* p. 24.

69. Meyendorff, *Christ in Eastern Christian Thought,* p. 25.

70. Meyendorff, *Christ in Eastern Christian Thought,* p. 27.

71. Marc Lienhard, *Martin Luther: Witness to Jesus Christ, Stages and Themes of the Reformer's Christology,* trans. Edwin H. Robertson (Minneapolis: Augsburg, 1982), pp. 231-35. For Luther, "the personal union does not result from the coordination of two metaphysical substances, a divine nature and a human nature, but from the movement of the Son, a free subject, who becomes incarnate

experience of Godforsakenness have to be acknowledged, thought together, and reconciled. The following excursus lays bare the problem.

## Excursus: "The Deity Has Withdrawn"[72]

We will examine a significant sample of Luther's preaching on the humanity and deity of Christ from the Smalcald Year of 1537 and its transmission a generation later at the hands of Andreas Poach (1515-1585): *The Eighth Psalm of David preached and explained by Dr. Martin Luther,* as Poach titled his edition of it in 1572. The sermon was originally preached in Wittenberg by Luther on All Saints, November 1, 1537.[73] Poach was a student in Wittenberg from 1530 to 1538. Presumably he listened to Luther's sermons there *viva vox.* In any case, he inherited George Roerer's stenographic records of Luther's preaching, the *Nachschriften,*

---

in order to save human beings, determining by this design of love the personal existence of the man Jesus. Luther was powerfully attracted by the christology of the Alexandrians, a christology which concentrates, in Athanasius, on the prolepsis, that is to say, the 'assumption' of the humanity by the Word. The human is thus 'surrounded' or 'carried' by the divine person, whose instrument it becomes for the realization of salvation. . . . Luther takes certain images or expressions from a christology founded on the *enhypostasis* . . . [John of Damascus] . . ." (pp. 231-32): ". . . the *enhypostasis,* that is to say, on the new and unique *Wesen* (being) which is Jesus Christ himself, a humanity united indissolubly to the divine hypostasis. . . . [Luther] refused to consider the Logos asarkos. . . . It is this union itself, says Luther, which saves us because this is what accomplishes the work of salvation . . . the saving work is not realized by the Word alone — occasionally united to the humanity — but by the Word and the humanity intimately linked. . . . [I]t is not a question of a coexistence of two natures, but of an intimate union, which requires the possession in common of a certain number of properties. We touch here on the conception of the communication of attributes" (p. 233). "When Luther speaks of the suffering of God in Jesus Christ, he is concerned with the communication of a human property to the divinity, and when he speaks of the ubiquity of Christ it is the other way around, because he then makes the divinity communicate one of its properties to the human nature. . . . There would be no unity of the person if there were not the activity of the Word, assuming a human nature . . ." (p. 234). Is the result a third thing? "[T]he person of the Son unites in itself the two natures, but in this hypostatic union a history begins, an intimate communion which Luther calls personal, in which the divine nature participates in the human suffering, and reciprocally the human nature participates in the divine ubiquity. The divine *hypostasis* thus truly descends into the history of human beings. It does not remain beyond them as an unchanging concept, but participates entirely in the history of Jesus of Nazareth. This is why Luther uses the term person in a double sense: on the one hand, to designate the eternal author of the act of redemption founded on the *enhypostasis,* namely the Logos; on the other hand, to designate the *concretum* in which, on the basis of the *enhypostasis,* the Logos and humanity are intimately united for our salvation" (pp. 234-35). In other words, for Luther, the Trinitarian Person is just what appears as the human figure Jesus in His obedience as the true subject.

72. This excursus derives from a paper presented at the 11th International Congress for Luther Research, July 2007 in São Paulo, Brazil for the seminar conducted by Prof. Bo Holm on the Relation between Doctrine and Life in Luther and Melanchthon.

73. *WA* 45:205-50; *LW* 12:95-136.

after Roerer's death in 1557. After his expulsion from his pastorate in Erfurt in 1569, he took the pastor's office in Utenbach in 1573. Poach tells us in his preface that he prepared Luther's Psalm 8 sermon from the Roerer notes for publication during his "exile." It is thus one of his first efforts in what proved to be his life's work. After settling down again in Utenbach, he was able to go on to produce a number of important editions of Luther's sermons.[74] These editions reconstructing Luther's sermons required of him considerable expansion of the minimal, sometimes cryptic notes that he had inherited.

This material is of interest for the question of the relation of doctrine to life on several levels. First, it is well established that the life and work of the Christian for Luther is first of all the life and work of Christ, e.g., from the early Heidelberg Disputation: "Actually one should call the work of Christ an active work and our work a passive one, and thus a passive work pleasing to God by the grace of the active work."[75] The latter, however, is communicated to the believer by means of doctrine, or, if you will, in doctrinal preaching, since one cannot *know* the life and work of Christ to entrust oneself to it apart from statements of belief that identify the agent, Christ, i.e., "doctrines." The sermon examined in this excursus is exemplary in this regard. Second, the sermon is interesting on account of Luther's provocative analysis of the *spiritual* suffering of Christ in Gethsemane in distinction from the physical torment that followed. The former Poach paraphrased as *"das rechte, hohe, geistliche Leiden."* Luther correspondingly portrayed a "Gethsemane of the soul" in the believer's own experience of Godforsakenness, biblically modeled on Job or Paul. Doctrine and life are correlated here not only, or chiefly, in regard to the activity of Christian love, but rather in connection with suffering, especially the spiritual suffering of the witness to truth, including the experience of martyrdom. This latter accent may have attracted the exiled Poach to this particular sermon in difficult days of his own life.

A third reason requires more elaboration. Poach himself became a major controversialist in the so-called Second Antinomian controversy concerning the validity of the law for the Christian life. He sharply opposed George Major's doctrine that "good works are necessary for salvation";[76] he even criticized friend[77]

---

74. Susan Siebert, "Andreas Poach," *Biographisch-Bibliographisches Kirchenlexikon* (Herzberg: Verlag Traugott Bautz, 1994), VII:762-63.

75. *LW* 31, p. 56, translation modified.

76. Poach smartly inverted Major's arguments in three theses: *"1. Iustitia et salus esse necessaria ad bona opera, quia nulla opera possunt dici bona, nisi quae fiunt a persona iustificata et salvata. 2. Lex et vetus testamentum non habent promissionem iustificationis et vitae aeternae sed promissiones praemiorum cum conditione. 3. Universa scriptura sancta legem in proprio suo usu docet ad mortem et damnationem. Nam Deus neminem iustificat et salvat, nisi prius damnatum et mortificatum."* Matthias Richter, "Andreas Poach und sein Anteil am 2. Antinomischten Streit," *Archiv für Reformationsgeschichte* 85 (1994): 132. All translations from this article are my own.

77. Oliver K. Olson, *Mathias Flacius and the Survival of Luther's Reform* (Wiesbaden: Harrassowitz Verlag, 2002), pp. 147-48.

and fellow Gnesio-Lutheran, Flacius, for conceding to the Majorists that, *abstractly* speaking, the fulfillment of the law is necessary for salvation, as the first thesis of the Eisenach synod had determined: "abstractly and regarding the idea as such it is possible to tolerate the thesis that 'good works are necessary for salvation.'"[78] Thus Poach is an important witness in second-generation Lutheranism to difficult problems that endure to the present day about the relation to life of doctrine, especially in respect to the decisive distinction of law and gospel.

The distinction between law and gospel is drawn here by Trinitarian Christology, that is, by the personal sojourn of Christ from humiliation to exaltation, a sojourn that renders the dispensation of the law temporary and the promise of the gospel everlasting. For Poach, the law is fulfilled *concretely* when its preaching exposes sin and effects despair before God of the helplessly indebted sinner. Then its work is finished. Correspondingly, Poach argued that the righteousness of the gospel is eschatological and heavenly. For this distinction Poach drew on Luther's second Galatians commentary. As Richter puts it, Poach's appeal to the distinction between "the *'iustitia activa terrena'* and a *'iustitia coelestis passiva'* that we do not possess but receive from heaven [as gift] is found in Luther almost verbatim."[79]

Poach's greatly expanded 1572 version[80] of Luther's 1537 sermon, however, did not directly take the opportunity to polemicize against the Majorists. Jaroslav Pelikan was right to state in 1955 that "comparison of Poach's work with Luther's sermon [i.e., the *Nachschrift*] indicates that he did his work conscientiously and did not consciously read into Luther ideas that were not there. . . . There appears to be no trace here of his position in the Majoristic and Antinomian controversies."[81] Yet as Richter maintained in his 1994 study, research had not determined precisely enough the nuance of Poach's position on the temporal delimitation of the law's ministry in distinction from the eschatological scope of the promise of the gospel.[82] This eschatology turns out to be a central concern in Luther's 1537 sermon and thus provides yet another motive for Poach's selection of it, since the Majorists, following Melanchthon, inclined toward a protological theology of *lex aeternitatis*.[83]

---

78. *Bona opera sunt necessaria ad salutatem, in doctrina abstractive et de idea tolerari potest.* Richter, "Andreas Poach und sein Anteil," p. 122. Against this, Poach took the position: "In abstracto & de idea könne diese These aber ebensowenig toleriert werden, da die lex et bona opera in der Kirche nicht abstractive oder speculative gepredigt werden, sonder so, dass die Menschen zur Erkenntnis der Sünde geführt werden . . . kein Spiel, sondern eine res seria. . . ." Richter, "Andreas Poach und sein Anteil," p. 127.

79. Richter, "Andreas Poach und sein Anteil," pp. 135-36, my translation.

80. In translator Jaroslav Pelikan's words: "Some of [Poach's] work is merely an expansion into complete sentences of ideas that were cryptically stated in a word or phrase; some of it is an exposition or quotation where Luther had only an allusion." *LW* 12, p. ix.

81. *LW* 12, p. ix.

82. Richter, "Andreas Poach und sein Anteil," pp. 123-24.

83. E.g., "Many ask, what is natural law? The answer is that it is precisely the eternal unchangeable wisdom in God which he proclaimed in the Ten Commandments." It is, like arithmetic, implanted in us and clarified through Christ and the Scriptures. It is the natural "light that

Luther's sermon of 1537 was a Christological exposition of Psalm 8; the sermon notes follow the course of the Psalm text. I will now provide a condensed paraphrase of pertinent selections from the sermon, based solely on Roerer's *Nachschrift,* followed with commentary. I have also provided some subheadings to outline the flow of the sermon. In this light, analysis of the theological nuances of Poach's appropriation and expansions in 1572 may be undertaken in which Luther's apparently Antiochene claim that in the spiritual suffering of Christ "the Deity had withdrawn" was placed firmly into the context of Luther's Alexandrian commitments in Christology. This indicates the way towards a "higher synthesis" in which the legitimate concerns of Antioch may be received without the cost of Christological dualism. Rather, the cost that must be paid for this "higher synthesis" is that believers receive Christ by joining the "women who watched from afar" the confrontation between the Father and the Son, when God was against God in order to surpass God.

### Synopsis of Luther's 1537 Sermon on Psalm 8

#### Trinitarian advent

> Psalm 8:1 — The Lord, our Ruler, how glorious is Thy name in all the lands! Thou to whom thanks are given in heaven.[84]

"This beautiful psalm is about the expansion of the reign of God from the little nook of Jerusalem to the entire world. The name of 'Lord' does not here signify the divine nature in its heavenly essence but rather his outward reign in relation to us. Thus Christ is indicated as true God with his Father and the Holy Spirit in the divine essence, and yet he comes here on earth to become our Lord and he is preached as God through the whole world as indicated in Romans 1:2-4: the Father awakened the Son from death and by the Holy Spirit let him be proclaimed so that this same one should be known as Lord, true God and also Lord according to his humanity, with all subject to him: angels, death, hell."

#### King of Truth

"Yet he is unlike all other authorities: Turk, Pope, Caesar, King, none of whom do the works ascribed to Christ. His is a miraculous kingdom, in that this kingdom is said not to be mortal yet those who are in it are mortal. Christ testified to this before Pilate, that he is 'the king of truth.' His kingdom is built by the Spirit, not

---

God is an eternal, omnipotent, wise, true, good, just, and pure being, who created all things, who wills that all rational creatures be like him in virtue and who will punish and remove the rational creatures who are repugnant to his wisdom and righteousness." *Melanchthon on Christian Doctrine: Loci Communes 1555,* trans. C. L. Manschreck (Grand Rapids: Baker, 1982), p. 128.

84. I am using Pelikan's rendering into English of the Psalm text supplied by Poach; it is lacking in the *Nachschrift.*

the sword. The world is full of guile and unfaithfulness, but Christ is the truth, namely, king in heaven and yet also on earth and even in hell, already now in heart and faith since believers believe in the resurrection, eternal life, and the holy catholic church. Here emperor and pope have nothing to do; here Christ is king. The believer looks ahead to rising on the last day, when this bag of worms will be cleansed. Even now on earth the believer gives thanks to God in heaven. Now we have the name of Jesus, not yet the person; nevertheless in His name we hear the promise of this future, when He will finally come and say to the dead: 'Come, and we will be gathered together in eternal life.' So the kingdom is on the earth yet not earthly. We are in the flesh but not fleshly. Our lives are hidden in Christ with God. The devil and unbelievers do not see this and so are hostile. The devil attacks the promise and faith. Who could defeat him?"

### The Foolishness of God

> Psalm 8:2 — Out of the mouths of babes and sucklings hast Thou ordained strength because of Thine enemies, that Thou mightest destroy the enemy and the avenger.

"Why not send Gabriel or Michael or another powerful angel? Amazing! God is pleased to be disdained and scorned. For that reason he becomes a poor worm, who had nothing. He undertakes weakness and absurdity, just as afterwards He makes the twelve apostles to be fools before the powers of the world, telling them to go preach to all creatures the news of the reign of Christ. He sends Peter to Rome to take on the most powerful people in the whole world, who thought no one in the world could hurt them, just as today the Turk and the Emperor hang their enemies by the noose or behead them. Is it not amazing? He does not use strong angels in heaven, who are powerful. He uses human nature, which the devil devours, in which the Lord dwells under sin and death, to bind the devil hand and foot. 'Go preach and raise up my kingdom and overthrow the devil.' Such are the works of God, whose nature is to make all things out of nothing. So God will make fools out of kings and emperors who travel about with gold and weapons according to the cunning wisdom of the devil. Out of the same infirmity, as out of the mouths of children, God makes those who are most foolish most wise, like the child in the Temple. The Boy confounds the sages."

### The Kingdom Prayer

"Just so also with us. The pope opposes us, what of it? Nothing happens, the Word alone goes out, the Our Father, the Creed, and kings and emperors are frightened. 'Out of the mouths of babes,' i.e., out of the folly of preaching, which they regard as nothing and as heresy. But so God is more powerful than the devil. So when God does nothing, He is most powerful, utilizing weakness. It is God's wisdom to establish His kingdom through the merciful Word, through oral preaching, which many hear, accept and believe, not at our urging, but moved by the Spirit they become again as children and learn to pray the Our Father. This enrages the devil, who embitters the world against the pious. God permits this. The babes have to deal with evil enemies. Paul asked three times to be delivered, but God answered him in His wisdom: 'You must be weak, that my strength may be manifest.' God's kingdom come, His will be done!"

### The New Heaven

> Psalm 8:3 — For I shall look at the heavens, the work of Thy fingers, the moon and the stars which Thou art establishing.

"There will be a new heaven. We will be there in heaven and everything will be heavenly. First God delivers from sin and death and then God binds the wounds. Then one is made entirely whole and pure in body and soul. Just as the cosmos fell into corruption with Adam's sin, so the promised kingdom of Christ is not temporal but celestial; yet it is coming here on the earth. The prophet David foresees it in faith and the Spirit, just as Peter does: we expect new things. We will be able to fly above and below in a new Paradise with a more beautiful heaven than before, with excellent lawns and roses — but no nettles. Christ will be the sun in it, as Malachi says, because where He shines the heart is enlightened and made righteous. Just as God made the sun to enlighten the first creation, in this new world Christ will shine as the sun, as Psalm 118 says. So the Son will be in this kingdom, the man and Son of Man."

### Accursed by God

> Psalm 8:4 — What is Man that Thou art mindful of Him, and the Son of Man that Thou dost care for Him?

"But now David looks upon him in a high, deep thought as the martyr of Isaiah 53, not even regarded as a man, from whom we averted our eyes. 'Phooey on you,' we say, 'whom God accursed!' Those who have it well, the rich, are the blessed of God. How can one believe that God embraces this worm as His beloved? How foolishly our Lord God acts that His Son should die and so be preached through-out the world."

### The Spiritual Suffering of Christ

> Psalm 8:5a — Thou wilt let Him be forsaken of God for a little while. . . .

"In amazement the prophet says: God has forgotten His own. So he describes the passion of Christ in a few words. He says nothing of the physical cross, but rather that for a little while the Son of man will be left hanging on the God who has deserted him. Who can understand that? To be deserted by God is more evil than death. Think of Job. God boasts of His servant. Satan replies: 'He has good things.' God permitted Satan to go after him, since he is able to do nothing unless the Lord allows. Now everything is burned away and the wife mocks him. Still the devil demands more: 'You have left him alive. Give me a piece of his soul.' That's the blow. Now Job is totally abandoned, in trial, feeling hell without help from either men or angels. There is nothing to do but abandon oneself to God. No one knows this like Christ in the Garden. He is left in death, as if it were eternal. David writes concerning this: the divinity thus will hide itself, so that it is possible to say that there is no deity here. There is only the devil, hell, eternal fire and eternal death. He is a man, who is thus deserted, so that the entire world says: God will never show Him regard. The deity has withdrawn, so that He fights all alone. In His agony there is not only sweat of blood but being abandoned, because He thought himself deserted by God. There are thus according to David two kinds of suffering, the physical thirst and also the absence of consolation. If God Himself is absent, no one is able to be consoled, be there all the dancing and music in the world. That is Christ's true suffering."

### Christ Adorned with His Saints

Psalm 8:5b — But Thou wilt crown Him with honor and adornment.

"Resurrection! All thought Him deserted by God and the world, but you, O Lord, will lead Him forth, and in place of His ignominy and disgrace, which He had on earth and before you, you will adorn Him. Not with expensive clothes and jewels but His body and soul will be beautiful and full of life, joy, blessedness, wisdom, power, full of deity so that all creatures, sun, moon and stars will laugh with Him, the victor over the devil. All the more will He be adorned by His saints and angels without end — His trophies of victory."

### The God-Man Reigns

Psalm 8:6 — Thou wilt make him Lord over the works of Thy hands; Thou hast put all things under His feet.

"This describes not only the man but also the God, who from eternity was born Lord. That is the divinity of Christ. God places no one above all creatures, except God. He alone is above angels, sun, moon. Therefore He is the man, who was stretched out on the cross and deserted by God so that He cried out, and yet, He should be called Lord over all creatures, i.e. God. Therefore He is true God and man according to His humanity. Killed, suffered, abandoned, raised. And nevertheless He the Crucified is Lord over all creation. Therefore the angels adore Him even as man, because He is one person, God and man inseparable. Thus Matthew 28: All authority is given to me. According to the deity, He had authority from eternity. So it is through the humanity which suffered and was raised from the dead and glorified that He becomes Lord over all. Therefore we know that Christ has two natures. Body and soul from His mother, being man like any other, yet without sin, He is the son of man. Yet also He is Lord over all, with the Father true God. So the child of man is made Lord over all. This is not said of Adam, who was placed on the earth to have dominion over all other creatures, as in Genesis 1. That man would rule over the beasts. That is an easy thing. But this man is Lord not only over beasts but over all men, angels, and whatever else may be said. Therefore He is greater than Adam to whom all are not subject. The world is His footstool. He is Lord over sins, death, life, angels and none other than true, natural God."

### Lord of Time and Eternity

> Psalm 8:7-8 — All sheep and oxen, and also the beasts of the field, the birds of the air, and the fish of the sea, whatever passes along the paths of the sea.

"In the new life when the heavenly kingdom comes, Christ will be the Sun, who on our account was deserted and raised, adorned and made Lord over heaven and earth. Now we have light in our hearts to invoke Him and the Father. And when death and sin take hold of us, we know that He holds us who is pleased to help us and obtains access to the Father. All things are in His power. Adam's kingdom too belongs to Christ. We do not reason: if Christ has His own kingdom, then He does not communicate with the kingdom of Adam. But that kingdom also will be under Christ. All both pious and impious must be under the king Christ. All things are in his hands."

### The Wonder of the Incarnation

> Psalm 8:9 — Oh Lord, our Ruler, how glorious is Thy name in all the lands!

"David concludes by repeating the first verse. The wonder of this kingdom is how the great Martyr has acquired it, not through worldly power but through His infirmities. Christ is called the new Light, replacing the Sun of the old creation, because this wisdom does not derive from human reason, but from the divine Sun, which came and died and was raised for us so that through Him we might be saved."

We turn now to commentary on the foregoing and then an account of Poach's expansion of the sermon for publication. Luther undoubtedly viewed his Christological reading of Psalm 8 as justified by the parallel of verse 6b, "Thou hast put all things under His feet," to Paul's statement in 1 Corinthians 15:27 about the reign of Christ. In general, Luther's Christological reading of the Psalms forms an essential component of his theology, with its scriptural hermeneutic.[85] The following aspects of the 1537 sermon are especially noteworthy.

---

85. Mickey L. Mattox, "From Faith to the Text and Back Again: Martin Luther on the Trinity in the Old Testament," *Pro Ecclesia* 15, no. 3 (Summer 2006): 281-303.

The sermon begins with Trinitarian advent. That is to say, the canonical narrative tells of God's eternal decision to send Christ in the flesh to redeem the lost and likewise to send the Spirit to incorporate the redeemed into Christ by repentance and faith. The anthropological transition from the state of sin to the state of righteousness is a function of this master Trinitarian narrative of which the coming of Christ in the flesh to redeem is the epistemic key. Here Christ appears as the *rex veritatis.* The action in the world which distinguishes this king of truth and His reign by Word and Spirit is that it employs no coercive tools nor conditional threats and rewards but only defenseless oral witness of an unconditional promise. That is a weakness that proves powerful on the basis of Luther's eschatological conception that stamps the entire sermon. Luther thus combines the Johannine theme of truth bearing witness with the Pauline motif of the foolishness of God through preaching the cross. These prove wiser than the wisdom of the world, which in its wisdom falsely thinks that those who have happiness now are blessed and close to God.

But through the word of truth, people learn to say the Kingdom Prayer, looking to the final future promised by God: *Thy kingdom come!* This is to invoke the New Heaven, the transformed cosmos in which Luther fancies the redeemed flying like birds in the sky — fanciful, yet an indication of the cosmic breadth of the Fall and of the scope of the Pauline "redemption of our bodies," that is, all the oppressed "creation now groaning in travail." Thus Luther insists that this final future of God is the future of this present earth, on which stood the cross of Christ. For the very same reason, however, the world in its wisdom enthroned upon the present reality and holding fast to it against God's coming mocks the Crucified as one accursed by God, since it does not believe, nor want to believe, this promised future.

Yet Christ actually was cursed by God. The spiritual suffering of Christ was not only that men and angels regarded him as nothing and as abandoned by God, but that Christ actually was abandoned, not only by the world but also by His God and Father. For Luther this must be so, though not in any modern sense of the cultural death of God. He is rather thinking after Paul in Galatians. Christ's death on the tree as one accursed gives the good reason why the saints — who otherwise would be abandoned to their sins and dead to God — will rise with Christ, whose faith and love and hope were vindicated on the third day. Because He was forsaken, He shared the plight of His people before God to make them His own, so that when God made the incarnate Christ, with this achieved solidarity, His own, Christ's own are included in the Easter inclusion. Thus the risen Lord is adorned with these same people, who have become His victory trophies. In His abandonment by God, He has gone to the depth of their predicament and laid claim to them and won the right over them for the final future in the heavenly kingdom.

From this root action of the gospel, i.e., the Easter vindication of the Crucified who now reigns on behalf of His people, we learn that Christ is the God-Man who reigns as Lord of time and eternity *on account of the passage He has made* from a state of humiliation to one of exaltation. Therefore the kingdom of Adam also comes into His possession and belongs to Him. There is no dualism of spheres, no separation of time from eternity, but only a provisional, ever-to-be-discerned practical distinction between "ultimate and penultimate" concerns (Bonhoeffer). There is, however, a sharp differentiation made between the sword and terror used by the kingdoms of this world with their rewards and threats and the Word of truth and Spirit of promise at work in the church in the field of conscience. The wonder of the Incarnation is that God the almighty who creates out of nothing confounds the regnant terrorists of this world astride structures of malice and injustice with a martyr, Jesus king of truth, defenseless in the world, speaking the truth that casts down the mighty but exalts those of low degree.

Poach is eager to appropriate Luther's Christologically modified apocalyptic eschatology because it restricts the dispensation of the law, that is, not with regard to its ethical content but with regard to its sovereignty by means of coercive threats and conditional promises, to a limited and worldly function in distinction from the gospel promise of inclusion in the Reign — God's eternal Word, unconditional in nature and universal in scope and finality. Poach was not antinomian, but in regard to the law he distinguished between a Major's *necessitas salutis* that must be rejected and a *necessitas debiti,* to be affirmed, that is, the necessity of good works as our creaturely debt to the Creator, based on Luke 17:10: "For God is not obligated to man but man to God."[86] The "sum of the controversy" with the Majorists according to Poach was "whether the law and Old Testament promise salvation or whether the promise of salvation, that is, of remission of sins and justification are properly of the gospel and the New Testament."[87] Here Poach accents the Christological modification of the apocalyptic eschatology as inaugurated eschatology. The New Testament does not promise a "king like the other nations" (1 Samuel 8) but a new kind of sovereignty altogether. Interestingly, this twist in the argument not only produced the tension with Flacius mentioned at the outset, who with "his Majoristic, abstract and concrete distinctions" justifies the "devilish doctrine" of the law's "necessity for salvation."[88] In the eyes of a semi-Majorist opponent, J. Moerlin, this argument about a new and eschatological righteousness brought Poach into the vicinity of Osiander, who notoriously had taught as Lutheran doctrine that righteousness is the essential quality of God infused into the hearts of believers.

Moerlin had in fact contended against Osiander in Königsburg in this dispute whether the righteousness of Christ was divine and essential righteousness or the righteousness acquired by His Incarnate obedience to the law. Moerlin did

---

86. *"Non enim Deus obligatus est homini, sed homo obligatus Deo."* Richter, "Andreas Poach und sein Anteil," p. 129.

87. *". . . lex et vetus testamentum promittat salutem . . . An vero promisso [sic] salutis, hoc est, remissionis peccatorum et iustificationis sit Euangelii et novi Testamenti propria. . . ."* Richter, "Andreas Poach und sein Anteil," p. 132.

88. Richter, "Andreas Poach und sein Anteil," p. 131.

not, however, concur with what he regarded as the "unfortunately" formulated first thesis of the Majorist Eisenach synod about the necessity of good works for salvation. For Moerlin, the heart of the controversy was rather whether the law taught of eternal life or not and thus expressed ethical continuity with God's saving purpose in creation and redemption and fulfillment. Thus for both Poach and Moerlin, there was agreement that the gospel of law-free grace is at stake in this difficult conflict, and that Major's formulation about good works as necessary for salvation was "Satanae doctrina" that evacuates the gospel as unconditional promise of God. Yet Moerlin objects to Poach that it is senseless to distinguish between the necessity of good works for salvation and the necessity of satisfying debt as creatures, since in fact God has created the human creature for eternal life. The works of the law are the works that ought to have led us to God, for the law is holy, just, and good. The "debt" we owe to God is the happy one of loving God and enjoying God forever. The law of God is ordered to our salvation. It is this law that Christ overfulfilled for us and so "merits" our salvation.

Poach sought to respond to this powerful objection in a way that genuinely advanced the argument. He agreed that the "merits" of Christ are the merits of our salvation: Christ is not simply savior as the incarnate Person, but it is the work that this incarnate Person accomplishes that saves by outbidding the law on its own terms. Thus the ground of Christ's "merit" is that, while we are debtors to the law, Christ in distinction from us truly is not such a debtor by nature but becomes one by grace — the grace of His forgiving solidarity with sinners whose sin He takes from them and upon Himself. The law was given to us creatures, not to Christ who is the Lord of the law. Nevertheless Christ spontaneously out of loving compassion subjected Himself to the jurisdiction of the law for our sake. As a voluntary act of love, which is not legally required, the forgiveness of sins and gift of justification come about as something *supra extra legem.* Christ is not to be conceived as a perfect human being who wins a prize and thus can share its benefits with his friends, as Anselm thinks. Christ is to be conceived of as the Incarnate Son who wins those dead in their sins for His Father's kingdom of life by fulfilling love's radical demand in taking their debt and death upon Himself, the very wages of sin. For Anselm, Christ is a punishment-bearer but for Poach, following Luther, Christ is more profoundly a sin-bearer. Richter calls this insight of Poach the highpoint of the entire debate. Moerlin could only ask in reply whether the righteousness or merit of Christ so conceived, *supra extra legem,* is not after all Osiander's essential righteousness.[89] Of course it may so appear if Western modalism controls Christological thinking: then the voluntary love of Christ is nothing but the expression of divine and essential righteousness. But if we are thinking in terms of Trinitarian personalism, Christ's incarnate love for sinners *supra extra legem* expresses the bold thought of God surpassing God.

In any event, in his edition of Luther's sermon on Psalm 8, Poach makes

89. Richter, "Andreas Poach und sein Anteil," pp. 133-34.

many expansions on Roerer's notes in this direction of the promise of the gospel as something *supra extra legem,* e.g.: "This is spoken according to the nature of Christ's kingdom, which is a strange and wonderful kingdom, not an earthly, perishable, mortal kingdom, but an eternal, heavenly, imperishable kingdom."[90] Verse 3 of Psalm 8, according to Poach's expansion of Luther's bare words, "speaks of the glory and revelation that we have to expect in that life. The kingdom of faith and the kingdom of future glory are one kingdom, but they are distinguished in that what is offered to us here in the kingdom of faith through the Word and what we receive and grasp by faith will be presented to us there in that revelation. . . . Therefore there is one kingdom, only there is a difference in knowledge. Now we believe and hope for it with all Christians on earth, then we shall possess it with all the holy angels and God's elect in heaven."[91] Particularly impressive is this addition: "We shall have an eternal Sabbath and holy day, be eternally satisfied in God, eternally joyful, safe and free of all sorrow. We shall see God and His work eternally, not hidden behind a veil. . . . It will not be an earthly, temporal life, but a heavenly, eternal life."[92] Thus David "believed in such a future glory of the children of God. . . . David looks into such a future."[93]

In all the foregoing, it should nonetheless be emphasized that Poach is building on thoughts actually expressed, however allusively, by Luther, as captured in the 1537 *Nachschrift.* Yet Poach's accentuation of the eschatological *Novum* comports well with his own position in the Majorist controversy: the promise of the gospel qualitatively surpasses anything envisioned in the dispensation of the law. The surpassing "merit" of Christ, who voluntarily out of love subjected Himself to the law, consists in the fact that this divine and personal condescension of love was not obligatory to the Lord of the law, although it was fitting for the Giver of the Law also to fulfill the Law in self-donation. Christ's "merit" was not then some act of the human nature on its own part, fulfilling its own natural debt of righteousness to the law.

Yet there is a problem for Poach in the *Nachschrift:* Luther's bold language about the withdrawal of the deity during Christ's spiritual suffering in Gethsemane might imply another view of Jesus' humanly autonomous obedience and hence quid pro quo "merit." Luther's troublesome words are: *"Divinitas sic occultabit se, ut dici possit nullam deitatem hic. Ibi Teufel, hell, ewig feuer und ewig tod."*[94] Or again: *"Die Gottheit hat entzogen. . . ."*[95] Such notions might imply along

---

90. *LW* 12, p. 103; cf. also pp. 108, 113. "My kingdom is not established, strengthened, or preserved by external force and the physical sword, as the kingdom of the world is. . . ." *LW* 12, p. 103. "Today the Jews are still waiting for Messiah to come with a great army and many soldiers and to establish a secular empire." *LW* 12, p. 104.

91. *LW* 12, pp. 103, 118.

92. *LW* 12, p. 120.

93. *LW* 12, p. 120.

94. *WA* 45, p. 239.

95. *WA* 45, p. 240.

Antiochene lines that the merit of Christ was indeed that of autonomous man who boldly abandoned himself to the God who had abandoned him. In this way he fulfilled *in extremis* the legal demand for faith in God in every trial and so morally compelled, as it were, God's recognition and reward. In that case, Major's doctrine would be validated: *bona opera sunt necessaria ad salutatem.* Christ's human merit in His bold, voluntary, and trusting death would be the supererogatory meritorious work par excellence. Here is a portrait of the naked human Christ that has much appealed to existentialist theologians of the twentieth century.

There is no express textual evidence that can be discerned in Poach's editorial expansions in his 1572 edition of the 1537 sermon for the preceding reconstruction of a motive in the polemics of the Majorist controversy. Yet it is striking how Poach strives to contextualize Luther's remarks about the withdrawal of the deity. He does this by introducing the distinction between the immanent and economic Trinity on the one hand, and the anti-Nestorian Christological doctrine of the *communicatio idiomatum* on the other hand. Luther, as we may recall, at the outset commented briefly on the meaning of the "Lord as our Ruler" to indicate that the psalm is about the economic advent to us of the Trinity. But Poach takes the opportunity here on the basis of Hebrew terminology to fill out Luther's tacit distinction between immanent and economic trinity as something required by the Incarnation. The deity is on the one hand "ascribed to no creature on earth . . . but only to God . . . a special and proper name of God [which] means the 'right, true, and eternal God . . . ,' the Divine majesty in its secret, heavenly being, as the Father is and is called Lord and God, and the Son is and is called Lord and God, and the Holy Spirit is and is called Lord and God."[96] But on the other hand, the eternal Son "came to earth and became man to deal with us and be our Ruler, Sovereign, and Authority, and we His dominion and subjects. He is Lord and God by His eternal and divine nature and being. He is Ruler by His human nature and by the office and kingdom in which He is our overlord and we are His subjects."[97]

That vital distinction sets the stage for what Poach is evidently most concerned to emphasize: "But David keeps the unity of the person firm and sure." As just mentioned, he "indicates the two natures in Christ . . . yet he speaks not of two, but of one single Lord and Ruler." This anti-Nestorian move, generally well grounded in Luther's theology, has but scant basis in the *Nachschrift.* There, towards the end, Luther is reminded to say: "Thus true God and man, according to the humanity dead, suffered, and abandoned and resurrected and nevertheless this one crucified is the Lord above all creations. Thus the angels adore Him, even the human being, because of the one person; [David] does not sever God and man."[98] Yet Poach recurs to the doctrine of the one person and the communi-

---

96. *LW* 12, p. 99.
97. *LW* 12, p. 100.
98. *WA* 45, pp. 240-41, my translation.

cation of idioms in his theologically corrected edition of Luther's sermon at the decisive point where Luther speaks of the deity withdrawing. Thus far Luther: "And in fact he was forsaken by God." Poach adds immediately: "This does not mean that the deity was separated from the humanity — for in this person who is Christ, the Son of God and of Mary, deity and humanity are so united that they can never be separated or divided. . . ."[99] Poach resorts to Philippians 2 and the personal, not natural account of the kenosis teaching to account for this apparent contradiction, interpreted in the sense of Christ's penal suffering.[100] The unity of the person who is in sequence humiliated and exalted is thus stated and reinforced at the beginning and end of Poach's edition of Luther's sermon.[101]

It would be unscholarly to make the remark about the withdrawal of the deity into an independent theme of Luther's mature Christological teaching, yet it is striking how close he comes here to Theodore of Mopsuestia's Son of Mary who could not have tasted "the trial of death if [the Godhead] were not cautiously remote from Him." As inept as the language is — as noted Luther corrects himself at the end of the sermon just as Poach makes abundant use of Luther's own correction in his expanded edition — there is something struggling to find expression here that the one personhood of the divine Son expressed in the *communicatio idiomatum* does not, or at least had not yet, perceived. This is the something that Poach tried to express with the notion of a righteousness *supra extra legem* achieved in the decision of obedience made by Jesus in His life's way, climaxing in this Beloved Son's decision *supra extra legem* to own our Godforsakenness as His own place before God. That entails not only a communication of the glorious divine properties to the human nature, as Cyril envisions and Luther also embraces, but a communication of the most miserable human properties to the divine, so that it is true to say of this Person: The Son of God was crucified, dead, and buried. More precisely — and this was Luther's special point in the sermon regarding the "spiritual" suffering — the Son of God was forsaken by His Father. Not naturally, but personally, where personal existence is the only real existence there is. A chasm opens here within the divine life of love, when the Father's love turned against what is against love just as the Son's love embraced just those who are against love. In this way, the Son of God suffered spiritually not pathetically, as Creator not creature, as God albeit in the way of being the Son, in the divine way of being the Son who is Jesus in Gethsemane. And in just this way He was, or rather became the righteousness of God in a new way, *supra extra legem*. And it is as this novel righteousness in the world that Jesus Christ the Son of God is the object of faith revealed in the gospel.

---

99. *LW* 12, p. 126.

100. *LW* 12, p. 127. On "penal suffering" in Luther's sense, see Heinrich Bornkamm, *Luther's World of Thought,* trans. Martin H. Bertram (St. Louis: Concordia, 1958), pp. 173-75.

101. *LW* 12, pp. 101, 132, 135.

## The Christological Way between Schleiermacher and Barth

The characteristic modern options in Christology between Schleiermacher and Barth are alike reductions that take the difference between divine and human natures as opposing starting points for reflection on the person of Christ. It does not matter here that modern Christologies are rightly critical of substance ontology as a way of thinking that tacitly divinizes creatures and also critical of the deceptive employment of a common concept of nature, taken as a substance, that eclipses the incomparability of the Infinite nature that cannot be contained in or made proportional to the finite. Schleiermacher pioneered such criticism, as we shall shortly note. Barth continues it by taking "nature" as event according to his ontology of act. Bruce McCormack has very carefully laid this out. The decisive modern question is, "How is it possible that God can take up a creaturely medium and bear witness to Himself in and through it without ceasing to be God? What is the condition for the possibility of revelation in God Himself?"[102] Barth asks the Kantian question, then, about the condition for the possibility of divine self-revelation. And Barth answers, according to McCormack, in the same Kantian idiom: "What must God be in eternity if He can reveal Himself in time without ceasing to be God? Barth's derivation of the Trinity is thus the fruit of an analysis of a *concrete* act of a *concretely existing Subject*."[103] God is the one, free, self-determining Subject, the Thinker who knows Himself and wills Himself as pure act and eternal event. As such, God is able to "repeat" Himself in time in the creature, Jesus, where and when Jesus is the "witness" of this free event and so of grace for us. Thus substance gives way to subject, and thing to event.

In modern Christology, also at its most profound as in Barth (as McCormack shows), the person is the noumenal Subject, an Ego transcendent to what is manifest in the work visible to our eyes. This is the causal agent that we deduce of the visible deed and assume as the praiseworthy or blameworthy initiator of deeds into the causal nexus. How could the person of Christ be grasped other than by a transcendental deduction from the work that is visible in history to its hidden agent? Yet Bonhoeffer objects: "Even Christ's work is not unequivocal. It remains open to various interpretations." To accentuate the point with reference to the preceding: Jewish perplexity at the allegedly messianic work of the Jesus whose life-work terminated at the cross accordingly now becomes a principle of self-questioning internal to Christology, so that, returning to Bonhoeffer, only "when I know who he is, who does this, I will know what it is that he does."[104] In turn, knowledge of what Christ truly does fills out and reinforces knowledge of

---

102. Bruce L. McCormack, *Karl Barth's Critically Realistic Dialectical Theology: Its Genesis and Development 1909-1936* (Oxford: Clarendon, 1995), p. 261.

103. McCormack, *Barth's Critically Realistic Dialectical Theology*, p. 354.

104. Dietrich Bonhoeffer, *Christ the Center,* trans. Edwin H. Robertson (New York: Harper & Row, 1978), pp. 37-39. See also Pannenberg, *ST* 2, pp. 334-43.

the Who that He is. Problematically, however, for Bonhoeffer's objection to the epistemological approach to Christology: only God knows who one is, since only God knows and searches the heart — only God knows the person.

For the "person" is not simply or even principally the *prosopon* who appears in the world or the posited agent/subject of free moral actions in the world. The "person" is finally, that is, eschatologically who anyone is in relation to God, as settled in the eschaton of judgment, even as the Sonship of Jesus Christ is settled (Rom. 1:2-4) in the prolepsis of that eschaton that is His resurrection from the dead. Personhood cannot then be reduced to some natural substantiality, but is rather the coherence of a life span, whether in default or in fulfillment of the human vocation to live before God, conscientiously in co-humanity as *imago Dei*. As recipient of that calling, the person is patient-agent, first formed before ever arising to action in the complex dynamics of creation continuing, albeit oppressed and distorted by the structures of malice and injustice. Hence knowledge of the person too, it seems, is blocked from us. It is God's knowledge of the person, of Jesus as well as of us, which is decisive. The person of Jesus becomes the object of knowing faith only when He is revealed by the Spirit to faith as the Father's Beloved Son. The "ambivalence was set aside only by the resurrection of the Crucified."[105] For just that reason, "Christology is not soteriology."[106] Epistemically, we can know Jesus Christ, present for us — truly, as Bonhoeffer will go on to say, *for* us, *the* Man-for-Others — only as a function of God's apocalypse, that is to say, of the Father's sharing with us already now His knowledge of His Crucified Son by the sending of His own Spirit to make us theological subjects who know this theological object.[107]

Trinitarian Christology is the procedure that follows the creeds that arose, as discussed above in Chapter Three, to form the theological subject in this knowledge of the theological object. Following upon the opening attestation of faith in the almighty Father, the baptismal creed turned to the Son of the just-named Father, "Jesus Christ, His only Son, our Lord." This statement of identity is the

---

105. Pannenberg, *ST* 2, p. 343.

106. Bonhoeffer, *Christ*, p. 39. Bonhoeffer hastens to clarify: "[T]he Christological question by its very nature must be addressed to the one complete Christ. This complete Christ is the historical Jesus, who can never in any way be separated from his work."

107. Wolfhart Pannenberg made the same argument. "There is no reason for the assumption that Jesus' claim to authority taken by itself justified faith in him. On the contrary, the pre-Easter Jesus' claim to authority stands from the beginning in relationship to the question of the future verification of his message through the occurrence of the future judgment. . . . Thus has been shown the proleptic structure of Jesus' claim to authority. . . . This means, however, that Jesus' claim to authority cannot by itself be made the basis of a Christology, as though this involved only the 'decision' in relation to him. Such Christology — and the preaching based upon it — would remain an empty assertion. Rather, everything depends upon the connection between Jesus' claim and its confirmation by God." Wolfhart Pannenberg, *Jesus: God and Man*, trans. Lewis L. Wilkins and Duane A. Priebe (Philadelphia: Westminster, 1975), p. 66.

presupposition for understanding the outline of His history that follows; likewise, the history that follows specifies in tersest outline the narrative content of this person as incarnate, identified by certain actions and passions as a particular individual in the world. Jesus Son of God is He "who was conceived by the Holy Spirit, born of the Virgin Mary, suffered under Pontius Pilate, was crucified, dead, and buried . . ." and so on. This procedure in Christology thus stands in marked, not to say categorical contrast to the dominant alternative in modern Christology, which takes the functional view that the "person" is to be known in its "works" in the way that a "cause" is deduced from its "effects" by a method that in principle is open to any neutral observer — transcendental deduction of the condition of the possibility of the moral performance of Jesus' supposedly manifest good works. This way of thinking about the person of Christ reduces person to an agent, the Kantian "transcendental subject." But this take on personhood is not adequately trinitarian since the essentially social nature of the self in relation to other selves in community disappears from view, as does the construction of agency as always coterminous with patiency — also in the divine Life. For just this reason it is not adequate to the *persona/prosopon* figured in the pages of the New Testament. As a result, the objectivity of Jesus Christ the Son of God as faith's knowledge of the Father's determination in the Spirit to love us in the Beloved Son cannot but over time dissolve into a variety of soteriologies conscripting Jesus as a usable savior.

Behind this sad devolution lies a commonplace of the neo-Platonic doctrine of God, namely, that while God's mysterious essence is incomprehensible it is manifest in its radiant energies at work in the creation. This essence-energy distinction, already at play in the West through the influence of Pseudo-Dionysius,[108] was transferred wholesale to Christology after the Kantian critique of reason, which in seeming parallel also denied the possibility of insight into things in and for themselves and limited knowledge to what appears to us by way of the bodily senses. If not already eclipsed by this essence/energy distinction, what is forgotten in this transfer, as we have been arguing, was the crucial Trinitarian distinction between nature and person. Or rather, the person-in-community of Trinitarianism was extracted from its habitat in the community of love and transformed into the single, active, synthesizing subject of knowledge, the posited Ego transcendent to every statement of purported factual knowledge, the "I think that" that must be thought in general as the condition for the possibility of constructing any statement of objective fact. These transfers eclipsed the Trinitarian notion of person in community of self-giving love in accord with the longstanding modalist tendencies of the Western tradition to sharply qualify personal distinctions by assertion of a common nature. So an ineffable divine "nature" — unknowable in its pure simplicity — yet supposedly radiating love into the world like the sun shining was posited as the noumenal cause or ground of the visible world, where according to various schemes it can be sensed or felt by its effects and its transcendental cau-

---

108. On this critique of Palamas, see Jenson *ST* 2, pp. 342-43.

sality deduced and its dignity recognized. Salvation is then thought to come about when this felt effect is lifted up from its preconscious state to articulate consciousness. This happens in the God-consciousness of Christ. Trinitarian modalism and Christological Nestorianism hence became the operative theologies of modernity.

All this was enunciated as a principle by Schleiermacher: "We could treat the whole doctrine of Christ either as that of His activity, for then the dignity must naturally follow from that, or as that of His dignity, for the activity must then result of itself."[109] The latter procedure, however, is unworkable. The creedal designation of the "person" of Jesus as God, which Schleiermacher takes modalistically as affirming the "dignity" of "the divine nature of the Redeemer from all eternity," he warns, results in a "very confusing description," i.e., that tacitly confuses the natures. He argues that the confusion arises when "the expression 'nature' is used indifferently for the divine and human" at the same time. How, he asks, can the term "nature" be used as a common concept covering both the infinite and the finite, that is, how "can divine and human be thus brought together? . . . Over against this divided and conditioned we set God as the unconditioned and the absolutely simple."[110] With this the longstanding Western tendency towards modalism crystalizes. *Das Unbedingt* manifests itself in the complex and conditioned world of appearances not in its infinite and simple "nature," which cannot be contained by the finite, nor by an impossible fusion with a finite nature, but in its energies apprehended in a variety of figures under various conditions as known by their effects in the world.

So in Christology we begin with Christ's apprehended activity, from which the dignity of His person will be deduced. Retrieving thereby the Antiochene Christology of the Indwelling Logos, Schleiermacher thus regarded "the theory of a mutual communication of the attributes of the two natures to one another" as something "also to be banished from the system of doctrine and handed over to the history of doctrine," since in such a communication "nothing human could have been left in Christ since everything human is essentially a negation of omniscient omnipotence."[111]

Calling Jesus God is thus not a cognitive grasp of an objective fact, but represents a judgment of "value" regarding His dignity made by the believer as one who experiences salutary effects of God's love radiating to her by the medium of His God-consciousness. It is an ascription of divine dignity to His agency on the basis of the effect of simple consciousness of unconditioned love encountered in Him, a love that may rightly be praised as divine. It is thus the believer who treats Jesus as if God in an act of devotion based upon the experience of Jesus as medium of simple and unconditional divine love. The difficulty of course is squaring this

---

109. Friedrich Schleiermacher, *The Christian Faith,* 2 vols. (New York: Harper & Row Torchbooks, 1963), #92, 3; 2, p. 375.

110. Schleiermacher, *The Christian Faith,* #96, 1; 2, pp. 391-92.

111. Schleiermacher, *The Christian Faith,* #97, 5; 2, p. 412.

with the actual figure that appears on the pages of the New Testament — a point raised against Schleiermacher in most devastating fashion not by orthodox opponents but by the radical arch-critic, David Friedrich Strauss.[112] Strauss's critique has Christological merit. Schleiermacher had to hold that Luther's Christology is naïvely docetist, but the reverse accusation might better be made. Cyrilian Christology, as we have seen, also claims that mantle of "anti-docetism." But Schleiermacher knew that admitting the Cry of Dereliction would fatally compromise his doctrine of the human Christ's perfect God-consciousness as medium of the ceaseless radiance of divine love: "I cannot think of this saying as an expression of Christ's self-consciousness."[113]

A generation later Albrecht Ritschl wrote in further development of Schleiermacher's Christological modernism — in express rejection of the Council of Chalcedon's pretension to a putatively "disinterested scientific knowledge" of Jesus' "nature" as the substantial Son of God. Here the correct critique of the ideal of knowledge as theoria and its object, the substantial form, by the gospel aborts into a mere negation of knowledge of God, whereby the thesis of theoria lives on in the antithesis of ontological apophaticism. Thus Ritschl affirmed, "every cognition of a religious sort is a direct judgment of value. The nature of God and the Divine we can only know in its essence by determining its value for our salvation . . . [we must understand] the Godhead of Christ, if it is to be understood at all, as an attribute revealed to us in his saving influence upon ourselves."[114] Note how here divinity becomes again a quality that may be possessed in varying degrees and recognized by a knowing and valuing subject. For all the supposed anti-metaphysical or anti-Platonic airs of modern Christology, the rival Platonic theologies of Arianism and modalism come flooding back unrecognized.

Only a little later, Wilhelm Hermann perfected this entire line of thought with what has proved to be the most influential argument of modern Christology because of the Reformation insight with which he coupled it. Hermann savaged the very desire for doctrinal knowledge of the creedal Christ as antithetical to saving trust in Christ: "No one can be made sure of his own redemption by hearing a doctrine of redemption and then endeavoring to hold it true and apply it to himself. . . . That Jesus Christ has the power to redeem us can only mean that our present experience of the reality of his Person convinces us as nothing else does that God will accept us."[115] Indeed, "we can be saved only by a reality presented

112. David Friedrich Strauss, *The Christ of Faith and the Jesus of History,* trans. Leander E. Keck (Philadelphia: Fortress, 1977), p. 120.

113. Friedrich Schleiermacher, *The Life of Jesus,* ed. J. C. Verheyden (Philadelphia: Fortress, 1975), p. 423.

114. Albrecht Ritschl, *The Christian Doctrine of Justification and Reconciliation: The Positive Development of the Doctrine,* trans. H. R. MacIntosh and A. B. Macaulay (Clifton, NJ: Reference Book Publishers, 1966), p. 398.

115. Wilhelm Hermann, *Systematic Theology,* trans. N. Micklem and K. A. Saunders (New York: Macmillan, 1927), p. 115.

to us as a fact of our own experience, a reality indubitable as our need. . . . If he is our Redeemer we must have discovered in him that one thing which awakens pure love and pure fear in us, or which can have complete sway over our soul."[116] Certainly Hermann is right that it is the lived encounter with Jesus Christ that redeems and assures and convinces of God's acceptance. But this is all too easy a critique of long-defeated Orthodoxy, all too easy a mere modernization of Pietism on the way to Existentialism (as happened in Hermann's students). In critical dogmatics, however, doctrine is not doctrine for theory but for life. Christological doctrine is for knowing the One in whom faith trusts, apart from which faith wanders in the dark.

To be noted throughout the foregoing is the Kantianism: theoretical knowledge of objects pertains only to worldly phenomena and in any case is misapplied to the divine, which cannot be an object in the world of human knowledge. To know *a priori* that God cannot be an object in our world, however, is to know a great deal about God. This presumption, moreover, is itself and as such a theology that appears in Arianism, or Nestorianism or Modalism in various iterations, provided that it can separate what God has united according to the Easter Word of God concerning the resurrection of Jesus. A Kantian form of negative or apophatic natural theology thus sets the agenda for modern Protestant theology. Theological reasoning about the dignity of Christ's person proceeds from the putative effect to the transcendental cause, transforming the person into a transcendental subject. Christology in this fashion fundamentally answers the question, "What do *we* think of him?" Christology inevitably becomes a function of soteriology and soteriology a function of contextually construed perceived need. By the time this journey of theological thought has reached Ruether, traditional piety's reverence for Jesus has sufficiently eroded that His privileged place as sole, or at least chief mediator of saving effects itself dissolves — which was not yet the case for Schleiermacher, Ritschl, or Hermann, though this trajectory is already manifest in them. Hence we see once again why a division of the divisions becomes necessary today in a new theological convergence around the objectivity of faith that is Jesus Christ the Son of God.

Still, the troubling question persists whether in this objectivity of faith we still meet *Jesus*. Does Jesus remain Jesus when named by faith confessing His resurrection the Christ, Son of God? At its best, the question goes back to Theodore of Mopsuestia. While we have interpreted the epoch of liberal Christology as a capitulation, more or less, to Kantianism, it is important to acknowledge the proper, Antiochene theological interest in the question of Jesus in Christology. Indeed, it is important for critical dogmatics to take this question more earnestly and consequently, as we propose to do in the second part of this chapter, than in the invention, on analysis, of what proves to be a convenient Christ for modernity — Gore's Nestorian Christ for Pelagian man who is the "sovereign self" of modernity.

116. Hermann, *ST,* p. 116.

We can articulate Luther's third way between Schleiermacher and Barth by recalling here the remarkable scheme Luther developed in 1538 following his intensive study of patristic Christology, "The Three Symbols or Creeds of the Christian Faith."[117] "I have perceived and noted in all histories of all of Christendom that all those who have correctly had and kept the chief article of Jesus Christ have remained safe and secure in the right Christian faith" — a notable qualification to the claim he also made for the doctrine of justification by faith as the *Hauptartikel*. Or rather, as per the present argument, we have here a notable clarification that his doctrine of justification is not reducible to anthropology but rather works as applied Christology. "For whoever stands correctly and firmly in the belief that Jesus Christ is true God and man, that he died and has risen again for us, such a person has all other articles added to him and they firmly stand by him." The reason this equivalence of Trinitarian Christology and justification by faith alone holds, according to Luther, is the divine self-determination. "For here I will dwell (says God), in this humanity, born of Mary the virgin, etc." If God is indeed the One who determined to redeem the creation through the mission of the Son incarnate, then "all error, heresy, idolatry, offense, misuse, and evil in the church originally came from despising or losing sight of this article of faith in Jesus Christ. And if one looks at it correctly and clearly, all heresies do contend against this dear article of Jesus Christ." Jesus Christ is the center of theology's cognitive claim.

From this vantage point Luther developed a schematization around the three poles of Christology regarding Christ's true deity, true humanity, and unity of person. "Some have attacked his deity, doing this in various ways." Luther singles out Ebionitism, modalist Patripassianism, and Arianism as examples and comments, "It is a marvel, a marvel, to see how discerning minds have fairly writhed here in their attempt to avoid believing in Christ as a real, true God!" Interestingly for us today, he regards Mohammed, "who came and nearly led the whole world in the East astray and away from Christ," as standing in the line of Christological heresies denying the Son's true deity. Others "have attacked Christ's humanity, and how strange their antics have been!" There were the Docetists, who said the Son "was a specter or a shadow who had passed through Mary like a phantom having neither a real body nor soul." He next mentions the followers of Apollinaris who taught "the deity ruled his body in place of a soul." Others said that he was not Mary's real, natural son. He then comments: "They have hit the mark unusually well in contriving how there cannot be three Persons in the Godhead, saying that these cannot be brothers or relatives, and what other way would there be of reckoning how the three Persons are equal?" With this observation, Luther connects the right perception of the true humanity of Christ with Trinitarian personalism. That is to say: knowing Christ as the Son of Mary and simultaneously as the Son

---

117. *LW* 34, pp. 201-29. All citations in the next four paragraphs are taken from this short work.

of God somehow profoundly correlate. There is a fittingness or correspondence, not necessary but contingent yet all the same real, between the One born from His Father in eternity and the same One born from Mary, Theotokos, in order to become her and our redeeming Lord. To know Christ is to know Him as One of us but also as One of the Three, as true God with them yet other than His Father and their Spirit. In this way we see the unity of the person Jesus Christ the Son of God in His distinct mission to seek and find and thence restore to His Father's own favor by the gift of that Spirit.

According to this redemptive purpose of the Incarnation — not of God in general but of the Son sent by the Father, not in humanity in general but by the flesh from the Jewish maiden sanctified by the Spirit — Luther's Christological scheme turns to the present. "We have confessed that he is God and man," he claims in the (mock) voice of his papist opponents. "But, that he is our Savior, who died and rose again for us, etc. — this we have denied and persecuted with all our might, and still do not cease." He lifts up here the "semi-Pelagian" teaching especially, that Christ died only to remove original sin so that our religious works must compensate for actual sins. The result is that "if we sin after our baptism, then Christ is no longer of use to us" and we must now try "to propitiate Christ himself, as if he were not our advocate, but on the contrary our judge, before God." Consequently, the "only honor left to Christ is that he has begun the work; but we are the heroes who complete it with merits. For us, Christ must mean his dying at the beginning and also the forgiveness of sins; but we are able to attain salvation with works." The semi-Pelagian way leaves Christ in the past as the Redeemer who has already done God's part. The present and future then belong to religious man or pious woman. In this way, Christ's past work as the prophet of God's reign is eclipsed. His present priestly work as intercessor is obscured. His future work, already operative but incognito in the world, as messianic king who completes the redemption of the creation and brings it to fulfillment at the eschaton of judgment is turned into a private fear of hell rather than a public hope for the earth on which His cross once stood.

In sum, "the devil has work to do and attacks Christ in three lines of battle. One will not let him be God, another will not let him be man, and the third will not let him do what he has done. Each of the three wants to reduce Christ to nothing. For what does it profit you to confess that he is God, if you do not also believe that he is man? Then you do not have the whole, real Christ with that, but only a phantom of the devil's. What does it profit you to confess that he is man, if you do not also believe that he is God? What does it profit you to confess that he is God and man, if you do not also believe that he has become everything and done everything for you?" Though this belief in Christ can be weak and faltering, it is a whole and cannot "remain at all when the three parts are severed." Nor is Christology a theologian's academic puzzle when taken in this holistic way as doctrine for life; here it is a matter of life and death: "To be weak does no harm, but to be false — that is eternal death." Luther predicts that the future work of

Christ as hope of the earth and judge of the nations is about to be abandoned "and the world will think nothing of a future life. In that case Christ is nothing any more. For whoever has no hope for a future life needs Christ just as little as the cows and other beasts in paradise did. . . ."

In sum, for Luther the saving righteousness of God in Christ *supra extra legem* is the work of the Son of God incarnate that saves from sin now and death eternally. One begins in Christology with this unity of Person because if, on the contrary, one starts with either the deity, or the humanity, or the work, one can never unify them again by theoretical reasoning since theory itself is the ambition *(sicut Deus eritis)* of fallen humanity to comprehend in place of God rather than to understand in and under God. Theoretical reasoning itself is thus invalid here; it is the old thinking of philosophy, not the Spirit's new thinking in theology. Theology knows that one never — not in all eternity — comprehends the "how," the mystery of Christ's person, which is rather to be adored. Faith thinks theologically after the Word incarnate, presented in the gospel's narrative by Word and Sacrament, for the sake of the saving work of the Word incarnate that is still under way and just so contested to the last day in the apocalyptic battle of the ages. Par excellence, Christology is the new thinking of the Spirit, who unifies the sign and the thing signified for faith in presenting the object, Jesus Christ the Son of God, for the work of creation's redemption. Faith thinks in and after this unification — or it is not faith's thinking at all no matter how much it sings Hallelujahs to Jesus.

With this foundation in Luther's Christological legacy as the proposed alternative to modern Christologies we now turn to a protracted conflict in Luther's tradition in our search for a higher synthesis that can appreciate properly the human, all-too-human cry of dereliction as the true spiritual suffering of the one Son of God incarnate and see in just this depth of the descent of divine love the ground for the new righteousness *supra extra legem* that He gains. That way was pioneered in early Lutheranism by the "second Martin," Martin Chemnitz.[118] Chemnitz clarified Luther's reluctantly speculative exploration of the deity's "repletive presence" (of the divine immensity or omnipresence) as a property communicated to the body of the glorified Christ as providing the possibility of Christ's promised Eucharistic presence. Were there such a metamorphosis of the human nature in Christ, however, it would seem to follow that the man Christ would be everywhere present *as* His personal promise of His Body given for us, just as God is present everywhere by divine nature. The New Testament meal would no longer demarcate the invasive and subversive presence of the new creation amid structures of malice and injustice. The distinction between God's work by His general omnipotence in continuous creation and His redemptive work in Christ would be annulled, and God's freedom in election would be sub-

---

118. Martin Chemnitz, *The Two Natures of Christ,* trans. J. A. O. Preus (St. Louis: Concordia, 1971).

sumed into a general determination of all things. Above all, God's righteousness in Christ *supra extra legem* would resolve back into the lawful ordering of things both physically and morally in creation. Everything could be called grace but would in fact be reward and punishment. Such "pan-Christism," so to speak, is *not* Luther's intention; he drew back from this evident implication of his own speculation already during the controversy with Zwingli by making this distinction: "It is one thing if God is present and another if he is present *for you*."[119] Or again, "both God and Christ are not far away but near, and it is only a matter of revealing themselves...."[120] To be present whether anyone knows it or not is a fact of nature; to be revealed "for you" is a free act of personal will that specifies the improbable presence *sub contrario* of the One who gave Himself, the innocent for the guilty. "He is free and unbounded wherever he is, and he does not have to stand there like a rogue set in a pillory, or his neck in irons."[121]

To substantiate Luther's distinction here, Chemnitz therefore spoke of the *ubivolipraesens* of Christ,[122] i.e., that Christ the divine-human *person* is present *personally,* as He *freely* wills to be for us in His body given for us, according to His promise. With this move, Chemnitz was also correcting his teacher Melanchthon in Luther's direction. Fearing the confusion or mingling of divine and human natures proscribed by the Fourth Ecumenical Council at Chalcedon, Melanchthon had already retreated in Luther's lifetime from the latter's Christological doctrine of the communication of idioms. For the mature Melanchthon, the ascription of suffering to the incarnate Son of God or of divine glory to His human body is a way of talking, not of being.[123] In Christ and in His sacraments we have not the Person at work but an efficacious sign of the Person at work. Melanchthon's overcorrection, however, all but reverts to standard Augustinianism's dualism of the sign and the thing signified. We can have the Person at work in Christ and His sacraments, however, when "person" is understood strongly as the agent who freely acts according to its own purpose in accord with other persons in its community of love. Thus the danger both of confusing the natures and of dividing the person can be addressed with a vigorous application of the Trinitarian distinction of nature and person in Christology, just as Luther attempts in saying: "It is one thing if God is present and another if he is present *for you*." Indeed, that distinction is precisely the Trinitarian distinction between nature and person.

Along these lines of the strong Trinitarian distinction between nature and person, Chemnitz made a threefold classification of the attribution of divine and human properties in the one person, Jesus Christ, by virtue of the personal or hy-

---

119. *LW* 37, p. 68.

120. *LW* 37, p. 66.

121. *LW* 37, p. 68. "... since Christ's body is outside the realm of creation," i.e., in the way the divine omnipresence is not spatial extension throughout creation, "it can assuredly be wherever he wishes...." *LW* 37, p. 217.

122. Chemnitz, *The Two Natures*, p. 278.

123. On this, see further *PNT*, pp. 162-69.

postatic union. First, he considered properties of divine and human natures that are alike attributed concretely to the one person that is Jesus Christ the Son of God. Here it may be said concretely: Jesus Christ is Creator of heaven and earth. Christ Jesus suffers and dies on the stake. Second, he added a category of inter-penetrating properties of both natures that are attributed to the concrete person in the performance of His messianic work, so that it is possible to say: This man gives His body for the forgiveness of sins. This God dwells in loving fellowship bodily with sinners and tax collectors. Third, Chemnitz held that properties of the divine nature are truly communicated to the human nature so that it is possible to say: This Body gives life. This Man is omnipresent. It is the last classification that was most controversial in its time, but in Chemnitz it is qualified by personal will, so that it will be more precisely stated, This Body gives life where and when its Head wills and promises; this Man-for-others is present personally where and when the Son of God wills and promises.

Broadly speaking, all of this categorization builds upon Cyril, and Luther's appropriation of Cyril, to make the fundamentally anti-Nestorian Christological point that "Christ, according to His human nature and insofar as this nature is personally united with the Logos, differs from the other saints not only by reason of His gifts, which by comparison excel the others in number and degree, but also by reason of the union He differs totally from the saints."[124] The person of Jesus Christ the Son of God is this union of the sign and the thing signified by the Holy Spirit; it is a "miracle" given to faith. Precisely as miracle, this person is not a fact of history there for anyone to see but must be revealed. All that is seen naturally is the sign. The unification of the sign and the thing signified for anyone to apprehend remains the sovereign work of the Spirit. Correspondingly, the self-donation of the Son of God is the free act of the person and so is there for us as He wills and promises, namely in the Eucharist of the ecclesia in mission to the nations. Otherwise Chemnitz writes, citing John of Damascus against the Nestorians, one actually makes "the union into something temporary and a mat-ter of indwelling, as when God dwells in the saints"[125] and thus the saving miracle of the person of Jesus Christ is obscured. Or, conversely, one makes this union ubiquitous and thus abolishes the distinction between the sinful and dying world and the new creation Jesus brings as the gift not other than His very self-donation. Not surprisingly, as Bertram pointed out, the soteriological consequence is not so much that saints are elevated to Christ's status as that Christ is demoted to theirs. Or, conversely, one evacuates eschatological salvation altogether in a mystifica-tion of present experience in the manner of the sentimental gobbledygook of religion in decay: everything is grace.

It is thus Chemnitz's strong Trinitarian personalism that makes it possible for him cogently to refute those that "speak falsely who assert that the force of the

---

124. Chemnitz, *The Two Natures*, p. 263.
125. Chemnitz, *The Two Natures*, p. 264.

term, *koinonia,* communion or communication, lies in the fact that whatever is said to be communicated becomes in itself a proper, essential, formal, subjective, or inherent part of that to which it is said to be communicated." Communication is an event of sharing, not of metamorphosis into another category. In all three classifications, the *communio idiomatum* is a personal and so free communication by the divine Person who is the one and only agent of the Incarnation and just so, the communion "by no means includes or implies in its meaning a comingling, conversion, abolition, or equating" of the natures, human or divine.[126] Arguably, we have here a competent retrieval of Cyril's own Christology with the same advantages but also the same difficulties.

No one in the classical tradition of theology after Luther worked through these difficulties with such acumen as did Johann Gerhard, the towering figure of Lutheran orthodoxy. The Trinitarian distinction between nature and person is raised up from the outset of his Christological presentation and made its *sine qua non:* "The confusion of this distinction in this article is the target against which all heretics once struck."[127] While the term "nature" designates the "essence" or definition of a thing and may be contrasted with "existence" as possible contrasts with actual, in this latter connotation of actual existence a "nature" is virtually identical to "hypostasis" as the specific way that any "nature" is actualized in its existence. The important point here is that "nature" has no real existence; it works semantically to classify sets of possibilities for the efficient sorting of information. What actually exists are hypostases that in turn are always specific ways of being in a world. Hence "the hypostasis of the Son and His divine nature do not differ in reality,"[128] since Sonship is His way of being in the divine world of the Beloved Community, the eternal Trinity. Moreover, hypostasis as the specific actualization of an abstract set of possibilities gives something "characteristic, by which a person in the Godhead is distinguished from the other persons inwardly, and it is supremely proper to each person."[129] So the Father is God but in the way of being a Father; the Son is God but in the way of being a Son; and the Spirit is God but in the way of being the Spirit of the Father breathed upon the Son. So "God" does not exist except as the Father, the Son, and the Holy Spirit, who each instantiate "God" personally, where "personally" entails each one's essential relations of communion with the others, what in conclusion we will articulate as *consistent perichoresis.*

Thus between these persons, Gerhard writes, there is an eternal and *"essential communication."*[130] All that the Father has and possesses as true God — that is to

126. Chemnitz, *The Two Natures,* p. 309.

127. Johann Gerhard, *On the Person and Office of Christ, Theological Commonplaces,* trans. Richard J. Ginda (St. Louis: Concordia, 2009), p. 38.

128. Gerhard, *On the Person and Office of Christ,* p. 162.

129. Gerhard, *On the Person and Office of Christ,* p. 172.

130. Gerhard, *On the Person and Office of Christ,* p. 273.

say, all divine possibilities other than the Father's hypostasis as the unoriginated origin in the divine life — are generated as the Son and breathed as the Spirit and thence returned in the loving praise of God the Father. This essential communication is proper to the life of God and strictly speaking incommunicable, as it is the eternal life that God alone is. Human beings as creatures come to participate *"proximately and spiritually"* in the divine nature; this theosis is not a fusion into deity, but a union of human persons with the person of the Son incarnate by the person of the Spirit to the praise of God the Father. Theosis is this personal participation in the eternal life of the Three, not natural fusion of humanity and deity, which would be for creatures an impersonal absorption into the ocean of divinity.[131] That being said, theosis is the very goal of the Trinity in the economy: "The redemption of the human race includes not only privative goodness — that Christ freed us from sin, the wrath of God, from death and hell — but also positive goodness, that He brought us to perfect righteousness, the grace of God, the gift of the Holy Spirit, and eternal life."[132]

All this bears directly on Christology in that "the Son of God assumed the human nature so that in and with it He might perform the office of mediation, redemption and salvation"; the Son thus communicated to His own humanity whatever divine capabilities were required to perform the "prophetic, priestly and royal office."[133] This assumption of humanity is and ever remains the *personal* work of the Trinitarian person, the Son of God, by which the Son's "natural properties" as God are communicated to the assumed humanity not, so to say, *carte blanche* but for the performance of the messianic office committed to the Son in the eternal self-determination of the Trinity. In this way Gerhard carefully fends off modalistic renderings of Christology that assert a confusion of natures or, if assuming critically that Christology does assert a confusion of natures, deny it. In either case, the journey of the Son of God to the far country and the narrative of His humiliation and exaltation by which the messianic office is accomplished are obscured. One then either affirms abstractly that Jesus is God, as if that were the gospel as such, or denies this as Christian idolatry, as if this denial hit a true target. But the personal union is and remains the personal act of the particular person, the Son of God, and is not an "essential union"[134] which, as Gerhard points out following Chemnitz, would have to be some sort of "physical transfusion and subjective inhesion" of divine properties in the human nature.[135] But adhering to the gospel narrative instead allows Gerhard to affirm that just as "Christ did not have a glorified body until in His state of exaltation after the resurrection, so also He did not have a glorified soul perfectly endowed with angelic gifts until

131. Gerhard, *On the Person and Office of Christ*, p. 220; cf. 267.
132. Gerhard, *On the Person and Office of Christ*, p. 138.
133. Gerhard, *On the Person and Office of Christ*, p. 266.
134. Gerhard, *On the Person and Office of Christ*, p. 272.
135. Gerhard, *On the Person and Office of Christ*, pp. 260-61.

in His state of exaltation," thus allowing for the true finitude, the growth and the ignorance of the assumed soul.[136]

The personal or hypostatic union of natures in Christ, as the Son of God's own and unique agency, may be sharply contrasted with the medieval "suppositive" Christology[137] that carries over into Melanchthon and some versions of Reformed Christology.[138] According to this, the union is a "bare sustenance and carrying of the flesh in the hypostasis of the Word"[139] — a formulation striking in its resemblance to Theodore's picture of the divine Son remote from Jesus' suffering yet near enough to help. But Gerhard points out that "carrying" and "sustenance" are merely external relations, whereas the hypostatic union "is an internal work" that forms the soul of Jesus from conception as it advances in its life's journey.[140] Thus the "Son of God is the Son of Man not through the bare sustenance of the human nature but through the fullest communication of the hypostasis, through the intimate communication of the natures, through closest interpenetration and passing-into."[141] Indeed, this union cannot be the work of the Word alone as modalism imagines, picturing the Logos as supernatural spirit carrying about the human individual. The personal union, Gerhard notes, "is especially ascribed to the Holy Spirit, who Himself is 'the indissoluble bond of love between the Father and the Son. . . .' "[142] The Incarnation is of the Second of the Three, but it is an action involving the Father who sends the Son who goes and the Spirit who unites these actions in presenting the one person, Jesus Christ the Son of God, in the narrative of redemption — not least to the human soul of Jesus who believed His Sonship, and in this concrete faith took responsibility before God for the sins of others that freely He had forgiven.

The personal action of communicating the natures in Christ in and for the work of redemption is the very sense of the personal union, understood in the foregoing nonmodalist way of Trinitarian personalism. In Gerhard's language, "the communication of properties, properly and accurately speaking, is not the *form,* but the *consequence and effect.*" The "form" here, in Aristotelian idiom, is the person who takes to Himself human nature in the Incarnation. To be certain, "Holy Scripture describes this very great mystery of the personal union *a*

136. Gerhard, *On the Person and Office of Christ,* p. 286.
137. Gerhard, *On the Person and Office of Christ,* p. 155.
138. Gerhard charges that the "real communication of divine properties in Christ's flesh is denied both by the Papists and the Calvinists, like Samson's foxes here tied together by their tails [cf. Judg. 15:4], though in other chief parts of doctrine they disagree with each other . . . [vindicating Luther's assertion that] 'Among the Papists are hiding many Nestorians who deny in Christ the real communication both of the natures and of the properties.' " Gerhard, *On the Person and Office of Christ,* p. 256.
139. Gerhard, *On the Person and Office of Christ,* p. 123.
140. Gerhard, *On the Person and Office of Christ,* p. 123.
141. Gerhard, *On the Person and Office of Christ,* p. 155.
142. Gerhard, *On the Person and Office of Christ,* p. 101.

*posteriori* through the communication of attributes, because we are unable to understand it *a priori* and scientifically in the weakness of this life."[143] We note again here at this critical juncture the nontheoretical and pragmatic nature of doctrine. What we see in the figure of Christ presented in the gospel narrative is the active communication of attributes that raises the question, Who is this that stills the storm and forgives the sinner? The affirmation that this is Jesus Christ the Son of God indicates the mystery of the personal union and describes it as a personal act but does not explain the phenomenon. Nor does Christological doctrine aspire to explanation, to probing the How; its task is rather to formulate propositions that somehow express "that supreme mystery, which is beyond the mind, beyond expression, beyond every comprehension not only of men but even of angels" as indeed it must be if *in truth* it is *God* who unites with flesh in the person of the Son. Because theology is not philosophy,[144] such propositions "are to be explained solely from the mystery of the union" as safeguards of it and not to be "turned about by so many twists and turns of tropes, and referred to the usual modes of predicating that are without any mystery . . . done with the whip of logic."[145]

Granted, there is a danger here of fideistic obscurantism where muddle is put forward as mystery and paradox asserted as a solution rather than as a command to think in a new way. But a danger is not a necessity. As we shall see, in a sober and cautious way Christology must venture some thoughts on the "how" of its mystery — a problem raised within Christology in Luther's tradition by the more radical Christological idea of Johannes Brenz that the communication of idioms is not the consequence of the personal union but itself the very "form" of the Incarnation, i.e. a dynamic exchange-event occurring universally in place of the mediating notion of personal agency. Although this proves in the end to be wrongheaded, Brenz's speculation was a salutary one that pushed the inherited and retrieved patristic Christology forward in the direction of the higher synthesis we are seeking. There we must find in Christ's woe the ground for the new righteousness *supra extra legem* of God surpassing God.

Before coming to that consideration, however, let us fully understand Gerhard's contention that the mystery of the personal union is the "form" that precedes its consequences and effects in the active communication of natural properties in Christ's performance of His messianic labors and thus for us Christ's free self-presentation in the joyful exchange.[146] The alternative would be a fusion of natures, Gerhard argues, contrary to faith (i.e., Chalcedon). Once again, he draws on the Trinitarian distinction of nature and person to make the case. "Just as in the article on the Trinity I do not say, because of the distinction of persons,

---

143. Gerhard, *On the Person and Office of Christ*, p. 136.
144. Gerhard, *On the Person and Office of Christ*, p. 166.
145. Gerhard, *On the Person and Office of Christ*, p. 169.
146. Gerhard, *On the Person and Office of Christ*, p. 174.

'The Father is the Son, the Son is the Father,' so also in the article on Christ I do not say, because of the distinction of natures, 'The deity is the humanity, and the humanity is the deity.' "[147] Such an abstract identification of general sets of divine and human possibilities is no good news. It is nonsense or profound confusion. "If the union were essential, the communication of properties that arises from the union would also be essential; thus the human nature according to its essence would be omnipotent." But, citing Leo, the personal union is not to be generalized this way; it is the "unique and singular" glory of the one person Jesus Christ "and there is no example of it in the entire universe."[148] "It is a union of *natures,* but not a *natural union;* it is a *personal* union, but not *of persons.*"[149] Its mystery resides in this singularity that makes it strictly speaking incomparable. Theological formulations get at it piecemeal by way of description and analysis, not by way of a comprehending theoretical synthesis. What they are getting at, however, is something affirmed to be real and not merely a way of talking.[150] In the personal union "the communication happened immediately in the first moment of the incarnation and will last through eternity, even if there were no one actually to enunciate it in the predication." The reality is prior, the predication posterior.[151] This prior reality is the Son of God's assumption of "the human nature into the unity of His hypostasis," taking assumption as an act of "appropriation."[152]

This is a deliteralizing move on Gerhard's part. The figurative language in which the mysterious figure of Jesus Christ the Son of God is presented in the New Testament is misunderstood in its communicative intention when taken literally rather than spiritually. It is to be decoded theologically, in accord with the Spirit's intention, not taken literally according to philosophical understandings of the cosmos and its workings. In principle, "[j]ust as Christ was sent by the Father and came into the world not by a change of place but by the assumption of the flesh and visible appearance in it, so also He departed to the Father and left the world not by a change of place but by putting aside the form of a servant and by the use of the complete majesty communicated to Him."[153] The *movement* told in the Incarnation — the Word *became* flesh — is the one person's *passage* through humiliation to exaltation (even if John condenses, so to speak, the passage already now into Christ's paradoxical exaltation on the cross).

The assumption of the flesh is depicted, as argued above, in Mary's conception as *Theotokos;* she is the icon of believing Israel, who gives us Christ according to the flesh, to be the New Adam, God's new beginning in the midst of creation's frustration and ruin. But the deliteralized reality is that from conception this man,

147. Gerhard, *On the Person and Office of Christ,* p. 153.
148. Gerhard, *On the Person and Office of Christ,* p. 112.
149. Gerhard, *On the Person and Office of Christ,* p. 115.
150. Gerhard, *On the Person and Office of Christ,* p. 147.
151. Gerhard, *On the Person and Office of Christ,* p. 174.
152. Gerhard, *On the Person and Office of Christ,* p. 188.
153. Gerhard, *On the Person and Office of Christ,* p. 271.

in his true humanity as lived from Bethlehem to Golgotha, simply is the Christ, the Son of God who as such carries out the messianic purpose of the Father who sent Him and the Spirit who endowed Him. Precisely as decoded theologically this personhood of the Son incarnate remains a mystery with regard to its "How"; if the Virgin Birth from Mary is taken as a literal answer to the question "How," the doctrine is piously but poisonously misunderstood. That is the point of theology that turns its back on the idolatrous pretensions of theoretical reason — also appearing in theology — in order to know God deep in the flesh, and so from Mary's sinful flesh, one with us all — or not at all. Admittedly, this reserve regarding the How of the Incarnation was *not* Gerhard's own thought, but under our conditions of knowledge, it is consistent with his line of Christological thinking.

Returning now to Gerhard: he takes up Chemnitz's *ubivolipraesens* of the glorified humanity and fully integrates it into Trinitarian personalism. In this way, the "*communication* should be distinguished from *the use of what has been communicated.* The communication of divine properties to the humanity occurred from the first moment of the Incarnation, but Christ put off the full use of them until His ascension into heaven and His placement at the right hand of God. From that observation flows the distinction between the state of emptying [*status exinanitionis*] and the state of exaltation [*exaltationis*]." Modern criticism, as we recall from our discussion of the messianic secret in Mark, has regarded this Christology as an *ex post facto* apologetic construct to explain away the historical Jesus' lack of messianic self-consciousness. But we have seen that it is the anachronistic imposition of the very notion of self-consciousness that causes the mischief here. Here the motive is entirely different: it is to affirm that the communication of properties in the Incarnate Son is and remains the personal and voluntary act of the agent who is agent in His personal relations with the Father and the Spirit, not a fusion of natures that now proceeds, as it were, naturally, as if on automatic. The kenosis of Philippians 2, then, is not a metaphysical or substantive emptying of the divinity, but the humility of compassion in the Son's personal obedience. And in this humility of love Gerhard, with Luther,[154] sees the true "glory of our God who comes down to the depths" to redeem His own creation fallen prey to the structures of malice and injustice. Citing Nazianzus, "the power of His might remained in the power to empty Himself, and to have passed into servant's form is not to have lost the nature of God," but rather to be true God in the way of being the Son also now in this Son's true humanity.[155] In becoming human, the divine Son is enacting His own proper and divine Sonship in the time and space of the creature, as this particular human being[156] in His act of loving obedience that is the way to His cross on behalf of others.

So it is fitting that of the Three it is only the Son who became incarnate so

---

154. Gerhard, *On the Person and Office of Christ*, p. 301.
155. Gerhard, *On the Person and Office of Christ*, p. 308.
156. Pannenberg, *ST* 2, pp. 389-96.

that "in this respect God and man would be one son in the unity of person."[157] As in the beginning all things were created through the Son, so also the new creation belongs to Him who mediates its coming in His own Person at work. As the substantial image of God, it was "fitting for the image of God to be renewed in us through Him." It was fitting that "we receive the adoption of sons through Him who is the natural and only-begotten Son of God." It was fitting that we who were estranged by the enmity of sin should be reconciled by Him "who is the beloved Son." It was fitting that we who had lost the life of God should be restored to life by "Him who is the Word of life." And it was fitting that we learn again to know God "through Him who is the Word and Wisdom of the Father."[158] What is "fitting" is not something absolutely necessary, but rather what is contingently necessary, that is, necessary under conditions that are not themselves necessary. The contingency here is this world, taken as the creation of God destined for redemption and fulfillment by the missions of the Son and the Spirit but fallen prey to structures of malice and injustice that obstruct the coming of the Beloved Community. Under these conditions, the mission of the Son is fittingly found incarnate, the object in the world that is the son of Mary, Jesus Christ, at work as Israel's prophet, priest, and king.[159] Christ, known in this "fitting" way as the Son in the unity of His person, is thus "necessary" under these dramatic conditions of the canonical narrative.

Centrally and presently His "fittingly necessary" work of redemption is Luther's joyful exchange: "This taking of our sins is so true, so real, and effectual that Christ is forced to endure the punishments for our sins. . . . In turn, Christ grants His righteousness to believers, and the heavenly Father imputes it to believers. . . . This imputation, too, is true, real, and most effective. . . ."[160] Justification by faith in this "true, real, and most effective imputation" is practical Christology, where Christology is "true, real, and most effective" Incarnation, not merely a way of talking; such is the personal union, and the fitting use in the Spirit of the natural properties of deity and humanity, in fulfillment of the Son's mission of redemption spoken at the climax of the promissory narrative, "This is My Body, given for you."

In all this there is in Gerhard a subtle intra-Lutheran polemic going on against Johannes Brenz's position that the human properties are also communicated to the divine nature, so that the statement "The Son of God suffered in the flesh" is not merely predicated of the person, but of the divine nature itself so that we can say: "God died on the cross." The implication is an ontology that would have to account for a true, albeit divine way of suffering. Gerhard opposes this: "[I]t is better to abstain from these abstractive propositions," as he acutely terms them, of the

157. Gerhard, *On the Person and Office of Christ,* p. 99.
158. Gerhard, *On the Person and Office of Christ,* pp. 98-99.
159. Gerhard, *On the Person and Office of Christ,* pp. 318-30.
160. Gerhard, *On the Person and Office of Christ,* p. 187.

Württemberg theologians descending from Brenz. For it is wrong Christologically to "abstract" from the existential actuality of the personal Son of God's suffering in the flesh speculatively to formulate unbecoming, if not self-contradictory metaphysical reifications. Gerhard holds with the patristic tradition from which he has drawn that by nature the "deity is impassible, immutable, and unalterable. Therefore suffering cannot be attributed to it."

Today we are quick to ask whether this criticism of Brenz by Gerhard is simply a reassertion of the impassibility axiom of Hellenistic metaphysics. Perhaps it is in a way, but not simply. Interestingly, Gerhard immediately connects this false, "abstractive" inference to divine passibility to the Trinitarian error of modalism: "The deity is common to the whole Trinity or to all three persons of the Godhead. If the deity were said to have suffered in itself, the entire Trinity would have suffered, and the error of the Sabellians and Patripassians would be brought back into the Church."[161] Gerhard is thinking that the suffering of God is specifically to be attributed, not only to the assumed humanity, but to the voluntary act of the Incarnate Son qua person who humbled Himself; yet to generalize from this concrete and voluntary divine suffering of a particular divine person to divine suffering in general erases the very personal property of filial obedience by which this One of the Three is fittingly incarnate and as such known and recognized in the first place. It was only the Son sent from His Father and endowed by their Spirit who became incarnate obediently to suffer and die for others. To "abstract" from this concrete way of the Son of God thus threatens to disrupt the narrative coherence of the utterly generous divine life in its tri-personal self-determination to give all in the redemption and fulfillment of the creation for the victory of Beloved Community. The Father gives His Son who gives Himself for sinners in order to give them the Spirit. The suffering in the flesh of the Son who gives Himself for sinners mediates between the Father's giving of the Son and the Spirit's coming to unite with the Son and return to the Father. If we abstract from these particular ways of divine giving into a suffering deity in general, we fatally disrupt the logic of the theology of gift and turn God from Father of the Son in the Spirit into God in general, as hapless, even pathetic Bystander, who feels terrible but does nothing.

There can be no doubt, hermeneutically, that Gerhard construes divine "impassibility" in the best patristic sense as divine freedom from need, hence also from greed and envy as moral possibilities and hence freedom for superabundant, self-surpassing generosity. *Esse Deum dare:* to be God is to give. Hence Christologically "nothing is added through the union to the divine nature (which is self-sufficient, unchangeable, and utterly perfect), but the human nature acquires divine excellencies from the hypostatic union beyond and outside its own essential properties."[162] The communication is one-way traffic from God the giver to

---

161. Gerhard, *On the Person and Office of Christ,* p. 195.
162. Gerhard, *On the Person and Office of Christ,* p. 176.

the recipient creature, also in the gift to receive the gift by the Spirit's return in the sacrifice of praise. Because "the divine nature is highest and unchangeable, therefore it cannot be exalted in itself to a higher position nor can it be brought down to a more humble position"; rather it is the weak and mutable human nature that now enjoys divine gifts.[163] True as this is, here we see the force of the simplicity axiom at work in a way that obfuscates the divine suffering of the eternal Son who humbled Himself. Gerhard writes in a strangely Nestorian-like way that humiliation and exaltation apply strictly speaking only to the human nature of Christ[164] and in this regard there is no "reciprocation" between them: "The Word assumed the flesh; the flesh did not assume the Word but was assumed by the Word."[165] Quoting Cyril, Gerhard concludes: "It is the mark of the human nature to receive from God. . . ."[166] True enough, but the divine Word gives to the creature in bondage to sin and unable to free itself by humbling itself in the merciful solidarity of love for them, taking their place as His own. This is a suffering of love that is divine, a divine deliverance into the hands of sinners, a divine abandonment and utter humiliation. Certainly to be God is to give, and to be human is to receive; that precisely is the Christological doctrine of the two natures; but the personal union of these two natures in Christ entails the personal humiliation of the Word who truly comes in the flesh, who appears in the likeness of sinful flesh and also dies in this likeness.

By contrast, a truly kenotic theory of the Incarnation — not Luther's "the deity has withdrawn" spoken in Trinitarian reference to the Son's forsakenness by the Father at the cross — but a metaphysical construction of the Incarnation as a natural, not personal "emptying" is traced by Gerhard to Beza — he exempts Calvin.[167] Gerhard sets it against the exegesis of Philippians 2: "According to the nature by which Christ was emptied, according to that nature He was also exalted."[168] In this way, Gerhard links natural kenoticism in Christology to the axiom *finitum non capax infiniti*,[169] which would make the very possibility of God for the creature something unknowable, unimaginable, indeed impossible. But this possibility is given as something actualized in the way of being the Son that is Jesus Christ in the narrative of redemption, when taken as fitting expression and so true incarnation of God. What is must be possible. Then one must reason *a posteriori,* thinking after revelation, not theoretically and *a priori* to what revelation can or cannot be according to the abstract philosophical dialectics of the finite and infinite. "It is not glorious but shameful for Christ to be in the Supper, therefore, he surely is not there and cannot be there, for Christ must be glorious. Now if I ask

163. Gerhard, *On the Person and Office of Christ*, p. 179.
164. Gerhard, *On the Person and Office of Christ*, p. 186.
165. Gerhard, *On the Person and Office of Christ*, p. 204.
166. Gerhard, *On the Person and Office of Christ*, p. 205.
167. Gerhard, *On the Person and Office of Christ*, p. 162.
168. Gerhard, *On the Person and Office of Christ*, p. 215.
169. Gerhard, *On the Person and Office of Christ*, p. 261.

them, "Who says it is not glorious?" they answer, "We do!" If I ask further, "Who are you? How do you know this?" and "How do you prove it?" "Ho!," they retort, "isn't it enough that *we* say so? *You* always have to be answered with Scripture!"[170]

In the tradition of Luther those following Brenz in Christology would hardly concede that they are thinking *a priori* and metaphysically. Rather, they conceive of their program as drawing fully and radically the Christological consequences of the communication of natures in Christ over against what they perceive to be an artificial barrier erected in the notion of a "personal" union. Gerhard cites with approval Athanasius: "Yet that thing was extremely strange — that the same one was suffering and not suffering. Indeed, He was suffering insofar as His own body, in which He was, was suffering, but not suffering insofar as God by nature is impassible."[171] But just this "Platonic axiom" of impassibility — reified or mythologized in the notion of a personally mediated union — blocks the full, radical, and eminently generalizable conclusion that ought to be drawn from Luther's Christology: that divine-human exchanges are at the throbbing heart of creation itself, exemplified rather than merely actualized in the particularity of Jesus Christ.

Such Christological insight would break to pieces the false and static antinomy of the "two natures" scheme and break through to free-flowing cascades of exchanges at the beating pulse of universal life-processes. Thus the followers of Brenz zero in on Gerhard's crucial notion of the hypostasis as something in distinction from nature. This blockage, as they see it, is visible when Gerhard writes: "Just as the divine nature of the Word is incapable of suffering, so also the simple hypostasis of the Word, that is, the hypostasis of only the divine nature, is also incapable of suffering" in that He is eternally and immutably the Son of the Father on whom He breathes the Spirit.[172] But if this hypostasis is as immutable as the divine nature, how can it, in supposed distinction from nature, "become" human, not to mention become sin and become dead? Isn't the blockage here caused by the notion of divine hypostasis? Isn't the true force of Jesus' actual experience of Godforsakenness moving Christology in the opposite direction of imputing His human passion to the divine life itself and so breaking to pieces the very distinction of divine and human natures?

Now we are in position to ask whether Gerhard was right in just this narrowly focused point. Taken at its best, Brenz's Christology requires a decision whether we are to take the notion of divine simplicity that Gerhard invokes as (1) a rule of faith instructing reverence before the ineffable mystery of the unity of the Three, *or* (2) as a putative metaphysical insight into the self-identity of perfect being (that in the end modalistically neutralizes Trinitarian personalism). Can it, in other words, make no difference to the Son's eternal identity that in the fullness of time He was born of a woman, under the law, even as this *Novum* is taken as a

---

170. *LW* 37, p. 72.
171. Gerhard, *On the Person and Office of Christ*, p. 189.
172. Gerhard, *On the Person and Office of Christ*, p. 195.

"fitting" expression of that way of being God that is the eternally begotten Son? If it makes some difference, how can that difference be expressed at the cost neither of modalism nor of subordinationism? If we can overcome the modalist tendencies and speculative proclivities at work in Brenz's school, must we not concede that they have a precise point — the very one raised by Theodore, and repeated virtually verbatim in Luther, about the specific humanity of Jesus at the dramatic juncture of the Cry of Dereliction expressing this true *Novum* in the Son's eternal life become temporal, bringing about a real, not apparent crisis within the life of the triune God? If so, must that not take us in the end to a gospel, theologically decoded, that tells of God surpassing God?

In his study *Was There a Lutheran Metaphysics?*, the Norwegian philosopher Joar Haga has recently provided the other side of this intense intra-Lutheran debate from the tradition of Brenz and taken up especially in recent theology by Jörg Baur.[173] In Haga's formulation, targeting the personalism of Chemnitz and Gerhard and made in criticism of the teaching of the Formula of Concord: "The divine of Christ is not emptied through the communication of attributes, but keeps its features intact. Obviously, the tradition of God's apathy is too strong to be modified through the movement or event of *communicatio idiomatum.* Again, it is the logical identity of the [divine] person [the eternal Son] which prevents the real communication of the natures,"[174] where by "real" Haga means unrestricted and reciprocating. Haga's splendid study not only makes available to the English-speaking world the demanding argumentation of Baur on behalf of Brenz's Christology but provides a wealth of analysis in primary sources, as Haga traces the interpretation of the *communicatio idiomatum* through early Lutheranism on into the period of Orthodoxy. While his study vigorously presents the Brenz-Baur Christological argument and often seems to favor it over against the Christological line that he sees flowing from Melanchthon through Chemnitz to Gerhard, the work falls short of advocacy. In the end the author indeed expresses a definite ambivalence about the choices he has excavated, as we shall see.

That ambivalence commences with the recognition of Luther's own Trinitarian personalism that Haga concedes in view of direct textual evidence from the *Haupttext* of Brenz's Christological line, Luther's *Confession concerning Christ's Supper.* Here Luther quite expressly attributes the suffering of God in Christ to the *person* incarnate, *not* to the nature.[175] Exasperated by the evidence, Haga exclaims, "What has happened here? Is the suffering and death, indeed some of the most fundamental properties of human nature, limited from their communication to the divine nature?" Apparently, for Luther himself, "Yes." Haga regards

---

173. Jörg Baur, *Luther und seine klassischen Erben: Theologische Aufsätze und Forschungen* (Tübingen: J. C. B. Mohr [Paul Siebeck], 1993).

174. Joar Haga, *Was There a Lutheran Metaphysics? The Interpretation of the communicatio idiomatum in Early Modern Lutheranism* (Göttingen: Vandenhoeck & Ruprecht, 2012), p. 175.

175. See notes 104-6 above.

this, however, as a problem. "The problem for Luther's unionist Christology is that the person of Christ can now be understood as a fixed *tertium,* an alternative to the communication of the natures themselves." Thus Luther appears here as a mere exponent of the patristic Christology of Cyril, operating with its strong Trinitarian nature — person distinction, rather than the religious genius who overcame it. As Haga further acknowledges, "There are, after all, some features of the idea that God is impassible which seem important for to [sic] for Luther's theology, too. As a theologian of Scripture in general, and the Old Testament in particular, Luther confirms that God as the living God is not surrendered to the decays and sways of this world, but faithful to his promises."[176]

While it is indeed true that Melanchthon draws back from Luther's *communicatio idiomatum* when taken realistically rather than verbally,[177] this retreat can hardly be parsed as a relapse to Trinitarian personalism from a modalist breakthrough in Luther. Haga unfortunately indulges in the familiar trope that lays all failure of theology in Luther's tradition at the doorstep of Melanchthon. He draws from Melanchthon (falsely, as we have seen) the alternative Christology of Trinitarian personalism. Thus instead of advancing with Luther to the "*terminus ad quem,* where the main emphasis is laid upon both natures and their common exchange of properties, Melanchthon retreats to the *terminus a quo,* where Christ is defined from his personal unity."[178] Even assuming for the sake of argument that such a distinction in supposed tendencies between Luther and Melanchthon is viable, this characterization misses the mark. What disturbs Melanchthon is not the exchange but taking the change realistically instead of verbally, since this implies to him a confusion of divine and human natures contrary to the Bible's axiomatic distinction between Creator and creature. And it is as well by no means clear that Luther's bold attribution of human sufferings to God in Christ implies a "*common* exchange of properties" — a kind of decentered ebb and flow between divinity and humanity tantamount to pantheism rather than the personal act of divine love that in compassion voluntarily takes to itself the sorrow and burden of the creature.

But it seems that this is the direction that Haga wants to go, namely, to "the extremes [taken] by Brenz":[179] "This relation is not seen as a static thing within a particular metaphysics. It is rather an event where there is a continuous exchange of properties. This radical perichoretic understanding of the relation between the natures is mirrored in the understanding of the [joyful exchange] metaphor, where sin and holiness are exchanged in Christ."[180] We will leave without comment the extension here of the technical term *perichoresis* from its native habi-

176. Haga, *Was There a Lutheran Metaphysics?,* p. 63.
177. *PNT,* pp. 162-70.
178. Haga, *Was There a Lutheran Metaphysics?,* p. 104.
179. Haga, *Was There a Lutheran Metaphysics?,* p. 210.
180. Haga, *Was There a Lutheran Metaphysics?,* p. 88.

tat in Trinitarianism to account for the eternal unity of the divine persons to a pantheistic vision of divinity and humanity flowing in and out of each other, as represented in the figure of Christ. The dubious benefit that Haga sees in this is that a natural exchange of properties is not "limited" to the particular "person" of Christ or to communication by His Spirit in the external Word and sacrament,[181] but becomes generalizable, "open[ing] up for a more speculative approach which reconnects theology to philosophy in a creative way"[182] — as if the teaching on the *Verbum externum* against enthusiasm were somehow Melanchthon's regrettable deviation from Luther's own cosmic-Christological tendencies! In more sober moments, however, Haga duly acknowledges that his favored Christological line from Brenz "is far from a mere repetition of Luther's interpretation. It marks a profiled expansion of the metaphysical implications already present in Luther's Christology."[183] Perhaps. But what we have in historical fact is an "oscillation" in the Christology descended from Luther between "the de-centered self in the tradition of Brenz, where the event of the natures' *communicatio idiomatum* opens up a space between God and human beings, and the more traditional emphasis on the will of the Christ-agent by Chemnitz"[184] that ghettoizes the God-human relation in a personal Christ and thus to the Spirit's ecclesia drawn from the nations.

This "oscillation" is a fact. Brenz's generalizing of ubiquity not only goes beyond Luther but depersonalizes Christ into a process of exchange funded by natural divine omnipresence,[185] while it is the alternative Christology of Gerhard that maintains that Christ's "humanity is only omnipresent *personaliter*."[186] Yet Haga's account of this oscillation errs in attributing what is in fact Christological confusion to "an unresolved understanding of how the anthropological notions from philosophy should be integrated in Christology."[187] Here are both the strength and the weakness of Haga's study. Its strength is limning out the Western medieval philosophical options current and debated in early Lutheran Christology. But its weakness lies in neglecting the simultaneous retrieval of patristic theology as an alternative theological resource[188] precisely against the modalistic framework of the medieval Christological debate. Haga regularly interprets the personhood of Christ in terms of Boethius' notion of an individual substance,[189] as the autonomous and active agent of its own effects.[190] Additionally, he treats

---

181. Haga, *Was There a Lutheran Metaphysics?*, p. 97.

182. Haga, *Was There a Lutheran Metaphysics?*, p. 210.

183. Haga, *Was There a Lutheran Metaphysics?*, p. 210.

184. Haga, *Was There a Lutheran Metaphysics?*, p. 174.

185. Haga, *Was There a Lutheran Metaphysics?*, p. 134.

186. Haga, *Was There a Lutheran Metaphysics?*, p. 148.

187. Haga, *Was There a Lutheran Metaphysics?*, p. 174.

188. Manfred Schulze, "Martin Luther and the Church Fathers," in *The Reception of the Church Fathers in the West* (Leiden and New York: E. J. Brill, 1997), pp. 573-626.

189. Haga, *Was There a Lutheran Metaphysics?*, p. 134, cf. 147.

190. Haga, *Was There a Lutheran Metaphysics?*, pp. 61, 174.

the "natures" as if they were really real things with timeless, quiescent, essential properties that may somehow surge forth outside of themselves into other such "natures" in processes of exchange. He thus treats abstractions from reality (according to the strong nature–person distinction in Trinitarianism, where "natures," i.e., abstract sets of possibilities are only actual as things or persons) as something real.[191] And he commits this hermeneutical transgression because he takes medieval philosophical notions in anthropology as suppositing, as it were, the notion of personhood in early Lutheran Christology. In this way, Haga fails to detect the vigorous retrieval of patristic Christology, with its crucial Trinitarian distinction between nature and person, on its own terms and to see how that distinction informs Luther, let alone Chemnitz and Gerhard. Here, as we recall, person is not reducible to a causal agent or subject of knowledge, but is person in community, hence always a patient-agent engaged in an intersubjective task involving reciprocating roles.

Ironically, however, in treating a final flower in Lutheran Orthodoxy of the line from Luther through Chemnitz to Gerhard in Balthasar Mentzer, Haga (albeit in a footnote) finally articulates the import and relevance of Trinitarian personalism (as opposed to medieval philosophical "supposit" anthropology) to his Christological topic. It is a passage worth quoting at length. Because "Mentzer insists on the real distinction between the persons of the Trinity . . . he lays another foundation for Christology in the doctrine of God than his adversaries in the reformed camp, who generally show more eagerness to preserve the *unity* of the Trinity":[192]

> This is partly an effect of a stronger *theistic* notion in the Reformed tradition, if we compare it to the Lutheran: God is placed outside the world, as the interpretation of a *spatial* transport of Christ's body in the ascension gives witness to. The Trinity as a unity confirms the structural difference between God's relative presence here, and his absolute presence in heaven. In the Lutheran tradition, however, there is an insistence of the Creator as being placed *in* and *with* the creatures. There is no spatial distance between creation and Creator, as the interpretation of a non-spatial heaven affirms. But if the Creator's presence among the creatures is seen as absolute, the existential misery caused by sin is radicalized: The Creator is not only a judge, but an adversary. That misery is overcome by the merciful Trinitarian *difference* — and not a unity — which opens up between God and God's Son in the incarnation, namely the difference between the Sender and the One being sent. The Lutheran tradition of *Dreifaltigkeit* — Trinity as diversity — reflects that dogmatic point.[193]

191. Haga, *Was There a Lutheran Metaphysics?*, p. 100.
192. Haga, *Was There a Lutheran Metaphysics?*, pp. 224-25.
193. Haga, *Was There a Lutheran Metaphysics?*, p. 225, n. 41.

Would that the analysis in *Was There a Lutheran Metaphysics?* had begun with this searching insight and used it to explore Luther's Christological breakthrough in the Eucharistic controversies! Then we would have seen that the real breakthrough is not a fall back into modalism and pantheism but the *Novum* of God surpassing God by the personal incorporation in Christ of the sinners of the world on the way to the coming of the Beloved Community to them and for them!

Haga is certainly right to contend broadly that Christology in Luther's tradition demands a revision of classical metaphysics in that Luther's "interpretation of the incarnation has fundamental philosophical implications or premises, as his opposition to Zwingli reveals."[194] But this revision was begun already with the patristic doctrine of the Trinity and in this way continued on through the "compromise" at Chalcedon; it was relitigated at the second council of Constantinople and seeped into the West in the synthesis of John of Damascus. Luther's actual Christological contribution was to retrieve the nature-person distinction and deploy it critically over against the medieval philosophical anthropology that had come to inform the modalistic "supposition" Christology, that imagines a man undergirded, grounded, in a particularly intense way by Deity-in-general.[195] Haga himself seems aware of the problem with the Brenz-Baur proposal in this regard, as he puts it on behalf of Mentzer's contention that a framework of personhood is necessary for salvation: "Divine presence cannot become a reality solely because of a Christological necessity. Christ must have the will to be present, a gracious presence [of] Christ eventually can withdraw from the world. If this is not the case, a kind of Christological[ly] secured automatic healing of sin is inevitably inscribed in the relation between man and God, and its soteriological tension would be suspended . . . a threat for a possible Protestant version of *ex opere operato* [emerges] if the voluntary aspect of presence is reduced."[196] That very devolution portends what Bonhoeffer was to name the Lutheran heresy of "cheap grace": the ideology of Christendom, replete with a depersonalized Christ turned into a universally operative metaphysical principle such that everything is grace and nothing in history decides anything that matters.

Thus Haga ends with a definite ambivalence, still caught in the "oscillation" he has described. How much better it would be to contend for the universality of the joyful exchange by thinking Christologically of the *heavenly session* of the *person* of Christ at work incognito in the world, as hinted in the Creedal article on His *descent into hell* to harrow it. That would be the kind of "exchange," not of natures, but of life for death and righteousness for sin that grounds hope without undermining the mission to the nations by turning everything, contrary to experience, into grace.

194. Haga, *Was There a Lutheran Metaphysics?*, p. 59.

195. To this extent, Haga's criticism of the later Melanchthon is justified, *Was There a Lutheran Metaphysics?*, pp. 108-9. But he is just wrong in construing the translation of *hypostasis* as *subsistentia* as equivalent to supposition Christology, pp. 96-97.

196. Haga, *Was There a Lutheran Metaphysics?*, p. 251.

The oscillation persists, however, because the question provoked to Cyrilian Christology by Theodore remains like an undigested lump: just how is the humanity in Christ communicated to the deity so that it is truly and personally the divine Son of God who prays, Thy will be done!, and cries out in dereliction when His prayer is granted? In what sense is it "fitting" that only the Son be incarnate, but incarnate just as the Jesus who was crucified and experienced there forsakenness by God such that "the deity withdrew"? If the kind of answer to this question given by the Brenz-Baur-Haga line is modalistic in tending to abolish the real personal distinctions of the Three, the alternative answer given today by a theologian like Pannenberg who intends continuity with the line from Luther through Chemnitz and Gerhard has unfortunate subordinationist tendencies. If I may somewhat flippantly reduce Pannenberg's rather elaborate conceptual construction in Christology, it amounts to the claim that the man Jesus is the one human creature who gave God the honor of His deity by utterly denying that He, a creature, was God,[197] in this dialectical fashion demonstrating true Sonship.[198] This is too clever by far, in spite of the truth it captures that divine Sonship, as filial receptivity, must be thought capable of giving itself away in obedience, even to death on a cross, in order to receive again. Criticism of Pannenberg here is not a matter of resisting the necessary theological deliteralizing of the mythic forms of New Testament language, but rather concerns proper decoding which cannot do without the semantic, if not metaphysical distinction of the two natures in Christ to express generally the difference between divinity and humanity but also to express thereby the concrete unification of that difference that is the Incarnation. The point is to say that the man Jesus is God in the way of being a Son, where and when the Spirit wills.

Jenson too seeks to overcome the "two natures" conceptuality with its Doppelgänger effect[199] in Christology and to see in Jesus' humanity the very eternal

197. Pannenberg, *ST* 2, pp. 230-31.
198. Pannenberg, *ST* 2, p. 325.
199. Jenson, *ST* 1, p. 132. Jenson can very precisely articulate Cyril's need for distinguishing the natures for the sake of the unity of person: "the one Christ is everything required to be God the Son and everything required to be this particular human being, that he instantiates the full attribute-set that specifies each" (*ST* 1, p. 130). His point is that under the influence of the Tome, Chalcedon fails conceptually to follow Cyril in unifying the person, that its affirmation "in one hypostasis" is thus empty, mere "verbiage" (*ST* 1, p. 132). This is as much to say that the "compromise" at Chalcedon cried out for "further creative thinking" that, at least for those following Cyril's Christological intentions, leads to the "neo-Chalcedonian Christology" (*ST* 1, p. 133), the position adopted in the present work. I do not wish to exaggerate my differences with either Pannenberg or Jenson, whose work in Trinitarian Christology I regard as crucially important modernizations of the tradition I share with them. Where I differ most probably lies in skepticism regarding the potential of the tradition of German idealism to be of service to postmodern theology, and an even greater skepticism about the nineteenth century's critique of the "two natures doctrine." If we follow out the trajectory of the Cappadocian distinction, we take "nature" semantically as specifying in ordinary language how *concepts* of Creator and

Sonship of God: the "second identity of God is directly the human person of the Gospels, in that he is the one who stands to the Father in the relation of being eternally begotten by him."[200] There is an ambiguity in this formulation, whether we are to take the "human person" as (1) the narrative figure *(prosopon)* or (2) the *hypostasis* that is the eternal Son/Logos made human or (3) the so-called historical Jesus. But according to the present argument, the human being of the Gospels is already the Son of God (Mark 1:1!), as we have seen, and does not exist as a "human person" at all, according to Cyril's *enhypostasis*. We can, however, take Jenson's statement as presupposing a perspectival dialectic between the natural man's perception of Jesus as one of us only, and the believer's, who no longer knows Christ according to the flesh, knowing Him also as a member of the set, the divine Three. Then an event of unification of the sign and the thing signified has transpired in the Spirit giving the correspondence of theological subject and theological object. Taken in this way as a statement of the unity of person for faith, there would be nothing objectionable about Jenson's formulation of God's "second identity": it is the equivalent of Barth's denial of a *Logos asarkos,* an affirmation of the man Jesus Christ as the Lamb slain from before the world's foundation, the *Logos incarnandus.*

But Jenson, as we recall from the earlier discussion, had inferred from Luther a teaching of divine passibility and ridiculed the Tome of Leo's claim for the two natures distinction at Chalcedon, *Agit enim utraque forma cum alterius communione quod proprium est,* which in "mild disrepect" he translated as, "Each nature does its own thing, in cooperation with the other," although admittedly he was "tempted to translate: "Each nature does its own thing, so long as it doesn't hurt the other."[201] Thus he imputes a tacit Nestorianism to the Tome that treats the natures as quasi-personal agents and fails to unify these as the one person who is and appears as the "human person" of the Gospels. In this way, the preconceived ideas of divine and human "natures" go unrevised, he argues, i.e., "unbaptized" in our theological thinking instead of being reconceived according to their perichoresis in the one person of Christ (i.e., their reality as a dynamic *communicatio idiomatum*). His concern in this is in a way parallel to Haga's, due no doubt to the fact that both claim inspiration from Brenz's reading of Luther's Christology. But if Haga thinks to abolish the person to open up universally the Christological exchange of natures, Jenson wants to attribute passibility to the divine nature by equating the human person of Jesus with the divine nature in its second identity.

Ironically, as Meyendorff pointed out, and as Gerhard also noted, Jenson's

---

creature are to be properly distinguished and related but we restrict reality statements to the hypostases. I am agreeing with Bruce Marshall in this specific point about the importance of sustaining the "two natures" doctrine in this conceptualist way, as I wrote at the conclusion of *DC,* pp. 237-38.

200. Jenson, *ST* 1, p. 137.

201. Robert Jenson, *Unbaptized God: The Basic Flaw in Ecumenical Theology* (Minneapolis: Augsburg Fortress, 1992), p. 123.

kind of mock translation of Leo is a sample of the underappreciation of the force of the word *communione* in Leo's Latin.[202] What Leo actually wrote is that each "nature" performs what is proper to it *in communion with* the other. While Jenson has a point in arguing that a "nature," as an abstract set of possibilities, does not *do* anything at all, the question may be posed whether he does not in this way also disregard what Gerhard called the "form" of the communication, the divine person (not "identity") whose personal act is to appropriate the humanity to utilize its properties, as also divine properties, for the accomplishment of the messianic mission. We have seen how carefully Gerhard exposits this "formal" union of the Son with human nature in the incarnation as the "fitting" expression of the divine Sonship in its mission of redemption. In the present view, then, it seems that Jenson misdiagnoses the problem along Brenz's line by thinking that it is the doctrine of divine impassibility as such that is the problem[203] rather than the equally ambiguous but more invidious doctrine of divine simplicity that works to efface the personal distinctions and relations presented in the gospel narrative.

The ambiguity of the impassibility doctrine can be sorted out to say that the divine suffering in Christ is voluntary, hence personal expression of divine Sonship, and so a truly divine and creative act of love; or, what is the same, that Sonship truly is a divine way of being, where to be God is to give, as one has first received. Simplicity, however, forces modalism into Christology the moment it ceases to operate as a rule of faith to take the Three of the gospel narrative as ineffably One and thus to await in faith the eschatological demonstration of this unity. But if we take simplicity as a metaphysical insight into the self-identity of perfect being according to the protological metaphysics of antique cosmos-piety, we have to deny that there is any "real" difference between the three ways, that is, hypostases, in which God is God for God — or treat these real differences as a dumb fact from above, a mystery revealed that does and can do no theological work.

The attempt in the line of Johannes Brenz to destabilize the concept of the person in Christology, no more than the attempt to smear the concept of the two natures with the label "substance ontology," should not lull us into think-

202. Jenson regards the doctrine of the hypostatic union as "vacuous" in the sense that it reasons in a circle, grounding the communication of attributes in a personal union that is only known, however, through the communication of attributes as evidenced in the gospel narrative's presentation (Jenson, *Unbaptized God,* p. 124). In defense of Gerhard above, however, we have rejected the demand here for a theoretical explanation of the Christological "How," even as we grant to Jenson the important points that (1) read through the Western tendency toward modalism, Chalcedon cannot but be read as positing two natures working side by side as quasi-agents, i.e., substances, and (2) it is right to read Luther's Christology as tending toward the real attribution of Jesus' suffering "to the Logos, also as God" no less than "God's infinite 'energies' to the man Jesus" (Jenson, *Unbaptized God,* p. 129).

203. See Jenson's contribution, "Ipse Pater non est impassibilis," in *Divine Impassibility and the Mystery of Human Suffering,* ed. J. F. Keating and T. J. White, O.P. (Grand Rapids: Eerdmans, 2009), pp. 117-26.

ing that such tinkering with the conceptual apparatus solves the true problem of Christology. Taken as Trinitarian Christology, the true problem is the one raised by Theodore's contention for Jesus' humanity, and raised anew by Luther from within the Cyrilian Christological framework: How can Jesus' experience of Godforsakenness be attributed to God as an event within the life of God? Here Christological reflection on the Person who is Jesus Christ the Son of God must pass into reflection on this Person at work not only towards us but at the same time in relation to the One whom He called Abba, Father. Here we must not be misled by the expression "at work" to think of a transcendental subject, a noumenal agent causing effects within the causally determined world, rather than a patient-agent, the person in community, receiving an identity to perform a role in concert with others. The "work" of Christ the Son incarnate is centrally His *passion as the divine passion of love,* a moment in the movement that is God surpassing God to bring the Beloved Community even to dying sinners. In this work of the Son, whom the Father sends and the Spirit brings to completion, we discover a "self-relationship which in freedom goes beyond itself, overflows itself, and gives itself away. It is pure overflow, overflowing being for the sake of another and only then for the sake of itself. That is love. And that is the God who is love: the one who always heightens and expands his own being in such great self-relatedness still more selfless and *thus* overflowing" (Jüngel).[204] To see this person in faith is to see this person at work, or better, in mission. So we now turn from the Cyrilian teaching of the person, Jesus Christ the Son of God, to His redemptive mission on behalf of Augustinian humanity.

## Salvation in Christ

The Son of man came on earth to forgive sins. The Son of man came to seek and to save the lost. The Son of man came to call sinners, not the righteous. The Son of man came that they might have life abundant. The Son of man came not to be served but to serve and lay down His life a ransom for many. In these and like designations from across the entire range of New Testament literature, Jesus "combines the *ebed Yahweh* [suffering servant of the Lord] and *barnasha* [apocalyptic Son of man] — titles of humiliation and exaltation respectively. . . . This is the unheard-of new act of Jesus, that he united these two apparently contradictory tasks in his self-consciousness, and that he expressed that union in his life and teaching."[205] Setting aside as irrelevant to Christology Cullmann's claim to have

---

204. Eberhard Jüngel, *God as the Mystery of the World: On the Foundation of the Theology of the Crucified One in the Dispute between Theism and Atheism,* trans. D. L. Guder (Grand Rapids: Eerdmans, 1983), p. 369.

205. Oscar Cullmann, *The Christology of the New Testament,* trans. S. C. Guthrie and C. A. M. Hall (London: William Clowes, 1963), p. 161.

insight into Jesus' "self-consciousness," the union of these two scriptural offices in the New Testament's narrative objectifications of the public *persona,* Jesus Christ the Son of God, signifies that His life-work is the *redemption* of the creation. The seemingly paradoxical combination of exaltation and humility characterizes the gospel narrative of Him "who, though He was rich, for your sakes He became poor, that you through His poverty might become rich" (2 Cor. 8:9). Salvation in Christ[206] is the beating heart of Christian theology and can be so wherever this knowledge of the person in mission according to Trinitarian Christology remains vital and soteriology has not decayed into monotheism and morality.

For that very reason, however, the crippling disunities of the divided churches are nowhere more evident than in the contrasting, if not competing and contradictory conceptions of salvation that necessarily drive these churches apart into diverse missions other than the Spirit's gospel mission to the nations. Unity in mission, theologically, is unity in the doctrine of salvation in Christ. For example, one could hardly imagine conceptions of salvation as evidently opposed as the extrinsic imputation of alien righteousness in Lutheranism and the deification of the saint growing in holiness according to Orthodoxy. To the extent that such diverse soteriologies actually hold, common mission is impossible. The partners would be at cross-purposes. Such contradictory theologies of salvation reflect a fall on every side of the divided churches from Trinitarian personalism; in this case, the missions of the Son and of the Spirit are set against one another or assimilated one to the other and so understood in one-sided and falsely exaggerated ways for the purposes of Christian tribalism settling down into the world in some territorialized space, each claiming its own turf. Tribalism and territorialism come in the default of ecclesial existence in the Spirit's mission to the nations. The way forward in the task of realignment therefore lies in mutually attentive theological experimentation among all who intend orthodoxy, in acknowledging that they fall short of it, on the way back to the mission to the nations, also within the formerly Christian place of Euro-America.[207]

The North American bilateral volume *Salvation in Christ: A Lutheran-Orthodox Dialogue*[208] brims with new theological possibilities for the construction of an evangelical and orthodox theological mission in our post-Christendom world. It will be by doing theology together that we will, in Orthodox theologian John Breck's words, "transcend our differences of history and culture, in order to discover the depth and breadth of theology that does in fact unite us."[209] We can

206. An earlier version of this section appeared as Paul R. Hinlicky, "Theological Anthropology: Towards Integrating Theosis and Justification by Faith," *Journal of Ecumenical Studies* 34, no. 1 (Winter 1997): 38-73.

207. See Kenneth Paul Wesche and Paul R. Hinlicky, "Theses from Sväty Jur," *Pro Ecclesia* 4, no. 3 (Summer 1995): 265-67.

208. *Salvation in Christ: A Lutheran-Orthodox Dialogue,* ed. John Meyendorff and Robert Tobias (Minneapolis: Augsburg, 1992).

209. *Salvation in Christ,* p. 106.

in this way learn to integrate the concerns of each theological tradition by turning together to the common matrix. "The native tongue of Christians, for theological expression as well as for speaking of the Christian life, is the Bible," the dialogue reported.[210] "Both traditions have continued to employ the language of the Bible as the primary vehicle of theological expression and spiritual understanding."[211]

To be sure, abiding in the language of the Bible as the matrix of Christian theology is not so simple today, nor may it so simply be taken for granted. Speaking from the Lutheran side in the time of a profound crisis of faith and Christian identity after the collapse of Protestant biblicism, there is a perceived need to recover the orthodox, that is, the early Catholic understanding of the authority of Scripture in the church.[212] As argued above in Chapter Two, the vision here is of a historical process of Holy Tradition arising from the inaugurating tradition of the resurrection of the Crucified (1 Cor. 15:1-8), guided by the Spirit who leads to all truth by recalling the word of Jesus (John 16:13-14), who gives both the biblical witness and its believing reception; here what the Bible witnesses is the Trinitarian economy, the canonical salvation history reaching out to include the nations, as parsed by the baptismal creed. The Agreed Statement on Revelation of the Lutheran-Orthodox International Joint Commission stated: "The revelation of God, even as contained in Scripture, transcends all verbal expressions. It is hidden from all creatures, especially from sinful man (Greek: the 'old man'). Its true meaning is revealed only through the Holy Spirit in the living experience of salvation, which is accomplished in the church through the Christian life. This catholic experience of salvation in the church is at the same time the only authentic expression of the true understanding of the Word of God."[213] If we take this statement not as a lame blessing of the ecclesiastical status quo ("reconciled diversity," as criticized above), but in fact as a probing indictment of Christian tribalism and territorialism that makes "true understanding of the Word of God" into the Spirit's contemporary accusation of deficit in every direction among the divided churches, we are prepared to turn to the matrix of the Scriptures to understand afresh the messianic work of Jesus Christ the Son of God. Here we meet Him in the power of the Spirit as Israel's prophet, priest, and king, as shortly we shall study.

Our claim has been that nothing less than a Cyrilian Christ is soteriologically adequate to facing, engaging, and in the end overcoming the predicament of Au-

---

210. *Salvation in Christ,* p. 17.

211. *Salvation in Christ,* p. 24.

212. On the Orthodox side, see chapter 8, "Tradition and the Traditions," in Vladimir Lossky, *In the Image and Likeness of God,* ed. John H. Erickson and Thomas E. Bird (Crestwood, NY: St. Vladimir's Seminary Press, 1985), pp. 141-68. On the Protestant side, see chapter 12, "Quo Vadis, Petre? Tradition from Irenaeus to Humani Generis," in Heiko Oberman, *The Dawn of the Reformation: Essays in Late Medieval and Early Reformation Thought* (Edinburgh: T. & T. Clark, 1986), pp. 269-96.

213. *Lutheran-Orthodox Dialogue: Agreed Statements 1985-1989* (Geneva: WCC, 1992), p. 15.

gustinian humanity that is sinfulness, that is, blind yet willing captivity of desire to malice structuring injustice. The ecumenical purpose in this second part of the present chapter is to work out Christologically an Eastern answer (theosis) to a Western question (justification): the man Jesus Christ, in his person the divine Son of God coming in the flesh to flesh, works our righteousness, the righteousness of living by faith that is simultaneously also the righteousness of God's coming reign overtaking us here and now to fulfill the lost promise of creation. For Jesus Christ is the one who in filial obedience to His Father personally assumed the sin and death of humanity and therewith triumphed over the structures of malice and injustice that held humanity captive, helpless, and perishing. Vindicated and installed as the saving Lord of creation, Jesus Christ bestows on His justified and liberated people His own Spirit, so that they become by the ecstasy of faith already now the holy children of God living together in love in prospect of the world's new creation, that is, the cosmic redemption and fulfillment of the Beloved Community.

While not asking the same question as in the West about divine righteousness, Orthodoxy's doctrine of theosis offers a genuinely theological anthropology; that is, it strictly thinks of the human being as the broken and unfinished creation of the triune God. The decisive point, as we have learned, is that a human being is never to be reduced to his or her "nature," that is, to an immanent set of general possibilities, but is called as a person by the Person of Jesus Christ in view of *His* possibilities (i.e., His personal relations with His Father and Spirit) to become concretely the new person united in love with other persons within the infinite, tri-personal life of God that is the Beloved Community. This calling to deification — of the created image to likeness to God by the uncreated image of God who came in the likeness of sinful flesh — consists in cross-bearing discipleship to Christ. This is the path of true holiness.

Integrating these two forms of theological thinking, we see that justifying faith wholly involves the human will in its uncoerced desire and obedient participation, yet not in any Pelagian sense in which the will retains its Adamic form of would-be autonomy over against God but rather is formed as discipleship to Christ the saving Lord. Justifying faith is the concrete, nonmeritorious, Spirit-worked synergy of the new person in Christ[214] that receives from God in order

---

214. That justifying faith comes as *regeneration* in the social sense of baptismal adoption into the ecclesia by conformation to Christ's cross and resurrection was the original teaching of the Augsburg Confession; when Osiander took this to refer to an individual religious experience or the later Melanchthon came to think of the individual will's contribution of "non-resistance" to grace, incipient Lutheran orthodoxy within this individualistic and psychologizing frame of reference had to insist on the miraculous monergism of divine grace. For these good reasons, it landed itself in a muddle. For the detailed argument see Paul R. Hinlicky, "Staying Lutheran in the Changing Church(es)," Afterword in Mickey L. Mattox and A. G. Roeber, *Changing Churches: An Orthodox, Catholic and Lutheran Theological Conversation* (Grand Rapids: Eerdmans, 2012), pp. 281-314.

to give from God. On this side of the Kingdom's coming in fullness, however, the new person in Christ is and remains until dying day also a member of the common body, that is, the Christian remains Augustine's perishing sinner in the bleeding and broken world. Jesus therefore is and remains Savior of the Christian from baptism day to resurrection day, also in the believer's new obedience and discipleship. The theological subject is and remains the growth into grace by the Spirit of grace that begins in baptism but endures forever. The believer's righteousness, taken as the individual who is still afflicted within and without by structures of malice and injustice in this life, consists for the most part, as Augustine affirmed, in the forgiveness of sins. By the same token, this believer's participation as member in the Body of Christ puts her to work in structures of love for justice, as we shall see especially in the next chapter.

To make this case for the integration of theosis and justification, I will be drawing on a forgotten work today from the so-called second quest for the historical Jesus,[215] Friedrich Gogarten's *Christ the Crisis* (German: *Jesus Christus Wende der Welt*), especially in exploring the priestly work of Christ. Gogarten, erstwhile comrade in arms with Barth in the early dialectical theology, broke ranks and entered into the "decision" for the National Socialist claim to a revolutionary "turning-point" (German: *Wende*)[216] — a breach that had no little influence on Barth's own turn towards the objectivity of faith in Jesus Christ as "the one Word of God whom we are to trust and obey in life and in death," as he put it in the opening salvo of the Barmen Declaration. In some oblique sense, *Christ the Crisis* is a penitential work, now attributing the true "turning point" of historical humanity not to Hitlerism but to the decision of Jesus to take responsibility *for* others *before* God — a "historical" Jesus that theology can uncover critically — so Gogarten thought — to know its object in the world.[217] It is also a kind of culminating work in the tradition of Theodore of Mopsuestia in its vigorous repudiation of the "metaphysical" and "dogmatic" Christology attributed to Cyril and his tradition in the name of Troeltsch's "historical method" in theology,[218] with appeal to Luther's own insistence that Christology account for the dereliction of the crucified man Jesus.[219] Interestingly, Gogarten is even able to draw Karl Rahner into this avowedly revisionist Christology.[220] So this text provides a fitting denouement in this chapter's quest for a higher synthesis in Cyril's tradition that accounts for the dereliction of Jesus as God's own experience in the movement of God surpassing God. At the same time it addresses Cyrilian Christology foursquare to the predic-

---

215. Friedrich Gogarten, *Christ the Crisis,* trans. R. A. Wilson (London: SCM, 1970). See especially chapter 4, "A New Quest of the Historical Jesus," pp. 23-43.

216. Jack Forstman, *Christian Faith in Dark Times: Theological Conflicts in the Shadow of Hitler* (Louisville: Westminster John Knox, 1992).

217. Gogarten, *Christ the Crisis,* pp. 38, 132.

218. Gogarten, *Christ the Crisis,* p. 28.

219. Gogarten, *Christ the Crisis,* pp. 281-98.

220. Gogarten, *Christ the Crisis,* pp. 285-86.

ament of Augustinian humanity of bondage in sin to death, what we have para-phrased consistently through this work as our inescapable belonging by virtue of the common body to prevailing structures of malice and injustice that have formed our subjectivities long before any of us had any say in the matter.

Gogarten gave as apt a theological description of that "doom" — no doubt crystallized in his mind by his own seduction to Hitlerism — as may be found in twentieth-century theology. He developed Bultmann's anthropological decod-ing of the Pauline language of the apocalyptic dualism of the ages. This dualism "refer[s] to one and the same world, which is good or evil depending upon how it is understood by the men who live in it. If it is understood as God's creation, then in it, in accordance with its created being, the invisible nature of God, his eternal power and deity, which calls nothingness into being, can be apprehended (Rom. 1:20, 4:17). In this case it is good. But if it is understood as a world, the nature of which is that it supports and maintains itself in existence, so that the creature is exchanged for the creator, and the honour and worship which belong to the creator alone is given to the creature, it is evil, and subject to ruin and futility (Rom. 8:20). For then it bars men who venerate and trust in it from access to God the creator."[221] This latter "secularist" self-understanding is humanity's default position, even if not especially in its religiosity, whether modern or classical. It issues in a kind of "cosmos piety" that repudiates responsibility *to* God *for* the world in the name of a moral claim of responsibility *to* the world *against* putative words from beyond it.

While the reliance on anthropological decoding from Bultmann is not finally adequate for overcoming the individualism in Bultmann that Gogarten himself criticizes[222] (but also finally resorts to),[223] Gogarten's analysis of the predicament of Augustinian humanity under the thrall of the *libido dominandi,* compelled to defend the world as it is from the world that is promised by God, gives us a theo-logically exact understanding of sinfulness. As a state or condition of humanity, sinfulness is not individual misdeeds or legal transgressions, but thralldom "to this world" in its total claim on conscience from which self-extraction is barred until Someone breaks into the strong man's house and binds him in order to plunder his goods. In order to understand this break-in, and binding, and plundering, as the messianic work of Jesus Christ, we turn first in the matrix of the Scriptures to the prophecy of Jesus, especially as presented by Luke. In its light, with Gogar-ten's aid, we may understand Jesus' priestly act of self-offering when once and for all He took responsibility before God for all in their sinful secularism.

221. Gogarten, *Christ the Crisis,* p. 58.

222. Gogarten, *Christ the Crisis,* pp. 52-53.

223. Gogarten, *Christ the Crisis,* pp. 267, 275. What is changed in faith is not the world, but the believer's attitude towards it. But against this reduction, we are arguing the believer's atti-tude towards the world changes because in the believer, God's relation to the world is changing redemptively. In this mediation, the world too changes.

## The Prophet of the Reign of God

On account of its use of the Jewish background sympathetically to exposit New Testament messianic belief, Oscar Cullmann, in his still-illuminating study, *The Christology of the New Testament,* observed that "in later Christian theology we find remnants of the Christology of the Prophet in the essentially altered form of the so-called *munus propheticum Christi,* the prophetic office of Christ."[224] Indeed, Cullmann began his investigation with a study of the title "*the* Prophet, the final Prophet who should 'fulfill' all prophecy at the end of time."[225] One can immediately see the pertinence of the category of "the prophet" for the figure of Jesus: "The function of the eschatological Prophet in the Jewish texts consists primarily in preparing the people of Israel for the coming of the Kingdom of God. He fulfills this function, not simply as the former Old Testament prophets did, but in a much more direct way as the immediate Preparer of the way for the Kingdom of God itself. He comes endowed with unique eschatological authority. His call to repentance is final and requires final decision.... [J]udgment is actually executed already in the present with the decision of each individual in response to this prophet ... he brings the last word, the final possibility.... For when he speaks, he points to the Kingdom of God already approaching."[226]

Cullmann argued that the title was not taken up by Jesus or by his disciples, since they regarded John the Baptist (Matt. 11:13-14) as the eschatological Prophet.[227] Cullmann acknowledges, however, that we hear "of other acts of the Prophet in the Jewish writings: he is to raise up the nation of Israel, overthrow the world powers, struggle against the Antichrist, work miracles"[228] that would not have applied to John. As the One who, not like John, baptizes in the Spirit, Jesus is regarded as the Prophet whose word is deed. Thus Hans Conzelmann could write: "at the same time Jesus' radical new approach is immediately evident"[229] by contrast with John, in that Jesus prophesies the good news of the Kingdom's coming in Galilee. Jesus Himself does not call out from but enters into the profane world. His is a summons not only to repentance but also to faith in news that is good. It consisted not only in a washing clean but a new anointing. It issues in a gracious and powerful summons to discipleship. "Now after John was arrested, Jesus came to Galilee, proclaiming the good news of God, and saying, 'The time

---

224. Cullmann, *Christology,* p. 50.

225. Cullmann, *Christology,* p. 13.

226. Cullmann, *Christology,* p. 43.

227. Quite in contrast, John's Gospel has the Baptist refusing this title for himself (John 1:21). This reflects the extended debate between Jewish disciples of John and Jesus in a later period. Cf. Cullmann, *Christology,* p. 38.

228. Cullmann, *Christology,* p. 45.

229. Hans Conzelmann, *Jesus,* trans. J. R. Lord (Philadelphia: Fortress, 1973), p. 32. Just so, Conzelmann argues, the title of the eschatological Prophet, who suffers as a martyr, passes over to that of the Suffering Servant of God.

is fulfilled, and the kingdom of God has come near; repent, and believe in the good news'" (Mark 1:14-15).

Whatever the application of the technical term historically, when we consider the teaching and preaching of Jesus, we can conceptualize the man and His message readily as prophet of the Reign of God. For Christian theology the "remnant of the Christology of the Prophet" by which Jesus speaks with authority to bring God near to the godless and thus to subvert the anti-divine powers that hold them in thrall constitutes the first movement in His saving work. It is a role, be it noted, in which there is absolutely no distinction possible between Jesus' so-called "ethical" message and His so-called "miraculous" deeds of power. Both enunciate the same prophetic word, liberating from Satan by issuing the powerful call to discipleship that gives what it demands (Mark 1:18, 20).

In pre-critical Lutheran dogmatics, Jesus is also named Prophet (Matt. 21:11; John 6:14; Luke 7:16, 24:19), a Rabbi or Teacher (Matt. 23:8, 10), Bishop of souls (1 Pet. 2:25), or Shepherd (John 10:11; Heb. 13:20 passim) in that He proclaimed the imminent reign of God. His prophetic office is His teaching "of those things necessary to be known and to be believed for salvation," i.e., "the gratuitous promise of the remission of sins, of righteousness and life eternal, by and on account of Christ" and therewith the "declaration and true interpretation of the Law." This prophetic function of Jesus continues in the church "by the establishment of the sacred office of the ministry."[230] What falls out of consideration in the old dogmatics, however, is the dimension of power. Jesus' prophetic office as it is conceived in the New Testament is a word-work of liberation from the contra-divine powers; here His "miraculous" deeds, as previously argued, are not to be taken as "proofs" of His authority for neutral observers, but as "signs" indicating His redemptive mission in the Spirit as the Son sent by the Father to do this good work of deliverance. In the grip of the Holy Spirit, Jesus goes to war with the unholy spirits: "What is this? A new teaching — with authority! He commands even the unclean spirits, and they obey him" (Mark 1:27). With the same teaching authority, Jesus calls the fishermen to follow Him, the diseased to health, the leper to cleansing, the sinner to righteousness — just as it is this proclamation of God's nearness to those who are far from God that flushes the demons from hiding and puts them to flight. "They were astounded at his teaching, for he taught them as one having authority, and not as the scribes. Just then there was in their synagogue a man with an unclean spirit, and he cried out, 'What have you to do with us, Jesus of Nazareth? Have you come to destroy us? I know who you are, the Holy One of God.' But Jesus rebuked him, saying, 'Be silent, and come out of him!'" (Mark 1:22-25).

Since Gustaf Aulén's influential book, *Christus Victor,*[231] this traditional ne-

---

230. Schmid, *Doctrinal Theology,* pp. 340-41.

231. Gustaf Aulén, *Christus Victor* (London: SPCK / New York and Toronto: Macmillan, 1931).

glect of the prophetic Christology of liberation in favor of the priestly theology of the reconciliation of the sinner with God has been much discussed. The old Lutheran dogmaticians so emphasized reconciliation, which they conceived in a modified form of Anselmian satisfaction theory as Christ's passive obedience satisfying God's just judgment on the sinfulness that makes ruin of creation, that the liberating word of the prophetic Christ from the powers and principalities (as also the royal work of Christ in bringing the renewed creation to fulfillment) was eclipsed. The centrality of reconciliation filled the circle and became the entire content of salvation in Christ. This neglect had its own peculiar cost. The orthodox Lutherans were never able to bring the deepest import of their teaching on reconciliation — the harrowing of hell as present, prophetic proclamation — to fruition; instead in this narrowness they succumbed to the much-lamented individualism, moralism, and otherworldliness that Aulén attacked, in spite of themselves reducing the gospel to the popularly understood good deal of "ortho-dox" belief in the doctrine of the vicarious atonement in exchange for heavenly reward. Nevertheless, the almost universal abandonment of Anselm today has had its cost as well.

By abandoning Anselm wholesale,[232] we do not on the whole recover the dialectic that Aulén actually saw in the classical patristic theory as recovered by Luther: "The deliverance of man from the power of death and the devil is at the same time his deliverance from God's judgment. God is reconciled by His own act in reconciling the world to Himself."[233] Absent reconciliation by the atoning death of Jesus on the cross, the demonic powers are rather accorded a de facto sovereignty that rivals God's when our words naming them prove powerless to liberate desire from captivation to them. Such is the despair into which recent theologies of liberation are falling at "the end of history," while self-identified prophetic Christians, who think it in their power in imitation of Jesus to defeat the demonic powers by symbolic political interventions, all the more stridently preach "the politics of Jesus" as the authentic Christian possibility. They have not yet learned Augustine's prayer that so offended, and had to offend Pelagius, "Command what you will, O God; but give what you command!" On the other side of the spectrum of the divided churches, Pentecostal Christians, endowed with the same Spirit as Jesus, would also imitate Him, quite literally finding the world of the twenty-first century as populated with demons as was first-century Galilee. As Jesus Christ is no longer fundamentally conceived as the helpless sinner's representative who by His innocence overcomes their guilt before God, Jesus Christ becomes little more than a model, howsoever "liberating," for victims to imitate in their own struggles to achieve agency and overcome the passivity indoctrinated by oppression. Mimesis soteriology forgets that imitation is what

---

232. See the incisive but little-known study of Burnell F. Eckhardt Jr., *Anselm and Luther on the Atonement: Was It "Necessary"?* (San Francisco: Mellen Research University Press, 1992).

233. Aulén, *Christus Victor*, p. 59.

the serpent seduces to: *sicut Deus eritis!* Certainly, as criticized above, a theology of the cross, taken as an *imitatio Christi,* falls to the same critique. A theology of the cross that amounts to nothing more than *imitating* the apparent self-hatred of the self-crucifying God would be only more of the world's sickness.

In any case, apart from His sacrifice on the cross and vindication by His Father, Jesus truly perished defeated in the faith that He had proclaimed and lived, His hope in God's reign dashed. For this reason, playing the New Testament's varying models of atonement against one another is decadent and schismatic theology; discovering their deeper unity in a higher Christological synthesis on the way to the visible unity of the realigned ecclesia in the Spirit's mission to the nations is the ecumenical task today of soteriology in critical dogmatics. Jesus is the prophet of God's imminent season of grace, the proclaimer of His Father's favor. Therefore discipleship to Jesus is the relation to Him in which this grace is effective as the Spirit's liberating power in conflict with the unholy spirits of malice and injustice. Let us look in the matrix of Scripture and see where this is a major theological theme, the central section of Luke's gospel.[234]

"Do not be afraid, little flock, for it is your Father's good pleasure to give you the kingdom," Jesus declares, adding immediately as if in consequence, "Sell your possessions, and give alms" (Luke 12:33). The free gift of the Father through Jesus the Son works in disciples a joyful self-abandonment to the cause of the kingdom. "See, I have given you authority to tread on snakes and scorpions, and over all the power of the enemy; and nothing will hurt you. Nevertheless, do not rejoice at this, that the spirits submit to you, but rejoice that your names are written in heaven" (10:19-20). The power of the reign of God is conferred upon those who follow Jesus. Yet disciples who have done all remain "unworthy servants" (17:7-10) who never cease utterly to depend on the Lord whom they follow. Discipleship requires a rigorous personal discipline: "Carry no purse, no bag, no sandal!" Yet this discipline is demanded for the sake of the missionary cause of the kingdom. Disciples are not cultivating their own garden, so to say, but are sent into a "plentiful harvest" which they are to gather in the name of the Lord (Luke 10:1-12). Disciples are therefore always to find their own joy in the joy of that father in Jesus' parable who maintained to the elder son, "We had to celebrate and rejoice, because this brother of yours was dead and has come to life; he was lost and has been found" (15:32). Joy in the salvation of others is the infallible sign that disciples are in fact following Jesus (10:21).

The evangelist Luke's teaching on grace and discipleship is worked out in

---

234. An earlier version of the following exegesis was published as "Grace and Discipleship in the Kingdom of God," *Pro Ecclesia* 4, no. 3 (Summer 1995): 356-63. See also Joseph A. Fitzmyer, S.J., *The Gospel according to Luke,* volumes 28 and 29 in the Anchor Bible (New York: Doubleday, 1979/1985); Walther von Loewenich, *Luther als Ausleger der Synoptiker* (Munich: Chr. Kaiser Verlag, 1954); I. Howard Marshall, "Luke and His 'Gospel,'" in *The Gospel and the Gospels,* ed. Peter Stuhlmacher (Grand Rapids: Eerdmans, 1991).

the course of the nine central chapters that narrate Jesus' sojourn to Jerusalem. The Evangelist's unusual verb in 9:51, "When the days drew near for him to be *taken up,* [Jesus] set his face to go to Jerusalem," alludes to the heavenly dominion, which the crucified and risen Lord will gain through the events that take place in Jerusalem (cf. 24:26). From 9:51 onward, the Evangelist regularly supplies notices of Jesus' itinerary that mark His progress there (e.g., 9:57; 10:1, 38). Everything presses towards Jerusalem. The use of this artificial framework to organize a variety of traditional materials is a clue to the catechetical purpose of the Evangelist. Readers had been prepared earlier to understand the journey with Jesus as a time of training for disciples in the mission of the kingdom of God (9:1), a motif repeated in 10:2. In Jerusalem, the disciples will be told definitively that the call to discipleship is Jesus' call to service in the kingdom, just as He Himself has been present among them as one who serves (cf. 22:27). In the same vein the call is sounded on the way: "If any want to become my followers, let them deny themselves and take up their cross daily and follow me" (9:23). "Whoever does not carry the cross and follow me cannot be my disciple" (14:27).

In broadest perspective, the Gospel of Luke tells what Jesus "began to do" (Acts 1:1), while the Acts tell what Jesus continues to do by His Word and Spirit, through disciples who have now become apostles. The same mighty deeds of salvation witnessed in the journey with Jesus to Jerusalem, the post-Pentecost apostles will themselves do "in the name of Jesus" (Luke 24:47; e.g., Acts 2:38; 3:6, 16). In either case, now is the time when "the good news of the kingdom of God is preached" (Luke 16:16). Thus the special literary function of the Journey to Jerusalem is to portray the approach of the kingdom of God in Jesus' words and deeds as the foundational and paradigmatic event of the church's mission: "When the crowds found out about [his location], they followed Jesus; and he welcomed them, and spoke to them about the kingdom of God, and healed those who needed to be cured" (9:11). Passages about missionary activity speak of the pressing in of the kingdom itself. "Cure the sick who are there," Jesus tells the seventy whom He sent out in pairs ahead of Himself, "and say to them, 'The kingdom of God has come near to you!'" (10:9). This is the cause to which disciples are enlisted. Disciples are to follow Jesus with respect to Jesus' complete devotion to the mission of the reign of God. Thus Jesus can explicate His call of discipleship with exclusive demands: "Let the dead bury their own dead; but as for you, go and proclaim the kingdom of God," or, "No one who puts a hand to the plow and looks back is fit for the kingdom of God" (9:60, 62).

Thus in Luke's own day, the call of the exalted Lord Jesus to follow after Him is sounded as readers are instructed by His earthly way to Jerusalem under the leading of the same Holy Spirit. This coming and calling through the gospel is the primary theology: "When Jesus came to the place, he looked up and said to him, "Zacchaeus, hurry and come down; for I must stay at your house today" (Luke 19:5). In the story of Zacchaeus, the central section of Luke's Gospel has reached its goal. Here we witness the salvation of Zacchaeus in that, having been sought and found by Jesus, he makes peace with the poor and whomever he had defrauded in a public act of repentance (19:1-10).[235] We are thus provided with a vivid image of the presence of salvation, a literary icon of the ultimate feast with "Abraham, Isaac and Jacob and all the prophets . . . ," with those who come "from east and west, and from north and south and sit at table in the kingdom of God" (13:28-29). "Blessed is anyone who will eat bread in the kingdom of God!" (Luke 14:15). The gift of salvation and the call to discipleship are alike expressions of the reign of God which breaks into the world in the coming of Jesus Christ. But what is their precise relation?

To answer that question, we must free ourselves from the habit of thinking in terms of a divine initiative followed by the option of human response in varying degree. For Luke, the gift of salvation in Christ and the task of following Jesus are equally expressions of the reign of God, the "task" given disciples being the sovereign work of the Holy Spirit, the "power from on high" (24:49) which Jesus promises and His Father sends. In precisely this connection, however, Luke's eschatology has been criticized. Luke's development of the theology of the Spirit is said to have "historicized the eschatological," i.e., transposed the early expectation of the Lord's imminent coming into the intra-historical facts of the time of Jesus and, even worse, of the church as the interim mission to the nations between Jesus' historical ministry and His parousia. If Ruether's Christological complaint of historicizing the eschatological were not bad enough, Luke compounds it by making Jesus' mission to Israel into His Spirit's mission in Jesus' name to the nations! This transposition is visible in the fact that according to Luke both the historical Jesus and the apostolic church are determined by one and the same divine Spirit (e.g., 4:18; Acts 2). This, so the criticism goes, obscures the terrible discontinuity between them: Jesus promised the reign of God. What history got was the church.

Indeed it is so according to Luke that in Jesus' mission the reign of God approaches. This is how Luke understands the kingdom parables of the mustard seed and the leaven hidden in the dough (13:18-21). In missionary activity one can speak properly though not yet finally of the presence of the reign of God in time and space. "But if it is by the finger of God that I cast out the demons, then the kingdom of God has come to you" (11:20). "The seventy returned with joy, saying, 'Lord, in your name even the demons submit to us!' He said to them, 'I watched Satan fall from heaven like a flash of lightning'" (10:17-18). "Today salvation has come to this house . . ." (19:9; cf. 4:21). "Today you will be with me in Paradise" (23:43). At the same time, Luke emphatically rejects imminent expectation of the Lord's public return (19:11). For Luke, this rejection goes hand in glove with criticism of any kind of reckoning about the time of the Lord's public coming (17:20-21). It is precisely to the point for Luke that the Lord's public coming is incalculable (12:35-48). The real question is whether, "when the Son of Man

---

235. *Pace* Fitzmyer, *Gospel according to Luke*, pp. 1220-21.

comes, he will find faith on earth" (Luke 18:8), concretely, whether He will find His own servants vigilant in their callings (19:12-26).

The first believers — so Luke depicts — regarded Jesus' exaltation as the first step in the restoration of the political fortunes of the Israelite nation (Acts 1:6). Luke has perceived this as a problem and tackled it with a depth that escapes his detractors. The story of the return of the one thankful leper (17:11-19) is an allegory of the turn away from such nationalistic expectations toward the mission to the nations. On the way to the Temple in Jerusalem (as Luke conceives matters), one leper, who turns out to be an alien, notices his healing. Instead of showing himself to the priest for verification that he might be restored to the community of Israel according to the instructions in the Law, this Samaritan returns to Jesus, falling prostrate before Him and glorifying God. The story signifies the end of the Temple as the center of Israel's faith (including that of the earliest, exclusively Jewish Christians) and its replacement by the apostolic mission in Jesus' name to the nations (a supersession of the Temple, not of the Jewish people, as discussed above in Chapter Five).

Luke's reserve in regard to apocalyptic calculations and imminent expectation is stamped no doubt by the trauma of the Temple's destruction in the year 70 (21:20-24). Nevertheless he not only preserves the realism of the eschatological expectation of final salvation as the resurrection of the body (21:27-28) but gives it a markedly anti-docetist cast (24:36-42). Indeed, Luke's chief idea is that the salvation of the future kingdom becomes present already now in the life of discipleship and the mission of the church because the promise of the resurrection elicits and enables joyful self-abandonment and unreserved commitment in bodily life. The scriptural promise of the divine reversal of this world's injustice in the resurrection constitutes the act of faith for Luke. The life of faith is the life that ventures to live now on the basis of that coming divine reversal: "But when you give a banquet, invite the poor, the crippled, the lame, and the blind. And you will be blessed, because they cannot repay you, for you will be repaid at the resurrection of the righteous" (14:13-14). On the one hand, such faith in the resurrection has been established in the Easter vindication of Jesus who had been crucified. On the other hand, Jesus showed Himself the Righteous One when on the cross He thrice refused the Satanic temptation to "save himself" (Luke 23:35, 37, 39; cf. 4:1-13), trusting instead the Father's promise of resurrection. Thus even now Luke sees Jesus paradoxically reigning from the cross, promising life to the repentant criminal whose faith is faith precisely in the dying Jesus' righteousness, that is, in His coming vindication by God and hence everlasting kingship.

The imminent apocalyptic hope of the earliest Christians was, in Luke's view, immature and inadequate. It valued the public appearance of the Son of Man as the day of vengeance upon God's enemies. But already at the beginning of Jesus' Journey to Jerusalem, Luke's revisionism in this regard is expressed in the rebuke of James and John who wanted "to command fire to come down from heaven and consume" a village of the Samaritans that had refused to receive Jesus (9:54). Everything that follows leads us to see that Jesus has come to "seek and to save the lost" (19:10). Wherever on the earth forgiveness of sin and repentance are proclaimed in His name (24:47), it is the Lord Jesus Himself who speaks this word of mercy and transformation which is uniquely His own to say. That is why, "whoever listens to you listens to me, and whoever rejects you rejects me, and whoever rejects me rejects the one who sent me" (10:16). If this act of the exalted Lord's self-identification with the message of mercy for all that is spoken in His name by disciples "historicizes the eschatological," so be it. In Jesus and in the church's ministry in Jesus' name, God's word of mercy is extended to the nations and God's coming reign is powerfully inaugurated in the alternative order that is the new life together of disciples (22:25-27).

Luke knows the distinctively Pauline usage of the term "grace" (Acts 15:11; 18:27; 20:24, 32) as a virtual summary of the Christian message, but he reserves that usage to the second half of the book of Acts. In the Gospel, his preferred term is "mercy." This usage is drawn from the Scriptures of Israel and indeed in the birth narratives, "mercy" supplies the divine motive for all that follows (1:50, 54, 58, 72, 78). In the course of the narrative, accordingly, Jesus Himself becomes the source of mercy. He shows compassion at every opportunity. At length even the traditional salutation of lepers, "Unclean! Unclean!" is displaced by the cry in Luke 17:13, "Jesus, Master, have mercy on us!" Hoisted upon the cross amid transgressors, the Lucan Jesus implores of His Father the forgiveness of His tormentors (23:34). On route to Jerusalem, Jesus teaches this mercy both in word and deed.

"Grace," we may say, is the active (10:37), seeking and finding love of the Lord (15:3-10). Grace is the undeserved favor of this God now demonstrated afresh and established anew in Jesus' table-fellowship (15:1-2) with the lost children of Abraham (13:16; 19:19), who are the sinners and publicans. This is a practice that at once anticipates the everlasting feast of the kingdom of God (13:28-29; 14:15) and culminates in the final Passover meal with his disciples (22:14-15). Grace is the right of God by which Jesus forgives sinners their sin (7:36-50) and the power of God by which Jesus frees these oppressed from their diseases and liberates them from the unclean spirits that have overtaken them. Grace restores humanity to wholeness (11:20). Grace is the Word of God which Jesus Himself serves, the service which any disciple must first receive before she can render in turn any true service in the kingdom (10:28-42). Grace is the joyful revelation in the Spirit of Jesus' filial relation to his Father (10:21-24), for this relation extends itself to encompass disciples as well. Disciples are bidden to call upon Jesus' Father as their own, to implore the coming of His reign, and to commend themselves body and soul to His care — in short, to receive the same Spirit from the heavenly Father (11:1-13). If grace is thus demonstrated and established in the Son's obedient life and death in solidarity with the disgraced of Israel, this grace simultaneously manifests the irrepressible joy and good pleasure of the Father of Jesus (15:6-7,

9-10, 32) in giving free place in His kingdom to all who are lost and helpless (18:13-14), if only they "come to their senses" (15:17).

This then is radical hospitality. Yet it is not so called because it is "unconditional," for in fact it is not unqualifiedly so. The grace of God which Jesus lives out is radical because it is for the helpless — only the helpless. It is for the lost — only the lost. It is for children — and "truly I tell you, whoever does not receive the kingdom of God as a little child will never enter it" (18:17). But just this latter requirement qualifies the unconditional nature of grace as grace for the "repentant," that is, for those who come to their senses in coming to understand their true need — not for bigger barns (12:18) — but for mercy and solidarity. It will therefore be of no help to recall, "we ate and drank with you and you taught in our streets" (13:26). What matters is that all who encounter the grace that Jesus is and brings become as its result such poor, lost people whom grace in fact can aid. That is the singular but indispensable repentance demanded of them by the prophetic ministry of Jesus, the conversion that grace requires in order to be *in us* the unconditional favor that it is in God's fatherly favor *for us.* That is the one "condition" on which the radical grace of Jesus depends, if it is to have free course to go to the root, like the axe the Baptist foresees in Messiah's hands, of the human predicament (3:9). "For all who exalt themselves will be humbled, and those who humble themselves will be exalted" (14:11; cf. 18:14). It does not avail here to protest that this repentance itself is the work of grace, as surely it is. The point is that the self-sufficient of this world have no need of the grace of Jesus and that for this very reason Jesus Himself becomes their mortal and implacable enemy.

Jesus' act of grace cannot then but effect a certain, i.e., penultimate conflict and division (12:49-53) in the world, since love must be against what is against love. Prophet Jesus works a division of the divisions. The mercy of the one and only God is jealous; it brooks no rivals, least of all that of human self-righteousness. The Lucan Jesus reiterates the twofold command for love absolutely and without qualification (10:27-28) as if it were the very substance of God's reign. Luke has Jesus correspondingly singled out for attack by one sin as the sin in all sins: envy, greed, covetousness, or concupiscence (12:15; even self-righteousness is understood by Luke as but a manifestation of greed, 16:14-15). The worldliness or "secularism" of those "who lay up treasure for themselves but are not rich toward God" (12:21) is a fortress wall thrown up against the coming of God's reign. The notion that we are alone in this world, not responsible *to* the Creator *for* our *lives in solidarity with other lives,* is both folly and idolatry. Life and all that pertains to it is a trust from the only Owner of all things. Human beings are but stewards who must someday render an account (16:10-12; 19:11-27). Wisdom therefore teaches, "Make purses for yourselves that do not wear out, an unfailing treasure in heaven, where no thief comes near and no moth destroys" (12:33). True blessedness is "to hear the Word of God and keep it" (11:28). Discipleship also begins with such reflection about the way the world really is under

God and reckons on what is truly of value (14:28-32; 16:8-9). Because the grace of God in Jesus Christ creatively values human beings in spite of lowliness and undeserving, "no slave can serve two masters; for a slave will either hate the one and love the other, or be devoted to the one and despise the other. You cannot serve God and wealth" (16:13).

The Lucan Jesus offers but one remedy of human greed: its extirpation by cross-bearing (9:23), self-renunciation (14:26), and prayerful trust in God's provision (11:1-13; 18:1-8a). "So therefore, none of you can become my disciple if you do not give up all your possessions" (14:33). Discipleship, for Luke, is not any kind of autonomous human response to Jesus. It is not the bargain a believer strikes with God, how he or she will respond to the divine initiative — so *little* merit has the uncomprehending criticism of Luke as a bourgeois theologian of *Heilsegotismus!* Discipleship for Luke is the victory of grace alone, already now, on earth and in history manifest in conversion, the transvaluation of values that Nietzsche most perceptively detected and most perceptively opposed. Discipleship is the surrender of autonomy as much as its liberation from heteronomy. Discipleship is assuming the yoke of the kingdom in theonomy. The disciple is the new person whom grace creates, the person who "sits at Jesus' feet" and in this very receptivity has "chosen the one thing needful" (10:38-42). So it will be the Lord Himself who is at work in the obedience of disciples. Discipleship is the gracious Lordship of Jesus Himself, extending by His Spirit through the realm of the human conscience before God into the web of human relations in space, through the changes and chances of time, where the believer learns from Jesus to live for others. This new service of servants of the Lord is as such divine deliverance from consumptive greed that rends the web of created life in spasms of cruelty and ruin (15:12-16).

Under no circumstance then is the absolute demand of discipleship to be spiritualized away. The truth of salvation itself is at stake in this. A real change in what human beings value is both offered and expected, for "where your treasure is, there will your heart be also" (12:34). Rather, the gift of the Spirit must be promised and offered to capture again the heart's desire for the reign of God. Rather, the true consolation of the life of discipleship is to be lifted up. "Truly I tell you, there is no one who has left house or wife or brothers or parents or children, for the sake of the kingdom of God, who will not get back very much more in this age, and in the age to come eternal life" (18:29-30). The new community of the disciples of Jesus, where mutual submission (17:10) and forgiving forbearance (17:3-4) reign, is their consolation and true treasure on the missionary way. For this fellowship in love is the beginning of eternal life, the very divine reality of the Spirit of the Son and the Father forming in space and time the Beloved Community of God.

By contrast, whoever wants to justify the existing self in the very act silences not only the infinite claim of God for love (10:29; cf. 18:9) but also the infinite promise of divine mercy. Paradoxically the threat of eternal death recoils upon those who have met grace but despised it. There is "a great chasm fixed" between eternal life and death (16:26). The injustices and ambiguities of the present order will not last forever. So all are warned by Moses and the prophets (16:29-31). "Some are last who will be first and some are first who will be last" (13:30). Not even God will be gracious to those who willfully reject grace and never come to sorrow over their sins. The single pound of the worthless steward is torn from his hands and given to the other who made good on ten, for "I tell you, to all those who have, more will be given; but from those who have nothing, even what they have will be taken away" (19:26; cf. 19:27!). The life of the rich fool is suddenly taken and the barns he had filled fall into another's hands (12:13-21). Dives shamelessly pleads that Lazarus be sent to do for him the very act of kindness that in his own lifetime he never once did for that beggar who pathetically begged at his doorstep every day. Not even in torment, then, does the rich man come to his senses, that is, to any true self-knowledge or sorrow over sin. He thirsts for water to abate his punishment, not for the repentance to see himself truly, nor then for the mercy that might yet forgive his life's way of lovelessness. Even in torment, he seeks only self and thus evidently remains forever a prisoner to self. Such evidently eternal human incurvation, as Jesus depicted in this haunting parable, is the very reason, to be sure, why the grace of Jesus cannot and does not depend in any way on human seeking but only on God's. That is what makes it grace. That Jesus has "come to seek and to save the lost" (19:10) is the good news of the kingdom that is now being spread abroad. Yet the prophetic edge of this proclamation of grace is that grace is grace only for the disgraced. So grace can be frustrated. It can fail to reach its goal. In that it is and eternally remains grace for the disgraced it is *resistible.* Therefore the word of warning is spoken above all to disciples who rejoice in the Lord's unfailing mercy: "Strive to enter through the narrow door; for many, I tell you, will try to enter and will not be able" (13:24).

The Lucan Jesus' message of repentance is thus essential to the gospel of grace. "When our Lord Jesus Christ said, 'Repent!,' He meant for the entire life of the believer to be one of repentance" (Luther). The good news of the gospel is the news of conversion to, as well as inclusion in, the merciful Reign of God. It is as prophet of the coming kingdom of God that Jesus announces the grace of God, and it is as such that Jesus collides with the forces that obstruct the coming of God's reign, as happened to the prophets before Him. Jesus, to be sure, is more than a prophet; but He is not less than a prophet, and whatever He does for human salvation that is more than announcing the judgment and mercy of God presupposes this prophetic ministry in all its radical urgency. Antinomian versions of Christianity, for which the prophetic preaching of the law is simply annulled, superseded or, worst of all, denounced and repudiated as so much "Jewish legalism," fail to situate Jesus in Judaism and in continuity with the Hebrew prophets, as Luke the evangelist requires. Yet in fact, Jesus' prophetic message of repentance is also a powerful act of liberation. Jesus is the Prophet who gives what He commands by sharing His own Spirit. But this gift to which His prophetic ministry ultimately points first costs His life in a "marvelous duel, when the law battled the law in order to become liberty for all" (Luther).

## The Intercession of Christ

The Father's grace, as prophet Jesus proclaims it, can be and in fact was refused in the figures of Caiaphas and Pilate and Judas; in the figures of Peter and the other followers it proved inefficacious in the hour of trial. It is only as Jesus passes from Israel's office of Prophet to the office of High Priest — yet outside the walls of the city — that His intercession avails before God (Luke 23:34) to prevail already now in giving true repentance and faith (Luke 23:39-43). In this office of Israel's priest, Jesus offered Himself as the victim, in this way interceding on behalf of sinful humanity before the holy God. Like baptism, indeed as baptism itself is grounded in this event, this intercession remains forever. It is offered and effective once and for all. For it is an event within the life of God by which God determines God. It is the event of God surpassing God, giving and receiving again His righteousness in place of human sinfulness as the saving righteousness of mercy. "Now the point in what we are saying is this," the Letter to the Hebrews states, "we have such a high priest, one who is seated at the right hand of the throne of the Majesty in heaven" (Heb. 8:1). The First Epistle of John similarly assures, "My little children, I am writing these things to you that you may not sin. And if anyone sins, we have an Advocate with the Father, Jesus Christ the righteous" (1 John 2:1).

Yet what in all eternity, we have asked, has God to do with rich Dives? Not even news of the resurrection penetrates the darkness of his incorrigible incurvation (Luke 16:30-31). "Indeed, God did not send the Son into the world to condemn the world, but in order that the world might be saved through him. . . . And this is the judgment, that the light has come into the world, and people loved darkness rather than light because their deeds were evil" (John 3:17, 19). Johannine theology at times takes this indubitable observation of the manifest inefficacy of Christ's intercession in the direction of a doctrine of double predestination: "For all who do evil hate the light and do not come to the light, so that their deeds may not be exposed. But those who do what is true come to the light, so that it may be clearly seen that their deeds have been done in God" (John 3:20-21). In this mode of theological reflection, the *krisis* that comes with the prophetic proclamation of Christ actually brings to the surface and exposes a hidden but preexisting division of humanity into camps of the children of light and the children of darkness. On this basis, judgment is announced: "Those who believe in him are not condemned; but those who do not believe are condemned already, because they have not believed in the name of the only Son of God" (John 3:18). The mediation of Christ as prophet of grace might thus be understood as *instrumental* to an absolute divine decree from eternity foreseeing and so also willing humanity into the two camps of the elect and the reprobate, as Augustine and later Calvin reluctantly thought, but as Zwingli argued in principle in his treatise against Luther, *On the Providence of God.*[236] What is to be noted critically, however, is that no historical passage that matters takes place in this theological reflection. Christ remains what He was, a superior prophet in whom the timeless Word indwelled in a superior manifestation, so that His priestly work is but an outworking of His proclamation of a timeless truth, just as its effect only brings to the surface a preexisting election and reprobation.

J. K. S. Reid puts his finger on the precise Christological problem in this otherwise rigorous, not to say dauntless reasoning: the tacit unitarianism underlying it. Christ "is clearly the very instrument of God in our election. But this is not to secure for Christ a place in the framing of that divine purpose to election. . . . [If] there is a real difference between the *manner* of our election which is Christ and the *cause* of our election which is the divine eternal purpose, then Christ after all is not the *fundamentum* of our election. He is not there as God frames His purpose to elect."[237] The alternative is to think of Christ's intercession in the fullness of time as the fundament not only of our election but of God's self-determination from all eternity to redeem and fulfill the creation by the mission of the Son as delivered in the Spirit. This is to think of Christ as "the Lamb slain from before the foundation of the world," as Rev. 13:8 states in the King James Version's rendering of the Greek. Joseph Mangina explains, "there is no Jesus who is not slain, and John is hardly imagining a 'second person of the Trinity' in abstraction from the incarnation. God's electing purpose is eternal, and it intends history — precisely the history enacted at Golgotha and in the lives of Jesus' followers, whose names are written in the book of life."[238] Then the passage from eternity to history in the Incarnation, as Jesus' passage in time from the office of prophet of grace to priest of grace, matters. At Golgotha, He enters the Holy of Holies and opens the doors once and for all.

The Formula of Concord's article on predestination makes exactly this point[239]

---

236. For a fuller account of these questions, and the interpretation of Luther's *De servo arbitrio,* see *LBC,* pp. 139-78.

237. John Calvin, *The Eternal Predestination of God,* trans. and ed. J. K. S. Reid (Louisville: Westminster John Knox, 1997), p. 40. Reid is following Karl Barth's acclaimed revision of the doctrine of election: "Christ must be allowed to occupy his rightful place where Predestination is being determined. He Himself is the elect and becomes the reprobate." *CD* II/2, p. 43.

238. Joseph L. Mangina, *Revelation* (Grand Rapids: Brazos, 2010), p. 164.

239. The following discussion of FC XI in *BC,* pp. 640-56, from which all citations are taken, is excerpted from Paul R. Hinlicky, "Law, Gospel and Beloved Community," in *Preaching and Teaching the Law and Gospel of God* (Delhi, NY: ALPB Books, 2013), pp. 91-114. Unfortunately, FC XI has never settled the perpetual conflict between the Gnesio-Lutheran and Philippist tendencies within Lutheranism. See Robert Kolb, *Bound Choice, Election, and Wittenberg Theological Method: From Martin Luther to the Formula of Concord,* Lutheran Quarterly Books (Grand Rapids: Eerdmans, 2005), pp. 281-90. According to the present argument that failure is due to the fact that neither has been willing to draw out fully the Trinitarian, communitarian,

as it surveys the incipient schism in the ranks of the Reformed that will emerge between free-will Arminians and double-predestination Calvinists. FC XI expressly states that it does not propose to settle any intra-Lutheran disputes as do the preceding articles. Rather it expresses an early Lutheran consensus. Looking out at the looming schism among the Reformed over predestination, FC XI attempts preventative medicine, "to prevent disunity and schism over these issues" of "the eternal election of the children of God." But that is not the only motive. The formulators are just as convinced that "no one should ignore or reject this teaching of the divine Word [concerning predestination] just because some have misused and misunderstood it." Thus they propose to "explain the proper understanding of it on the basis of Scripture." As we shall see, that "proper understanding" is that the beloved community in Christ is God's very goal in creating, redeeming, and fulfilling the world; the proper distinction and relation of divine law in the prophetic office and divine gospel in the priestly office is thus a distinction made within this divine economy in order to say No to the sinful world structured by malice and injustice but Yes to its redeemed as gathered into new structures of love and justice. This gathering of the ecclesia by the intercession of Christ through the Holy Spirit's proclamation of the Word concerning Him and His cross inaugurates the Beloved Community of God on the earth. To accomplish this, Jesus must appear in both offices, as prophet and as priest, yet in this historical sequence to this particular purpose, namely, to afflict the comfortable and to comfort the afflicted.

FC XI begins with Luther's pastoral counsel, forbidding pride and despair alike. "By instructing people to seek eternal election in Christ and in his holy gospel as the Book of Life, this teaching gives no one cause either for faintheartedness or for a brazen, dissolute life. For this teaching excludes no repentant sinners. Instead, it calls and draws all poor, burdened, and trouble sinners to repentance, to the recognition of their sins, and to faith in Christ. It promises the Holy Spirit for purification and renewal. Thus, it gives the most reliable comfort to troubled, tempted people, that they may know that their salvation does not rest in their own hands . . . [but] in the gracious election of God." The Formulators, citing the Apostle's statement that all Scripture is written that we might have hope, stipulate that any presentation of the doctrine of election that produces pride or despair rather than repentance and hope "is not being presented according to God's Word and will but rather according to reason and at the instigation of the devil."

The Formulators advance the case for this ordering principle of law to gospel against pride and despair beyond the rudiments worked out by Luther. They do so by several crucial moves. They begin with a daring argument that violates the venerable principle of divine simplicity that had driven Zwingli and now con-

---

and supralapsarian implications — the very step into critical dogmatics for which contemporary theology is indebted to Karl Barth (provided we take Barth as a pioneer of post-Christendom theology).

temporary followers of Calvin by logical necessity to the doctrine of the eternal divine reprobation of the wicked. Divine simplicity means that God is simply one in knowing, willing, and doing. So if anyone is damned, God has known it, willed it, and done it. At best, one can dodge the frightful implications of this insight into the divine authorship of eternal damnation with a scholastic distinction between God's antecedent will (that all be saved) and His consequent will (that all be saved through Christ), that thereby attributes reprobation to the sinner's failure to meet the condition of salvation through Christ. Against this principle of divine simplicity as such, however, the Formulators demand that we "carefully note the difference between God's eternal foreknowledge and his eternal election of his children"; the first, foreknowledge, is understood as an act of divine intelligence that knows all things in advance but the second, election, is taken as an act of divine love by which God determines Himself towards creation in one way and not another. The Formulators say there is a difference here, so that *God is not simply one in knowing and willing.* Thus, according to these early Lutherans, God can know and permit that Adam will sin but not properly will it, just as God can foresee and determine that Jesus will be crucified for all but not desire or author the malice and injustice of His crucifiers.

The motives at work in this distinction are not simply ones of rational theodicy, as if to get God off the hook for authoring evil, though the theodicy of faith must find the way to affirm with Paul that all things work together for good — also the cross — for them that love God and are called according to His purpose. Rather, the motive is to make clear the potential universalism of God's eternal self-determination. God truly wills the salvation of all, even if God foresees the condemnation of some. According to the (metaphysical, not regulative) doctrine of simplicity, however, this distinction is quite impossible. There can be no real difference between God's knowing and God's willing; in God both are simply one and the same eternal act. God knows what He wills and wills what He knows, otherwise He would not be God. God is timelessly one simple love that timelessly saves the worthy and timelessly damns the unworthy.

If divine simplicity is true in this metaphysical way, there are indeed only limited options. One would be to limit God's governance, as Plato did, and say that God cannot help it. God is only good, not powerful; God is limited by the material He has to work with, which is at fault by virtue of its recalcitrant materiality that resists the good shaping of God. Or, as Christian Platonism argued, for example, in Luther's beloved Augustine, one could say that God alone is really real, hence evil is unreal to Him and thus cannot affect God. At the same time, if one sees that evil is actual on the earth, and if one is unwilling to give up God's governance over all things, there seems to be no other conclusion to be drawn from the evident fact that many are called but few are chosen than that God properly wills also the loss of those not chosen.

The Lutheran Formulators, however, mock this conception of God's election and reprobation as an absolute eternal decree. They compare it to a military "muster, in which God said, 'this one shall be saved, that one shall be damned; this one will remain faithful, that one will not remain faithful.'" This depiction makes God into the heavenly *Decimator,* so to say, in which one of every ten is singled out arbitrarily for punishment (though the ratio of 1 to 10 is inverted in the doctrine of double predestination, in that "many are called but few are chosen"). The Formulators assert instead that God's preordination "does not apply to both the godly and the evil, but instead only to the children of God, who are chosen and predestined to eternal life 'before the foundation of the world'" as elaborated in Ephesians 1. Thus, while God surely foresees sin and its evil consequences, God hates and rejects the sin He foresees and does not desire it, will it, purpose it, or author it. Yet it happens. God "permits" it.

Note then what this view of the divine permission of evil entails: strictly speaking, God suffers. Not of course in the pathetic way of human creatures, but in the divine way that befits God as Creator of creatures other than Himself and thus with wills of their own. In creating a world that is genuinely other than God, God suffers the contradiction of wills other than His own that are actual and do actual violence to God's name on the earth (hence the second commandment and the first petition of the Lord's Prayer), not to mention violence to fellow creatures, in the wayward project of being God without God that disrupts the web of life and assails the creation's true goodness as gift of God and promise of fulfillment in God. That is why Paul the Apostle speaks of the longsuffering patience of God, even to the neglect of divine justice, until the priestly intercession of Christ who, in taking the mercy seat, shows God at once just and the One who justifies those who have faith in Jesus (Rom. 3:25-26).

God is not surprised by sin, but sin occurs as a real effect in the world, e.g., the crime of the brothers in selling Joseph into slavery as discussed in the great tale of divine providence ruling and overruling the sins of sinners for the sake of Beloved Community (Genesis 37–50). Sin, as actual evil, does real damage, not only to creatures, but to God's name and authority in the world where His patience appears as indifference or incompetence, as lovelessness or powerlessness. In such a world, the victory of the triune God is the accomplishment of His determination from the beginning in Christ by the Spirit that effectively turns human evil to His good. This community of triumphant love, according to the Formulators, is what God predestines, the final victory of the Beloved Community, including even us ungodly brothers of Joseph, as nevertheless beloved children. God is not surprised by the sin that He does not will. But reckoning with it from all eternity as the very cost to Him of creating beings such as us, God's own self-determination is to redeem and fulfill the very earth on which the crime of Joseph's envious brothers transpired. God permits the evil that He does not will in order to accomplish His own good purpose from out of its ruins. Whoever comes to this judgment in faith by the Spirit's calling — that God receives me, the sinner, for the sake of Christ — experiences divine election. Whoever holds on to their victimhood in preference to Christ's self-offering for them plays with divine reprobation. But Christ the high priest can exorcise even that demon and defeat any horror (as we shall discuss Marilyn McCord Adams's Christological thesis below at the conclusion of this chapter).

Building on Luther, the approach of the Formulators thus articulates four new things. First, "God's counsel, intention, and preordination in Jesus Christ (who is the genuine, true 'Book of Life') is revealed to us through the Word. This means that the entire teaching of God's intention, counsel, will, and preordination concerning our redemption, calling, justification and sanctification must be taken as a unity." Jesus Christ is not God's second thought, His, "O gee! Adam sinned, what do I do now?" Creation is not a neutral, empty stage on which a human drama unfolds one way or another. But creation is part and parcel of the one will of God in Jesus Christ to redeem and fulfill a world other than God for communion with God. Second, in Jesus Christ, accordingly, there is and can be no deception, no pretense as if outwardly God calls by the gospel but inwardly were play acting with someone already secretly fated to death. God is true in His self-giving in Christ and self-revealing by the Spirit. Third, the "human race has been truly redeemed and reconciled with God . . . ," the "promise of the gospel is *universalis,* that is, it pertains to all people." The notion of a limited atonement only for the elect gets things precisely backwards: all are included in Christ's atoning death though some may refuse to be reconciled. Election in this One rejected for all is universal. Only the mystery of final fatal self-exclusion that persists in owning sin, rather than surrendering sin to the Lamb of God who bears it away, remains as the dreadful final possibility of eternal death. Fourth, God's permission of evil in the kenosis of creation, so to say, is just this mysterious final possibility of God's divine suffering of sinners to have their way eternally, letting them exercise their powers just as they see fit, forever. That would be hell.

This is the most difficult point. The Formulators allow this kind of human freedom, if such it be called, our freedom in sin to sin forever. "Thus the Apostle very carefully distinguishes between the work of God, who alone makes vessels for honor, and the work of the devil and of human beings, who, at the instigation of the devil and not of God, have made themselves vessels of dishonor." Indeed, "as God is not the cause of sins, so he is also not the cause of punishment or condemnation." Following the Apostle's teaching in Romans 1:18, they teach that God abandons the wicked to their wickedness, "God punishes sin with sin." God permits the evil that He does not will. Yet the reverse does not hold; they deny that there is "something in us" which is "a cause of God's election." So we have a true paradox, that is, a surd. We are unfree in our election, as Jesus says, "You did not choose me; I chose you" (John 15:16). But we are "free" in our rejection, in the *sicut Deus eritis* project, playing Prometheus, wanting to be God without God. In wanting to be the free causes of our existence, we do act as true agents and do cause our own condemnation as we persist in refusing God's election of those rejected in this sinfulness to new life in Jesus Christ.

Of course, even more paradoxically our unfreedom in election promises the glorious liberty of the children of God, while the so-called freedom to reject the grace of Christ threatens persistence, even eternal persistence, in bondage to sin in undying death. Difficult as that paradox is, it gives the reason why Jesus in Johannine idiom brings the *krisis* of the world, its ongoing, provisional but actual *division* — also within the relics of Christendom in the realigning churches of Euro-America. Just this *krisis* of Jesus, who elects in the gospel only those who will to be rejected by the divine judgment on sin, makes and marks the division between the ecclesia as harbinger of the Beloved Community and the dying world that flees from God, including the flight from God that is institutionalized in the nominally Christian churches of Euro-America. The church that in this sense of Johannine *krisis* is not in conflict with the world is neither holy nor temple of the Spirit. For the holiness of the church is nothing other than Jesus' saving solidarity with real, not imaginary, sinners whose great high priest He will be in the temple that the Spirit is making of them.

When we follow out the theologic of Formula of Concord XI fully, we come to the eternal counsel and proper will of the triune God: "for the Holy Spirit wills to be present with his power in the Word and to work through it. This is the drawing of the Father." We see that this "eternal election of God should be considered in Christ and not apart from or outside of Christ. For in Christ, the holy apostle Paul testifies, we have been chosen before the foundation of the world, as it is written, "He has loved us in his Beloved. . . . Thus the entire Holy Trinity, God the Father, Son and Holy Spirit, directs all people to Christ as the Book of Life, in whom they should seek the Father's eternal election." This beloved community of God, then, is the intention, the purpose, the goal of the Trinity for the creation, the Trinity's own proper self-expression in and for creation. Notice what has happened: in the course of thinking out God's purpose in Christ, the framework of religious individualism in the late medieval quest, whether for a good deal or for a gracious God, has been transcended, without however abandoning the existential and personal dimension of faith. Rather the redeemed individual has been correlated essentially with the Beloved Community; God's action has been correlated with God's final purpose, shedding light on the church's battle in the fog and friction of human history.

The doctrine of election arose in the early theology of the martyrs, who needed to know that when they had fallen into the hands of the persecutors, they had not fallen out of the hand of God. This motive is palpable in Calvin: "Hence in all violent assaults, all kinds of peril, almighty storms and agitations, the perpetuity of our standing consists in this, that God will constantly defend with the strength of His arm what He has decreed in Himself concerning our salvation. If anyone of us should regard himself, what can he do but tremble? . . . But since the heavenly Father allows none of those whom He has given to His Son to perish, our assurance and confidence are as great as His power."[240] So

---

240. Calvin, *The Eternal Predestination*, p. 75.

also Luther: ". . . the Christian's chief and only comfort in every adversity lies in knowing that God does not lie, but brings all things to pass immutably, and that His will cannot be resisted, altered or impeded."[241] In this martyriological light, the primitive Christian experience of the world's rejection of the grace that Jesus had brought can lead in another direction than that of an absolute, proto-logical double decree of election and reprobation. This is a direction that early Christians, perhaps Jesus Himself in His passion predictions (i.e., the mysterious divine passive, "it is necessary"), discovered in meditation on the second Isaiah's Suffering Servant of the Lord: "Who has believed what we have heard? And to whom has the arm of the LORD been revealed? For he grew up before him like a young plant, and like a root out of dry ground; he had no form or majesty that we should look at him, nothing in his appearance that we should desire him. He was despised and rejected by others; a man of suffering and acquainted with infirmity; and as one from whom others hide their faces he was despised and we held him of no account. Surely he has borne our infirmities and carried our diseases; yet we accounted him stricken, struck down by God, and afflicted" (Isa. 53:1-4). Here it is the elect one of God who is selected by God for vicarious rejection in place of and on behalf of the unbelieving world. The elect servant suffers rejection *on behalf of* the unrighteous world that persecutes him for this very — to them, un-welcome — intercession. It is this possibility for understanding the priestly work of Christ that we now explore.

Oscar Cullmann rightly wrote that the title, the *Suffering Servant of God,* is "especially important because the main thought behind it, vicarious repre-sentation, is the principle by which the New Testament understands the whole course of *Heilsgeschichte* . . . the thought of the representation of the many by a minority, progressing to the representation by the One. . . ."[242] Cullmann held that "the concept High Priest is closely related to that of the Suffering Servant" since it too was an "ideal figure in Judaism."[243] Cullmann suggests that the con-fession of Jesus before the Sanhedrin at His trial — "you will see the Son of man sitting at the right hand of Power and coming with the clouds of heaven" — in reply to the accusation that He would destroy the Temple is a similar clue. "Is it not significant that Jesus applies to himself a saying about the eternal High Priest precisely when he stands before the Jewish high priest and is questioned by him concerning his claim to be the Messiah?"[244] Cullmann believed that this title for Jesus "goes back to Jesus himself and therefore opens to us most clearly the secret of his self-consciousness."[245] This valuable exegetical insight here does not depend

241. Luther, *Bondage,* p. 84.
242. Cullmann, *Christology,* p. 51.
243. Cullmann, *Christology,* p. 83.
244. Cullmann, *Christology,* p. 89.
245. Cullmann, *Christology,* p. 81. This is a position that Peter Stuhlmacher has tried to corroborate by his study of the *Verba* in *Jesus of Nazareth, Christ of Faith,* trans. Siegfried Schatzmann (Peabody, MA: Hendrickson, 1993), pp. 49-57.

on a claim to penetrate Jesus' "self-consciousness," assuming that He had one. At the same time, if we drop the historicist apologetics, there is no reason to doubt that Jesus, facing His fate in Jerusalem, would and could have understood His mission in just this way. In any case, that was surely how the earliest Christians objectified His fate.

"Indeed," Karl Barth wrote in the crowning achievement of his theological journey in the *Church Dogmatics,* "every 'individual' in himself and as such would be rejected if it were not that his own election is incorporated in that of Jesus Christ, if it were not that Jesus Christ was elected for the very purpose of taking his rejection upon Himself, and therefore of removing it from him."[246] Barth went on to develop the notion of Christ's universal representation of the lost in his doctrine of the atonement as the public office of Christ (not then as an expression of Jesus' "self-consciousness"). He calls this the "decisive statement: What took place is that the Son of God fulfilled the righteous judgment on us men by Himself taking our place as man and in our place undergoing the judgment under which we had passed."[247] He was the Judge judged in our place.

Barth, however, understands this representation under the rubric of the kingly office of the judge: the representation is a royal act of power, not a priestly offering in service, of Christ the Son of Man present "as a man among men."[248] Just so, "He not merely demanded decision from them, but introduced and made it . . . as the Judge, bringing about and bringing to light the final divisions in and among men. And yet, of course, in a final sense He was also present to unite them, His death being the judgment on the sin of the whole world which He, the Judge, did not execute on the world but Himself."[249] In being judged, He is the active and sovereign agent, the royal Judge who judges Himself in place of those deserving judgment.

We see once again how in Barth the true subject in Jesus Christ is the divine Son assuming, as the knowing subject, the judgment on sin by assuming the place of the human sinner, knowing Himself as this object. The divinity abased, the humanity exalted, Barth's peculiar Christological doctrine sees, as it were, a double helix in the descending Son of God and the ascending Son of Man; a dynamic Nestorianism, so to speak, stands behind this unusual interpretation of the threefold office. "We have now realized the fact and the extent that in His self-humbling in Jesus Christ the true God became and was and is also true man, and therefore the exaltation of man to fellowship with God as it took place in him."[250] The narrative sequence of the one Christ's humiliation followed by His exaltation is therefore deliteralized and decoded by Barth to indicate the logical priority

246. *CD* II/2, p. 351.
247. *CD* IV/1, p. 222.
248. *CD* IV/2, p. 156.
249. *CD* IV/2, pp. 157-58.
250. *CD* IV/2, p. 155.

of the divine Subject's initiative that produces immediately and simultaneously its human counterpart in the human Jesus' royal freedom. One can accordingly view Christ from the vantage of either of His natures, each regarded as subject (even though the divine subjectivity precedes and causes the human subjectivity), and thus allocate, so to say, the threefold office to the exalted humanity of Christ. Already in His earthly sojourn (as the "Synoptic" Jesus) we can see Jesus as the royal Man who was free: "who came and went with absolute superiority, disposing and controlling, speaking or keeping silence, always exercising lordship . . . [even as] He entered and trod to the end the way of His death and passion."[251]

In this peculiar way, Barth wants to respond to the problem going back to Theodore's demand to preserve in Christology the new and true humanity of Jesus that by its own free decision willed the will of God so that, as Barth puts it, in His human obedience as the royal Son of Man "the presence of the man Jesus of Nazareth meant the presence of a kingdom — the kingdom of God. . . . This is what made Him absolutely unique and unforgettable."[252] The Nestorian penumbra, however, is inescapable: the self-humbling Son of God and the exalted Son of Man appear, as it were, side by side, as cause and effect, united then in a close community of moral will and action, not "personally" integrated as the one Jesus Christ the Son of God who passed through a history of humiliation to exaltation.

Barth's effort here to integrate the human Jesus in Christology is valuable and to be appreciated, all the more so his dramatic revision of the Reformed doctrine of predestination in the direction of the old Lutheran teaching of universal atonement. Nevertheless an important difference from the present proposal is indicated in his decision for a dialectical theology of the two natures over against a Christology of the unity of person as that touches upon the teaching of Christ's saving work, namely, that universal atonement cannot without further ado be equated with a royal decree of universal salvation. The neo-Platonic teaching of Origenism on the *apokatastasis* of all things, lest "God's dominion would fall short of being absolute and God's love would fail of its object,"[253] had been ecumenically rejected at the same ecumenical council that also affirmed the theopaschite thesis that One of the Three suffered.[254] The two judgments stand and fall together.

For Western theology, Augustine's insightful judgment here is decisive: it is hardly a matter of "compassion" for "the Devil and his angels, who," as (Augustine perhaps incorrectly thinks) Origen taught, "will be rescued from their torments and brought into the company of the holy angels." Rather, the "good reason" for

251. *CD* IV/2, p. 161. That is of course how John and Luke see things, but not Matthew and Mark.

252. *CD* IV/2, p. 161.

253. J. N. D. Kelly, *Early Christian Doctrines,* revised edition (San Francisco: Harper, 1978), p. 474.

254. See John Meyendorff's penetrating analysis of the neo-Platonic theology of Evagrius Ponticus that stands behind the "heresy" of "Origenism" in *Christ in Eastern Christian Thought,* pp. 47-68.

the rejection of this teaching is that *apokatastasis* reduces Christian salvation to a mythological return to origin that renders the intervening history a senseless falling away from undifferentiated unity rather than a true origin surfeit with the promise of the Beloved Community that comes to be fulfilled in a history that matters. The only apparently optimistic neo-Platonic narrative must not be allowed to replace the canonical one, because in the former we have a myth of restoration that actually resolves in the swastika, the eternal return of the same. There is here, in other words, a most profound pessimism right below the surface. There is and never can be any resolution to the eternal cycle of disremption and reconstitution: the "theory of the incessant alterations of misery and bliss, the endless shuttling to and fro between those states as predetermined epochs."[255] The eschaton of judgment, however, is really an end corresponding to a real beginning; hence it is really a judgment on what is done and left undone in the unique, unrepeatable, unidirectional flow of time — a beginning of creatures that comes to an end of creating. It is the judgment anticipated already now in justification by faith but not displaced by it. The priestly offer of Christ's intercession for one as for all in this interim between His atoning sacrifice and His Parousia does not entail its reception by one and all. More profoundly, to make universal salvation into the royal fiat of the triumphant Son of Man (and to take this as the eschaton of judgment already perfected and finished) is to make the suffering love of the Son of Man ultimately *coercive*.

Thus the immediate objection that arose against Barth's teaching here was that — without reverting to a serious doctrine of purgatory (such as Pannenberg has proposed)[256] or the annihilation of the incorrigibly wicked (such as Jenson entertains)[257] — it simply dissolves by the royal fiat of an accomplished reconciliation the excruciating tension of good and evil at work in the apocalyptic interpretation of human history with its promised resolution at the eschaton of judgment. Emil Brunner put the objection clearly and decisively: "Barth goes much further" than "Origen and his followers." For "none of them ever dared to maintain that through Jesus Christ, all, believers and unbelievers, are saved from the wrath of God and participate in redemption through Jesus Christ. But that is what Karl Barth teaches. . . . Hell has been blotted out, condemnation and judgment eliminated."[258] This is "in absolute opposition, not only to the whole ecclesiastical tradition, but — and this alone is the final objection to it — to the clear teaching of the New Testament."[259] Brunner asked how it was possible for Barth to come to such "a fundamental perversion of the Christian message of

---

255. Augustine, *Concerning the City of God against the Pagans,* trans. H. Bettenson (London and New York: Penguin, 2003), XXI:17:17; p. 995.

256. Pannenberg, *ST,* 3, pp. 619-20.

257. Jenson, *ST* 2, p. 365.

258. Emil Brunner, *The Christian Doctrine of God,* trans. O. Wyon (Philadelphia: Westminster, 1974), p. 348.

259. Brunner, *The Christian Doctrine of God,* p. 349.

Salvation," and answered that it was due to Barth's characteristic "objectivism," i.e., "the forcible severance of revelation and faith. . . ."[260]

Brunner thus wanted to preserve the *ephapax* of historical existence, both Calvary's and ours: "If the decision of faith is not deadly serious, then salvation through Jesus Christ is not deadly serious either; everything has already been decided beforehand."[261] In this objection, Brunner sided with Bultmann and spoke for many in the existentialist mood of the mid-twentieth century in pointing to the theological subject who never attains a theoretical superiority over the object of faith, but is rather put by it — objectively — into the risk and decision of faith in Jesus Christ as the coming, not yet visible king of creation: "Only the renunciation of the logically satisfying theory creates room for true decision: but the Gospel is the Word which confronts us with the summons to decision."[262]

We have in Part One of this work diagnosed this standoff between objectivists and subjectivists as due to a Pneumatological deficit on both sides of this quarrel where each is thinking of individual subjects, "self-consciousness" and all, rather than persons in community as subject and object of theological knowledge in unending acts of interpretation, pending the eschaton of judgment. In that case, at the heart of the objectivity of Jesus Christ is His own Spirit-given but truly human decision of faith, His own theological subjectivity as a historical event of sharing in joyful exchange. Just this we must uncover in understanding the priestly passion and action of His Messiahship as the center of the atoning or reconciling work, prepared by His prophecy and fulfilled by His coming again in glory to judge the living and the dead as king of creation.

We have argued throughout this work that the gospel confronts us with the *persona,* Jesus Christ, narratable as the story of His merciful decision for the sinner, thus also in His powerful word of forgiveness, life, and salvation setting the creature free from contra-divine powers by undertaking its burden and sweeping the liberated creature up in the Spirit into His own doxological self-offering to the Father. Only as such does the gospel also summon us to decision, as a kind of echo in choral response, the "Amen!" of our own "proper righteousness" in consequence of the primary and to us "alien" righteousness of Christ given and received as a gift.[263] Strictly speaking, even this summons through the gospel is

---

260. Brunner, *The Christian Doctrine of God,* pp. 349-50.

261. Brunner, *The Christian Doctrine of God,* p. 351.

262. Brunner, *The Christian Doctrine of God,* p. 33.

263. "There are two kinds of Christian righteousness. . . . The first is alien righteousness, that is the righteousness of another, instilled from without. This is the righteousness of Christ by which he justifies through faith, as it is written in I Cor. 1[:30]: 'Whom God made our wisdom, our righteousness and sanctification and redemption.' In John 11[:25-26], Christ himself states: 'I am the resurrection and the life; he who believes in me . . . shall never die.' Later he adds in John 14[:6], 'I am the way, and the truth, and the life.' This righteousness, then, is given to men in baptism and whenever they are truly repentant. Therefore a man can with confidence boast in Christ and say: 'Mine are Christ's living, doing, and speaking, his suffering and dying,

the work of the Holy Spirit who speaks through it; thus it is no less a "perversion of the Christian message of salvation," if an anxious and ever-so-serious "decision of faith" supplants the work of the Spirit who calls, gathers, enlightens, and sanctifies. "For no one can say, 'Jesus is Lord,' except by the Holy Spirit" (1 Cor. 12:3).

As we saw in the first part of this system of theology, the actual work of election to faith on the earth is to be discussed under the topic of the person and work of the Holy Spirit; what is at issue here is the universal atonement of Christ in fulfillment of Israel's sacerdotal office: "My house will be called a house of prayer for all nations" (Mark 11:17, citing Isa. 56:7). Barth takes this universality not only *extensively* to include all peoples, but above all *intensively,* to include the damned, the godless, the Godforsaken, the rejected, the reprobate. This move to the depths is surely correct, if indeed Christ was made to be sin so that in Him we might become the righteousness of God, if indeed God consigned all to sin in order to have mercy on all. Indeed, this move paves the way forward towards the higher synthesis we are seeking that incorporates the Cry of Derelicton as the very moment in the self-surpassing life of God when God incorporated human sinfulness in order to still wrath. That is a pathos in God scarcely imaginable, though like the second Isaiah the prophet Hosea anticipated it.[264] What is not correct, however, is to regard this divine pathos as availing coercively by a royal act of power (let alone *not* availing, pathetically wishing but helplessly watching, as in kenoticism). It avails in the act of priestly oblation, as promise not demand, as gift not reward, as the impassible passibility of redemptive love gracefully received, where and when the Spirit gives grace to receive grace.

The old Lutheran theologians understood the priestly office of Christ, in which Christ "is both priest and sacrifice in one person . . . that He may reconcile man with God," to consist in the satisfaction He renders and the intercession He makes on behalf of the sinner. The satisfaction in turn consists both in the active obedience of His life in fulfillment of the law and His passive obedience by which He suffered the penalty the sinner deserved "to the praise of divine justice and mercy, and for the procurement of our justification and salvation." The intercession is perpetual: "Christ is not content merely in silence to await the effect of His satisfaction, but . . . He actively, effectively, really avails Himself of His merit

---

mine as much as if I had lived, done, spoken, suffered, and died as he did.' Just as a bridegroom possesses all that is his bride's and she all that is his . . ." (LW 31: p. 297). "The second kind of righteousness is our proper righteousness, not because we alone work it, but because we work with that first and alien righteousness. This is that manner of life spent profitably in good works, in the first place, in slaying the flesh and crucifying the desires with respect to the self. . . . In the second place, this righteousness consists in love to one's neighbor, and in the third place, in meekness and fear toward God" (p. 299).

264. See Oswald Bayer, *Martin Luther's Theology: Its Historical and Systematic Development,* trans. Roy A. Harrisville (Minneapolis: Fortress, 1999), pp. 214-25; and Christine Helmer, *The Trinity and Martin Luther: A Study on the Relationship between Genre, Language and the Trinity in Luther's Works (1523-1546)* (Mainz: Verlag Philipp von Zabern, 1999), pp. 121-81.

with the Father in such manner as becomes Him in His divine dignity." As Hollaz summarized: "The redemption of the human race is the spiritual, judicial, and most costly deliverance of all men, bound in the chains of sin, from guilt, from the wrath of God, and temporal and eternal punishment, accomplished by Christ, the God-man, through His active and passive obedience, which God, the most righteous judge, kindly accepted as the most perfect ransom (Gk: *lytron*), so that the human race, introduced into spiritual liberty, may live forever with God."[265] It is evident that behind this old Lutheran teaching stands Anselm, even though he lacked the notion of the passive, penal suffering of Christ by which God incorporates human sinfulness, which is the new doctrinal development ensuing from Luther's reformation theology, as I have shown elsewhere.[266]

It is right in theological reflection to ground Christ's once-and-for-all sacrifice on the cross, and His perpetual intercession on that basis as the risen and ascended Lord, in "the Lamb who was slain before the foundation of the world" (Rev. 13:8 KJV), i.e., in the triune God's eternal self-determination to redeem the creation fallen prey to malice and injustice that the dwelling of God may be with people and people with God. Yet the Christological question before us is whether we may also know that objectively in the man of our common body in the little piece of His history with us, and, if so, whether we can know this man in His decision to take responsibility for us before God as one and the same thing in the world as that eternal Son's coming in the fullness of time to "be born of a woman, born under the law, to redeem those under the law . . ." (Gal. 4:4-5). Then we would have the unity of the person *of* the Son of God's coming to us *as* the Son of Man's obedience for us in its linear progression, according to Philippians 2.

Of course, this too is to be deliteralized and theologically decoded, though not in the fashion attempted by Barth that makes a timeless simultaneity out of a true historical passage. The movement of God is not, of course, a local change of place, a descent and ascent as pictured in Philippians 2. The motion of the one Son at work sent from the Father in the power of the Spirit to be for us prophet, priest, and king on behalf of the Beloved Community rather tells of God surpassing God in the movement from wrath to mercy. In this movement in the life of God, Christ's prophetic preaching of the reign of His Father's grace and His coming victory as King on behalf of His Father's mercy integrate as the reign in preparation and fulfillment respectively. They are so integrated by the work of that Priest who in His human history with us once and for all mediated by offering Himself for us all in our state of enmity and willful ignorance, the innocent for the guilty. Though it was not Friedrich Gogarten's intention to put the matter so, his research, analysis, and argument serve to validate this objectivity of faith in the priestly work of Jesus Christ the Son of God,

It is striking, to begin with, how the charge of neo-docetism was registered

---

265. Schmid, *Doctrinal Theology,* pp. 342-46.
266. See *LBC,* pp. 66-104.

(and not without merit) against Bultmann by the second Questers. Gogarten cites Käsemann's complaint that, as the primitive church regarded the exalted and earthly Lord as identical, "we, too, cannot abandon the identity of the exalted and the earthly Lord without falling into docetism."[267] Jesus cannot serve as the narratively empty cipher, *"das Dass,"* i.e., the mere fact of His coming does not suffice either to give sense to the claim of the risen One to speak or to test the spirits who venture to speak as this risen One. Gogarten acknowledges the historical-critical problem: since we cannot take the gospel plot line that structures the narrative presentation of Jesus of Nazareth as the Christ, the Son of God by progression through the turning points of His baptism, transfiguration, prayer in Gethsemane, and Resurrection appearances as providing a historically credible framework, we have no choice but to seek and find our own historically credible framework that follows the anti-docetist theological intention of the canonical gospels. That is critical dogmatics: critical in that it proceeds with rigorous intellectual honesty before God; dogmatic in that it receives in faith the theological intention of this literature, also before God.

It is not only anti-docetism that requires this. Bultmann's own profound insight that in the kerygma the "proclaimer became the proclaimed" does so. For Bultmann himself realized that belief in the Jesus who is present in the proclamation "does not only promise salvation like the historical Jesus, but has already brought it."[268] That entails a knowledge of Jesus in His proclamation that is more than a *das Dass* — precisely, then, for the sake of Christian proclamation that graciously gives what it commands. Asserting the mere fact of this transition does not at all make it intelligible as gift. "What gave the kerygma the right to make this 'change' [from Jesus as proclaimer to Jesus proclaimed]?" That is the question of the historical Jesus that theology really has to ask and answer if it wants, not only to prevent docetism's Christological speculation and soteriological escapism, but to understand what salvation it is that the present Christ brings as the gift of that for which the historical Jesus had lived in obedient faith. That reflection yields Gogarten's chief thesis: "Jesus in his characteristic historical reality is only known when one apprehends in him and in his teaching the salvation he has not merely promised in his preaching, but has also brought about by promising."[269]

This "historical" Jesus is akin to Theodore's: "not, as in the traditional christology of the church, the second person of the triune God, in whom divine and human nature are united, and who in the power of this union of God and man, understood in this sense, redeems the world." Neither is He the Jesus produced by modern pietism and its decay into the personality cult of liberalism, "a savior concerned in the first instance with the salvation of the soul of individual human beings, a savior in whose visible concrete images and individual personal features

267. Friedrich Gogarten, *Christ the Crisis,* trans. R. A. Wilson (London: SCM, 1970), p. 27.
268. Gogarten, *Christ the Crisis,* p. 38.
269. Gogarten, *Christ the Crisis,* p. 38.

it is believed 'the fatherly countenance of God' can be perceived." Allowing, then, for Gogarten's modern conviction that "the Christ of the traditional thinking of the church [has] ceased to be credible, and [that] the quest for the Jesus who was a real historical human person became increasingly urgent"[270] — his search for the "historical" Jesus is a cognate of Theodore's: "a man who, in the obedience towards God which determines and sustains his whole existence, has the power and authority to take upon himself responsibility for the fate which is imposed upon man and his world, and, by taking it as his own, to allow it to be fulfilled in himself and so to avert it."[271] This is Jesus as a "true historical person," not "an unhistorical heavenly being."[272]

As with Theodore, this very Jesus is personally close to God and indeed unintelligible in His historical reality apart from this closeness to God. Gogarten avers that we "cannot avoid including Jesus' relation to God in his historicity" even if this relationship is inaccessible to "modern historical scholarship as long as it clings to its usual methods" and does not move toward hermeneutical understanding of Jesus' faith "in the way in which he understood it himself." But "if there is anything which is characteristic and essential in the historical figure of Jesus it is that he understood himself as one whose thinking and action were determined by the will of God, and therefore as one who knew himself to be responsible to God for the world." Whatever historical-critical accounts of Jesus that modern scholarship comes up with, if they fail to understand this relation with God, the Abba Father, they concoct a Jesus without His "own true historicity, and therefore as something different from what [He] is."[273] Granted that we have here the man Jesus and God — not yet the Son and the Father — but two persons, one by nature a creature and another Creator, yet the man and His God are bound together by the greatest intimacy imaginable in a lived history. Just so, how is this not — with the exception of the (for Gogarten) superfluous mediation of the divine Logos — Theodore's Christology?

Like Theodore, Gogarten turns to the Bible, of course with the modern difference of historical-critical consciousness. A genuinely historical Jesus therefore can be known — not from the artificial plot line supplied after the fact by the evangelists — but from the historical-critical correlation of His preaching and His fate. His preaching of God's merciful nearness to the outsider, the lost, the marginal, the diseased, the tormented in soul "was only possible insofar as he directly took for himself in the act of this preaching the decision that must be made in the face of the irreconcilable alternative which . . . opposition produces. With this decision he at once placed himself on the side of those who were excluded from the present world. For with this decision, he excluded himself

270. Gogarten, *Christ the Crisis,* p. 96.
271. Gogarten, *Christ the Crisis,* p. 95.
272. Gogarten, *Christ the Crisis,* p. 97.
273. Gogarten, *Christ the Crisis,* p. 161.

from this world. . . ."[274] He can give signs of this decision, but not proof of its rightness or divine authority. He can only live this decision of His faith in God in freedom for the others, namely, for those who are excluded. That freedom is double-sided. It is freedom from the responsibility that this world claims in place of God: "[W]e call the existence of Jesus historical because for him there is no world *to* which he could be responsible for his existence . . . it is not possible to be responsible to that *for* which one is responsible."[275] The freedom of Jesus, which may be known historically and hermeneutically, is rather the freedom of responsibility *to* God *for* the world as God's rebellious creation. The decision of the historical Jesus to take responsibility for the sinful world hostile to God and His coming reign is the decision to take upon Himself and before God the impending judgment of "doom."

Of course, this decision of Jesus "before God" is no more accessible to the modern historian than are the narrated epiphanies of the Baptism and Transfiguration episodes in the Gospels. In fact, these are theologically one and the same thing. Gogarten in this way deliteralizes and decodes these episodes as "events which by [their] very nature take place between Jesus and God in a way which is not historically ascertainable."[276] All that the historian might ascertain is that the historical Jesus believed in God and acted on such beliefs. The theological task then, according to Gogarten, builds on this historical-critical clarification but goes beyond it to the hermeneutical way of knowing, "to render this event intelligible to ourselves" in light of a series of "concepts of faith" that are likewise historically ascertainable. He lists these concepts excavated from detailed analysis of Jesus' preaching: "obedience, responsibility, fate, the exchanging of the creator for the creation, doom, futility, and faith in the God who calls into existence the things that do not exist."[277] We discover in the process something that will become important in the next chapter's explorations in patrology of life *coram Deo* (before God), namely that "virtually nothing remains in modern historical thought of responsibility *to* God, whereas for Jesus it is what principally determines responsibility *for* the world."[278] We also learn something else little known in modernity with its easy conscience, that responsibility for the world demands penitent solidarity with it in its sinfulness before God. Just this solidarity is Jesus' priestly office — though Gogarten himself does not put it that way.

Jesus "thereby took responsibility upon himself for men, who by exchanging the creator for the creation had transformed God's creation into a world subject to wickedness and transitoriness. As their brother he took this responsibility upon himself, by accepting as one of them his part in the fearful sentence of doom that

274. Gogarten, *Christ the Crisis*, p. 132.
275. Gogarten, *Christ the Crisis*, p. 143.
276. Gogarten, *Christ the Crisis*, p. 82.
277. Gogarten, *Christ the Crisis*, p. 83.
278. Gogarten, *Christ the Crisis*, p. 157.

they had drawn upon themselves, and united himself to them not as a lord who seeks to be served, but as one who accepted lordship "to serve, and to give his life as a ransom for many" (Matt. 20:28)."[279] This "is the reality of an event which has taken place in the relationship between a man, the man Jesus of Nazareth, and God. This relationship is not a metaphysical relationship between two natures, a human and a divine nature, but one which is exercised in the obedience of the man towards God. This obedience actually takes place between Jesus and God."[280]

Thus Jesus' obedience actually took place, and it can be known historically when history becomes hermeneutical and understands Jesus as He understood His own baptismal calling in faith up to the uncanny obedience that calling required of Him at Gethsemane. Certainly Gogarten is right to deny that this obedience is "a metaphysical relation between two natures," though he is quite mistaken to think that with this aside he has struck the target as he imagines. Only one thing actually prevents him from seeing this human decision of faith lived in obedience to death on the cross as the loving humility of the Son of God who counted not equality with God a thing to be held onto but so undertook His own human life and obedience. What blocks this is Gogarten's unbaptized notion of "nature" as substance, not yet distinguished from "person," hence revised to denote nothing but an abstract set of general possibilities in distinction from what is real as a concrete way of being in a world. The Son of God is God, as we have argued, but concretely in the way of being Son, within the eternal life of God in relation to His Father and their Spirit; and this same eternal Son of God comes into our world as the Son of Mary Theotokos, that is, as true man among men and women and children in Adam. He thus comes concretely in the way of freedom *from* the world's idolatrous claim for totality and freedom *for* those crushed under the impossible weight of this total claim. And in Jesus Christ the Son of God, these two are just one and the same way of being in the world, one concrete person in the mission that culminates not in being served, but serving like a slave at table, the priest who offers His own body and blood as ransom for all.

This is the higher synthesis for which we have been seeking: the unification of the sign, the Cry of Dereliction, with the thing signified, the incarnate Son of God, effecting the new meaning in the world of Mark 10:45. But it is a synthesis that can only be had by Trinitarian Christology, where the Son who gives His life as a ransom for many is the Son sent by His Father from above and revealed as such to repentance and faith by the same Spirit who sustained Jesus in this obedience by which He took responsibility for the world before God. This is the same Spirit then that vindicated this obedient faith when He raised Jesus bodily from death and installed Him at the right hand of God as priest and coming king.

So it is that He can be in His death on the cross the tearing of the veil of the Holy of Holies in the Temple: "the veil is rent asunder, the glory of God hidden

279. Gogarten, *Christ the Crisis,* p. 60.
280. Gogarten, *Christ the Crisis,* p. 61.

behind it begins to radiate out into the world, and as an initial reflection on this unveiling, a human being, and a Gentile at that, acclaims Jesus' divine sonship for the first time in the Gospel" (Marcus).[281] The apocalypse of this mystery of Jesus' true identity is the Christological mystery of His person at work in a passion; it is this to which we argue in theology because when we come to it, we grasp the redemptive work that He, so unexpectedly, has undertaken (Mark 10:45) and accomplished (Mark 14:24). When we come to this understanding we have nothing more to do than refuse it or receive it and be changed by it, as was Thomas (John 20:28), not only momentarily, but daily from baptism day to resurrection day to all eternity.

This once-and-for-all intercession continues in the exalted Christ in the interim between His sacrifice and His Parousia that begins with His descent into hell/Hades. It is nothing other than this same intervention of the incarnate Son on behalf of the doomed now extending to the depth and breadth of creation. He is the One whom we all come to know like Thomas when in the Spirit we combine the sign of the wounds with the thing signified, the Victorious Lamb; and we know Him truly then as this One who intercedes for all who do not yet know Him, *incognito,* as the tradition that made its way into the Credo regarding Christ's descent *ad inferna* (to hell) or *inferos* (to the underworld) attests. Beyond the sin and limited vision of the church and in ways unknown to us, Christ the Great High Priest intercedes for all. George Murphy has neatly laid this out. "The cry that God had abandoned him meant that he was dying in separation from the source of life, in the darkness where God cannot find God. Yet it was the person of the Son of God, the one through whom all things were made, who cried out. By taking on human dying, God goes into the deep, the nothingness that threatens creation." So this descent into death and hell is at once "the nadir of the passion and in a sense the first act of the resurrection . . . because in the utter dereliction of Christ sinners see the end of their 'wrong road' and in his resurrection we are given a vision of the goal that God desires for them. This is a dramatic way of saying that God truly 'made him to be sin who knew no sin, so that in him we might become the righteousness of God' (2 Corinthians 5:21)."[282] As Murphy argues, because of its unbounded scope, the divine Son of God's intercession knows no limits; nothing in all creation can separate from this love of the Son of God incarnate who gave Himself for us as for all and forever.[283]

Thus we may conclude this treatment of the priestly office of Christ: if we follow this line of interpretation of the descent into hell as the termination of

281. Marcus, *Commentary on Mark,* p. 1067.

282. George L. Murphy, *Models of Atonement: Speaking about Salvation in a Scientific World* (Minneapolis: Lutheran University Press, 2013), pp. 101-2.

283. Murphy, *Models of Atonement,* pp. 116-18. The final chapter, pp. 116-29, in a useful and disciplined fashion speculates on the scope of salvation in Christ in vistas opened up for us by modern science.

Christ's passive obedience as "at once both priest and sacrifice" as the Lamb of God bearing away the sin of the world, and at the same time as the dawning of Messiah's royal rule as the coming judge and king of all creation, then we can affirm with the theodicy of faith in Romans 8: there is no hell, no Godforsakenness, nothing in all creation that can separate from the love of God in Jesus Christ. Christ entrusts the preaching of this gospel of His own, all-victorious love to His church, but does not abandon it to the church. The scope of salvation cannot be limited to what is visible under the fog and friction of this battle of the ages.

Yet this affirmation does not entail, as Barth's theology seems to entail, universal salvation, but only that salvation is potentially universal. For Barth, as we recall, since it is in His office as king and judge of creation that Christ atones, the love of Christ must appear as something inevitably triumphant. Among other anomalies that result from this is the untoward implication that divine love in this way finally becomes coercive. This cannot be. There remains to the reprobate (who is each of us), the ultimate danger that, like Dives, we remain reprobate, since the universality of Christ's atoning love both in its breadth and in its depth consists in His priestly act of offering like a slave at table, not in a royal act of commanding. As Prophet Christ demands; as Priest Christ gives what He demands; as King Christ judges the living and the dead with the righteousness of mercy that is His own achievement, gift, and standard. Christ enters hell defeated by Satan, there to arise in victory over Satan, rob him of his claim, and so empty his domain, victoriously leading its denizens forth. The devil is thus not reconciled but defeated. History therefore matters. The battle is real. Consistent with this, we can thus imagine those who, beginning with ourselves, will never surrender even in all eternity to the victorious Lamb of God. Consequently some, beginning with ourselves, may be forever lost. So far as we can imagine, for cautionary and heuristic purposes the church must therefore warn any who prefer to hold onto their sin as though to their own true and personal identity achieved in their once-and-for-all historical biography that they resist the Spirit; just this resistance to change is the unforgivable sin (Mark 3:28-30).

This is dramatized for us in Luke's account of the two thieves crucified with Christ in Luke 23:39-42. "One of the criminals who were hanged there kept deriding him and saying, 'Are you not the Messiah? Save yourself and us!' But the other rebuked him, saying, 'Do you not fear God, since you are under the same sentence of condemnation? And we indeed have been condemned justly, for we are getting what we deserve for our deeds, but this man has done nothing wrong.' Then he said, 'Jesus, remember me when you come into your kingdom.' He replied, 'Truly I tell you, today you will be with me in Paradise.' " We do not transcend this place, side by side with the Crucified. This is our place, where the Son of God incarnate finds us, as truly we are before God. Here we are not yet in the kingdom of heaven, only on the way when change takes place so that repentant faith already now knows Jesus who intercedes for us as coming king of all creation. Our redemption thus remains incomplete. The body of the penitent thief dies and is planted in the ground, awaiting its perfection at the coming of Christ as King. Christian wisdom requires that we see the solidarity of Christ with the sinful world as the very depth of the love of Him who gave Himself, the innocent for the guilty — yet only victorious in those willing to be guilty in order to be justified, dead in order to be made alive, sick in order to be healed.

### An Alternative: Marilyn McCord Adams's *Christ and the Defeat of Horrors*[284]

Marilyn McCord Adams's recent treatise is a brilliant, witty, and tough-minded case for Christology as a contemporary contender for the hearts and minds of postmodern and post-Christendom Euro-Americans whose despair of Christianity is intertwined with our increasingly unavoidable awareness of the horror of life on this earth, both natural and moral (for notable instance, the ecclesiastical brutality that Radner insists that we face in the corresponding discussion of an alternative position at the end of Chapter Four). Recognizing this spiritual situation, McCord Adams unabashedly speaks out of her own Anglican confessional tradition, yet in a nonsectarian and ecumenically constructive spirit. This honest acknowledgment of her theological subjectivity in several dimensions enables her to abandon useless pretensions to universality to speak to our spiritual situation concretely and with philosophical rigor, laying out a compelling Christological proposal that is unusual and provocative in being at once metaphysically high and materially low.

That is to say, McCord Adams argues that none less than the metaphysically real God appears in Christ and that the Jesus in whom this true God appeared is nothing other than a finite and even sinful human being fully immersed in the sinful particularities of His time and place. Indeed, in just this way the true God can and does connect also with us as "ensouled matter." Though placed differently in the vast sequence of time and space, we are each *placed* just as *particularly* as Jesus was. And this non-transcendable particularity of bodily placement somewhere, sometime in the world entails *each one's own* peculiarly human horrors. Horrors arise, that is to say, from the basic mismatch of being ensouled matter: thrown into the world where ridiculously we have to make meaning as soaring minds that shit daily — if not, we cannot think straight at all.

This existential point of connection with the human predicament as ensouled matter provides McCord Adams a contemporary context for establishing a Christological pattern for the defeat of horrors in a three-stage process. First,

---

284. Marilyn McCord Adams, *Christ and Horrors: The Coherence of Christology* (Cambridge: Cambridge University Press, 2008). See also Sarah Hinlicky Wilson, "Jesus Christ, Horror-Defeater," *Lutheran Forum* 47, no. 1 (2013): 2-10. My thanks to her for calling McCord Adams's work to my attention.

connecting "organically" and "intimately" with Jesus by the Word; then, second, healing by His Spirit to make new meaning of ruined lives with this organic connection; and ultimately, third, the resurrection of the wounded body to eternal life in the true, eternal God that is not worthy to be compared to the sufferings of the present age.[285] In these Christological ways, God saves creation from the horrors that attend it and would otherwise defeat God's creative purpose for it. Notably, at her first stage, McCord Adams connects Christologically with what we have identified as the real advancement of Luther's Christology from within the framework descending from Cyril. "Certainly," she writes, "the systematic desideratum of horror-identification [by God] encourages a Lutheran reading of the cry of dereliction (Matthew 27:46; Mark 15:34), which understands the crucified Jesus to have shared in our sense of abandonment by God and of Divine condemnation — which is surely incompatible with beatific intimacy, and plausibly at odds with any simultaneous face-to-face vision at all."[286] Yet somehow this identification with us happens in and with, not over against, God — only so could it both meet us in the horror and there overcome it.

McCord Adams's book deserves a full and wide-ranging discussion, but it is selected here to articulate an alternative to the Christological and Eucharistic proposal that has been developed to this point regarding the theological object. Hence we can isolate that feature of McCord Adams's thesis that is relevant to this purpose, as we did previously with Radner. As with Radner, the point here of engaging McCord Adams in this way is not to refute her but to advance the argument to which she has so ably contributed. Disputation in critical dogmatics is about what we believe in knowing Whom we believe through a process of conceptual clarification aimed at ecumenically converging formulations of teaching — *intending* orthodoxy (not claiming it as an established possession), as McCord Adams too explicitly affirms. This engagement is possible because of an agreement between us on the Christological nature of the problem regarding the objectivity of faith. We agree, summarily, that Christ is the saving answer to the horrors, "horror-defeater" in her words, Aulén's *Christus Victor* as I would put it. How we disagree in this agreement is a matter of some subtlety.

It would be too easy to state the obvious, but for the sake of clarity let us do so. Whereas this work in systematic theology has defended the interpretation of the human predicament as Augustinian sinfulness that makes difficult natural life morally horrible, McCord Adams argues something almost the reverse, namely, that sinfulness is our moral dysfunction arising inevitably with evolutionary human emergence from the natural world of scarcity, competition, and predatory horrors.[287] This is the source of the mismatch between the soul's thirst for God and the body's bond to nature. Ultimately, this alternative narrative of the human predicament

285. McCord Adams, *Christ and Horrors*, p. 66.
286. McCord Adams, *Christ and Horrors*, p. 67.
287. McCord Adams, *Christ and Horrors*, p. 37.

follows Hobbes rather than Augustine on the "state of nature." Equally obvious, I have argued accordingly for a Cyrilian Christ whose union with humanity climaxes in the Son's abandonment by the Father on account of His incorporation of our sinfulness into the divine Life in a once-for-all moment of dereliction; the redemptive purpose is at once to judge sin in the flesh and at the same time free our bodies for their promised material fulfillment. But McCord Adams, following the modalist tendency of Western theology, argues for a Nestorian Christ; this is especially evident in her treatment of Eucharistic impanation and the medieval suppositional Christology that stands behind it. That is to say, just because the metaphysically high Logos is not personally identical with the materially low Jesus, the same Logos who identified with Jesus once upon a time can and does come to the Eucharist to identify with the blessed bread and cup — after the same pattern, to be sure, as disclosed in Jesus. She argues this in express critique of Luther's "ubiquitism"[288] that supposedly stretches Jesus out everywhere. I have cashed out Christology in the joyful exchange of Christ's righteousness for our sinfulness, His divine life for our perishing, a soteriology that turns Christologically not on Brenz's ubiquitism but on Chemnitz's and Gerhard's *ubivolipraesens.* But she has God sacrificing to us in an exchange of horrors: "Horror for horrors!"[289] The result is that the divine Son of God gives Himself to defeat our horrors after that pattern but not in and ever as the historical person, Jesus Christ the Son of God, who comes to us personally as bodily in the Eucharist or not objectively at all.

But clarifying our differences this way is too easy, especially when our strong convergences are kept in mind, beginning with her "Lutheran" reading of the Cry of Dereliction. Let us list them, using her words. We agree that the theological subject or human person is "ideally inclusive. Who we are is a function of our relationship to others, in interaction with whom we become more fully ourselves" — and this in express rejection of "the scholastic philosophical tradition that defined personality primarily in terms of separation or distinction from others,"[290] i.e., as substance with autonomous agency. Drawing on a different current of medieval scholasticism, we agree that the Trinity is the Beloved Community[291] so that "in the world to come, all friends of Christ will be friends to one another, so that God will be all in all."[292] We agree that the human vocation of the image of God aims at maximal similitude while remaining a creaturely, material, and finite image.[293] We agree that soteriology is only understood theologically in view of an eschatological fulfillment since sin is only understood theologically as a defection from this divine purpose;[294] in the same vein, we agree that the miracle of the

288. McCord Adams, *Christ and Horrors,* pp. 302-7.
289. McCord Adams, *Christ and Horrors,* p. 281.
290. McCord Adams, *Christ and Horrors,* p. 145.
291. McCord Adams, *Christ and Horrors,* p. 157.
292. McCord Adams, *Christ and Horrors,* p. 159.
293. McCord Adams, *Christ and Horrors,* p. 208.
294. McCord Adams, *Christ and Horrors,* p. 214.

resurrection of the body is not only scientifically conceivable, but that it is the only way in a scientifically informed world to think intelligibly of persons gifted with the eternal life of God. Perhaps above all, we agree that "all creatures are made for the church triumphant, but for the sake of the God-man as their ultimate end and God's principled aim. Because the end is prior in intention to those things that are for the sake of the end, Christ *qua human and Divine* is the 'first born of all creation' (Colossians 1:15)."[295] Given these strong agreements on the Lamb slain before the foundation of the world, not to be gainsaid in the climate of contemporary theology, the more interesting question is, how is it possible that we disagree, as in fact we do, as shown above?

It is interesting to observe here that McCord Adams takes crucially important positions that find parallels and have precedent in the early Enlightenment philosopher, Gottfried Leibniz, although this parallelism undoubtedly derives from the common sources of McCord Adams and Leibniz in the later medieval philosopher theologians. With regard to the origin of moral evil, McCord Adams takes the position that what Leibniz called "natural evil," i.e., the finitude of any conceivable creature and hence its endemic vulnerability, is the necessary but not sufficient condition of moral evil. McCord Adams develops this basic insight by accentuating the metaphysical "mismatch" between the immateriality of the true and eternal God and the embodied souls that human beings are. This mismatch leads with virtual inevitability, though not logical necessity, to sinful anxiety and all the havoc it weaves into the web of life when the temptation to be like God without God and in place of God becomes overwhelming.

In regard to the possibility of the Son of God's presence in the Eucharist, McCord Adams takes a position actually worked out by Leibniz in his negotiations with Catholic theologians for the reunification of the churches, namely the classical impanation doctrine that the omnipresent Son of God incorporates the Eucharistic bread and makes it therewith His body, His objectivity for us in the world.[296] The theory of impanation does not need to haul the finite body of Jesus of Nazareth from heaven and multiply it like the loaves to feed the multitudes or stretch it across space to make it proximate. The Son of God is thus in principle separable from the body of Jesus, born of Mary and crucified under Pontius Pilate and resurrected to a heaven that is place other than this earth where the Eucharist takes place. It is by *the pattern* established in the Incarnation as the body of Jesus once upon a time (not then *as* this *one person*) that the Son of God according to His divinity comes and establishes a true union with bread for us at the Eucharist. In this way, the union of the Logos of God with the humanity in Jesus can be described as the late medievals did, as one of suppositing it — in plainer language,

295. McCord Adams, *Christ and Horrors*, p. 180.

296. Gottfried Wilhelm Leibniz, *New Essays concerning Human Understanding,* trans. Alfred Gideon Langley (LaSalle, IL: Open Court, 1949), pp. 611-12. G. J. Jordan, *The Reunion of the Churches: A Study of G. W. Leibniz and His Great Attempt* (London: Constable, 1927), p. 86.

undergirding or carrying it. Surely, this echoes Theodore's view that the Logos undergirds the humanity of Jesus without being personally identified with it.

We can put it this way: for McCord Adams the divine nature manifests paradigmatically as Jesus and can be recognized universally in analogy to Jesus; just this the Eucharist illustrates. That is indeed the only way within Western modalism to have a "high" Christology: "Christ is in person impanated in the bread *just as* God was in person incarnate in human flesh."[297] The Logos indwells the man and analogously the Eucharistic bread. Soteriologically that is all that is necessary for establishing the traumatized creature's already metaphysically organic but not-yet-known relationship to God's loving will, solidarity, and purposes of redemption and fulfillment.

A visible realignment of the churches along these lines would be, as Leibniz once sought, a significant step in Euro-America, all the more so in our desperate times of post-Christendom. We might even agree on that. But would that agreement align us again in the Spirit's mission of repentance and faith in the name of Jesus to the nations? McCord Adams has an insightful discussion of the problem here: "By sharing the horrors, Christ binds Himself to the human race in a mutuality of horror-defeat . . ." that can be conceptualized as the church universal, the wrestling church, the congregating church, and the missionary church.[298] At the same time, like Radner, she sees with unflinching clarity that "the Body of Christ (whether church or cosmos), [is] both headed by Christ and directed by the Spirit of Christ, and yet [is] riddled with systemic evils and productive of horrors."[299] Yet, also like Radner, she seemingly resigns herself to this ecclesiastical status quo: "We will all have to live this tension until God acts to bring horrors definitively to an end."[300] Is that the best theology, specifically Christology, can do?

As one reviewer noted, Christology actually does all the work in McCord Adams's essay; her proposal is not articulated as Trinitarian Christology. "Oddly enough, Adams does not elaborate this proposal [of the three stages of horror-defeat] along Trinitarian lines, connecting the first stage of divine horror defeat with the Son, the second with the Spirit and the third with the Father."[301] Certainly, as shown above, the Trinity as Beloved Community is far from an afterthought in her theological thinking. Yet if, as we have contended, Christology is a function of the doctrine of the Trinity, in this respect the Trinity in fact fails to do any soteriological work at a critical juncture. In one incautious moment, McCord Adams comments that the incarnation of *any* divine person would do the *same*

---

297. "Ita personaliter in pane impanatum Christum, sicut in carne humana personaliter incarnatum Deum." *The Oxford Dictionary of the Christian Church*, 2nd edition revised (Oxford: Oxford University Press, 1990), p. 694, cited from Alger of Liège (PL, clxxx, 754 B).

298. McCord Adams, *Christ and Horrors*, p. 201.

299. McCord Adams, *Christ and Horrors*, p. 204.

300. McCord Adams, *Christ and Horrors*, p. 204.

301. Gijsbert van der Bink, *Journal of Reformed Theology* 1 (2007): 125.

work of horror defeat. In that case the way of being God that is Sonship makes no particular difference to horror-defeat; rather, it is divine incarnation as such that does all the soteriological work. What matters, it seems, is that Jesus is God, not that Jesus is God in the way of being the Son. Just this expresses, as argued throughout these two chapters of Part Three, Western modalism.

It is perhaps too global an explanation of our disagreement — also then on what the actual realignment of the churches in Euro-America would or could mean — but this analysis of our divergence would instantiate the charge against Western theology that I have sustained throughout, namely, that it is tacitly modalist in accentuating the unity of God and further in taking that unity metaphysically as timeless self-identity of substance. If this metaphysical notion of divine simplicity holds, we cannot attend to the personal distinctions revealed in the gospel narrative as something really real in God, rather *as* God, nor conceive of divine unity as something truly jeopardized in the Incarnation of the Son who was made to be the sin of the world — albeit at His Father's will and command. Nor can we think of divine unity as something established in a new way by the resurrection of the Son's sin-bearing body, hence now revealed to faith by the Spirit of the resurrection as the justification of the sinner, in turn to be revealed visibly in the coming of Jesus Christ the Son of God to judge the living and the dead. If we cannot see these Trinitarian differences, neither can we see just how the Body of Christ proceeds in its *particularly redemptive mission* to the nations. And if we cannot see that, is it any wonder that we resign ourselves to the shameful status quo of the broken and unfaithful churches of Euro-America, as if God's solidarity with our sinfulness were not for the purpose that in Christ we *become* instead His righteousness in the world?

## A NOTE ON THE PAROUSIA OF CHRIST

According to the testimony of Luke, on which we have drawn so heavily in this chapter, Jesus now reigns — that is, in this interim awaiting His parousia — from the cross, and so incognito to the world, though already able from there to assure inclusion to those who in faith desire His manifest reign. With this, of course, the well-grounded expectation of political Messiahship in Israel was fundamentally reconceptualized (not depoliticized): the disciples on the road to Emmaus "had hoped that he would be the one who was going to redeem Israel." The risen Christ, reverting to "all that the prophets have spoken" — in Luke this means especially the priestly office of the Suffering Servant of Isaiah 53 — asks them in turn, "Did not the Christ have to suffer these things and then enter into his glory?" (Luke 24:21, 26). His work as Messiah of Israel and King of Creation is thus indicated as something still future, arising from His past work as Prophet and His present work as Priest. This futurity of Kingship is also evident in the Risen Lord's commission in Matthew 28:18-20. "And Jesus came and said to them, 'All authority in heaven and on earth has been given to me. Go therefore and make disciples of all nations, baptizing them in the name of the Father and of the Son and of the Holy Spirit, and teaching them to obey everything that I have commanded you. And remember, I am with you always, to the end of the age.'"

As this kingship over creation was deferred during His earthly ministry in order that He not be served but rather serve as a slave at table, it now is hidden to the world in the sad, sorry, and harassed face of the church of the poor, of sinners and collaborators, where Christ rules by the gospel in the Spirit: "collecting, governing, adorning, and preserving the Church, His defense of it against the enemies of grace, and His ruling in their midst."[302] The horizon of Christ's kingship is the final future; in the interim He reigns as one still at battle. "Then comes the end, when he hands over the kingdom to God the Father, after he has destroyed every ruler and every authority and power. For he must reign until he has put all his enemies under his feet. The last enemy to be destroyed is death" (1 Cor. 15:24-26). "Just as a general, after having destroyed all his enemies, presents to the king, who through him has waged the war, the victorious and triumphant army, the saved citizens, and the free people, and tenders them to him, that he may judge and approve his deeds, and nevertheless does not lay down the power which he had over the army; so much more, when the world is ended, and all enemies have been suppressed shall Christ, as the Son, place His immaculate (Eph. 5:27) ecclesiastical army in the presence of God the Father. . . ."[303] The church in mission under Christ the servant Lord who ever intercedes and rules as this intercessor is in this way militant, not with the sword of steel but of the Spirit in the Word.

The future King of all creation reigns as in battle through His Word and Spirit until He presents a liberated creation to His Father for its eternal fulfillment. Yet "despite this fundamental identity between Christ's lordship and the Church with regard to their temporal nature," Cullmann rightly notes, "the area covered by Christ's lordship" covers all creation. "Christ rules also over the invisible powers which stand behind empirical institutions"[304] — even those that "do not necessarily know the role assigned to them within his lordship."[305] Christians consequently can in good conscience cooperate with political sovereignty except when it "abandons its proper role and deifies itself."[306] They can also marry and raise children. They can also labor and go to market. In just these "arenas of responsibility" (Benne), they can pursue their baptismal vocation as priests of Christ in service to their neighbors. In the process, they serve under Christ to transform structures of malice and injustice into counter-structures of justice and love.

Since this kingly reign of Christ consists in His sending of the Spirit to publish

302. Schmid, *Doctrinal Theology,* p. 374.
303. Schmid, *Doctrinal Theology,* p. 375.
304. Cullmann, *Christology,* p. 227.
305. Cullmann, *Christology,* p. 230.
306. Cullmann, *Christology,* p. 230.

the gospel to the nations and create the new humanity in the gathering of the church, it is as such manifest only to faith in the sphere of Christ's manifest lordship, the ecclesia in mission to the nations. It will finally be visible only upon the fulfillment of creation when Christ comes publicly as king of creation to resolve forever the conflict of good and evil as judge of the living and the dead. Hence, as we reserved for fuller discussion the Spirit's final work of the resurrection of the dead, so also here we reserve fuller discussion of Christ in His parousia at the eschaton of judgment to the concluding chapter on the eternal Trinity and life eternal.

# PART FOUR

# Patrology

Jesus believed conscientiously before His heavenly Father, making the God of Israel the audience of His self-interpretation as the Son. Whoever believes does so by the Spirit-communicated conviction of adoption as a child of the heavenly Father through Jesus Christ the Son of God, living in expectation of the glorious liberty of the creation redeemed and fulfilled.

# CHAPTER SEVEN

# The Audience of Theology

## Conscience and Theology

The familiar epistemological scheme of modernity regarding the constructing subject and its constructed object is a scheme without conscience, insofar as it systematically forgets that knowledge is always responsible as knowledge for someone, the interpretation of experience to a particular audience. The theological relevance of this critique of criticism, however, is not merely to expose the conceit of the Tribunal of Reason, salutary as that debunking is. It is rather to recall that the heavenly Father, whom Jesus proclaimed, is the audience of theology, before whom the Spirit-born theological subject knows its object, Jesus Christ the Son of God. For theology to have an audience indicates that inquiry and knowledge in theology is hermeneutical, that is to say, it is the pragmatic knowledge of a community of interpretation in the world that not only intends to interpret experience but to interpret it for someone, namely, from faith for faith (Rom. 1:17). What makes this interpretation theological, however, is that it partakes *in* God's own self-interpretation, naturally, of course, *as* creatures in the world of creatures.

The "conscience" of knowledge is its audience, to whom its knowledge is responsible, for whom its knowledge is constructed. Recent "contextual" theology has not been wrong to insist upon this sociology of knowledge, though it has been wrong so far as it reduces this sociology to pure immanence — such politicization of theology "all the way down" makes theology but a function of a worldly context where the dynamics of malice and injustice "go all the way down" as well. Here theology does not merely lose its object, but conscripts the object of theology, Christ and Him crucified, into the ideological service of one worldly partisanship or another. Denominational theologies of the divided church, interestingly, are even guiltier of the same sin. Here the theological object is captured by contrastive identity machines, staking out a competitive market niche in the sordid business of religion. But the context of Christian theology in the world is nothing less than that triune life of God; in living this life, God the

Father appears as the One to whom "responsible talk about God" (Jüngel) is owed in the Son's return of praise. As the audience of theology is none less than God the Father, so the conscience of theology is formed by His promise of His coming Beloved Community, the end for which He created the world and called humanity in His image to become His likeness. At stake in this contention for the conscience of theology is what is precious, each little one's faith in Jesus, the Spirit-born theological subject's knowledge of its object before God. "Whoever causes one of these little ones who believe in me to sin, it would be better for him to have a great millstone fastened round his neck and to be drowned in the depth of the sea" (Matt. 18:6).

The Greek, *syneidesis,* and the Latin, *conscientia,* are both compound words that indicate this "knowledge with others" that becomes a "knowledge of one-self," the Pauline "witness of conscience" (e.g., 2 Cor. 1:12). When Paul says that the Gentiles, who do not know the Torah of the LORD, are nevertheless a "law unto themselves" and "show that what the law requires is written on their hearts, while their conscience also bears witness and their conflicting thoughts accuse or perhaps excuse them" (Rom. 2:15), he indicates this distinctly social sense of human responsibility that formally judges attitudes and behaviors more than any specific code of conduct.[1] Conscience excuses or accuses because it is knowledge of relations of moral debt to the larger whole of one's community and corresponding obligation to repay or to be paid; the economic metaphor is apropos, since embodied life on the earth turns economically on just exchanges of labor even as all social relations depend on just exchanges.[2] Transgressions of community life in this respect do damage to its ecology; real defenses against transgressors and/or reparations are needed in turn to protect and/or to restore community. It is indicative of this ecology of the common body that the biblical writers describe the experience of conscience or take up the notion of con-science without any special grounding. Conscience may be clouded, confused, or torn in reflection of the conflicts besetting human communities organized by structures of malice and injustice, but nothing seems more self-evident than the blessings of a good conscience and the curse of an evil one. "Adam, where art thou?" (Gen. 3:9).

Citing Leviticus 26:36, "The sound of a driven leaf shall put them to flight," Luther famously observed that a "dry leaf shall terrify an evil conscience in such a way that it thinks this is sheer thunder and lightning."[3] Even so, conscience in general is not as such the voice of God. Rather, "it is the strict distinction between the coram Deo and the coram hominibus that leads to Luther's new conception of conscience" as responsibility to God for the world, a distinction that comes upon

1. Stephen Westerholm, *Perspectives Old and New on Paul: The "Lutheran" Paul and His Critics* (Grand Rapids: Eerdmans, 2004), pp. 409-11.

2. Gary A. Anderson, *Sin: A History* (New Haven: Yale University Press, 2009).

3. *LW* 7, p. 271.

the "natural man."[4] Luther writes of Joseph's brothers, whose "hearts failed them" upon their discovery that the viceroy of Egypt is the brother whom long before in their envy they had sold into slavery, "Yet they do not confess their sin. But this is a strange situation. Conscience feels the judgment and wrath of God. Yet it is ashamed to repent of and confess its transgression, even if it must remain in everlasting condemnation and torments. This is the fault of original sin, as is clear in the case of Adam. . . . Adam is terrified. He quakes and trembles. He knows that he has sinned. Nevertheless he does not confess his sin." The reason Luther gives for this "strange situation" is that "it is completely contrary to the nature of sin to confess that one has sinned."[5] For Luther, the true confession of sin is a virtue and gift of the Holy Spirit. Only the conscience captive to the Word of God hears the voice of God truly and replies responsibly. Yet the phenomenon of conscience singles out the dimension of human life in which the claim of God is heard, whether to be ignored and suppressed or believed and obeyed. The voice of God addresses conscience, because the God of the gospel summons to conscientious life in allegiance to the promised coming of the Beloved Community; the Word of God enters into this contested field of human life on the earth, there to claim and to gain the conscientious obedience of faith.

What is distinctly biblical, then, is that the *imago Dei* text of Genesis 1:26-28 grounds the human vocation in the call *from* God to assume responsibility *to* God *for* the world; as we have learned with the help of Friedrich Gogarten, Jesus is this new and true Adam, image and Son of the Father, who in true human obedience has taken responsibility for the world before God. His assumption for us of human responsibility before God initiates a radical, divisive, but ultimately salutary conflict with "the world," when and where "the world" claims this human responsibility to and for itself, the creature in place of, rather than under, the Creator. Just this responsibility *to* God *for* the creation forms the "conscience" of Christian theology in Christ, the new Adam. In Christ, by the Spirit God the Father becomes the audience of Christian knowledge of God which is at work in the world interpreting experience. In that case everything depends ethically in critical dogmatics on the knowledge of God the Father before whom faith lives in assuming responsibility for the world in union with Jesus Christ by the power of the Spirit.

Who is this heavenly Father? He is the God of Israel, the character made known in the Hebrew Scriptures, the Judge who judges the world in righteousness at the eschaton of judgment, whose will is righteous and is to be willed by His creatures.[6] Jesus' proclamation of Israel's God of election, exodus, and covenant

4. Berhard Lohse, "Conscience and Authority in Luther," in *Luther and the Dawn of the Modern Era: Papers for the Fourth International Congress for Luther Research* (Leiden: E. J. Brill, 1974), p. 165.

5. *LW* 7, pp. 271-72.

6. Philip B. Harner, *Understanding the Lord's Prayer* (Philadelphia: Fortress, 1975), pp. 35-46.

as His heavenly Father and ours is preserved preeminently among the Synoptic Gospels in the Gospel of Matthew's "Sermon on the Mount," chapters 5–7. This composite text, compiling and catechetically organizing traditional sayings of Jesus, evidently had its roots in a community of Jewish Christians. It appears to be consciously organized as the first of five units of teaching material in Matthew — perhaps to present Jesus as the New Moses teaching the New Pentateuch.[7] While the presentation of God as the heavenly Father is spread throughout the Gospel of Matthew, it is thematically introduced in the first of the five units, the celebrated Sermon on the Mount.

Here readers are introduced to "your" Father "in heaven" who "is" in secret and "sees" in secret (6:18). Unlike human judges, He does not judge superficially but searches the human heart; He knows the person in the work, not merely the work behind which the person hides all the while claiming agency. "Heaven" is not then some distant galaxy, but the "secret" place in our midst from which God sees into what hides behind the appearances of the phenomenal world visible to human eyes. Heaven is the divine perspective on the shared world of the common body. Heaven is thus the hidden palace of God's royal power, the veiled seat of just judgment, from which God "reveals" judgment in the words of prophets, and which judgment finally will appear openly on the Day of the Lord when accounts are settled and secrets revealed. Standing in the background of Jesus' usage is a forensic conception of history drawn from the Hebrew Scriptures, after the prophets who conceive of historical events as God's trial of the world. "Heaven" is both the secret present and the public future of this world, the coming of the Last Judgment already proclaimed in prophetic speech-acts of judgment and mercy.

Yet this "heavenly" Father whom Jesus proclaims as also "yours" is first of all Jesus' own, whom He addresses in His own prayers as *Abba,* the Aramaic word for father.[8] "Abba as a form of address to God expresses the ultimate mystery of the mission of Jesus. He was conscious of being authorized to communicate God's revelation, because God had made himself known to him as Father."[9] Jesus' relation to the God of Israel as son to father is thus a matter of revelation, a judgment disclosed from heaven. "Blessed are you, Simon son of Jonah! For flesh and blood has not revealed [Jesus' true status] to you, but *my* Father in heaven" (Matt. 16:17, emphasis added). What God reveals is that, despite His lowly appearance, Jesus is the coming heavenly Son of Man to whom divine sovereignty is delegated to execute judgment that forgives and retains sin (an authority further delegated to the

---

7. Günther Bornkamm, Gerhard Barth, and Heinz Joachim Held, *Tradition and Interpretation in Matthew,* trans. Percy Scott (Philadelphia: Westminster, 1963).

8. Joachim Jeremias, *New Testament Theology: The Proclamation of Jesus,* trans. J. Bowden (New York: Charles Scribner's Sons, 1971), p. 67.

9. Jeremias, *New Testament Theology,* p. 68. The allusion is to Jesus' baptism: "At his baptism, Jesus experienced his call . . . it is clear that Jesus attached supreme importance to the moment of his baptism" (p. 55).

church, 16:19).[10] As Jesus proclaims the heavenly Father, the heavenly Father in turn reveals to disciples this secret judgment of Jesus' heavenly standing already during His earthly sojourn. "I thank you, Father, Lord of heaven and earth," Jesus prays, "because you have hidden these things from the wise and the intelligent and have revealed them to infants; yes, Father, for such was your gracious will. All things have been handed over to me by my Father; and no one knows the Son except the Father, and no one knows the Father except the Son and anyone to whom the Son chooses to reveal him" (11:25-27). The human judgment made in faith or unbelief regarding Jesus' Sonship thus anticipates the last judgment: "Everyone therefore who acknowledges me before others, I also will acknowledge before my Father in heaven; but whoever denies me before others, I also will deny before my Father in heaven" (10:32). But what does acknowledging Jesus' Sonship entail?

As the heavenly Father is already secretly present on earth seeing where human vision does not penetrate, Jesus urgently admonishes to truthfulness: "Beware of practicing your piety before others in order to be seen by them; for then you have no reward from your Father in heaven" (Matt. 6:1). The promise of heavenly reward, "where neither moth nor rust consumes and where thieves do not break in and steal" (6:19; cf. 18:10), is the life of the resurrection, life in the radiance of the Father's own imperishable life, to which the "blessed" of Jesus are appointed heirs (5:3-12). The "reward" of eternal life is the gift inheritance of children, not merit earned by hires. These true children have come to know the heavenly Father and do not live falsely. "Not everyone who says to me, 'Lord, Lord,' will enter the kingdom of heaven, but only the one who does the will of my Father in heaven" (7:21). The idea, however, is not that these children are sinless, for daily they pray for forgiveness of their sins. They have become children because of the mercy shown to them. As recipients of mercy, they are obliged to show the same generosity towards others. "For if you forgive others their trespasses, your heavenly Father will also forgive you; but if you do not forgive others, neither will your Father forgive your trespasses" (6:14-15).

So "conscience" formed by life before God as "our heavenly Father" at Jesus' invitation is the forum of the Christian knowledge of God; it necessitates but also sharply qualifies the relation to the proximate audience of theology in every new generation. Theology is to relate to its *coram hominibus* context in the same Spirit who spoke by the prophets, responsible *to* God the Father for confessing *His* Word *in* the world. Put cognitively, God the Father is the audience of the interpretation by the theological subject of the object of theology in and for the neighboring world, where and when it asks *God's* question and answers *before Him:* Who is Jesus Christ for us today? Theology that purports to be Christian

---

10. Günther Bornkamm, "The Authority to 'Bind' and 'Loose' in the Church in Matthew's Gospel: The Problem of Sources in Matthew's Gospel," in *The Interpretation of Matthew,* ed. Graham Stanton (Philadelphia: Fortress / London: SPCK, 1983), pp. 85-97.

will be judged for intending, or failing to intend, this object before these audiences in this way.

For theology in the tradition of Luther it is not the "faculties" of reason or will or passion individually or in some order but the filial relation of "conscience" that marks the whole human creature as made in the image of God for likeness to God.[11] Conscience picks out the human creature as the fundamentally *social* creature called to live responsibly, *coram Deo,* before God. This claim is easily misunderstood, because the nature of a "relational ontology," as Luther scholars have tried to articulate, is easily misunderstood. A relational ontology is not claiming, theologically, that creatures have no natural capacities, faculties, or species-characteristic possibilities but that these properties emerge, exist, and persist in time *(in-esse)* by the grace of God's *creatio continua;* for this natural being human creatures are bound conscientiously to thank, praise, and obey the Creator with free, joyful, and intelligent lives of service, as Luther famously exposited the First Article of the Creed.[12] Thus "relational ontology" is the nature-person distinction; it claims that human creatures, in distinction from creatures not so endowed as *imago Dei,* rightly relate to their Creator *(ad-esse)* in the conscientious obedience of personal faith that is love for others and hope for the world. In this way, they fill the image that they are with harmonies reflecting divine power, wisdom, and love.[13] Wherever the dignity of the human person is thus acknowledged the natural image of God is known and acknowledged, even if there is little if any personal likeness to God.

Naturally, responsible living involves intelligence, choice, and desire; but it is not these natural endowments as such, then, that relate the human creature to God as *His* image. These natural endowments just as readily deliver human creatures to other claimants to deity than the God of Exodus and Easter. It is rather the calling of this God addressed to the person and binding her as a whole of body, soul, and mind to the Word spoken from God for the new being worked by the Spirit that is the coming of the Beloved Community into the world. The universal scope of this calling is indicated theologically by the "hope projected backward" of the *imago Dei* text of Genesis 1:26-28; under the conditions of existence fallen under the sway of the power of malice structuring injustice, however, the call to conscience is actualized in Jesus' summons to discipleship which is heard in the Spirit where and when the gospel is proclaimed. Likeness to God in turn progresses where and when the stations in life, groaning under the structures of malice and injustice, become sites of baptismal vocation for new ways of love structuring justice. This is in fact the theologic at work in Israel's Decalogue and

---

11. *LW* 1, p. 337.

12. *BC,* pp. 354-55.

13. Sammeli Juntunen, "Luther and Metaphysics: What Is the Structure of Being according to Luther?," in *Union with Christ: The New Finnish Interpretation of Luther,* ed. Carl E. Braaten and Robert W. Jenson (Grand Rapids: Eerdmans, 1998), pp. 129-60.

in Jesus' appropriation and radicalization of it in the Sermon on the Mount. First, the God who claims conscience self-identifies as the liberating God who has delivered from bondage. Then His exclusive claim, "I am yours and you are mine" sounds. Next, the ramifications of that exclusive claim *coram Deo* are elaborated in the so-called First Table. Finally, in the "Second Table" an elementary moral sociology *coram hominibus* is sketched for love to work at justice in the world.

There are several notable implications of this view of God's creating continuously and judging immanently. The first is theological. Creation is not to be viewed in a merely theistic or deistic way as if once upon a time a divine Mind set up a stage of nature and then retired to watch human individuals work out their otherworldly salvation on the premise of their independent or autonomous substantiality-cum-agency — perhaps intervening when entropy threatens the system with breakdown. Creation is rather to be viewed eschatologically as the triune project of the Beloved Community initiating, redeeming, and fulfilling creatures, in which God by grace gives time and space for creatures freely and joyfully to repent of rival projects that have seduced them and come instead to entrust themselves to God's. That giving of "nature" is the giving (not necessitating) of permission to "evil," that is, to those very rival projects, as figured generally in Adam's *sicut Deus eritis*. To those in the thrall of rival projects, naturally, that makes the putative God of the gospel the author of their "evil," who has set them up to sin in order to save them. To those in the thrall of the Trinitarian project of Beloved Community, however, that permission makes them the fallen authors of the evil of which they now repent. There is no creaturely transcending of this perspectival either/or. Conscience is *either* being in Adam *or* being in Christ: Either/or! In either case, however, one relates *conscientiously* to the gospel's claim to truth, whether in faith or in offense.

Thus the other implication is anthropological. With respect biographically to her existence antecedent to the new calling to discipleship through the gospel, it is not as if the human person were incomplete or broken but rather that she as a whole lived conscientiously as a member of some other whole than the Beloved Community of God, however inadequate or indeed sinful that previous commitment comes to be considered in the new perspective of repentance and faith. Abstractly considered, conscience thus marks the relation of the person to the whole to which she gives allegiance as a whole; conscience indicates that to which one wholeheartedly clings in every need and trouble, for which one lives and in the case of necessity is willing to sacrifice, even to die. Conscience is social loyalty, allegiance and obligation by which a human "nature" becomes the concrete biographical person within the larger whole of its community. Conscience is thus a social concept for the knowledge of persons in relationship to the wholes greater than themselves to which they essentially belong as persons, belonging that if violated injures not only the whole but also degrades the member — dehumanizes, as we say. The very notion of a "private" conscience, in this light, is oxymoronic. "Private" conscience rather refers in a convoluted way to the actual fact of the polytheism of fallen creation, where contending gods organize contending ways of life beneath the surface of some official and superficial monolatry. In this polytheism, moreover, torn and fragmented consciences are commonplace.

As it was famously said at the outset of this tradition of Christian theology: "Unless I am convinced by the testimony of the Scriptures or by clear reason (for I do not trust either in the pope or in councils alone, since it is well known that they have often erred and contradicted themselves), I am bound by the Scriptures I have quoted and my conscience is captive to the Word of God. I cannot and will not retract anything, since it is neither safe nor right to go against conscience. May God help me. Amen." Luther is bound by certain, "quoted" words of Scripture, understood by "clear reasoning,"[14] through which he has heard the "captivating" Word of God. "Conscience" appears here as but the knowledge of an obligation that has overtaken him and made him member of the new whole that is the theological subject adhering by faith to the theological object, Jesus Christ, conscientiously, before God the Father, as the court that matters in the contestation of life upon the earth. It is the knowledge, now internalized, of the God who has spoken, the Father of the Son who by the Spirit convicts the world concerning sin and righteousness and judgment. It is the conscience that defies a judgment poised to fall against it by secular and religious powers claiming authority, indeed ostensibly claiming the same authority as that to which Luther appeals.

Ephraim Radner rightly skewers the cliché that "Luther especially inaugurated a modern turn to individual conscience over and against communal authority."[15] In Luther's case, he writes, "conscience is bound to God's own commands as given in Scripture . . . like any human ruler, the conscience can err and is rightly set aside when it does . . . instruction is necessary . . . as a reasoning faculty, an instructed conscience, to be sure, can read the Scriptures correctly, and, when joined thereby to consciences of others, agreement can be reached among disputing Christians."[16] Such interpretation of *Christian* conscience *as captive to the Word of God,* then, provides justification for what Radner calls the "sacrifice of conscience" in the sense of a "certain abandonment, so that local loyalties, quite explicitly, and even convictions to forms of life, are necessarily exchanged for the sake of being able to place oneself literally 'next to the other' in the solidarity of Christian love."[17] "Conscience, understood as the consciousness that forms a

14. See the important clarification that Bernhard Lohse derives from comparison with Luther's 1521 Judgment on Monastic Vows: ". . . in the Worms formula Luther intended to say that what clearly contradicts the *ratio evidens* is also against God's Word." Bernard Lohse, *Martin Luther's Theology: Its Historical and Systematic Development,* trans. Roy A. Harrisville (Minneapolis: Fortress, 1999), pp. 199-200.

15. Ephraim Radner, *A Brutal Unity: The Spiritual Politics of the Christian Church* (Waco, TX: Baylor University Press, 2012), p. 324.

16. Radner, *A Brutal Unity,* p. 325.

17. Thus when ecclesial unity is "rendered atemporal, undeveloping, bound to unchangeable selves of this or that commitment, it is only division that can be described historically,

value-laden world, is thus not only penultimate and provisional; it is dispensable and must be for the sake of God's own movement" in Christ, who first became a neighbor to us, "next to" us in the divine movement of love incarnate for sinners.[18] So it is Christ who first sacrificed His conscience to befriend "real, not fictitious sinners," as Luther would have put it, the Holy One who was made to be sin, as said the apostle Paul. In Radner's words, "Jesus leaves behind his conscience as he moves towards those who would take it from him."[19] As we shall see, this sacrifice of Jesus in God surpassing God is the act of the Father's own conscience, the Father's resolution of Athanasius' divine dilemma, the resolution of Hosea 11:9.

Biographer Martin Brecht likewise comments that Luther here does not appear as "an emancipated man, relying freely on himself. . . . For him, the Scriptures were not just a theological and scholarly source, but they rather held his conscience captive in the ultimate depth of his existence. . . . [I]t was precisely the Word of God which had freed him from guilt and then also from false human impositions. He could not repudiate the Word which promised him salvation. In no way could the academic theologian and the believing Christian be separated at this point. 'One must fear God,' he had said earlier. From his fear of God courage grew. . . ."[20] This scriptural "beginning of wisdom" that is the "fear" of the LORD (Prov. 1:7) is yet another paraphrase for "conscience" as life "before God," that is, the knowledge in the Spirit with the Son of the heavenly Father whose name is holy and is to be hallowed in and above all things. To fear this God alone, then, is to be set free from all other fears by the forgiveness of sins, as Lohse noted in passing, that "freed him from guilt and then also from false human impositions." The moral debt that is weighed out as guilt is the leverage of the religion business, the traction of political sovereignty, the power of the devil over consciences. Its forgiveness by the One truly offended delivers from the cruel tyranny of those falsely offended. This fear of the Lord who forgives thus gives the courage of the martyrs: "We will never be able to abandon the Christ who suffered for the salvation of the whole world of those who are saved, the blameless on behalf of sinners, who is the Son of God. . . ." (*The Martyrdom of Polycarp*).[21] This fear of the Lord is still sung (whether consciously or conscientiously, who can say?) in memorial of the stand that Luther took at Worms: "take they goods, fame, fortune, child or spouse, they yet have nothing won. The kingdom ours remaineth."

"Conscience" appears here as the human field of battle where the call of God contends with the powerful claims of the structures of malice and injustice (for

---

given contours and detail, and so granted an engaging personality. Discord, in such a view, can be judged (usually in the other); the Church itself, never." Radner, *A Brutal Unity*, p. 396.

18. Radner, *A Brutal Unity*, p. 396.

19. Radner, *A Brutal Unity*, p. 351.

20. Martin Brecht, *Martin Luther: His Road to Reformation 1483-1521*, trans. James L. Schaaf (Minneapolis: Fortress, 1993), pp. 460-61.

21. *The Apostolic Fathers:* Revised Greek Texts with Introductions and English Translations, ed. J. B. Lightfoot and J. R. Harner (Grand Rapids: Baker, 1984), p. 241.

Luther, "devils filling the land, all eager to devour us"). Yet, as argued above, conscience is "natural." The claim for conscience as the mark of the human creature in relation to the social wholes to which it belongs is nothing especially theological (or it is theological in the secondary sense of a theology of the natural); the phenomenon of conscience is everywhere visible. The modern "monster," the "sociopath" who feels no co-humanity, or the living-dead "zombie" of popular horror fantasy, is the nightmarish exception that proves the rule. Indeed, if we accept the body as the place of the human, and the web of language as the social mediation of such bodily selves needing in their proximity as neighbors to live together justly through time, conscience is a "natural" knowledge of co-humanity with little mystery about it. The organization of bodies for tasks in common purposes is mediated by language in the sense that it is address that names and summons; address is the power to initiate and sustain such social relationships. Names call us out and summon us to response. It is such address in turn that evokes the experience and the consciousness of responsibility. Conscience, we could argue naturalistically, is rooted in the biological "instinct for reciprocity" (Ridley)[22] that flowers into the civilized, that is, cultivated goods of good will and just relations to fund social trust for life together on the earth. Noting again that there need be no uniquely biblical basis for these rather formal observations regarding human sociality, it is *not* the case, as is sometimes argued today against the nihilistic turn of contemporary culture, that human beings cannot be responsible or self-critical or fund social trust without God — that "without God anything is possible." This imprecise and inflated claim overshoots the mark. It misses the polytheistic situation of postmodernity, our reversion in Euro-America to the status quo ante of paganism.

Or, perhaps better said, this too-dire alarm as such misses the gospel and its honest situation in the world. That God whose primary function is protologically to anchor the cosmos and thus provide a morality of mere order is the God of the "myth of the origin"; here religion is always trying to impose order on the chaos or return from the dissipations of historical existence to the primal order.[23] While the God of the gospel is also the origin, and intends orders of justice and love for the continuation and preservation of creation on the way to Beloved Community, this God originates in order to achieve an eschaton that surpasses the origin; this eschaton, in turn, needs time and space with and for creatures to attain this surpassing goal of Beloved Community through the conscientious obedience of faith.[24] This God claims conscience as its own image for tasks of

22. Matt Ridley, *The Origins of Virtue* (London and New York: Penguin, 1998).

23. Mircea Eliade, *The Sacred and the Profane: The Nature of Religion,* trans. Willard R. Trask (New York: Harcourt, 1987). Paul Tillich faulted the rationalism of the Left that missed the seductive appeal in Fascism of "the myth of origin" in the symbols of blood, soil and tribe. "Ontologically this means being is holy." Paul Tillich, *The Socialist Decision,* trans. Franklin Sherman (New York: Harper & Row, 1977), p. 17.

24. Jenson, *ST* 2, pp. 29-49.

love and justice in anticipation of the coming of the Beloved Community.[25] For God too, personally God *the Father,* has a conscience that makes this person self-surpassing, as we shall see. Self-surpassing is just what a conscientious person *is.* It is rather true, in any case, that "without the gospel" a human being will be responsible to something other than to the God of the gospel, self-critical in ways other than the way of His commandments, and fund social trust on some other basis than the *esse Deum dare* of biblical creation faith. In that case, however, it is not the "sincerity" or even viability of other ways to responsibility in the world, but what these alternative moral allegiances might signify for life together that constitute the interesting and indeed decisive questions in critical dogmatics. In other words, theology must provide good reasons amid rival claims for its assumption of responsibility in the world *to* God *for* the creation, that is, for Jesus Christ as the image and likeness of the conscientious God and the concrete form of conscience before Him.

The theological command "to have no other gods before me" purports, for example, to spell out the difference between the moral authority of Pharaoh and that of the LORD who called and sent Moses in His name to demand from Pharaoh, "Let my people go" (Exod. 5:1 et al.). What else could the LORD's demand be to Pharaoh than the imposition of a moral heteronomy requiring a betrayal of his royal responsibility to the well-being of the Egyptian empire? Is that not good reason that the demand of the LORD multiplied wrath and hardened Pharaoh's heart (Exod. 4:21 et al.)? What else could the Lord's demand be to the oppressed Hebrews than the summons to risk themselves in the obedience of faith, leaving behind the "fleshpots of Egypt" (Exod. 14:11 et al.)? Is that not the good reason that the wanderings in the wilderness that followed revealed impotence? The Word of God coming as a claim on conscience initiates these kinds of *moral* conflict in the world, for "no one can serve two masters" (Matt. 6:24). It is essentially controversial in this, cutting through and reorganizing not only the affects of the individual organism but all its social relations, e.g., "He who loves father or mother more than me is not worthy of me; and he who loves son or daughter more than me is not worthy of me" (Matt. 10:37). Just as in any non-utopian moral claim, this controversial claim of the God of the gospel comes about and gains a hearing in the world on the basis of some warranted pledge of solidarity; its "ought" is grounded in the "is" of covenant: "I *am* the LORD your God, who brought you up from the land of Egypt, out of the house of bondage." Therefore, "have no other gods. . . ." "This *is* my body, given for you." Therefore, "do this in remembrance of me." The conscience-binding imperative of grace is grounded in the indicative of grace, just as grace performs a claim on conscience of that Giver who gives *Himself* in and as the gift.

Thus the much-discussed passage of Romans 2:14 concerning conscience does not indicate "an innate sense of right or a guiding moral ideal" in the private

25. Jenson, *ST* 2, pp. 6-9.

shrine of the individual heart as such but rather that "in his innermost being a person is not his own master"[26] and answerable to another. The "witness" of conscience is the voice of this other within, internalized sociality, Freud's "superego." Käsemann is in this way pointing to the deep contradiction of modern claims to moral autonomy in the name of "conscience," which, as the etymology indicates, is in fact internalized social knowing, a "knowing with others" that has become a "knowing within" about one's place, role, and duty in the social whole to which one belongs. In appealing to the right and power of *private* conscience, however, modern moral autonomy saws off the branch of sociality on which it sits. Its claim to authority in fact represents the internalization and sublimation — that is, the rationalization — of some heteronomy rather than expresses, as Kantianism imagined, some mysterious freedom of agency. Noumenal freedom is a mystification of this internalized heteronomy. This is especially true today of allegedly "free" thinking, which has long since settled into its own highly ritualized tradition, mouthing the shallow platitudes of its own conceited narrative in what is in truth a smug and deeply uncritical dogmatism. "Free thinking" is surely not the *freed* thinking of Christian theology that is not ashamed to call Jesus *Lord;* it is rather the deep illusion of the centered self of modernity, where Adam's *sicut Deus eritis* has been heralded as liberation rather than despised as folly. One may prefer the tale of Prometheus to that of Adam, but clarity demands that we acknowledge here nothing but the exchange of one myth of conscience for another.

Ephraim Radner writes in this connection that "the notion that only a 'collective' procedure can uphold cohesion and peace, but only 'conscience' itself — individual if need be — can maintain the moral accountability for collectivities and individuals alike, presents a classic conflict in decision making and a formidable challenge to the very notion of moral agreement in the standard understanding of the term. . . . What is involved in these kinds of conflicts is not *simply,* nor can it ever be, an encounter between "group" and "individual," institutional demand and personal conscience, tradition and truth. . . ." Radner exposes a classical aporia of liberalism. Think of Henry David Thoreau's retort to Ralph Waldo Emerson, who had exclaimed, "Why are you in there?" to the jailed Thoreau after Thoreau had conscientiously refused to pay the war tax in support of Polk's Mexican adventure; to which Thoreau replied, "Why are you out there?" That is my illustration, not Radner's, of the aporia of supposedly private conscience against the rule of lawful procedure under liberalism. In other words, what divides Thoreau and Emerson is not Thoreau's stand of conscience over against Emerson's social conformism, but Emerson's conscientious commitment to lawful democratic procedure and Thoreau's democratic commitment to regard also Mexicans as bearers of rights. Both stands are conscientious. In this light, a "moral agreement," Radner argues, is a matter of "deliberated subtraction, conscience retired from a

---

26. Ernst Käsemann, *Commentary on Romans,* trans. and ed. G. Bromiley (Grand Rapids: Eerdmans, 1980), p. 66.

host of often cacophonous conscientious demands working at once in collective and individual together. In Christian and Christian ecclesial terms, there is no agreement without sacrifice of conscience."[27]

Theologically, if we are not "indoctrinated" by the gospel to *its* sacrifice of conscience, which is God surpassing God in the gift of His Son that was the Son's abandonment into the hands of sinners, we will be indoctrinated by some other doctrine into some other sacrifice. That is what is at stake in the formation of the theological subject. What else then could those whose consciences are bound objectively to the Word of God incarnate say, for near contemporary example, to a "sincere" Nazi other than a Moses-like witness, "Cease and desist in the name of the LORD"? Confusion about this formal point of the binding, because essentially social, nature of conscience to something external to the self is not least of the reasons for the largely miserable performance of Christians accommodated to the modern world of Euro-America, who have excused or even justified the Gulag, or the concentration camp, or the incinerations of Dresden, Hiroshima, and Nagasaki on the confused grounds of responsibility *to* the world in its tragic conflicts. But the very same confusion attends those shocked and awed by this failure of Christian conscience, who imagine that an all the more strident and exclusive claim for responsibility *to* the world would prevent accommodation rather than perpetuate it. At the heart of the deep contemporary confusion in claims for "contextual" theology is precisely this confusion of the proximate and ultimate audiences of theology, where contextual responsibility *for* the world is possible and necessary theologically only as responsibility *by* the Word of God *to* the judgment of God. How could attention to context be called "theology" otherwise? Where is the text in con*text*ual theology?

In any event, even the well-intentioned desire to defend personal dignity in the name of "autonomy" simply fails, as the deep cynicism of the "whatever" generation amply attests and must attest as the progressive decentering of the sovereign self of modernity proceeds apace, fueled by the scientific knowledge of human materiality "all the way down" and the new metaphysics of naturalism without remainder. Precisely now at the apogee of modern "autonomy," the rising generation has come to understand how profoundly manipulated they are, paradoxically, in being told that they are free. That awakening can launch a dangerous vertigo spinning into nihilism, or it can present a new opportunity for the knowledge of God the Father before whom life can be lived with integrity and so in a good conscience by the forgiveness of sin, as we see sketched out in the Lord's Prayer, shortly to be discussed.

If Reinhold Niebuhr spoke rightly of "the easy conscience of modern man," there are numerous plausible candidates in the modern self-consciousness of Euro-America that could account for the phenomenon. This "easy" conscience of the would-be sovereign self can be loosely characterized, as Gogarten put it,

27. Radner, *A Brutal Unity*, p. 315.

as the one that disowns God's royal claim to judge at the eschaton of judgment in the name of assuming responsibility to the *saeculum,* this "present age," as if it were the really real. That precisely is the total claim of secular-*ism,* quite to be distinguished from Christianity's belief in holy secularity, the sanctification of the profane. Human beings are according to secularism not fallen angels but rising beasts. Sins are the product of immaturity and ignorance, not rooted in the malice of envy animating structures of injustice that bear fruit in words and deeds of violence. The structures of malice and injustice, if they are acknowledged as endemic at all, are thus regarded as anachronisms destined to pass away with more of the same — the real fantasy of our times. The unholy trinity of Hitler, Hiroshima, and Stalin mark but growing pains on the way to secular happiness. The pursuit of happiness is natural, normal, and easily generalized. In hard reality, this easy conscience of "secularism" as "worldly responsibility" always founders on the universal claim it makes for what in fact prove to be partial and interested perspectives.

The young Marx, still thinking philosophically with Hegel and not yet the positivist, famously put the question to the Enlightenment, *Quis custodiet custodem?* (who will guard the guard?). So, earlier and theologically, did Hamann put the question, as Oswald Bayer reconstructs: "Kant does not perceive the character of simile or analogy in 'maturity' [in his essay, 'What Is Enlightenment?']. [Hamann] illuminates what Kant, more likely unaware than aware, leaves in the dark, that is, the correlate of the immature, namely, the guardian who is Kant himself . . . ," not a politically innocent correlate, but rather one betrayed by "the partisanship [of] Kant's *Laudatio* of Frederick the Great . . ."[28] to Prussia's enlightened despotism. What distracts from facing this immanent contradiction, and the malice and injustice this very distraction masks, is the manufactured and highly manipulated memory of the supposedly theocratic medieval past[29] — a specter stridently if no longer plausibly evoked whenever the total critique of the Christian doctrine of sin is prophetically made and totally resisted. Yet, even under any contemporary Frederick the Great, "[w]hat modern state would hesitate to extinguish an individual who threatened its very existence?"[30] With kill-lists, predator drone strikes, and National Security Administration spying on citizens under the auspices of the most politically "progressive" regime in recent memory, for example, how is the United States of America really different from medieval crusaders and Inquisitors except that it crusades in the name of other goods and gods? Only the ideologies have changed. That medieval Europeans did such things in the name of the political ideal of Christendom, and that we

---

28. Oswald Bayer, *A Contemporary in Dissent: Johann Georg Hamann as a Radical Enlightener,* trans. Roy A. Harrisville and Mark C. Mattes (Grand Rapids: Eerdmans, 2012), p. 118.

29. *SF,* pp. 144-45.

30. Roland H. Bainton, *Hunted Heretic: The Life and Death of Michael Servetus 1511-1553* (Boston: Beacon, 1953), p. 42.

today do such things in the name of the political ideal of secularism, is nothing but a change in costume. Christians, of course, have their own — Reformation — reasons for repenting of the sin of Christendom for misapplying the adjective Christian to the sword of steel rather than the sword of Word and Spirit.

To mention only the two great rival schools of secular modernity, Anglo-American liberalism and Continental socialism: one can speak of modern conscience in liberalism as the happy bourgeoisie's upwardly mobile aspiration that secures *the right* to possess property as a new fundament of economic organization or of conscience in socialism as the quest of the alienated bourgeoisie for human meaning in a world without purpose in collective or individual *projects* that make emancipatory history. Ownership or agency: the ecological and moral ruination that these rival claims for the conscience of the sovereign self of Cartesian-Lockean-Kantian modernity have worked is increasingly evident today as is the metastasis of it spreading across the face of the groaning earth in runaway, massively unsustainable formations. This is the juggernaut of the sovereign self that funds its own polarized but immanent critics in liberalism and socialism, the modern "left-right" binary that distracts us from the common root and thus serves to keep the system alive and growing, when even a child can see that it is lunging blindly into catastrophe.

Over against these rival philosophies of "excarnation" stands the Christian view of "incarnation," in words of the late Jean Bethke Elshtain from her Gifford Lectures: "Within a framework that stresses our sociality and that couches an account of the human subject as a being who exists in a body in and through definite, specific relations, human beings can be understood not so much as self-interested bearers of rights, certainly not as sovereign selves, but as beings whose sufferings and joys, pains and pleasures, triumphs and tragedies, make them members of a human community, participants in a social compact."[31] Such is the theology of the Beloved Community of God that takes anthropological form in the ecclesia in mission to the nations to call political sovereignty to its conscientious responsibility to God (Rom. 13:5) for the justice of love in the world. To be sure, the antecedent Christendom of Euro-America had in its own way so confused Christian conscience before God for the creation with self-interested responsibility for Christendom that moral discredit was inevitable. From the post-Christendom Christian perspective of this system of theology, however, the modern rivals of liberalism and socialism (not to mention the elite conscience of Epicurean libertarianism) equal each other in disowning responsibility *to* God *for* the world. Responsibility to God for the world, beginning with each one's responsibility for his own body as a member of the common body and object together with all others of God's redemption and fulfillment, is living by faith in hopeful experiments to structure love and justice in this still-contested reality.

---

31. Jean Bethke Elshtain, *Sovereignty: God, State, and Self,* The Gifford Lectures (New York: Basic Books, 2008), pp. 224-25.

This experimentation is the subject matter of theological ethics, which we will sketch at the end of the next chapter.

Christian conscience is Christian and theological in being infinitely responsible as responsible to God. Again, in Radner's words: "Christian conscience is unceasingly relearned as the Christian him- or herself is restlessly reordered in and for the sake of 'life together . . .' a reordering that brackets aspects of its apparent claims, dismisses others, and rearranges the rest. Let us call this process of learning the act of the conscience sacrificing itself in the ineluctable engagement of life with others. That at least captures some of the combination of intentionality and self-abandonment that a Christian will face in recognizing the limits of any stable consensus and the demand to go beyond it as means of apprehending the truth 'with others.'" As this is the specifically Christian ethos in the Spirit's refashioning of the self on the basis of specifically Christian knowledge of Christ, Radner comments sharply in passing that "it has been a source and result of sin that Christian conscience has been thought of in any other terms. . . ."[32] There is no one to whom one cannot at any moment become neighbor (Luke 10:36). Before God who casts a neighbor in one's path one ought to become neighbor, as encountered in the particularity of each one's existence. This massive burden sensitizes conscience, though apart from Christ being first and Himself the neighbor showing mercy to the believer, it crushes it; this infinite burden of bearing one another's burdens (Gal. 6:2) is the Pauline "end of all boasting" (Gal. 6:14) that boasts only in the Lord who has been neighbor to us. Far from settling the experience of the divided self as depicted in Romans 7 (as though this reflection on life between baptism, Romans 6, and expected consummation, Romans 8, were recalled from the natural agony of coming to self-consciousness from which now faith delivers), baptism *inaugurates* the *conflicted* conscience and *sustains* this battle of the Spirit and the flesh up to the Lord's Day.

This new orientation of conscience to the redeeming judgment of God in the cross of Christ (Gal. 6:14) bears decisively on the knowledge of God that systematic theology produces, both proximately and finally. Proximately, God is to be justified in His judgment at the time and place of the believer; here the audience of the theological subject in confessing Jesus Christ, the Son of God, is one's own generation. One knows God in prophetic dispute with one's own time and place, beginning with one's own "self-consciousness." To be sure, in assuming this embattled stance, temptation to illusions of moral superiority is profound, plentiful, and ever present. Consequently, "hypocrisy" becomes the sin of the believer not at her worst but at her best; this unconscious fault that fails to see oneself truly, as God sees, is the deep reason why in this life the Christian's righteousness for the most part consists in the forgiveness of (unknown) sins. Anyone who is knowingly a hypocrite, however, is no longer a hypocrite but has become either a fraud or a penitent. To know penitently one's hypocrisies is progressively to see

---

32. Radner, *A Brutal Unity,* 379.

oneself in Another's eyes, those not deceived by outward appearances but rather knowing and judging the heart. Thus, God is ever to be justified, also here and now, in knowing oneself concretely as the sinner for whom Jesus lived and died and reigns. God therefore is to be justified as the Father in heaven who sent His Son, Jesus, who in turn proclaimed His Sender as the One who "sees in secret." In this way, the eschaton of judgment already now protrudes into this present evil age in the field of Christian conscience, accompanying and encompassing the proximate moments of dispute with and critique of this self-aggrandizing world of which the theological subject remains a part by virtue of the common body.

But the ultimate audience of theology is the eschatological judgment of the God whose kingdom comes so that His will be done on earth as in heaven. Jacques Derrida both recognized this claim and critiqued it in a fashion that usefully articulates a certain, important objection to the claim of this chapter for the heavenly Father as ultimate audience of theology that in Christ is conscientiously responsible to Him for the world by the gift of Christ's own Spirit. At the concluding juncture of his stimulating essay *The Gift of Death*,[33] Derrida finally made explicit his own *apophatic* theology in contrast to Jesus' presentation in the Sermon on the Mount of the heavenly Father who sees in secret: "[I]n order to eschew idolatrous or iconistic simplicisms, that is, visible images and ready-made representations, it might be necessary to understand [the Father who sees in secret] as something other than a proposition concerning God. . . . Then we might say ['at the risk of turning . . . against' the theological 'tradition']: God is the name of the possibility I have of keeping a secret that is visible from the interior but not from the exterior." "God" then names a "structure of conscience . . . a witness that others cannot see, and who is therefore *at the same time other than me and more intimate with me than myself.*" "God is in me, he is the absolute 'me' or 'self'" that Kierkegaard calls "subjectivity." This "heretical" but "internal critique of Christianity," nontheistically or apophatically refuses as idolatrous the iconic heavenly Father with His heavenly reward whom Jesus proclaimed and who in turn proclaimed the self-forgetting Jesus victor on the third day by vindicating His afflicted faith in the Father He had proclaimed.

This apophatic move beyond patrology, moreover, is in keeping with the "Pagan School," Derrida continued, which, sniffing out "the slightest hint of calculation," calls the evangelical bluff with a critique of mystification and a reproach of its counterfeit currency: one must give without knowing, without recognition, without thanks, without any audience for the conscientious gift of death. So long as "God sees in secret," Someone knows, and thus sacrifice is hedged and turned into the tawdry wager. "We have to *believe* that he knows. This knowledge at the same time founds and destroys the Christian concept of responsibility and justice

33. Jacques Derrida, *The Gift of Death,* trans. D. Wills (Chicago and London: University of Chicago Press, 1995). An earlier version of this material appeared as Paul R. Hinlicky, "Sin, Death, and Derrida," *Lutheran Forum* 44, no. 2 (Summer 2010): 54-59.

and their 'object.'" Betting on God? Can one imagine anything more unworthy of God than to reduce Him to supernatural compensation for earthly repressions resentfully posing as genuinely ethical sacrifices? It was Nietzsche of the "Pagan School," who detected here a root cruelty hidden in supposed Christian altruism. That cruelty is the "self-destruction of justice by means of grace." In fact such grace (the reward expected in Pascal's wager) is but "the privilege of the strongest" masquerading as pious sacrifice; what it really does is effect a self-exemption from responsibility. It is an *egodicee,* a cunning manifestation of the will-to-power.

The Christian theological retort to this Nietzschean critique no doubt ups the ante. Derrida sees what Nietzsche exposes as Christianity's sacrificial *hybris:* the notion of grace going beyond justice in God surpassing God; this excess of generosity is the very thing that "takes this economy to its excess in the sacrifice of Christ for the love of the debtor." That is a substitution that at once fulfills the law and goes beyond it. *"Can one credit that?"* Nietzsche asks incredulously. Derrida does not answer Nietzsche's open question, but takes leave suspended between Nietzsche's protest at the injustice of grace and "the irreducible experience of belief."

That is the state of the question in contemporary Euro-America. Can we conscientiously think once more with Luther of God the Father as God surpassing God by sending Christ made to be sin, at once fulfilling the Law as love and surpassing it as judgment? Can we think so while distinguishing the Law of God from the Jewish people whose gift and calling are irrevocable? Can we think of Goodness which not only forgets itself in time *for us* but also remembers itself *with us* now conjoined in eternity, for salvation that saves not least from our easy consciences in delivering us from our sin? Can we overcome the Cartesian and Kantian dualism of the so-called *Zweireichelehre* to think of a Christian polity and politics that is not, however, the strident utopianism of those who have no Derridean sense of the irresponsibility that attends all our political responsibility for the common body this side of the coming of the Beloved Community? Can we articulate the sense of the doctrine of original sin to complicate, indeed to burden and oppress the easy conscience of modern man without the literalism that makes temporal death the consequence rather than a source of faithless anxiety? Can we teach that true humanity is not decided in conscientious being-towards-death, but in conscientious being-towards-death-and-resurrection (Luke 14:12-14)? Can we confess in faith the promise of Jesus, "Be of good cheer, little children! It is your Father's good pleasure to give you the kingdom!" (Luke 12:32), which raises to life before God already now? Such confidence is the good conscience of the theological subject before God, the same conscience that is, as consciousness of sinfulness in the world, an infinitely bad conscience before others. This being *simul iustus et peccator* in the interim between Ascension and Parousia becomes possible for us, if the God of the gospel is in fact the self-surpassing Father, who is "God after God" (Jenson).[34]

---

34. Robert Jenson, *God after God: The God of the Past and the God of the Future, Seen in the Work of Karl Barth* (Indianapolis and New York: Bobbs-Merrill, 1969).

## God after God

Nietzsche proclaimed the death of the Christian God — who in his reading is also the God of Parmenides and Plato — in the same book in which he proclaimed, in the dead God's place, the (re)new(ed) divinity of Dionysus as he figured his great metaphysical insight into the Eternal Return of the Same. "Have you not heard of that madman who lit a lantern in the bright morning hours, ran to the market place, and cried incessantly: "I seek God! I seek God!" — As many of those who did not believe in God were standing around just then, he provoked much laughter. Has he got lost? asked one. Did he lose his way like a child? asked another. Or is he hiding? Is he afraid of us? Has he gone on a voyage? emigrated? — Thus they yelled and laughed." Notice that Nietzsche's madman is put into conversation, not with theists hanging on against the tide, but with self-satisfied atheists, who casually dismiss belief in God and do not understand the implications of their own disbelief. But the madman makes this explicit. "The madman jumped into their midst and pierced them with his eyes."

> "Whither is God?" he cried; "I will tell you. *We have killed him* — you and I. All of us are his murderers. But how did we do this? How could we drink up the sea? Who gave us the sponge to wipe away the entire horizon? What were we doing when we unchained this earth from its sun? Whither is it moving now? Whither are we moving? Away from all suns? Are we not plunging continually? Backward, sideward, forward, in all directions? Is there still any up or down? Are we not straying, as through an infinite nothing? Do we not feel the breath of empty space? Has it not become colder? Is not night continually closing in on us? Do we not need to light lanterns in the morning? Do we hear nothing as yet of the noise of the gravediggers who are burying God? Do we smell nothing as yet of the divine decomposition? Gods, too, decompose. God is dead. God remains dead. And we have killed him."[35]

Vertigo, chaos in place of cosmos, random matter in motion violently colliding, combining, and again colliding to pieces and recombining *ad infinitum* — that is the visage of the world after the death of God who grounded space in a sacred center and ordered time into a meaningful cycle of life. Even worse, somehow we modern humans have committed this crime of crimes. What such human criminality could mean will occupy us in a moment. For now we entertain Nietzsche's question whether we are capable of owning up to — taking conscientious responsibility for — the deed.

---

35. *The Portable Nietzsche,* trans. W. Kaufmann (New York: Viking, 1969), p. 95. I am indebted to my colleague, coauthor, and conversation partner of many years, Brent Adkins, for the following deliberations, though he rejects the metaphysical interpretation of the Eternal Return. On this see *RPTD,* pp. 109-14.

How shall we comfort ourselves, the murderers of all murderers? What was holiest and mightiest of all that the world has yet owned has bled to death under our knives: who will wipe this blood off us? What water is there for us to clean ourselves? What festivals of atonement, what sacred games shall we have to invent? Is not the greatness of this deed too great for us? Must we ourselves not become gods simply to appear worthy of it? There has never been a greater deed; and whoever is born after us — for the sake of this deed he will belong to a higher history than all history hitherto.[36]

As our antecedent definition of the human depended on the antecedent definition of "God," so now "after God" a new self-defining, self-determining, value-creating *Übermensch* must arise to own up to the murder. "Must we ourselves not become gods simply to appear worthy of it?" But the madman is met with silent, uncomprehending astonishment. "I have come too early," he said then; "my time is not yet. This tremendous event is still on its way. . . . This deed is still more distant from them than most distant stars — *and yet they have done it themselves.*"[37]

*They have done it themselves.* What can this actually mean? If we are at all correct thus far in this presentation of the Christian faith in God, it might mean that they have come to disbelieve the One whom Jesus proclaimed as the heavenly Father in the specific sense of disbelieving His deed as Father of the Son, namely, the sending of the Son, anointed in the Spirit, to the destination of Golgotha, thence resurrection of the Crucified vindicating His faith and revealing His Sonship. So they must also leave Jesus behind, as dead in the grave and not the vindicated Son of that Father. Henri de Lubac acutely wrote along these lines: "Whatever the antecedents may have been, the meaning Nietzsche attaches to this phrase, 'the death of God,' is new. On his lips it is not a mere statement of fact. Nor is it a lament or a piece of sarcasm. It expresses a choice"[38] against "the great convenience that belief in God too often affords." Note that de Lubac indicates critically a self-serving "convenience" of belief, an unconscientious belief that is decided against. This rejection of convenience is *a conscientious choice for choice,* "saying No to everything that was dear and estimable to him, in order that he might free himself from everything."[39] By *this* proclamation of the *murder* of the convenient God, Nietzsche offers in its place a gospel of inconvenient freedom; as this alternative message of costly liberation, Nietzsche's "death of God" indeed articulates the root question for theology in contemporary Euro-American culture. "Already at work in the preceding generation, the urge to do without God now became a greater ferment than ever in souls which were not at all lacking in

36. *The Portable Nietzsche,* pp. 95-96.

37. *The Portable Nietzsche,* p. 96, emphasis original.

38. Henri de Lubac, S.J., *The Drama of Atheist Humanism* (San Francisco: Ignatius, 1995), p. 53.

39. De Lubac, *The Drama of Atheist Humanism,* p. 54.

nobility and which would have been the first to reject an atheism of the ordinary complacent type."[40]

"Why atheism today?" Nietzsche once asked; and he answered: " 'The father' in God has been thoroughly refuted; ditto, 'the judge,' 'the rewarder.' "[41] This person of God is refuted by modernity's experience with random evils against which God as father, judge, and rewarder was a convenient hedge; paternalistic theism, of the kind that Gottfried Leibniz represented philosophically, founders on the very problem of theodicy that Leibniz himself so acutely articulated. The protological God of monotheism and morality, i.e., the One simultaneously for and against the many, the Father of the cosmos who once set things in motion to run their course according to a predetermined plan but now waits at the finish line; distant, then, without affect if not disapproving in visage, emotionally absent, finally only there to punish the lazy and reward the achievers — this "father god" is outgrown and discarded in the adulthood of the human race.

We may let this verdict stand with the following qualification: the fateful development of so-called atheism in contemporary Euro-American culture, to which Nietzsche bore seminal witness, is the fruit of inadequate Trinitarianism in the antecedent Christianity, namely, of taking the "fatherhood" of God in the first place as a general similitude for God's relation to the cosmos rather than the gospel's telling of the God of Israel's self-surpassing in relation to Jesus by the Spirit of their love for the redemption and fulfillment of the creation. As similitude the fatherhood of God is but another version of the cosmogonic myth. As per the analogy, Jesus is to the Creator as a son is to his father, the Trinitarian fatherhood of God strips the cosmogonic myth of its eternity and necessity. In disruption of cosmos-piety, it renders the earth on which the cross of Jesus stood the place where in time the Beloved Community is to come. In this light, paternalistic theism is, in T. F. Torrance's words, the "failure to give clear-cut ontological priority to the Father/Son relation in God over the Creator/cosmos relation."[42] A regression to a general God-cosmos frame of reference had to eclipse "the mighty act of God [the Father] in raising Jesus from the dead[, . . . where] the absolute power of God over life and death, over all being and non-being was uniquely exhibited . . . "; the gospel of the resurrection had in fact been "the real starting-point for the doctrine of creation,"[43] i.e., as Bonhoeffer's "hope projected backwards." "Creation," taken radically as creation *out of nothing* in light of the resurrection of

---

40. De Lubac, *The Drama of Atheist Humanism*, p. 58.

41. Friedrich Nietzsche, *Beyond Good and Evil: Prelude to a Philosophy of the Future*, trans. W. Kaufmann (New York: Vintage, 1966), p. 66.

42. Thomas F. Torrance, *The Trinitarian Faith: The Evangelical Theology of the Ancient Catholic Church* (Edinburgh: T. & T. Clark, 1993), p. 85.

43. Torrance, *Trinitarian Faith*, p. 97. So Torrance calls attention to key trinitarian affirmations of Athanasius, "the revelation is not of the Father manifested as God but of God manifested as the Father," and of Hilary, "the centre of saving faith is belief not merely in God, but in God as Father." Torrance, *Trinitarian Faith*, p. 77.

the Crucified and the justification of the ungodly, is not even a possible thought in standard theism which naturally thinks instead of a First Mover or Necessary Being of the cosmic system that is itself infinitely extended in time.

To the contrary, as Torrance suggests, the notion of "creation" itself is eschatological through and through. Proceeding from the faith-inaugurating resurrection narrative of the Crucified, Trinitarianism cannot regard "creation" as some neutral, self-secured common ground, but only as the eschatological project from the beginning of making all things new by the missions of the Son and the Spirit. Trinitarianism's "cosmological principle," as it were, holds that "while God was always Father, he was not always Creator or Maker."[44] The almighty Creator of creation is from eternity the Father of Jesus Christ through whom as well as for whom all things are made and so hang together for the sake of the coming of the Beloved Community. This is the One who creates a world — through and for His Son, in and by their Spirit. Creation is undertaken purposively in prospect of redemption and fulfillment; what "creation" really means, therefore, is unknowable apart from its redemption by the Son and fulfillment in the Spirit. Apart from the Son incarnate and the hallowing Spirit, creation is hidden under the mask of nature groaning in travail. "Creation" to be sure continues as a promise in the making, redeemed in principle but yet to be fulfilled in the redemption of our bodies. Creation is the promise of the coming of the Beloved Community. It is this promise at work incognito that still elicits the basic forms of human life in structures of love and justice: structures of doxology, of marriage and family, and of labor and creative exchange. "Creation" as we sinners know it, however, is fallen under structures of malice and injustice where worship becomes religious bribery, marriage turns into ownership, labor reduces to rote drudgery, and exchange is legalized as a pretext for thievery backed by a state that claims the sovereignty belonging to the Creator alone.

When we take Trinitarianism all the way down, as it were, into the properties that comprise our concept of divine nature, God the Creator's sovereignty is anything but the convenient and arbitrary claim to power of the powerful as we experience it under political sovereignty. God the Father's almighty *power* as creator of all things other than God is at work in accord with the *wisdom* of the Logos/Son's incarnate and crucified existence in and for the world by the *love* of the Spirit in which the Father gives all authority into this Son's hands and the Son returns all whom he has won with this authority back into the Father's waiting arms of mercy. As God is the Father that He is only by the self-surpassing of eternally begetting the Son on whom He breathes His Spirit, so God is all powerful in creating the world only in harmony with the wisdom of the *Logos incarnandus,* the Lamb slain from before the foundation of the world, a giving that in pure love only costs God. Divine "nature" is thus a concept that is to be

---

44. Torrance, *Trinitarian Faith,* p. 87. The point is a logical priority, not a temporal one, which would be question-begging.

gained *a posteriori* by relating power, wisdom, and love as attributed to the Three respectively in their economic roles, yielding then a conception of divine nature as living and dramatic harmony in being. More on this topic of the eternal nature is to come in the conclusion of this systematic theology. For the present, the point is that it is in just this light and only in this light that church and world divide into city of God and earthly city for the present time of the economy. At root, this is the division over the estimation of their shared space and time in the common body, whether to take it ultimately as "nature" as per the cosmogonic myth of the eternal return of the same or as "creation" on the way to glory as per the gospel promise of the resurrection of the Crucified. A corresponding division over God "the Father" ensues.

Yet such a stark juxtaposition is not quite adequate to the situation. Decisive even for this economic division of the world that longs to return to its pristine origin and the ecclesia that lives in anticipation of the Parousia in glory of the Crucified One is the matter of epistemic access for those living in exile from Paradise, as *fallen* creation, groaning and sighing for liberation in a state of frustration. Bonhoeffer, as we shall see, points us to the redemption of "the natural" as that which, after the Fall, is oriented to Christ. We do not understand this economic division in any case as a scientific one that sets up a foolish conflict between evolution and creationism, so called, but as something beyond science, something "metaphysical" from the one side and "theological" from the other. We are not talking about how the cosmos works piece by piece, part by part, discipline by discipline, but about how the concept of the cosmos as a whole may be taken by us as interested members of it who cannot live on the bread alone of principled and consistent agnosticism. While scientific disciplines work on the assumption of the uniformity of nature, this assumption would have to have access to the whole to be itself empirically demonstrated. Even though "the world" may thus understand itself "naturalistically," religiously then in terms of the cosmogonic myth, that construal of the whole indicates its own leap of faith.

Because of Christ who comes in freedom into the middle of time, always concretely to a particular place, however, the church cannot regard our shared space and time in the common body as a necessary unfolding or emanation of a principle of origin, not to mention some tragic self-alienation at the origin, as various iterations of the cosmogonic myth indicate. The Christian, theological notion of a creation that we commonly inhabit exhibits the notion of *the choice* of a world that would fall into sin yet be redeemed in Jesus Christ and fulfilled in the Spirit. That is certainly not the random play of all possible combinations of being in infinite succession as Spinoza and Nietzsche metaphysically imagined the divinity of sheer "naturalistic" becoming. What is the eternal return of the same, whose ancient symbol is the *Hakkenkreuz,* but the cosmogonic myth philosophically comprehended, *deus sive natura?* It is a misuse of language to call such a world "creation" at all, though it is the rival, today powerful, alternative conception of deity secretly but more and more openly believed as the genuine alternative to the Father who *creates* by his Son in his Spirit a world other than Himself; the *reward* that He showers upon these creatures as a place within His own eternal life by the coming of the Beloved Community that He eternally is; and the *judgment* of this love that He finally executes against what is against love.

To call upon God as Father, then, is to worship in union with the Son by the power of the Spirit the One who makes all things new. As Torrance put it, "This is a revelation of God's almightiness that conflicts with the ideas of limitless arbitrary power which we generate out of our worldly experiences, make infinite, and attribute to God, for the divine power manifest in Jesus Christ is of an altogether different kind. It is not in terms of what *we* think God *can do,* but in terms of what God *has done and continues to do* in Jesus Christ that we may understand something of what divine almightiness really is."[45] It is, as we shall see in conclusion, holy power as the infinite possession of possibilities always in creative conjunction with wisdom and love — *holy* in that it comes from the One and only Father, yet *living* in that it *comes* through the Son in the Spirit to *enliven* all that is not God.

We are "in the middle," as Bonhoeffer observed.[46] The canonical story of the Genesis-to-Revelation Bible, including its depictions of the origin and of the end, was itself constructed by extrapolating from the central events of redemptive history, the Exodus from Egyptian bondage and the resurrection of the Crucified.[47] The canonical story accordingly is not the dominant narrative of the status quo ante, i.e., the cosmogonic myth or its philosophical rationalizations, but exhibits the definite alternative story of *creatio ex nihilo,* deliteralized and theologically decoded as the coming of the Beloved Community. This biblical story and its theological understanding always work a division of the divisions by which the cosmos is cosmogonically structured: promising homeland to nomads by dispossessing the wicked, liberating the enslaved but hardening the heart of slavemasters, casting down the mighty from their thrones but exalting those of low degree, embracing lepers, teaching with authority to expel demons, pouring out the Spirit on little ones not wise in the foolish wisdom of the world. The beginning must lead to such a redemption, so theology reasons, and the end must follow from it, and in this way come together to make one story of the one God's creation in redemption and fulfillment — this creation being the earth on which the cross of Jesus stood, the common body in which we live and move and have our being.

God is God the Father who creates ex nihilo, and that creating pertains not only to the act of origin but also to its faithful continuation during the exile, its redemption — the justification of the ungodly — and fulfillment in the resurrection

---

45. Torrance, *Trinitarian Faith,* p. 82.

46. Dietrich Bonhoeffer, *Creation and Fall,* Dietrich Bonhoeffer Works, vol. 3, trans. D. S. Bax (Minneapolis: Fortress, 1997), pp. 8-31.

47. Gerhard von Rad, *Old Testament Theology,* vol. 1, trans. D. M. G. Stalker (New York: Harper & Row, 1962), pp. 136-39.

of the dead to the life eternal of the city of God. In these three "mysteries" of the works "which God reserves to Himself alone" (Luther), God shows Himself the almighty Father, the creator of all things other than God through His own Word in His own Spirit. In the Creed's three-act drama, creation is the *proprium,* the divine work especially attributed to the Father, who is the Father of the Son Jesus through whom He speaks-works *all* things past, present, and future in the Spirit.

The "almighty Father" of the Creed is, then, clearly *not* the cosmogonic father of the cosmos. The God of the Bible is not the sky god of ancient cosmogonies. That deity rather appears as the rival, the Baalim of Old Testament Scripture; his rain, like semen, fertilizes mother earth and brings forth fruit from it. "The fatherhood of YHWH is . . . a means of creation that shatters and completely replaces the sexual creation metaphor."[48] His altar is not a phallus, His cult is not sympathetic magic by means of imitative rites and/or expiatory sacrifices. For this almighty Father is precisely the Creator, who cannot be bought or bribed, neither controlled nor manipulated, but only feared, loved, and trusted above all as the one and only true God who lives eternally His own self-surpassing life and hence is free to give being and life to what is not. The fruit of His creative act is not the result of cooperation with other powers or capacities, but rather all other powers and capacities spring into being at His command and must willingly or unwilling serve His sovereign purpose of the coming of the Beloved Community. His purpose is life, true life, abundant life overcoming the anti-divine powers, redeeming the sinner, fulfilling the promise of creation in the coming of the Beloved Community that is antecedently and eternally the Almighty Father with His Son and Spirit.

If by "God" we indicate the principle or *arche* of the cosmos, then according to Christian theology "God" is this almighty Father — the "mon-archy." As *simply* self-surpassing, that is, *without loss* infinitely, unrestrictedly, boundlessly, and eternally generating the Son *from* His own being *as* His own being and breathing the Spirit *from* His own being *as* His own being upon the Son, the Father is *arche* in the divine life and so also fittingly of the creation *ad extra.* In just this particular way, the Father receives His own personal identity, eternally becoming the Father of the Son in the Spirit, that is to say, the Father receives His personal identity in the Spirit's return of the Son to Him in love, crying, Abba, Father! So "God" lives as this infinite cycle of giving and receiving that can infinitely fund all things that are not God.

Hence one might also say that in the fullness of time the Father's sending of the Son expresses this simple and eternal self-surpassing of divine life. In the Incarnation we creatures then have a "repetition" in time of what God eternally is, as the Father who so loved the world that He gave His only Son that we might receive and believe this gift and enter into its eternal life as those so gifted. That

---

48. Paul Mankowski, "The Gender of Israel's God," in *This Is My Name Forever: The Trinity and Gender Language for God,* ed. Alvin F. Kimmel Jr. (Downers Grove, IL: IVP, 2001), p. 58.

insight would be true, but it would not yet quite express the gospel that seeks and finds and wins us in *our sinfulness.* The incarnate Son's redemptive mission with us and for us is not simply the self-surpassing God repeating itself in time, for in fact this repetition in time is repetition into our "body of this death" (Rom. 7:24). The Son's identification with the sinfulness of the world at the cross is a true and fit expression of the eternal being of the self-surpassing Father, but it is self-surpassing, so to say, in a new way. The incarnation would have come about, hypothetically speaking, even if there had been no fall into sin. God the Father is self-surpassing, and so the sending of His Son to unite with humanity simply would have been the culmination of God's creation from its origin in fit expression of the infinite generosity that the almighty Father is. But the incarnate Son's identification on the cross with the sinful world is self-surpassing in a new and complex way that requires God to become our Father in a new and complex way.

Oswald Bayer has captured this view of *Deus actuosissimus* ("the most actual God") of *creatio continua* who "comes to the world only as the one who is always and already present in the world: *among* all creatures and *in* all of them. . . ." To speak of God "who comes," so Bayer deliteralizes and theologically decodes, is to say that "God's presence in the world is not self-evident and is not deserved."[49] It is to say that the coming of God is not a physical movement in space, as the mythical language of the Bible cannot but figure it, but rather another kind of movement within the divine life in its most actual relation to creatures. This divine movement makes evident to us an undeserved presence whereby the eternal Father of the Son becomes our Father too by the cross of His incarnate Son: "But God proves His love for us in that while we still were sinners Christ died for us" (Rom. 5:8). Just as we speak of the Spirit's formation of the theological subject by the death of the sinner in union with Christ and from this watery tomb His raising to newness of life, we have correspondingly to speak of God the Father "in motion" of love from wrath to mercy by new creation. In this way we have to describe and understand a new and complex episode in God's history with us, not simply as Incarnation taken as a repetition in time of a timeless love, but rather complexly as the timely reiteration of eternal love to create anew.

Bayer argues accordingly that "according to the Greek way of thinking, what belongs to the essence of God as essence itself is immortality, impassibility, and along with it the inability to experience emotions, which is known as apathy." Whether Bayer in this formulation thinks through the evangelical revision of divine "apathy" in patristic theology adequately or sufficiently is a question for the moment that we can leave to the side. Surely the paradox of "impassible passibility" that is formulated as early as Ignatius of Antioch resists any consistently kenotic reduction of God's being to sheer pathos. Bayer, at any rate, continues, "The deepest conflict with Greek metaphysics and ontology must of necessity

---

49. Oswald Bayer, *Martin Luther's Theology: A Contemporary Interpretation,* trans. Thomas H. Trapp (Grand Rapids: Eerdmans, 2007), p. 105.

come at the point where the biblical texts are taken with utter seriousness." Theologically we take the biblical text seriously when we deliteralize mythical accounts of divine motion and decode them as referring to the change that attends the life of God in relation to His creatures in the self-surpassing passage from wrath to mercy. So Bayer cites Hosea 11:7-11 for the "ontologically unthinkable": an "overthrow" (German: *Umsturz*), a "change within God himself: God is not the one who is identical with himself, who corresponds to himself" but is self-surpassing. He cites the biblical text: "My heart has changed within me; my remorse grows powerfully, I will not execute my fierce anger; I will not again destroy Ephraim; for I am God, not a human being."[50] One may say that this God — the reconciled God of God surpassing God in transit from wrath to mercy in His history with us made, and hence made known in Christ the Son's way to Golgotha — this God is truly the "God after God." Notably, Bayer draws Luther's "happy exchange" from the same prophetic resource in Hosea.[51]

Bayer has put his finger on the problem, but it is questionable whether he solved it (he would not think that "solving" it is a proper theological task). The Hebrew word translated "man" in 11:9, "for I am God, not a human being," is not *'adam* but *'ish,* i.e., not a human being as such but a male. In the context of Hosea's prophetic preaching, that would imply something like, "I, YHWH, the Holy One am not like a jealous husband enraged at an adulterous wife, intent on destructive revenge." So God's holiness, God's wholly otherness, the simplicity of divine being demarcating the incomparable One, apophatically qualifies the dramatically kataphatic language likening God's relation to Israel to a troubled marriage. So James Luther Mays wrote in his commentary on this text: ". . . in v. 8 Yahweh speaks as a man incapable of action because of his divided feelings. . . . But now the resolution of Yahweh is grounded on his utter difference from man. The apparent inconsistency is a warning that Hosea's many anthropomorphisms are meant as interpretative analogies, not essential definitions. . . . In the dramatic metaphor the personal reality of Yahweh's incursion into human life and history is present and comprehensible. But he transcends the metaphor, is different from that to which he is compared, and free of all its limitations. He is wrathful and loving *like* man, but *as* God."[52]

The familiar analogical doctrine of language regarding God appears here in Mays's sophisticated interpretation in which the similitudes by which God is made comparable with familiar things in our world is granted. But the comparison is then qualified by God's transcendent simplicity in being as Holy One. True so far as it goes, this too does not quite resolve the problem that Bayer identifies; indeed, it rather obscures it in another way. We have to wonder whether the unknowable distinction, "*like* man, but *as* God" is anything more than a pious gloss.

50. Bayer, *Martin Luther's Theology*, p. 215.
51. Bayer, *Martin Luther's Theology*, pp. 225-30.
52. James Luther Mays, *Hosea: A Commentary* (Philadelphia: Westminster, 1969), p. 157.

Do we in this way all too "simply" evade Bayer's insight into the "overthrow" in the God who does not remain identical with Himself but rather surpasses Himself? Do we all too "simply" return in this way to unbaptized Greek metaphysics in which the metaphysical notion of divine simplicity-cum-apathy renders unthinkable Hosea's account of the cost to God of God's true incursion into sinful human life and history that puts God in conflict with God?

We take the biblical text seriously when we deliteralize it and decode it theologically to tell about movement in the uniquely divine life: God is God as self-surpassing not only as font or origin in the eternal Trinity but also in relation to us when by costly grace He becomes our Father too "while we were yet enemies" (Rom. 5:10). Bayer is content to suggest; he declines to move fully towards the revision of metaphysics entailed by the gospel, theologically understood. Mays neutralizes the pathos of God in the name of divine simplicity. Between the two positions, we can see that the manifest difficulty in taking the biblical text seriously as theology is real. As we shall see, Walter Brueggemann has profoundly explored this problem at the heart of Christian patrology, as pinpointed in Hosea 11: "these two characterizations of Yahweh" — that is, as wrathful and as merciful, are both present in the biblical texts, but "are in profound tension with each other" and indeed "finally they contradict each other." And, he adds, "if we take these statements as serious theological disclosures, then the tension or contradiction here voiced is present in the very life and character of Yahweh."[53]

In this light, the faith of Jesus in the heavenly Father is a defiant faith in the reconciled God of Hosea 11:8-9, YHWH of Israel. Jesus heard Him calling Him "beloved Son," whom He in turn called Abba, and in filial obedience to His will He took responsibility before Him for us, just as Hosea did for Gomer. In the obedience of this faith of Jesus in God the Father, the tension in the life of the God of love between wrath and mercy was met and resolved once and for all by God in God, so that wherever and whenever the Spirit wills, it is resolved on earth as in heaven by baptism into Christ's death and resurrection. The "fatherhood" of God, as a result, can so little be assumed or taken for granted as the complacent similitude of cosmos piety; it is something gained for us as also for God in the singular act of supreme, self-surpassing life that is the sending of the Son into the likeness of sinful flesh.

"God after God" is the God surpassing God, the almighty Father who begets the Son and breathes the Spirit. To come to such faith in God as "the Father" concretely, already now in the travail of the creation, is to regard the Father as the reconciled God of Hosea 11:9 in the teeth of contrary experience, hence as the *final* audience of theology; this regard of God as the Father in faith is to pray as Jesus taught His disciples, in the power of Jesus' own articulated obedience, as that is given to them as gift by the Spirit. So we now turn to the *teaching* of Jesus

---

53. Walter Brueggemann, *Theology of the Old Testament: Testimony, Dispute, Advocacy* (Minneapolis: Augsburg Fortress, 1997), p. 227.

on the fatherhood of God. Jesus *taught* His disciples to live before God, already now, in anticipation of the eschaton of judgment. He could succeed in *teaching* them this way not only if He Himself lived and died in just this faith but if, and only if, this lived act of obedient faith in "our heavenly Father," even to death on a cross, was vindicated, and can hence be given to disciples by the Spirit as the completed gift of His vindicated faith.

As we saw in Part Two of this work, the teaching of Jesus forms a seamless garment with His destiny and constitutes an object in the world that, under the proper conditions of epistemic access, can and must be known if Jesus is to be present and active to us, like Hosea to Gomer, in the joyful exchange of His righteousness for our sinfulness, His prayer of trust displacing our religious bribes. The proper Christological condition of our hearing and receiving the teaching of Jesus regarding the heavenly Father, then, includes the theological subject's own venture of faith in living conscientiously before God.

This venture comes with all the attendant possibilities of habituated and habitual bad faith, e.g., where the "fatherhood" of God is taken as pretext for masculine privilege or imperial domination, for absence or for intrusion as the case may be. Bad faith occurs when we displace the strictly Christological analogy of divine fatherhood and take it instead as theism's similitude, the highest good within cosmos-piety, that is accordingly to be understood by the more familiar term of our own experience of fatherhood (warped as that is by structures of malice and injustice). But faith takes the Christological analogy for what it is in the gospel narrative that gives it: the evident contradiction of the Father of the particularly beloved Son, Jesus, who gives Him into the hands of sinners, over to shameful death and abandonment. "Divine child abuse," indeed. There is nothing obviously commendable here yet, nothing "self-evident" and "deserved." Like "Christ crucified," the appeal to "Abba, Father" in the Gethsemane of our own souls is an evident contradiction whose paradoxical sense, if it is not nonsense or illusion, must be decoded by discovery of its novel reference in the world, as in the revelation of Mark 9:7-8.

The unspoken bias of theologically naïve modern quests for the "historical Jesus" — enunciated with clarity more than a century ago by Adolf von Harnack — is that the "fatherhood" of God is an unproblematic articulation of the simple goodness of the deity, so that if only we could get back behind the early Christian mythologizing of Jesus as the divine Son, we could have His own human faith in God's fatherly goodness as a foundation for our faith. In the process, much critical doubt has been cast upon the fidelity of the primitive Christian traditions, as codified in canonical Scriptures, in conveying the historical faith of the man Jesus. The bias, as just argued, is ungrounded. It is highly problematical in principle and even more problematical in fact to join Jesus in calling upon God as our heavenly Father. No one can, unless drawn by the excruciating Spirit into Jesus' own faith, hence into His own righteousness, hence into His own destiny in the conflicted world by the Gethsemane of that believer's own soul.

If, moreover, as Luke 11:1 suggests, the Lord's Prayer was given to disciples to identify them as followers of Jesus in distinction from the Baptist's disciples, the Lord's Prayer was already assuming a creedal function in the most primitive Christianity, namely, to identify God in the world and enable knowledgeable life before Him by union with Jesus the Son who invites disciples to pray with Him. In that case, wherever and whenever the ecclesia joins Jesus in the kingdom prayer, it takes upon itself the yoke of the very faith of the man. So little should modern pretensions to an alternative knowledge of the "historical Jesus" trouble theological subjects, who by the Spirit of the Son sent into their hearts, cry, "Abba! Father" (Gal. 4:6). With Jesus, to know God as our heavenly Father — before whom those united with the Son live in the power of the Spirit — brings upon believers an entirely different world of trouble.

## The Faith of Jesus in the Heavenly Father

Can God truthfully be named, as in the address, "Our Father in heaven"? Should not this gender-biased and one-sidedly "transcendent" perspective on God be balanced with feminine immanence, say as some have proposed, "Our Mother who is within us"? If "fatherhood" is intended as the similitude of cosmos piety, the question is surely apt; the father sky god cannot be fertile without mother earth. Baal needs Ashtoreth. But the assumption at work in the question — that naming God is expressive of our own spiritual aspiration to find our niche in the cosmic order rather than doxological confession of the Word that God has spoken to us in Jesus Christ and given His Spirit that we may hear, trust, and obey in the passage from wrath to mercy on the way to the Beloved Community of God — is massively inept, Christianly speaking. Still, there is genuine difficulty here.

In his *The Divine Name(s) and the Holy Trinity: Distinguishing the Voices*,[54] R. Kendall Soulen takes up an "unhappy paradox" that Jacques Derrida found in Exodus 3:14-15, the gift of the divine Name to Moses at the Burning Bush. He cites Derrida's puzzlement over the divine name, Yahweh: "Translate me, don't translate me. On the one hand, don't translate me, that is, respect me as a proper name. . . . And, on the other hand, translate me, that is, understand me, preserve me within the universal language, follow my law, and so on." Soulen notes Derrida's perplexity at the puzzling coalescence of apophatic and kataphatic ways in the text only in order to assert that the apparent contradiction is "simply transcended" when the purely referential proper name, YHWH, and the inter-

---

54. R. Kendall Soulen, *The Divine Name(s) and the Holy Trinity: Distinguishing the Voices*, vol. 1 (Louisville: Westminster John Knox, 2011). The following discussion is in part excerpted from Paul R. Hinlicky, "Quaternity or Patrology? A Response to Soulen," *Pro Ecclesia* 23, no. 1 (Winter 2014): 46-52.

pretative paraphrases of it as "I AM," or "I AM WHO I AM," are *"taken together."*[55] The kataphatic assertion of the unintelligible proper name, YHWH, described as the Tetragrammaton, is reverenced apophatically by its nonpronunciation and the substitution of surrogate terms for it in Jewish piety. This yields, according to Soulen, a real albeit mysterious Subject who nevertheless comes to own and bless by the many names creatures ascribe to it, by virtue of the interpretative I AM who will be for them Shepherd and King, Friend and Lover, Rock and Womb, as creaturely need contextually requires.

This key move of qualifying the kataphatic apophatically has promise. Such kataphatic predicates, variably refracted in the finite language of the creature's praise and thanksgiving by the Spirit's evocation, are determined in turn by their contextual suitability to articulate the constant of the divine *coming* and *blessing* of this uncanny, ever-elusive *Subject*. The divine Subject, as indicated by the oblique Tetragrammaton, *causes* that Name (YHWH) to be remembered in order to *come* and to *bless* in all the variegated situations of creaturely need. Soulen mines this threefold articulation of God as causal agent, advent, and blessing from Exodus 20:24b ("... in every place where I cause my name to be remembered I will come to you and bless you"), and he conceives of it as the primary or "theological pattern" of Trinitarian discourse. It tells the divine uniqueness from the vantage point of the first of the Trinitarian persons, the One who causes. After sorting out how subsequent Christological and Pneumatological patterns and their relations also articulate the divine uniqueness of the first person, each in their respective ways, Soulen concludes that the "most appropriate way of naming the persons of the Trinity consists precisely in the three patterns together, as mutually illuminating, nonidentical repetitions of each other."[56]

The innovative and critical edge of Soulen's argument lies in his claim that the first pattern, with its basis in the Hebrew Scriptures, has as such gone unacknowledged in Christian theological history, even though it is silently operative throughout, even in the Nicene Creed. The church has never ceased also to speak of "the LORD" in this way with Israel reverencing the divine Name by a surrogate term. Jesus Himself and the apostles regularly employ the divine passive to the same end. When Jesus addresses God as Abba-Father, He is speaking of none other than this unutterable God of Israel, just as Gentile believers adopted into His filial relation with God turn from idols to the true and living God (1 Thess. 1:9), who gave His Name at the Burning Bush, who causes this Name to be remembered in order to come and to bless. But loss of articulate awareness of this primary pattern of Trinitarian naming due to the original schism of Jews and Gentiles has had debilitating consequences. Loss of it has worked to pit the other two subsequent patterns of Trinitarian naming against each other, when their harmony in fact depends on the one causal Subject who comes in Christ to bless by the Spirit.

---

55. Soulen, *The Divine Name(s)*, p. 273, n. 11, emphasis original.
56. Soulen, *The Divine Name(s)*, p. 255.

But when this monarchy of this Subject is forgotten, the second, Christological pattern of "kinship terms," namely of Father, Son, and Holy Spirit, claims for itself a stifling exclusivity at the price of kataphatic absurdity (as in contemporary perceptions of Father and Son as privileging masculine gender or, more seriously, the objection to the present proposal that it verges on tritheism). The third Pneumatological pattern of open-ended ternaries (as in Augustine's "vestiges" or as in contemporary experimentation, e.g., McFague's "Mother, Lover, Friend") liberates itself from Christological exclusivity and kataphatic absurdity at the terrible price of an ultimate agnosticism: we can play with many names for God just because no name names God truly or adequately. But, Soulen proposes, when we recover awareness of the primary "theological" pattern, we learn anew how to let all three patterns have their proper place and play in mutually enlightening ways. This is so because the Jewish apophaticism — of reverencing the divine Name of the Subject by referring to it obliquely — honors divine uniqueness not in spite of but on account of the gift of the Name. Thus it does not point in the dark, signing a "God beyond God," but believes God as self-giving in advent and blessing. In the threefold sequence of cause, advent and blessing, the patrological point is that God as Subject is the *fons divinitatis* in the divine life and just so the Sender of the Son and the Spirit in the economy, who in these latter patterns can be named Christologically the Father of the Son upon whom He breathes His Spirit, or Pneumatologically as say, "Life, Life Bestowed, Life Imparted," or "Source, Well-Spring, Living Water,"[57] or "God Speaks, God Is Spoken, God Is Heard," et cetera as context requires and the Spirit gives utterance.

Soulen's contribution is enormous, not least in specifying the personhood of the Father, the God of Israel: this is a needed step, as Jenson called for, towards the "patrology" that overcomes the Western tendency toward modalism.[58] Yet in an unfortunate formulation, Soulen can also write: "While the uniqueness of the first person can be represented by a variety of linguistic tokens (Father, Font of Divinity, etc.), there is only one of these whose role consists solely in pointing, in gesturing away from itself to the transcendent, unfathomable mystery of its bearer,"[59] namely, the Tetragrammaton. Such formulations would seem to sketch a rather different argument, namely, that the mystery of divine being lies beyond in some unknowable transcendence rather than, as Soulen has for the most part argued, in *causing* presence and blessing. Yet this other line of argument is not without a significant role in Soulen's book. The gift of the apophatic sign points away to the thing signified, namely a transcendent and incomprehensible divine Subject to which our naming of God in turn is accountable. This, let us say, "Barthian" move serves to preclude the Feuerbachian reduction of God as Subject to

---

57. Soulen, *The Divine Name(s)*, pp. 249-50.
58. Jenson, *ST* 1, p. 115.
59. Soulen, *The Divine Name(s)*, p. 254.

the empty cipher on which the religion business hangs human projections (the great vulnerability of the unhinged Pneumatological pattern). To the extent that Soulen follows this Barth-against-Feuerbach line of thought, however, we are set back again on the horns of Derrida's dilemma, where the kataphatic Name refers apophatically to a Great Unknown, a sign absent of the thing signified.

We are rightly commanded not to take the name of God in vain as a first principle in theology (Exod. 20:7; Deut. 5:11). Does Soulen propose obedience to this rule by means of apophatic reserve in respect of the divine singularity and in this sense incomparability of the kataphatic Name caused by God in order that God come and bless? Or does he propose obedience by construing the Name itself as the apophatic sign of an unknown Thing Signified (yet inconsequently attributing causal agency to it)? The latter cannot actually be attributed to God's self-donation without knowing what cannot be known (God as causal agent in the world); it in fact arises out of the chaotic polyonymy of divine names for seeking God beyond the gods, beyond language, by direct intuition in the mystics, or by arising to a beatific vision in heaven, or even in infinite resignation, as in Derrida. It is the way of human ascent, not divine descent. This latter apophaticism stems from the tradition of Pseudo-Dionysius, which asserts an infinite divine "essence" beyond essence, existence, and all naming.[60] In this neo-Platonic tradition, not only St. Thomas (as Soulen discusses), but also the Lutheran Thomas, Johann Gerhard, takes the Tetragrammaton to indicate metaphysically the absolutely simple divine substance or ousia,[61] not then, if I understand Soulen's intention correctly, the hypostasis of the First of the Three, the causal agent of His own coming and blessing. Unbaptized, or insufficiently catechized, the Dionysian train of thought at work here leads either to open modalism or to the more subtle error of teaching a quaternity, where the unknowable divine essence is de facto hypostasized as God beyond the named persons of Father, Son, and Holy Spirit.

Indeed, Soulen — inadvertently, if I have correctly grasped the true thrust of his argument — names the first pattern "theological" rather than "patrological." Citing Thomas, he rightly avers that the very *gift* of the divine Name means that *deus non est in genere,* but surely he ought to continue as the argument would seem to indicate, *sed in nomine.* The very opacity of the divine Name, YHWH, indicates a Who, a Subject, that is, an inscrutability, a God hidden also in this revelation, thus a *deus absconditus,* just as the first half of John 1:18 concurs: "No one has ever seen God." But this inscrutability is asserted so that we may "come and see" (John 1:46), eyes open and ears alert for the coming and blessing this very questionable God promises in giving this unutterable name to be remembered in all its mystery. Surely then, just on this basis, Christian theology must

---

60. Soulen, *The Divine Name(s),* pp. 62-67.

61. Johann Gerhard, *On the Nature of God and On the Most Holy Mystery of the Trinity, Theological Commonplaces,* trans. Richard J. Ginda (St. Louis: Concordia, 2007), p. 21.

continue in all offensive exclusiveness to make the anti-Arian claim: "It is God the only Son, who is close to the Father's heart, who has made him known," that is, who has made the mysterious Subject of the Tetragrammaton known as the Father of Jesus Christ, just as John 1:18 concludes. Christian theology accordingly takes the Tetragrammaton given at the Burning Bush as God's own question for us about God's identity in time and space; this is a self-introduction that summons to come and see and so to discover the manifestation of the self-surpassing Father as God's answer to God's own question about who God will be for us in the fullness of time in the space that Jesus bodily occupies "full of grace and truth" (John 1:14). This construal of salvation history reflects both the continuity and the novelty between the Testaments. What Soulen contributes to such a construction is fresh awareness that the question indicated by the gift of the Tetragrammaton is to be preserved so that the patrological answer is received as a living one, i.e., that the uncanny "subjectivity" of God who will be who God will be is revealed in the self-surpassing "fatherhood" made known in the filial obedience of Jesus and so received by us through grant of their Spirit making us the children of God by baptismal adoption.

The Christian theological subject, as we recall, is formed by baptism in the name of the Father, the Son, and Holy Spirit. Baptismal seeing and hearing gives a *deus revelatus,* albeit for faith alone and so ever against the background of divine inscrutability, as this dialectic may be seen in Luther's catechetical teaching on the baptismal Creed: "For in all three articles God himself has revealed and opened to us the most profound depths of his fatherly heart and his pure, *unutterable* love [*unaussprechlicher Liebe,* emphasis added]. For this very purpose he created us, so that he might redeem us and make us holy, and, moreover, having granted and bestowed us everything in heaven and on earth, he has also given us his Son and his Holy Spirit, through whom he brings us to himself."[62] Here we have an apophatic qualification, unutterable, of the kataphatic affirmation at the heart of the gospel, divine self-donation and self-communication. The inscrutable Name of God opens its mystery as a fiery furnace of love for us in the divine self-donation of the Son sent from the Father's self-surpassing heart to reclaim us in the self-communicating Spirit for the Beloved Community. It is this kataphatic self-giving of the God whose essence is to give, and this alone as it named and confessed and so believed, that overcomes Derrida's unhappy paradox, not by "transcending" it but by deliteralizing and decoding it. It is not overcome in any case merely by asserting the univocity of the canonical text in its final form, which begs the question of how the unity of the Testaments is to be conceived and who it is who so perceives their unity — questions that we have explored in Part One of this book.

Soulen is rightly concerned with the post-Holocaust problem for Christian theology of its supersessionist tradition, and is seeking to overcome it. Yet, as

62. *BC,* p. 439.

Jacob Neusner has taught us[63] and none other than Richard L. Rubenstein has recently acknowledged,[64] there can be neither normative Judaism nor early catholic Christianity without supersessionism in *some* sense, *carefully* to be defined. For *both* Jew *and* Christian, the LORD has put an end to the sacrificial system of worship in the Jerusalem Temple. For the rabbis this happened on account of the sins of the Jewish people in neglecting Torah with the result that Judaism in diaspora must now become a living temple, making a true sacrifice of praise and good works. For Catholics[65] this has happened on account of Messiah's cross, which once and for all fulfilled and thus in one sense preserved and in another abrogated the instituted rites of atonement in the Temple, with the result that the mission of the gospel to the nations proceeds, founding Eucharistic communities in anticipation of Messiah's coming in glory. It is, then, *quite another thing* to continue on from these foundational Jewish and Christian convictions on the supersession of the Temple to the teaching that God has rejected His people, Israel. Wherever triumphalist Christian or despairing Jewish thought comes to this, it errs.

Soulen himself thus acknowledges that "[i]n the final analysis, the reliability of God's presence is not a function of the temple per se, but of the name that he has caused to dwell in it. Just as God once freely chose the temple, so he remains free to abandon it."[66] By the same token of divine freedom, God may give His Name as a question and in the fullness of time give His Name anew as an answer to His own question. But, Soulen argues, naming the first person as Father articulates God's uniqueness not "as such [i.e., as supposedly does the Tetragrammaton], but rather [as] presence: the first person is the *Father* of the Son,"[67] "the One whose very being is in coming."[68] But this is inept. Characteristically in the New Testament, the Father sends the Son who speaks in His name. Otherwise, we are taking the Tetragrammaton as an apophatic sign that articulates the first person as absence, as infinite *beyond* the named God of the second and third patterns rather than *in* them. In Trinitarian terms, then, the question is whether Soulen's first "theological" pattern names God as ousia or as hypostasis. Soulen surely intends to speak of the first divine person as hypostasis, not ousia. But the question remains whether an abyss opens here between hypostasis and ousia, if His name is

63. Jacob Neusner with William Scott Green, *Writing with Scripture: The Authority and the Uses of the Hebrew Bible in the Torah of Formative Judaism* (Minneapolis: Augsburg Fortress, 1989).

64. Richard L. Rubenstein, "Religion and the Uniqueness of the Holocaust," chapter 2 in *Is the Holocaust Unique? Perspectives on Comparative Genocide,* ed. Alan S. Rosenbaum (Philadelphia: Westview, 2009), p. 40.

65. The depth of this ecumenical conviction is visible in Matthew Levering's study, *Christ's Fulfillment of Torah and Temple: Salvation according to Thomas Aquinas* (Notre Dame: University of Notre Dame Press, 2002).

66. Soulen, *The Divine Name(s),* p. 154, cf. p. 172.

67. Soulen, *The Divine Name(s),* p. 231.

68. Soulen, *The Divine Name(s),* p. 178.

and evidently remains the unutterable question mark, YHWH, pointing beyond itself to the unknowable that as such is only made utterable for us as the Father through the coming to us of the Son and blessing of the Spirit. Against this danger, critical dogmatics has to maintain that there is no divine essence existing apart, transcendentally causing things in general, which may or may not be connected to its own presence in the Son and blessing in the Spirit. It is the eternal Father who sends the Son and the Spirit. If that is so, the divine essence *is* the Father of the Son and Breather of the Spirit, who is essentially related to Son and Spirit as Begetter and Breather respectively.

If we resolve the ambiguity in Soulen's presentation in this direction, we indeed find Soulen's repeated paraphrases of the "theological" first person amounting to kataphatic patrology insofar as they avoid agnostic essentialism: "as a kind of *fons divinitatis*,"[69] "whose voice sounds the mystery of divine uniqueness at the source of the divine life,"[70] "the sourceless source of all the music of the divine life."[71] We are in such deliverances given the first person in its divinely self-surpassing uniqueness — not as a purely abiding Question Mark, as the Arian-Eunomian reification of a negation, an *Agennetos* or its modern equivalent, *das Unbedingt*. But we are given the Person, the very Subject who took the name, Yahweh, as a self-introduction to "come and see," hence in the fullness of time revealed as the Father of our Lord Jesus Christ, the unbegotten begetter of the Son and unbreathed breather of the Spirit. This is God's revealed uniqueness as the eternal Father strong to save, which remains a mystery also in its revealedness as faith awaits and can only await its eschatological confirmation. That this Father is not my father or your father, but our Father by virtue of baptismal adoption into the family of God, hence our *heavenly* Father, suffices to preserve the penumbra of mystery that from the beginning of salvation history was indicated by gift of the divine Name to His people, Israel. The sense of this gift, according to Christian faith, is spelled out in the prayer by which Jesus invited disciples to enter into His own filial relation with the God of Israel who sent Him, and thus who, by His Spirit, now also sends them in mission to the nations to proclaim and enjoy and suffer the coming of the Beloved Community.

*"Our Father, who art in heaven, hallowed be Thy name . . ."*

Jesus' prayer invites hearers into His own relation with the heavenly Father (we will exposit the version in Matt. 6:9-13).[72] As faith in promised mercy at Jesus' command-and-promise, the address to God as "our Father" expresses His own

69. Soulen, *The Divine Name(s)*, p. 23.
70. Soulen, *The Divine Name(s)*, p. 177.
71. Soulen, *The Divine Name(s)*, p. 173.
72. Harner, *The Lord's Prayer*, p. 55.

faith in the God of Israel as well as in their own new status as beloved children and heirs. "The reason He commands [us to pray this way] is, of course, not in order to have us make our prayers an instruction to Him as to what He ought to give us, but in order to have us acknowledge and confess that He is already bestowing many blessings upon us and that He can and will give us still more. By our praying, therefore, we are instructing ourselves more than we are Him. . . . When my heart is turned to Him and awakened this way, then I praise Him, thank Him, take refuge with Him in my need, and expect help from Him . . . more and more acknowledg[ing] what kind of God He is. . . . It is the truest, highest, and most precious worship which we can render to Him; for it gives Him the glory that is due Him."[73] The petitions thus mold those who pray this way into the particular way of life of the new family of God which Jesus gathers. "For whoever does the will of my Father in heaven is my brother and sister and mother" (Matt. 12:50).

It is imperative for understanding that the prayer not be detached from the address of Jesus to disciples: "Come, follow me and I will make you fish for people" (Matt. 4:19). This way together seeking others is *new*, in that those regarded as least by the skewed values of the present order — the fishermen of Galilee — have become instead the most precious here: "So it is not the will of your Father in heaven that one of these little ones should be lost" (Matt. 18:14). The gathering of such unlikely people and their formation into the new, out-reaching family of God *is* the saving event of "God with us" (Matt. 1:23) already now at work on the earth, as pronounced in the Beatitudes (Matt. 5:3-12). "No other Gospel is so shaped by the thought of the Church as Matthew's, so constructed for use by the Church; for this reason it has exercised, as no other, a normative influence in the later Church" (G. Bornkamm).[74] The heavenly Father's will is done on earth as in heaven through the ecclesia, which dares even to execute the judgment of mercy in Jesus' name: "I will give you the keys of the kingdom of heaven, and whatever you bind on earth will be bound in heaven, and whatever you loose on earth will be loosed in heaven" (Matt. 16:19; 18:18). Therefore, the unlikely community of the least, this most improbable heir of the kingdom, already now shares in the secret of God's royal rule on the earth, though not by means of earthly sword of steel. It rules with words that forgive and retain sin — it rules in the arena of *conscience*. This is the secret of its true power, the power of the Spirit who in love unites the Father and the Son, and so unites believers with the Son before the Father by the forgiveness of their sins — and in the very act also judges what is against this love, not least the merciless failure to forgive in turn the sins of others.

As disciples are to know God in this improbable community that Jesus gathers, so they are disciplined in prayer to know the heavenly Father as "ours," not

---

73. *LW* 21, pp. 144-45.

74. "End Expectation and Church in Matthew," in *Tradition and Interpretation in Matthew* (Philadelphia: Westminster, 1963), p. 38. So Matthew also has pride of place in the canonical ordering of New Testament writings.

"mine," thus in an inclusive way that begins with the community but acknowledges no human identity boundaries. Only the beloved Son Jesus by right speaks of God as "my" Father; it is by grace that His relation to God is extended to others and becomes also theirs and thus may become that of others equally as improbable as one's own self. Thus God is to be invoked *by the community* (i.e., by the individual too, of course, but *as* a member of the community) in a peculiar combination of intimacy ("Father") and distance ("in heaven"), of "immanence" and "transcendence." Yet the transcendence of "heaven" here is to be deliteralized and decoded, as argued above, just as the immanence of the name, father, is to be taken strictly by the analogy with Jesus as son, not as a general similitude.

The heavenly Father exists as the Personal Difference generating all other differences, both divine and human; He is the self-surpassing Father of His own Son Jesus, and through Him, becomes the Father Creator who gives life to each and all by His own Word in His own Spirit. God the Father is personally present as the One who gives being in these generative and creative actions that individuate persons and at the same time summon them into the harmony of charity with other persons, returning to Him only the glory that is due in praise of gifts, acknowledgment as "our Father." This summons of difference to charity is the "transcendence" of heaven, deliteralized and decoded theologically. By that token, we may say in a way reminiscent of Levinas that this Father God hides Himself under the mask of each unique other encountered in the evident contingencies of historical existence, there summoning charity. His heavenly being "in secret" among us is this self-hiding in presenting Himself in the face of the other person cast on our path. By this the Creator commands concrete love *of His creation in the face of some particular other,* summoning difference to charity, creatively making harmony out of chaos. Being "thrown into the world" (Heidegger), for the believer, is not an absurd fate but rather experience of the infant asking for and the adult being asked for love, in the continuous creation that makes neighbors.

As inclusively "our" heavenly Father, the Father is "the Lord of Heaven and earth," the cause of all causes who "throws" each and all into the world next to others, calling and being called to love. Thus God the Father is "the Creator of all natures . . . the giver of all powers — though He is not the maker of all choices" (Augustine).[75] The distinction Augustine urges here is a difficult one, but crucial; it is the distinction discussed previously on several occasions between the *Alleswirksamkeit Gottes* and the *Alleinwirksamkeit Gottes,* that is, the Creator as universally operative and the Creator as alone operative, respectively. Both constructions of God's continuous creativity destabilize exaggerated claims for human and political sovereignty, but the former permits moral evil to creatures and the latter makes God the moral author of evil. There can be no genuine conception of sin in the latter, then, unless one is willing to speak of the sin of God

---

75. Augustine, *The City of God,* ed. Vernon J. Bourke (New York: Doubleday, 1958), V.9; p. 107.

in making beings like us, intelligent creatures with wills of our own. Nor then can there be any sense to salvation as deliverance from sin (Matt. 1:21), both its guilt by forgiveness and its power by the Spirit's grant of new life together in the ecclesia, as parsed in the "Our Father." To be sure, only in the light of redemption in Christ promising fulfillment in the Spirit can faith glimpse how God is not weak but powerful in creating a world of intelligent creatures with wills of their own, including the permission of moral evil that gift entails.

The almighty Father is powerful because to respect conscience, also erring conscience, requires the restraint of Hosea 9:11, a self-surpassing mastery holy and divine that expresses the patiency of love and exhibits conscience in respecting conscience. Only intelligent creatures can sin willingly and in their sinfulness exercise conscience sinfully to justify their sin as precisely their own feeling, apathy, or deed. As you believe, so you have. God's creating of creatures manifestly enables their sin, but does not commit their sins, which are properly the failures, omissions, and deeds of intelligent creatures with wills of their own to own or disown them. The differentiation between image and likeness of God tells how God's *creatio continua* calls every individual in every moment to free, joyful, and intelligent service and just so empowers the creature to rebel against this vocation as well as surrender to it. Paradoxically, then, one is unfree in election, for it is God who universally creates and calls, but therewith freed for service or rebellion, for sin or righteousness. The decisive difference between sin and righteousness, then, presses beyond this initial paradox in the direction of eschatological creation. It cannot be resolved on the basis of a static theism where God creates free will and watches passively to see whether creatures will merit reward or punishment.[76] The paradox of free will bound in Adam to sinful self-assertion resolves in coming to know "our" heavenly Father with the true limitlessness of this predication that is shown in Christ the Son — He who first becomes a neighbor to us and makes us neighbors one to another, rather sisters and brothers, in the newborn family of God. Such is the righteousness of God for all who believe.

There is a decisive difference in the conscience of the priest and Levite of Jesus' parable (Luke 10:29-37) who pass by the stricken man on the road and the Samaritan who becomes a neighbor to him. "Our" heavenly Father is limitlessly operative in the face of such an other, especially the other who is stricken, there summoning each one to charity; but as hidden in the small face of the stricken, this infinite summons of God to charity does not and will not physically coerce the passerby to this righteous will of His (as natural laws "force" natural happenings like gravity "forcing" the falling apple to the ground). The dignity of the human person, who conscientiously chooses and persists in the choice of filling the image of God that he is with unlikeness to God by religious narrowness or

76. Frances Young, "'Creatio ex nihilo': A Context for the Emergence of the Christian Doctrine of Creation," *Scottish Journal of Theology* 44 (1991): 139-51.

ethnic bigotry or loveless apathy, is respected in this way of its choice, that is, in the permission of God that enables the sinner's lovelessness. He may pass by the stricken with no physical consequence and even, so far as he is concerned, with a "good conscience." God acts as God in this very permission, respecting the dignity of the evildoer even in his actual evil that harms the other by failing to help. The almighty Father summons only by a word of obligation spoken in the face of the broken and crushed; as an ethical instruction to charity it is truly fulfilled only as it is obeyed freely and joyfully. But this is the obedience of faith that arises from the revelation of the righteousness of God in Christ who first became a neighbor to loveless sinners.

The heavenly Father does this righteousness conquering sinfulness in the person of His Son, the One who in turn identified Himself with the naked, the imprisoned, the hungry (Matt. 25:40), the One who becomes a neighbor even also to the bystander and the passerby by taking their place before God who damns Dives to hell for his merciless hardness of heart. Charity — that is to say, infinite generosity — is the moral law of God who gives that now reigns in the new conscience of the children of "our" heavenly Father, who receive the burdens of others as providentially given opportunities for creative acts of love and justice.

Those invited by Jesus to address God as our Father hallow His name, then, by charity on the earth that fills the image of God that each one is with true likeness to God who gives. At the beginning of the Sermon on the Mount, Jesus instructs: "Let your light shine before others, so that they may see your good works and give glory to your Father in heaven" (Matt. 5:16). Disciples learn that they are so to act towards enemies and persecutors that they "may be children of your Father in heaven" (Matt. 5:45). The heavenly Father's perfection is *generosity,* the capacity by which God surpasses God in giving, even to reconciling enemies by giving His Son into their hands, yet for their sakes. So the heavenly Father is perfect (Matt. 5:48), *esse Deum dare.* This perfection of love is manifest in the heavenly Father's care for them, which they are to know and to trust on Jesus' saying so ("But I say to you . . ."; Matt. 5:22, 28, 32, 34, 39, 44; 6:25; 7:24-27, 29). In saying so, Jesus presciently attacks the unbelieving materialism of His listeners — not in this case, the wealthy who will not listen to Him at all who blesses the poor, but also the poor who would be rich: "Therefore do not worry, saying, 'What will we eat?' or 'What will we drink?' or 'What will we wear?' For it is the Gentiles who strive for these things; and indeed your heavenly Father knows that you need all these things. But strive first for the kingdom of God and his righteousness, and all these things will be given to you as well" (Matt. 6:31-33). So the name by which the all-mighty, all-knowing, all-good God who gives is to be invoked, "Father," is to be used reverently. It is to be invoked inclusively with respect to all others to whom one can be brother or sister, but exclusively with respect to deity: "And call no one your father on earth, for you have one Father — the one in heaven" (Matt. 23:9). That is how God's name as "our" Father is hallowed.

God's name is sanctified, not by the pretentious silence of those who will not know anything in faith, not to mention do anything obedient in the body, but by its proper use, which is to believe God in this way of concrete obedience that Jesus proclaims and exemplifies as the true Son of this Father in His own life of faith. The proper use of God's name is based upon its proper meaning, and the proper meaning of God's Fatherhood is given and made known in Jesus' Sonship, the Father's gift making the Giver known. Because of Jesus, the proper meaning of the invocation, *our heavenly Father,* is an instruction to include all, even, indeed especially enemies, and so the proper use of God's name is the worship of God which in thanksgiving for His gift *reaches out and brings in the nations* "according to the command of the eternal God, to bring about the obedience of faith," as Matthew concludes (28:19-20) in harmony with the doxologies of the Pauline tradition: "to the only wise God, through Jesus Christ, to whom be the glory forever! Amen" (Rom. 16:25ff.); " . . . so that grace, as it extends to more and more people, may increase thanksgiving, to the glory of God" (2 Cor. 4:15); ". . . so that God may be glorified in all things through Jesus Christ. To him belong the glory and the power forever and ever. Amen" (1 Pet. 4:11).

Theologians like Jonathan Edwards[77] and his modern follower, H. Richard Niebuhr,[78] understood that the inclusive ethic of charity is grounded in Jesus' faith in God the Father in the sense that it is this dogma that provides *universal* scope to charity. "For if you love those who love you, what reward do you have? Do not even the tax collectors do the same? And if you greet only your brothers and sisters, what more are you doing than others? Do not even the Gentiles do the same? Be perfect, therefore, as your heavenly Father is perfect" (Matt. 5:46-48). Apart from this ultimate ground in God who gives, moreover, charity loses its *public* character in the aspiration for *social* justice and becomes the merely private option of goodwill giving alms to the poor, even when this privatized charity is collectivized into love of our own kind. The commonplace critiques of private charity today in the name of such collectivized self-love, on the other hand, are deeply malevolent and profoundly cold-hearted. If we fasted from charity until social justice arrived, we would more starve the poor in the name of utopia than hasten the day of righteousness. But the "ethics of Jesus Christ, as the way of life of the one who responds to the action of the universal God [= *our* heavenly Father] in all action, in whatever happens, is an ethics of universal responsibility."[79] This "responsible self" of conscientious life in the world and before God finds echoes in all religions and cultures. It finds echoes in all religious cultures and often articulate awareness in their philosophies, because it is the secret operation and

---

77. Jonathan Edwards, *The Nature of True Virtue* (Ann Arbor, MI: University of Michigan Press, 2001), p. 19.

78. H. R. Niebuhr, *The Responsible Self: An Essay in Christian Moral Philosophy* (New York: Harper and Row, 1963).

79. Niebuhr, *The Responsible Self,* p. 172.

hidden presence of God the Father as Creator of all that is not God, who individuates in order to summon to charity, who hides in the face of the poor asking for love that structures life in new orders of justice.

Another latter-day Augustinian, Gottfried Leibniz, argued that most questions about right and wrong are confused because people "do not agree on a common conception of justice," i.e., which for Leibniz meant that they have excluded "our heavenly Father" from consideration in determining the scope of justice, and thus cannot include all others. "There are those who believe that it is enough if no harm is done to [others] and if no one has deprived them of their possessions, holding that no one is obligated to seek the good of others or prevent evil for them, even if it should cost us nothing and give us no pain. Many who pass in the world for great judges keep themselves within these limits. They content themselves with harming no one, but they are not inclined to improve people's condition. In a word, they believe one can be just without being charitable. . . ." But consider the case of a little child drowning, Leibniz continues in a thought experiment. Use your imagination to put yourself in the other's place. All the cost of her rescue to you would be a hand extended to draw her out of danger. Would we not be angered *morally* at one who lovelessly refused such help? "Led by degrees, people will agree not only that men ought to abstain from doing evil but also that they ought to prevent evil from being done and even to alleviate it when it is done, at least so far as they can. . . ."[80]

Why is this so? Why should one be able to awaken people to the obligation of charitable human solidarity, valuing one's neighbor as oneself? Why is something like this Golden Rule of human equity found in all religions and cultures, not only Jesus' Sermon on the Mount? And why, on the other hand, is the Sermon on the Mount not just a supposed "ethic" of Jesus, separable from His person, but the proclamation of His heavenly Father as also ours, just so revealed "dogma"? The intelligent creature of God has the natural capacity to imagine itself in another's place and to recognize its own regard for self in the other, even if this rational capacity is corrupted in the egocentric self by countervailing inclinations of willful ignorance, cold-hearted sloth, envy, and greed.

Leibniz is following in the tradition of Luther's exposition of the Golden Rule as the natural law inscribed on the human heart, as in Romans 2:15.

> Christ himself (Matt. 7[:12]) includes all of the law and the prophets in this natural law, "So whatever you wish that men would do to you, do so to them; for this is the law and the prophets." Paul does the same thing in Rom. 13[:9], where he sums up all the commandments of Moses in the love which also the natural law teaches in the words, "Love your neighbor as yourself." Otherwise, were it not naturally written in the heart, one would have to teach and preach

---

80. Gottfried Leibniz, "The Common Concept of Justice," in *Leibniz: Political Writings,* ed. P. Riley, 2nd ed. (Cambridge, UK: Cambridge University Press, 2001), pp. 45-64.

the law for a long time before it became the concern of conscience. . . . However the devil so blinds and possesses hearts, that they do not always feel this law. Therefore one must preach the law and impress it on the minds of people till God assists and enlightens them so that they feel in their hearts what the Word says.[81]

Rational people who must live together can thus be "led by degrees" to see themselves in others, experience empathy, and aspire to charity; but they will not so be led — given the corruption of human nature, the incurvation of its desire from charity to self-regard — until they learn and are persuaded of the good reason for this obligation to value others as themselves: the one and same heavenly Father whom Jesus proclaims as inclusively "ours." The decisive question of an ethic of charity is who counts as my neighbor and why (Luke 10:29, 36). The answer that the scope of charity is infinite and without exception begs the question of the critical dogmatics of charity: our heavenly Father, the self-surpassing God who counts us all together as His creatures, chosen in Christ and so beloved on the way to the Beloved Community. The sufficient ground of the ethic of charity is the Father's personal being as the originating cause of all things, taking the good-pleasure of love in each thing and for all things together in a harmony of maximal diversity that is the eschaton of this origin.

So Leibniz continued: "In general, if someone asks you to do something or not do something, and you refuse his request, he has reason to complain if he can judge that you would make the same request if you were in his place. And this is the principle of equity or, what is the same thing, of equality or of the identity of reasons, which holds that one should grant to others whatever one would himself wish in a similar situation. . . ." Strict insistence on right or limitation of duty to "do no harm" *fails to do the good* because, lacking the sense of human equity under our heavenly Father, it lacks the motive of charity: " . . . not to do evil to another, *neminem laedere,* is that precept of the law which is called strict Right *(ius strictum),* but equity demands that one also do good when this is fitting. . . . This is the rule of reason and of our Master [Christ]: Put yourself in the place of another, and you will have the true point of view to judge what is just and unjust."[82] This "ought" of charity does not derive from the factual "is" of the fallen world, where *homo lupis homini* (man a wolf to man) prevails. Here the minimal requirement of public order to do no harm serves minimally to arrest this dying world from its recurring spasms of violence. Yet groaning in frustration beneath this travail, the "ought" of charity is revealed as the "natural" desire of creation. Aspiration for shalom is "natural," if "nature" itself is social and historical because creation is from the origin the promise of the Beloved Community. The "ought"

---

81. *LW* 40, p. 97.
82. Gottfried Wilhelm Leibniz, *Philosophical Papers and Letters,* ed. Leroy E. Loemaker (Chicago: University of Chicago Press, 1956), p. 921.

of charity is natural, if human imagination is constantly reckoning with the future and just as constantly complicated by the other cast providentially on its path. The command of God to love the neighbor as oneself is the "natural" law "written on every human heart" (Rom. 2:14-15) in the sense that to be a true self at all is to recognize oneself socially, in *the face* of the other (Levinas) that is the "mask of God" (Luther), making each one a *restless* conscience until it rests in the fulfilled city of God. Not self-consciousness, then, but other-consciousness, that is, *conscience,* is the ecstasy of life on the way to the Beloved Community of God.

Around the same time in early modern Euro-American history, Jonathan Edwards explained: "True virtue most essentially consists in benevolence to being in general . . . [i.e.,] that consent, propensity and union of heart to being in general, and is a part of the universal system of existence; and so stands in connection with the whole; what can its general and true beauty be, but its union and consent with the great whole."[83] The failure to imagine oneself in the other's place, and unite oneself with that other in charity under God, does not fail to do harm. Apathy devalues the other, mistreats by slothful neglect the other to whom we owe love as equally valued creature of the One God and Creator, the almighty Father who gives. The universal failure in Adam *to become* the concrete good of active love — this failure in being — "falls short of the glory of God" (Rom. 3:23). *Sin* is most profoundly understood, not as the commission of this or that transgression, but as *the failure to become* in charity the creature whom God wills, a living member of the Beloved Community, whose prayer of faith and rule of doctrine is an invocation and doxology, "*Our* Father in heaven"! Jesus' instruction to love the other, as one loves the self, in and under our heavenly Father is no arbitrary imposition of a law alien to our being, if what is truly natural to the human as creature made in the image of God for likeness to God is aspiration for the Beloved Community; rather this law exposes a total human failure to become what truly it is called to be. Just so, it *makes* this human failure a "matter of conscience."

Therefore instruction in charity under "our" heavenly Father corresponds with the deepest nature of things: God's *good pleasure* in His works, the divine aesthetic pronounced in blessing upon all that God has made (Gen. 1:31–2:3). The pleasure God takes in others initiates and sustains a rich world of maximal diversity in harmony of love. It is a world of human diversity ordered to "adoption as his children through Jesus Christ, according to the *good pleasure of his will* . . . his *good pleasure* that he set forth in Christ, as a plan for the fullness of time, to gather up all things in him, things in heaven and things on earth" (Eph. 1:5, 9-10). This "regard" of divine good pleasure is the deepest nature of things, as we have learned from the gospel's critique of epistemology and revision of metaphysics. Created things do not have intrinsic being in and for themselves, least of all in the self-consciousness of modernity's sovereign self; only God the Trinity exists in and for Himself as the uniquely divine being, and even so this divine being is a

83. Edwards, *True Virtue*, pp. 3-4.

living being of mutual valuations, the love of the Father for the Son and the Son for the Father in the Spirit that is the surplus of its love spilling out spontaneously to give all things. Thus creatures exist in and for others and so by valuations other than their own, having substantiality as being valued and only so also then in their own active valuations of others.

To love is to value, to treasure, to regard as precious. To love divinely is to value creatively, to make valuable by a gift. We may note in passing that the "forensic" conception of God's Word as such sovereign and creative regard of love has often been impugned for setting up a legal fiction, e.g., that God declares by fiat that the sinner is righteous when in fact the sinner remains sinful. No doubt a deformed and Spirit-less Protestantism of cheap grace has thought so. But this is a caricature of the insight that God in speaking the sinner righteous speaks by identifying her as the sinner for whom Christ lived, died, and now reigns so that in unification with Christ by Spirit-worked faith God creatively re-values the sinner and so effectively, if inchoately, makes the now gifted sinner righteous. An opponent no less savvy than Nietzsche grasped this power from out of his Lutheran heritage, for instance, when he had Zarathustra proclaim: "To esteem is to create: hear this, you creators! Esteeming itself is of all esteemed things the most estimable treasure. Through esteeming alone is there value: and without esteeming, the nut of existence would be hollow. Hear this, you creators! Change of values — that is a change of creators. Whoever must be a creator always annihilates."[84] Recaptured theologically, what is this but to say that God kills in order to make alive, as the true Creator must, when God devalues our loveless devaluations of His creation to redeem and fulfill it by speech-acts of creative charity revealed in the righteousness of God the Father who sent His Son to become a neighbor to us in need.

This love of the world in and under God, who in creating it, loves it, is entailed by the invocation of God as "our" heavenly Father; as argued above, this love can be, and notoriously is, repudiated. The human choice to hear and obey this command of love is declined by the creature that does not by faith value itself as God's own beloved by grace (Eph. 1:6-8) and so hope in Him for the redemption of "our" bodies and thus regard every other on the way as the precious one created, redeemed, and destined for fulfillment. This is the creature that refuses to receive its own life as gift and so to place this specifically given life rightly into the ecology of things earthly and heavenly, which God wills for it in its own time and place. When the creature refuses this divine evaluation of itself in unbelief, it also — in the very social nature of things — refuses it for others, objectively withholding the service of love for others. In the very social and ecological nature of things private sin is never private: it wreaks havoc on the nexus of creation by actualizing possibilities for itself other than the ones God wills. This is *actual* evil, disrupting the orders of community in love and justice that God has in fact

84. *The Portable Nietzsche*, p. 171.

willed in creation and transforming them into structures of malice and injustice. If the creature refuses its solidarity with others and its destiny in the Beloved Community, if it finds the divine and creative evaluation of its true self in Christ repugnant to its dignity, autonomy, and freedom; then it mimics the very Creator (as we saw in Zarathustra's summons above) whom it refuses and asserts itself in its celebrated act of "free will" for some other self outside of Christ than the one "our" heavenly Father gives and takes pleasure in. But the only place outside of Christ before God is Adam.

This is the acute judgment that must be pronounced over our greediest generation of Euro-Americans ever to have afflicted the earth. Whoever will not pray God as "our" Father in the Beloved Community of the ecclesia as our Mother, will have no other as "brother" or "sister," but seeks self in all things, also in the enlightened self-interest of allegedly progressive politics. The inclusive ethic of charity can hardly be sustained in face of actual evil except as the act of faith in our heavenly Father to which Jesus summons and so as a *dogma,* howsoever *critically* accessed and gained, of the world as the promise of the coming of the Beloved Community. The enlightened self-interest that would replace the lost faith is a masquerade. Behind its surface, hidden structures of malice work injustice. The apostate creature, posing as its own creator, as Karl Barth so acutely analyzed, "chooses a freedom which is no freedom." Refusing human solidarity under "our" heavenly Father, it becomes "a prisoner of the world-process, of chance, of all-powerful natural and historical forces, above all of himself. He tries to be his own master, and to control his relation with God and the world and his fellow-man. And as he does so, the onslaught of nothingness prevails against him, controlling him in death in an irresistible and senseless way and to his own loss. This is the *circulus vitiosus* of the human plight presupposed and revealed in and with the grace of God."[85] As such, Jesus bids next to pray . . .

*"Thy kingdom come! Thy will be done on earth as in heaven . . ."*

As an eschatology, Christianity's appeal to God as our heavenly Father at the invitation of Jesus is governed by an orientation, not to what is or was but to what will be. In praying as Jesus taught, the church speaks into the world the promise of its destiny by telling the canonical story of the Almighty Father, who in fulfillment of the promise of origin through His Son Christ Jesus brings about by his Spirit the resurrection of the dead and the life everlasting, i.e., the "reign of God" that is the Beloved Community, the redemption of our bodies, the eternal fulfillment of the earth on which the cross of Jesus stood. Just this redemption and fulfillment is the will of God that is to be done upon the earth, first of all in praying this prayer, *Thy kingdom come!* Manifestly, the invocation of the coming of God's kingdom

85. *CD* IV/1, p. 173.

is faith's hope for the real theodicy, the theodicy of faith giving way to sight of glories to be revealed that are not worthy to be compared to the sufferings of the present time (Rom. 8:18). This is *the belief* in God's reign that comes from God to the earth groaning under the curse, longing in eager expectation for the revelation of the glorious liberty of the children of God (Rom. 8:21). It is the dogma of dogmas, the end for which God created the world, the claim to truth embedded in the Christian knowledge of God — but, when the Son of Man comes, will He find this faith on the earth (Luke 18:8)?

Dietrich Bonhoeffer observed in an acute analysis of this petition that we Euro-American Christians today "are otherworldly or we are secularists, but in either case we no longer believe in God's kingdom,"[86] for this is to believe what comes as gift from God to this earth upon which the cross of Jesus stood, as "the new Earth of the promise, on the old Earth of the creation. This is the promise: that one day we shall behold the world of the resurrection . . ." where "God alone will be the Lord as the Creator, the crucified and resurrected One, and the Spirit that reigns in his holy community. Thy kingdom come[!]"[87] As he analyzes our *"lack of belief in God's kingdom,"*[88] Bonhoeffer asks, "Why should we be ashamed that we have a God who performs miracles, who creates life and conquers death . . . ? If God is truly God — then God is God, then God's kingdom is miraculous, the epitome of miracles. Why are we so anxious, so cautious, so cowardly? God will shame us all one day. . . . We will feel shame before the miraculous God."[89] If this be not so, there is indeed no sense to Jesus' petition, *Thy kingdom come!*

The problem here is less the God who as almighty has all possibilities than the almighty God who now permits such evils as afflict the creation subjected to frustration (Rom. 8:20) and under the curse (Gen. 3:17-19) in order to hope — precisely — for the coming of the reign of God. The eschatological orientation thus solves certain of the kinds of problems denoted by the term "theodicy" — a philosophical topic that arose in the disputes between Stoics and Epicureans regarding the universe's "intelligent design"[90] — but it by no means resolves theoretically the so-called "problem of evil." In some ways it accentuates it, as the discussion of God's permission of moral evil above shows. The point of the theodicy *of faith* in Romans 8, however, is not to resolve what can only be resolved by the fulfillment of the promise of God's creating that comes with the eschaton of judgment; it is rather to clarify now the problems of evil that presently afflict. This clarification is needful to discern what must be endured, what may be resisted,

---

86. *Dietrich Bonhoeffer: Berlin: 1932-1933,* Dietrich Bonhoeffer Works, vol. 12, ed. L. Rassmussen (Minneapolis: Fortress, 2009), p. 285.

87. *Dietrich Bonhoeffer: Berlin: 1932-1933,* p. 296.

88. *Dietrich Bonhoeffer: Berlin: 1932-1933,* p. 33.

89. *Dietrich Bonhoeffer: Berlin: 1932-1933,* p. 346.

90. R. W. Sharples, *Stoics, Epicureans and Sceptics: An Introduction to Hellenistic Philosophy* (London and New York: Routledge, 1996), pp. 53-58.

and what should be stopped. But even such triage is possible only because, and precisely because, the coming of the Beloved Community alone provides the true resolution of "the problem of evil," so that in the interim patience endures, hope springs eternal, and zeal does not flag. In any event, a theology that has at its very center the resurrection of the Crucified can hardly evade engaging the problem of evil; the petition, *Thy kingdom come!,* makes this plain already in the faith of the man Jesus, whose belief was vindicated if, but only if, He was indeed loosed from the grave's grip on Him. Then the petition deliteralized and theologically decoded will be seen to have the present sense of imploring that God kill in order to make alive, beginning with each believer's sinful self. That will be the doing on earth of God's will as in heaven, the blessing that is bearing the cross.

---

## A NOTE ON THE FAITH OF THE "HISTORICAL" JESUS FORMULATED IN THE LORD'S PRAYER

As an aside, we recall here how the canonical story was shaped by the cross-and-resurrection gospel, which functioned as a hermeneutic of prophetic and apostolic traditions as well as memories of Jesus. This fact about the rise of creedal Christianity raises the much-discussed problem in modern theology of the continuity between the church's faith in Jesus Christ and the faith of Jesus of Nazareth. There is a real issue here, even though liberal theology framed the question on the misleading assumption that what is involved is epistemologically founding the church's faith on Jesus' private opinion about Himself on the quixotic supposition that Jesus had a modern "self-consciousness." Liberal theology is simply, massively wrong about that for the simple reason that the church's faith in Jesus is faith in His Father's Easter vindication of Him as the beloved Son. Not to hold resurrection faith as the epistemic access to Jesus is simply to have some other relation to Jesus than that of Christian faith in Him as the revealed Son of God. That is surely possible, but it is not Christianity in its orthodox theological intention.

Yet it is not wrong within the theological intention of orthodoxy to ask about Jesus between Bethlehem and Golgotha, even to ask as Schleiermacher did about His "God-consciousness" (properly understood, i.e., precisely not *self-*consciousness) as a matter of critical historical inquiry that tests church practice in Jesus' name for fidelity to Jesus. This is a matter, as we have previously argued, of the self-critical testing of the church's Easter faith in Jesus by the standard of Jesus' own faith in His heavenly Father which somehow — the details reconstructing this remain controversial — led him to Golgotha. "Given man's infinite capacity to rationalize as well as the fact that Jesus has been made the warrant for every sort of theological or social program, it is utterly essential to press the historical question against the church and its kerygma"[91] — to be sure, for Keck,

---

91. Leander E. Keck, *A Future for the Historical Jesus: The Place of Jesus in Preaching and*

for the sake of the church and its kerygma. This "historical question" is, by present lights, simply the critical function of dogmatics, where dogmatics is not ecclesiastical ideology, but prophetic and apostolic testing of the spirits precisely but not exclusively in the field of the church and its kerygma. Edwyn Hoskyns rightly stated in this regard that the "whole spiritual and moral power of the primitive church rested ultimately, not upon a mystical experience, but upon its belief that what Jesus had asserted to have been the purpose of his life and death was in very truth the purpose of God. Further than this the historian dare not and cannot go."[92] But this far historical inquiry can and must go.

Presupposing critical historical work that can ascertain Jesus' confession of His own calling that implicated Him at His trial (Mark 14:62) — His so-called "claim to authority" that expresses at least an "implicit Christology" — we can proceed on the basis that this belief of Jesus about His purpose is conveyed in the Lord's Prayer that He gave disciples for the purpose of following Him in faith before God and identifying them in the world. It concludes by asking God to preserve from the time of trial and save from the Evil One. That is what presently concerns us. Jesus' faith in the God of Israel as His Abba-Father was articulated in His kingdom prayer, thus as the *public* faith which He taught His disciples to pray *together*. It was just this confession of faith by this act of public prayer that somehow brought Him as a public person petitioning the coming of the reign of God into conflict with the Temple in Jerusalem and the occupying authorities. It thus brought him into the "time of trial" in terrible contradiction to His prayer's

---

*Theology* (Philadelphia: Fortress, 1981), p. 71. "My own concern is to show that, out of the obscurity of the life story of Jesus, certain characteristic traits in his preaching stand out in relatively sharp relief, and that primitive Christianity united its own message with these. The heart of our problem lies here: the exalted Lord has almost entirely swallowed up the image of its earthly Lord and yet the community maintains the identity of its exalted Lord with the earthly. The solution of this problem cannot, however, if our findings are right, be approached with any hope of success along the line of supposed historical *bruta facta* but only along the line of the connection and tension between the preaching of Jesus and his community." Ernst Käsemann, "The Problem of the Historical Jesus," *Essays on New Testament Themes,* trans. W. J. Montague (London: SCM, 1971), p. 213. Yet, is it really "preaching" — particularly in the way that Käsemann's teacher, Bultmann, understood preaching as the existential "call to decision" without the narrative that warrants the announcement — that can parse the continuity between Jesus' faith and the faith of the church? Cf. Hans Conzelmann, *Jesus,* trans. J. R. Lord (Philadelphia: Fortress, 1973), p. 89. Peter Stuhlmacher, heir to Käsemann's chair, tried rather to locate the continuity in Jesus' act of faith and obedience as a Jew who believed in God — in parallel to our resort to Gogarten above in Chapter Six. Pointing to the Last Supper narrative, he concluded: "Jesus is willing to undertake his earthly pilgrimage as Son of man, and is ultimately able to stand his ground, only because he understands himself to be God's servant and the ransom, in person, chosen by God as the existential representative of Israel and of all the lost." *Jesus of Nazareth, Christ of Faith,* trans. Siegfried Schatzmann (Peabody, MA: Hendrickson, 1993), p. 35.

92. Edmund Hoskyns, *The Riddle of the New Testament* (London: Faber & Faber, 1936), p. 177.

climactic petition, just as Jesus acknowledges: "But this is your hour and the power of darkness" (Luke 22:53).

In receiving the Lord's Prayer as its own and in making it central to its liturgical and devotional life — *mediated by the narrative link of the petition, "Thy will be done!," with Jesus' reception of His destiny in the account of His Agony in the Garden of Gethsemane* — the church has always in this decisive way echoed the very faith of the man Jesus in His heavenly Father. Jesus teaches disciples who do not know what they, as *His* disciples, are to pray (Luke 11:1-4). The "just as" clause in the disciples' request ("teach us to pray *just as* John taught his disciples"), as Jeremias pointed out, shows that the Lord's Prayer was meant as "a prayer that will characterize Jesus' followers [as] the community of salvation. Thus, right from the beginning, the Lord's Prayer was meant not only as a model for proper prayer, but as a formula, a token of recognition — which is the way in which the church has used it down the centuries."[93] Indeed, we could even call it the *Credo* of Jesus of Nazareth, so that if all that the church possessed from Jesus of Nazareth was this brief Kingdom prayer, it would have all that is requisite for its confession of faith in the moral agent of common human history, Jesus of Nazareth, as the One identified as the Christ, the Son of the heavenly Father who is the God of Israel. For the *historical intention* of Jesus as a public *persona* is nothing other than this publicly articulated faith in the heavenly Father, also with respect to His personal destiny. The praying of this prayer brought Jesus to Gethsemane; it is the theological key to His destiny, even as the riddle of the so-called "historical Jesus" is irreducibly theological[94] — whether or not the faith by which He lived this prayer out to the final surrender to His Father's will in the Garden of Gethsemane is true, i.e., whether Jesus has in fact been raised from death's grip to live and reign by the One whom He addressed as Abba, Father.[95] In any case, the Lord's Prayer displays the historical continuity between the faith of Jesus in God the Father and the faith of the church in Jesus as God's Son.

---

## *"Thy kingdom come . . . !" — Continued*

"Hear the word of the LORD, O nations, and declare it in the coastlands far away; say, 'He who scattered Israel will gather him and will keep him as a shepherd a flock'" (Jer. 31:10). The LORD scatters in order to gather, afflicts in order to heal,

93. Jeremias, *New Testament Theology,* p. 197.

94. When the historian has reconstructed the public agency of Jesus in *this* sense of the particular convictions of faith that guided Jesus in His mission and fate, he or she is faced at this point "by the problem of theology, just as, at this same point, the unbeliever is faced by the problem of faith." Hoskyns, *The Riddle,* p. 182.

95. E. F. Scott, *The Lord's Prayer: Its Character, Purpose, and Interpretation* (New York: Charles Scribner's Sons, 1951), pp. 72-73.

kills in order to make alive, does an alien work *ut faciat opus proprium* (in order to do a proper work). Historically, it was the gospel narrative's unification of the cross and resurrection of Jesus that established this *divine purpose clause* that constituted in turn early Catholic theology's firewall against docetism and dualism. Gnosticism — the original deviation, the first heresy — in turn bursts into flame (as Tertullian would observe) whenever the problems of evil seem unbearable — as already in Jesus' crucifixion. The petition, *Thy kingdom come! Thy will be done!*, is but the prayer that this proper purpose of God be accomplished.

Thus the answer of Christian faith to the burning question of our affliction is nothing other than, and so just as unbearably difficult as, the faith of Jesus in His heavenly Father at Gethsemane. Yet the question about affliction is not as such deviant. It takes shape from the very first page of canonical Scripture, where the Creator is portrayed as commanding into existence by His Word a world that He adjudges "good" at every step along the way. The "Behold, it was very good" of Genesis 1:31 is a "concluding formula of approval for the entire work of creation. . . . This statement, expressed and written in a world full of innumerable troubles, preserves an inalienable concern of faith: no evil was laid upon the world by God's hand; neither was his omnipotence limited by any kind of opposing power whatever."[96] That God is depicted as at once all powerful and all good — namely, then, as our heavenly Father — in His work of creation makes the problem of the origin and reality of evil in the world unavoidable and indeed central for theology. For good reason, Augustine called it the "all-embracing question"[97] just as the prayer, "Thy kingdom come!" is this question's all-embracing answer.

As mentioned, the Greeks also knew the question of theodicy, and the Epicurean formulation of the theological dilemma became classical also in Christian theology. If God is good, He cannot be powerful — else He would remove the evil. If God is powerful, then He cannot be good — since He permits evil and so is complicit in it. Left out, as previously noted, is consideration of the wisdom of God in the selection of this particular world out of the infinitely possible worlds available to the divine mind. Wisdom brings into consideration therefore the notion not usually entertained in philosophy, namely, of the Creator as author, and the creation as narrative displaying the cunning of the author in devising a plot, and further, as the director in seeing to the narrative's performance. Philosophical theodicies — with the exception of Leibniz under the influence of Christian theology in the tradition of Luther and Melanchthon — leave divine wisdom to the side just because they do not take the world as a narrative that begins with a promise and pledge aimed at a fulfillment. Instead they take the world more or less as a fixed stage upon which human beings play out their destinies, where indeed the question as to whether the stage has been designed intelligently, that

96. Gerhard von Rad, *Genesis: A Commentary*, revised edition (Philadelphia: Fortress, 1973), p. 61.

97. Augustine, *City of God* II:2; p. 67.

is, made convenient to their human purposes or not, makes an ethical difference. In an important sense, however, Christian theology does not have a dog in that philosophical fight. The divine wisdom revealed in the economy of God made known in Christ crucified and risen (Ephesians 1) tells of God who creates all things in order to fulfill them in the Beloved Community. Here in theology the wisdom that philosophy loves is indeed divine, the mediator between the power of God and the goodness of God. This mediation does not resolve the problem of evil theoretically but it does put it in the different light of the coming of God's kingdom. It moves the question of evil in the world from the light of nature to the light of grace on the way to the light of glory.

Thomas Reinhuber has smartly underscored this very point: "In Luther's doctrine of the Lights [of nature, grace, and glory] the concern is less with general knowledge of God as much more with the problem of theodicy and predestination . . . both are problems about the righteousness of God. . . ." Reinhuber explains that the question of theodicy arises philosophically, in the light of nature. Honest reason is led there by the course of events to Epicurus, that is, either to doubt about God's existence, that is, divine power, or doubt about God's justice, that is, divine goodness. The light of grace comes and provides a "solution" to these questions of natural theology by the promise of "eternal life after this temporal life." But this very answer that assures both of God's power and goodness raises a new problem of theodicy: "Why are not all people destined for this eternal life?" Faith cannot in the mere light of grace yet answer this question; it can only believe in the righteousness of the electing God to be revealed fully in the light of glory.[98] Hence the light of grace resolves one kind of question in theodicy, namely, assurance to those gifted with faith of God's fatherly care, since faith is union with God's own Son, Jesus Christ, by the Holy Spirit who bears witness that believers are indeed the children of God and heirs of divine life (Rom. 8:16). But simultaneously the sovereign Spirit's election to faith evokes a new kind of question in theodicy, the problem of divine justice in the apparent reprobation of those from whom faith is withheld.

Luther is eager to concede that it is incomprehensible also to believing reason how it can be just for God to crown some who are unworthy with saving grace, but then to abandon to punishment those who are no more unworthy. But believing reason, he says, trusts on the basis of the mercy revealed in Christ in spite of what cannot yet be comprehended; incomprehension will give way to understanding God's justice when faith gives way to sight.[99] Thus Luther summons his readers to trust in the future revelation of the "God whose justice is most righteous and most evident" — a trust the good reason of which is evident already now in the *deus revelatus in Christo*. In the light of glory, the presently

---

98. Thomas Reinhuber, *Kämpfender Glaube: Studien zu Luthers Bekenntnis am Ende von De servo arbitrio* (Berlin and New York: Walter de Gruyter, 2000), p. 199, my translation.

99. Luther, *Bondage,* p. 234.

perceived contradiction between faith and experience will be resolved. That is the gist of Luther's eschatological theodicy of the just who live now by embattled faith. Hence the petition, *Thy kingdom come!* What Luther leaves unclarified, however, is whether in glory the redeemed shall be satisfied at the righteousness of the reprobation of the wicked or be surprised at the wideness of God's mercy. In any case, Luther must tell the plot line of creation through the lights of nature, grace, and glory to affirm a divine wisdom, albeit still beyond our ken, that will mediate divine power and goodness at the sight of divine justice "most righteous and most evident."

On the horns of the Epicurean dilemma (that had already been anticipated by the pre-Socratic Democritus), the classical solution of philosophical theology (in significant contrast to Luther) was executed by Plato in Book II of *The Republic:* "[S]ince a god is good, he is not — as most people claim — the cause of everything that happens to human beings but of only a few things, for good things are fewer than bad ones in our lives. He alone is responsible for the good things, but we must find some other cause for the bad ones, not a god."[100] This becomes a theological rule for Plato: "This then is one of the laws or patterns concerning the gods to which speakers and poets must conform, namely, that a god isn't the cause of all things but only of good ones."[101] This move of Plato to save God's goodness by limiting God's power is remarkably fashionable today, even among theologians who would not otherwise be caught dead in Plato's company. To be sure, Plato removes one horn of the dilemma. Yet this solution, if it may be called that, does not satisfy and cannot satisfy any theology that intends to confess the Father almighty, creator of heaven and earth. A God of limited power is not God at all according to the biblical conception of the Creator of everything other than God, the "matter" as well as the "form." A God of limited power is in fact a creature, like all the rest caught up in the fatal necessities of the eternal cosmic system — which is taken as the real, operative deity.

As a result, there can never be in such cosmos-piety any resolution to the conflict of good with the evil that preys upon creation and corrupts it — which eschatological resolution of evil is what the biblical tradition means by salvation at the eschaton of judgment.[102] In fact, as Augustine realized, if one "admits God's existence while denying His foreknowledge [i.e., the wisdom attending God's authorship in creation, cf. Eph. 1:3-14], what [one] says amounts to nothing more than what 'the fool hath said in his heart: There is no God.'"[103] The limited deity of Plato turns out to be an internally incoherent being, a stopgap erected against the threat of honest Epicurean "atheism." The contemporary alternative to the

---

100. Plato, *The Republic* II:378c, trans. G. M. A. Grube, revised C. D. C. Reeve (Indianapolis: Hackett, 1992), p. 55.

101. Plato, *The Republic,* II:380:c, p. 56.

102. Cf. Revelation 18:21–19:2, timely words for those with ears to hear.

103. Augustine, *City of God* V:9 (Bourke), p. 110.

almighty Father whom Jesus proclaimed and the ecclesia confesses takes theology all the way with Nietzsche "beyond good and evil" to embrace "this world: a monster of energy, without beginning, without end . . . this, my Dionysian world of the eternally self-creating, the eternally self-destroying, this mystery world of the twofold voluptuous delight, my 'beyond good and evil,' without goal, unless the joy of the circle is itself a goal. . . . *This world is the will to power — and nothing besides!* And you yourselves are also this will to power — and nothing besides!" That is indeed, as Nietzsche thought, a kind of *theological* liberation.[104]

Yet, it is not the gospel's liberation which by Jesus' vindication delivers us to faith in His heavenly Father, whose kingdom comes. The gospel tells that Jesus had met and endured once for all the powers of evil *at His Father's own behest,* at the hand of the One *who spared not His own Son.* One cannot make the problem of evil more acute than the gospel itself makes it in this uncanny confrontation between the Father and the Son. As the Nietzsche citation above about going beyond "good and evil" indicates, it is a curious implication of this, which we must now note and assess, that "evil" is not universally perceived as a "problem," as *the* problem of *theodicy.* If we differentiate philosophical theodicy as the Platonic or Stoic rationalization of cosmos piety from the eschatologically oriented theodicy of faith, the impossibility now of closing the gap between faith and sight or between the lights of grace and glory makes an "extraordinarily clear demonstration of the necessary brokenness of all theological thought and utterance" (Barth).[105] In theology too we are beggars, like the poor man at Dives' gate, waiting, not in control, trusting and praying, *Thy kingdom come!* The gates to Paradise are truly barred; we in exile still wandering cannot conceptually close the experienced gap between the God hidden in majesty who indifferently works all and all under the mask of nature and the God revealed in cradle and cross who passionately desires not the death of the sinner nor the loss of any of the least. Although Barth railed against Luther's articulation of this experiential gap just enunciated, in speaking of the brokenness of all theology on the hard rock of the realities of evil he acknowledged the substance of Luther's concern in making that distinction. What faith knows remains faith in face of God's hiddenness and so "all theology is *theologia viatorum*"[106] — on the way by light of grace, not yet arrived and enlightened in glory.

On another level, however, the problem of evil in theology is not merely one of the inadequacy of the human mind to comprehend the ultimate harmonization of things which it believes on the basis of common morality and the

---

104. Friedrich Nietzsche, *The Will to Power,* ed. W. Kaufmann (New York: Vintage Books, 1968), pp. 548, 550. With this "nothing besides," Nietzsche succumbs to the very nihilism he set out to oppose. See Rudiger Safranski, *Nietzsche: A Philosophical Biography,* trans. S. Frisch (New York: W. W. Norton, 2002), pp. 223-44.

105. *CD* III/3, p. 293.

106. *CD* III/3, p. 293.

gospel promise, as for example Leibniz thought. Rather, as Barth also saw and daringly explored, from the outset faith is and remains particularly afflicted with the perception of something *impossible* under the sovereignty of the God of love: the reality of moral evil as that bizarre, uncanny event erupting into creation as that — precisely as that — which God does not will. How can such a surd be at all — something that God, taken rigorously as Creator of all that is not God, does not will? This question, obviously, cannot even arise for the limited deity of Platonism. The limited deity of Platonism was invented to dodge this question of life on the earth in which the will of God is not done and must rather be hoped for and implored, *Thy kingdom come! Thy will be done!*

In Platonizing theologies, even, as we saw, in McCord Adams's metaphysical mismatch between embodied souls and divine immateriality — the natural evil of incorrigible matter resists the divine will, much as the chaotic, cutting, grinding atomic "triangles" in the Receptacle bend to the Demiurge's formation only so far as their indivisible geometries allow. Recalcitrant materiality just belongs to the way things are in this cosmic system, always have been, and always will be. Biblically, however, the saints suffer actual evil not as a limitation emanating from their embodied condition but rather commit it as a spiritual aspiration erupting from their higher powers — the *sicut Deus eritis* against *the Creator God*. This is God who is all powerful and all good but also all wise, the very One who truly knows good and evil, if He is to fulfill His promise in the act of originating this world. How can that *contradiction* of wills, not merely verbal, actually be in a world created from nothing and adjudged indeed very good?

Virtually making a mythical figure out of an abstract concept in a dialectic that stretches the imagination, Barth radicalized the patristic doctrine of evil as privation of being when he wrote of *das Nichtige,* the Nothingness, *that which exists as what God does not will. Das Nichtige* is "the comprehensive negation of the creature and its nature. And as such it is a power which, though unsolicited and uninvited, is superior, like evil and death, to all the forces which the creature can oppose to it."[107] I have taken Barth's idea[108] here to indicate all the abstract possibilities that God in His eternal omniscience possesses, but declines to actualize in choosing to enact a particular world of harmonious compossibilities in which God will be the God of grace for humanity. These alternative ideas, whether taken individually or as comprising alternative worlds, are nothing actual, as is this world on which the cross of Jesus stood. They are nothings, nothing but unreal logical possibilities. Yet somehow these nothings refuse their primal rejection in the mind of God; Leibniz had pictured them as quasi-living elements within the divine Mind, jealously or enviously pressing to be admitted into existence. For Barth, they erupt unexplained within our world as utterly destructive forces, as biblical chaos unleashed (Gen. 8:2). Sin, death, and devil are such projections of

107. *CD* III/3, p. 310.
108. *PNT,* pp. 87-126.

*das Nichtige,* that which God does not will nevertheless asserting itself into the ordered cosmos of the creation and so tearing apart the fabric of things that God has actually willed. Barth is trying in this paradoxical way to avoid interpreting the evil — that must honestly be admitted as the surd of true contradiction of the good will of God — as a logically necessary part of a cosmic system that would, as in Hegel and Leibniz, make evil less bizarre and less dangerous, something domesticated, even justified in the overall scheme of things, in this way anesthetizing Christian conscience to what should not be.

While Barth's intention is well taken, having admitted the surd of *das Nichtige,* it is a sheer act of will on his part when Barth affirms that even this evil remains under God's sovereignty: "God Himself comprehends, envisages and controls it" from the beginning — since, by my interpretation, the *das Nichtige* is nothing but God's own infinite treasury of possible thoughts from which God has wisely selected only some for the particular actualization that is this world on which the cross of Jesus stood, rejecting the rest. As the Noah story indicates (Gen. 6:5–9:18), however, a flood unleashing the watery powers of chaos that had been bounded in the construction of a world fit for human habitation (Gen. 1:6-7) would be nothing other than God's repentance that He had ever made humanity (Gen. 6:5-6). While the "never again" conclusion of the Noah story (Gen. 8:21) would support Barth's faith in God's mastery, more precisely, in God in the act of His decision to be the God of grace for humanity, still "we have not yet reached this point"[109] of seeing His mastery visibly displayed and without ambiguity. The rainbow is but a sign not yet unified with the thing signified. One must ask, indeed, not merely whether God is master of *das Nichtige,* but whether God is master of His own self.

Notwithstanding Barth's impressive clarification of the unnatural nature of undomesticated evil, he has hardly mastered the theological problem of the theodicy of faith (if he even so desired). We must return in the conclusion of this system of theology to the neuralgic question that we leave hanging at this point: the "horrible" thought (Calvin) whether the world that God chooses to create and redeem and fulfill through Jesus Christ does not entail — to put it concretely — the reprobation of Judas Iscariot by whom Jesus was betrayed in order that He might redeem — the very doctrine of the double decree (even if only applicable in the one case of Judas) that Barth had labored to overcome. Can we pray, *Thy kingdom come!,* if it entails the reprobation of even one person scripted to betray in order that others be delivered by the betrayal? Can the redeemed rejoice in the damnation of the wicked? Or is there an eternal sorrow also to be sung in the tents of the righteous?

Many who followed Barth this far, however, shook their heads at such aporia and took the more practical and activist turn represented by Moltmann's influential interpretation of Christian hope. The perception of realities that God does not

109. *CD* III/3, p. 302.

will but are nevertheless active in the world puts believers into a state of contradiction with the world as it is on this side of the eschaton; this contradiction propels them to make history in anticipation of the Reign. "Christian hope is resurrection hope, it proves its truth in the contradiction of the future prospects thereby offered and guaranteed for righteousness as opposed to sin, life as opposed to death, glory as opposed to suffering, peace as opposed to dissension. . . . In the contradiction between the word of promise and the experiential reality of suffering and death, faith takes its stand on hope and 'hastens beyond this world,' says Calvin."[110] The very perception of the anti-divine powers as evil is evoked by the promise of God for righteousness, Moltmann stresses; apart from Easter faith we would consider what is morally evil as necessary components of the unchangeable cosmic system of things — as Nietzsche did in his Shiva-like embrace of the eternal return of the same. Faith accordingly never transcends this state of active contradiction to the evils of this world until it gives way to sight at the coming of the Kingdom; it now lives and acts in hope for the victory of the kingdom over the evil powers. "The man of hope who leaves behind the corrupt reality and launches out on to the sea of divine possibilities, thereby radically sets this reality of his at stake — staking it on the hope that the promise of God will win the day."[111]

So far as it goes, Moltmann's practical resolution of the problem of theodicy in *The Theology of Hope* is surely right; it is a position that the present system of Christian doctrine gratefully recognizes and in large part adopts. Such ethical *practices* of reconciliation are the practical answers that Christian faith gives to the problems of evil here and now. Any theoretical resolution, moreover, that domesticates moral evil as anything other than sinful contradiction to the God of Beloved Community, and so defunds the energy of hope at work in love to structure justice in the world, would to that extent somehow be also theoretically false. Whatever else there is to say theologically about moral evil, it is practically to be resisted and ultimately to be defeated as per the petition, taken seriously, *Thy kingdom come!* Notwithstanding this summons to hope, in his *The Crucified God* Moltmann evidently felt the need to develop a comprehensive theology of the suffering of God: not only of the Son's incarnate suffering, but the suffering of the Father who knows His own infinite grief of loss. The difficulty here is whether Moltmann's patripassianism re-mystifies the problem of evil. In place of God's wrath against sin we meet God's helplessness at his Son's victimization. That is a far cry, so to speak, from Moltmann's earlier claim that it is ". . . this world [that] cannot bear the resurrection and the new world created by the resurrection."[112] Here, in hope rather than in bathos, the theodicy of faith strengthens courage to live by faith in the contradiction of hope to the way things are.

---

110. Jürgen Moltmann, *The Theology of Hope*, trans. J. W. Leitsch (New York: Harper & Row, 1967), pp. 18-19.

111. Moltmann, *The Theology of Hope*, p. 227.

112. Moltmann, *The Theology of Hope*, p. 226.

The contradiction of hope to the structures of malice and injustice is real and may be eternally real. Recall once again the parable of Jesus that Luke preserved for us. Not in all eternity does Dives lament over his perdition issue in repentance. He never sees the wickedness of his lifelong lovelessness. In Dives we see unvarnished the old Adam, making himself the measure of all things, so that others are experienced, assessed, deployed to his advantage, or disposed of as obstacles in his path — God included. But God is *truly* love, where divine "love must be against what is against love" (Tillich). For "love [must be] sincere: hate what is evil; cling to what is good" (Rom. 12:9). In this improper and "alien" way, the God of love, who hates what is loveless, "hands over" the loveless to the loveless choices made (Rom. 1:24, 26, 28). In this active, providential disposing of what is not love to its own destinies, the false self of loveless self-love experiences the true God of love as mortal enemy. Thus Luke in his version of Jesus' preaching of the heavenly Father issues also the "woes" corresponding to the eschatological "blessings" in the Sermon on the Plain: "But woe to you who are rich, for you have received your consolation. Woe to you who are full now, for you will be hungry. Woe to you who are laughing now, for you will mourn and weep. Woe to you when all speak well of you, for that is what their ancestors did to all the prophets" (Luke 6:24-26). *Opus alienum, ira Dei.*

Against this backdrop of God's wrath at the greed that ruins His earth, consider Luke's dramatic image of the spontaneous forgiving love of the rejoicing father in the parable of the lost son, who in his greed had wasted all. Spontaneous, forgiving love extends even towards the resentful elder brother, who in his envy towards his brother's redemption withheld reconciliation (Luke 15:11-32). So the father's self-surpassing love stands out as a contradiction of the contradiction that is self-sustaining lovelessness. We have additionally the express word in Luke of the Father's generosity, "Do not be afraid, little flock, for it is your Father's good pleasure to give you the kingdom" (Luke 12:32). For Luke, the gift which the Father gives is His own Spirit: "If you then, who are evil, know how to give good gifts to your children, how much more will the heavenly Father give the Holy Spirit to those who ask for him!" (Luke 11:13). So here, as well as in Matthew, the address, *Our Father in heaven,* calls to participation in Jesus' own filial relation to God by the gift of the same Spirit in earnest of the coming Reign. Yet this gift also indicates a definite *Novum,* a divine self-surpassing that works a negation of the negation, a division of the division, a contradiction of the contradiction. That too is what is prayed in the petition, *Thy kingdom come!*

On account of His solidarity with us, Jesus' faith in the coming reign of His Father is an afflicted faith (Luke 9:41). The revelation of Jesus' standing before God at His baptism forms the basis in Luke for the testing questions by the unholy spirit regarding the nature of Jesus' Sonship (Luke 4:5-13), which follow immediately upon the baptism and then recur in the taunting of the mob at the crucifixion (Luke 22:53b; 23:35-37). In this way of trial, the evangelist Luke sets before us the truly *human* obedience of *faith* in the *almighty Father* which appeared once and for all in the journey of Spirit-anointed Messiah Jesus (Luke 4:18-19) to Jerusalem (Luke 9:31), by which obedient faith He loved the ungodly to the end (Luke 23:34) and died in hope of that Father's reign, "Father, into your hands I commit my spirit" (Luke 23:46), establishing in Himself this way of inclusion also of the wicked who turn to him, "Today you will be with me in Paradise" (Luke 23:43).

The one who proclaimed God as the heavenly Father, who knows in faith that He is His beloved Son, who brought Him mercifully near to the undeserving goes finally to ignominious death as one disgraced before the world and abandoned by the Father into the hands of sinners, all his claims to speak in God's name and bring Him near publicly refuted with the finality of death. Yet still, by Luke's testimony, this Afflicted One dies trusting in this Father (Luke 23:46). The heavenly voice that set Jesus on this path will now have to leave Jesus dead, deceived, and refuted, or vindicate His trust and call Him anew from that state of defeat and humiliation as victor over it on behalf of those others for whom He has lived and died. The Father will have to proclaim His Son Jesus who had proclaimed and believed Him, the heavenly Father. In this way the kingship that Jesus proclaimed actually comes to power in the coup d'état of the ages.

We may also see from John's Gospel how Jesus' proclamation of the God of Israel as the heavenly Father entailed for early Christians Jesus' own identity as the Son who has come down from heaven to inaugurate the reign of God. John 6:32-33 has Jesus saying, "Very truly, I tell you, it was not Moses who gave you the bread from heaven, but it is my Father who gives you the true bread from heaven. For the bread of God is that which comes down from heaven and gives life to the world." Jesus is the Son whom His Father gives for the life of the perishing world. Several verses later, Jesus makes the direct identification: "I am the bread of life" who has "come down from heaven, not to do my own will, but the will of him who sent me. And this is the will of him who sent me, that I should lose nothing of all that he has given me, but raise it up on the last day. This is indeed the will of my Father, that all who see the Son and believe in him may have eternal life; and I will raise them up on the last day" (John 6:35, 38-40). The natural objection sounds at once: "Is not this Jesus, the son of Joseph, whose father and mother we know? How can he now say, 'I have come down from heaven'?" (John 6:42). Yet, this objection lacks true force, since admittedly "no one can come to me unless drawn by the Father who sent me" (John 6:44) as it is "written in the prophets, 'And they shall all be taught by God.' Everyone who has heard and learned from the Father comes to me. Not that anyone has seen the Father except the one who is from God; he has seen the Father" (John 6:45-46).

This Johannine dialectic between the Son's proclamation of the heavenly Father and the heavenly Father's attestation of the Son seems maddeningly circular until we realize that access, not epistemology, is the point and that accordingly the circle in question is the divine life itself, which is not interested in demonstrating itself to neutral observers but in opening itself to include lost creatures in its own eternal life. Here the circle of the Father's love for the Son and the Son's love for the Father opens to include estranged creatures by the Spirit's procession to them. The question therefore hangs as much upon whether they come to know God's Fatherhood as Jesus' Sonship — this patrological knowledge comes only by the Spirit of the Father that rests upon the Son. Therefore, the climactic statement of Johannine theology has Jesus asking for the enacting in time, inclusive now of the lost of the world for whom Jesus has come, of the relation of mutual esteeming that obtains eternally. According to John 17, "After Jesus had spoken these words, he looked up to heaven and said, 'Father, the hour has come; glorify your Son so that the Son may glorify you, since you have given him authority over all people, to give eternal life to all whom you have given him. And this is eternal life, that they may know you, the only true God, and Jesus Christ whom you have sent. I glorified you on earth by finishing the work that you gave me to do. So now, Father, glorify me in your own presence with the glory that I had in your presence before the world existed. . . . All mine are yours, and yours are mine; and I have been glorified in them. And now I am no longer in the world, but they are in the world, and I am coming to you. Holy Father, protect them in your name that you have given me, so that they may be one, as we are one.'" The eternal love of the Father and the Son in the Spirit now gathers and keeps and brings to the fulfillment of eternal life all those for whom the Son was given and gave Himself, for whom — *in this Johannine version of the petition of Lord's Prayer, "Thy kingdom come!"* — Jesus himself intercedes as priest of the reign that He petitions.

The theme of God's kingship spans the Bible from beginning to end. "The Lord will reign forever and ever," Miriam concludes in her hymn of victory to the One who triumphed gloriously, casting horse and rider into the sea (Exod. 15:18). The seer sees One who sits upon the throne exulting, "I am making all things new. . . . It is done! I am the Alpha and the Omega, the beginning and the end. To the thirsty, I will give water as a gift from the spring of the water of life. Those who conquer will inherit these things, and I will be their God and they will be my children. But as for the cowardly, the faithless, the polluted, the murderers, the fornicators, the sorcerers, the idolaters, and all liars, their place will be in the lake that burns with fire and sulfur, which is the second death" (Rev. 21:6-8). The drama of the biblical salvation history, unfolding between this beginning and this end, consists on the one hand in humanity's persistent refusal of God's proffered kingship: "They have not rejected you [Samuel], but they have rejected me from being king over them. Just as they have done to me, from the day I brought them out of Egypt to this day, forsaking me and serving other gods . . ." (1 Sam. 8:7-8). On the other hand, the biblical story depicts the Shepherd King all the more persistently seeking and finding, calling and redeeming those lost to His reign that its ranks may be filled to overflowing (Luke 14:23).

In answering the prayer that He Himself has us pray at the Son's invitation, *Thy kingdom come!,* the Father proves faithful to His creative purpose. In summation of the biblical whole, the Pauline school can state doctrinally: "The saying is sure: If we have died with him, we will also live with him; if we endure, we will also reign with him; if we deny him, he will also deny us; if we are faithless, he remains faithful — for he cannot deny himself" (2 Tim. 2:11-13). There are, then, things which the *almighty* Father *cannot* do in bringing about His kingdom, if He is to be faithful to His own purpose. The paradox is only apparent. God is *not* the arbitrary tyrant that the egocentric mind projects apart from knowing Him in the Spirit as the self-surpassing Father of the Son, Jesus Christ. This God cannot undo His promise in the act of origin without denying Himself; He is almighty in making and keeping commitments, not by "freely" walking away from them. The Noah tale of the primeval history conducts a theological thought-experiment that brings out the possibility lurking in the background that has been henceforth and forever rejected in the divine resolution to redeem sinful humanity (Gen. 8:21-22). There is in God's assertion of rule, therefore, a "happy necessity" (Leibniz) consequent upon God's free but now-resolute self-determination to redeem and fulfill His creation, the same insight behind Luther's adamant rejection of Ockham's speculation that God can save apart from the gift of His justifying grace. There is thus a divine wisdom at work mediating God's power and love beyond what human imagination can conjure that has found the way in the cross of the incarnate Son to redeem the promise of origin and bring in God's saving reign on behalf of all, even the "faithless." The Father's almighty power shows forth in this inexhaustible and inexpressible generosity — so Jesus has proclaimed Him as the heavenly Father — and just this patrological good pleasure in all things created establishes the *right* by which He is to be sought and *ought* in turn to be acknowledged by creatures. Staying in character, it is the Father's *good pleasure* to give the kingdom to all who at Jesus' invitation and command implore its coming. This chief petition in Jesus' prayer implores the kingdom's victory for *me* as *for all*.

To pray the *kingdom* of God's coming is therefore to acknowledge doxologically the *two natures* in the eternal *hierarchy* of Creator and creature, by *right* of which the *creature* petitions the *Creator* who patrologically gives all things freely, whose superiority does not consist merely in power but also in the right and righteousness that delivers power in harmony with wisdom and love. "If a mortal man should pronounce his will and command and make his volition a sufficient reason, I admit it would be tyrannical. But to transfer the principle to God is sacrilegious folly. For no immoderation may be attributed to God, as if desire surged in Him as in men. Rather such honor is rightly ascribed to His will that it constitutes a sufficient reason, since it is the origin and rule of all righteousness . . . so far from there being anything unordained in God, rather all order, traceable in heaven and earth originates in Him. When, therefore, we carry the will of God to the highest level so as to be higher than all reason, we do not at all imagine that He does anything but with the highest reason. . . . Hence Augustine's word should never be forgotten: Attend to who God is and who you are. He is God, you are man."[113]

---

113. John Calvin, *Concerning the Eternal Predestination of God,* trans. J. K. S. Reid (Louisville: Westminster John Knox, 1997), pp. 117-18.

The eternal hierarchy so construed, God's kingship is not despotism, as Calvin affirms, although he could not, for lack of adequate Trinitarianism, fully substantiate this theologically by patrological interpretation of it.[114] God's almighty power is faithful and righteous, wise and good, not capricious, willful, arbitrary, but motivated by the good pleasure of the Father that rests upon the Son on whom the Spirit descends: "This is my Son, the Beloved, with whom I am well pleased" (Matt. 3:17). Jesus Christ is the right and righteousness of the God who is Father. It follows that there are things that this Father, precisely as almighty Creator and rightful King over all creation, will not and cannot do. God cannot be motivated by anything other than His own good pleasure, which He takes in His Son upon whom He breathes His Spirit. God therefore cannot deny His own wisdom or love in the almighty assertion of His coming reign. God exercises almighty power in conjunction with wisdom and love. His kingdom comes in the harmony of power, wisdom, and love — and never apart from it. Apart from this harmony, it is not the kingdom of God but that of some pretender.

And pretenders abound. Spirits must be tested, exposed, and sometimes opposed. There can be no doubt that Jesus of Nazareth viewed the coming of God's kingdom as the routing of a superhuman usurper, whom he named Satan, and from whose cruel grip His mighty words-and-deeds inaugurating His Father's reign by the power of the Spirit released suffering human beings. "No one can enter a strong man's house and carry off his possessions unless he first ties up the strong man. Then he can plunder his goods" (Mark 3:27). The progressive theology of the nineteenth century rightly seized upon the New Testament's rhetoric of the kingdom of God as central to Jesus' proclamation of His Father, but minimized this crucial aspect for Jesus of its mortal combat with the *regnum diaboli;* this it regarded as a remnant of primitive mythology. Therefore, unlike McCord Adams, it had no real need for an Incarnation in Christology to enter into the strong man's house there to face and defeat the horror-maker. It took the kingdom of God in Kantian fashion as the progressive establishment of an ethical kingdom of ascending freedom over the brute force of nature — "the victory of the good principle in the founding of a Kingdom of God on earth."[115]

In so doing, liberal theology understood the socio-ethical progress of humanity (such as it is) as the erection of the kingdom of God on earth, ascribing to

114. Reid says in criticism of a kind of a crypto-Unitarianism operative in Calvin: "To accord Christ an important place in the execution of the decrees falls short of what is demanded. Instrumentality is not a concept that adequately conveys the role that Christ must here be deemed to play. . . . Where and when the counsels of God are determined, there and then Christ is present. . . . The incarnation gives us the key to all God's nature, or it is not the complete revelation which Christianity has always considered it to be." Calvin, *Concerning the Eternal Predestination,* p. 41.

115. Immanuel Kant, "Religion within the Boundaries of Mere Reason," in *Religion and Rational Theology,* trans. A. W. Wood and G. Di Giovanni (Cambridge: Cambridge University Press, 2001), pp. 130-32, 146-53.

its ethical ascent the eschatological "work which God reserves to himself alone" (Luther) as the almighty Father who creates all things by his Word in his Spirit. It was not wrong in principle to make a correlation here, to see in struggling structures of justice and love on the earth an in-breaking of the Kingdom's righteousness that prepares the way of the Lord who comes. What is questionable is whether "progress," so understood along Kantian lines as the ethical humanization of brute nature, was a proper conceptualization of the kingdom that comes from *above,* from the *heavenly* Father, by *His* Word incarnate and His preaching Spirit in this present interregnum through the ecclesia in mission to the nations.

The discovery by Johannes Weiss at the turn of the last century that Jesus did not think in a "thetic" way about the kingdom, but "antithetically," i.e., that God's kingdom comes to vanquish Satan's kingdom, still unnerves. For, it means that we are blinded by and captive to structures of malice and injustice; until the strong man is bound before our eyes, we cannot realize that we had been in his grip. Sinners have grown fond of their oppression; our world is one vast Stockholm syndrome. To believe with Jesus in this petition for the coming of His Father's kingdom, one therefore has also to be more than merely enlightened. One must be disenchanted, so that one now disbelieves Satan's promises as false, sees through the manifold seductions, and indeed comes to see in this one disguised as an angel of light (2 Cor. 11:14) the usurpation of creation in pervasive corruption — all this as knowledge of God, to boot, accessed by the powerful "interruption" (Jüngel) of the Word in the Spirit. Theology that intends orthodoxy thus finds its true place in the modern world of Euro-American self-consciousness by return to the renunciation that prefaces early Christian baptism. The forgiveness of sins rather than the "value of personality" (taken as "self-consciousness") again becomes the key opening the kingdom's gates. The entire "apocalyptic fantasy" about the future returns, deliteralized to be sure and theologically decoded to tell the movement of God beyond wrath to a self-surpassing mercy that in its coming transforms the theological subject by conforming it to the theological object, the crucified and risen Son incarnate, in conscientious new life before God, hence *contra mundum* (against this world). But in the crises of the twentieth century, liberalism instead turned to existentialism to avoid this unsavory prospect of embracing apocalyptic theology in critical dogmatics.

According to Luke's revision of Mark, Christians live in apocalyptic time, i.e., not the end of time but the time of the end pressing in and pressing Satan back. In a sermon on Luke 21, Luther thought it worthwhile for sixteenth-century Germans to hear the "testimony" of the fourth-century "Christian Cicero," Lactantius, who suffered for the faith. Luther quoted at length as follows.

> When the end of the world draws near, the condition of human affairs must materially change and take on a more wicked form. Then will malice and wickedness prevail to such a degree that our age, in which malice and wickedness have almost reached their highest pitch, will be looked upon as happy and treasured,

as golden in comparison with that time when no one will be able to help or give advice. Then will righteousness become practically unknown, and blasphemy, covetousness, impure desires, and unchastity become common. Then will the godly become a prey to the most wicked and be vexed and grieved by them. At the same time only the wicked will be rich and well to do, while the godly will be driven hither and thither in shame and poverty. Justice will be perverted, law will be overthrown, and no one will have aught else but that which is secure by his own strength. Daring and strength will possess all. There will be neither faith nor confidence left in man, neither peace, nor loveliness, nor shame, nor truth, and as a result, no safety, no government, no rest of any kind from the reprobate. For all lands will become rebellious, everywhere men will rage and war with one another, the whole world will be in arms, and bring destruction to itself.[116]

If we follow Luther following Lactantius following Luke, we know that Christians have been living with apocalyptic times for a very long time. Thus, according to Luther, they ardently pray, "Thy kingdom come," and "Deliver us from evil." "If we are true Christians we will earnestly and heartily join in this prayer. If we do not so pray, we are not yet true Christians. . . . If we really wish to be freed from sin and death and hell, we must look forward to this coming of the Lord with joy and pleasure."[117] In the *Confessions,* the yet unconverted Augustine had half-heartedly prayed, "O Lord, give me chastity — but not just yet." Luther borrows the witticism and charges "false" Christians with praying, "May thy kingdom not come, or not just yet."[118] Living in the tension between the already and the not yet, Christians live *with* apocalyptic crises, bearing a double witness to the wrath of the God of love against all that is against love and to the surpassing mercy of the God of love, who comes into these times with us and for us in Christ by the Spirit, who teaches us earnestly to pray, *Thy kingdom come!,* hence to live on the earth that God's will be done as in heaven — apocalyptic times!

Classical theology in any case allows for an economic, though not an onto-logical dualism here. That is to say, it is a stubborn fact of historical human expe-rience that God's will is refused and resisted with such force and depth as virtually to require the supposition of a superhuman force behind it. The figure of Satan, in this way, is rhetorically necessary. Deliteralized and theologically decoded, we may say that whatever this superhuman evil may be, it is and only can be a creature. God the Father who creates *ex nihilo* by His own Word and Spirit has no equal and opposite opponent — not the chaos of Genesis 1:2 nor the chaos of Satan, whose only power is privative envy of what God by good pleasure wills and gives. Satan erupts and destroys like Noah's flood by God's permission but then is

116. *Sermons of Martin Luther,* ed. John Nicolas Lenker, 8 volumes (Grand Rapids: Baker, reprinted 1983), 1:70-71.

117. *Luther Sermons,* 1, p. 75.

118. *Luther Sermons,* 1, p. 79.

sent back into its hole, so that once purged, life on the earth may be renewed. Its seduction of humanity with false promises; its assault on the innocent; its tyranny over the blinded minds and hardened hearts of the Pharaohs of this world are matters of urgent concern in the life of faith and pastoral theology. Just because ontological dualism is and must be rejected, the economic dualism embedded in the petition *Thy Kingdom come!* is theologically unavoidable.

Nevertheless, the critical issue for dogmatics is not merely to acknowledge the actual evil of the demonic; it is to articulate the *theodicy* of this divine permission of evil, that is to say, God's making of this particular world in which rain falls on the just and unjust alike (Matt. 5:45); where indeed the just suffer and the wicked prosper under structures of malice and injustice; where the superhuman power of envy fuels the malice that works injustice. God's kingdom comes in the end, whether creatures pray it so or not, though Jesus' prayer asks that petitioners be enlisted in its cause by new lives of love and justice. Yet rebellion against the will of God is something foreseen and thus permitted from the origin on the way to the eschaton, and so in the fullness of time is made to serve God's reign. "You meant it for evil," says Joseph to the brothers who had sold him into slavery, "but God meant it for good" (Gen. 50:20). This knowledge of God whose kingdom comes in the apocalyptic time of trial steels the petitioner to perseverance in the righteousness of faith.

> But later Joseph got what he did not understand and never had the courage to hope or ask for. These are truly lofty and wonderful examples which we ourselves should learn and also set before others, in order that we may recognize the divine *wisdom, goodness, mercy, and power* which are most certainly near us. The *goodness* is certainly there; the *wisdom* is certainly there; the *power,* etc. But God does not act according to our wish when He governs according to His goodness, wisdom, etc. Then we do not understand; for we think that God does not know us and does not want to concern Himself with or think about the outcome of our trial. This is the way reason judges. But this is not in accordance with the doctrine of Christians or with the knowledge of God in the Spirit. Nor can I boast of perfection. . . . Accordingly, these matters should be thought of and practiced more often, in order that we may prove what is the good, acceptable, and perfect will of God (cf. Rom. 12:2). [For what it is that God is wise, good, powerful, merciful, no one understands except speculatively and metaphysically], just as one can conceive some idea of the goodness or wisdom of a prince that is pure speculation. But when it comes to practice, when God snatches Joseph from the embrace of his parents, his grandfather, father, and the whole household, and he is hurled into prison in a foreign land on the charge of adultery and remains there [in fear and] in constant expectation of death — [surely this will not be interpreted to anyone as the good will of God]?[119]

119. *LW* 7, p. 175, emphasis added. Brackets indicate my emendation of the translation. For fuller discussion of this text, see pp. 848-49 below.

Like Hegel's Owl of Minerva that takes flight only at dusk, Luther's faith that trusts the promise of God only sees in hindsight. "We, however, do not understand [God's promises] until His counsels are carried out."[120] There is and must be then a principled agnosticism regarding the "how" of the fulfillment (1 John 3:2), an openness to the surprising folly of God that is wiser than human wisdom (1 Cor. 1:25). In this classic theodicy of faith the example of Joseph, in Luther's reading, makes this point again and again. But faith then *sees.* Luther therefore expects that experienced faith will progress in knowledge of God and with the help of biblical narrative learn to recognize God also in times of testing. "Accordingly, these matters must be taught for our instruction, in order that we may know what the theology of the Gospel is."[121] God is God whose reign surely comes, though we know not how (Mark 4:27). But what can this mean?

As the Luther citation shows, the knowledge of faith is not other than the "speculative" knowledge of God in the positive attributes by which God relates to the world as Creator who governs events so that His kingdom come. These are the trinity of attributes — power, wisdom, and love. God is present to the creation at all times in power, wisdom, and goodness, having available all possibilities to actualize intelligently for the good by the ever-innovating Spirit of the Word. But the divine subject of these predicates does not act according to our understanding of their sense. The unity of God as the harmony of these predications indeed seems to fall victim to Epicurus's dilemma. Given the evils that afflict creation, if God is good, then God seems powerless to prevent them. If God is powerful, then God seems not to care for us in our affliction and that is not good. Such appearances of God lead to incomprehension of the divine subject as a unified subject possessing these predicates in the simplicity of His transcendent being. For Luther, then, the speculative knowledge of God as Creator jars with the experiential knowledge of creatures and cannot but lead to the false judgment of *ratio:* God neither knows nor cares for us but abandons us in the time of trial.

This judgment of *ratio,* however, conflicts with Christian doctrine and the knowledge of God in the Spirit, according to Luther, which knowledge of faith is resisted by the flesh (according to Paul's antinomy, not Plato's). The flesh is spiritually operative in the false judgments of *ratio.* The knowledge of God as power, wisdom, and love is what speculative metaphysics attains in thinking abstractly the condition of the possibility of a free act of creation and preservation of all that is other than the Creator. As speculative metaphysics, it does not know God's wisdom in the cross of the Messiah — how even actual evil is made there to serve the coming of God's reign. In contrast to this speculative knowledge, the recipient of God's messianic promise, Joseph, encounters God in the experience of God permitting great evils to happen to him. He surely cannot understand these evils as the good will of God. God's permission of evil makes the question of theodicy

---

120. *LW* 8, p. 30.
121. *LW* 8, p. 30.

a question precisely for the faith of the elect Joseph, heir of messianic promises. But Joseph exemplifies true faith precisely in the time of trial and in this way prefigures the Messiah to come. He suffers God's will to be done.

This scriptural conviction of God's overruling of the wayward creation in the course of events is at the heart of Jesus' scriptural faith in the heavenly Father in respect to His own person and messianic role. He prayed in Gethsemane that God's will be done on earth, not only absolutely in the sense of the final events, but particularly in relation to the here-and-now circumstances of impending torture and utter spiritual humiliation. In facing that destiny, Jesus knew Himself handed over by His own Abba Father "into the hands of sinners," who meant to destroy Him who had brought that same heavenly Father mercifully near to the godless. Jesus nevertheless trusted in this ordeal that the evil of His passion would become in the hands of the Father the occasion of the redemption of those sinners and all other sinners.

*Thy will be done on earth as in heaven* is probably the first church's gloss of Jesus' original and simpler petition, *Thy kingdom come!* It gives the correct understanding of Jesus' petition in the light of Jesus' destiny, specifying that this very earth on which stood His cross is the place of redemption. "The greatest prayer ever uttered was that of Jesus in Gethsemane." *"Abba Father, for you all things are possible. Remove this cup from me. Yet, not what I want, but what you want!"* (Mark 14:36). "Perhaps it is this one [in Gethsemane] rather than the other which ought to be called preeminently the Lord's Prayer."[122] If Jesus was not spared the cup by the God who spared not His own Son, nor saved from the time of trial, neither can the kingdom's coming be hurried by our prayers nor the time of trial on the other hand delayed by them. "God's kingdom comes on its own without our prayer. . . . [But] we ask in this prayer that it may also come to us" by the gift of the Spirit, "so that through his grace we believe his Holy Word and live godly lives here in time and hereafter in eternity" (Luther).[123] To believe God's holy Word in the power of the Spirit is to persevere in time of trial and thus all the more ardently to pray, *Thy kingdom come!*

Luther's theological exposition of the Lord's Prayer, just cited, was virtually cribbed from Augustine's treatise "On the Gift of Perseverance," who in turn virtually cribbed it from Cyprian. The petition, *Thy kingdom come!,* is the biblical seat of anti-Pelagian doctrine. This consists in three points according to Augustine: "One of these is that the grace of God is not given according to our merits; because even every one of the merits of the righteous is God's gift, and is conferred by God's grace. The second is that no one lives in this corruptible body, however righteous he may be, without sins of some kind. The third is that man is born obnoxious to the first man's sin and bound by the chain of condemnation, unless the guilt which is contracted by generation be loosed by regeneration."

---

122. Scott, *The Lord's Prayer*, p. 17.
123. *BC,* pp. 356-57.

Did these truths not obtain, there would be no point to the petition, *Thy kingdom come!* When the church of forgiven sinners petitions the hallowing of God's name and the coming of His kingdom, it asks that it "may persevere in those good things which they have acknowledged that they have received . . . perseverance itself, the great gift of God whereby His other gifts are preserved." This perseverance is not, however, mere conservatism. It is the prayer of the church to persist in mission to the nations, and in baptismal vocations within them, "since the holy Church prays not only for believers, that faith may be increased or may continue, but, moreover, for unbelievers, that they may begin to have what they have not had at all, and against which, besides, they were indulging hostile feelings."[124]

At Jesus' invitation, the *ungodly,* who do not know how to pray nor to deal in faith with the Difference that is God the heavenly Father, who permits evils but works all things to good for them who love God according to God's own purpose, are taught to seek first the kingdom and its righteousness (Matt. 6:33) in this new life before God that is prayer and so to become in the Spirit *holy* people, i.e., just those who pray with Jesus in the Spirit for the coming of the Father's reign. *That comes first.* Jesus' faith in His heavenly Father is *primary.* Only on this basis does Jesus' prayer now turn attention to the doing of that will on earth for the interim physical and moral needs of earthly and historical life in the community of disciples and beyond.

*"Give us this day our daily bread; and forgive us our trespasses as we forgive those who trespass against us . . ."*

In this petition one daily receives biological life — and all that pertains to it[125] — as gift and so shares bread with the hungry; in precise parallel, one receives one's moral life as gift and in turn remits the moral debts of others. Prayer at Jesus' invitation is the act of welcoming other such biological lives in their personal otherness as gifts from above meant for our good, even when one cannot by one's own lights see the human community with them or indeed has reason to be offended by them. The two petitions belong together. That unity of physical and moral need is made clear by the striking economic similitude[126] for moral

124. *NPNF* V, pp. 527-28.

125. "What is meant by daily bread? Answer: Everything required to satisfy our bodily needs, such as food and clothing, house and home, fields and flocks, money and property; a pious spouse and good children, trustworthy servants, godly and faithful rulers, good government; seasonable weather, peace and health, order and honor; true friends, faithful neighbors, and the like." Luther, "Small Catechism," in *BC,* p. 357.

126. Gary Anderson, *Sin: A History* (New Haven: Yale University Press, 2009). One can therefore speak of the merit of Jesus Christ gained by His obedience and accredited to us in justification, though it will not be the preferred way of articulating His decision to take responsibility for us before God.

need given in parallel to physical need. Transgressions of the legal-moral order are not the sinfulness of sins but rather the deeds of sinfulness, the distrust of the Father's Word that declines the Spirit and so fills the soul with envy that breaks out in injury. As such, sinful people do injury and in failing to do the good, also do injury. The continuum between the physical and the moral, the natural and the social is seamless. As we need bread daily biologically to live, to live socially we need forgiveness from God for the injuries our irresponsible lives have done to His Name and the coming of His Reign and need in turn to repair the injury by remitting the debts incurred by others who have actually injured us.

These are not our perceived needs, for who is satisfied with daily bread and forgiveness? These are our true needs, learned from praying at Jesus' invitation, if God is truly our heavenly Father whose reign approaches. The prayer for satisfaction in daily bread and forgiveness has one take the world and the others in it, like oneself, on faith in the almighty Father's generosity. The opposite of this faith that takes world, self, and others together as gifts from "our" Father's generosity, is the evil passion that fills faith's void: *concupiscence,* "inordinate desire," rapacious self-love, incurvation, love of self in all things whether in the form of envy for what one does not have or greed for more of what one already possesses.

The evangelist Luke especially has Jesus single out *greed* for attack (12:15; even self-righteousness is understood by Luke as but a manifestation of greed, 16:14-15). The materialism or secularism of those "who lay up treasure for themselves and are not rich toward God" (Luke 12:21) throws up a fortress wall against the coming of God's reign. Greed distorts right understanding. Greed is the folly of the godless who think themselves cunning and wise in the way of the world. The notion that we are alone in and against the indifferent order of nature, and that nature in turn is but the inanimate stage on which solitary minds dance to their own tunes, not responsible to the Creator for the gift of life and its stewardship for future generations, is both folly and idolatry.

Biological life and all that pertains to it link one generation to another; it forms what Edmund Burke called a "covenant of the generations." The covenant of the generations is the fundamental structure of love working justice in creation, the trust from the only Owner of all things, who commands and blesses the human couple to be fruitful, multiply, and fill the earth, subduing the wilderness to make of it a garden in a loving dominion corresponding to the Creator's own dominion. "[W]e are gardeners of someone else's garden. We are to tend our area of creation on behalf of the Creator to whom it continues to belong. . . . Nothing could be more opposed to exploitive modernity's understanding of the world as a conglomerate of 'natural resources' available for our use as we feel a need and technology enables."[127] Beginning with their own bodies, human beings are but *stewards* in this dominion of God; as such they must someday render an account (Luke 16:10-12; 19:11-27). Worldly cunning of avarice is not true wisdom, since

127. Jenson, *ST* 2, p. 115.

it fails to reckon conscientiously with God and His good pleasure, esteem, valuation, judgment. Wisdom therefore teaches the true value or treasure of things: "Make purses for yourselves that do not wear out, an unfailing treasure in heaven, where no thief comes near and no moth destroys" (Luke 12:33). Disciples are wisely to reckon with the way the world really is under our heavenly Father and so learn to love what is truly of value (Luke 14:28-32; 16:8-9). True blessedness is "to hear the Word of God and keep it" (Luke 11:28). Because the grace and good pleasure of the heavenly Father announced in Jesus' word values human beings in spite of their lowliness and undeserving, wisdom forms conscience by instruction regarding the two natures, the hierarchy that is Creator and creature. Consequently, "no slave can serve two masters; for a slave will either hate the one and love the other, or be devoted to the one and despise the other. You cannot serve God and wealth" (Luke 16:13). Daily bread and mutual forgiveness are sufficient satisfactions for those who conscientiously follow Christ into the kingdom of His Father. The experience and knowledge of His generosity has remade them from greedy into giving people who daily pray not for more but for enough, not to avenge but to forgive.

This self-denying of the old Adam in cross-bearing discipleship is a spiritual following, of course, a hearing with self-entrusting faith of the Word in the Spirit. The only "literal" way to follow Jesus of Nazareth would be to enter some science-fiction time machine and join Him on the dusty byways of Galilee in the time of Herod and Pontius Pilate. Luke understands this. One follows Jesus *spiritually,* i.e., in the same *Spirit* as the One who once and for all had led Jesus on His messianic way through the cross to the crown. The Lucan Jesus therefore offers the Spirit to effect the one and only remedy of greed in new lives of discipline: cross-bearing (Luke 9:23f.), self-renunciation (Luke 14:26) in prayerful trust of God's provision (Luke 11:1-13; 18:1-8a). "So therefore, none of you can become my disciple if you do not give up all your possessions" (Luke 14:33). The radical appropriation is spiritual, not a literalistic imitation that can actually turn a vow of poverty into the occasion for religious boasting (cf. 1 Cor. 13:3). Christ comes from the Father to take away our "possessions," that is, our possessiveness, to make us His own, His "property," His "slaves," by giving the Father's Spirit that we should will on earth His will as it is willed and done in heaven. He comes offering the true riches of God for those who will be poor; life to those who will die; righteousness to those who beat their breasts and do not even lift up their eyes to heaven (Luke 18:13-14). His call to discipleship in this way excludes the fatal misunderstanding of bourgeois Christianity that "discipleship" is some kind of autonomous human response to Jesus, more or less rigorous, but essentially a religious option on the smorgasbord of inconsequent pluralism, so finally a bargain struck on the basis of the gospel taken as a good deal. But following Jesus is not about how lucky individuals respond to a divine deal too good to be refused (or so cheap that we cannot give it away), as if now to make themselves worthy of the offered grace and thus undo the giftedness of the Spirit to make us truly new beings.

As discipleship for Luke is the work of the Spirit, it is the victory of the Father's good pleasure, already now, on earth and in history in the astonishing wisdom of the "joyful exchange" Jesus brings about. This is precisely not economy as usual, even an eminently just and equitable *quid pro quo;* it is joyful in its utter generosity, thus radical in the regenerative exchange it effects. In this exchange, discipleship surrenders autonomy to Jesus and assumes from Him the yoke of the kingdom. The disciple is not the old person using Jesus as he or she pleases, but the new person whom grace creates, the person who "sits at Jesus' feet" and in this attentive receptivity has "chosen the one thing needful" (Luke 10:38-42). Precisely this choice of the disciple by the Spirit's grant is divine deliverance from consumptive greed — salvation from sinfulness that leads to cruelty and ruin (Luke 15:12-16) — the just wages of spiritual death.

Under no circumstance then is the demand of discipleship to be spiritualized away, but rather it is to be deliteralized in the sense of being decoded theologically as the gift of the Spirit that it may be fulfilled radically, that is spiritually, in new lives of generosity on the earth. The truth of salvation itself is at stake in the Spirit-ed petitions for daily bread and mutual forgiveness. A real change of what human hearts take pleasure in — a radical reorganization of affects — is offered by Jesus and expected, for "where your treasure is, there will your heart be also" (Luke 12:34). Thus Augustine rightly prayed against every moralizing Pelagianism, howsoever "literal" it claims to be: "Command what you will, O God, but give what you command!" With this change in what the heart treasures by the Spirit's regeneration of the disciple's heart, the true treasure and consolation of the life of discipleship is lifted up, inclusion in the Beloved Community. "Truly I tell you, there is no one who has left house or wife or brothers or parents or children, for the sake of the kingdom of God, who will not get back very much more in this age, and in the age to come eternal life" (Luke 18:29-30). This true treasure manifests in the struggling new community of the disciples of Jesus in mission to the nations, where mutual submission (Luke 17:10), common provision (Acts 2:44-45), and forgiving forbearance (Luke 17:3-4) reign, because here Jesus already reigns, though from His cross. Jesus with His people is the one true consolation in life and in death. Whoever loves the church (not the corrupt institution, the religion business of decaying Christendom, but the Beloved Community that sighs and groans beneath that heavy load) is made content with daily bread and mutual care. This temporal foretaste of the eternal Reign satisfies as manna in the wilderness. The Bread of Life shared here in the holy Eucharist of Christ's body and blood suffices on the way to that best of all possible worlds.

Yet, one might still object that the petition to forgive others, as a condition of one's own forgiveness, demands the impossible. Who can let go of the right against the wrongdoer, without letting go of the right as well, that is, the very ground for distinguishing the innocent from the victimizer? Does forgiveness of sin condone sin? Does table-fellowship with sinners make one guilty by association? Does grace overthrow the law? Does forgiveness unloose a moral chaos upon the world that tenuously holds onto the rough but visible justice of the *quid pro quo* and the order of merit, the *suum cuique* (to each her own)? Should Christians simply forget the African slave trade, the Trail of Tears, the Gulag, the Holocaust? Should perpetrators get away with murder and molesters with abuse? It is a serious objection; indeed, it is the one legitimate reason of living Judaism for honest disbelief in Jesus' proclamation of the Kingdom, just as contemporary Judaism rightly maintains that forgiveness of the sincere and persistent Nazi is an impossible moral contradiction and that in this dramatic case one is right to speak of the "virtue of hate."[128] For Christians too, love must be sincere in *hating* what is evil (Rom. 12:9).

For it is not merely a question of giving up the right to avenge the wrong, to punish the evildoer, to require reparation of the injury suffered. There is a temporal and temporary place for these rights under the rough justice of political sovereignty, by which God preserves the creation from its self-destructive tendencies (Rom. 13:1-8), however corruptly this rough justice is in fact administered. But as a spiritual act, forgiveness seems to demand of the forgiver a kind of moral suicide in which a true victim is asked to give up the right to the victimizer, to let the perpetrator get away morally. The demand to abolish the right of the innocent against the wrong of the guilty is offensive enough to price Jesus' petition of forgiveness right out of the moral marketplace of historical life. Even worse, the demand of Jesus to forgive seems theologically impossible. Who can forgive sins but God alone, since sins (in distinction from crimes) offend God as Creator by despising His moral will, bringing ruin on His own precious work and creation and disgrace to His Name? What right has a mortal to forgive the sin that has been committed against God? One could hypothetically pardon a crime committed against one's own person, release from the debt, forget the transgression — all this is imaginable, however difficult. But even in one's own case, concerning one's own person, the sin against oneself that one may forgive remains sin against the creature of God that one is, and injury therefore against the name, the honor, the office of God. How can anyone forgive that? If the disciple presumes to forgive, does not the disciple, just like Jesus himself, take issue with God, *as if God were not the just judge, the avenger of the innocent, who casts down the mighty from their thrones but exalts those of low degree?*

Luke's account of Jesus' death on the cross edits out the scandalous cry of Godforsakenness from Jesus' dying lips that Luke had found in Mark. Luke does this, like John, in his generation's new situation in order to model martyrdom; he presents Jesus as the model martyr (cf. the parallelism with Stephen's death in Acts 7:54-60). Yet in another way, Luke preserves Mark's witness to the Godforsakenness of Jesus' death. Luke's Jesus is reckoned among transgressors; hoisted, He forgives His executioners. In this narrative way, Luke theologizes to the same

---

128. Meir Y. Soloveichik, "The Virtue of Hate," *First Things* (February 2003), accessed online 10/26/13 at http://www.firstthings.com/article/2007/05/the-virtue-of-hate-26.

effect as Mark, when Mark tells that the veil separating the Holy of Holies in the Temple was torn in two at the moment Godforsaken death transpires. Is not this, whether in Mark's telling of the rending of the veil or Luke's of Jesus' intercession amid the guilty, the true stone of stumbling? It is surely the one good reason, as mentioned, of living Judaism, *not* to believe the teaching of the Christian gospel, and, as argued previously, a principle that should become internal to Christian theology. For, it was also and first of all a stone of stumbling for *the Jew* Jesus in that agony of faith, which he endured in the Garden, to give up the right of the Beloved Son, sacrificing His conscience (Radner) truly to die seeing His persecutors triumphant over Him, abandoned by all, forsaken, utterly alone. Conscientiously to die such a spiritual death before God in which there is no more difference between the innocent and the guilty, the murderer and the murdered, the hater and the lover, meant for Christ Himself His own most devastating loss of identity, a true and spiritual death that obliterated the line between His righteousness and the persecutor's sin, the very line that had marked out and specified His own personal integrity and public identity in the world. Accursed and Godforsaken — in obedience to God! — Luke's Christ too resolved to be "reckoned among transgressors," descending into total darkness, His light extinguished, His truth crushed down, His voice silenced, the strange and awful action of giving by dying. "Father into your hands I commit my cause."

If the petition, "Give us this day our daily bread and forgive us our trespasses as we forgive those who trespass against us," is to be fulfilled, it is fulfilled when, by the same Spirit that led Jesus through Golgotha to await in a state of extinction His vindication by the almighty Father, believers must participate in Jesus' own afflicted faith. It is important, however, to recall again that conscientious participation in Jesus' afflicted faith by followers is only possible if by the resurrection that affliction has been vindicated and thus exists as something that can be given as the gift of a new way of life, not imposed or demanded as a way of death. A self-chosen theology of the cross that imagines itself closer to God by self-imposed self-hatred is nothing but a peculiarly sick twist on the sinful narcissism from which the resurrection of the Crucified sets free. The theology of the cross has its moment on the way to the joyful exchange; if not, it gets stuck in a sick and joyless exchange of self-hatred for God's approval.

Johann Anselm Steiger has brought out the peculiar dialectic of mutability and immutability involved in prayerful participation in the afflicted faith of Jesus, prefigured, as Steiger explores, in Luther's interpretation of the prophet Jonah's "three days in the belly of the whale."[129] Christologically, this is, as we may recall

---

129. Johann Anselm Steiger, *Jonas Propheta: Zur Auslegungs- und Mediengeschichte des Buches Jona bein Martin Luther und im Luthertum der Barockzeit,* mit einer Edition von Johann Matthäus Meyfarts "Tuba Poenitentiae Prophetica" (1625) (Stuttgart-Bad Cannstatt: Frommann-Holzboog Verlag, 2011). The following material first appeared in a book review in *Lutheran Quarterly* 26, no. 4 (Winter 2012): 453-55. Translations are my own.

from Chapter Six, the peculiar ambivalence that attaches to the motif of the descent into hell, at once the downward nadir of Christ's affliction and at the same time the beginning of His victory on behalf of those in bondage. Luther's passive obedience of Christ in His atoning death is typologically anticipated by the guilty Jonah who was cast overboard to spare the innocent shipmates.[130] This theology of atonement, moreover, couples seamlessly with the Christus Victor motif, prefigured in Jonah's "resurrection," i.e., being "spewed forth" from the whale/tomb.[131] "The swallowed swallows the swallower"[132] — a picture Steiger relates to the theology of baptism and indeed finds engraved upon baptismal fonts from the Reformation period,[133] recalling the formation of the theological subject argued in Chapter One of this book.

Hermeneutically, Steiger fastens Luther's key onto contemporaneous theological exegesis: identification with Jonah's *tentatio* (trial) in his history with God.[134] Some distinctive discoveries made with this approach stand out in comparison to the antecedent history of exegesis. The church fathers generally regarded the "whale" as a savior sent from God to rescue the drowning Jonah,[135] but Luther, on the basis of Jonah's prayer from its belly, regards the place instead as a figure of hell;[136] typologically then, Jonah here figures Christ's descent into hell. Typology is not one-for-one allegory. Luther does not exculpate Jonah, who, he avers, had sinned as gravely as Adam.[137] Insisting on Jonah's true sin under true judgment allows Luther to bring out the "contrafacticity" of Jonah's faith in the prayer uttered from the whale's belly, faith's "nevertheless."[138] Jonah's audacious faith can *alter God;* faith's prayer is a "hammer,"[139] which can turn hell upside down[140] and move God from wrath to mercy.[141] "God is also in hell, that is, in the place of absolute distance from God. Put otherwise: Even in hell, where God is not praised (Isa. 38:18), where indeed God is not, the divine promise is and remains valid that faith has the power even here to claim the promise and through its petition (be it only a breath) to overcome hell."[142] Steiger is careful to note: this power to "alter God" is for Luther not a capability of the pious subject,[143] the bribery of the religion business in one form or another. No, it is the very power of the Word

130. Steiger, *Jonas Propheta,* pp. 116, 121.
131. Steiger, *Jonas Propheta,* p. 127.
132. Steiger, *Jonas Propheta,* p. 133.
133. Steiger, *Jonas Propheta,* p. 139.
134. Steiger, *Jonas Propheta,* p. 16.
135. Steiger, *Jonas Propheta,* p. 18.
136. Steiger, *Jonas Propheta,* p. 17.
137. Steiger, *Jonas Propheta,* p. 24.
138. Steiger, *Jonas Propheta,* p. 31.
139. Steiger, *Jonas Propheta,* p. 32.
140. Steiger, *Jonas Propheta,* p. 34.
141. Steiger, *Jonas Propheta,* p. 37.
142. Steiger, *Jonas Propheta,* p. 36.
143. Steiger, *Jonas Propheta,* p. 38.

of God preached back to God. Here God's identity disclosed as promised in the Word is not the philosophical abstraction of standard theism, but God *is* the One who is determined to redeem and fulfill His creation for the Beloved Community. By the power of His *own* Word, as revealed for *this* purpose, God lets Himself be besieged and overcome in the conscientious prayer of faith. Hence a dialectic of immutability and mutability takes place in a real history with humanity.

God is not a frozen block of ice; God is no "Stoic,"[144] but manifests divine freedom, just as the Biblical text says in response to Nineveh's eventual repentance, also "to repent"[145] when Jonah cries out to Him from his experience of eternal death. Calvin could still retain from Luther the motif of Jonah's sin and experience of hell,[146] but at just this juncture of the mutability of God before conscientious prayer at God's own invitation for God's own immutable purpose, exegesis in the Reformed tradition sharply separated from Luther and his followers. God's immutability demanded, according to the Reformed, that the report of God's repentance be taken as "improper language."[147] Steiger's discussion of natural and spiritual omnipresence that arises from Luther's seminal exegesis[148] in this regard comes to the proposition we recall from Chapter Six. It is one thing for God to be present, even in hell, as the place of His spiritual absence; it is another for God to be present for you, also in hell, at the depth of His self-surpassing mercy. To live conscientiously before God is to wrestle, like Jacob at the Jabbok,[149]

---

144. Steiger, *Jonas Propheta*, p. 65.

145. Steiger, *Jonas Propheta*, p. 207.

146. Steiger, *Jonas Propheta*, p. 18.

147. Steiger, *Jonas Propheta*, p. 58.

148. Steiger, *Jonas Propheta*, pp. 34, 37, 123, 168-69, 202.

149. "This passage is regarded by all as among the most obscure passages of the whole Old Testament," Luther writes. "Nor is this strange, because it deals with that sublime temptation in which the patriarch Jacob had to fight not with flesh and blood or with the devil but against God Himself. But that is a horrible battle when God Himself fights and in a hostile fashion opposes His opponent as though on the point of taking away life. He who wishes to stand and conquer in this struggle must certainly be a holy man and a true Christian." Jacob's foe, Luther opines, "the wrestler, is the Lord of glory, God Himself, or God's Son, who was to become incarnate and who appeared and spoke to the fathers." When God appears in hostile form — that is, as disincarnate, not as the baby in the manger, the man on the imperial stake — Luther writes, "the afflicted heart complains that it has been forsaken and cast off by God. This is the last and most serious temptation to unbelief and despair, by which the greatest of the saints are usually disciplined. . . . But before we reach this stage [of Jacob who prevailed by faith in the incarnate God], life may be a trying experience. . . ." Luther imaginatively depicts the spiritual struggle: "Undoubtedly, the [attacker] sounded forth with terrifying voice, saying: "You must perish, Jacob; you are in for it!" To this Jacob would have replied: "No! that is not God's will. I shall not perish!" Yes and no there assailed each other very sharply and violently. Such things cannot be adequately expressed by word of mouth, especially when God Himself is saying: "You will perish!" and the spirit shouts back: "I shall not perish, but live. . . . I may be pushed, assailed, and thrown down, yet I shall not die." So they struggled with arms and words alike as two wrestlers usually do. But in the meantime, faith, too, joined the struggle by praying and crying. . . . This was the crisis of the struggle, in

with God in prayer, that is, in the Spirit till God surpasses God also on the earth as in heaven, that is, until the heavenly Father becomes our Father too, just as He wills, already now on earth, also in the time of trial.

*"And lead us not into temptation, but deliver us from evil. For Thine is the kingdom, the power and the glory, forever. Amen."*

It is foolhardy, in light of the foregoing, to seek out the trial of faith, which in any case comes on its own with or without our prayer as birth pangs of the creation, signals of the time of the end and the coming of the Reign. But the faith of Jesus, which is the faith of the Suffering Servant of God in the LORD, the faith of believing Israel that is also the faith of the martyrs,[150] comes into its own through the trial of conscience, because it anticipates in just these depths God's promised victory over the contra-divine powers of sin, death, and evil.

> It was Passover, 1944. A transport had arrived from Vittel, France. There were many worthy Jewish notables on it, including the Rabbi of Bayonne, Rabbi Moshe Friedman of blessed memory, one of the greatest Polish Jewish scholars, a rare figure of a patriarch. He removed his clothes together with the others. Then a certain Obersturmfuhrer came in. The rabbi went up to him, took hold of him by the lapels of his uniform and told him in German, "Don't imagine, you low fiends, murderers of humanity, that you will really extinguish our nation. The Jewish people will live eternal. We will not disappear from the world stage. But you, you low butchers, will pay dearly, ten Germans for every innocent Jew. You will disappear not only as a power, but as a separate nation. The day of reckoning is coming. Our spilt blood will cry out for retribution. Our blood will not rest until the consuming fire of wrath sweeps over your nation and annihilates the blood of all of you — beasts!" It was with enormous energy, with the voice of a lion that he spoke these things. Then he placed his hat upon his head and cried out the Shema Yisroel with great fervor. All who were there lifted up their voices with him, "Shema Yisroel . . ." and an extraordinary rapture of faith swept through everyone. It was an extraordinarily sublime moment, never equaled in our lives, a confirmation of the undying spiritual power of the Jews. [From the notes of an unknown Jewish inmate, found in the Auschwitz camp after the war][151]

---

which faith exerted itself more than the arms did by urging and repeating: "No, no, etc.! God has given me orders, called me, and sent me to return to my father-land; I shall not believe you nor agree with you. Even though God kills me, well, let Him kill me, but I shall still live." *LW* 6:24-28.

150. Daniel Boyarin, *Dying for God: Martyrdom and the Making of Christianity and Judaism* (Stanford, CA: Stanford University Press, 1999), pp. 123-24.

151. *Auschwitz: Voices from the Ground*, ed. Teresa and Henryk Swiebocki (Panstwowe: Muzeum Oswiecim-Brzezinka, n.d.), p. 48.

The First Epistle of John (5:4) can, in this way, go so far as to say: "this is the victory that conquers the world, our faith," in the sense that faith already now appropriates the promised victory of God in taking courage to refuse obeisance now, on the earth, no matter what the cost. That is why the just *live* by their *faith*, as Habakkuk proclaimed and Paul retrieved. So Paul: "[Abraham] did not weaken in faith when he considered his own body, which was already as good as dead (for he was about a hundred years old), or when he considered the barrenness of Sarah's womb. No distrust made him waver concerning the promise of God, but he grew strong in his faith as he gave glory to God, being fully convinced that God was able to do what he had promised." Therefore his faith "was reckoned to him as righteousness" (Rom. 4:19-22), not because Abraham was otherwise righteous but because in face of all contrary experience he entrusted himself to the righteousness of God that prevails in the coming of the Kingdom.

*For thine is the kingdom!* What faith anticipates in this doxology may be glimpsed in the vision of the vindicated martyrs at the heavenly court: "After this I looked, and there was a great multitude that no one could count, from every nation, from all tribes and peoples and languages, standing before the throne and before the Lamb, robed in white, with palm branches in their hands. They cried out in a loud voice, saying, 'Salvation belongs to our God who is seated on the throne, and to the Lamb!' And all the angels stood around the throne and around the elders and the four living creatures, and they fell on their faces before the throne and worshiped God, singing, 'Amen! Blessing and glory and wisdom and thanksgiving and honor and power and might be to our God forever and ever! Amen'" (Rev. 7:9-12). In this doxological way, faith under trial gives God all the glory, for faith is a *defiant* act that refuses the idols and demons at work in malice and injustice and instead anticipates and appropriates the promised victory of the God of the gospel already now to spite the usurpers of the earth. Faith does not bow down in obeisance to the pretenders to the throne. It does not ascribe to the persecutors the predicates of sovereignty, power, and glory forever.

*Soli deo gloria* was once upon a time such a defiant doxology sung in the church of the Reformation against the world, the devil, and our sinful selves in echo of the doxology appended to the Kingdom prayer of Jesus. Wherever now it is still sung this way, perhaps among the despised Pentecostals or the "born again" evangelicals or even the papists, there the being of the true God as the Almighty Father of His own Son and Breather of His own Spirit for one and all in Jesus Christ is truly known. In this ethically costly ascription, the predicates of majesty, power, wisdom, and love are given to the Father alone. This robs the idols of their glory and the demons of their claim. The briefest survey of Scripture illustrates this. "For I will proclaim the name of the LORD; ascribe greatness to our God! The Rock, his work is perfect, and all his ways are just. A faithful God, without deceit, just and upright is he . . ." (Deut. 32:3-4). "Sing to the LORD, all the earth. Tell of his salvation from day to day. Declare his glory among the nations, his marvelous works among all the peoples. For great is the LORD, and greatly to be praised; he is to be revered above all gods. For all the gods of the peoples are idols, but the LORD made the heavens. Honor and majesty are before him; strength and joy are in his place. Ascribe to the LORD, O families of the peoples, ascribe to the LORD glory and strength. Ascribe to the LORD the glory due his name; bring an offering, and come before him. Worship the LORD in holy splendor; tremble before him, all the earth. The world is firmly established; it shall never be moved. Let the heavens be glad, and let the earth rejoice, and let them say among the nations, 'The LORD is king!'" (1 Chron. 16:23-31). "Ascribe to the LORD, O heavenly beings, ascribe to the LORD glory and strength. Ascribe to the LORD the glory of his name; worship the LORD in holy splendor" (Ps. 29:1-2). "Now to him who is able to keep you from falling, and to make you stand without blemish in the presence of his glory with rejoicing, to the only God our Savior, through Jesus Christ our Lord, be glory, majesty, power, and authority, before all time and now and forever. Amen" (Jude 24-25). "To him who loves us and freed us from our sins by his blood, and made us to be a kingdom, priests serving his God and Father, to him be glory and dominion forever and ever. Amen" (Rev. 1:5-6). "And the four living creatures, each of them with six wings, are full of eyes all around and inside. Day and night without ceasing they sing, 'Holy, holy, holy, the Lord God the Almighty, who was and is and is to come.' . . . the twenty-four elders fall before the one who is seated on the throne and worship the one who lives forever and ever; they cast their crowns before the throne, singing, 'You are worthy, our Lord and God, to receive glory and honor and power, for you created all things, and by your will they existed and were created'" (Rev. 4:8-11).

To God alone the glory! With the Son, in the Spirit, the church of the martyrs, grafted into living Judaism,[152] defiantly ascribes to the almighty Father the kingdom, the power, and the glory forever (Rom. 15:8-13): the predicates of majesty belong to creation's one and only and coming King. In so doing, the church strips the Leviathan of political sovereignty of its claim to ultimacy while at the same time, for the time being of the not yet, "acquiesc[ing] in the sinful determination of human beings to live apart from God . . . recogniz[ing] that they are not fitted for such a task [as Christianizing society], that they are sinful themselves."[153] It is the *right* of the church's worship that is politically significant, not the ambiguous righteousness of Christians which is theirs as gift not as possession. This *right* is founded upon *knowledge* of the almighty Father as the one true God, that is, the God who gives, which is ours by faith (not sight) through His Son Jesus Christ, when by the Spirit we come into the very faith of Jesus, a faith that is one with

---

152. Boyarin, *Dying for God*, p. 117.

153. Glenn Tinder, *The Political Meaning of Christianity: An Interpretation* (Baton Rouge and London: Louisiana State University Press, 1989), p. 95.

the faith of believing Israel, the Israel that receives in faith its vocation of suffering service and light to the nations. We receive this vocation of conscience as children of God when we come to know God our Father, that is, as God surpassing God. This is true because God surpassing God expresses the very "conscience" of God; it is the conscientious deed of God in sending the Son and the Spirit in order to become the Father of us sinners.

## God Surpassing God

The motif of God surpassing God is not Hegelian philosophy of religion, but Trinitarian patrology, corresponding to the motifs of the self-donating Son and the self-communicating Spirit. God the Father is personally God surpassing God in eternally begetting the Son and breathing the Spirit upon the Son. This is the almighty Father who hides Himself in creating a world for creatures under the mask of "nature," who in the fullness of time gives up the beloved Son into profoundest solidarity of love with the ungodly, who sends the Spirit to dwell with forgiven sinners patiently to make them righteous by giving life to the dead already now and to eternity. God the Father is God surpassing God antecedently in the divine life, who eternally begets the Son of His own inexhaustible being and breathes the Spirit of His own being on Him, so eternally becoming the Father of the Son as the Spirit returns the Son to Him in joyful and obedient love. God the Father is God surpassing God in the event of Jesus Christ for us and in us, in whom the sin of the world was undertaken and God's wrath against it satisfied in the clearing operation that makes way for the coming of the Beloved Community. So the Father surpassed His righteous wrath and came into His own righteous mercy in order to settle once for all who God is as the Father of this Son incarnate for us and so who the Father will be for us, unified with the Son by the Spirit, our Father and Father of all for whom the kingdom comes, the Beloved Community of God. God the Father of Jesus Christ is by no means the emblem of carnal patriarchy and vainglorious machismo! This blasphemous smear, however, is the forgivable sin of those who know not what they do, think, or say.

The revelation of God's Fatherhood in this dynamic way by the Father's gifts in the self-donation in the Son and self-communication in the Spirit, together with the problem of theological understanding of this self-surpassing self-revelation, arises above all in the doctrine of the atonement, which in accord with our approach of Trinitarian Christology cannot only be considered in the doctrine of the work of Christ. If God reconciles Himself by reconciling us, then God the Father is said at once to be the source of reconciliation and at the same time the object of reconciliation, both the origin and the audience of the saving deed. This is a genuine problem for theological understanding that the modalist tendency of the Western theological tradition can only resolve *either* by making God the Father the divine but passive object of Christ the man's perfect sacrifice on behalf of others *or* by making God the Father the loving and active subject of Christ the man's sacrifice for others, the so-called objective and subjective theories of the atonement respectively. The decisive thing here is that the main operators are abstractly conceived divine and human natures. Natures, however, cannot do anything; they are not agents at all, but only abstract sets of possibilities available to particular classes of agents. The alternative to the objective and subjective "theories" of the atonement, therefore, in a return to patristic and Trinitarian personalism would have to conceive of God the Father reconciling humanity to Himself in the person of the Spirit subjectively by reconciling Himself to humanity in the person of His Son objectively; here the Father is the audience of His own conscientious act of conciliation in sending the Son and the Spirit into a world held captive by structures of malice and injustice.

Gustaf Aulén clarified the difficulties here with great acumen, not chiefly in his well-known *Christus Victor*[154] but rather in his lesser-known yet more mature dogmatics, *The Faith of the Christian Church*.[155] Here Aulén articulated more clearly the development that patristic Christology experienced in Luther: "It is significant that Luther not only regards the ancient triad, sin, death and the devil, as destructive powers, but includes also the law (as Paul did) and wrath, the divine wrath."[156] Through this peculiar insight of Luther into the penal suffering of Christ (a thought unknown to Anselm though not, as we shall see, to Athanasius),[157] "Christian faith is able to view the work of Christ in the most profound perspective . . . ,"[158] namely, that of God surpassing God in the Father's sending of the Son to sinners, to their place on the cross, in order to bring the sinner with Christ by the Spirit of the resurrection to the new time and place of the reconciled Father in the dawning Beloved Community of God. "Wrath," Aulén argues, "is God's direct and immediate reaction to sin. But at the same time it is, according to Luther, a destructive power and a tyrant, even the worst of all tyrants. When wrath is separated from love it assumes this character. Thus, the conflict is carried into the divine nature itself." The conflict in the "divine nature" — rather, we

---

154. Gustaf Aulén, *Christus Victor* (London: SPCK / New York and Toronto: Macmillan, 1931).

155. Gustaf Aulén, *The Faith of the Christian Church,* trans. Eric H. Wahlstrom (Philadelphia: Muhlenberg, 1960).

156. This claim about Luther is massively corroborated by Marc Lienhard's *Martin Luther: Witness to Jesus Christ, Stages and Themes of the Reformer's Christology,* trans. Edwin H. Robertson (Minneapolis: Augsburg, 1982). Luther takes up a "reality which the early church only glimpsed — namely, the anger of God. . . . One can never insist enough on this aspect of Luther's theology. The work of Christ stands out against this background. The terrible uneasiness of human beings does not come from the fear of death as physical reality, but from the fact that after death comes the anger of God, the last judgment, the rejection. In such a perspective, Christ appears as the only salutary reality . . . where they can shelter as in a safe hiding place" (p. 70).

157. *LBC,* pp. 73-91.

158. Aulén, *The Faith,* p. 200.

would say, between the Father and the Son as willed by the Father and the Son for the justification of the ungodly — is overcome on Easter morn, when the Father at the Spirit's beckoning recognizes His own completed love for sinners in the Son who has totally perished before Him in solidarity with them. The judgment of wrath is thus "satisfied" — not simply abolished or canceled but executed, so that a new beginning can be made out of its annihilation, a virtual second *creatio ex nihilo*, yet in time and space, hence a redemptive *creatio ex vetere* (out of the old). The devil's tyranny is not overthrown simply by power, then, but by right. "The overcoming of wrath means, according to this analysis, that the inmost nature of God, the divine love, the 'blessing,' makes a way for itself through wrath, 'the curse.' This overcoming takes place concretely through Christ's 'self-giving sacrifice of love.'"[159]

While it is not utterly wrong to conceive of a tension in divine "nature" between attributes of wrath and love so far as this presses against a falsely conceived axiom of divine simplicity as metaphysical indivisibility, it is misleading and can be simply false if modalistically it personifies wrath in the Father and love in the Son. Rather it is the Father who in love for us sends the Son into the maw of the structures of malice and injustice under His wrath to seek and to find the lost creation of His own making, just as it is the Son who in wrath goes like a lamb to the slaughter bearing witness of truth against the mendacity of sinful humanity. The divine dilemma cannot be captured on this level of treating an abstraction, the concept of "nature," as if it were something real. Rather, concretely, the conflict on the divine level is the conflict shared by the Father and the Son and resolved in their Spirit, as we shall see.

Luther was not purely innovating in this line of thought, as reconstructed by Aulén. The church father, Athanasius, had already explored the divine dilemma and the victory of love over wrath by the cross and resurrection in his seminal treatise *On the Incarnation of the Word*. What was God in His goodness to do, at once to assert His righteous rule against the usurpation of sin and its lethal effects on the creation and yet to reclaim the lost and sinful creature and put it again in the right? It happened in "no other way save on the cross . . . [since] no other way than this was good for us. . . . For if he came to bear the curse laid upon us, how else could he 'become a curse' unless he received the death set for a curse? and that is on the cross."[160] Furthermore, "he accepted on the cross, and endured a death inflicted by others, and above all his enemies, which they thought dreadful and ignominious and not to be faced; so that this also being destroyed, both he himself might be believed to be life, and the power of death be brought to naught. So something startling and surprising has happened. . . ."[161] The astonish-

---

159. Aulén, *The Faith*, p. 204.

160. Athanasius, "On the Incarnation," in *Christology of the Later Fathers*, ed. Edward R. Hardy (Philadelphia: Westminster, 1954), p. 79.

161. Athanasius, "On the Incarnation," pp. 78-79.

ing thing is that, moved by irrepressible divine love for humanity, the Logos in a unique historical act took all human woe upon Himself, up to and including the ultimate woe, "the curse" laid upon the sinner by God's own judgment of wrath that excludes from the coming reign. This suffering of love does not happen to the Logos in a pathetic fashion.[162] The origin of this event is the holy God's holy love. It is a peculiarly divine suffering, not in God for God as in heaven, but by God for others on earth.

Luther reasons following the Eastern fathers in just this way, according to Aulén. On the one hand, "[s]ince the divine will is radically antagonistic to evil, and since God cannot therefore be reconciled to evil, this reconciliation entails the destruction of the power of evil and its dominion[,]" that is to say, the execution of divine wrath upon Luther's "real, not fictitious" sinner, the one captive to malice and obedient to structures of injustice by the fault of its own envy in place of trust in God and obedience to humanity's divine calling. Luther's Christ is not a mere punishment bearer who gets such sinners off the hook, but leaving them as such unrepaired. Christ is rather their sin-bearer, in whom their own sin is stolen away from them and made Christ's own in order on the cross to be damned, dead and buried once and for all. Yet, Aulén "hasten[s] to add, this sin-bearing of the Son is at the Father's own will and command, who is 'the acting subject in reconciliation,' so that it is equally true to say that in personal perspective the Father's 'wrath is stayed,' 'is turned away,' and so on. . . ." (In terms of Trinitarian personalism, it would be clearer to say God's wrath is surpassed.) Thus the whole complex thought is that "God is reconciled in and through his reconciliation of the world unto himself,"[163] that is, the atoning sacrifice is a self-propitiation of God for the sake of others.

Aulén in this way sought to unify the virtues of all three atonement motifs from the Bible and its subsequent theological tradition: the one liberated from the wrath of God by the Christ who perished Godforsaken to satisfy it has nothing to fear in life and death but may live boldly and even "sin boldly" in the teeth of the structures of malice and injustice that still cling to power but have lost all right; the one liberated from the wrath of God by Christ's sin-bearing self-sacrifice of love may as one so profoundly beloved confess one's own sins conscientiously and no longer protest them by rationalizations of self-justification, entering into the clean, fresh air of a new life of truthfulness before God; the one liberated from the wrath of God by Christ's magnanimity of love descending even to the depths of hell, *a patre derelictus,* may follow Christ in the descent of love into the woe of any neighbor in need, there to befriend and aid. What goes underdeveloped and hence unclarified in Aulén's own presentation — despite his crucial insight that God reconciles us by reconciling Himself — is, as indicated above, the Father's self-surpassing movement in just this passage from the wrath of His love to the

---

162. Athanasius, "On the Incarnation," pp. 60-62.
163. Aulén, *The Faith,* pp. 201-2.

mercy of it. If God *is* simply love, and if *that* wrath is *divine* that is love against what is against love, however, it remains obscure how there can be an *actual* conflict, as Aulén dramatically puts it, carried over into the "divine nature" itself. For then God, who is timelessly love, would simply be the same love in time against what is against love and for what is for love, depending on the temporal state of various creatures. That would not be news, nor would it be good news, but the mere revelation of an eternal verity, the judgment of the law but not yet the *Novum* of the gospel. That is to say, as in the classical Lutheran terminology, it would be only a truth that merely *demands* rather than a surpassing truth that *gives* what it demands.

Aulén senses the difficulty, but cannot clarify it because the modalist tradition of the West inclines him to think in terms of the essential and indivisible properties or attributes of a divine nature, rather than persons who are in their mutual relations and history with us claimants alike to the title of divine "nature." He goes on to talk about a "fusion" of wrath with love in reconciliation, reflecting his prior notion that wrath is a tyrant when separated from love in God. But this notion of "fusion" is even more obscure than that account of the conflict between wrath and love in the divine "nature" that it tries to resolve. One worries, accordingly, that this dramatic rhetoric from Luther and Athanasius that tries to account for genuine movement in God's history with us is pure mythology that, following Gerhard Forde,[164] following Karl Barth[165] (as we shall shortly examine), "swallows" up the act of reconciliation in a "sea of cultic imagery, pictures, and anthropomorphic and mythological language."[166] Is a "mythologically" conflicted God true God? Is God not purely and timelessly the act of mercy, also and indeed above all self-revealed as such in the cross and resurrection of the Incarnate Son, where this eternity of love is asserted in time, as Forde following Barth claims, as the "event" of "actual atonement," as subject that becomes object without ceasing to be subject by a self-repetition of its eternal subjectivity in time? On the other hand, has Aulén carried through fully on his own insight into the revision of metaphysics demanded by theology that takes the cross and resurrection of the Incarnate Son as decisive for the knowledge of God the Father as God surpassing God? In that case, as we following Jenson have throughout argued, "it is divine personhood, not divine being, that is metaphysically primary."[167] Or has he remained captive at the

---

164. Gerhard O. Forde, The Seventh Locus, "The Work of Christ," in *Christian Dogmatics,* vol. 2, pp. 1-99.

165. Forde, "The Work of Christ," p. 69.

166. Forde, "The Work of Christ," p. 83, written in criticism of Frances M. Young.

167. Jenson, *ST* 2, p. 96. I note in passing that either I do not follow, or do not share, Jenson's misguided affection for Kant's transcendental Ego, which I take to indicate the condition for the possibility of any cognitive claim that supplies the universal "I think" to any putative statement of fact. Jenson seems to take it however as the claim that "all consciousness is perspectival" (*ST* 2, p. 97), a notion I would endorse but find much more compatible with Leibniz's (supposedly) pre-critical account of knowledge. Jenson claims in the name of the Transcenden-

decisive juncture to the modalist tendency of the Western theological tradition to privilege the concept of nature at the expense of the concept of person?

We turn now to Forde's source. Barth's important answer to these questions shows that the modalist tendency of Western theology is also at work here, insofar as it is the deity of Christ that provides Barth the framework for understanding God's self-surpassing in the atonement. "That God as God is able and willing and ready to condescend, to humble Himself in this way [of the cross] is the mystery of the 'deity of Christ' "[168] — so Karl Barth answers the question, *Cur Deus homo?* God reveals His deity, according to Barth, in a surprising and liberating way at the cross. By the self-humiliation of taking on flesh to be crucified for us God reveals His deity as the event of freedom for love. Thus, in words that could have been targeted at Aulén, Barth continues: "As God was in Christ, far from being against Himself, or at disunity with Himself, He has put into effect the freedom of divine love, the love in which He is divinely free. He has therefore done and revealed that which corresponds to His *nature*."[169] Needless to say, despite the dynamism of Barth's "ontology of act," the conception of divine nature as simple is operative here and with it the modalist tendency of the Western tradition in attributing agency to nature as such. Barth senses the difficulty, however, and labors valiantly to make the notion of divine simplicity dynamic by conceiving of God's being or deity as the event of freedom for love. But this involves Barth in a difficult dialectic of the *simultaneity,* rather than the *sequence,* of humility and exaltation in "the journey of the Son of God into the far country," as he thus narrativizes the doctrine of the Incarnation. "God does not have to dishonour Himself when He goes into the far country, and conceal His glory. For He is truly honoured in this concealment"[170] in that the "mystery reveals to us that for God it is just as *natural* to be lowly as it is to be high, to be near as to be far, to be little as to be great, to

---

tal Ego that the church and the world have the "same abstract structure" of knowledge. What differentiates them, he writes, is that to "avoid God, modernity and its precursors posited a focus of consciousness that was itself this abstraction, the same for all by virtue of its pure formality. No such thing subsists. . . . I can, to be sure, pretend I am self-existent, the condition of my own hypostasis. And I can try actually to live by that pretense. . . . A great deal of Western epistemology is simply Eve's and Adam's error" (*ST* 2, p. 99). I emphatically share *this* judgment with Jenson on Western "epistemology," but I apply it above all to the invention of the "abstract structure" that is the transcendental ego of Cartesian-Kantian subjectivity in distinction from Spinoza's and Leibniz's deeply embodied subject that knows perspectivally only from its location within space and time. Such a subject knows theologically by union with Christ in the Spirit before God in the world, when access is provided to it. This creation of access, however, is hardly the same formal structure claimed in epistemology in that *persons are not to be equated with subjects.* Persons arise from the calling of God. Epistemological subjects supposedly know impersonally, transcending personal embodiment. Theological persons know subjectively, by union with their objects, in some social relationship, in relation to some audience.

168. *CD* IV/1, p. 177.

169. *CD* IV/1, pp. 186-87, emphasis added.

170. *CD* IV/1, p. 188.

be abroad as to be at home."[171] The condescension in Christ does not contradict, but rather expresses the "natural" being of God as freedom to love. As such, this condescension in Christ objectively reconciles the world to God by revealing in time and space the eternal and hence universal event of God's being as freedom to love — an event to which the church witnesses, but does not contain either in its own being or in its ministry of Word and sacraments.

Thus far it would appear that Barth indeed thinks in modalist fashion in that the subject of the divine condescension appears to be the "nature" or "being" of God, His "deity," the mystery of which as freedom for love the Incarnation actualizes and displays. Moreover, as noted, right understanding of this mystery explicitly disallows any thought of disunity in God's nature as something that would subvert the very objectivity of divine reconciliation that Barth is so urgent to maintain in regarding the Incarnation as the true repetition in time of what God eternally is. Yet Barth is careful to explicitly deny modalism and subordination-ism alike,[172] that is, according to his own understanding that models the Trinity psychologically. The Trinitarian argument here is that there is in God's nature or being essentially "an above and a below, a *prius* and a *posterius,* a superiority and a subordination . . . [so] that it belongs to the inner life of God that there should take place within it obedience." God's unity "consists in the fact that in Himself He is both One who is obeyed and Another who obeys."[173] He is and can be these two as the One God "without any cleft or differentiation but in perfect unity and equality" because God is also "a Third, the One who affirms the one and equal Godhead through and by and in the [other] two modes of being" in "their con-crete relations of the one to the other, in the history which takes place between them." In the event of reconciliation, this eternal divine history of the Father and the Son by the Spirit becomes "identical with the very different relationship between God and one of His creatures, a man" — namely, Jesus Christ, who is the heavenly and eternal event's repetition in time and space.[174] Thus, Barth argues, it can be the case that God "does not change in giving Himself. He simply activates and reveals Himself ad extra, in the world. He is in and for the world what He is in and for Himself" as the triune God. And such is the "true deity of Jesus Christ, obedient in humility, in its unity and equality, its *homoousia,* with the deity of the One who sent Him and to whom He is obedient"[175] and thus "not another, a second God, but the Son of God, the one God in His mode of being as the Son."[176] So the atonement begins with the sending of this Son of God into the far country of our ruin, with the One who obediently goes.

---

171. *CD* IV/1, p. 192, emphasis added.
172. *CD* IV/1, p. 199.
173. *CD* IV/1, p. 201.
174. *CD* IV/1, p. 203.
175. *CD* IV/1, p. 204.
176. *CD* IV/1, p. 209.

Barth accordingly turns attention to the passion of this action of the obedient Son, which he narrativizes under the rubric of "the Judge judged in our place." This paradoxical judgment is the very deed of redemption and reconciliation that "embraces us" and as such becomes the "basis of fellowship" quite prior to any question of human faith or unbelief. In undergoing judgment for us, the condescending Son of God "represent[ed] us without any co-operation on our part."[177] In His very passion, He actively, indeed with supreme divine action, represented humanity — sinful humanity, that sinned in wanting to judge like God, knowing good and evil, hence "in trying to be as God: himself a judge."[178] But this sinful posture of assuming a godlike pseudo-sovereignty in claiming judgment is stolen away from us by Christ's sovereign divine deed of representation. The Judge judged in our place is the One who "has taken the place of every man" by "penetrat[ing] to that very place where every man is in his inner being supremely by and for himself." Therefore, as represented by Christ, this sinful being is displaced, "no longer judge. Jesus Christ is Judge," not only externally, "over" us, but rather now as the One who is there "radically and totally for us, in our place" whether we know it or not. God in Jesus Christ in this way of humiliation and cross reclaims His usurped sovereignty, not "by a prohibition," but by "an action," the sovereign action of His being utterly for us who are against Him.[179]

We may accordingly experience this representation of us by the Son of God as an "abasement": "Before this Judge I obviously cannot stand." But also we may experience it as "immeasurable liberation and hope" that comes when "a heavy and indeed oppressive burden is lifted from us when Jesus Christ becomes our Judge,"[180] i.e., when the whole of "the evil responsibility which man has arrogantly taken to himself is taken from him" so that "it is no longer necessary that I should pronounce myself free and righteous."[181] Indeed "I," who am represented and displaced therewith from the office of judge by the Judge judged in my place, am revealed as the sinner who wanted to judge and not be judged. In sum, the judged Judge judges us by being for us when we were against Him. Love asserts itself triumphantly against what is against love. Conscience is abased and at the same time liberated by the conscience of God in giving the Judge to be judged in our place. God surpasses God in becoming what He is in Himself also for us.

The difficulty in following Barth's highly dialectical account here is one that he himself anticipates when he considers an objection: How can Christ come into this "strange place" and take "our place as the enemies against God"? He does so, Barth answers, by an act of conscience, "accepting responsibility for that which we do in this place," making our "evil case His own," thus "expos[ing] Himself

---

177. *CD* IV/1, p. 230.
178. *CD* IV/1, p. 231.
179. *CD* IV/1, p. 232.
180. *CD* IV/1, p. 233.
181. *CD* IV/1, p. 234.

to the accusation and sentence which must inevitably come down upon us in this case." And, "as He does that, it ceases to be our sin. . . . He is the man who entered that evil way, with the result that we are forced from it; it can be ours no longer."[182] This, let us say, "forcible exchange" — this divine thievery, stealing our sins, sovereignly taking our place — is "undoubtedly the mystery of the divine mercy" but also of the "divine righteousness," for He did not will to "overcome and remove [sin] from without, but from within [human nature] . . . to do right at the very place where man had done wrong, and in that way to make peace with man." This sovereign and divine exchange of divine right for human wrong dare not be taken "as an exchange only in appearance," but "in bitter earnest it is the fact that God Himself in His eternal purity and holiness has in the sinless man Jesus Christ taken up our evil case in such a way that He willed to make it, and has in fact made it, His own."[183]

The affirmations here that Christ was "sinless" in His representation of our "evil case," that just here He did the right where we had done the wrong, indicate that Barth is *not* saying that Christ makes our evil His own by doing our evil. Rather, Christ makes our evil His own in the sense of assuming its guilt before God — taking responsibility before God for us whom He has forgiven; so also and on this account taking our place as those liable to wrath for judging the Judge rather than being judged by Him. Hence Barth — here explicitly with Luther — pronounces reconciliation on account of Christ's conscientious deed, that is, on account of the exchange of responsibilities and places that occurs in Christ's Incarnation: reconciliation is the accomplished fact that "[o]ur sin is no longer our own. It is His sin, the sin of Jesus Christ."[184]

The fact of this reconciliation in Christ has implications in three directions, which Barth now lists. First, we see ourselves in Christ truly as the sinners whom He represented. Second, we see ourselves in Christ as those sinners forgiven, even more, as *liberated* from the old sinful posture of the would-be judge, hence a new creation out of the sinful humanity. "What we are He Himself willed to become, in order to take and transform it from within, to make of it something new, the being of man reconciled with Himself." Third, there is accordingly — since really our sins are Christ's — "nothing more that we can seek and do there even as evil-doers."[185] In Christ we are already converted, the new creation. In Christ the old man is robbed of his claim and divested of his sinful possessions, whether he knows it or not, surrenders to his victor or not. Indeed, the old man who judged is now judged and put to death by the Judge who was judged in his place, paradoxically by the One who judges purely and totally for us while we were still sinners.

182. *CD* IV/1, p. 236.
183. *CD* IV/1, p. 237.
184. *CD* IV/1, p. 238.
185. *CD* IV/1, p. 242.

Following the dialectics of identity here is, to be sure, a challenge. There is a danger, moreover, of a vicious ambiguity or equivocation in the claim Barth makes that in Christ's divine and objective deed of representation the old man is already in his own sinful subjectivity converted, slain and raised to new life. The logic of Barth's claim that the sinless Christ was made to be sin representatively, so far as it follows *Luther,* requires a distinction between the nonimputation of sin and the defiantly persisting subjectivity of Adam by virtue of the newborn believer's persisting membership in the common body. This is a distinction, then, between the guilt of sin forgiven and sin's concupiscence now resisted by the gift of the Spirit in its continuing battle with the flesh. The claim that in Christ the old Adam, taken as sinful desire rather than personal identity, is already dead, buried, and so rendered incapable of return cannot in any case be based upon Christ's penal representation. The latter provides for the nonimputation of sin to the new person in Christ, since the burden of guilt otherwise bars the fellowship of sinful persons with the holy God. Christ's representation of the sinful person by assuming her sin as His own must not only be validated by the Father but also communicated by the Spirit to become effective in her by the external Word creating faith. Taken as the new birth of the person in Christ, the gift of the Spirit takes to battle against the sinful desires of the flesh that remain alive and at work in the forgiven sinner who is not yet risen from the dead, whose "nature" is still bodily subject to the last enemy, death. This work of the Spirit is the inauguration of a new, inchoate subjectivity of persons in community, the ecclesia in mission; it is a summons to battle, not already its victorious conclusion.

But the active passion of the Incarnate Son that objectively reconciles is, for Barth, the "comprehensive turning in the history of all creation" — "the reconciliation of the world with God." It can be this, if indeed it is *divine* action, as Barth repeatedly stresses the *deity* of the passion, the *active* in the passive: "He gives Himself to be the humanly acting and suffering person in this occurrence. He Himself is the subject who in His own freedom becomes in this event the object acting or acted upon in it . . . in this humiliation, God is supremely God." For here, at the cross of Jesus, "[w]e are not dealing merely with any suffering, but with the suffering of God and this man in face of the destruction which threatens all creation and every individual, thus compromising God as the Creator." The threatening destruction is sin, the would-be sovereignty of man who has left the posture of the creature to know and to judge as if God, and has thus separated from the true God and Creator. But in Christ, God has "Himself borne the consequence of this separation to bear it away."[186] The two natures are thus now rightly reordered. So it is the "passion of Jesus Christ itself and as such which has to be believed and proclaimed as the act of God for us." This is the very "truth" of God's deity — not a mere appearance that may be relativized by opposing it

---

186. *CD* IV/1, pp. 246-47.

to a hidden essence — "but the disclosure and recognition of that which is as it appears to man."

Thus it is now apparent how Barth interprets "modalism" in a modern way, a Kantian way, as positing a cognitive gap between the phenomena and noumena, the thing for us and the thing for itself. In the name of true deity, Barth closes this gap with the proviso that it closes as an event, not a settled thing that can come under human control. Thus truth in the event of its disclosure "only needs to be indicated. And faith only needs to confess that it has happened. It happened for us, but it happened without us, without our co-operating or contributing."[187] The utter objectivity of the event of revelation by Christ's representation of the sinner, in which the dynamic love of God asserts itself for the human creature and prevails by being against its sinful pride, does not merely offer reconciliation but, as stressed above, already *is* and *effects* reconciliation, also subjectively: "In the suffering and dying of God Himself in His Son, there took place the reconciliation with God, the conversion to Him, of the world which is out of harmony with Him, contradicting and opposing Him"[188] so that "in Him the world is converted to God. . . . Representing all others in Himself, He is the human partner of God in this new covenant."[189] It is, as said above by way of mild parody, a "forcible exchange."

This thematic of the New Adam revealed in Christ's divine deed of representation becomes increasingly important in Barth's exposition. Not wrath, but sin (i.e., not its imputed guilt but its root in evil desire, concupiscence) is already now the "obstacle which has to be removed and overcome," and indeed "the very heart of the atonement is the overcoming of sin" which is accomplished by "delivering up sinful man and sin in His own person to the non-being which is properly theirs." The sinner in this real sense is put to death, crucified with Christ, annihilated. Once again there is similarity with Luther and yet a subtle but consequential divergence. God's wrath is "satisfied" with nothing less than the death of the sinner — "not out of any desire for revenge" but out of true and holy love, as the end of ruin and the necessary presupposition for resurrection to a new humanity. Like Luther in distinction from Anselm, then, Barth avers that the "decisive thing" is not that "He has suffered what we ought to have suffered so that we do not have to suffer," but rather by His suffering Christ "has made an end of us as sinners and therefore of sin itself by going to death. . . . He has removed us sinners and sin, cancelled us out. . . ."[190] Yet, unlike Luther for whom this mortification of the sinner in Christ is the work and office of the Holy Spirit who forms the theological subject by baptism that inaugurates a life of struggle between the flesh and the Spirit, for Barth this execution of the sinner has already

187. *CD* IV/1, p. 249.
188. *CD* IV/1, p. 250.
189. *CD* IV/1, p. 251.
190. *CD* IV/1, pp. 253-54.

transpired in principle and in power on Golgotha, in the new humanity of the New Adam — as our true humanity, whether we know it in Luther's way by the Spirit forming subjects in baptismal union with Christ in time and on the earth by the mission of the ecclesia to the nations — or not.

In this utter objectivity of Christ's representation, not only as bearer of our guilt, but as the very doer of God's will, our old Adam "was taken and killed and buried in and with Him on the cross"; thus atonement is radical, going to "the source of our destruction." Barth reminds again at this juncture "why it is so important to understand this passion as from the very first the divine action . . . the activity of the second Adam who took the place of the first, who reversed and overthrew the activity of the first in this place, and in so doing brought in a new man, founded a new world and inaugurated a new aeon — and all this in His passion." We might say that for Barth, Christ has not merely represented humanity by assuming its sinfulness but has actually replaced the humanity of sin, not only in His own person but in the person of all others, objectively. Hence, for Barth, it is not enough to think that Christ *bears* away sin as guilt before God; He *takes* away sin and the sinful being itself and *replaces* it with Himself. The "forgiveness of sins" is far too weak an expression for the radical surgery of the cross. "The suffering and death of Jesus Christ are the No of God in and with which He again takes up and asserts in man's space and time the Yes to man which He has determined and pronounced in all eternity." This taking away of sin by the objective righteousness of God in Christ manifests as the man Jesus' human obedience, "true to his own nature as the creature of God."[191] In the Son's willingness "to take our place as sinners," God "has brought about in the man who is the child of this God, this new and obedient and free man. As this man, He has revealed and made operative the righteousness of God on earth." This righteousness is the assertion of the Creator's right that returns humanity to proper order, "to the place which is proper to him as a creature in relation to God, [thus] reversing the fall which consists in his usurpation" of the place of the Creator.[192] Christ as New Adam *is* already now our humanity. We may only awaken to this reality and act upon it. Our being as Old Adam is finished and done with.

We may fairly conclude that for Barth the reconciliation occurs in the divinely active passion of Jesus Christ, whereby God the Creator newly asserts His right against the sinful creature by creating in this man a representative obedience that takes the place of sin, both forgiving its guilt and displacing its power. It is not, then, the Father as God surpassing God who reconciles Himself by reconciling sinners, strictly speaking, but God as Creator who eventuates Himself in time to reestablish the proper order of Creator to creature. This critical differentiation is confirmed by the curious fact that the next section to come in Barth's unfolding of the doctrine of reconciliation bears the title "The Verdict of the Father," even

191. *CD* IV/1, p. 257.
192. *CD* IV/1, p. 258.

though that section in fact says very little about the Father as such coming to the speech-act of Easter morn. Rather, we hear once again of a contradiction between proud creature and the humble Creator overcome by the superior contradiction of grace: "Note that on the one hand it is God for man, on the other man against God. These are two orders (or, rather, order and disorder), two opposite world-structures, two worlds opposing and apparently excluding each other"[193] that the Creator overcomes in asserting His freedom to love in and as Christ for us, indeed Christ in place of us.

In this passage, Barth takes up in passing the problem of the contemporaneousness of Christ, that is, how the event of reconciliation that transpired on Golgotha 1900 years ago can have traction for us today. But Barth regards the problem of contemporaneousness as a pseudo-problem, an evasion from genuine encounter with the content of event, *Christus pro nobis praesens* (Christ present for us). The "question of historical distance," he maintains, "is not a genuine problem,"[194] if we have grasped the truth of the atonement as the revelation of the *true deity* of Jesus Christ who is, as God in action for us, just so objectively and universally present for us, provided we understand this as the event that it is. His divine work in "the conversion of man and the world to God has become an event . . . a completed fact."[195] Easter morn is not "a miracle accrediting Jesus Christ, but the revelation of God in Him . . . the perception that God was in Christ (2 Cor. 5:19), that is, that in the man Jesus, God Himself was at work, speaking and acting and suffering . . . *the mediation of a perception hitherto closed and inaccessible. . . .*"[196] This is a telling passage in that it speaks of the resurrection not as a causal event but as a disclosure event.[197] It would not be unjust, accordingly, to call Barth's conception of Easter and the misleadingly named "verdict of the Father" a "disclosure" event rather than a "causal" one, that is, a newly given insight into what is, rather than the new creation of reality. The Father's verdict thus discloses "that the action and passion of Jesus Christ were not apart from or against Him, but according to His good and holy will . . ."[198] even though Barth can also phrase this disclosure as "God's decision concerning the event of the cross."[199]

Thus here again equivocation threatens. "Disclosure" unveils a state of affairs that already obtains. A disclosure can certainly be eventful; coming to knowledge of a hitherto unknown truth causes the knower to rearrange her world to accommodate the new information. "Decision" indicates a division between unactualized possibilities that causes one course of action to unfold rather than another; a decision may be disclosed in the event of its actualization as a deed in

193. *CD* IV/1, p. 290.
194. *CD* IV/1, p. 292.
195. *CD* IV/1, p. 296.
196. *CD* IV/1, p. 301.
197. See *DC*, pp. 31-49.
198. *CD* IV/1, p. 305.
199. *CD* IV/1, p. 309.

the world, or in the telling of this deed. In the same way knowledge causes the recipient of it to reorganize its world. The two events are not the same, however, and the ambiguity matters.

God, we have argued, is determined to redeem and fulfill the creation by the mission of the Son and the Spirit, a decision executed in the resurrection of Jesus Christ from the dead because the resurrection is the actuality of this divine self-determination in time and space, its passage from intention to deed. Further, this election of God is extended causally to affect recipients in the telling of this news, where and when the Spirit wills to grant it. Disclosure of an existing but unknown state of affairs may be melodramatically figured in a historical narrative that is then comprehended in its timeless truth, leaving the narrative behind as so much scaffolding. Decision by contrast produces truth as a *Novum* of the historical narrative that tells of it; understanding of this decision in its temporal particularity cannot be accessed at all apart from the event that tells of the event. The former has God the Father asserting the preexisting order of Creator-creature in Jesus Christ that is valid and obtains timelessly quite apart from the work of the Spirit in communicating it. The latter has God the Father surpassing wrath to come to mercy, indeed, to come to a new unity of Creator and creature in Christ. This is the Spirit's unification of the sign and the thing signified in proclaiming the theological object, Jesus Christ for us, hence also and essentially an integral work of the Spirit in the gospel's mission to the nations where He forms theological subjects accordingly.

In his study of some years ago, *Christology in Conflict*, Bruce Marshall put his finger on the difficulty now under consideration, the ambiguity in Barth between accounts of God surpassing God as (1) eternal election and/or (2) historical reconciliation. This, wrote Marshall, "seems to create a dilemma. (1) If fellowship with human beings in the particular life of Jesus Christ is God's original purpose, and the particular life of Jesus Christ is identical with the reconciliation of the world, then it would seem that in willing the particular life of Jesus Christ, God must necessarily will sin. . . . (2) This undesirable result can be avoided, it seems, only by discarding either 'election' or 'reconciliation' . . . ; they cannot, it seems, both be necessarily true of the same person."[200] Marshall noted the problem, and left it aside, since his purpose in that study was to demonstrate the subordination of soteriology to the theological identification of Jesus Christ in His historical particularity. This latter stance of Barth's, in terms of the present system of theology, Marshall rightly vindicated over against Karl Rahner (as argued above in Chapter Three). But the difficulty of reconciling election and reconciliation remains within this Christological consensus in which the *Heilsbedeutsamkeit Christi* (the saving significance of Christ) is to be learned from the historical particularity of Jesus Christ.

---

200. Bruce Marshall, *Christology in Conflict: The Identity of a Saviour in Rahner and Barth* (Oxford: Basil Blackwell, 1987), pp. 122-23.

The problem appears this way: How can God's self-determination in freedom to love be Jesus' friendship with sinners, without making God antecedently the author of sinners for Him to love? We are arguing, however, that just this difficulty cannot be solved by an abstract dialectic of deity and humanity in Christ, where election represents, according to Barth's ontology of act, the eternal decision of God to be the God of grace for us in the humility and obedience of the eternal Son, so that reconciliation occurs in the human decision and obedience of the man Jesus as a temporal repetition of the eternal decree. We are arguing here, with Robert Jenson, that this unity of election and reconciliation is rather a problem of "patrology,"[201] that is, how God who is antecedently Father of His own Son in His own Spirit becomes our Father too — precisely by giving us His Son in His Spirit, where we are those who have sinfully refused His calling of us as image made for likeness to God. In that case, Jesus' solidarity with sinners is "an event in God's triune life," hence an *"eternal"* event, i.e., that *"settles* what sort of God he is over against fallen creation."[202] If this is right, in other words, the problem of the Western modalist tendency in Barth lies in conceiving of eternity as a merely "original event," as a protological "time before time" that predetermines our time by God's self-determination in electing to be the God of grace in the primal act of His freedom to love. While this thinking secures the primacy of grace, both the difficulty of Judas's unbelief, and the appearance that God's saving self-repetition in time for some entails the reprobation of others, i.e., Judas, are in this way obscured by Barth's solution.

If we have only conceptions of divine and creaturely nature with which to think, we will naturally have to think of God the Creator as "before" the creature, as preceding the creature, as grounding the creature, so that revelation can ultimately only disclose what God already is and does according to this right order of His precedence. But if we subordinate ideas of divine and creaturely nature — abstractions that they are — to the personal identities of the Three in their actual history with us, we have to think of eternity as the Father's time with the Son in the Spirit, a time that can and does anticipate its own history, as any living God must be conceived above all to be ever its own future. Then God's self-determination for a history with us on the way to the Beloved Community is actualized in creation by making time for creatures, in redemption by finding time to seek and to save the lost and in fulfillment by the gift of a place in God's own eternal life. In that case, moreover, the object of God's eternal predestination is not so much Jesus as elected to be rejected in our place, taken, as we have seen, as the New Adam who by grace displaces us. Rather it is the Beloved Community of the Father who sends the Son to sinners who triumphs in the Spirit in triumphing for the estranged, for the enemy, for the sinner. It is *us* as actually we are whom He had loved in the Beloved; *we* are the object of divine self-determination, as a

201. Jenson, *ST* 1, p. 115.
202. Jenson, *ST* 1, p. 189, emphasis added.

careful reading of Ephesians 1:3-14 shows. And this triumph for us is the promised future, yet to be fulfilled in the redemption of our bodies.

So also, God's deity is God's own future for us, genuinely at risk in loving creatures such as we are in Adam. Thinking in this way of strong Trinitarian personalism, then, we think of "God after God," of God after the creature's fall into the nothingness of sin and of God after the condemnation of this fall at the cross, of God who will give life to the dead and calls into being worlds that do not yet exist. This is what is entailed when we take the eternal election of the Beloved Community in Christ, not as a mere repetition in time of an eternal verity, but rather as the execution in time of a costly divine decision that binds the conscience of God.

Barth's view that the content of the event is the revelation of the deity of Jesus Christ, if taken modalistically, tips the balance towards disclosure over against decision. Polemically Barth can now with his considerable rhetorical arsenal array himself against "recollection, tradition and proclamation" as the material and historical means of the Spirit in making Christ present in Word and sacraments in execution of the divine decision in favor of the universally operative divine event of reconciliation as disclosed in Christ. "His history did not become dead history. It was history in His time to become as such eternal history — the history of God with the men of all times, and therefore taking place here and now as it did then. He is the living Saviour."[203] For this reason the problem of the contemporaneousness of Christ is for Barth a pseudo-problem. With this move to the *extra-Calvinisticum* (though qualified by Barth's accompanying rejection of any *Logos asarkos*), Barth has a difficult time, however, fending off the accusation that the perfected work of reconciliation on Golgotha as the repetition in time of the eternal event that God simply is amounts to a realized eschatology, that is, where the only difference between the already and the not yet is that the latter is the "definitive manifestation" of the former. That the exalted Christ still has real work to do now as intercessor and embattled king subduing enemies, as the One to whom the Father has given all authority for the mission to the nations to gather the ecclesia as harbinger of the Beloved Community — these redemptive but not-yet-completed works of Jesus Christ cannot receive the recognition they merit and the theological attention they deserve. Nor by the same token can the Spirit's work of communicating and so effecting the redemptive work of Christ as the very making of this living Christ's own new history with new peoples in and as the community of His body in the gospel's mission to the nations receive the recognition and attention it deserves.

But, as per the critique being made here, the cause of this neglect is that Barth, surprisingly, has taken the Fatherhood of God for granted, just like the liberal theology of the nineteenth century which he inherits and against which he otherwise contends. Barth to be sure wanted Christian hope to be securely fixed

203. *CD* IV/1, pp. 313-34.

on Jesus Christ, so that hope is strictly hope for *His* "definitive manifestation," and is not hijacked by other anxieties inspiring other utopias. "The one crucified and risen Jesus Christ is the object of New Testament faith and the content of New Testament hope."[204] Surely he is right about that, and this accent reflects his rejection of any *Logos asarkos*. But the decisive argument Barth marshals on behalf of atonement as the disclosure of the deity of Jesus Christ in His passion may be found in a certain polemic, again surely right on one level, against the theology of the cross. "There is no going back behind Easter morn,"[205] taken by Barth, as we have argued, as the disclosure of the deity of Christ in His passion. Therefore, Barth insists, "in Him we have life before us and not death" as already we are objectively converted from sinfulness and reconciled as creatures to Creator, whether we know or do not know this, believe or do not believe this. Driving this point home, a revealing statement follows: "The way of God the Father, Son and Holy Spirit, the way of the true God, is not a cycle, a way of eternal recurrence, in which the end is a constant beginning. It is the way of myth which is cyclic, an eternal recurrence, summoning man to endless repetitions, to that eternal oscillation between Yes and No, grace and judgment, life and death. We must not mythologize the Gospel of the way of the true God (not even in the name of Kierkegaard or Luther himself)."[206] This is indeed a *crux intellectum*. For what else does the doctrine of the immanent Trinity as an account of the divine life assert other than an eternal becoming of God as God for God, beginning with the Father, as the person of God surpassing God so that the Son may return in the Spirit the praise of His deity as the God who gives?

Barth's attempt to fuse eternal election and historical reconciliation Christologically, then, renders reconciliation the disclosure of a universal *Heilsontologie*, and by the same token presses towards an ontologizing of the economy according to the so-called "ontology of act," i.e., that the Trinitarian being of God is itself an implication of the primal decision of God to be for creatures the God of grace; this is the (overly) bold position that Bruce McCormack draws from Barth, that "the covenant of grace is the ground of God's triunity" (criticized above in Chapter Four). As indicated by the peculiar attempt at a synthesis in Barth of the *extra Calvinisticum* and the *Logos ensarkos*, we enter here upon the most difficult problem in Christian theology of the relation of time and eternity, of heaven and earth. We can begin to sketch out a position on this in anticipation of the conclusion of this system of theology by the following reflection.

If God's eternity is not to be thought as the mere negation of sequenced time, as the sheer timelessness of the eternal present of the single creative consciousness (that is nevertheless asserted *to have come* to create a world other than itself that *now* unfolds all at once before it), what else could God's eternity be but in

---

204. *CD* IV/1, p. 328.
205. *CD* IV/1, p. 344.
206. *CD* IV/1, p. 345.

some living or dynamic sense the eternal becoming from the Father of the Son in the Spirit returning to the Father, i.e., an "eternal recurrence of the same"? And so, if *this* eternal God's history with His creation is ordered to the eschatological outcome of the Beloved Community, what else could creaturely time be than the gift of a sequenced existence destined and appointed heir of that eternal life? And if the eternal God is in sequenced time and indeed comes in sequenced time, what else could reconciliation be but the unification of Creator and creature in the Beloved Community — the resurrection of the dead at the eschaton of judgment, the eternal fulfillment of the temporal sequence? If God is eternally the Father and just so and only so *becomes* the Creator, then the "natural" order, Creator-creature, is temporal and not eternal, abstract and not real, a way to the goal not the goal itself. If the creature by grace inherits the eternal life that is God's alone by nature as the infinite life of the Three, then the Fatherhood of God does not consist in sustaining *ad infinitum* the temporal boundary between Creator and creature, but in surpassing it in the Incarnation and thence in the Spirit's resurrection of the *totus Christus* to eternal life. The anxiety that arises here — that any such theosis abolishes the natural distinction between Creator and creature — is met, however, with the observation that persons remain the persons they have become in their creaturely history even when they participate by the resurrection in God's eternal life.

Building, then, on Barth's not inconsiderable contribution to the theology of the atonement but taking this contribution as formulating a *patrological* question, Robert Jenson follows the narrative course of the gospels more rigorously and more patiently than did Barth. He follows Barth in claiming that "the Man for Others died rather than seek his own kingdom" and that this death for others "settles that he *is* the Man for Others," and that this settlement of His identity as the Son who came to serve thus "determines the salvific import that he lives as Lord." But to this Jenson adds the thought from Luther that the death of the Man for Others "transform[s] his promises to us into a testament," i.e., "[w]hat Jesus' death did was to remove the promise from the possibility of retraction or qualification." At least, it does this so far as it pertains to the person of the Son, who sealed His promises with the new testament of His body and blood, just as we heard Gogarten articulate the very same point in the previous chapter in the claim that Jesus took responsibility before God for us and our world in His filial obedience. But unlike Barth, this active passion of the Son is not taken simply as an act of the divine nature as freedom to love, a revelation of the deity of the Son as the humility of God. Rather, according to Jenson, "[w]hat Jesus' death did was to put the implicit claim made by his life and teaching to a final test . . . [that] posed the issue to the Blessed One himself, which is of course where it belonged: Would he act to acknowledge his Son?" So in Jenson's limning of the gospel narrative's dramatic plot, the "verdict" of the Father cannot be a mere disclosure of the antecedent deity of Jesus in His obedient way; the obedient Jesus is truly dead and can act no more. Now, "it would not be Jesus but his Father who could act,"[207] if there was to be any verdict at all surpassing condemnation and death.

The subtle but significant difference from Barth here is that, for Jenson, the point of departure is neither the deity nor the humanity in Christ but the Spirit-born Man for others, the earthly Jesus as a person alongside us, who lives His human history in anticipation of His vindication as God the Son, or, what is the same, it is the person, Jesus alongside of us, who lives as the beloved Son by faith in the Father as the reconciled God of Hosea 11. For Barth, as we have seen, it is as God the Son journeying to the far country, that is, as the mysterious deity of Jesus, the man who represented sinners in their guilt and replaced them in their sinfulness as the new creature, once and for all. The difference here is rooted in the difference, in classical terms (from which both Barth and Jenson would each in their own ways demur), between the *extra Calvinisticum* in Barth and the *unity of person* in Jenson. It is not possible for Jenson, then, to relate resurrection to crucifixion as but a disclosure event. "The Crucifixion is God's salvific action just in that God overcomes it by the Resurrection."[208] The overcoming here is causal in the sense of God causing God to be God in a new way; it is not merely the overcoming of human malice and injustice by an unveiling of divine power timelessly asserting love and justice against them in a "superior contradiction." Rather, "we must understand the Crucifixion, precisely as Jesus' human doing and suffering, as itself an event in God's triune life." As such, the resurrection of the Crucified discloses *because* it decides; it does not merely unveil and thus put into consciousness a preexisting and timeless truth, no matter how dramatically figured or how eventfully experienced. What it decides is the very Fatherhood of God: "[T]his is the event in God that settles what sort of God he is over against fallen creation." Jenson then does not shy from involving the Father fully in the Son's time: "The Crucifixion put it up to the Father: Would he stand to this alleged Son? To *this* candidate to be his own self-identifying Word? Would he be a God who, for example, hosts publicans and sinners, who justifies the ungodly? The Resurrection was the Father's Yes."[209] But as the Father's temporal act, then, it is the Yes of a decision that affirms one possibility to the exclusion of others; it is the decision that causes the person who makes it to go forward in one way rather than another. In it the Father, who eternally surpasses in begetting the Son and breathing the Spirit on Him, now surpasses Himself in creaturely time by acknowledging the Son's incarnate-to-death-on-a-cross love for sinners as His own. He surpasses by receiving the Spirit, who remained on dead and buried Jesus but now raises the Son, presenting Him in whom all have died to the Father's welcome and the joy of heaven.

Every decision involves cost. There is an economy here that involves even

207. Jenson, *ST* 1, p. 181.
208. Jenson, *ST* 1, p. 182.
209. Jenson, *ST* 1, p. 189.

God in the exercise of His deity, if God's deity is a concrete life claiming universal scope in the redemption and fulfillment of creation, and not a reified abstraction. We pay for decisions by giving up some possibilities for the sake of doing some one thing in particular. God in eternity is the almighty Father who has all possibilities, but God in time is God who has decided on some and not others. Moreover, we decide who we particularly are to be in making such decisions, that is, not by realizing a predetermined essence but by acting on the array of possibilities before us in choosing our best of possible worlds and thus effecting in time and space a narrative identity that tells our story from decision to outcome. The crucifixion of the beloved Son, Jenson writes in this light, "is what it cost the Father to be in fact — not just in somebody's projected theology or ideology — the loving and merciful Father of the human persons that in fact exist" — a point at which Jenson acknowledges with gratitude the aforementioned contribution of Gerhard Forde[210] (itself borrowed from Barth, as we have seen). But further, this cost to God the Father in the self-surpassing act of giving over His beloved Son into the hands of sinners there to satisfy the wrath of His love against the ruin of the creation, yet moving beyond that to decide for the mercy of His love for the redemption of His creation is the necessary but not sufficient account of the Father's reconciliation, who reconciles Himself by reconciling us.

"Jesus' sacrifice accomplishes our reconciliation only when we are actually brought together with him and his Father in one community; that is, in that their communal Spirit becomes that of a community in which and by which we live."[211] That is to say, the "objective" sacrifice of Christ obtains objectivity for us not above us but within us by the Spirit's work of creating theological subjects in the dawn of the Beloved Community of the Father. It is by participation in the Eucharistic community, entered through Baptism, that the Spirit unites us, and sustains that union, with the Son, who offered Himself for us, so that in the Son, we may offer ourselves to the Father's praise and glory. Free and joyful life lived conscientiously before the Father, *coram deo,* is the life the just live already now by faith. Note well, then, how the entire Trinity of persons is at work in Jenson's account of the atonement, and, as pertains to our present topic, how the eternal Father becomes our Father too as God surpassing God not in eternity alone, but already now also in time. "It is the Crucifixion as the completion of the life lived in Palestine that settles what sort of God establishes his deity at the Resurrection; and the question does not reopen because Jesus lives anew."[212]

What then of time and eternity? "God's eternity is temporal infinity," Jenson avers, not in the sense of endless physical time, but in the sense of the tensed structure of reality, divine and thus also fittingly creaturely. Father and Spirit are to each other as Alpha and Omega, as past and future, even though in God this

210. Jenson, *ST* 1, p. 191, n. 79.
211. Jenson, *ST* 1, p. 192.
212. Jenson, *ST* 1, p. 200.

difference is immaterial and thus indivisible: "[N]othing in God recedes into the past or approaches from the future." God's tensed life, then, is somehow simple, not composite. It does not fall apart into past and future as with creatures, but in the divine life the Father's past and the Spirit's future are ever present to one another by the mediation of the Son. Nevertheless, in this inseparability there is a sequence that is directed and irreversible: "[T]he arrow of God's eternity, like the arrow of causal time, does not reverse itself." This is among the more daring and difficult speculations in Jenson's theological project; nor is it easy to understand what it means. On the surface, it does not cohere with the characterization of God's eternity as the true "eternal recurrence of the same" that has been elaborated step by step in this system of theology, according to which the Father who begets the Son on whom He breathes His Spirit welcomes the returning Son in the ecstasy of the Spirit to the praise of His deity. So it was in the beginning, is now, and will be forever more, amen. But Jenson's attempts to explain his meaning here fairly reeks of the German Idealism that also attends Jenson's account of the Trinity; nor is this in self-evident harmony with the less speculative doctrine of the social Trinity he develops from the Cappadocian reading of the New Testament narrative. We will critique it more fully in the conclusion of this work, where our concern will be to elaborate eternal life as the life of the Three to which the redeemed creation is raised. For the present, what matters is that even in this speculation Jenson understands God, and particularly the Fatherhood of God, as ecstatic, as God surpassing God, as God on the way to His own future, even at the cost to Him in time of the Son's cross, so that by it His future becomes our future too, in the grant of "the Spirit of Him who raised Jesus from the dead" (Rom. 8:11). For this contribution to an articulate patrology against the trajectory of Western modalism, Christian theology is greatly in Jenson's debt.

## Missio Dei

If God the Father is God surpassing God in eternity, hence also in time as almighty Creator, who sends the Son to redeem and the Spirit to fulfill His creation, what is the mission that comes from the self-surpassing Father by the self-donating Son in the self-communicating Spirit? The divergence between Jenson and Barth here is subtle; once again, God asserts His deity in the Son's way into the far country by the superior contradiction of grace to Adam's presumption to judge, according to Barth; the Spirit anticipates Jesus' Sonship in His earthly life and attests the Sonship of the dead and buried Jesus, friend of sinners, to the Father, who by His resurrection receives the Son together with His redeemed, according to Jenson. This divergence matters immensely in terms of the theological understanding the *missio Dei;* each theologian accordingly parses the work of the ecclesia in mission to the nations differently. Without doubt, moreover, in reflecting on this both theologians are post-Holocaust, historically probing witnesses of the end of

Christendom in Euro-America in which the ecclesia must rediscover the Spirit's mission to the nations or simply and deservedly vanish. But what *missio Dei* is and must be have been and remain a matter of no little contention.

Elsewhere[213] I have traced the peculiar fate of "political Barthianism" in which, as I showed, the German Christian thesis for a wholly acculturated *Volkskirche* "coordinated" with the National Socialist worldview lived on in the "Christians in Socialism" antithesis that emerged from the increasingly radicalized Dalhemite Front following the war and the division of Europe. In *either* case, in the same *undifferentiated* way, the "world set the agenda for the church." For the German Christians this was theologically possible because the world as created by God was to be known as the contest of the races for *Lebensraum* (living space) according to cutting-edge anthropological science; for the Christians in Socialism this was possible because the reconciliation of the world in Christ is a completed fact, and the ascended Christ — quite apart from the church and its ministry of the Word — is creating shalom in revolutionary movements for humanization as these may be understood by cutting-edge sociological science. It is not fair wholly to burden Barth's theology with such appropriations, but neither were these followers wholly mistaken in their reading. Neither will it be right to link Jenson's theology with a merely conservative reaction against political Barthianism. We can trace out this latter line of thought in a 1967 document of the World Council of Churches, "The Church for Others and the Church for the World."[214]

The study takes its point of departure in rejecting as "nostalgia" the "hope" of "refill[ing] the empty pews." The end of the privileged place of the church of Christendom is upon us. It is a fact of history, not to be lamented but affirmed as a step on the way to Christian authenticity. "The missionary Church is not concerned with itself — it is a Church for others." Only by radically listening to the other, i.e., "what modern man is saying in suffering and in success," can theology have contemporary meaning. This radical contextualization is theologically warranted because — and here we can hear the echo of Karl Barth's theology — "in the person of Jesus Christ there were united inseparably and indivisibly the truth concerning God and the truth concerning the world," not ecclesiastically as Head to body in the ecclesia, but cosmic Christologically as the event of reconciliation occurring where God happens in the world. Sociology therefore can inform theology as it seeks "new forms of Christian responsibility in a changing world"[215] in which God is happening Christologically in the event of reconcilia-

---

213. See *BA,* pp. 141-54.

214. *The Church for Others and the Church for the World: A Quest for Structures for Missionary Congregations,* Final Report of the Western European Working Group and the North American Working Group of the Department on Studies in Evangelism (Geneva: WCC, 1967). I am grateful to Sarah Hinlicky Wilson for calling this text, and Krusche's critique of it (see below), to my attention, and for the invigorating discussion of these texts by the Younger Theologians Working Group of Lutheran CORE and the NALC in Pittsburgh, August 2013.

215. *The Church for Others,* p. 7.

tion. In the same key, "de-churching" is affirmed as a change of function under God, not a loss; "secularization" is likewise embraced as the very fruit of the gospel in making state and society responsible for love and justice. *Missio Dei* at all costs, then, must not be "misunderstood as a counter-attack to restore the *corpus Christianum* of former times."[216] Christendom is finished. Rather, Christians must seek and find *Christus extra muros ecclesiae* (Christ outside the walls of the church),[217] wherever the event of reconciliation is happening. The document, again in echo of Barth, affirms that it is *Christ* who is sought there, hence it is a "very specific kind of change" that can be recognized as His. Thus this summons to mission in the world does not "identify God with the flow of events, nor say that every change is a sign of his activity, but it is to recognize him in his action in events," prophetically.[218] Discernment is therefore the crucial contribution of theological thought.

The arena of discernment is secular history, "because our knowledge of God in Christ compels us to affirm that God is working out his purpose in the midst of the world and its historical processes." The biblical notion of *shalom* as a "social happening, an event in interpersonal relations," discerned as "God's gift in actual situations," is what we have called Beloved Community: "the ultimate end of his mission" involves "the realization of the full potentialities of all creation and its ultimate reconciliation and unity in Christ."[219] The affinities here with the present proposal in critical dogmatics, according to which the chief cognitive claim of Christian theology is that God is to be identified as the One who is determined to redeem and fulfill the creation by the missions of His Son and Spirit for the coming of the Beloved Community, are patent, no doubt due to the present proposal's debts to Karl Barth's theology. The divergence from the WCC document that follows therefore is all the more significant. This divergence, parallel to the discussion of ecumenical realignment in Part Three of this work, has its basis in the critique running through this chapter of the modalist tendency of the Western tradition, instead to derive the understanding of *missio Dei* from the vigorous Trinitarian personalism at work in Jenson's theology.

In the WCC document *missio Dei* employs far too vague a notion of deity in general, reifying an easily manipulated abstraction, in place of understanding mission as participation in specific works of the Three in their personal particularity and inseparable mutuality. As we shall see in the next chapter, these works are (1) the Father's creating structures of love for justice by labor, marriage, and organized religion that nurture conscientious life before Him on the way to the best of all possible worlds; (2) the Son's redemption by wedding Himself to sinners in the joyful exchange, and thereby joining each to all the others in the ecclesia

216. *The Church for Others*, p. 10.
217. *The Church for Others*, p. 11.
218. *The Church for Others*, p. 13.
219. *The Church for Others*, pp. 14-15.

as a good in itself within the Trinitarian economy; just this binding unbinds the grip of the structures of malice and injustice so that conscientiously Christians gathered as church may "live under him in his kingdom, and serve him in eternal righteousness, innocence and blessedness, just as he is risen from the dead and lives and rules eternally" (Luther); (3) the Spirit's unification of the sign and the thing signified wherever truth occurs as an event in the world of mendacity and is attested by the signs of truth that are confessions of (1) sin, (2) of Christ as Lord, and (3) of the Father's glory in the sacrifice of praise and thanksgiving.

We distinguish these distinct works of the Three that are the one God in mission in the world in order to be able to praise with Christian praise the prayers of the Muslim who bows down in surrender, as did Jesus in Gethsemane, to the will of God; or to celebrate the marriage of the Hindu couple as graced incognito with the presence of the Incarnate Son; or to acknowledge and learn from the truth of a Confucius not other in wisdom than Solomon, or the skepticism of a Socrates no less than the Preacher of Ecclesiastes, or the labor of an Edison or an Einstein in subduing the earth for human dominion in fulfillment of the mandate of creation, or the grace made known wherever and whenever "truth pressed down rises again" (King). All this Christians are to praise in true praise of the Father through the Son in the Spirit in all His various works (Phil. 4:8; 1 Thess. 5:21), even if these goods are not and cannot be recognized together as works of the one God until by repentance and faith in Jesus Christ they are made known by the Spirit's unification of these signs with the things signified. As the works of the one true God, these works of the Three pertain universally; but as unknown they cannot be held together in conscientious hope for creation's redemption from corruption and its fulfillment in eternal life. Unrecognized as the works of the One who is determined to redeem and fulfill the creation, they fall apart as isolated goods, fragmented and so weakened, goods captured and at the mercy of the structures of malice and injustice which exploit them. Needless to add the same fate falls on Christendom, where the works of the Three have been obscured in the eclipse of the Trinity by unbaptized notions of deity.

The evangelical mission to the nations, so far from being a matter of bringing civilization to the barbarous, is a matter, then, of redeeming the civilization already mandated and operative according to Genesis 1:26-28, liberating it for fulfillment in the ways just indicated by the baptismal vocations of the redeemed people of God within the nations. So far from being a Gnostic mission plucking individual souls from out of history and materiality, it works the redemption and liberation of this earth on which the cross of the Son of God stood. So far from founding funeral societies, its gathering to faith and uniting in love in the ecclesia as a good in itself with the economy of God foreshadows the Sabbath rest already now breaking in to celebrate what God has done for the lost world in Christ. The church thus sings the Spirit's hope into the groaning world, always on the cusp of despair, "to keep on keepin' on." The evangelical mission to the nations is thus indispensable within the broader scope of the Trinitarian economy. It is the redemptive key that holds creation and fulfillment together as one work of the Three on the way to the best of all possible worlds. Such ecclesiology demands theologically the differentiations between potential and actual universalism, between inaugurated and realized eschatology, between Trinitarian personalism and modalism, and between a one-kingdom progressivist and a two-kingdom apocalyptic parsing of the economy of God in history and nature.

The WCC document's *missio Dei* by contrast reduces the ecclesia from its New Testament being as the living Body of Christ in His mission of redemption to that of a human witness to an event essentially other than itself. "The Church," the document maintains, "is always tempted to believe that the activity and presence of God are confined within the boundaries it draws round itself and to think that shalom is only to be found within them. But the whole world was implicated in the death and resurrection of Christ."[220] The critique of Christendom here slips into a critique of Christ in His earthly Body, an uninhibited Zwinglianism. The paradigm "God-Church-world . . . has been understood to mean that God is primarily related to the Church and only secondarily to the world by means of the Church." But this paradigm should be reversed "so that it reads instead God — world — Church."[221] In this proposed paradigm shift to Zwinglian political theology, the church is now to understand itself as part and parcel of the "world, albeit one which confesses the universal Lordship of Christ." This shift in self-understanding is said urgently to be required if the alleged distortion and perversion of the *missio Dei* into missionary "propaganda," i.e., "into the attempt to make man in *our* Christian image and after our ecclesiastical likeness,"[222] is to be overcome for the sake of joining up with what God is doing in the world now.

Hence, the document's famous claim to truth for contextual theology: "The World Provides the Agenda."[223] This claim makes even the "confession of faith" a contextual variable of "worldly experience."[224] The traditional notion of the confession of the faith, subscribed especially by the ordained ministry *to* the Word as confessed by the church for the training and equipping of the laity in their baptismal vocation in the world, is said to be "misleading, because it conveys the impression that there are in the churches those who train or equip and others who need to be trained or equipped."[225] Lest anyone think in this connection of misled readers of this document that had been prepared for their enlightenment by professional theologians, we are assured that would be a mistake, since "theological competence cannot be handed down in the form of packaged doctrines by theological experts."[226] The reality is the collapse of Christendom. In this loss

220. *The Church for Others,* p. 15.
221. *The Church for Others,* p. 16.
222. *The Church for Others,* p. 18.
223. *The Church for Others,* pp. 20-23.
224. *The Church for Others,* p. 24.
225. *The Church for Others,* p. 25.
226. *The Church for Others,* p. 25.

of inherited certainties, we may not understand the lost relevance of traditional "symbols and concepts, dear to the ecclesiastical and theological tradition" as a loss of the "witness to the event to which these symbols and concepts pointed,"[227] the happening of shalom in the world that God is as the event of reconciliation. This reference to the Event remains, purified from ecclesiastical-historical baggage.

Thus, in a perfectly modalist articulation of the doctrine of the Trinity as the external functions of Creator, Christ, and Guide, together with a Nestorian affirmation of the Son of Mary as a "real man" whose "life corresponded completely to the will of God"[228] (though how anyone would know that dogmatic assertion remains unclarified), along with the thorough instrumentalization of the church[229] into a tool of political-theology agitprop, the document urges, as Konrad Raiser expressed in the 1990s, that we have transcended the old theological arguments. They are no longer relevant. The demand of the hour is to give witness in political deeds rather than in theological words to the "Event."

The companion document from the North American working group honestly acknowledges the fear that contextual theology "runs the danger of assuming a 'second source of revelation' (in 'the world' and its 'events') uncontrolled by the theological criteria provided by the given revelation in Christ." But it comes to the conclusion that the "greater danger" is "theological reductionism" — the notion that only theologians can talk about "church" and "mission."[230] Theological reductionism assumes "that 'church' can first be defined in some theological realm above and outside the sociological," but this assumption "overlook[s] the historical character of the Christian faith and the fact that all traditional formulations arose in particular historical situations."[231] It would not be wrong to see in this "North American" iteration of "Church for Others" the relatively greater import of Ernst Troeltsch's thought[232] as compared to the European group's echo of Barthianism. Yet the North American report acknowledges the need to test the spirits: "Where Christ is present, the demons gather." The critical contribution of theology remains discernment. "Can we see where God is at work in such a way that we can join the secular struggles as the people of God, witnessing to the presence of our Lord?"[233] It is a genuine question, left hanging.

It must be left hanging. The very engagement with the world required by the collapse of Christendom indicates a "breakdown of that sense of 'Christian security' over against a 'bewildered' world." As part and parcel of that bewildered world in which change is the only constant, "[q]uestioning has become the piety

227. *The Church for Others*, p. 36.
228. *The Church for Others*, p. 37.
229. *The Church for Others*, p. 38.
230. *The Church for Others*, p. 64.
231. *The Church for Others*, p. 64.
232. *The Church for Others*, e.g., p. 94.
233. *The Church for Others*, p. 78.

of thinking. Nothing remains outside the act of questioning. Even the fundamental datum and presupposition of our theology, God, is no longer self-evident. . . ." One wonders then how the critical contribution of theology to discernment of the spirits, affirmed above, remains possible. But the report concludes dialectically that "openness very often reflects the discovery of the *world* with all its perplexities as the arena of God's action and therefore the authentic locus of *theology*,"[234] even as now bereft of its own theme and presupposition. Open theology in an open church open to the world open to God as a happening now means that we "must say that theology has no subject-matter of its own. It reflects on the history of the whole world and seeks to understand the saving acts of God within and through the secular events."[235] The *petitio principii* (question begging) is too obvious to further comment.

Since 1989 this optimistic, North American reading of "secular events" is no longer possible. But it never was theologically viable, as becomes obvious today in the profound pessimism that haunts the thoughtful. God's love for the world in Christ, hence the coming of the Beloved Community, is not yet fulfilled, and secular events therefore can as readily structure malice for injustice as serve justice and love. Justice and love in any case are concepts normed theologically by the *Verbum externum* of the Son of God's way to and through Gethsemane; thus claims, inherently precarious, to know the incognito work of the Ascended Lord can and must be tested for conformity to Jesus Christ the Son of God. The Beloved Community in any case cannot be actual under present conditions, as Jenson put it, until "we are actually brought together with him and his Father in one community; that is, in that their communal Spirit becomes that of a community in which and by which we live." Here again we see the indispensable role of the manifest gathering to faith in Jesus Christ by which the Spirit signs to the world its destiny in God's promise of His coming as Beloved Community; just so, we are as well reminded that we have this promise now by faith, not yet by sight, on the way to reconciliation and not yet arrived. The promise of the Beloved Community is not and cannot be fulfilled until the promise of the redemption of our bodies is fulfilled; and this fulfillment only comes from above, at the Parousia of the world's still embattled and hidden Lord.

At the time of the WCC document's publication, Werner Krusche issued a decisive critique of the WCC statement from theology in the tradition of Luther, which, to be sure, included important elements of affirmation and approbation.[236] He came to the heart of the matter when he identified the gravamen of the document's understanding of reconciliation as an accomplished event: "[T]he whole

234. *The Church for Others*, p. 91.
235. *The Church for Others*, p. 94.
236. Werner Krusche, "Parish Structures — A Hindrance to Mission?," in Herbert T. Neve, *Sources for Change: Searching for Flexible Church Structures* (Geneva: WCC, 1968), e.g., pp. 81-82.

world is drawn into the death and resurrection of Jesus Christ, that thus the whole of mankind has been led out of captivity and every man has been made a member of the new mankind. . . . Church and world are thus not ontically different — to the contrary, they are precisely therein united, in that they are reconciled through the same reconciler and form the new mankind — , the peculiarity of the Church is rather that it *knows* all this." Accordingly, the church "in the know" may take its place in the world as the "*avant-garde* of its contemporaries." The church is the "perceptive" part of the world, when it is "clear that its job is not to clarify to this world its lostness without Christ from a position over against the world,"[237] but rather from within the world to discern the reconciliation already at work in it. What in Barth had been the highly dialectical "event" of God's love for His enemies in Jesus Christ by the Word's address as witnessed by the church's proclamation thus slips into an uncritical and undialectical optimism about the world as the place where shalom happens. The result is that New Testament texts "describing the world as the epitome of hostility to God have no important role in the discussion." Likewise the apocalyptic *regnum diaboli* is "not to form the point of departure in determining the relation of the Church to the world." Instead the world is entirely regarded under the aspect of God's good creation and thus as "a promising arena of responsibility for men."[238]

Krusche thus critiques the WCC's one-kingdom *missio Dei* theology as wholesale retreat from the recovery of the apocalyptic conflict of the ages that frames the theology of the New Testament in the course of twentieth-century theology, as a reversion, then, to nineteenth-century historical progressivism. "God's action is one, i.e., His historical action, with which He moves the world towards its goal . . . *shalom*." Thus history acquires an "irresistible tendency" and does "not run towards its end, but its fulfillment; the new world does not break into history by breaking it off, but it breaks out of history," revealing the Lordship of Christ, who in turn is understood continually if anonymously to seize power in secular events "to rule against the principalities and powers."[239] Thus, "if Christ is already at work outside the Church, the Church-in-mission does not have the task of bringing Christ to the world, but rather of discovering Him in the world"[240] by joining its movements towards humanization.

Skeptical as Krusche was of such progressivism, he acknowledged passages in the WCC document that also allow for the critical function of theology in testing the spirits: if it "becomes separate from the Gospel the free relationship to the world becomes distorted to a new enslavement to sacred-like powers." The church accordingly keeps watch over the "liberation from the demons by Jesus Christ, and thus [guards] against the danger of subordination to false authority" claimed by

237. Krusche, "Parish Structures," p. 61.
238. Krusche, "Parish Structures," p. 62.
239. Krusche, "Parish Structures," pp. 64-65.
240. Krusche, "Parish Structures," p. 66.

secular powers[241] — a salient point no doubt in the Leipzig of 1968 where Krusche was writing. But the question returns about how this necessary watch can be kept when, according to the WCC document's understanding of reconciliation, "all are beyond danger because there is no judgment,"[242] i.e., so far as an undialectical version of Barth's theology of the Judge judged in our place stands behind the WCC document, according to which God is not only not counting trespasses any longer, but has actually replaced the transgressor with the New Man converted to God. Against this, Krusche points to the Spirit's work of forming the theological subject by baptism into Christ's death and resurrection: "[N]owhere in the New Testament does it say that everyone, as a result of the salvatory death of Jesus Christ which took place for all, already belongs to the new mankind, i.e. without judgment, and that this must merely be confirmed by baptism"[243] (i.e., as in Barth's teaching that water baptism is the believer's testimony confirming God's grace, not the Spirit's grace making the believer). Over against an undifferentiated *missio Dei,* that restores the thetic as opposed to antithetic ( Johannes Weiss) understanding of the nineteenth century, what is needed, says Krusche following the American Lutheran theologian Martin Kretzmann, are the differentiations of Trinitarian personalism that would allow for speaking more precisely of "the Church as the *missio Christi*" rather than of "*missio Dei* so broadly."[244] Then it would be clear that the order "God — Church — world" is "justified, as long as it is kept in mind that God acts in the world in a *saving* way exclusively through the Gospel proclaimed by the Church,"[245] forming there the theological subject by baptism into Christ. In gathering and unifying the church in this way, the Spirit indirectly aids the world by enabling a church that is competent to test the spirits.

Krusche thus relies here on a traditional Lutheran "Two Kingdoms" theology that distinguishes God's temporal preservation of this world from the ravages of sin's ruin and God's eternal salvation of sinners for heavenly life. Writing from the bosom of the Worker's Paradise, and in the aftermath of Hitler's ruinous political messianism, it is surely salient that on this basis Krusche could call for genuine "prophecy" that would oppose the sacrifice of human beings to "programs and utopias"; that instead of trying to discover Christ in messianic movements in secular history, theology would discern "that through His law God is already at work in world occurrences and that there He repeatedly forces men to reason and objectivity"[246] in the creative works of love and justice that structure marriage and family, labor and organized religion, and resist the temptation to totality in political sovereignty.

---

241. Krusche, "Parish Structures," p. 68.
242. Krusche, "Parish Structures," p. 82.
243. Krusche, "Parish Structures," p. 83.
244. Krusche, "Parish Structures," p. 84.
245. Krusche, "Parish Structures," p. 84.
246. Krusche, "Parish Structures," p. 91.

A flatfooted scheme of Two Realms, however, is not adequate to the theology of the Beloved Community, in that the creation of God the Father is the object of the Son's redeeming and the Spirit's fulfilling such that neat separations into mutually delimited social realms are not possible in theological reality. Dividing the world into spheres of creation and law over against church and gospel is false to the one cognitive claim of Christian theology. The distinctions Krusche intended are better understood as distinctions between kinds of divine power and rule in the one world that the one God is creating in order to redeem and fulfill. Nonetheless the protest Krusche makes by means of the traditional Two Kingdoms doctrine, with his biting observation on how the German Christian thesis now lives on in the Christians in Socialism antithesis, was and surely remains spot on. "The Church should be warned once for all by the bad example of the German Christian prophets of lies who in 1933 pretended that National Socialism was the great movement of liberation. . . . The danger of finding Christ precisely in those movements for freedom, peace, unity and humanity of which we ourselves approve and in which we would like to see Christians involved is very great indeed."[247] But the true people of God are those who bring the judgment of the cross upon themselves; this happens in the faithful church and it is its indispensable political contribution in the contested world. Here sin is confessed rather than protested. Being this conscience in the world and before God, the church in mission to the nations makes the one political intervention that is salutary just because it is not the intervention that the world wants or thinks it needs. As for the church's specifically redemptive mission, then, what the gospel of Jesus Christ delivers from above all is our sin (Matt. 1:21), both its guilt and inchoately its power. This is central. From this center the Father's continuous creating for the sake of the Spirit's final fulfilling is both discerned and held together in hope as the works of the one God who gives, the self-surpassing Father of the self-donating Son in the self-communicating Spirit.

## A Note on Islam as the Judgment of God on Christendom

Since September 11, 2001, Euro-America has faced a conundrum. Lacking genuine knowledge of its own sinfulness, it has vastly and compulsively overreacted to the despicable attack of that dark day. Since that time it has spent blood, treasure, and its own precious legacy of civil liberties in a vain effort never again to be vulnerable to "terrorism" — an impossible aspiration trading on a conceptually vacuous term, "terrorism," that can and has now been deployed by every and any political sovereignty in the world facing the wages of its own sins in the rising wrath of its dispossessed. Recognizing this hypocrisy, many of us in theology have worked double-time since 9/11 to learn about Islam, to appreciate it as an Abrahamic faith, and to seek ways for Christians and Muslims to live together on

247. Krusche, "Parish Structures," p. 91.

our shrinking planet, where Islam claims more than a billion adherents.[248] On the plane of critical dogmatics, this requires Christian theology to embrace a difficult anomaly.

Western Christian theological generosity in this regard is still too tangled up in the convoluted hypocrisies of Christendom, also under liberal democratic regimes, according to which Christian attention to Islam has tried to narrow the difference between Islam and Christianity to the person of Jesus Christ — not a difficult or costly gesture on the part of liberal theology that had already and for its own Nestorian reasons reduced Jesus to the prophetic Son of Mary, as we shall shortly examine in the case of Karen Armstrong's scholarship. Indeed, Muslims may be said to honor Jesus, "peace be upon Him," with a religious devotion that exceeds that of contemporary theological liberals. In any case, the dodge attempted here does not work; that is to say, it fails to get at the genuine critique of Christianity in which Islam was born, and the judgment of God on Christianity which this birth and growth of Islam meant and still means. To be sure, Islam also has been judged in turn by God: in the schism of Sunni and Shia, in the centuries of Ottoman hegemony over the Arabs, followed by European colonial occupation with continuing political dysfunction to this day, not to mention the contemporary notoriety that its fanatics bring upon Islam in the eyes of the world. All this is true, but beside the point of the present note.

When the early Luther argued that Islam is God's rod to punish us wicked Christians for our sins,[249] and even later when the mature Luther argued against the holy crusade as a fanatical way of forging a false political unity as Christendom against the invading Turks (yet at the same time obligated secular authorities to defend the European people against aggression),[250] he executed in principle the kind of complex judgment spiritually and politically that conscientious life before God the Father demands. For us today to interpret this judgment of Luther's correctly and fruitfully, however, we must bear in mind that Luther, like all Christians until recent times, regarded Islam as a Christian heresy, just as the early rabbis had regarded Christianity as a Jewish heresy.

The ironies of supersessionism play out in these ways. Moreover, there is a grain of historical truth in this traditional view, since Muhammad in fact offered Islam to the world as a pure retrieval of the uncorrupted faith of the Abraham who surrendered to God's will — purged, then, of self-serving corruptions by Jewish election ideology and the polytheism of Christian Trinitarianism. What is "heresy" and what is "purification" are relative in such ways to the basic claim to truth in a theology. In any case, we are not helped today unless we can hear

---

248. Exemplary in this regard is the Muslim initiative and Christian response, *A Common Word: Muslims and Christians on Loving God and Neighbor,* ed. Miroslav Volf, Gharzi bin Muhammed, and Melissa Yarrington (Grand Rapids: Eerdmans, 2010). Volf's contribution, pp. 125-42, is an exception to the generalization made about liberal theology in the following paragraphs.

249. *LW* 31, p. 92.

250. *LW* 46, pp. 161-205.

Islam's claim to truth in such fashion that Islam at its best would say of our interpretation, "Yes, that is what we mean. You have spoken well." Only then may we, as with human sisters and brothers in equality before God, proceed conscientiously into the kind of rational disputation (Peter Ochs's "scriptural reasoning") that achieves disagreement and so bears fruit not only in civil tolerance but also in forms of friendship and co-humanity. Surely that is and must be the hope of Christian theology. For Christians must hold to their truth and its claim in such a way that its reference remains the coming of the Beloved Community, not our own triumphs within the contested reality that is history between the times, where this truth that we claim is effective already now as the confession of sin that brings the judgment of the cross to bear upon ourselves — not against others.

Along these lines we can offer a short reflection here as food for thought by way of bringing this chapter on God the Father as the audience of theology to conclusion. Inasmuch as Islam regards Jesus as truly born from His virgin mother, Mary, it holds, abstractly speaking, to a "higher" Christology than do many contemporary liberal Christians. This demonstrates that Christology, especially when taken in the decadent modalist fashion of Western tradition as a register of intensities, "higher" and "lower," in divinizing Jesus as God in general, is not and cannot get to the true theological divergence between Christianity and Islam. Rather, when the holy Qur'an announces that "God neither begets nor is begotten," we have a knowing, intelligent, and logically forceful rejection of Christian *patrology.* God is father for Islam only (if at all) metaphorically, as one of many ways of naming the One that is in itself utterly transcendent and thus whose Will is incommunicable in its self-determination, knowable only as what was dictated and then purely recited by the Prophet in delivering the holy text. What else is Islam's theological claim to truth than this?[251]

Well-intentioned Western scholars like Karen Armstrong, however, argue a speculative, historical-critical reduction of this claim to truth that makes Islam unintelligible to its own adherents by making it all-too-intelligible to secularized Western liberals.

> The story of the night journey reveals Muhammad's longing to bring the Arabs . . . into the heart of the monotheistic family. This is a story of pluralism. Muhammad was abandoning the pagan pluralism of Mecca, because it had degenerated into the self-destructive arrogance and violence of *jahiliyyah,* but he was beginning to embrace monotheistic pluralism. In Jerusalem, he discovered that all the prophets, sent by God to all peoples, are "brothers." Muhammad's prophetic predecessors do not spurn him as a pretender, but welcome him into their family. They do not revile or try to convert each other; instead they listen to each other's insights. They invite the new prophet to preach to them. . . . The

---

251. So also as liberal and Westernized an Islamic scholar as Khaled Abou el Fadl, *The Great Theft: Wrestling Islam from the Extremists* (San Francisco: HarperCollins, 2007), pp. 112-27.

fact that this appreciation of other traditions is written into the archetypal myth of Muslim spirituality shows how central this pluralism was to early Islam.[252]

If fact, we might rather say that such "monotheistic pluralism" is the myth of *our* times. That is to say, it is the mythologizing of religion as still a force in the world that matters insofar as its particular claims to truth do not matter.[253]

For Christian theology, Islam confronts its claim to truth with a massive factual as well as theological anomaly that cannot so wistfully be swept under the rug, reinventing Christianity along Pelagian, Nestorian, and Modalist lines in the process. If God is God in His self-surpassing determination to redeem creation by the redemptive and fulfilling missions of His Son and Spirit, then God in God's own reality is eternally the Father who begets the Son on whom He breathes the Spirit. He is the self-surpassing origin of the life that is the holy Trinity, who reaches out from eternal blessedness to enter human unblessedness in Jesus Christ, born from the Theotokos to die for our sins. Since this outreach of God is God, evident anomalies dare not be swept under the rug. Anomalies press adherents of a claim to truth to deeper knowledge that will succeed, as Lindbeck put it, in redescribing the anomalous phenomena adequately or they will amount to the de facto falsification of the claim to truth. Genuine theological dialogue with Islam along these lines is a task in theology that has hardly begun.

Corresponding to its God, Christian conscience is complex in living before the judgment of God surpassing God, where the transition from the wrath of love to the mercy of love is ever at stake among conscientious creatures. The right kind of distinction between Christ and Caesar in the claim on conscience (e.g., Paul's pointed reference to conscience in Rom. 13:5) turns on the hard theological work of distinguishing the structures of love and justice from their perversion into structures of malice and injustice. This need for criteria to test for God the Father's continuous creating in this contested reality should move theology towards an ecumenical doctrine of confession in the following threefold form: (1) confession of sins by the Spirit, (2) confession of the Son incarnate as saving Lord, and (3) confession of praise to the Father with the Son in the Spirit in the Eucharistic doxology of the ecclesia on behalf of all nations. To come to that inquiry — really the task of a Christian ethics — as a continuing gift and task rather than the mere preservation of a fixed deposit, however, entails clear insight into God the Father as God surpassing God before whom the just live in faith by waiting on the coming of His Beloved Community. That has been the argument of the present chapter.

---

252. Karen Armstrong, *Muhammad: A Prophet for Our Time* (New York: HarperCollins, 2006), pp. 97-98.

253. My colleague Gerald McDermott comments: "Armstrong's repetition of the night journey story (to Jerusalem) is not properly historical-critical: the word Jerusalem is not in the Qur'an, and the original reference to "the furthest mosque" (S 17.1) probably refers to a mosque outside Mecca" (personal correspondence, 8/27/2013).

# CHAPTER EIGHT

# The Almighty Father

## Toward the Ecumenical Doctrine of Confession — I

In the contribution of the Norwegian theologian Peder Nørgaard-Højen to the ecumenical study of Petrine ministry considered above in Chapter Four, he made note of a perspective on doctrine that is congruent with the pragmatic ideal of knowledge embraced in this system of theology: "Lutheran theology raises objections where indefectibility is perverted into infallibility, where the fragmentary and approximative are absolutized, and where the historicity of the church and the truth is in this way rejected in favor of an ahistorical fixation and codification, where normativity is misunderstood statically instead of historical-dynamically. The church or rather the truth is infallible, not the pope — neither as authority nor (even less) as an individual."[1] The danger flagged here of claiming to have palpably achieved orthodoxy as a possession rather than to intend orthodoxy within the parameters of the ecumenical tradition of the gospel is a danger, however, that is recognized in the light of a specific construal of Christian truth. It is the one that we have articulated by the claim that God is to be identified as the One who is determined to redeem and fulfill the creation by the missions of His Son and Spirit, namely, then, as the self-surpassing Father, the almighty Creator of all that is not God and the unoriginated Origin within the life that is eternal.

This allegation of danger reflects the familiar Protestant denial that the essential qualities of the ecclesia in oneness, holiness, catholicity, and apostolicity are visible attributes of a substance in the world, that instead the visibility of the ecclesia is noticed by the "marks" of the Head appearing in its earthly Body, namely, pure preaching of the Word and administration of the evangelical sacraments in accordance with the pure understanding of the gospel as mercy for "real, not fictitious" sinners. This construal of Christian truth must be acknowledged and warranted; it is itself disputable and in its own way vulnerable to the danger

---

1. *How Can the Petrine Ministry Be a Service to the Unity of the Universal Church?*, ed. James F. Puglisi (Grand Rapids: Eerdmans, 2010), pp. 199-200.

of ahistorical absolutization when it is asserted as a given and fixed dogma, or a historically given "identity," without contemporary warrant. Without this more penetrating inquiry, indeed, we do not reach the underlying issue whether the earthly Body of Christ is rightly conceptualized as a substance recognizable by essential qualities rather than as the Pauline Body of its Head.

More broadly, we do not ask with genuine perplexity what a "body" is in Christian theology where its resurrection can in one and the same breath be proclaimed with the denial that "flesh and blood" can inherit the kingdom of God (1 Cor. 15:50-56). For it would seem that such a body is (at least temporally) a persisting pattern of material becoming or (at least temporally) an enduring organization of material affects within the material world of becoming; consequently, the information that patterns or configures its being in the world of becoming is not yet settled but still in dispute until the life span of this body is complete. If that is so, "orthodoxy" in the sense of the information known and appropriated that conforms the Body of Christ to its Head, must be taken as an intention rather than an achievement (Phil. 3:8-16), a work in progress, a working knowledge.

It is perplexing, to be sure, to claim to bind consciences to truth with historically relative formulations of God's Word in this fashion, but the necessary perplexity here reflects another theme embraced in the present study. God's Word comes to form theological subjects into the Body of Christ as the promise of an eschatological future, disputable therefore until God, and God alone, proves true to His word of promise, settling its truth definitively before us at the eschaton of judgment. For our part, we do not know how God will fulfill His promises; "it does not yet appear what we shall be" (1 John 3:2), and this principled agnosticism, this necessary apophatic qualification of our *knowledge* of God, must be sustained if it is indeed to be claimed here and now as knowledge of *God*. The deep reason for this is not a metaphysical principle about the incapacity of the finite for the infinite but rather that the kingly work of Christ, of Him who is known in the objectivity of faith, is not yet finished, not to mention also the work of His Spirit in the resurrection of the dead. Thus again with Nørgaard-Højen, "The concept of *infallibilitas* runs an unnegligible risk of de-eschatologizing the truth, which remains historical and becomes only tangible and perceptible in history, and of wresting the truth-finding process from history and thus of depriving God, i.e., truth itself, of the final word . . . [so that] critical, constructive, and disquieting discernment is now perverted into ideology."[2] This construal of Christian truth contends, then, for an ecumenical "doctrine of doctrine" out of the tradition of theology that stems from Luther within the contemporary brokenness of Euro-American Christianity; but it is made with the intent of a division of the divisions on the way to the new formation of the Body of Christ that will be "post-Christendom."

---

2. *How Can the Petrine Ministry Be a Service?*, p. 200.

To put the point positively: timely confession of Jesus as the self-donating Son of the Father who is self-surpassing, not the mere preservation of a timeless deposit, is the always contemporary formulation of doctrine that concretely anticipates the eschaton of judgment in the relativity of the present moment.[3] "Jesus Christ is the same, yesterday, today and forever" (Heb. 13:8), to be sure, and the conscience of this concrete and timely confession of Jesus Christ the Son of God is the eternal God and Father in whom and before whom account is rendered for the hope that is in us. Confession of the gospel is made public at every moment in time before God, who is the final forum of this ultimately doxological act; it is concrete, however, as the confession of sins and ecstatic as the confession of praise. As in Nørgaard-Højen's reflection in dialogue with Roman Catholic theologians on the Petrine office, such "doctrine of doctrine" is put forward here for the sake of a new unity of divided Christianity on the way to renewed mission post-Christendom. It is also, then, a critical rejection of tribal versions of doctrine in confessionalism or orthodoxy, not to mention the loss of doctrinal theology in pietism and liberalism. To speak of doctrinal theology "in the tradition of Luther" this way is to claim Luther as a teacher in faith alongside others, not a hero or prophet, but the teacher who taught us all that the saving righteousness of God in Jesus Christ saves the real, not fictitious sinner or its saves none at all. To articulate this saving reach of the Son sent from the Father into the world, however, so that in context it penetrates to precisely this depth, there to grasp hold and win free, is always a matter of fresh confession on the way to the Beloved Community of God.

What is heresy and what is purification of doctrine, in any case, are relative to some such claim to truth. Far from a reduction to the epistemically lazy bonhomie of "monotheistic pluralism" or "reconciled diversity," the pragmatic ideal of knowledge requires something far more taxing, namely, timely confessing the truth of God in and for one's own place. Doctrine as confession, precisely in the freshness of timely reformulation, stands therefore under a twofold test of recognizable continuity with the preceding tradition of the gospel and contextual aptness, where the continuity is Jesus Christ ("the same yesterday, today and forever") and the variable is apt articulation of the salvation that He alone brings to the contemporary audience — remembering of course that, as *His* salvation, this articulation may well offend and be a stone of *stumbling*. "Relevance" is no one-way ticket to religious success in the world according to the business of religion as usual.

Indeed, since in every new situation the ultimate audience of the claim to truth made by the theological subject in confessing Jesus Christ the Son of God is the One whom He called "Abba, Father," the fresh articulation of doctrine can perform nothing less than an offensive claim upon and against modernity's sov-

---

3. Robert W. Bertram, *A Time for Confessing,* ed. Michael Hoy, Lutheran Quarterly Books (Grand Rapids: Eerdmans, 2008).

ereign self that would bind its conscience and in just this way subvert its putative sovereignty. Theology is not free thinking but freed thinking, thinking therefore bound to its Liberator, if it would remain free in the still-contested reality of the apocalyptic conflict He conducts against the structures of malice and injustice. That is because, concretely, timely confession gives the good reason for the forgiveness of sins in the saving Lordship of Christ as the Father's final Word already now appearing in the justification of the sinner who surrenders by the Spirit to His merciful reign. But who and what the sinner is in any concrete case must be discerned by the venture of a pastoral and prophetic judgment, if saving truth is to be formulated truthfully in context.

Nørgaard-Højen thus very helpfully goes on in his contribution to explore the Reformation notion of *casus confessionis,* "the case requiring confession," from an early Lutheran dispute regarding the witness required when the gospel is under persecution. What is under examination here is the problem of novelty in the church's historical experience (e.g., the shock in the sixteenth century of finding the church's hierarchy, rather than the pagan state, persecuting the gospel). Whether for good or for evil, novelty requires something "far beyond a mere repetition of the [past] confession within the community of tradition," a tradition, however, that by no means has become "obsolete or even meaningless," but now requires "an explicit consideration" of the "new situation and its difficulties."

The Book of Acts teaches nothing else. Christian theology must both preserve its evangelical institution as mission to the nations in the confession of Jesus Christ the Son of God before God and at the same time receive in the Spirit its experience in the world, including novelties, also the painful novelties of persecution, as the continuing creation ruled and overruled by the same Father of Jesus Christ, the almighty Creator of all that is not God, the Lord of history. If docetism and dualism are to be rejected, and if the tension-filled unity of creation and redemption is to be maintained against the perennial seduction of Gnosticism, as in fact the paradigmatic battle-lines in the early history of orthodoxy were drawn in the second century, then mundane experience must be received from the hand of God and trumped by the concrete confession here and now of the gospel of God. Thus theology in the Spirit comes to articulate in an "exceptional decision" a "new version of at least some of the traditional confessional statements, lest the credibility — or even the very existence — of the church as a community of faith and obedience should be endangered."

One may think here of the conciliar judgment of Acts 15, but also for painful counter-instance, as Melanchthon ventured to judge against medieval warlords dressed in copes, that *"persecutors* of the gospel are *not bishops."*[4] In turn, such

---

4. Philipp Melanchthon, *On Christian Doctrine: Loci Communes, 1555,* trans. C. L. Manschreck (Grand Rapids: Baker, 1982), p. 262. Indeed, the binding nature of the claim to truth requires that "all men are obliged by divine command to abandon untrue teachers and bishops as accursed" (p. 258, cf. Matt. 7:15).

critical turning points in the history of doctrine themselves become, according to Nørgaard-Højen, "part of its permanent witness." This is evident, to continue for contemporary example with Melanchthon's doctrinal judgment just mentioned against a mechanical understanding of apostolic succession as transmission of a legal title, in the convergence statement of Lutherans and Anglicans that "apostolic succession is a sign, not a guarantee" (that is, *of* an *intention,* not *to* the *possession*) of fidelity in teaching by the standard of the historical apostolate as codified in the New Testament writings. It is, we have argued throughout, the Spirit's sovereign work to unify the sign and the thing signified; the Spirit is not any spirit that the ecclesiastical apparatus swallows whole, "feathers and all" (Luther), so that in turn whatever flows forth from its sanctified lips is ipso facto Word of God. But the Spirit, who may sovereignly speak even through Balaam's ass (Num. 22:30), may as freely withhold this unification for faith and obedience in frightful judgment upon an unfaithful hierarchy "holding to the form of religion but denying its power" (2 Tim. 3:5).

To judge a hierarchy unfaithful, however, is not to reject hierarchy but to uphold it against abuse. By the same token, conscientious ecclesiastical disobedience is not an innovation of Melanchthon. It actually finds its evangelical precedence in the long period of the semi-Arian emperors-cum-episcopate between the first and second ecumenical councils.[5] Ecclesiastical obedience or disobedience, in any case, is relative to the intention for orthodoxy in accord with the truth of the gospel; as the gospel has a history in the world, and thus also a legacy of such decided decisions, Christian theology that intends orthodoxy inherits theological traditions of binding ecumenical beliefs with continuing force that define the parameters of orthodox belief. These dogmatic decisions are few in number and broad in scope, but they are binding on theology that intends to be orthodox. These are, in bare-boned sum: the canonical Scriptures, the Trinity of divine persons, the personal unity of divine and human in Christ, and salvation by grace. Within these parameters, the point for Nørgaard-Højen is that theology in the "Lutheran" idiom of "the case of confession" also and necessarily teaches in ways that bind conscience, formally resembling not only the Petrine claim to magisterium,[6] but also the creedal dogmas of the ecumenical councils. In all of these ways, the church dares to bind conscience by the "power of the keys," as the Augsburg Confession Article 28 actually teaches, by judging doctrine for its accord with the gospel.[7]

Confession as a model of the theological life is broader than the epistemic concerns of critical dogmatic theology, just as the theological "subject" abstracts

---

5. Oyvind Nordeval, "The Emperor Constantine and Arius: Unity in the Church and Unity in the Empire," *Studia Theologica* 42 (1988): 113-50.

6. *How Can the Petrine Ministry Be a Service?*, pp. 204-5.

7. See Paul R. Hinlicky, "Authority in the Church: A Plea for Critical Dogmatics," in *New Directions for Lutheranism,* ed. C. Braaten (Delhi, NY: ALPB Books, 2010), pp. 123-53.

from the theological person in respect to epistemic concerns, i.e., the true knowledge of God and self. Doctrinal confession is embedded in the holistic practices of the confession of sin and the doxology of the corporate community in the Eucharist. In this living whole of corporate Christian practice, however, the confession of faith in the timely formulation of doctrine holds pride of place in the way that knowledge, as opposed to ignorance or benightedness, holds pride of place in any human form of life. Thus, in accord with Romans 10:9-10, Luther observes that "confession is the principal work of faith."[8] In the Apology, Melanchthon speaks along the same lines. On the one hand, "confession does not justify or save mechanically, but solely on account of the faith of the heart," but on the other hand, "it is not, however, a firm faith which does not present itself in confession."[9] Once again, with Luther: "Truly, if faith is there, he cannot hold back; he proves himself, breaks out into good works, confesses and teaches the gospel before the people, and stakes his life on it."[10] The "case" of confession arises in the mission to the nations and in the service of the baptized within the nations whenever and wherever the public question arises, "By what right? On what grounds? In whom really do you believe and why?" In that case, one answers repeating (Greek: *homologizein,* to "same say") the authorizing and hence authoritative Word from God spoken in one's formation as a theological subject by baptism into Christ, acknowledging union with Christ and new life in the Spirit in praise of the Father as the good reason for the new corporate life of the ecclesia and its disruptive practices of grace in Jesus' name. So Günther Bornkamm wrote at the time of the German Church struggle as the model of theology as confession was being retrieved in those apocalyptic times: "The content of confession is always that which is decisive for the relation to another . . . confession contains nothing other than the name of Jesus . . . encounter with the world proceeds because they are bearers of the name of Jesus."[11]

---

## A NOTE ON PASTORAL AND LITURGICAL THEOLOGY

The confession of Jesus Christ in the world as before the Father is already now prolepsis of the eschaton of judgment; prolepsis is the epistemic relation of access that especially interests systematic theology. But as doctrine for life, the confes-

---

8. *LW* 25, p. 411.

9. *BS,* p. 232, my translation from the "quarto" edition, omitted by *BC,* p. 172, n. 232. The opponents are said to understand faith as "acknowledgement of history or dogma, not this power that apprehends the promise of grace and of justice that vivifies the heart in the terrors of sin and death." *BC,* p. 232.

10. *LW* 35, p. 361.

11. Günther Bornkamm, "Das Wort Jesu vom Bekennen," *Geschichte und Glaube,* Erster Teil, Gesammelte Aufsätze, Band III (Munich: Chr. Kaiser Verlag, 1968), p. 32; all translations are my own.

sion of faith cannot be separated, as just mentioned, from the integral partners of conscientious life before God in the confession of sin and communal worship in the confession of praise. The following brief comments on pastoral and liturgical theology bear this out.

By the divine imperative "Believe the gospel!" (Mark 1:15) one is commanded to live as forgiven and united people of God or de facto to deny Christ (cf. Luke 5:8). In this light, we have to ask whether pastoral theology today has turned away from the nurture of conscientious life before God. We have to ask whether the increasingly desperate attempt of chaplaincy in the Euro-American religion business only bandages and sends back into battle sovereign selves in would-be pursuit of happiness, yet in an increasingly vicious and predatory social environment that exploits this greed for its own greedy purposes. The confession of sins before God, in that case, is caricatured as some kind of torture, a medieval self-abasement for purposes of ecclesiastical policing rather than the Spirit's gracious work of liberation from internalized structures of malice and injustice. As you believe, so you have. Throwing off the yoke of Jesus Christ and the discipline of discipleship to Him (Matt. 11:30), we are yoked instead to the needs and requirements of the global juggernaut that wants to make of each and everyone an easily replaced cog in its machinery, bribing with bread and circuses in exchange for the surrender of lives of personal integrity before God.

The confession of sins is the fruit of the Spirit: "all the godly, as many as there are of them, have this virtue in them, that they confess their sins to God"; this work of the Spirit is grace, that is, when, and only when, such confession is "not a matter in which it is in our power to take or to give, but it is a gift which has come down from heaven."[12] Confession of sins, in other words, is nothing in principle that can be extorted out of a person by threats or force; it can only come forth freely as the affections of the heart are reorganized by the Spirit's infusion of the love of God through the Word of the love of Christ. In that case, the concrete application of the "judgment of the cross" to oneself in the theological interpretation of personal experience is painful only to the old Adam, for by faith "Christ carries all sins, if only they are displeasing to us, and thus they are no longer our sins but His and His righteousness in turn is ours."[13] That sin becomes displeasing to us is therefore the infallible sign of the presence and work of the Spirit who is holy. Whoever so battles is to be comforted with just this evangelical interpretation of her experience. To minister this joyful exchange personally is, by the same token, the pastoral ministry of the gospel. For if "Christ himself is made guilty of all the sins that we have committed" in the very act of forgiving them in the name of God, then "we are absolved from all sins, not through ourselves or through our works or merits but through him."[14] Entering pastorally into

12. *LW* 36, p. 360.
13. *LW* 25, p. 254.
14. *LW* 26, p. 280.

this Christological place of costly mercy, believers are to be personally freed by sacramental absolution from Adam's congenital self-justification. The therapy of the confession of sins is a veritable exorcism of the powers of internalized malice and injustice that have penetrated bodies to form subjectivities in ruinous ways. Pastoral theology is this ministry to souls *in terroribus peccati et mortis* ("in the terrors of sin and death").

By the forgiveness of sins that comes concretely and personally through confession, moreover, the believer united with Christ is further united through Christ in the Spirit with all other sinners whom He forgives. This is the "spiritual" unity of the ecclesia that should also be a "visible" unity of mutual love and burden-bearing before the world (John 17; Gal. 6:2). And this union in the Spirit is true; it is not merely a removal of sins from the individual but a conferral of righteousness that binds together in love; for where there is forgiveness of sins, there also is life and salvation. "The essential feature of redemption — forgiveness of sins — being once obtained, everything belonging to its completion immediately follows. Eternal death, the wages of sin, is abolished; and eternal righteousness and life are given ... everything in heaven and earth ... is in turn reconciled to us. The creatures are no longer opposed, but at peace with us and friendly: they smile upon us and we have only joy and life in God and his creation."[15] The Eucharistic gathering of the new creation people of God on the day of the Lord's resurrection manifests this new life in the Spirit that sings praise to His Father who has thus become our Father as well. Here His "uniting *is* His forgiving them, and vice versa" (Bertram).[16] This palpable unification of bodies to form the earthly body of Christ in their common life erupts into the doxologies that anticipate the final victory of God and the Lamb for one and for all. So Luther put it in the divine voice: "thankoffering confers upon me my divine glory; it regards me as God and lets me remain God."[17]

Clarity on this critical point — how it is that the church is part of the gospel — has long bedeviled Protestant theology in its justified concern to insist that only the hearing church can become the teaching church, the receiving church the ministering church. Lutheranism has frequently regarded any worship of God in the corporate return of selves in Spirit-filled thanksgiving precisely in and on account of the unification with Christ that is the communal eating and drinking of His body and blood as some Romanizing move that threatens the purity of God's gracious self-donation in the gospel. As we saw above in Chapter Six, the new Scandinavian theology of gift works out an analysis that shows just how wrongheaded this often-unconscious assimilation of

---

15. On Colossians 1:14, *Sermons of Martin Luther*, ed. John Nicolas Lenker, 8 volumes (Grand Rapids: Baker, reprinted 1983), 8:375-77.

16. Robert Bertram, "Our Common Confession and Its Implications for Today," *Concordia Theological Monthly* 39 (1968): 719.

17. *LW* 38, p. 106.

the Spirit to the Word truly is, why a dialectic in divine giving of the Word *and the Spirit* is required to articulate the grace of God's redemptive *and fulfilling* gifts. As R. David Nelson has shown in this regard in his excellent appreciation and critique of Jüngel, a theologian without equal in championing the interruptive work of the Word of God incarnate in Word and Sacrament, the grace to receive this interruption and be made new by it and to grow together in its newness of life is the corresponding grace of the Spirit who returns the Son to the Father.[18] For Luther the actual alternative here is not between God's works and human works, when the contrast "God and human" is made in the tacitly unitarian and modalist way of modern theology. It is rather formulated by Luther as one between self-chosen works and the works instituted and commanded by God; it is "self-chosen worship" of Adam who wants to be God and does not want God to be God that makes a "sacrifice of human works rob[bing God] of His glory, mak[ing] an idol of Him."[19] The commanded worship of God is the one given by the New Adam in the Lord's Supper, who wants to be God for us and succeeds in being God for us precisely in giving in the Spirit "a sacrifice of thanksgiving, for by this very remembrance we confess and thank God that we have been saved and become righteous and blessed by sheer grace through Christ's suffering."[20] The Trinitarian distinction of persons and their characteristic operations is manifest.

Liturgical theology has its post-Christendom task laid out in embracing this dialectic of the gift of the Son *for us* in the proclamation of the Word pointing to the Spirit's gift *of us* to the Father in union with the Son in the Eucharistic doxology. For if also the gift to receive the gift of the Son from the Father is thus given by the Spirit's unification of the believer with the Son in His own self-offering to the Father (as Rom. 12:1-2 indicates), there is no place at all left for the sovereign self of modernity in the ecclesia. That is the timely truth for today — no place for modernity's sovereign self, not even the disguised place that claims "unconditional grace, no matter what," but thus turns the costly grace of God in Christ into a cheap ideology of conformity with the world; its "unconditional" acceptation along with its phony "reconciliation" of "diversity" in doctrine succeeds so far as doctrine is made inconsequential because it can make no claim to Christian truth that concretely binds conscience. In this way too the coming division of the divisions will cut through the confusion that is the abject and obsequious church of dying Christendom.

---

18. R. David Nelson, *The Interruptive Word: Eberhard Jüngel on the Sacramental Structure of God's Relation to the World* (London and New York: Bloomsbury T. & T. Clark, 2013), p. 139.

19. *LW* 38, p. 107.

20. *LW* 38, p. 117.

## Toward the Ecumenical Doctrine of Confession — II

The unity of these two forms of confession, personally of sin and corporately of thanksgiving, is the confession of Jesus Christ the Son of God in the world as before the Father: "Thereby a person thanks and praises not only God in Christ ... but he also confesses his Lord Christ openly before the world and confesses that he is a Christian and wants to be one."[21] The confession of Jesus Christ acknowledges Him as true Son of God in His messianic works that the ecclesia in mission performs in His name. It is first of all "confession that Christ is a Priest who intercedes between God and us," so that confessors "are undismayed in the face of every sin and the wrath of God, through faith in Christ."[22] It "confesses and praises Christ as Lord ... the great, mighty, courageous and fearless trust of all Christian believers, in the face of everything that is against them."[23] Confession of Christ as Lord is not mere exuberance or enthusiasm; it is doctrinal knowledge of "the great price and work which it cost Christ to be our priest and king."[24]

While this confession is made in the world, its true audience is God the Father, as may be seen in the text of Matthew 10:32/Luke 12:8-9. Bornkamm noted the eschatological correspondence claimed in the text: it "brings into precise harmony God's activity in judgment and human activity before the last judgment," so that the promised eschaton of judgment ceases to be a supra-historical threat but becomes already now an event in which "what is applied to a person is what the person him/herself has done."[25] Bornkamm fills out the picture by indicating the subversion of the total claim of political sovereignty that is effected by public confession of the crucified King of the Jews: "Human beings call the disciples before their tribunal ... the world gives itself a public legitimation in which it carries through in its organization of legal power its battle against Jesus and his society of disciples. ... By this commitment to order, in which from the beginning the roles of judge and of accused have been established, the world documents that it denies any responsibility here, yet it takes over — indeed at the same time against its will — all responsibility."[26] But where the "world exalts itself in its anti-godly resolve, there the Spirit of God comes on the scene" to give utterance to those who bear the name of Jesus so that boldly and intelligently they confess it. And since it will be God who judges finally and definitively, "denial which ensures acquittal and peace for the disciples on earth is damnable before God, and the confession which allows them to be ruined before the earthly court means redemption before God."[27] Justification by faith is the personal prolepsis already

21. *LW* 38, p. 111.
22. *LW* 52, p. 279.
23. *LW* 52, p. 278.
24. *LW* 52, p. 280.
25. Bornkamm, "Das Wort Jesu vom Bekennen," p. 30.
26. Bornkamm, "Das Wort Jesu vom Bekennen," p. 31.
27. Bornkamm, "Das Wort Jesu vom Bekennen," p. 34.

now of the eschaton of judgment; so also this concrete confession of Jesus Christ as saving Lord is the social and public prolepsis of the eschaton that casts down the mighty from their thrones and exalts them of low degree.

In all this what is at issue is the grace of Jesus' calling of disciples and the new freedom of responsibility *to* God *for* the world — as opposed to the world's assertion of its freedom from God in the name of responsibility to the world. Jesus is confessed, then, as the reason good enough for the disciples following Him in His mission, now by the Spirit, to all nations, there to gather the church as the Spirit's sign of the unification of God with humanity in the coming of the Beloved Community. Put on trial by the world for just this *disruption,* the confession of Jesus Christ puts the world on trial before God. In demanding an account of confessors, the account given by the confessors justifies the hope that the earthly court excludes in its own claim to sovereignty. The disruption of this grace in the world's business inaugurates, then, a salutary conflict of God against the world for the sake of the world. Confession that concretely formulates this disruption of grace, as Melanchthon put it in the Apology, shows "the reign of Christ, whereby he shows his rule before the world. For in these works he sanctifies hearts and suppresses the devil. And in order to keep the Gospel among men, he visibly pits the witness of the saints against the rule of the devil."[28] The Father's conscientious confession of His Son, Jesus Christ, before the world by the resurrection proclamation of His vindicated faith thus disarms tyrants that preside in structures of malice and injustice and puts the worldly power that they exploit back under God's law of love and demand for its justice on the earth. Confession reorders the powers. This political purpose of the Father is actualized through the concrete confession of that ecclesia that hears, believes, and teaches this Word from God.

Doctrinal confession then is the insignia of the ecclesia free in Christ to be in mission to the nations for the true service within them of love for justice. This confession should be standard, operating procedure, ordinary and catechetical, not any kind of extraordinary thing — although it becomes dramatic in the apocalyptic moments of the "case requiring confession." Such doctrinal theology indeed always presupposes the apocalyptic framework of New Testament theology with its question, in Käsemann's celebrated formulation, "Who owns the earth?"[29] Confession that answers "the God and Father of our Lord Jesus Christ," then, is not at all a matter of preserving Christendom but rather of a post-Christendom church emerging from those ruins bearing faithful witness to the identity of the world as claimed by God for the Beloved Community: judged, pardoned, and being returned to the true political sovereignty of the Father, through His Son Jesus Christ, by the Spirit of their love for the destiny of life, righteousness, and peace. Confession is theology that knows in God the Father the true cause for

---

28. *The Book of Concord,* ed. Theodore G. Tappert (Philadelphia: Fortress, 1959), p. 133.

29. Ernst Käsemann, *Perspectives on Paul,* trans. Margaret Kohl (Philadelphia: Fortress, 1978), p. 25.

which it labors and the final court to which account is rendered. Confessing theology identifies God as the One who is self-determined as the Father to redeem and fulfill His creation through the missions of His own Son and Spirit; it must do this in every new situation concretely, knowing that its own time and place will be superseded as the gospel mission moves on to new peoples and new generations; just so, fully engaged in the here and now, it contributes its little chapter to the history of the gospel's way through the world, until its promise is fulfilled and all the chapters are integrated at the eschaton of judgment.

---

### A NOTE ON CREATION FAITH AND THE
### SCIENTIFIC UNDERSTANDING OF NATURE

A manifest objection to the foregoing account of the apocalyptic-confessional (not denominational-confessionalistic) posture of critical dogmatic theology is common today in the complaint, often urged against Barth's theology (as Robert Bertram, in the spirit of the University of Chicago Divinity School where he was trained, once put it) for "abjuring Christian theology's accountability to the world, for insisting — positivistically, as Bonhoeffer complained — on the privileged immunity, the arbitrary givenness of Christian revelation. . . . [Barth's] 'retreat to commitment.' "[30] There is a genuine issue here, but only after the conceit of epistemology to know knowing universally and necessarily is itself "abjured" for what in gospel truth it is, the *libido dominandi* of post-Christian Euro-America's putative Tribunal of Reason. An account of theology's epistemic access, on the other hand, puts theology itself along with its inquisitors under the judgment of the Word of God; to appeal to the Word of God is no "privilege." The disruptive event of the advent of the Word indeed puts the one who appeals to it into the vulnerable position of the martyr in the world.

If there is any "privileged" claim here in the claim to truth that God has spoken in Jesus Christ and that the spoken God has been heard in the Spirit giving faith, it is in any event *never* a claim that contests in principle our best available accounts of experience in the common body. It is rather always a demand that minimally the theological claim to truth be shown to cohere with all other truths we hold by virtue of abiding membership in the common body. It is *ever* a claim, maximally, to interpret those best accounts alongside other interpreters in the pluralistic disputation that is our *modus vivendi* in the common body (at least so far as minimum standards of justice and equality are secured by the state in obedience to its divine commission, Romans 13:1-8, that undergirds such progress of science by way of free disputation; see below the discussion of structures of love working justice). Being itself a science in civil society, what Christian theology disputes is never science but rather bad science, that is, science that exceeds

---

30. Bertram, *Time for Confessing*, p. 37.

its finitude and finite location in the world. Alongside philosophy (sometimes with philosophy, sometimes against philosophy) as academic heir of the *studia humanitatis* (in the particularity of the Euro-American tradition of the West) Christian theology proffers interpretations of natural and social science on behalf of the promise to all of the coming of the Beloved Community of God.

When, in turn, its own claim to the knowledge of God along these lines is disputed by others, Christian theology can give no other reasons than scientific ones, pragmatically understood, for its epistemic access. That is to say, the account demanded of the new theological subjectivity by the Spirit conforming to the cross and resurrection of Christ makes no appeal to special intuitions, mystical experiences or supernatural exceptions to regular mechanisms of experience (even if believers should enjoy such events, they "prove" nothing publicly). Rather it gives a sober description of the *Wirkungsgeschichte* (the efficacious history) of the external Word of the gospel in mission to the nations, where and when it elicits repentance and faith in the coming of the Beloved Community of God. "Faith comes by hearing" (*fides ex auditu,* Rom. 10:17) of the (putative) word from God. This truthful account of the grounds for the Christian claim to truth also does not "prove" its truth, which only the divine fulfillment of the promise can do. But it does account for the conviction of it without the bad faith of impugning others who are not convinced by supposed "evidence that demands a verdict." Christian theology is precisely *not* the "true" version of epistemological foundationalism. Rather, Christian theology takes the message of the "resurrection of the Crucified," not as a supernatural proof that provides exceptional justification for its claim to truth, but rather as the historical event of God surpassing God in the disruptive speech-act of the gospel — extraordinary in its own way, to be sure, but not an epistemological miracle proving or demonstrating the truth of faith as if to neutral observers. Only the Spirit works conviction concerning "sin and righteousness and judgment" — no "privilege," as we have stressed, but a heavy cross laid upon the one who comes to faith.

Contemporary dialogues of faith and science, accordingly, are culturally important in several dimensions, especially to remind the sciences of the limits they meet in metaphysics and to disqualify the fundamentalisms at work in the religion business. The best available scientific thinking constrains theology in the sense that it provides the material of the book of nature that theology as the book of Scripture interprets as God's continuous creating. At a minimum, theology that fails to receive this best available thinking makes itself contextually unintelligible in Euro-America today, no matter what truths it otherwise thinks to preserve. So-called "creationism" is a prime example of uncritically dogmatic tone-deafness in this regard; theologically, it succeeds in misunderstanding Scripture as much as it willfully misrepresents nature. On the other hand, theological interpretation cannot but challenge any tendency to absolutize scientific understandings by reminding one and all that science works by assuming what cannot be demonstrated until the hypothetical completion of natural history (the epistemic "eschaton" of pragmatism), namely, the categorical uniformity of nature.[31] This posit of the uniformity of nature is an axiom, a powerful and valuable one; yet as an axiom, it betrays the fact that inquiry into nature on natural grounds alone is metaphysically a *petitio principii.* It is not surprising, as a result, that scientific discovery repeatedly finds any domain of nature studied in a discipline embedded in some supervening order, we know not what (e.g., the "initial condition" antecedent to the Big Bang in physics, the "irreducible complexity" discovered in biological evolution). Metaphysics asks about this ultimate coherence that the sciences come up against but that, on account of methodological assumptions and disciplinary limitations, science itself cannot account for. This limit is the domain of metaphysics, taken as interpretation of the whole in which the sciences study parts. Consequently, contra Kant, metaphysics cannot but be speculative, however disciplined it is and well informed scientifically. Yet it is arbitrary to exclude speculative metaphysical interpretation of the whole because it cannot in principle acquire the certainty of concrete knowledge that is gained within the disciplinary study of the parts by aid of the powerful assumption of uniformity that is not itself demonstrable. Metaphysics queries the why of this powerful assumption.

To speculate about the uniformity of nature as a whole, then, is to step past scientific procedure into metaphysics. The cognitive significance of such speculation is evident to historians of science. Ironically enough, modern Western science nurtured on Aristotle's biological-organic metaphysics came into its own in the seventeenth century when it rejected Aristotle's version of naturalism for another speculation, specifically, that of mechanistic metaphysics in the tradition of Democritus and Lucretius, as in the atomism of Hobbes or the modalism of Spinoza. This new metaphysical thinking, of course, is as licit as any other metaphysical speculation, so far as it recognizes that it goes beyond the procedures of science in quest of the ultimate coherence. Classically theology has engaged in disputation with metaphysics, rather than the individual sciences (from which, as per this argument, it cannot dialogue or dispute but only learn), in that philosophy (at least before or apart from Kant) knows that metaphysics transgresses and must transgress the limits of scientific procedure to speculate (in however disciplined a way) about first or final causes, necessary or perfect beings, and so on. In a culturally maturing scientific age, there is nothing to prevent the resumption of this classical dialogue, as Adkins and I endeavored in *Rethinking Philosophy and Theology with Deleuze.*

---

31. E.g., "biological process requires the availability of a stable planet, irradiated by an energy source capable of chemical conversion and storage, and the existence of a diverse array of core chemical elements, with certain fundamental properties [i.e., carbon chains], before life can begin, let alone evolve. Biology has become so used to the existence and aggregation of highly organized attributes that they are seen primarily as core assumptions of evolutionary theory, rather than something that requires explanation in its own right. There is an implicit assumption that life would adapt to whatever hand of physical or chemical cards were dealt to it. Yet this is untested and intrinsically questionable." Alister E. McGrath, *A Fine-Tuned Universe: The Quest for God in Science and Theology* (Louisville: Westminster John Knox, 2009), p. 180.

Alister E. McGrath, on the other hand, has said what is necessary and possible for Christian theology with respect to the natural sciences in his Gifford Lectures, *A Fine-Tuned Universe;* we stipulate his position here as the operating assumption in what follows: "I believe in design because I believe in God; not in God because I see design," that is, concretely, that "the teleonomic [not teleological] disclosures of evolutionary biology can be reconciled with a Christian vision of reality."[32] By "teleonomic" McGrath is ultimately referring to the "origination of a potentially multileveled reality, whose properties *emerge* under certain conditions, which did not exist at the origin of the universe."[33] Metaphysical or theological interpretations of this most salient "disclosure of evolutionary biology," i.e., the *emergent* properties that constitute the human, cannot not be a matter irrelevant to theological subjectivity. So McGrath himself concludes: "a fundamental theme of the Christian gospel is the transformation of humanity, traditionally and rightly articulated in terms of atonement and salvation. Yet a part of that transformation is intellectual: the Christian faith gives rise to a renewal of the mind (Rom. 12:1-2), which inevitably leads to seeing things in a new way . . ."[34] including "a new way of 'seeing' the natural world."[35]

Questions about the dating and mechanics of cosmic origin and the evolution of life remain ongoing questions of natural science, and in any case, it is the *fundamental error* of modern theisms and deisms (and their atheistic opponents) to restrict the notion of the world as creation to the past matter of origin, or tacitly, to ask about God as only or chiefly this God of the Past.[36] As Adkins and I argued in *Rethinking Philosophy and Theology,* the metaphysical orientation of classical philosophy is protological, the search for the initial condition that conditions all other conditions; but the metaphysical orientation of Christian theology is eschatological, the anticipation of the future disruptively promised in the putative Word from God spoken in the resurrection of the Crucified. This orientation distinguishes Christian theology from natural theology and accounts for the regular polemic against the business of religion as so much idolatry as also against the metaphysics of the *summum bonum* as the "ontotheological" rationalization of religious idolatry. That is, to be certain, a partisan Christian construction of things.

In philosophical or natural theologies, as the highest level of interpretation of the world, i.e., as metaphysics, we find rational interpretation of archaic religious or mythological beliefs with their eternities making sense of time, anchoring the immanent in a transcendent. This continues. Only a primitive literalism equal to the fundamentalism it thinks to debunk thinks that modern science replaces these

---

32. McGrath, *A Fine-Tuned Universe,* p. 196.

33. McGrath, *A Fine-Tuned Universe,* p. 206.

34. McGrath, *A Fine-Tuned Universe,* p. 218.

35. McGrath, *A Fine-Tuned Universe,* p. 219.

36. The useful popular books of Paul Davies, *God and the New Physics* (New York: Simon & Schuster, 1983) and *The Mind of God: The Scientific Basis for a Rational World* (New York: Simon & Schuster, 1992), betray this theological tendency.

protological myths and their rationalizations in philosophical theologies. The bookstores today are filled with cosmological and anthropological speculations, all claiming the prestige of natural science, which rather continue in the primeval religious motive of finding and fixing the human place in the cosmos. In this light, the so-called conflict of science and religion on examination can be shown to reflect conflicts between rival paradigms in science or rival theologies interpreting science, as John Hedley Brooks has shown.[37] Thus generally, reflecting differing religious traditions, theologies interpret the world abysmally, chaotically, teleologically, eschatologically, or otherwise. Science provides knowledge of the world to be so interpreted.

More specifically, the Jewish, Christian, and Islamic theological interpretations of the world by way of radical monotheism were instituted in the Book of Genesis in that this text — composed in the trauma of Israel's exile in Babylon six hundred years before the time of Christ — takes the humanly inhabited world as the great creature of the Exodus God, the One "who is more than necessary." Following this precedent of Genesis 1, this "taking as" is the ongoing task of theological interpretation in the light of ever-new discovery and ongoing experience until the cosmic story is confirmed (or falsified) when (or when not) the harmony of nature and grace is revealed in all its glory by the defeat of actual evil in the eternal Sabbath of God (Gen. 2:1-3). In this perspective, there is indeed an interest in scientific questions — howsoever primitively posed by Babylonian astrological science — in the first chapter of the Bible, which rightly understood justifies the interest of Christian theology in learning the discoveries of natural science today along the lines of McGrath's Trinitarian Natural Theology.[38]

The "mistake" of a "narrowly existentialist theology," George Murphy writes from within the theological tradition of Luther, "is the idea that we can understand ourselves adequately as individuals isolated from the rest of the universe. We exist only as parts of humanity and of the whole world."[39] Murphy approvingly cites Thomas's stricture on the play of worldviews in theology: ". . . the opinion is false of those who asserted that it made no difference to the truth of faith what anyone holds about creatures . . . error concerning creatures, by subjecting them to causes other than God, spills over into false opinion about God. . . ."[40] Theology cannot ignore the best available thinking of science about the world, if it wants to speak of the revealed God as the creator, redeemer, and fulfiller of the same; science provides the material that theology interprets, and material always constrains form, which organizes it into contemporary understanding of the world as

---

37. John Hedly Brooks, *Science and Religion: Some Historical Perspectives* (Cambridge: Cambridge University Press, 1991), pp. 33-42.

38. McGrath, *A Fine-Tuned Universe,* pp. 61-82. See also Mark William Worthing, *God, Creation, and Contemporary Physics* (Minneapolis: Fortress, 1996), p. 32.

39. George L. Murphy, *The Cosmos in the Light of the Cross* (Harrisburg, London, New York: Trinity Press International, 2003), p. 82.

40. Murphy, *The Cosmos,* p. 74.

created by God, though subjected to futility and groaning for the glorious liberty of the children of God. In this act of interpretation, moreover, Christian theology, which in historical fact nurtured the rise of the modern sciences in the West,[41] also today nurtures the scientific vocation as a central element of the divine calling of humanity to subdue the earth and have dominion over it. This incredible power is, to be sure, highly ambiguous morally; it can be used to kill cancer but also to napalm villages. *Which* theology embeds the scientific calling, *which* dominion of God science emulates, matters immensely to the fate of the earth.

## The Almighty Agent of Eschatological Creation

According to McGrath's "new way of seeing" nature, all things are *from* God, even as they are also *through* God and *to* God (1 Cor. 8:6), so that that there is one God coming, who is personally determined from the origin to redeem and fulfill the creation by the missions of His own Son and Spirit. This One is, following Augustine, the cause of all causes *(Alleswirksamkeit Gottes)* but not the maker of all choices *(Alleinwirksamkeit Gottes)*, since from this origin He has chosen to be the God of grace for humanity, even for sinful humanity in the Lamb slain before the foundation of the world; consequently, humanity's salvation, which is its love for God and all things in and under God, will be won to the Beloved Community freely and willingly as love must if it is to be love. Thus the one God is the initiating agent of an *eschatological* creation. What is entailed in this eschatological affirmation of the Father's agency as the almighty Creator of heaven and earth, as the Nicene Creed puts it, of all things both visible and invisible?

To initiate is to have a possibility that can be actualized and actually to do so and to continue in this decision, faithfully, through to its accomplishment, so that the divine will is done on earth as in heaven. To honor God as almighty Creator of all that is not God, minimally, is to honor God as actualizer of the very world in which I write these words and you read them, so that we are talking of one and the same world of the common body in its continual becoming. This world taken as God's eschatological creation refers to the journey of becoming, therefore, not a stable thing, fixed being, substance. For one implication of eschatological creation (Heb. 13:14) is that it divests of substantiality what exists in the world of creatures and affirms that God alone is "substantial" in the specific sense of being *a se, per se* and *ad seipsum,* that is, that God alone is God from God, through God and to God, the one, true eternal return of the same. In this light to speak of a "created substance" is at best to speak paradoxically or metaphorically in order to indicate the human creature as made in the image of God for likeness to God.

41. Sachiko Kusukawa, *The Transformation of Natural Philosophy: The Case of Philip Melanchthon* (Cambridge: Cambridge University Press, 1995).

Otherwise, that is, taken literally this contradiction in terms falsely divinizes the creature and blesses its sinful aspiration to be God without God — the sovereign self of modernity with its roots in the ancient serpent's *sicut Deus eritis.*

By the same token, however, to honor the almighty Father as the creator of this fragile and temporary creation without substantiality of its own but in the flux of God's continual creating is not to affirm that God can do just anything; least of all is it to affirm that God has already done everything in one timeless act that is simply now unfolding. What God has determined is Himself in relation to His creature as the One who will have mercy on all (Rom. 11:32); this self-determination or "election" constitutes the divine intention carried out in the history of the Son incarnate yet still to be fulfilled at His Parousia, the eschaton of judgment. God's foresight in this regard does not necessarily entail anything among creatures, since, as we have previously argued, it is conceivable that God's mercy be consciously refused by that creature of envy that wants to be God and does not want God to be God, demanding for itself a substantiality that will not "be changed" (1 Cor. 15:51), hence an eternal death in relation to God who makes all things new. The point of this reflection is not, of course, to populate hell but to indicate that what God is deciding and doing now in the work of eschatological creation constitutes the latent drama of history that includes human obedience in faith or disobedience in unfaith to the God who is faithful in working and willing the coming victory of the Beloved Community as the end for which He creates the world.

The almighty God cannot in any case make a circle square nor, more pertinently, contradict Himself without ceasing to be one and the same personal agent, i.e., without self-destructing as the one self-determining God who has in fact from the origin resolved in Jesus Christ to be merciful. Apart from accepting the sinner by the merciful provision of justifying grace, God would be turned into a many-headed Gorgon or a two-faced Shiva. Rather, God as this Creator can do any logically possible thing, and God, as Creator of all that is not God, has this infinite range of logical possibilities at His disposal in pursuing His purpose in the victory of the Beloved Community, though in fact not all possibilities are compatible with this divine purpose. In fact this God of the gospel can and does act on, to us, improbable possibilities, just as Jesus appealed, "Abba, Father, with you all things are possible" (Mark 14:36), having previously assured disciples despairing of their salvation that "with God all things are possible" (Mark 10:27). The almighty God is the One who is "more than necessary" (Jüngel), an excess that, as revealed in the disruptive message of grace by the resurrection of the Crucified, already now puts the regularities and continuities of natural being into the new light of coming glory.

As discussed already in Chapter One, no contemporary theologian in the tradition of Luther has in such sophisticated fashion worked through the biblical testimony to the "miraculous" power of the almighty Father God, "who gives life to the dead and calls into being what is not," as has Eberhard Jüngel. The coming of God already now in and as the *Sprachereignis* (the event of the word) opens the creature up to divine possibilities not immanent in her situation, yet now accessible in repentance and faith. In just this way, the coming of the Incarnate Son for us by the Word in the Spirit reveals the one true God as the almighty Father, creator of heaven and earth, of all things visible and not visible, on the way in His continual creating to the best of all possible worlds. Jüngel is surely right in this contention for the "miraculous" God, no matter how embarrassed modern theologians are to understand God as "more than necessary," *supra extra legem.* To believe in God the Father almighty is to believe in what is more than necessary to the "natural man," who wants to be God and does not want God to be God. Setting that objection of unbelief aside, the genuine difficulty within the theological circle lies in believing God who makes all things new ahead of time, already now, in the midst of the dark and tragic "necessities" of the strong man's house in which we are held captive with the common body, if not already now in soul and spirit won to conscientious responsibility to God for our world.

Jesus' prayer was uttered in the midst of time and space in the conviction that the Father's almighty and creative will is operative continuously in the here and now. Consequently prayer personally addresses God as this Father with this praise of His deity as "more than necessary." In this act of faith prayer only preaches back to the Father His own promise made and vouchsafed in the Son, trusting at the Spirit's encouragement (Rom. 8:26) that God can and does respond to wills other than His own in innovative ways insofar as they are compatible with God's self-determination (8:28) to redeem and fulfill the creation. It is just this prayer of faith that already now receives experience as God's continuous creating and directing, and thus believes that "God has created me and all that exists . . . out of pure, fatherly, and divine goodness and mercy without any merit or worthiness of mine at all! For all of this I owe it to God to thank and praise, serve and obey him."[42] As baptism is our practical Pneumatology and the Lord's Supper our practical Christology, the trusting prayer of thanks and praise is our practical Patrology. In prayer faith becomes active, invoking the almighty power of God in accord with God's own Word in the power of God's own Spirit. Whoever believes in this way of prayer believes in God the Father almighty, not as her own possibility but as the possibility of God for us that has come upon us in the Spirit by the Word. Whoever does not pray in the Spirit, with Jesus, "Our Father who art in heaven . . . ," does not believe with the intention of orthodoxy. Here the law of faith and the law of prayer are one and the same. Here then another fault line opens to view upon which the coming division of the division will fall.

The One who initiated all things is working still (John 5:17). He has not built a stage on which to let demi-gods work out their self-chosen destinies as would-be substances/agents. Nature is history and history is natural and the triune God initiates and preserves, redeems and fulfills this one world on the way to the

---

42. *BC,* pp. 354-55.

best of all possible worlds, *sub contrario,* in the agony of spiritual battles with principalities and powers. Here, in this history on the earth, God enters the lists in true partnerships with human creatures; these are characterized from the side of God by calling and from the side of creatures by the conscientious obedience of faith in the active passion of prayer, as exemplified in Jesus' kingdom prayer.

Two features of this view of creation as *creatio continua* with respect to God's eschatological purpose, not often recognized, are worthy of special attention. First, as hinted above, what distinguishes Creator and creatures is that they have their being *a se* and *per aliud* respectively. "God comes from God" (Jüngel) and no one or nothing else, as the Spirit and the Son come from the Father, who is the Unbegotten but just so self-surpassing Father. To say that God is *a se,* then, is not to imagine a divine substance or generic deity as such but to specify the personal being of the Father who self-surpasses. This crucial point was established for Christian theology in Gregory of Nyssa's great argument against Eunomius and his cohorts; these hyper-Arians "deify the idea expressed by this 'ingeneracy' of theirs, as not being only a certain relation in the Divine nature, but as being itself God, or the substance of God."[43] This hyper-Arianism makes absoluteness, or beyondness, or unconditionedness God — in fact the reification of nothing but *ideas* of creatures about the Infinite. This in-truth empty screen or sky imagined in the way of nature, not of grace, is the horizon of the natural man's experience of finiteness. It knows nothing of the true and concrete, hence personal "transcendence" of the God who begets His own Son on whom He breathes His own Spirit. The Trojan Horse in which this "unbaptized God" (Jenson) sneaks even into Trinitarian theology is the reified notion of the one divine *ousia* or essence or substance, as if it were a fourth God, somehow common and basic to the Three persons, like a foundation on which a superstructure is built. That would give a quaternity, not a trinity. Its deleterious effect would be to relocate God beyond God, turning the attention of faith away from this earth on which the cross of Jesus stood as the becoming meant for the eternal being of the Beloved Community, this earth to which God is coming to make forever His own. But the God of the gospel comes from God as God to bring us to God who is coming to us. Consequently, "there will be nothing whatever transcending this cause of all things"[44] that is the self-surpassing Father of the self-donating Son and breather of the self-communicating Spirit. This God is *not* the idea of a creature thematizing its ineluctable experience of self-transcendence but the *a se* and *per se* reality of the eternal Father revealing Himself by the sending of the Son and the Spirit into the creation and as such as the One working in continuous creation on the way to His eschatological kingdom.

Creatures as creatures of God's continuous creation come from creatures, both naturally by biological mechanisms and socially by the mediation of per-

---

43. *NPNF,* V, p. 260.
44. *NPNF,* V, p. 312.

sonal address in language — a position taken up in modernity by the anti-Kantian, Hamann.[45] So the continuous creating of God gives daily bread and forgiveness by which human life, once initiated, is nurtured and sustained so far as it is also delivered from evil. A being that has its being *per aliud* in this way is radically creature; it does not have life of itself but only in essential relations within the ecologies of life and of human sociality. Whatever agency it acquires is acquired out of this patiency of *natura naturata*. Second, then, the being of creatures "is a matter of continuous reception of being from God. Human beings exist only because they receive God's gifts from outside themselves, such as life, being *(esse)*, reason, intellect, nourishment, and clothing" (Juntunen). This continuous reception, whether it comes impersonally by nature or personally by grace, is not accidental, but essential both in creation and in redemption. "Christians are comparable to the Son of God, who is continuously born of the Father. In a similar way we must at all times be born, renewed, and generated *(nasci, novari, generari)*. The *esse gratiae* of a person, like the *esse naturae,* is a continuous reception of the gifts of God...."[46]

Contemporary "[p]hysics posits no entities that satisfy the concept of substance.... That does not eliminate the question What, finally, are physical equa-

45. Oswald Bayer, *A Contemporary in Dissent: Johann Georg Hamann as a Radical Enlightener,* trans. Roy A. Harrisville and Mark C. Mattes (Grand Rapids: Eerdmans, 2012 from the German original, 1988). Hamann's two key moves are the theological critique of epistemology and the Trinitarian revision of metaphysics. The theological self is *matter* addressed by God *through matter:* "the transient and voided human being who is nonetheless immortal because God has addressed him and thus will have to do with him in eternity, whether in anger or in grace..." (p. 33). In the place of Kantian transcendentalism comes instead the auditory event of being addressed by God as matter through matter. Kant would object to this: How could one ever tell that some finite and material word is the word of the Infinite? Kant is thus thinking that the issue is one of epistemological justification for an outrageous, "enthusiastic" claim to know the infinite in the finite. For Hamann, however, the biblical text on the *imago Dei,* Genesis 1:26-28, is the "historical a priori." It decodes all human experience, most basically the child's experience of being addressed by elders and parents and hence summoned to adult dignity and responsibility. God thus speaks to the creature through the creature continuing, enjoying, preserving, and expanding the work of creation, eminently and decisively in the new man Jesus Christ, in whom creation is redeemed. The epistemic warrant of this theological interpretation of nature and history is biblical narrative, which displays the structure of Trinitarian advent: "the condescension of the triune God who has interlaced his eternity with time, not only with his incarnation and death on the cross but as the Creator who addresses the creature, and as the Spirit who kills and makes alive through modest, particular, temporal events, as narrated by the Bible" (p. 196). "Creator and creation, eternity and time are not separated but united in Christ, and thus Christ is the Bible's key to interpreting nature and history." Paul R. Hinlicky, Review of *A Contemporary in Dissent* in *Lutheran Quarterly* 27, no. 1 (Spring 2013): 94-96.

46. I am indebted to Sammeli Juntunen for these insights. See his "Luther and Metaphysics: What Is the Structure of Being according to Luther?," in *Union with Christ: The New Finnish Interpretation of Luther,* ed. Carl E. Braaten and Robert W. Jenson (Grand Rapids: Eerdmans, 1998), 138-40.

tions *about?* It only throws the question wide open." So Robert Jenson acutely registered the import of taking "creation out of nothing," not as the once-and-for-all erection of a solid stage on which demi-gods would then play out their sovereignty projects, but as the initiation of a divine relationship with creatures that continues to its eschatological finale. He made this incisive comment against metaphysical atomism-cum-mechanism in his "recommendation" of the innovative Jonathan Edwards, whom he acclaimed as "America's theologian."[47] According to Stanley J. Grenz, we can indeed add Edwards to Hamann as one who worked a "thoroughgoing reconceptualization of the nature of reality itself. He replaced the traditional Western metaphysics of substance and form with a conception of reality as a dynamic network of dispositional forces and habits."[48] For Edwards, "God is creatively present and directly communicative everywhere and at all times. This God does not simply speak creation into existence in the primordial past. Rather, creation emerges out of the divine infinity, and it does so continuously, as God expresses himself in an outgoing movement" — all this, as with Luther out of divine fatherly goodness and mercy, in "a glorious and abundant emanation of his infinite fullness of good *ad extra.* . . . [T]he disposition to communicate Himself, or to diffuse his own Fullness [is] . . . a perfection of his nature [that] moved Him to create the world."[49] So daring was Edwards in thinking *creatio continua* out in this way that he could take Newtonian space as the analogue of the "all-inclusive Being" of God's immensity-cum-omnitemporality, "the very thing that we can never remove or conceive of its not being."[50] Like Jenson,[51] Grenz too connects this time-space physics of the creation with the Trinitarian "spiral" (as we have pictured it) in Edwards: "creation emerges from God as the repetition in space and time — that is, ad extra — of the everlasting process of God's self-enlargement of what God already is" as the eternal love of the Father and the Son in the Spirit, now becoming temporal and spatial for creatures.[52] Grenz's analysis shows, then, that in place of substance and essential attributes in the doctrine of God, we have the Trinitarian *esse Deum dare* with its intrinsic "disposition" to surpass itself *ad extra* in the harmony of power, wisdom, and love that will accomplish the love of God above all and all things in and under God, the Beloved Community. The tacit distinction made here between the incommunicable essence of the Trinity as infinite Giver and His communicable properties revealed in gifted creatures will become important later in this chapter.

47. Robert W. Jenson, *America's Theologian: A Recommendation of Jonathan Edwards* (New York and Oxford: Oxford University Press, 1988), p. 29. See chapter 2, "God against the Machine," in this connection, pp. 23-34.

48. Stanley J. Grenz, *The Named God and the Question of Being: A Trinitarian Theo-Ontology* (Louisville: Westminster John Knox, 2005), p. 73.

49. Grenz, *The Named God,* p. 75.

50. Grenz, *The Named God,* p. 77.

51. Jenson, *America's Theologian,* pp. 91-98.

52. Grenz, *The Named God,* p. 79.

As noted previously, however, the theological price of this view of continuous creation on the way to the eschaton is to make God the apparent author of evil (as Jesus acknowledges in Matt. 5:45), certainly of the "natural" evils that necessarily accompany the "ensouled matter" (McCord Adams) that is the creature, vulnerable to other forces and other persons precisely as it exists *per aliud* not *per se.* But God the almighty Father is also "responsible" for such creatures (He knows their need even before they ask, Matt. 6:32), also for the "moral" evil that His choice to initiate this world necessarily permits, even though God does not positively will it or necessitate it bur rather passionately opposes moral evil and vows finally to defeat it forever. The Father conscientiously assumes this responsibility for moral evil in the sending of the Son for that redemption of creation that saves creatures morally by saving them from their sins (Matt. 1:21). Accordingly, we see the Son by the Incarnation making His own the natural evils that afflict creatures as also by His cross owning the moral evils that they commit in the despair and envy occasioned by natural suffering, where faith in the Almighty Father has failed. The sending of the Son by the Father is thus the deed of God surpassing God, conscientiously taking responsibility for His creation to redeem and fulfill it, in the resolve to be the reconciled God of Hosea 11:9.

*Creatio continua,* in this reading, belongs to the canonical narrative of Trinitarian advent; it cannot be split off from it as an independent insight. If it is split off seriously, it becomes Spinoza's pantheism or, if lightheartedly, process metaphysics, not Christian theology of the Trinitarian advent.

Now as the eternal world of the triune God within which all things are possible is God's own divine life as the Father of the Son in the Spirit, so also this temporal world is God's determinate choice of "the best of all possible worlds." This notorious Leibnizian thesis, however, is not demonstrated rationally and philosophically *a priori,* as Leibniz thought, but only *a posteriori* by faith and faith's transition to sight at the fulfillment. For, according to the canonical narrative, we are on the way to the best of possible worlds; we have not yet arrived. This destination, however, is already now vouchsafed in the resurrection of Jesus Christ from the dead. As the self-surpassing Father's newly gained recognition of His incarnate Son, the One bonded in the solidarity of death with the sinners whose sins He had forgiven in His Father's name, Easter turns the ancient promise of creation into Christ's new testament. This is Christ's testimony that recurs in every Eucharist where and when He speaks over bread as the risen Lord, "This is my Body given for you." In this way, at His address, the obedient and faithful gathering of the ecclesia to eat and drink proclaims the Lord's death until He comes. That still-future public verification at His Parousia brings the glory that is not worthy to be compared to the sufferings of this present time, the best of all possible worlds. The unity of these two perspectives on one and the same earth is the Lamb slain from before the foundation of the world, that is, the Father's self-determination in giving the Son for sharing by the Spirit their Beloved Community with a world of creatures.

The crucial point is this: the powers of actual evil in the moral sense, unleashed by divine permission, are *known* as both potent and wicked in Adam's *sicut Deus eritis,* that is, in envious imagining and actualizing of those possibilities that God has rejected in determining upon this blessed earth as the time and place of His eschatological creation. Since Kierkegaard, modern theology has often thought of anxiety at finitude as the occasion of moral evil, and this deliteralizing reflection is apt so far as it goes. But it does not go far enough in interpreting anxiety theologically. What is more disturbing and insightful is how in the story of Adam, God permits evil by apparently absenting Himself from the creatures, leaving them with only His Word, just as the wily serpent, taking advantage of the apparent divine absence, immediately assaults the good will of God in the command that limits the creatures. Left only with the memory of His Word, the particular accent in the exposé of the *sicut Deus eritis* falls, then, not on the desire for power as such but rather on the desire for one's own knowledge of good and evil, for another conscience, that is to say, than the one bound to the Word of God. It is the desire to have a conscience other than one formed essentially by the relation to the Creator who relates to creatures by His Word. It is the desire to have a conscientious self-relation, "*self*-consciousness," one might say, that is other than God-consciousness.

But what of God's disappearance? What of God who is "present as absent" (Jüngel) in His Word, i.e., as the incarnate Son who speaks for the Father whom no one has ever seen (John 1:18)? The trial of history is a trial of faiths, of commitments to putative words from God or the renunciation of them for other words making similarly divine promises (Gen. 3:4). God's "disappearance," God's resolve to relate to creatures by His Word alone, means that no creature transcends this situation of self-risking faith where the issue is not ever whether to believe but what is to be believed. That God makes a trial of history, however, is an inescapable implication of the teaching that the almighty Father alone is substantial, and that His intelligent creatures live or die, "not by bread alone but by every word that comes from the mouth of God" (Matt. 4:4). So Christ by the obedience of faith undid the fateful deed of Adam.

As self-conscious creatures innovate in the destructive way that is the actual realization of possibilities that God the Creator has rejected, so also the ever-innovating Spirit of God improvises ways forward through the ruins and impasses of history in a creation that has lost its way. It is no accident, then, that the prophecy of Joel, taken up in the Pentecost narrative of the Book of Acts (Acts 2:17), sees the gift of the Spirit in the dreaming of dreams for moral good within the nightmare that sin has made of the creation. Prayer, as we have heard, is this Spirit-moved dreaming of dreams for good and against evil (Rom. 8:26-27). Distinguishing these novelties of Adam's violent imaginations and the Spirit's dreaming new dreams of righteousness, life, and peace is the spiritual act of discernment that takes place in every sermon, every testimony, and every pastoral act of consolation or rebuke. Theology can so discern since the Spirit who is Holy is the Spirit of the Almighty Father who breathes Him on the Son, by which relation to the incarnate Son the Spirit who is Holy is known and distinguished from all other spirits. The Holy Spirit can hence be recognized as the Spirit of the almighty Father, just as already now in the Spirit the ecclesia sings praises with Jesus Christ to God the Father almighty, creator of heaven and earth in anticipation of His manifest victory over all the contra-divine powers that besiege it. The Father is the audience of theology, the origin to which the Son in the Spirit returns.[53]

Thus in the eternal triune life, the First of the Three is the personal principle of origin, and hence of ontological unity, in and as the ecstasy of the self-surpassing divine life. As such, the almighty Father is the Alpha and Omega of the temporal world (Rev. 1:8, 17; 21:6; 22:13), which is His initiation and work and His gift, redeemed and fulfilled. In the present time of discernment and expectation the church worships the Father with the Son in the Holy Spirit in that its faith is a participation in the faith of Jesus from whom it learns to live conscientiously before God; only as such does it also worship the Spirit with the Father and the Son, that is, worship the eternal and co-equal Trinity whose kingdom shall have no end. The worship of the co-equal Trinity is worship *in anticipation* of the end of the economy, when God will be all things to all people (1 Cor. 15:24-28), as we shall discuss further in the conclusion of this system of theology. For the moment, the point is that in either case, the Spirit-ed faith of Jesus in the heavenly Father is primary. It is faith in that Person who is the first and the final mystery of it all; to the Father, Alpha and Omega, the kingdom in its power and glory is ascribed in doxological anticipation of the promised fulfillment. As God the Father is the font of the deity by generation of the Son and spiration of the Spirit, God the Father is also the initiating agent of creation from origin to eschaton. This first Person of the divine Life exists in His own eternal and supreme act of personal being, precisely of self-surpassing in generation and spiration. *This* eternal act of God's being is the self-determination of the Father to be God for God (generation) in God (spiration) and so also subsequently but truly for us in time in sending Jesus Christ to us by the Holy Spirit. Neither in eternity nor in time is there any divine nature that exists in abstraction from this personal act of origin in God the eternal Father. The divine nature exists concretely in this act of its personal being by which its possibilities are shared and communicated in generation and spiration, thus also with creatures in the Incarnation and by the coming of the Spirit to create repentance and faith and community of love. The Father is the agent of this act of personal being and so the one and only principle of unity in the dynamic life of the eternal Trinity. It is as the Father of the Son, but not with the Son *(filioque),* that the Father eternally breathes the Spirit on the Son; it is because of the Spirit that the Son returns all glory to the Father, giving God this praise of His specific deity as the almighty Father. As the Holy Trinity, the Three

53. Jenson, *ST* 2, p. 227.

live in this consistent *perichoresis* of concrete and mutually referred ways of being because, and only because, God the unoriginated Father is sole origin of this eternal life that consists in His personal act of sharing.

What is a constant source of confusion in this matter is the temptation to think the concept of nature substantively, as something really real, more real than surface appearances, which in the case of the Trinity are the Three of the gospel narrative. Not even Nyssa, whose eminent and pioneering struggle was to break free of such Platonism, entirely succeeds in this so that subsequently the Eastern tradition became vulnerable to a Platonizing dualism between the unknowable hyper-essence of deity and its radiant energies. This Platonic distinction between appearance and reality, to be sure, is the precious charter of all critical thinking, also in critical dogmatics. It has its own place in the world, but that place is not theology, where in God's economy "what you see is what you get" (Luther: "As you believe, so you have"). Hence in theology it is rather the "you who sees" that must be changed to see God as nothing other than this consistent perichoresis of the eternal Life. In any case, the concept of nature in theology is properly "baptized" when its use becomes purely semantical and we are no longer bewitched into reifying what remains a concept, that is, a way by abstraction of organizing the data of perception according to general possibilities for interested subjects.

That confusion became possible due to the fact that in the history of Christian theology the concept of nature has been used loosely, although permissibly and usefully, to indicate something real that exists in its own right apart from our interest and use of it, as Christopher Stead argued in *Divine Substance*,[54] rather than in the technical metaphysical sense as an *ens per se*. As we have just seen, however, strictly speaking only the Creator God can be *ens per se*. And if that abstraction is all we have with which to parse the relation of God to creatures, then a pantheism in which creatures are but modes of God's being seems unavoidable (if we do not resort to the contradiction in terms in speaking literally of "created substances"). Of course, the intention in this usage to indicate God as really real is not wrong, only confusing. For the really real God exists only personally as the Father who generates the Son and breathes the Spirit and as this Person creates all things; only personally as the Son who obeys the Father and accomplishes His will; only personally as the Spirit who unites the Son with the Father and the Father with the Son in love; only personally also for us "our Father in heaven." Aside from these personal relations, there is no divine "nature," as it were, freestanding and independent. All that is divine — to give wholly, to create out of nothing, to forgive sins, to raise the dead — is equally and rightly attributed to each of the three persons, but according to each one's personal way of being this one divine "nature," thus according to their constitutive relations to the others. And constitutive of these relations is the first in the sequence of divine becoming, the Father.

In particular then, we are not to imagine an undifferentiated divine nature

---

54. Christopher Stead, *Divine Substance* (Oxford: Oxford University Press, 2000).

at the origin, which differentiated itself from the nothingness from which it was indistinguishable, by generating and spirating; this is the Gnostic-Hegelian version of the doctrine of the Trinity as self-positing Ego bootstrapping itself out of the darkness that became so influential in modern theology.[55] When we come in faith to the reflective insight of the eternal Trinity as anticipation of the victory of the Beloved Community, theology has rather reached its doxological goal beyond which it can think no more but only adore. When we thus come to the ultimate mystery of the almighty Father as the font of the deity to whom we are returned by the Spirit in union with the Son, we have no further place to go. Here truly we meet the Alpha and Omega, the beginning and the end of all that is and can be.

Faith in the Almighty Father is faith in the God who in the beginning of the creation that continues to its eschatological denouement originated out of nothing, and so recognizably in the history of salvation justifies the ungodly and gives life to the dead. These are those works of divine majesty that the Father shares with no creature but alone accomplishes and in just this way declares and manifests His deity that brings in the Beloved Community. Indeed His divine promise of the eternal Sabbath of the eschaton is intimated in the very origin of things, as we shall see; as the promise of fulfillment it underlies all ensuing reality and is universal in scope. This universality of the divine command-and-promise in Genesis 1, as we shall see, permits no ontological dualism of spheres, as became characteristic of modern thought under the influence of Kant: law, nature, determinism, godlessness to be known by science on the one side and grace, miracle, freedom, godliness to be known by ethics on the other, with art vainly trying to mediate this tragic (but in reality constructed) chasm between the two realms of theoretical and practical reason. That Christian theology as knowledge of God is excluded by this dualistic scheme of modernity is hardly an accident.

Against this scheme, theology, so we have argued, asserts simply and radically the *hierarchy* of the *basileia tou theou:* God is Creator and coming King of creation and the creature is not, since the Creator creates *ex nihilo* all that is not God, making us through time and space fit subjects of and partners in His city not made with hands. Here "creation" is not being but becoming, not health but healing, not rest but labor. In this very distinction, however, the Creator immediately encompasses the creation, working in all things *(Alleswirksamkeit* but not *Alleinwirksamkeit Gottes).* The "natural" order of the (fallen) creature is embedded in the encompassing order of grace and so is open to innovation from it, just as the order of nature is also vulnerable to choices of actual evil when creatures in envy's pride or despair seize for themselves possibilities that God has rejected in determining this world for the coming of the Beloved Community. In the light of glory, the now-hidden harmonies of nature and grace will become transparent,

---

55. Cyril O'Regan, *The Heterodox Hegel* (Albany: State University of New York Press, 1994); Lewis Ayres, *Nicea and Its Legacy: An Approach to Fourth-Century Trinitarian Theology* (Oxford: Oxford University Press, 2006), pp. 384-429.

when actual evil is revealed for what it really is and so defeated and excluded forever in a just and final judgment. In the interim, the ultimate harmony of nature and grace is hidden by the fog of battle with actual evil. This requires of theology a penultimate, economic distinction between the earthly city and the city of God, being in Adam and being in Christ, and therefore also a theology of creation that distinguishes temporal orders or structures of love working justice from their perversions by malice into structures of injustice.

## Genesis as Promise

When we survey New Testament usage regarding creation, we quickly discover that the creative act of God can hardly be confined to the act of origin. Jesus speaks of an act of origin which continues in Mark 10:6, "... But *from the beginning of creation,* 'God made them male and female,'" from which He draws the conclusion that God continues so to join together in marriage; and again in Mark 13:19, "For in those days there will be suffering, such as has not been *from the beginning of the creation that God created until now,* no, and never will be" — a locution that intimates that creation is the continuous repetition of the same command as known in the regularities and continuities of nature. The second Epistle of Peter uses the same phrase in 3:3-8 to embed nature in the history of God with His creation:

> First of all you must understand this, that in the last days scoffers will come, scoffing and indulging their own lusts and saying, "Where is the promise of his coming? For ever since our ancestors died, all things continue *as they were from the beginning of creation!*" They deliberately ignore this fact, that by the word of God heavens existed long ago and an earth was formed out of water and by means of water, through which the world of that time was deluged with water and perished. But by the same word the present heavens and earth have been reserved for fire, being kept until the day of judgment and destruction of the godless. But do not ignore this one fact, beloved, that with the Lord one day is like a thousand years, and a thousand years are like one day.

The act of creation had an origin such that it continues to the eschatological finale, itself an act of new creation. Creation is history, natural history too. In this regard the venerable idea of preservation — that God preserves what He has made in a fixed state against the threat of change — must be subject to criticism and revision. In the dynamism of eschatological creation God preserves creation against the destructive forces of malice and injustice, not only by conserving what is good and just, but also by innovating in accord with the divine aim of His determined purpose of bringing creation to the fulfillment of Beloved Community.

So Paul teaches in the decisive passage, for this system of theology, from

Romans 8:19-23: "For the creation waits with eager longing for the revealing of the children of God; for the creation was subjected to futility, not of its own will but by the will of the one who subjected it, in hope that the creation itself will be set free from its bondage to decay and will obtain the freedom of the glory of the children of God. We know that the whole creation has been groaning in labor pains until now; and not only the creation, but we ourselves, who have the first fruits of the Spirit, groan inwardly while we wait for adoption, the redemption of our bodies." Käsemann comments:

> For all the mythical form of expression it brings, it concerns here the core of the Pauline message. This is what necessarily makes him a world missionary. In these verses the justification of the ungodly appears in a new cosmological variation as salvation for the fallen and groaning world. . . . *The world makes sense as creation only if it is oriented constitutively to Christian liberty,* which is not to be equated with autonomy. . . . If Marcion was forced by the inner logic of his theology to cut out vv. 18-22, he is followed today by an existentialism which individualizes salvation and thereby truncates Paul's message. . . . [It] no longer knows what to do with Pauline apocalyptic, allows anthropological historicity to conceal the world's history, obscures the antithesis of the aeons of 1:20ff by natural theology and here through the assertion of mythology, and for this reason can no longer speak adequately of the dominion of Christ in its worldwide dimension.[56]

*The world makes sense as creation only if it is oriented constitutively to Christian liberty.* God in freedom creates *the world* by calling life forth from nothing. The creature arises to freedom in the surrender of faith to this liberating act of God. The liberty to which the world is oriented as creation is the liberty of the God who will send His Son in the likeness of sinful flesh to suckle at Mary's breast only to die tortured on the Roman gibbet. This is the liberty of the Spirit of the Father and the Son, the liberty of love for others that defies death believing in the life of God that the vindicated children of God inherit forever at the coming of the Beloved Community.

So freedom is not understood here as rational autonomy, based upon a human capacity for acquisition according to private taste in a world that grants an abundance of consumer choices. Rather, Paul sees believers as having been called out of such illusory freedom of the dying world of bread and circuses into the liberated sphere of Christ to form the *ecclesia,* the *representative* church, God's *priestly* people, the church *vicarious* — the true "church for others" because it has been set free by the love of Christ for others. In this interim, the eschatological finale of the new creation already takes place in faith by incorporation into Christ

---

56. Ernst Käsemann, *Commentary on Romans,* trans. G. Bromiley (Grand Rapids: Eerdmans, 1980), pp. 234-36.

through baptism. So 2 Corinthians 5:17: "If anyone is in Christ, there is a new creation: everything old has passed away; see, everything has become new!" Or again, Galatians 6:14-15: "May I never boast of anything except the cross of our Lord Jesus Christ, by which the world has been crucified to me, and I to the world. For neither circumcision nor uncircumcision is anything; *but a new creation is everything!*" The Deutero-Pauline Letter to the Ephesians (which affirms the traditional association of creation with the act of origin, 3:9: "And to make everyone see what is the plan of the mystery hidden for ages in God who *created* all things . . .") nevertheless repeatedly speaks of God's new creative act in the redemption in Christ, as in 2:10: "For we are what he has made us, *created* in Christ Jesus for good works, which God prepared beforehand to be our way of life. . . ." Or again, 2:15: "He has abolished the law with its commandments and ordinances, that he might *create* in himself one new humanity in place of the two, thus making peace. . . ." Finally, 4:24: "And to clothe yourselves with the new self, *created* according to the likeness of God in true righteousness and holiness." *The world makes sense as creation only if it is oriented constitutively to Christian liberty,* i.e., by understanding the creation of the world *eschatologically,* and the act of origin accordingly as *promise* to humanity, and the nonhuman world under its dominion (not domination), to inherit a treasured place in God's own eternal life of love.

One virtue of the doctrine of eschatological creation is the disassociation of the knowledge of the almighty Father as Creator of heaven and earth with knowledge of the origin. It makes the starting point of Christian knowledge of God to be God's Trinitarian self-revelation in the gospel. This starting point makes it all the more clear that the doctrine of creation is in the first place about *who* the Creator is, not *when* or *how* the world began (or ends).[57] Basil the Great commented on Genesis 1:1,

> What a glorious order! He first establishes a beginning, so that it might not be supposed that the world never had a beginning. Then he adds "created" to show that which was made was a very small part of the power of the Creator. In the same way that the potter, after having made with equal pains a great number of vessels, has not exhausted either his art or his talent; thus the Maker of the Universe, whose creative power, far from being bounded by one world, could extend to the infinite, needed only the impulse of His will to bring the immensities of the visible world into being. If then the world has a beginning, and if it has been created, *enquire who gave it this beginning, and who was the Creator. . . .*[58]

What is decisive in the early creeds' teaching about the "almighty Father," who is Creator *of all,* is the "that" of the act of origin, insofar as it raises the

---

57. T. F. Torrance, *The Trinitarian Faith: The Evangelical Faith of the Ancient Catholic Church* (Edinburgh: T. & T. Clark, 1993), p. 76.

58. *NPNF* 8, p. 53.

question of "who" this Originator is. For Basil the "that" of the origin points as sign to the person of the Creator, i.e., to the *free personal decision* actualized in the world's very existence among the infinite possibilities imaginable, as the citation above shows. What matters theologically is that the world's origin be understood as this *free* action of a "who," not when and how the "that" of the origin happened. Coming to the knowledge of this *free* Person is what matters today, in the time between origin and fulfillment. Luther thus rightly emphasized that one believes the Almighty Father, Creator when one confesses here and now the *creatio continua:* "I believe that God has created *me* and all that exists. . . ."[59] For as the First Article is about "who" the Creator is, it is correspondingly about "who" the human creature is that lives as God's image in order to become God's likeness in each one's particular history that must be lived out on the earth. But let us look in the matrix of the Scriptures and see.

The primeval "saga" of Genesis 1–11, as Gerhard von Rad named the genre of this literature,[60] is an act of prophetic *interpretation* of the world in which *presently* we live — prophecy projected backwards in time. The biblical story of the act of origin is critically understood as an inference in faith back to the original state from the future goal of God revealed presently in the history of salvation. The signature of this history is the Exodus from the land of bondage and the journey through the wilderness to the land of promise; and the catalyst of this interpretation of the origin is the exile of Israel, in default of its vocation, and its consequent need of new creation ("Can these bones live?" Ezek. 37:3). In analogy to Israel's experience of the sovereign initiative of divine grace in the Exodus, the Genesis saga represents the act of origin as one of divine command-and-promise, bringing being of nothing, life out of death and freedom out of slavery. As such, the etiological narrative of the primeval history sets the stage for the covenantal history commencing with the call of Abram (Gen. 12:1-3) that is to proceed by the obedience of faith in hope of the universal fulfillment. Speculative interest in the past becomes here forward looking; the "etiological" question about origins is refashioned from providing justification of the *status quo ante* to providing hope for the coming transformation: "Why are things the way they are and must be?" becomes "How have we come to the present state of affairs? Is this violence natural? Or is it not rather a fall from 'nature' that has become 'second-nature'? Can 'nature' be redeemed as a promise and still be fulfilled? Is there ground for hope?" At the same time, however, we may not overlook the fact that the primeval saga interprets the present *by positing an origin* of the world and of life, revealing the sovereignty of God in His Word that calls, especially humanity as image of God for likeness to God; as well it posits therewith a *sin of origin* and thus an interpretation of the present as a situation of exile. The peculiar and fateful default of

59. *BC,* p. 354.
60. Gerhard von Rad, *Genesis: A Commentary,* revised edition (Philadelphia: Westminster, 1972), p. 33.

the human vocation may as a result be identified now, as the false path taken by Adam, and the hope for the coming of a new Adam can be generated.

Christian theology is not bound to a historically literal reading of Genesis; on the contrary, it cannot proceed today without abandoning that pre-critical reading. Only a deliteralized and theologically decoded reading is entitled to speak *of God* as the author of the origin, and consequently of (1) cosmos as creation, i.e., of nature as history and history as natural, and, (2) in such a world of ordered contingency, of humanity made in the image of God for Christ-likeness, although still burdened and defaced by the sin of origin, figured as Adam. Deliteralized and thus decoded theologically, this interpretation of origins is canonical for Christian theology. It is Scripture, rightly read. Dietrich Bonhoeffer's reading of Genesis as "hope projected backwards" accordingly made "being in Adam" and "being in Christ" the keys to the social interpretation "of the basic Christian theological terms."[61] This contest of Adam and Christ, hidden or manifest, constitutes the true drama of the historical present from the origin onward. Christ as the New Adam is correlated with the first Adam by Paul in the important and influential passages of Romans 5. Karl Barth commented: ". . . although Adam has no power to identify himself with Christ, Christ has the power to (Rom. 5:15-17) identify Himself with Adam, and so to establish the formal identification upon which the parallel rests. The close relation of the two sides is established, not by trying to find a way from Adam to Christ, but by seeing that Christ has found the only way to Adam by His cross. And since Christ has passed from His side into the world of Adam, Adam is now free to pass into the world of Christ; Christ has removed the barriers and opened the doors. . . ."[62] The distinction between the two humanities, like the conflict it represents, is penultimate; just so it does mark an economic division of humanity, pending the eschaton of judgment.

We may say the same about the economic distinction, indeed, contradiction between the law that accuses the naked sinner and the promise that justifies the believing and penitent sinner clothed and covered in Christ. William Lazareth, following in part Paul Althaus, sorted out the convoluted discussion of the relation of law and gospel in relation to the primal divine command-and-blessing in creation's opening act. He cites the later Luther against the antinomians: "What Paul says about the Law which came in after (Gal. 3:17), [the antinomians] deceitfully and blasphemously apply to the Law which was given in Paradise. . . . Paul is speaking strictly of a Law for which there was need after nature had become corrupted by sin."[63] Thus Luther distinguishes "the primal and eschatological law

61. Dietrich Bonhoeffer, *Sanctorum Communio: A Theological Study of the Sociology of the Church,* Dietrich Bonhoeffer Works I, trans. Reinhard Kraus and Nancy Lukens, ed. Joachim von Sooten and Clifford J. Green (Minneapolis: Fortress, 1998), pp. 61-62.

62. Karl Barth, *Christ and Adam: Man and Humanity in Romans 5* with an Introduction by Wilhelm Pauck (New York: Macmillan, 1956), p. 63.

63. William Lazareth, *Christians in Society: Luther, the Bible, and Social Ethics* (Minneapolis: Fortress, 2001), p. 73.

of creation *(lex non scripta)"* from the office of Moses.[64] This distinction bespeaks "the multiple forms of God's eternal will to different persons in different situations in different epochs of the biblical drama of salvation . . . to defend the binding nature of God's pre-fall command against the antinomian ('lawless') denial of original sin, but without thereby capitulating to its replacement by the retrojected legalism of any alleged eternal law *(lex aeterna)* . . . the divine command of love in primal creation *(mandatum)* becomes the divine law of wrath in fallen creation *(nomos)."*[65] The ethical content is the same — holy, just, and good.[66] Luther: "the Law before sin is one thing, the law after sin is something else *(alia lex)."*[67] Primarily, "in ethically responsible opposition to all simplistic forms of antinomianism, it was God's intention that this command should provide man with an opportunity for obedience and outward worship . . . a sign by which man would give evidence that he was obeying God."[68] Again citing Luther: "For Adam this Word was Gospel and Law; it was his worship; it was his service and the obedience he could offer God in this state of innocence."[69] The ethical substance of the divine command is the imago's summons to "dominion-sharing love"[70] by which likeness to God is acquired in a genuine history of the obedience of faith.

Indeed the divine command-and-blessing spoken in the act of origin is renewed in the Book of Genesis after the catastrophes of sin and judgment in the primal history (Genesis 2–10) by the calling of the first "historical" figure. Abram turns away from his homeland of pride, rebellion, and violence, the way of life that had become second-nature to the Adamic humanity expelled from Paradise (Gen. 6:5, 11-12), in order to journey to the new land that God would show him (Gen. 12:1-3). The election of Abraham from this wicked mass of fallen humanity represents God's new beginning in a creation gone astray from the sin of origin. In this way the divine command-and-blessing spoken in the very origin of things is now renewed within the history of salvation as a *promise* of blessing; this "indicates that the expected future does not have to develop within the framework of the possibilities inherent in the present, but arises from that which is possible to the God of promise. . . . It is not evolution, progress and advance that separate time into yesterday and tomorrow, but the word of promise cuts into events and divides reality into one reality which is passing and can be left behind, and an-

64. Lazareth, *Christians in Society,* p. 73.

65. Lazareth, *Christians in Society,* pp. 74-75.

66. Lazareth, *Christians in Society,* p. 76; cf. 89.

67. Lazareth, *Christians in Society,* p. 89.

68. "Before their fall into original sin (Genesis 1–2), Adam and Eve were governed by God's gracious command of holy love. In the absence of any sin, strictly speaking, God's eschatological will as command was explicitly expressed neither as law (to condemn sin) nor as gospel (to conquer sin). At most, the law and the gospel were latently united in command and grace as the governing will of God for righteous human beings." Lazareth, *Christians in Society,* p. 89.

69. Lazareth, *Christians in Society,* p. 93.

70. Lazareth, *Christians in Society,* p. 224.

other which must be expected and sought."[71] The God of promise is "more than necessary." The "Yahwist" accordingly sees "God's leading in the facts of history as well as in the quiet course of human life, in the sacred things, but not less in the profane, in great miracles as well as in the innermost secrets of the human heart."[72] So after the Fall, the original Word of command and blessing, as it were, acquires the twofold form of divine command that curses sin by the measure of merit and of divine promise that blesses the undeserving by the plenitude of grace.

In such a world under the rule of the twofold form of the one Word of God working judgment and mercy, the human being has a singular status and dignity as well as the corresponding degradation and misery. Of all the creatures, the Priestly writer teaches, human beings are the ones who may intelligently hear and willingly answer the call of God in the act of faith that sojourns to the promised future. "Just as powerful earthly kings, to indicate their claim to dominion, erect an image of themselves in the provinces of their empire where they do not personally appear, so man is placed upon earth in God's image as God's sovereign emblem . . . summoned to maintain and enforce God's claim over the earth. The decisive thing of man's similarity to God, therefore, is his function in the non-human world."[73] To image God is to care for one's body in the common body, with the earth to which organically it belongs, as the thing personally entrusted to one's care, just as God cares for the universe: ". . . the *imago Dei* means for man a relationship with, and dependence upon, the one for whom he is only the representative. To wish to be like God, the temptation suggested by the serpent, is to desire to abandon the role of image . . . in behaving thus man degrades himself and falls to the animal level instead of raising himself: to desire to become an angel is to prepare to become a beast."[74] The young Wolfhart Pannenberg similarly wrote: "What the environment is for animals, God is for man. God is the goal in which alone his striving can find rest and his destiny be fulfilled."[75] The very act of interpreting the origin as the commanding call of God in promise to humanity, and through humanity to the world that humanity governs, singles out the human couple, the community of persons made of the male and the female, as the creature destined for God — but also as the creature who in unfaith closes the ear to God's command-and-promise, who thereby forfeits divine destiny and wreaks havoc on the earth in falling into a godless *causa sui* project under the curse of divine law.

The projection back to origins made in this way by the opening chapters of

---

71. Jürgen Moltmann, *The Theology of Hope: On the Ground and the Implications of a Christian Eschatology,* trans. James W. Leitch (New York: Harper & Row, 1967), p. 103.

72. Moltmann, *Theology of Hope,* p. 29.

73. Moltmann, *Theology of Hope,* p. 60.

74. Edmond Jacobs, *Theology of the Old Testament,* trans. A. W. Heathcote and P. J. Allcock (New York: Harper & Row, 1958), p. 171.

75. Wolfhart Pannenberg, *What Is Man? Contemporary Anthropology in Theological Perspective,* trans. D. Priebe (Philadelphia: Fortress, 1970), p. 13.

Genesis is thus not idle speculation. The urgency that attended this prophecy projected backwards — and still does — may be seen in the fact that it emerged in Israel in conflict with competing etiological myths inspired by despair of God's command and promise to humanity, i.e., the cosmogonic myths that claimed to tell the truth of origin but in the process fated humanity to faithless servility and futile violence. Even Eliade acknowledges this: "Judaism presents an innovation of the first importance. For Judaism, time has a beginning and will have an end. The idea of cyclic time is left behind. Yahweh no longer manifests himself in *cosmic time* (like the gods of other religions) but in a *historical time,* which is irreversible."[76] Of course, this "innovation" creates its own problem — when history is unidirectional and unrepeatable it comes to bear the crushing burden of what Josiah Royce called the "hell of the irrevocable." Therefore, in Eliade's words (as Royce also saw): "Christianity goes even further in valorizing *historical time.* Since God was *incarnated,* that is, since he took on *a historically conditioned human existence,* history acquires the possibility of being sanctified"[77] — true enough, but this is also a possibility for living Judaism which conceives the yoke of Torah as nothing other than the task of the sanctification of profane existence.

Bernhard Anderson brought out the way in which Israel's knowledge of God as savior in redemptive history entailed the de-divinizing of the cosmos and corresponding to that the elevation of universal humanity (the name Adam means literally "Earth Man," and the name, Eve, we are told, means "Mother of us all") as God's partner in the care of life for the sanctification of historical time.[78] Genesis 1, according to his historical-critical exposition, originated as a radical reworking of the New Year Festival *Enuma Elish* of Babylon, probably the work of Israelite priests from Jerusalem during the time of the Exile. The Babylonian myth, recited before the king annually at the time of Spring's arrival (by which the new year was reckoned), told of the victory of one of the sons of gods, Marduk, over Tiamat, the sea monster (whose body is made of saltwater; she is also the mother of these sons of the gods by her union with Apsu, the god of freshwater). Incensed at all the noise they make and wanting to get some sleep, Tiamat created monsters to destroy her children. The desperate sons look for a hero whose powerful word commands authority and they fasten upon Marduk, who goes forth to slay. In one of history's first instances of the social contract theory, Marduk takes on sovereignty in exchange for his siblings' fealty. In battle, he cuts his mother, Tiamat, in two and seals the heavens above and the dry earth below from the slaughtered, now-entombed parts of watery chaos. To memorialize his victory Marduk builds

76. Mircea Eliade, *The Sacred and the Profane: The Nature of Religion,* trans. Willard R. Trask (Orlando: Harcourt, 1987), p. 110.

77. Eliade, *The Sacred and the Profane,* p. 111.

78. For the following summary of Israel's redaction of the Babylonian creation myth, see Bernhard W. Anderson, *Creation vs. Chaos: The Reinterpretation of Mythical Symbolism in the Bible* (Philadelphia: Fortress Press, 1987) and *From Creation to New Creation: Old Testament Perspectives* (Minneapolis: Fortress, 1994).

a temple in Babylon. But not wanting his sibling gods to be burdened with caring for it, Marduk carves up Kinga (Tiamat's general) and mixing the deity's body parts with mud, fashions human beings to be a race of servants for the gods in caring for the temple. The sons of the gods crown Marduk their king and acclaim themselves his servants. In Babylon at the New Year's festival the earthly order is ritually renewed in the reciting of the *Enuma Elish*. As Marduk overcomes Tiamat and manifests his reign in the return of Spring as the winter floods recede in defeat, so also the Babylonian king reasserts his rule over subjects as the living image and representative of the heavenly king Marduk. Likewise, all present are renewed in servile devotion to him.

The parallels with Genesis 1 are significant and interesting: (1) the representation of God as a king, whose royal word commands and so it is; (2) creation as an act that puts the world in order and suppresses the threatening powers of watery chaos to make a habitable place for mortal beings; (3) the division of heaven above and dry earth below as the fundaments of cosmic structure holding back the chaos of watery flood; (4) the creation of man as the climax of the process and etiological conclusion of the myth. All this stands in common and brings out a measure of theological continuity between ancient Near Eastern religion and the Biblical tradition. That continuity is elementary but important: humans know that they are products of the world, not their own creators. And they know as a result that they are obligated beings, in debt to life-giving forces but just so exposed to death-dealing ones. In Israel's redaction, we once again see how the gospel works revision of the antecedent metaphysics (in the narrative form of mythology) on account of Israel's epistemic access to the God of Exodus. When we thus understand Genesis 1 as redaction of contemporary knowledge of the world (however primitive the myth appears to us) by Exodus faith, what is entailed by faith in God as Creator *ex nihilo* is set into sharpest relief.

According to Genesis 1, this world does not originate in any kind of conflict among the gods, but as the free and solemn act of the LORD. How much of *Enuma Elish* therefore just disappears in the sovereign words of Genesis 1:1-2! God creates by His commanding Word and so it is — unlike Marduk who also commands, but must go forth to war to enforce his word against co-equal divine powers in order to establish the dry earth and humanity upon it. But no one and no thing (not even the *tohu wabohu* of Genesis 1:2 in which a remnant of the watery chaos of the Babylonian myth survives)[79] lays down any kind of resistance that threatens to recur without God's permission. With the seven "days" of creation, a genuine interest in and attention to the emergent properties of the evolution of increasingly complex forms of organization up through organic life appears in place of the battles of the gods. The creation of humanity in the image of God — not

---

79. The Genesis 1 redaction of *Enuma Elish* does not expressly teach "creation out of nothing" (any more than John 1:1 expressly teaches the *homoousios* of the Nicene Creed). But the tendency is entirely in this direction.

the king, but the first couple as partners — is the climax of the story. Moreover, humanity here does not exist to serve God (in need of relief!) as priests in the temple but rather to serve under God as priests to the world over which they mediate the blessing of divine dominion. Here human beings are established as responsible *to* God *for* the world.

Indeed, this is the theological point of this act of prophetic interpretation: the world in which we live, and move, and breathe, the world upon which the cross of Jesus stood, *this world* is taken unequivocally as the good creature of God for a destiny that must be lived out in a history; it is not the precarious product of divine forces in perpetual conflict whose blessing must be leveraged by sacrifice. The cosmos comes into being not as an emanation out of God's own (inwardly conflicted) being, nor as mere shaping of rude matter by divine intelligence. The Babylonian myth understands events in human history in the framework of the cycle of recurring natural events in which order emerges from chaos, as Spring follows Winter. The Genesis story by contrast depicts a linear series of unique events authored by the God whose purpose supervenes the seven "days" of Genesis 1 to culminate in the Sabbath rest. Here time is, as Eliade saw, linear and irreversible. In time God accomplishes something genuinely new. The end is greater than the beginning, not the eternal recurrence of the same. And the symbol of this irreversibility of time as God's creature will be the cross of Jesus, not the *Hakkenkreuz*.

Genesis 1 retains, however, an echo of the mythical motif in order to indicate that even in this directionality of created time a deep, mysterious resistance to the purpose of God arises from within the creation itself: somehow chaos (the *tohu wabohu*) may reassert itself against God's purpose of a habitable earth in the custodianship of humanity, for example, when at God's permission the "fountains of the deep" are opened in the flood that destroys wicked humanity in the time of Noah. Likewise, the devious serpent that tempts the first couple in the second creation story originally represented the allure of nature-fertility cults for the people covenanted to the Lord alone. Israel's late apocalyptic traditions eventually focused this resistance to God from within creation upon the figure of Satan, the rebel Angel who attacks the faith of the faithful by introducing moral chaos: targeting the innocent, protecting the wicked, and accusing the righteous with the knowledge of their sins. Early Christian theology further developed ideas of the prehistorical fall of Lucifer, the angel of Light, who in pride envied the exalted destiny planned for the lowly race of Adam and out of malice determined to thwart it. The power of chaos is here represented as the joker in the deck of actual evil, a willful act of spiteful destruction of self-and-world, a contra-divine destructive fury. This personification of opposition to God from within the creation does not locate evil either in matter or in another deity of equivalent power, like Tiamat. It depicts Satan's defection from God personally;[80] it represents the

---

80. Jenson, *ST* 2, pp. 131-32.

bizarre but real choice of a creature for death and destruction, with all the chaos this works, including incitement of the fall of Adam.

In all these iterations, moral evil in the good creation arises from refusal to suffer in faith the natural "evil" of creaturely limitation by trust in God's command. Moral evil arises as opposition to God's good will for creation in a harmony of maximal diversity; sin arises as refusal of a creation of mutually limiting others that presses one and all in an irreversible historical movement towards Beloved Community and just so accuses them of sin when they refuse and resist that destiny. The act of origin is the "that" of giving existence to genuine, indeed maximally diverse others. It institutes the hierarchy of the reign of God with the corresponding metaphysical principle that it is better to be, even as an insubstantial creature of "ensouled matter," than not to be at all,[81] even as creaturely being as such is vulnerable and subject to spiritual as well as physical pain as member of the common body. The sin of origin, in this light, arises from resentment of this "natural" evil of bodily, not substantial existence and consists in the decision of primal envy to make oneself *sicut deus,* like God, deciding what is good and what is evil rather than suffering one's own body, let alone other bodies in faith that "all things work toward good to them that love God and are called according to His purpose" (Rom. 8:28) — which purpose is the redemption of our bodies (Rom. 8:23).

Genesis is promise. This in sketch is the teaching of the first chapters of the Book of Genesis, taken Trinitarianly. What, then, is this sovereign act of the personal God, the Father almighty, to which Genesis 1 attests in the mighty refrain, "Let there be . . . and there was!," on the basis of which early creedal Christianity refused Gnosticism and affirmed the almighty Father as the God of Abraham, Isaac, and Jacob, the God of the Exodus and of the House of David, of Sinai and the prophets, Israel's only God who will be God of all? How could a contemporary confess that faith and how can it be understood in relation to the origin? What rejections are entailed by that affirmation? And who finally is the creature that does, and the creature that does not, want to be the creature of this Creator, the creature who wants God to be God?

## God's Time, Created Time, and the Divine Decree

An enormous perplexity intervenes at this critical juncture. Process theologians are only the latest in the long line of those who have pointed out in objection to the doctrine of *creatio ex nihilo* that the idea of a beginning of time seems to be contradictory. "Even a beginning is a change, and all change requires something changing that does not come to exist through that same change. The beginning of the world would have to happen to something other than the world, something

81. Augustine, *Confessions* VII, 6, trans. Garry Wills (New York: Penguin, 2006), p. 139.

which as the subject of the happening would be in a time that did not begin with the world."[82] Hartshorne is thinking with the ontological tradition, *ex nihilo nihil fit* ("out of nothing comes nothing"), itself the philosophical rationalization of the ancient cosmogonies.[83] An ordered world comes into being out of the preexistent chaos; the chaos is rude matter in random motion on which intelligence imposes form. As the chaos of disorganized things in random motion (sheer manifold "becoming"), matter has only the potential for being something definite within an ordered whole ("cosmos"), in the sense that persistence through time in a self-identical way (as a "being") requires the ordering of internal consistency in things, a rational entelechy that lends substantiality and agency to matter. This order, supposedly, is not immanent in the chaos but the work of intelligence that designs and imposes it. Time as such stretches infinitely backwards and forwards, albeit in the motion of a circle. Space is imagined as a definite container or receptacle of the equally eternal material chaos within an infinite void. In Plato's classic *Timaeus,* the Demiurge appears at some point (*ex nihilo,* as it were) within the endless cycle of time as an architect to design the transition from material chaos to formal order and to initiate its implementation; this is the origin of our cosmos, an island in the sea of chaos that must henceforth maintain its self-identity against the tides or revert to chaos. The Demiurge, having set things in order, leaves the cosmos to run on its own. Process metaphysics, today, continues in this tradition of Platonic theology.

If linear time itself, however, is a creature, as the Christian faith in the creation *ex nihilo* has classically held, what could be "before" time? Nothing can be before time without time already there to register before and after. It must be in some analogical sense that the Creator precedes, who initiates physical time as the space for creatures other than the Creator to come into existence and pass from it, each in its own linear sequence. As mother is before daughter in time, so God is before creation in eternity. Here "before" indicates a logical, not chronological priority. Or does it? By this reasoning, in what sense can "being" be ascribed to the One who exists before time is created as the space for beings? Clearly, this cannot be the "being" to which creatures are accustomed; a God who temporally passes in and out of existence is another corporal creature, not the Creator of all that is other than God. The analogy only serves to indicate the difficulty, that God's place above or beyond physical time is also thought analogically. As the beer is in the stein, so the cosmos is in God. The notion of God's eternity-cum-immensity is the central difficulty, as we shall offer resolution at the conclusion of this system of theology, though the line of thought that considers God's space as the Beloved Community of the Father and the Son in the Spirit and God's time

---

82. Charles Hartshorne, "The Divine Self-Creation," in *A Map of Twentieth Century Theology: Readings from Karl Barth to Radical Pluralism,* ed. Carl E. Braaten and Robert W. Jenson (Minneapolis: Fortress, 1995), p. 351.

83. Eliade, *The Sacred and the Profane,* pp. 68-113.

as an infinite Trinitarian return, the origin and goal of which is the Father, will be developed in this section.

For the moment, the question before us is whether, if we take the doctrine of creation out of nothing consequently, we are not required to think that form and matter arise together out of nothing, so that in view of the perpetual change in continuing creation, any emergent creaturely being is but a temporary organization of becoming. Then the probing question, why something exists rather than nothing, indeed reflects the Christian challenge to naturalistic metaphysics of the world's eternity, yet it remains misleading in its subtle bias, also inherited from Aristotle, to regard really existing "things" (substances) as such as the mystery in need of explication. Rather, the mystery to be explained by the theological interpretation of nature that is creation from nothing is why any particular something rather than something else emerges in its place and time, that is to say, not only the protological act of origin but also its continuing execution through time in space. Furthermore, as Jüngel has argued, the world as creation, theologically decoded, privileges *potential* over what is actual, regular, and continuous. It gives knowledge of the *almighty* Creator, who consequently cannot be imagined ever ontologically to leave the scene of the creation, the inertia of which in the very persistence of things as temporal extension is ever a matter not only of His immediate power but also of His wise decisions for this, rather than that, cosmic development and evolving harmony. "God will reign forever" — His creating is His governance and His governance is His creating in accord with His originating command and blessing, as we have argued above for *creatio continua,* following Luther.

Yet Luther himself urged that it "is folly to argue much about God outside and before time, because this is an effort to understand the Godhead without a covering, or the uncovered divine essence. Because this is impossible, God envelops Himself in His works in certain forms. . . . If you should depart from these, you will get into an area where there is no measure, no space, no time, and into the merest nothing, concerning which, according to the philosopher, there can be no knowledge."[84] Can theology be satisfied with Luther's undoubtedly wise pastoral counsel here?

Not today. We may take Luther's insight that "nature" is the mask of God, since the insight here concerns the immediacy of God's creativity to the creature's being, its self-identical persistence through time in accord with God's purpose. Yet echoing Luther's very thought that apart from space and time, one gets into an area "where there is no measure, no space, no time, and into the merest nothing," Nietzsche drew the atheistic conclusion that the absolute God presupposed here "above" and "before" time is indeed a "nothing," nothing but a "nothing," that is, the religious reification of a nothing, a mystification of the creature's flight from time, a religiously sanctioned but imaginary place ("heaven") secured from the perils of authentic becoming. Under press of this atheistic challenge to the most

84. *LW* I, p. 11.

basic concept in theology, the eternal God, pious pleas of ignorance regarding things "above us" do not much help. Christian theology has to meet this atheistic challenge in Euro-America today or fold up shop and go out of business.

Neither does the apophatic critique much help in this regard. Apophatic theology unmasks the relativity of the concept of eternity as "heaven" above corresponding to earth below, two parts of the cosmic whole as grasped in the perspective of the creature, Eliade's *homo religiosus*. In this kataphatic "ontotheology" God is taken as the supreme or perfect being within the cosmic whole, certainly then the creature's *summum bonum*. Apophatic theology outbids Nietzsche in the sense that it already conducts an atheistic critique (Marion's "God without being") within theology against this construction of a humanly convenient deity, yet unlike Nietzsche for the sake of reverencing God's wholly otherness. Apophatic theology follows the critical philosophical advance of Parmenides beyond polytheism's contending gods and kataphatic myths into transcendence as "what-is . . . , ungenerated and imperishable, a whole of a single kind, unshaken, and complete. Nor was it ever, nor will it be, since it is now, altogether one, holding together: For what birth will you seek out for it . . . ? What need would have roused it, later or earlier, having begun from nothing, to grow?"[85] In Parmenides' footsteps, apophatic theology asks whether the Christian notion of the beginning of time as God's creature, taken literally rather than symbolically, lands us back in the pre-critical world of polytheism's cosmogonies. Is biblical monotheism in fact no more than monolatry? Does holding to a genuine act of God in the origin violate divine simplicity by implicating God's being ontologically in time?

As Parmenides' last question indicates — it was the selfsame taunt that Spinoza threw up against the incoherency of Jewish and Christian Platonisms,[86] or again, the same bafflement that Augustine himself expressed at the first verse of the Bible[87] — whatever is gained for Christian theology by Parmenides' alleged insight into divine simplicity is lost the moment we consider that adopting it in Christian theology quite literally makes God into a "something, we know not what," out of this world, a God beyond God. But the biblical origin by God of the creation as something other than God for fellowship with God, together with the Incarnation and the coming of the Beloved Community by the resurrection of the dead in execution of that original intention, are the mysteries that reveal the being of the triune God coming into the world as "more than necessary." If God *is* God in His becoming the Creator of all, and *is* His divine Word's becoming flesh, and *is* the Spirit's giving God's own life to the dead, then God *is* in time in God's own divine way, or what is the same, time *is* divine in a Trinitarian way, so that the creature's time is the fitting creature of the *living* God.

---

85. *A Presocratics Reader: Selected Fragments and Testimonia,* 2nd edition, ed. Patricia Curd (Indianapolis and Cambridge: Hackett, 2011), p. 59.

86. *RPTD,* p. 161.

87. Augustine, *Confessions* XI, 5, p. 260.

The difficult alternative to Parmenides here means embracing the situation of immanence classically parsed by Heraclitus (if not his way through it): "War is the father of all and king of all, and some he shows gods, others as humans; some he makes slaves, others free."[88] This way of Heraclitus is, on its own terms, fraught with perils; it gives in the first place, theologically, nothing but the *Deus absconditus.*[89] It appears, as Milbank especially has maintained, to script violence right into the nature of things.[90] Just so, however, it is truer to life as experienced shorn of mystifications and illusions, that is, theologically, to life in exile groaning under the structures of malice and injustice. Here according to Heraclitus, the divine Logos is key to the riddle of history,[91] key to the riddle of becoming, key to the riddle of change, yet not as insight into a putatively timeless transcendence beyond the fray that renders the fray in turn an unreal and inferior realm, Nietzsche's "slander against life."

As mentioned, the way of Heraclitus, taken on its own terms, is fraught with peril, just as thinkers like Milbank see. In the *Science of Logic,* Hegel famously argued that absolute being is indistinguishable from absolute nothing, and so is, as it were, motivated to differentiate itself from nothing by becoming something that it was not, hence a self-estrangement that is reconciled in yet a further coming to self-consciousness; so, he seemed to conclude, the world exists as God's self-unfolding, thought thinking itself and willing itself as such not in a Prime Mover, but in a progressive, if dialectical, temporal history. Significant contemporary theology thinks along such (right-wing) Hegelian lines: to be God is always to be open to and always to open a future, surpassing all past-imposed conditions. History occurs not only in Him but as His being-in-becoming; history is God's self-revelation, as the young Pannenberg and his circle proclaimed. The objections are quick in coming. Is the cost of this construal to make God temporal in a superior, not strictly supreme way? Does time in this way consequently become a God over God, the Greek *nemesis,* to which God too is finally subject? Is the divine exception of Sophocles, then, no longer valid? "Oh Theseus, dear friend, only the gods can never age, the gods can never die. All else in the world almighty Time obliterates, crushes all to nothing . . . infinite Time, sweeping through its rounds gives birth to infinite nights and days."[92] Is it so? Not long ago Mark Worthing, a student of Pannenberg, posed the question along these lines whether God could survive the heat death of the universe.[93] If not, then God too is a creature, and

88. *A Presocratics Reader,* p. 47.

89. *RPTD,* pp. 105-42.

90. John Milbank, *Theology and Social Theory: Beyond Secular Reason* (Oxford, UK and Cambridge, MA: Blackwell, 1997), pp. 278-325.

91. Drozdek, *Greek Philosophers as Theologians,* pp. 32-35.

92. "Oedipus at Colonus" (lines 685-700) in *Sophocles: The Three Theban Plays,* trans. Robert Fagles (London: Penguin, 1984), p. 322.

93. Mark William Worthing, *God, Creation, and Contemporary Physics* (Minneapolis: Fortress, 1996), pp. 160-98.

Time, slowing down to an infinite crawl, proves enduringly to be lord over all in the cosmic finale of endless night. How can God originate time and participate in time and bring time to fulfillment in the mutual indwelling of Creator and creature of the Beloved Community without being at the mercy of time — without making time God over God?

That is the serious, indeed decisive concern behind the traditional theological denial in Christian Platonism of God's temporality; it resolves the problem by arguing that God does not cease to be God in involvement in time since this involvement is not immediate and actual as in *creatio continua,* but analogical, that is, by means of mechanisms of secondary causality through which creatures participate in God's transcendent causality. The mechanism is replication. All actual things in motion exist as materialized copies of ideas in the mind of God, which as copies of the things themselves (God's thoughts) may be said to "participate" in God's creative thinking that as such wills the world into being.[94] Thus God's involvement in time is the once-and-for-all decree in the act of the origin that ordains the creaturely replication or sign of His creative will by means of which material creatures participate in God's works and ways. The dualism of the sign and the thing signified here is essential to establish the distance in being of the timeless God from His temporal creature and to relate them only in a way that strictly maintains this ontological difference. In turn it lends to the creature the high status of a created substance with a definite autonomy and agency of its own as secondary cause, so that its fate in actualizing its own essence as replica of God lies in its own hands.

Thus here, as argued above, the problematic gap remains between creaturely similitude and divine reality that threatens the entire approach with instability, even as the entire orientation of this approach remains protological rather than eschatological, privileging actuality over possibility, things over persons, and merit over grace. The question before us, therefore, is whether there is a fittingly divine way to be God in time, that is, a way of God's eternal being that is conceivable apart from creaturely time and yet open for it so that the mysteries of God's creating, redeeming, and fulfilling are now understood as free but fitting realizations of God for us. What could such an "eternity" be?

This concrete way of self-surpassing being is the almighty Father. In the kenosis of creation — that is, in deciding for this world on which the cross of His Son would stand rather than an infinity of other worlds — the Almighty Father gives time as the place for genuine, albeit creaturely, others with wills of their own, albeit finite, in order to win them as such, freely and voluntarily, to the Beloved Community. This eternity is the Almighty Father, who ever gives His inexhaustible being to the Son and the Spirit from whom He ever awaits personal return in acknowledgment of His Fatherhood. This is God the Father's protological act of self-giving and corresponding stance of eternal patiency. To be sure, this implies that

94. Plato, *Timaeus,* 48e2-53b5.

God's eternity is not sheer timelessness but that, as creaturely time is tensed, so also God's eternity consists in a sequence, eternally renewed, of giving, receiving, and returning of love, hence ever enriched, an abundant life from God for God in God back to God that infinitely expands — perhaps a spiral rather than circle pictures this. Strictly speaking, what is not communicable to creatures is this radical giving as such, the *esse Deum dare,* such that creatures in their deification would ever cease to be recipients of blessing. But deified creatures rather only adore this eternal self-surpassing of the unoriginated origin as fount of gift and every blessing flowing to them from God the Father through the Son in the Spirit. Only God the Father is and has eternal life in this ecstatic way of inexhaustible giving, and only God the Son and Spirit receive and return this divine giving by their own personal giving in self-donation and self-communication. If creatures attain to eternal life, as here understood, it is only by personal (not "analogical"!) participation, not by natural confusion, by unification of love not fusion of natures, by ecstasy not by assimilation. More on this will follow in the conclusion. For the present, it is clear that deification is not a natural fusion of creature with Creator, but a specific personal union with the Son in the Spirit to live to the Father, even as God's eternity is not sheer timelessness, but this life in motion of giving, receiving, and returning now turning *ad extra* in the act of eschatological creation.

The divine decree, then, is not to be conceived as the once-and-for-all creative intuition of Augustine's "eternal now," as if Jesus Christ just happened to be one important, indeed instrumental character by which God determines others. The divine decree is rather the Trinity's *self*-determination to be the God of grace for sinful humanity. According to Ephesians 3:9, building on Romans 16:25-27, it comes as news of the boundless riches of Christ that makes the divine decree visible for all to see, "the plan of the mystery hidden for ages in God who created all things." One should thus talk about God's time and the time of the creature as united by Jesus the Lord of Time, as Karl Barth did.[95] To affirm this Christological "time of God" for us, however, is to agree with Luther that properly speaking free choice is *the* divine prerogative[96] so that, as Robert Jenson has lifted up and advocated in recent theology, "God's history with us is one integral act of sovereignty, comprehended as his decision to reconcile us with himself in Christ Jesus. The existence and specific membership of the community are predestined in this decision, with the 'pre-' appropriate to the biblical God."[97] What "pre-" is that?

"The LORD will reign forever and ever" (Exod. 15:18). This way of becoming God in the creature's time characterizes Scripture from beginning to end. It is

---

95. *CD* III/2, pp. 437-40.

96. A "power of freely turning in any direction, yielding to none and subject to none." Luther, *Bondage of the Will,* p. 105. The freedom of God's commitment to His creature that is the decision made in the divine decree of the economy entails that God limits God, not a weakness in the case of God, but power to decide and commit, Barth's "freedom to love."

97. Jenson, *ST* 2, p. 178.

evident already in the ancient poem preserved in Exodus 15, where God's victory over Pharaoh's army at the Red Sea is hymned with mythical elements drawn from the ancient Near Eastern story of the cosmogonic emergence of the habitable order from the threat of watery chaos. "The LORD is a warrior; the LORD is his name. Pharaoh's chariots and his army he cast into the sea; his picked officers were sunk in the Red Sea. The floods covered them; they went down into the depths like a stone. Your right hand, O LORD, glorious in power — your right hand, O LORD, shattered the enemy. In the greatness of your majesty you overthrew your adversaries; you sent out your fury, it consumed them like stubble. At the blast of your nostrils the waters piled up, the floods stood up in a heap; the deeps congealed in the heart of the sea" (Exod. 15:3-8). In the same way, Psalm 77:16-20 celebrates the Lord's victory in political history by ascribing to Him the predicates of majesty drawn from ancient Near Eastern cults: "When the waters saw you, O God, when the waters saw you, they were afraid; the very deep trembled. The clouds poured out water; the skies thundered; your arrows flashed on every side. The crash of your thunder was in the whirlwind; your lightnings lit up the world; the earth trembled and shook. Your way was through the sea, your path, through the mighty waters; yet your footprints were unseen. You led your people like a flock by the hand of Moses and Aaron." The biblical pattern is the same throughout. From the promise in which it originated God works the world through every natural evolution, human failure, and supra-human obstacle of the eruption of actual evil to the fulfillment of the Reign, as the Spirit of the Father and the Son includes human beings, representatives of the whole creation by virtue of their bodily solidarity with nature, into the very history of the Father with the Son until God is all things to everyone (1 Cor. 15:28). "Being God" is thus "becoming" God for creatures in the act of giving and realizing the Reign: creation is eschatological, God comes into time. In that case, of course, the question redoubles in intensity: Comes *from where?* God comes from God. The Patrological answer to the question is from the unoriginated Father of the Son and breather of the Spirit. What can this mean? What "pre-" is that?

The early creeds ascribe this work of creation, taken as the possibility of God for us in realizing the Reign, to the Almighty Father as the uncaused cause of all causes and effects. The unoriginated person of the Father is thus rightly associated with the act of origin, when "in the beginning" the world was first called into existence out of nothing. As there is an unoriginate origin in God, so also there was an originating act of the created cosmos. *Ad extra,* "facing outward," the Father creates everything other than God out of nothing by his own Word of Command in his own Breath of Life, as Genesis 1:1-2 depicts in Trinitarian perspective. In this Christian-biblical depiction, the "ultimate origination of all things" (Leibniz) occurs as a free act of the will or good pleasure that the almighty Father properly possesses in conjunction with wisdom and love. How are we to understand this originating divine decision? What kind of spontaneity or for that matter necessity attends it? Or is this entire line of inquiry by far too anthropomorphic? How could there be a decision between all possible worlds before time existed in which a decision could transpire, before space existed in which any possible world could even be imagined to unfold?

Since "something rather than nothing exists," Leibniz held, we[98] creatures who are something, not nothing, are entitled to infer that "there is a certain urge for existence or (so to speak) a straining for existence in possible things," just as we experience the strain or press of possibility in our own existence. Moreover, we creatures may further infer that "of the infinite combinations of possibilities and possible series, the one that exists is the one through which the most essence or possibility is brought into existence" to make up a maximally rich world. This principle of plentitude, of maximal diversity so far as it admits of harmony, accounts for the metaphysical goodness of the actual creation. Thus we are entitled to the assumption of an intelligent choice, both good and wise, in the powerful act of origin, i.e., "that at *some time* being is to prevail over nonbeing, or that *there is a reason why* something rather than nothing is to exist" (emphasis added). This inference is admissible, not because "the world is . . . metaphysically necessary" but because "its contrary implies imperfection or moral absurdity . . ." in the Creator, i.e., that the "Creator" would be but an anthropomorphic cipher for random exploration of all possibilities rather than a morally accountable person. In other words (although Leibniz was not always clear on this point), it is the rational and so *believing* creature who is entitled to such inferences in that she believes the Creator to be wise and good as well as powerful in His work, a work that is a true or at least fitting expression of His own being. She has epistemic access in the fact of her own mere existence so far as it instantiates her being this "something" rather than nothing or anything else. The one who in faith understands her self-and-world as creature in this way is entitled to this confidence in God's wisdom and moral goodness as well as power as her Creator. These warranted inferences constitute an interpretation of the fact of existence, which is also a doxological justification of this fact in praise of God's free, wise, and loving work of giving creation, for it shows how "the Author of the world can be free, even though everything happens determinately, since he acts from a principle of wisdom or perfection."

Of all conceivable worlds residing in the logical space of the divine mind, God freely chooses in the eternal time of His triune life *this one, in which I am writing and you are reading* these words, as the *particular* something being created in order to be redeemed by Christ and fulfilled in the Spirit. That, in the view of the present proposal, is the vista that Leibniz helps to open to us for progress in the knowledge of the God who is determined by the missions of His Son and

---

98. G. W. Leibniz, "On the Ultimate Origination of Things," in *Discourse on Metaphysics and Other Essays,* trans. D. Garber (Indianapolis and Cambridge: Hackett, 1991), pp. 43-44. Leibniz's "we" speaks in the name of natural reason, or philosophy, but I take it to be the case that he in fact speaks in the tradition of Christian philosophy.

Spirit to redeem and fulfill this creation in these ways. In this creative decision for us, the almighty Father absolutely originates all that is other than God, sustains it in being, preserves it from decay, orders it purposefully, innovates within it, responds to and defeats the vicious incursions of actual evil, and in all these ways leads it to His goal of life in His kingdom, eschatologically effecting "the best of all possible worlds." This decision and its faithful execution and accomplishment in time is the divine decree. Theologically decoded, then, *the* act of origin is the free and gracious decision of God the Father of His Son Jesus Christ in the endless love of the Spirit personally to *become* the Creator of others, and so to initiate this space-time of the world and to involve Himself concomitantly with it from this moment of origin onward and indeed forever. God is not eternally creator, nor does the world exists eternally. But rather by a definite act of origin that can and must be theologically decoded as a free, wise, and loving choice, it remains actual as divine decision mandating continuing creation at every moment of continuing time. The Almighty Father thus *becomes* the Creator in the act of creating "at some time," having "reason why there is [to be] something not nothing" other than God, more precisely this *particular* something of the coming of the Beloved Community in Christ, as revealed according to Ephesians 3:9.

If we grant this re-theologized reading of Leibniz that makes explicit his tacit Trinitarianism,[99] the question presses: What kind of divine movement constitutes an eternal decree — not its temporal execution, but the antecedent decision-making? How is that to be measured? Time is the measure of motion. By what time is the movement measured of this One who *becomes* the Creator with the origination of space-time, yet *remains* antecedently the eternal Father begetting His own Son and breathing His own Spirit without beginning or end who as such comes to a decision? Simply put, how can this *Novum* of the decision come about in the eternal God? In Jüngel's words interpreting Barth: ". . . God's being is capable of possessing historical predicates, although these as such are not capable of predicating the being of God. In that God in revelation interprets himself, God's being is *reiterated* with the help of historical predicates."[100] That is an apt description of the movement *ad extra* in question. God as God for God iterates Himself in time as Creator, Redeemer, and Fulfiller; yet the prior question involved here, that we are pressing with Leibniz's aid, is how in eternity God as God for God comes to such a resolve to reiterate Himself in time for creatures without attributing temporality to God.

In a sense, we are asking for the reason why the distinction, not separation, of the immanent and economic Trinity is to be sustained. How can the immanent

99. Maria Rosa Antognazza, *Leibniz on the Trinity and the Incarnation: Reason and Revelation in the Seventeenth Century,* trans. G. Parks (New Haven and London: Yale University Press, 2007).

100. Eberhard Jüngel, *The Doctrine of the Trinity: God's Being Is in Becoming* (Grand Rapids: Eerdmans, 1976), p. 95.

Trinity be conceived to come to a decision that *freely* as well as wisely and benevolently reiterates itself in the physical time of creatures, i.e., as the economic Trinity. Trinitarianly, the unique being of the Creator of all that is not God is God the Father's infinitely self-surpassing personal being; this personal identity of God as God is not strictly speaking communicable as it is the source of communication *ad intra* and *ad extra;* thus the distinction, once made by God in eternity between Creator and creature, or between the "two natures," as also between the immanent and economic Trinity remains forever. What kind of motion is the making of such distinctions and relations that is divine resolve, decree, election in the eternal Trinity, in the divine time "before" the creation of cosmic time for creatures that thus also marks the becoming of God as Creator, Redeemer, and Fulfiller of creation and therewith the commencement of our world on the way to fulfillment?

Clearly we do not have here a simple identity but a complex event of identification. The relation between the economic and immanent Trinity is not fully convertible; it is and must be asymmetrical.[101] This is the differentiation that makes creation intelligible as a divine choice. Jenson hangs on here by the barest of threads: "It might not have been so. God might have been the God he is without this world to happen to . . . how God would have described his own being had he been without the world, we cannot even inquire."[102] Is this asceticism a version of Luther's pastoral advice? Is it a (rare) moment of apophatic reserve in Jenson? Or is it a right-wing Hegelianism that slams on the brakes against left-wing Hegelianism's inexorable slide into pantheism? Hegel acknowledged that the

---

101. The deeper difficulty in Jenson's attempt to think, according to Rahner's rule, the immanent and economic Trinity together so tightly may be seen in the fact that Jenson holds the historical human creature, Jesus, simply to be the second identity of God, that is, without the mediation of an event, namely the Incarnation of the immanent or eternally preexistent Son by the Spirit — a mythology that he would deliteralize and decode as a simple identity. This difficulty arises inescapably at just this admittedly difficult point of the "pre-" of the biblical God. Here it appears, in a fashion similar to Bruce McCormack, and in keeping with right-wing Hegelianism, that Jenson must make the Father as origin the "decider" of the reconciliation that will be carried out by the Son incarnate, hence instrumentalizing the Son, just as had occurred in the classical Calvinist doctrines of the divine decree, only now as executing a universal rather than a limited atonement. It is not the counsel of the immanent Trinity, but the decision of the One who thus becomes the Father in so deciding for us by generating the *Logos ensarkos* for us in "the one integral act of sovereignty" that takes place in the economy. In Michael Allen's words, "The immanent life of the Son within the eternal Trinity has been entirely reduced to the economic foreshadowings of his earthly imprint." R. Michael Allen, *Justification and the Gospel: Understanding the Contexts and Controversies* (Grand Rapids: Baker Academic, 2013), p. 83. I agree with Allen's judgment here: "Theology [i.e., the doctrine of God] really is manifest in the economy; theology really does precede the economy" (p. 83), though *with* Jenson I would hasten to qualify, so as not to privilege "precedence," "precedes, accompanies and fulfills the economy." Jenson is certainly aware of the difficulty, but his solution rests in his doctrine of the metaphysics of anticipation over against metaphysics of persistence, to be discussed in the conclusion of this work.

102. Jenson, *ST* 1, p. 221.

abstract, eternal idea of God in and for Himself "prior to or apart from creation" is "expressed in terms of the holy Trinity." Hegel thus knew that the classical theological function of the doctrine of the eternal or immanent Trinity had been to account for God's transcendence of creation as its free author by virtue of His fulfilled life as the eternal love of the Father and the Son in the Spirit, while at the same time affirming this God's immanence in creation as its actual, immediate, and committed author. Yet in criticism of this very theological function, Hegel added that "insofar as [God] is not the creator, he is grasped inadequately. His creative role is not an *actus* that 'happened' once; [rather] what takes place in the idea is an eternal moment . . ." since "it belongs to his being, his essence, to be the creator."[103] Hegel here confounds a justified rejection of the notion that creation is only or even primarily a completed act of the past with denial of the free act of origination as such. To make God Creator by nature, however, is radically to immanentize God in a pantheism on the way to atheism, as Kojève[104] has persuasively argued and Žižek in recent times has championed against Milbank.[105] With Hegel, we have theologically returned to Origen's doctrine of God's natural creativity, and so to all the difficulties that attend the neo-Platonic theology of *apokatastasis* (the universal reconciliation of all things), specifically, the danger of compromising the decisiveness of historical time — also for God — in the interest of a comic resolution of the tragedy of history. (Corresponding to his pre–Arian crisis theology, Origen's "natural" creativity is subtly but sharply to be distinguished from Edwards's Trinitarianly grounded divine disposition of the personal surplus of Trinitarian love freely deciding to communicate itself *ad extra.*)

Time, to take a classical definition, is the measure of motion, and so the criterion by which we discern the motion of life and distinguish it from the stillness of death. In this abstract sense, the concept of time applies to the eternity of the Trinity as the living God, for love is motion occurring between persons. The infinite love of the Father and the Son in the Holy Spirit is the divine life in the eternal motion of giving, receiving, and returning — as we are picturing, a spiral not a circle, the true eternal return of the same that returns ever more enriched by the experience it freely generates within its own life. The Father eternally generates His Son and breathes on Him the Spirit just as the Son eternally cries, "Abba, Father," in the return of the Spirit. So it was in the beginning, is now, and ever will be. But the wonder of the gospel is that this God makes time for the creature and incorporates its place into His own. God's own eternity is this motion of the divine self-donation and self-communication: the Father of the Son and Son

103. G. W. F. Hegel, *Lectures on the Philosophy of Religion: The Lectures of 1827,* one-volume edition, ed. P. C. Hodgson (Berkeley: University of California Press, 1988), p. 417.

104. Alexandre Kojève, *Introduction to the Reading of Hegel: Lectures on the Phenomenology of Spirit,* trans. James H. Nichols Jr. (Ithaca, NY and London: Cornell University Press, 1996).

105. Slavoj Žižek and John Milbank, *The Monstrosity of Christ: Paradox or Dialectic?,* ed. Creston Davis (Cambridge, MA and London: MIT Press, 2009).

of the Father in the Spirit who searches the depths of God (1 Cor. 2:10) but now bears witness to our spirits that we are indeed the children of God (Rom. 8:14-17). Thus we can say with Garrett J. DeWeese that God the Trinity's eternity is to be conceived of, not as timelessness, but as "omnitemporality."[106]

The God of the Bible is transcendent in such a way that He can be radically immanent to the world as His creation. The latter affirmation entails that "God does experience a succession of states in his being and, subsequent to the creation of a (temporal) world external to himself, God stands in real temporal . . . relations to that world."[107] In DeWeese's terminology, God has accordingly both relational and nonrelational properties,[108] or, in classical terminology, communicable and noncommunicable attributes. This is in accord with the classical distinction between the immanent and economic Trinity, as just argued, where the former is the possibility but not the necessity of the latter, which latter exists as the former's free choice to be related to a creation other in being than its Creator. In such a relation, given God's free choice for it, temporal change in God is both natural and necessary. This relative mutability is particularly demanded by the most elementary considerations of Christian theology: if time is dynamic and truly tensed, and if God is immediately related to temporal changes in His creation as Creator, then "there has been a real change in God's internal mental state (his 'regarding' of Paul as rebellious and later as forgiven) as well as in his relation to Paul (from 'angry with' to 'loving')."[109] Following Wolterstorff, DeWeese writes that Christian redemption "is a multifaceted event which includes at least God's forgiving the sinner, changing from an attitude of wrath to one of love towards the sinner, adopting the sinner as his child and imputing to the sinner the righteousness of Christ."[110] The evangelical idiom here of God and creature entering into "personal relationship"[111] may be off-putting to the liberal theological establishment, yet it remains qualified in DeWeese's presentation by his equal attention to God's nonrelational properties. Nonrelationally, that is, impersonally or naturally, we might well state that God simply *is* love and that wrath thus appears as but the shadow sign of this love that God simply is in handing over to nothingness what is against love. So God is timelessly angry with Paul when this creature is in the state of rebellion and timelessly loving to Paul when he enters into the state of repentance and faith. The advance in thinking that DeWeese arguably provides is to combine the two insights, so that the latter consideration of God's nonrelational, incommunicable, natural attributes serves as the presupposition of God's entering into temporal relations with creatures.

106. Garrett J. DeWeese, *God and the Nature of Time* (Aldershot, UK and Burlington, VT: Ashgate, 2004), pp. 239-76.

107. DeWeese, *God and the Nature of Time*, p. 209.

108. DeWeese, *God and the Nature of Time*, p. 261.

109. DeWeese, *God and the Nature of Time*, p. 261.

110. DeWeese, *God and the Nature of Time*, p. 212; cf. 255.

111. DeWeese, *God and the Nature of Time*, p. 213.

Yet even this proposed combination infects, as it were, God's own being with "metaphysical time" since for "the Father, the Son, and the Holy Spirit to enjoy dynamic relationality in any sense analogous to the relationality of human persons would be to experience change."[112] Such "metaphysical time," as DeWeese tags it, is a notion that this analytic philosopher of religion expressly correlates to Trinitarianism: "the causal succession of mental states in God's conscious life grounds the flow and direction of metaphysical time. . . . [This] would not be a limitation on God, since he is the cause of his own being, including his own mentality. Further, it would aid our understanding of the dynamic relations among the persons of the Trinity prior to creation (cf. the doctrine of *perichoresis,* the "interpenetration" of the persons of the Trinity)."[113] As sequence (and alterity), then, there is indeed a divine time (and space), if the divinity in question is that of the Holy Trinity, when, as we shall argue in the conclusion of this book, the eternal Life of the Three is to be conceived as consistent perichoresis.

While DeWeese's formulations may be somewhat too mentalist for the social Trinitarianism of the theology of the Beloved Community, he has advanced the theological argument by exposing the view of timeless eternity as incompatible with creation, Incarnation, and the coming of the Beloved Community as the true self-determination of God the eternal Father in the missions of His Son and Spirit to redeem and bring to fulfillment of communion with Himself a world of created persons other than Himself. Timeless eternity rather coheres with a static view of created time where, by a once-and-for-all act of external determination, God casts in concrete a four-dimensional universe, in which the physical future is already fixed, rigorously entailed by what already is and has been. There is correspondingly a price to be paid either way. Even if we grant a coherence not apparent to the classical Augustinian "eternal decree," for which timeless decision we utterly cannot account, timeless eternity determining all things ad extra in a single all-determining act entails, given our best available knowledge of physics, the death of God along with the universe when the Big Bang whimpers into eternal night. Or rather, this death of the creature entails the death of God *as Creator.* This is not so farfetched an interpretation of Augustine's pessimism about the creation, always hovering on the brink of his former Manichaeism. On the other hand, omnitemporality has God in His own time coming in and through His creature's time to an outcome of cosmic events that is truly contested on the way to a salvation that is and can be nothing less than the Pauline redemption of our bodies. Of course, if the universe ends as contemporary physics now projects, here too creation dies, but *God as God* also. That would the real "death of God," if God is the One who has pledged by His very deity to redeem (Gen. 15:17).[114]

---

112. DeWeese, *God and the Nature of Time,* p. 280.

113. DeWeese, *God and the Nature of Time,* p. 253.

114. I note that this is my own take on DeWeese's proposal, not anything that he has suggested in his book.

On this view, as in Leibniz, "God's governance is based on his foreknowledge of Middle Knowledge of all possible futures, not his foreseeing of the actual future that already exists."[115] God's eternal decree is His self-determination to create, redeem, and fulfill that enables His immediate presence to and action on creatures, thus in their time (and space) as ever-innovative in fidelity to His own freely chosen purpose, as ever-patient with fallen creatures making ruin of His work and disgrace of His Name. The "actual" future of this earth is therefore a matter of no little urgency because it can go either way. The fate of the earth is something that hangs in the balance between God's fidelity and God's patience, just as Paul sees in Romans 3:6, 21-26. This lends eschatological urgency to the mission to the nations, as it did for Paul (Rom. 16:25-26) proclaiming God's determination to be for us in Jesus Christ so that by the Spirit we are turned with all our hearts to "the obedience of faith" in the Father who sent Him by the Spirit who proclaims Him. It is the urgency of intercessory prayer by the ecclesia on behalf of all nations. It is the urgency of new priestly lives of intercession in baptismal vocation within the nations. It is the urgency of Spirit-steeled resistance to the juggernauts of malice and injustice during this time of trial, in Spirit-driven experimentation in new structures of love and justice by the daily gift of bread and mutual forgiveness.

Omnitemporality is analogous to the traditional notion of omnipresence: as the immeasurable God is present to every actual point of space, without thereby being circumscribed in physical space, so the immeasurable God is present in every actual moment of time, without thereby being captured in any moment or series of moments of physical time.[116] The price of this interpretation of God's timely eternity is that God cannot be present to unreal, that is to say, not-yet-actual future moments of physical time for the simple reason that they really do not yet exist (or do not exist in our world but only in another — imaginary — world).[117] God can be present to, but not encompassed within, the present moment of physical time because God's own time is the Trinitarian sequence by which the self-determined God is immediately present faithfully to give each place and every moment as a gift from its author and governor. Thus physical time, interpreted as God's creature, exists in the execution of God's plan for a world unfolding as space made into the habitable place for humanity and humanity in turn growing into maximal compossible diversity fit for translation into the eschatological kingdom at the fulfillment of time. This temporal emergence of humanity in a fit habitation calling for its care and development under their stewardship in structures of love and justice — making wilderness into park and garden and city into brother-sisterhood — is what creation faith deems "very good"; it is the same judgment of value to which humans are summoned by faith in the Creator in order that the works they do are truly good in loving all creatures

---

115. DeWeese, *God and the Nature of Time,* p. 275.
116. DeWeese, *God and the Nature of Time,* p. 240.
117. DeWeese, *God and the Nature of Time,* p. 242.

in and under God their Creator. Created time then becomes humanity's dramatic history with God to bring about the obedience of faith (Rom. 16:26); in humanity chronology is turned to history and becomes "day" upon "day" (Genesis 1), epoch upon epoch, dispensation following dispensation in God's continuously creative work of structuring the world to love and justice in mandates for creative labor, marriage and family, and organized religion, as more complex and beautiful things emerge in this cumulative process.

Unbelief can of course reduce these "teleonomic" or emergent properties of increasingly complex things to their components and the mechanisms underlying their natural production and thus interpret them as nothing but accidental epiphenomena of those impersonal processes, as in fact they appear in the perspective, precisely, of unbelief. This reduction is theologically useful insofar as it deflates another kind of unbelief — the arrogant anthropocentrism of modernity's sovereign self. But reductionism is sinful so far as it wishes to discredit the human calling by God as His image to acquire in history His likeness by assuming conscientious responsibility to Him for the creation. Materialist reductionism in any event commits what William James identified as the "genetic fallacy." The genetic fallacy holds that the "worth of a thing can be decided by its origin"[118] rather than its utility for life in receiving and achieving a destiny, thus by its protology rather than by its eschatology. According to James, the worth of a thing is to be measured by its "fruitfulness for life," a criterion that itself arises out the same evolutionary process and reflects its "teleonomic" dynamism organically.[119] "Fruitfulness for life" in turn depends on a theological judgment that James himself sought in his philosophy to avoid, though the need for theology haunts him: whether the immanent valuation of life as good is but a survival-illusion or in fact dim awareness of the promise of God in the decision and act of *creatio continua* for a fulfillment.

We have argued throughout that the "nature" or "essence" of the triune God is "to give," a giving that begins eternally as the Father's self-surpassing in begetting the Son and breathing the Spirit and continues forever in the return of the Son in the Spirit; this is a divine motion in a space of its own, as it were, a mutual indwelling that glorifies God in God for God. Consequently in creating a world *extra se,* God is not motivated by need or greed but only by surplus, fully cognizant of, but disregarding, the cost to Himself in patiently suffering the contradiction of His will by sinful creatures, even to giving to sinful creatures the eternity without Him that they have chosen for themselves in knowing good and evil. We have suggested accordingly that the essential properties of the *esse Deum dare* are known as the complex harmonies of power, wisdom, and love, so that God as God for God is able, wise, and free to grant a world of creatures time and space in order, for His part, to bring the creatures that emerge in creation through

118. William James, *The Varieties of Religious Experience: A Study in Human Nature* (Mineola, NY: Dover, 2002), p. 237.

119. James, *The Varieties of Religious Experience,* pp. 327-29.

creation freely and joyfully to the gift of Beloved Community. Jenson is right in this connection in citing Peter Brunner. We "'must abandon . . . all pictures of God . . . [as] fixed perfection . . . , so that talk of new judgments, new reactions, new deeds, and new words in God . . . appears naïve and anthropomorphic.'"[120] Creation "out of nothing," taken here as expressive of the agency of the Trinity who freely, knowingly, and lovingly decides for this world rather than any other and commits Himself without reserve to its redemption and fulfillment, is the endeavor to affirm and thence to understand in critical dogmatics how this eternal God can do such new things, also for God, not at the expense of His divinity but in true expression of it.

In Christian understanding, God's free, wise, and loving decision to become God for others means that something happens also for this eternal Trinity that can happen just because the deity of God is that of the eternal Trinity. God writes Himself into the story of the created world by the Lamb slain before the foundation of the world. In accord with this Christological self-determination, creative improvisations on God's side will anticipate and respond to destructive improvisations on the side of creatures. Yet the tide of battle between actual good and actual evil will ebb and flow by which decisiveness of history there will be loss and casualty as well as liberation and victory. Nonetheless, in this entire affair God is supreme in the sense that God is not limited in His creativity by a material alter ego, equally eternal, that intrinsically resists formation. God is rather, and freely, limited by His moral commitment to love "ensouled matter," as McCord Adams rightly holds, conscientiously to respect created persons as His own precious and fragile, because emergent, creatures. As Augustine rightly noted, God who created us without our will nevertheless will not redeem us apart from our willingness. This open world with its sorrows does not happen, then, as something unforeseen, but rather as something intelligently foreseen and personally willed in generous, indeed inexhaustible self-giving that continues, fittingly, through the conscientious divine deed of the redemption of the sinful and sorrowing creature to the Spirit's fulfillment of the oft squandered promise of this creation. The order of nature mysteriously erupted from the order of grace at the movement in God's eternity constituted as this divine decree; this was the origin of the world "out of nothing" other than the surplus of the Trinity. How this theology overlaps with contemporary physics and biology we may leave to specialists. That act of origin is, in any case, but half the wonder.

Simultaneously with this divine decree — the economy of God hidden from the ages but now made known in Christ — God implicates Himself personally to live within created time as a *localized* participant, not only as the Father "in heaven," but in the fullness of time the "Word made flesh," and the Spirit "poured into our hearts" to form the elect body of Christ. This localization is not "natural," but "personal"; yet as personal, it is and must be bodily reality in the world of

---

120. Jenson, *ST* 1, p. 221.

the common body. The former is the truth that Calvin ineptly defended in his Christology, when he denied that the natural deity of Christ was locally confined to the finite body of Jesus of Nazareth. But the mistake here, as we have argued, is to be attributed to the modalist tendency of the Western tradition that fails to think consequently in the way of Trinitarian personalism. The Son of God qua person is wholly and without reserve the man Jesus, not qua divine nature since neither the Spirit nor the Father, wholly the same divine nature, is incarnate. The creature Jesus is wholly and without reserve this person, the Son of God, not God in general because the Son who He is is not God in general but God in the way of being Son. When that is clear, it is also clear that God's redeeming mercy becomes spatially and temporally concrete in the particular history of redemption made by the preaching of the gospel in mission to the nations, where the personal promise of Jesus Christ the Son of God, "This is My Body for you," is spoken and heard in personal repentance and faith "for me" as for all. The Spirit's preaching of the Son calls to faith, in this way gathering from the nations the ecclesia as body to its Head, Jesus Christ. By this gathering, the Spirit reorders the powers and principalities by the concrete, indeed localized presence of the living Christ in His gathered people, as His Body moving into the world.

Or to put the same matter Patrologically: in the act of origin, God out of good pleasure of grace promises Himself ("'I have sworn by my name,' says the Lord") to become the heavenly Father of all humanity, i.e., to ransack the pits of hell by His Son's descent so that by His ascent He may bring forth His heavenly reign on the earth. As the temporal world exists by grace because it is originated out of nothing but the free decision of God to become its *Creator,* so also God *becomes* in the fulfillment "the cosmic transformation just adduced"[121] in a manner befitting the infinity of love which the Father of the Son in the Spirit is. The creation exists as the promise of the coming of the kingdom of God. Time unfolds as the execution of the Creator God's determined "plan" of what the world is to become, notwithstanding the intrinsically incalculable incursions of actual evil and the spontaneously divine improvisations in response.

Hence, as suggested above in DeWeese's notion of eternity as omnitemporality, we must speak in Christian theology in a careful way of the *temporality* of God.[122] Here we speak of the mysterious "metaphysical" time of the infinite life of the Trinity without beginning or end (which we continue to call "eternity" provided that we understand by that word nothing but the *circumincessio/perichoresis* of the unlimited but internally sequenced life of the Three). And we speak this way of God's time because, and only because, God calls forth the theological subject to know God objectively in created time on the way to the final forum,

---

121. Jenson, *ST* 1, p. 222.

122. This problem of the temporality of God has occupied me from the beginning of my theological work. See Paul R. Hinlicky, *The Gospel and the Knowledge of God: St. Mark's theologia crucis* (Ph.D. thesis; Union Theological Seminary, New York, 1983).

the eschaton of judgment. Such temporality implies that God is not "perfect" in the sense of the philosophical perfect being descended from Parmenides' simplicity and thus incapable of what is imperfect as an object of its own will and knowledge. The triune life is perfect in the living way of giving and returning love, and so creatively capable of what is not perfect either in giving or receiving love. The God of the gospel does not exist ideally, delimited in this way — really imprisoned in its perfection in this way — from all that is temporally real, the concrete, the particular, the finite, the imperfect, the weak. God lives infinitely, *thus also in the finite,* which exists at all only because of the reality of God's free decision and decided commitment in the act of origin that we have deliteralized and theologically decoded as the divine decree.[123]

The infinitely self-surpassing personal being of God the almighty Father is the ultimate, non-transcendable mystery, in that He lives eternally in generating the Son and breathing the Spirit; just so, as living, the real personal being of God the Father moves out from its eternity of joy to create the world and therewith to undergo sorrow (Gen. 6:5-6), to love the enemy in the Son's taking the sinner's place (Rom. 5:8, 10), and to embrace the ungodly in the Spirit's grant of life to the dead (1 Cor. 6:15-20), already now forming of them His own Temple. The Father is author of the world-drama, into which script He writes His Son and Spirit as eminently real participants among creatures, so that in the contingencies of determinate improvisations, the real and present Father is leading to His good end, also through the invited prayers of His people, the church vicarious, the priestly people of God who cry out, Abba! Father (Gal. 4:6).

From the beginning the world is something new for God, as is also the Incarnation, and at last the fulfillment — the newness, however, of His own free, joyful, and intelligent decision.[124] In this way the *infinite is capable of the finite:* "This is the life, the deed, the activity of God; he is absolute activity, creative energy [*Aktuosität*], and his activity is to posit himself in contradiction, but eternally to resolve and reconcile this contradiction."[125] The "right-wing" reading of Hegel is based upon this significant remnant and radicalization of classical Trinitarianism that overcomes the abstract alternative between transcendence and immanence

---

123. "When we view the characteristic of finitude as something contradictory to God, then we take the finite as something fixed, independent — not as something transitional, but rather as something essentially independent, a limitation that remains utterly such. . . . If God has the finite only over against himself, then he himself is finite and limited. Finitude must be posited in God himself, not as something insurmountable, absolute, independent, but above all as this process of distinguishing what we have seen in spirit and consciousness. . . ." Hegel, *Lectures on the Philosophy of Religion,* p. 406. We decline the latter point but affirm the former.

124. Thomas F. Torrance, *The Trinitarian Faith: The Evangelical Theology of the Ancient Catholic Church* (Edinburgh: T. & T. Clark, 1993), p. 89.

125. Hegel, *Lectures on the Philosophy of Religion,* p. 413. That is why two decades ago Milbank could dialectically write both "for" as well as "against" Hegel in *Theology and Social Theory,* pp. 147-76. One fears the dialectic is giving way to the analogy of being.

in modeling God's relation to the world. It lacks only, but decisively, the eschatological orientation recovered since Hegel's time and the patristic retrieval of the patrological teaching that God's self-surpassing is not exhaustive of God, a metaphysical kenosis, but infinitely generative, revealing the *esse Deum dare*. Infinite generosity is the personal mystery of the Father, the unoriginated origin both *of* God and *for* the creation: *of* God for what is personally other as the Son and the Spirit; in creation *for* what is naturally as well as personally other, the world of physical persons emerging from natural evolution claimed by the Son and united by the Spirit for the coming of the Beloved Community.

How is it possible for God to experience time by undertaking something new to God without becoming subjected to time? Love "suffers all things, believes all things, hopes all things, endures all things" (1 Cor. 13:7) and ultimately, so the Christian faith trusts, triumphs over all things. "And I heard a loud voice from the throne saying, 'Behold, the dwelling of God is with men. He will dwell with them, and they shall be his people, and God himself will be with them; he will wipe away every tear from their eyes, and death shall be no more, neither shall there be mourning nor crying nor pain any more, for the former things have passed away.' And he who sat upon the throne said, 'Behold, I make all things new'" (Rev. 21:3-5). This, finally, is the divine decree.

As surely as this promise of the triumph of the God of love at the eschaton of history gives the existential and social sense of the Christian claim to truth, it therewith makes the problem of theodicy here and now in the travail of creation fallen under structures of malice and injustice all the more acute and acutely felt. Why evil at all? In order that it be overcome? What are we to make of this thought — the *felix culpa* — the "happy fault" of Adam by which so great a redemption was achieved in Christ as the New Adam? Patrick Riley, in his exemplary Leibniz study, fairly skewers Leibniz for drawing near to Malebranche in giving this classical theological interpretation of the economy of God. In Part 49 of the *Causa Dei*, the Latin appendix summarizing the argument that Leibniz had made in his *Theodicy*, Leibniz gave the appearance in history of the New Adam (hence, logically, also the antecedent divine permission of the old Adam) as the "sufficient reason for the real existence of the world: 'The strongest reason for the choice of the best series of events (namely our world) was Jesus Christ, God become man, who as a creature represents the highest degree of perfection.'" In reality, says Riley following Mark Larrimore, according to this logic (said to be borrowed from Malebranche), God "can have no motive to create a 'ruined' finite world" unless "the *débris* of that world is redeemed by the Crucifixion, by the 'blood sacrifice' of a 'perfect victim.'" No doubt as well, so Riley continues, the optimist Leibniz "wants to avoid blood, crosses and victims" in the *Theodicy* to "offer Christ as successful institutionalizer of the rational moral imperatives which underpin universal jurisprudence" and "the horrors of Golgotha do not advance that kind of reading."[126]

---

126. Riley, *Justice as Charity*, p. 115.

Howsoever muted the witness, Leibniz in fact wrote what he wrote (as none other than Karl Barth also recognized and appreciated).[127] But we can leave aside the peculiar matter of Leibniz's attempt at a *rational* theodicy, confused as it is in arguing philosophically what can only be argued theologically. Once again, what then of the *felix culpa?* Is it entailed in the divine decree as we have exposited it? Does it then entail, on the most generous reading, the reprobation of the few, say, Judas, for the sake of the many? That would provoke a morally conscientious objection to the Christian teaching that the goodness of the almighty Father is to be found in His self-surpassing gift of the Incarnate Son to redeem sinners, if that gift can only be given by fating Judas to play the villain in the drama.

The theodicy *of faith* derives from Paul's great meditation in Romans 8; it is not meant as a speculative reconciliation with the way things are and must be, as though the permission of evil were God's affirmative will that could be understood and justified as instrumental to the greater good of the cosmic system here and now. It is rather meant as praise of the God who outfoxes the enemy, as with Moses before Pharaoh, and makes good out of evil, as in raising the Crucified, thus as encouragement and consolation for the suffering righteous that live by the concrete faith here and now in God who promises forgiveness to sinners and life to the dying. Against the pretensions of rational or philosophical theodicy, Leszek Kolakowski was right in his study of Jansenism[128] to affirm that "God owes us nothing" (Luke 17:10), unless and until we are changed to know the Creator as the Father of our Lord Jesus by the gift of His own Spirit, thus as the One who surpasses Himself in freely giving all things in creation, yet once again in the very gifts of the Son and the Spirit. To be sure, just this is what we Euro-Americans no longer know. As Pascal saw about us, in Kolakowski's telling, "people have lost their ability to trust God and thereby to trust, to accept, and to absorb their own destiny."[129] That concretely is what it means to trust God in the patiency of faith: to receive one's destiny in time and space, tangled up as it is with one's own malice and injustice as well as that of others under anti-divine structures of malice and injustice, yet nevertheless the continuing creation of God, object of His redeeming love for its destined fulfillment. The theodicy of faith is not interested in speculatively justifying the existing world as God's will, but in justifying the sinner who justifies God in His judgment on the way to the best of all possible worlds. It is thus interested in reframing the problems of evil so that she who learns to trust again can *know* what must be borne, what must be resisted, and what may be overcome.

The God of the gospel is *internally* committed to the redemption and fulfillment

---

127. *PNT,* p. 97. In the interim Riley's case for Leibniz's deism has been profoundly complicated, if not overthrown by Antognazza, *Leibniz on the Trinity.*

128. Leszek Kolakowski, *God Owes Us Nothing: A Brief Remark on Pascal's Religion and on the Spirit of Jansenism* (Chicago: University of Chicago Press, 1998). Kolakowski attributes the transformation of Augustinianism into Jansenism to the intervening role played by Cartesianism, i.e., in the neo-Gnostic movement toward dualism (p. 86).

129. Kolakowski, *God Owes Us Nothing,* p. 186.

of *this* world, because the glory of this *real* God is *to become* in time that which His own infinite love decides, creatively imagines, and faithfully executes. In one of the most sophisticated early Christian theological reflections on the biblical account of the origin in the first chapter of Genesis, Basil admonished in his *Hexaemeron:* "Do not then imagine, O man! that the visible world is without a beginning; and because the celestial bodies move in a circular course, and it is difficult for our senses to define the point where the circle begins, do not believe that bodies impelled by a circular movement are, from their nature, without a beginning. . . . Although we are not sensible of it, [a circle] really begins at some point where the draughtsman has begun to draw it at a certain radius from the center. Thus seeing that figures which move in a circle always return upon themselves, without for a single instant interrupting the regularity of their course, do not vainly imagine to yourselves that the world has neither beginning nor end." Basil in this way challenged the cosmic supposition of the immanent eternal recurrence of the same, a notion derived from the regular cycles of nature and the circular motion of the heavens. Instead Basil assimilated these observed phenomena of the regularities of nature into the biblical world with its linear history of salvation, positing a beginning and an ending. Consequently, Basil immediately pointed to the eschatological goal promised in the act of origin: "For *the fashion of this world passeth away* and *Heaven and earth shall pass away.* The dogmas of the end, and of the renewing of the world, are announced beforehand in these short words put at the head of the inspired history: *In the beginning God made.* That which was begun in time is condemned to come to an end in time. If there has been a beginning do not doubt of the end."[130]

From its origin creation is eschatological; just this is the theodicy of faith, the way of life now that looks to the promised future. As stewards of the earth, believers live towards the eschaton of judgment. Their own personal identity through time consists finally in the word which God as Judge pronounces over them for their fidelity to His calling, and, as this judgment concerns their history *in and as the body,* the conviction entails that the natural world itself finally yields to the supervening order of grace by the resurrection of the dead and the redemption of our bodies.

The Greek philosophers, Basil concluded in the aforementioned passage, "have discovered all except . . . the fact that God is the Creator of the universe, and the just Judge who rewards all the actions of life according to their merit. They have not known how to raise themselves to the idea of the consummation of all things, the consequence of the doctrine of judgment, and to see that *the world must change if souls pass from this life to a new life.* In reality, as the nature of the present life presents an affinity to this world, so in the future life our souls will enjoy a lot conformable to their new condition. But they are so far from applying these truths, that they do but laugh when we announce to them the end of all things and the regeneration of the age."[131] Enduring this ridicule, the

130. *NPNF,* 8, pp. 52-53.
131. *NPNF,* 8, p. 53.

theodicy of faith points with Basil to the coming of the Beloved Community as the actual justification of God in His judgment of the living and the dead: *"There is a life after this life; and all that is not punished or repaid here will be punished and repaid there; for this life is nothing more than a precursor, or, rather, a beginning, of the life that is to come"* (Luther).[132] Precisely in this light of God the Father's self-determination to redeem and fulfill the creation by a just judgment of mercy, faith knows what evils are, how to bear them, resist them, and overcome them just because faith knows that God's fatherhood consists in "giving life to the dead and calling into existence the things that do not exist" (Rom. 4:17) — *creatio ex nihilo* that becomes eschatologically *creatio ex vetere* (out of the old).

The redemption of this earth on which the cross of Jesus stood, then, is not the outworking of its own immanent possibilities, which are in any case captivated by structures of malice to make a walled fortress against the reign of God, the *civitas terrena*. Its redemption rather comes as a prolepsis of its promised fulfillment, the in-breaking of its translation into the eternal life of God that already now frees from the guilt of sin by which we are captivated to empower new life in the filial, not servile obedience of faith. The risen Lord greets His cowering disciples with the claim of victory, "Peace to you!" and breathes on them His own Spirit, "As the Father has sent me, so I send you" ( John 20:21-22) into the mission to the nations. In this way, the divine decree of creation is newly articulated within history in the Great Commission (Matt. 28:19-20). As Adam is united with the Son by the gift of His own Spirit to live before the Father, the "problem of evil" is as well reframed by the theodicy of faith. The fault of Judas, in this light, was our willingness to know good and evil and so take destiny into our own hands. The conscience of God the Father respects this willing sinfulness of Adam and out of his betrayal of its calling gives the New and faithful Adam. It is not Adam's fault that is happy, but the New Adam's joyful exchange with him, taking on his betrayal to give His fidelity in its place. As the God who gives in this way His own Son is the Father who gives eternally, the one who conscientiously objects to this exchange does so eternally as well. That *need* not be the case, though it in fact may be.

## Problems of Evil[133]

In the light of resurrection grace, then, we have problem*s*, not *a* problem, with evil. The pastor engaged in the care of souls is engaged first of all in a process of

---

132. *Bondage of the Will*, p. 316, emphasis original.

133. The section was originally published as "Problems of Evil: For Julius Filo on his Sixtieth Birthday," in *V Službe Obnovy: Vedecký zborník vydaný pri príležitosti 60. Narodením Dr. h.c. prof. Th.Dr. Júliusa Fila* [*In the Service of Renewal: A Scholarly Collection Published on the Occasion of the 60th Birthday of Dr. Julius Filo*], ed. M. Jurík and J. Benka (Bratislava: Evanjelická bohoslovecká fakulta, Univerzita Komenského v Bratislave, 2010), pp. 65-74.

discernment. Evil is one word but not one thing, and the care extended to the suffering must accordingly be discerned. This is particularly true of Christian care, if Luther was right in his *theologia crucis* to teach us that what is evil to the natural person is good to the spiritual person, and vice versa. Luther's truth is especially pertinent today, where so many are in misery, or are makers of misery, just because of their seduction to the modern view of the sovereign self, with its practical imperative to regard every and any kind of suffering as a meaningless evil to be overcome. Over against this illusion of a life without a body, and the special miseries it causes for oneself and for others, Augustine, and a contemporary Augustinian, Diogenes Allen, help us to understand the problems, not problem, of evil. Such knowledge of evils is what makes practical theology theological: not chaplaincy to the modern self-understanding of the sovereign self, i.e., who tries to live *incurvatus in se* with a happy conscience, but as the promise and nurture of an alternative, an "ecstatic" self, i.e., the theological subject who lives by faith in God, love for others, and hope for the world to be redeemed and fulfilled, including one's own self.

What *Luther* meant by the theology of the cross is that God heals by first afflicting morally evil disputants whose egocentric unhappiness fueled by envy or greed drives them to rend the web of life in aggressive acts of expropriation *(amor concupiscentiae)*. The theologian of the cross "knows that it is sufficient if he suffers and is brought low by the cross in order to be annihilated all the more. It is this that Christ says in John 3[:7], 'You must be born anew.' To be born anew, one must consequently first die and then be raised up with the Son of Man. To die, I say, means to feel death at hand."[134] The death of the centered self and the birth of an ecstatic self by union in faith with the crucified but risen Jesus Christ — that is what Luther meant by the *theologia crucis.* The negatives of human experience are accordingly to be lived with and engaged because, taken from our hands and restored to God's, they become the "severe mercy" (Augustine) of "costly grace" (Bonhoeffer) that changes us in the aforementioned way.

There can be no doubt, however, that Luther's *theologia crucis* raises dangerous and sensitive questions of theodicy,[135] which theology cannot in turn refuse to consider.[136] The world in which the cross of Jesus stood is a world in which the One He called Father permits the natural evils of flood and famine no less than the moral evil of created wills actually contravening His own. In such a world,

134. *LW* 31, p. 55.

135. In criticism of this author, Daphne Hampson identified a "Lutheran" anthropology of the "breaking of the self," and calls it a "profoundly masculinist description" of the human relation to the divine. *Christian Contradictions: The Structures of Lutheran and Catholic Thought* (Cambridge: Cambridge University Press, 2001), pp. 239-40. But alas, in our liberated age how many women have become these "masculinist" sovereign selves? Indeed, what else did Simone de Beauvoir summon women to when she told them to abandon immanence for transcendence?

136. I deal with such objections, particularly from some Feminist theologians, in the conclusion of *LBC,* pp. 358-78, from which this paragraph is adapted.

affliction belongs to life, and from birth day to death day human beings can no more disown their pain than the bodies by which they experience it. The gospel never delivers us from natural evil and does not easily or cheaply deliver us from moral evil. Indeed, even to understand this much as a theologian of the cross is to have owned one's affliction in faith as the birth pangs of God's new humanity.[137] Such insights cannot be shared with the old Adam, who lives to repudiate them. *Theologia crucis* is wisdom for those who boast "in the cross of our Lord Jesus Christ, through which the world has been crucified to me and I to the world" (Gal. 6:14). For such, this present world-order is not ultimate, but passing away, and only so can it be redeemed at the eschaton of judgment and fulfilled as God's new creation.

Diogenes Allen, a Princeton philosopher of religion who has written on Leibniz,[138] is one contemporary thinker for whom theodicy as faith which justifies God in His judgment is key to the "postmodern" theological possibility.[139] The Incarnation of God in the Crucified Jesus calls into question the assumption that this present world-order is its final reality, to which even God is subject. Reminiscent of the fundamental pre-Kantian question posed by the alternatives of Spinoza and Leibniz,[140] Allen asks whether "this universe [is] ultimate or not." This, he argues, "is the real question"[141] that "cannot be settled scientifically or philosophically,"[142] because this "controversy is between a theological view and a rival theological view, that is, between saying, 'God is the reason we have a universe' and saying, 'The universe just is.' "[143] Both views, Allen argues, are metaphysical in the broad sense of speaking to ultimate matters of interpretation, how to take the cosmos as a whole. Moreover, one of these two basic views is inevitably adopted by every human person, insofar as she is a purposive agent who must live a historical life, seeking to realize goals and fulfill duties in the physical reality of the common body. Living historically in the world, the question of whether it is to be taken as ultimate is inescapable. It is the question of responsibility, whether to the world (but then, for whom?) or for the world (but then, to whom?). Moreover, the kinds of goals we adopt, and the priorities we assign when conflicts arise among various goods in face of physical necessities and moral duties, are decided by this basic epistemic choice, certainly if we are following the Jews Jesus and Paul.[144]

---

137. Is that a "masculinist image" of the human relation to the divine?

138. Diogenes Allen, "The Theological Relevance of Leibniz's Theodicy," *Studia Leibnitiana. Supplementa* 14 (1972).

139. Diogenes Allen, *Christian Belief in a Postmodern World: The Full Wealth of Conviction* (Louisville: Westminster John Knox, 1989).

140. Matthew Stewart, *The Courtier and the Heretic: Leibniz, Spinoza, and the Fate of God in the Modern World* (New York and London: W. W. Norton, 2006).

141. Allen, *Christian Belief,* p. 67.

142. Allen, *Christian Belief,* p. 154.

143. Allen, *Christian Belief,* p. 82.

144. See Luke 14:11-15. "If the dead do not rise, 'Let us eat, drink and be merry, for tomor-

According to Allen, this is a question that contemporary science itself is coming to pose. The discoveries of contemporary physics have sealed the fate of modern rationalism by uncovering the radical contingency of all that exists. This discovery that "it might have been otherwise" — that even the uniformity of nature (as we know it) was contingently organized in an apparently improbable way that could lead to the evolution of life during the first nanoseconds of the Big Bang — underscores the "postmodern situation" of thought characterized by a loss of the "modern" confidence in the "power of reason alone," which had, as in Spinoza,[145] based itself upon the presumed timelessly rational necessity of all things. Allen points to four breakdowns in this confidence.

First, there is the emergence of scientific cosmology which "actually points toward God" as an answer to the questions, "Why does the universe have this particular form (which led to the evolution of humanity) instead of some other? Why does the universe exist at all?"[146] Second, there is the failure of the Enlightenment to find a rational basis for morality in social life that is not parasitic upon the Judeo-Christian legacy.[147] Third, there is the collapse, after Hitler, Hiroshima, and Stalin, of the rationalistic faith in inevitable progress with the renewed perception of moral evil as a deeply rooted and powerful force that cannot be overcome merely by education.[148] Fourth, the idea that knowledge is inherently good has become questionable. When we consider the new technological possibilities for mass destruction that the growth of knowledge facilitates, confidence evaporates in the proposition that all knowledge is beneficial and that all change is for the good.[149] All these "breakdowns" of rationalism make for a "postmodern" situation that provides Christian theology with a tremendous opportunity, provided that it faces the challenge to warrant its faith rationally, i.e., not to demonstrate faith, but rather to make faith intelligible as an response to the promissory narrative of God in Christ as interpretation of contemporary experience.[150] In that case,

---

row we die'" (1 Cor. 15:32b). But if the dead do rise, "Be steadfast, immovable, always abounding in the work of the Lord, knowing that your labor is not vain in the Lord" (1 Cor. 15:58).

145. Jonathan I. Israel, *Radical Enlightenment: Philosophy and the Making of Modernity 1650-1750* (Oxford: Oxford University Press, 2001).

146. "The question remains, however: how or why were the laws and the initial state of the universe chosen?" Stephen Hawking with Leonard Mlodinow, *A Briefer History of Time* (New York: Bantam Dell, 2005), p. 140.

147. In corroboration, see Alasdair MacIntyre, *After Virtue: A Study in Moral Theory,* 2nd edition (Notre Dame: University of Notre Dame Press, 1984), p. 51. Now — surprisingly — further corroborated by Jürgen Habermas, *Time of Transitions,* trans. Ciaran Cronin and Max Pensky (Cambridge, UK and Malden, MA: Polity, 2008), pp. 140-69.

148. In corroboration, see Reinhold Niebuhr, *Moral Man and Immoral Society: A Study in Ethics and Politics* (New York: Charles Scribner's Sons, 1960).

149. In corroboration, see Martin Heidegger, *The Question concerning Technology and Other Essays,* trans. William Lovitt (New York: Harper & Row, 1977).

150. Ronald Thiemann, *Revelation and Theology: The Gospel as Narrated Promise* (South Bend, IN: University of Notre Dame Press, 1987).

theology shows how Christian faith "makes sense" provisionally of the whole cosmic story by telling of the justice of God which justifies the ungodly, that is, as theodicy of faith.

When Allen argues that the fundamental question is whether this world is ultimate, then, he is not (*pace* Nietzsche) denigrating this world as inferior or bad any more than when Luther contests secularism to speak of this world as precursor to the life to come. That would be to interpret them as (bad) Platonists,[151] or rather as Gnostics, not as Paulinists and Augustinians. Allen's purpose is quite the contrary. He wants to affirm the world, but the world as it really is: as becoming not being, as fragile and contingent, as a precious and passing state that had a beginning and will have an end, as a natural order that operates lawfully, bound by physical possibilities, in which humanity has emerged and will someday disappear. He does not want to proffer a false, rosy picture of the world as a "steady state," secure and permanent, populated with substantial agents without internal relations to others and free to act on their own sovereignty projects, which we may then take for granted, as if it all existed for the sake of this massively inordinate egoism and we had license to use and consume all for wholly immediate and selfish ends — the next generation be damned. He wants to expose the crypto-theologies of naturalism and secularism, which affirm this world as if it were a god.

Allen accordingly does not want to obscure the necessity with which the laws of nature both bless and afflict us.[152] He insists that we take the world as it really is, where the vast universe that modern science has discovered does not exist just for human beings, where a single asteroid colliding with earth could end humanity's existence in the twinkling of an eye in an uncannily literal fulfillment of Jesus' talk about the end of the world (cf. Mark 13:24-27). Existentially it is the age-old human question of "meaningless" suffering inflicted by the happenstance of natural evils; just this raises acutely the question of whether this natural-world order is the ultimate reality.[153] If there is an answer to the question, stuttered from the lips of the afflicted, if there is a "purpose, and not just a cause [of 'meaningless' suffering], this purpose must reside outside the universe"[154] — in what we have delineated as the divine decree. As in Augustine, natural evils in this way point to the Creator God, whose work is nature but whose purposes just so transcend

151. Ancient Platonism set itself against the Gnostic devaluing of this visible world of becoming. That is evident in the pagan critic Celsus, to whom Origen eventually responded. See Celsus, *On the True Doctrine: A Discourse against the Christians,* trans. R. J. Hoffmann (New York and Oxford: Oxford University Press, 1987). Closer to Augustine, see Margaret R. Miles, *Plotinus on Body and Beauty: Society, Philosophy, and Religion in Third Century Rome* (Oxford: Blackwell, 1999).

152. So Ned Wisnefske, *Preparing to Hear the Gospel: A Proposal for Natural Theology* (Lanham, MD: University Press of America, 1998).

153. Allen, *Christian Belief,* p. 92.

154. Allen, *Christian Belief,* p. 93.

His instrument as His free and conscientious decision to become the God of grace for humanity.

To understand this perhaps surprising[155] theological argument for the "indifference of nature" (but note Jesus' statement in Matt. 5:45), one must recall the background of the question in modern philosophy and theology. David Hume devastated the so-called cosmological proof for the existence of the Cosmic Engineer, on which so many Enlightenment-era theologians of Deism (heirs of Plato's *Timaeus*) tried to build their theological systems. Hume pointed out that even if we grant that some Cosmic Engineer designed the world, "we cannot infer that the alleged designer of nature is either purely benevolently or purely malevolently disposed" toward humanity. The existence of so many natural evils alongside natural blessings prevents either inference. The more likely inference is that nature's "alleged designer is unconcerned with or indifferent" to human welfare (as Cicero's Cotta skeptically concluded in *On the Nature of the Gods*). This inference of course constitutes "an insuperable barrier to a rational belief in the goodness of God."[156] Allen embraces Hume's argument. It exposes the false theological premise of Deism's natural theology. The God of the Bible is not at all adequately represented in the figure of the Cosmic Engineer — this idea is nothing but a personification of the mechanism of the natural order, which anthropomorphically lends to the mechanism a teleological cast. But natural mechanism, taken as it is and unfigured, betrays no moral purpose and indeed operates indifferently to humanity's moral purposes. By the same token, the goodness of the biblical God is not demonstrated by anything less than the grant of eternal life — life in God, with God, before God — to a created nature which is inherently or naturally mortal. The equation of the biblical God and the Cosmic Engineer falsely robs the former of the moral purpose of the Beloved Community for which the world is created, according to the divine decree revealed in Christ (Eph. 3:9), and by which measure divine goodness is to be assessed — essential, not accidental markers of this God's identity as the God who is capable of His creature. On the other hand, it can be rightly said that the Nazi death factories were "intelligently designed."

Thus Allen insists upon the "bitter truth" that Hume uncovered in his refutation of the proof of Deism's God from the design of the world: ". . . to come to terms with our vulnerability to [indifferent] nature is to come to terms with the

155. It might be objected, in the words of Jonathan Sorum (personal correspondence, 8/9/09), that "the church has traditionally taught that pain, sickness, and death are a consequence of human sin (i.e., the curses in Genesis 3). I certainly cannot look on death, even in faith (especially in faith) as a 'natural part of life.' It is not wrong to hate death as the negation of all God's goals for us. Jesus himself hated death and even feared it. Can natural evil be justified because it supposedly teaches us to live by faith? I wouldn't try that on any of my parishioners. All of this applies to . . . Allen's apologetic." But contemporary biological science *constrains,* as we argued above, the theological interpretation of death and pain as consequences of sin. I take Allen's argument, not as "apologetics" but in service to critical dogmatics.

156. Allen, *Christian Belief,* p. 112.

truth about ourselves: we are natural beings and, like all natural beings, we are mortal and vulnerable to disease, accidents, and natural catastrophes."[157] We thus encounter once again the same difficult but crucial distinction between natural evil and moral evil, i.e., the ontological vulnerability as such of all created beings as temporal-spatial ensouled bodies in relation to other forces and persons in time and space. Here we are endemically exposed to whirlwind as to the existential aggression human creatures undertake as souls or moral agents to secure their threatened existence at the expense of others. No genuine creature can be conceived apart from such intrinsic bodily and psychological vulnerability — the "evil" that is "natural" to anything that has come into being. Indeed, its unique, creaturely freedom as moral patient-and-agent lies precisely in how it responds to its intrinsic vulnerabilities in the changes and chances of its own unique life. Natural evil, we can say following Leibniz, provides the possibility of, but does not necessitate, moral evil.

In this light, the true force of Allen's basic question, "Is *this* world ultimate?," becomes apparent. "Only when we face the fact that nature operates by regular laws, that it is indifferent to our welfare and causes both good and evil, and allow it to break our egocentric and anthropocentric perspective, can we even conceive of One whose goodness is beyond" natural evils and natural blessings[158] — in the way that the resurrection of the Crucified by God surpassing God is "beyond" the continuities and regularities of nature. Only when we are shocked into awareness that this world and we in it are not ultimate do we realize that the good "which God seeks to give us is the good which is God himself."[159] This leads Allen to the (perhaps too sweeping) claim that the "indifference of nature" is ordered by God to lead us to God. Better put: if nature's blessings have not led us, as they ought, to lives of joyful praise and thankful service (as per Luther's explanation of the First Article), its afflictions shock us into awareness of our own fragility and need. As the idols crumble, we may be led to seek our true good, not in any other creature, but in the Creator alone. But we may also be led to a not-salutary despair.

When we are opened by the experience of suffering to this truth about ourselves, we may at last apprehend the "good of the cross," the strange salvation which the Christian gospel offers in telling of the obedience of Jesus in faith towards His heavenly Father. Otherwise "we are inclined to think that because Christ suffered for us, we do not have to." But "the good which God would do to us is not available apart from suffering, but is achieved precisely in and through suffering. Much of our suffering is useless. It springs from our egocentric and anthropocentric illusions and our acts of injustice." But the suffering of the Incarnate Son of God, who takes the violence of human greed, envy, and deception upon Himself rather than perpetuate it in returning evil to the evil, forces us to

157. Allen, *Christian Belief,* p. 113.
158. Allen, *Christian Belief,* p. 114.
159. Allen, *Christian Belief,* p. 115.

learn — not merely intellectually — the distinction between natural and moral evil. He who was under no necessity to suffer naturally took upon Himself the creature's condition of suffering. He who had the authority to destroy evildoers rather endured their evildoing that even they might be pardoned. In encounter with this Jesus Christ we learn the difference between "the suffering which results from egocentrism, anthropocentrism, and our own injustices, and that suffering which is the inevitable result of being a creature and a victim of injustice."[160] This penitential learning about the natures of evil is the good of the cross. The good of the cross is not that the sinner escapes, but that the sinner dies; not that the victim avenges, but that the victim is vindicated. The good of the cross is that dying with Jesus, "we can truthfully say [that we are just], if we are loved by one who loves us in spite of our failure to be just. This love enables us to speak truthfully about ourselves because it is the love of one who is wholly just, who innocently suffers the consequences of other people's injustices, and who as the creative Word of God has the power and authority to identify itself with every victim of injustice and, as the one who suffers at our hands, grants us absolution for our evil. In our self-evaluation we may truly believe that we are filth because we believe that we can be changed and in fact are being changed."[161]

This is the theodicy of faith, which justifies God in His judgment, where God's judgment is taken as "a saving revelation, that is, [which] shows and mediates a path to righteousness. . . . Jesus Christ reveals the full depths of God's saving mercy since it is the actual endurance of suffering which is the cost of God's mercy toward human unrighteousness, a suffering which is borne by very God."[162] But, Allen concludes, "the problem is: do Christians who address others about God so understand the cross themselves?"[163] Allen's rhetorical question formulates the practical problem of Christian theology, taken both as critical dogmatics and as a pastoral theology within the life of the pilgrim church. So also the young Luther, drawing upon Augustine's *Confessions* and his treatise *On the Spirit and the Letter:* "This is the [true] people of God: it constantly brings to bear the judgment of the cross upon itself."[164] The just live by this faith that justifies God in His judgment in this world, in the structures of creation, in the workaday Galilee to which the risen Christ summons Peter and the disciples (Mark 16:7) as to the proper place of their discipleship and of the priesthood of all believers. This must be the place of meeting the crucified and risen Lord, and by His Spirit the discernment of evils, if creation is to be in fact the object of the Father's redeeming and fulfilling love.

160. Allen, *Christian Belief,* pp. 118-19.
161. Allen, *Christian Belief,* p. 109.
162. Allen, *Christian Belief,* p. 208.
163. Allen, *Christian Belief,* p. 196.
164. *Luther: Lectures on Romans,* trans. Wilhelm Pauck (Philadelphia: Westminster, 1961), p. 120. I insert the word "true" because in context Luther is distinguishing "the new people, the believing people, the spiritual people" from the false and hypocritical.

## Structures for Justice and Love

The repeated divine command of Genesis 1, "Let there be . . ." (Gen. 1:3, 6, 9, 11, 14, 20, 24, 26) is to be understood as *mandating* certain lines of continuous development for the world culminating in humanity, and then through humanity in anticipation of the Beloved Community. Careful study of the chapter reveals considerable ancient science at work in thinking about the evolution of life. Of course, this is not Darwinian evolution in any modern sense. But neither are the seven "days" of creation "days" in any ordinary sense (the earth's sun, by which a day was calculated even then, is not created until the fourth day). A genuine sense of the ecological interdependence of life, of the continuity of humanity with the rest of animate and inanimate creation, and of cumulative complexity in organization evolving step by step over time is provided by the scheme of the seven "days." The divine ordering, however, is governed not by inherent natural powers but by the wise arrangement of natural powers by the Creator's command and blessing. The wisdom of the Word by which God speaks with almighty power to create what is good reflects Israel's conviction about *who* God is. This is above all evident in the recognition of the status of humanity in the creation as God's royal image, i.e., the partnered couple of male and female (*pace* Paul's ad hoc and reckless argument in 1 Cor. 11:7) are given the mandate as God's kingly representative in the care of the earth.

This gift and task assigned to humanity in Israel's "hope projected backwards" derives from the knowledge of God who had chosen and rescued Hebrew slaves and made them partners in covenant to build a new society in the Promised Land. In Israel, *pars pro toto,* humanity therefore will be blessed in making and keeping the earth a paradise fit for the flourishing of human life, as the Creator expressly declares at the conclusion of each of the days of creation and in sum at the climax: "Then God said, 'Let us make humankind in our image, according to our likeness; and let them have dominion over the fish of the sea, and over the birds of the air, and over the cattle, and over all the wild animals of the earth, and over every creeping thing that creeps upon the earth.' So God created humankind in his image, in the image of God he created them; male and female he created them. God blessed them, and God said to them, 'Be fruitful and multiply, and fill the earth and subdue it; and have dominion over the fish of the sea and over the birds of the air and over every living thing that moves upon the earth'" (Gen. 1:26-28). This passage is the *Haupttext* of theological anthropology, when we interpret the notions of image and likeness in accord with the commandment and blessing given with it and then relate this gift and task to Jesus Christ, the new Adam, the *eikon tou theou* (2 Cor. 4:4; Col. 1:15).

In this command-and-promise, humanity finds its vocation to rule the earth in love and justly to tame the wilderness, to marry and multiply, and to worship God in thanksgiving; these three are the formative tasks of human social development, what Bonhoeffer called the creative mandates of God. In this development, they are conscientiously to structure love to justice by institutionalizing creative labor, marriage and family, and public worship, constructing society on earth in anticipation of the promised kingdom of God in the eschatological fulfillment. Christian theology, especially in Luther's tradition, on this basis has traditionally spoken of labor, family, and church as "estates," "orders," or "arenas of responsibility" mandated by God in the very act of the creation and calling of His human partner. It has implicitly therewith taken creation not as the given, set stage fixed at the origin but rather as the ever-new gift and ever-new task of the *creatio continua.* These ever-renewed structures are given and enacted to provide for the co-humanity by means of which humanity socially collaborates with the Creator, that life in harmony with nature, between humans, and before God may flourish. Of these various and contested terms, Bonhoeffer's "mandate" is to be exegetically preferred, in that it derives from the divine *fiat* ("Let there be!") and accentuates the temporally extended task therewith laid upon the creature; Robert Benne's "places of responsibility" captures the spatial dimension of social life together in the common body in sexual, economic, and religious arenas as the places of conscientious care and accountability under the mandates.[165]

*Mandatum Dei* and arenas of responsibility are complementary conceptions that avoid the static connotations of fixed "estates" or "orders," as if the point of the doctrine were to define social existence in a rigidly fixed way so that any development seems like a fall away from origin or to segregate life into compartments rather than to provide for social integration on the way to the Beloved Community of God. For, clearly, exploited workers make poor spouses and parents, and poor parents raise children less capable of creative labor, and poverty disorganizes the worship of God and makes worship life vulnerable to the hucksters of the religion business. But if we take creation as *creatio continua,* the mandates institute certain directions for integrated social development and summon human cooperation in these tasks for the obedience of faith. "We speak of divine mandates rather than divine orders because the word mandate refers more clearly to a divinely imposed task rather than to a determination of being. . . . This means that there can be no retreating from a 'secular' into a 'spiritual' sphere. There can be only the practice, the learning, of the Christian life under these four mandates of God." The discrepancy between Bonhoeffer's mention of *four* mandates and the *three* that are listed above will be clarified shortly.[166]

The *static* notion of the "orders of creation" in fact was deployed as a reactionary ideological defense against progressive social change in nineteenth-century Germany. But even worse, it was redeveloped *dynamically and progressively*

---

165. Robert Benne, *Ordinary Saints: An Introduction to Christian Life* (Minneapolis: Fortress, 2003), pp. 63-79; 131-223. See further *LBC,* pp. 331-54.

166. Dietrich Bonhoeffer, *Ethics,* ed. E. Bethge (New York: Macmillan, 1978), p. 207. Bonhoeffer includes government, i.e., the state, which for reasons given below I separate from the three creative tasks of labor, family, and worship.

during the church struggle in Nazi Germany by significant "mediating" theologians like Paul Althaus,[167] who took "race" (German: *das Volk*, "the people," conceived here as an ethnic-racial group) as a newly disclosed order of creation discovered by allegedly "scientific" anthropology for our intentional cultivation and development. Race, it was claimed, evolved according to God's providential purposes and now imposed the ethical responsibility upon people and state for preserving biological health and purity. Evolution was now to be taken responsibly into the People's own hands. Christians too had a conscientious duty to *Volk* in the competition for *Lebensraum* with other races on the shrinking planet. Aside from the utter lack of exegetical standing for this claim to a racial interpretation of the orders of creation, and the theologically violent severance of it from the Christological-baptismal unification of the nations in the ecclesia,[168] the Nazified rendering of the "orders" obscured and rendered suspect the fundamental correctness of the Reformation teaching about the social nature of the image of God doctrine. But in the act of origin God intends community in the manifold, mutually delimiting forms of marriage, labor, and worship in anticipation of His own eschatological fulfillment of creation in the Beloved Community.

Christian theology takes the existence of this material world, now under the fateful and possibly fatal dominion of the troubled being that is humanity, as the decision of the Father's free and loving valuation of "ensouled matter." This is the Father's will for fellowship with the common body of humanity by exercising a shared dominion, a partnership, so ordered in wisdom by God the Word for justice and unified by God the Spirit in love. As such the created world of human society is neither necessary nor arbitrary, but exhibits contingently created forms of social life corresponding to (or more dynamically, "imaging") God's triune life in its missiological actions. In human obedience, where and when the image becomes like God, these social relations become true formations of love in structures of justice in the historical development of nature that is humanity in its history with God.

Labor reflects the mission of God the Father in creating a world; marriage reflects the mission of God the Son to redeem the creation by the joyful exchange

---

167. As Nathan Yoder has recently shown, moreover, it was precisely the progressive and social orientation of the Reformation doctrine of the "three estates" that made plausible Althaus's development of the doctrine to keep current with the latest, allegedly scientific insights into anthropology, a point I have labored to make intelligible in *BA*, pp. 21-25. See Nathan Howard Yoder, "*Ordnung in Gemeinschaft:* A Critical Appraisal of the Erlangen Contribution to the Orders of Creation" (Ph.D. Dissertation, Regensburg, 2011).

168. Prior to these developments, Heinrich Schmid's *Doctrinal Theology of the Evangelical Lutheran Church,* 3rd edition (Philadelphia: Lutheran Publication Society, 1899) does not speak of the orders *of creation* but of the "Three Estates in the Church," indicating the status of the doctrine as serving the *redemption* of the creation, not *the preservation of the fallen world* (pp. 604-5). Steven Ozment, *When Fathers Ruled: Family Life in Reformation Europe* (Cambridge, MA: Harvard University Press, 1983), has poignantly argued for this kind of orientation.

between Christ and His bride, the ecclesia gathered from the nations for service in the nations; public worship reflects the mission of God the Spirit to bring the redeemed creation to fulfillment in the eternal praise of the Father by union with the Son. Perhaps better: these forms of human social life *can* reflect, or image, God's Trinitarian acts and participate in God's missiological agencies. They can also be perverted into structures of malice and injustice; the image that the basic social relations of humanity in labor, marriage, and worship in fact are can be filled with idols and demons, not like the one true God. Though likeness may come about incognito by the hidden reign of the exalted Christ, it is only by the redemption won in His incarnation that these created forms of life are rightly recognized. Reordered in the Spirit and integrated together, they are reattached to the Head, as dimensions of Christ's body in the world, and thus reconciled to the Father's will for fellowship in the coming of the Beloved Community. A difficult task of scrutiny and discernment is thereby laid upon theological ethics, the criteria for which, however, systematic theology lays out in this teaching of actual creation as the continuous social formation of humanity by the mandates of labor, marriage, and worship as ordered to and by Christ for the coming of the Beloved Community.

The image of God grows to maturity in Christ by way of these forms of sociality: "It is God's will that there shall be labor, marriage, government and church in the world; and it is His will that all these, each in its own way, shall be through Christ, directed towards Christ, and in Christ."[169] Bonhoeffer provided Christological content in this way to the doctrine of creation's mandates in order to provide the "likeness" to God with which the "image" is to be filled, i.e., to provide the Christological norm for ethical direction in genuinely "progressive" social change. Christ as Lord also over the creative mandates empowers social obedience without the terrible costs (unfolding all around Bonhoeffer) of utopian illusions on the one side or cynicism and despair on the other. In this, Bonhoeffer was following what he found in his Luther-studies: ". . . this image of the new creature begins to be restored by the Gospel in this life, but it will not be finished in this life. But when it is finished in the kingdom of the Father, then the will will be truly free and good, the mind truly enlightened, and the memory persistent . . . the godly have within themselves that unfinished image of God which God will on the Last Day bring to perfection in those who have believed his Word."[170] The mandates for humanity created in the image of God are conscientious tasks for the redeemed in Christ to acquire likeness to God, even as the status of image remains gift and thus an alien dignity without regard to the performance.

Thus the mandates sign human dignity in the social dimensions of existence — the dignity of work, of marriage, of worship — that does not yet correspond to the reality they anticipate as a task. This is the counterfactual truth captured in the

---

169. Bonhoeffer, *Ethics,* p. 207.
170. *LW* 1, p. 65.

modern tradition of liberalism, that all are equally valued because each one is, as Jefferson wrote in the Declaration, "created equal and endowed by their Creator with certain, inalienable rights; that among these are life, liberty and the pursuit of happiness." Yet this right conferred and awarded as an alien dignity by the Creator is also *mandatum Dei,* thus the gift of a task to be responsibly undertaken in full awareness that it can only be completed by God at the eschaton of judgment.

As mentioned, this social intention of the original Reformation teaching on the "orders of creation" has largely been lost from memory in Protestant history, eclipsed by the dark new sociology of Hobbes and his followers on the one side and by the theological individualism and optimism of Protestant liberalism on the other. John Witte Jr. in his superb study[171] of the Reformation social teaching from the perspective of the history of jurisprudence argues that the truly innovative thing that occurred under the impact of the Reformation teaching of the three estates (in his rendering: church, family, *and state*) was the new theological legitimation given to the temporal authority of the state and the specific reforms in civil law, political theory, and judicial practice this produced. This argument is important and insightful, particularly in showing how the early modern state could be conceived in republican, rather than absolutist and monarchical ways, in analogy to the Trinitarian Fatherhood of God rather than the *Deus exlex* of nominalist metaphysics. Yet a criticism of Witte is indicated by the preceding omission of the state from the list of the structures of creation in favor of labor, that is to say, that human beings govern the earth in created likeness to God not by political sovereignty but by creative labor, as close reading of the Genesis text shows. In historical fact Witte takes from Melanchthon and his students (rather than Luther) the notion that the state is a positive and creative order that exists in analogy to the Fatherhood of God. This development, as we shall see, is highly problematic.

What were the reforms in the understanding of state and law? In short, the Ten Commandments provided the divinely clarified teaching of the natural law inscribed by God on creation (Rom. 2:15) and for this reason replaced the sacramental system, codified in canon law, as an overarching moral framework for the organization of civil law. This was possible because the Decalogue in fact presents a moral sociology governing worship, family, and labor relations in what we call today "civil society." In political theory, the papacy's claim to hold the two keys of church and state was thus replaced by the new doctrine of the Protestant magistrate, who not only held the sword as God's "lofty viceroy" on earth, but was to represent God's paternal care for His children in works of public welfare (the community chest and public education particularly). In judicial practice, the rule of law was strengthened, not subverted, by the further development of the theory of equity under God the Father creator of all, which encouraged both new schol-

---

171. John Witte Jr., *Law and Protestantism: The Legal Teachings of the Lutheran Reformation,* with a Foreword by Martin E. Marty (Cambridge: Cambridge University Press, 2002).

arly research in law and a definite judicial activism. Equity — the rational capacity to put oneself in the place of another, according to the Golden Rule — provided a meta-rule for applying written rules; it formed the conscience of rulers in their official duties before God the Father, indeed as analogues of God the Father.

Witte's detailed case goes a long way toward reframing Troeltsch's tendentious judgment that the Lutheran reformation "simply continued the medieval conditions," was "no watershed in the Western tradition, and certainly not the font of modernity," but only gave "new solutions to medieval problems."[172] The new legitimacy accorded to temporal power was generative of progressive political thought and reform — something that can be seen at length in Leibniz's politics of "justice as the charity of the wise." Witte assigns that new legitimacy given to the state in the Reformation to Luther's two kingdoms doctrine, which he keenly characterizes as a horizontalizing of the traditional, vertically imagined notion of a "great chain of being." God is not to be depicted remotely at the pinnacle, whose governance is then mediated by natural hierarchies of descending links in the great chain so that creatures "participate" in God's works by the analogy of being. Rather Luther's God, the continuous Creator of all that is other, is for that very reason immediately present to all levels as Potter to the clay, or better,

---

172. Witte, *Law and Protestantism,* pp. 23-26. Witte sees the origins of modern republicanism in a student of Melanchthon's, Johannes Eisermann (1485-1558), whose 1533 tract *On the Common Good,* later expanded and retitled *On the Good Ordering of a Commonwealth,* was "the first detailed social contract theory of the Christian commonwealth to emerge in Evangelical Germany" (p. 153). Eisermann was concerned "to construct a theory of the common good out of a theology of total depravity." In Eisermann's view, "the state of nature began as a perfect realm of Paradise . . ." (p. 143). "They were by their natures 'civil and communal.' They lived in perfect communion with God and perfect community with each other. . . . In the perfect state of nature in Paradise, human life had been lovely and long. In the sinful state of nature after the Fall, human life had become 'brutish' and 'short' *(ferus et brevis).* Despite the fall into sin, however, God has allowed all people to retain a glimmer of those 'inborn sparks' of honesty, virtue, and community with which they were created: an innate knowledge of a natural law of love of God, neighbor, and self, and a natural sense of equity by which these laws must be applied. . . . They could quickly be extinguished and forgotten through depraved and debased living. But they could also be ignited to give greater light if they were subject to 'careful study.' Throughout history, Eisermann argued, 'God has always lifted up wise men,' who have undertaken such 'careful study' of these 'inborn sparks' of natural law. . . . Egyptians, Greeks, Romans and other ancient peoples of the West all saw that 'man is by nature sociable and aspires to society and community of life, in order to curb vice and embrace virtue, to help others, and to find a way to help himself and his community.' Accordingly, each of these ancient peoples has formed a 'covenant of human society *(foedus humanae societatis)* . . .'" (p. 144). "A commitment to the rule of law was the most essential provision of all these early social covenants" (p. 145). According to Witte, Eisermann drew three conclusions for the construction of the new Christian republic: (1) "Christians have no monopoly on the understanding of natural law and natural reason," (2) "there is no single foreordained or natural system of society, politics, and law . . . ," and (3) "there is no single person — far less a single dynasty — in a commonwealth that should naturally rule" (p. 146).

presently impelling organizations of being in the various "masks" He adopts and by which He moves creation onward to His own goal. The two kingdoms, then, are not two parallel magnitudes of heavenly and earthly things stacked one upon another in a vertical series. Rather the kingship of God the Creator manifests its *temporal* rule in the earthly masks of three co-equal estates established at the creation: the domestic economy, the church, and the state (as Witte renders them). Before God these three estates are equal, just as they are autonomous in relation to each other. Each has its own specific mandate, which collaborates with the others for earthly and heavenly welfare. In this view, temporal power is not chiefly the state, nor is it chiefly characterized by possession of the sword. Rather all three estates comprise the *temporal* kingdom and mutually limit each other to preserve the creation, while God's *eternal* kingdom is at work through the gospel of redemption. Witte can use this horizontal rendering of the two kingdoms scheme to describe legal reforms affecting not only the church, consequently, but also public morality, marriage, education, and poor relief.[173]

Witte is well aware of the problem his scholarship uncovers here in linking church and family with the state as orders of creation to the neglect of labor. On the positive side, he can conclude that "a good deal of our modern Western law of marriage, education, and social welfare, for example, still bears the unmistakable marks of Lutheran Reformation theology."[174] He emphasizes that ". . . the state has a role to play not only in fighting wars, punishing crime, and keeping peace, but also in providing education and welfare, fostering charity and morality, fa-

---

173. There is a very dark side to this fusion of state paternalism with the monopoly on the means of coercion. The ancient commonwealths were, in the view of Melanchthon and Eisermann, "incomplete. They can speak only to a 'civil goodness,' not to a 'spiritual goodness.' . . . For none of these classical civilizations had the full biblical revelation of the heavenly kingdom on which the earthly kingdom must be partly modeled" (Witte, *Law and Protestantism,* p. 147). "For Eisermann, this meant that the law of the prince must coerce citizens to a 'civil goodness,' and also cultivate in them a 'spiritual goodness'" (p. 151). Eisermann was following his teacher, Melanchthon, who "went beyond Luther . . . in articulating the divinely imposed task of Christian magistrates to promulgate what he called 'rational positive laws' *(rationes iuris positivi)* for the governance of the earthly kingdom" (p. 129). Melanchthon regarded the Christian magistrate as "the 'custodian' of both tables of the Decalogue, 'a voice of the Ten Commandments' within the earthly kingdom . . . magistrates must pass laws against idolatry, blasphemy, and violations of the Sabbath — offenses that the First Table prohibits on its face. Magistrates are also, however, to pass laws to 'establish pure doctrine' and right liturgy, 'to prohibit all wrong doctrine,' 'to punish the obstinate,' and to root out the heathen and the heterodox" (p. 131). Witte rightly notes that "Melanchthon's move toward the establishment of religion by positive law was a marked departure from Luther's original teaching . . ." (p. 131). The *cuius regio, eius religio* principle of the Leipzig Interim, and at length "the Peace of Westphalia (1648), rested ultimately on Melanchthon's theory that the magistrate's positive law was to use the First Table of the Decalogue to establish for his people proper Christian doctrine, liturgy, and spiritual morality" (p. 132).

174. Witte, *Law and Protestantism,* p. 295.

cilitating worship and piety . . . law has not only a basic use of coercing citizens to accept a morality of duty but also a higher use of inducing citizens to pursue a morality of aspiration."[175] But, on the negative side, he notes that ever since the Reformation times "Germany and other Protestant nations have been locked in a bitter legal struggle to eradicate state establishments of religion and to guarantee religious freedom for all. . . ." In the end, Witte appreciates "an instinct for egalitarianism" rooted in the Reformation view of the equal value of all persons before God the heavenly Father as grounded theologically in the baptismal "priesthood of all believers." This is "the Lutheran gene in the theological genetic code of Protestantism,"[176] an emphasis that links together rights and duties, gospel and law in Christian republicanism.

A problem with Witte's account, however, is that Luther does not regard the state, that is, political sovereignty, as a co-equal structure of love and justice along with family and religion. In principle, the state is a coercive order that cannot be a structure of love working justice, though love and justice may and must make use of it in a fallen world where love must be against what is against love. So Luther and decisively: "There was no state before there was sin, since it was not yet necessary. The state is the necessary means for dealing with the depraved condition of nature."[177] The rendering of social ethics Witte gives therefore cannot but founder on the problem of freedom of conscience: as a version of Christendom, the renewed political order of Reformation Germany (undertaken, as Witte's source material actually betrays, after Luther's death by Melanchthon and his students) could tolerate much in the way of vice, but it could not tolerate conscientious dissent in religion, as Anabaptists and Jews quickly learned and as Muslims experience today. The truth is that the early Luther well understood that justifying faith in principle cannot be coerced as inevitably the attempt is made when Christianity is privileged by the support of the state. The failure of the Reformation to reform the ecclesiastical order, that is, to persuade Rome to its view of an evangelical episcopacy (Augsburg Confession 28) is missing in Witte's account. The consequent resort to the emergency episcopacy of secular power for support of a truncated church, Christologically decapitated, led progressively to the nationalization of the church for purposes of political sovereignty (cf. Quentin Skinner's *bon mot:* "The Church *in* England became the Church *of* England"). The denouement of this fall of the church in Protestantism in the past century was its thoroughgoing secularization as the *Volkskirche;* all this is a profoundly sad tale of tragedy, unintended consequences, and "decay" (to use Bonhoeffer's precise evaluation)[178] that goes missing in Witte's account. The concomitant neglect of creative labor as a mandate of creation, moreover, could give little theological

---

175. Witte, *Law and Protestantism,* p. 296.
176. Witte, *Law and Protestantism,* p. 303.
177. *LW* 1, pp. 103-4.
178. Bonhoeffer, *Ethics,* pp. 88-109.

scrutiny to the transformations occurring in the capitalist revolution that was shortly to evolve out of mercantilism; this left theology in Luther's tradition ill-prepared to deal with the rise of "economic man." It left theology in the reaction-ary position of trying to maintain an outmoded form of "domestic economy" that no longer served love and justice in marriage or marketplace.

The difficulty involved in thinking of the human community intended in the act of origin is not simply a matter of replacing a static concept of fixed orders with that of mandates that develop. The difficulty is more profound: in a fallen world it is not so obvious what kind of social change is actually for the better. After Hitler, Hiroshima, and Stalin, it is indeed unconscionable theologically to advo-cate for "change" as such and in abstraction from the concretely inherited forms, howsoever perverted, of social organization that are nevertheless the products of God's creative mandate and objects of His redeeming and fulfilling love. It is important thus to note that in the canonical story the mandates of creation are issued before the disobedience of Adam by the commandment and blessing of Genesis 1:26-28 and remain valid and in force (Gen. 9:6-7) despite affliction (Gen. 3:14-19) of the ensuing exile of the first couple from the Garden (Gen. 3:24). The mandates are not canceled, any more than God's continuing creation is canceled, by sin and its punishment; they continue to be in effect, even as the image, taken as God's calling humanity to responsibility as His partner in the tasks of love and justice in the world, persists, despite the human default into irresponsibility before God for the world and the corresponding affliction.

Now in exile from the original possibility of innocent, trusting obedience of faith, these mandated social structures operate under the distortion of coercive force pressing against the egocentrism of sin. Paradise is lost. "Because of your hardness of heart, [Moses] wrote this commandment for you" (Mark 10:5). So the divine command and blessing becomes demand and curse laid upon sinful Adam. Divorce accompanies marriage, contract accompanies labor, and bribery and superstition accompany worship and prayer. In the Genesis tale, the fallen couple no longer rules together in partnership over the creation on the way to the best of all possible worlds. Now the man rules the woman, even as the man is ruled by the earth; that is, in rough and poetic justice each is now ruled by the material of its origin. The man and the woman no longer simply rejoice in each other, but the woman suffers the husband and the husband suffers the soil in sweat and toil to make bread for her and her child from out of thistles and thorns. The praise of thanksgiving in the Garden transforms into a lament and a cry for redemption in the wilderness — if not into the bribes and magic conjured in the religion business, a competition in sacrifice that immediately brings brother to the murder of brother (Gen. 4:1-16). The original structure of co-humanity in love for justice is not dissolved but warps, so to say, into coercive structures that extract by reward and punishment minimal levels of social coexistence, so that life is not utterly destroyed by the egocentric turn of the exiled human race after the fall. The teaching about structures of creation must articulate both the precariousness of preservation and the urgency of redemption in the art of discernment in any ethical context that would identify the Father's creative mandates for the obedience of faith in social responsibility.

We cannot read out God's creative will from our experience of social organization, which has warped into structures of malice and injustice; we can read only the nude fact that God as Creator places us in concrete social stations, there demanding that we become the creatures of His love that we continually fail to be. In this dark placement into a fallen world, God's Fatherhood is hidden. Our lot in life appears as cruel destiny or lucky privilege. On account of that deep ambiguity, Bonhoeffer insisted that the mandates "each in its own way, shall be through Christ, directed towards Christ, and in Christ." For it is in Christ that God's Fatherhood is revealed, and our placement in life redescribed accordingly as the place of God's intended redemption and transformation. Most basically, in Christ we learn that the distorted experience we have of human community due to sin is temporary and extrinsic, not God's affirmative will but His permissive will, permitted in the patience of God for the sake of repentance and redemption. Human community in living structures of love for justice is God's affirmative will, the very object of God's redemption and the content of God's fulfillment. That is why, for Luther according to Oswald Bayer, it is "God's Word [that] offers clarity of purpose to the chaotic natural forces that drive human life and . . . [gives] a person specific guidance concerning a different way to life" as worker, as spouse and parent, as worshiper.[179]

Oswald Bayer's probing interpretation confirms the foregoing analysis, in both its appreciation and criticism of an interpretation like Witte's. The difference is stated summarily by Bayer: "Luther's own testimony shows that the teaching about the three estates carries much greater weight for him than the teaching about the two realms of God."[180] Under modern political economy, we are accustomed to denigrating static "stations" in life in favor of the dynamic mobility the capitalist juggernaut requires for the easily substitutable cogs it makes of human beings for utilization in its machinery.[181] Self-understood "progressives" need to become more deeply aware of how their advocacy for "change" is and remains parasitical upon this capitalist leveling of traditional sources of resistance in the creative labor of craftsmanship and the wonder of science, in the commitment to lifelong and exclusive sexual partnership for the sake of children in the covenant of marriage that is the covenant of the generations, and in the organized form of life for the public worship of God, not private bribery. Only by the Marxist dialectical trick of regarding capitalism teleologically as the brutal but logically necessary step in the unfolding logic of progressive history that creates the wealth and technology

179. Oswald Bayer, *Martin Luther's Theology: A Contemporary Interpretation*, trans. Thomas H. Trapp (Grand Rapids: Eerdmans, 2007), p. 144.

180. Bayer, *Martin Luther's Theology*, p. 124.

181. Bayer, *Martin Luther's Theology*, pp. 120-21.

necessary for socialism[182] could one conscionably advocate change at any cost, without regard to its content and immediate cost in physical and cultural carnage.

In any case, theologically, we are bodily creatures. Each one of us is placed somewhere, uniquely, with an attendant perspective of our own that reflects our individual "station" in life, the place in space where God has created and formed us even now under the structures of malice and injustice. "Conservatives" consequently need to become more deeply aware of how their resistance to "change" is readily confused with an ideological defense of perverted structures that are not stable and enduring but highly precarious because deeply coercive insofar as they are motivated by malice reeking social injustice in the eyes of others. "Careers" involve selling one's soul to corporate greed or political graft or academic herd-mentality; marriage yokes women to male privilege and children to parental ambitions; religion becomes a carnival of bribery and superstition. And democratic politics gives vent to the *libido dominandi,* forming parties of greed and envy, the Republicans and the Democrats in the United States, respectively. In any case, the "station" in life is only the place in the fallen world to which redemption in Christ comes, reordering the powers with the creative task imposed upon the newly baptized to make the station in life a vocation of the priesthood of all believers, transforming structures of malice and injustice into new structures for love and justice by the concrete work of being Christ to others.

Bayer puts his finger here on the main thing: the theological function of the Incarnation is to affirm materiality and the common body as the creative labor of God, betrothed, if not yet wed to Jesus Christ for the consummation of the Beloved Community. This "holy secularity" (Lazareth), of course, is sharply to be distinguished from modern, ideological secularism that reifies and absolutizes "this world" as if it were something fixed and permanent, an old-fashioned substance, rather than a fragile and passing episode in the history of nature that is itself bounded by the mysteries of origin and end. Bayer sets the point in italics for emphasis: *"After Luther was thoroughly convinced, because of his new understanding of Word and sacraments, that the spiritual is constituted in the form of what was earthly — not only negatively but also positively — the spiritual importance of all things earthly was opened to him in a positive sense as well."*[183] It would be the labor of an entire volume of social-ethical theology to develop the insights here and make them fruitful for our increasingly desperate situation today in late capitalism, with no "utopia *ex machina*" on the horizon, but human survival itself at stake on the groaning earth. What Bayer contributes to this as-yet-unfulfilled task is a new interpretation in the tradition of Luther of the theology of the state, or, as I prefer to put it following Giorgio Agamben, of political sovereignty.

---

182. Jonathan Sperber, *Karl Marx: A Nineteenth-Century Life* (New York and London: Liveright, 2013), powerfully makes this point, how Marx's capitalism was precisely Smith's and Ricardo's capitalism, pp. 408-52. See also the analysis in *LBC,* pp. 323-30.

183. Bayer, *Martin Luther's Theology,* p. 141, italics original.

We have already noted that Witte errs in attributing to Luther the view that the state is an order of creation; far more, he regards the state as a *Notordnung,* an emergency order to constrain violence with violence that paradoxically violates the rule of the law to establish a limited zone of legality against barbarism. As mentioned, this analysis of political sovereignty should underscore the precariousness of preservation and the urgency of redemption, not devolve into an ideological justification of the powers that be or the powers that would be. Of course, this insight into the intrinsically coercive nature of the state can be taken in a merely Hobbsean way, to justify the status quo ante by fear-mongering scenarios of social chaos if "law and order" break down. It can also be taken in a Leninist-Trokskyite way to justify revolutionary rage and its preservation at any cost. Recent experiences, for example, in Somalia or the former Yugoslavia, show that this fear in any case is not purely manufactured. The Hobbsean state of nature remains as a latent possibility, the nightmare of civilizational breakdown.

On the other hand, ignoring the essentially coercive nature of the state blinds progressives to their complicity in the imperial lust for domination, and the malice and envy that motivates them in this complicity, when they deploy the machinery of the state to engineer "social justice" without a trace of Derrida's "bad conscience." To be sure, the state is the only institution that has the power as well as the right to put the market back in the marketplace and protect life from the commoditization of all things.[184] Equally true, free markets are the engine of creative labor, by just exchange ever giving birth to new forms of human community under the mandate to subdue the earth and have dominion over it. Such developing human community is both the command and blessing of God the Father in continuous creation, and its progress gives grounds for the political hope, as Bayer puts it, that "human beings can strive for a consensus that will eventually be cosmopolitan."[185] In this way Bayer marshals a neglected theme of theology in the tradition of Luther away from the "Two Kingdoms" scheme in either its conservative or liberal readings to that of the "Three Estates" in order to coordinate social and public ethics with liberal democracy, conceived here as a new aspiration for a cosmopolitan world order where the state domesticates the capitalist economy (rather than the other way around). Given the catastrophe of German Lutheranism in the twentieth century, and given the alternative post-Holocaust stance of political Barthianism for "Christians in Socialism,"[186] Bayer's stance here is understandable and relatively justified.

In a way that is conceptually, though not terminologically reminiscent of Hannah Arendt's important distinction between force and violence,[187] Bayer fur-

---

184. Michael J. Sandel, *What Money Can't Buy: The Moral Limits of Markets* (New York: Farrar, Straus & Giroux, 2012).

185. Bayer, *Martin Luther's Theology,* p. 148.

186. See *BA*, pp. 141-54.

187. Hannah Arendt, *On Violence* (San Diego: Harcourt Brace Jovanovich, 1970).

ther argues (emphatically, in italics) that *"[w]hatever power is exercised because of force and whatever aims to stop the exercise of force, so that life can go well, is to be considered legitimate and responsible, accountable governmental rule, dominion."* Political sovereignty, in this view, "opposes naked force, prevents fratricide, aims to limit street justice and private recrimination."[188] But this very legitimacy of the use of coercive force by the state depends on its limitation to just use by a just state as tested by "the consensual affirmation of a large majority of its citizens, a moral consensus."[189] Hence, Bayer moves the insight of Luther into the essentially postlapsarian nature and task of the inevitably coercive state from its deployment on behalf of conservative and authoritarian political ideology to service in contemporary democratic theory. This is possible, if Witte is right about Christian republicanism and moral egalitarianism as equally essential convictions of theology in the tradition of Luther's doctrine of the Three Estates. But doubts remain whether this modernization is adequate to the gravity of our postmodern situation. Majoritarian consensus begs the question whether such "democratic" majorities are but products of widespread capitulation of popular sovereignty to oligarchs that keep peace with bread and circuses.

Here John Milbank's seminal account of the rise of social theory in modern secularism as pioneered by Hobbes, Machiavelli, and Spinoza demands attention. These authors beginning with Hobbes displaced what Milbank calls the "metanarrative" status in the antecedent European culture of the gospel story of Jesus and His church as a work in progress, constructing the City of God from out of the ruins of the rival city of fallen humanity.[190] Fundamental to this modern liberal, sometimes democratic, but emphatically secularist, i.e., "this-worldly" thought is the notion that the original state of nature was populated by "the isolated, self-conserving individual" from which political and economic interrelationships could only artificially be constructed in transition to "the state of society."[191] In this way the biblical social thinking of humanity fallen "in Adam" (the Augustinian "city of man") but restored "in Christ" (the "city of God") could be turned on its head in the name of a more "realistic" and "scientific" social thought under the "progressive" motto, if I may put it this way: "we are not fallen angels but rising beasts."[192]

In the *Leviathan,* Hobbes inverted the biblical story of origin to imagine a state of nature in which, so to say, "alpha males" war themselves into exhaustion seeking gain and glory, finally transferring each one's natural right to self-preservation by means of violence into the hands of an absolute sovereign, ceded a monopoly on the means of coercion, for the sake of constructing a zone of

---

188. Bayer, *Martin Luther's Theology,* p. 151, emphasis original.

189. Bayer, *Martin Luther's Theology,* p. 152.

190. Milbank, *Theology and Social Theory,* pp. 387-88.

191. Milbank, *Theology and Social Theory,* p. 51.

192. As I once heard Arthur Peacocke put it, thinking to affirm the superiority of the Darwinian narrative to the Genesis story, but de facto endorsing Hobbesianism.

social peace: the state of society. In Hobbes, one does not "in the beginning" fall morally from God into an exile where brother murders brother, thus falling from paradise to jungle. Rather from the beginning all is fratricide and from out of this violent anarchy ordered human society arises by the instrumentality of political sovereignty and social contract. Hobbes's new story of origin, as told in the *Leviathan,* is a sustained attack on the legacy of Augustine,[193] and Augustine's biblical-theological interpretation of *imperium* with its *libido dominandi* from the new perspective of the Spirit-rendered ecclesia in mission to the nations. With Hobbes a new "naturalistic" metanarrative was born and came eventually to dominate modern social theory, though it had roots in the voluntaristic metaphysics of medieval nominalism. Milbank insightfully draws from Hobbes's *Leviathan* a citation that locates precisely the theological departure from the biblical narrative in the rise of the sovereign self: "The right of Nature, whereby God reigneth over men, and punisheth those that break his Lawes, is to be derived, not from his creating them, as if he required obedience as of gratitude for his benefits; but from his *Irresistible Power.*"[194] One cannot imagine a theological statement as insightful

---

193. E.g., "For notwithstanding the insignificant distinction of *temporal* and *ghostly* [i.e., the two cities of temporal and spiritual loves], they are still two kingdoms, and every subject is subject to two masters. For seeing the ghostly power challengeth the right to declare what is sin, it challengeth by consequence to declare what is law . . ." Thomas Hobbes, *Leviathan,* with selected variants from the Latin edition of 1668, ed. E. Curley (Cambridge, UK and Indianapolis: Hackett, 1994), p. 215.

194. Milbank, *Theology and Social Theory,* p. 15, cited from *Leviathan,* Part II, ch. 31, p. 397. In *Reflections on the Common Concept of Justice,* Leibniz made this significant argument against Hobbes. "It is generally agreed that whatever God wills is good and just. But there remains the question whether it is good and just because God wills it or whether God wills it because it is good and just; in other words, whether justice and goodness are arbitrary or whether they belong to the necessary and eternal truths about the nature of things, as do numbers and proportions." "To say, *Stat pro ratione voluntas* — 'Let my will stand for the reason' — is definitely the motto of a tyrant. Moreover, this opinion would hardly distinguish God from the devil . . . some people, overly devoted to the absolute right of God, have believed that he could justly condemn innocent people and even that this may actually happen. This does violence to those attributes which make God love-worthy and destroys our love for God, leaving only fear. . . ." "The Sacred Scriptures also give us an entirely different idea of this sovereign substance, speaking, as they so often and so clearly do, of the goodness of God and presenting him as a person who justifies himself against complaints. In the story of the creation of the world, the Scripture says that God considered all that he had done and found it good; that is, that he was content with his work and had reason to be so. This is a human way of speaking which seems to be used explicitly to point out that the goodness of the acts and products of God does not depend on his will but on their nature. . . . All our [i.e., evangelical] theologians, therefore, and most of those of the Roman church, as well as the ancient Church Fathers and the wisest and most esteemed philosophers, have favored the . . . view, which holds that goodness and justice have foundations independent of will and of force," namely, as members of the eternal verities they are founded in the divine mind. Gottfried Wilhelm Leibniz, *Philosophical Papers and Letters: A Selection,* trans. Leroy E. Loemker, 2 volumes (Chicago: University of Chicago Press, 1956), 2:911-13.

as it is hostile to the Genesis narrative as read by the Trinitarian conjunction of almighty power with wisdom and love.

There is a complication to the story that Milbank overlooks, however, in his justified zeal to expose Hobbes's theological decision for arbitrary power as God. This zeal sometimes leads Milbank to elide a viable liberalism (i.e., a genuine affirmation, as in Leibniz or Bonhoeffer, of personal freedom in and for community life) into the mere stalking horse for the totalist agendas of modernity. For example, Milbank can write that "Hobbes was simply more clear-sighted than later apparently more "liberal" thinkers like Locke in realizing that a liberal peace requires a single undisputed power, but not necessarily a continued majority consensus, which may not be forthcoming."[195] Two qualifications are in order here.

Granted that Locke's moral philosophy is not wholly congruent with Locke's epistemology and metaphysics, it remains the case that Puritan theology and canonical narrative still inform his social theory. Lockean moral philosophy, like Leibnizian metaphysics, has a patent claim to stand within the biblical tradition in the movement of European modernization as alternative paths to the line that led to Kant's dualism of the spheres of nature and freedom — Kant's sophisticated Frederick-the-Great-enlightened-despotism version of Hobbseanism, one might say. It is in particular relevant to point out that in the *Second Treatise of Government* (from which Jefferson drew in penning the words of the *Declaration* on human equality before God, upon which Lincoln drew to critique the slave-system codified in the Constitution of the United States),[196] Locke sought philosophically to refute Hobbes[197] by restoring again the canonical narrative of the state of nature: "The state of nature has a law of nature to govern it, which obliges every one: and reason, which is that law, teaches all mankind, who will but consult it, that being all equal and independent, no one ought to harm another in his life, health, liberty, or possessions: for men being all the workmanship of one omnipotent, and infinitely wise maker; all servants of one sovereign master, sent into the world by his order, and about his business; they are his property, whose workmanship they are, made to last during his, not another's pleasure. . . ."[198] The cited text forms a perfectly biblical rebuttal of the Hobbesian-Occamist thesis that God rules by the sheer irresistible might of power, not by the right of being the creature's wise and loving Creator.

So we may fill out the truncated thought of liberalism theologically: the almighty Father of the Son in the Spirit who gives human life as made in His image

195. Milbank, *Theology and Social Theory*, p. 13.

196. Harry V. Jaffa, *A New Birth of Freedom: Abraham Lincoln and the Coming of the Civil War* (Lanham, MD: Rowman & Littlefield, 2000), pp. 69-70.

197. Nicolas Jolley, *Locke: His Philosophical Thought* (Oxford: Oxford University Press, 1999), p. 194.

198. John Locke, *Second Treatise of Government*, ed. C. B. Macpherson (Indianapolis and Cambridge: Hackett, 1980), p. 9.

and commands accordingly its respect and protection (Gen. 9:6)[199] summons all by the "natural law" of "reason" to acquire likeness to God in care for one another. One does not, therefore, need theologically to refute modern liberalism categorically; arguably there are within it significant remnant traditions of co-humanity informed and inspired by the biblical narrative of Christ as the creation's redeemer that can be reconnected with the city of God in contest with the *civitas terrena.* Democratic political theory increasingly recognizes the crucial cultural presuppositions of democratic politics in so-called civil society. Where institutions of family, labor, and religions flourish, people are empowered for democratic citizenship. Patrology in turn conceives of labor, marriage, and religion as mandated forms of social life from, to, and in Christ; as such they limit political sovereignty in its coercive apparatus to the police function as servant and protector of these forms of civilized life in a fallen world that still awaits its fulfillment in the coming of the Beloved Community.

The question before us in Euro-America today, where predator drones and spying on the private life of citizens have become the preferred means of sustaining Western political regimes against the wrath of the dispossessed (made fanatical to be sure by their own culpable indulgence in religious bribery and superstition), is whether this dogmatic liberalism and reactionary secularism can open itself again to the Fatherhood of God.[200] The mandated task of government as a divine *Notordnung* opens itself to the Fatherhood of God, not to claim sanction for its social discipline and policing, but rather to hear and conscientiously obey the summons to use its coercive powers justly to safeguard creative labor, as well as to care for future generations in humble acknowledgment of the authority over political sovereignty that is recognized by the free practice of conscience in the world, and in particular by the free exercise of public worship in civil society. The theological default of this cultural ministry by mainline Protestant traditions in the catechetical formation of the theological subject today is complicit with ideological secularism and makes this cultural achievement of holy secularity less and less likely. In the interim, the juggernaut rolls on, with quarreling liberalisms ("conservative liberals, liberal liberals and radical liberals")[201] diverting attention from the approaching precipice with no hope of a Marxist happy ending but not a little fear of Leninist-Stalinist revanchism. But the groaning of the oppressed creation bears witness to the promise of the faithful Father, even as its cry of conscience goes up, "How long?"

199. Paul R. Hinlicky, "Luther and Liberalism," in *A Report from the Front Lines: Conversations on Public Theology,* A Festschrift in Honor of Robert Benne, ed. Michael Shahan (Grand Rapids: Eerdmans, 2009), pp. 89-104.

200. Derek R. Nelson in his "Inquiry, Conversation and Theistic Belief: William James and Richard Rorty Get Religion," *The Heythrop Journal* (2009): 495-507, pries the door open.

201. Alasdair MacIntyre, *Whose Justice? Which Rationality?* (Notre Dame: University of Notre Dame Press, 1988), p. 392.

## Whether God Exists . . .

As it is now clear that when we say "God" in Christian theology we are talking in the first instance about the Father of His Son, Jesus Christ, on whom He breathes His Spirit, we are finally prepared to deal properly with the question "whether God exists" that was raised above in Chapter Two. It is not the case that anyone can answer this question in a way that evades the decision of faith or unfaith; rather, we can now clarify far more precisely what the question means and what is at stake in the adult decision to believe in God or not. We are speaking here in the popular sense of the notion of substantiality, i.e., whether God is real, existing apart from His relations to those who come to know God, such that this God is not reducible, as Feuerbach influentially accused, to the projection of the human subject. What is the divine existence such that it can *come* to be known and understood? Only *as that,* can *God* be disbelieved, as opposed to disbelieving particular human claims about God; critical dogmatics, as we have seen, is especially keen *to join* with the alleged "atheists" in debunking idols and exposing demons and in applying these same critical questions to its own affirmations in faith about God.

Clearly, if we come to know God by His coming in the Spirit to conform us to the Son so that we return in Him to the Father, then this God must be understood to exist antecedently as the eternal love of the Father and the Son in the Spirit as that "than which nothing greater can be thought," as Anselm of Canterbury classically clarified the status of the question. This "immanent Trinity" is what God is in and for God and apart from His relation to creatures; the eternal existence of God who may freely come to creatures to be known and understood exists as just this One who comes in grace to give and to bless and thus be known and understood in love. The subtle but key problem here is in understanding this coming as a *free* coming, not in any sense necessitated, yet at the same time "fitting" with respect to what God is as "being in communion" — what Edwards called a "disposition."

What is at stake in this question? The previous century, according to one of Robert Jenson's early studies, has been characterized by a two-sided cultural and theological event: the self-cancelation of the Christian religion and the meaninglessness of the word "God"[202] in that it had come to express the pure "negation of the creature."[203] Note well: not the negation of the perverted creature and so the conversion and fulfillment of this troubled being in Christ as the Spirit's new creation, a newborn child of the heavenly Father in mission to the nations. Rather, "God" had become apophatic theology's "pure negation" raised to the level of pseudo-reality, the chimera of absoluteness, nonbeing regarded as Supreme Being and highest good, God's existence affirmed as the pure negation of

---

202. Robert Jenson, *God after God: The God of the Past and the God of the Future, Seen in the Work of Karl Barth* (Indianapolis and New York: Bobbs-Merrill, 1969), p. 24.

203. Jenson, *God after God,* p. 3. The reference is to the early Barth's rhetoric in his *Epistle to the Romans.*

life on the earth. Rather than the word "God" speaking the great biblical hope of the redemption of the Father's creation by Christ in the Spirit, as we have traced through the chapters of this work, the word "God" to most Euro-Americans had come to conjure up ghostly, disembodied ineffability of the great Beyond. In costly versions, true believers followed Pascal into bargaining excruciating worldly denial for heavenly reward; in cheap versions, God in heaven backs the progress of European world mastery on earth and, for those who need it, going to heaven when you die.

Under these conditions, the gospel of God can hardly be spoken with clarity and force. Embarrassed at the cheap version, but unwilling to sacrifice body, soul, and intellect with Pascal, "God" died the death of a thousand apophatic qualifications (recall from Chapter Two, Tillich's "God does not exist"). Nor does the true transcendence of the Trinity as the Creator of everything that is not God ever come to be spoken, which transcendence is such that it connects God immanently with everything that happens in space-time as the immediate cause of all causes, also the evil causes of the evildoers who choose what God rejects. Appalled with Plato at this implication of the Creator in His real, not imaginary creation, negative theology makes God only the cause of the good by distancing God through the trick of analogy: when human beings do good, they "participate" in God's causality, but when they do evil they do their own thing as the sovereign selves they sinfully presume to be. This theodicy does not work; it dodges the question, for it sacrifices the almighty power of the Father as the immediate cause of all causes. It succeeds therefore only in handing the actual world over to the devil. Consequently, after Hitler, Hiroshima, and Stalin, so it seems to contemporary atheism, for good or for ill human sovereignty for the fate of the earth stands over against the putative claim of God, although from Christian perspective just that secularist claim of responsibility to this world is what inspired Hitler, Hiroshima, and Stalin.

Jenson's diagnosis of the relentless dialectic of negative theology leading to contemporary atheism in this sense of a claim against the apophatically beclouded Christian God in the name of responsibility to this world was intended to clear ground for recovery of the word "God" in its gospel meaning and so to lead to a revitalization of the ecclesia in mission to the nations. The task before us now is to understand how his diagnosis is true and how as a result, faith in God the almighty Father can affirm that God exists in the sense that God is not reducible to His relations with creatures but rather exists precisely in such a way that He can and does relate truly, to Himself and to them, as their present and faithful Redeemer and future Fulfiller in the life everlasting by the resurrection of the dead.

The preface to the Decalogue in Deuteronomy 5:6 has God asserting His existence and its sense as such for His chosen creature, Israel: "I am the LORD your God, who brought you out of the land of Egypt, out of the house of slavery; you shall have no other gods before me." This declaration, as it stands, is not metaphysically monotheistic but historically monolatrous. That is to say, it acknowledges the existence, real or imagined, of rival claimants to the title LORD. In turn, it is precisely as the One depicted in the narrative of the Exodus that the self-identifying declaration warrants an ensuing command: "You shall not make for yourself an idol, whether in the form of anything that is in heaven above, or that is on the earth beneath, or that is in the water under the earth. You shall not bow down to them or worship them; for I the LORD your God am a jealous God, punishing children for the iniquity of parents, to the third and fourth generation of those who reject me, but showing steadfast love to the thousandth generation of those who love me and keep my commandments" (Deut. 5:8-10). This prohibition of graven, i.e., constructed images seems to step in the direction of ontological monotheism, if we take it as critiquing the inadequacy of all human representation of the ineffable divine being. But the emphasis may rather lie on the human crafting rather than on the inadequacy of the sign to the thing signified; it is the self-chosen theological imagination of the creature that is then prohibited, not an image that God is free to make and give to make Himself known and understood to creatures.

As we shall see at the end of this chapter, the deep challenge in the text of Deuteronomy 5:8-10 to an all-too-apophatically habitual and thus thoughtless move from salvation history monolatry to philosophical monotheism, or, as it may also be said, from mythology to ontology,[204] or as I prefer, from divine complexity to divine simplicity, lies in the manifest tension of the cited biblical text in depicting the zeal of the LORD, whose wrath and mercy stand here side by side unreconciled, just as if this very ambivalence ran through the divine heart of God. The classic story of the Golden Calf in Exodus 32 lays out the visitation upon idolatrous iniquity that has forgotten or rather misplaced the claim of the God of the Exodus for the obedience of faith. "When the people saw that Moses delayed to come down from the mountain, the people gathered around Aaron, and said to him, 'Come, make gods for us, who shall go before us; as for this Moses, the man who brought us up out of the land of Egypt, we do not know what has become of him.'" Aaron, as a mediating theologian, hastens to accommodate the apostasy. "He took the gold from them, formed it in a mold, and cast an image of a calf; and they said, 'These are your gods, O Israel, who brought you up out of the land of Egypt!'" Aaron tries to co-opt the idol and claim it as another, equally valid sign of the God of the Exodus than remembrance of His salvation and the corresponding commandment to have no other gods. But the God of the Exodus, the would-be thing signified by Aaron, is not impressed. The LORD tells Moses on the mountain that "they have acted perversely; they have been quick to turn

---

204. David Bentley Hart, *The Beauty of the Infinite: The Aesthetics of Christian Truth* (Grand Rapids: Eerdmans, 2003), p. 213. Ironically, this move by Hart is a Hegelianism. Or it allows that Hegel the foe simply does continue in the Anselmian tradition of *fides quaerens intellectum.* Compare to Torrance's construal of the relation of ontology to the Christian narrative, *Trinitarian Faith,* p. 134.

aside from the way that I commanded them; they have cast for themselves an image of a calf, and have worshiped it and sacrificed to it, and said, 'These are your gods, O Israel, who brought you up out of the land of Egypt!'" More outrageous than the inadequacy of the sign is the displacement of the thing signified and the corresponding misuse of the name of the LORD, which attributes to a product of human hands the salvation wrought by the LORD's outstretched arm.

It is not the image that sins, which may be icon as well as idol, depending on the use to which it is put and by whom. It is the Holy Spirit who unifies the sign with the thing signified, where and when it pleases God, for the obedience of faith (or for offense). It is the idolater who unifies the sign and the thing signified to capture God with sacrifices, i.e., the bribes of the religion industry. Behind the idol is the profoundly sinful substitution for the narrated God, the One who had alone rescued Israel as good as dead. As Luther saw, in the idol saving faith in human works is replacing the saving work of God alone, since the agency of salvation is now predicated of what is, with only the shallowest veneer of self-deception, the product of human manufacture. The narrated God of the Exodus reserves to Himself the work of salvation and requires from His people just this faith alone in Him alone as savior. In the idol the narrated God of promise is forgotten as the One who can save just because He is not reducible to His relation to creatures, who as such is not manipulated by religious bribes, but is rather able freely to come and to deliver. Or, more subtly, when His remembered Name is taken in vain, false consciousness covertly attributes the work of salvation to human hands that have fashioned a symbol of their own choosing. But "this is the work of God, that you believe in him whom he has sent" (John 6:29).

In Romans 1:18-32, accordingly, Paul analyzes idolatry as a self-deceiving folly that darkly "exchanges" the promise of creation by God for the *sicut Deus eritis* of Adam, the glory of God for crafted images, the truth of God for lies, the knowledge of God for boundless descent into depravity that erodes cultured distinctions between male and female, human and animal. In Thessalonians 1:9-10, Paul commends his Gentile converts: "you turned to God from idols, to serve a living and true God, and to wait for his Son from heaven, whom he raised from the dead — Jesus, who rescues us from the wrath that is coming." Faithful waiting in hope and love on the promised salvation of God from the coming wrath of God is the true worship of God that has turned from dead idols. That eschatological confidence vouchsafed by the resurrection of the Crucified is the reason why Paul can say that "we know that 'no idol in the world really exists,' and that 'there is no God but one'" (1 Cor. 8:4): the idol is alive as the form of false consciousness that claims responsibility for the world against the claim of God alone to save. The irreducibility of the one, true God to His relations with creatures, then, is affirmed in the biblical writers as an implication of His claim to save, not least of all from His own wrath. Indeed, God's freedom to reject His own is the infallible insignia in time of the irreducibility of God to His relations with creatures, as Deuteronomy 5:8-10 indicates (but see also Amos 3:2; Luke 3:8; Rom. 11:20-22; Rev. 3:15-16).

By the same token, the false consciousness of the *sicut deus eritus* is a real force of actual evil at work in the world; thus Paul goes on to acknowledge, reverting to the historical situation of the monolatrous form of the putative word of God in history, "indeed, even though there may be so-called gods in heaven or on earth — as in fact there are many gods and many lords — yet for us there is one God, the Father, from whom are all things and for whom we exist, and one Lord, Jesus Christ, through whom are all things and through whom we exist" (1 Cor. 8:6). The deutero-Pauline Colossians 1:13-16 can accordingly point to Christ as the image — the "true idol," if you will — of God given by God: "He has rescued us from the power of darkness and transferred us into the kingdom of his beloved Son, in whom we have redemption, the forgiveness of sins. He is the image of the invisible God, the firstborn of all creation; for in him all things in heaven and on earth were created, things visible and invisible, whether thrones or dominions or rulers or powers — all things have been created through him and for him." The Fourth Gospel in the same way points to Christ as the "true idol" of God given by God in the gospel narrative. So also the thematic John 1:14-18: "And the Word became flesh and lived among us, and we have seen his glory, the glory as of a father's only son, full of grace and truth. From his fullness we have all received, grace upon grace. The law indeed was given through Moses; grace and truth came through Jesus Christ. No one has ever seen God. It is God the only Son, who is close to the Father's heart, who has made him known." Should not Christians concede that their claim for Jesus is patently idolatrous in the eyes of others, if not also their own — unless and until the Spirit unifies the sign with the thing signified for repentance and faith (or offense)? If Jesus is the icon of God, in other words, and not the Christian's tribal god, what makes the idol in distinction from the icon is not representation as such; indeed, the man Jesus saves from sins by representing us to His Father and His Father to us. What makes an idol, even out of Jesus, is to think one relates truthfully to God without this Spirit-given Mediator, who as the man afflicted saves us from our sins.

With the Seventh Ecumenical Council[205] and Martin Luther,[206] Jenson was right to argue that idolatry has been misunderstood along Platonic lines, culminating in Barth's ferocious assault on the nineteenth century's "domestication of transcendence" (Placher) recorded in his *Epistle to the Romans.* It is no solution, however, simply to reassert against the nineteenth century's all-too-easy coziness with "the God who is in heaven" the metaphysical thesis that the finite is incapable of the infinite. Hegel was not wrong to see in the classical doctrine of

---

205. "What was going on in the making of icons was not circumscription, since Christ was not bodily present, but depiction. . . . The real issue, as the iconophiles saw it, was the reality of the history of Christ, which the icons sought to portray." Pelikan, *TCT* 2, p. 130. Furthermore, "Only a truly human Christ could save, and it belonged to true humanity to be susceptible of portrayal." Pelikan, *TCT* 2, p. 133.

206. *LW* 40, pp. 84-117.

the Trinity an ontological description of the living God of the Bible as the true infinite. The true infinite is not limited by the finite; such a limit would make the supposed infinite a finite. A true infinite is capable of the finite (what Hegel, and Hegelianism, made of this insight in reducing God to negative dialectics is another question). It *is* a false infinite that confronts the creature on the same ontological plane demanding total capitulation; that is not the claim of the God of the Exodus and of Easter, but of Pharaoh the slavemaster, the claim of a tyrant; it is Leviathan's claim. As irreducible to His relation to us, the claim of the God of the Exodus comes from God as the liberating claim that sets free for committed lives of love working justice in the world. Where this liberation and commitment do not follow, it follows that the claim of the God of the Exodus has not been heard, believed, and obeyed. This clarification notwithstanding, the difficulty of course remains: "God comes from God" (Jüngel). The self-surpassing Fatherhood of God indicates the substantiality or irreducibility of God. What can this mean?

It ought to mean, as we have just underscored the monolatrous field of this putative word from God, Christian "atheism" according to the classical theology of the martyrs. In the words of Justin Martyr: "We certainly confess that we are godless with reference to the beings like those who are commonly thought of as gods, but not with reference to the most true God, the Father of righteousness. . . ."[207] But instead, disillusioned of the idols in the Platonic way of negative theology, for the most part "atheism" today amounts to helpless silence before the ineffable; it is theologically agnostic. It is not that modern people do not believe in some final reality other than the endless death of the universe in dark, cold silence that science is now predicting, but that (1) they have no idea how to affirm anything positive about it and are abashed by fundamentalists who all too easily make positive affirmations that on examination seem more absurd than the problems they allegedly solve, so that (2) even the classic creedal claims of the confessing church seem to them not only unlikely, but, so far as they are intelligible, unseemly (Virgin birth? God incarnate in a crucified man? Resurrection from the dead?).[208] Soft-pedaling the total critique made in Christian theology on human sinfulness, and the corresponding soteriological radicalness in the proclamation of the Christ crucified, the equally radical implication of Christian "atheism," i.e., Paul's disbelief in the so-called gods and lords, is hardly known in Euro-America, where mediating theologians are still trying to keep the churches open by co-opting the culture's golden calves.

True atheism over against the God of the gospel — for example, Nietzsche's tragic view of life transcended by art, on the other hand, would be in Christian perspective the radical and consequent denial of hope, which is — at least in one

207. *ANF,* p. 164; cf. *DC,* pp. 128-33.

208. See the reply of Stanley Fish to Richard John Neuhaus in *First Things* (February 1996), accessed online at http://www.firstthings.com/article/2007/09/003-stanley-fish-replies -to-richard-john-neuhaus-10.

historically influential reading of Nietzsche — nihilism. Nietzsche went through his "positivist" stage in which he drank to the dregs the cup of the emerging worldview in the nineteenth century of matter in random motion. This latter ontological despair — truth be told, never far below the surface of life classical or modern — is what is contested when the Christian says with the Creed, "I believe *in God*," i.e., as God not reducible to our relation to Him, so that even if we are on some level matter in random motion we can nonetheless relate to the God who "is more than necessary" in hope as the one, true God who can freely and ably come to be redeemer and fulfiller of this creation that we are. The way to the ontology of hope is through the mythology (despite its negative connotation, a "myth" is but a "story" or "tale," a "narrative"), or more precisely, the contending mythologies, essentially, Dionysus versus the Crucified (as Nietzsche put it).[209]

Nietzsche's iconoclastic metaphor was "philosophizing with a hammer." He takes the ax from John the Baptist's hand and lays it to the very root of biblical hope by his renewal of the pagan myth of the eternal recurrence of all things — symbolized in the swastika adopted in this spirit by Nazism.[210] Consideration of this alternative mythology exposes what is truly at stake in maintaining the substantiality of God (in the sense of irreducibility to creaturely relations with Him) by the distinction, not separation, between the immanent and economic Trinity, even as we take the Trinity as eternal becoming rather than a timeless being. Nietzsche's myth proposes a thought experiment: Imagine that the time of the world runs in a big circle, so that in infinite ages everything that has been eventually, inevitably repeats itself, again and again to infinity, along with all the madness of senseless suffering. Ontologically, it will never get better. There is no hope of betterment beyond the little surd that appears to be in our momentary control, that is, in the attitude we adopt to the tragedy that life is. Myths that suggest otherwise are illusory; the love of Jesus was dashed on the cross, end of story, not backed finally by the way reality turns out because reality never turns out but only turns around in an eternal circle. We cannot now anticipate our future as the victory of Jesus' love, nor remember and evaluate our past on this basis, nor in conversation with others reconcile and repair and move forward in love's power of repentance and forgiveness for reparation and innovation. In fact there is no future that is not a return to the same senseless criminality, the violent clash of impersonal forces, and so on, again and again *ad infinitum*. There is only the eternal recurrence of the logos of becoming — a logos that Nietzsche names "the will to power." In the ebb and flow of this law of being, ironclad necessity reigns over beings that must will their own power (even in the self-deception of altruism) in contest with myriad other such forces. "The world exists; it is not something that becomes, not something that passes away. Or rather: it becomes,

209. *RPTD,* pp. 109-14.

210. Steven E. Aschheim, *The Nietzsche Legacy in Germany 1890-1990* (Berkeley, Los Angeles, London: University of California Press, 1994).

it passes away, but it has never begun to become and never ceased from passing away — it maintains itself in both — it lives on itself: its excrements are its food. We need not worry for a moment about the hypothesis of a created world. The concept 'create' is today completely indefinable; unrealizable; merely a word, a rudimentary survival from the ages of superstition. . . ."[211]

That is Nietzsche's thought-experiment. If you can stomach this myth of the eternal return of the same, and still affirm your life, you are, or rather in the very act of so valuing your tragic existence, you become the human being who overcomes, the self-creator. In affirming the tragedy of your existence you achieve Adam's dream to be as God, or rather more than God, "beyond good and evil." Nietzsche's laser-guided attack on the notion of "creation" in the passage just cited is telling. His objective doctrine of despair is nihilism with respect to the divine purpose of creation as the coming of the Beloved Community; this atheism, which is in fact an alternative mythology to the gospel's narrative of the resurrection of the Crucified, constitutes the true antipode today of Trinitarian faith in the God whose project is eschatological creation. It is through these contests in mythologies that we may find the way in Christian theology to the divine ontology, the immanent and co-equal Trinity that has its source in the mystery of the self-surpassing Father, singing "Glory to the Father and to the Son and to the Holy Spirit, as it was in the beginning, is now and ever will be. Amen."

## Divine Being

The Father is the unbegotten God *a se* and so is the *fons divinitatis,* "the font of the deity."[212] We must accordingly be Christian "atheists" also ontologically in the sense that we deny that there is any divine substance that is not the exclusive predicate of the almighty Father. There is not a divine substance in general, of which Father (or Son or Spirit) are predicated as possible instantiations, but it is the other way around. The almighty Father possesses aseity as the primordial and irreducible instantiation of deity. Christians do not believe in God in general. Indeed, they disbelieve deity in general and regard it as a conceptual idol, the reification of a nothing. The God of Israel, of Exodus and of Easter, the almighty Father of His own Son, Jesus — not some divine substance or hyper-substance conceived along other lines — is the font of the deity and the principle of its unity in being as the Three. Whatever deity is as a nature or *ousia,* it exists only as the unique and concrete reality of what the Father has of Himself and just so eternally donates to His Son and Spirit, who return to the Father in the eternal becoming of divine tri-personal Life. This way of life can be described, as we have already

---

211. Friedrich Nietzsche, *The Will to Power,* trans. W. Kaufmann and R. J. Hollingdale (New York: Vintage Books, 1968), p. 548.

212. Torrance, *The Trinitarian Faith,* p. 79.

indicated, as the perfect harmony of power, wisdom, and love, which we can conceive discursively and imaginatively, but never in all eternity comprehend.

Within the divine life the Father is primary personal possessor of deity, that is, the first divine agent. "Throughout the early Church the Father was understood in a two-fold but indivisible way, as the one being *(mia physia)* of the Godhead, and as the Father of the Son . . . precisely as Father = Godhead is the one supreme, almighty being, uncreated, self-sufficient, all-perfect, who is the transcendent Fount *(pege),* Source *(arche)* and Author *(aitios)* of all other being. It may even be said that in the fullest sense he alone is being . . . inherently productive and creative in his very being as God. . . ."[213] Speaking from the Eastern tradition, John Zizioulas made this point in his celebrated and justly influential study: the ultimate mystery of the Divine Life is that "God, as Father, and not as substance, perpetually confirms through 'being' His *free* will to exist. And it is precisely His trinitarian existence that constitutes this confirmation: that the Father out of love — that is, freely, begets the Son and brings forth the Spirit. . . . Thus God as person — as the hypostasis of the Father — makes the one divine substance to be what it is: the one God. This point is absolutely crucial."[214] The singular "act of God's being" (to borrow a concept from Thomism), then, is the Father's free and perpetual donation of His being in begetting the Son and breathing the Spirit. The Father *is* God personally *as* God who *a se* and so *freely,* so Zizioulas emphasizes, begets and spirates, imparting His own divine nature once to the Son and again to the Spirit in one indivisible act that returns and so circulates eternally.

What is slippery about this account is that it appears to be saying that already the Father has a divine nature that can be communicated to the Son and the Spirit, and, at the same time, that the Father's divine nature, taken as the Father's free and personal act of being, is to give this divine nature to the Son and the Spirit without ceasing to be the God and Father. That would seem to be an equivocation between nature, taken as possession of a set of possibilities that can be given and shared, and nature, taken as an act of actualizing a set of possibilities that as personal is unique and incommunicable. We can reverently resort here to an ineffable mystery: to be God is wholly to give, and this giving which God is *simply* begins with the Father who wholly gives the power, wisdom, and love to give, without ceasing to be this power, wisdom, and love, to the Son who also wholly gives in the way of being the Son, and the Spirit who also wholly gives in the way of being the Spirit of the Father who rests upon the Son. To posit this simple but unfathomable beginning of divine giving in the ungiven Father who gives, then, is what is meant when the Creed has us say, "We believe in one God, the Father almighty. . . ."

In our understanding, as a result, God's nature or deity as power, wisdom, and love of wholly giving is a concrete determination of God's personhood as

213. Torrance, *The Trinitarian Faith,* p. 79.

214. John D. Zizioulas, *Being as Communion* (Crestwood, NY: St. Vladimir's Seminary Press, 1985), p. 41.

the almighty Father, so that the Father irreducibly exists in and as His Trinitarian community with the Son in the Spirit. While in our sinful desire to be God and not wanting God to be God, we manufacture idolatrous conceptions of deity (always stingier than wholly giving), and while in our conversion from idols to serve the true and living God we proceed through a contestation of mythologies, we cannot begin our theological thinking in Christian theology with a general idea of deity that abstracts from this contestation or settles for less than *esse Deum dare.* For Christian theology, there *exists* only the particular concrete deity of God of the self-surpassing Father who exists in no other way than in being communicated and returned in the eternal Life.[215] The almighty Father exists as the unoriginate origin of all that is, the simple beginning, self-existent, unbegotten begetter, unbreathed breather, ungenerated generator, uncreated creator, the unique and ultimate reality beyond which there is not nor can be thought anything greater, the ultimate mystery of all that is. Ultimate, that is to say, non-transcendable substantiality (in the sense of simple or incomparable irreducibility) is therefore rightly ascribed to Him with the Son in the power of the Spirit in the doxology of the church — and accordingly refused to any other conceivable claimant.

What then can be said of this incomparable *deity* of the Father and how can it be sufficiently if never adequately or comprehensively *described,* that it may be recognized, worshiped, and glorified in distinction from all that is not God? The classic kataphatic answer to this question in Western theology goes by the misleading name "the ontological proof" for the existence of God, which is not meant as a demonstration that convinces a skeptic rationally that some Supreme Being exists but rather as theological reflection that instructs believers about what existence is God's as the Creator of all that is not God, the being which is *supreme* ("greater than") in relation to the being of each and all creatures, that is, the One who exists in an eminent sense.[216]

Note that the argument is not philosophical, without presuppositions, *solo ratione,* as Anselm misleadingly claimed and since Descartes has been errone-

---

215. Augustine too knows this: "Thus it is clear that the Son has another from whom he is and whose Son he is, while the Father does not have a Son from whom he is, but only whose Father he is." Augustine, *On the Trinity,* trans. E. Hill (New York: New City Press, 1991), II, 1.2; p. 98.

216. The "ontological proof" had a prehistory in Augustine's theology. The source of the *via eminentia* is in Augustine, *De doctrina Christiana,* I, vii: "For when God is thought of, our thought tries to reach something than which nothing is better or more sublime," who in turn borrowed the idea from Seneca's *Quaestiones Naturales* (R. W. Southern, *Saint Anselm: A Portrait in a Landscape* [Cambridge: Cambridge University Press, 1993], p. 129). The presuppositions of the ontological proof are: (1) "there must be degrees of being"; (2) the hierarchy or gradation of being must be "strictly related as ascending powers in the scale of existence" such that "things have their highest degree of being in the mind of God. . . . This is of course a form of Platonism" (pp. 133-34). Thus the argument involves "acceptance of a concealed philosophical principle which commits the unbeliever to a view of knowledge which necessitates the existence of God. . . . The argument returns, and must always return, to the faith from which it starts" (p. 134).

ously understood. For Anselm the *solo ratione* method intended to disbar the oppressive resort to unprincipled, conversation-stopping proof-texting in theology and rather to enable believers to understand the dogmas that they receive on the authority of revelation. Anselm is thus a father of the critical method in critical dogmatics.[217] Karl Barth's study of Anselm's so-called ontological proof of God's existence in the *Proslogion* came at a critical moment in his own struggle for the renewal of dogmatics. "In faith we are given and by faith we recognize, a designation for God which is not totally inadequate, not just a symbol . . . for the simple reason that it expresses nothing about the nature of God but rather lays down a rule of thought which, if we follow it, enables us to endorse the statements about the Nature of God accepted in faith as our own necessary thoughts."[218] In other words, Anselm's so-called proof provides a rule for understanding the use

217. At a time when the mere authority of tradition stifled theological inquiry and thus had brought the gospel sense of that tradition into obscurity, Anselm determined to inquire *solo ratione,* "by reason alone" into the meaning of the faith once delivered to the saints. According to R. W. Southern, this was a methodological decision that had its "origin in talking." Anselm excluded "the quotation of authorities" played like trump cards to end discussion. As the method of dialogue, *solo ratione* was "a determination to leave no objection unanswered." To uncomprehending traditionalists who cared only about the authority claims of the church as an institution, "the whole theological method appeared misguided, freeing the subject from the authorities which were the proper guides both to the questions to be asked and the answers to be given. . . . But in outlining this radical programme of inquiry, Anselm was not speaking as a searcher for new truths, but as a conservative, who reached old conclusions by new methods" (Southern, *St. Anselm,* p. 119). The procedure is thus reminiscent of Irenaeus's seminal introduction of the question, Why?, to discern the unity of God's acts in the Scriptures (see *DC,* pp. 140-45); for Anselm, "the Christian ought to progress through faith to understanding, and not through understanding to faith" (p. 123). Like Irenaeus centuries before, Anselm was convinced that *theology as faith's rational form of inquiry* discovers the good reasons of the good news of God: ". . . careful meditation on the content of faith by a competent inquirer will lead to reasons which are satisfying and true. . . . This understanding will add nothing to, and subtract nothing from, the adhesion of mind and will, to which the baptized person is irrevocably committed. But it will add a justifiable pleasure: a warmth of adhesion, one might say . . ." (p. 124) of the one who now worships God knowingly, as an adult human being. Thus "the concepts of faith, in becoming clearer in the understanding, become more active in the soul, more systematically interrelated in the mind, more joyfully embraced. This is the whole aim of meditation: to lead the inquirer forward along the road towards the final beatitude of the immediate experience of the object of faith" (p. 127). Of course, for Anselm, reason is not logic chopping but the summit of humanity created by God for God; reasoning is a kind of *meditation* in which the image of God, deformed by sin, is rekindled: "For reasoning on these subjects, therefore, it is not enough to perform a plodding series of mechanical acts; it requires a kindling of the spirit, a throwing-off of the chains of the flesh, a rising above the world of material things, all of which are the fruits of a long process of purification . . . only through prayer that he could reach the state at which reasoning on these subjects could be profitable" (p. 125). Meditation, contemplation is "the proper exercise of the religious mind" (p. 131).

218. Karl Barth, *Fides quaerens intellectum,* trans. Ian W. Robertson (New York: World Publishing Company, Meridian Books, 1960), p. 80.

of the concept of nature in theology rather than a claim for insight into the divine nature. Far then from trying to prove God's existence or define God's essence in a philosophical way, as if to take a human mind beyond the stance of faith, Anselm's so-called "ontological proof" does *not* according to Barth's exposition seek to demonstrate God's existence to "the fool, who says in his heart 'there is no God.'" The fool cannot be persuaded, but the believer who says in her heart that God exists needs to understand what it is she thus affirms. Anselm's so-called "ontological proof" might then be better named *the doxological analytic of the reality of God,* that is to say, an analysis of the reality ascribed to God in faith's act of worship. This approach is justified not only, as Barth pointed out, because Anselm's *Proslogion* takes the literary form of prayer, but because the analysis here (and in the *Monologion*) is faith's own attempt to understand the uncanny reality to which a believer entrusts herself in the act of addressing the person of the Almighty Father as the one true God.

Moreover, Anselm was very clear in the first part of his argument, the *Mono-logion,* that "although the [Supreme Nature] can be spoken of relationally as *supreme* over, or as *greater* than, all the things that it made . . . [these utterances] do not, it is obvious, designate its natural being . . . clearly 'supreme' does not signify unqualifiedly *that* Being which is in every way greater and better than whatever is not what it is."[219] *That* natural being of God "in and for itself" remains infinitely beyond our capacity to comprehend, and thus irreducible to its relation to us, even when it is clear that that relation is one of ontological supremacy. Thus, in designating God's being "supreme," we venture nothing about what it is in itself, only that whatever it is, it is supreme in relation to us and thus capable, we know not how, of just this relationship to creatures as Creator. Anselm thus intends only to speak of the existence of God relatively, not absolutely, i.e., in relation to creatures as understood by faith. His argument does not claim metaphysical insight, but in faith wants to identity for faith what exists as God and what does not, as that than which we creatures can think nothing greater.

This being supreme in relation to us is, as Anselm argues, the being which is *a se,* "from itself," having the quality of *aseity* in relation to creatures, and so able to grant existence to beings that are not *a se,* but have their being derivatively, whether by nature within the divine life of the Trinity *per alium,* or contingently as gift in the creation, *per aliud.* The supreme being will consequently be said in the *Proslogion* to "exist necessarily" or "by nature" *in relation to us* who do not exist necessarily: as such, the ontological proof demonstrates analytically that "God cannot be thought not to exist,"[220] namely to exist for us as the Giver of the gift of life that we thinking creatures are who want to know the One in whom we believe. If we think of God at all correctly in the biblical relation of the uncreated

---

219. Anselm, *Monologion,* chapter 15:10 in Jasper Hopkins, *A New Interpretive Translation of St. Anselm's Monologion and Proslogion* (Minneapolis: Arthur J. Banning Press, 1986), p. 93.
220. Anselm, *Proslogion,* ch. 32, in Hopkins, *A New Interpretive Translation,* p. 227.

Creator to all that is not God we must think — it is an analytical truth — of God as what is supremely real in relation to us. The creature who comes to understand the supreme existence in this way as the being of the Creator in relation to the creature, therefore, cannot and need not and indeed dare not form any notion of what this necessary divine existence is in itself except that it is, again in relation to us, so "simple, complete and absolute" that it "can in a certain respect rightly be said alone to exist."[221]

Divine "simplicity" then is an apophatic qualifier of the kataphatic demonstration of God's existence to us as Creator to creature, an important qualifier that points to an existence that is unique and strictly speaking incomparable, *not like* any creaturely existence we know or imagine. This too is an analytical truth that merely brings out the singularity of the relationship of creature to Creator. As argued previously, if we must use the concept of substance in theology at all, it is to be taken as a concept that properly speaking applies only to God in the sense of affirming that God is the One and only that is not reducible to His relations with others that are not God, as creatures are in fact reducible to their relations to other persons, forces, and things. Yet this negative, virtually annihilating conclusion of pantheism should not be drawn, since *ex hypothesi,* "created beings do not altogether lack existence, since from nothing they have been made something through this Spirit, which alone exists absolutely."[222] This standing as creatures who want to know the One in whom they believe is something, not nothing, a particular something (the image of God called to likeness to God by the gospel). As such this exemption from what seems to be the pure force of the argument towards pantheism is valid, if the entire argument in fact unfolds from the epistemic access of the believing creature wanting to understand what the word "God" means as that eminent reality, so to speak, that lends reality to the creature and does not annihilate it but comes to redeem and fulfill it.

Consequently, Anselm is able now to shift his argument from the — if I may so express his thought precisely — the *relatively absolute* or the *simply complex* being of the Creator to its self-expression "though which all things were made." Anselm now reasons out the instrumental and perfecting causalities of the Creator in His intelligent Word and animating Spirit, drawing the conclusion that "whatever the Supreme Spirit is in relation to creatures this Spirit's Word is also,"[223] and likewise the Spirit's Spirit of love. In relation to us, the Simple Being's Word and Spirit are Creator, not creature. This allows Anselm a further reflection: "[I]f there never had been a creature — i.e., if nothing had ever existed other than the Supreme Spirit, who is Father and Son — nonetheless the Father and the Son would still have loved themselves and each other. Hence, it follows that this Love is identical with what the Father and the Son are, viz., the Supreme Being . . . that the Father,

---

221. *Monologion,* ch. 28:30, in Hopkins, *A New Interpretive Translation,* p. 133.
222. *Monologion,* ch. 28:30, in Hopkins, *A New Interpretive Translation.*
223. Ch. 37:4, in Hopkins, *A New Interpretive Translation,* p. 149.

the Son, and their Love be the one Supreme Being."[224] So Anselm reasons to the immanent Trinity as the truth of God's eternal being not reducible to its relation to creatures.

Anselm's argument has attained to some truth about the eminently real being of God in this way, yet this truth remains relative, not absolute; that is to say, it is a truth accessed by reasoning in faith to faith's basis in God, while the matter thus discovered, God's substantial reality as eternally triune, remains ineffable.[225] Nonetheless the human mind has been enabled in this "relative" way truly to approach the thought of God as its truly existing and hence supreme good; the *Monologion* has shown that "the rational creature was made for this end, viz., to love above all [other] goods the Supreme Being, inasmuch as it is the Supreme Good. Or better, [he was made] so that he might love nothing except the Supreme Being or on account of the Supreme Being. . . ."[226] That is what the argument thus far establishes. The *Monologion* has shown that "this Being which we call God is not nothing. . . . Indeed, everyone who affirms that a God exists . . . understands [thereby] nothing other than a Substance which he believes to be above every nature that is not God. . . ."[227] The "relative" approach of the believing creature to the knowledge of the substantial being of God succeeds in establishing this because it has epistemic access in that, in relation to us, "all things were made through, and are sustained by, this Spirit's supremely good and supremely wise omnipotence."[228] This too is an analytical truth; it merely makes explicit what is implicit in the given relationship of the intelligent creature wanting to know the Creator in whom it believes. In Anselm's list of perfections — power, wisdom, and love — we have genuine, though relative, insight into the being of the Creator who can and does create the very creature who has come to believe in Him. What is forever hidden to the creature is not that God exists as this infinite harmony of power, wisdom, and love but *how* these perfections perfectly cohere as one in God's mysterious life "in and for itself." This ineffable coherence of the Three, like their simple beginning in the self-surpassing Father, is the mystery of God's eternal being that remains mystery to the creature even in all eternity.

The paradoxical result of this analysis is that we have to speak of God as the "relatively necessary being," understanding the so-called ontological proof in a modal or hypothetical way. It affirms that, if God as Creator exists to us as creatures, this God must be conceived to exist eminently, or exist necessarily, that is *a se, per se,* and *ad seipsum,* in order to be just this Creator of intelligent creatures who come in faith to the knowledge of Him who loves us freely, that

224. Ch. 53:5, in Hopkins, *A New Interpretive Translation,* p. 171.
225. Ch. 65, in Hopkins, *A New Interpretive Translation,* p. 189.
226. Ch. 68:15-20, in Hopkins, *A New Interpretive Translation,* p. 195.
227. Ch. 80:5, in Hopkins, *A New Interpretive Translation,* p. 211.
228. Ch. 80:5, in Hopkins, *A New Interpretive Translation,* p. 211.

is, loves us without being reducible to this creaturely experience of being loved. This is *all* that Anselm's so-called ontological proof in the *Proslogion* goes on to claim, in that it is a *theological* effort to make the ontology of the word "God" manifest to faith. God is to us the concretely and supremely real in relation to which we are His passing and temporary beings, whose "substantiality" derives from His calling of us as His image to acquire likeness to Him. But the "necessary existence" here predicated of God as the creative harmony of the power, wisdom, and goodness that gives a world to creatures for the sake of their inclusion through history into the Beloved Community, gives us no positive insight whatsoever into the how of God's being in and for itself; this life of God in its simple beginning and ultimate coherence remains ineffable. What is thought is *that* God's being in and for itself is *somehow* the perfect harmony of power, wisdom, and love, beginning with the mystery of the self-surpassing Father generating the Son on whom He breathes His Spirit, though we can never grasp *how* this is what it is — that mystery indicates the irreducibility of God to His relations with creatures.

This *something* provides the pragmatically required distinction, indeed hierarchy in natures divine and human as supreme to subordinate, that is given with the notion that Nietzsche so incisively targeted but remains irrevocable for theology: creation as the free gift of the God whose deity is manifest in giving wholly. The ineffable being of God as One in power, wisdom, and goodness so to give is to be acknowledged, then, by the creature in the act of adoration that acknowledges the Difference in purely receiving its gifts, including the gift of the Spirit to graciously receive in faith the gift of creaturely existence that personally returns to the Giver in ardent thanksgiving. "Deity" is thus known in its giving but known only as the ultimate mystery of the self-surpassing Father of the Son whose gift is the creature's life in the Spirit; to Him the predicates of majesty (power, wisdom, goodness) are doxologically ascribed without pretension of grasping how internally they cohere. The modest task of ontological description in theology, with the deliberate refusal of metaphysical insight lest the deity of God be profaned with a theoretical explanation, or the focus on the salutary receiving of divine gifts on the earth be obscured, is undertaken in theology strictly in order that God's Name not be taken in vain by ignorant or misguided creatures. The church's proclamation of God in its worship of the God who is not reducible to His relation to us is thus to be kept true to God who gives in a world that still bows down to idols that in truth are the products of its own self-chosen works.

God's divine nature is thus recognized and distinguished from other natures that are not God by *attributions of being,* just as in worship such perfections are actively ascribed to God alone in an eminent or infinite sense. As "God surely wishes to be recognized and worshipped as He has revealed Himself, that description of God is to be held, to which the mind reverts in prayer; for adoration is nothing but a confession, whereby we ascribe to the essence addressed in prayer all the attributes comprised in the definition [rather, description]."[229] Again, the point is neither to prove God's existence to a creature that lacks epistemic access in the Spirit's gift of faith to receive the Father's gift in the Son's self-donation nor to make this mystery of whole and divine giving ultimately comprehensible. The point is to say here on the earth what is *not* God, namely, the idol that is the manufacture of Adam who wants to be God; the point is to affirm what *can be* God, who *became* the afflicted object in our world, the man Jesus Christ, the cruciform icon of God. That task entails a descriptive, not speculative ontology.

Yet if we look carefully at the previous citation, we can see that Lutheran orthodoxy nonetheless presupposed in its otherwise worthy account of the doxological location of attribution in theology that the essence of God can be "defined." In spite of all emphatic disclaimers, it ventured to define God as a "spiritual being, subsisting of himself," i.e., as "an independent Spirit"[230] — that is, an immaterial, spiritual, or intellectual substance in the metaphysical traditions of Plato and Aristotle. If for a moment it is forgotten that "supreme being" is a relative, not an absolute notion, providing for a description of the irreducibility of the divine Being of the Trinity not an essential definition, the danger arises in this subtle way of displacing the personal distinction of the self-surpassing Father, and thus coming to think of the generic "Supreme Being" as in essence, that is, by definition, the First Cause of the eternal cosmos. Lutheran orthodoxy could actually fall from grace in this way. "By the term, God, is understood the first Being, because He is of himself and is the cause of all other things, and because He preserves and governs all things."[231] On this basis Lutheran orthodoxy then went on to distinguish between the quiescent or immanent attributes of the First Being in and of Himself, and then the operational attributes that apply to the causation, preservation, and governance of all the rest of the created beings. This procedure is highly problematic, as Pannenberg has brilliantly exposed: "A distinction is here made between God's essence and his causal relation to the world, since he brings forth the world freely and not by any necessity of his nature. Yet the qualities that are ascribed to him rest on his relation to the world which corresponds to the relations of creatures to him. This is not less true of negative attributes like infinity and eternity, which are negatively related to finitude and temporality. . . ."[232] What had been critically acknowledged by Anselm was now taken for granted. The conceit of insight replaced the poverty of humble description. The so-called quiescent attributes of divine aseity too, like eternity or immensity, become insights into the timeless, spaceless Ghost, not the apophatic qualification of relative and kataphatic affirmation of the exis-

---

229. Heinrich Schmid, *The Doctrinal Theology of the Evangelical Lutheran Church,* 3rd edition (Philadelphia: Lutheran Publication Society, 1899), citing Chemnitz, p. 114.

230. Schmid, *The Doctrinal Theology,* p. 115.

231. Schmid, *The Doctrinal Theology,* p. 116.

232. Pannenberg, *ST* 1, p. 364.

tence of God for us as the Creator of all the rest, as we saw above in our analysis of Anselm.

The essential point against the ambiguity of the theological tradition here is that a metaphysical First Cause cannot give us what is promised, the divine irreducibility of the triune God who relates to us freely in grace; it can only give us a false infinite, a finite god, a god defined, i.e., limited essentially by the causal role it plays in the cosmological totality, along the lines of the clear-thinking Spinoza's *natura naturans* in distinction from *natura naturata*. Sensing this slippery slope to pantheism when the metaphysical notion of substance is consistently applied in theology, if one should nonetheless want to revise Aristotle by the Bible, it seems that one must maintain God's irreducible "essence in its own unrelated and transcendent self-identity apart from all relation to the world" (Pannenberg); yet the only available category to accomplish that is Aristotle's very notion of substance, "that which remains the same beneath all change." So you get the God of philosophical monotheism dressed in biblical garb, for instance, Lutheran orthodoxy's "spiritual being, subsisting of himself," "an independent Spirit." Compounding one error upon another, the independent Spirit's engagement with His creature, the world of time, change, and becoming, becomes fundamentally aporetic, i.e., God's relation to this world becomes something purely "accidental" to God. One makes a virtue of necessity here by invoking analogy, so that God, remaining substantially above the fray, can be imitated by creatures here below, when by revelation they come supernaturally to know what God the Substance is like. Jesus is the revealer (why He is better at this than other candidates who actually undertook this work, like Moses, Muhammad, the Buddha, et cetera, goes unspoken). He does not save creatures from their sins. He shows them "what God is like" so that they can save themselves from their sins. And the total critique on a world captive to structures of malice and injustice that is the cross of the Son of God goes by the wayside. Jesus becomes the Golden Calf of Christendom.

Pannenberg stresses that in the process of working out the divine attributes in this dualistic way of essential attributes of the independent spiritual substance and the accidental attributes concerning its relation to the cosmos, the eschatological character of creation was eclipsed by protology and the agency of creation was credited to generic divine substance rather than to the Father of the Son in the Spirit. In the course of time what begins in theology in this way could only lead through deism on to today's atheism; for "the essence is real only in its attributes, without which it is an empty idea. If there are no qualities, there is no divine essence to bear them. If the cloak falls, the duke falls with it."[233] In genuine Trinitarianism, Pannenberg argues, the essence of God to whom the attributes are ascribed in worship simply *is* the almighty Father, whose very same being of giving, moreover, is begotten in the Son and breathed in the Spirit and so eternally returned to the Father in the ectypal love — worship, if you will, self-

---

233. Pannenberg, *ST* 1, p. 364.

offering — of the triune life.[234] It is the Son in the Spirit who eternally gives His God and Father all the glory. This active ascription of the predicates of majesty to His God and Father by the eternal Son *is* the properly doxological identification of the being which God is, as in the Kingdom prayer's doxology: "Thine is the kingdom, the power, and the glory forever." This ascription of the predicates of majesty within the life of the Trinity by the Son who in the Spirit gives the glory to His Father does not indicate an impersonal, self-standing divine substance, but it does provide theology with its description of divine being, the predicates of majesty: wisdom, power, and love *ad intra* and so also *ad extra.*

Under the influence of the substance/accident scheme of Aristotle, however, the divine attributes have been divided into the two categories of immanent and operational, or metaphysical and moral, respectively. On the surface this division corresponds to the two accents of distance and intimacy in the appellation "heavenly Father." God's being is "heavenly," i.e., transcendent, in a category of its own without analogy to anything earthly other than the analogy of heaven itself as that which is beyond the earthly. As ungraspable, God's being may only be characterized negatively by saying what it is not: not visible, not tangible, not mutable, not measurable, not bounded, not compounded, in a word *infinite.* As discussed above in Part One of this work, Pannenberg is willing in this connection even to concede a general notion of deity as the horizon presupposed in finite self-awareness, a *sensus divinitatis* more or less criticized, refined, and articulated in philosophical theology "with its statements about the unity, immutability, and eternity of God [which in turn] is a sophisticated form of the general idea of God which is more or less vaguely presupposed in all religious talk about God and all proofs of God." He is quick to add, however, that philosophically to "formulate conditions for consistent talk about God in general" is "not to describe the concrete reality of God with the essential attributes which come to light in his specific acts in history."[235] That God is "heavenly," in other words, represents little more than an intelligent awareness of God as what is beyond us, *not* like us, so that the condition for the possibility of meaningful speech about God is provided by such negative concepts — whatever these may actually mean.

To know that the "heavenly" One beyond us in being is concretely "our Father," on the other hand, depends on revelation of God in His specific acts of history; and this further entails stipulating positive attributes like righteousness *(tsedaqah)*, faithfulness *(chesed)*, the pathos of love and wrath, or wisdom. These give knowledge of the "heavenly" being as the concrete *individual,* indeed true singularity, the *particular, though unbounded* existence of the one, true God. The two kinds of attribution will then be complementary in a dialectical way, so that when we speak of God's being we speak of holy righteousness, holy love, holy wisdom, and so on to describe (not define) the unique being of the heavenly Fa-

234. Pannenberg, *ST* 1, p. 389.
235. Pannenberg, *ST* 1, p. 394.

ther of the Son in the Spirit so that it can be identified on the earth, in space and time, without confusing it with earthly imposters — the idols and the demons, the "so-called gods and lords."

Thus far we have Pannenberg's revision of Lutheran orthodoxy's division of divine attributes into quiescent and operational in favor of a dialectic of apophatic and kataphatic ways. Recalling the critique of Pannenberg in this connection from Chapter Two, however, it must be underscored here that biblically the negative characterizations saying what God is not are summed up under the notion of *holiness*, i.e., the utter, uncanny uniqueness of being that separates the "wholly other" God in His own *gravitas* from all creatures: "Who can survive before Yahweh, the holy God?" (1 Sam. 6:20). Yet, at the same time, this God is revealed as the holy One *in our midst* (Hos. 11:9) and not beyond us, that is to say, in the zeal of His exclusive claim to be our God and that we be His people: "Because he is the God of the covenant, Yahweh does not jealously keep his holiness for himself, shielding it from all contamination by making it the barrier between the spheres of the divine and human. His jealously impels him, on the contrary, to manifest his holiness . . . Yahweh sanctifies . . . ," i.e., calls and makes holy to Himself.[236] In Israel's characterization of God's holy otherness by such active, outreaching, ingathering zeal of love the revision of the antecedent metaphysics of the ancient cosmogonies is underway (including, then, the merely apophatic critique of the cosmogonic myths as initiated by the pre-Socratics and turned into a program of philosophical theology by Plato). Von Rad emphasized in this connection the "zeal" of Yahweh's holiness (Exod. 20:5; 34:14; Deut. 6:14ff.; Josh. 24:19) "so much so that his zeal is simply understood as an expression of his holiness . . ."; consequently, "the holy was experienced as a power, and not as something in repose. . . ."[237] The zeal of the Lord, "this most personal of all the manifestations of his being,"[238] results in the "intolerant claim to exclusive worship," something "unique in the history of religion, for in antiquity the cults were on easy terms with one another . . ."[239] (much like today in Euro-America). The radical monotheism of the Bible, with its exclusive claim as enunciated in the First Commandment and recapitulated in Jesus' proclamation of the kingdom of His heavenly Father (Matt. 6:33), has its primal roots here: general ideas of God — the eternal, the other, the beyond — are predicated only of Yahweh to qualify His historical actions as zealous and exclusive because alone saving.[240] God's holiness is thus not a sanctuary in the

---

236. Jacobs, *Theology of the Old Testament*, p. 89.

237. Gerhard von Rad, *Old Testament Theology*, two volumes, trans. D. M. G. Stalker (New York, Evanston, San Francisco, London: Harper & Row, 1962), 1:204-5.

238. Von Rad, *Old Testament Theology*, 1:207; citing Eichrodt: the zeal represents an "emotion sprung from the very depths of personality: as the zealous one Jahweh is a person to the highest possible degree."

239. Von Rad, *Old Testament Theology*, 1:208.

240. Thus even "the way in which Jahweh introduces himself, 'I am Jahweh, your God,' presupposes a situation of polytheism" (von Rad, *Old Testament Theology*, p. 210).

Beyond marked off from the world but rather manifested in it in contestation with unholy powers of malice and injustice usurping God's reign over His creation. Thus God's holy otherness may and indeed must be positively described, named, articulated, even imaged and conceptualized.[241]

The Decalogue's prohibition of images (which are "first and foremost the bearer of a revelation"),[242] as argued above, is not to be understood as a Platonic-Kantian rejection of revelation in and through finite forms, but of the "worship of other gods" telling other stories of the world and its salvation by means of other images than cruciform Jesus. To be sure, "in her relation to God Israel, unlike the other nations, is not directed to a cultic image, but to the bare word of God."[243] It is the word, however, which pictures the outstretched and mighty arm of the LORD rescuing from bondage and in the fullness of time, the Father who spared not His own Son but gave Him up for us all. Being heard, this Word gives sight as we saw in the Johannine resurrection narratives discussed in Chapter Three. This new seeing of faith both sees through imposters and sees into the plan and purpose of God given in the *icon of God,* Crucified Jesus as the Christ of Israel, the Logos of God incarnate. The prohibition of images understood in service of the Word of God works a "relentless shattering of cherished concepts of God"[244] even more than of graphic representations, since by its revision of classical cosmogonies the obedient human couple living in conformity to the covenant by doing God's will on the earth now forms the image of God on earth. Ultimately this new and true Adam is Jesus Christ, the image of God, betrothed to the ecclesia to form the new human couple, in whom God makes Himself known in an iconic image, when and where the Spirit unifies the sign and the thing signified for the obedience of faith. Iconic revelation should warn interpreters "against a philosophic misunderstanding of the commandment. Its intention was not by any means to debar the people from representing Jahweh in concrete form,"[245] but to direct them away from the vague, general deity of fixed notions and pre-

---

241. Von Rad acutely criticizes the tacit Platonism of "the older critical school" of the nineteenth century: "Starting from an antithesis between visible and invisible, material and spiritual, which, while quite generally held, is quite alien to the Old Testament, the critics thought that the second commandment had to be understood as the expression of a special spirituality in the worship of God, as the signal, important overcoming of a spiritual and cultic primitivism, and so as the attainment of a decisive stage in the education of the human race . . ." (von Rad, *Old Testament Theology,* 1:213). Since biblical speech about God is surfeit with literary images that may function to refer to Yahweh, the prohibition would cancel out the Word itself, if the intention were to ban graphic depictions or theological concepts, anything but literal speech. But biblical metaphor can and does refer to the being of God, which however must always be qualified as the holy other infinite being in community.

242. Von Rad, *Old Testament Theology,* 1:214.

243. Von Rad, *Old Testament Theology,* 1:216.

244. Von Rad, *Old Testament Theology,* 1:218.

245. Von Rad, *Old Testament Theology,* 1:219. It is no less anthropomorphic to think of God as Mind than as matter!

conceived ideas that undergirds the cosmic order of the cosmogonies and to direct them toward the zealous holiness of the One and Only who had brought them up out of the land of Egypt and the house of bondage. "In the midst of the changes inherent in a revelation of God in history *chesed* represents the permanent element which allows Yahweh always to be faithful to himself."[246] The holy zeal of Scripture's passionlessly passionate God of love is manifest in Yahweh's *faithfulness* — to Himself, to His own goal, to the coming of His kingdom, and just so also to His chosen people that in fullness of time realizes the promise of the Beloved Community by which all nations of the earth will be blessed. This One who sets the oppressed free and zealously, jealously lays claim to them in love is the holy God, God alone, the one, true God. God's faithfulness to Himself, *this* divine substantiality through the physical time of creatures, is made known to creatures in and through time. For God's holiness is manifested in this fidelity, not compromised or distorted by it.

As God's holy being is manifested in His fidelity through created time, we recall once again with Pannenberg that "the eternal essence of God is not itself a subject alongside the three persons. It is not the one subject that includes the persons so that they are reduced to mere aspects of the divine subjectivity. Only the three persons are the direct subjects of the divine action."[247] Divine nature is not a quasi-personal agency, but the abstract condition for the possibility of agency, the set of possibilities that must be available to an agent for it to do what it intends. God's "being" proceeds from the Father through the Son in the Spirit and in return of the Spirit with the Son to the Father. Once again, then, we ask: if divine substantiality consists in the one life of the Three that can be without creatures, but freely chooses rather to be with creatures, what difference does it make to locate the agency in God in His works *ad extra* in the collaboration of the Three from origin to eschaton rather than in one timeless and generic substance? The early Pannenberg pointed out that in Israel "the God of history is essentially person because events occur at his initiative in unforeseeable ways. If, on the contrary, the totality of reality is conceived under the idea of law, then the ground of all events can hardly be understood as Creator and thus as person. This is shown by the depersonalization of the divine in the history of Greek religion. . . ."[248] This depersonalization happened precisely by the Platonic move from mythology to

---

246. Jacobs, *Theology of the Old Testament,* p. 105.

247. Pannenberg, *ST* 1, p. 384.

248. Pannenberg, *Basic Questions in Theology,* two volumes, trans. G. H. Kehm (Philadelphia: Fortress, 1972), 1:233. Following the lead of the nineteenth-century theologian H. Cremer, the mature Pannenberg sustains this criticism: although "the statements about God's attributes in traditional theology were backed up by scripture . . . in reality they were based on the functions of God as first cause of the world," which "purely causal relation" necessarily overlooks the "purposeful nature of action" involving choice, i.e., the "selection and fulfillment of the goal" (*ST* 1, pp. 368-69). One cannot safely infer from effect to cause to ascertain the purpose of a personal agent, unless the causality itself is understood as personal agency revealing itself in its action.

ontology, the critique of the idolatrous personal deities of polytheism and re-placement of them by abstract conceptions of the divine nature,[249] such as Mind (Pannenberg's "law"). Reasoning from effect to cause delivers the impersonal "ground of the present world," the First Cause, the one perfect substance, *actus purus,* the agency of all agencies presupposed by the many imperfect substances forming our world in their own acts of being. But the "biblical conviction that *the creation is still underway* to its proper reality and that the essences of all things will finally be decided simultaneously with the final end by which God will defi-nitely be revealed . . ."[250] requires a different, doxological kind of ontology, which confesses God not only as Origin, but also as Goal and Mediation. For Pannen-berg, the resurrection of Jesus from the dead warrants "worshipful speech [that] anticipates ultimate revelation,"[251] so that the point of talk about God's being or nature is not only to ground the status quo in its Origin, but also to move the status quo towards its Goal.

A virtue of Pannenberg's pragmatic point here — that theology's cognitive work is not merely to understand the world, but to change it — is that one is de-livered by it from the perpetual oscillation in classical theology between divine transcendence and immanence, in favor of divine imminence — not the end of time but the in-breaking of the time of the end. Some such dialectic to guard speech about God from profanation and the world from self-worship is necessary in any event; but in thinking of God who comes from God as the imminence of the Kingdom of God, this needed dialectic of the already and the not yet is derived from Trinitarian advent rather than the abstract opposition of the divine and created natures. In gospel revelation, God is at hand, not in hand. The Son brings the Father near, but the Father alone can validate the Son. The Son promises the Spirit, but the Spirit bestows faith in the Son's promise of the Spirit by the Word concerning Him. The Spirit incorporates believers into the life of God, but only the Father sends the Spirit. And so on. The positive attributes of that one holy divine and eternal Life in its coming to us, by which we distinguish it from, but also properly relate it to, creatures appears under the three distinct personal ways of being God that mutually refer to each other, so that a creature can "possess" or "have" God only in faith being constantly circulated through this living peri-choresis. The almighty Father refers us to the wisdom of the Word made flesh, but the dying Son refers us to the Father's almighty promise of life, and these two are held together in dynamic unity by the Spirit's loving movements of *katabasis* (descent) and *anabasis* (ascent).[252] One cannot get a handle on this such as to

249. I call to attention in this connection a little-known work in defense of Homer against Platonic criticism, "Preface to Homer," in Philipp Melanchthon, *Orations on Philosophy and Education,* ed. Sachiko Kusakawa (Cambridge: Cambridge University Press, 1999), pp. 38-59.

250. Pannenberg, *Basic Questions,* 1:237, emphasis added.

251. Pannenberg, *Basic Questions,* 1:237.

252. This perichoresis, which Pannenberg unfortunately seemingly identified with the no-tion of a field of force in contemporary physics (e.g., *ST* 1, p. 383), would be the proper version of

possess it like a thing as a piece of property. One has it only in faith that ventures to live in this circulation.

In such Trinitarianism the holy attributes of the divine Life belong first to the almighty Father and are revealed as Jesus proclaims Him the coming king of creation, prays to Him, obeys Him, and surrenders His life to Him, ascribing to Him alone the kingdom, the power and the glory. Just so and only so the man Jesus receives these very predicates of divine majesty from the Spirit who raised Him from death and exalted Him as Lord, to whom now is given all authority in heaven and on earth (Matt. 28:18). In the latter two movements of the Son's obedience and the Spirit's vindication, the Father's almighty divine power appears under the aspects of wisdom and love. The wisdom of God, which is folly to the world, is revealed in Jesus' obedient suffering. The creative love of God, only for the weak and ungodly, is revealed in the Holy Spirit's vivification of smitten Jesus who surrendered to God for us into the solidarity of death. This is the love which unites anew the Father who sent and the Son who went into the teeth of this most drastic diastasis in order to unite the sinful creature with the holy Creator.

Pannenberg, however, still developed his teaching on the divine attributes in a version of the traditional but ambiguous twofold categorization, concretely, as the attributes of infinity and the attributes of love respectively — a descendant of Barth's distinction of divine attributes of freedom and love. In substantial sympathy with this aspect of Pannenberg's (and Barth's) theology, I wish nevertheless in what follows to develop the trinitarian dialectic of divine attribution somewhat differently than they. In the self-giving of the Father of the Son in the Spirit, God's holy act of being may be described by essential attributes appropriated to the persons in the project of eschatological creation in the threefold categorization that has been tacitly employed throughout this work: power, wisdom, and love respectively. That is to say, with deference to the lost contribution of Leibniz and in distinction from Hegel's kenotic disremption of it into the "cunning" of reason, the *wisdom* of God which mediates power and love to bring forth justice on the

---

the dialectic that Barth sought in order to sustain the subjectivity of God as the free Lord in the very act of His self-objectification for us in Jesus Christ. Barth's Christology finally foundered on the "diastasis" of the substance doctrine: "World remains world. But God is God." Bruce McCormack, *Karl Barth's Critically Realistic Dialectical Theology: Its Genesis and Development 1909-1936* (Oxford: Clarendon, 1995), p. 129. Hence a genuine personal, hypostatic union must finally be regarded as a way of talking, not a communication of being. The diastasis may be traced through Kant (p. 130) to ". . . the impossibility of identifying the Word of God with either the secular form in which the divine content veils itself or the divine content in absence of the secular form — for both content and form belong to the event of the Word. But here a problem immediately arises. The event of the Word occurs only where a synthesis of content and form take place, but this is a synthesis which no human being can bring about" (pp. 464-65). True, so far as it goes: the Christological personal union is the Spirit's unification of the sign and the thing signified; but this unification as the Spirit's work means that here, concretely, the world becomes God and God becomes the world.

earth has been strangely neglected in modern theology. The folly of the cross has been treated as mere folly, as sheer paradox of nonsense and not as the folly of God which is wiser than the world in its wisdom. In any event, let us now see how these predicates of power, wisdom, and love are ascribed to the unique being of God in the doxology of worship that anticipates the eternal and co-equal Trinity.

## Doxological Analytic of the Holy Existence

God's eternal "act of being," we are arguing, should not be conceived along naturalistic and hence inevitably modalist lines, as in the argument Thomas inherited and adapted from Avicenna. Rather, the act of God's being in Christian theology that makes God to be One is the irreducible mystery of the almighty Father's self-surpassing donation of all that He is and has, save this agency as the Father, to the Son and to the Spirit, so that they as personal agents in turn can as freely and as wholly return what they have received, thus constituting one eternal Life of giving, receiving, and returning — a circle of divine eros, if you will, that becomes a creative spiral of agape in relation to what is not God, that is, to creatures. So according to this doctrine of God's eternal being as consistent perichoresis (John 17:20-24), the God who exists by way of mutually indwelling persons can give Himself purely to the creature, indeed to the sinful creature, without giving Himself away[253] but rather, in the act of coming to exist for them in Jesus Christ, restoring the lost creature to the rejoicing of all heaven (Luke 15:7, 10). God, being the event of finding love to be enjoyed within its own eternal circulation, becomes in its outward spiral coming to creatures "the love of the cross, born of the cross, which turns in the direction where it does not find good which it may enjoy, but where it may confer good upon the bad and needy person."[254]

Infinity, too, is not to be conceived along naturalist lines, the *apeiron* of Anaximander, who conceived of the divine as deathless and indestructible infinity without an origin but origin of all the rest. "The best description of the *Apeiron* is in its privative name: something with no limit, and any attempt to be more specific could be considered by [Anaximander] presumptuous."[255] Like all the alpha-privatives, infinity cannot in Christian theology tell us anything affirmative of God; it rather stipulates a warning to come no closer, but to take off one's shoes when treading on holy ground (Exod. 3:5). It is quite another story, however,

---

253. Following with appreciation, if also the by-now-standard reservation regarding the modalistic tendency of Western theology, Nico den Bok, "Always Working Always Resting, Jan van Ruusbroec: An Original Contribution to Western Trinitarian Theology," in *Trinitarian Theology in the Medieval West,* ed. Pekka Kärkkäinen (Helsinki: Luther Agricola Society, 2007), pp. 188-225.

254. *LW* 31, p. 57.

255. Adam Drozdek, *Greek Philosophers as Theologians: The Divine Arche* (Aldershot, UK and Burlington, VT: Ashgate, 2007), p. 11.

when infinity and simplicity construed in the biblical sense of the Holy come to modify the affirmations of God made in the literal sense of ordinary human language. The divine Life of love is as such unlimited, simple, and holy in its eternal giving, receiving, and returning, not then as the putative metaphysical insight into a merely timeless self-identity, nor even as neo-Platonism's mind knowing itself and willing itself in the event of coming to self-consciousness (least of all does the triune God need creatures as a means to achieving divine self-consciousness).[256] Therefore, this *unbounded* event of divine becoming, circulating eternally, *can and may and in fact does* spiral forth from its peace and blessedness to work blessing and bring peace for all that is other than itself, as we have pictured the matter following Edwards.

According to its own "metaphysical time" (DeWeese), the triune God spirals forth in the mask of the physical space-time of creatures, immediately operative everywhere working and giving life, in the fullness of time to sanctify the profane and justify the ungodly by making place for such creatures in this "enlargement" of divine life. This unbounded God does not "necessarily" create; nothing binds Him other than Himself. Yet as the unbounded Trinity, in so doing this God manifests a "disposition" to create, indeed to take the good pleasure of love in the creation (Gen. 1:31) as also the pain of love's wrath at the violence, degradation, and death of these creatures (Gen. 6:5-6), and by these divine dispositions united in the cross and resurrection of the Incarnate Son to accomplish the purpose in, and not apart from, the creature of the coming of the Beloved Community. *Esse Deum dare.* It is *fitting* that this God create and faithfully redeem and fulfill what He has created.

Here we must face a significant objection. How is this ascription of infinite, hence innovative vitality to the God of the gospel to be understood, so that God's being or nature is understood as life and never as less than life? T. F. Torrance, who has been our guide in these matters, argued that if we take *hypostasis* or person to indicate life in relation to *other* living persons, and *ousia* or being or nature to indicate reality in the relation of identity to oneself, then "in God one and the same identical 'substance' or object, without any division, substitution, or differentiation of content, is permanently presented in three distinct objective forms . . . in the light of God's self-revelation as the Creator who is beyond all created being or *ousia,* and who alone is *ousia* [= self-identical] in the strict sense . . . he is the only one who really and truly *is.* . . ."[257] But tacitly, we have been critical of this interpretation which, in rightly wanting to affirm the substantiality of God in the sense of irreducibility in relation to His creatures and also in denying in turn such substantiality to creatures, slips imperceptibly into the error of reifying a concept and, in Trinitarian terms, creating a quaternity that thinks in modalist fashion of nature as if an agent rather than an abstract set of possibilities that

256. Hart, *Beauty of the Infinite,* p. 165.
257. Torrance, *Trinitarian Faith,* citing Prestige, p. 310.

may characterize a particular class of agents. In any case, such slippage makes the crucial nature-person distinction on which strong Trinitarian personalism rests vacuous. It is vacuous to say that God is one and the same identical object that is permanently presented in three distinctive objective forms. Either this is incoherent or it is that Western tendency to modalism reappearing yet again in the theologizing of a great theologian who has done so much to recover the authentic sense of Eastern Trinitarianism for the West. The key here, as Torrance himself also recognized, is to move away from all reifications of the concept of nature *by which to secure divine unity,* especially by the muddle of ascribing alpha-privatives to erase the evident contradictions. The way forward is rather to discover divine unity in consistent perichoresis, so that the irreducible reality or substantiality of God in His eternal Trinitarian life consists strictly and solely for us in the coming of the Beloved Community. In Paul's pointed words, "if Christ is not raised, your faith is futile and you are still in your sins" (1 Cor. 15:17).

The unification of the triune God, given its free involvement and hence commitment in human history, is event for us and so cannot now be less than this fulfillment of His Word incarnate by which the Spirit demonstrates the Father's own truthfulness in the time and space of creatures. And this demonstration of the truthfulness of God's putative Word is God's existence in the time and space of creatures, as all the Scripture proclaims in promising nothing less and therefore settling for nothing less. God's existence in another possible world does not concern us, who are creatures of time and space, who cannot leave behind the body to go there ("to heaven") without ceasing to be who we are, whose salvation can only be the redemption of the body that is the coming of God. We have, however, the earnest of this demonstration already now in the gift and work of the Holy Spirit who raised Jesus from the dead and proclaims Jesus to us as the Christ, the Son of God, to vouchsafe to us eternal life with Him before the Father. In repentance and faith, we have the Spirit "who mediates to us the life of God, glorifies Christ as the Son of the Father, by throwing his radiance upon him, who thus actualises among us the self-giving of God to us in his Son. . . . He is the bond *(syndesmos)* of the Holy Trinity in the midst of the Father and the Son, but also the bond *(syndesmos)* of truth and faith who creates unity among us and brings us into communion with the Father, the Son, and the Holy Spirit, into whose one name we are baptised."[258] In this way already now we attribute vitality to God as Lord and Giver of life in the person of the Spirit, who unifies what otherwise disintegrates and dies.

Because faith looks to the demonstration of God's existence at the eschaton of judgment, it already now ascribes existence to God. In similar fashion Anselm's *Monologion,* as pointed out above, presupposes God's moral faithfulness as Creator to the world, taken as His creation, in which the thinker, taken as a believer, actually lives. The faith that takes this actual world up to and including

---

258. Torrance, *Trinitarian Theology,* pp. 249-50.

the creation of the believer as the one created by the good God who does not lie or deceive in His works, thus believes in God's *goodness* and *wisdom* in the powerful work of creating the human creature in His image for His likeness. Anselm's reasoning proceeds on the supposition of the unity of truth and value in the judgment, articulated by Augustine in *Confessions* Book X, that it is better to be than not to be. Because of this supposition *of faith* (a Buddhist, for example, may not share it and a Nietzsche wants deeply to question it) that takes this world in spite of all perversity and corruption as the good creation of the wise God, with the correlate now drawn out that even perverse and corrupt being is better than nonbeing, it follows that "only the being who exists outside as well as in the [human] mind satisfies this definition [of that than which nothing greater can be thought] . . . if the argument is valid, the predicate 'does not exist' contradicts the subject 'God,' of whom non-existence cannot be predicated without contradiction."[259] That is all that Anselm claims in his so-called ontological "proof," which is rather a doxological analytic of God's existence as that than which nothing greater can be thought by the creature who has come to believe in God and to understand what she believes. The argument shows that theological statements that make no cognitive reference to God under truth-conditions, that is, that make no statement about God that are true or false depending on what and how God is,[260] self-destruct into pure vacuity, even though the truth of their claims cannot finally be settled by any other than God as His eschaton. Thus this latter is what it means already now to affirm that God exists. And this affirmation of God's existence is the conscience of theology that lives before the heavenly Father who sees in secret, before whom no secrets are hid, who knows and judges the heart.

What then is demonstrated other than the seeming triviality — not, however, to be taken for granted today — that believers believe in God as something not reducible to His relation to them? Anselm has argued analytically that this God to whom the Christian prays must be conceived as the bearer of the perfections requisite for a Creator of the good creation. Southern explains: "[T]his proof was not intended to be a proof of the existence of God, but a proof that the essences of Goodness, Truth, Justice, etc., which he had shown in the *Monologion* to be the necessary attributes of God, must cohere in a single Being, and that this Being, properly understood, cannot be thought of as non-existent."[261] The "necessary" being of the Creator of the good creation — that is to say, a consequent not an antecedent "necessity," given the freedom of God to create or not, to create this world rather than some other — exists as the personal harmony of this power or freedom with wisdom and love. When the believer affirms that God exists, this trinity of perfections is what is being affirmed. And such knowledge of God is not trivial, nor is it to be taken for granted. The God who promises to fulfill the cre-

---

259. Southern, *St. Anselm,* p. 130.

260. On truth-conditions in theology, see here Dennis Bielfeldt, chapter 2 in *SF,* pp. 59-130.

261. Southern, *St. Anselm,* p. 128.

ation by the coming of the Beloved Community must be conceived as personally able, competent, and willing to do what He has promised.

Kant famously thought he had refuted the "ontological proof" when he pointed out that "existence" is not a predicate, i.e., that the copula only serves to put some predicate in relation to a subject within the phenomenal world structured by space and time.[262] This is indeed a refutation, but not of Anselm. As we saw earlier, Anselm expressly noted that God's supreme or most real existence is affirmed in relation to us, not in and for itself, in his demonstration that the believer's God must be thought as the subject who properly owns and in whom thus harmonize the Creator's properties of power, wisdom, and goodness. Anselm's ascription of supreme reality to God is the doxological adoration of faith ascending by way of eminence from creation to its Creator by the access granted to the believer who wants to know what it is that she believes. He is not claiming that something in her mind — howsoever perfect — just so exists in reality. He claims that the theological subject in its act of praise intends the supremely real in relation to the ephemeral reality of the creation. It is an act that de-divinizes the world and restores it as creation precisely by glorifying the One to whom alone the predicates of Creator are worthily attributed. Fools, however, who foolishly say that there is no God are foolish because they end up divinizing some passing state of affairs when they fail to praise the Creator who is not reducible to their wants and needs. They do so because they use words like "God" in an unexamined way and construct sentences about "God" without understanding this meaning of the term "God exists" as irreducibility that summons the creature's prayer, praise, and thanksgiving. It is the wise creature, by contrast, who does not want to be God, but wants God to be God; this wisdom is the access given to the theological subject by the Word incarnate who invites her to pray, "Our Father in heaven." "[B]y meditation, the right-thinking person has risen from understanding the meaning of the word, 'God,' to understanding the thing ('a Being outside the mind') for which the word ('God') stands and further, to understanding that God cannot not exist."[263] In this way, the sign and the thing signified are united for the theological subject already now in ascribing existence to the God whose existence is to be demonstrated at the coming of the Reign.

So the critically dogmatic theologian Anselm's "proof" is a work of conceptual *analysis* that takes its point of departure, that is, its epistemic access, in certain contents given by faith (the Credo's "I believe in God, the Father almighty, Creator . . .") and sees that these contents entail significant *theological* commitments: God's existence is external to the mind, i.e., irreducible to it; God's existence is necessary for any coherent thought about the world as the good creation; God as Creator cannot be thought of as nonexistent without self-contradiction;

262. Immaneul Kant, *Critique of Pure Reason,* trans. J. M. D. Meiklejohn (Mineola, NY: Dover, 2003), p. 335.

263. Southern, *St. Anselm,* p. 131.

God as Creator is to be thought existing as the proper subject of the predicates of divine glory by which the Father almighty is understood as able, competent, and willing to do what He says in creating all that is not God, up to the believer who prays, and unto the coming of the Reign.[264]

If Anselm's argument had seriously intended a proof that would convince nonbelievers *solo ratione* that the Christian God really exists, it could thus be faulted for begging questions taken on faith: for example, whether God must be conceived as *the one bearer of all perfections pertinent to the Creator in a true and dynamic coherence,* i.e., as the Trinity, that is, not as God according either to atheism, theism, or polytheism; or that this reality in which I write these words and you read is indeed the immediate creation of the God who does not lie or deceive, not the miscarriage imagined by Gnostics or the cosmic fluke the Epicureans theorize or the web of necessity the Stoics spin. In fact, Descartes' famous and influential modern version of the "ontological proof" discards precisely the personal aspect of address to God the Father, Lord of heaven and earth, which is key to Anselm's epistemic access. For Descartes, it is the notion of perfect being that is demonstrated to exist in the sense of *the necessary ideal* of thought, foreshadowing Kant's regulative idea of God, which imperfectly thinking things require to gain clear and distinct conceptions. "And when I take note of the fact that I doubt, or that I am a thing that is incomplete and dependent, there comes to mind a clear and distinct idea of a being that is independent and complete, that is, an idea of God. And from the mere fact that such an idea is in me, or that I who have this idea exist, I draw the obvious conclusion that God also exists. . . ."[265]

In spite of Pannenberg's unfortunate dependence on Descartes in this connection (due to his own idealist appropriation of Cartesian infinitude as the horizon of finite self-conscious understanding), he provides a sketch, useful in part, of the implications of faith's analysis of God's unbounded reality as "external to the mind" and "necessary for any coherent thought about the world": "God is always present already in all human life. He is there for us and our world even though he is not known as God. He is there as the undefined infinite which is formed by

264. Southern, *St. Anselm,* p. 132.

265. *Meditations on First Philosophy,* 3rd edition, trans. Donald A. Cress (Indianapolis: Hackett, 1993), p. 36. It is true of course that Descartes bows before the altar of traditional theological descriptions of God as "a certain substance that is infinite, independent, supremely intelligent and supremely powerful, and that created me along with everything that exists." But his decisive consideration is that "the perception of the infinite is somehow prior in me to the perception of myself. For how would I understand that I doubt and that I desire, that is, that I lack something and that I am not wholly perfect, unless there were some idea in me of a more perfect being, by comparison with which I might recognize my defects." Hence, "the idea that I have of God is the most true, the most clear and distinct," and consequently, given Descartes' epistemology, therewith "necessarily exists" (pp. 30-31). *Pace* Pannenberg, *ST* 1, p. 352. Leibniz's account of divine infinity is far more amenable to Christian theology, indeed to Pannenberg's own concerns, as we shall see below.

the primal intuition of our awareness of reality, as the horizon within which we comprehend all else by limitation . . . the undefined mystery that is present and active in our lives . . . the mystery that embraces all things and that never comes to an end with the march of time." Therefore "we can and do call [the undefined infinite] God in the process of concrete revelation. . . ."[266] It is true that, if God exists as we have now determined according to analysis of the Christian faith, God is "already present already in all human life." But presence as "undefined infinite" is pure incognito and anonymity. Little is gained by this affirmation, and the price of construing God's unknown presence in the idealist fashion that serves to isolate human self-consciousness from the natural processes in which it remains embedded is too high for the theology of the Beloved Community.

The "undefined infinite" is the boundless Chaos saturating the phenomenal world; it is the *Deus absconditus* of the natural man's holistic experience of life as dark strife of superior forces. As you believe, so you have. Behind this incognito works the self-surpassing Almighty Father who is creating all things, unmasked and revealed by the faith of Jesus Christ in Him at the cross, in the power of the same Spirit who first inspired and then vindicated His faith now given to believers. In this epistemic shift, we differentiate the present approach from Pannenberg's Cartesian horizon of infinity for the acquisition of self- and world-consciousness (still a version of Protestant progressivism) in favor of the imminence of God who breaks into the strong man's house to bind him and plunder his goods. We discern instead apocalyptic conjunctions of power, wisdom, and love as events breaking in and breaking up the structures of malice and injustice by working new, ecstatic existence of faith in hope for the world by the love of God above all and therewith for all creatures in and under God, that is, the Beloved Community. Only in this way can we affirm already now that God exists, lest we say that this existing reality is God, necessity, dark fate, repetition of the same, eternal death.

Anselm's analysis of the act of praise makes clear what is involved in Jesus' ascription of the kingdom, the power and the glory to His heavenly Father alone, whose kingdom comes. Faith in the almighty Father is faith in the divine Person who exists ecstatically from Himself but for others, and so is able to grant life to others as from the surplus of an inexhaustible act of being. This act of power is by the same token no act of arbitrary self-assertion; as the Almighty Father is the eternal Father of His own Son on whom He breathes His own Spirit, His Reign comes wholly as gift in the conjunction with divine wisdom and love. Pannenberg himself holds dear the fundamental point here that would differentiate Christian knowledge of God from a strict and consequent Cartesianism: "The three persons of Father, Son and Spirit are primarily the subject of divine action. By their cooperation the action takes form as that of the one God. This must be the starting point of a Christian answer to the totalitarian implications of a single divine sub-

266. Pannenberg, *ST* 1, p. 356.

ject acting without restriction."[267] Yet Pannenberg takes his theological point of departure from the Cartesian horizon of infinitude — the modern domestication of transcendence in the interest of the assertion of the sovereign self — rather than from the Spirit-born, Christ-united believer's praise of the almighty Father whose eminent existence affirmed makes the world the gift of His creation again. Thus he still follows the Western tradition's tendency toward a twofold (freedom to love), rather than threefold (freedom to love wisely) articulation of the attributes of divine being. In this way, Pannenberg fails to follow through on the implications of his own strong distinction between the Son and the Spirit.

Karl Barth, we should note here, had in fact gone on from his starting point in the Anselm book to break new ground in liberating the God of the gospel from the prison-house of Greek naturalism by redescribing God's Being in Act as the "event" of "freedom to love." In his usual "dialectical" fashion, Barth summed up the "almighty power" of God, the traditional "immanent" or "ontological" predicates of the divine majesty, under the notion of "freedom," which he then correlated with the self-giving love of the Son, the traditional "operative" or "moral" predicates. He thus made this correlation of freedom and love to correspond with the personal relations of the Father and the Son. He wanted in this way to overcome the tendency in traditional "substance metaphysics" to think of God's reality as some static thing-like substance, some "spiritual stuff" underlying the personal relations, like a solid stage on which the persons extemporize. But if one is thinking in this way about self-identical spiritual stuff as the foundation, God's feet, as it were, get stuck in concrete and God's performance is profoundly constrained. It becomes theologically incomprehensible how this primary simple substance, the point of which is to ground, can at the same time live, move, act, reach out, and innovate in love as love must do. God is by nature then caught in the cross-tides of apparently contradictory "qualities" like irresistible power and condescending love. Barth saw the culprit here as the classical metaphysical notion of deity as impassible or immutable *substance,* which fails to think out the biblical depiction of God as the free subject of the *event* of His own being: ". . . with regard to the being of God, the word 'event' or 'act' is final. . . . To its deepest depths, God's Godhead consists in the fact that it is an event."[268]

For Barth this being in act is what characterizes personal being, and he can go so far to say that "the real person is not man but God. It is not God who is a person by extension, but we. God exists in His act. God is his own decision. God lives from and by himself. . . . Every statement of what God is, and explanation how God is, must always state and explain what and how He is in His act and decision."[269] This ontology of act parallels Zizioulas's claim that the almighty Father constitutes deity in the act of being which is the generation of the Son and

267. Pannenberg, *ST* 1, p. 388.
268. *CD* II/1, p. 263.
269. *CD* II/1, p. 272.

spiration of the Spirit (though that is not exactly how Barth takes it). If we take our very notion of deity from the Bible, in either case we understand the deity of God spiritually, as the event of a life, indeed as eternal Life itself, and so economically as the *coming of the kingdom,* the redemption of the body, our incorporation into the Beloved Community. When we analyze this event, we understand that "God is He who, without having to do so," i.e., in majestic freedom, "seeks and creates fellowship between Himself and us," so that in condescending love, it is in "an overflow of His essence that he turns to us."[270] He *is* the Father of the Son in this free act of love for us. Freedom and love thus provide the two basic categories of the attributes of God conceived dialectically as the event of the divine Life. God truly is the free event of love; where this happens on the earth, God comes. God happens.

Christian theology does well to adopt Barth's approach against the ghostly being designated by the Platonic alpha-privatives; yet today we need to develop it more fully in the manner of the doctrine of consistent perichoresis. Barth especially wanted to avoid the danger of generic notions of divine perfection like "omnipotence" hijacking the gospel's presentation of the Father's almighty power in the sending of the Son. In the gospel the Father displays His almighty power by sending His Son small in the manger, thence weak and defeated on the cross. Barth wanted theology to derive its concrete descriptions of God's almighty power *from this very act* in which God determines Himself to be God *in Christ,* as God *for us.* Barth's pioneering effort, however, is in need of fuller trinitarian development. As it stands, the dialectic of freedom and love is inadequate and reflects what Robert Jenson (in another connection) called a de facto "binitarianism" in Barth. In his dialectic of freedom and love, Barth often seems to deprive the Spirit of genuine agency and the result is to collapse the *proprium* of the Spirit's action of divine self-communication in salvation (i.e., as the One "who calls, gathers, enlightens and sanctifies the whole Christian church on earth, etc." — Luther) into the "love" objectively manifest in the Son's self-donation as Word incarnate. These two are inseparable but not the same. Only the Son is incarnate to bear the sin of the world and thus to rise victorious over the tyrants. This is the cunning of the Word made flesh, the folly of God that is wiser than the wisdom of the world, the wisdom of the divine economy of salvation hidden from the ages but now revealed. Only the Spirit raises Jesus to new life and the believer in Him to newness of life. This is the goodness of God that makes good even on what is dead, lost, estranged, disgraced, and ruined. The Word is received in the Spirit; the Spirit is given through the Word. If we keep these personal operations distinct and related in this way, then we have to conceive the event of God's coming, the advent of Beloved Community, as the freedom that loves — neither recklessly nor timidly — but wisely.

Barth tended to assimilate the Spirit to the Son for fear of "enthusiasm," lest

270. *CD* II/1, p. 273.

the "objectivity" of the Son's universal act of reconciliation be compromised by inflated claims for human subjectivity, be those claims either the wishful thinking of political utopianism or triumphalistic political-ecclesiastical claims of believers for Christendom.[271] In order not to reduce the gospel to the church establishment, the pious believer, or the political zealot, Barth tended to fuse together what are actually the distinct personal operations of the Son's oblation once for all and the Spirit's election to faith by the mission of the ecclesia to the nations. Thus the difference between them is eclipsed into the doctrine of universal reconciliation that we examined and critiqued in the previous chapter. Jenson detailed the ecumenical and ecclesiological price Barth paid in losing sight of the ecclesia in mission as the Spirit's earthly and public anticipation of the coming reign of God by the march of the gospel in world history. I would emphasize here another aspect in line with Jenson's critique: the *wisdom* of the Father in exercising power through weakness in Christ's lowliness and in showing forth love by the Spirit's calling of humanity (i.e. election in history, as in Romans 9–11) into this faith of Jesus through the "folly" of concrete space-time preaching of the gospel (1 Cor. 1:18–2:16). As previously argued, the Spirit in Barth sometimes seems little more than a religious cipher for the subjective appropriation in adult decision of what objectively obtains in the event of God's self-revelation. Preaching (not to mention baptism and Eucharist) becomes a merely human witness to this divine event other than itself, rather than being in public act the Spirit's own calling and enlightening, divinely doing the electing to faith that forms every believer into a living member of Christ's body for a concrete and particular way on the earth, as argued above in Part Two of this work. New creation in the Spirit in this way has a diminished reality in Barth's account — always for fear of falsely objectifying and capturing the free subjectivity of God. Barth's entirely legitimate concern is that "God gives himself, but He does not give Himself away. He does not give up being God in becoming a creature, in becoming man. He does not cease to be God."[272] Barth clearly wishes to safeguard the *freedom* of God in the *love* of Christ, so that God's love does not become the proud possession of the exclusivist Christian and/or triumphalist church.

The better way to safeguard the freedom of God's love in Christ, however, is to point to the *wisdom* of this love in the "joyful exchange," so that the Christian's *possession* of God's love is always in the event of faith's surrender of sinful self-love at the coming of the Lamb of God, which the Spirit works in conforming the believer to Christ's cross and resurrection where and when the Spirit unifies the sign and the thing signified. Instead of this, Barth occasionally speaks of the "carelessness" of God's grace, an "antinomian" gospel to the effect that the world in all its godless secularity simply *is* reconciled, even though it does not yet know

---

271. Robert W. Jenson, "You Wonder Where the Spirit Went," *Pro Ecclesia* 2, no. 3 (Summer 1993): 296.

272. *CD* IV/1, p. 185.

it — the view criticized at the end of the previous chapter. As Krusche pointed out, Barth's doctrine of objective reconciliation tends to reduce the Spirit's historical action of calling to faith and repentance to a merely noetic matter: some know themselves to be saved, while others do not yet know that they are saved. The outpouring of love by the Spirit in the hearts of believers disappears from sight as the crucial event of election on the earth, as history, dying and rising with Christ as God's own passage from wrath to mercy. Being called into the new life of the community appears to make no *ontic* difference, only a *noetic* one. The strange fate of postwar European political Barthianism, which gave up on the church after the Church Struggle and turned to radical politics to chase after the ever-elusive revolution of God in utopian politics yet ended up collaborating with Stalinism, reflects the great irony of antinomianism; those who deny in principle the law's authority to condemn sin end up as all the more strident and self-deceived moralists.

But "the foolishness of God is *wiser* than the wisdom of men" (1 Cor. 1:25). The cross of Christ reveals the *wisdom* of the self-surpassing God, not the recklessness of an antinomian grace; and it is this *wisdom* that forms and informs the church as the pilgrim people of God. "For our sake, he made him to be sin who knew no sin, so that in him we might become the righteousness of God" (2 Cor. 5:21). The power of God the almighty Father is exercised in love *and wisdom,* which cannot leave the creature in its spiritual ruin of lawlessness, with a happy conscience to boot, as if carnal folly were as good as philosophical wisdom, as if philosophical wisdom at its best were as good as the righteousness that comes from God to lead forward to the Beloved Community, beyond both law and lawlessness, not a *deus exlex* but the self-surpassing *deus supra legem.*[273] "It is clear that when we live according to God," Augustine writes, "our mind should be intent on invisible things and thus progressively be formed from his eternity, truth and charity, and yet that some of our rational attention, that is to say, some of the same mind, has to be directed to the utilization of changeable and bodily things without which this life cannot be lived; this however not in order to be *conformed to this world* (Rom 12:2) by setting up such goods as the final goal and twisting our appetite for happiness onto them. . . ."[274] The cast of Platonic rhetoric here should not obscure Augustine's fundamentally eschatological point, nor should it obscure an eschatological interpretation of the *ordo caritatis* (a notion that will become important in the conclusion of this system of theology). God's love does not simply, recklessly bless the "secular," but complexly, wisely weans from conformity to this dying world under judgment to grow into the form of the new humanity in Christ. "Our knowledge therefore is Christ, and our wisdom is the same Christ. It is he who plants faith in us about temporal things, he who presents

273. *RPTD,* pp. 179-86, 200-206.

274. Augustine, *The Trinity,* trans. Edmund Hill, O.P. (Brooklyn, NY: New City Press, 1996), p. 331.

us with the truth about eternal things. . . ." Christ is "one and the same person by whom deeds were carried out in time for us and for whom we are purified by faith in order that we may contemplate him unchangingly in eternity."[275] Christ by the Incarnation offers "a model of return to man who had fallen away and was unable to see God on account of the impurity of sin and the punishment of mortality[;] he emptied himself (Phil 2:6), not by changing his divinity but by taking on our changeability." This *great exchange* manifests the *wisdom* of God in the otherwise foolish conjunction of almighty power and suffering love.[276]

To put it in a formula, then: God the Father exercises almighty power through this wisdom of the Word incarnate in the love of the Spirit poured into human hearts. The wisdom of the incarnate Word is the "astonishing commerce," the "joyful exchange" by which the Son became the slave in order that the slave might become child and heir. The justification of the ungodly in this transaction is no arbitrary fiat, not even the fiat of love. It creates what it declares because it enacts what it tells in the cross and resurrection narrative, once for all in Jesus and accordingly in every newborn believer who now follows Jesus, as a disciple, by the same Spirit that once led the Lord into battle with the powers of malice and injustice. By this wisdom, God works the conversion of radical or exclusive monotheism. That this exchange between creature and Creator in and by the Incarnation is a free act of love, of course, is true, just as it is the creative act of divine power. Yet, in its wisdom divine love does not recklessly set aside justice to redeem the sinner, but rather fulfills all righteousness, just as it does not magically cancel death but supersedes its reality with an act of new creation. Consequently, whoever is in fact elected by the Spirit of the Father and the Son is, and must be, transformed by this election since election is not arbitrary fiat but consists in God's cunning exchange of sin with righteousness, death with life, woe with blessing. Established as it is in the once-and-for-all sacrifice of Christ, the Spirit's electing call of the sinner to faith is not and cannot be a love that leaves the world as it is, let alone asserts the counterfactual of its objective reconciliation, if it is truly *God's* love working in conjunction with power and wisdom in the project of eschatological creation.

## An Alternative: Brueggemann's Conflicted Yahweh

Walter Brueggemann's magisterial *Theology of the Old Testament* is a wide-ranging work that is worthy of considered and considerable attention in systematic theology for a number of crucial contributions. Not least of these, in the perspective of the present work, is that Brueggemann lifts up the skeptical counter-testimony of the Wisdom traditions within the canon over against its core testimony to Yah-

275. Augustine, *The Trinity,* p. 363
276. Augustine, *The Trinity,* p. 223.

weh's saving deeds in history. This represents the canonical precedent for critical dogmatics. In this way, that is, with the Bible itself, Brueggemann demolishes the false antithesis between theology and philosophy that biblicists, both left and right, employ to evade the work of systematic theology for hermeneutical appropriation, logical consequence, and epistemic warrantability of the Christian and biblical claim to truth in a contested world, where disputability attends claims to truth until the eschaton of judgment. That contribution of Brueggemann in itself ought to be a game-changer.[277] We will probe this insight more fully below. But in itself that is not the contribution that is relevant here as a helpful and illuminating challenge to this chapter's claim to truth, namely, the case for God the Father as God surpassing God in Christ for us all, where and when the Spirit moves in mission to the nations to unify the sign and the thing signified for the confession of the Lordship of Jesus Christ. Rather, it is Brueggemann's courageous and insightful depiction of the conflicted character, Yahweh,[278] that claims attention.

*"The substance of Israel's testimony concerning Yahweh,"* Brueggemann writes in italics for emphasis, *"yields a Character who has profound disjunction at the core of the Subject's life. This disjunction, moreover, is the engine that drives Israel's testimony. . . . [It is] not a mark of erroneous, primitive religion that later 'concepts of God' can leave behind."*[279] He finds this disjunction baldly stated in the text of Exodus 34:6-7, which begins with a summary of Yahweh's all-forgiving intent to be in solidarity with Israel come what may, yet ends in an "abrupt about face," simply contradicting the former will to forgive with a determination to visit iniquity on children to the third and fourth generation. "I can find no evident way in which the two parts of this formulation can be readily and fully harmonized." There appears to be a double will in God, indeed an arbitrary will to forgive some but to harden others, both asserted with equal force and in immediate proximity to each other.[280] If this text is to be taken as bearing witness to the reality of Yahweh, "the ground of the dispute is not to be found simply in modern, undisciplined pluralism or in Israel's ancient disputatiousness, but in the very character of Yahweh."[281] In Israel's testimony, "Yahweh moves back and forth between self-regard and regard

---

277. For an important, and contrary assessment of Brueggemann's achievement that decries his default to postmodern relativism and lifts up the epistemological primacy of historical criticism, see Paul D. Hanson, "A New Challenge to Biblical Theology," *Journal of the American Academy of Religion* 67, no. 2 (1999): 447-59. Revealing, from the perspective of the present work and its engagement with Brueggemann, is Hanson's claim that "conflicting views of God will be traced to the struggling efforts of finite humans to understand the Infinite in their midst . . ." (p. 455).

278. I will use this English language transliteration, Yahweh, in this section following Brueggemann's usage.

279. Walter Brueggemann, *Theology of the Old Testament: Testimony, Dispute, Advocacy* (Minneapolis: Fortress, 1997), p. 268.

280. Brueggemann, *Theology of the Old Testament*, p. 270.

281. Brueggemann, *Theology of the Old Testament*, p. 715.

for Israel, between sovereignty and pathos."[282] There is in Yahweh an "intense self-contradiction between norms and yearning . . . ,"[283] betraying "an unsettled interiority of fidelity and sovereignty."[284] This self-contradiction is manifest in the pervasive tension found in Israel's witness to "the conditionality of Torah and the unconditionality of royal ideology" that stand side by side "in deep tension."[285] The law that rewards and punishes according to human merit and the promise that unconditionally secures blessing by divine compassion and mercy are in conflict.

Brueggemann tends to sketch this tension psychologically, as a conflict between pathos for Israel and jealous self-regard, an oscillation in affects between altruism and narcissism. Yet he comes close in other passages to Barth's doctrine of *das Nichtige,* the "Nihil" in Brueggemann's rendering, which is a device for externalizing Yahweh's jealous self-regard in its destructive effects as the "onslaught of negation," the "power of death still on the loose in creation."[286] Yet here too it is Yahweh "who abandons" — also to these powers of negation, howsoever figured. This, he acknowledges, makes for a *"massive Holy Problem. . . .* Yahweh's sovereignty does not everywhere and always converge with fidelity, even though fidelity is finally powerfully affirmed."[287] This latter reflection makes it plain that the conflict in Yahweh is chiefly to be understood as a conflict of *conscience,* that is, between obligations incumbent upon Yahweh who has elected Israel in love yet for His own sovereign purpose of blessing to all nations, thus putting affection and purpose into not-infrequent conflict. This happens when Israel takes election as a pretext for privilege rather than the summons of love to justice. But even with this clarification, there are uncanny turns in Israel's vexed history with Yahweh that cannot be sorted out: surds, anomalies, episodes of chaos and evil from the Lord's hand.[288]

Brueggemann claims in sum that the preponderance of testimony is that "Yahweh is, perhaps at great cost, resolved to maintain creation as a system of blessing, and so will not give in, even to Yahweh's own propensity to enraged destruction. Israel ponders this terrible interiority in Yahweh, and Israel dares to give it voice. Yahweh is deeply torn about the future of the world." Brueggemann dares further to suggest, however, that this very conflictedness "constitutes the hope of creation."[289] Recalling the creative, prelapsarian commands of Genesis 1, Brueggemann writes that because the "command authority" of Yahweh "is not coercive but generative, not repressive but emancipatory," the heart of true human desire is for the free obedience of faith. "Yahweh is indeed the ultimate

---

282. Brueggemann, *Theology of the Old Testament,* p. 309.
283. Brueggemann, *Theology of the Old Testament,* p. 366.
284. Brueggemann, *Theology of the Old Testament,* p. 459.
285. Brueggemann, *Theology of the Old Testament,* p. 609.
286. Brueggemann, *Theology of the Old Testament,* p. 537.
287. Brueggemann, *Theology of the Old Testament,* p. 311.
288. Brueggemann, *Theology of the Old Testament,* p. 271.
289. Brueggemann, *Theology of the Old Testament,* p. 546.

joy of human desiring."[290] His Sabbath-rest is the rest in which the restless heart of the groaning creation of Romans 8 finds peace.[291] So the conflict of divine conscience manifest in Yahweh's dealing with Israel is indeed hope *for God surpassing God* by the Spirit finding ever-new ways to reconcile the affection of election with the sovereign purpose of universal blessing, the coming of the Beloved Community.

Thus I venture to suggest at this juncture that Brueggemann's suggestion that the tension in Yahweh issues in hope constitutes the *Christian* theological nature of Brueggemann's account. As the very title of the book indicates, an "Old" Testament Theology is by definition a work of Christian theological reflection that takes the perspective of the New Testament in constituting the Hebrew Scriptures as its own "old." The superiority of Brueggemann's endeavor precisely in this regard is that he strives to listen to the chorus of voices in the Old Testament in each one's particular testimony, and counter-testimony, not too quickly or too easily harmonizing them as fodder for the obviously superior New Testament perspectives. He thus comes to this discovery of the tension in Yahweh immanently, from immersion in the text itself, closely read according to the various voices. Nothing, in turn, so helpfully challenges complacent, not to say smug Christian assurances of their kind and loving God in invidious comparison to the vengeful Jewish deity as Brueggemann's probing presentation of the "divine dilemma" — the words we used earlier to speak of Athanasius's and then Luther's biblically informed grasp of the problem for God that Israel, *pars pro toto,* that *we* troubled beings are as His own precious creation seduced by structures of malice and injustice and thus justly but destructively abandoned to our adulterous lusts (Rom. 1:18-32).

In spite of this challenge to complacent Christianity, and in spite of deep reservations about contributing to a theological reduction of complex texts to simplistic platitudes or hegemonic dogmatisms, Brueggemann ventures "materials for a metanarrative." He overcomes his hesitations in this regard because he is "impressed" with the Old Testament's "profound tension with the regnant metanarratives of our society" in relation both "to Enlightenment liberalism" and the "standard claims of classical Christianity." Interestingly, Brueggemann's charge against classical Christian theology is that it obviates the conflict in Yahweh with a "tilt towards closure" by a "transcendental" move that closes off the "genuine unsettlement" between Yahweh and Israel in their history.[292] Hand in glove with supersessionism goes the view that Israel's negative engagement with Yahweh in history is the shadow side of Christian achievement. We will return to this important critique of classical Christian theism below.

290. Brueggemann, *Theology of the Old Testament,* p. 200.

291. I would turn this Augustinianism back against Brueggemann's unfortunate indulgence of the Krister Stendahl canard about the "introspective consciousness" of Augustine and Luther on the preceding page, p. 199. See the critique of Stendahl in *LBC,* pp. 233-36.

292. Brueggemann, *Theology of the Old Testament,* p. 563.

The first of the material elements from Old Testament Theology for the construction of a counter-narrative in systematic theology today at the end of Christendom is the claim that "at the root of reality is a *limitless generosity* that intends an extravagant abundance."[293] *Esse Deum dare.* This is indeed, according to the argument of this chapter, the proper way of conceiving God's "transcendence" relative to His "immanence," as the self-surpassing Father of the Son in the Spirit. "Will not He who spared not His own Son give us with Him all things?" (Rom. 8:32). The second element, already much discussed above, is the "deep, radical, painful, costly fissure" at the core of this reality that remains "complicated and unresolved," reflecting a human brokenness that cannot be illuminated or aided by moral stridency. Conflicted Yahweh over his conflicted creation points forward in messianic expectation to the coming "in pathos into the brokenness" of an "incommensurate Power and Agent" who "by coming there makes the brokenness a place of possibility"[294] — Agamben's "new possibility for the fallen." This is, according to the argument of Part Three of this work, the liberating work of the incarnate Son sent from His Father to harrow hell. And this messianic work gives, in place of rationalistic optimism based upon the calculation of immanent probabilities, the Holy Spirit as down payment on the coming Beloved Community of God. "Israel's speech witnesses to *profound hope,* based in the promise-maker and promise-keeper for whom all things are possible"[295] — Jüngel's "more than necessary" God. In sum, in the figure of Yahweh, Brueggemann finds a trinity of *"generosity, candor* in brokenness, and resilient *hope"* as alternative to contemporary *"scarcity, denial,* and *despair,* surely the ingredients of nihilism." But receiving this Trinity of love in exchange for our unholy trinity of nihilism entails a fresh embrace of this continuing Jewish dialectic of solidarity and sovereignty in the experience of Yahweh — the same formation of the theological subject articulated by dying and rising in Christ as described in Chapter One. Such a synthesis of materials from Old Testament theology "stands as a fragile alternative to the embrace of the Nihil," just as nihilism is, in Brueggemann's analysis, the consequence, not of the death of God but of His attempted murder, i.e., "the elimination of this incommensurate, mutual One in the interest of autonomy and self-sufficiency."[296]

The faith of Jesus in the God of Israel as His and our heavenly Father, and the Christian faith in the vindicated faith of Jesus, is faith in the God of Israel as the *reconciled* God of Hosea 11:9, the *self-surpassing heavenly Father* who has determined Himself in His decision in Christ and made Himself known in this way by the Spirit, namely, as seeking and finding the lost and the estranged for life gathered into the Beloved Community. This gospel faith is neither intelligible apart from God's continuing history with Israel nor apart from the disruption of

---

293. Brueggemann, *Theology of the Old Testament,* p. 559.
294. Brueggemann, *Theology of the Old Testament,* pp. 560-61.
295. Brueggemann, *Theology of the Old Testament,* p. 561.
296. Brueggemann, *Theology of the Old Testament,* p. 564.

that continuing history with Israel — the departure from Jerusalem in mission to the nations and a return that comes from above. Brueggemann's work powerfully demonstrates the truth of the first statement but in curious ways leaves the second hanging in an undecided state of continuing aporia. As already mentioned, Brueggemann demonstrates the first claim in showing how the "divine dilemma" that frames the theological thinking of an Athanasius and a Luther is not some imposition of pagan polytheism on the monotheistic text of the Hebrew Scriptures, but rather reflects the closest and most careful theological reading of it. Indeed, it is rather the suppression of this theme of divine conflict that reflects the imposition of a pagan notion of divine simplicity on the text.

This insight has ramifications on multiple levels, beginning with the fact that the biblical canon itself gives us "no way out of this competitive, conflictual situation" of selection and counter-selection, interpretation, and interpretation of interpretation in the trial of history that is also materially a history of the divine dilemma, the torn conscience of God over His torn creation. Relativity in the account of knowledge is not only indexed to the finitude and corresponding plurality of our creaturely perspectives, in other words, but to conflicted and contested states of sin and grace, despair and hope, unfaith and faith. Our sin and our limited vision interpenetrate, as do Yahweh's wrath and His love for creatures willingly seduced by malice to injustice. This "no exit" sign posted theologically over history by Brueggemann is thus due only in part to our postmodern criticism of criticism. We know indeed today that "there is no interest-free interpretation," that is, the "illusion of the Enlightenment that advocacy-free interpretation can exist" by recovering with scientific objectivity what really happened in criticism of the text. Certainly this post-critical insight means for theology as a disciplined reading of the Bible according to its theological intention that "there can be no right or ultimate interpretation" short of the eschaton of judgment since only conscientious submission to that final court actually talks theologically now about God. In the interim there are "only provisional judgments for which the interpreter is prepared to take practical responsibility and which must always yet again be submitted to the larger conflictual conversation." In this epistemic situation of interminable yet conscientious disputation pending the eschaton of judgment, a "faithful interpretation" is not one that presumes to settle the matter by reconstruction behind the text of what really happened (let alone by biblicist proof-texting), on the naïve assumption that the historian (or the fundamentalist) has some kind of unproblematic access to actuality that is not the product of another set of highly precarious ethical commitments or metaphysical posits. Rather a faithful interpretation is one that is "congruent with the text being interpreted" and thus, in this tentative appropriation of meaning for audiences today, is willing "to stay engaged in such an adjudicating process and not to retreat to a separated interpretive community." In short, in the language of this system of theology, theology as *critical dogmatics* is warranted by the specific material collected in the biblical canon, when taken theologically as testimony to the divine dilemma, the *conscience* of God the Father, who spared not His own Son, but gave Him up for us all. Indeed, as Brueggemann claims, the, if I may say so, *meta-critical* "warrant for such an interpreting process" as described above "is that precisely this kind of process is evident in the biblical text itself."[297]

But this evidence in the text does not just fall off the pages to commonsense reading. The biblical text gives this evidence when we take the text in the light of the gospel — also the "gospel" of the Old Testament, the promise given to Abraham and to the House of David and renewed in the preaching of the second Isaiah and crystallizing in Israel's messianic hope. For it is the same "gospel," whether in anticipation or in retrospect, that resolves the divine dilemma in the news that "Yahweh is, perhaps at great cost, resolved to maintain creation as a system of blessing, and so will not give in, even to Yahweh's own propensity to enraged destruction." Then, indeed, as Paul affirms theologically of the Old Testament, "whatever was written in former times was written that we might have hope" in the reconciled God, the self-surpassing Father who gives the Son in the Spirit into the hands of sinners to put sinners back into the hands of the Father. In that case, we receive the canonical collection in critical dogmatics as the writings selected from a range of candidates by the Spirit at work in the synagogue, as also in the selection of Israel's canon by the New Testament ecclesia deciding in the Spirit against docetism in Christology and dualism in theology. These selections, as such constituting the canon and forming together its metanarrative and so the matrix of Christian theology, construe God as conflicted in conscience, with Christ as the *krisis* in the life of God that resolves on Easter morn in the reconciliation. Thus we know God as *one* God, rather than dualizing the conflict that drives human history or dualizing God. That is the theological decision at the root of the Bible and of theology that would be biblical.

Hence there is no *epistemic* need to remain in a troubled state of aporia regarding the Christian nature of Brueggemann's powerful construction of the theology of the Old Testament, even as baptism into Christ grafts the Gentile into Israel's history with God along with all the *existential* aporias attending it that Brueggemann so powerfully exposits. As we have argued above in Chapter Four, Jewish unbelief in the messianic office and work of Jesus therewith becomes a principle internal to Christian theology after Christendom, so that faith remains faith. And faith that remains faith lands Christians anew in the company of Abraham and Moses and David and Elijah and Hosea and Jeremiah and all the others singing in that maximally rich, sometimes interestingly dissonant choir of the Israel of God. In this contested reality, congruence with the text is not and cannot be the work of haphazard, reader-response opinionating that only manifests the preconceived and preformed subjectivity of those innocents still in the thrall of structures of malice and injustice, including the hopelessly shallow structures of contemporary theological education that resort to such silliness in

---

297. Brueggemann, *Theology of the Old Testament,* p. 63.

place of serious theological scholarship. Rather, congruence with the text comes by a loss of innocence not less than the Pauline "the world is crucified to me and I to the world" as also by the disciplined and creative labor of scholarship that Brueggemann so skillfully exhibits. Lost and done with for us today is the not so innocent innocence of Christian triumphalism in order that we may claim anew the triumph of the Father's love for us troubled beings that is the justification of the ungodly, their costly inclusion in the Beloved Community, the "Israel of God" (Gal. 6:16). What does *this* affirmation of God's existence mean as "doctrine for life," that is, for living justly by faith already now in the God who exists for us in the event of breaking in and breaking up structures of malice and injustice to set us on the path of righteousness, life, and peace?

We turn again to the matrix of the Scriptures, with Luther as our guide. For the book of Genesis is not only or even chiefly about origins; in the great saga of Joseph (Genesis 37–50), it tells what belief in God who exists means for holy living in a world subject to the contra-divine powers of malice and injustice. The theodicy of faith is our practical Patrology.

## The Theodicy of Faith

Following longsuffering Joseph's elevation to viceroy over Egypt by Pharaoh (Gen. 41:40), Luther made the following comment on the theodicy of faith. *Luther's Works* translates as follows:

> But later Joseph got what he did not understand and never had the courage to hope or ask for. These are truly lofty and wonderful examples which we ourselves should learn and also set before others, in order that we may recognize the divine wisdom, goodness, mercy, and power which are most certainly near us. The goodness is certainly there; the wisdom is certainly there; the power, etc. But God does not act according to our wish when He governs according to His goodness, wisdom, etc. Then we do not understand; for we think that God does not know us and does not want to concern Himself with or think about the outcome of our trial. This is the way reason judges. But this is not in accordance with the doctrine of Christians or with the knowledge of God in the Spirit. Nor can I boast of perfection. And I hate my flesh, which continually fights against the Spirit. Accordingly, these matters should be thought of and practiced more often, in order that we may prove what is the good, acceptable, and perfect will of God (cf. Rom. 12:2). [For what it is that God is wise, good, powerful, merciful, no one understands except speculatively and metaphysically], just as one can conceive some idea of the goodness or wisdom of a prince that is pure speculation. But when it comes to practice, when God snatches Joseph from the embrace of his parents, his grandfather, father, and the whole household, and he is hurled into prison in a foreign land

on the charge of adultery and remains there [LW omits: in fear and] in constant expectation of death — [surely this will not be interpreted to anyone as the good will of God]?[298]

Some observations and questions about this passage arise immediately. For Luther, faith sees in hindsight. "We, however, do not understand [God's promises] until His counsels are carried out."[299] The example of Joseph, in Luther's reading, makes this point again and again. But faith then *sees*. Luther therefore expects that experienced faith will progress in knowledge of God and with the help of biblical narrative learn to recognize God in times of trial. "Accordingly, these matters must be taught for our instruction, in order that we may know what the theology of the Gospel is."[300] The knowledge of faith is knowledge of God in the positive attributes by which God relates to the world as Creator and Governor. These are the trinity of attributes — power, wisdom, and love. God is present to the creation at all times in power, wisdom, and goodness. But the divine subject of these predicates does not act according to our understanding of their sense and this leads to incomprehension of the subject and the false judgment of *ratio*, that God neither knows nor cares for us but abandons us in the time of trial. With *ratio* here, Luther is thinking of Epicurus: Given the evils that afflict us, if God is good, then God is powerless to prevent these evils. If God is powerful, then God does not care for us in our affliction. This evident judgment of *ratio*, however, conflicts with Christian doctrine and the knowledge of God in the Spirit, which is resisted by the flesh (according to Paul's antinomy, not Plato's). The flesh is operative in the false judgments of *ratio*. The knowledge of God as power, wisdom, and love is what Christian metaphysics attains in thinking the condition of the possibility of a free act of the creation and preservation of all that is other than the Creator. In contrast to this speculative knowledge, however, Joseph as recipient of God's messianic promise encounters God in the experience of God permitting great evils to happen to him, which evils he surely cannot understand rationally as the good will of God. God's permission of evil makes the question of theodicy a question precisely for the faith of elect Joseph, heir of messianic promises. Joseph consequently is seen by Luther to exemplify true faith in the time of trial. In just this way Joseph prefigures the Messiah to come.

From where has Luther acquired the trinity of attributes — power, wisdom, and goodness — and what is their logical status in his theology? No doubt from his close reading of Augustine's *City of God,* from which so much of his theology tacitly draws. There Augustine had analyzed: "[T]here are three questions to be asked in respect of any created being: 'Who made it?,' 'How?,' and 'Why?' I put forward

298. *LW* 7, p. 175; *WA* 44, p. 429. Passages in brackets are my emendations to the LW translation.

299. *LW* 8, p. 30.

300. *LW* 8, p. 30.

the answers: 'God,' 'through His Word,' 'Because it is good.' Now whether this formula is to be regarded as a mystical revelation of the Trinity, the Father, the Son and the Holy Spirit . . . is a question meriting extended discussion."[301] Moreover, it seems evident in this text that Luther does not reject the three metaphysical attributes or play them off one against another but rather affirms them, for emphasis switching to German from Latin: *divinam sapientiam, bonitatem, misericordiam et potentiam, quae certissime adsunt nobis. Bonitas ist gewisslich da. Sapientia ist gewisslich da, potentia, etc.* After Kant, we today tend to hear the words "metaphysical speculation" as indicating uncertain opinionating about matters beyond the capacity of sense-bound knowledge. Is this Luther's criticism? If not, what value does he assign to metaphysical knowledge in forming an idea of God as Creator and Governor? And what, if any, revision does he make of such ideas of God?

Luther thinks the biblical God is the subject of these predicates; this is evident in his sharp contrast between two human subjectivities, that of the Spirit and that of the flesh. The flesh resists the Spirit, *its* reasoning judges otherwise than God judges and thus concludes falsely about God, especially in time of trial, denying to God either power to save or goodness to care. But the Spirit judges according to Christian doctrine, that is to say, according to the crucified Messiah. It knows that God, "who spared not His own Son," permits great evils. Indeed, Luther switches from the divine passive to the active voice, depicting God "snatching" Joseph from his home and family and "hurling" him not only into an alien land but into prison on a false charge. What is this divine permission of evil? And just who is the one unable to interpret it as the good will of God? Spirit or flesh? This poses of course the neuralgic question of *theodicy,* just as the Genesis narrative intends. Or more precisely, it poses the alternative of a theodicy of reason and a theodicy of faith. It is thus also a question about epistemic access, a questioning of *ratio*'s access (MacIntyre's "Whose justice? Which rationality?") or, as we might say in anti-Kantian fashion, the critique of epistemology given with the gift of theological subjectivity as Luther sees on display in the person of Joseph. Let us probe further.

At the heart of Luther's exposition of the Joseph story is a claim about the knowledge of God: "But that indeed is the true knowledge by which we recognize that God has the will, the wisdom, and the power to help and to have mercy. . . . This, then, is the true knowledge of God: to know His nature and will, which He reveals in the Word, where He promises that He will be my Lord and God and orders me to take hold of this will in faith. . . . Therefore I commend and surrender myself to the Lord, my God, who alone is wise, powerful and good."[302] We note here the recurrent refrain, "power, wisdom and love," which attributes to God as subject or agent the ability, the intelligence, and the good will to perform what is promised in the Word.

301. *City of God,* XI, 24, p. 456.
302. *LW* 8, pp. 17-18.

This trinity of attributes is traditional in patristic and medieval theology. We thus find it, for example, in the noncontroversial Article I of the Augsburg Confession, where it comes after the trinity of negative attributes: *quod sit una essentia divina, quae et appellatur et est Deus aeternus, incorporeus, impartibilis, immensa potentia, sapientia, bonitate, creator et conservator omnium rerum* (the "one divine essence which is called and which is God, eternal, incorporeal, indivisible, immeasurable power, wisdom, goodness, Creator and preserver of all things"). The apophatic adjective, *immensa,* summarizes the preceding three negative attributes saying that the immeasurable divine being is without beginning or end, not located in space, and hence incapable of division. God is immeasurable in terms of the created parameters of time and space, and this immeasurability qualifies our three positive attributes of power, wisdom, and goodness, such that there is no proper proportion that can be ascertained between our ideas of these things and God's possession of them, since there is no proportion between the finite and the infinite. We only have an idea here, Luther says in the Joseph commentary, like a peasant imagining the lifestyle of a great prince. Nevertheless, the positive attributes give us some notion of how God can be creator and preserver of all things.

While this trinity of attributes is traditional, its logical sense and theological status is not at all settled. One question that troubled Luther's medieval predecessors is how three distinct attributions can belong to the one simple God. According to Peter Gemeinhardt, Abelard took up the refrain of "power, wisdom, and love,"[303] but applied the notion of divine simplicity radically to it. This produced an apparently unitarian or at least subordinationist doctrine of God: "if three persons are predicated of God as distinct in property [i.e., as power, wisdom, and love respectively] but not in number, he is still one person and one essence!"[304] Consequently the three positive attributes fade into incomprehensible unity and cease to work as identifying the divine nature in particular ways. In reaction to Abelard, Gilbert of Poitiers penetrated to the heart of the problem: given the axiom of divine simplicity, "defining the persons by their properties or by their relations in order to derive the three relations from the divine unity" implied that, since "the three persons participate in the same divine essence, the relations cannot be substantial to them, nor can they be accidental, for in God accidents do not exist."[305] As the result, even triunity now seemed inconceivable, if not impossible. But if the church's faith is true, the problem created here must lie in the supposition of unqualified divine simplicity. For the persons are numerically three. The three substantial agents exist in their own relations and have their own corresponding properties.[306] Quite in contrast to Abelard, then, is Hugh of St. Victor, who finds the "ternary *potentia,*

---

303. *Trinitarian Theology in the Medieval West,* ed. Pekka Kärkkäinen, Schriften der Luther-Agricola-Gesellschaft Vol. 61 (Helsinki: Luther Agricola Society, 2007), p. 29.
304. *Trinitarian Theology in the Medieval West,* p. 32.
305. *Trinitarian Theology in the Medieval West,* p. 41.
306. *Trinitarian Theology in the Medieval West,* p. 42.

*sapientia* and *benignitas* in the created world," which allows him "to deduce personal properties of the Trinity out of the structure of creation." Hugh combines this cosmological perception with Augustine's psychological analogy of the Trinity, with the result that despite the danger to the doctrine of simplicity caused by the personal appropriation of attributes in the Three, Hugh could provide a "lively description of the loving relationship of the persons including their joint operation concerning redemption." The Trinity thus finds its way back to the "economical aspect of the history of salvation."[307] The Father expresses almighty power in sending the Son, the Word and Wisdom of God incarnate, as also the Spirit of their love in the hearts of believers. Power, wisdom, and love respectively now appear in the unified operations of the Three for human salvation.

As a student commenting on the *Sentences,* Luther could make the somewhat daring marginal note that I translate as follows: "I, unless blessed Augustine would say otherwise, but I would say, that the Father is not the Father except from the Son or by filiation. Thus neither by Himself is He wise, but through the Son who is His wisdom by which He is wise. Neither by Himself is He good, but through the Holy Spirit who is His goodness. Thus it is that whenever He is called powerful, wise, good, always at the same time all three persons are named. The reason is that 'father' is relative. And, as Ambrose puts these things: He is not able to be named or called Father, unless the Son is also co-named. Thus being wise and wisdom are relative. And He is not able to be named such, unless the Son also is co-named."[308] The young Luther here, perhaps knowingly, challenges the crucial turn in the argument of Augustine in *De Trinitate,* Book VII (as Luther's own allusion to 1 Cor. 1:24 may indicate). Since the substance of each person is the one God, and since by the principle of simplicity power, wisdom, and love as essential divine qualities apply equally, wholly, and indistinguishably to each of the three, it followed for Augustine that statements like "Christ is the wisdom of God" or the "Holy Spirit is the goodness of God" can only be a way of speaking accommodated to creatures, not a true declaration of God's being and as such also true for creatures. With this result, however, all of Augustine's labor to render the trinity of persons intelligible for faith in the preceding six books became nugatory: the distinctions between the persons are intra-divine, hence utterly simple, and thus incomprehensible to us for whom consequently there is no discernible reason why in the economy of salvation the Son became flesh instead of the Spirit or for that matter the Father.

So Augustine actually concluded: "What are we left with then? Perhaps we just have to admit that these various usages were developed by the sheer necessity of saying something, when the fullest possible argument was called for against the traps and errors of the heretics."[309] This is a doubly bad result. It renders the

---

307. *Trinitarian Theology in the Medieval West,* p. 48.
308. *WA* 1, p. 38, my translation.
309. Augustine, *The Trinity,* VII: 9; p. 227.

trinity of persons-cum-attributes in the economy of salvation unintelligible and renders those who find it unintelligible heretics. As the young Luther perhaps intuited, it was the inevitable result of the introduction of a strong doctrine of divine simplicity already in Augustine, a problem exacerbated after knowledge of the Muslim philosophers Avicenna and Averroes enter medieval theology in the twelfth century. By a "strong" doctrine of divine simplicity, recall, is meant the putative metaphysical insight of natural theology that the necessary being which grounds all contingent beings must itself be pure actuality, the simple identity of essence and existence, to which and for which no possibilities remain. A "weak" doctrine of simplicity is the stipulation of holiness, that God's singularity as Creator of all that is not God, makes God strictly speaking incomparable so that only God can speak truly of God.

Luther returned to Trinitarian problems late in life, now applying his mature Reformation theology to them. For example, in the first seventeen theses of the *Promotionsdisputation of Petrus Hegemon,* Luther discusses the trinity of attributes along traditional Augustinian lines: while each person as wholly divine possesses all three of these predicates, the individual "common names, which are called attributes, were spoken about them to discern and manifest the person. So because in the Son the wisdom and power were shown through the flesh, the wisdom and power of God are attributed to Him. So the virtue or power of the person of the Father is attributed from the creation. . . . Thus goodness, as well as vivification, are attributed to the Holy Spirit. . . ."[310] Thus there is an appropriation or attribution that is proper to the economy of salvation: the almighty Father out of boundless love creates *ex nihilo,* the incarnate Word exchanging righteousness for sin in the cunning of love, the Spirit pouring love into human hearts to make the Beloved Community. Luther certainly uses the notion of divine simplicity here and elsewhere, but with Luther it works generally as a rule of faith respecting the Divine Majesty in its mystery, not as an insight into how ontologically God is the one God.

Moreover, according to Luther, there is a natural knowledge of God (or better, an awareness, a *sensus divinitatis* as Calvin would put it) available to all. From around the same period late in life in the *Promotionsdisputation of Erasmus Alberus,* Luther forces Aristotle to concede that "infinite power both exists and can be known. . . . St. Paul says rightly in Romans 1: 'The knowledge of God is manifest to all people, that is, his eternal power and divinity.' But this knowledge is obscure and partial (although the knowledge of faith is also in its own way partial), as a line touches the whole sphere but at a point, and thus does not comprehend the whole thing."[311] Note that for Luther both the knowledge of reason and the knowledge of faith are partial and perspectival and to that extent obscure. They are so in differing ways. Clarity as such does not distinguish the two ways from

310. *SF,* pp. 205-6.
311. *SF,* p. 197.

each other; each in its own way deals finitely with the infinite and each knows one and the same world as the other.

In sum, Luther inherited a knot of theological problems in the traditional refrain celebrating the Creator's "power, wisdom, and love." In his commentary on the Joseph story, as we shall now see, his criticism of metaphysical speculation is not that it grasps nothing true of God, but that it cannot grasp these very truths truly. One is reminded of the twenty-fourth thesis of the Heidelberg Disputation: "Yet that [philosophical] wisdom is not of itself evil, nor is the law to be evaded; but without the theology of the cross man misuses the best in the worse manner."[312] The connection with the *theologia crucis* is apropos: Luther sees in Joseph's sufferings a type of Christ the crucified. Indeed, Joseph, betrayed and sold by his brothers and falsely accused by Potiphar's wife, typifies Christ abandoned and delivered to death and hell.[313] So Joseph "cries out, groans, and is tormented in death and hell without any comfort or hope of rescue. For no one is present to console him in his affliction and to tell him to trust in the goodness and presence of God, who will be his Protector in his worst and saddest troubles, but he remains in the extreme misery of solitude and hell."[314] In the time of trial, the *truth* of metaphysical knowledge of God turns against the sufferer; it only taunts the abandoned with *knowledge* of abandonment, indeed *doubt* that the subject of the predicates exists at all.

Commenting on Genesis 45:3, Luther writes that the example of Joseph is set before us "in order that we may know what God is. Philosophers argue and ask speculative questions about God and arrive at some kind of knowledge, just as Plato looks at and acknowledges the government of God. But everything is merely objective; it is not yet that knowledge which Joseph has [as a theological subject], that God cares, that He hears the afflicted and helps them. Plato cannot determine this; he remains in metaphysical thinking, as a cow looks at a new door."[315] At the end of this section of his commentary, Luther makes this criticism of metaphysics more precise when he writes that "in a Christian school it is the chief and highest knowledge to learn what God is, not speculatively but in a practical manner."[316] Two items are noteworthy here. First, Luther esteems practical knowledge, that is, know-how over theoretical comprehension, that is, over gazing, contemplation that he likens to the cow that sees the gate but won't walk through it to greener pastures. Second, practical knowledge is knowledge of God's care, that God governs not only species but also individuals; it is the existential knowledge that God cares "for me." At stake in Luther's criticism of metaphysics is the acquisition of a new theological subjectivity, which goes beyond Plato's merely *obiectiva* knowledge of power, wisdom, and goodness.

312. *LW* 31, p. 55.
313. *LW* 6, pp. 379, 385, 392.
314. *LW* 6, p. 380.
315. *LW* 8, p. 17; *WA* XLIV, pp. 391-92.
316. *LW* 8, p. 28.

At the climax of the Joseph story, when Joseph declares to his brothers: "You meant it for evil but God meant it for good" (Gen. 50:20; cf. 45:5), Luther comments: "This is what Paul says in Romans 8:28. . . . And somewhere Augustine says: 'God is so good that He does not permit evil to be done unless He can draw great good from it.' "[317] This puts Luther in the train of Paul and Augustine at the center of the great Western debate between Epicurean, Stoic, and Skeptic, which had been staged by his beloved Cicero centuries before in his dialogue *On the Nature of the Gods* on the question of theodicy, whether the gods care for humanity. Cicero represented his own skeptical views in the figure of his character Cotta, who concluded that "divine Providence is either unaware of its own powers or is indifferent to human life. Or else it is unable to judge what is best."[318] Impotent, ignorant, or uncaring, the gods cannot in human experience be known to be powerful, wise, and good. Augustine had joined this debate centuries later in the opening chapters of *City of God*, when he confronted the accusations against Christianity that its God brought on the fall of Rome and consoled the Christian women who had been violated by the invaders.

Taking his part in this great debate, Luther feels the force of the skeptical and Epicurean objections profoundly — so profoundly that meeting it requires, he says, "speaking with new tongues" in language that is "unnatural." This latter "way of speaking is peculiar to and customary for God. Moses does not speak in this way. Nor do the jurists and the philosophers. But it is a theology of promises."[319] Promise creates narrative, the tense tale of fulfillment, in which God's purpose comes to supervene human purposes. Impersonating Joseph speaking to his brothers, Luther continues: "You have destroyed and killed me. This cannot be denied. But this destruction and killing of yours, what has it been in the eyes of God? For in the same work God's plan is one thing, and your plan is something else. God has used your plan and your exceedingly evil intentions for life, not only mine, which would be a matter small enough, but universally."[320] Thus it is "earthly language to say: 'Joseph perished after being sold.' But in heavenly language that same thing is called a sending for salvation and life. This is our Lord God."[321] Indeed, this *is* the Lord God and thus also the true Christian *knowledge* of the Lord God, as Luther drives the cognitive point of the *theologia crucis* home: "Before the world Christ is killed, condemned, and descends into hell. But before God this is the salvation of the whole world from the beginning

---

317. *LW* 8, p. 328; *City of God*, XIV: ch. 27 or *Enchiridion*, VIII, 27. Luther had earlier made the same citation from Augustine commenting on Genesis 45:5 and added: "Thus from the captivity, servitude, and exile of Joseph He brought about the salvation, life and the glory of all Egypt" (*LW* 8, p. 37).

318. Cicero, *On the Nature of the Gods*, trans. C. P. McGregor (London: Penguin, 1972), p. 234.

319. *LW* 8, p. 30.

320. *LW* 8, p. 28.

321. *LW* 8, p. 29.

all the way to the end."[322] "This, then, is a special and heavenly language, to send a savior and to appoint a king by hurling him into a pit and hell."[323] Just so, "Christ subjects those who are His to the cross. . . . For it is not a physical blessing to die, to be crucified, to be destroyed by fire and sword, is it? Indeed, we shall more correctly call it a curse. Therefore there is a new language in that abundance of the Spirit according to which the godly speak with new tongues,"[324] like the martyrs who "were compelled to hear the same thing, as though they were insane and mad because they dared despise the Roman Empire and laugh at prisons and whips."[325]

So things in one and the same world and history appear differently in two perspectives. Thus there are also two subjectivities, Spirit and flesh, faith's reason and unfaith's reason with two languages. But they are talking about one and the same world and history. That is why Luther's position, like Paul and Augustine before him, raises the acutely painful question, especially for us today, of theodicy, as we have had to emphasize in these chapters. For the question of the existence of God is above all a practical question of theodicy. Faith justifies *God* in His judgment; just this is what unfaith cannot and will not ever do, not in all eternity. But faith justifies God in *His* judgment, which is the resurrection of the Crucified. Commenting on the conspiracy of Simeon and Levi to sell Joseph into slavery, Luther had written: "This God permits to be done while He is silent, asleep, deaf, and insensitive without any mercy and recognition of such a beloved son. . . . What is our Lord God doing with His elect? What sort of government is this for the elect of God? Why is it that He forsakes and afflicts them in this way?"[326] Likewise, commenting on Jacob's fatherly pain when later the brothers demanded that Benjamin accompany them back to Egypt to acquire grain, Luther asks:

> But why does God permit this to happen? Did Jacob not have God's promise: "I will be your Protector; grow, and multiply"? . . . But in spite of all these promises, Jacob is brought into the greatest distress, so that most certain danger threatens his life and his household. Where now is his faith in the promises? Why does he not perform miracles . . . ? Surely the outcome and existing state of affairs do not seem to agree with the abundant and rich promises which God has heaped upon him. A miracle should certainly have been performed in such distress and extreme necessity. But he is in the same danger, and he is oppressed by the same famine by which other men, heathen and idolaters, are oppressed.[327]

322. *LW* 8, p. 29.
323. *LW* 6, p. 397.
324. *LW* 8, p. 255.
325. *LW* 8, pp. 260-61.
326. *LW* 6, p. 405; *WA* XLIV, p. 303.
327. *LW* 7, p. 307.

Luther repeats this latter thought several times in what follows: Jacob and his sons "are in peril of their lives here, just as if they had been deserted and cast off by God." "Jacob endures all extremities in no other way than others, who are godless idolaters, endure them."[328]

The godly Jacob, like the godly Joseph, is member of one and the same world with the ungodly with whom he shares the common body. Theological subjectivity does not remove them from the common world. Here they must play by the same rules as all others so "that the means ordained for sustaining this life and avoiding dangers should not be despised" either by fatalist despair or by tempting God and demanding a miracle. God sends the famine to fall on the just and the unjust alike (cf. Matt. 5:45) and they are to use their own powers to seek relief. "Or is the bread of the Egyptians not God's creature just as much as other food and nourishment? Thus we enjoy the same marketplace, land, water, air, and sun that, as we know, godless men also use. God will not send you an angel from heaven to nourish you in a special manner, since He supplies you abundantly with the means of livelihood on the earth."[329]

Notice the work that raising the question of theodicy has done for Luther theologically. The question about God's permission of evil allows Luther both to clarify that the new, theological subject does not live in a religious Disneyland but in one and the same world where hardship and famine befall without respect to persons. As a result, Luther is able gradually to shift the question from God's permission of evil to Jacob's faith: "But it was by far the greatest miracle that they lived in faith in the promises, since it seemed that the promises had vanished completely and were invalid."[330] The theodicy of faith "is a doctrine only for Christians and the children of God, who are able to swallow and devour whatever evils confront them and confidently to expect a thousand advantages for one disadvantage or loss. For we believe in that God who is the almighty Creator, produces things from nothing, the best things from those that are evil, and salvation from what is despaired of and lost."[331] Thus, it follows that the experience of God "deaf and dumb, taking no thought of the things that are done and not knowing them" in His permission of evil, is, for Luther, the very place of faith in the world: "But faith is present, and God is still speaking to his heart, saying: 'O Joseph, wait; be patient; believe! Do not despair! Cling to the promise which you heard from your father!'" The theodicy of faith specifies Christian faith itself as "endurance in afflictions."[332]

By enduring or persisting faith, Joseph is for Luther the very model of the "sanctified" life, i.e., when it is clear that holiness is not desertion of the one and same world, as Luther regularly parodies monastic tradition and ascetical

---

328. *LW* 7, p. 307.
329. *LW* 7, p. 309.
330. *LW* 7, p. 307.
331. *LW* 8, p. 39. *WA* XLIV, pp. 607-8.
332. *LW* 6, pp. 405-6; *WA* XLIV, p. 303.

disciplines, e.g.: "We proceed on our way with shaven heads and girded with cinctures. We, who do not eat meat, who abstain from the delights and pleasures of matrimony, from civil affairs, and all association with the human race — we are truly saints and Baalites. We are not in any way concerned with the common herd, which understands nothing beyond the duties of ordinary life."[333] As if the narrative were speaking directly to his own situation, Luther rather finds holy Joseph abandoned to the life of the world on account of God who cares even for heathen Egypt. There Joseph learns *sinlessness* in the *patiency* of faith. "For he who is patient does not sin; 'he who has died is freed from sin,' we read in Rom. 6:7. He who is patient in faith in Christ is truly holy. No sin remains in him. For whatever he suffers is sheer righteousness as pure as it can be."[334] These are those who can rebuke evildoers and yet endure in turn their "unjust violence without desire for revenge."[335] Thus it is "certain that a life of suffering is the best and most precious life, and so much so that it does not need the remission of sins because it is without sin. I am saying these things of the godly, that is, of those who suffer in their faith in Christ. These do not sin, but they endure and bear the sins of others."[336] For in the patiency of faith, God is creating His creature anew in and according to Christ, and this new creation is true holiness or sanctification. "For such is the nature of God's poems, as Paul neatly says in Eph. 2:10: 'We are His *poiema.*' God is the Poet, and we are the verses or songs He writes."[337]

Ever since the dispute after Luther's death between the followers of Melanchthon and those of Flacius over the relation of nature to grace, theology in Luther's tradition has oscillated between an optimistic resolution of the theological subject into the natural goodness of God's creation and a pessimistic isolation of the theological subject at a countercultural remove from the ungodly world. Luther's own ambiguous usage of the traditional binary "nature and grace" is in part to blame for this; each side has its list of Luther texts in support. In the Joseph commentary, for example, Luther explains the dying Jacob's curse on Levi as a curse on the old nature: ". . . you follow nature and boast of being descended from Abraham. . . . Therefore it is necessary for you to put on another nature. . . . Nor should you place confidence in your paternal blood if you want to teach correctly and keep the commandments of God. . . . Therefore you must become another man and pay no attention to your grandfathers, fathers, and your whole flesh and nature."[338] Theological subjectivity simply is for Luther the new creation in Christ by the patiency of faith, a radical break with the old subjectivity of Adam's

---

333. *LW* 7, p. 344; *WA* XLIV, pp. 555-56.

334. *LW* 6, p. 402; *WA* XLIV, pp. 300-301.

335. *LW* 6, p. 402; *WA* XLIV, pp. 300-301.

336. *LW* 6, p. 398; WA XLIV, pp. 297-98. Luther can here even cite Socrates' "excellent statement" that "it is better to bear injustice than to commit it."

337. *LW* 7, p. 366; *WA* XLIV, pp. 572-73. See Oswald Bayer, *Gott als Autor: Zu eine poietologischen Theologie* (Tübingen: Mohr Siebeck, 1999).

338. *LW* 8, p. 232; *WA* XLIV, pp. 748-49.

would-be sovereignty, the language of philosophy, the judgment of *ratio*. There is no Luther apart from this new birth. At the same time, however, there is for Luther a definite sense in which this new creation in Christ is a redemption and indeed vindication of God's good creature. This sense appears in his commentary on the Joseph narrative above all in the running polemic against Stoic apathy and corresponding defense of human affectivity.

Luther expresses astonishment at the pitiless brothers, who care not that their bereft father should "die and descend into hell without any pity and without all feeling of humanity and *storges* ('of affection') such as has been implanted by God in all living creatures towards a father and a grandfather."[339] "Why," he demands, do such people "not remember that they had sucked their mother's milk and that they were human beings brought into this light from that mother?"[340] He says the same about grieving Jacob: "But grace and the Holy Spirit do not strip human nature of its emotions in such a way that Jacob, the father, does not lament the death of his son. For this would conflict with nature, which has been created in such a way by God that it has affections."[341] Luther describes the invented sanctity of the pope and violent schismatics, like Müntzer, as "Stoic," boasting of "strength in suppressing grief and overcoming creatures . . . not [being] affected by things that existed. . . . But God abominates this apathy. . . . He seeks such persons as have godly and loving feelings . . . love towards one's neighbor is commanded, and this is surely not fulfilled without feeling or affection. . . . [True saints] are affected by their own disasters and by those of others. . . ."[342] "God also hates and rejects the exceedingly harsh apathy of the Stoics, which robs a man of all his senses and emotions and goes along in wonderful things that are too high for it."[343] In Luther's understanding of the grief and struggle of Joseph and Jacob, "the natural affections and feelings of the saints are praised."[344] Indeed, in the saints feelings are "increased . . . [they] are aglow with the most ardent feelings,"[345] while repression is "Stoical pretense. Among the Stoics no one does what he pretends."[346]

Joseph's offer of peace and reconciliation to his brothers shows that "his heart burns with natural affection and spiritual love; for faith and the Holy Spirit do not corrupt or destroy nature but heal and restore it after it has been corrupted and destroyed. Accordingly, the most natural affections remain in parents, brothers, and wives; they are awakened through grace, not removed."[347] Joseph is "overwhelmed" at the sight of his family at long last before him; "his heart and eyes

---

339. *LW* 8, p. 403; *WA* XLIV, pp. 301-2.
340. *LW* 7, p. 342; *WA* XLIV, pp. 553-54.
341. *LW* 7, p. 261; *WA* XLIV, pp. 492-93.
342. *LW* 7, p. 315; *WA* XLIV, p. 533.
343. *LW* 7, p. 354; *WA* XLIV, pp. 562-63.
344. *LW* 7, p. 342; *WA* XLIV, pp. 553-54.
345. *LW* 7, p. 343: *WA* XLIV, pp. 554-55.
346. *LW* 7, p. 345; *WA* XLIV, pp. 556-57.
347. *LW* 7, p. 261; *WA* XLIV, pp. 492-93.

melt and are dissolved in tears." He is "stunned and speechless because of the exceedingly great compassion he feels. . . ."[348] Here Luther sounds like Thomas Aquinas. "See how great the power of nature is. The better and purer it is, the more excellent and ardent are its natural affections. Nor do grace and the Holy Spirit remove or corrupt it, as the monks have dreamed; but the Holy Spirit heals it and restores it to a healthy state when it has been corrupted."[349] "Healthy" — this for Luther appears at the sight of the viceroy of all Egypt withdrawing to another room "to break down and weep. He had to cry his heart out."[350] Luther immediately connects this to holy secularity, worldly godliness.[351] True holiness is formed by being abandoned by the Spirit to the world for the sake of the world, in conformity to Christ who believed in God where and when it mattered, in the time of trial, under the aspect of hiddenness and abandonment.

Luther's uncanny God, as limned from the Joseph story, is good, wise and powerful, immeasurably more than we imagine, a "fiery furnace of love."[352] The ontotheologians are not wrong to imagine in their speculation that the Creator of all that is not God must be a perfect harmony of power, wisdom, and love. But they do not understand this in the Spirit and according to Christian doctrine, namely, that God the almighty Father is the *free* Subject of these predicates (not then subjugated to them according to the human creature's incurvated reasoning) in the revealed way of Trinitarian advent by the resurrection of the Crucified. Thus they miss the conflict of the Spirit and the flesh; at their best, these philosophers are flesh and remain flesh in the Pauline sense: not body as opposed to mind (so Plato), but in would-be human mastery *(sicut Deus eritis)* resisting the cunning coming of God's messianic reign of endless peace for the throne of David and his kingdom, established and upheld with justice and with righteousness from this time on and forevermore (Isa. 9:6-7). The Spirit overcomes this human resistance by the baffling word of Messiah's cross, a message with its own *ratio* prefigured in the sufferings of holy Joseph. In him, believers see not only the creative power of God at work in the patiency of their faith, not only the wisdom that thwarts evil intentions and retools them for divine and saving purposes, but above all the love which affects and transforms the human heart, redeeming and fulfilling nature. "You meant it for evil, but God meant it for good." So God as the intentional subject of the predicates of power, wisdom, and love is justified in enduring faith (Mark 13:13). But this divine subject is the Three, a holy Complexity, not a philosophical simplicity, as befits the eternal life of a fiery furnace aflame with love for us, brothers of Joseph that we are.

---

348. *LW* 7, p. 340; *WA* XLIV, p. 552.
349. *LW* 7, p. 340; *WA* XLIV, p. 552.
350. *LW* 7, p. 341; *WA* XLIV, p. 552.
351. *LW* 7, pp. 340-44; *WA* XLIV, pp. 552-56.
352. *LW* 7, p. 260; *WA* XLIV, p. 492.

## The Circle Spirals

"I believe in God" — the real God who does not reduce to His relations with creatures but freely and decisively lives in His relations to creatures for the sake of creatures. This does *not* mean only or chiefly the "God of the Past," God as the Riddle of the Origin, God as Naked Power "which the heathen know . . . evidenced by the fact they have set up gods and arranged forms of divine service" (Luther). But the Credo's "I believe in God" sings *the Father Almighty . . . [of] Jesus Christ his only Son . . . [in] the Holy Spirit,* the harmony of power with wisdom and love who will demonstrate to all what He now intimates to repentance and faith. So the God who is believed in this putative word from God is the coming of His Reign, when He will make all things new and just so demonstrate that He has been the Creator from the beginning. Then all will know that He was, is, and will be the eternal Life that could in His own divine time become Creator, become flesh, become the Temple of the redeemed. God surpassing God freely *exists* in the realization of His own decision to create, redeem, and fulfill the world in Jesus Christ. God's *being* is this particular *becoming* spiraling forward from its eternity, breaking in and breaking up becoming that pretends to being. Space-time is then taken in faith as the intentional outworking of the Trinity, even as it masks to Adam who wants to be God, and does not want God to be God, to appear as a dark force and enemy. Nevertheless, from its origin space-time was made a habitat fit for the growth to maturity of the human image of God (Gen. 1:28) in attaining likeness to God. In humanity's redemption God became a space-time creature among others dwelling on the earth (John 1:14), the new Adam. In fulfillment of the frustrated promise of creation, God will be all things to everyone forever (1 Cor. 15:28b). So we turn in conclusion to the eternal Trinity and the Life eternal.

# Doxology

In Christian faith to know God is daily to die to sin, daily to rise to new life of love seeking justice, living in hope of the promised inheritance of one's place and time in the eternal life of the Father and the Son in the Spirit at the coming in power and glory of the Beloved Community at the Parousia of Jesus Christ.

# The Eternal Trinity and the Life Eternal

## God Is the Eschaton of Judgment

The fulfillment of the promise of creation in the redemption of our bodies is the gift of life eternal, which is to be understood as full participation in the risen life of Jesus Christ that has already begun in faith. "Beloved, we are God's children now; it does not yet appear what we shall be, but we know that when he appears we shall be like him, for we shall see him as he is" (1 John 3:2). According to this text, there are things we can say, and things we cannot now say, about how the God of the gospel will fulfill His promise of life eternal vouchsafed in Christ. The manifest meaning is that at the public Parousia of Christ, when faith becomes sight so that the body may adhere with its eyes to what its soul now believes through the "Word of life" (1 John 1:1), those already now called God's children by the Word of the Father's love for them attain to the likeness to God that is Christ. We cannot, however, say *how* this happens, not in all eternity, for "the vision of God exceeds the natural capacities of human beings and represents impossibility so long as they are bound to their earthly existence."[1] Perhaps, therefore, the most important thing here is said tacitly, in the words of commentator Georg Strecker: "The existence of those born of God, those accepted as God's children, is not yet complete. It is open to a future reserved to God, but without ceasing to be present." That of course is to deliteralize the Parousia and decode theologically: God, whose signature is *creatio ex nihilo,* is the One who reserves to Himself the accomplishment of the good that He promises in a fashion according with His own cunning. So it was in the beginning, is now, and shall be forever. Amen.

To come to believe in this way in the God who exists, not reducible to His relation to creatures but rather free, wise, and good to relate to creatures as God who gives wholly, makes believers in the interim responsible to God for their lives now in the body that is His claimed creature, as the Epistle emphat-

---

1. Georg Strecker, *The Johannine Epistles: A Commentary on 1, 2, and 3 John,* trans. Linda M. Maloney (Philadelphia: Fortress, 1996), pp. 90-91.

ically goes on to teach (1 John 3:4-24). Moreover, this hopeful faith and love in the body is precisely what organizes the community of the beloved children of God in the midst of the unbelieving world as a disciplined community of belief (1 John 4:1-6), as the Epistle's author had noted in the preceding chapter. "See what love the Father has given us, that we should be called children of God; and so we are. The reason why the world does not know us is that it did not know him." Strecker comments, "The world neither knows nor acknowledges God. That is what shapes its very being. The dualism of community and world cannot be more clearly expressed . . . wherever God is not acknowledged, the sphere of the world's hegemony expands."[2] This is the hegemony we have interpreted as ideological secularism, old and new, claiming responsibility *to* the world against God, or the putative Word of God, where the affirmation of "this" age has become an ideology making a total claim on conscience, as an "-ism," secular*ism* also in the religion business, in the ecclesiology of the "people's church," as if *vox populi* were *vox dei* (cf. Mark 15:13).

To be sure this willful ignorance of God that wants to be God, and does not want God to be God, can only "shape," not comprise the world in its "very being"; it can achieve only the corruption of creation, as a parasite feeds on God's *creatio continua.* The theological opposite of "this world" is not, then, religious otherworldliness, or ecclesiastical authoritarianism, or theological stick-in-the-mudism, but "holy secularity," the fulfillment (or "sanctification") of the redeemed creation already now in love's hopeful works of justice in marriage, in creative labor, in public worship, and even also in the just deployment of political sovereignty. There is, in these ways, a Christian responsibility *for* the common body, based upon the Incarnation that can and must also claim the social conscience of the believer. There can even, and indeed must be, a *conscientious* Christian cooperation with political sovereignty, as Romans 13:5 expressly states (just so, there may also be a *conscientious* civil disobedience). Having said that, the Christian knowledge of the eternal God with hope in a share in God's eternal life is unintelligible except as the conviction expressed here, shared with Paul, that the sufferings of this present age are not worthy to be compared to the glory that is to be revealed (Rom. 8:18) at the "redemption of our bodies" (Rom. 8:23). To live life now on this basis — Luke 14:12-14 tells us to invite those to the party who cannot repay — without knowing *how* it can be that the messianic banquet comes that feeds all infinitely — is the justice of living by faith in the God who is not reducible to His relation to creatures but rather freely summons one and all to His own eternal feast.

In the preceding chapters we have left a series of important questions dangling along the way that must now be settled. We have affirmed, but not explicated, what we can say now in faith on account of "Christ, as the righteous one, [who] intercedes for us and thus reveals God's justice towards us (cf. 1 John

2. Strecker, *The Johannine Epistles,* p. 87.

1:9) [as] nothing other than the revelation of the love of God."[3] This belief in Christ binds the Christian community together conscientiously as harbinger of the promised victory of the Beloved Community of God for all. We have accordingly affirmed the hope in the exalted Christ who still has work to do as the embattled and coming king of creation; that at His Parousia in the eschaton of merciful judgment His victory, not an *apokatastasis* because it is not a return to origin, brings forth *ex vetere* (out of the old) the new creation of the dying cosmos already now inaugurated in the faith of the Beloved Community (1 John 3:1); that the eternal triumph of the Beloved Community in its gift given and received by personal union with the Son of God incarnate through faith consists in a place in the eternal life that is the Trinity; that this personal place in eternal life is the redemption of the body and the fulfillment of the earth in which the tomb was dug that once held fast the slain corpse of Jesus.

Yet we have also affirmed that the final victory of Jesus Christ does not bring a comic ending. Neither of course is it a tragedy. But the biblical narrative in its apocalyptic denouement is not a comedy. It is neither a tragedy nor a comedy, because it is *sui generis* gospel, good news, of the true son of David, the Messiah of Israel. It is precisely, that is to say, news of a victor and His victory, *Christus victor,* with which endures eternally as well the memorial of the sacrifice of the Lamb who was slain but has now begun His reign. According to this hope, then, there is and will be to eternity an accompanying grief, healed and surpassed but never forgotten, over the "destroying [of] those who destroy the earth" (Rev. 11:19) that this victory entails, as recorded in the great end-time lamentation of Revelation 18, "Fallen, fallen is Babylon the great!" If ontology, thinking to spare God's hands from the dirtiness of Babylon and its destruction, erases this grief and turns Christ's victory into comedy, it itself becomes guilty, all abstraction notwithstanding, of mythmaking of an all-too-happy ending. "Music, craftsmanship, food, light, marriage — the things that make up a habitable world," observes commentator Joseph Mangina; "Babylon's destruction would seem to mark the end of civilized existence, indeed of the city as such. It is tempting to say that the passage invites the hearer to mourn. . . ."[4]

We may indulge this temptation, eternally, even as Mangina goes on rightly to argue that there can be no resurrection without first Luther's "real, not fictitious" death, accompanied, then, with corresponding "real, not fictitious" lamentation. "God wishes to bestow on human beings the gift of freedom — negatively, freedom from the enslavement of Babylon, positively, freedom for God and for the life in the coming city."[5] But the coming of the Beloved Community for the denizens of Babylon is a "severe mercy" (Augustine). It cannot be without grief of a wrenching loss, as the heart of human desire is wrenched free from its idol.

---

3. Strecker, *The Johannine Epistles*, p. 86.
4. Joseph L. Mangina, *Revelation* (Grand Rapids: Baker, 2010), p. 211.
5. Mangina, *Revelation*, p. 211.

The only question is whether the grief of this loss is grief only of the lost or also of the redeemed; whether, then, the redeemed are finally in human and indeed bodily solidarity with the lost; whether the very real "dualism between world and community" is temporary division or already final judgment. It is as important to explore this question as to realize that only God who makes all things new can answer it, for this too is faith that recognizes the God who is irreducible to His relations to creatures yet who wills all the same to relate to them by grace.

We asked above in Chapter Seven whether the teaching of the divine decree concerning the Lamb slain from before the foundation of the world *entailed* the reprobation of Judas — focusing on the traitor of Christ in this pinpoint way Calvin's (but also Augustine's and Luther's) admittedly "horrible thought." The horror here outbids McCord Adams by one little but significant degree and disallows her, or her casual readers, too happy an ending. It gives theological ground for the suggestion that an eternal sorrow accompanies the victory of the Beloved Community; that Christ the Horror-Defeater is, as McCord Adams indeed admits with refreshing candor, Himself implicated in the horrors He defeats; that the holy Hands of God get dirty with the dirt from which we are fashioned also in the redemption of the same body now polluted, as the Seer of the Apocalypse sees, with the spiritual pollution of idols.[6] It is the same antinomy that Brueggemann discovered in Deuteronomy 5:9-10. Who can smoothly bridge the juxtaposition between the lament in Revelation 18:19, "Alas, alas, the great city . . . in one hour she has been laid waste," and the commandment immediately following in 18:20, "Rejoice over her, O heaven, you saints and apostles and prophets! For God has given judgment for you against her"? Why must the saints in heaven be *commanded* to rejoice at the sight of wasted Babylon? Is it, perhaps, more justice than they wanted or desired or imagined? Perhaps they too grieve, as also grieved the Lord in the days of His flesh (Matt. 23:27). Can the reprobation of Judas, then, not come but at the cost of God's eternal grief?

Mangina is surely right to note that we "are not told what finally happens to these people . . . ," that is, to the earthly spectators of Revelation 18:9-19, bemoaning Babylon's demise, the politicians and businessmen who eagerly had collaborated with Babylon, willingly captive to its great malice, happy-go-lucky cogs in the machine of the great Leviathan of injustice on the earth. Mangina is also right to insist that the "end of Babylon" ultimately comes about as "an act of divine grace, resulting in God's refusal to let this be the definitive embodiment of the human story."[7] But penultimately, let us adjudge, believers too grieve over the fall of Babylon as truly as they grieved on September 11, 2001 and will yet again and often grieve in this fashion in the apocalyptic times ahead for Euro-America. As there can be no resurrection without death, nor forgiveness without sin, there

---

6. Marilyn McCord Adams, *Christ and Horrors: The Coherence of Christology* (Cambridge: Cambridge University Press, 2008), pp. 276-77.

7. Mangina, *Revelation,* p. 212.

can be no eternal rejoicing of Revelation 18:20 without the sorrow sung to all eternity of 18:9-19. The final defeat of the Righteous One would be tragedy, but His victory in war is not comedy. It is precisely *gospel* for a world fallen prey to the usurpation of malice in structures of injustice. If that is so, then, the difficult question remains whether the saints also mourn, or, what goes with that, whether "the city descending is for the sake of the city doomed, or at least for the sake of its inhabitants."[8]

We should emphatically answer both of these questions today in the affirmative because of the Lamb who was slain, "Christ, the righteous one, [who] intercedes for us and thus reveals God's justice towards us as nothing other than the revelation of the love of God" also for Luther's "real, not fictitious sinners," that is to say, also for those denizens of Babylon who willfully defend their addiction and will not see themselves as God sees them in the judgment that is spoken in the justification of the ungodly. If that is so, the question is refined to whether this heavenly city descending from above, also for the sake of the inhabitants of Babylon, to give the gift of eternal life comes without the surd possibility of invincible willfulness, knowing persistence in the *sicut Deus eritis,* eternal refusal of grace, an envy of the gift of eternal life gratis consummated in the perverse self-coronation that awards to itself the crown of eternal death. We have said that this absurdity cannot be excluded because of God's own identity for creatures as the God of the gospel is constituted in this triumph over evil, and that God's merciful triumph in this respect is for sinners, who cannot be sinners except as God's intelligent creatures called in His image to become His likeness. Just so, this mercy cannot prevail in them apart from their human willingness to be changed in true repentance by this mercy for them. The divine query spoken to Cain, the fratricide, remains to all eternity. "Why are you angry, and why has your countenance fallen? If you do well, will you not be accepted? And if you do not do well, sin is crouching at the door; its desire is for you, but you must master it" (Gen. 4:6-7). This query *is* the eschaton of judgment.

The willingness of the redeemed is, to be sure, a passive willingness, modeled in the "Let it be to me as the Lord has spoken" of the *Theotokos.* It is a Spirit-worked willingness graciously to receive the gift offered. Yet it is a truly human willingness that in all eternity God who has created it will not violate or annihilate. It constitutes each one's personal identity, such that it would be simple nonsense to speak of the redemption and fulfillment of one unwilling to be redeemed and fulfilled. God who wrenches all free by shattering the great idol, Babylon, to assert His reign on the earth does not just so force to Himself the hardened heart that is each one's own by the love that makes anybody the historical person that she is and remains to eternity. Only theologians who invent a purgatory — a judicial sentence, let us say, to an extended Twelve Step process — see an alternative here. Yet in the process they dodge the difficulty that even the success of Twelve

8. Mangina, *Revelation,* p. 213.

Step programs turns on the mystery of the addict's true and willing repentance. We reiterate: What in all eternity is God to do with rich Dives, who is exceedingly sorry for his punishment but never for his sin? We can hope in Christ that Babylon is emptied of its population; the final lamentation of its people may be the grief of repentance, as we saw depicted in the one of two thieves crucified alongside Jesus in Luke. But, with Black theologian James H. Cone, we must warn that hell may not be so easily or fully emptied.[9] That is where the church militant must leave the matter. That is all that can be said now by the ecclesia that remains in mission to the nations. It does not judge but announces the coming and merciful Judge, the Lamb who was slain also for the people of Babylon. Just so it summons all to the repentance of the justification of the ungodly, a prolepsis of the eschaton of judgment that includes this divine judgment on the sinner.

David Bentley Hart, however, acutely objects that "if God's identity is constituted in his triumph over evil, then evil belongs eternally to his identity, and his goodness is not goodness as such but a reaction, an activity that requires the goad of evil to come into full being." The biblical narrative, as we have now followed it through the Johannine epistles into the Apocalypse of John, must be taken as "analogical," then, as myth at a step removed from the thing it signifies. Needed, he argues, is an "analogical interval" between the immanent or ontological Trinity and economic or historical Trinity to preserve God from being the active and immediate agent (say, as depicted in the Apocalypse) of "every painful death of a child, every casual act of brutality, all war, famine, pestilence, disease, murder . . . [as] aspects of the occurrences of his essence . . . [thus] converting the Christian God into a god of sacrifice." Hart invokes here the test of Ivan Karamazov: "If the universal and final good of all creatures required, as its price, the torture of one little girl," that bargain would be morally unacceptable.[10] Is it not the same judgment that falls on a theology according to which the redemption won at the cross of the Son of God *for all* had, paradoxically, to be gained at the price of the reprobation of Judas? That there is accordingly a grief carried into eternity where eternity is the victory of the Lamb who was slain from before the foundation of the world?

Of course, Judas was not innocent. Judas willingly betrayed his Lord. God did not choose Judas's choices for him, but permitted his evil as part and parcel of His handing His own Son into the hands of sinners. So the story tells. But must we not, then, take this very narrative, this "myth," not as God's way of being, but only our way of talking about God's way with us? not, then, as the way of the Son of God on the earth in the flesh, but the flesh made into a simile of God above in heaven? showing us what God is like, not telling us what God is who comes to His creature in just this way, "handed over into the hands of sinners"?

9. James H. Cone, *Black Theology and Black Power* (Maryknoll, NY: Orbis, 1999), pp. 43-56.

10. David Bentley Hart, *The Beauty of the Infinite: The Aesthetics of Christian Truth* (Grand Rapids: Eerdmans, 2003), p. 165.

Hart's is a powerful argument, although it is far too easily made against the negative dialectics of Hegel, (1) when theologically speaking, Hegel has on his side the Cry of Dereliction from the lips of the crucified Son of God incarnate, not to mention the lamentation of Revelation 18 that credits the desolation of Babylon to the wrath of God; (2) when the ostensible target of Hart's critique in this passage is not the actual one (namely, Hegel), but Jenson's rejection of Hart's "analogical interval" (the "gap," in Jenson's language, between the immanent and economic Trinity that serves as an empty screen on which we project our idols, especially the idol of Platonic apathy); and (3) when Hart's alternative points up, up, and away and thus fails to unify the sign and the thing signified *on the earth* for repentance and faith, that is, *in history* where the actual change of human subjectivity that is repentance and faith is decided in the mission of the ecclesia to the nations. A revelation of a pure love of God happily above the fray in heaven is not gospel at all. It is only law, an indictment of what we are here below and an incitement, as if to climb Jacob's ladder, that fuels either religious self-deception or, in rigorous honesty, despair. Analogical intervals spare God the blame for the evil; they also remove God from the action and leave the derelict forever abandoned. What is a better path forward?

We have agreed with Hart that the distinction, but not separation of the immanent and economic Trinity is necessary to preclude, in accord with the non-technical sense of "substantiality," the reduction of God's being to His relations to creatures. The notion of an "immanent" or "ontological" Trinity does this by affirming that God's eternal act of being consists in the self-surpassing Father's generation of the Son and spiration of the Spirit by which God eternally becomes the Father of His Son on whom He breathes His Spirit so that the Son, in the Spirit, returns to the Father in an eternal circulation of mutual indwelling. We have called just this way of conceiving God's eternal unity of being in becoming the doctrine of consistent perichoresis, founded as it is on John 17.[11] The divine "self-consciousness" of the triune God is each person's ecstatic other-consciousness, and the unity of this triad of other-consciousnesses is the ultimate mystery of the Father's self-surpassing giving as the beginning and point of return of this endless circulation. Because of this immanent, that is, eternal self-relation of perfect love in endless circulation, the triune God is ontologically the complete or perfect life that has no need, hence no temptation to greed, but is rather wholly free, wisely and lovingly, to give creatures their existence with His blessing in the perichoretic spiral *ad extra* that is the act of eschatological creation. To the (limited) extent that this distinction is beclouded in Jenson's *Systematic Theology,* Hart's critique is salient. Yet Hart's critique of Jenson is not without its own problems.

First, it is guilty of the kind of scholastic hermeneutical failure described in Part One of this work. Hart extracts Jenson's critique of impassibility as unbap-

---

11. Stanley J. Grenz, *The Named God and the Question of Being: A Trinitarian Onto-Theology* (Louisville: Westminster John Knox, 2005), pp. 199-206.

tized Platonism from its context in the critique of Western modalism and sets it into his own preferred frame of reference (see below) to subject the resulting caricature of his own manufacture, not to an immanent and illuminating critique, but rather to a frontal assault. This sheds more heat than light. Second, Hart minimizes the Regnon thesis[12] that Western Trinitarianism, especially after Augustine, manifests a modalist tendency because of its starting point in the philosophical doctrine of divine simplicity over against the Eastern starting point in the Three of the gospel narrative, who, in Meyendorff's words, "are met and experienced first *as divine agents of salvation,* and only then are they also discovered to be essentially one God."[13] Hart's own theological agenda is to work a synthesis of later Eastern Patristic Trinitarianism with themes from St. Thomas regarding the simplicity of the act of God's being, the *actus purus* by which God simply is all that God could be in heaven above, and in consequence of this metaphysical difference to maintain "the analogical distance" between God and creatures who are never all that they could be, but can be their best by participation in God's beauty when Jesus shows them what God is like.[14] In service of this theological agenda, however, Hart assimilates Jenson to Hegel *tout court,* even while conceding grudgingly that Jenson intends none of what Hart insists are the inevitable implications (such as providing "the metaphysical ground of Auschwitz") of his argument.[15] This is a kind of polemical theology for which we in the tradition of Luther are learning to repent. One can, on the other hand, really learn from St. Thomas the principle of charitable reading that is no less pointed in critique for assuming the burden of understanding words in light of an author's context and intention.

More broadly, there is an element of bad faith involved in attributing to Hegel all the problems of modern theology that really should be laid at the door of Kant's claim to a Copernican revolution in his vaunted "turn to the subject," which we have interpreted from the outset of this work as the not benign ideology of modernity's sovereign self. Given this Kantian context of "modern" theology, Hegel may be *both* appreciated for working out a dynamic ontology that attempts to retrieve the Trinity *and* faulted for failing to penetrate to the idolatrous "turn to the subject." It is this latter that inevitably makes an idol out of the human event of coming to self-consciousness, also if not especially in Hegel's putative retrieval of the doctrine of the Trinity. In that light, moreover, we can see profound continuities in Hegel, as previously pointed out, both with Anselm's *fides quaerens intellectum* and with Augustine's psychological model of the Trinity (itself borrowed from neo-Platonism). There are considerable ironies involved in seeing

12. Hart, *The Beauty of the Infinite,* p. 169.

13. John Meyendorff, *Byzantine Theology: Historical Trends and Doctrinal Themes* (New York: Fordham University Press, 1979), p. 180.

14. Hart, *The Beauty of the Infinite,* p. 213.

15. Hart, *The Beauty of the Infinite,* pp. 161, 166.

the muddles perpetuated by Hart's learned, but polemical diatribe against Jenson in this light. On the present reading, Jenson is guilty, if anything, of spoiling his own achievement in retrieving the social model of the Trinity from the Eastern fathers precisely by trying to synthesize this retrieval with an idealist philosophy of the event of coming to self-consciousness[16] (yet just this dynamism is the very thing that Hart in turn defends in his collateral assault on Rahner in the follow-

16. Inter alia, *ST* 1, p. 220, though Jenson seems here and elsewhere to be reasoning to the "immanent" Trinity in his own sense of the "temporal infinity" of the divine self-consciousness. Thus he can write in an essentialist way, "To be God is always to be open to and always to open a future, transgressing all past-imposed conditions" and claim that this is "the eternity appropriate to the gospel's God" (p. 216). Jenson has defended his position in a contribution, "Ipse Pater non est impassibilis," in *Divine Impassibility and the Mystery of Human Suffering*, ed. J. F. Keating and T. J. White, O.P. (Grand Rapids: Eerdmans, 2009), pp. 117-26. He reminds that his position is resolutely anti-Arian (p. 121, something that can at least be questioned regarding his critics who analogically distance the earthly Jesus from the heavenly Son) and that his way of unifying God with humanity in Christ makes petitionary prayer theologically possible (p. 125, again, something that can at least be questioned regarding his critics' embrace of Augustine's eternal now). He expressly rejects the inflated criticisms that he has said any such "pseudo-Hegelian thing" as that God actualizes His being in history (p. 117), and he denies that his position is implicated in "Moltmann's theatrically suffering God, or the God of 'open theism . . .'" (p. 120). Very helpfully, he clarifies his stance by arguing that the question, whether God in Himself is passible or impassible, posits a pseudo-question that cannot be answered just because such "an abstraction cannot be performed on the biblical God" (p. 123). If we take that to mean that such an abstraction performed on the biblical God is nothing but an abstraction, and that the status of the doctrine of the immanent or ontological Trinity is that of an abstraction, and that by the metaphysics of anticipation one expects the final revelation of the co-equal Trinity along the lines that this "abstraction" deduces and hence projects, then Jenson has indeed cleared his teaching of suspicion of pseudo-Hegelianism. But it is by the same token not clear that this is in fact a doctrine of the immanent Trinity, other than by Jenson's assertion that God could have expressed His identity (the event of His coming to self-consciousness) otherwise (we know not how) than He has in fact done in His history with us. Further, in parallel with his theoretical ambitions, Jenson wants to revise notions of divine and human nature as "communal concepts" in order to overcome their oscillation between "unhelpful abstraction" and "disastrous concretion" (Jenson *ST* 1, p. 138). But "abstraction" is just how the notion of "nature" is helpful, while it is clear that treating nature concretely as if an agent is exactly the problem of modalism in Western theology that must be exposed and eradicated. Yet instead, "natures" in Jenson become living "mutualities," just as divine life becomes temporally plotted: "in God's eternal life Christ's birth from God is the divine *future* of his birth from the seed of David," where the infinity of God is God's own unbounded future (*ST* 1, p. 143). Allowing for the obscurity of the language, this seems to be an equivocation and not an innocent one. If "nature" is communal and mutual, in what "natural" respect can it be affirmed to be infinite or unbounded, when precisely communal and mutual existence seems to indicate mutual boundedness as the condition of relationship? Overcoming the two natures doctrine in Christology, like overcoming the "gap" between immanent and economic Trinity, can only be achieved by the strong Trinitarian personalism of consistent perichoresis, not Jenson's unfortunate resort to the dialectics of self-consciousness via German idealism where "natures" become flows and so confusion of natures becomes inevitable.

ing section of his book).[17] The truth that the Western tradition of theology that intends to be orthodox must still maintain with Augustine is the difficult one (in reality, not in thought) that God in His *creatio continua,* in the ubiquity of His Almighty presence, in the mask of nature is immediately the cause of all causes, though not the maker of all choices.

As to God's righteousness, who, according to the Bible, hardens wicked Pharaoh's heart (Exod. 4:21; 7:3; 14:4) and therefore admonishes, "Do not harden your hearts" (Ps. 95:8), the reprobation of Judas (Acts 1:16-20) comes after-the-fact; his moral suicide decided his own fate to which he is "handed over" (the divine passive of Rom. 1:24, 26, and 28), fitting him to play his role in Jesus' way to the cross, when His Father also "handed over" His Son into the hands of sinners. This moral suicide preceded his final reprobation, one committed in his right mind though possessed of false consciousness (Matt. 27:5). In Christian imagination, Judas persisted in wanting to be God and not wanting God to be God, even at the paradoxical cost of self-assertion by self-destruction. Judas therefore remains as a type, not of the damnation of others but of the damnation of those within who betray the Beloved Community. Beyond this figure of warning, however, the evangelist Luke was concerned to display the innovative and redemptive possibilities of the Spirit so that the persevering ecclesia can survive betrayal by counting on the God who makes good out of evil (Acts 1:21-26). The proper emphasis here, as Karl Barth taught us, is Christological: "the Son of Man goes as it is written of Him but woe to that man by whom the Son of Man is betrayed" (Mark 14:21). That is to say, it is Jesus Christ who was reprobated, i.e., "handed over" for all; but the one so elected by Christ taking his reprobate place, who nonetheless betrays this self-donating grace of Christ, culpably sins the unforgivable sin. That in substance is "the horrible" thought. We cannot erase it. We may grieve it through all eternity as the fateful sin of our own sister or brother. And, so long as we live, we fear it as our own fatal possibility.

Hart argues, rightly, that apart from ontology, theology remains mired in mythology, mere storytelling, with one anecdote as serviceable as any other, so long as "it preaches." We have derived exactly the same methodological rule from Luther's controversy with Zwingli, who without warrant preferred the "myth" of the Ascension to the "myth" of Christ's bodily coming in the Eucharist according to His personal promise. Appealing to divine simplicity as to a rule that forbids thinking of God traversing space in local motion, Luther, as we saw in Chapter Five, interpreted the "myth" of the Ascension as Christ's exaltation as coming

---

17. Hart, *The Beauty of the Infinite,* p. 169. One can read Jenson, and I hope the present effort, charitably as also wanting nothing other than to "abide the irreducible mystery of God's oneness in the persons' distinctions, or a single and infinitely complete divine utterance that is one precisely as already eminently embracing reciprocity. One obviously must resist the lure of purely social trinitarianism, which is, if pure, nothing but tritheism . . ." (p. 169). But this latter notation against "pure" social Trinitarianism is merely to observe that *models* in theology give contextually apt concepts for understanding the thing itself in union with its sign and do not replace it.

King of creation, such that He who is everywhere at work as coming King of creation can become present bodily, where and when He wills, according to His personal intention and promise in the Eucharistic meal, as the sanctified bread and cup. We have referred to this methodological procedure as one of deliteralization and theological decoding; in contrast to Bultmann's version (so-called "demythologization") this procedure holds that biblical narrative ("myth" if you prefer) has reference to the being of God in becoming our God and that understanding this reference for the praxis of the ecclesia in mission to the nations is what constitutes theology as the discipline of critical dogmatics. So decoding is ontology, as Hart demands, though of a pragmatic and descriptive, not theoretic and speculative, sort.[18]

Yet *what* myth it is that we take as canonical for theological interpretation is not a matter of indifference, and the problem of analogical theologies, such as Hart advocates, is the borderline Arianism and/or Nestorianism that shies from the full ontological implication of the *homoousios* of the incarnate Son with the Father in heaven. The deeper point of Jenson's critique of divine impassibility in this light is that the unbaptized doctrine of divine impassibility reflects another myth than that of canonical Scripture (e.g., telling of the God who *reacts* with wrath to human violence, Gen. 6:5-6, 11, but is *moved to compassion* and action by the cries of the afflicted, Exod. 3:7-8, and who finally *resolves* by divine holiness not to destroy, Gen. 8:21; Hos. 11:9). Jenson traced this other mythology to the revelation received by Parmenides[19] that becoming is illusion and only being is real, a doctrine nuanced and theologically worked out by Plato's systematic critique of Homer. Here God, as in the cosmogonies, emerges from battle, or is demythologized, as the transcendent anchor of the precarious order of political sovereignty. That is to say, Jenson argues, that here God is the God of Pharaoh rather than the God of Moses. Here God represents *escape* from the biblical calling of the image of God to attain likeness to God by the promise of God in a lived history of faith active in love and hope. Ontology cannot stand aloof over this *contestation* of the myths (Exod. 7:1–11:10), providing a Tribunal of Reason; it can only help in explication of it. In helping, ontology is servant and canonical Scripture is the Lord. The First Commandment, as we have seen, stipulates monolatry in a contested world, not philosophical monotheism that reposes sweetly above in the clouds, whispering "Come hither." The great message of the Second Isaiah is not that God is the One Being above the fray, but that the God of the Exodus alone demonstrates the unity of His divine being, contested by the human experience of His diverse judgments of wrath and mercy in the world, by the victorious coming of the Beloved Community through the atoning work of the Servant of the Lord.[20] This God *is* the eschaton of judgment.

18. Or perhaps, "theo-ontology," as Stanley J. Grenz contends in *The Named God*.
19. Jenson, *ST* 1, p. 7.
20. Grenz, *The Named God*, pp. 161-73.

To be sure, from within this monolatrous community, "theo-ontology" (Grenz) explicates the canonical "myth" to mean that there is one, true God, who is not reducible to His relation to creatures, as we witnessed Anselm discover in Chapter Eight. But that is the achievement to which Christian theology comes and in which it rests in adoration before the eternal oneness of the co-equal Three. The unity of God as the One who exists eternally but is known temporally by faith in the gospel is never to be taken for granted as a pseudo-philosophical axiom on the basis of which to speculate in ways that turn the human story into a comedy to avoid despair at its ample tragedies. By this Trojan horse other ontologies of other mythologies sneak in and subvert the primacy of Scripture as the narrative of God and matrix of Christian theology for the ecclesia in mission to the nations until the Parousia of Christ that brings the true conclusion of theology at the eschaton of judgment.

More interesting than the mere reaffirmation here of the classical doctrine of the ontological Trinity is the parsing of its own time and space, the "heaven" where God dwells and the "eternity" in which God lives. Corresponding to the criticism of Jenson's apparent application of the irreversible arrow of physical time to God's time in Chapter Seven, we put forward (in our own attempt to out-bid Nietzsche) a conception of God's eternity as "being in becoming" (Jüngel), an endless circulation that begins in the almighty Father and returns in the Son by the Spirit; just so it can and does spiral *ad extra,* most daringly, giving eternity as the "true" eternal return of the same. In this context, Jenson's critique of the metaphysics of persistence was received. A block of granite persists (relatively speaking), but it does not live, and the kind of eternity ascribed to the God of the gospel must think of the living God of the Bible, not an act of being that merely and formally stays the same (through time, or, as opposed to time). But the eternal act of being of the God of the Bible is one that, following Edwards, is immanently disposed to enlarge its own space and enrich its own life through its own outward passage. Just this immanent disposition is the "metaphysical time" (DeWeese) of the eternal Trinity who thus fittingly becomes the economic Trinity, creating, redeeming, and fulfilling our creaturely time by making it a place of His own dwelling in the eschatological fulfillment.

In the process, Jenson's solution of a metaphysics of anticipation was found wanting for a tendency towards instrumentalizing the Son in the curious repetition of Calvin's error that is fully worked out in McCormack's proposal that the Trinity itself is a function of the divine decree to be the God of grace for humanity. The question thus remains how God's eternity is to be conceived, if not as simple and timeless self-identity. In this question, we agree with Jenson's fundamental claim: "The Christian eternity is not silence but discourse, and spiritual progress in the gospel does not take place by the progressive abandonment of speech."[21] What is the time and space of God's eternal discourse such that it can be true of

---

21. *ST* 1, p. 223.

the eternal God in time to say: "Thou art my Son; this day have I begotten Thee!" And to have us pray, "Our Father in heaven, hallowed be Thy Name! Thy Kingdom come!" And to say about us, "God has sent the Spirit of His Son into our hearts, crying, Abba! Father!"

If we take Origen's great contribution to the development of Trinitarian doctrine but conceive of the eternal begetting of the Son as a timeless act, we conceive a muddle, not a mystery. There can be no such thing as a timeless act; it is a contradiction in terms. As such it fails to provide a theologically lucid description of the being of the God revealed in the gospel by illuminating the personal distinction of the Son and the Father as an eternal act, that is, as an eternal becoming. Origen himself conceived this begetting as everlasting, in the same way that he conceived of God's creativity as everlasting. While that latter idea of everlasting creation generated the problem for Christian theology of making the cosmos the completion of the triad in a way that displaced the Spirit both economically and ontologically,[22] the present point is that eternal begetting for Origen was not the nonsense of asserting an act that can in principle make no difference between a prior and posterior. This was exactly the difference he parsed by conceiving the hypostases of Father and Son. This had for Origen the good sense of asserting an act that ever[23] makes the Father Father and so the hypostatic or personal prior in ever making the Son Son and so the hypostatic and personal posterior. This hypostatic act of being in becoming, to be sure, leads us to the baffling idea of the self-surpassing Father as the origin and end of all things, persons, and thoughts in wonder before the irreducible mystery of an irreducible beginning without end. But that is as it should be.

Following the study of DeWeese in Chapter Seven, we have argued therefore for omnitemporality as the sense of the eternity of the triune God, by this indicating the everlasting *succession* in God's being that *originates with the Father* yet returns in the Son by the Spirit without end. The act of the Father's being in this becoming without end is what DeWeese calls God's own "metaphysical" time. We can properly distinguish accordingly between incommunicable and communicable properties of the triune God. Just this conception of a beginning that endlessly yields in turn the *proper* distinction between immanent and economic Trinity. Because God is irreducibly the act of His own being as the self-surpassing Father of the self-donating Son in the self-communicating Spirit in the heavenly space and in the time of His own eternal return, spiraling outward this God can wholly give Himself in creating a world of creatures, undertaking the lost creature's sin and death, making of the redeemed creation His own holy Temple and everlasting dwelling.

22. Robert W. Jenson, *The Triune Identity: God according to the Gospel* (Philadelphia: Fortress, 1982), p. 77. Wolfgang A. Bienert, "The Significance of Athanasius of Alexandria for Nicene Orthodoxy," *Irish Theological Quarterly* 48, no. 3-4 (1981): 190.

23. Joseph W. Trigg, *Origen* (London and New York: Routledge, 2002), pp. 24, 136.

In sum, then, the economic/immanent distinction in Trinitarian theology is a necessary one, although there is confusion about its status. According to this system of theology, the immanent and co-equal Trinity of the one eternal God is the *induction* to which theology comes from its place in the economy; there theology stops in wonder at being given this much understanding of what it praises when it lifts praises in the Spirit, with the Son, to the Father. In anticipation of glory, regarding this abduction as a prediction, it praises the Father and the Son and the Holy Spirit, one God, now and forever, the co-equal Trinity. Here theology ceases with reflection in due reverence before the eternal and incommunicable mystery that is precisely not a comprehension as spelled out by Parmenides' ontology of metaphysical simplicity. Here, the ontological test of "that than which nothing greater can be thought" is and remains eternally a *relative* determination — a "great*er* than which we beloved creatures can think nothing." Here "we" are and eternally remain the baptized creature, the theological subject united with the theological object before the eternal Father as the *terminus ad quem* of the doxology of love.

"The proleptic character of statements about God is closely connected with the element of doxological structure in dogmatic statements. To speak about their proleptic character means that dogmatic statements rest entirely on an anticipation of the eschaton, that they have, so to speak, a prophetic tendency."[24] The pragmatic knowledge of theology comes to its rest in praise of the irreducible mystery of the self-surpassing Father who lives eternally with the Son and Spirit, the one eternal God, the co-equal Trinity, when praise is understood as anticipation by grace of the light of glory. In this way the present affirmation of the doctrine of the immanent and ontological Trinity differs from traditional formulations, under the influence of the simplicity axiom borrowed from Platonist metaphysics, in thinking rigorously from the access bestowed in theological subjectivity to its validation in divine fulfillment of divine promise. The unity of God is not assumed philosophically, but it is held up as that which God demonstrates when He makes all things new, just so showing that He has been the one Creator all along.

## The Co-Equal Trinity in Anticipation of Glory

Human history is, so the Bible testifies from Genesis to Revelation, an excruciating contest between many so-called gods, lords, and saviors; each answers the question about the destiny of the world and of humanity in it also in the form of its own myth, with speculative interpretations about origin and destiny. Christian theology is born in this disputation and does not transcend it. That is

24. Wolfhart Pannenberg, *Basic Questions in Theology*, two volumes, trans. G. H. Kehm (Philadelphia: Fortress, 1972), 1:204.

the real meaning of the contemporary affirmation of pluralism in an emerging global civilization. Between the Scylla of imperial secularism and the Charybdis of reactionary fundamentalisms, the stakes for the common body on the earth are very high and the outcome very uncertain. The gospel of the coming Beloved Community of God does not depend on Euro-America's successful traversing of this passage, but theology in this Babylon cannot fail to attempt the navigation, also for the sake of Babylon's inhabitants. That is to say theologically that the fulfillment of creation in the coming of the Beloved Community surely comes in a way that surprises just as the coming of the Messiah in the flesh for impalement on an Imperial stake surprised and had to surprise and continues to surprise the faithful of Israel with an aporia, we have argued, that should be acknowledged as a principle internal to Christian theological reflection. Christianity, predictably, will be "superseded" by the coming of the Beloved Community, but also fulfilled, although that supersession cannot be less than the reconciliation of Jew and Gentile forever (Rom. 11:25-32). Just like persisting Israel, the ecclesia must persist in its Christ-commissioned and Spirit-empowered mission to the nations until over-ruled by the revelation of glory. Then it will come to pass that all nations will be blessed by the fulfillment of the promise to Abraham (Gen. 12:1-3).

We have seen that creedal Christianity acknowledges the Father at work by the Son in the Spirit as Creator of *all* things. God did not just once upon a time set things in motion upon a spatial stage on which an autonomous drama would play out according to its own inexorable laws; nor demythologized, does God preside above and beyond at an ontological distance so that God is credited as Creator only of what enlightened creatures deem good. Rather, "out of nothing" God is the continuing Creator of space-time itself, where the physical world of space exists as the temporal extension and actualization of God's creative command of origin, "Let there be!" This command continues, immediately, to the eschaton when it is superseded by the shout of triumph, "Behold! I make all things new!" Here nature is historical, just as history is natural, and in both spatial and temporal aspects creation will be finished and perfected in the fulfillment of the Creator's promise from the origin of all things to bless, "that they may have life, and have it abundantly" (John 10:10). The promise of origin is the coming of the Seventh Day, the eschatological Sabbath of God, when God sees that everything He has made is indeed very good (Gen. 1:31; Rev. 21:1-22:7) so that all the blessed rejoice in an accomplished goodness. Hence, by "hope projected backwards," we are to understand the mysterious origin in faith as God's promise of a fulfillment so that we conceive of creation itself eschatologically. The work of the Father in the origin points forward to the work of the Spirit at the consummation, and the mediation of these works is the redemption that is in Christ Jesus. So in the economy the Father works all things through the Son in the Spirit, so that in the Spirit, with the Son, creation renders the eternal sacrifice of thanksgiving to the Father that is its doxological place in the eternal Life.

If the gospel is true, that is to say, if God is true as the Father in the seeking self-donation of Christ the Son and the finding self-communication of the Spirit for His self-surpassing grant of eternal life to His redeemed creation, then God in His eternal being is not static, but ecstatic, just as His eternity is alive as an eternal becoming. Eternity is not timeless self-identity, but a sequenced life that eternally recurs, in ways that are consistent but not purely predictable in the outward spiral of its engagement with creatures through time. Here possibilities rejected by God in deciding for us may nevertheless be seized by intelligent creatures who also act upon these vain imaginings. In the ecstasy of divine Life, the spiraling God *ad extra* is capable of redemptive novelties with which to counter and defeat these novelties of evil; so the "good news" at the heart of Christian theology enacts the resolve of the LORD, anticipated from the foundations of the world in the Lamb to be slain, to maintain creation as a system of blessing over against the LORD's own righteous wrath at creation's seduction to, and the usurpation by, structures of malice and injustice.

To alternative conceptions of deity, most influentially those in the West that descend from Parmenides, such capacity for novelty is a sign of defect that makes God a finite creature alongside of other creatures, thus a reactionary God that provides the metaphysical ground for the absurdity of sin as that which God does not will but rather needs to overcome in order to become fully what He could be. For the Bible, however, this capacity for novelty is the signature of the living God who is real in His tri-personal vitality, and real for us in giving life, His own life, eternal life, and real yet again in inviting us already now to prayer and to live in expectation that this invited prayer is truly heard and answered. As the younger churches in the two/thirds world know, the Father in the Son by the Spirit is making all things new because the creature's sin and death are real, and so must really be defeated in the real, not sham battle that is found in, with, and about human history. This real battle is invoked in the petition, *Thy kingdom come!* As Euro-America slides into neo-paganism, the remnant of Christianity within it may also come again to know the apocalyptic battle-line demarcated by the cross of the Messiah and its proclamation of the God incarnate who enters in just this fashion the strong man's house to bind him and plunder his treasures. It may come to know again without shame (Rom. 1:16) this divine thievery that gives what is not deserved as the very righteousness of God (Rom. 1:17), neither tragedy nor comedy, but *sui generis* gospel (Rom. 1:16), news — *novelty* of God who as the living God shows His true deity by new doing.

In the economy we know God in a definite sequence, as the structure of this system of theology presents: in the Spirit we are conformed to Christ in whom we are given to the Father. That order of knowledge may, however, suggest a subordination in the order of being, as if rising through an ascending scale of intensity in divine being. Likewise, when we think theologically of this economy, we conceive of the origin in the Father who sends and its execution in the Son who is sent and the Spirit, sent by the Father and the Son, to bring the redeemed creation to fulfillment. Here too a definite subordination in being seems implied (as Schleiermacher cunningly observed),[25] from the one true agent to its subordinated instruments, as Irenaeus pictured the Word and the Spirit as the "two hands" of God. If thinking this way, theologians today who hold to Rahner's rule that the economic Trinity *is* the immanent Trinity, are led to the view that McCormack is now notorious for, that in God's primal act of being, the constitution of the Trinity and the divine self-determination in Christ by the Spirit to redeem and fulfill a creation of creatures other than God are one and the same event. That is the theology of God as freedom to love driven to its ultimate consequence.

This development seems incongruous, however, with the Trinitarian argument, also as old as Irenaeus, that God's antecedent eternal life as the communion of love of the Father and the Son in the Spirit provides the divine ontology of infinite generosity that can freely fund extravagant abundance for creatures. Moreover, this account of infinite generosity in the eternally Trinitarian communion of love grounds the *freedom* of the divine decision to create, as also the *wisdom* of its choice for *this* creation on which the cross of the Son would stand rather than any other in the decree concerning the Lamb slain from before the foundation of the world. It thus avoids the necessitarian implication of right-wing Hegelianism that God, in order to be God, *had* to create a world of creatures. It is the co-equal divine personhood of the Spirit that completes the triad in the doctrine of the ontological Trinity, recognizing God's eternal reality in His own right in the circle that begins in the self-surpassing Father but never ends of God for God in God that is as such the divine Life. If that is so, we have, as the Christian claim to truth, the eternal Trinity as the true eternal recurrence of the same, all the more wondrous for spiraling forth *ad extra* to create, redeem, and fulfill the world of creatures that gains God nothing but the trophies of His love, "a great multitude that no one could count, from every nation, from all tribes and peoples and languages" (Rev. 7:9). Consequently, God's eternity and creaturely time cannot be simply identified as one and the same event, howsoever intimately they now connect as creature to Creator or as sign to thing signified by the free Spirit's advent. The complication that prevents any ontological identification of God's time and the creature's time is that they may also divide by what Irenaeus called the Great Apostasy, the Satanic rebellion that dualizes the sign and the thing signified by wanting to be God and not wanting God to be God. We live in this contestation. But wherever already now the Spirit unifies the sign and the thing signified for repentance and faith to gather into the ecclesia in mission to

---

25. Friedrich Schleiermacher, *The Christian Faith,* 2 volumes, ed. H. R. Macintosh and J. S. Steward (New York: Harper & Row, 1963), p. 747. Of course, the present system of theology is nothing if not a categorical repudiation of Schleiermacher's claim that "the main pivots of the ecclesiastical doctrine — the being of God in Christ and in the Christian Church — are independent of the doctrine of the Trinity" (p. 741). We turn Schleiermacher's claim to expose the true sense of the Trinity on its head: modern Protestantism conceives of Christ and the church independently of the doctrine of the Trinity — an error far graver than a theoretical miscue in theological speculation.

the nations, wonder breaks out at the free, wise, and loving choice of the Eternal to become temporal that is the redemption of the creation and its fulfillment (Rev. 21:2-4).

In anticipation of this unification of all things in Christ (Col. 3:1-4), praises arise (Col. 3:15-18) in the power of the Spirit to God and the Lamb. This praise ascribes by anticipation the co-equal deity of the persons, the Father, and the Son, and the Holy Spirit, as it was in the beginning, is, and will be forever. The reason for the co-equal unity, we have argued, is not a common nature, since "nature" is nothing real in itself, but rather consistent perichoresis. The Holy Spirit, who eternally unifies the Son with the Father in love, in time unifies the dying sinner with the Son and at last this total Christ with the Father in the resurrection of the dead. Basil, the Cappadocian church father, made just this argument against those who maintained exclusively the economic formula of adoration, "Glory to the Father through the Son in the Spirit." True as this order of knowledge is in the economy, the economy itself brings us to the doxological anticipation of God in glory at the consummation of creation. So even now the church sings the order of being, "Glory to the Father and to the Son and to the Holy Spirit."[26]

Of course, it can be forgotten that this latter is doxological anticipation of the coming of the Beloved Community in power and great glory on the lips of the theological subject formed by union with Christ in baptism. It can be taken for granted, as if here and now in the still-contested time and place between the already and the not yet we already had arrived in that blessed land of promise. Or it can be imagined that God in Himself, in heaven, above it all in timeless eternity, simply is by nature one and the same effortless, because dead, thing, precisely not the fractured reality experienced in time, where divine wrath and divine grace and demonic chaos erupt without clear narrative connections, where absurdity and meaninglessness, not without God but precisely before God (Mark 15:34) assail, if not crush faith. What can this trial mean theologically but the Son's continuing gathering to Himself of the ungodly athwart the Father's continuing wrath on all ungodliness and wickedness of humanity? These are not yet historically reconciled; their historical reconciliation indeed would simply be the Parousia of the Son of Man at the eschaton of judgment. So the Spirit has not yet finished His great work of uniting humanity with Christ and of uniting the total Christ with the Father. Only then will the co-equal deity of the Three become visible *to us,* that is, as a historical undertaking truly and fully achieved. Only then will it be true for creation to sing without reserve, "Glory to the Father and to the Son and to the Holy Spirit."

So the normal use of the economic formula, despite its subordinationist appearance, reminds the baptized they are and still remain the pilgrim people of God, *homo viator,* whose access is on the earth and in history, in the Spirit, with the Son, on the way to the Father. "This life therefore is not righteousness but

26. "De Spirtu Sancto," *NPNF* 8, pp. 1-50.

growth in righteousness, not health but healing, not being but becoming, not rest but labor. We are not yet what we shall be but we are growing toward it, the process is not yet finished but it is going on, this is not the end but the road. All does not yet gleam in glory but all is being purified" (Luther). The eternal glorification of God the Father, co-equal in deity with the Son and Holy Spirit, one God, henceforth and forever as all things to everyone (1 Cor. 15:28), is ours now by anticipation in the light of grace of that light of glory still to be revealed at the redemption of our bodies. But just this is what is anticipated. What is the relation of the creature's life in time, personal and social, to this eternal life? This is the concluding topic considered in this system of theology.

## Eternal Life

The believer's personal hope in eternal life is wholly bound up with the victory of Christ in the coming of the Beloved Community, as previously described. Thus we will consider first the social dimension of the gift of eternal life, the Beloved Community, which we have affirmed as the eschatological interpretation of the *ordo caritatis* (order of love). "But seek ye first the kingdom of God, and his righteousness; and all these things shall be added unto you" (Matt. 6:33, KJV). As the discerning reader will have long since realized, the theology of the Beloved Community presented in this work is at once an appreciative appropriation of Augustine's "City of God" and a certain criticism of it that accords with the broader critique of Western modalism sustained throughout this work. Carol Harrison captures the gravamen of Augustine's interpretation of the *ordo caritatis*. "The argument revolves around a distinction between *res* (or 'things' which signify nothing other than themselves), and *signa* (or 'signs' which signify something beyond themselves). God, the eternal, immutable Trinity, is the *res* which is to be loved and enjoyed *(frui)* for its own sake, everything else — creation, man, God's temporal revelation — is to be used *(uti)* and referred to this end."[27] Harrison thus correlates the duality of thing signified and sign with the order of love, so that God alone is loved above all and all creatures are loved accordingly, in and under God. This is the social ordering of love in the kingdom of God, its righteousness. "Man's attitude," she continues, "to created reality, his love, is therefore ordered by the created and revealed order of God: it is to be used towards, and referred to, its maker and orderer, and created reality is only to be enjoyed, if at all, in God, and towards the final end of love and enjoyment of Him. It is this which Scripture authoritatively states in the double commandment of love of God and neighbor."[28] In the obedience of faith, this order of love or Beloved Community

27. Carol Harrison, *Augustine: Christian Truth and Fractured Humanity* (Oxford: Oxford University Press, 2000), p. 63.
28. Harrison, *Augustine,* p. 63.

of God with creatures breaks in already now. When faith turns to sight, it is established forever.

Criticisms of Augustine's conception of salvation as translation of creatures to the love of God above all and all creatures in and under God are of two types, particularly in theology in the tradition of Luther, especially as that is articulated in modern theologies under the spell of Kantianism. The first critique is the classic argument of Anders Nygren that Augustine's notion of *caritas* has the redeemed creature enjoying its beloved, God, and that this enjoyment of God in love represents a compromising synthesis of selfish eros with altruistic agape. "Luther then is not so much the man in whom Augustinianism finds its fulfillment, as the man who vanquishes it."[29] The second critique is an argument made on the basis of the Luther dictum, also very important for the present effort in systematic theology: "In philosophy the sign marks the absence of the thing; but in theology the sign marks its presence." Use of this dictum to distance Luther from Augustine's distinction of sign and thing, however, arguably misunderstands the apocalyptic sense of Luther's opposition between the "old" language of philosophy and the "new language" of the Spirit. In any case, the modern Lutheran notion here is that the *efficacy* of the *thing signified* is what is communicated in the performance of the peculiar language of promise, so that the sign is not, for example, "this," the liturgically designated bread and the wine, nor is the thing signified the Body and Blood. Rather, the linguistic event telling Christ-for-us elicits the event of existential faith in "Christ-for-me."[30] Jüngel, to take the example of an outstanding theologian in modern Lutheranism, argues that "Jesus Christ is the one sacrament of God," i.e., subordinating sacraments like baptism and Lord's Supper to the Christ-event, taken as language-event, making sacraments word-events and word-events efficacious as the communication of promise, not as the presentation of a substance.[31] This word-event may happen in association with bread and wine, or course, and be pictured as Body and Blood, but these traditional sacramental accouterments are incidental to the real action of God in coming *as* language.

There is a grain of truth in each of these critiques, but they do not suffice to sustain Nygren's judgment, or more importantly, to undermine the theology of the Beloved Community; rather, they can be seen to refine it. The first critique misses the mark because it fails to see that agape characterizes for Luther the cre-

29. Anders Nygren, *Agape and Eros,* trans. Philip S. Watson (New York and Evanston, IL: Harper & Row, 1969), p. 562. Perhaps no one in recent memory has quite so resolutely prosecuted this agenda as Steven D. Paulson, "God Is Not True Love's Goal," *Lutheran Theology* (London and New York: T. & T. Clark International, 2011), p. 147.

30. This view has myriad modern followers, but it begins already with Philipp Melanchthon. See Ralph W. Quere, *Melanchthon's Christum Cognoscere: Christ's Efficacious Presence in the Eucharistic Theology of Melanchthon,* Bibliotheca Humanistica & Reformatorica, vol. 22 (Nieuwkoop: B. De Graaf, 1977).

31. Eberhard Jüngel, *Theological Essays I,* ed. J. B. Webster (Edinburgh: T. & T. Clark, 1989), pp. 189-213. See Webster's critical comment in Chapter Two, note 191.

ative love of God for what is not God, that is, according to Augustine's *ordo*, the love of the superior for the inferior. Presumably such critics do not wish to evacuate the difference between Creator and creature and to this extent must accept some order that regulates our understanding of this difference — just as we have received and interpreted the doctrine of the "two natures." So if agape is divine love for creatures, what kind of love do beloved creatures have for God, assuming also that such critics will not disagree with Jesus' commandment of love to God and to neighbor as, in Luther's teaching, the very command that faith alone fulfills. Certainly, then, they should not love God instrumentally, making use of God for other ends than God, His kingdom and righteousness. That would not even be the mutually fulfilling reciprocity of just eros. That would be rather concupiscent love for God, the grievous sin that fuels the religion business. Certainly, as well, creatures cannot be rightly ordered toward God with agape love. They should certainly love God for God's sake, but they cannot love God creatively, that is, love God in a way that creates God or makes the unworthy God worthy. Rather, they can only love God in a way that honors God who creates them and makes them worthy by His agape love. They do so by *taking pleasure;* this is what *bodily* creatures do when they "treasure from their hearts" (Matt. 6:21) the God who has first loved them. Creatures love God in taking their own good pleasure in God's good pleasure and according to God's good pleasure as made known in Christ. That is to say in Lutheran lingo, they love God "when they believe that they are received into grace and that their sins are forgiven on account of Christ." What else is Augustine saying? When he denies that the beloved of God *should* love God with concupiscent love and denies that creatures *can* love God with agape love, what else can this ordering, or sorting out, of love be but critical theology by which true and appropriate love is discriminated from false and abusive love? Or is this minimum of conceptual clarity scholastic logic-chopping?

The underlying bone of contention, perhaps, is Augustine's conviction that grace heals and does not destroy nature by condemning and putting to death the corruption of nature. "For man cannot lose the will to happiness . . . ," Augustine writes. "By sinning we lost our hold on piety and happiness; and yet in losing our happiness we do not lose the will to happiness."[32] "Where your treasure is, there your heart will be also" (Matt. 6:20). Creatures live as desire, taking pleasure as they can and averting from pain, in order to live at all. To despise this irreducible corporeality as *Heilsegoismus* is not to despise the eminently despicable religion business, but to despise our creatureliness. This desire of all conceivable creatures, this hunger and thirst, is the law of our nature; it is what it means to be a creature, not having life in oneself but always in other things and other persons. Now Augustine reads, again on dominical authority, and at the very heart of the contestation, that "one does not live by bread alone . . ." (Matt.

---

32. Augustine, *Concerning the City of God against the Pagans,* trans. H. Bettenson (London and New York: Penguin, 2003), XXII, 30; p. 1089.

4:4). The command to love God above all, or, what is the same, to seek first His Kingdom and His righteousness, or again, to harken alone with the obedience of faith to the Word of God, then, cannot be anything other, if it is addressed to creatures, than the command to purify desire in true repentance, to cease with the anxious desiring of the Gentiles over "what we shall eat, what we shall drink, what we shall wear" (Matt. 6:31) and to find instead true pleasure and enduring satisfaction in the "treasure in heaven where neither moth nor rust consumes and where thieves do not break in and steal." The command is not only warranted on dominical authority; theologically understood, it penetrates to the "willingness" of desire that makes every creature in becoming voluntarily the person that she will be in her own historical journey. So Augustine puts all this together: "[I]t is better to struggle against vices than to be free of conflict under their dominion. Better war with the hope of everlasting peace than slavery without any thought of liberation. Our desire is, indeed, to be free even of this war; and by the fire of divine love we are set on fire with longing to attain that orderly peace where the lower elements may be subdued and the higher in a stability that can never be shaken."[33] *Ordo caritatis.* The integration of the person comes as integration into the Beloved Community of God, or the converse, its eternal disintegration, its eternal fracturing, its eternal death.

If one wishes to argue against Augustine's ordering of loves in this way so that believers can practically "know what they must do and what has been given to them" (Bonhoeffer, citing Luther),[34] one is really arguing with the Jesus of the Sermon on the Mount in the name of a Paul read through the eyes of a Marcion or a Kant. Moreover, to imagine that Luther does not hold to exactly the same position in this respect[35] — his entire theology is but an assault on the greed of concupiscent love by the assertion that faith alone in Christ alone worships God above all, honors God truly, loves God as the God who has loved creatures creatively in agape love — must be suspect as but knee-jerk polemical theology assuming modern form in the barren formalism of Kantian ethics with its profoundly misogynist suspicion of "inclination," bodily desire and emotionally intelligent affectivity. It is quite astonishing, otherwise, to witness how a Nygren can make the *doctor gratiae* (the teacher of grace) into the Pelagian he opposed. Augustine affirmed at the conclusion of the *City of God* that all our truly good works now done, "when they are understood as being [Christ's] works, not ours, are then reckoned to us for the attainment of that Sabbath rest," when "[w]e ourselves shall become that seventh day"[36] in the eternal rest of the City of God. When God rewards the Christian's merits, He crowns His own gifts. To come

33. Augustine, *City of God*, XXI, 16; p. 993.

34. Citing Luther, in his collaborative work with Franz Hildebrandt, "As You Believe, So You Receive: Attempt at a Lutheran Catechism," in Dietrich Bonhoeffer Works 11, p. 258.

35. *LW* 21, pp. 200-209.

36. Augustine, *City of God*, XXII, 30; p. 1090.

by way of the fiery love of God for us that purifies desire to the fulfilled ecstasy of body-and-soul love for God above all and all things in and under God is the eschatological salvation of those already now justified by faith operative in love and hope. The heavenly "reward" is our change; it is to become *non posse peccare* (not able to sin any more). "There we shall be still and see; we shall see and we shall love; we shall love and we shall praise."[37] If this love of the creature for God is false to Luther, so much the worse for Luther! But in fact, so much the worse for modern Lutheranism!

With a little bit of magic borrowed from Wittgensteinian theories of performative utterance, it is also argued that Luther abandons signification or reference altogether in order to do God as language; in these anti-Augustinianisms of modern theology, God happens, not in objectifying discourse about Him, but rather God happens as event in the language spoken that liberates or comforts or exalts according to the felt needs of contemporaries. This second line of criticism takes to task Augustine's philosophically indisputable observation that linguistic signs refer to things other than themselves. Contemporary deconstruction disputes that signs succeed in doing this, but it hardly denies that this is what signs attempt. Why else would a deconstruction be called for? In any event, Reinhard Hütter showed conclusively, in the present view, that one cannot remove the referential aspect of theological language in Luther's undoubted accentuation of its performative qualities without turning the performance of theological language into a circus side-show of clever illusions.[38] Dennis Bielfeldt has likewise contended against the reduction to absurdity that occurs when the epistemic primacy of the conversion of the theological subject by the Spirit working through the Word replaces, rather than correlates with, the semantic primacy of Christ as the theological object to whom the subject is converted.[39]

Luther in any case never disputes the philosophical truth that signs are precisely the absence of the things to which they refer; that ability to speak of things in their absence by signs is exactly the power of language to transcend the immediacy of sense experience. To think that Luther impugns this natural function of language as "objectifying" God constitutes a breathtaking misreading. It is not Luther, but such misreading interpreters who want to evade making the cognitive claim to truth in Christian theology. Luther, in any case, presupposes this "natural" truth[40] of the referential function of signs on the basis of which he articulates the advent of the new language of the Spirit that is new, not in ceasing

---

37. *City of God,* XXII, 30; p. 1091.

38. Reinhard Hütter, *Suffering Divine Things: Theology as Church Practice,* trans. D. Stott (Grand Rapids: Eerdmans, 2000).

39. *SF,* pp. 59-130.

40. Paul R. Hinlicky, "Luther's Anti-Docetism in the Disputatio de divinitate et humanitate Christi (1540)," in *Creator est creatura: Luthers Christologie als Lehre von der Idiomenkommunikation,* ed. O. Bayer and Benjamin Gleede (Berlin and New York: Walter De Gruyter, 2007), pp. 139-85.

to refer, but in unifying the sign with the thing signified to refer to the new thing coming into the world, the *Christus praesens pro nobis,* where and when it pleases God. In the same context, moreover, Luther emphatically affirms the Augustinian maxim, *res non verba,*[41] in Harrison's words: "things not words: it is the meaning of the passage, not the expression that is important; the intention, not the literal statement — the object, not the formulation."[42]

What Luther adds to the development and refinement of the Augustinian tradition in these connections, corresponding to his retrieval of Trinitarian personalism and Trinitarian Christology in criticism of the Western tendency to modalism, as argued in earlier parts of this work, is the clarity and necessity of the sequence of agape and caritas, that is, of the precedence of the Father's love for the Son from which arises the Son's love for the Father in the Spirit. For Luther it is not a matter of indifference which of the Three became incarnate for our salvation. It is fitting that we, who were dead in our sins, become the objects of the Father's unconditional good pleasure by union with His beloved Son, and only so, as united in this way with the Son as objects of the Father's free and unconditional favor, arising in the Spirit to glorify God with love for Him above all and all His beloved creatures, as loved together in the way of Beloved Community. Likewise, for Luther, it not a matter of abolishing the distinction between sign and thing signified in order to reduce signs to performances without any specific content, as prevails in our contemporary decadence of "doing God as language" where whatever is "creative" or "loving" or "stirring" is *ipso facto* hailed as constructive theology and worshiped as a new deliverance of deity. What matters is the unification of the sign and the thing signified so that *here* on the earth and in history, at Christ's Word and Command and not elsewhere, the Spirit comes to accomplish *His* incarnate work, not some other would-be savior's.

These refinements by Luther could actually still work to save Western Augustinianism from its own internal decay, and if so, the theology of the Beloved Community could also lead beyond the contemporary despair of those who "attempt without Christ to fulfill the promise made by Christ," as Étienne Gilson put it in some of the darkest days of the last century.[43] Gilson spoke of the gods that were failing, the "diverse philosophies of history" since Augustine's time, as "so many attempts to resolve, with the light of natural reason alone, a problem which was first posed by faith alone and which cannot be resolved without the faith."[44] That is the faith described in this system of theology, again in Gilson's words, that "the whole world, from its beginning until its final term, has as its unique end the constitution of a holy Society, in view of which everything has been made, even the

---

41. "Theologia non spectat tam verba, quam sensum." *WA* 39/II, p. 109.

42. Harrison, *Augustine,* p. 64.

43. Étienne Gilson, "Foreword," in Augustine, *City of God,* ed. Vernon J. Bourke (New York: Doubleday, 1958), p. 35.

44. Gilson, "Foreword," p. 31.

universe itself. . . . Everything that is, except God Himself whose work the City is, is for the City and has no meaning apart from the City. . . ."[45] Secularism, unconsciously to be sure, lives on the evaporating fumes of Christendom. A new way beyond Christendom and secularism is the marching order of the global future.

The victorious coming of the Beloved Community of God is the final work of the Spirit, the unification of the sign that is every personal life lived from birth day to death day with the thing signified that is the eschatological creation of God; this unification is the resurrection of the body to everlasting life. The body, as organized desire, is the sign of our common humanity and solidarity with nature in this fractured age, and the thing it signifies in the darkness and confusion of sin is the renewed cosmos for which it groans where no one will hunger in body or soul, where all will be fed with daily bread and the Bread of Life. Already now and despite all, even apart from repentance and faith, the despised body remains God's creature under His blessing and command to be fruitful and multiply; as such it can be the wellspring of compassion and the innocence of desire that rises up by God's *creatio continua* to defy our depraved captivity to structures of malice and injustice and bridge our ethnic, economic, and gender divisions; it can function as this sign whenever we hear the cries of the afflicted as the calling to become neighbor to the one in need. The body with its pleasure and pain in this way created and governed by God refers us, unconsciously or consciously, to all the other bodies to which we belong: the body of the vast cosmos and our local spiral galaxy and our little, out-of-the-way solar system on our speck of dust, the good earth, from which each of us specks of this speck is formed and nourished and to which we each return in the body's disintegration at death. The body, a temporary organization of space on the earth, thus learns that it is not a substance, a thing in itself; it is rather a sign that has lost its reference, a sign that is searching for its signified. The body is, as Leibniz argued, a "well-grounded phenomenon," from the perspective of which each item of "ensouled matter" (McCord Adams) that has emerged from the evolution of matter, looks out upon the whole vast body of the cosmos in motion and apprehends it for its little moment in some particular, hence partial yet uniquely personal way. It thus finds fragments of meaning in our fragmented humanity in our fragmented world, but without faith and in the light of natural reason alone, it cannot find the community of everlasting love to which all fragments of meaning refer, nor bind itself to it in hopeful faith.

If the body bearing its soul is a sign in this way, not the thing itself but a well-grounded reference to the thing, to what does it refer? What is the thing itself? Perhaps nothing, as contemporary nihilism affirms; perhaps it achieves only self-reference, as deconstruction thinks. The contestation of history disputes just about this. The thing itself, by the argument of this system of theology, is the coming promised from the origin, now vouchsafed in Christ, that Beloved Community where "God shall wipe away all tears from their eyes; and there shall be

---

45. Gilson, "Foreword," p. 21.

no more death, neither sorrow, nor crying, neither shall there be any more pain: for the former things are passed away" (Rev. 21:4, KJV). The body that each one is, and the body that we, fractured, nevertheless are together, signs this longed-for compassion. The God of the gospel is this compassion becoming present that the body signifies as wanting, as absent, as utterly needed. The resurrection of the body, already now anticipated in justification of the ungodly and the sanctification of the profane, is the final unification of the sign and the thing signified. It is the salvation that is anticipated already now in every healing work of compassion, giving form to every new structuring of justice on the groaning earth.

We face a final difficulty. We have affirmed repeatedly, in words taken from Bonhoeffer's abortive *Bethel Confession* against the Nazification of Christian faith in the tradition of Luther that the redemption of the body comes in fulfillment of the earth on which the cross of Jesus stood. We see today here too how contemporary knowledge constrains our understanding of this affirmation of faith and requires its deliteralization and theological decoding. For the "earth" on which the cross stood, like the river into which Heraclitus asks us to wade, is not today what it was yesterday. This body of mine, recognizable through time by a certain genetic pattern of information that governs its life cycle, becomes, in terms of molecular composition, an entirely new composite every seven years or so. The body, with the whole vast cosmos and our little earth and the common body of humanity on it, is but a temporary organization in the great flux of becoming. The irony of secularism in this light is that, in its proper turn of attention to "this world" as the creature that God redeems and fulfills, it divinizes as if an absolute what is in fact a fleeting moment in the perpetual change that is God's *creatio continua* on the way to the eschaton of judgment. In this way, secularism can become the ultimate reactionary force and an anti-divine ideology. There is nothing perpetual about the hegemony of Euro-America. The United States is not the *novo ordo seclorum* (new order of the ages). Prescient eyes already now see its decline and fall from this pretension, not without the grief of compassion and the solidarity of the common body. But secularism's emphatic "this" in "this world" is not today what it was yesterday or will be tomorrow. It is a polemical "this." It is a construct, then, that only makes theological sense as a descendant of the Reformation protest against an otherworldly interpretation of Christian eschatology as pie in the sky in the sweet bye and bye. But today, this battle long since over, by ferociously defending at the expense of others our partial "this" as if it were a universal, presently triumphant secularism becomes the *civitas terrena*. It becomes the unholy Babylon that is to be laid waste at the in-breaking of the Beloved Community of God.

Yet what then can it mean to speak properly of the redemption of this earth on which the cross of Jesus stood? Pannenberg makes the essential point against all chiliastic interpretations of the redemption and fulfillment of the creation as "this worldly utopias of a form of social fulfillment that will be achieved by human action. . . ." These can be "only very imperfect expressions of the hope of a future consummation of humanity. The consequences of the related functionalizing of individuals have also come to light especially in the case of Marxism in the ruthless sacrificing of the happiness of those who are now alive in the name of the supposed goal of humanity."[46] Redemption of creation must include all those who have gone before, who have died before entering the Promised Land, who have lived in obscurity and toiled in dark places humanly forgotten, who have been violently cut off from fulfillment. Redemption of creation is not found, then, in the prospect of this-worldly victory but rather generates and sustains *hope,* not optimism based on rational calculation, but the *hope of faith in the living God* that issues in conscientious living in love here and now that works for justice still in the maw of structures of malice and injustice.

If it is by now clear that the Christian hope can only refer to the social salvation of the Beloved Community coming down out of heaven in place of fallen Babylon but also for the sake of its stricken inhabitants, it can mean nothing less, then, than the promised act of the God, who is "more than necessary," whose knowledge is of each and every person in its own historical and biographical uniqueness, to be purified at the eschaton of judgment and reconciled with all the others whom God knows, assembled together as Temple of the Spirit where each one "will know fully, even as [each] has been fully known" (1 Cor. 13:12). The body sown perishable at its burial into the earth is in this way raised imperishable (1 Cor. 15:42), as it sees and knows and enjoys the One in whom it has believed. The affirmation here, Christologically not anthropologically grounded (1 Cor. 15:45), is thus that "we shall be changed" (1 Cor. 15:51) by the One who is making all things new. So the affirmation is that we shall as individual persons experience, know, and enjoy this great change — in communion with others.[47]

To ask, as Paul asks in 1 Corinthians 15:35-56, "how" the dead are raised is to entertain a foolish question, if the thought is to explain scientifically how God can do what God alone can do. It is, however, permissible and even imperative, if the import of the question is rather to ask why and in what sense the body is the object of divine redemption, which is that actual objection in Corinth with which the Apostle was dealing. In Luke 20:27-38, Jesus had proclaimed the God of Israel as the God of the living. Those whom the living God remembers therewith live in His memory and do not objectively perish. This is itself the wonder of the God that is the living God of the Scriptures; it is the wonder that we are fully known, that the very hairs on each one's head are numbered, that not a sparrow falls to the ground without the Father's knowing. In our fleeting reality we are known fully, loved nevertheless, and eternally remembered. This knowledge of God, of course, is beyond all creaturely comprehension. Never in all eternity does the creature comprehend how God comprehends the creature. All Christian reflection on the question of "how" the dead are raised begins and ever returns to this primary

---

46. Pannenberg, *ST* 3, p. 586.
47. So also Pannenberg, *ST* 3, pp. 573-74.

wonder of the Father in heaven who sees in secret and knows in secret. The Christian hope of eternal life is theocentric in this way.[48] There is no Christian theology of the resurrection that does not center on the wonder that God is the living God and so the God of the living. Following Luke 20, the theology of eternal life begins with the Life that is eternal, the almighty Father who knows each one fully and remembers each objectively and judges each truthfully and reconciles each with all the others so known, remembered, judged, and reconciled.

Only to the extent that that is clear, may we ask in what way will this become one's own body's knowing and rejoicing in what it knows. The physicist turned theologian, John Polkinghorne, has helpfully speculated about how this bodily experience may be conceived in the light of our best scientific thinking today.

> My understanding of the soul is that it is the almost infinitely complex, dynamic, information-bearing pattern, carried at any instant by the matter of my animated body and continuously developing throughout all the constituent changes of my earthly life. That psychosomatic unity is dissolved at death by the decay of my body, but I believe it is a perfectly coherent hope that the pattern that is me will be remembered by God and its instantiation will be re-created by him when he reconstitutes me in a new environment of his choosing. That will be his eschatological act of resurrection. Thus, death is a real end but not the final end, for only God himself is ultimate.[49]

It is interesting to observe that Luther, without the benefit of Polkinghorne's contemporary science, reasoned in a similar way.

> It is enough for you to know that [souls] are in God's hands and not in the care of any creature. Though you do not understand how it happens, do not be led astray. . . . The Scripture says, "Father, into your hand I commend my spirit," and so let it be. Meanwhile there will arise a new heaven and a new earth, and our bodies will be revived again to eternal salvation. Amen. If we knew just how the soul would be kept, faith would be at an end. But now we journey and know not just whither; yet we put our confidence in God, and rest in his keeping, and our faith abides in all its dignity.[50]

Luther obviously still thinks that the very matter which was our body at death will be collected and revived; Polkinghorne knows that a carbon atom is a car-

---

48. Gustaf Aulén, *The Faith of the Christian Church,* trans. Eric H. Wahlstrom (Philadelphia: Muhlenberg, 1960), p. 393.

49. John Polkinghorne, *The Faith of a Physicist: Reflections of a Bottom-Up Thinker* (Princeton: Princeton University Press, 1994), p. 163.

50. *Sermons of Martin Luther,* ed. John Nicolas Lenker, 8 volumes (Grand Rapids: Baker, reprinted 1983), 1:83.

bon atom whether on Mars or on Jupiter, while soul and body form one complex informational whole of the temporally organized organism that lives a personally unique life on the earth as a historical event that originates at conception and terminates in death. Yet both make the wonder of the resurrection the wonder of God who not only remembers each one as such a body but in the fulfillment re-creates this remembered one to enjoy Him in His fulfilled creation forever.

The Christian's hope in the resurrection of the body to eternal life is hope in the almighty God who remembers each one personally and so can re-create each one bodily. The point of any biblical "miracle," we have affirmed, is simply to indicate that God the Father is the almighty, the One who has possibilities beyond our power, including the power of our imagination. If you grant the premise about God's "almightiness," then the hope in the resurrection is at least, as Polkinghorne affirms in our scientific age, "coherent." Moreover, it is meaningful in the sense that it specifies life now in the body with its various societies as the very object of redemption and fulfillment. Such trust in the almighty Father who knows and remembers each one personally matters now for living life on the earth, where human minds go mad with the absurdity of being "thrown into the world" as a "being-towards-death," as Martin Heidegger famously put the experience of "chance governing all things at random" (Luther) that profoundly demoralizes modern people. Against this threat of madness, Luther prescribed medicine for the soul that cannot live without its body at the end of his great treatise against Erasmus: "There is a life after this life . . . for this life is nothing but a precursor, or, rather, a beginning, of the life that is to come."[51] Polkinghorne says the same when he argues that resurrection is new creation *ex vetere,* that is, out *of the old* so that, "quite to the contrary to the jibe about pie-in-the-sky, it invests the present created order with a most profound significance, for it is the raw material from which the new will come."[52] The Father remembers us better than we can remember ourselves, so that, purified by final conformation to Christ, in the resurrection the Spirit makes us all together new forever in His love. The gift of eternal life is this membership in the life that is eternal. So it is that already now the church sings in anticipation, "Glory to the Father and to the Son and to the Holy Spirit, as it was, is now and will be forever. Alleluia. Amen."

51. Martin Luther, *The Bondage of the Will,* trans. J. I. Packer and O. R. Johnston (Grand Rapids: Fleming H. Revell [Baker], 2000), p. 316.
52. Polkinghorne, *The Faith of a Physicist,* p. 168.

# Works Cited

*A Common Word: Muslims and Christians on Loving God and Neighbor.* Edited by M. Volf, G. bin Muhammad, and M. Yarrington. Grand Rapids: Eerdmans, 2010.

*A Map of Twentieth Century Theology: Readings from Karl Barth to Radical Pluralism.* Edited by Carl E. Braaten and Robert W. Jenson. Minneapolis: Fortress, 1995.

*A Presocratics Reader: Selected Fragments and Testimonia,* 2nd edition. Edited by Patricia Curd. Indianapolis and Cambridge: Hackett, 2011.

Adorno, Theodor W., and Max Horkheimer. *Dialectic of Enlightenment.* Translated by John Cumming. London and New York: Verso, 1997.

Agamben, Giorgio. *Homo Sacer: Sovereign Power and Bare Life.* Translated by D. Heller-Roazen. Stanford, CA: Stanford University Press, 1998.

——. *The Time That Remains: A Commentary on the Letter to the Romans.* Translated by P. Dailey. Stanford, CA: Stanford University Press, 2005.

Aland, Kurt. *Did the Early Church Baptize Infants?* Translated by G. R. Beasley-Murray. Philadelphia: Westminster, 1963.

Alfsvåg, Knut. *What No Mind Has Conceived: On the Significance of Christological Apophaticism.* Leuven, Paris, and Walpole, MA: Peeters, 2010.

Allen, Diogenes. *Christian Belief in a Postmodern World: The Full Wealth of Conviction.* Louisville: Westminster John Knox, 1989.

——. "The Theological Relevance of Leibniz's Theodicy," *Studia Leibnitiana. Supplementa* 14 (1972).

Allen, R. Michael. *The Christ's Faith: A Dogmatic Account.* London: T. & T. Clark, 2009.

——. *Justification and the Gospel: Understanding the Contexts and Controversies.* Grand Rapids: Baker Academic, 2013.

Anatolios, Khaled. *Athanasius: The Coherence of His Thought.* London and New York: Routledge, 2005.

Anderson, Bernhard W. *Creation vs. Chaos: The Reinterpretation of Mythical Symbolism in the Bible.* Philadelphia: Fortress, 1987.

——. *From Creation to New Creation: Old Testament Perspectives.* Minneapolis: Fortress, 1994.

Anderson, Gary A. *Sin: A History.* New Haven: Yale University Press, 2009.

Anselm of Canterbury. *Why God Became Man,* and *The Virgin Conception and Original Sin.* Translation, introduction, and notes by Joseph M. Colleran. Albany, NY: Magi Books, 1969.

Antognazza, Maria Rosa. *Leibniz on the Trinity and the Incarnation: Reason and Revelation in the Seventeenth Century.* Translated by G. Parks. New Haven and London: Yale University Press, 2007.

*Apocalyptic and the Future of Theology: With and Beyond J. Louis Martyn.* Edited by Joshua B. Davis and Douglas Harink. Eugene, OR: Cascade, 2013.

Aquinas, St. Thomas. *Summa Theologiae: A Concise Translation.* Edited by Timothy Mc-Dermott. Allen, TX: Christian Classics, 1991.

Arendt, Hannah. *On Violence.* San Diego: Harcourt Brace Jovanovich, 1970.

Armstrong, Karen. *Muhammad: A Prophet for Our Time.* New York: HarperCollins, 2006.

Asad, Talal. *Formations of the Secular: Christianity, Islam, Modernity.* Stanford, CA: Stanford University Press, 2003.

Aschheim, Steven E. *The Nietzsche Legacy in Germany 1890-1990.* Berkeley: University of California Press, 1994.

Augustine. *Concerning the City of God against the Pagans.* Translated by H. Bettenson. London and New York: Penguin, 2003.

———. *Confessions.* Translated by Garry Wills. New York: Penguin, 2006.

———. *The Trinity.* Translated by E. Hill, O.P. Brooklyn, NY: New City Press, 1996.

Aulén, Gustaf. *Christus Victor.* London: SPCK / New York and Toronto: Macmillan, 1931.

———. *The Faith of the Christian Church.* Translated by Eric H. Wahlstrom. Philadelphia: Muhlenberg, 1960.

*Auschwitz: Voices from the Ground.* Edited by Teresa and Henryk Swiebocki. Panstwowe: Muzeum Oswiecim-Brzezinka, n.d.

Ayres, Lewis. *Nicea and Its Legacy: An Approach to Fourth-Century Trinitarian Theology.* Oxford: Oxford University Press, 2006.

Bainton, Roland H. *Hunted Heretic: The Life and Death of Michael Servetus 1511-1553.* Boston: Beacon, 1953.

*Baptism and the Unity of the Church.* Edited by Michael Root and Risto Saarinen. Grand Rapids: Eerdmans, 1998.

Barth, Karl. *Christ and Adam: Man and Humanity in Romans 5.* Translated by T. A. Smail with an Introduction by W. Pauck. New York: Macmillan, 1968.

———. *Epistle to the Romans.* Translated by E. C. Hoskyns. London: Oxford University Press, 1972.

———. *Evangelical Theology: An Introduction.* New York: Holt, Rinehart & Winston, 1963.

———. *Fides quaerens intellectum.* Translated by Ian W. Robertson. New York: World Publishing Company, Meridian Books, 1960.

———. *The Word of God and the Word of Man.* Translated by Douglas Horton. New York: Harper & Brothers, 1957.

Bauer, Walter. *Orthodoxy and Heresy in Early Christianity.* Edited by R. Kraft and G. Krodel. Philadelphia: Fortress, 1971; reprint Sigler Press, 1996.

Baur, Jörg. *Luther und seine klassischen Erben: Theologische Aufsätze und Forschungen.* Tübingen: J. C. B. Mohr (Paul Siebeck), 1993.

Bayer, Oswald. *A Contemporary in Dissent: Johann Georg Hamann as Radical Enlightener.* Translated by Roy A. Harrisville and Mark C. Mattes. Grand Rapids: Eerdmans, 2012.

———. *Gott als Autor: Zu eine poietologischen Theologie.* Tübingen: Mohr Siebeck, 1999.

———. *Schöpfung als Anrede.* Tübingen: J. C. B. Mohr (Siebeck), 1986.

———. *Theology the Lutheran Way.* Edited and translated by Jeffrey G. Silcock and Mark C. Mattes. Grand Rapids: Eerdmans, 2007.

Beiser, Frederick C. *The Fate of Reason: German Philosophy from Kant to Fichte.* Cambridge, MA: Harvard University Press, 1987.

Bell, Daniel M., Jr. *Liberation Theology after the End of History: The Refusal to Cease Suffering.* London and New York: Routledge, 2001.

Bellah, Robert N., Richard Madsen, William M. Sullivan, Ann Swidler, and Steven M. Tipton. *Habits of the Heart: Individualism and Commitment in American Life.* Berkeley: University of California Press, 1985.

Benne, Robert. *Ordinary Saints: An Introduction to the Christian Life.* Minneapolis: Fortress, 2003.

Bertram, Robert W. *A Time for Confessing.* Edited by Michael Hoy. Lutheran Quarterly Books. Grand Rapids: Eerdmans, 2008.

―――. "Our Common Confession and Its Implications for Today," *Concordia Theological Monthly* 39 (1968).

―――. "The Human Subject as the Object of Theology: Luther by Way of Barth." University of Chicago Ph.D. Dissertation, 1964.

*Biblical Studies: Meeting Ground of Jews and Christians.* Edited by Lawrence Boadt, C.S.P., Helga Croner, and Leon Klenicki. Mahwah, NJ: Paulist, 1980.

Bienert, Wolfgang A. "The Significance of Athanasius of Alexandria for Nicene Orthodoxy." *Irish Theological Quarterly* 48, nos. 3-4 (1981): 190.

*Biographisch-Bibliographisches Kirchenlexicon.* Herzberg: Verlag Traugott Bautz, 1994.

Bobik, Joseph. *Aquinas on Being and Essence: A Translation and Interpretation.* Notre Dame: University of Notre Dame, 1965.

Bonhoeffer, Dietrich. *Christ the Center.* Translated by E. H. Robertson. New York: Harper & Row, 1978.

―――. *The Cost of Discipleship.* Translated by R. H. Fuller. New York: Simon & Schuster, Touchstone Edition, 1995.

―――. *Creation and Fall.* Dietrich Bonhoeffer Works, vol. 3. Translated by D. S. Bax. Minneapolis: Fortress, 1997.

―――. *Ethics.* Edited by E. Bethge. New York: Macmillan, 1978.

―――. *Sanctorum Communio: A Theological Study of the Sociology of the Church.* Dietrich Bonhoeffer Works, vol. 1. Translated by Reinhard Kraus and Nancy Lukens, edited by Joachim von Sooten and Clifford J. Green. Minneapolis: Fortress, 1998.

Bornkamm, Günther. "Das Wort Jesu vom Bekennen." In *Geschichte und Glaube,* Erster Teil, Gesammelte Aufsätze, vol. 3. Munich: Chr. Kaiser Verlag, 1968.

―――, Gerhard Barth, and Heinz Joachim Held. *Tradition and Interpretation in Matthew.* Translated by Percy Scott. Philadelphia: Westminster, 1963.

Boyarin, Daniel. *Dying for God: Martyrdom and the Making of Christianity and Judaism.* Stanford, CA: Stanford University Press, 1999.

Braaten, Carl E. "Sixth Locus: The Person of Jesus Christ." In *Christian Dogmatics,* vol. 1, ed. Carl E. Braaten and Robert W. Jenson. Philadelphia: Fortress, 1984, pp. 465-579.

―――. *The Flaming Center: A Theology of Christian Mission.* Philadelphia: Fortress, 1977.

Brecht, Martin. *Martin Luther: His Road to Reformation 1483-1521.* Translated by James L. Schaaf. Minneapolis: Fortress, 1993.

Brooke, John Hedley. *Science and Religion: Some Historical Perspective.* Cambridge: Cambridge University Press, 1993.

Brown, Raymond E., S.S. *The Community of the Beloved Disciple: The Life, Loves and Hates of an Individual Church in New Testament Times.* Mahwah, NJ: Paulist, 1979.

―――. *The Gospel according to John, xiii–xxi.* Garden City, NY: Doubleday, 1970.

Brueggemann, Walter. *Theology of the Old Testament: Testimony, Dispute, Advocacy.* Minneapolis: Augsburg Fortress, 1997.

Brunner, Emil. *The Christian Doctrine of God.* Translated by O. Wyon. Philadelphia: Westminster, 1974.

Brunner, Peter. *Worship in the Name of Jesus.* Translated by M. H. Bertram. St. Louis: Concordia, 1968.

Bultmann, Rudolf. *Faith and Understanding.* Translated by Louise Pettibone Smith. Philadelphia: Fortress, 1987.

————. *The Gospel of John: A Commentary.* Translated by G. R. Beasley-Murray. Philadelphia: Westminster, 1976.

————, and Five Critics. *Kerygma and Myth.* Edited by H. W. Bartsch. New York: Harper & Row, 1961.

Burleigh, Michael. *The Third Reich: A New History.* New York: Hill & Wang, 2000.

Burrell, David B., C.S.C. "Creator/Creatures Relation: 'The Distinction' vs. 'Onto-theology,'" *Faith and Philosophy* 25, no. 2 (April 2008): 177-212.

————. *Freedom and Creation in Three Traditions.* Notre Dame: University of Notre Dame Press, 1993.

Busch, Eberhard. *Karl Barth and the Pietists: The Young Karl Barth's Critique of Pietism and Its Response.* Translated by D. W. Bloesch. Downers Grove, IL: InterVarsity, 2004.

Calvin, John. *Institutes of the Christian Religion,* 4 volumes. Edited by J. T. McNeil, translated by F. W. Battles. Philadelphia: Westminster, 1975.

————. *The Eternal Predestination of God.* Translated and edited by J. K. S. Reid. Louisville: Westminster John Knox, 1997.

*Canons and Decrees of the Council of Trent.* Translated by Rev. H. J. Schroeder, O.P. St. Louis and London: Herder, 1960.

Carabine, Deirdre. *The Unknown God: Negative Theology in the Platonic Tradition: Plato to Eriugena,* Louvain Theological and Pastoral Monographs, 19. Louvain: Peeters / Grand Rapids: Eerdmans, no date.

Carter, Guy Christopher. *Confession at Bethel, August 1933 — Enduring Witness: The Formation, Revision and Significance of the First Full Theological Confession of the Evangelical Church Struggle in Nazi Germany.* Ph.D. Dissertation, Marquette University, 1987.

Carter, Jimmy. "A Cruel and Unusual Record." *New York Times,* June 25, 2012.

Cary, Phillip. "The Mythic Reality of the Autonomous Individual." *Zygon* 46, no. 1 (March 2011).

*Catholic and Reformed: Selected Theological Writings of John Williamson Nevin.* Edited by C. Yrigoyen Jr. and G. H. Bricker. Pittsburgh: Pickwick Press, 1978.

Celsus. *On the True Doctrine: A Discourse against the Christians.* Translated by R. J. Hoffmann. New York and Oxford: Oxford University Press, 1987.

Chemnitz, Martin. *The Two Natures of Christ.* Translated by J. A. O. Preus. St. Louis: Concordia, 1971.

*Christian Dogmatics.* Edited by Carl E. Braaten and Robert W. Jenson. 2 vols. Philadelphia: Fortress, 1984.

*Christianity and Revolution: Radical Christian Testimonies 1520-1650.* Edited by Lowell H. Zuck. Philadelphia: Temple University Press, 1973.

*Christology of the Later Fathers.* Edited by Edward R. Hardy. Philadelphia: Westminster, 1954.

Cicero. *On the Nature of the Gods.* Translated by C. P. McGregor. London: Penguin, 1972.

Clayton, Philip. *Transforming Christian Theology for Church and Society.* Minneapolis: Fortress, 2010.

Clement, Keith W. *Friedrich Schleiermacher: Pioneer of Modern Theology.* London: Collins, 1987.

Clifford, W. K. *The Ethics of Belief and Other Essays.* Amherst, NY: Prometheus Books, 1999.

Cone, James H. *Black Theology and Black Power.* Maryknoll, NY: Orbis, 1999.

Congar, Yves. *The Word and the Spirit.* Translated by David Smith. San Francisco: Harper & Row, 1986.

Conzelmann, Hans. *A Commentary on the Acts of the Apostles.* Translated by James Limburg, A. Thomas Kraabel, and Donald H. Juel. Philadelphia: Fortress, 1987.

Cragg, Kenneth. *Jesus and the Muslim: An Exploration.* Oxford: Oneworld, 1999.

Cranfield, C. E. B. *A Critical and Exegetical Commentary on the Epistle to the Romans.* Edinburgh: T. & T. Clark, 1975.

*Critical Issues in Ecclesiology: Essays in Honor of Carl E. Braaten.* Edited by Alberto L. Garcia and Susan K. Wood. Grand Rapids: Eerdmans, 2011.

Cullmann, Oscar. *Baptism in the New Testament.* Translated by J. K. S. Reid. London: SCM, 1964.

———. *The Christology of the New Testament.* Translated by S. C. Guthrie and C. A. M. Hall. London: William Clowes, 1963.

Cyril of Alexandria. *On the Unity of Christ.* Translated by John Anthony McGuckin. Crestwood, NY: St. Vladimir's Seminary Press, 1995.

Dahl, Nils Alstrup. *Jesus in the Memory of the Early Church.* Minneapolis: Augsburg, 1976.

———. *Jesus the Christ: The Historical Origins of Christological Doctrine.* Edited by Donald H. Juel. Minneapolis: Fortress, 1991.

Davies, Paul. *God and the New Physics.* New York: Simon & Schuster, 1983.

———. *The Mind of God: The Scientific Basis for a Rational World.* New York: Simon & Schuster, 1992.

de Lubac, S. J., Henri. *Augustinianism and Modern Theology.* Translated by Lancelot Sheppard. New York: Crossroad, 2000.

———. *The Drama of Atheist Humanism.* San Francisco: Ignatius, 1995.

Del Colle, Ralph. "The Triune God," chapter 7 in *The Cambridge Companion to Christian Doctrine,* ed. C. E. Gunton. Cambridge: Cambridge University Press, 1997.

Deleuze, Gilles, and Felix Guattari. *What Is Philosophy?* Translated by H. Tomlinson and G. Burchell. New York: Columbia University Press, 1994.

Dennett, Daniel C. *Darwin's Dangerous Idea: Evolution and the Meanings of Life.* New York: Touchstone, 1996.

Derrida, Jacques. *The Gift of Death.* Translated by D. Wills. Chicago and London: University of Chicago Press, 1995.

Descartes, René. *Meditations on First Philosophy,* 3rd edition. Translated by Donald A. Cress. Indianapolis: Hackett, 1993.

Dewart, Joanne. *The Theology of Grace of Theodore of Mopsuestia.* Washington, DC: Catholic University of America Press, 1971.

DeWeese, Garrett J. *God and the Nature of Time.* Aldershot, UK and Burlington, VT: Ashgate, 2004.

Dieter, Theodor. *Der junge Luther und Aristoteles: Eine historisch-systematische Untersuchung zum Verhältnis von Theologie und Philosophie.* Berlin and New York: Walter de Gruyter, 2001.

*Dietrich Bonhoeffer: Berlin: 1932-1933.* Dietrich Bonhoeffer Works, vol. 12. Edited by L. Rassmussen. Minneapolis: Fortress, 2009.

Di Giovanni, George. *Freedom and Religion in Kant and His Immediate Successors: The Vocation of Humankind 1774-1800.* Cambridge: Cambridge University Press, 2008.

Dillon, John. *The Middle Platonists: 80 B.C. to A.D. 220,* revised edition. Ithaca, NY: Cornell University Press, 1996.

*Divine Impassibility and the Mystery of Human Suffering.* Edited by J. F. Keating and T. J. White, O.P. Grand Rapids: Eerdmans, 2009.

Dodd, C. H. *The Interpretation of the Fourth Gospel.* Cambridge: Cambridge University Press, 1995.

Drozdek, Adam. *Greek Philosophers as Theologians: The Divine Arche.* Aldershot, UK and Burlington, VT: Ashgate, 2007.

D'Souza, Dinesh. *The Enemy at Home: The Cultural Left and Its Responsibility for 9/11.* New York: Doubleday, 2007.

Dupré, Louis. *Passage to Modernity: An Essay in the Hermeneutics of Nature and Culture.* New Haven and London: Yale University Press, 1995.

*Early Judaism and Its Modern Interpreters.* Edited by Robert A. Kraft and George W. E. Nickelsburg. Philadelphia: Fortress, 1986.

Ebeling, Gerhard. *Word and Faith.* Translated by J. W. Leitch. Philadelphia: Fortress, 1964.

Eckhardt, Burnell F., Jr. *Anselm and Luther on the Atonement: Was It "Necessary"?* San Francisco: Mellen Research University Press, 1992.

Edwards, Jonathan. *The Nature of True Virtue.* Ann Arbor: University of Michigan Press, 2001.

Edwards, Mark U. *Luther's Last Battles: Politics and Polemics, 1531-46.* Ithaca, NY: Cornell University Press, 1983.

Elert, Werner. *The Structure of Lutheranism.* Translated by Walter A. Hansen. St. Louis: Concordia, 1962.

el Fadl, Khaled Abou. *The Great Theft: Wrestling Islam from the Extremists.* San Francisco: HarperCollins, 2007.

Eliade, Mircea. *The Sacred and the Profane: The Nature of Religion.* Translated by Willard R. Trask. New York: Harcourt, 1987.

Elshtain, Jean Bethke. *Augustine and the Limits of Politics.* Notre Dame: University of Notre Dame Press, 1995.

———. *Sovereignty: God, State, and Self.* The Gifford Lectures. New York: Basic Books, 2008.

Ericksen, Robert B. *Theologians under Hitler: Gerhard Kittel, Paul Althaus and Emanuel Hirsch.* New Haven and London: Yale University Press, 1985.

Farmer, William R. *The Formation of the New Testament Canon: An Ecumenical Approach.* Mahwah, NJ: Paulist, 1983.

Feuerbach, Ludwig. *The Essence of Christianity.* Translated by George Eliot. New York: Harper Torchbooks, 1957.

Fiorenza, Elisabeth Schüssler. *The Book of Revelation: Justice and Judgment.* Philadelphia: Fortress, 1985.

Fish, Stanley. "Reply to Richard John Neuhaus." *First Things* (February 1996), accessed online at http://www.firstthings.com/article/2007/09/003-stanley-fish-replies-to-richard-john-neuhaus-10.

Fitzmyer, Joseph A. *The Gospel according to Luke, I–IX,* The Anchor Bible, vol. 28. New York: Doubleday, 1979.

Flett, John G. *The Witness of God: The Trinity, Missio Dei, Karl Barth, and the Nature of Christian Community.* Grand Rapids: Eerdmans, 2010.

Forde, Gerhard O. *On Being a Theologian of the Cross: Reflections on Luther's Heidelberg Disputation, 1518.* Grand Rapids: Eerdmans, 1997.

Forell, George. *Faith Active in Love*. Eugene, OR: Wipf & Stock, 2000.

Forstman, Jack. *Christian Faith in Dark Times: Theological Conflicts in the Shadow of Hitler*. Louisville: Westminster John Knox, 1992.

Frank, Günther. *Die Theologische Philosophie Philipp Melanchthons (1497-1560)*. Erfurter Theologische Studien, vol. 67. Benno.

———. *Die Vernunft des Gottesgedankens: Religionsphilosophische Studien zur fruehen Neuzeit*. Stuttgart-Bad Cannstatt: Frommann-Holzboog, 2003.

Frei, Hans W. *The Identity of Jesus Christ: The Hermeneutical Basis of Dogmatic Theology*. Philadelphia: Fortress, 1975.

*Friedrich Heinrich Jacobi: The Main Philosophical Writings and the Novel Allwill*. Translated by G. di Giovanni. Montreal and Kingston: McGill-Queen's University Press, 2009.

Gäbler, Ulrich. *Huldrych Zwingli: His Life and Work*. Translated by Ruth C. L. Gritsch. Philadelphia: Fortress, 1986.

Gadamer, Hans-Georg. *Truth and Method*. New York: Seabury, 1975.

George, Luke Timothy. "Interpretive Dance: How the Brazos Biblical Commentary Falls Short." *Commonweal* 2, no. 18 (2012), accessed online at commonwealmagazine.org.

Gerhard, Johann. *On the Nature of God and On the Most Holy Mystery of the Trinity, Theological Commonplaces*. Translated by Richard J. Ginda. St. Louis: Concordia, 2007.

———. *On the Nature of Theology and Scripture, Theological Commonplaces*. Translated by Richard J. Dinda. St. Louis: Concordia, 2006.

———. *On the Person and Office of Christ, Theological Commonplaces*. Translated by Richard J. Ginda. St. Louis: Concordia, 2009.

Gilbert, Martin. *The Holocaust: A History of the Jews in Europe during the Second World War*. New York: Holt, Rinehart, & Winston, 1986.

Gillespie, Michael Allen. *Nihilism before Nietzsche*. Chicago: University of Chicago Press, 1996.

Gilson, Étienne. "Foreword," in Augustine, *City of God*. Edited by Vernon J. Bourke. New York: Doubleday, 1958.

Girard, René. *Violence and the Sacred*. Translated by Patrick Gregory. Baltimore: Johns Hopkins University Press, 1979.

Gogarten, Friedrich. *Christ the Crisis*. Translated by R. A. Wilson. London: SCM, 1970.

*Great Debates of the Reformation*. Edited by Donald L. Ziegler. New York: Random House, 1969.

Gregersen, Niels Henrik. "Deep Incarnation and *Kenosis:* In, With, Under, and As: A Response to Ted Peters." *dialog* 52, no. 3 (Fall 2013): 244-62.

Greggs, Tom. *Theology against Religion: Constructive Dialogues with Bonhoeffer and Barth*. London and New York: T. & T. Clark, 2011.

Grenz, Stanley J. *The Named God and the Question of Being: A Trinitarian Onto-Theology*. Louisville: Westminster John Knox, 2005.

Grillmeier, Aloys, S.J. *Christ in Christian Tradition*, vol. 1, *From the Apostolic Age to Chalcedon, 451*, 2nd, revised edition. Translated by J. Bowden. Atlanta: John Knox, 1975.

Gritsch, Eric W. *Born Againism: Perspectives on a Movement*. Philadelphia: Fortress, 1983.

Guitton, Jean. *The Virgin Mary*. Translated by A. Gordon Smith. New York: P. J. Kennedy & Sons, 1952.

Gundry, Robert H. Review of Marcus, *Mark 1-8*, in *Review of Biblical Literature* 3 (2001): 386-91.

Gunton, Colin. "Augustine, the Trinity and the Theological Crisis of the West," *Scottish Journal of Theology* 43, no. 1 (February 1990).

Gustafson, David A. *Lutherans in Crisis: The Question of Identity in the American Republic.* Minneapolis: Fortress, 1993.

Habermas, Jürgen. *Time of Transitions.* Translated by Ciaran Cronin and Max Pensky. Cambridge, UK and Malden, MA: Polity, 2008.

Haga, Joar. *Was There a Lutheran Metaphysics? The Interpretation of the communicatio idiomatum in Early Modern Lutheranism.* Göttingen: Vandenhoeck & Ruprecht, 2012.

Hampson, Daphne. *Christian Contradictions: The Structures of Lutheran and Catholic Thought.* Cambridge: Cambridge University Press, 2001.

Hanson, Paul D. "A New Challenge to Biblical Theology." *Journal of the American Academy of Religion* 67, no. 2 (1999): 447-59.

Harner, Philip B. *Understanding the Lord's Prayer.* Philadelphia: Fortress, 1975.

Harrison, Carol. *Augustine: Christian Truth and Fractured Humanity.* Oxford: Oxford University Press, 2000.

Harrison, Verna. "Perichoresis in the Greek Fathers." *St. Vladimir's Theological Quarterly* 35 (1991): 53-65.

Hart, David Bentley. *The Beauty of the Infinite: The Aesthetics of Christian Truth.* Grand Rapids: Eerdmans, 2003.

Hauerwas, Stanley. *The Peaceable Kingdom: A Primer in Christian Ethics.* Notre Dame: University of Notre Dame Press, 1983.

Hawking, Stephen, with Leonard Mlodinow, *A Briefer History of Time.* New York: Bantam Dell, 2005.

Hays, Richard B. *The Faith of Jesus Christ: The Narrative Substructure of Galatians 3:1–4:11,* 2nd edition. Grand Rapids: Eerdmans, 2001.

*Healing Memories: Reconciling in Christ.* Report of the Lutheran-Mennonite International Study Commission. Geneva and Strasbourg: Lutheran World Federation and Mennonite World Conference, 2010.

Heckel, Johannes. *Lex Charitatis: A Juristic Disquisition on Law in the Theology of Martin Luther.* Translated by Gottfried G. Krodel. Grand Rapids: Eerdmans, 2010.

Hegel, G. W. F. *Lectures on the Philosophy of Religion: The Lectures of 1827,* one-volume edition. Edited by P. C. Hodgson. Berkeley: University of California Press, 1988.

Heidegger, Martin. *The Question concerning Technology and Other Essays.* Translated by William Lovitt. New York: Harper & Row, 1977.

Helmer, Christine. *The Trinity and Martin Luther: A Study on the Relationship between Genre, Language and the Trinity in Luther's Works, 1523-1546.* Mainz: Verlag Philipp von Zabern, 1999.

Hendrix, Scott H. *Luther and the Papacy: Stages in a Reformation Conflict.* Philadelphia: Fortress, 1981.

Hengel, Martin. *Judaism and Hellenism: Studies in Their Encounter in Palestine during the Early Hellenistic Period.* 2 vols. Translated by J. Bowden. Philadelphia: Fortress, 1981.

Henriksen, Jan-Olav. *Desire, Gift, and Recognition: Christology and Postmodern Philosophy.* Grand Rapids: Eerdmans, 2009.

Hermann, Wilhelm. *Systematic Theology.* Translated by N. Micklem and K. A. Saunders. New York: Macmillan, 1927.

Heschel, Susannah. *The Aryan Jesus: Christian Theologians and the Bible in Nazi Germany.* Princeton: Princeton University Press, 2008.

Hinlicky, Paul R. *A Contemporary in Dissent,* review. *Lutheran Quarterly* 27, no. 1 (Spring 2013): 94-96.

———. "A Leibnizian Transformation? Reclaiming the Theodicy of Faith." In *Transforma-*

*tions in Luther's Reformation Theology: Historical and Contemporary Reflections,* vol. 32. Arbeiten zur Kirchen- und Theologiegeschichte, ed. C. Helmer and B. K. Holm. Leipzig: Evangelische Verlagsanstalt, 2011.

———. "A Lutheran Contribution to the Theology of Judaism." *Journal of Ecumenical Studies* 31, nos. 1-2 (Winter-Spring 1994): 123-52.

———. "Authority in the Church: A Plea for Critical Dogmatics." In *New Directions for Lutheranism,* ed. Carl Braaten. Delhi, NY: ALPB Books, 2010.

———. "Christ's Bodily Presence in the Holy Supper: Real or Symbolic?" *Lutheran Forum* 33, no. 3 (Fall 1999): 24-28.

———. "Confessional Subscription Today." *Lutheran Forum.*

———. "Grace and Discipleship in the Kingdom of God." *Pro Ecclesia* 4, no. 3 (Summer 1995): 356-63.

———. "Havens from the Heartless Home." *dialog* 28, no. 3 (Summer 1989): 175-82.

———. "Irony of an Epithet: The Reversal of Luther's Enthusiasm in the Enlightenment." In *A Man of the Church: Festschrift for Ralph Del Colle,* ed. Michel Barnes and Mickey L. Mattox. Eugene, OR: Wipf & Stock, 2013.

———. "Law, Gospel and Beloved Community." In *Preaching and Teaching the Law and Gospel of God.* Delhi, NY: ALPB Books, 2013, pp. 91-114.

———. "Leibniz and the Theology of the Beloved Community." *Pro Ecclesia* 21, no. 1 (2012): 25-50.

———. "Luther against the Contempt of Women." *Lutheran Quarterly* 2, no. 4 (Winter 1989): 515-30.

———. "Luther and Liberalism." In *A Report from the Front Lines: Conversations on Public Theology.* Festschrift in Honor of Robert Benne, ed. Michael Shahan. Grand Rapids: Eerdmans, 2009, pp. 89-104.

———. "Luther's Anti-Docetism in the *Disputatio de divinitate et humanitate Christi* (1540)." In *Creator est creatura: Luthers Christologie als Lehre von der Idiomenkommunikation,* ed. Oswald Bayer and Benjamin Gleede. Berlin and New York: Walter de Gruyter, 2007.

———. "Luther's Atheism." In *The Devil's Whore: Reason and Philosophy in the Lutheran Tradition,* ed. J. Hockenberry Drageseth. Minneapolis: Fortress, 2011, pp. 53-60.

———. "Problems of Evil: For Julius Filo on His Sixtieth Birthday." In V Službe Obnovy: Vedecký zborník vydaný pri príležitosti 60. Narodením Dr. h.c. prof. Th.Dr. Júliusa Fila [In the Service of Renewal: A Scholarly Collection published on the Occasion of the 60th Birthday of Dr. Julius Filo], ed. M. Jurík and J. Benka. Bratislava: Evanjelická bohoslovecká fakulta, Univerzita Komenského v Bratisalve, 2010, pp. 65-74.

———. "Resurrection and the Knowledge of God." *Pro Ecclesia* 4, no. 2 (Spring 1995): 226-32.

———. "Secular and Eschatological Conceptions of Salvation in the Controversy over the Invocation of God." In *This Is My Name Forever: The Trinity and Gender Language for God,* ed. Alvin Kimmel Jr. Downers Grove, IL: InterVarsity, 2001.

———. "Sin, Death, and Derrida." *Lutheran Forum* 44, no. 2 (Summer 2010): 54-59.

———. "Status Confessionis." *The Encyclopedia of Christianity,* vol. 5. Grand Rapids: Eerdmans/Leiden: Brill, 2008, pp. 198-201.

———. "Staying Lutheran in the Changing Church(es)." Afterword in Mickey L. Mattox and A. G. Roeber, *Changing Churches: An Orthodox, Catholic and Lutheran Theological Conversation.* Grand Rapids: Eerdmans, 2012, pp. 281-314.

———. "The Doctrine of the New Birth: From Bullinger to Edwards." *Missio Apostolica* 7, no. 2 (November 1999): 102-99.

————. *The Gospel and the Knowledge of God: St. Mark's theologia crucis.* Ph.D. Thesis, Union Theological Seminary, 1983.

————. "The Lutheran Dilemma." *Pro Ecclesia* 8, no. 4 (Fall 1999): 391-422.

————. "The Presence of Jesus the Christ." *Pro Ecclesia* 4, no. 4 (Fall 1995): 479-85.

————. "The Spirit of Christ amid the Spirits of the Post-Modern World: The Crumley Lecture." *Lutheran Quarterly* 14, no. 4 (Winter 2000): 433-58.

————. "The Use of Luther's Thought in Pietism and the Enlightenment." In *Oxford Handbook to Martin Luther,* ed. Robert Kolb, Irene Dingel, and Lubomir Batka. Oxford: Oxford University Press, 2014, pp. 540-50.

————. "Theological Anthropology: Towards Integrating Theosis and Justification by Faith." *Journal of Ecumenical Studies* 34, no. 1 (Winter 1997).

————. "Tough-Minded Augustinianism: Some Guidance for Christian Apologetics in Our Day." *Glaube und Denken* (Sonderband 1999): 157-72.

————. "Verbum Externum: Dietrich Bonhoeffer's Bethel Confession." In *God Speaks to Us.* International Bonhoeffer Interpretations 5, ed. R. Wüstenberg and J. Zimmermann. Frankfurt: Peter Lang, 2013, pp. 189-215.

————. "Whose Church? Which Ministry?" *Lutheran Forum* 42, no. 4 (Winter 2008): 48-53.

Hobbes, Thomas. *Leviathan* with selected variants from the Latin edition of 1668. Edited by E. Curley. Indianapolis and Cambridge: Hackett, 1994.

Holifield, E. Brooks. *A History of Pastoral Care in America: From Salvation to Self-Realization.* Nashville: Abingdon, 1983.

Hopkins, Jasper. *A New Interpretive Translation of St. Anselm's Monologion and Proslogion.* Minneapolis: Arthur J. Banning, 1986.

Hoskins, Sir Edwyn, and Francis Noel Davey. *The Riddle of the New Testament.* London: Faber & Faber, 1949.

Hoskyns, Sir Edwyn Clement. *The Fourth Gospel.* Edited by Francis Noel Davey. London: Faber & Faber, 1947.

*How Can the Petrine Ministry Be a Service to the Unity of the Universal Church?* Edited by James F. Puglisi. Grand Rapids: Eerdmans, 2010.

Hultgren, Arland J. *The Rise of Normative Christianity.* Minneapolis: Fortress, 1994.

Hultgren, Stephen J. "Holy Scripture and Word of God: Biblical Authority in the Church." In *Seeking New Directions for Lutheranism: Biblical, Theological, and Churchly Perspectives.* Delhi, NY: ALPB Books, 2010, pp. 53-108.

Hunsinger, George. *Disruptive Grace: Studies in the Theology of Karl Barth.* Grand Rapids: Eerdmans, 2000.

Hütter, Reinhard. *Suffering Divine Things: Theology as Church Practice.* Translated by D. Stott. Grand Rapids: Eerdmans, 2000.

*In One Body Through the Cross: The Princeton Proposal for Christian Unity.* Edited by Carl E. Braaten and Robert W. Jenson. Grand Rapids: Eerdmans, 2003.

*In Search of Christian Unity: Basic Consensus/Basic Differences.* Edited by Joseph A. Burgess. Minneapolis: Fortress, 1991.

Israel, Jonathan I. *Radical Enlightenment: Philosophy and the Making of Modernity 1650-1750.* Oxford: Oxford University Press, 2001.

*Is the Holocaust Unique? Perspectives on Comparative Genocide.* Edited by Alan S. Rosenbaum. Philadelphia: Westview, 2009.

Jacobs, Edmond. *Theology of the Old Testament.* Translated by A. W. Heathcote and P. J. Allcock. New York: Harper & Row, 1958.

*Jacques Ellul: Interpretative Essays.* Edited by Clifford C. Christians and Jay M. Van Hook. Chicago: University of Illinois Press, 1981.

Jaffa, Harry V. *A New Birth of Freedom: Abraham Lincoln and the Coming of the Civil War.* Lanham, MD: Rowman & Littlefield, 2000.

James, William. *The Varieties of Religious Experience: A Study in Human Nature.* Mineola, NY: Dover, 2002.

Jenson, Robert W. *America's Theologian: A Recommendation of Jonathan Edwards.* New York and Oxford: Oxford University Press, 1988.

———. "An Ontology of Freedom in the *De Servo Arbitrio* of Luther." *Modern Theology* 10, no. 3 (July 1994): 247-52.

———. *God after God: The God of the Past and the God of the Future, Seen in the Work of Karl Barth.* Indianapolis and New York: Bobbs-Merrill, 1969.

———. "Ipse Pater non est impassibilis." In *Divine Impassibility and the Mystery of Human Suffering,* ed. J. F. Keating and T. J. White, O.P. Grand Rapids: Eerdmans, 2009, pp. 117-26.

———. *The Triune Identity: God according to the Gospel.* Philadelphia: Fortress, 1982.

———. *Unbaptized God: The Basic Flaw in Ecumenical Theology.* Minneapolis: Augsburg Fortress, 1992.

———. *Visible Words: The Interpretation and Practice of Christian Sacraments.* Philadelphia: Fortress, 1978.

———. "You Wonder Where the Spirit Went." *Pro Ecclesia* 2, no. 3 (Summer 1993): 296.

Jeremias, Joachim. *Infant Baptism in the First Four Centuries.* Translated by David Cairns. Philadelphia: Westminster, 1962.

———. *New Testament Theology: The Proclamation of Jesus.* Translated by J. Bowden. New York: Charles Scribner's Sons, 1971.

Johnson, Elizabeth A. *She Who Is: The Mystery of God in Feminist Theological Discourse.* New York: Crossroad, 1994.

Johnson, Paul. *A History of the Jews.* New York: Harper & Row, 1987.

Jolley, Nicolas. *Locke: His Philosophical Thought.* Oxford: Oxford University Press, 1999.

Jordan, G. J. *The Reunion of the Churches: A Study of G. W. Leibnitz and His Great Attempt.* London: Constable, 1927.

Juel, Donald H. *Messianic Exegesis: Christological Interpretation of the Old Testament in Early Christianity.* Philadelphia: Fortress, 1988.

Jüngel, Eberhard. *God as the Mystery of the World: On the Foundation of the Theology of the Crucified One in the Dispute between Theism and Atheism.* Translated by D. L. Guder. Grand Rapids: Eerdmans, 1983.

———. *Justification: The Heart of the Christian Faith.* Translated by J. F. Cayzer. Edinburgh and New York: T. & T. Clark, 2001.

———. *The Doctrine of the Trinity: God's Being Is in Becoming.* Grand Rapids: Eerdmans, 1976.

———. *The Freedom of a Christian: Luther's Significance for Contemporary Theology.* Translated by R. A. Harrisville. Minneapolis: Augsburg, 1988.

———. *Theological Essays I.* Edited by J. B. Webster. Edinburgh: T. & T. Clark, 1989.

Juntunen, Sammeli. "Luther and Metaphysics." In *Union with Christ: The New Finnish Interpretation of Luther,* ed. Carl E. Braaten and Robert W. Jenson. Grand Rapids: Eerdmans, 1998, pp. 129-60.

"Justification and the Church." Joint Evangelical Lutheran–Roman Catholic Commission (1993), accessed on-line at http://www.prounione.urbe.it/dia-int/l-rc/doc/e_l-rc_church.html.

*Justification and the Future of the Ecumenical Movement.* Edited by William G. Rusch. Collegeville, MN: Liturgical Press, 2003.

Kaiser, Otto. "Traditionsgeschichtliche Untersuchung von Genesis 15." *Zeitschrift für die alttestamentlische Wissenschaft* 70 (1958): 107-26.

Kant, Immanuel. *Critique of Pure Reason.* Translated by J. M. D. Meiklejohn. Mineola, NY: Dover, 2003.

————. *The Conflict of the Faculties.* Translated by Mary J. Gregor. New York: Abaris Books, 1979.

Kärkkäinen, Veli-Matti. *One with God: Salvation as Deification and Justification.* Collegeville, MN: Liturgical Press, 2004.

Käsemann, Ernst. *Commentary on Romans.* Translated and edited by G. Bromiley. Grand Rapids: Eerdmans, 1980.

————. *Essays on New Testament Themes.* Translated by W. J. Montague. London: SCM, 1971.

————. *Perspectives on Paul.* Translated by Margaret Kohl. Philadelphia: Fortress, 1971.

Kavanagh, Aidan. *The Shape of Baptism: The Rite of Christian Initiation.* New York: Pueblo, 1978.

Kay, James F. *Christus Praesens: A Reconsideration of Rudolf Bultmann's Christology.* Grand Rapids: Eerdmans, 1994.

Keck, Leander E. *A Future for the Historical Jesus: The Place of Jesus in Preaching and Theology.* Philadelphia: Fortress, 1981.

Kelly, J. N. D. *Early Christian Creeds,* 3rd edition. New York: David McKay, 1972.

Kerr, Fergus. *After Aquinas: Versions of Thomism.* Malden, MA: Blackwell, 2002.

King, Martin Luther, Jr. *Strength to Love.* Philadelphia: Fortress, 1987.

Kirk, J. R. Daniel. Review, *Horizons in Biblical Theology* 32 (2010): 99-127.

Klenicki, Leon, and Richard John Neuhaus. *Believing Today: Jew and Christian in Conversation.* Grand Rapids: Eerdmans, 1989.

Koester, Craig R. *The Word of Life: A Theology of John's Gospel.* Grand Rapids: Eerdmans, 2008.

Kojève, Alexandre. *Introduction to the Reading of Hegel: Lectures on the Phenomenology of Spirit.* Translated by James H. Nichols Jr. Ithaca, NY and London: Cornell University Press, 1996.

Kolakowski, Leszek. *God Owes Us Nothing: A Brief Remark on Pascal's Religion and on the Spirit of Jansenism.* Chicago: University of Chicago Press, 1998.

Kolb, Robert. *Bound Choice, Election, and Wittenberg Theological Method: From Martin Luther to the Formula of Concord.* Grand Rapids: Eerdmans, 2005.

Kroetke, Wolf. *Sin and Nothingness in the Theology of Karl Barth.* Translated by P. G. Ziegler and C.-M. Bammel. Studies in Reformed Theology and History, New Series, Number 10. Princeton: Princeton Theological Seminary, 2005.

Kuhn, Thomas S. *The Structure of Scientific Revolutions,* 2nd edition, enlarged. Chicago: University of Chicago Press, 1973.

Kuklick, Bruce. *Josiah Royce: An Intellectual Biography.* Indianapolis: Hackett, 1985.

Kusukawa, Sachiko. *The Transformation of Natural Philosophy: The Case of Philip Melanchthon.* Cambridge: Cambridge University Press, 1995.

Lapide, Pinchas, and Peter Stuhlmacher. *Paul: Rabbi and Apostle.* Minneapolis: Augsburg, 1984.

Lazareth, William H. *Christians in Society: Luther, the Bible and Social Ethics.* Minneapolis: Fortress, 2001.

Lee, Philip J. *Against the Protestant Gnostics.* New York: Oxford University Press, 1987.

Leibniz, Gottfried Wilhelm. *Discourse on Metaphysics and Other Essays.* Translated by D. Garber. Indianapolis and Cambridge: Hackett, 1991.

———. *Philosophical Papers and Letters: A Selection,* 2 volumes. Translated by Leroy E. Loemker. Chicago: University of Chicago Press, 1956.

———. *Theodicy: Essays on the Goodness of God, the Freedom of Man and the Origin of Evil.* Translated by E. M. Huggard. Chicago and La Salle, IL: Open Court, 1998.

*Leibniz: Political Writings,* 2nd edition. Edited by P. Riley. Cambridge: Cambridge University Press, 2001.

Levering, Matthew. *Christ's Fulfillment of Torah Temple: Salvation according to Thomas Aquinas.* Notre Dame: University of Notre Dame Press, 2002.

Lienhard, Marc. *Martin Luther: Witness to Jesus Christ, Stages and Themes of the Reformer's Christology.* Translated by Edwin H. Robertson. Minneapolis: Augsburg, 1982.

Lietzman, Hans. *A History of the Early Church.* New York: World Publishing Co., 1961.

Lindbeck, George A. *The Nature of Doctrine: Religion and Theology in a Postliberal Age.* Philadelphia: Westminster, 1984.

Lindberg, David C. *The Beginnings of Western Science: The European Scientific Tradition in Philosophical, Religious, and Institutional Context, Prehistory to A.D. 1450,* 2nd edition. Chicago and London: University of Chicago Press, 2007.

Lischer, Richard. *The Preacher King: Martin Luther King, Jr. and the Word That Moved America.* New York and Oxford: Oxford University Press, 1995.

Locke, John. *Second Treatise of Government.* Edited by C. B. Macpherson. Indianapolis and Cambridge: Hackett, 1980.

Lohse, Bernhard. *A Short History of Christian Doctrine.* Translated by F. Ernest Stoeffler. Philadelphia: Fortress, 1978.

———. "Conscience and Authority in Luther." In *Luther and the Dawn of the Modern Era: Papers for the Fourth International Congress for Luther Research.* Leiden: E. J. Brill, 1974, pp. 158-83.

———. *Martin Luther's Theology: Its Historical and Systematic Development.* Translated by Roy A. Harrisville. Minneapolis: Fortress, 1999.

Lösel, Steffen. "The *Kirchenkampf* of the Countercultural Colony: A Critical Response." *Theology Today* 67 (Fall 2010): 279-98.

Lossky, Vladimir. *In the Image and Likeness of God.* Edited by John H. Erickson and Thomas E. Bird. Crestwood, NY: St. Vladimir's Seminary Press, 1985.

Louth, Andrew. *Maximus the Confessor.* London: Routledge, 1996.

*Luther: Lectures on Romans.* Translated by Wilhelm Pauck. Philadelphia: Westminster, 1961.

Luther, Martin. *The Bondage of the Will.* Translated by J. I. Packer and O. R. Johnston. Grand Rapids: Fleming H. Revell (Baker), 2000.

*Lutheran-Orthodox Dialogue: Agreed Statements 1985-1989.* Geneva: WCC, 1992.

*Lutherans and Catholics in Dialogue I-III.* Edited by Paul C. Empie and T. Austin Murphy. Minneapolis: Augsburg, n.d.

*Lutherans and Catholics in Dialogue IV: Eucharist and Ministry.* USA National Committee of the Lutheran World Federation and the Bishops' Committee for Ecumenical and Interreligious Affairs, 1970.

Luz, Ulrich. *Matthew 1-7: A Commentary.* Translated by Wilhelm C. Linss. Minneapolis: Augsburg, 1989.

MacIntyre, Alasdair. *After Virtue: A Study in Moral Theory,* 2nd edition. Notre Dame: University of Notre Dame Press, 1984.

―――. *Three Rival Versions of Moral Inquiry: Encyclopedia, Genealogy and Tradition.* Notre Dame: University of Notre Dame Press, 1990.

―――. *Whose Justice? Which Rationality?* Notre Dame: University of Notre Dame Press, 1988.

Mack, Burton L. *A Myth of Innocence: Mark and Christian Origins.* Philadelphia: Fortress, 1988.

Mangina, Joseph L. *Revelation.* Grand Rapids: Brazos, 2010.

―――. "The Cross-Shaped Church: A Pauline Amendment to the Ecclesiology of Koinonia." In *Critical Issues in Ecclesiology: Essays in Honor of Carl E. Braaten,* ed. Alberto L. Garcia and Susan K. Wood. Grand Rapids: Eerdmans, 2011, pp. 68-87.

Mannermaa, Tuomo. *Der im Glauben Gegenwärtige Christus: Rechtfertigung und Vergottung zum ökumenischen Dialog,* Arbeiten zur Geschichte und Theologie des Luthertums, n.s. 8. Hannover: Lutherisches Verlagshaus, 1989.

Marcus, Joel. *Mark 1–8, A New Translation with Introduction and Commentary.* The Anchor Bible, vol. 27. New Haven and London: Yale University Press, 2000.

―――. *Mark 8–16.* The Anchor Yale Bible. New Haven and London: Yale University Press, 2009.

Marion, Jean-Luc. *God without Being.* Translated by Thomas A. Carlson. Chicago: University of Chicago Press, 1995.

―――. "Resting, Moving, Loving: The Access to the Self according to Saint Augustine." *The Journal of Religion* 91, no. 1 (January 2011): 32.

Marshall, Bruce D. *Christology in Conflict: The Identity of a Saviour in Rahner and Barth.* Oxford: Basil Blackwell, 1987.

―――. "Faith and Reason Reconsidered: Aquinas and Luther on Deciding What Is True." *The Thomist* 63 (1999).

―――. "Justification as Declaration and Deification." *International Journal of Systematic Theology* 4, no. 1 (March 2002): 3-28.

―――. *Trinity and Truth.* Cambridge: Cambridge University Press, 2000.

Martyn, J. Louis. *History and Theology in the Fourth Gospel,* 3rd edition. Louisville and London: Westminster John Knox, 2003.

―――. *Galatians: A New Translation with Introduction and Commentary,* The Anchor Bible, vol. 33A. New York: Doubleday/Random House, 1997.

Marx, Karl. *On Religion.* Translated by Saul K. Padover. New York: McGraw-Hill, 1974.

Mattes, Mark C. *The Role of Justification in Contemporary Theology,* Lutheran Quarterly Books. Grand Rapids: Eerdmans, 2004.

Mattox, Mickey L. "From Faith to the Text and Back Again: Martin Luther on the Trinity in the Old Testament." *Pro Ecclesia* 15, no. 3 (Summer 2006): 281-303.

Mauer, Wilhelm. *Historical Commentary on the Augsburg Confession.* Translated by H. George Anderson. Philadelphia: Fortress, 1986.

Mays, James Luther. *Hosea: A Commentary.* Philadelphia: Westminster, 1969.

McCord Adams, Marilyn. *Christ and Horrors: The Coherence of Christology.* Cambridge: Cambridge University Press, 2008.

McCormack, Bruce. "Grace and Being," chapter 6 in *The Cambridge Companion to Karl Barth.* Edited by John Webster. Cambridge: Cambridge University Press, 2000, p. 103.

―――. *Karl Barth's Critically Realistic Dialectical Theology: Its Genesis and Development 1909-1936.* Oxford: Clarendon, 1995.

McCoy, Charles S., and J. Wayne Baker. *Fountainhead of Federalism: Heinrich Bullinger and the Covenantal Tradition.* Philadelphia: Westminster, 1991.

McCumber, John. *Time in the Ditch: American Philosophy and the McCarthy Era*. Evanston, IL: Northwestern University Press, 2001.

McDermott, Gerald R. *Jonathan Edwards Confronts the Gods: Christian Theology, Enlightenment Religion, and Non-Christian Faiths*. Oxford: Oxford University Press, 2000.

McGrath, Alister E. *A Fine-Tuned Universe: The Quest for God in Science and Theology*. Louisville: Westminster John Knox, 2009.

Melanchthon, Philip. *On Christian Doctrine: Loci Communes, 1555*. Translated by C. L. Manschreck. Grand Rapids: Baker, 1982.

———. *Orations on Philosophy and Education*. Edited by Sachiko Kusakawa. Cambridge: Cambridge University Press, 1999.

Meyendorff, John. *Byzantine Theology: Historical Trends and Doctrinal Themes*. New York: Fordham University Press, 1979.

———. *Christ in Eastern Christian Thought*. Crestwood, NY: St. Vladimir's Seminary Press, 1975.

Meyer, Harding. "The Ecumenical Dialogues: Situations, Problems, Perspectives." *Pro Ecclesia* 3, no. 1 (Winter 1994).

Meyer, R. W. *Leibniz and the Seventeenth Century Revolution*. Translated by J. P. Stern. Cambridge: Bowes & Bowes, 1952.

Milbank, John. *Theology and Social Theory: Beyond Secular Reason*. Oxford: Blackwell, 1997.

Mildenberger, Friedrich. *Theology of the Lutheran Confessions*. Translated by E. Lueker. Philadelphia: Fortress, 1986.

Miles, Margaret R. *Plotinus on Body and Beauty: Society, Philosophy, and Religion in Third Century Rome*. Oxford: Blackwell, 1999.

Miller, Michael J. *What Are They Saying About Papal Primacy?* New York/Ramsey: Paulist, 1983.

Moltmann, Jürgen. *Der gekreuzigte Gott*. Munich: Chr. Kaiser Verlag, 1976.

———. *The Theology of Hope: On the Ground and the Implications of a Christian Eschatology*. Translated by James W. Leitch. New York: Harper & Row, 1967.

———. *The Way of Jesus Christ: Christology in Messianic Dimensions*. Translated by Margaret Kohl. San Francisco: Harper, 1990.

Morse, Christopher. *Not Every Spirit: A Dogmatics of Christian Disbelief*. Harrisburg, PA: Trinity Press International, 1994.

———. *The Logic of Promise in Moltmann's Theology*. Philadelphia: Fortress, 1979.

Müller, Christine-Ruth. *Bekenntnis und Bekennen: Dietrich Bonhoeffer in Bethel, 1933: Ein lutherischer Versuch*. Munich: Chr. Kaiser Verlag, 1989.

Muller, Richard A. *Dictionary of Latin and Greek Theological Terms: Drawn Principally from Protestant Scholastic Theology*. Grand Rapids: Baker Academic, 1985.

Murphy, George L. *Models of Atonement: Speaking about Salvation in a Scientific World*. Minneapolis: Lutheran University Press, 2013.

———. *The Cosmos in the Light of the Cross*. Harrisburg, London, New York: Trinity Press International, 2003.

Nelson, Derek R. "Charles Finney and John Nevin on Selfhood and Sin: Reformed Anthropologies in Nineteenth-Century American Religion." *Calvin Theological Journal* 45 (2010): 280-305.

———. "Conversation and Theistic Belief: William James and Richard Rorty Get Religion." *The Heythrop Journal* (2009): 495-507.

———. *What's Wrong with Sin? Sin in Individual and Social Perspective from Schleiermacher to Theologies of Liberation*. London and New York: T. & T. Clark, 2009.

Nelson, R. David. *The Interruptive Word: Eberhard Jüngel on the Sacramental Structure of God's Relation to the World.* London and New York: Bloomsbury T. & T. Clark, 2013.

Nesbitt, Paula D. *Feminization of the Clergy in America: Occupational and Organizational Perspectives.* New York and Oxford: Oxford University Press, 1997.

Neusner, Jacob. *Judaism and Christianity in the Age of Constantine.* Chicago: University of Chicago Press, 1987.

———. *Judaism in the Beginning of Christianity.* Philadelphia: Fortress, 1984.

———, with William Scott Green. *Writing with Scripture: The Authority and the Uses of the Hebrew Bible in the Torah of Formative Judaism.* Minneapolis: Augsburg Fortress, 1989.

Neve, Herbert T. *Sources for Change: Searching for Flexible Church Structures.* Geneva: World Council of Churches, 1968.

Newbigin, Lesslie. *The Household of God: Lectures on the Nature of the Church.* London: SCM, 1953.

Niebuhr, H. R. *The Responsible Self: An Essay in Christian Moral Philosophy.* New York: Harper & Row, 1963.

Niebuhr, Reinhold. *Moral Man and Immoral Society: A Study in Ethics and Politics.* New York: Charles Scribner's Sons, 1960.

———. *The Nature and Destiny of Man,* volume 2: *Human Destiny.* New York: Charles Scribner's Sons, 1943.

Nietzsche, Friedrich. *Beyond Good and Evil: Prelude to a Philosophy of the Future.* Translated by W. Kaufmann. New York: Vintage, 1966.

———. *The Will to Power.* Edited by W. Kaufmann. New York: Vintage Books, 1968.

Nordeval, Oyvind. "The Emperor Constantine and Arius: Unity in the Church and Unity in the Empire." *Studia Theologica* 42 (1988): 113-50.

Norgate, Jonathan. *Isaak A. Dorner: The Triune God and the Gospel of Salvation.* London and New York: T. & T. Clark, 2009.

Norris, Richard. *Manhood and Christ.* London: Exford Press, 1963.

Novak, David. *Jewish-Christian Dialogue: A Jewish Justification.* New York and Oxford: Oxford University Press, 1989.

Nygren, Anders. *Agape and Eros.* Translated by Philip S. Watson. New York and Evanston: Harper & Row, 1969.

Oakes, Edward T. *Pattern of Redemption: The Theology of Hans Urs von Balthasar.* New York: Continuum, 2002.

Oberman, Heiko A. *Luther: Man between God and the Devil.* Translated by Eileen Walliser-Schwarzbart. New Haven and London: Yale University Press, 1989.

———. *The Dawn of the Reformation: Essays in Late Medieval and Early Reformation Thought.* Edinburgh: T. & T. Clark, 1986.

———. *The Harvest of Medieval Theology: Gabriel Biel and Late Medieval Nominalism.* Grand Rapids: Baker Academic, 2000.

———. *The Roots of Anti-Semitism: In the Age of Renaissance and Reformation.* Philadelphia: Fortress, 1984.

Ochs, Peter. *Another Reformation: Postliberal Christianity and the Jews.* Grand Rapids: Eerdmans, 2011.

Oden, Thomas C. *Classical Christianity: A Systematic Theology.* Previously published in three volumes. New York: HarperOne, 1992.

Oehlschlaeger, Fritz. *Procreative Ethics: Philosophical and Christian Approaches to Questions at the Beginning of Life.* Eugene, OR: Cascade Books, 2011.

Olson, Oliver K. *Mathias Flacius and the Survival of Luther's Reform.* Wiesbaden: Harrassowitz Verlag, 2002.

*On the Dormition of Mary: Early Patristic Homilies.* Translated by Brian E. Daley, S.J. Crestwood, NY: St. Vladimir's Seminary Press, 1998.

O'Regan, Cyril. *The Heterodox Hegel.* Albany: State University of New York Press, 1994.

Ozment, Steven. *When Fathers Ruled: Family Life in Reformation Europe.* Cambridge, MA: Harvard University Press, 1983.

Pannenberg, Wolfhart. *Basic Questions in Theology,* 2 vols. Translated by G. H. Kehm. Philadelphia: Fortress, 1972.

————. "Catechism of the Catholic Church: An Evangelical Viewpoint." *Pro Ecclesia* 4, no. 1 (Winter 1995).

————. *Jesus: God and Man.* Translated by L. L. Wilkins and D. A. Priebe. Philadelphia: Westminster, 1975.

————. *What Is Man? Contemporary Anthropology in Theological Perspective.* Translated by D. Priebe. Philadelphia: Fortress, 1970.

*Papal Primacy and the Universal Church.* Edited by Paul C. Empie and T. Austin Murphy. Minneapolis: Augsburg, 1974.

Paulson, Steven D. *Lutheran Theology.* London and New York: T. & T. Clark International, 2011.

Peacocke, Arthur. *Theology for a Scientific Age: Being and Becoming — Natural, Divine and Human,* enlarged edition. London: SCM, 1993.

Pelikan, Jaroslav. *Christianity and Classical Culture: The Metamorphosis of Natural Theology in the Christian Encounter with Hellenism.* New Haven and London: Yale University Press, 1993.

Perkins, Judith B. "The Passion of Perpetua: A Narrative of Empowerment." In *Latomus: Revue d'Études Latini,* vol. 53.

*Peter in the New Testament.* Edited by Raymond E. Brown, Karl P. Donfried, and John Reumann. Minneapolis: Augsburg / New York, Paramus, Toronto: Paulist, 1973.

Peters, Ted. "Happy Danes and Deep Incarnation." *dialog* 52, no. 3 (Fall 2013): 244-62.

Peterson, Cheryl M. *Who Is the Church? An Ecclesiology for the Twenty-First Century.* Minneapolis: Fortress, 2013.

Piepkorn, Arthur Carl. "What Does 'Inerrancy' Mean?" *Concordia Theological Monthly* 36, no. 8 (September 1965): 577-93.

Plantinga, Cornelius, Jr. "Gregory of Nyssa and the Social Analogy of the Trinity," *The Thomist* 50, no. 3 (1986): 325-52.

Plato. *The Republic.* Translated by G. M. A. Grube, revised by C. D. C. Reeve. Indianapolis: Hackett, 1992.

Poder, Christine Svinth-Voerge. "Why Read Regin Prenter?" *Lutheran Forum* 47, no. 3 (Fall 2013): 52-55.

Polkinghorne, John. *The Faith of a Physicist: Reflections of a Bottom-Up Thinker.* Princeton: Princeton University Press, 1994.

Prenter, Regin. *Spiritus Creator.* Translated by John M. Jensen. Philadelphia: Muhlenberg, 1953.

Quere, Ralph W. *Melanchthon's Christum Cognoscere: Christ's Efficacious Presence in the Eucharistic Theology of Melanchthon.* Bibliotheca Humanistica & Reformatorica, vol. 22. Nieuwkoop: B. De Graaf, 1977.

Radner, Ephraim. *A Brutal Unity: The Spiritual Politics of the Christian Church.* Waco, TX: Baylor University Press, 2012.

Rahner, Karl. *Foundations of the Christian Faith: An Introduction to the Idea of Christianity.* Translated by William V. Dych. New York: Seabury, 1978.

Raitt, Jill. *The Colloquy of Montbéliard: Religion and Politics in the Sixteenth Century.* New York and Oxford: Oxford University Press, 1993.

*Ralph Waldo Emerson Texts* at http://www.emersoncentral.com/lordsupper.htm.

Raunio, Antti. *Summe des Christlichen Lebens: Die "Goldene Regel" als Gesetz der Liebe in der Theologie Martin Luthers von 1510 bis 1527.* Helsinki: Reports from the Department of Systematic Theology XIII, 1993.

Rauschenbusch, Walter. *A Theology for the Social Gospel,* with an Introduction by Donald W. Shriver Jr. Louisville: Westminster John Knox, 1997.

Reinhuber, Thomas. *Kämpfender Glaube: Studien zu Luthers Bekenntnis am Ende von De servo arbitrio.* Berlin and New York: Walter de Gruyter, 2000.

*Religion and Rational Theology.* The Cambridge Edition of the Works of Immanuel Kant. Translated by A. W. Wood and G. Di Giovanni. Cambridge: Cambridge University Press, 2001.

Reno, R. R. *Genesis,* Brazos Theological Commentary on the Bible. Grand Rapids: Baker, 2010.

Reumann, John. *The Supper of the Lord: The New Testament, Ecumenical Dialogues, and Faith and Order on Eucharist.* Philadelphia: Fortress, 1985.

Rice, Daniel F. *Reinhold Niebuhr and John Dewey: An American Odyssey.* Albany: State University of New York Press, 1993.

Richardson, Alan. *Christian Apologetics.* New York: Harper & Brothers, 1947.

Richter, Matthias. "Andreas Poach und sein Anteil am 2. Antinomistichen Streit." *Archiv für Reformationsgeschichte* 85 (1994).

Riley, Gregory J. *Resurrection Reconsidered: Thomas and John in Controversy.* Minneapolis: Fortress, 1995.

Riley, Hugh M. *Christian Initiation.* Washington, DC: Catholic University of America Press, 1974.

Riley, Patrick. *Leibniz' Universal Jurisprudence: Justice as the Charity of the Wise.* Cambridge, MA: Harvard University Press, 1996.

*Rite of Christian Initiation for Adults.* Chicago: Liturgy Training Publications, 1988.

Ritschl, Albrecht. *The Christian Doctrine of Justification and Reconciliation: The Positive Development of the Doctrine.* Translated by H. R. MacIntosh and A. B. Macaulay. Clifton, NJ: Reference Book Publishers, Inc., 1966.

Robeck, Cecil M., Jr. *Prophecy in Carthage: Perpetua, Tertullian and Cyprian.* Cleveland: Pilgrim Press, 1992.

Rohls, Jan. *Reformed Confessions: Theology from Zurich to Barmen,* with an Introduction by Jack L. Stotts, translated by John Hoffmeyer. Louisville: Westminster John Knox, 1998.

Rorty, Richard. *Philosophy and the Mirror of Nature.* Princeton: Princeton University Press, 1979.

Roth, John D. "Mennonites and Lutherans Re-Remembering the Past." *Lutheran Forum* 44, no. 1 (2010): 38-42.

Royce, Josiah. *The Problem of Christianity.* Washington, DC: Catholic University of America Press, 2001.

Ruether, Rosemary Radford. *Faith and Fratricide: The Theological Roots of Anti-Semitism.* New York: Seabury, 1979.

Russell, William R. *The Schmalkald Articles: Luther's Theological Testament.* Minneapolis: Fortress, 1995.

Saarinen, Risto. *God and the Gift: An Ecumenical Theology of Giving.* Collegeville, MN: Liturgical Press, 2005.

Safranski, Rudiger. *Nietzsche: A Philosophical Biography.* Translated by S. Frisch. New York: W. W. Norton, 2002.

Saler, Robert C. "Paul Hinlicky's Critical Dogmatics: Triune Redemption and Hope in the Beloved Community." *dialog* 52, no. 2 (Summer 2013): 151-57.

*Salvation in Christ: A Lutheran Orthodox Dialogue.* Edited by John Meyendorff and Robert Tobias. Minneapolis: Augsburg, 1992.

Sandel, Michael J. *What Money Can't Buy: The Moral Limits of Markets.* Farrar, Straus & Giroux, 2012.

Sanders, E. P. *Paul and Palestinian Judaism.* Philadelphia: Fortress, 1977.

Schillebeeckx, Edward. *Jesus: An Experiment in Christology.* Translated by H. Hoskins. New York: Seabury/Crossroad, 1979.

Schleiermacher, Friedrich. *The Christian Faith,* 2 vols. Edited by H. R. MacKintosh and J. S. Stewart. New York and Evanston: Harper & Row Torchbooks, 1963.

———. *The Life of Jesus.* Edited by J. C. Verheyden. Philadelphia: Fortress, 1975.

Schmid, Heinrich. *The Doctrinal Theology of the Evangelical Lutheran Church,* 3rd edition. Philadelphia: Lutheran Publication Society, 1899.

Schnelle, Udo. *Antidocetic Christology in the Gospel of John: An Investigation of the Place of the Fourth Gospel in the Johannine School.* Translated by Linda M. Maloney. Minneapolis: Fortress, 1992.

Schweitzer, Eduard, and others. *Spirit of God.* Translated by A. E. Harvey. London: Adam & Charles Black, 1960.

Scott, E. F. *The Lord's Prayer: Its Character, Purpose, and Interpretation.* New York: Charles Scribner's Sons, 1951.

*Seeking New Directions for Lutheranism: Biblical, Theological, and Churchly Perspectives.* Edited by Carl E. Braaten. Delhi, NY: ALPB Books, 2010.

*Sermons of Martin Luther,* 8 volumes. Edited by John Nicolas Lenker. Grand Rapids: Baker, reprinted 1983.

Sharp, Hasana. *Spinoza and the Politics of Renaturalization.* Chicago and London: University of Chicago Press, 2011.

Sharples, R. W. *Stoics, Epicureans and Sceptics: An Introduction to Hellenistic Philosophy.* London and New York: Routledge, 1996.

Shewring, W. H., translator. *The Passion of Perpetua and Felicity.* London: Sheed & Ward, 1931.

Smith, James K. A. "Re-Kanting Postmodernism? Derrida's Religion within the Limits of Reason Alone." *Faith and Philosophy* 17, no. 4 (October 2000): 558-71.

Smith, Leonard S. *Religion and the Rise of History: Martin Luther and the Cultural Revolution in Germany, 1760-1810.* Eugene, OR: Cascade Books, 2009.

Soloveichik, Meir Y. "The Virtue of Hate." *First Things* (February 2003), accessed online 10/26/13 at http://www.firstthings.com/article/2007/05/the-virtue-of-hate-26.

*Sophocles: The Three Theban Plays.* Translated by Robert Fagles. London: Penguin, 1984.

Soskice, Janet. *Metaphor and Religious Language.* Oxford: Clarendon, 1987.

Soulen, R. Kendall. *The Divine Name(s) and the Holy Trinity: Distinguishing the Voices,* vol. 1. Louisville: Westminster John Knox, 2011.

Southern, R. W. *Saint Anselm: A Portrait in a Landscape.* Cambridge: Cambridge University Press, 1993.

Spener, Philip Jacob. *Pia Desideria.* Translated by T. G. Tappert. Philadelphia: Fortress, 1964.

Sperber, Jonathan. *Karl Marx: A Nineteenth-Century Life.* New York and London: Liveright, 2013.

Spinoza, Baruch. *Ethics, Treatise on the Emendation of the Intellect and Selected Letters.* Translated by S. Shirley. Indianapolis: Hackett, 1992.

————. *Theological-Political Treatise.* Translated by S. Shirley. Indianapolis: Hackett, 1998.

Stead, Christopher. *Divine Substance.* Oxford: Oxford University Press, 2000.

Steiger, Johann Anselm. *Jonas Propheta: Zur Auslegungs- und Mediengeschichte des Buches Jona bein Martin Luther und im Luthertum der Barockzeit,* mit einer Edition von Johann Matthäus Meyfarts 'Tuba Poenitentiae Prophetica'. 1625. Stuttgart-Bad Cannstatt: Frommann-Holzboog Verlag, 2011.

————. "The *communicatio idiomatum* as the Axle and Motor of Luther's Theology." *Lutheran Quarterly* 14, no. 2 (2000): 125-58.

Stewart, Matthew. *The Courtier and the Heretic: Leibniz, Spinoza, and the Fate of God in the Modern World.* New York and London: W. W. Norton, 2006.

Stout, Jeffery. *The Flight from Authority: Religion, Morality and the Quest for Autonomy.* Notre Dame and London: University of Notre Dame Press, 1981.

Strauss, David Friedrich. *The Christ of Faith and the Jesus of History.* Translated by Leander E. Keck. Philadelphia: Fortress, 1977.

Strecker, Georg. *The Johannine Epistles: A Commentary on 1, 2, and 3 John.* Translated by Linda M. Maloney. Philadelphia: Fortress, 1996.

Stuhlmacher, Peter. *Jesus of Nazareth, Christ of Faith.* Translated by Siegfried Schatzmann. Peabody, MA: Hendrickson, 1993.

————. *Reconciliation, Law, Righteousness: Essays in Biblical Theology.* Translated by Everett R. Kalin. Philadelphia: Fortress, 1986.

Taylor, Barbara Brown. *Leaving Church: A Memoir of Faith.* San Francisco: HarperSanFrancisco, 2007.

Telford, W. R. Review, *Journal of Theological Studies* 53 (2002): 191-96.

*The Apostolic Fathers: Revised Greek Texts with Introductions and English Translations.* Edited by J. B. Lightfoot and J. R. Harner. Grand Rapids: Baker, 1984.

*The Beginnings of Dialectical Theology,* vol. 1. Edited by James M. Robinson. Richmond, VA: John Knox, 1968.

*The Book of Concord.* Edited by Theodore G. Tappert. Philadelphia: Fortress, 1959.

*The Cambridge Companion to Christian Doctrine.* Edited by C. E. Gunton. Cambridge: Cambridge University Press, 1997.

*The Cambridge Companion to Karl Barth.* Edited by John Webster. Cambridge: Cambridge University Press, 2000.

*The Christian Theology Reader,* 3rd edition. Edited by Alister E. McGrath. Oxford: Blackwell, 2007.

*The Church for Others and the Church for the World: A Quest for Structures for Missionary Congregations.* Final Report of the Western European Working Group and the North American Working Group of the Department on Studies in Evangelism. Geneva: World Council of Churches, 1967.

*The Complete Writings of Menno Simons c. 1496-1561.* Translated by L. Verduin, edited by J. C. Wenger. Scottdale, PA and Kitchener, ON: Herald Press, 1984.

*The Devil's Whore: Reason and Philosophy in the Lutheran Tradition.* Edited by J. Hockenberry Drageseth. Minneapolis: Fortress, 2011.

*The Gospel and the Gospels.* Edited by Peter Stuhlmacher. Grand Rapids: Eerdmans, 1991.

*The Interpretation of Matthew.* Edited by Graham Stanton. Philadelphia: Fortress and London: SPCK, 1983.

*The Latin Works of Huldreich Zwingli,* 2 vols. Translated by Samuel Macauley Jackson. Philadelphia: Heidelberg Press, 1922.

*The Lutheran Book of Worship.* Minneapolis: Augsburg / Philadelphia, Lutheran Church in America, 1978.

The Martyrdom of Perpetua and Felicitas. Translated by Herbert Musurillo, Oxford, 1972, accessed online at http://www.fordham.edu/halsall/source/perpetua.html.

*The New Church Debate: Issues Facing American Lutheranism.* Edited by Carl E. Braaten. Philadelphia: Fortress, 1983.

*The One Mediator, the Saints, and Mary: Lutherans and Catholics in Dialogue VIII.* Edited by H. George Anderson, J. Francis Stafford, and Joseph A. Burgess. Minneapolis: Augsburg, 1992.

*The Oxford Dictionary of the Christian Church,* 2nd edition revised. Oxford: Oxford University Press, 1990.

*The Oxford Handbook of Evangelical Theology.* Edited by Gerald R. McDermott. Oxford: Oxford University Press, 2010.

*The Pietists: Selected Writings.* Translated by P. Erb. Classics of Western Spirituality. New York: Paulist, 1983.

*The Pietist Theologians: An Introduction to Theology in the Seventeenth and Eighteenth Centuries.* Edited by Carter Lindberg. Oxford: Blackwell, 2005.

*The Portable Nietzsche.* Translated and edited by W. Kaufmann. New York: Viking, 1969.

*The Reception of the Church Fathers in the West.* Leiden and New York: E. J. Brill, 1997.

Theissen, Gerd. *The Miracle Stories of the Early Christian Tradition.* Translated by Francis McDonagh. Philadelphia: Fortress, 1983.

Theodore of Mopsuestia. *Catechetical Homilies,* Woodbrook Studies, vol. 5. Translated by A. Minguna. Cambridge: W. Heffer & Sons, 1932.

―――. *On the Incarnation,* Fragment 6 from the unpublished translation of Richard Norris.

Thielicke, Helmut. *The Evangelical Faith,* vol. 1. Translated by G. W. Bromiley. Grand Rapids: Eerdmans, 1974.

Thiemann, Ronald. *Revelation and Theology: The Gospel as Narrated Promise.* South Bend, IN: University of Notre Dame Press, 1987.

*This Is My Name Forever: The Trinity and Gender Language for God.* Edited by Alvin F. Kimmel Jr. Downers Grove, IL: InterVarsity, 2001.

Thoma, Clemens. *A Christian Theology of Judaism.* Translated and edited by Helga Croner, with a Foreword by David Flusser. Mahwah, NJ: Paulist, 1980.

Tillich, Paul. *The Courage to Be.* New Haven and London: Yale University Press, 1976.

―――. *The Socialist Decision.* Translated by Franklin Sherman. New York: Harper & Row, 1977.

Tinder, Glenn. *The Political Meaning of Christianity: An Interpretation.* Baton Rouge and London: Louisiana State University Press, 1989.

Torrance, Thomas F. *Atonement.* Edited by Robert T. Walker. Downers Grove, IL: InterVarsity Academic, 2009.

―――. *Incarnation.* Edited by Robert T. Walker. Downers Grove, IL: InterVarsity Academic, 2008.

―――. *The Trinitarian Faith: The Evangelical Theology of the Ancient Catholic Church.* Edinburgh: T. & T. Clark, 1993.

————. *Theology in Reconstruction.* Grand Rapids: Eerdmans, 1975.

*Transformations in Luther's Reformation Theology: Historical and Contemporary Reflections,* vol. 32. Arbeiten zur Kirchen- und Theologiegeschichte. Edited by C. Helmer and B. K. Holm. Leipzig: Evangelische Verlagsanstalt, 2011.

Trigg, Joseph W. *Origen.* London and New York: Routledge, 2002.

*Trinitarian Theology in the Medieval West.* Edited by Pekka Kärkkäinen, Schriften der Luther-Agricola-Gesellschaft, vol. 61. Helsinki, Finland: Luther Agricola Society, 2007.

*Trinity, Time, and Church: A Response to the Theology of Robert W. Jenson.* Edited by Colin E. Gunton. Grand Rapids: Eerdmans, 2000.

Troeltsch, Ernst. *Religion in History.* Translated by James Luther Adams and Walter F. Bense. Minneapolis: Fortress, 1991.

*Union with Christ: The New Finnish Interpretation of Luther.* Edited by Carl E. Braaten and Robert W. Jenson. Grand Rapids: Eerdmans, 1998.

Vainio, Olli-Pekka. *Justification and Participation in Christ: The Development of the Lutheran Doctrine of Justification from Luther to the Formula of Concord (1580).* Leiden and Boston: Brill, 2008.

Vanhoozer, Kevin J. *The Drama of Doctrine: A Canonical Linguistic Approach to Christian Theology.* Louisville: Westminster John Knox, 2005.

Vilhauer, Monica. *Gadamer's Ethics of Play: Hermeneutics and the Other.* Lanham, MD: Rowman & Littlefield, 2010.

von Balthasar, Hans Urs. *Theo-Drama: Theological Dramatic Theory, IV: The Action.* Translated by G. Harrison. San Francisco: Ignatius, 1994.

von Harnack, Adolf. *What Is Christianity? Sixteen Lectures delivered in the University of Berlin during the Winter Term, 1899-1900.* Translated by Thomas Bailey Saunders. New York: G. P. Putnam, 1901.

von Loewenich, Walther. *Luther als Ausleger der Synoptiker.* Chr. Kaiser Verlag, 1954.

von Rad, Gerhard. *Genesis: A Commentary,* revised edition. Philadelphia: Fortress, 1973.

————. *Old Testament Theology,* 2 vols. Translated by D. M. G. Stalker. New York: Harper & Row, 1962.

Wallman, Johannes. *Luther, Lutheranism and the Jews.* Edited by J. Halperin and A. Sovik. Geneva: Lutheran World Federation, 1984.

————. "The Reception of Luther's Writings on the Jews from the Reformation to the End of the 19th Century." *Lutheran Quarterly* 1 (Spring 1987): 73-74.

Warns, Johannes. *Baptism: Studies in the Original Christian Baptism in Its History and Conflicts to a State or National Church and Its Significance for the Present Time.* Translated by G. H. Lang. London: Paternoster, 1962.

Weikart, Richard. *From Darwin to Hitler: Evolutionary Ethics, Eugenics, and Racism in Germany.* London: Palgrave Macmillan, 2004.

Wengert, Timothy J. "The 'New' Perspectives on Paul." *Lutheran Quarterly* 27, no. 1 (Spring 2013): 89-91.

Wesche, Kenneth Paul, and Paul R. Hinlicky. "Theses from Sväty Jur." *Pro Ecclesia* 4, no. 3 (Summer 1995): 265-67.

Westerholm, Stephen. *Perspectives Old and New on Paul: The "Lutheran" Paul and His Critics.* Grand Rapids: Eerdmans, 2004.

Westhelle, Vítor. *After Heresy: Colonial Practices and Post-Colonial Theologies.* Eugene, OR: Cascade Books, 2010.

White, Graham. *Luther as Nominalist: A Study of the Logical Methods Used in Martin Luther's Disputations in the Light of Their Medieval Background.* Schriften der Luther-Agricola-Gesellschaft 30. Helsinki: Luther-Agricola Society, 1994.

Wilson, Sarah Hinlicky. "Jesus Christ, Horror-Defeater." *Lutheran Forum* 47, no. 1 (2013): 2-10.

———. "Joyful Exchanges, Part I." *Lutheran Forum* 44, no. 2 (2010): 2-6.

———. "Joyful Exchanges, Part II." *Lutheran Forum* 44, no. 3 (2010): 2-6.

Wingren, Gustaf. *Luther on Vocation.* Translated by Carl C. Rasmussen. Philadelphia: Muhlenberg, 1957.

———. *Theology in Conflict: Nygren, Barth, Bultmann.* Philadelphia: Muhlenberg, 1958.

Wisnefske, Ned. *God Hides: A Critique of Religion and a Primer for Faith.* Eugene, OR: Pickwick, 2010.

———. *Preparing to Hear the Gospel: A Proposal for Natural Theology.* Lanham, MD: University Press of America, 1998.

Witte, John, Jr. *Law and Protestantism: The Legal Teachings of the Lutheran Reformation,* with a Foreword by Martin E. Marty. Cambridge: Cambridge University Press, 2002.

Wolterstorff, Nicholas. *John Locke and the Ethics of Belief.* Cambridge: Cambridge University Press, 1996.

*Word-Gift-Being: Justification-Economy-Ontology.* Edited by Bo Kristian Holm and Peter Widmann. Tübingen: Mohr Siebeck, 2009.

Worthing, Mark William. *God, Creation, and Contemporary Physics.* Minneapolis: Fortress, 1996.

Wright, N. T. *The Climax of the Covenant: Christ and the Law in Pauline Theology.* Minneapolis: Fortress, 1991.

———. *The Resurrection of the Son of God.* Vol. 3 of *Christian Origins and the Question of God.* Minneapolis: Fortress, 2003.

Yeago, David S. "The Church as Polity? The Lutheran Context of Robert W. Jenson's Ecclesiology." In *Trinity, Time, and Church: A Response to the Theology of Robert W. Jenson,* ed. Colin E. Gunton. Grand Rapids: Eerdmans, 2000, pp. 201-37.

Yoder, John Howard. *The Politics of Jesus.* Grand Rapids: Eerdmans, 1972.

Yoder, Nathan Howard. "*Ordnung in Gemeinschaft.* A Critical Appraisal of the Erlangen Contribution to the Orders of Creation." Ph.D. Dissertation, Regensburg, 2011.

Young, Frances. " 'Creatio ex nihilo': A Context for the Emergence of the Christian Doctrine of Creation." *Scottish Journal of Theology* 44 (1991): 139-51.

Zimmermann, Jens. *Recovering Theological Hermeneutics: An Incarnational-Trinitarian Theory of Interpretation.* Grand Rapids: Baker Academic, 2004.

Žižek, Slavoj, and John Milbank, *The Monstrosity of Christ: Paradox or Dialectic?* Edited by Creston Davis. Cambridge, MA and London: MIT Press, 2009.

Zizioulas, John D. *Being as Communion: Studies in Personhood and the Church.* Crestwood, NY: St. Vladimir's Seminary Press, 1993.

*Zwingli and Bullinger: Selected Translations.* Edited by G. W. Bromiley. The Library of Christian Classics, vol. 24. Philadelphia: Westminster, 1953.

# Index

CPSIA information can be obtained
at www.ICGtesting.com
Printed in the USA
LVHW110323080223
738987LV00005B/157